D0498515

CHARLES IVES

CHARLES
IVES

A Life with Music

JAN SWAFFORD

DISCARD LCCC LIBRARY

W · W · *Norton & Company* · *New York* · *London*

Copyright © 1996 by Jan Swafford. *All rights reserved.* Printed in the United States of America.

FIRST EDITION

The text of this book is composed in Galliard with the display set in Centaur. Composition and manufacturing by The Maple Vail Book Manufacturing Group. Book design by Marjorie J. Flock. Genealogy chart on pages xvi and xvii by Ben Gamit.

Photographs courtesy of the Danbury Scott-Fanton Museum and Historical Society, Inc. appear on pages 8, 13, 42, 47, 63, 71, and 174.

Photographs from Charles Ives papers, courtesy of Yale Music Library, appear on pages 8, 11, 20, 22, 31, 41, 50, 56, 59, 79, 84, 106, 109, 114, 120, 133, 148, 192, 199, 215, 267, 275, 341, 370, 401, 412, 417, 424, 426, and 436.

Credits for music examples:

Page 81, from *Psalm 67:* Copyright © 1939 (Renewed) by Associated Music Publishers, Inc. (BMI). International Copyright Secured. All Rights Reserved. Reprinted by Permission.

Page 83, from *Psalm 24:* © 1955 Mercury Music Corporation. Used by Permission.

Page 123, from Symphony No. 1: © Copyright 1971 by Peer International Corporation. International Copyright Secured. Printed in USA. All Rights Reserved. Used by Permission.

Page 162, from *Three Harvest Home Chorales:* © 1949 Mercury Corporation. Used by Permission.

Page 180, from *The Unanswered Question:* © Copyright 1953 by Southern Music Publishing Co. Copyright Renewed by Peer International Corporation. © Copyright 1984 by Peer International Corporation. International Copyright Secured. Printed in USA. All Rights Reserved. Used by Permission.

Page 240, from String Quartet No. 2: © Copyright 1954 by Peer International Corporation. International Copyright Secured. Printed in USA. All Rights Reserved. Used by Permission.

Pages 246 and 248–49, from *Three Places in New England:* © 1935 Mercury Music Corporation. Used by Permission.

Pages 258–59 and 265, from *Concord* Sonata: Copyright © 1947 (Renewed) by G. Schirmer, Inc. (ASCAP). International Copyright Secured. All Rights. Reprinted by Permission.

Pages 349, 350, 354, and 358–59, from Fourth Symphony: Copyright © 1965 (Renewed) by Associated Music Publishers, Inc. (BMI). International Copyright Secured. All Rights Reserved. Reprinted by Permission.

ML
410
.I94
S93
1996

Library of Congress Cataloging-in-Publication Data

Swafford, Jan.
    Charles Ives: a life with music / Jan Swafford.
        p.   cm.
    Includes bibliographical references and index.
    ISBN 0-393-03893-9
    1. Ives, Charles, 1874–1954.   2. Composers—United States—
Biography.   I. Title.
ML410.I94S93   1996
780'.92—dc20
[B]   95-22549

W. W. Norton & Company, Inc., 500 Fifth Avenue, New York, N.Y. 10110
http:// web.wwnorton.com

W. W. Norton & Company Ltd., 10 Coptic Street, London WC1A 1PU

1 2 3 4 5 6 7 8 9 0

In Memoriam

JOHN KIRKPATRICK

Contents

Contents

Preface

FROM CHARLES IVES'S first advent before the public until now some seventy-five years later, his music has often baffled listeners, musicians, and critics alike. He has never fit the picture of "great" composer, creator of "masterpieces." In one page of the Fourth Symphony he stacks up a roaring brass-band march, "Turkey in the Straw," "The Irish Washerwoman," a piano whose right hand is atonal and left hand ragtimey, and assigns everyone else wildcat tunes in sundry rhythms and keys, all of it adding up to a pandemonium like nothing else ever heard in the genteel confines of a concert hall. Obsessed by the past, he wrote a music of the future. As a person he was volatile yet much loved. He flayed commerce in art while getting rich around the corner from Wall Street. He exalted a sense of community while remaining of all important composers the loneliest. And likewise his music—at once so familiar and so peculiar, complex and naive, rude and gentle.

For seventy-five years critics have tried to capture this slippery specimen and attach a label to him. We read—roughly in order—of Ives the Ultra-Modernist, the Nationalist, the amateur, the primitive, the atavist, the neurotic, the sly fabricator of his own myth. These themes, of course, track the concerns of their times, from the Modernist obsession with novelty down to the present affinity for biography as pathology. All these approaches have found some resonance with Ives and his music. None has contained him; none speaks adequately to what he perceived himself as trying to do, and how well he succeeded at it.

Some time ago Ives's champion John Kirkpatrick attached to him the word "paradoxical," and that suits him. I have proposed that the best category for Ives is simply *Ivesian*. These ideas became a starting point for this book: to examine Ives's paradoxes and how, sometimes, he made them work for rather than against him; and to ponder what is singular about him and his work, in the context of the European classical tradition that was the only milieu available to him. The broader goal has been to find, beneath the protean surface, the consistencies that contained—for a time—the centrifugal paradoxes of his psyche and his art.

To put it another way, this is an Ivesian biography of Charles Ives. Fortunately, and paradoxically, to be Ivesian means first of all to be yourself, to keep your own counsel. It therefore means to be critical, as Ives was among his own least forgiving critics. To be Ivesian is to be an enthusiast and a humanist, to look for the social value in things, to recognize flaws and failures without letting them cloud what is good and true. To be Ivesian is not to play safe; it is to look always for the big picture and not submit to categories, such as biography "scholarly" or "popular." To be Ivesian is to see music and life as one story. Some of his most eloquent words concern that matter: "The fabric of existence weaves itself whole. You cannot set an art off in the corner and hope for it to have vitality, reality and substance. . . . It comes directly out of the heart of experience of life and thinking about life and living life." To his wife and muse he wrote more succinctly: *Music is life*. Ives knew that music contains abstractions and he dealt with them as such. But he also teaches us that in its essence music is not abstract but spiritual and humanistic: music is something people do for the benefit of people.

So this book treats music and life together, holding up each to the mirror of Ivesian ideals to see how well they reflect each other. I call the book a parallel biography: the story of Ives's music unfolds alongside his life, the music developing with its own logic and trajectory but not wholly distinct from his experience. And thus the subtitle, *A Life with Music*. After decades of experiment and growth, in the end—with the Fourth Symphony, to be exact—Ives's music, his philosophy, his politics, and his autobiography converged.

More specifically, this book is about Ives the musician and man of his time. This approach may seem obvious, but has been scarce in the Ives literature. No one has presented him as a prodigy who spent much of his childhood sitting at a keyboard and, as organist and composer, received the best professional training available in the country. In the literature we do not find Ives at desk or piano working over a piece until it comes out right, playing chamber music with friends, painstakingly shaping form and meaning out of the inchoate matter of sound that all composers begin with. Peter Burkholder first alerted us that Ives had a development like that of any other artist, that he was not born Transcendental. Here you will find the first extensive examination of Ives's artistic development, the years of thinking and experimenting with musical materials that brought him to his late maturity.

Ives will be set in the context of his era. We cannot adequately understand him without reference to the spirit of his age: Progressive, Pragmatist, and Realist. His concept of the social background of music comes not only from his small-town youth but from a Progressive vision of social responsibility and evolution. Usually portrayed as a social prophet and pioneering insurance man, Ives is better seen as a product of his time, even if an extreme product.

Those are some of my (Ivesian) goals—to interweave life, music, criticism, and context. To that purpose this book contains three kinds of chapters and several kinds of endnotes. The regular numbered chapters largely concern his life, with some shorter discussion of pieces. The chapters called "Entr'acte" are centered on the music, its growth and its consummation. (The chapter "Entelechy" and the following one deal mostly with his mature music, with the excuse that, in those years, there was little going on in his life outside the insurance office other than composing.) Since the intention is to show the essential outlines of his musical development, not every piece is mentioned, but rather those that best represent his work and its progress (which includes only a few of his songs). Since this is a book for general readers and music lovers no less than for musicians and scholars—a democratic book for a democratic artist—technical terms are kept to a minimum. It begins and ends with chapters called "Prelude" and "Postlude."

The endnotes, beyond serving their usual function of citation, contain technical details for musicians, glosses, speculations, asides, jokes. The endnotes are designed to be browsed and even enjoyed. Once in a while they also spell out my own preconceptions, when those inflect the text. (I aspire to objectivity, but not fake objectivity.) As Ives used "shadow lines" in his music, the notes form a shadow text to the book. The "Postlude" is my own reflection on Ives at the approach of the millennium. This would not be an Ivesian book if I did not finally stand up and say my piece.

One of the innate dilemmas of biography is that life is not much like a book. It rarely contains a clearly stated thesis, coherently developed. Life sprawls, stumbles, advances, retreats, gropes for the light switch, and once in a while makes intuitive leaps whose import is barely understood until later, if ever, by the leaper. Life seems to me an *improvisation*. For a genius like Charles Ives it is an inspired one, but an improvisation all the same. This biography tries to be less like a book and more like life; while it does not lack structure, it unfolds like life and at times resembles an improvisation. Here and there, in italics, I improvise a scene. Even then little is invented—the record is so full.

Perhaps because I am a composer myself, the logic of a person's life strikes me as lying mainly in its characteristic themes and improvisatory variations on them. That is the primary structure of the book: it is thematic. (As it happens, Ives was a master of thematic development in music.) The themes are many and their variations continuous. To mention some of the leading ones: the musician and man of his time; the wholeness beneath the paradoxes; his major influences, especially his father and his wife; his crowded, energetic lifestyle; his career as insurance executive and its effect on his music; his adolescent anxieties; his relationship to vernacular and cultivated genres, and his creation of an American art music; his philosophy of art and life; the lack of a milieu for his mature music; his health; and his relationship to his hometown of Danbury and his vision of community. The last, the most valuable part of his philosophical legacy, is here examined more thoroughly than anywhere else.

This biography follows no schools or theories but rather the material at hand and my understanding of it. Stanley Cavell wrote, "The way to overcome theory correctly, philosophically, is to let the object of your interest teach you how to consider it." Rather than theories I have facts and materials, and I tried to draw no conclusions until the facts and materials demanded them. When I speculate—usually in the notes—I say so. I admit to being skeptical of much biography as currently practiced in the United States, an approach that has been called "pathography" and "the revenge of the small on the great." If the attitude of the Romantic biographer tended to the worshipful, our age puts the famous on a pedestal so they will make an easier target. We seem no longer to believe much in art and its powers. Artists are fair game for dissection not because they are great or admirable but because they are stars, like Elvis. That some believe language is mainly about language, art about art, biography about the biographer, and "quality" a matter of hegemony and public relations deepens a crisis of belief that has tended to demolish art, artists, and writing about art together. If those things are thus demolished, sure enough there is nothing left but to loiter in the rubble, to quibble over personality, power struggles, and the like, as if that were mainly what art is "about."

These attitudes are far from the art and ideals of Charles Ives. In only a few studies of Ives does one get the least sense of the value of his work and his ideals and why they have made an impact on the world. Nor do we get much sense of why so many people were devoted to him. Those are facts like any others, important ones, and to omit them is to distort the picture.

Certainly biography bears much blame for the Romantic cult of personality depreciating into the present cult of celebrity, its glitter and malaise. I persist in believing both in art and in biography. In spirit if not in quantity, this book keeps Ives's art and its value in the center of the picture. That Ives was an infinitely fascinating man is icing on the cake.

With Ives, a biographer has an unprecedented collection of material to work from. Perhaps the modern age of musical biography begins with him. He threw out little (though he lost a lot), and after he died archivists and historians pounced. We have his published music and prose, recordings of him playing and singing, a mountain of manuscripts, memos, and marginalia, reminiscences of friends and family, scrapbooks, library, his house and study and barn and kitchen sink. For this book I had unique access to a collection of letters from Ives's fiancée to her future husband that fills in one of the most significant and least understood chapters of his life and music. Of course, a mountain of material can both illuminate and obscure a subject. It may be a general rule of biography that the more material on your subject, the more contradiction. With someone as contradictory as Charles Ives the problem is compounded. In that thicket I have kept to my intention to find the consistency beneath the contradictions.

The scholarly literature on Ives has proliferated apace. Older works include Henry and Sidney Cowell's pioneering *Charles Ives and His Music,* Frank Rossiter's sociological study *Charles Ives and His America,* Vivian Perlis's oral history *Charles Ives Remembered,* John Kirkpatrick's compilation of Ives's *Memos,* and H. Wiley Hitchcock's brief but valuable *Ives: A Survey of the Music.* All have been important sources for me. The past ten years have seen the appearance of Peter Burkholder's admirable two volumes on the music and the ideas behind it, and Stuart Feder's psychobiography *Charles Ives, "My Father's Song."* I think of these three recent books and mine as complementary even if occasionally contradictory. Together they create a multifaceted perspective on their subject that I hope will last for a while as something approaching a consensus.

Here my own ideas are interwoven with what seems most valuable in all the writings. I have tried not to emphasize my own interpretations at the expense of others, but to give each point its proper weight in the story. Like Ives, I enjoy collaborators and quotes—starting with my subject's own exuberant prose. The intention, however unattainable, is to be comprehensive, reasonably objective, and relentlessly accurate. It is a hoary platitude of our time that the search for truth is futile. That may be "true" as far as it goes, but futile does not necessarily mean useless. It has seemed to me more productive to set off in the direction of truth and see how far I can get (something one learns from Ives). To that end I will use any idea that does the job, original or borrowed, without favor. What is new here is sometimes a matter of new material and interpretation. More important, it is a fresh perspective that takes shape cumulatively: a thoroughgoing study of Ives as musician and man of his time.

One symptom of the confusions inherent in the material Ives left us is Maynard Solomon's much-noted 1987 article "Charles Ives: Some Questions of Veracity." In it Solomon suggests that Ives sometimes lied about when his pieces were composed, backdating them to make himself appear more the prophet. The article set off a good deal of research and rethinking about Ives's dating of his works. Among those efforts were a Yale dissertation by Gayle Sherwood, a *Musical Quarterly* article by Carol Baron, one in *American Music* by Thomas Brodhead, and, from a psychological perspective, an appendix to Stuart Feder's book. None of these studies, nor any other, supports Solomon's suggestion that there was a "systematic pattern of falsification" in Ives's datings (more on this in the endnotes).

This is not to say that Ives's datings have been cleared up, or ever will be, or that he never fibbed. Ives quoted dates for all kinds of things off the top of his head and was often wrong (including, sometimes, about the date of his father's death). When we catch him in a deliberate transposition of dates, he is as likely to be late as early: Brodhead discovered that Ives backdated the Fourth Symphony *Comedy* to its roots in the *Hawthorne* Concerto; at the same time,

Ives claimed the date for the same symphony's Fugue as some twenty years *after* it was composed. Theories about why Ives did that are possible, but they are not in line with Solomon's. Meanwhile there is decisive evidence that Ives explored prophetic musical materials from his teens on. The datings here are the best available: Ives's, refined by John Kirkpatrick in *The New Grove Dictionary of Music and Musicians,* with corrections by Sherwood and Brodhead. More often than not, Sherwood has determined, Ives's stated dates were in the ballpark. All the same, we owe Maynard Solomon gratitude at least for spotlighting the question of what Ives was doing after he supposedly had wound down as a composer. Several people have turned up information that we might not have looked for without Solomon's startling—if misleading—charges.

This book has been a labor of love. Ives and I go back a long time. As a teenager I noticed Leonard Bernstein's recording of the Second Symphony. The composer was then new to me. I looked at the picture of Ives on the cover and thought: *I like that face. I like that name. I bet I'll like that music.* The first recording I owned was *Three Places in New England,* Howard Hanson's account. After some initial bemusement I liked it as much as I'd expected. I'd play it for friends and they'd laugh—usually with scorn or disbelief, rarely with pleasure. I didn't care. When I left Chattanooga for college the only book in my suitcase was *Essays Before a Sonata.*

I didn't really understand the *Essays* then or for a long time after, but they helped shape my creative consciousness all the same. Today in an old underlining I read Ives's warning about "the Byronic fallacy: that one who is full of turbid feeling *about himself* is qualified to be some sort of an artist." That warning seems sound now; it was revelatory to an eighteen-year-old composer. Likewise Ives's words on substance and unity. My Ivesian interests were a standing joke in the Harvard Music Department. In 1966 I conducted what may have been the first all-Ives concert in the Boston area, for an audience of twenty. It took another two decades of being a desultory and amateur Ivesian before it occurred to me that if I were going to be writing about music, I should write about him. Though my own background, religion, aesthetics, and music diverge from Ives's, there are few composers with whom I could so happily have spent seven years. Ives has never stopped interesting or moving or enlightening me.

Among other things this book amounts to a sustained meditation on Ives's achievement as an artist. That achievement I take to be manifestly flawed but in the end gigantic. His achievement, in other words, is one more Ivesian paradox. Its scope is so large that it has been hard to perceive. This is partly because of generations of misunderstandings and misrepresentations by critics both for and against him, too many studies of what is wrong with Ives and not enough of what is right, plus his own obfuscations and misrepresentations and cross-purposes (he could be his own worst enemy). Maybe the flood of recent

Ives recordings and studies shows that as the end of the century approaches—the millennium his generation anticipated—the scope of his achievement has finally begun to sink in. This book tries to capture that moment in our journey with his music.

Of those to whom I owe thanks for help, I begin with John Kirkpatrick: superb performer of Ives and longtime carrier of the flame, whose work with the manuscripts and papers will be fundamental to Ives and Ivesians for as long as the music lasts. I thank Vivian Perlis, whose oral history and meticulous compilation of the Ives Papers make a scholar's job so much easier. (I used to sit in the Yale rare book library leafing through the pages, wondering how this pleasant journey through well-marked territory could be construed as work.) During the research I had much help from Ken Crilly at the Yale Music Library, and from Lucie Boland of the Scott-Fanton Musuem and her knowledge of Danbury. Town historian William Devlin was a great help with the first chapters.

Thanks to Michael Tilson Thomas and James Sinclair for ideas and inspiration, both as conductors and as sages when it comes to Ives. Thanks to the Harvard Mellon Faculty Fellowships, the Ingram Merrill Foundation, and the Sinfonia Foundation for funding. Thanks to my Harvard Freshman Seminar in American Music for ideas and enthusiasm, to Charles Ives Tyler for his hospitality and reminiscences in West Redding, and to friend and composer Larry Moss for his analytical insights. Todd Vunderink at Peer-Southern, Ives's publisher and mine, provided scores. Dr. Richard Spark helped much with medical matters. In a series of conversations, Gayle Sherwood refined my sense of Ives's datings.

Finally, thanks to the readers of the manuscript, each of whom contributed indispensable advice: Mordecai Gerstein in the early stages, then James Sinclair, H. Wiley Hitchcock, my brother Charles Johnson, and Mary Frakes, all of whom read the whole manuscript and culled it of innumerable weeds. Ives teaches us to value collaborators: every page is better for their help, and the remaining faults are mine alone.

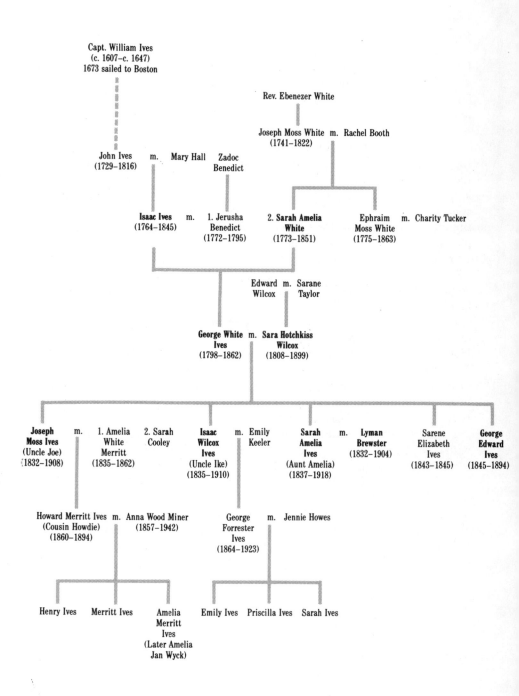

IVES FAMILY GENEALOGY

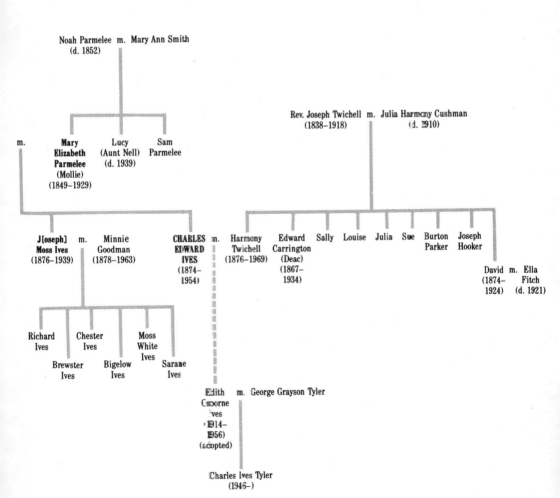

Noah Parmelee m. Mary Ann Smith
(d. 1852)

m.   **Mary   Lucy   Sam
     Elizabeth   (Aunt Nell) Parmelee
     Parmelee   (d. 1939)
     (Mollie)
     (1849–1929)**

Rev. Joseph Twichell m. Julia Harmony Cushman
(1838–1918)   (d. 1910)

J[oseph] m. Minnie   **CHARLES** m. Harmony   Edward   Sally Louise Julia Sue Burton   Joseph
Moss Ives   Goodman   **EDWARD**   Twichell   Carrington   Parker   Hooker
(1876–1939)   (1878–1963) **IVES**   (1876–1969) (Deac)
                              (1874–   (1867–
                              1954)   1934)

                                                                                                    David m. Ella
                                                                                                    (1874–   Fitch
                                                                                                    1924) (d. 1921)

Richard   Chester   Moss
Ives   Ives   White
                               Ives
     Brewster   Bigelow   Sarane
     Ives   Ives   Ives

                              Edith   m. George Grayson Tyler
                              Osborne
                              Ives
                              (1914–
                              1956)
                              (adopted)

                              Charles Ives Tyler
                              (1946–)

Prelude

IN THE OLD IVES HOUSE in the middle of Danbury, Connecticut, in 1874, among the warren of rooms smelling of beeswax and fruit, these sounds were familiar: the intimate patter of rain, the measureless pealing of thunder; the jingle of sleighs in winter, the chirr of spring peepers from streams and ponds; the clatter and clop of buggies down dusty Main Street, and the deeper rolling rumble of wagons on their way to shops and factories; from the Congregational church next door, the muffled sounds of choir and organ and the great bronze booming of the bell, and all day Sunday the sound of distant bells like intimations of a presence beyond the horizon of this moment, of this life; at holidays the brass bands marching past, the rattle and crump of fireworks, the clang of the firebell; in summer the cries of icemen and boys selling newspapers; inside the house the groaning of old floors, the antiphonal voices of a big family's comings and goings; and every day the bright rising and falling of music, cornet or piano or violin or bands or little orchestras, playing in the parlor or outside in the shed or in the barn, playing quicksteps and hymns and Beethoven and Stephen Foster.

On October 20, 1874, from the large bedroom over the south parlor rose the keening wail of newborn Charles Edward Ives, who would register the myriad sounds of home as few people have, and who would never forget them, in the intimacies of their timbres and in their deeper human resonances.

Word went out around Danbury. Joe Ives announced in his Main Street housewares store that brother George had a son. Spring Street clerk Sam Parmelee rejoiced that sister Mollie had delivered safely. Bluff, extravagant Ike Ives roared the news at his lumberyard on the corner of Ives and White Streets. Word spread through the parlors and factories of the Whites and Merritts and Hoyts and Tweedys. If spirits can commune, the birth was noted on the heights of Wooster Cemetery, where the graves of a century's Iveses, Whites, and Merritts gathered around the marble monument to George White Ives, the new baby's legendary grandfather. "The Danbury News Man," who kept the town apprised of the notable, made his wry commendation of the event in the town paper: "Ives' Brass Band has included among its soloists an infantile performer on the *vox humana*."[1] And all over Danbury the question was doubtless raised in one form or another: Would this new Ives follow that musical quirk of his father's, or would he be a real Danburian and a real Ives? Which is to say: business, both feet.

A prince had been born to the clan that everyone knew to be tireless, shrewd, extravagant, unpredictable, maybe a little crazy. Whatever Charles Ives later became, there remained the constants of his family and his town. Though he would be the only one of his clan to leave Danbury for good (eventually settling just over the hill, in West Redding), the town was in his blood as with all the Iveses. From childhood he knew that he would find his resting place among the great families on the heights of Wooster Cemetery. Even though he assimilated his own era and wrote a music of the future, the grown-up Charles Ives would never quite be at home, except in memories.

At Home

THE MUSIC OF CHARLES IVES, which on first acquaintance generally strikes listeners as willfully eccentric, grew from "a long foreground"—as Emerson said of Walt Whitman's equally eccentric *Leaves of Grass*. Ives well understood how insistently the past remained present in his work. In a 1940 letter he wrote of himself that his art "came not only from folk music he was brought up with but to a very great extent from the life 'around & in him' . . . a kind of 'inheritance' from his forbears & father—a natural interest in wanting to make his own paths around the hills & mountains—a trait all native if not all national."[1] By "native" he meant Connecticut Yankee. That inheritance traces back three centuries, to the time of his town's founding and his first American ancestors.

The history of Danbury's founding is like the stories a family tells about itself, or the stories told in Charles Ives's music: a quilt of fact and fancy and forgetting. The facts are patchy. Seventeenth-century chroniclers took little note when a few Norwalk families thrashed into the wilderness and raised a small muddy settlement. The story goes that in 1684 John Hoyt set out on foot from Norwalk, looking for farmland in the endless forest. Having found a promising stretch with a good stream about twenty miles to the north, an area the Indians called Pahquioque or Paquiack (meaning "open land"), Hoyt headed back to Norwalk and then returned leading several families. The town would commemorate them as the Original Eight. They included names of families still leading Danbury 200 years later: Hoyt, Taylor, Barnum, Benedict, Beebe, Bushnell.[2] Legend adds the price of purchase from the Potatuck Indians as thirty pounds in cash, twelve axes, twelve knives, four kettles, ten overcoats, one piece of cloth, and small goods.[3]

The settlers laid out Towne Street, the future Main, along the Indian trail that had brought them there. They erected their spare houses along it and planted crops, and the land proved fertile. Other families arrived, some bearing names also destined for local renown: Starr, Wildman, and Wood.[4] In 1687 the twenty families in the settlement petitioned the General Court for a charter under the name Swampfield, which described much of the land. Governor

Robert Treat granted the charter but decreed the more propitious name of Danbury, after a town in his native Essex.[5]

As New Englanders did in those days, the people of Danbury worked together raising houses, pulling stumps, planting and harvesting. Most were Congregationalist, also like most New Englanders; the entire community co-operated to erect the first meetinghouse in 1695.[6] In the next century a dispute erupted around First Congregational Church and Reverend Ebenezer White, father of Joseph Moss White, who would be father-in-law of Danbury's first Ives. Another Yankee determined to find his own way up the mountain, Reverend White denounced church control of government and the doctrines of original sin and infant damnation. The imbroglio around his dismissal in 1764 divided the citizenry and led to the formation of White's New Danbury Church. Some disaffected Congregationalists joined the Episcopal church, founded in 1762.[7] This spiritual controversy and its outcome boded a town relatively diverse in religious makeup and, in the end, relatively tolerant as well.

By that time Danbury was prospering modestly and exporting a variety of foodstuffs, had become a trading and milling center for surrounding communities, and so had accumulated roads—all features useful in a war. In December 1774, when Danbury had some 2,500 souls,[8] town meeting voted to support the Continental Congress and revolution.[9] Before two years were out Danbury had units in the field and was storing up food and turning out shoes and wagons for the rebel army. This naturally attracted the attentions of the British. Redcoats and Tories marched into Danbury on April 26, 1777, and torched military provisions and over forty buildings. Fat from burning pork ran ankle-deep in the street. Marching out next day, the troops ran afoul of rebel general David Wooster, who attacked near Ridgefield and made good progress before he was wounded and carried back to Danbury to die. Forces under Benedict Arnold harried the British back to their ships.[10]

Danbury's monument to General Wooster would be erected in 1854, near his grave in the new Wooster Cemetery. The procession to dedicate the monument began at the Wooster House Hotel, in Wooster Square. (The town has a short list of heroes, but has done well by them.) The camp of General Israel Putnam, whose troops spent the winter after the raid in nearby Redding, would also remain a local landmark. Among its commemorations would be Charles Ives's *Putnam's Camp*.

After the war, town and state settled back to their perennial concerns of getting and having. Already the character of the region was definable, and that character would abide. Two centuries after the Revolution, Brewster Ives dubbed his late Uncle Charlie "a real old-fashioned Connecticut Yankee."[11] He added that Charles Ives had "a sense of humor and eccentric ways" and was a "talented businessman." The traits typified the breed. Historian W. Storrs Lee writes that from the state's early Puritans "descended the generations of shrewd bargainers, conscientious pietists, and resourceful craftsmen; the outspoken individualists and inquisitive inventors, the enterprising traders, the stable scholars, the intellectuals, and the droll humorists. And through them all was a strain of respect for expediency . . . , that the attainment of a glorious end could justify the employment of an opportune means."[12] In his music Charles Ives would employ the means at hand, in memory, toward the attainment of a glorious end.

The Puritans pursued wealth as a sign of industry and divine favor; at the same time, they disdained money as a temptation.[13] A later symptom of this paradox was the New England philanthropical tradition—finding satisfaction in giving away the tainted products of worldly ambition.[14] Eventually sects proliferated while sectarianism declined; Yankees became relatively unconcerned about which roof and rubric you worshipped under, as long as you remained Christian in good standing. Connecticut nonetheless retained a streak of Puritan religiosity unto mysticism, and it was this affinity that responded to revivalists and to the pantheistical raptures of Emerson and the Transcendentalists. In the end, the mercantile impulses usually overrode the spiritual. In *From Puritan to Yankee,* Richard L. Bushman summarizes, "The Yankee's religious character, like his attitudes toward authority and wealth, is best described as a polarity." The word most often used to describe Charles Ives, the old-fashioned Connecticut Yankee, is *paradoxical*. A parochial streak is regularly noted in Yankee stock too. Writes historian Van Wyck Brooks, "The Connecticut mind . . . was keen, strong and witty, but usually narrow, educated rather than cultivated. It abounded in prejudices that were often small. . . . It was a village mind, in short, that had never breathed a larger atmosphere."[15]

In the story of Charles Ives one happens on these traits time and again. In crucial respects, however, Ives escaped his native mold: in being an artist of immense ambition, a businessman driven by values spiritual and grandly humanistic, with his mind on his village but nonetheless breathing a larger atmosphere. Creative artists were something that, for the most part, old-fashioned Connecticut Yankees notably were not. Practical musicians they were; the state had a robust performing tradition going back to the hymn-singing schools of the 1720s and continuing in the next century with its embrace of the brass-band movement. In the first half of the nineteenth century Hartford's Elam Ives, a distant relative of the Danbury branch, compiled hymn books for use in singing schools and collaborated with Charles Ives's favorite hymn composer, Lowell Mason.[16] Hymns were the most characteristic expression of Yankee musicality; Charles Ives would bring that tradition to its apotheosis in his Fourth Symphony. The rare composers of concert music, however, had to justify their profession to dubious countrymen. Connecticut organist and composer Dudley Buck, with whom Ives studied, got his training in Europe; afterward Buck quit his first job in Hartford and headed for more congenial New York City. Connecticut men of letters were less likely to write imaginative fiction than to be teachers, such as Yale's Timothy Dwight, or nuts-and-bolts scholars like Noah Webster, the dictionary man. The splendid painter John Trumbull was an exception among dozens of workaday crafters of likenesses.[17]

Which is to say, old-fashioned Connecticut Yankees were on the whole a pragmatic and uncreative breed, their imagination tending to the sort useful for commerce and scholarship. Born both a Yankee and an artist, Charles Ives was predestined to a divided nature.

For some time after the Revolution the population of Danbury grew at a relaxed pace—3,180 in 1800, 3,873 in 1820, 5,964 in 1850. At midcentury it seemed appropriate to organize a Cemetery Association.[18] The boom in population started in the 1860s, commencing a prosperous era that peaked in the 1880s.

What brought this golden age was a new business that added a major industry to the town's farming base, and in the process gave Danbury its character, its particular slant on the Yankee pattern. There exists, naturally, a pleasant fable concerning the inception of the town's principal trade. Sometime around 1780 townsman Zadoc Benedict was discommoded by a hole in his shoe and plugged it with a wad of fur he happened to have in his pocket; later he discovered that friction and sweat had kneaded the fur into a sort of felt.[19] After a few experiments demonstrative of Yankee ingenuity, Zadoc was shaping felt into hat forms over his bedpost. Soon he opened a shop on Main Street, turning wool and rabbit fur into hats at the rate of three a day.[20] Twenty years later Danbury was making 20,000 hats annually, more than anyplace else in the United States; by 1887 five million hats a year emerged from some thirty factories in the city.[21] Anyone who appeared in Danbury without a hat on was asking for trouble. Besides, this was the great age of hats in America; by the time of the Civil War, few men, women, or children would leave the house without one. The town's motto: DANBURY CROWNS THEM ALL. One never saw Charles Ives outdoors without "that crazy hat," as Brewster Ives and others described it—the hat or its battered descendants, which he wore in a 1913 Battery Park photo and in the photos of 1950.

It was around the hatting industry that the fortunes of Danbury and the Iveses intersected, when Charles Ives's great-grandfather Isaac came to Danbury following his 1785 graduation from Yale. Isaac was descended from Captain William Ives, first of the clan in America, who in 1637 sailed from England to Boston on his ship *Truelove* and became one of the first planters in the New Haven colony. William Ives's sons established a family seat in the region of Wallingford, Connecticut, where Isaac was born in 1764.

In Danbury Isaac Ives married Jerusha Benedict, daughter of first hatter

Zadoc and descendant of Samuel Benedict of the Original Eight. Isaac's early business ventures in town faltered, however, and Jerusha died. He married again in 1796, this time to Sarah Amelia White, daughter of fellow Yale man Joseph Moss White and Rachel Booth and granddaughter of Reverend Ebenezer White the dissenter.[22] The Whites were among the main developers of the hatting industry; in the early nineteenth century they owned the largest shop in the country.[23] Isaac Ives would involve himself in business with various Whites for the rest of his career. With both marriages he wove himself into the center of town life and commenced the family interminglings that would produce generations of Iveses with given names a muddle of Whites, Mosses, Merritts, Amelias, Sarahs, and Josephs. In 1795–96 Isaac represented Danbury in the state legislature[24]—the last Ives to hold political office for more than a century. His descendants would be civic-minded, but tending to sit on boards and commissions rather than stand for election.

In 1802 Isaac Ives established the first wholesale hat warehouse in New York City,[25] which became a conduit for Danbury factories. His son George White Ives was born in New York in 1798 but grew up largely in Danbury living with his maternal grandfather Joseph Moss White. George White Ives attended school in a house on Danbury's Main Street built just after the Revolution.[26]

Isaac's New York warehouse burned in 1828. The next year he retired to Danbury and bought his son's onetime schoolhouse, which he enlarged enough to contain three generations of the family and their servants and guests. Settling into a role as town elder and Congregational deacon, Isaac intended the house to become the family seat forever. The Ives House would be that for four generations, then become a white elephant literally carted all over town. Next to the plain but handsome old house, with rooms that smelled of beeswax and fruit and of lilies in summer, stood a giant pear tree that had survived the town's burning by the British and was regarded nearly as a member of the family.[27] In his retirement Isaac busied himself with civic endeavors and with planting his property—roses and lily of the valley and star-of-Bethlehem in the yard, to the north a vegetable garden in the plot where the new First Congregational Church would later rise. He dammed a brook to pipe water to the house and installed the first indoor bathroom in the county. People came from miles around to admire it.[28]

Isaac Ives set patterns for his descendants in more than business and civic matters. In his features he was a model for his bloodline: high oval face, long straight nose, lips thin and straight. He was also the first of several generations of Ives men to get his start out of town and then be drawn back by the magnetic attraction of Danbury. He died in 1845, after his son, George White Ives, had taken his place among town leaders.

That son, Charles Ives's grandfather, got started working for his father in

George White Ives, father to George and Amelia, grandfather to Charles, and Danbury's leading businessman and entrepreneur. Right: Sarah Hotchkiss Wilcox Ives, the composer's grandmother, whose endeavors ran from militant abolitionism before the war to orphanages after the war.

Isaac Ives, first of the Danbury branch of the family.

New York.[29] George White Ives returned to Danbury around 1830 to live with retired Isaac in what the town now called the Ives House, and before long the old Ives House: on Main Street, half a block from the town's principal intersection at Main and Liberty, in the middle of a growing business strip that would render the house an anachronism, a relic of quieter times. In 1831 George White married schoolteacher Sarah Hotchkiss Wilcox, an energetic and idealistic woman who would survive her husband by nearly forty years.

Four years after his marriage, in 1835, George White Ives and a group of associates (including two Hoyts, a Tweedy, a Benedict, and a Wildman) secured a charter for a railroad; it became the Housatonic line to Bridgeport; George White served as secretary of the line. Later he helped create and run the Danbury and Norwalk, completed in 1852. The D&N, connecting to New York, might stand as the turning point in the fortunes of Danbury. It brought in coal to run factories and sent hats in a steady stream south to New York and the rest of the country. The number of hatting workers in town tripled in the decade after 1850. Placing the railroad station north of the town center created a boom around Wooster Square, where Iveses and Hoyts and Tweedys owned property. In turn, all this progress demanded new industries; George White helped create and manage the Danbury Gas Light Company in the later 1850s.[30]

His obituary describes George White Ives as "foremost in every public improvement designed to benefit and adorn our village." His wife Sarah matched him. Both campaigned for the abolition of slavery. Charles Ives would endlessly retell the family story of his grandmother leading a group of women to rescue a fugitive slave caught in New Fairfield[31]; his piano piece "The Anti-Abolitionist Riots" echoes that era. Sarah was a stalwart among the women who started the Danbury orphanage, and helped found Hampton Institute, a "colored school" in Virginia.[32] She had a passion for Emerson.[33] The sons and grandsons of Sarah Hotchkiss Wilcox Ives would inherit her ardor for Transcendental ideas and her social conscience. Charles Ives would also inherit her large, baggy eyes.

In the 1850s, near the end of his life, George White Ives became director of the Cemetery Association and laid out the eighty-three-acre Wooster Cemetery.[34] There he prepared his resting place among the other Iveses, leaving room for future tenants. He had his White ancestors exhumed and moved to the cemetery's heights to lie alongside his family and the Merritts, all of them situated to keep an eye on their town.

Of all George White Ives's contributions to the life of Danbury, the most renowned was his bank. Years later, the town history by James Montgomery Bailey, "The Danbury News Man," began the story of the bank with an evocation of the time before the Civil War: "Nearly a half century ago, when Danbury had no electric lights, no pavements, no street railway, but was a pretty town with grand old trees and beautiful gardens, one of her venerated citizens,

Horace Bull, suggested to George W. Ives that a savings bank would be a blessing to many of the town people."[35] And so in 1849 George White established the Danbury Savings Bank in his house, a wooden chest in the dining room serving as safe. Sometimes townsfolk made deposits by handing money to George White in the street, trusting him to take care of the particulars. In 1852 he moved the bank to a tiny Greek Revival building built at the south corner of his yard. There it stayed until 1866, after his death, when a new brick Savings Bank with elegant arches was erected next to the old homestead.[36]

George White Ives's endeavors tended not only to his own benefit; they rose from the growth of the town and in turn accelerated progress of all kinds. In those days, progress seemed an unalloyed good, and many of the new ideas spread benefits among the citizenry. When George White Ives and his fellow entrepreneurs greased the wheels, the hatting business changed and that changed Danbury from a village to a booming town on the way to a city. Banks helped nudge the economy from barter to cash, and financed railroads and factories. Business growth attracted workers for those factories, many from among the waves of immigrants pouring into the United States—Irish from the late 1840s, and after the Civil War Italians, Germans, Swedes, Polish Jews, and smatterings of other groups. St. Peter's Catholic Church, focal point of many immigrants, became active in the community, sponsoring among other things a Library Association and a band (which Charles Ives's father would lead).[37] Despite resistance from manufacturers, hatting unions grew from the time of the United True and Assistant Society, formed in 1800. In 1885 a closed-shop agreement between unions and manufacturers demonstrated the power workers had attained.[38] In that decade the population exploded from 11,466 to 19,473.[39]

By the time Charles Ives was born, Danbury had become a mix of ethnic groups working side by side in the hatting factories. The old Yankees—still generally running things—and the polyglot immigrants celebrated holidays together in the streets and sat together on summer evenings listening to their friends and families play in bands. This relatively pluralistic, thriving, and tranquil Danbury was shaped to a large degree by Charles Ives's grandfather and a few of his family and associates. The day George White Ives died in December 1862, all Danbury closed in mourning. His memorial in Wooster Cemetery reads, *This monument is erected to George White Ives by his friends as a testimonial of his services in laying out and beautifying this cemetery, and in remembrance of his public and private worth*. His newspaper obituary concluded:

His purse was ever open to assist the needy, and no one was ever sent away from his door empty-handed. Unostentatious in his manners and social intercourse, . . . he regarded every man his equal. . . . An unflinching hater of wrong and oppression of every kind, he was always found in defence of the weak and oppressed. A firm friend, a kind neighbor, an honest man has passed away.[40]

In George White Ives and his wife Sarah, more than anyone else in the clan, we find united the motifs that were to separate out in various strands and mixtures in the next generations of his family: ambition tempered by kindness and generosity, innate leadership mixed with an authentic democratic spirit, visionary imagination fixed on the long term, an embrace of progressive ideas

The four homes of the Danbury Savings Bank—the Ives House in the middle, where George W. Ives kept depositors' money in a trunk. Then the smaller and larger buildings to the left, and the marble edifice at the right, which replaced the Congregational Church, which had replaced old Isaac Ives's vegetable garden.

practical and philosophical. In many ways George White's sons and his grandson Charles Ives would be more interesting men. All the same, in many ways they were chips, and George White Ives the block.

George White and Sarah Hotchkiss Wilcox Ives had five children, two girls and three boys. One of the girls, Sarene Elizabeth, died in childhood. The other, Sarah Amelia Ives, would find a late but fortunate match with lawyer Lyman Brewster and make him a family member in all but name. The commanding and feared Sarah Amelia would be called Amelia, or Millie. She would long survive her husband and do her best to run the family in detail. The first two of George White's sons were born close together—Joseph Moss Ives in 1832, Isaac Wilcox Ives in 1835. Third son George Edward Ives, father of Charles, came along in 1845.

Joseph Moss became the stolid merchant of the brothers even though he never liked business and aspired to philosophy. Though George White Ives had not attended college, he packed son Joe off to Yale, alma mater of old Isaac and various Whites. It turned out badly. In his sophomore year Joe and some friends attempted to silence the hated morning chapel bell by filling it with plaster, and got caught. He was not expelled, but his father was so enraged that he decreed Joe would not return to Yale but go to Boston, to work in a branch of the family hat business. For several years there Joe did his job, grudgingly, but gave his main energy to the ideas and people turning Boston and Concord into an intellectual center of historic import. He made the acquaintance of Ralph Waldo Emerson and James Russell Lowell; in the 1850s, after his return to Danbury, he brought them to town for lectures at the Congregational church. According to family legend, both men stayed at the house, where Joe was living.[41] He and his mother, Sarah, would fill Charles Ives's childhood with talk of Emerson and the Transcendentalists. The boy grew up on those soaring, cloudy ideas.

Swallowing his distaste for business, Joe opened a store in Danbury that grew into a Main Street mainstay. By 1879 the J. M. Ives Company Inc. had stockholders and twenty-five workers.[42] Joe's first wife, Amelia White Merritt, died in 1862, two years after giving birth to their son Howard Merritt Ives (known to family youngsters as Cousin Howdie). After his brother-in-law Jacob Merritt died, Joe courted the widow and married her in 1875.[43] They would have no children. The siblings were unprolific for the time—Joe had only one child, brother Ike one, George two; Amelia and Lyman Brewster had none.

Like the rest of his family, Joe Ives involved himself in civic matters; among other things he helped start and manage the famous Danbury Fair.[44] Joe was noted as much as anything for his personality. His 1908 Danbury *News* obituary implies with gleeful irony that he could be a pain in the neck: "There was a rare quality of gentleman in spite of a certain brusqueness and violence of language in which he often indulged rather to amuse than to shock his listeners. He . . . frequently used an easy banter and chaff to conceal the depth and sincerity of his feeling. His favorite device was to oppose every proposition started by others, and so develop life and earnestness in the conversation." This could have been part of his nephew Charlie's obituary.

By no means was Joe the choice eccentric among the children of George White Ives. That honor goes to Isaac, Charles Ives's Uncle Ike, who barnstormed through life with the kind of manic energy we will find reappearing in his nephew. George White sent this son not to Yale but to New York, where from age seventeen to twenty-one Ike worked in a Wall Street office. Apparently fired by the ambition of making millions and having a whale of a time, he returned to Danbury to start, in 1856, a lumber business at Ives and White Streets that would be a fixture for the next twenty-five years.[45] Lumber, building, hatting, and real estate would be the foundation of Ike's fortune, or rather his several fortunes, but these were hardly the sum of his interests. His 1910 *News* obituary recalled,

[His] business activities had been more numerous and more diversified than those of any other who had lived in Danbury in the last half century. . . . The name of "Ike" Ives . . . was almost a household word in Danbury and many of the neighboring towns. . . . In those days it was "Ike" Ives who was interested in the biggest real estate deal, who drove the turnout that attracted the most attention at the Danbury Fair, who promoted the newest industry, had the biggest advertisement in the newspapers, or was the brains and energy of the latest scheme to revolutionize something or somebody.[46]

Ike ran his lumber company and speculated in land and building and railroads and hatting. An 1870 newspaper ad of his shouts in crescendos: "LARGEST STOCK! GREATEST VARIETY!! LOWEST PRICES!! SHINGLES! SHINGLES!! SHINGLES!!!" For a time he and his two brothers ran coordinated operations in town that would provide you a house from the ground up: Ike might sell you the land, or at least the lumber and shingles; brother George (during the early 1870s) would add the builders' supplies and water pump; and brother Joe would fill up the place with stoves, plumbing, furniture,

Isaac W. Ives with one of his characteristic rigs in downtown Danbury. Ike is in the rear of the carriage.

carpets, and sleighbells. By 1870 the family operation was flourishing and Joe and Ike were among the biggest taxpayers in Danbury.[47]

Perhaps two stories concerning Ike Ives tell us most succinctly about the man, and why he was held in the collective mind of Danbury with such high regard, mixed with an undercurrent of something less well-disposed. The first story results from Ike's fascination with George Francis "Express" Train, prophet of rapid transportation, partner in clipper ships and the Union Pacific, self-proclaimed Great American Crank, and model for Jules Verne's Phineas T. Fogg. (In the 1870s he circled the world in record time.) George Francis Train was something like Ike Ives on a grander scale. Ike brought Train to Danbury for some appearances, drumming for them with his usual extravagance. However, for one of the programs the lecturer failed to show up. The town would never forget what Ike pulled that day: he disguised himself as the lecturer and gave the promised wild-eyed oration to a full house, declaiming that he/Train considered Danbury "a dead place, eaten up by fogyism," and that he was coming here to live, to shake the place out of its lethargy. At the end of the show Ike revealed his identity to the crowd, to general astonishment.[48]

The second story concerns an enterprise that Ike ran for some years. In the early 1870s he became president of the Moses Dame Company, manufacturer of a patent medicine called "Wine of the Woods." In 1873 he gave a perhaps self-parodying address at the Danbury Fair entitled "Wine of the Woods, and Its Effect on the Agricultural Interests of the World." The label proclaimed his concoction a guaranteed cure for constipation, indigestion, liver and blood complaints, and an impressive further list of ailments and epizootics.[49] Literally and figuratively, Charles Ives's Uncle Ike was a snake-oil salesman.

Biographers have naturally concentrated on the influence of Charles Ives's bandmaster father, the youngest of the brothers. George Ives would grow up with music and endow his son with great natural gifts, practical training, a sense of the meaning of music in the community, and revolutionary perceptions of musical materials. But the story of Charles Ives's ancestors reveals something of equal importance in his life: a family and community and cultural tradition that powerfully shaped him. He grew up a favored child in a town at the zenith of its prosperity and optimism. The Iveses were big fish in a small pond, but to a large extent it was *their* pond. In Danbury they knew who they were and what they amounted to; by birthright they were in the thick of things. From that heritage came Charles Ives's mostly unspoken but immense confidence in himself, his powers, and his identity that marked him through life. He called it the " 'inheritance' from his forbears & father" that created an "interest in wanting to make his own paths around the hills & mountains." Aaron Copland, knowing that the life Ives led would have destroyed an artist less endowed, called it "the courage of a lion."[50]

Beyond George Ives's musical side, scholars have stressed George's break with his business-oriented family and community, painting him as an eccentric, the black sheep of the family. From that angle he and Charlie appear as a world to themselves in a town that neither understood nor appreciated them. That seems overstated. George Ives would be one of the best-known and best-liked citizens of Danbury. With whatever incomprehension the town viewed his profession, they still recognized a leader and an inspired cornet player when they saw one. The social position of the Iveses *was* ambiguous, but not just because of George. The town watched the Iveses incessantly and read about one or another of them in every issue of the paper. They watched with admiration and sometimes amusement, and sometimes with darker suspicions. We find these suspicions cropping up between the lines, recalled in old puzzled memories. In January 1874 a note in the Danbury paper recounted an overheard conversation:

"Where did you buy your lumber?" "From that crazy fellow at White Street bridge." The reply to this query would hardly seem to mean Mr. Isaac W. Ives, yet it did.

Seventy years later, when a young man was preparing to marry an Ives girl, an old lady from among the town bluebloods (a higher aristocracy than the Iveses, perhaps of the DAR sort) called the suitor into her parlor and, as he recalled in the 1970s, "tried desperately to convince me that there was insanity in the Ives family and that I should not marry that girl."[51] He married her anyway, but did not forget the experience.

It is unlikely that the meddling society lady was thinking only of George Ives or of his son, the composer of peculiar music. She was thinking of all the Iveses, what the town had probably been whispering about them through the years, an undercurrent to the admiration and amusement. Charles Ives's wife would say, with characteristic charity, "All the Iveses are a little odd, but in a nice way."[52] The whole clan seemed touched somehow, at least after George White's generation. They were too enthusiastic, too eruptive. There was some wildness in their blood that expressed itself differently in each of those brilliant and idiosyncratic individuals, from the Transcendental business-hating businessman Joe to Ike's epic booms and busts to George's musical obsessions. The women of the family were legendarily strong-minded as well. And of course there would be Charles Ives, who would exalt his family's imagination and idiosyncrasies to a plane of visionary genius and then inflame them further, to the point of burnout and collapse.

The Music of War

GEORGE EDWARD IVES, last child of George White Ives, future father of Charles Edward Ives, was born on August 3, 1845, a week before his grandfather Isaac died and four years before his father founded the Danbury Savings Bank. The first story that survives about George is of the day his vocation announced itself out of nowhere, like a calling.

Well-brought-up children in those days were taught French and Latin and a little art and music. In 1849 George White Ives bought the square piano that stood in the parlor for the next two generations.[1] Music lessons for the first three children availed little, however, so with his youngest son George White didn't bother. Then one Fourth of July, as the family got ready to leave for a picnic, George declared that he wasn't going: "If you don't mind, I'd rather stay home and pick cherries to earn some money to buy a flute." His parents were amazed, but agreeable.[2] George got his flute and music lessons. In the next few years he went on to study violin, piano, and cornet, the latter becoming his specialty.[3] George proved not only to have a mysterious compulsion to learn about music, but also possessed perfect pitch,[4] considerable intelligence, and tireless curiosity.

He got his first training in Danbury, in a musical milieu that had never had much focus or professionalism. There was nominally a Danbury Band, but it was mostly an ad hoc outfit. A few locals gave lessons and people fooled with instruments in their spare time; little groups were scraped together for parades and such, and fiddlers played for dances. Now and then touring ensembles appeared at the Concert Hall, among them minstrel shows and popular groups including the Baker Family and the Hutchinson Family Singers, purveyors of sentimental tunes and temperance ditties: "My Mother's Bible," "The Inebriate's Lament."[5] The music most familiar during George Ives's boyhood was heard in church and outdoor camp meetings—Protestant hymnody pale and saccharine on the page, but vibrant in the voices of worshippers moved by the spirit.

"Cultivated" music struggled for a foothold in a United States where the majority of citizens lived in small towns and pursued small trades and farming.

Symphony orchestras ephemerally formed and dissolved in a few urban centers. The first orchestra that still survives, the New York Philharmonic Society, was founded three years before George Ives was born; the second, the Boston Symphony, did not appear until 1881, when Charles Ives was seven. Mostly foreign-born musicians stocked these orchestras. Professional cultivated music was generally held to be the preserve of European men, its appreciation the preserve of women and the rich. In the Danbury of the 1850s training was scant, and likewise perspectives versed in the larger musical world.

George probably first studied with Emile Gaebler, a conductor, church organist, and occasional composer. Part of Gaebler's support came from the usual public-spirited families, including the Whites and Iveses. In 1852 Gaebler rehearsed his local chorus over six months for a performance of Mendelssohn's *Saint Paul*. Mounted in Danbury with the accompaniment of New York's Jenny Lind Orchestra,[6] it was a spectacular event for the time. By the spring of 1860, George, now fifteen, had advanced enough to play cornet in the newly reorganized Danbury Band. Their first concert featured a minstrel in blackface and a black fiddler named Judge Peters. Reported the paper: "The exercises were frequently applauded by the *slim* audience in attendance and, considering everything, we have had many worse entertainments."[7]

In 1860 an ambitious young musician needed more than what Danbury could offer. George being an ambitious young musician from a well-to-do family sympathetic to the arts, he was able at fifteen to convince his parents to send him to New York to live on his own and study music. He would also study German, the indispensable language for a musician, and the language *of* many musicians in America. What did George White and Sarah Ives have in mind in agreeing to their boy's leaving? Did they deem this a pastime and expect he would outgrow it, then take his place in business alongside his brothers? Or were they agreeable to George's becoming a professional musician? In either case, the family seems not to have pressured George to do anything else, though out of necessity he would involve himself occasionally in business.

In August 1860, George began studying music theory and German full time at Morrisania (later part of the Bronx) with a German-born music master named Carl (or Karl, or Charles) Foepple. At the same time he took cornet lessons from one Franz Schreiber, also German-born.[8] He returned home regularly to visit the family and play in concerts. With Foepple George studied traditional European harmony, counterpoint, and orchestration—all useful to a future band director wanting to teach, arrange pieces, maybe compose a little. George's notebooks survive, dutifully labeled "Lessons on Musical theory and thorough base Taken in the Winter of 1860–1 at New York, From Prof. Chas. A. Foepple by Geo. E. Ives." They contain featureless but competent fugues and chorales he composed in Bach style, sections copied from works by composers including Bach and Mozart, and assorted marches and dances.[9] A family legend, much dressed up by Charles Ives in later years, related that George once came across Stephen Foster lying drunk in the street, and helped home the composer of "Old Black Joe," "Camptown Races," and dozens of other favorites.[10] George would remain a lover of Foster's songs and pass on that taste to his students, including his son.[11]

During those years George regularly attended New York Philharmonic concerts, the highest level of music one could aspire to in the America of that time. Did he aspire to it? There is no indication he did, that he ever planned to do anything beyond what he did pursue. As much as he admired and studied European cultivated music, George Ives was destined for a more modest setting than the glamorous one of urban concert halls. Like his son, he would never be an insider in that milieu.

Usual life went on around the country in 1860: farmers harvested, businessmen hustled, politicians contended, musicians played. Within the days' ordinary rounds, inexorably as a nightmare, civil war coalesced in the winter of 1860 and 1861. In November anti-slavery candidate Abraham Lincoln won the presidency; in December South Carolina seceded from the Union, followed by most of the other slaveholding states; on April 13, 1861, after a day of virtually ceremonial trading of cannonfire without casualties, Fort Sumter's commander surrendered. Next day the Northern soldiers paraded out of the fort, band playing and banners streaming, and the South proclaimed its first victory. President Lincoln declared a state of insurrection and called for troops to put it down. On both sides, thousands of volunteers signed up to fight. Country boys and city boys and wealthy young gentlemen posed for photographs grinning fiercely over rifles and pistols and knives. It was the most exciting thing that had ever happened to them, and for most of them it would remain so to the end of their days, whether that end came sooner or later.

It was an era of parades and bunting, of patriotic orations, of grand phrases loved for how they rang the heartstrings. In towns across the country great benedictions were declaimed over squares filled with roaring crowds and green young volunteers and officers, all of them delirious with the thrill of impending battle. After the fall of Fort Sumter, Connecticut volunteers rallied to the flag. Some seventy men of Danbury's Wooster Guards went to war within a week under Captain E. E. Wildman. The scene of their departure was a cathartic event in the history of the town. After a final dinner the Guards marched in ranks down the street, accompanied by a band and hundreds of citizens. At the Concert Hall (later the site of the Soldiers' Monument) the men listened to an impassioned prayer, then proceeded to the Danbury and Norwalk station amidst a growing multitude. At their departure, "wives, mothers, fathers, and children stood in tearful mood, but withal imbued with firmness and patriotism and heroism. . . . Here amid the huzzas of the crowd, the bursts of martial music, the waving of flags, the boom of cannon, the Wooster Guards went forth the first company in the State of Connecticut to pledge itself to the defence of the untarnished honor of the commonwealth and the nation."12

Danbury's Fourth of July that year was a roaring spectacle of crowds, fireworks, gunfire, and bells pealing all over town. From a platform vaunting a statue of George Washington swathed in bunting and topped by a rampant eagle, young lawyer and poet Lyman Brewster gave the featured address. The day ended with a torchlight parade. (The band was borrowed, however. A letter writer complained to the paper, "Where was the Cornet Band? . . . I sincerely hope on all occasions when music is needed that strains of victorious music may come floating from our own Band and no other."13) Those marching to battle would soon be disabused, but the veneer of glory remained for the boys left behind. Among the remaining was George Ives, writing his fugues in New York during the battles of First Bull Run and Shiloh.

At the beginning of 1862 a group of three-year enlistees was organized into a regiment that became the First Connecticut Volunteer Heavy Artillery. Their lieutenant-colonel was Nelson L. White, a cousin of the Iveses.14 On a furlough home in September, White proposed to George Ives the idea of organizing a band for the First Connecticut "Heavies," as such artillery outfits were called. Dazzled by the idea, the boy set about recruiting members from musicians he knew, mainly in New York. Half the band turned out to be from German families.

When George enlisted in September 1862, shortly before his father's death, he was just seventeen and the youngest bandmaster in the Union army.15 He and his players reported to Fort Richardson, near Washington, D.C., at the end of July 1863. Rather than staying there with the Heavies, he was first attached to the Third Brigade of the Army of the Potomac, also languishing in garrison duty in the area.16 At the beginning of that July the Union Army of the Potomac, decimated at Fredericksburg and humiliated at Chancellorsville, had pulled itself together and whipped Robert E. Lee at Gettysburg. That victory, and Grant's the same month at Vicksburg, decided the war, but there would be two more years of sparring before Lee gave up. The Heavies spent nearly a year guarding Washington before being transferred to more active duty with the Army of the Potomac, pursuant to Grant's siege of Petersburg. There George saw his fill of war, and maybe more than his fill. With one startling exception he would show remarkable leadership for a teen-age boy, holding together his group—mostly immigrants older than their leader—for the duration, and training them until they were called, on at least one occasion, the best band in the army.

Soldiers of the Civil War lived and fought to the accompaniment of music. During the first year, each regiment (around a thousand men) was allowed a band; in the first months of the war perhaps one out of forty Union soldiers was a musician.[17] In the summer of 1862 the War Department trimmed this extravagance, allowing only one band per brigade (a brigade being two or more regiments). Federal soldier / bandsmen lived relatively well;

Teenaged George Ives as leader of the Second Connecticut Heavy Artillery Band.

players made about $20 a month and leaders such as George Ives $86—a salary near princely in those days given that the army provided tent, cot, and sustenance.[18] To the bandsmen were added the buglers, drummers, and fifers needed to coordinate operations of the army from getting up in the morning to marching in line of battle.

George Ives's days in the garrison ran according to regulation. Soldiers jumped to the cries of bugles, from the 5 A.M. "Assembly of Buglers" through the stations of the day to the final "Extinguish Lights."[19] (Better known as

Taps, this most eloquent of bugle calls served also for soldiers' last extinguishing of lights.) Every soldier knew the calls as he knew the sounds of home; they were his clock and his spur. They would resound in soldiers' memories and reunions and dreams for the rest of their lives, and beyond that into history: *Reveille* sparks the climax of Charles Ives's Second Symphony, *Taps* separates the mournful and joyous halves of his *Decoration Day.*

The presence of musicians in camp and on the march was indispensable to armies on both sides. A Union private wrote his family from Mississippi in 1862, "As I write the splendid brass band of the 15th Michigan is practicing about a quarter mile from here. The stirring notes of the 'Red, White and Blue' swell triumphantly through the still night air. . . . We have a perfect surfeit of music here."[20] Evening concerts for the troops and serenading of officers and their ladies were a regular feature of military camps, but bandsmen and drum corpsmen had more important duties. They played at recruitment rallies and led troops at the full-dress parades that kindled the morale of soldiers and citizenry. Music eased the long dusty slogs from camp to camp and battle to battle. Because brass bands usually marched ahead of the troops, most were outfitted with over-the-shoulder horns that aimed the sound backward. (Soldiers cracked that these also came in handy when the band led the skedaddling on a retreat.) A stereopticon slide of George Ives's band shows his men with over-the-shoulder instruments; it is labeled "Siege Arty Brigade Band Drewry's Bluff on Bank of Jas [James] River near Richmond."

As music graced the moments of glory and pageantry, no less did it accompany the dismal expediencies of war. Units were called into line of battle by bugles and drums; drumtaps marched them in ranks toward the enemy's guns. Troops filed into place for military executions to Hance's "Dead March"; after the firing squad had done its job, the band led the way back to camp with "a merry tune . . . designed to take some of the weight from the men's hearts."[21] Sometimes, needing inspiration, generals sent their bands into the fight. In the Battle of Antietam, Confederates found a line of bluecoats charging at them with a brass band right behind. After the guns finished, musicians formed stretcher parties to pick up the wounded and bury the dead. Many assisted surgeons at the operating tables, holding down the patients while the saws worked. All these monstrous and commonplace experiences of wartime George Ives endured, along with many of his generation.

Music was woven into every part of it, into the glory and the horror. Fighting is a matter of spirit, of hearts and minds. Trifles and amenities, however intangible, are part of the formula for victory—a splendid uniform, a barrel of rum, an intoxicating speech, a stirring march. Courage can rise on a tune, a drum, a blaring bugle. After battle, music can soothe soldiers' anguish, give voice to the ecstasy of victory or dilute the bitter taste of defeat.

The Civil War produced more enduring music than any American war before or since. Within three days of the battle at Fort Sumter, George F.

Root, the time's most celebrated composer of war songs, had in print "The First Gun is Fired."[22] Root went on to write several beloved melodies, from the jaunty recruitment song "The Battle Cry of Freedom" to the marching tune "Tramp! Tramp! Tramp!" to "The Vacant Chair," one of the favorite weepers of the war. In our ears the marches of the time tend to sound sprightly and slight, the songs of mourning damply sentimental. To soldiers and their families, to George Edward Ives and later to his son, they were an authentic expression of feeling and experience. Time and again in veterans' recollections we find this sense of everyday music having powers that seem hyperbolic to those who have never seen the comradeship and shared suffering of war. One soldier told a writer,

Don't forget to put in the book how we boys used to yell at the band for music to cheer us up when we were tramping along so tired that we could hardly drag one foot after the other. That good old tune . . . "Hell on the Rappahannock" had enough music in it to make a man who was just about dead brace up, throw his chest out and take the step as if he had received a new lease on life.[23]

George Ives's Civil War band at Drewry's Bluff during the siege at Petersburg. George is on the left.

In the long sieges, such as the one George Ives observed at Petersburg, bands played during truces and soldiers of both sides sat listening and singing. The night before the battle of Stone's River in Tennessee, a Federal band struck up "Home, Sweet Home." Recalled a Southern participant,

Reader, I tell you this was a soul-stirring piece. During the still of the night, each soldier of both armies was holding communion with his soul, his mind occupied with the thought of what tomorrow would bring . . . when the notes of this inspiring tune came floating on the stillness of the night. Immediately a Confederate band caught up the strain, then one after another until all the bands of each army were playing "Home, Sweet Home." . . . What a thrill of memories was brought to minds of all that night.[24]

Often in the evening before battle, another strain swelled from hundreds of men gathered around tents and campfires, in need of solace:

> We're tenting tonight on the old campground.
> Give us a song to cheer
> Our weary hearts, a song of home
> And friends we love so dear.

> Many are the hearts that are weary tonight,
> Wishing for the war to cease;
> Many are the hearts that are looking for the right
> To see the dawn of peace.

Besides quicksteps and war-related tunes, there were soldiers' favorite hymns and popular songs—"Nearer, My God, to Thee," "The Sweet By and By," "Kathleen Mavourneen," "The Girl I Left Behind Me," "Aura Lee," and the songs of Stephen Foster that remain today as sentimental relics, but then were connected to the heartstrings. All the songs of glory, death, mourning, hope, remembrance, forgetting, victory, and finally of return: "When Johnny Comes Marching Home." Just after Lee's surrender President Lincoln asked a Union band to play "Dixie," saying it had always been one of his favorites. Everyone understood the symbol of reconciliation in that gesture.

The music of the war was a different kind of art, for different purposes, from the European cultivated tradition George Ives had studied in New York. This was an ingenuous American vernacular claimed by masses of people as the voice of their experience and feelings. Though the writers were usually commercial tunesmiths living far from the battlefield, soldiers and their families transmuted these songs into a folk art that helped sustain them. While the horrors of the war asked only to be forgotten, the music would remain with the veterans, resonating with the comradeship that was the sweetest part of the memories. For nearly all who took part in it, the Civil War shaped their lives more than any other experience. It would be that way for Charles Ives's father and for his future father-in-law, a chaplain in the Army of the Potomac. George Ives's years in the army shaped his sense of music and its meaning to communities—whether communities of soldiers, of worshippers, or of towns-people.

Charles Ives would grow up with his father's wartime melodies and his understanding of them. At Grand Army of the Republic reunions Charlie watched old men gathering around campfires to sing old songs and weep. He saw meadows filled with worshippers pouring their hearts into "The Sweet By and By" and "Nearer, My God, to Thee." In his childhood Charlie experienced time and again how fervent and inspiring this vernacular music could be in comparison to the soirées of genteel Danbury. When the grown-up Charles Ives, who never saw war, quoted these songs in his music, he added to them the feelings of veterans and of worshippers in campground or church, singing from their souls. Painstakingly he taught himself to create a context that made everyday music sound forth as the voice of the common heart.

Like his father, Charles Ives would not on that account repudiate culti-vated music in favor of vernacular. He was devoted to the classics and to performing them, and he was too ambitious in his expressive goals to be satisfied writing popular tunes. But the classical masterpieces were somebody else's tradition. Father and son respected the American vernacular as much as the European cultivated, refusing to draw lines between them—as the "cul-tured" aesthetics of their time insisted they must. In contrast was the world of bands, which mingled classical and popular in their repertoire. Beyond matters of technical training and experimental imagination, this wartime-shaped dem-ocratic vision of music would be the heart of George Ives's legacy to his son. As he matured artistically, Charles Ives would go further, enlarging his father's communal sense of music to embrace the whole human community: "some-thing personal, which tries to be 'national' suddenly at twilight, and universal suddenly at midnight."[25]

In May 1864, the war was poised for its final act. George Ives and the First Connecticut Heavies were transferred to active duty with the Army of the Potomac, playing a supporting role in the catastrophic but inconclusive battles that climaxed Grant's summer-long hammering of Lee. In the trenches of Petersburg Lee made his last stand, protecting the rail line to Richmond. From June 1864 to early April 1865, when the Confederate army bolted and were run to ground at Appomattox, there would be siege and stalemate in the trenches around Petersburg. As the siege first took shape in June 1864, George's unit was planted at Broadway Landing on the Appomattox River, to protect the main Federal supply depot. The fighting line at Petersburg was some seven miles away. There, finding himself once more on garrison duty, something snapped in young George Ives.

At this distance we cannot say what the matter was—a typically Ives enthusiasm to get into the middle of things, a teenager's craving for glory, a falling-out with his band, or something more hysterical or self-destructive. On

June 29, 1864, George sent a letter to the First Connecticut's commander asking to be made a soldier of the line. The same day he smashed his cornet. Two days later he failed to show up for guard duty.

The authorities arrested George pending court-martial for neglect of duty, "conduct prejudicial to good order and military discipline," and for destroying military property—the cornet. The offense was minor as offenses went, but there could be nasty consequences. Soldiers could be strung up all day by their thumbs for this sort of thing, or lashed to the back of an artillery caisson. There was every reason to expect, at least, that George would be demoted. In the event, the trial was handled as a family affair. Heading the July 3 court-martial was George's cousin, Lieutenant-Colonel Nelson White, who two years before had encouraged the boy to form the band in the first place. Doubtless everyone understood that things were to be smoothed over, and they were: George got a ten-day arrest, forfeited a month's pay, and returned to lead the band.[26]

Something worse happened at the beginning of 1865. While George was on furlough home to Danbury he slipped on ice and injured his back badly enough, a doctor reported, to make him unfit for duty.[27] With this development, the outlines of the story become blurred, perhaps because the record of George's injury conflicts with one of his son's favorite stories. After a review of the Army of the Potomac during the siege of Petersburg, the story runs, General Grant and President Lincoln were discussing the various elements of the army when, in regard to George Ives's outfit, Lincoln exclaimed to Grant, "That's a good band." Grant replied, "It's the best band in the army, they tell me. But you couldn't prove it by me. I know only two tunes. One is 'Yankee Doodle' and the other isn't."

Possibly something like that happened, to somebody, at some point. Those present were entertained by Grant's crack and it became famous, an expression men used to demonstrate their manly indifference to music. (Or it may already have been current when Grant used it.) Among those hearing the exchange was an orderly from Connecticut, who reported it to Ira Wildman of the Danbury Wildmans, who presumably relayed it to George and the band. From there it took a leading place in Ives family legends. It was revived by Colonel Wildman for a Danbury newspaper article of 1932.[28] To the end of his life, Charles Ives (and biographers after him) would produce the story like an heirloom: Pa and Lincoln and Grant, and the best band in the army.

The problem is, that military review must have taken place near the end of March 1865, when Lincoln was in Virginia for the City Point conference at which he discussed reconstruction with Grant and Sherman.[29] At that time, according to notes from his doctors, George Ives was home in Danbury nursing his back. Which is to say, he was not in attendance for his greatest moment of glory. The simplest conjecture is that the band marched without their leader; splendid family stories often have these kinds of unmentioned details.

It seems, anyway, that George returned to his unit by June, apparently still ailing; one of his later musical notebooks contains the entry, "A space of three years servitude as Leader . . . and one year sick, from Sept / '62 to Sept / '66."[30] This is odd, too, both that he would describe himself as "sick" rather than "injured" or some such, and that the records show him as laid up less than nine months. There may have been another sickness, rather than or in addition to the fall on the ice.

During the last weeks of the war the First Connecticut Heavies were busy shelling enemy ships at Dutch Gap and the James River. On April 2, 1865, Grant flushed Lee from Petersburg. Next day the Confederate government fled and Richmond surrendered. The day after that Abraham Lincoln walked through the streets of the enemy capital and sat pondering at Jefferson Davis's desk. Five days later, Lee surrendered to Grant at Appomattox. The Connecticut Heavies were transferred in July to Washington, too late for the triumphal Grand Army of the Republic review down Pennsylvania Avenue. That day, for the first time in four years, flags flew at full mast in the capital.

George Ives was discharged on September 25, 1865. In December of the next year, after his convalescence, he went back to New York and spent several months completing his musical studies with Carl Foepple. George's father had left him an inheritance of $2,000, enough to live on for two or three years. He remained in New York for a while, performing now and then in Danbury. Then in the spring of 1868 George collected his army enlistment bounty of several hundred dollars and got on the train for home.[31] He brought with him an ex-slave servant named Henry Anderson Brooks, who would practically be adopted by the Iveses. While the prospect of ordinary town life seemed for many veterans drab and female-ridden after the excitement of war, George Ives would spring back into civilian life with the same enthusiasm and resourcefulness he had brought to the army. Like his father and brothers, after his apprenticeships and adventures out in the world, George returned home for good.

A Place in the Soul

IN A SONG LYRIC Charles Ives would write, "I think there must be a place in the soul, all made of songs of long ago." The setting of his own long ago was always Danbury. His family and his town, like all families and towns a mixture of the singular and ordinary, were the foreground of his art. Ives's lifelong affinity for his hometown went deeper than nostalgia, though nostalgia played a part. Whatever the town might objectively have been, in his mind it grew into a myth, a symbol of the human community. His family and their feeling for the Danbury of long ago, the prewar pastoral vision of itself the town sustained well into its industrial boom, would be the foundation of Ives's vision of life, his soul, his song. No less would they be the source of his frustration and rage. His volcanic genius and his final creative burnout flowed from the same inheritance.

When Charles Ives's father returned home from schooling and war in 1868, still young and living again in the old Ives House on Main Street, Danbury was primed for its golden age. Accordingly, it was primed for what George Ives wanted to do, which was to provide for a family by playing and teaching music.

The Iveses had helped prepare the town's ascent after the war, and at the same time helped destine it to stagnation. As Danbury gradually tore down the elms and elegant houses that had graced Main Street, the town would consume its past in search of its future, betting too many of its chips on the hatting industry. Danbury never had the feeling for its past that Charles Ives would, the reason why in later years he could not bear to walk down the streets of his childhood. But in the decade after the Civil War most things seemed promising in the life of the town, and in a country filled with peace and new railroads, with time and money for music and the other embellishments of life. The golden age of Danbury kept pace with the Gilded Age of the United States.

After Johnny had come marching home and peace settled in, the town did not change dramatically in the years before Charles Ives was born. In winter, sleighs jingled through the streets and men harvested blocks of ice from the ponds. Tall elms still shaded Main Street, where in summer vendors sold ice cream from carts and circuses paraded to the glorious cacophony of bands and calliopes and crowds. On the verandas of the Wooster House and the Pahquioque Hotel the winter's ice harvest cooled August's mint juleps and brandy smashes. At the height of autumn the Danbury Fair spread its array of blue-ribbon cows and pigs and pumpkins, of prize domestics, of horticulture, orators, bands, and beer. In winter boys skated on the ponds, in spring they flew kites; baseball teams arrived with warm weather like butterflies. From the edge of town spread still unsullied the immemorial green Connecticut hills.

Through town every day floated its recording angel, James Montgomery Bailey, owner and editor of the weekly *News* and known nationwide as "the Danbury News Man."[1] His paper's motto: "News and Gossip without Politics." In his prime Bailey was nearly as famous a humorist as Mark Twain. His main subject, expressed in his newspaper column of small anecdote and observation, was his town and its people. In 1878: "It appears that the general idea . . . of an appropriate observance of the [Fourth of July] is to dress up, make a noise, or get drunk. The man who doesn't get drunk or make a noise goes on a picnic. . . . The four prominent ingredients of a popular Fourth are Starch, Ice Cream, Gin and Powder."[2]

After the war the Ives clan continued in prosperity. Sarah, George White's widow, anchored the family. Joe expanded his housewares store. Ike and his fellow entrepreneurs put up their factories and businesses mostly to the east of Main Street and north of the Wooster Square depot. The southwest part of town remained for a time like old Danbury—quiet streets with churches and handsome residences with well-kept lawns.[3] The Ives House lingered on Main Street as another relic of old Danbury, while elsewhere commercial buildings replaced one venerable house after another. In 1875 the house in which General Wooster died, perhaps the most hallowed place in Danbury, was razed in pursuit of Progress.[4]

In 1870 Danbury bustled, but still moderately; the boom began in the 1880s. Hatting factories hummed, there was little overt poverty, and wealthier citizens were disinclined to show off. At least a veneer of equality remained among the citizens.[5] The change from a pastoral village to a manufacturing center penetrated townsfolk's awareness only slowly. They still imagined their village to be the "pretty town with grand old trees and beautiful gardens" that it had been before the war. This nostalgia defined what Ike Ives called "fogyism," a lack of entrepreneurial spirit. In the long run, "progress" would triumph.

Seeming largely contented and cheerful in the pages of the *News*—and in the memory of Charles Ives—Danbury was also full of meannesses noted but not dwelled on. Pollution was endemic to the hatting industry; from the 1870s factory effluents increasingly clouded the streams that had drawn the original settlers to Pahquioque. Poisoned by the mercury used in felt processing, men went crazy in steady numbers or developed "hatter's shakes." In saloons, a man with bad shakes had to tie a rag to his wrist, loop it around his neck, and reel the glass to his lips. By the 1890s Danbury had become one of the thirstiest towns in Connecticut. At all hours in some eighty-five unregulated watering holes a man could get good and drunk and then be pitched into the street to sleep or roar it off. By way of competition to the saloons, the town boasted six temperance societies in 1883 Every day or so a runaway horse would run its berserk race through town. Wrote the Danbury News Man, "If there is one thing we glory in above another it is our manner of conducting runaways. . . . Our horses can run farther, breaking more wagons, kick higher, shatter more knee pans, and raise more dust than the horses of any other place in Connecticut."[6] Each season harvesting machinery claimed fingers, limbs, and a life or two from the ranks of farmers and curious children. Every few years an epizootic took its harvest of horses or cattle or townspeople. Said the *News* in 1870, "Small pox and scarlet fever are traveling together this summer." Rabies made regular appearances.[7]

None of this implies a shortage of fun. The grandest amusements were found in the streets at holidays and parades, and at Fair time. Charles Ives conjured up Danbury Fourths of July in a chain of images and sounds:

Cannon on the Green, Village Band on Main Street, fire crackers . . . Church bells, lost finger, fifes, clam-chowder, a prize-fight, drum-corps, burnt shins, parades (in and out of step), saloons all closed (more drunks than usual), Baseball game . . . pistols, mobbed umpire, Red, White and Blue, runaway horse,—and the day ends with a sky-rocket over the Church-steeple, just after the annual explosion sets the Town-Hall on fire."[8]

He wasn't exaggerating: in 1874 the *News* reported four fires on the Fourth, including the Danbury and Norwalk depot, plus fights and a stabbing and a man wounded by exploding powder. Earlier, at the end of May, came the relatively solemn ceremony of Decoration Day (later Memorial Day), which Charles Ives saw throughout his childhood: bands on the march and his father's cornet sounding over the graves of the Union dead. He wrote of that day,

After the Town Hall is filled with the Spring's harvest of lilacs, daisies, and peonies, the parade is slowly formed on Main Street. First come the three Marshals on plough horses (going sideways), then the Warden and Burgesses in carriages, the Village Cornet Band, the G.A.R., two by two, the Militia . . . , while the volunteer Fire Brigade, drawing the decorated hose-cart, with its jangling bells, brings up the rear—the inevitable swarm of small boys following. The march to Wooster Cemetery is a thing a boy never forgets. The roll of muffled drums and *Adeste Fidelis* [*sic*]* answer for the dirge. A little girl on the fencepost waves to her father and wonders if he looked like that at Gettysburg.

After the last grave is decorated, "Taps" sounds out through the pines and hicko-

---

* Occasionally in Ives's writings it seems appropriate to alert the reader to a misspelling or other irregularity in the original. Most have not been marked, however, so as to allow Ives expression uninterrupted by scholarly comment.

ries, while a last hymn is sung. Then the ranks are formed again and "we all march back
to town" to a Yankee stimulant—Reeves' inspiring *Second Regiment Quickstep*. . . . The
march stops—and in the silence the shadow of the early morning flower-song rises
over the Town, and the sunset behind West Mountain breathes its benediction upon
the Day.[9]

Such a day in springtime became one of the transforming experiences of
Ives's youth and one of the most beautifully realized works of his maturity. He
was to place his *Decoration Day* second in a four-season set called *Holidays*. The
others are *Washington's Birthday* (winter), *The Fourth of July* (summer), and
Thanksgiving (autumn). In those and its other festivals Danbury lived and
celebrated in harmony with the calendar, to each season its proper activities
and mood, from riotous excess to somber commemoration.

George Ives returned home from the Civil War in fine fettle. He had
founded and trained a first-rate army band; friends and musicians all over town
liked him. People might wonder why he was fooling around so much with
music to the detriment of his career, but for twenty years they would enjoy his
playing and turn out for his productions. An article in the *News* after George's
death would recall, "A soldier of the armies of the Republic in his seventeenth
year, he was always ready with reminiscences of the three years of the great
struggle . . . one of the raciest of story tellers, open minded, hearty, and frank
almost to bluffness, he had probably as many friends, endeared to him by
personal ties as any man, old or young, in our city."[10]

Three generations of the family lived with George in the old house. His
widowed mother Sarah had rooms upstairs over the kitchen, where she could
keep an eye on things. George settled into the big bedroom over the south
parlor; his bride would join him and their sons be born there. Brother Joe and
son Howard lived downstairs behind the north parlor; when Joe remarried,
his wife moved in and Howdie took a bedroom upstairs. Later, Charles Ives's
Uncle Lyman Brewster and Aunt Amelia came to live in the house. There
were always guests, visitors, wandering souls to be taken in. These included
George's black servant from the war, Henry Anderson Brooks, who had
chronically shaky health. George taught him music, the family helped support
his education at Hampton Institute in Richmond (Sarah had helped found the
school), and for twenty years the Iveses traded letters with him and sent barrels
of clothes.

Visiting friends might stay for a week or for months. Sometimes they
shared the guest rooms with strangers. One night an ailing and destitute
farmer and his wife appeared at the door during dinner (this story may be
from George White's time) having heard the Iveses would help them. The
couple lived with the family until the husband could return to work. Another
time a passing wagon train deposited a sick little girl with the family. Nursed
back to health, she was placed on the next wagon train west.[11] Charles Ives's

cousin Amelia Ives Van Wyck would jokingly call the family seat "an expandable house."[12]

Photos record the Victorian look of the interior: patterned wallpaper and rugs, fringed antimacassars on the chairs and mantels, rocking chairs, velvet sofa, old china and clangorous clocks, brass andirons, George White's square piano, and pictures upon pictures—historical, patriotic, and inspirational subjects, paintings and photographs of the family from old Isaac down to the current inhabitants. The house was filled with relics and with time, with voices

Uncle Ike and wife in front of the Old Ives House.

and echoes, and at night with a deep silence unknown to later town dwellers. Generations of Iveses grew up in that resonant texture of family living and legendry, of friends and supplicants and servants.

As brother Joe was rapt in his Transcendental reveries and brother Ike in his business schemes, and both knowing the value of publicity, George brought the family style to his own productions. A newspaper ad blared "GEO. E. IVES' POPULAR CONCERT" for July 2, 1869, at the Concert Hall. (A church refurbished into an auditorium by George White Ives among others, the little Concert Hall would be superseded in the center of town by the barrel-roofed Opera House, built in 1871.) The Danbury News Man, invariably a booster of local endeavors, cheered George's production. "[It will] undoubtedly prove the finest entertainment given to our public. His extensive acquaintance in the musical world, and his excellent knowledge of what is desired by the play going people of Danbury, will enable him to produce a programme that will be attractive in every feature."[13] The show involved a chorus of forty voices and an orchestra, plus George's New York teachers— Charles Foepple at the piano and Franz Schreiber on cornet. The program included a cornet duo "Zephyrs" played by George and Schreiber, Suppé's light-classical warhorse *The Poet and the Peasant,* and a novelty number arranged by George: a "Railroad Galop 'Across the Continent' with Imitations by Chas. Schleyer."[14] The concert finished with a glorioso rendition of "America" by the full forces, the audience invited to join in.[15]

With this production George introduced himself to the town as a concert artist and promoter, mounting the sort of entertainment for which he would become known—light classics, popular vocal and instrumental items, virtuoso cornet solos, and novelties sometimes imaginative, sometimes cheesy: his "burlesque opera" on Romeo and Juliet, the "Humanophone" that his son would fondly remember.

George involved himself in every sort of musical activity. Most visibly he directed bands, several of them over the years in the fluid milieu of amateur and semiprofessional music in Danbury. First he pulled together what had been for years an erratic situation with smatterings of financial support. In the 1860s some citizens had written letters to the paper expressing outrage that the band expected to get paid for playing at events. Music was something you were supposed to do for fun, and for free.[16] This attitude gradually gave way to something approaching professionalism. In January 1870 the Danbury News Man groused, " 'What has become of our Cornet Band?' is a very pertinent conundrum. Here is the Brewster band getting a professor from New York, and the Carmel band importing a live somebody from England. Why can't our band secure somebody equally remote and grand?" Somebody unremote, probably George Ives, replied testily to the paper, signing himself "A Member":

A brass band, like many other institutions, is not self supporting. Let Danbury take as much interest in her band as Brewster and Carmel do in theirs and you will not have to ask, *"Where is our band?"* . . . With one single exception no citizen has ever given directly one cent for the support of the same. . . . [The town-owned instruments] will not execute music without somebody behind them, and somebody to teach those who get behind.[17]

For a while after that George directed his own Ives Cornet Band and occasionally a group sponsored by its namesake, the Bartram & Fanton Sewing Machine Company.[18] By 1874 that company had failed and George's group was officially styled the Danbury Brass and Quadrille Band. usually called simply the Danbury or Ives Band.[19] The paper commenced its "remarkable progress," but in September 1874 George wrote to the paper in some frustration,

At present Danbury is "afflicted" with only one brass band. It seems necessary on the part of the band, to explain to a part of the public, how it is that they can't always play "for fun!" In the first place, it costs somebody almost one hundred dollars for the first outfit (uniform and instrument) of each member. . . . The present Danbury Band have never asked or received any help from the public, except as in pay for services rendered; yet it has survived for quite a while by its own personal endeavors . . . and made the thing pay for itself after a fashion. . . . So please talk up a good price even if you don't pay it individually, and if we don't play as well as the prize band of this world, don't help us downhill with your mouths and we'll endeavor to deserve whatever praise or pay we may get.

In 1875, George teamed up with drummer John Wilson of the rival Wheeler & Wilson Band and solidified his group with a number of the area's best players.[20] Rival outfits would come and go, but the ones George led would remain *the* Danbury Band.

In July 1876 the *News* advised, "The town is large enough and there are occasions enough for the employment of a band." With that, Danbury jumped on a nationwide bandwagon. Musical propagandist G. F. Patton wrote in 1875, "In this age the horn blowing organizations are recognized as essential elements in the great march of popular enlightenment, and a town that . . . must send off and hire assistance from its neighbors on all public occasions, cannot lay claim to having reached a very high standard of advancement."[21] A Chicago paper editorialized in 1911 that a band was "as great a blessing and almost as much a necessity to real civilization as fresh air or pure water."[22]

Wind bands had existed around the country before the Civil War, but their heyday came after. Brass groups had been involved in the glorious part of the war, the part people chose mainly to remember. The bright clamor of horns and drums and cymbals and groups of men marching in splendid array became essential to civic pomp and pride. The groups went under various monikers, most commonly *brass band* or *cornet band*. Outside church and home, they were most often what one heard of instrumental music in towns.

Beyond popular enthusiasm, thousands of musical veterans wanted to keep playing and to hang on to the masculine camaraderie they had found in the army. In an age of joiners, bands took their place among a potpourri of lodges and societies—Masons, Moose, Elks, Red Men, and similar fauna—as a means for men to socialize and drink and enjoy themselves, to escape from the feminized world of family, church, temperance, and sissified Culture. One did find the occasional ladies' band, usually regarded with patronizing irony. (At one point George Ives formed an all-girl cornet band.)

Writes onetime band director Jonathan Elkus: "Typically, bandsmen are big-hearted, fair minded, well read, resourceful, and fun loving. They are a tough, resilient, all-weather breed and the legs, lungs and ears are remarkably hardy. They have almost insatiable appetites for novelty as well as for tradition. . . . They are almost fanatically devoted to their own band, which 'is not an organization,' as the saying goes, 'but a way of life.' "[23] George Ives, an enthusiast, a man's man ready with a war memory or a racy story, who ruled by means of good spirits and competence and commitment, was the ideal director for these collections of amateurs and semiprofessionals.

A good time was the galvanizing idea, in the playing or otherwise. In summer 1878 the paper reported George's band and orchestra enjoying "a bivalvular repast" in Brookfield, as guests of fiddler John Starr. Next month George and a nine-member group working on the Newark steamer *Adelphi* were so busy admiring lady bathers on Rockaway Beach that they missed the boat home.[24] On an earlier evening, in 1873, George's band and a group of townsfolk went to Brookfield for some playing and dancing, and there were joined by the Newtown Cornet Band. With the evening going fine and about 400 folks busy singing and dancing, one of the bands tried marching past the other, each playing away on its own. Reported the News Man: "the two bands fused and the music that vibrated among the halls of old Brookfield ["Hail, Columbia"] was of an inspiring nature."[25]

The holding-your-own game between bands happened often in parades, sometimes by accident and sometimes by design. A player of the era wrote, "The band's idea of musical superiority was to blow louder than an oncoming band on the countermarch, and thereby drown it out."[26] It was characteristic of George Ives that once in a while he would set two groups marching past each other, to see what would happen. Danburian Philip Sunderland recalled George sending one contingent around the park playing one tune and another in the opposite direction with another tune, the two repeatedly passing each other on the march, the din becoming more strident as they approached.[27] Probably George stayed in the middle, listening to the clashes rising and falling. *How,* he would be thinking, *does distance affect dissonance?* It was part of his curiosity about sound, the experimental streak that would find historic responses in his son.

There was another dimension to bands that went beyond their civic and fraternal roles and spoke for larger American ideals. Part of the point of bands was that they existed for everybody. The Minneapolis *Tribune* wrote in 1875, "These concerts are the contribution of art to the people, to be enjoyed by the occupant of the humblest cabin and by the master of a mansion, and harmonizing all classes in the democracy of music." After the concert, of course, rulers and ruled returned to their places. But bands existed as a model of democracy in action, and that tradition would contribute its part to the dreams of Charles Ives.

He and his father also appreciated that town bands integrated all levels of ability. If the notes and the beat got the worst of it in this democracy of competence, at least everyone was enjoying himself. Ives's riotous *Fourth of July* features drunken cornet players falling off the beat and mixing up the crook attachments that changed the horns' key, so some end up blaring away in the wrong key. *Country Band March* ends revealing a hapless saxophonist playing an extra couple of beats. "Bandstuff," Ives wrote to one of his long-suffering copyists; "they didn't always play right & together & it was as good either way."[28]

In larger cities bands could number fifty or more members—up to thousands in some of the jubilees of the day—but towns like Danbury tended to have a group of around fifteen men wielding some assortment of cornets, trumpets, trombones, alto, tenor, and baritone horns, tubas, and drums. Usually the first cornetist led. Instrumentation was serendipitous; you made do with who you had and the more the merrier. If a couple of fiddlers were handy they joined in, and woodwinds made their way increasingly into town bands: a flute or clarinet can't sound out on the march like a brass horn, but they're useful for sitdown occasions. By 1889 George's band had grown to twenty-four regulars, including two piccolos, six clarinets, and a saxophone.

The group matched the occasion. In the course of a couple of days, George might lead an afternoon parade with his full band, conduct his theater orchestra that night, play a church social next noon with his String Band or Quartette Brass Instrumentalists, then board an excursion boat or a D&N passenger train with a small group, everywhere playing roughly the same repertoire of popular and light-classical numbers—polkas, galops, waltzes, songs. Around his hectic playing schedule, George also taught a good percentage of the town's children piano, violin, cornet, music theory, and whatever else was called for.

In other words, as a proper bandmaster he had to do considerably more than man his horn and keep the beat. He had constantly to arrange and rearrange pieces for the shifting groups under his command, and if possible compose things for special occasions. George Ives's training in theory and orchestration had prepared him for that job. He would teach the bandmaster's crafts to his son, who from then on viewed his material and its instrumental garb as malleable, like band music. Charlie grew up watching his father at his desk nearly every day, grunting and humming to himself as he wrote out his arrangements.[29] That appeared to the boy a normal and exemplary way tᴏ live.

In the 1870s George Ives settled into a cluttered and sometimes exhilarating life of directing music, teaching, and performing on cornet and violin and other instruments ranging from trombone to basset horn to slide trumpet. (He had the latter made so he could follow the wandering pitch of a church congregation. It was their right to get off pitch, he believed, and his job to follow them.[30]) One or another outfit of his might turn up at most any public occasion, sacred, secular, or verging on sinful: parades, concerts in Elmwood Park or at the Wooster House bandstand, Opera House productions, weddings, church services and socials, camp meetings, store openings, dances, horse races, ball games, the Fireman's Strawberry Festival, the skating rink, Grand Army of the Republic campouts, Women's Christian Temperance Union theatricals, the Fat Man's Clam Bake, extravaganzas and jubilees of all varieties, and excursions of the steamer *Adelphi* (until the ship's boiler blew up in September 1878, killing fifteen, when George didn't happen to be aboard).[31] On Sundays for ten years starting in 1878, George played cornet and later conducted the choir at the Methodist church.[32] In the 1880s he conducted the Danbury High School orchestra.

Every year or so George mounted a show in the Opera House, among them Gilbert and Sullivan productions with all-local talent. The level of performance seems often to have been beyond what anyone thought possible. "One time a visiting orchestra came to Danbury to give a concert, and something happened to the conductor," recalled George's grand-niece Amelia Van Wyck, "so George took over and conducted the strange orchestra, much to the nervousness of the family. They wondered how it would go, but it went very well. George was more capable than Danbury expected him to be."[33]

In his accustomed musical settings, though, George's contributions were credited, his skills eulogized in the pages of the *News:* "Geo. E. Ives' cornet solo had to be repeated as a matter of course, for George is a master at the cornet, and its clear sweet tones were heartily welcomed."[34] "For a band of fifteen pieces we do not hesitate to pronounce [the Danbury Cornet Band] the best in the State."[35] "The concert at the Opera House last night was, as is always the case when Mr. Ives undertakes anything of the kind, a complete success."[36] "We had the pleasure, yesterday, of hearing Mr. George E. Ives play the new Distin light-action cornet, with their patent echo, and were pleased with the beautiful effect it produced . . . in fact, a perfect echo. . . . Mr. Ives played us the 'Sweet By and By,' echoing each strain of the chorus."[37]

Charles Ives's memories of his father's playing, especially of George's trademark hymn "Sweet By and By," amplify these reports:

[There was] something about the way Father played hymns. Even if some of the choir could read music readily at the rehearsals, he always liked to play each part over with his horn, and have them get it entirely through listening. . . . He had the gift of putting something in the music which meant more sometimes than when some people sang the words. . . . Somebody heard him play the *Erlking* (Schubert) and felt that he sang it (through the basset horn or trombone, I forget which it was) and carried him away with it, without the words.[38]

Until nearly the end of his life, George would function in town as "that moving and controlling spirit in our musical matters," as the paper called him in 1872. A New York *Herald* article of January 5, 1890, headlined "Danbury's Delight is All for Music," notes that George "has probably done more for instrumental music than any other man" in the most musical town in Connecticut.

George moved and controlled, did more than anyone else, and Danburians applauded his programs with delight. Then they went home and wondered when he would get a life. Many years later his grand-niece Amelia Van Wyck observed, probably echoing her businessman father, "George became the bandmaster. Of course Danbury thought that that was just kind of foolishness. Music and art were not things that you really worked at. They were entertainment."[39] A 1910 obituary of brother Ike mentions George, who "by reason of death was not permitted to enjoy the benefit of his study and labor."[40] The study and labor in question were not in music but rather in the Danbury Savings Bank, where George worked as a teller in his last, frustrating years. The town had little notion of how seriously he took music, how hard and imaginatively he worked at it, how much he really knew. He would be remembered as someone who, unlike the other Iveses, never found his place or his fortune.

With father and son alike, it seemed to take a long time to sink in that hardly anyone took their art seriously, that they were only the bandmaster or only the organist or the Sunday composer. Their marginality was among the things that held them together. Until these debilitating truths fully sank in— in their forties for both—they would flourish in their work, bringing the family enthusiasm to everything they pursued, and consider themselves a vital force in their community just like the rest of the Iveses.

As a bandmaster's son meanwhile, Charles Ives inherited that medium, or rather an idealized version of it, as part of his fundamental inspiration. Near the end of his creative life he wrote, "In 'thinking up' music I usually have some kind of a brass band with wings on it in back of my mind."[41]

So in Danbury after the war, between 1869 and 1874, George Ives pulled together a sort of career and started his family. By the time of his first big concert in 1869, his inheritance and army bounty had nearly run out and he could not find enough musical piecework to support him. For the time being

George did what everyone doubtless expected him to—he went into the family business. In March 1870 the Danbury *News* announced, "George E. Ives has taken the business of Ives Brothers on White Street, where he will promptly serve all in want of builders' hardware, etc." His relatively modest ads would appear in the paper along with Ike's and Joe's showy ones. In October 1870 "a brass band, a song, several teams and a brace of men" drew attention to Bartram & Fanton sewing machines at George's store.[42] Occasionally he would do freelance bookkeeping for companies. Like musicians through the centuries, he made his living on a little bit of this and that.

It's a good guess that for those few years in business George conformed to the family mold without enthusiasm. He had observed brother Joe's frustration at spending his days running a store when his heart lay in books and ideas. Chances are that the better music paid, the less George was seen around the Ives Brothers store. One way and another, he was earning his way now. It was time to contemplate a family.

George had probably worked with Mrs. Mary Smith Parmelee, Danbury's leading church singer. Widow Parmelee possessed an available daughter, named Mary Elizabeth but called Mollie—tiny and doeishly pretty, with dark hair and luminous eyes. Born on a Redding farm, Mollie was one of six children of Mary and a square-jawed storekeeper named Noah Parmelee, who had died when she was three. (Noah spent his spare time tinkering with perpetual-motion machines, a fact that intrigued his composer grandson.[43]) Socially the Parmelees were somewhere en route from the country to a more sophisticated town life. Most of Mollie's family lived in Danbury including her mother, merchant brother Sam, and spinster sister Lucy. Mollie and George began courting, became engaged, and were married on January 1, 1874, at the Methodist Episcopal Church. He was twenty-eight, she twenty-four.

Mollie remains a mystery in the Ives chronicles, surprising in a family usually loquacious about itself. Her sons faithfully saw to her needs to the end of her life, but Charles Ives rarely mentioned his mother and neither did the rest of the family. What we know of her comes from scattered scraps of stories. It appears that Mollie's concerns turned entirely around family and household and garden. Henry and Sidney Cowell's biography, based on information from their subject, describes her as "a staunch friend, a conscientious New England housewife forever trying to keep rubbers on her husband and sons, and to inveigle them into starched collars."[44] She was not particularly interested in music or learning or ideas: that was men's stuff. Her letters reveal her as semiliterate. Charles Ives's wife would describe Mollie as "a determined little woman . . . only 90 pounds."[45] She was not afraid to flag down the New York train between stations (the incident became family legend)[46] or to interrupt her son's musical practice to send him on an errand.[47] When in 1924 the old Ives House was moved up the hill out of the way of commerce, it moved with stubborn Mollie Ives sitting inside.[48] In later life she proclaimed herself prouder of her son's musical accomplishments than of his success in business.[49] One would like to know how she felt at the time those accomplishments were taking shape, and if she contributed to them.

What attracted George to Mollie? One can only speculate. He saw a handsome woman on his arm and a good homemaker, and maybe that was all he wanted. Her family was well below the Iveses on the social scale. On the whole the Iveses were no snobs, but certainly Mollie's background was noted, especially by his sister Amelia. George, for his part, was more an extroverted sort than a thinker like Joe, and had no social ambitions like Amelia. While his son would paint a picture of George as a thoughtful and innovative musician, that seems only partly to fit the original. Amelia Van Wyck remembered her great-uncle as "a very genial person, but . . . you wouldn't think of him as being a deep philosopher."[50] He was a remarkable musician for his setting, but Charles Ives did not recall, or did not know, his father the racy storyteller, the admirer of bathing beauties on outings with the band.

Perhaps Mollie suited George also because he was too busy for intellectual stimulation at home, given his practicing and rehearsing and performing and conducting all over the map, making a living where he could, spending his spare time experimenting with the materials of music—his multiple ensembles, his quarter-tone instruments. George was not creative but rather curious and inquiring and skeptical of tradition. Something like Noah Parmelee but on a more sophisticated level, George was a Yankee tinker, a maker of gadgets that never quite pulled together. From Mollie he asked for forbearance and a smooth-running family, and apparently he got them.

On October 20, 1874, less than ten months after the wedding, their first son, Charles Edward Ives, made his appearance in the bedroom over the south parlor. Unlike most Iveses he was not named for an ancestor; his given name may have been chosen in honor of George's teacher, Charles Foepple. Father and son shared a middle name and the family sometimes called both "Eddy."[51] On his scores the composer would sign his name Charles E. Ives, echoing his father's George E. Ives. Of course there is symbolism here: the son inheriting the substance of his father and family but his own man too, unique in a clan full of singular characters.

Charles Ives grew up amidst a big close family and his father's incessant music-making, with a good part of the town streaming past his house every day. His surroundings, his upbringing, his lifestyle, and his music would all be notable for their crowdedness.

In the Danbury *News* we read that in October 1874, the month of Charles Ives's birth, the sixth annual Danbury Fair provoked the usual excitement. Businessmen and Fair visitors filled the Wooster House and Turner House. One afternoon a team of horses bolted through town, apparently spooked by the playing of Bacon's Band; when the band stopped, so did the horses. New regulations decreed gas streetlamps must be lighted whenever moonlight was weak and be turned off at 11 P.M. The Flora Myers dramatic troupe and Blind Tom, the Musical Wonder, drew good crowds at the Opera House. The current population was around 9,000.[52] Hat factories raced to satisfy the new fashion for ladies' fur bonnets; the Tweedy Co. was shipping 500 dozen a day. Ives & Hoyt—Joe had a partner at the time—advertised carpets, furniture, kitchenware, wallpaper, parlor stoves, ranges. Ike Ives's lumberyard blazoned "Dry Lumber Way Down." The Golden Stars baseball club whipped the Young Americans 20 to 2. A new team was being organized, to consist exclusively of men weighing over 200 pounds. The Bartram & Fanton Sewing Machine Company, sponsor of George Ives's band, went bust (eventually St. Peter's Catholic Church would become his sponsor). A peculiar white bat was observed flitting about the streets. A young lady attempted to hang herself from a lamppost, "but only succeeded in hanging her bonnet." Passersby foiled a robbery on Main Street. Mrs. Folsom advertised musical instruction. "Miss Borie, the gifted *soprano* who recently made such a favorable impression at the Opera House, sings at Mrs. Folsom's concert at the Turner House tomorrow evening. . . . A *soiree dansante* follows." Genteel Danburians were fond of *soirée*s.

When Charlie was one and a half and Mollie ready to deliver her second baby, she ordered George and his violin out of the house to practice in the family barn up the hill. Day after day the toddler sat in Uncle Joe's buggy playing with the whip while his father fiddled.[53] Aunt Amelia wrote approvingly to her mother that "Charlie will sit for an hour at a time" listening.[54] His brother and only sibling came along on February 5, 1876, and was christened Joseph Moss Ives after his uncle Joseph Moss, who in turn had been named for old Isaac's father-in-law Joseph Moss White. Once more needing to distinguish which generation they were talking about, the family called the new baby Mossie. Danbury would know him in adulthood as Judge J. Moss Ives. For some time, as his older brother presumably had been, Mossie was decked out in the era's standard boy-toddler outfit of dress and Little Lord Fauntleroy ringlets. Pictures survive of one-year-old Mossie in that getup, one of them with three-year-old Charlie posing by his side with the same bright, self-possessed expression he would have in photographs for the rest of his life (though without his later sheepishness before the camera). Moss's looks were a bit of a sport in the family—thick-lipped, heavy-lidded, and lugubrious. As a baby he already looked like a judge.

By the time Moss was born, George Ives seems largely to have extricated himself from his brothers' businesses—no longer advertising in the paper, and looking to sell the store on White Street.[55] Now he would see if he could make a go of it in music; there was always bookkeeping to fall back on. He appeared regularly in town with his band, at the Opera House with his Standard Orchestra, and here and there with other detachments. Since he could not get along playing and teaching and bookkeeping only in town, he worked all over the area and into New York State. Just after Charlie's second birthday in 1876, George went out on the first of six annual tours with minstrel shows.[56] A couple of years later he traveled for a month and appeared in Danbury with the Swedish Lady Vocal Quartette, "The Finest Company of Lady Quartette Singers Known."[57] For long stretches of his sons' boyhood, George would be out of town.

He remained nonetheless an overwhelming presence. Charlie probably saw the grand ceremonies led by his father at the reopening of Elmwood Park, with its new bandstand, in the summer of 1879. Some 4,000 Danburians showed up. The paper described the evening in words resembling some of Charles Ives's later reminiscences:

On the arrival of the evening train of the Danbury and Norwalk Railway there was quite a throng of people and teams in front of the station. The two Bethel bands came by this train and were met by the St. Peters band. [George directed all three.[58]] The

Charlie and Moss Ives around 1878.

three bands consolidated and . . . appeared on Main Street playing a march . . . flanked by a throng of delighted people and followed by an army of teams. Approaching the Park the sight ahead was an inspiring one. The dark outline of the trees, the moving masses beneath the colored lanterns, the lights in the buildings and the spray from the fountain formed a spectacle that was very pretty and called forth involuntary exclamations of delight.[59]

The next May saw another of the spectacles this pre–radio-and-television era delighted in, when the new memorial to the town's Civil War dead was dedicated on May 27, 1880. Much of the town was decked with flags and bunting. In spite of rain and muddy streets, everyone turned out to see the new thirty-two-foot-high granite column, covered with streamers and wreaths. George's band led the parade. The *News* noted that the Ives House sported a large flag, and "a little son of G. E. Ives, dressed in national colors, sat in front

The Soldiers' Monument in the middle of Danbury, decorated for a holiday in 1888.

and saluted the colors."[60] Standing in the space once occupied by the Concert Hall, the Soldiers' Monument had been erected after a long campaign by Iveses and other prominent townsfolk, mostly ladies. It would become the omphalos of Danbury, the center of its consciousness.[61]

Another day, smaller in scale but more prophetic, appears among the earliest memories of Charles Ives's life: *Papa is standing in the back garden in the middle of a thunderstorm, listening to the ringing of the bell from the Congregational church next door. Papa runs inside to the piano and tries to make the sound, but he can't find the notes to make the piano sound like the bell. With growing exasperation he runs outside over and over again, listening hard, trying again and again to find it on the piano, and Mama shouting at Papa for his foolishness.*

In the 1930s Charles Ives added a postscript to the memory: George decided that to re-create the bell he needed notes "in the cracks between the piano keys." He began to experiment with microtones, and to hell with his inborn perfect pitch. He tried tuned glasses, a clothespress strung with violin strings. "Everything in life is relative," George would explain. "Nothing but fools and taxes are absolute."[62] His son's music would be full of the sounds of bells, near and faraway.

Boyhood. Flying through doors into summer's sun or into winter's crackling chill, playing in cricket-loud fields, joining clubs and teams, sleeping over at Gramma's. The names of people and places and holidays full of music and magic, like eternal forms: *Main Street. The Soldiers' Monument. Danbury Fair. The Fourth of July. Wooster House Bandstand. Darien. Bridgeport. Aunt Amelia. Uncle Lyman. Starr. Parmelee. Ives. Papa.*

Charlie and Mossie grew apace, family life changing around them. About 1880 Aunt Amelia decided that she and Lyman were going to take over George and Mollie's room in the family house. Amelia did not appreciate opposition to her wishes. George was obliged to establish his family a few blocks away in a house at 16 Stevens Street.[63] Amelia would live in the old house until she died in 1918, at which point widowed Mollie finally moved back.

By the time they moved out, George had probably begun teaching music to Charlie.[64] Many years later the composer was to tell the story, gussied up a little probably, of how it began. His father arrived home one day to find his five-year-old (or thereabouts) trying to play the band's drum parts on the parlor piano with his fists. Maybe George had been waiting for that moment. "It's all right to do that, Charles," Ives remembered his father saying, "*if* you know what you're doing." George sent his son downstreet for drum lessons at the barbershop of Charles Schleyer, the First Connecticut bandsman from the war. Between customers Schleyer taught the boy drum technique on an upended tub.[65] Presumably Charlie's studies with his father began soon after that, with piano. He would go on to study organ, violin, cornet, orchestration, and music theory.[66] George started Charlie on keyboard and then handed him over to other teachers, but he remained Charlie's mentor in music theory, conventional and otherwise.

In August 1882, just before his eighth birthday, Charles Ives made what may have been his public debut as a musician: he played bass drum in a Methodist church concert by his father's all-girl cornet band.[67] Around then he also appeared in one of George's Gilbert and Sullivan productions, a little boy raising his voice in song: *Jack is every inch a sailor, / Five and twenty years a whaler.*[68]

From early on Charles Ives shared his father's musical life, developing a range of skills and applying them to whatever situations came along. From age twelve or so, already a good pianist, Charlie would occasionally play snare drum in George's band.[69] Two years after that he debuted as a professional organist. In deference to the neighbors, Charlie continued to practice drum parts on piano. Most children who study music outgrow the piano-banging stage, or are discouraged from it. Charlie was never discouraged and never outgrew it. His father had begun to teach him harmony, so for a while Charlie tried using standard chords to represent the drums—bass drum on the low keys, snare on the high. But that didn't seem to do the trick. "Triads and chords without bites were quite out of place, or any combinations that suggested fixed tonalities." So the boy began to make up his own chords, some of them involving handfuls of adjacent notes,[70] improvising drum music at the keyboard with these percussive harmonies. (Forty years later, Modernist composers would call them *tone clusters*.)

Charlie's intentions at that point were not avant-gardist but rather pragmatic and imitative: the father had tried to conjure a bell on piano, so the son tried a drum, which was easier anyway. Charlie also experimented with bell-like sounds at the keyboard. These complex sonorities would be a leading feature of his mature style—innovations used to conjure up something beyond the notes. For as long as harmony had existed in Western music, every composer had grown up writing the same chords. Charles Ives may have been the first to begin in childhood finding his own harmonies, not lost chords but ones never heard before. For him as for the coming generations of creators, harmonic discoveries would become an integral part of composing.

In these ways Charles Ives's involvement with tradition and with innovation began together, both stimulated and supervised by his father. It would be some time before Charlie began to understand the implications of his experiments. So far it was a boy's horsing around, his father alternately tightening and loosening the reins.

Fifty years later, Charles Ives would write of his father's "remarkable understanding of the ways of a boy's heart and mind."[71] George evolved his ideas of education and his expectations as he observed the results in his sons. Moss was not pressured toward music; he would play a little flute and banjo, but his interests seemed more literary, like Uncle Lyman Brewster's. George gave his spectacularly talented older son mounting challenges and responsibilities, but also allowed him room to be a boy.

Charlie started at New Street Public School in 1881, and did well at first. He seems to have learned his letters before he started school. From the year before, a note from Charlie to Aunt Amelia survives, written on letterhead from her husband's law office next door (Lyman was probably looking after Charlie). Charlie calls Amelia "Millie":

Aunt millie i have wrote to you for hte fun fo it. I have a sour toe. how is clams. I have nothing out of my garden. my name was in the newspaper for I worked for the school . my head aches for I mus leave you now. good by. Charlie Ives.[72]

Much of what remains of Charles Ives's day-to-day boyhood comes from Mossie's diary, begun in March 1885 and kept sporadically for a few years. In his brother's words we find a ten-year-old musician already juggling the conflicting demands of art and life:

This morning I went down street with Ben Mason and Charlie On the way I met Arthur Nut with his byecyicle and so we went with him Charlie and I stopped to grammas and Charlie got his Byecyicle and I got my velosipede And we all went up to my house Art Nut and Charlie went up to cousin Charlie Merritt's hat shop when they came back Charlie went into the house to pratis so Art Nut and I went down on West street to ride our velosipedes when Arthur Nut went home I rode home and when I got there he was starting to take his music lesson so I went over to play with [cousin] Sammie Parmelee an half of a xcur when the time come home I went home and got my dinner this after I went with papa and Charlie to East Danbury to buy some doughnuts.[73]

Next day, Sunday, Mossie "went to church with papa and blowed the organ." (Before organs were electrified, the wind chest had to be pumped by hand.) At the end of March there was a practice at the house for the old-folks concert and Mossie and Charlie built a snowman. At the concert on April 1 Charlie sang in a duet.[74]

The diary for that April of 1885 notes one of the games that absorbed the boys for a good deal of their childhood. Wrote Mossie, "Charlie and I made a Railroad Office Charlie rides his bycicle and I keep office. . . . After school Sammie Parmelee came over and Sam and I kept railroad office and Charlie was the cars."[75] In 1914, a midnight composer in a white-hot creative stretch and also a businessman commuting on trains, Charles Ives jotted down a meditation on his childhood pretend railroad, reaching characteristically from the nostalgic to the philosophical:

Travelling down & back to Redding now every day—a sleepless night when I was 10 years old or so always preceded a trip to New York in the cars from Danbury. The excitement & anticipation was greater than a trip to England would be now . . . the only hard part of commuting now is that each time I fear I may get further & further away from my boytime dreams . . .

So. Wilton, Winnipauk, Darien . . . names that had a mystical meaning in imagination. . . . Trains were run on the Ives Bros RR under the clothes line to these places & back a hundred times a week and every time we made a new acquaintance—Manlove the left fielder on the Danbury nine . . . said he had rather play a cornet like father than make a home run every inning. . . .

The two barrels on the wash bench, an old stove pipe & the dinner bell . . . the cab was part of a chicken coop a brass spittoon was the sand box but the most realistic touch was a medicine indicator clock for a steam gauge. The engineer had to jump up & turn the hands (when no one was looking) & then "sissle" until his siliva dissappeared. The whistle was the weak point we could find no substitute for our voices so we started by taking turns, Moss would whistle for the cross roads & I for the stations. Then one day we rec'd a blow—real engines only had one whistle & it always sounded the same. So I decided to do the "whistle" & Moss the "sizzling." . . . Somehow or other dinner time always came when we were in So. Norwalk & we couldn't make the folks at the table stop talking as if we were in Danbury—also town rumor had it that no one in So. Norwalk ate anything but clams & that made it necessary to turn bread & milk into shellfish but a sudden relief from this came when one day Moss saw a brakeman eating an apple pie in the So Norwalk Station restaurant.

Father never disturbed our mental processes when we were at play. He always entered into it seriously. He seemed to know when we were going slowly or a mile a minute & would just wave & never stop to talk while the train was going. At that time I remember, he was practicing the violin several hours a day . . . father discovered that staccato passages & arpeggios sounded like the clicking of the car wheels especially when they were going over switches. So he would come down of an afternoon in the rear passenger car for whole trips at a time. . . . I remember . . . the noise of the wheels always stop[ped] at the stations, sometimes 2 or 3 measures late—but we knew that was the fault of the air breaks. . . .

How thankful we feel now, that father dreamed with us, how circumspect our lives would be now if he hadn't.

I have an idea that we felt then sub-consciously the fun was when the sunrise would . . . start to throw its color & hope into our attic bedroom, we would lie a while & live ahead the day to come. It was our enthusiasm & plans seemed most inspiring & throughout the day an underlying stimulant was the hope of "grasping a real throttle."

If dualism is a true theory of the physical world of life there must be some similar theory in spiritual organization—faith—& the realization [of] ideals & their fulfillment. It is always the "minute after" that everyone lives. Immortality is a component substance we have now, that must be full of hope. Riding up and down from Redding, as I do now, might stifle it if we hadn't had our RR under the clothes line.[76]

A few months after Mossie's first diary entries about the train, he reports on another long-running game: "After breakfast our Orchestra meet. After that Charlie and I went down to grammas to play with our grocery store."[77] For several years the boys ran a make-believe store in the woodshed behind the Ives House. Charlie and Moss purveyed real goods and kept books, relying on family and neighbors for business. A photo shows the store in its glory, Charlie in hat and knickers examining the books, Moss posing sturdily in front, and stacks of goods topped by prices and ads ("PYLE'S PEARLINE for easy washing").[78] Here the boys revealed the salesman in their blood, which in Charlie would run truer than in his brother or his father.

George entered into this game too. In July 1886, when eleven-year-old Charlie was vacationing at "Cousin's Beach" (Lyman's vacation house on the coast at Westbrook), he wrote to his father back in Danbury,

Mama received your letter last night. I am very sorry you could not come Saturday and stay Sunday. I am having a nice time down here. Us boys have got an engine fixed up on the beach near the bath house. Mossie is the Conductor and brakeman, Joe King is the fireman & I am the engineer. I am glad the concert at Patterson was a success. . . . Moss & I are goining to change are firm Instead of Abbotts Bros [so it would be first in the town directory] we are going to have it Ives Bros. Will you please take the sign down & letter it on the other side Ives Bros 165 & 167 (like this).[79]

George did as requested; the photo of the play store shows a neatly painted sign, just as Charlie drew it on the page. A note from Charlie to Aunt Amelia that summer is on company letterhead: IVES BROS / GROCERIES / MAIN ST DANBURY.

It was just after this summer of 1886, it appears, that Charlie hit on another grown-up game to play. He began to write music.

Charlie and Moss Ives with their store in the woodshed, Charlie with the books. He already understands the importance of advertising.

An Apprenticeship

 On MAY 11, 1887, twelve-year-old Charles Ives made his debut as an emerging piano virtuoso, playing a showy, slight *Tarantella* in a recital by students of Misses Ella Hollister, Belle Fayerweather, and Florence Rice.[1] After studying piano with his father from about age five, for the past two years or so Charlie had been taking piano, and probably organ, with Miss Hollister, who was organist and choirmaster of the Disciples Church.[2] One imagines the evening as the archetypal American piano recital: an occasion of girls and a couple of embarrassed boys, long on middle-class gentility and short on skill. Other pieces on the program included "Chirping Crickets" and "Fire-Balls." Presumably Charlie made a good account of himself, but he was not yet receiving the newspaper reviews that would come with his mounting abilities. Within two years he would be a professional organist.

The previous autumn, between runs of his make-believe train, Charlie may have first tried composing. Only the title page survives of his "Schoolboy March" of September 1886. Grandly headed "OP.1," the page contains a few measures of a nebulous $\frac{6}{8}$ tune on hand-drawn staves (maybe those measures are as far as he got). In contrast to Charlie's letter handwriting, which was relatively neat in those years, this page shows unfamiliarity with his father's music pen; the notation begins with a blot and the writing is ragged and inexpert. By the end of 1886 he had composed at least two more pieces, the surviving copies in George Ives's hand—a fiddle tune called "New Year's Dance," and a minuetto. The next year he produced over a half dozen little pieces including a polonaise for two cornets and piano, vocal works for church, and pieces for organ. With his growing mastery as a keyboard player, an accelerating performance schedule, and his newfound game of composing, his musical career was gearing up.

When Charlie was eleven or so, George decided to aim his son toward a career as a concert pianist.[3] One cannot say how long a run this fantasy had, or when George's feelings evolved to the point that he would counsel his son to stay out of music entirely. Charlie would become an exceptional keyboard player during his apprentice years, but he specialized in the organ. Besides his attraction to composing, Charlie lacked a soloist's personality that loves striding onstage and playing for admiring crowds. He was painfully shy from the outset, likely more so as he moved into his teens. Said an acquaintance, "I heard him introduced to a young lady, and the result is very typical of Ives as a young man . . . he hemmed and hawed, and he said, 'Look at the salt on the tennis court,' and then he turned abruptly and ran away."[4]

Timid as he was, Charlie could sit on an organ bench, out of sight of the congregation and in his own world, and function in a familiar context. No one applauds in church anyway. He could also sit out of public view (for much of his life out of public hearing as well) and put notes on paper—for love of the work, in search of wisdom in music and in life, and in hopes that someday somebody might care to listen.

In May 1889 George Ives moved Mollie and the boys, for the second and final time, to a new home on Chapel Place just behind the Ives House on Main. Once the structure had been the family barn and Chapel Place the path to it. Matriarch Sarah Ives had proposed the idea of rebuilding the barn and probably paid for the job; true to form, George's sister Amelia daily supervised the carpenters' work. George's family would live in the lower two of the three floors and rent out the top. When it was finished, some months after they moved in, they had a roomy house for four, with a kitchen, dining room, two parlors, and bedrooms. The first floor contained a music room, made out of the carriage barn where the infant Charlie had once sat in a buggy listening to his father play violin.[5] George fitted the old family square piano with dummy organ pedals, so Charlie could practice at home.[6]

Except for George, who played Sundays at the Methodist church and from 1885 directed the choir, the Iveses attended the big white First Congregational Church built on the site of old Isaac's vegetable garden. After services the grown-up Iveses and Hoyts and Tweedys and other friends gathered in the house around matriarch Sarah and passed the time talking books and politics and gossip, while the children had their Sunday-school classes.[7] A photo of 1887 preserves what may be one of those Sundays: three generations pose at the front door around ancient Sarah, Cousin Howdie and his wife Anna and their two children, and in the back thirteen-year-old Charlie and his brother Moss. Charlie, skinny and tanned and sporting a snappy lace-up shirt, gazes warily at the camera and looks very bright, like the young virtuoso he was getting to be. Already he had to cope with a considerably more demanding life than most boys his age, and he looks to be handling it all right. His tan might have been acquired in a baseball outfield.

In August 1888, Charlie filled in at the organ for his teacher, Miss Hollister, at the Disciples Church. The following February he became the regular organist at Second Congregational, where Hollister had just become choir director.[8] His diary of that period, which mostly just indicates the pieces he

Iveses of four generations. Charles Ives, right rear, and brother Moss standing behind matriarch Sarah. To her side are grandson Howard Moss Ives (called Howdie), his wife, and children. Amelia Ives Van Wyck, the older girl, would become an artist and the main family chronicler.

played, notes about his debut, "Mossie pump." Critical observations on later Sundays include "TERRIBLE" and "Bad mistake."[9]

He was then the youngest salaried church organist in Connecticut, and would be still when he took over at the Baptist church on October 10, his fifteenth birthday. He would remain at that post until he left Danbury in 1893. Meanwhile he performed around town on piano and organ, and as a singer. A memo on one of his pieces says, "Concert 16 Stevens St by Paul [cousin Parmelee], Mossi, Will, & Ch E I."[10] (He was already in the habit of jotting notes on any handy piece of paper, which was often music paper.) On a program for a City Hall "Kinder Concert" of March 1888, Master Charlie Ives is noted as manning the drums and musical glasses in Haydn's *Toy Symphony*. Years later, at the bottom of his copy of the program, Ives wrote, "I remember father did all the work, rehearsing and organizing etc. for this, & showed Miss Hollister how to conduct—as this was a ladies Society concert!"[11] He resented that this decorous lady, his onetime teacher, got the glory for his father's labors.

Charlie jotted down a practice schedule for himself in July 1889, a detailed accounting of his time of a sort he would make for the rest of his life:

Morning 7.00 to 8.30 1 hr. ex[ercises] ¼ hr. Pedal ¼ Church m[usic.] Noon. ½ h. church ½ hr. fugue. Night 6.15 to 7.45 ½ hr. fugue 1 hr. C[hurch] Organ[.] S[chool] Les[son] 7.45 to 8.45.[12]

At age fourteen Charlie was practicing four hours a day, the regime enforced by his father.

During four months of 1888 Charlie learned the Bach Toccata and Fugue in C Major, a virtuosic piece with a spectacular pedal part. After getting his son started with Miss Hollister, George sought out more advanced teachers. Toward the end of May 1889, Charlie took the first of a dozen lessons, two a week, with J. R. Hall, who presided at First Congregational.[13] That October, as he was beginning at the Baptist church, he commenced thirty-six lessons with Norwalk organist Alexander Gibson, who tutored him in the highest level of the repertoire—Bach preludes and fugues, Mendelssohn sonatas, the Beethoven et al. orchestral transcriptions that were rife in those days, plus bread-and-butter items by Batiste and others used as filler in church services. With Gibson, Charlie spent five or six lessons working through a Dudley Buck transcription of Rossini's *William Tell Overture,* a grandstanding number that would turn up on recitals for the rest of his playing career.[14] By the age of fifteen or so, Charlie had some formidable organ works under his fingers and toes. He studied with Gibson probably through the Danbury School of Music, founded by Misses Hollister and Fayerweather in 1887. The school became the center of cultivated music in Danbury, producer of soirées and musicales and recitals like the one in which Charlie debuted.

He also studied briefly with an organist named Hans Raasch, until Raasch opined to George Ives that Rossini and Meyerbeer were better composers than Wagner, and George broke off the engagement. Ives later remembered "how mad his father used to get when so many German musicians would run down Richard Wagner—one of [George's] heroes of the time."[15] Along with much else, the son would pick up that taste; his organ repertoire included Wagner transcriptions. But this was one legacy from his father that did not last. In maturity Ives's devotion to his father's memory did not impede the development of a cold hatred for the German juggernaut of opera: "[The] boy of twenty-five was listening to Wagner with enthusiasm. . . . But when he became middle-aged . . . this music had become cloying, the melodies threadbare. . . . Those once transcendent progressions . . . were becoming slimy."[16]

Apprentice works composed in Charlie's first creative years include the fiddly "New Year's Dance" from 1886—spry but mechanical, its harmony and melodic shape as gawky as one would expect from a novice. The same applies to the "Hymn" and "Chant" denoted "Opus 2 Nos. 1 & 2" on the manuscript. (A memo from the grown-up composer is attached to them: "none of these any good, just kept for curiosity.") For a while, as Charlie's hand for notation developed, George wrote out his son's pieces as part of his copying and arranging chores. Charlie composed several elegies for departed pets,[17] lost except for the circa-1888 "Slow March" in memoriam a family dog, quoting Handel's "Dead March." Uncle Lyman Brewster supplied the text. Thirty years later Ives would include the "Slow March" in his first collection, *114 Songs*.

Charlie's first intensive studies in harmony must have come in those years, because his ensuing works are more sophisticated, in their conventional way. A polite church-style piece of around 1887 sets Psalm 42, "As Pants the Hart," for voice and organ; in a later memo Ives noted that this was done with "father's help." More expansive than his first pieces, and as blandly pious as most New England church music, "As Pants the Hart" was sung at the Methodist church, probably with the nervous composer at the organ.[18] Several other church pieces from these years are lost.

One early work that survives was the most visible of his first efforts—*Holiday Quickstep*, whose manuscript dates it "Xmas '87." This sprightly tune (a quickstep is a sort of march) includes a variant of Reeves's *Second Regiment Connecticut National Guard March*. The young composer was already making use of familiar melodies, this one being a favorite of his and his father's. Charlie may have written out *Holiday Quickstep* for piano; George arranged it for various ensembles. What strikes one about this piece is not only how astute it is technically, how much an advance on the halting pieces he was writing a few months earlier (George probably helped here too), but how sharp a feel it has for the genre: it is just the weightless, swinging-along kind of band piece that suits a spring parade.

The *Quickstep* was first heard in the theater pit, though. George played it at the Opera House on January 16, 1888, during a performance by the German Drama Association. Two days later this review appeared in the Danbury *News*:

The music was furnished by the popular Standard Orchestra, and it is not necessary to remark that it gave the best of satisfaction. . . . The feature of the evening . . . was the rendition of the "Holiday Quickstep," composed and arranged [actually the parts are in George's hand] for an orchestra by Charlie Ives, a thirteen-year-old son of George E. Ives. Master Ives is certainly a musical genius, being an accomplished performer on several instruments, as well as a composer and arranger. The "Holiday Quickstep" is worthy a place with productions of much older heads, and Master Charlie should be encouraged to further efforts in this line. We shall expect more from this talented youngster in the future.

They got what they expected from the talented youngster. The *Quickstep* received a lot of play around town. One performance was by Charlie at the piano and Moss on piccolo, at the Methodist church Sunday school; Charlie also contributed a xylophone solo on the program[19] Another performance came on Decoration Day, by George's full band on the march. Long after, the aged and ailing Ives was to create his famous account of that event: the agitated young composer was "too overcome" to play his snare drum in the parade but instead, when the band came marching by the Main Street house playing his piece, was observed facing the other way and hurling a hardball at the barn door. (To whatever extent the story is true, it reflects the terrors of performance for a composer young or old.) Likewise, the old Ives liked to relate what he said, or wished he'd said, when Danbury folks asked him what he played: "Shortstop."[20]

By 1889 the town knew Charlie well. He was that Ives boy at the organ, accompanying singers on piano, marching with the band, and now and then trotting out a little number of his own. The newspaper had dubbed this teenager a genius, but who knew what that amounted to in so strange a job as music. Though famous musicians visited the Opera House and the town had watched other talented youngsters grow up, the hatters and bankers and lawyers and club ladies of Danbury had never seen anything quite like Charlie. A performing and composing prodigy was even harder to fathom than was George Ives. It would have been the same in most towns in America.

Probably Charlie himself had little idea of what "musical genius" was supposed to mean. George had imparted to his son a good deal of European musical history and literature, and the boy soaked them up the way he did everything else; but those were other times, other places, far away.[21] Charlie was still mostly following his ears, his instincts, and his father. Besides their mutual fascination with music, their shared strangeness helped cement their bond, for the critical few years the sharing lasted. Their study of the classical tradition and their experimenting with its laws (which George only occasionally attempted in public) was a secret game between them Psychiatrist and Ives biographer Stuart Feder has written: "They were more like each other than like anyone else in their lives."[22] The veneration the adult Ives would feel for his father, which in our rootless age seems exaggerated unto neurotic, was in large part the simple recognition of a rare bond and an unrepayable debt.[23]

Now Charlie's days consisted of shuttling hurriedly from bed to piano, piano to school, at noon to church for practice on the organ and then back to school, after dinner settling in for hours of practice and homework. Sundays he presided at the Baptist church organ for choir rehearsals and services; often he appeared in evening performances during the week. From about 1890 father and son would occasionally take the train to New York for orchestral concerts in the new Carnegie Hall. Somehow amidst all this Charlie composed steadily and still managed, from his mid-teens on, to find a measure of glory in sports.

George kept the boy at it when he was home; when George was traveling, as he still often was, perhaps Mollie Ives oversaw practice. More important, George kept his son interested by provoking and prodding, allowing this and disallowing that, but always with a point: "Father was not against a reasonable amount of 'boy's fooling,' if it were done with some sense behind it."[24] So George approved, or maybe originated the idea, when Charlie varied his scale practice by "playing the chromatic scale in different octaves, and seeing how fast you could do it."[25] The resulting wide leaps were to be a trademark of Modernism and are found, here and there, in Ives's advanced scores.

The son picked up the father's war-honed sense of vernacular music and its significance in the lives of ordinary people. He also refined his father's technical explorations, such as singing a tune in one key while accompanying in another, or doing the same with two hands on the piano (musicians two generations later would call that bitonality). Taking the idea further, the boy wrote fugues that extended traditional practice in a direction technically logical, but unprecedented in effect: instead of sticking to the standard procedure of fugue entries (the fugue subject first in the home key, then transposed up a fifth, then returning to the home key), Charlie kept transposing entries up a fourth or fifth, keeping each voice in its own key, until he had polytonal fugues going in four keys at once. George's response, as his son recalled it: "If you know how to write a fugue the right way *well*, then I'm willing to have you try the wrong way—*well*.[26]

One can imagine the teenager sitting at the piano working with the intensity and quick intelligence one senses in his photos of that time, George looking over his son's shoulder as the boy does his exercises, practices assignments from his teacher, polishes his church-service pieces, and improvises and composes: *Here's a good chord, Charlie says, playing a chain of thirds hardly containable in traditional theory: C–E–G♯–B–D–F♯–B♭–D. George listens, his first thought bowing to convention: "If you will play this B [as] B♭, and stop at F♯ [on the] top, there won't be any half-tone dissonance." Then, listening again, George concedes that maybe the first chord sounds better.[27]*

The boy's childhood would be filled with this kind of dialogue. It was an extraordinary way of growing up, full of excitement and stimulation, and no less of humiliation and frustration.

The struggle for musical mastery is largely carried on in long hours in lonely rooms. In many ways that struggle and its effects on Charlie's psyche were the same for him as for any boy or girl subject to an intense discipline. This life arises from talent and inner compulsion; it is also enforced from the outside, by parental decree and unrelenting pressure. The life poses grueling obstacles for an adolescent who wants to be out with others, having fun and learning some colloquial wisdom. Some who have been reared as virtuosos suppress those instincts, or forget or deny the strains in their lives. Charles Ives never forgot and in some ways never forgave. In later life he would direct his resentment not toward his father but, startlingly, toward music itself:

As a boy [I was] partially ashamed of it—an entirely wrong attitude, but it was strong. . . . When other boys, Monday A.M. on vacation, were out driving grocery carts, or doing chores, or playing ball, I felt all wrong to stay in and play piano. And there may be something in it. Hasn't music always been too much an emasculated art?[28]

He was partly ashamed for being an artist, afraid other boys might call him sissy; he felt alien in an environment that rated almost anything else higher than artistic creativity. In later years he would say to cousin Amelia Van Wyck that "being an artist made me the other oddball in the family."[29] Likely his chronic shyness was only partly temperamental (he would shed it for a while in college). Otherwise it came both from embarrassment before peers and public, and from distraction: he always had a lot on his mind.

Social dilemmas were not unusual for an American boy growing up an artist, then or later. Some of Ives's solutions were common ones—lambasting sissies, playing sports, becoming profane and "manly" in personality. This pattern turns up time and again in male American artists—in Hemingway, Faulkner, Pollock, Carl Ruggles, and many others.[30] At length Ives would arrive at a perverse view of dissonance as a token of manliness in music.

His other solution, developed in childhood, was more individual. Charlie and his father were both determined that he would be a superior musician. For himself, he was also determined to be a boy among boys, to run the bases, to bull across the goal line, to *win*. That too his father allowed. Later, in characteristically American fashion, Ives would replace the drive to excel in sports with the same in business. His solution for this double allegiance to art and "normal" life was to compromise neither, to do it all at once. One finds the beginnings of this solution in Mossie's diary, ten-year-old Charlie running from games to music lessons. In his teens he played outdoors until he had to go practice, composed in off hours, crammed everything in. In college they would call him "Dasher." Boy and man, Charles Ives would be implacably in a hurry.

His favored games matured predictably, though not in a direction healthy for a keyboard player. In a letter of September 1886 eleven-year-old Charlie tells Aunt Amelia, "I do not play in the store every day but I keep it a going." He also mentions the pastime that superseded his career as a pretend store-keeper and railroad engineer:

Every body has the base-ball fever up here & I have it a little. We were playing base-ball up to Ned Tweedy's saturday Moss was 3rd base Ned fired the ball to Moss to have him put him out, but Moss dodged it, & the ball struck him & knocked him down that was Moss'is last playing of base-ball.[31]

The game, which predated the Civil War, became the national pastime
when soldiers took it up to while the hours between drills and fighting, then
brought it home with them. By the time Charlie was born it was a fixture of
summer across the nation. Baseball was the most popular element of a Gilded
Age boom in sports, when for the first time Americans considered it physically
and even spiritually salutary to hustle about outdoors rowing, pedaling, or
chasing some sort of sphere. In 1876 the National Baseball League formed
with eight teams.[32] The postwar period also saw the spread of football, tennis,
golf, rowing, and bicycling.[33]

As with its musical organizations, Danbury possessed a changing collection of amateur baseball teams, some for adults—often factory clubs—and
some for teenagers. The latter included a team called the Alerts, which Charlie
apparently joined in March 1889. A newspaper clipping preserved in one of
his grown-up diaries notes that the Alerts beat an ad hoc nine that month,
21–20; that may have been his first game. Though destined to be a pitcher

Charles Ives, center row on the left, happily among his baseball team the "Alerts."

and a pretty good one if a little wild, the next summer he played in the outfield through a busy season.

On June 11, 1890, fifteen-year-old Charlie soloed for the better part of a Baptist church program, playing pieces that would have challenged an organist of any age. The program included his showpiece *William Tell* arrangement, Bach's "Dorian" Toccata, Dudley Buck's *Variations on "Home, Sweet Home,"* and finally the Mendelssohn First Organ Sonata. The *News* headed its review "The Greatest Artistic Success of the Season."[34] At the end of the month, on the 28th, he played with the Alerts in an afternoon game and that night gave a full recital at the church, playing the Mendelssohn Second Sonata, a Bach Prelude and Fugue, pieces by Flotow, Batiste, and Guilmant, and finishing with Wagner's *Tannhäuser* Overture. This time the paper called his abilities "almost phenomenal." A couple of weeks later a photo of the Alerts appeared in the paper, fielder/recitalist Charlie posing amidst his teammates with a relaxed pride that he rarely showed in pictures.

The same jumble of music and sport prevailed during his vacations at "Cousin's Beach" in Westbrook, where Mollie and the boys (busy George only occasionally) spent part of every summer at Uncle Lyman Brewster's place, one of a row of vacation houses owned by Whites, Seeleys, and other Ives relatives. In August 1889, Charlie wrote home to his father of fishing, swimming, and playing tennis with Uncle Lyman, filling in with local ball teams, and daily practice on the Seeleys' piano. He plaintively asked George to substitute for him at church so he wouldn't have to come home early: "you might play cornet." Sports had strained his arm, but he wouldn't let that slow him down: "I can't write very well because I have to hold my sore arm up. I am going to play tennis now." His handwriting in those days was clear and delicate. George apparently demanded neat penmanship and correct expression; in one letter Charlie felt obliged to explain that the inkblots on the page were already there.[35]

Back in Westbrook the following August, Charlie had changed his tone in letters to his father. Before he had been boyish and chatty; this year he became more formal:

I found Mr. Spinning home after dinner and we then went up to his church. (Presbyterian) I tried the organ which is (he says) the largest in the state and of course a very fine one. It has 60 registers. Uncle Lyman, I suppose has told about the tennis racket.

In the letter Charlie in businesslike style arranges for a substitute organist at the church. Later that month his mother sent a note about the upshot of Charlie's cutting his hand, and begged off another Sunday for him:

Dear George
Charlie hand has prevented him from going in bathing, or rowing & he wishes to stay another week and he can, if you can get anybody to play for him Sunday the Miss Smith he speaks of is the one from Bethel I wish he had got her in the first place if you cannot

get any body of course he will have to come home Saturday but I hope you will be able to. Mossie & I expect to come home the last of the week
Mollie[36]

His mother worried about what sports were doing to his hands,[37] but Charlie was allowed to take up football later in his teens, and he tore into it with his usual energy. The American game was relatively new. Rules were codified in the 1880s by Yale's Walter Camp, but football remained wild and woolly, played with no helmets and little padding, the bone-breaking flying wedge the favored tactic. After ten years at New Street School, Charlie entered the private Danbury Academy in September 1891. Next month a newspaper article first mentioned his gridiron performance: a few days before his seventeenth birthday, Charlie played right halfback when the academy lost to New Street in a game the paper describes as "not brilliantly scientific, and no ribs were broken, but there was fun enough in it for the youngsters."[38] A week later Charlie's team beat New Street, Charlie scoring fourteen touchdowns.[39]

In 1892 he posed with the Danbury Academy team as its captain. The picture suggests that he was playing a lot. In contrast to his thin and rather ethereal look in earlier photos, in those years he looked like a football player, fleshy of build and thick of neck. In the 1892 season, his last in Danbury, Charlie played left end in a combined academy and high school team in their 56–0 thrashing of Bridgeport.[40] Also in those years, 1891–92, amidst practice and performing and sports, Charlie composed dozens of new pieces for organ, chorus, band, and voice, including the precocious *Variations on "America."*

He would keep to that pace. Increasingly during his teens the time he needed for music and fun was subtracted from studies. Charlie began as a good student at New Street School, making the honor roll as late as 1888.[41] In his later teens at Danbury Academy, and after that in prep school and college, he barely scraped by. His solution of crowding everything in would work, up to a point. An almost unnatural energy was the decisive element. Ives drew on that energy for some three decades as he roared full-throttle through life. When it deserted him, he crashed once and for all.

In Charlie's teens Lyman and Amelia Brewster took up the slack in looking out for George and Mollie's boys. George seems to have been busier than ever, on the road teaching and directing and playing, the prospect of two sons approaching college age adding to his concerns. George had always been closer to his sister Amelia than to his brothers Ike and Joe, and childless Amelia and Lyman were happy to indulge in some parenting. This aunt and uncle would loom larger in the lives of their nephews than Mollie Ives, especially for Moss but also for Charlie. Lyman was a brilliant man and warmly fond of his nephews, while Amelia was dictatorial and hypochondriacal,[42] but Charlie seems to have appreciated her all the same.

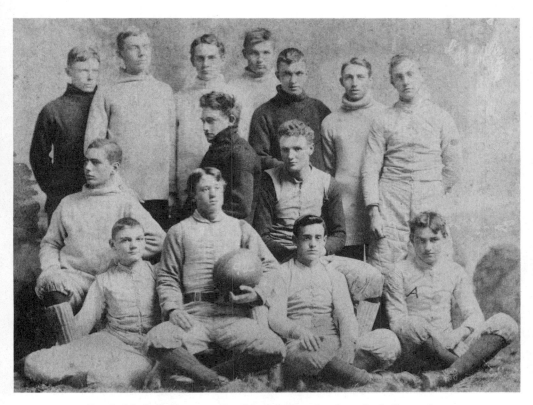

Ives holds the ball as captain of the Danbury Academy football squad.

Lyman Brewster had not only married into the Iveses; he adopted himself into the family and become the most prominent figure of his generation. Once class poet at Yale, he remained an amateur versifier. After college Lyman studied law in Danbury with his uncle Roger Averill, who went on to become lieutenant-governor of Connecticut. Having establishing himself in practice, Lyman married Sarah Amelia Ives in 1868, the year he first became a judge. Despite prospects for a national career in Republican politics, Lyman Brewster never considered leaving home. He cut a grand and glamorous figure as the town's leading lawyer and judge, and the prime shaper of the city charter.[43] With partners including Ives relative Samuel Tweedy, Lyman long held forth in his offices over the Danbury Savings Bank, next door to the Ives House. After a decade on the bench he served in the state senate and then became national chairman of the Committee on Uniform State Laws.[44] He would die in the Ives House in 1904 and be buried among the family in Wooster Cemetery.

Lyman spent much time with his nephew Charlie and that had its effect.

This lawyer was more bookish than George Ives and his influence on the boy's literary sense may have been considerable. Lyman would supervise the intensive cramming that proved necessary to get Charlie into college. But Charlie was already deep into music, and so Lyman's main attentions fell on Moss, who was interested in writing and soon picked up his uncle's fascination for the law. Moss Ives's life would become an echo of Lyman Brewster's. Moss graduated from Yale Law School after only one year and immediately passed the bar.[45] He practiced in Danbury, first as Lyman's partner and later with Samuel Tweedy, and eventually became the most prominent judge in town. Also following his mentor, Moss would be a Republican leader involved in all sorts of community affairs, and worked as secretary of Lyman's state-laws committee.[46] And like Lyman, Moss wrote on the side—toward the end of his life he published *The Ark and the Dove,* about the contribution of Maryland Catholics to American religious freedom.

It was characteristic of all the Iveses that the extended family cooperated in most things, including child-raising. Charlie and Moss spent much of their time in the care of relatives from the Brewsters to Gramma Ives to various Parmelees. (In later years most of Moss's children would live for long periods with their Uncle Charlie.) Presumably Mollie Ives did her share in raising the greater Ives and Parmelee brood. One of Moss's children, Chester, who stayed with Mollie in childhood, recalled, "She was a disciplinarian. I know because I had her. She used to call us all 'goosies.' "[47] Chester's brother Brewster said, "Uncle Charlie was extremely fond of his mother. . . . She would constantly remind all of us of his genius . . . and how she was even more proud of that than of his business accomplishments."[48] Never did her sons say much about Mollie. When Charles Ives visited Danbury in later years, he always stayed in the old house with Aunt Amelia, not with his mother.[49]

The 1880s and early 1890s, during which Charles Ives came into his own as a musician, were Danbury's glory years. In 1887 an old resident reviewed for the *News* the changes brought by the last decade or so: the new library ("our first public building of any account"), City Hall (its erection marked "the burial tablet of fossilism in Danbury"), the fireman's building, two banks, the expansive Treadwell and McPhelemy commercial buildings, and the forthcoming hospital. The last decade had seen the arrival of the telephone, electric streetlights and fire alarm, sewers, and the street railway; Main Street was paved in 1890. Optimism was epidemic, fogyism and fossilism on the retreat. The *News* article concluded that "Danbury has awakened from a lethargy . . . and our village has sprung into a new and healthy life."[50]

The impetus came from a hatting industry thriving within nationwide good times, at the height of the Gilded Age. In 1887 the town produced more than five million hats, mostly men's derbies.[51] Both businessmen Iveses were profitably incorporated—Joe moving housewares, Ike hawking "Wine of the Woods." The crash would arrive with the nationwide panic of 1893 and ensuing depression, which swept much away. That year nineteen hat factories closed in Danbury, and Charles H. Merritt, an owner and Ives relative, tried to break the union with a two-month lockout.[52] While the country would recover in a few years, Danbury never quite reclaimed its glory. The 1880s turned out to have been its zenith. It was at that zenith that Charles Ives would immortalize his hometown.

During the 1880s, with the growth in income and leisure time, music thrived under the efforts of George Ives, Misses Hollister and Fayerweather, and the town's other artists and teachers. The big Opera House, built in 1871, attracted more and better visiting artists than the town had heard before— Theodore Thomas's Orchestra,[53] the Fisk Jubilee Singers, minstrel shows, opera stars in recital, full-scale operettas, and chamber music groups. The influx of new workers and resulting population surge—from 11,666 in 1880 to 19,386 in 1890[54]—expanded audiences for all sorts of events. At the 1882 Fireman's Parade, always one of the grandest occasions on the calendar, the splendid uniforms and burnished carriages were accompanied by thirty-one bands and drum corps.[55] Charles Ives's *The Gong on the Hook and Ladder,* written around 1911, is an echo of those parades, with the hook and ladder speeding up on the downhill part of Main Street and slowing on the uphill.[56]

A New York *Herald* article of January 1890 headlined "Danbury's Delight Is All For Music" begins with this impressive summary:

> All Danbury loves music. Wherever you may go, no matter with whom you talk, ten chances to one music will become the topic of conversation. . . . There are no less than a dozen regularly organized societies, embracing nearly all of the best vocalists, and about as many orchestras, and bands. Of course there is besides a Salvation Army band, drum corps innumerable and kindred organizations. . . . The most prominent organization is the Choral Union. It was organized about a year and a half ago and now numbers more than one hundred members, nearly every one of whom is qualified to be a soloist. The Society is very successful, owing its prosperity chiefly to the zeal of the director, Professor Harry Rowe Shelley, of New York.[57]

The article cites the Choral Union's upcoming performance of Mendelssohn's *Loreli* and the presence of the Male Chorus, Musical Virtuoso Club, the German singing societies, the Apollo Banjo Club, George Ives's Standard and Philharmonic Orchestras and two other orchestral ensembles, George's Danbury Band, and Fayerweather and Hollister's School of Music. It was in this article that George was singled out as one who "has probably done more for instrumental music than any other man in Danbury," and his band "conceded to be one of the best in Connecticut."

Charles Ives wrote his first works in the context of a community throbbing with music in modes from provincial to sophisticated. Many of his early pieces show Charlie's innate audacity. A few show full-blown the experimental streak that first earned him, in Danbury, the laughter that would echo in his ears for the rest of his life.

His works from the late 1880s and early 1890s show not only imagination and precocious technique, but also canny intuitions about the sound and sense of musical genres familiar in Danbury. His marches are gay and swaggering, his church anthems as saccharine and uplifting as they were supposed to be. His "Hear My Prayer, O Lord," of 1888, exemplifies one species of unctuously sentimental church solo, a fact not lost on the adult Ives. With its publication in 1920 (as "A Song—for Anything") he included a sardonic footnote: "That music of this character is less frequently heard in religious services now-a-days is one of the signs of the wholesome progress of music in this country."

As with "A Song—for Anything," Charlie's work well into college is rife with chromatic fillips in the harmony, some conventionally sentimental à la Stephen Foster, some fresh and striking, some showing a determination to push chromatic chordal alterations beyond convention. Charlie liked to toss added notes into the harmony, the more piquant the better; one finds some of that as early as the "Slow March." For the moment, with George looking over his shoulder, Charlie resolved his dissonances like a good boy. All the same, from the beginning of his creative life his searching imagination prodded at conventions in ways sometimes clumsy, sometimes fresh and effective. Rarely, though, did he violate the spirit or context of a genre. His 1891 "When Stars are in the Quiet Skies," for example, does its job as a decorous little parlor song, its harmonic novelties worked in seamlessly.

The theme-and-variations genre was familiar to Charlie from his organ repertoire—he played both European ones and American extravaganzas on native tunes including Dudley Buck's *Variations on "Home, Sweet Home."*[58] Around the beginning of 1889 he composed a rather callow set of organ variations on the hymn "Jerusalem the Golden," and a band fantasia (now lost) on the same tune, one perhaps an adaptation of the other. A year or so later he performed some variations on "God Save the King" (the same tune as "America") by the German composer J. H. C. Rinck. Then early in 1891 Charlie premiered his own variations on that tune, a piece clearly influenced by Rinck but not unduly beholden to his model.[59] This product of the seventeen-year-old composer is a minor work in adult terms, but listenable enough to find a place on programs a century later.

Charlie first played *Variations on "America"* in a concert at the Brewster, New York, Methodist church, on February 17, 1892. At that point he was still improvising some of it.[60] As is clear in the first measures of the introduction (it was published fifty years later), the piece is European-genteel in the grand style, European too in its fashionable chromaticism. While Charlie may not have been familiar yet with Franck, perhaps he picked up the era's slippery-fingered chord changes from French pieces in his repertoire by Guilmant and Batiste (the sort of thing, in fact, that he denounced as "slimy" in Wagner). What Americanism lurks in the *Variations* comes mainly from the patriotic associations of the theme itself.

The general idea of the theme-and-variations form is to deck out the basic tune and/or its harmonies in a series of contrasting garbs. Charlie plays the game astutely, embellishing the theme and its harmonies with largely standard

Charles Ives at about seventeen—precocious organist, football captain.

but effective figuration, and shaping the whole piece in a series of contrasts: Variation I adding a nimble running line—eventually treacly chromatic 32nds—to the theme; Variation II an andante whose sliding close harmonies push the bounds of Romantic practice; III a sort of skating-rink march; IV a driving minor-key polonaise; V an allegro with skittering 16ths in proto-ragtime rhythmic patterns, and with a virtuosic pedal part that the adult Ives declared "almost as much fun as playing baseball."[61]

Much of what would bring the *Variations on "America"* to the attention of a later, novelty-obsessed age would be its startling departures from convention by way of two bitonal interludes. In the piece as published in 1949, there is a canonic interlude between Variations II and III that combines F major in the right hand and D♭ major in the left hand and pedals.[62] The other interlude, a brief one between IV and V, superimposes A♭ major on F major. The two interludes mark this work of circa 1891 as the world's first systematic use of bitonality. (Charlie had sketched earlier studies including several on "London Bridge is Falling Down" in various combinations of two keys, and played one of them in an 1891 Baptist church service.[63] The idea had come, as usual, from his father—the game of having the boys sing in one key while he accompanied in another.)

In a memo of the 1930s Ives writes of another interlude that does not survive, involving canons on the theme in three keys. He adds that his father did not let him play these at the premiere because "they made the boys laugh out loud."[64] (George also forbade playing the polonaise because he found it too European to hold court with an American tune.[65]) Probably because the interludes might sink its commercial possibilities, the surviving fair copy of the piece, which George copied and sent to a New York publisher,[66] does not contain the wayward interludes; Charlie penciled them in later.[67] The minor mystery of when he did that is another example of a situation that turns up time and again in Ives's work: an experiment that he held back from committing to a manuscript intended to be shown around, but which he restored later. In sound, the *Variations'* interludes are close to his other early polytonal studies— murky and ungrateful to the ear, in contrast to the elegant polytonal effects he would be shaping not long after. All the same, the interludes create a logical tonal linkage by superimposing the keys of the surrounding variations.[68]

Part of the *Variations'* appeal in light-classical concerts of the next century (often in William Schuman's orchestral arrangement) is their apparent irony. To our ears they seem a lampoon of an over-familiar tune. The irony is in ourselves, though, not in the music; the teenaged Charlie was probably in earnest. As the basis of a piece to flex his muscles as composer and performer, he chose this melody because he loved it and honored the patriotic sentiment it represented. Certainly Ives was capable of musical jokes, then and later, but most of them are broader and usually funnier than the *Variations*.

Around 1892 Charlie composed an enormous amount of work—finished and unfinished, some of it later lost—for an assortment of media: organ pieces, a couple of marches for piano or band, choral music, songs. Notable among that output is the organ Postlude in F,[69] now surviving only in an orchestration Charlie did in college. In style it clearly, if a little blandly, smacks of Wagner—say, the *Siegfried Idyll*. On the vernacular side came his March No. 2, quoting "Son of a Gambolier," later reworked as a McKinley campaign song.

In surviving sketches from his teens we see Charlie's radical ideas taking shape, in small studies of particular technical games: here whole-tone chords harmonizing whole-tone scales; here the bitonal "London Bridge" studies in various superimpositions of keys; here a melody harmonized with seventh chords rising in whole steps; here two handfuls of triads diverging in a chromatic wedge; here a chromatic polychordal organ cadenza (with a note at the bottom: "I played for Mr Gibson—it made him laugh!"). One sees in these now-faded pages (some from his father's old notebook) the beginning of a process of self-teaching that would continue over the next decades in little pieces written to find out things: What if you do this, what if you do that?

Already as a teenager Ives's creative pattern was set. He would explore new sonorities and effects with systematic formulas, let the results percolate into his ears and intuition, then compose freely with these new sounds in pieces he took more seriously.

By age eighteen Charles Ives had served much of his apprenticeship as performer and composer. He still had things to learn of tradition and technique, but he was already a professional organist and writer of shorter conventional genres. He would, in fact, sell some of his more commercial items. On the whole, however, a commercial tunesmith was not what Ives wanted to be, as he began to turn his thoughts toward life beyond Danbury. Charlie would finish his musical education in college with an intensive study of European Romantic techniques, genres, and ideals. At the same time he would mine his experimental vein, following his ears to see where they led him, turning up a rich supply of creative ore that he could hardly have anticipated amidst the games and hectic labors of his boyhood. He yearned for something bigger and he was born and reared for that. But it would take him a long time to discover what that bigger music might be.

Farewell

For more than two decades before 1890, while George Ives started his family and watched his elder son grow into a musician, he stood before Danbury on countless occasions. He marched with his bands on holidays, and on summer evenings played for throngs of townspeople from the bandstands of Wooster Square and Elmwood Park.[1] His cornet and violin and instrumental groups were ubiquitous at Opera House shows, ball games, skating rinks, picnics, church services, steamer excursions, camp meetings. Wherever there was music, George was likely to be around. But he was the kind of fixture that tends with time to fade into the woodwork, to become invisible in plain sight. George Ives had not changed much in two decades; the town and its music had. This evolution was due in part to his own playing and conducting and teaching that had inspired many of the musicians filling ensembles all over western Connecticut. Like many parents and teachers before him, George brought up a new generation that passed him by.

Among that generation was his son. George and Charlie may have resembled each other more than anyone else they knew, but the father did not bring up his son to follow his life. Even though Charlie spent his childhood hanging around his father's rehearsals and occasionally playing with the band, his advanced training was as a classical musician rather than a bandleader and jack-of-all-trades. The split in the direction of their careers was bound to create tensions. As a keyboard player and composer, Charlie was torn between his father and the more cultivated side of town musical life. That side was dominated in Danbury, as elsewhere in the country, by women.

Among the women's clubs in town were the Afternoon Musical Society, Classics, Monday Club,[2] the Daughters of the American Revolution, and the temperance societies for which women had always provided the impetus. These groups reflected a craze for joining that caught up both sexes after the Civil War. There was a difference in style and direction, though, between men's and women's clubs in the United States. Most proclaimed fellowship and community service, but the men's clubs tended to emphasize "manly" fellowship (that is, alcohol-enhanced male bonding) while the ladies tended to be more earnest about the service. Women's clubs of the era ranged widely in social concerns—temperance, pacifism, suffrage, public welfare, and self-improvement; but above all, literature and the arts.[3]

These efforts played out in contrary directions. The temperance movement, to name one, provided a counterforce in a hard-drinking age. At the same time, the hymn-singing self-righteousness of the movement tended to drive men even more desperately to the meetings of the Shriners or Red Men or Fat Men—or the Danbury Band. Women's clubs were both admired and deplored, and not only by men: Edith Wharton wrote of "ladies who pursue Culture in [clubs], as though it were dangerous to meet it alone."

With their School of Music, Charlie's keyboard teacher Ella Hollister and contralto Belle Fayerweather were prominent among the ladies heading groups that aspired to greater sophistication than the common run of music. That common vernacular was represented, as much as anything, by George Ives's brass bands and theater orchestras. George knew cultivated music as well as anybody in town, but that was not his main job or the context in which people regarded him. "Classical" music was represented by the School of Music and by clubs, most of them run by ladies—the Rossini Musical Soirée, the Mozart Musicale, the Mendelssohn Musicale, and the like. These groups sometimes met at the Ives House and on occasion Charlie and George joined in. In 1889 the leading musical ladies hired Harry Rowe Shelley, a celebrated New York organist and composer, to direct the Danbury Choral Society. Shelley began performing oratorios with this large, well-trained choir, and brought Victor Herbert to town for a program.[4]

The arts had an inescapable connection to the world of women, and the effects of that cut both ways. Professional classical music in the United States may have been performed mostly by European men, but its establishment was primarily the work of cultivated, well-to-do ladies. The major symphony orchestras are the most visible example. In this century, Gustav Mahler in New York, Leopold Stokowski in Philadelphia, and Serge Koussevitzky in Boston got their jobs partly by their appeal to the Symphony Dames; then they had to undertake exhausting power struggles with the same women. (Koussevitzky was the only one of the three to win the battle.[5])

The club lady was notoriously high-minded, but her tastes tended to the conservative, sentimental, and moralistic—in other words, Victorian. Wrote Frances Trollope in 1832, "I never saw or read of any country where religion had so strong a hold upon the women or a slighter hold upon the men."[6] Historian Ann Douglas has described the turn during the nineteenth century from a dogmatic Puritanism to a sentimental, feminized religiosity. The role of women—a role defined as much *by* women as by men—was to be passive and Christlike, a godly influence in the home and the world.[7] Women were held to be innately the more sensitive and spiritual sex; it was their task and burden in life to subdue the coarse passions of men and bring them into the fold as respectable, temperate Christians. Writer and editor Sarah Hale wrote in 1852,

[Woman] was not made to gratify [man's] sensual desires but to refine his human affections and elevate his moral feelings. Endowed with superior beauty of person and a correspondent delicacy of mind, her soul was to "help" him where he was deficient, namely in his spiritual nature.[8]

Catherine Beecher wrote that American women in particular had "the exalted privilege of extending over the world those blessed influences which are to renovate degraded man." J. C. Furnas writes, "The fashionable cant of the day was casting Woman as the princess yoked to the barbarian chieftain."[9] Thus the old syndrome of women dragging their boozing, profane, tobacco-chewing men to be elevated at the revival or the temperance meeting, the recital or the opera. As a result, notes Henry Steele Commager, an American man's "attitude toward culture tended to be at once suspicious and indulgent. Where it interfered with more important activities, he distrusted it; where it was the recreation of his leisure hours or of his womenfolk, he tolerated it."[10] Since the purpose of art was to elevate and enlighten, what was read, seen, and heard was expected to conform to feminine / Victorian tastes and sensibilities. Writes Commager:

Women not only controlled education and religion but largely dictated the standards of literature and art and clothed culture so ostentatiously in feminine garb that the term ["culture"] itself came to have connotations of effeminacy. Conformity and conventionalism in matters of morals sometimes assumed aggressive form, and the willingness to resign control of the whole field of culture to women combined with the tradition of Puritanism to encourage intolerance and justify censorship. Language was emasculated, literature expurgated, art censored.[11]

As elsewhere, the cultural activities of Danbury ladies cut both ways. Without them there would have been fewer concerts, less of the musical life on which Charles Ives's art was grounded. Inevitably, though, the same women threatened the teenager's fragile and developing sense of masculine identity. From the beginning, as he confessed, Charlie was "partly ashamed" of music because it took him away from a boy's life. Yet the more he became a "classical" musician and church organist, the more he worked with women. They were some of his teachers, his main co-performers in concerts, and the bulk of his audience.

In that dilemma—which he could mitigate only by playing sports and staying close to his father—lay the foundation of anxieties that would last a lifetime.[12] Among its themes, the story of Charles Ives includes his lifelong crescendo of vituperation against what he considered emasculated art, against the people he named lilypads, mollycoddles, Rollos, old ladies, aunties, pansies, pussies, and on through the wretched lexicon of invective much of which he shared with his time, but wielded more obsessively than most. His predicament was bitter, inevitable, and nobody's fault. During an age in which men and women cooperated in relentlessly circumscribing women's roles, Charlie grew up with an abiding interest in what was perceived as women's territory, irrelevant to the business of American males—still less of Connecticut Yankee males. That situation created paradoxes and contradictions in his psyche and potentially in his art.

In his teens music became life and breath to Ives; he played and composed daily from then on. He might have stuck with the masculine world of bandsmen and vernacular music, but that could not satisfy his instinctive creative breadth and ambition. More or less despite himself, he was drawn into the cultivated tradition, and so into the intimidating milieu of gentility and of women. Cultivated music fulfilled Charlie's creative drive at the same time that it threatened his masculinity. It also threatened the vital vernacular music that his father represented: Charlie felt the discrepancy in fervor and immediacy between the parade or the revival on one hand, the genteel parlor recital on the other. (Maybe later he sensed the class underpinnings of that divide—bands and revivals appealed more to working-class women and men, recitals more to the upper crust.) As a result, drawn to the cultivated tradition, he would not let go of the vernacular side of music.

On the surface, on a given day, much of Charles Ives's response to the psychological threat of feminization was predictably irrational (if we believe, from our perspective, that feeling unmanned by such circumstances is irrational). All the same, there was a more immediate foundation for his later anxieties and tirades, one not so irrational. Women's artistic tastes were notoriously conservative and sentimental. We see the tone in this lady's newspaper review of June 1890, headed "The Greatest Artistic Success of the Season," of the concert in which Charlie played several organ works:

"Welcome, Pretty Primrose." Pinsuti, as rendered by Master George Moore, the boy soprano, was a dream of delight, for his wonderful voice rung like a silver bell, and rippled along like the murmuring of a gently-flowing brooklet. In response to an encore, Master Moore gave the gem of the evening in "Angels Ever Bright and Fair," in so charming a manner that one could almost fancy he heard the flutter of white wings and heard the music of distant harps.[13]

One fancies one hears the same treacly tone in a good many Victorian parlor songs by Stephen Foster and his ilk—and by Charles Ives. Nor are Ivesian forays into the Victorian parlor song always satiric; like his father, Ives loved Foster's songs to the end of his life. For example, in the song pair "Memories" of 1897, Ives begins with a breathless and quite funny description of sitting in an opera house waiting for the curtain to go up and feeling "expectancy, a certain kind of ecstasy." Then, by way of the first number after the curtain, he lovingly sets his own maudlin lyrics to a Fosterish melody:

From the street a strain on my ear doth fall,
A tune as threadbare as that "old red shawl,"
It is tattered, it is torn, it shows signs of being worn,
It's the tune my Uncle hummed from early morn.
'Twas a common little thing and kind 'a sweet,
But 'twas sad and seemed to slow up both his feet;
I can see him shuffling down to the barn or to the town, a-humming.

Even though he was capable of perpetrating it himself, such Victorian manifestations by others could touch off an Ivesian barrage of "manly" obscenities and name-calling. Beyond matters of taste and adolescent sexual anxieties, there had to have been a good deal of humiliating personal experience behind these outbursts. No doubt his attempts to inject his experiments into recitals and church services regularly met with more grief from women than from men. On the manuscript of his organ prelude on "Adeste Fideles" of 1897, we find the note: "Rev. J. B. Lee, others & Mrs Uhler said it was awful".[14] On another sketch: "To hear the old girls scold brings up all the mean remarks up to the surface first crack."[15] For a teenager of hair-trigger sensibilities like Charlie, these must have been exquisitely humiliating moments.

These double binds, centrifugal tensions aesthetic, psychological, and sociological, threatened Ives's creative balance from beginning to end. They never defeated him, but they made his balance the more fragile, his achievement in maintaining it more a matter of courage than of confidence. Courage takes more energy than confidence; it costs more. But while the courage sustained him, Ives would not only transcend his ambiguities but find ways to make them enrich and even define his art.

In 1890, George Ives got his picture taken in his piped and braided uniform as leader of the Danbury Band. It is George's best photograph and probably was displayed in the house. Then at the end of that year he resigned as director. For over two decades he had led some of the town's finest musicians. Now, though he probably continued to play and direct here and there, he seemed to have given up music, the first and grandest dream he ever had.

The likeliest reason for this dramatic change is simple enough: George had two sons about to enter college and he could not make enough money in music to support them. He had long supplemented his income with bookkeeping; now he had to do more. At some point during those years he worked as a clerk under his nephew Howdie—Howard Merritt Ives, who kept the books for the hat factory of his maternal uncle Charles H. Merritt.[16] Probably it was depressing for George to be an employee of his nephew. Worse, as a liberal with friends among working people, George was hardly fond of his rich second cousin Merritt, whose crusade against unions included forming the American Anti-Boycott Association.[17] Danbury architect Philip Sunderland would remember George as an unhappy, muttering man around the office. One day, as

Merritt supervised some carpenters bridging a stream outside the factory, George snapped within earshot of Sunderland, "There you are, you damned old monopolist, you have to tell them how to build a bridge!"[18]

George E. Ives in his uniform as director of the Danbury Brass and Quadrille Band.

Around 1891 George took a position as a teller in the Danbury Savings Bank, which his father had founded[19]; in 1894 he became a director. By requirement or choice, George worked dutifully at the brick building next to the Ives House, often opening the doors in the morning and closing them at night.[20] He did what he had to for his family, but he seems to have taken little pleasure in it. Everything had come down on George at once. He had devoted his life to music and in the end had to submit to what he had spent all those years trying to avoid: clocks and bosses and suits. Certainly he realized that as far as most of the town was concerned he was finally getting a job, finally growing up. To them he was a failure because he had only been a musician. To himself he was a failure because he hadn't made a go of the job he loved. He had even become dated musically, a relic of the postwar years when bands were the glory of town musical life. Now Shelley's chorus and other cultivated organizations, the kinds of programs Charlie appeared in, got most of the attention.[21]

It is likely that George Ives was a disappointed man in those years, and maybe a bitter one. He became less the lighthearted enthusiast that had made him everybody's friend and an ideal band director.[22] Beyond that, there are hints that his health was failing. In a photo of 1893 he looks worn and sad and surprisingly aged since the portrait in his uniform three years earlier.

There was still more weighing on him: His relations with his elder son had changed for the worse. For reasons partly generational, partly temperamental, there appears to have been less of the sharing and closeness that had once been vital to both. From around 1890, nearly every surviving letter between them reveals more strain than affection. Charlie was growing up and about to leave home; like most teenagers on the brink of adulthood, he pushed for freedom. Though his rebellion would remain passive,[23] Charlie was as stubborn as all the Iveses. Just as stubbornly, George balked at giving up control. If anything he became more demanding: Charlie was to practice, he was to study, he was to write his letters neatly and correctly.

And Charlie was to go to Yale, like old Isaac and most of the ensuing Iveses, Whites, Merritts, and Brewsters who had gone to college at all. The family history there would help, but getting Charlie admitted was going to be a stretch; his grades had gotten embarrassing in the last few years. The first step was to put him into an institution that specialized in preparing boys for Yale—Hopkins Grammar School in New Haven. Charlie would be sent there in the spring of 1893.

In March of that year Charlie, presumably with his father, heard Paderewski play Bach, Scarlatti, Beethoven, Chopin, and Liszt at Carnegie Hall.[24] It may have been their last trip to New York together. On April 16 Charlie played at the dedication of the new Danbury Baptist Church. The program included his "Song for Harvest Season"; the manuscript notes that "father played the cornet, Mrs Smyth tried to sing & I played lower parts." The end of that month saw his last service as organist of the church.[25]

These were Charles Ives's farewell performances in Danbury. From then on he would be only a visitor in his hometown. The town began to recede in his mind into a nostalgic aura, finally to become the mythical Danbury that he would bequeath to the world as an image of the primal community. From that arose all his other conceptions of community: the nationwide bond of insured families, the national town meeting proposed in his 1920 constitutional amendment, the global joining he would call the People's World Union, and from there into the stars, humanity taking its destined place in the community of angels.

Hopkins Grammar School was founded in 1660, forty-one years before Yale. In Charles Ives's day it stood, rather shabbily, at the corner of Wall and High Streets. There was no dormitory, so Charlie and other boarding students stayed at rooming houses in New Haven. Though the school in those years was in a period of decline, it still managed to get a fair number of its graduates through the gates of Yale, a couple of blocks away. Hopkins mirrored New Haven's famous college in classroom style, in an emphasis on Greek and Latin, in its wooden fence where students perched and passed the time, and in its secret society (which took Charlie in).[26] Athletics were the main excitement; in 1876 a Hopkins baseball nine, with Walter Camp on the mound, had first beaten the Yale freshmen.[27] At Hopkins that was the pinnacle of success.

Amidst enrolling and looking for a flat, Charlie also found an organist position, at St. Thomas' Episcopal Church. The music director there was a forbidding British gentleman named Charles Bonney, whom Charlie didn't particularly like. A letter of Bonney's to his new organist, accompanying some music for services, suggests his style: "I hope you will carefully read the Psalter Preface, for therein lies the whole secret of my plan of chanting. . . . I want to urge you most strongly to study the Prayer Book thoroughly too. That after all is the rule and guide for everything and everybody in the Episcopal Church."[28]

Charlie was by then, at eighteen, an old pro, but this sort of high-church service was a continent away from the relatively unceremonious Baptists of Danbury. After his first Sunday at St. Thomas on May 7, 1893, he nervously wrote his father, "I had the most trouble with the chants, and found the best way to learn them was to commit the music [to memory] and follow the words. They sing their hymns faster than I have been accustomed to and it is rather hard to get used to it."[29] As usual in those days, his letter is addressed "Dear Father" instead of the onetime "Dear Papa," and is signed "C." He adds, "The nine goes to Bridgeport Saturday afternoon." He sat with the Hopkins team for their picture in July.

In the middle of that month an exciting proposal arrived from George: "Your Uncle Lyman has been appointed Commissioner on Equalization of Laws, & is to be paid expenses to attend convention at Milwaukee the first week in September. He could get a secretary's expenses & thought if you could go."[30] The real thrill was that Lyman and Charlie would have time to visit the World's Columbian Exposition in Chicago. At the end of the letter, George corrected some spelling and grammar mistakes in Charlie's last letter.

Lyman and his nominal secretary boarded the train west, and on August 20 sat listening to Theodore Thomas's Orchestra at the fairground in Chicago.[31] A few days later Charlie heard a recital by the French organist Alexandre Guilmant, whose music had long been in his repertoire.[32] At the time, Charlie and his uncle probably saw this visit simply as an adventure in the wide world. But the importance of the Columbian Exposition in Charlie's future, and in the country's, would be considerable. This would be one of the times that Ives made contact with a critical moment in American history. His appearance on the fairground along with Thomas and Guilmant—as well as John Philip Sousa, Scott Joplin, Augustus Saint-Gaudens, Stanford White, Henry Adams, Houdini, and Little Egypt—makes for irresistible symbolism.

On May 1, 1893, opening day of the World's Columbian Exposition celebrating the 400th anniversary of Columbus's voyage, President Grover Cleveland threw a switch and the giant fairground exploded into a panoply of light and towering fountains. It was the American public's first and perhaps most awe-inspiring experience of the power of electricity. In daylight and in the new man-made radiance of night, Frederick Law Olmsted's two miles of grounds spread along Lake Michigan, crowned by the White City of buildings by McKim, White, and other renowned architects, which fronted on an artificial lagoon. There came to be an aura almost of holiness around this radiant spectacle of American art and technology.

Atop the Agricultural Building flew Saint-Gaudens's notoriously naked sculpture of Diana the Huntress, intended for the Women's Building until protests of indecency forced a move. More unequivocally naughty was Little Egypt's hootchy-kootchy show on the Midway. Her supposedly authentic belly dance was commemorated in the popular tune "Streets of Cairo," which would intimate sin for generations to come. Fairgoers whisked around the 200-foot-tall wheel of George Ferris. On the Midway a teenager who had recently changed his name from Weiss to Houdini astounded audiences by shedding locks and chains as easily as Little Egypt shed her veils.[33]

Above all, the Exposition would live in history for the repercussions of the White City. Glowing like marble but made mostly of plaster of paris, it announced the triumph of the classical pastiche, derived from French Beaux-Arts style, that over the next decades inspired wedding-cake buildings all over the country.[34] But the Exposition's leverage on the future went beyond architecture into matters large and small, material and spiritual. Standing before the hulking dynamos that powered the fair, Henry Adams began the process of thought that led to "The Dynamo and the Virgin," in which he speculated uneasily on the new complexity of technology and life.

In America's past lay the old agrarian society; just ahead loomed an urban technological society. The fair heralded the future of architecture, technology, and the arts in the United States. Theodore Thomas, then conducting the Chicago Symphony, had been drafted as music director. He had planned a broad variety of presentations including popular and light-classical band programs, leading up in degrees of refinement to full-blown orchestral concerts. Within the first weeks of the fair, however, it became clear that the bands were getting most of the attention. The average attendance for the dollar-a-head classical concerts was 100, while the free band concerts drew thousands. At the beginning of August, Thomas resigned as music director of the fair and tersely counseled that "for the remainder of the Fair music shall not figure as an art at all, but be treated on the basis of an amusement."[35]

So it would be. John Philip Sousa's resident Military Band was the musical sensation of the fair. His programs established two tunes in the American ear: the lusty "Ta-ra-ra Boom-de-ay!" and the sentimental waltz "After the Ball is Over." Already famous as "the March King," Sousa played "After the Ball" at the end of every day; it became the theme song of the fair. On the Midway (the first to be so called) another kind of music evolved from its past as a bawdyhouse accompaniment to become a national craze: the syncopated style called ragtime, performed by a contingent of black musicians including, for a short while, young cornetist Scott Joplin. Within another decade, Joplin would be crowned "King of Ragtime."[36] With his resignation, Theodore Thomas conceded that all this rough royalty could draw the multitudes he had labored his entire career, with only modest results, to capture for refined music.

Charlie dashed from exhibit to exhibit, concert to concert, Midway attraction to attraction during the week or so he and Uncle Lyman spent at the fair, on two visits in mid-August and early September. Some of the consequences in his later music are clear, though incidental: in pieces of the next decade he quoted "Ta-ra-ra Boom-de-ay!" and "After the Ball," which he may have picked up from Sousa; he slipped "Streets of Cairo" into a quartet movement, so maybe he and Lyman had a gander at Little Egypt.[37] More important, Charlie could hardly have missed hearing ragtime on the Midway. It is intriguing to contemplate Charles Ives listening to Scott Joplin one summer night in Chicago. We will never know if that happened, but one cannot miss ragtime's impact on his music. It would give his rhythmic sense an infusion of fresh ideas without which he might never have found his voice.[38]

The triumph of "amusement" over cultivated music at the Exposition had its consequences on the future of music in the United States. "After the Ball" became the first popular song in history to sell over a million copies,[39] finally racking up sales of five million. With the Columbian Exhibition and its hit tunes we find the beginnings of Tin Pan Alley, of the big-time music business that was to feed on and accelerate the commercialization of the whole culture.[40] Heralding the international conquest of American popular music, ragtime would sweep the country and the world, paving the way for the success of blues, jazz, and rock 'n' roll.

The teenaged Charles Ives was not exactly a rube, but more sophisticated visitors than he were overwhelmed by the sights and sounds of the Columbian Exposition. Henry Adams wrote, "As a scenic display Paris never approached it . . . [it was] more surprising . . . than anything else in the continent, Niagara Falls, the Yellowstone Geysers, and the whole railway system thrown in." One can imagine that as the spectacle washed over Ives, it left a vision of the future that marked his life and work. The effect on him cut in contradictory directions, though. It showed him the most advanced ideas of his age and exuberant new kinds of music that would help remake his own. The coming urban culture was the setting of his business success. At the same time, the commercialization of music (different from the past not so much in kind as in scope) hastened the decline of the community music-making that was Charles Ives's creative wellspring.

In other words the cultural changes heralded by the fair simultaneously enriched and threatened him. The coming technologies of radio and recording would doom community music. As an adult, Ives detested radio, movies, and the other new mass media, seeing them as destroying the immediacy of contact between art and people. In his childhood anyone wishing to hear music had to play it or sit close by and listen to someone play it. He was to see the advent of entertainment that only required the faceless, distant listener to turn a knob, and that horrified him. Ives remembered "what imagination can do for the better amusement of fortunate children who have to do for themselves— much-needed lessons in these days of automatic, ready-made, easy entertain-ment which deaden rather than stimulate the creative faculty."[41] He never owned a radio and never saw, or admitted seeing, a movie. In his song "The Ruined River" Ives equates the babble of mass culture with the ruin of nature:

> Down the river comes a noise!
> It is not the voice of rolling waters.
> It's only the sounds of man,
> Dancing halls and tamborine,
> Phonographs and gasoline.
> Human beings gone machine.

All these developments would unfold in the future, after the World's Columbian Exposition sank into Charles Ives and into the country. At the time Charlie simply dashed, with Uncle Lyman in tow. Lyman wrote home to his wife, reassuring Amelia about their health and deportment:

Charley's task as "Secretary of the Com. Commission" was not very onerous, about four hours in all. . . . We have had a reception at the Schlitze [sic] Park Wednesday night of the regular German sort, sort of a Promenade Concert—music & Lager the characteristic ingredients. . . . You need have no apprehensions as to C's health. He has weighed at every stop & has found no deficiency in weight. If there has been any over-action it is in chewing gum—strictly confined to our room.[42]

By the second week of September 1893, Charlie was back in New Haven to take his exams at Hopkins. Having scraped by, he turned his attention to football and was elected manager of the team. In the letter home with that news, he concluded with a peevish note to his mother: "I wish you would please get somebody else to write your letters as I can hardly make them out."[43] Friction with his family would only get worse during the coming year.

Charlie was largely on his own now. He had found himself a church job and lodging with a Hopkins roommate, at 7 Park Street.[44] No longer did his life gravitate around Danbury and its elaborate but inbred musical life, or around the old house full to stifling of family history. For the time being, getting away from all that seems to have suited Charlie fine. Insulated by distance, he did what he wanted to do and deflected family complaints as best he could. What he wanted to do, mostly, was put off studying and have fun. This is a common theme in the biographies of prodigies: the time of breaking away from years of family-imposed discipline. Charlie's rebellion would be relatively quiet, but dogged. As always, he would do an able job at the organ on Sundays; by now that probably cost him little effort. And as always, he would be working steadily on new pieces.

At the end of October 1893, Charlie wrote his father a hedging letter, trying to put the best slant on a brutal afternoon of football. There is, though, a touch of pride at being part of the mayhem:

We rec'd your telegrams last evening, and answered both. I suppose you thought I was nearly killed, as all the papers here had accounts of horrible accidents, and how we had to be carried off the field etc, etc. They say that there were accts. of it in N.Y. papers. Cheny got the worst of it as he broke his collar bone, but I just bruised the cartilage of the lower part of the nose. [In fact, it was broken.] It pains quite a good deal, but Doct. Cheny says it will be all right in a week or so, and will not leave any scar of [*sic*] deformity. [He would have a crooked nose for life.][45]

That Sunday the organist of St. Thomas' Episcopal Church played services with a white plaster on his nose. Perhaps to see if he was more maimed than he admitted, Mollie Ives showed up in New Haven soon after. She and George were worried, for good reason, that he might injure his hands.[46] Charlie would tiptoe around the subject of football for a while. Increasingly in the next months he also begged off visiting home:

I doubt if I will be able to come home Thanksgiving, as there is to be services in the church on that day. I have been playing tennis this week, instead of football. . . . I am trying to finish up the fugue now, which I began last winter. [He was ordered home for Thanksgiving.]

I hardly think it would be worth while for me to come home Saturday, just . . . to try the clothes, as I see of no time now when I shall need to use them . . . and I am usually very busy Sat. [This letter to his father is starchily signed "Chas. E. I."]

I suppose I can come Wed. evening but there is a card party which I would rather like to go and then Thurs. the asst. organist wanted to have me play at the 4:00 Lenten service. . . . Then I have a debate Friday which I expected to work on. . . . Of course I would like to see you all, but it is such a short time to Easter. Please let me know if you still think I had better come. [Reply: He *had* better come.][47]

In March 1894, Charlie tried out for another organist position, in a more familiar kind of service, at the Baptist church. It was the first time on record that he didn't get a job, and he figured there had to have been a fix. In a letter home he prods Uncle Lyman to pull some strings concerning another position.

I have finally managed to find Dr. Walker the chairman of the Baptist Ch. committee and he says that the committee have decided on a Mr. Hogson, I don't know how the name is spelled nor have I ever heard of him before, except that he was the one that offered to do it for nothing and was the one that Mr. Wheeler, the former organist, critized [*sic*] the most. Dr. Walker told me himself that this one knew some of the committee personally, and that may [have] had something to do with it. . . . It seems as if everything here was run that same way, by a "pull", and that is one of the reasons that I think it would be better for Unc. Lyman to see Prof. Stoeckel [of Yale] and the sooner the better, as I heard that he is going away . . . and that also, Jepson [Yale organ instructor and Center Church organist] was going to Germany next fall to study, and that will probably leave the center church, and the Asst. organist at Chapel open . . . / I am bound that I will not let all of these things interfere, with my musical studies . . . although it does make one feel blue, etc. . . . The first thing I am going to get the best of [presumably in college] is the harmony & counterpoint, which I ought to get through with out taking much time to it with Dr. Stoeckel. There is some kind of a music course in college which I will look up . . . / I don't see now why things at school hadn't ought to go all right. . . . Mr. Fox . . . asked me how my arm was for baseball. . . . I don't quite see what you mean by the "appearances" it would make. It would be a means of regular out door exercise and don't take much time. . . . Of course if you decidedly think it would hurt me very much, why I won't. . . . I won't let the N.Y. trip interfere with work, but am very anxious to see what Wagner Opera is.[48]

He attended a performance of *Götterdämmerung* at the Metropolitan Opera. His letter home about it, written with due concern for the feelings of his Wagner-loving father, gives it a tortuously mixed review, with a blend of insight and naïveté appropriate, respectively, to his intelligence and his age:

I could easily see what Wagner tried to [do]. You wouldn't notice the music or the orchestra, as it all seems to be a part of and go along with the action and story. I don't mean that you wouldn't notice it . . . but, that it feels as if it was only made to help one pay attention to the action. I don't remember of any particular piece or song that you would notice simply for the music itself unless it was the "Song of the Rhinedaughter" at the beginning of the 2nd Act. There are some things that don't seem exactly natural. For instance in one place, Siegfried is supposed to be greatly furiated at Brünhilde and she has a long song in which she is greatly excited and upbraids him, but he, instead of interrupting her waits until the orchestra plays a long intermezzo, and then begins, and there were several other places like that struck me as being rather unnatural, although there was probably some reason for it. . . . And then the using so much horn and kettledrums, grows awful tiresome towards the end. . . . Of course I don't mean to criticize but this is just as it seemed to me, but probably if I had studied it more before, I would think differently. . . . I wish I had time to study and hear all of his operas. Everything all together is great and you can see just what his idea was, and it seems funny that nobody thought of it before. Although it does seem that if it had more rhymn [*sic*] or connected melody (you know what I mean) in his music, and if the action was more natural, and if the plot had more sense to it, as it was just a common fairy story, it looks like a great deal of work over nothing, or if it was a fact in real history, or taken from some noted book, so that some educational benefit could be gotten from it. Will send the program and libretto, when I send wash, as I want you to read it over and tell what you think.[49]

A few days later, on April 3, came an experience that unequivocally excited Charlie, and which he would recall proudly for the rest of his life: he pitched for Hopkins in their 10–9 defeat of the Yale freshman baseball team.

Pitcher Charles Ives, left, and catcher Franklin Hobart Miles, the winning combination that beat Yale for Hopkins Grammar School.

As a pitcher Charlie tended to be a little wild, but he was good at catching runners off-base.[50] It was only the second Hopkins victory over Yale. The college boys had been paying scant attention and confused the last inning for the eighth. A week later the Yalies got their revenge to the tune of 19–0, in a game called after seven innings on account of hopelessness.[51] That probably failed to dampen Hopkins' or Charlie's euphoria. Next month the team elected him captain.[52]

George was putting more dampers on Charlie's style, however. Replying to another critical letter (probably about baseball and bad grades), Charlie wrote on April 12, 1894,

Why don't you think that I don't understand your letters. Maybe I don't write as if I did but I think I understand what you have advised and what I have got to do. . . . The best I can do now is to study and exercise, with the church work. . . . I don't see how things could go better now either at church or school. Please send hat as soon as convenient, as I described in a letter to Moss.[53]

At the end of March, Charlie had ended the job at St. Thomas under the martinet Bonney. Still, he began to take singing lessons with Bonney and George criticized that too, this time apparently on the grounds of its being a waste of time and suspiciously sissy. George did not forbid the lessons and probably paid for them, but he instructed Charlie not to tell the rest of the family. Confused, Charlie wrote back, "I can't think of anything in my last letter that wouldn't do for the family to hear. Don't they know I'm taking singing lessons, and if they don't, don't you want them to know?"[54] Charlie continued to write George about the lessons: "[Bonney] believes that singing is only an extension of talking, and makes me say a certain sentence and then sing it with the same kind of voice." (That idea was to be a foundation of his mature songwriting.)

His grades continued to languish despite tutoring from a Mrs. Porter. She kept George apprised of Charlie's Yale chances, which were not looking so good. Finally the family hired another tutor for a summer's worth of cramming, supervised by Uncle Lyman. There were thirty-two hours billed in June, and considerably more into September, the subjects including Latin, English, and German, much of it done at the vacation place in Westbrook.[55] Charlie submitted, grudgingly; the subjects bored him to distraction and he wanted to swim and fish and play tennis. He had other concerns on his mind too. It may have been that summer that he sketched some of the most astonishing pieces of his life.

He sits at the piano trying out superimpositions of chords, looking for something that sounds right for this psalm, "God, be merciful unto us." He gets it finally, a rich complex made of a G-minor chord in men's voices, C major in the women's. With that sonority as a foundation, a home chord, he goes on, mainly following his ear (theory and history can help him little here), finding chords that seem to agree with that opening, that mystical sound, and setting the words in a kind of chant as in the Episcopal service.[56]

This was *Psalm 67,* one of his unforgettable miniatures.[57] George seems to have tried out the piece—at least an early version of it—with his church choir.[58] Its vibrant close harmonies explore chordal streams running in two keys between men's and women's voices (though Ives allows chromatic notes in both streams, perhaps to avoid dissonant cross-relations). Beyond its unprecedented sound, the psalm is an elegantly shaped arch with chanted sections that symmetrically frame a vigorous imitative episode reminiscent of the "fuging tunes" of colonial hymnody.[59] Oddly enough, what seems partly to have guided Charlie's ear through this new polytonal world are the close harmonies of barbershop music—like ragtime, a genre in its heyday during the 1890s.[60] The effect of *Psalm 67* resembles a sort of cosmic barbershop choir. When it slides into a cadence reminiscent of the style, it seems satisfyingly startling in a context of mystery and worship.

Like Stravinsky's *King of the Stars, Psalm 67* is a sport in Ives's work and in music generally. He never returned to its sound, and there is nothing anywhere quite like it.[61] As with all the short psalm settings of that period, it is an unprecedented musical world fully formed and confidently explored. In these works his childhood experiments with dissonance and polytonality begin to acquire shape and direction.[62] Even as a teenager, Ives must already have been haunted by a common specter of twentieth-century composers, which Stravinsky describes in the *Poetics* as "a sort of terror when . . . finding myself before the infinitude of possibilities that present themselves, I have the feeling that everything is permissible to me . . . if nothing offers me any resistance, then any effort is inconceivable . . . and consequently every undertaking becomes futile."[63] To a composer this terror is more than metaphysical. To leave the familiar foundation of diatonic harmonies and their rules and traditions is to suffer a paralyzing freedom. The response of a true composer—one for whom *composing* means what it says, putting things in order—is to erect boundaries in the void. Arnold Schoenberg responded to the specter of the arbitrary with the twelve-tone system. Stravinsky wrote: "My freedom thus consists in my moving about within the narrow frame that I have assigned myself for each one of my undertakings."[64]

When he wrote *Psalm 67*, Charles Ives was a small-town American teen-ager, hardly under the cultural onus and historical self-consciousness that afflicted Stravinsky and Schoenberg. Nonetheless, he felt the same drive to control his new freedom, and he began to find ways in psalm settings of the mid-1890s. For a while, his most elaborate experiments would be found in this series of choral psalms. They are etudes in new ways of ordering harmony, growing out of his earlier "research" pieces and presaging ones for the rest of his career.

All the same, as would be characteristic of all his music, Ives does not hesitate to adjust his patterns if they do not please his ear, or if they threaten to become mechanical. His early psalms prophesy serialism, but he would never accept the inflexibility of later composers in applying systems. Later we will find him setting up elaborate formulas and then deliberately introducing "mistakes" into them. He writes a credo about formalism in the margin of the song "Majority": "Occasionally something made in this calculated, diagram, design way may have a place in music . . . but generally or too much or alone . . . it is a weak substitute for inspiration or music. It's too easy, any high-school student (unmusical) with a pad, pencil, compass & logth table . . . could do it. . . . This wall paper design music is not as big as a natural mushy ballad."

The other three early psalms that survive are not so monumental in effect as *Psalm 67*, but reach the same level of ingeniousness and imagination. *Psalm 150*, "Praise ye the Lord," is a brilliant, fanfarish piece for adult chorus, four-part boy's choir, and organ. Here Ives creates layered effects, the boys holding sustained harmonies while the main choir declaims chords—still traditional triads—moving chromatically around them. He got the idea from the singing in camp meetings, when "the fervor of the feeling would at times . . . throw the key higher, sometimes a whole tone up," while the accompaniment stayed the same.[65] And so with Ives, the "unmusical" became music and symbol.

In *Psalm 54*, "Save me, O God," he plays another game with planes of harmonies, the women and men singing independent cycles of augmented triads, with the added fillip that now the women are rhythmically independent from the men (the men in half notes, women in triplets). Thus Ives adds a hint of polyrhythm to enhance the chordal independence of each plane.

Psalm 24, "The earth is the Lord's," is the thorniest and most revolution-ary of the lot. The other pieces experiment with novel superimpositions of traditional harmonies. In *Psalm 24*, Ives became perhaps the first composer in Western history to discard the old harmonies altogether and launch into chromatic space, finding fresh kinds of logic from which to derive sounds unknown to the past, and anticipating techniques Webern and Bartók arrived at decades later. In *Psalm 24* the outer voices fan out like wedges from a central middle C, the symmetry of voice movement creating a series of unique harmonies.

The fanning process is systematic, the first wedge opening at the smallest interval and each succeeding wedge one notch wider; finally the process roughly reverses to arrive back at the first pitch.[66] For all the wildness of sound, the tonal design is so logical that it arrives back on C with an inevitability nearly as strong as a traditional cadence. The piece also suggests other thumbprints of Ives's maturity—text-setting in free, prose-like rhythms, the sudden gospel harmony (on "O Jacob") appearing out of a dissonant context.[67]

Before these radical works of the mid-1890s, Charlie had composed two or three conventional pieces of more than passing interest and some tentative experiments. With the *Psalms* he leaped into the future in a way neither he nor anyone else could yet understand, because that future could not possibly be anticipated. In those years Schoenberg—the same age as Ives but a late starter—was just beginning to study counterpoint, and the teenaged Stravinsky was tinkering with piano and preparing to study law. (Meanwhile Brahms, in the twilight of his career, was writing his late clarinet sonatas. In a way, young Charles Ives had been invaded by the future, a future as strange as if he, or a part of himself, had been abducted to another time. What did the singers and congregations think when George Ives tried some of these psalms with his Danbury choir, or when Charlie later tried them out in New Haven and New York?

Charlie would not be forced to confront, quite yet, the implications of that question, which was to be one of the great dilemmas of his life: ordinary people, from whom he derived his music, consistently rejected it. He did not yet understand the significance of what he was doing, or its strangeness. He was still a teenager playing games, following his private train of logic where it led him while his father, still the listener whose response he most cared about, steadily encouraged him.

For the next several years, though, Charlie would have to put his experimental side—already capable of producing music both revolutionary and durable—on the back burner. He was about to get his wrist slapped, and would spend his college years backing up and filling in what he needed to know about shaping larger pieces. That process began with a blow that would change everything.

The fates were stalking Charlie and his father now, as the two played unheeding through the perennial script of adolescence, of boyish stretching for independence and parental resistance, all made worse by a careworn and ailing father.

George Ives in the last year of his life.

Somewhere in or just before 1894, George apparently sat Charlie down and told him to stay away from music as a career. Music had not supported George's family and he could not see how it would support his son's. He had tried to make a concert pianist of his boy, but Charlie never showed much interest in that. Certainly George recognized in his son a calling to music as strong as the one he had felt in boyhood, and a gift far beyond his own. But as a father who knew the musical life, he must have balked at the idea of his son's attempting a career as a composer of classical music. In the United States of those days, as today, the profession verged on chimerical. Of course, George would have added, Charlie should keep playing, maintain his church jobs, compose. But leave it a pastime, as they did, probably wisely after all, in Danbury. The gist of all this, which we may hope George Ives left unspoken, was: *Don't be a failure like me.*

Years later, Charles Ives would put the best face on what his father told him. Likely most of the words are the son's:

Father felt that a man could keep his music-interest stronger, cleaner, bigger, and freer, if he didn't try to make a living out of it. Assuming a man lived by himself and with no dependents . . . [he] might write music that no one would play, publish, listen to, or buy. *But*—if he has a nice wife and some nice children, how can he let the children starve on his dissonances . . . So he has to weaken (and as a man he should weaken for his children), but his music . . . more than weakens—it goes "ta ta" for money—bad for him, bad for music, but good for his boys!![68]

George Ives had been forced to weaken for his boys (the boys Charles Ives would never have), and left music. In a way his son would do the same, as advised.

Though Charlie proclaimed himself dutiful, through the spring and summer of 1894 the friction between him and his father continued. In March, Charlie wrote home with barely contained anger,

I don't see why you insist on blaming everything on ball, or at least because I didn't write a good letter last Sunday. . . . Mr. Fox has not complained to me at all for a long while, and I am sure he thinks I am doing all I can. . . . Sunday after I had gotten lessons out of the way, I was working on a little song. . . . I worked later than I expected to, and then wrote that letter. I was rather tired and probably that was the reason it was so poor. I will try to have better ones in the future. . . . The last part of this letter is not written perhaps as well as I can, but hope otherwise it is satisfactory.[69] [The end was cramped as the end of the page approached—he felt obliged to explain that to his demanding father.]

On the first day of September a tragedy put further strains on the family. Uncle Joe's only child, Howard Merritt Ives, Cousin Howdie, died at age thirty-four. Charlie was stunned; it was the first death in the immediate family he had seen. Finally at the end of that dismal month came two pieces of good news. Charlie had secured the most prestigious organ job in New Haven, at Center Church on the town green; and after a summer's tutoring he wired home that he had passed the entrance exam and been accepted to Yale. George's letter of congratulation is more relieved than enthusiastic. He and Mollie had not been well:

Dear Charles / Was glad to rec've Telegram. Want to know particulars but suppose you've been too busy to give details. As Mr. R. has gone to N.Y. I am to stay in Bank all day which will be the first day I have done so since last week Thursday. I feel awfully weak & shaky, but besides that & a cold & cough am about well I hope . . . Mother has another new Nurse, quite a young girl but starts off well.[70]

Charlie's life got very busy again, setting up in college, shopping for clothes and room furnishings. At the end of September he wrote his father:

Rec'd Moss' papers. [Moss edited the high school newspaper, and apparently put in a notice about his brother.] To read it, it would appear that I didn't often pass a successful examination (which is about right I guess). Ned is trying for foot ball team. Some of the fellows want to have me try, but of course have given up hopes of that. [The family had put its collective foot down about going out for the team, but Charlie would not be entirely denied:] They some times get fellows together later in the seasons and play scrub games, just for the fun of it . . . would like to play then if I get to it, and wish you send my football things.[71]

Classes began in early October. Charlie's letters home trace his way in these weeks. He moves into a dormitory room at 76 South Middle with roommate Mandeville Mullally, and writes his mother a list of things needed to fill out a comfortable, crowded Victorian dormitory room: bedstead, 12 × 15 rug, Franklin stove, desk chairs, easy chairs, curtains, lamps, washstand, accessories. He spends time practicing and learning the ropes at Center Church. His summer tutor writes to the parents that Charlie "will, I am sure, be better appreciated by his instructors here than by those at the Hopkins Grammar School." He buys tickets for a Beethoven series by the Kneisel Quartet and attends a New Haven Symphony concert. He plays intramural football nearly every day. His first Sunday at Center Church goes well. Horatio Parker, Yale's new music professor, gives an organ recital in Battell Chapel.[72]

In those hectic weeks of autumn, too, the fates indulged in their sense of irony, their literary flair. On October 29, 1894, Charlie wrote in haste to George,

I started a letter Sunday evening to you but left it before I had finished, to go over to Dwight Hall as Mullally wanted to have me go with him to hear the Rev. Mr. Twichell of Hartford. . . . Please send march, music sheet paper, & that book of B. Cornwallis, that Dr. Stoeckel used, "Harmony."[73]

Six days later the news arrived, however it arrived—by telephone, by telegraph, by a friend or a stranger walking up and speaking the terrible, unbelievable words: *Your father is dead.*

Entr'acte One:
The Music of the Ages

A LIFE HAS A SHAPE, a form, the beginning and end the same for everybody, the rest of infinite variety. An artist's life has a more predictable form than most, involving a coalescing around the production of work, which sometimes becomes a profession but is always a compulsion. An artist's lifework has its own shape, its own biography, paralleling that of its creator but also obeying the logic of the medium.

Amidst an extraordinarily busy life outside music, from around the age of twelve to his mid-forties, Charles Ives composed like breathing, turning out a steady stream of work of mounting audacity and confidence. His beginnings as a composer unmistakably foreshadow his maturity. Though he would struggle for years to forge his mature style, its beginnings can be heard in the first flurries of his creative life: the *Holiday Quickstep*, written at age thirteen, paraphrases D. W. Reeves's *Second Regiment Connecticut National Guard March*. Ives would quote the same march twenty-five years later in one of the most beautifully realized works of his maturity, *Decoration Day*, part of a symphony called *Holidays*. The two works mark the widely separated stylistic poles of his music, but the tune and title, and some of the spirit, are the same.

Few composers begin with composing. Like Charles Ives, most start by learning an instrument, often acquiring considerable skill. Then the young performer discovers a rankling dissatisfaction, a yearning to go deeper into music than listening and playing can take you. Composing may begin as play, imitation, doing what Daddy or Mommy does; eventually it becomes absorbing and finally consuming, in every sense of the word. The young artist acquires a drive to compose that outweighs all the dilemmas (especially pointed dilemmas in nineteenth-century America) of pursuing an endeavor so extraneous to the usual rounds of life. In turn, the discovery of a drive to compose begins another learning process, similar to mastering an instrument but more fickle. One learns relatively quickly what it is to play well; composing well is a far more enigmatic affair, and few ever become first-rate at it.

Even more than an artist's life, the lifework has a roughly predictable shape, coalescing toward an approach, a voice, a maturity—call it a style. Often that style moves toward some sort of zenith and consummation, sometimes followed by a decline. The mature voice, call it the style of an artist, may be suggested early but usually only later assumes a definable identity. In the case of the painter Wassily Kandinsky, over the years of his work one sees horses and hills and moons melt out of representation into a vocabulary of hiero-glyphic abstractions we call *Kandinsky*. His beginnings contain his end, his end his beginnings.

Predictably for a beginner imitating the adults around him, Charles Ives started composing the kinds of pieces he heard every day—marches, a fiddle tune, church anthems, a genteel minuet for the parlor. A later age would call such stuff *Gebrauchsmusik,* functional music. But from early on Charlie would also take up and expand on the experiments of his father, finding in them a direction that would take him, to all appearances, far from his hometown and its music. In the end, though, all his paths would lead back to his roots. From its beginnings to its consummation in the Fourth Symphony, the shape of Ives's lifework—its assumptions, sounds, genres, settings—flowed from and returned to its wellspring in the music-making of Danbury.

Ives's life with music would be filled with detours, but most of the essen-tial elements were in place by the time of his first works in 1886: an imaginative and inspiring father and a vital community musical life with its cyclic celebra-tions, working on the sensibilities of an uncommonly gifted youth. More specifically, George Ives's experiments and ideas and the life of Danbury shaped the boy's perception of nearly every dimension of music. Perhaps the most salient of those perceptions had to do with melody.

Melody

"Father, who led the singing, sometimes with his cornet or his voice, sometimes with both voice and arms, and sometimes . . . with French horn or violin, would always encourage the people to sing their own way. . . . If they threw the poet or the composer around a bit, so much the better for the poetry and the music."[1] In the same spirit was George's observation about stonemason John Bell's off-key bellow at camp meetings: "Watch him closely and reverently, look into his face and hear the music of the ages. Don't pay too much attention to the sounds—for if you do, you may miss the music. You won't get a wild, heroic ride to heaven on pretty little sounds."[2]

His father's cues turned these experiences of amateur music, especially hymn singing, into some of the elemental impressions of Charles Ives's boy-hood. He could not separate the music on the page from the way people sang or played it. Even the coarseness of amateur performance seemed to Ives a sign of authenticity. The mistakes were part of the music; sometimes the mistakes were the music of the ages. Humble melodies lay in his memory like icons, illuminated by the halo of spirit and emotion townsfolk had bestowed on them. Commonplace tunes came to represent the common heart itself, the tunes like a creation of the whole people. For Ives the value of vernacular music, and eventually of all music, had to do not with the notes or the polish of the performance, but with the fervor and conviction behind them: "I've heard the same hymns played by nice celebrated organists and sung by highly-known singers in beautifully upholstered churches, and in the process every-thing in the music was emasculated."[3] Writing about Hawthorne but also about himself, Ives would proclaim in the *Essays* an art "not about something that happens, but the way something happens."[4] Elsewhere he exclaims, "My God! What does sound have to do with music?"[5] The music of the ages is the underlying spirit, of which the sounds are symbol. At his most visionary Ives proclaimed, *Music is life.*[5]

The words of songs had the same kind of resonance. The boy was struck by the occasions when his father played hymns on an instrument while listeners silently followed the words; thus the strange indication on the choral hymn *Watchman* in the Fourth Symphony: "Trumpet Col voices (preferably without voices)." Ives would write many songs without words, and often use hymns with reference to their texts whether or not voices were involved. "Nearer, My God, to Thee," sings the orchestra wordlessly throughout the Fourth Symphony, and there is where he proposes to take us.

Harmony

George Ives allowed his son a certain amount of boy's fooling with novel harmonies, in piano-drumming or otherwise. Meanwhile George taught Charlie the conventional rules from Salomon Jadassohn's textbooks (which would be inflicted on Charlie again at Yale, to his undying disgust). In contrast to Jadassohn, who presented European conventions of harmony and counter-point as dogma, George took a freethinker's approach. Part of an article of his on music theory survives, perhaps written for his classes[7]; there George cautions students to take nothing for granted, to use their ears, to note the absurd-ities lurking in tradition. In his words we find the questioning, curious, blunt, and iconoclastic temperament his son admired:

While you have been playing and listening to [the] above notes, it seemed as if you must do something to make something sound satisfactorily. . . . If not, keep at playing, singing, and listening . . . till you feel you must do something else [that is, resolve a dissonance].

The chord that you've been learning to call the dominant is called (among other names) the "dominant chord of the seventh," more names than it has tones. Poor thing! . . . (I feel like apologizing every time I use one of these names and will use them only when I feel compelled to.)

This 7th note produces what all musicians call a dissonance but sounds in some cases to me only like a partial dissonance and is used so much that we get used to it and treat it as if it were as much of a consonance as our other tones.

Ives describes his father indulging in still more heretical speculations: "If one can use chords of 3rds and make them mean something, why not chords of 4ths? . . . If one has twelve notes in an octave, why not more or less? If you can learn to like and use a consonance (so called), why not a dissonance (so called)?"[8]

In part these departures from theoretical dogma in the spirit of *why not* found sanctions in European thought, sanctions proclaimed in a sedate and scientific but nonetheless revolutionary book that lay in George Ives's library, and which filled father and son with an exhilarating sense of freedom and new horizons: *On the Sensations of Tone, As a Physiological Basis for the Theory of Music,* the pioneering 1877 work on acoustics by Hermann L. von Helmholtz, who denied that the assumptions of Western music theory are as natural as they claim:

At every step we encounter historical and national differences of taste. . . . What degree of roughness a hearer is inclined to endure as a means of musical expression depends on taste and habit; hence the boundary between consonances and dissonances has been frequently changed. Similarly Scales, Modes, and their Modulations have undergone multifarious alterations. . . . Hence it follows . . . that *the system of Scales, Modes, and Harmonic Tissues does not rest solely upon inalterable natural laws, but is at least partly also the result of esthetical principles, which have already changed, and will still further change, with the progressive development of humanity.*[9]

Among the echoes of that declaration in both Europe and America were the iconoclastic ideas of George Ives and of his son. Charles Ives would write, "Unity is too generally conceived of . . . as analogous to form; and form as analogous to custom; and custom to habit. . . . Perhaps all unity in art, at its inception is half-natural and half-artificial, but time . . . inclines to make us feel that it is all natural."[10]

Counterpoint

George taught his son conventional counterpoint (the art of interweaving melodies) and the old contrapuntal forms of fugue and canon, along with introducing him to the Bach repertoire that became a lifelong daily study and recreation for Charlie. In addition to learning orthodox counterpoint in Bach style, Charlie acquired further notions from what he heard around him in Danbury. That collaboration of his schooling and his experience galvanized a central train of logic that would run from the beginning to the end of his music: *a steadily growing independence and integrity of contrapuntal lines.* Which is to say, Ives broadened the concept of counterpoint until he could take into his reach an enormous range of heterogeneous material.

An important source of this evolution was his bone-deep feeling for some melodies as potent iconic objects—not to be used blandly and uncreatively, but still to be respected and somehow preserved with reference to their original form and context. That led to his habit of using borrowed melodies, the quotes rarely done literally but usually recognizable as "Sweet By and By," "Columbia, the Gem of the Ocean," or one of his other favored tunes.

Beyond his use of tunes as found objects, from boyhood Ives was accustomed to the band-march device of the *countermelody.* The device appears in the familiar Sousa march *Stars and Stripes Forever:* the first time through the trio one hears the theme alone, then after a brassy break the trio is repeated with a piccolo countermelody added above. In March No. 3 of 1893, Ives works in "My Old Kentucky Home" as a countermelody to his own tune. Abstractly considered, a countermelody is simply a counterpoint added to the main melodic theme, usually a theme already stated in the piece. In practice, the trick is to try and make the countermelody compete in interest with the original theme.

Traditional counterpoint tends to subdue the individuality of lines in deference to the total effect. In contrast, a march-style countermelody results in something like *quodlibet.* That term indicates a game of older composers going back before Bach: a combination of preexisting tunes. The last of Bach's *Goldberg Variations,* for example, makes a quodlibet of two German popular songs. In the *Memos,* Ives mentions a piece he destroyed, an "organ sonata a la Mendelssohn (but with a movement . . . of three old hymns—in the coda ending with the three going together)" in quodlibet.[11] Because of his love of traditional melodies and his experience with march-style countermelodies, Ives often wrote counterpoint in quodlibet or approaching it. Each line, borrowed or original, has the effect of a freestanding melody.

The revolutionary techniques Ives developed from his teens onward enormously amplified the independence of his lines. He had already filled his ears with fresh, free harmonies that held the potential—when he finally realized it—to free counterpoint from its subservience to traditional harmony.[12] A similarly freeing innovation was *bitonality* or *polytonality*—combinations of two (bi-) or more (poly-) keys simultaneously.[13] The idea came from George's ear-building exercise of accompanying in one key and having the boys sing in another.[14] Around 1891 Charlie made his bitonal experiments on surviving sketch pages, among them "London Bridge is Falling Down" in various juxtapositions of keys.[15] In the same period he included polytonal episodes in *Variations on "America"* and sketched polytonal fugues. Among his experiments with piano-drumming and bell sonorities and his polytonal inclinations, by the end of his teens Ives had stretched his ears to encompass a harmonic vocabulary enormously broader than that of any other composer in history, and which in practice phased into atonality. That in turn allowed his contrapuntal lines more freedom and integrity—a dimension beyond one-key quodlibet. Later, Ives's discoveries in *polyrhythm* added another dimension to the independence of parts. Now melodies could be going on not just in different keys but at different tempos simultaneously. (He devised polyrhythmic exercises for himself at the keyboard: "in the left hand a 5—with the left foot, beat a 2—with the right foot, beat a 3—with the right hand, play an 11—and sing a 7."[16])

Another feature of his most advanced music grew from his father's experiments spreading out performing forces. Along with his unprecedented harmonic freedom and exploration of polyrhythm, this element added a third dimension to the integrity of lines in a composition: space.

Space

The writer remembers hearing, when a boy, the music of a band in which the players were arranged in two or three groups around the town square. The main group in the bandstand at the center usually played the main themes, while the other, from the neighboring roofs and verandas, played the variations, refrains, etc. . . . The bandmaster told of a man who, living nearer the variations, insisted that they were the real music. . . . Others, walking around the square, were surprised at the different and interesting effects they got as they changed position. . . . The writer remembers, as a deep impression, the echo part from the roofs played by a chorus of violins and voices.[17] [Ives is probably describing his own band fantasy on "Jerusalem the Golden," now lost.]

In addition to this experience of spreading out musical forces, each group having its own job, Charlie absorbed his father's investigations of the effect of space on timbre. George would play for Charlie at increasing distances, or from across a pond, so the boy could gauge the effect of space on the tone. Charlie had an indelible memory of the sound of his father's cornet floating across the water. That image of a sound receding into an echoing distance came to symbolize to Charles Ives his entire relationship with his father. His text for the luminous song "Remembrance" or "The Pond" runs: "A sound of a distant horn, O'er shadowed lake is borne—my father's song."[18]

Inspired by George's experiments with space—another being to march two bands past each other—Ives eventually arrived at unprecedented spatial effects in the Fourth Symphony, surrounding the main orchestra with distant choirs of instrumental groups and voices. Spatial separation would be the final element culminating the integrity and independence of groups that Ives ultimately achieved, to the degree of setting more or less self-sufficient pieces of music, in assorted styles, going together in what amounts to an aural collage.

So Ives's contrapuntal development only began with traditional contrapuntal technique. It was broadened by a new harmonic freedom and by polytonality, polyrhythm, and spatial separation, culminating in the riotous and ecstatic super-counterpoint of the Fourth Symphony. Ives's incompleted

Universe Symphony carried the independence of musical groups to the point of visionary impossibility in a work that proposed to set multiple choruses and orchestras playing from valleys and mountaintops, a kind of transcendent camp meeting.[19]

These were the prime technical elements of Ives's mature music that arose from his father's tinkerings. Beyond these there were other important elements in the foundation of his art, some learned from his father and others from elsewhere.

Program Music

The nineteenth century—the Romantic period—was the heyday of musical works built around a story, a scene, an idea. That trend, which by the end of the century marked the most advanced music, traced its immediate lineage from Beethoven's *Pastoral Symphony* through Berlioz's *Symphonie fantastique* (with its program of an artist's opium dreams) to the "symphonic poems" of Liszt and Wagner's "Music of the Future" agenda. In some writings Wagner claimed that music can *only* be properly motivated by ideas or stories, that being his answer to the Brahmsians and their doctrine of "abstract" or "pure" music. Wagner and other Romantic composers even supplied narratives to go with Beethoven symphonies and other abstract works. Though Brahms the abstractionist was still composing during Ives's apprenticeship, program music à la Liszt, written by Richard Strauss and his generation, was closer to the spirit of the times.

In addition to the influence of European-classical program music on young Charlie, some of his father's doings also involved musical illustration. Charlie always fondly remembered an Opera House whizbang of 1889, *A Musical Trip to Coney Island,* a whole evening involving George's band and orchestra, hundreds of choristers, and elaborate sets. The show represented a railroad trip, a concert aboard a shoreline steamer (selections ranging from Gounod's *Ave Maria* to "Home, Sweet Home"), a scene on the Coney Island beach complete with storm, an orchestral concert ending with the *William Tell Overture,* a band concert (the *Anvil Chorus* with fireworks), and concluding with a sing-along of "America" as the "travelers" arrived home.[20] These stunts of George's seem cheesy these days; maybe they did not amuse Danbury's more refined music lovers. But this kind of musical illustration was enjoyed by rank-and-file townsfolk, and by Charlie.

Charles Ives, echoing Wagner whom he despised, could never quite approve of music that was not *about* something more than the notes. Surely, the Connecticut Puritan in him whispered, there has to be more to it than the mere sensuous effect of musical tones. "Is not all music program music?" Ives writes in the *Essays:* "Is not pure music, so called, representative in its essence?"[21] He granted that music contained abstractions (he inherited his father's gift for theoretical speculation), but for him the essence of music was never abstract; it was humanistic and spiritual (just as Wagner said). Ives granted too that the language of tone as presently constituted was imprecise in expressing a specific idea: "A theme the composer sets up as 'moral goodness' may sound like 'high vitality' to his friend, and but like . . . 'nervous weakness' or only a 'stagnant pool' to those not even his enemies."[22] (He had heard terms like those from his own friends.) Yet he dreamed of a perfect program music, a universal language of tone, a great someday when music "will develop possibilities inconceivable now—a language so transcendent that its heights and depths will be common to all mankind." His mature music was conceived as a step in that direction. So one day in his crotchety old age, while visiting composer friend Carl Ruggles, Ives threw the manuscript of his *Robert Browning Overture* across the room, shouting that the goddamn thing was no good.[23] He had come to hate *Browning*'s fugues and canons, its abstractions. They had no connection to anything. They didn't tell the stories he wanted to tell.

Experimentation

We have seen how much George Ives's tinkerings with musical materials meant to his son, and how Charlie expanded on them. But there was more to George's tinkerings. From the day George tried to capture the sound of churchbells on piano dated his interest (or so Charlie surmised) in splitting the musical atom—the half step, the smallest written interval in Western music.[24]

My father had a weakness for quarter-tones—in fact he didn't stop even with them. He rigged up a contrivance to stretch 24 or more violin strings and tuned them up to suit the dictates of his own curiosity. He would pick out quarter-tone tunes and try to get the family to sing them, but I remember he gave that up except as a means of punishment.[25]

George also tried exotic tunings using water glasses, his slide trumpet, and so on, constructing scales without octaves.[26] In his career Charles Ives would produce only a few pages of quarter-tone music and an article on the subject. Still, his father's experiments with microtones would be one more inspiration to strengthen his imagination, stretch his ears, and examine musical materials from a fresh perspective. Likewise other of George's stunts, including the "Humanophone," in which a number of townsfolk were installed onstage inside mock organ pipes, each accounting for one note in tunes. Ives cited this as suggesting the leaps in some of his vocal music; he proposed they might be handled by multiple voices.[27] Naturally his father's experiments "made some of the townspeople call him a crank whenever he appeared in public with some of his contraptions (which was not often)."[28] From our perspective, we find in George Ives's teaching and example not eccentricity but instead the inquiring mind that would be a major part of his legacy. The ridicule George experienced was another prophecy of his son's career.

Community

Even beyond the experimental approach, momentous as it was, George kept Charlie's mind on the meanings and purposes of art to the community: the human dimension of vernacular music, the affection even for the mistakes and limitations of amateurs like stonemason Bell, as adumbrating the music of the ages. This was what had been revealed to George Ives about music in the campgrounds of the Civil War. Later as conductor of St. Peter's Parish Band, he spent much of his time with immigrant Catholic working people—mostly Irish, some Italian[29]—and from that experience likely came to a more democratic (and perhaps Democratic) view of society, in contrast to the other Yankee-Republican Iveses and Lyman Brewster.[30] The Iveses had always been leaders. Charles Ives ended up preaching that we must do away with leaders, help citizens acquire the knowledge and wisdom to lead themselves. His Twentieth Amendment proposal imagined running the United States like a New England town meeting, and his ideas for a People's World Union applied the same principles to the global community. His music and his politics would run in converging streams.

By his example and by his aphorisms George Ives inspired Charlie to stay true to the commonality and to his roots: "If a poet knows more about a horse than he does about heaven," George told Charlie, "he might better stick to the horse, and someday the horse may carry him into heaven." That may have been the most fruitful piece of wisdom he ever gave his son.[31]

Though Ives would later claim as much, his father's influence was not the only one shaping him and his art. George introduced Charlie to the European classical tradition and to basic instrumentation,[32] but as a composer George was a dilettante. He could help his son with a quickstep or an anthem, not much with a symphony or string quartet. For that kind of training, and for learning the ropes of the full Romantic orchestra, Charlie would have to wait for his Yale studies with the limited but nonetheless astute Horatio Parker. It would be Parker who taught Charles Ives to think the long, slow thoughts of a symphonist, and helped flesh out his student's Romantic ideals about music.

The Danbury influences outside the home were humble but still significant. One of Charlie's early heroes—probably the same to many Danbury youngsters—was fiddler John Starr of Brookfield, another son of a locally illustrious family who cast his lot with music. For a while Starr played first violin in George's groups; he went on to be the most popular of the men who provided jigs and reels and waltzes for barn dances and other sociable occasions.[33] Charlie's early "New Year Dance" may be an echo of John Starr's fiddle. Among Ives's memorials to this folk artist, who died at forty-eight in 1890, would be the country fiddling in the last movement of the Second Symphony and the Barn Dance in *Washington's Birthday*.[34] (The dissonant yawp that ends the relatively conservative Second was, Ives explained, a reflection of how barn-dance fiddlers used to cadence the last tune with a raking discord across the strings, to indicate the evening was over.[35])

The hymns that pervaded Charlie's childhood ranged from the decorous singing of church choirs to the more perfervid expression of camp-meeting revivals. Hymnody in America began with the imported sacred song of the Puritans. Then a rough, homespun tradition of sacred music grew up under the leadership of Boston's William Billings, who wrote a succinct credo later applied both to him and to other native artists: "I think it best for every Composer to be his own Carver." At length this untutored colonial tradition was suppressed, in part due to the activities of mid-nineteenth-century hymn composers such as Boston's Lowell Mason, who took European tradition as their model and produced hymns in the correct, decorous, generally insipid style that became standard in American Protestant churches. (Billings's and other native hymnody survived underground, in the southern "Sacred Harp" tradition and here and there in New England.) Among Lowell Mason's own tunes are some of the most popular in the hymnbooks, from his day to this: "From Greenland's Icy Mountains," "Work, for the Night is Coming," "Nearer, My God, to Thee."

For music both sacred and secular Mason championed the notion, centered in the aristocratic Northeast, that American standards must be raised by submitting to European standards. Charles Ives would be among the first generation to challenge that assumption. All the same, in his childhood Ives soaked up mainstream hymnody in small-town churches, and to the end of his life loved the melodies of Mason and his school. But there was another, lower-class subspecies of hymnody that Charlie heard throughout his youth—the gospel hymn, product of nineteenth-century revivals and camp meetings. Revivals had sprung up in the South in the early part of the century when charismatic ministers gathered crowds of faithful for orgies of religiosity, folks singing their hearts out and sometimes bawling and writhing on the ground from the sweet lash of the spirit. One echo of that kind of revival is Ives's *General William Booth*. A more temperate and middle-class variety of revivalism began in the mid-1870s with the crusades of Dwight Lyman Moody. By his endeavors, it was said, Moody "reduced the population of Hell by a million souls." (Revivalists have always been big on numbers; it's something of a statistical sport.) The Methodists of Danbury and environs began holding camp meetings in the later 1870s, multitudes tenting out for days in the countryside and participating in services that went straight for the spiritual jugular.

American-music scholar H. Wiley Hitchcock writes that gospel hymnody originated in the decorous style of Lowell Mason and his school, but "its harmony tended to be more chromatically engorged, its texts more sentimentally swollen."[36] Gospel music gained momentum from the revivals of Moody and his musical partner Ira D. Sankey. Though a commercial creation, gospel functioned more or less as folk music, and that is how Ives viewed it. Many nineteenth-century gospel hymns are still popular: "The Old Rugged Cross," "Just As I Am," "Shall We Gather at the River," and George Ives's trademark "Sweet By and By." The words of the latter would resonate mightily in the life of George's son:

> There's a land that is fairer than day,
> And by faith we can see it afar;
> For the Father waits over the way,
> To prepare us a dwelling-place there.
> In the sweet by and by,
> We shall meet on that beautiful shore.

Loving both the hymnody of Sunday services and the more heated and sentimental gospel style, Charlie responded not only to the notes but to the feelings, what his father called the music of the ages. Ives wrote of camp meetings,

I remember how the great waves of sound used to come through the trees—when things like *Beulah Land, Woodworth, Nearer My God To Thee, The Shining Shore, Nettleton, In the Sweet Bye and Bye* and the like were sung by thousands of "let out" souls. The music notes and words on paper were about as much like what they "were" (at those moments) as the monogram on a man's necktie may be like his face. . . . There was power and exaltation in these great conclaves of sound from humanity.[37]

George had primed Charlie for these moments of exaltation and the boy responded with fervor enough to fuel a creative life. Reticent as he was, the grown-up Ives could write passionately about those times. Another moment is evoked in the *Essays,* this one having to do with bands and marches. Written in the third person, it is clearly a memory of his own:

In the early morning of a Memorial Day, a boy is awakened by martial music—a village band is marching down the street—and as the strains of Reeves' majestic [*Second*] *Regiment March* come nearer and nearer—he seems of a sudden translated—a moment of vivid power comes, a consciousness of material nobility—an exultant something gleaming with the possibilities of this life—an assurance that nothing is impossible, and that the whole world lies at his feet. But, as the band turns the corner, at the soldiers' monument, and the march steps of the Grand Army become fainter and fainter, the boy's vision slowly vanishes—his "world" becomes less and less probable—but the experience ever lies within him in its reality.[38]

What transformed the young Charles Ives that morning as he listened to the approach of his father's band, what made a new and exalted world seem to lie at his feet, was something that happens now and again to most composers actual or potential: one has an uncanny musical experience and is inflamed by the desire to *do something like that,* to re-create the effect in one's own voice. Ives's recollection of that Decoration Day may well describe not only the inspiration for the *Holiday Quickstep* and *Decoration Day,* but also the moment he became a composer. In that radiant moment nothing seems impossible, and its echoes can resonate for a lifetime.

The trouble, as one finds out soon enough, is that one cannot literally re-create the exalted experience. Even in the unlikely event that the identical forces, the parade or the camp meeting, could be scraped together, they would lack the spontaneity that gave the original experience its radiance. When composers try to conjure specific scenes and memories in the cold medium of ink and paper, inevitably a stylized version of the experience, the attempt normally fails. There are exceptions, or partial exceptions: Maybe Beethoven succeeded in transmuting birdcalls and thunderstorms into workable music in the *Pastoral;* certainly in *La Mer* Debussy conveys a sense of the sea (which he in fact never sailed). But arguably only Charles Ives, and only in his later music, succeeded so consistently in transmuting the immediacy and intensity of human experience into his work. The working out of the stylization and symbolization he needed to accomplish that will be a long story, but it began in his teens, in Danbury, with the radiant moments he so lyrically recalled.

The final development of Ives's style, then, would have much to do with his embracing of dissonant harmonic structures and the extension of counterpoint by means of revolutionary techniques: polytonality, polyrhythm, spatial separation. His iconic sense of existing melodies led him to use quotes to evoke the power of the originals and their settings. Folk music, hymnody, and band music made their contribution, no less than the European tradition. In order for Ives to reach his maturity, however, two more currents from his childhood, independent at first, had to intersect with his harmonic and contrapuntal discoveries, his love of familiar melodies, his mediation with European genres.

The first of these currents was *chance:* musical and social collision, happenstance, misadventure. As the teenaged Charlie tickled his imagination with polytonality and his father's other notions, he could hardly foresee how he could put them to use, toward grander ends. Among other things, the new techniques he was discovering were going to be essential as a means of corralling the serendipitous musical effects that also fascinated him—two bands clashing on the march, or drunken cornet players getting their crooks mixed up, or a congregation declaiming assorted attempts at the pitch of a hymn. In the latter case, others heard only a tune out of tune; Charlie heard the moving tone clusters that had been there from time immemorial when large groups sang. The mistakes were part of the music. His imagination seized on these effects of emotion and serendipity; sometimes as he presents them they are comic, but always they evoke the communal context and meaning of the occasion—the parade, the revival, the church service. In college Ives would contrive accidents by throwing tunes roughly together, in theaters or at fraternity shows where it could be taken as a joke. But in the long run he was serious, he was a *composer,* and he could not be satisfied with simple accident. The carefully shaped illusion of serendipity would be a defining feature of Ives's maturity, especially of his teeming orchestral phantasmagorias conjuring the experience of great public events—*The Fourth of July, Decoration Day, Hanover Square,* the *Comedy* of the Fourth Symphony. His Yale experiments were slight and some of his early experimental pieces hardly get off the ground. It would mainly be his mature handling of dissonant counterpoint and the systematic application of polyrhythm that would bring these quasi-accidental effects under control.

The final significant current coming from Ives's childhood was not just the embrace of cultivated and vernacular music, but their synthesis. Or call them high and low art, or classical and popular—all terms that have been used for an elusive but nonetheless inescapable dichotomy in the artistic spectrum.[39] In late-nineteenth-century America, cultured taste erected a wall between the two; when it came to putting on a genteel concert or composing in a classical European genre, only cultivated, elevated music would do. Charlie's Yale professor Horatio Parker would embody this point of view, which was articulated in the nineteenth century above all by John Sullivan Dwight, Boston Transcendentalist and music critic. A selection from Dwight finds him characteristically deploring popular music and presenting classical music not as a feature of American life but as an alternative to it, an infusion of sweetness and light to temper American vulgarity:

[Americans] take to noise, to *sounding* demonstrations, as a duck takes to water. Stunned with all this glory, with breast full of patriotism, and ears full of "Yankee Doodle" and "Hail Columbia," what can we have to say, or what report of music as Art? And verily it is a bad time with us, in respect of music. . . . The Psalmody of the country choir and the dancing master's fiddle, the waltzes and variations of the music shop . . . and "Jim Crow" [i.e., Stephen Foster] . . . are not apt to visit the popular mind with deep emotions of true music. Handel should be heard more, and Haydn, and Mozart, and Beethoven. . . . [Liberty will] bring its own ruin unless there shall be found some gentler, harmonizing culture, . . . a sweet sense of reverence for something far above us, beautiful and pure. . . . We need this beautiful corrective to our crudities.[40]

Taking his cue from his father, Charles Ives would refuse to take sides between vernacular and cultivated, American and European genres and ideals. He loved "Hail Columbia," the dancing master's fiddle, Stephen Foster, the psalmody of the country choir. He grew up in a musical culture parochial but thriving, in the last generation of Western composers to experience as living traditions a number of musical genres both cultivated and vernacular that have since become, in effect, museum pieces. During his childhood and apprentice-ship the symphony and string quartet were still vital and developing in some-thing like their classical forms; so were the march, the hymn, the sentimental parlor song. These genres would persist in the twentieth century increasingly as anachronisms, learned rather than absorbed in the context for which they were intended. (Classical music, of course, remained European dominated, something of an orphan in the United States, but the Gilded Age of the late nineteenth century still saw its final establishment as a presence in the States.)

One could say that in maintaining allegiance to both sides of most musical divides, Ives remained a bandsman at heart. Bands always played all kinds of music. In the works of his apprenticeship Ives generally maintained the cultivated/vernacular dichotomy, writing marches, parlor songs, college songs, church anthems, a symphony, each in its accustomed mode. All these genres he knew from childhood; they were in his blood. Meanwhile, at first he kept his experimental ideas separate, in pieces such as the *Psalms*. Then the genres started to interpenetrate: the First String Quartet clinging to the famil-iar European format but based on revival tunes; the Second Symphony encom-passing both American-folk and European-symphonic material. Finally, integrating cultivated and vernacular influences with his own wide-ranging experiments, Ives arrived at his mature style and, moreover, the first truly native concert music, one that reexamined style, or ignored style, or (maybe best expressed) synthesized a meta-style that integrated the musical voice of the American people with the European classical tradition.

Thus the musical streams flowing from Ives's youth—the extension of harmony and counterpoint, quotes, program music, experiment, chance ef-fects, a polystylistic aesthetic—converged with the European genres he studied and composed at Yale. In college Ives absorbed the European concept of form and the traditional patterns of sonata, rondo, and the like. He would make much use of that knowledge, but also look for unique forms within his sub-jects, within the forms of dynamic human and natural phenomena, within *stories*. His stories would be transmuted into musical forms, often ones that avoided the kinds of literal repetition required by older forms. "Nature loves analogy and hates repetition," Ives writes in the *Essays*,[41] and in his maturity so did he. In his writings, the word and idea *natural* would be his touchstone.

The converging of all these elements shaped the voice we call *Ivesian*. Its uniqueness, its strangeness, came not from eccentricity willed or inherited, but from a merging of currents from his childhood, a merging and mediation among centrifugal elements, compelled at once by emotion, personality, and musical logic. As we found Ives writing of himself, his art "came not only from folk music he was brought up with but to a very great extent from the life 'around & in him' . . . something reflecting a kind of 'inheritance' from his forbears & father—a natural interest in wanting to make his own paths around the hills & mountains." (He leaves out the European contribution—

the Horatio Parker part of it.) Another, later, less noticeable but nonetheless galvanizing element in that merging was the African-American genre called ragtime. Still later, the aesthetic and technique of his music would converge with other once-independent but important streams in his life—his vision of business and politics and society.

(To this outline of Ivesian stylistic development a caveat: In practice, the process would hardly proceed as categorically as it is apt to in a book. Charles Ives demonstrates as well as anybody that in its logical trajectory an artist's development resembles more the butterfly than the arrow.)

These developments, these mergings, did not in themselves bring Charles Ives to maturity. A composer's work is more than a technical feat; it is a matter of personality, feeling, spirit—all intangibles, but ones without which there is nothing worth expressing in music at all. In his teens and early twenties Charles Ives served a traditional apprenticeship as a composer. For some time, perhaps until after college, he would derive some satisfaction from his work. Gradually, though, putting notes on paper year after year, the dots marching blandly left to right, the played results increasingly unsatisfactory, he sensed that the notes did not contain enough of himself, what he had experienced and felt. The orthodox musical language he had been taught, and even his formalistic experiments, came to seem a desiccated (his word was "emasculated") undertaking, keeping him from the language he wanted to hear but did not yet know how to speak. It is a common experience among young composers. Usually it leads either to a breakthrough or to giving up. Likely it was a sharper dilemma with Ives; and so his journey to maturity stretched longer than most composers'. And he would need help in that journey.

All artists work from an intersection of the external—say, experience of the world and of musical sound—and the internal. To an extent, becoming an artist is a way of claiming something, of participating more deeply than any other way in something that has powerfully moved you, of internalizing an experience from outside. In this sense, art is *The world according to . . .* In his early works, some of them striking but none first-rate, Charles Ives captured the everyday musical genres of parade and church and parlor. Later he would mimic the forms and gestures of European tradition with results from awkward to inspired, but never really his own. Somewhere in the process, memory and intuition began to remind him of what he had felt so powerfully in childhood, that this surface—the techniques, the skill, the genres, the styles, the notes—was not was he was after. He came to call this surface *manner,* the lesser value in art. His intuition drove him beyond that, somehow paradoxically to capture in notes the ineffable spirit behind notes: *not something that happens, but the way something happens;* the music of the ages that his father had discerned when stonemason Bell bellowed his hymns so "unmusically," his exaltation the substance of his music rather than the sound. Therefore this underlying spirit Ives called *substance,* and thus he wrote: What does sound have to do with music?

It would take him over two decades of growth and experiment to claim his experience in his music, to embody the substance in what he was trying to say. That achievement, the converging of his paradoxical experiences and intuitions and inspirations into a unified art, would require immense stylization, transmutation, analogizing, and the synthesis of a musical language at once singular unto eccentricity yet familiar as a tune whistled in childhood. It would also require a great outlay of courage and energy, drawn from a fund of both that was enormous but not inexhaustible.

At length, in the great works of 1909–23, Charles Ives would find the means to conjure up what he had heard and felt and remembered and imagined, from a dream-vision of black soldiers marching to battle, to the meandering waters of the Housatonic River in autumn, to Decoration Day and the Fourth of July in Danbury, to citizens joining in spontaneous song on the eve of war, to an evocation of the future of music. With little help from peers or tradition, with mainly his own experience and volcanic imagination to guide him, and with his wife as muse and virtual audience, Ives would assemble the palette with which to reclaim his past and paint it in universal colors.

A College

FOR CHARLES IVES, who had asked for nothing more complicated than to plunge into the adventure of college life, it was shattering: the terrible news, the bleak train ride to Danbury, his prostrate mother, the dreamlike service at his father's grave, the relatives and friends passing by as in a dream murmuring strained, sympathetic words. On Sunday evening, November 4, 1894, George Ives, apparently recovered from a bout of illness, had called on his mother Sarah at the old Ives House, accompanied his young cousins home to Farview Avenue, strolled back to Chapel Place, turned in beside his wife Mollie, and died. He had suffered a stroke that seemed to come from nowhere.[1] He was forty-nine.

At Wooster Cemetery the Danbury Band played at the funeral of their old leader. Attending were a multitude of Iveses and relatives and townsfolk who had always liked George, even if they were puzzled about what he had been doing in all those years of fooling with music. George was laid to rest in Wooster Cemetery near the memorial to his father, among the Iveses and Whites and Merritts. His pallbearers represented the town's other royalty—Wildman, Hoyt, Benedict, Seeley, Tweedy.[2] The Danbury News wrote, "The death of George E. Ives . . . removed one of the most familiar figures in Danbury. He has for years been one of the best known men of the middle or younger generations. His personality was so bright, so genial as to cast a gloom over the community by its removal." Later there appeared in the paper a Resolution by the directors of the Danbury Savings Bank, where George had become a director. Of his life's main love and labor the Resolution said only, "an artist in music all his life, he enjoyed its harmonies as only an artist can, and delighted to share its beatitudes with others." It went on to mention, in the same spirit, that he was "one of the raciest of story tellers" and added, "he had probably as many friends, endeared to him by personal ties as any man, old or young, in our city."[3]

George Ives had touched many with his character and his music, most of all the beloved son who stood numbly at the funeral, staring at the ground where he too would come to rest someday. Long after, with an anguish that survived the years, Charles Ives would write of the "awful vacuum I was carrying around with me" after his father died.[4] George had been woven into his son's consciousness and his daily experience of music. His passing left a hole that could never be repaired. The vacuum, when time is gray and flat and full of phantoms, enfolded Charlie's first months of college.

"Father died just when I needed him most," Ives would write.[5] For years he would try to find a mentor to take on his father's role. It was hopeless; there was no one like George, no one able to understand so well this particular boy and his gifts. But as a freshman in college Charlie had no way of knowing that. He knew only that he needed his father now that he was stumbling toward adulthood, trying to figure out what to do, how to work music into his life. Desperate for consolation, he began reading Thoreau, whom he would later call "that reassuring and true friend who stood by me one 'low' day, when the sun had gone down, long, long before sunset."[6]

What made his father's death unbearable was that George had died at the nadir of their relationship, in the cloudy valley between a parent's last struggles for control and a mature respect and friendship. Charlie had been trying to get away from his father—but not like this. There were too many unresolved issues between them that now could never be resolved. The valley had not been so terribly deep, the issues not so bitter, but the lack of resolution was enough to leave Ives feeling suspended and frustrated and guilty for the rest of his life. "How I want to see Father again!" he would exclaim over and over, in his dotage.[7] For Ives the main meaning of the afterlife seemed to be reclaiming the great love and inspiration of his childhood, at last to bring their relationship to the absolution life had denied him. Here we find a source (by no means the only source) of his regard for the incomplete, of the open-endedness of so much of his music. Ives became an artist of the unfinished, but he believed with all his heart that completion was possible, that someday humanity would get there. For himself, until then Charles Ives possessed only "the sound of a distant horn . . . my father's song."

His loss, eternally painful and inexplicable to him, shadowed his life at Yale and after, but he did not respond as one would expect. Ives had arrived at college a small-town youth of twenty, with few of the connections that helped one get ahead in the college's brutally competitive social scene. Charlie was involved in a kind of music that hardly interested his classmates, and to help pay his way he worked off campus in the most demanding organist job in town. He began his college career stricken, wandering, needy, overburdened with work, and chronically shy as always.

Yet Ives blazed through Yale as one of the most visible and popular men on campus, finally to be singled out as one of the "geniuses" of his class. In his grief and emptiness, he directed himself outward rather than inward. The system of achieving campus success was Byzantine, but Charlie mastered it, made his connections, and sailed to glory. As he had before and would time and again in the future, he would, with little overt sign of ambition, percolate to the highest rank of whatever endeavor he involved himself in.[3]

The Yale social system that Ives so unaccountably mastered is immortalized in Owen Johnson's strange, Balzacian novel *Stover at Yale,* a collegiate yarn superficially of the Frank Merriwell sort, but in fact an assault on the narrow elitism, conformity, and anti-intellectualism of Yale at the turn of the century. Johnson, who was graduated in 1900, drew on his own experience for this critique of the college's democratic ideals, which professed to elevate talent and achievement but in practice ran on hustling, connections, and relentless conformity in pursuit of a niche in the clubs that ruled campus life. At the top of the ladder lay three senior societies, social rather than functional, each of which elected fifteen men a year—Skull and Bones at the apex, Scroll and Key second, Wolf's Head third.

There were 350 or so men in each class; everyone knew most everyone else by name and by reputation. The senior-year tally of Ives's class of '98 counted 158 Republicans and 64 Democrats. The majority were Presbyterian, Congregational, or Episcopal; otherwise there were four Jews, ten Catholics, four Methodists, two Universalists. No one claimed to be without religion. Law was the favored professional goal, followed by medicine, the ministry, teaching. Ten years after graduation, nearly half the '98 class would be working in business or finance.[9]

This was the classic backward-looking, oligarchical Yale, the all-American boola-boola college whose football teams dominated the sport, whose students proclaimed, without irony and often with tears, their ideal of service "For God, for Country, and for Yale." A little elm-shaded world to itself, it was tucked away from the urban business centers where graduates confidently expected to find their fortunes, and to find them mainly through college connections. The little world of the college resembled the big world; to succeed at one was to succeed at the other: "Four years of Yale was not just a stretch of time. It was a career—a concentrated lifetime of experiences."[10] In spirit, this little lifetime continued into the ensuing lifetime: "Yale men are Yale men from the cradle to the grave."[11] The school was made of a singular history, with a language, a style, a framework of traditions to which one conformed or risked becoming invisible. "Ask a Yale man the reason for anything and he will give you the origin; and he thinks he has answered your question."[12] Tradition ruled college life, from the weird, ratcheting Greek Cheer of the football stadium, taken from Aristophanes' *The Frogs* (BREK KEK KEK KEX! KOAX! KOAX!), to the structure of student-run activities on campus, to the ceremonies of Ivy Day and graduation.

In contrast to scholarly Harvard, Yale proposed to cultivate in its students not so much knowledge as *character,* that grand, foggy notion beloved of conservatives. "Everything," wrote George Santayana, "is arranged to produce a certain type of man."[13] Since most of the faculty had come through Yale

Ives and roommate Mandeville Mullally strike unwontedly studious poses in their Yale dormitory room.

themselves, there was an easy complicity between the classroom and the livelier round of extracurricular life. All fostered the Yale Man, whom Owen Johnson observed at home in "the rarefied contending nervousness of the place . . . the nervous panorama of the struggle for position." Johnson's fictional hero Dink Stover, grabbing quick glory by way of the football field, is troubled by Yale's reflection of "the deadly seriousness of the American spirit, which seizes on everything that is competition and transforms it, with the savage fanaticism of his race, for success."[14] In the little world of Yale as in the big American world, *success*—in the conventional financial and social definition—was the goal of life. (Often enough, it worked. When a prominent Harvard alumnus of the era was asked why he sent his son to Yale, he said he had discovered "all the Harvard men are working for Yale men."[15])

While the college Charles Ives entered in the fall of 1894 remained the old school in spirit, it had begun a glacial process of change. Discreetly, Yale was following the lead of Harvard in bending the old classical curriculum, with its emphasis on Latin and Greek and mathematics taught in dreary recitation classes. That system still prevailed in a student's first two years, with everyone taking the same courses. but now juniors and seniors were offered a modest slate of electives. Somewhere in the offing, to the consternation of many faculty and alumni, awaited a university incorporating the kinds of professional disciplines that the college had traditionally kept quarantined in the Scientific School.[16]

Among new disciplines creeping into the curriculum was music. In early 1890, President Timothy Dwight, Jr., last of Yale's unbroken string of clergyman presidents, sanctioned a Musical Department. This brought a flurry of protest, exemplified by an alumnus who wrote the New Haven *Register*. "It is hard to repress disgust at finding the Corporation appealing to the community for $300,000 as an endowment for a ridiculous sideshow like a department of music."[17] When the *Yale Daily News,* the student newspaper, pointed out that money for the sideshow had come from private contributions, the fuss subsided. Music settled into a small but established curriculum, largely ignored by most of the students. The first Battell Professor of Music was German-born Gustave Stoeckel, who had been teaching non-credited music courses at the school since 1855. Stoeckel had concentrated on developing the Glee Club and Chapel Choir in a time when male voices in rich harmony were a cherished feature of college life. When the Musical Department began in the 1890s, students took little interest in cultivated music, but the school was already resonant with singing, especially of the lusty and sentimental college songs of the era.

As Charlie wrote his father early in 1894, he planned to take the few music courses Stoeckel offered. But arriving with Ives in the fall of that year was Stoeckel's successor in the Battell chair, a man of higher reputation and caliber, who during his tenure would expand the curriculum and professionalism of the department and go on to help create the Yale School of Music. This was Horatio Parker, the teacher whom Charles Ives would later acknowledge only with difficulty, and never forgive.

Parker came to Yale at age thirty-one with a bright new reputation as one of the premiere American composers of his generation. That reputation was founded mainly on his Latin oratorio of 1893, *Hora novissima*. British performances of that and other of his choral works were to bring Parker an overseas audience unusual for an American, and an honorary Cambridge University doctorate in 1902.

When Parker took charge of music at Yale, wrote his protégé and successor David Stanley Smith,

A good measure of the missionary spirit was needed. . . . The few men who were endowed with the gift of music had the task of converting an indifferent America to a due regard for the art as something worthy of a real man's life work. Poetry and painting had been established, though still slightly under suspicion, but music was good only for the ladies' seminary.[18]

This new professor had the missionary spirit; he also had considerable energy despite shaky health, and an iron sense of duty. As a teacher Parker would concentrate more on practical skills than theory. He expanded the curriculum to six courses: Harmony, Counterpoint, History of Music, Strict Composition (fugue, canon, and other contrapuntal genres), Instrumentation, and Free Composition. Other faculty took care of instrumental lessons.[19] Composition was the heart of Parker's curriculum; he built up the fledgling New Haven Symphony partly as a musical laboratory for his student composers.

In his person as in his music courtly and orthodox, a product of the old-Yankee cultural establishment, Parker suited the capacity assigned to him. It was his duty to convince Yale that music was a proper and disciplined field of study, and he carried off that assignment handsomely. In the process he trained several composers who made a name, among them Roger Sessions, Quincy Porter, and Douglas Moore. He became, in short, one of the leading American-born composition teachers of his time.

At the same time, Parker's own background limited his horizons and those of many of his students. He had been born in rural Auburndale, Massachusetts, his father an architect and his mother a piano teacher and high-Victorian poetess. He studied theory and composition with George Chadwick in Boston, and the two formed a lifelong friendship. Both were charter members of what has come to be called the Second New England School (the First being the colonial-era church composers led by William Billings). Also part of the group, most of them European trained, was Harvard's John Knowles Paine, who in 1875 had been named the first professor of music in the country.

Civil War attitudes persisted in the 1890s: professional cultivated music in the United States was considered to be something pursued mainly by Europeans. Aspiring composers tended to make a pilgrimage to Europe—Germany in the nineteenth century, later often to France—to get their final polish and to imbibe the classical tradition at its fount. George Chadwick said of his study in Germany, "They kept me at harmonizing chorales [in Bach style] for four years, but I've always been grateful for that incomparable discipline."[20]

In 1882, Parker made his way to the Hochschule für Musik in Munich, where for three years he studied composition, conducting, and organ with the famously dogmatic Josef Rheinberger. David Stanley Smith wrote that Rheinberger imparted to Parker "the greatest respect for fineness of detail and

Horatio Parker as a young composer and teacher. In college he taught Ives more than Ives was ever willing to admit.

the keenest appreciation of niceties."[21] (We have met, and will again, Charles Ives's enmity toward niceties.) Probably to general amazement, this American became Rheinberger's favorite pupil.[22] Parker also became engaged to a Munich woman and fellow music student, whom he married the next year. His wife might stand, and maybe did in his own mind, as a talisman of his connection to the great German tradition.

In 1885 Parker returned home to his country, which had little use for living composers of art music. The rent-paying jobs open to him were as an organist, choirmaster, and teacher; that is what he did in the next years, in New York. The early 1890s were a watershed in his life. In the space of one year Parker suffered the deaths of his father, a sister, a grandmother, and a baby son. His own health began to decline from that point. In 1891–93 he taught at the National Conservatory in New York. Directing the Conservatory was visiting Czech composer Antonín Dvořák, then trying to convince Americans to foster a national music as his own country had, and preparing to show them how with his Symphony *From the New World*. Dvořák chaired the committee that awarded a prize to Parker for the cantata *Dream-King and His*

Love.[23] The award, however, failed to warm Parker to Dvořák's call for a national music. Parker's entire training presumed that American music must be built on the European model. Shocked by Dvořák's suggestion that a national school could be based on Negro and Indian music, Parker proclaimed, in lectures of the 1890s, that there was no indigenous American music worthy of the name at all.[24]

The great event of those years for Parker, one that colored the rest of his career with a tinge of anticlimax, was the 1893 New York premiere of *Hora novissima,* his response to the tragedies in his family. Its text, Latin verses of Bernard de Morlaix, describes the glories of heaven. A relentlessly high-minded oratorio in the tradition of Mendelssohn and Elgar,[25] the work elevated Parker into the elite of American composers, and helped make his British reputation. After the 1894 Boston premiere of *Hora novissima,* critic Philip Hale (later dubbed by Charles Ives "Aunt Hale"[26]) wrote rapturously,

[Parker has] a talent that approaches genius, if it is not absolute genius. . . . Nor is it perhaps foolish to predict that the future historian of music in America will point back to "Hora Novissima" as a proof that, when there were croakers concerning the ability of Americans to produce any musical compositions save imitations of German models, a young man appeared with a choral work of long breath that showed not only a mastery of the technique of composition, but spontaneous, flowing, and warmly colored melody.[27]

Future historians did not take their cue. No doubt Parker's oratorio deserves better: it has discernible feeling and grace, a certain gloomy nobility, and discreet touches of boldness[28]: an operatic, Gounod-like flair that is striking for a religious work; an aria exploiting changing meters; occasional cross-rhythms and attempts at fresh harmonic patterns. (Some of these elements characterize Charles Ives's pallid facsimile of *Hora novissima,* the cantata *Celestial Country.*) But Parker had been trained, in Germany, in the niceties, and could not help but display them in high-flown fugues full of figures from the counterpoint books. A succinct description of Parker's music in those days is this one: "It was seldom trivial—his choral works have a dignity and depth that many of [his] contemporaries, especially in the [field of] religious and choral composition, did not have. Parker had ideals that carried him higher than the popular, but he was governed too much by the German rule."[29] The words are Charles Ives's. They are the nicest he ever wrote about his teacher. They are also accurate.

Much honored, Parker would die at fifty-six, in harness as dean of the Yale School of Music, having more or less worked himself to death. Given the sardonic irony of fate, his name would turn up most often in history books as the teacher who laughed off the experiments of his most famous student, who failed to recognize a genius who labored under his nose for four years. That unenviable reputation, at most half deserved, would be bequeathed to Horatio Parker by that student.

The first meeting of Ives and Parker, both of them new to Yale, went well enough. Parker observed that their fathers shared common first names George Edward.[30] Did that encourage unreasonable expectations? Parker agreed to let this clearly advanced freshman audit music courses, which could not be formally elected until junior year. Composition could be supervised in private lessons.

Then the trouble began. Asked to bring in something, Charlie produced his old song "At Parting." Parker took a look and pounced on an unresolved dissonance, snapping, "There's no excuse for that." Charlie knew the rules for resolving dissonances, but no one had ever belabored him with such a mundane rule in his creative work. He wrote home complaining about it and his father replied in words that became oracular to his son, given that they were written in George Ives's last weeks of life: "Tell Parker that every dissonance doesn't have to resolve, if it doesn't happen to feel like it, any more than every horse should have to have its tail bobbed just because it's the prevailing fashion."[31] Did Charlie have the good sense *not* to tell that to Parker?

When Charlie innocently brought in some of his experiments—they may have included *Psalm 67* and one or two fugues in four keys—Parker waved them off with a joke about "hogging all the keys at one meal." He ordered this apparently overindulged youth not to bring in any more manifestations of who knows what. This was a graver matter than criticizing an unresolved dissonance; it was a rejection of a founding element of Charles Ives's creative identity: the freedom to explore that his father had always allowed him, always taken seriously, always integrated into the boy's learning and thinking. After that experience, Ives wrote, "I kept pretty steadily to the regular classroom work, occasionally trying [experiments] on the side." In the next years he still plied his teacher now and then with something beyond the pale, only to be met with a patronizing smile at best[32]; sometimes Parker would "get a little bothered or puzzled,"[33] then change the subject.

By training and by inclination, Parker was not equipped to comprehend musical prophecy. In other words, he had the attitude of nearly all professional musicians. This was an era when many considered Wagner a dangerous radical, and Brahms, still alive, as harsh and intellectual. (Philip Hale once proposed that an exit in Boston Symphony Hall be labeled "Exit, in Case of Brahms.") Few contemporary musicians or listeners could have countenanced Ives's extraordinary *Psalms*. Though he had certainly met resistance to his radical ideas before, Charlie, saturated with the experience of working with his father, had never quite absorbed how strange his ideas appeared to the mainstream. And Horatio Parker was the personification of the mainstream.

Worst of all for Charlie was how their relationship developed after George Ives died, those lonely months when

I went around looking and looking for some man to sort of help fill up that awful vacuum I was carrying around with me—the men among my classmates—the tutors program, etc.—and a kind of idea that Parker might—but he didn't—I think he made it worse—his mind and his heart were never around together.[34]

All Parker could give to his teaching was his mind, not his heart. The latter he did not give easily to anyone. In recalling Parker most people mentioned his reserve, his dignity despite bursts of temper, his elegant and precise diction. He was often taken for an English gentleman. His hectic schedule was eventually the death of him: he taught six different courses at Yale, saw private students, ran the Musical Department, conducted the New Haven Symphony and local choruses, served as organist/choirmaster of the distinguished Trinity Church in Boston, gave frequent lectures and organ recitals in New Haven and New York, and composed constantly (much of it on the train). Parker had neither the temperament nor the time to be a substitute father for a needy youth. Nor could he afford, as head of a new and controversial department, to encourage what might be seen as undisciplined experimentation by his students.

Parker possessed a fine knowledge of the European musical tradition and a fastidious skill at imparting it. He expected to do that, and only that; surely that was enough. As a pupil, Ives would absorb a good deal of this tradition, plowing through the Jadassohn harmony book again and writing fugues and canons, in much the same spirit as he had dealt with his father in the last few years: dutiful, but passively resistant.

Though he learned more than he ever admitted, Ives would never forgive Parker's orthodoxy, his coldness, his failure to recognize talent, and most of all his failure to fulfill the impossible expectation of becoming George Ives's successor. Two years after Charlie arrived at Yale, David Stanley Smith began studies with Parker and became his favorite and eventually heir apparent. Ives never wrote a jealous word about Smith, who was more or less a friend, or about his friend and classmate William Haesche, another Parker favorite who began teaching at Yale in 1902. But Ives rarely wrote an overtly jealous word about anyone; we must look between the lines for his feelings. Most notably we see his feelings in the steady refusal to acknowledge what Parker gave him, his insistence that his father was his only real teacher, and his unforgiving comparison of the two: "Parker was a composer and widely known, and Father was not a composer and little known—but from every other standpoint I should say that Father was by far the greater man."[35]

Luckily for his music and his self-confidence, Ives did not entirely fail in his search for a mentor. John C. Griggs, the new choirmaster at Center

Church, admired and encouraged his young organist. It was to Griggs that Ives, nearly forty years later, would write his anguished lines about the awful vacuum, and continue, "You didn't try to superimpose any law on me, or admonish me, or advise me, or boss me, or say very much—but there you were. . . . I didn't show how or what I felt—I never seem to know how."[36] It was a circumscribed relationship, reticent on both sides, and John Griggs was not a composer. But there he was; he sufficed. Artists have to do their work themselves and ultimately rely on their own resources, but they do not develop without help. Unusual people are shaped by encounters with unusual people. Griggs was another fortuitous encounter that helped make Charles Ives what he became.

This choirmaster was a sophisticated musical thinker and a first-rate baritone. As a Yale student Griggs had studied philosophy and physics in addition to music, and ended up editor of the *Yale Literary Magazine*. In 1893 he received a musicology Ph.D., magna cum laude, from the University of Leipzig. During Ives's New Haven years, Griggs commuted from his Center Church job to teach Music History and Singing at Metropolitan College in New York; in 1897 he began teaching voice at Vassar.[37]

His doctoral thesis, written and published in German, was called *Studies in Music in America*. In it Griggs speculates on the most pressing musical question of that day, the requirements for building a cultivated tradition. In his conclusion Griggs astutely summarizes the artistic dilemma of a country still mostly rural and a cultural patchwork:

If musical composition does develop . . . it will not be hampered by the traditions of any one country or school, for America has received, and is receiving, impulse from many countries. . . . But this very breadth of outlook, and the lack of any musical history of importance, are the two great reasons why American music cannot, for the present, have any distinctive national character.[38]

Despite that pessimism, shared by many, these issues were boiling in the 1890s, heated up by Dvořák's calls for a native music. Probably Griggs, still fresh and open-minded in his profession, contemplated his young Center Church composer / organist with considerable interest for that reason.

Charles Ives was lucky enough, then, to work under one of the rare musicians of the day possessing the openness and imagination to respond to whatever ideas were thrown at him. After listening to the superimposed C-major and D-minor chords that opened Charlie's 1897 *Thanksgiving Prelude* for organ, "Parker made some fairly funny cracks about it, but Dr. Griggs said it had something of the Puritan character, a stern but outdoors strength, and something of the pioneering feeling. He liked it as such, and told Parker so. Parker just smiled and took him over to Heublein's for [a beer]" [39] Ives recalled Griggs's reassurance (though the words are certainly Ives's) after one of Charlie's wilder pieces was aired in a church service: "Never you mind what the ladies' committee says; my opinion is that God must get awfully tired of hearing the same thing over and over again, and in His all-embracing wisdom he could certainly embrace a dissonance—might even positively enjoy one now and then."[40]

Griggs was sometimes critical, but never dismissive like Parker. Ives, as he always would, seized on any honest response he could get. Griggs was forgiving when the boy slipped some of his trademark harmonies into hymn accompaniments.[41] He also paid Ives the compliment of performing a number of his songs and choral pieces, and he allowed Ives to play, in services, his organ works from the conservative to the revolutionary. Perhaps the main memorial to this mentor is Ives's German-Romantic lied "Feldeinsamkeit," one of the most beautiful songs an American has created, which Ives wrote for a Griggs recital in 1897.

Most of the time in the choir loft, Charlie was a good boy. He would

John C. Griggs, Ives's choirmaster and mentor at Yale.

never lose a job over his dissonances. He was a manifestly fine organist and learned to parcel out experiments judiciously; most of his composing was mild enough. For Center Church he wrote around two dozen anthems and other pieces in orthodox style. Then and for some time after, he remained a competent producer of conventional music for practical purposes.

Griggs and Parker were the central figures in Charles Ives's creative life at Yale.[42] The music he would write in college, much of it with their guidance and advice, included two large works, dozens of songs and choral pieces, a pile of light music, and experiments from the slight to the enduring.

These were the settings and the dramatis personae of Ives's last years of formal training, the platform from which he launched his paradoxical careers. As to the particulars, much of his four years at Yale would teem with the sorts of doings that do not leave traces: fun, private labors, chimes at midnight. Few letters survive. He probably wrote his mother less than he had his father and did not keep her letters; there was little to say anyway, little to ask her advice about. Uncle Lyman was still supportive, but he was concentrating on getting brother Moss into Yale Law.

From his freshman year at age twenty, Charles Ives had to find his own way. In examining his time at Yale, we will see that in most respects he did that well, and characteristically. In college Ives discovered, as Arnold Schoenberg was to write of him, "how to preserve himself and to learn."

Dasher at Yale

ANYONE WHO WAS ANYONE lived a particular life at Yale, with particular goals. Morning was the domain of studies, perceived by most students, wrote Owen Johnson, as "a sort of necessary evil, the price to be paid for the privilege of passing four years in pleasant places with congenial companions."[1] Every school day began at 8 A.M. with the chapel bell, summoning the spectacle of 1300 students erupting from entry doors and sprinting across Old Campus, pulling on clothes as they went, and crowding through the doors of Battell Chapel. The chapel service was overseen by President Dwight; as the minister of the day droned on, students discreetly perused textbooks or browsed the morning papers. At the end of the service Dwight made his way down the center aisle and the seniors, who by tradition occupied aisle seats, bowed as the president passed. Superstition had it that to touch Dwight's humpback during the bow bestowed good luck in recitations. Some skill was required for this grotesque maneuver; one could not be too flagrant, but must imperceptibly brush the nap of the president's coat as he strolled serenely past.[2]

The main luck one hoped for in recitations was not to be called on. At 8:30 everyone sat down in one of the plain, shabby classrooms and anxiously regarded the professor on the lectern. Henry Seidel Canby recalled the teachers of that day as "bearded men, a little dusty. . . . Men sure of themselves, severe, arid, uncompromising, uninventive, uninterested in the constantly new thing which we call life."[3] Questions were directed from the lectern, each unlucky student standing to recite a canned answer, to bluff, or to pass. Years later, Charles Ives would write of the experience: "I found a pleasure browsing in my father's library that I never found in college. My mind seemed to stop, at my first freshman recitation, as soon as I felt smothered by the . . . compulsory ideas of tutors, compulsory traditions of professors, compulsory courses, compulsory freedom of thought, compulsory chapel—I learned not a thing that I ought."[4]

Indeed he did not. With the rest of his class, freshman Ives took Greek, Latin, mathematics, modern language (he continued with German), and English literature—the latter with the legendary William Lyon "Billy" Phelps.

The sophomore schedule was similar; Charlie elected French. His last two years would branch into logic, political science, history, philosophy, and music electives. The breadth of learning this implies is illusory. Only in his music classes and in those with Phelps—with whom he became friendly during three years of courses—would Ives's grades rise above minimally passing. In modern terms, his overall four-year average, outside music, was D+.[5] In music he earned a middling B average—not bad, for Horatio Parker's grades, but not so excellent as David Stanley Smith et al.

After the ordeal of morning recitations the intensive part of Yale set in, much of it a matter of jockeying for position. At lunch, students spread out to eating clubs in restaurants and rooming houses; the clubs, of course, were ranked in prestige and a means of making connections. Afterward, some men might socialize on the railings of the Yale Fence, with its divisions for each of the upper classes (freshmen were allowed a place only when their baseball team beat Harvard). Afternoons one could find ranks of derby-hatted, choke-collared young men perched like sparrows along the Fence. Once it had faced the pathways and elms of New Haven Green, but as President Dwight tore down the old Brick Row and erected a grim neo-Gothic fortress of buildings around campus, the Fence was moved inside the new quadrangle. For four years, Ives roomed with Mandeville Mullally at 76 South Middle, the present Connecticut Hall and only remnant of Brick Row.

For Yale underclassmen with any ambition—and waves of ambition surged around campus—most afternoons and evenings were spent "heeling," which is to say, working for one of the organizations that ran much of student life. Even the football team was coached largely by its captains. The week Ives registered as a freshman, the Yale *Daily* editorialized,

Freshmen must clearly understand that a man is judged here for what he is, and that abundant opportunity will be offered to all. No matter where distinction is to be attained—be it in the class room, on the athletic field or in literary work—there must be a corresponding amount of self-sacrifice and persevering effort.[6]

One heeled for any of the organizations—an athletic team, the Football Association, the *Daily,* the *Lit,* the Glee Club, the Class Deacons, and so on, each post ranked in a hierarchy of consequence. For plum positions competition was ferocious; men going out for the *Daily* might spend months sleeping four hours a night and wearing out shoes and bicycles hustling around campus for news.[7] The social and organizational skills cultivated at Yale were the same as one needed later, in professional life; each post was a step toward the next and eventually to big-city boardrooms. Henry Seidel Canby recalled,

No one that I remember did anything that was regarded as doing, for its own sake. No, the goal was prestige, social preferment, a senior society which would be a springboard to Success in Life. And all gilded, made into illusion, by the theory that in such strenuosity we demonstrated loyalty to our society, which was the college, that thus the selfish man transcended his egoistic self-seekings, and "did" something for . . . Yale.[8]

Charlie kept his serious music confined to church and quarters. His classmates would not understand what was to be gained by composing a symphony; at that point, maybe, neither did he.[9] In his first year he landed a spot in the Freshman Glee Club, from which he had a leg up to the regular Glee Club; he composed ten partsongs for the group.[10] For whatever reason—lack of time or interest or voice—Ives did no choral singing after that. In fact, he would rarely heel the sorts of activities that got one ahead at the school. Ives inherited an individualism closer to Thoreau than to the ideal Yale man, what he would call his "a-association" instinct.[11] A classmate, writing of Ives's senior society chances, mentioned "becoming independence" as a character trait.[12] So why and how did he rise in a school preoccupied with conformity and group endeavor?

Ives later wrote, "I went to college for athletics . . . the one thing that interested me in those days."[13] His participation would be mostly from the bleachers: Charlie tried out for pitcher of the Yale freshman team and was cut. Probably he held down positions in occasional fraternity or scrub games, and in his last year he played on the senior-class football team and rowed for class crews.[14] Still, all four college years would be marked by steady involvement in the school's sporting and social life. The friends who enjoyed "Dasher" Ives's exploits (everybody at Yale had a nickname) knew little about the midnight oil he was burning with his musical projects. His classmates simply watched him go, this whirligig who seemed to be everywhere at once, who could pound out any song you asked for on piano and would occasionally produced a number of his own. He had an inimitable style, too: "In playing the songs . . . I used to play off-beats on black keys, etc., and often men would ask to have those 'stunts' put in. Some said . . . that it made the music stronger and better, after he had got used to it."[15]

Everyone knew Dasher had brains and talent, but they did not run in the usual grooves, and he took pains to wear them lightly. The label of "amateur" that would attach itself to Ives's music for decades would be created as much as anything by his own writings. Ives led the way in painting himself as a small-town rube who learned everything he knew from his pa. Following a habit formed in childhood, when he wanted to be one of the boys, Ives concealed his real sophistication and his real feelings. He seemed to want somehow to lead the crowd and at the same time not stand out in it. Much of the time he succeeded in those paradoxical goals. Then as later, no one seemed to suspect how knowing and ambitious he was—socially, professionally, and creatively.

Biographers Rossiter and Feder speculate that at Yale Ives was a "lame duck," the term for a student who rose up the ladder by attaching himself to the "big men" who controlled student life. There is something to that. Ives's gabby, Kentucky-born roommate "Mull" Mullally was a big man. More important was another friend—David Twichell, son of a popular Hartford minister who often preached on campus. (In his last letter to his father, Charlie wrote of his intention to go hear Reverend Twichell.)Dave played freshman football, was a Class Deacon, and ended up as president of the Football Association, one of the plum posts on campus. His popularity seemed to be based mainly on hard work and a kind of moral radiance; in senior year Dave Twichell would be voted among the most admired—and best-looking—men in the class of '98.[16]

While Mull Mullaly and Dave Twichell and a few others helped Charlie climb, there was more to his popularity than their influence. If no big man, he was not entirely a lame duck either.[17] The Yale social system was riddled with inequities and hypocrisies, but its democratic ideal—to foster an elite of character, ability, and enterprise rather than (as at Harvard) money and family—was not entirely imaginary. A talented, attractive, tireless classmate like Charlie, a small-town boy who had made a name for himself, was exactly the sort on whom, at its best, Yale smiled. He was a loyal and hilarious friend, an ideal companion for a night on the town, ready to listen to your poems at midnight and to catch the dawn from the top of East Rock.[18] With a few drinks and a piano in front of him, Dasher could be the life of a party. Wrote a Yale buddy: "I had not the slightest intimation that Charley was a musical genius. . . . I regarded him as a most delightful man and companion, completely unpredictable . . . one never knew what to expect next."[19]

Charlie may have been inhibited by his fear of girls, but girls were distant foreign creatures anyway. They were brought in for dances and socializing largely from Miss Porter's finishing school, "the honorable legion of Farmington"[20] where many Yale men's sisters got their polish, and where many Yale men hoped to find their mates (as did Ives, eventually). Girls appeared at picnics or as dates or at concerts; a photo of an outing survives, showing Charlie sitting at the feet of some wistful young ladies. Women and love came later. Girls were ornaments to the real concerns and pleasures of manly Yale.

Most of those pleasures were innocent, by later standards. Charlie gravitated to the New Haven theaters where students spent many of their evenings, where one might observe a naked female ankle or a stockinged leg. It was a familiar setting for Charlie; he had grown up hearing his father's orchestra accompanying shows in the Danbury Opera House. Besides the acts onstage, he enjoyed the unpretentious spirit and skill of the musicians in the pit. The elegant Hyperion Theater, across Chapel Street from Yale, presented anything from plays to traveling opera troupes, oratorios, and recitalists.[21] "Professor" Frank A. Fichtl led the house orchestra. Charlie sometimes sat in, and for

Fichtl's group composed a number of pieces that took advantage of resourceful musicians who, hours a night, had to grind out all kinds of music for all kinds of shows. Ives affectionately recalled the pit orchestras of those days:

The make-up of the average theatre orchestra of some years ago, in the towns and smaller cities . . . depended somewhat on what players and instruments happened to be around. Its size would run from four or five to fifteen or twenty, and the four or five

Ives, lower left, amid a picnic group during the Yale years.

often had to do the job of twenty without getting put out. Sometimes they would give as much support 'during the rescue' as the whole town band. Its scores were subject to make-shifts, and were often written with that in mind. There were usually one or two treble Woodwind, a Trombone, a Cornet, sometimes a Saxophone, Strings, Piano and a Drum—often an octave of High Bells or a Xylophone. The pianist usually led—his head or any unemployed limb acting as a kind of Ictusorgan.[22]

Domed, ornate Poli's Theater, also next to the Yale campus on Chapel Street, was the favored vaudeville house, a place to take in acrobats, magicians, dog acts, chanteuses, and blackfaced comedians singing the ragtime tunes that were the sensation of the day. At Poli's students traditionally carried on a boisterous byplay with the performers onstage.[23] Among the seven or so musicians holding forth from the pit sat George Felsburg, renowned for his ability to play piano while reading the paper. "When I was in college," Ives wrote, "I used to go down there and 'spell him' a little if he wanted to go out for five minutes and get a glass of beer, or a dozen glasses."[24]

As a performer, Ives would be experienced and at home in only two venues—in church and in the theater orchestra pit. In the world of symphony orchestras and urban concert halls he would be only a spectator, on the outside looking into a milieu he could never entirely accept, yet which his grandest dreams required.

Within weeks of his father's death, Ives was swallowing his grief, bustling in all directions, and thinking about the future. In January 1895 he wrote his mother Mollie of "taking a few lessons this winter with Dudley Buck as I haven't taken any lessons at all for quite a while. I think it almost necessary that I should and if I don't get any other good from it, just being a pupil of Buck's would be very helpful. . . . Mr. Griggs who advised me to do it has made arrangements."[25] His desire to have a famous name on his résumé implies that he was thinking about later church positions. Besides being a composer, Buck was one of the two leading organists and teachers in the country, the other being Harry Rowe Shelley. Ives took lessons with both men, probably at Metropolitan College in New York, where Center Church choirmaster Griggs was teaching.[26] The music of Shelley and Buck served as models for Ives's more conventional church-choir pieces.[27]

At the end of March 1895 Ives played a recital in Westville, Connecticut. Two weeks later came what may have been his debut as a composer in New Haven: his choral *Easter Carol,* from 1892, was sung at the Center Church Easter service. "The Light that Is Felt" was premiered there two months later. Already he had made his music part of his new church, and he would do the same on campus and in local theaters—to each venue its appropriate music.

Ives played two services at Center Church each Sunday, the 4:00 worship service the more musically elaborate. When he began, music director John Griggs had only a quartet for the singing, himself and three others, all of them professional. Then Griggs put together a volunteer choir and kept them interested by giving free voice lessons.[28] That made for a sophisticated music program in the town's leading church, the middle of the three on New Haven Green.[29] Center Church is a brick Federal-style building patterned after London's St. Martin in the Field; in those days it sported ten splendid Tiffany windows. Pastor Newman Smyth was liberal for the time's Congregationalists, a believer in evolution and the ultimate unity of faiths. The choir and organist held forth from the balcony in back. In contrast to the cave-like sound of many churches, the acoustics in Center Church are dry and lucid. That characteristic, plus the encouragement of Griggs and the skill of his singers, would have much to do with the kinds of music Ives wrote for services there—the particular blends of harmonies appropriate to a well-defined acoustic space. A chorister remembered Ives: "He was thin and tall and dynamic in his handling of the organ—he was all over the thing."[30] His repertoire ranged from his own pieces to the Bach and Mendelssohn he had studied in Danbury, to works by Schubert, Liszt, Fauré, Shelley, Buck, and Horatio Parker.[31]

Now and then two students from Miss Porter's School sat in for Center Church services—Sally Whitney, granddaughter of inventor Eli Whitney, and her roommate Harmony Twichell, sister of Dave, daughter of Reverend Joseph Twichell. When Dave's friend at the organ struck some of his peculiar harmonies in a hymn accompaniment, Sally would smile and nudge Harmony.[32]

As a freshman Ives continued the staggering schedule he had pursued since childhood. He played in church, went when necessary to classes (probably auditing Parker's harmony course), played for Griggs's lectures on religious music at the Divinity School, frequented music halls and lent a hand in the pit, attended chamber and orchestral concerts in town, commuted to New York for organ lessons, played ball, socialized with friends until all hours, and composed piles of music. Rarely did he crack a book. Creatively, his major medium through college would be songs, some fifty of them,[33] mostly conventional, written for class, for student shows, for theaters, for church.

Around the time George Ives died, Charlie began his first major work. On a surviving sketch one sees him begin tentatively with a melody in G, then start over in D, extending a theme that would see little change in the final version. So began his First Symphony, a big piece in European Romantic style that would occupy him off and on throughout his time at Yale.[34] He composed fast, as usual, long stretches apparently struck off at one sitting, probably after being worked out in his head or at the piano. (Ives seems generally to have composed at the piano if one was handy, but he could work without it and often did on vacations in the country.) The draft of the first movement was ready to be shown to Parker at the end of freshman year. Parker certainly made suggestions: in the short-score draft the opening theme was originally marked "oboe & Bassoon," then "oboe & clar," but maybe with Parker's help was reduced to the quiet clarinet solo over murmuring strings that now begins the symphony.[35]

The main Parker criticism that Ives remembered and resented was that the movement went through too many keys. Parker demanded a more orthodox version and Ives obediently drafted a new one, which seemed weaker. "I told him that I would much prefer to use the first draft," Ives recalled. "He smiled and let me do it, saying 'But you must promise to end in D minor.' "[36] In fact, the first draft rambles aimlessly through the keys, pausing to hit the correct harmonic bases at the correct points according to the rules of sonata form. This restless chromaticism shows Ives's acquaintance with Franck and Wagner; he can easily roam from key to key, and in this symphony he prefers to.

If the movement is in the style of another place, it is still an up-to-date piece for 1895, when the symphonic genre was still thriving. Dvořák's *New World Symphony* and Tchaikovsky's *Pathétique* date from the first half of the decade, and Ives's symphonic debut shows familiarity with both.[37] Like Tchaikovsky but more so, his first movement does not lack for padding and hackneyed stretches. All the same, this symphony would end up quite a remarkable homework assignment. For all the immaturity there is a voice arguably more distinctive, if less sophisticated, than Horatio Parker managed in his celebrated *Hora novissima*. Ives had launched a big Romantic symphony and done well at it—and that before the influence of his new teacher had fully sunk in.

Most striking and genuinely Ivesian in the first movement is the meditative central section, based on a sequence of minor chords rising melodically while harmonically descending in whole steps. This section cost Charlie much effort in the drafts before he struck out most of the melodic material and simply let the chords drift quietly upward, in a magical endless sequence. It is tempting to look at this part of the movement as a prayer in memoriam George Ives.[38] Ives would return to this chord sequence thirty years later, in his recomposition of *Psalm 90*.

The symphony movement done, freshman year over, and the immediate mourning for his father past, Ives gathered his forces during the summer for the coming school terms that would be as productive a period as any in his life. One finds little trace of what he did during this or later college vacations. The best guess is that he spent part of the summers in New Haven—he still played at Center Church on Sundays—part in Danbury, and perhaps part at the family vacation spot on the coast in Westbrook.[39] Likely he did a good deal of composing.

During the 1895–96 school year he would write quite a few occasional items, some for publication and some designed to smooth his progress through the social system. Along with Dave Twichell and his roommate Mullally, Ives belonged to the sophomore society Hé Boulé, the first step in the winnowing process that everyone hoped would lead to a senior society. Charlie responded to his elevation with a flood of practical pieces, and bestirred himself to send the more commercial items to publishers. The year 1896 would see the printing of his barbershop chorus "For You and Me!," the *March Intercollegiate* for band, the song "Scotch Lullaby" (published in the *Yale Courant*), and "William Will," a McKinley campaign ditty.[40] Over the next years he would get a few more pieces in print, before the long drought.

"William Will" is a revealing item. It is partly based on Ives's older March No. 3, now supplied with words (beginning "What we want is honest money") by Danbury writer Susan Benedict Hill.[41] Ives probably put it together in the summer of 1896, as the presidential contest heated up between William McKinley and populist William Jennings Bryan. The song reveals that Ives's politics had not yet taken the leftward turn that marked his adulthood. McKinley was a Republican lawmaker whose protectionist bills gained him the blessing of big business, but his policies went hard on working people. Given that he was an affable man and Civil War veteran who had pulled himself up from a limited background, McKinley was bound to be admired at Yale and in the Ives family. For the moment, "Bill McKinley and the McKinley Bill" were good enough for Charlie, too. Bryan, "the Great Commoner," meanwhile, was shouted down by students during an 1896 speech on New Haven Green.[42] "William Will" brought Ives some glory: the New Haven Band apparently took it with them to Washington in 1897, and joined the Marine Band in playing it at McKinley's inauguration.[43]

The published pieces were a fraction of Ives's output in those years. Others included a set of overtures (now lost) called *In These United States;* one, *Town, Gown, and State,* played by the New Haven Band, became the kernel of the Second Symphony finale. He supplied bands in New Haven, Bethel, and Danbury with new pieces. Several organ works (also lost) were later rearranged and parcelled out into the Second Symphony and First String Quartet. (Ives would retain his bandsman's—and theater musician's—habit of adapting pieces for varying instrumental combinations.) His campus music included "A Song of Mory's," a paean to the legendary off-campus tavern, the delightful piano march "Here's to Good Old Yale," and the fraternity-show tune "Pass the Can Along." Certainly the First Symphony lay heavily on Ives's mind during his sophomore year, and he may have worked on the later movements. The Hyperion Theater orchestra, perhaps under Ives's direction, played an arrangement of the second movement and part of the last in 1897.[44]

The major work of his sophomore year was the First String Quartet, subtitled "From the Salvation Army," finished in May 1896. Ives put it together from church pieces, as he would most of his larger works. Three of the movements, arranged for organ and strings, he played at a Center Church revival service. Appropriately to that service, they were based or gospel hymns—thus the Salvation Army subtitle. Having arranged the pieces for string quartet, Ives grafted onto the beginning a fugue on the hymn *Missionary Chant* ("From Greenland's Icy Mountains"), originally written as an exercise for Parker's counterpoint class.[45] Over a decade later, Ives removed the fugue and retooled it toward the Fourth Symphony.[46]

Like the First Symphony, the First String Quartet is no "masterpiece," but neither is it negligible. It rambles and essays some dubious experiments, but it stands up a century later as a work of precocious individuality and charm. For the student Ives it represents another leap in imagination and sophistication, and a step closer to his mature voice.

In Ives's relations with Horatio Parker, though, the First Quartet represents a step backward. He could have found few better ways to abrade his teacher's sensibilities than writing a fantasia on revival hymns. Ives recalls Parker sermonizing, "In music they should have no place. Imagine, in a symphony, hearing suggestions of street tunes like 'Marching through Georgia' or a Moody and Sankey hymn!"[47] If that is all Parker said, he was biting his tongue. In a lecture of 1900 Parker denounced revival music as "vulgar with the vulgarity of the streets and the music hall. If sentimentality is evil . . . what shall we say of vulgarity? . . . Let the stuff be confined to the mission where it may do good. Among people of any appreciable degree of refinement and culture it can only do harm." Parker even deplored the more mainstream hymns of Lowell Mason and his school as "vulgarity tempered by incompetency . . . the lowest form of music."[48] It is as if he were thinking, with a shudder, of his former pupil Ives.

In contrast to the way history would tend to paint the situation, it is here, rather than in Ives's experimental notions (which Parker rarely saw anyway), that we find the main divide between teacher and pupil. To Parker, Ives's string quartet was redolent of the street and the music hall, of bad air and cheap religiosity—far removed from the splendid theaters, the cultured old-Yankee salons, the wealthy Boston church that delineated Parker's milieu. Given Parker's ideal of artistic purity, the revival service itself reeked of some obscure sin, "evil music . . . harmful to our sense of beauty, to our aesthetic sensitiveness."

Beyond his hatred of the revival and music hall, Parker took an odd position for a composer specializing in vocal and dramatic works: he allied himself with the doctrine of "pure music," of abstraction as represented by Brahms, as opposed to the programmatic tradition of Liszt, Wagner, and Richard Strauss. "We can profit enormously in technical details," Parker wrote, "from Strauss and his long train of followers, but I do not think that we, the Anglo-Saxon race, need be among them." Against the dramatic scenarios that underlay Strauss's orchestral music, Parker placed "the impersonal, abstract serenity of the great classic masters."[49] Music "loses some of its purity when called upon to support any other than musical ideas or suggestions."[50]

(Of course, Parker wrote program music himself, including the overture *Count Robert of Paris* and the symphonic poem *A Northern Ballad*. When he did compose on a subject, in vocal or instrumental works, he often resorted to a sort of pre-Raphaelite fantasy: *Fairyland, Cáhal Mór of the Wine-red Hand, King Gorm the Grim*.[51])

Inconsistent or not, this was Parker's vision of the great task of Anglo-Saxon composers in Britain and America: to revive the Brahmsian spirit of pure music that appeared, by the turn of the century, to have been exhausted in corrupt old Europe.[52] What could Parker do, then, with this student who seemed incurably infested with crude hymnody and program music, who without shame could title a string quartet, that purest of genres, "From the Salvation Army"?

Yet if the tainted sources of Ives's First Quartet offended Parker, the execution has his stamp all over it. We see his gifts as a teacher, his understanding of form and development, in the subtlety of thematic derivations and relationships, and in Ives's inconsistent but still resourceful aptitude for planning and holding together a long work. The First Quartet—excepting the extraneous opening fugue—weaves together a collection of supple and apparently original themes derived from gospel tunes, mainly *Beulah Land* ("I've reached the land of corn and wine"), *Nettleton* ("Come, thou Fount of every blessing"), *Webb* ("Stand up, stand up for Jesus"), and, lingering in the background throughout like a distant echo, *Shining Shore* ("My days are gliding swiftly by").[53] Ives would take up these tunes again and again over the decades.[54]

Did Parker respond to this student's quartet with one of his exasperated little smiles? Did he swallow his outrage and help Ives with the thematic development, perhaps suggesting a contrapuntal combination of themes at the end? (Parker ended several of his own works that way,[55] and Ives used the device in the First Symphony and First Quartet.) In any case, the quartet conforms to Parker's requirements in more ways than not. Even if the material is derived from hymns, they are recast into open-ended themes suitable for long pieces. As for the first-movement fugue on "Greenland," though the key scheme is untraditional and the counterpoint intermittent,[56] it is a beautiful piece with an impressive climax—a stretto on a "new" theme (actually the refrain of "Greenland"). As the First Symphony would be, the First Quartet is "cyclic"—melodic themes recur from movement to movement, a nineteenth-century formal device going back to Berlioz and Schumann. On the whole, personal as they are, both quartet and symphony arise from late-Romantic European tradition. As David Eiseman summarizes,

Mahler, Dvořák, Ives, and other composers born in the 1860s and '70s inherited as their contrapuntal models the polyphonic and polyrhythmic designs of Brahms and the continual contrapuntal interweaving and alternation of . . . *Leitmotiven* in the late music dramas of Wagner. The resulting contrapuntal writing in the latter part of the century, rather than being restricted to the inner parts, began spreading throughout all the melodic lines, thus becoming the main generating force within the music.[57]

Did Parker see the penetrating musicality and imagination running through the quartet and symphony, for all their weak pages? What did he make of this precocious, infuriating student? One may speculate that at some point—say, the point Ives laid the First String Quartet on his desk—Horatio Parker gave up. He had not the time or the energy to lead such a student to the light. He had other students, less talented perhaps but more tractable, less threatening to his dreams for the Anglo-Saxon future of music. For Ives's part, he wrote his exercises and pieces, doggedly followed his own inclinations, and did not, so far as we know, fight with his teacher. His passive resistance is seen in a note on a sketch for a classroom assignment: "Organ Fugue for Prof. H. W. Parker, a stupid fugue on a stupid subject."

Outside the classroom Charlie continued to experiment and enjoy himself. For his more novel ideas he had two outlets. One, for things not too obstreperous, was Center Church, where in July 1896 (or 1897) the brilliant polychordal exploration *Psalm 150* had, at least in excerpt, its premiere.[58] In the theater orchestra pit he took advantage of the adventurousness of those musicians to try some bolder games. He recalled,

While in college, some things were written and played by the Hyperion Theater Orchestra . . . some short overtures and marches, some brass band pieces, and short orchestra pieces. Some had old tunes, college songs, hymns, etc.—sometimes putting these themes or songs together in two or three differently keyed counterpoints (not exactly planned so but just played so)—and sometimes two or three different kinds of time and key and off-tunes, played sometimes impromptu. For instance, a kind of shuffle-dance-march (last century rag) was played on the piano—the violin, cornet, and clarinet taking turns in playing sometimes old songs, sometimes the popular tunes of the day, as *After the Ball*, football songs, *Ta-ra-ra-boom-de-ay*. . . . The pianist (who was I, sometimes) played his part regardless of the off-keys and the off-counterpoints, but giving the cue for the impromptu counterpoint parts etc. . . . Some similar things were tried in the [fraternity] shows, but not very successfully, as I remember. Marches with college tunes in the trio against the original themes went better,—though Prof. Fichtl, in the theater orchestra, would get students in the audience whistling and beating time (sometimes) to the off-key and off-time tunes.[59]

Ives whipped up these serendipitous quodlibets in a situation where he could play for laughs, and filed the results in his steel-trap memory for sounds and their contexts. He never switched off his judgment; some things went better, some worse. We hear approximations of these experiments in a few of his quirkier pieces from the next decade—say, in *Country Band March*; or in the middle movement of the Piano Trio, called "TSIAJ" for "This Scherzo Is A Joke," and subtitled "Medley on the Campus Fence." What strikes one about these pieces probably resembles what struck Ives, listening to his stunts in the theater: interesting, funny, potentially useful, but not particularly good music.[60] He had years of experimentation and learning to go before he could succeed in creating the effect of accident while keeping his hand on the tiller. At least in the context of a theater he could get away with things that would be forbidden in Parker's classes and out of place in church, and could even draw some enthusiasm from the audience: *Imagine a theater full of rowdy students whistling and singing away at class and club songs, like a musical version of their intramural games and wrestling matches; and amidst the melee Ives rocking at the keyboard, ragging the tunes, touching off musical effects like fireworks in competing keys and times; and all the while listening, listening.*

Another variety of stunt created a kind of aural photograph. One night each spring Yale erupted in an eerie ceremony. Members of the junior fraternities, robed like monks and roaring their songs to the accompaniment of ragtag bands, paraded through the campus holding up glaring red and green calcium lights (a.k.a. limelights). From one procession would be declaimed, "When in after years we take our children on our knee / We'll teach them that the alphabet begins with DKE," while from another, "And again we sing thy praises, Psi U. Psi U / We don't give a damn for DKE."[61] En route, the marchers tapped fraternity members for the next year.[62] On such a night in May 1896, sophomore Ives was elected to Delta Kappa Epsilon. He turned this Yale tradition into a piano improvisation for laughs; we hear the procession approach, pass by, fade into the distance. At some later point he wrote it down for chamber orchestra as *Calcium Light Night*. Several similar "cartoons or take-offs" would join it over the years, the subjects ranging from sports (*Yale-Princeton Football Game*) to current events (*"Gyp the Blood" or Hearst!? Which is Worst?!*) to memories (*The Gong on the Hook and Ladder*). These imitations of events or people or ideas are mostly scraggly, unfinished pieces. From them Ives gleaned technical lessons toward the works he really cared about.

In August 1896, at the end of summer vacation, Dave Twichell invited friends to Keene Valley in New York's Adirondacks, where Hartford minister Joseph Twichell had long vacationed with his family. For all of them this was an interlude pleasant and prophetic, in the eloquent mountain landscape that over the years, as it happened, was to witness great joy and great sorrow in the Ives and Twichell families. Charlie spent the weeks at Keene Valley in the company of the big family and their friends, including Yale classmates Ned Ware and Bart Yung. How much did Charlie notice Dave's sister Harmony? Then twenty and a famous Hartford beauty, how did she regard him? Did his shyness clog his tongue and even his fingers at the keyboard? Did he perhaps consider this exquisite woman, with her elegant manner and easy laugh, as out of his league? Did Harmony Twichell have time, given the crowd of men always around her, to think about him? If anything clicked in either of their minds, they did not speak of it. This was the Victorian era; as Harmony would say in later years, "We were very *formal* then."[63] After vacation they went their ways. At the end of the next school year Charlie would work up his courage and ask Harmony to the Junior Prom. They danced a little, she was crowned queen of the prom, and they parted with no apparent repercussions.[64] Charlie would take another classmate's sister to the Senior Prom.

Charlie returned to school as a junior in the fall of 1896 to a musical and social life more heated than ever. Among other things, he directed and composed music for his fraternity's productions, which strengthened his portfolio of social stock. The DKE spring show was a romp called *Hells Bells*. As the program indicates, it dispensed college wit in the form of bloated clichés, a style that would characterize some of Ives's adult whimsies:

For the last time the '98 extravaganza company presents the rib-fracturing phantasy of which the headlines appear above. This mammoth production over which no time and expense have been wasted, brings to a culminating climax the apex of our efforts. . . . Mr. C. E. Ives has furnished much original music for this play; his latest masterpiece will be sung at the close. . . . You are all requested to join in the chorus, but kindly wait until it sounds familiar.[65]

Ives signed up for music electives he could now take officially. Having probably audited the Harmony and Music History courses earlier,[66] in his junior year he took Counterpoint and Instrumentation, in his last year Strict Composition and another year of Instrumentation. During these terms with Parker, Ives set several German and French songs in Romantic style, some of them successful and "Feldeinsamkeit" remarkable. Music classes were held in the old marble Treasury Building in the center of campus, downstairs from the college's financial offices. Classes were practical, Parker correcting exercises and working out solutions at the blackboard.[67] In his senior music courses Ives received grades of 325 and 340 (roughly a B) out of 400, the highest he ever managed at Yale.[68] (His composition lessons were ungraded.) The best he did otherwise was the 295, a gentleman's C, he received in Billy Phelps's American literature course.

The supreme event on the Yale calendar arrived in spring 1897: Tap Day, when fifteen juniors were elected by each of the three senior societies, Wolf's Head, Scroll and Key, and, at the summit, Skull and Bones. Each society resided in a windowless mausoleum, compulsively secretive and pervaded by arcane traditions and rituals.[69] For three years most men in the class had fought for advancement, found some posts, and avoided getting "queered" by conspicuous displays of eccentricity or wickedness. To be elected to a senior society was to become a prince of the campus, and to connect with other men likely to be allies for life. To fail more or less obliterated three years of single-minded effort.

On a Thursday afternoon in May nearly everyone in school gathered for the tap. Hundreds of students and visiting alumni thronged across the Old Campus, hung from windows and roofs, all watching the anxious juniors clumped by the Yale Fence. At the stroke of the five o'clock bell society men

appeared, all hooded or masked; they fanned through the crowd to stride up
to one elected man after another, slap him hard on the back, and command,
"Go to your room!" Each tap was greeted by a roar, the name of the lucky
man racing through the crowd.[70] Ives was tapped for Wolf's Head, the least
prestigious but still a distinction, given that only forty-five men from the junior
class were chosen at all. He would spend much of his senior year in the society's
rooms, with their stuffed wolves at the entrance, their outlandish Egyptian
decor, their chart of tappers and tappees. Mullally and Dave Twichell were
received into Scroll and Key. Ives and his best friends were made men now,
and they would carry that notion, or that illusion, with them for life.[71]

After another summer of vacation, composing, and Center Church services, Ives returned for his last year of school. His main job for Parker was to
complete the First Symphony, by way of a senior thesis.[72] He would submit
the final version in May 1898.[73] The last three movements do not quite come
up to the level of the first. That movement, padding and all, generates some
genuine symphonic excitement from the elegant opening theme to the adroit
rhythmic crescendo of the final pages, which lay on the faux-Tchaikovsky
fatalism with a dripping brush. (Conductor Michael Tilson Thomas has described the symphony as "going for the jugular of the listener.") The second
movement's opening English horn melody recalls the slow movement of the
New World Symphony, though the Dvořák-like scoring may have been Parker's
idea.[74] The movement spins out variations including some beautifully atmo-
spheric textures for muted strings, perhaps owing something to the slow
movement of Beethoven's Ninth. The third movement scherzo begins with a
nimble canonic theme, brilliantly scored, and has a trio rather coy à la Tchaikovsky's ballet music. For a finale comes a grand march punctuated by Tchai-
kovskyan whirlwind figures, but the brass bands of Ives's childhood put in
regular appearances.[75] The symphony winds up, quite satisfactorily, with an
expanse of bracing trombonic banality.[76]

With this high-European work Ives made a remarkable beginning as a
symphonist, but not as the Charles Ives the world knows. Here he plays, not
for the last time, Horatio Parker's game. It could not satisfy him, but for the
moment he knew no other way to shape big works. For some time his more
innovative pieces would be relatively short.

In his struggle to find a mature voice, rhythm was hampering Ives as
much as anything. In the First Symphony and First Quartet he achieves a good
bit of rhythmic variety and energy, even if he sometimes falls into fits and
starts. Already he strains at the confines of conventional rhythmic figures in
regular measures; the quartet has frequent meter changes, and in both symphony and quartet he uses sustained two-against-three effects—simple polyrhythms. (Quintuplets, a feature of his mature polyrhythm, function in the
quartet's first movement only as written-out rubatos.) More intriguing, the
second and fourth movements of the quartet show systematic games with

phrasing, superimposing metric divisions on the basic pattern. These games logically wind up with a polymetric section near the end—one of his climactic quodlibets, the integrity of the tunes now reinforced by simultaneous $\frac{3}{4}$ and $\frac{4}{4}$ meters.[77]

The ingenious phrasings of the First Quartet were another step toward Ives's mature rhythmic style; soon polymeter would become true polyrhythm. But to drum up excitement in a long allegro he still had no other means than writing some sort of march, heavy on the stiff rum-te-dum-te-dum of "dotted" figures. He had yet to discover that the syncopated African-American style called ragtime, which he was already playing in music halls and bars, could be adapted to large works. Only when Ives had absorbed and adapted ragtime could he write a true Ivesian allegro. In the faster music of the First Quartet and first three symphonies, his imagination would still be confined in march rhythms.

Amidst finishing the First Symphony during his senior year, Ives also wrote what he would later call (ignoring several revolutionary earlier works) "the first piece that seems to me to be much or any good now"—the organ *Prelude and Postlude for a Thanksgiving Service*.[78] They are lost except for a page of draft, but the two pieces, joined and arranged for orchestra, survive as *Thanksgiving* (1904), the last movement of the *Holidays Symphony*. The *Prelude*'s opening superimposition of C-major and D-minor triads[79] is the sort of polychord by then a regular feature of Ives's innovative pieces. The same applies to its polytonality—as he put it, "some free counterpoint in different keys." He plays with rhythmic ideas, carrying them further than does the First Quartet, in sections "with two rhythms going together . . . a scythe or reaping Harvest Theme, which is a kind of off-beat, off-key counterpoint." This music is close to the mature Ives in spirit and substance, but still simpler in rhythm and counterpoint than his later work. The eventual *Thanksgiving* also contains, in its gentle, folklike interludes based on hymn tunes, some of the most beautiful lyrical writing of Ives's life.

Another piece from his senior year is a piano stunt later orchestrated, the *Yale-Princeton Football Game*. It was inspired by the epic conclusion of the 1897 season, when the Yale Bulldogs ground down the favored Princeton Tigers and finally scored the game's only touchdown, securing an unbeaten season.[80] Going beyond the simpler takeoff *Calcium Light Night,* Ives reduced the game to two sets of downs, picturing everything from the crowds in the stands (the Greek Cheer in trombones) to the flying wedge play (wedgelike note patterns) to the Yale quarterback's legendary fifty-five-yard run (zigzag trumpet line) to the referee's whistle (picolo trills).[81]

As Ives's senior year wound up along with his frustrating and indispensable studies with Horatio Parker, an event supplied him, for once, with a victory over his teacher.

The date, most likely, was March 31, 1898. Parker's old mentor and friend George Chadwick had come to town for a performance of his *Melpomene*

Overture by Parker and the New Haven Symphony. In those days Chadwick was a celebrated figure, head of the New England Conservatory. After the two men had a jolly lunch at Heublein's beer hall, Chadwick sat in on a composition class and listened to Ives's songs "Ich Grolle Nicht" and "Feldeinsamkeit." The former text had been famously set by Schumann, the latter by Brahms. In style, Ives's settings of these high-Romantic lyrics echo those models. Presumably on this occasion Ives handled the accompaniment, and perhaps John Griggs sang. At the end, Parker declared his preference for "Ich Grolle Nicht" (a stodgy song, in fact), saying it was closer to the model of Schumann; and anyway, "Feldeinsamkeit" modulated too much.

This time it was Parker rather than Ives who received a patronizing grin from his teacher. As Ives recalled the splendid moment, Chadwick said he preferred "Feldeinsamkeit": "The melodic line has a natural continuity—it flows—and stops when [rounded out] as only good songs do. . . . In its way [it's] almost as good as Brahms." Winking at Parker, Chadwick added, "That's as good a song as you could write." It would be a long time before Ives again received an endorsement so perceptive on all points. The song is a little masterpiece, with a supple melody full of fresh harmonic relationships to the piano. Meanwhile the surging accompaniment conjures up the clouds of a summer's day and the soul's exaltation. Ives rushed back to his room and wrote down the incident on the manuscript.[82]

That was nearly his farewell to Horatio Parker. Ives would return to campus often in the next few years, and kept up with Griggs for the rest of Griggs's life. There is no record that he ever stopped in to say hello to Parker, ask his advice, show him a piece. Yet before Ives left Yale he was already working on the cantata *Celestial Country,* so close to Parker's *Hora novissima* that it would seem almost an homage to his teacher. Why?

Ives's last months of school were filled with valedictory doings. In January he visited friends in New York, to sound things out in the city. With Griggs's recommendation he secured an organist/choirmaster job, to begin the next summer, at Bloomfield Presbyterian Church in New Jersey, commutable from Manhattan. For March vacation he sailed to Virginia's Old Point Comfort with brother Moss, who was due to start at Yale Law the next term (and would, after Uncle Lyman's tutoring, earn his law degree and pass the bar in one year).[83]

At the end of the term the Yale '98 class historian started his survey of the seniors with this portrait:

I begin with this charming pair [Ives and Mullally] because I believe them to be the two greatest geniuses in our class. Quigley, known also as Sam, and the Dasher of Danbury (he yonder with the volcanic face), is our Paderewski. Let me tell you the romance of his life. It happened down in Center Church, where Quigley manipulates the organ so gloriously that a maiden who sat in the galleries loved and pined although she never had seen more than the back of Quigley's explosive head, and when one cruel day the heartless Quigley left Center Church never to return, his broken-hearted girl—I cannot go on—the tale is too sad—but I do think these Paderewski people ought to be, Oh so much more tender of the frail hearts they crush. And Mull, good ol Mull . . . we love your plantation ditties and those extraordinary true stories of the South you tell. But as for Quig, the squirrels are after him. Let him go.[84]

A biographer would like to know the identity of that girl, if she existed. What the story does reveal, at least, is some of the reasons the explosive Dasher (also "Quigley" et al.) had become so well liked on campus. Beyond his winning personality, music had been a large part of his popularity. Classmates had ears enough to admire his organ and piano playing, and probably his original stuff too. His sentimental song "The Bells of Yale" had become a Glee Club favorite that year; they sang it through a countrywide tour, and it would be published in a 1903 Glee Club collection. His popularity was confirmed when at the end of senior year Ives was elected chairman of the Ivy Committee, which managed the ceremonial planting of ivy on Class Day.[85]

Ives's Yale graduation photo. Early in his career as head of an insurance agency, he used this as a reassuring face in a newspaper ad.

As the graduation ceremonies commenced, Charlie escorted Ella Fitch, perhaps sister of his friend Ash Fitch, to the Senior Prom.[86] (Dave Twichell had left school early as a volunteer for the Spanish-American War; maybe that was the reason Charlie did not ask Harmony again.) On June 28th, at a Hyperion Theater concert of the Glee and Banjo Clubs, Charlie's "Bells of Yale" was featured. Next day Mollie Ives, Aunt Amelia, Uncle Lyman, and

Moss arrived for graduation. Some of Ives's friends were surprised, given his approach to studies or rather flight from them, that he had made it out of the gate at all.[87]

Then Ives packed up his successful little career at Yale, said goodbye to John Griggs after four years together in the choir loft, and headed for Danbury. He would rejoin many of his friends soon, in New York. At home during the summer of 1898 he composed as usual, and with Moss and old friends enjoyed some last games in the sunny playing fields of his youth. He apparently spent part of the summer living at the Yale Club in New York, having begun his new church job in New Jersey around the end of June.[88] Then or sometime after, Ives claimed a weathered wooden sign that he would keep with him for the rest of his life, as a talisman of his childhood: it simply says "BALL FIELD." It was time to put away childish things. The question was how to proceed with his life.

As musician and composer, Charles Ives had grown remarkably in college. By graduation he was as well set up as one could want for a career in music. He had studied with the leading teachers in the country; he was one of the finest American organists of his generation; he could dash off light-classical and popular and church-service pieces with little effort; he was well on his way to becoming that rarity in American musical life, an accomplished symphonist. As a professional composer all he needed was a little final polish—say, at a *Hochschule* in Germany. Certainly then he could have made his way on organ playing, teaching, and hackwork, and had plenty of time, by his standards, for serious composing and for exploring his radical ideas (if, after the polishing, he still dabbled in such things). With less imagination and no more resourcefulness, Horatio Parker had lived more or less that life and thrived. It was not that Ives had much competition, either; serious composers were scarce in America at that time, few if any with Ives's talent or energy. A promising musical career lay ahead of him. All he had to do was embrace it.

But Charles Ives declined to take Horatio Parker's route to becoming a successful and forgotten composer. He had spent four years contemplating Parker the successful composer, and Parker had spent the same time trying to tame this renegade student, and neither of them had much liked what they saw. As his father had told him to do and his college experience only confirmed, Ives turned onto another path, one that would call on every resource he possessed.

In September 1898 Ives moved into a New York apartment with some Yale friends. He had signed on as a clerk with the Mutual Life Insurance Company. With what time he had to compose he would continue groping in his own direction, toward something that Emerson had once called for: an art new, self-reliant, independent of "the courtly muses of Europe." Emerson had also warned, however, that anyone answering such a call must expect a life "full of renunciations and apprenticeships."

Entr'acte Two:
Graduation

WHAT HAD CHARLES IVES learned in college, what had he accomplished, what hurdles confronted him?

The main thing he would carry out of Yale was what he had carried in: a boiling creative imagination primed by his father, and far exceeding that of his teacher Horatio Parker. He had written a good deal of music from "low" to "high" in style and scope, and on his own had worked his experimental vein in venues from the choir loft to the music hall. He had not equaled his teacher's command of musical technique, orchestration, and shaping large works, but he had gone a considerable distance in that direction.

Ives's task in the next years, like that of all artists finally free of masters, would be to sift through what he had learned and see what of it he could use. He had more or less finished a conventional apprenticeship as a composer and church musician. Now he would begin another sort of apprenticeship.[1] In pursuing that he would discard much of the technique Parker had taught him and strike off in another direction, whose requirements he would have to discover for himself. No one had charted that territory. But he would retain some of the most important things Parker taught him: great skill in thematic development, a practical command of the orchestra,[2] and above all, the ability to ride herd over thousands of notes for long stretches of time. Even at its most radical and chaotic, Ives's best music knows where it is going and when it gets there, and conveys that to the listener. His sense of form and continuity would be as inconsistent as everything else about him, but in the largest view Ives was a symphonist, which is one of the rarest gifts on earth. Ives owed the shaping of that gift primarily to Horatio Parker.

Though Parker taught practical skills and was not much of a philosopher, he still confirmed Ives as a Romantic in his outlook toward music and life. It had been Wagner above all who declared the artist a kind of high priest, leading his people toward redemption. The grandiose belief that art can help redeem a people, and ultimately all humanity, underlay Parker's windy ambitions for Anglo-Saxon music. Parker also proclaimed, despite his concern for technique, the Romantic doctrine of the primacy of individual creative intuition: "The past has shown that cultivated feeling and educated intuition are . . . the only guides for [artists'] essentially unlogical wishes."[3]

Ives would slip into jingoism on occasion, but on the whole he did not swallow Parker's conventional Yankee chauvinism. Ives would draw from the better part of Parker's ideals, from the Wagnerian vision of the artist-priest blazing his own trail, and from his own Puritan and Yankee heritage the faith that music can accomplish something of profound moral and spiritual value, and so be a vehicle of human evolution and redemption.[4] Corollary to that vision was that among the means of redemption were the great musical genres as conceived and shaped by Beethoven, Brahms, and the European Romantics: the symphony, the sonata, the tone poem. "Whoever truly understands my music," said Beethoven, "is freed thereby from the miseries that others carry about in them." "A symphony," said Mahler, "must be a world." Ives could have said the same of his Fourth Symphony. He might have added, as might Mahler and Beethoven, that the ultimate goal of a symphony is to help remake and redeem the world.

As Ives's ideals developed over the years, this high-Romantic motivation kept him writing sonatas and finally brought him back to the symphony so called, even as he rejected the cultural and financial milieu that had always sustained such genres, and the "abstract music" ideal that lay behind some of them.[5] He was determined to put more of the world into big musical forms than they had ever contained, more of the experience of average men and women and the unpretentious music that expressed and exalted their lives.

Besides Parker there was another Yale figure who made his mark on Ives during three years of classes in English and American literature: irrepressible Billy Phelps, the prototypical modern Yale professor, who in the next decades would keep track of Ives as he did hundreds of other alumni. Many of the authors Ives later read and set to music he first studied with Phelps, especially Browning, Tennyson, and other Romantic poets. Ives's unfinished set of overtures called "Men of Literature," the origin of works including *Robert Browning Overture* and the *Concord Sonata,* arose from Phelps's classes and ideas. So does much of the *Essays Before a Sonata;* the "Emerson" chapter of the *Essays,* in fact, probably began as a paper for Phelps (submitted to the *Yale Review,* who "promptly handed it back").[6]

If Parker and Phelps confirmed Ives's Romantic ideals, the nineteenth-century concern with nationalism arose inevitably in their train. As Ives's choirmaster John Griggs had concluded in his doctoral dissertation *Studies in Music in America,* the pursuit of a national art music in the United States had little to go on: no thriving tradition, no clear sense of what sort of folk music might be a basis for a national school. In melting-pot America, unlike the smaller and less diverse countries of Europe, one had to ask, *Which* people is *the* people? *Which* music is *the* American music? Griggs had thrown up his hands at these dilemmas. Horatio Parker largely repudiated nationalism and pursued his King Gorm and Cáhal Mór of the Wine-red Hand, who existed only in fantasy.

Antonín Dvořák, innocent of the dilemmas of American composers and the racism of his host country, had suggested that "inspiration for truly national music might be derived from the Negro melodies or Indian chants." These seemed, after all, the only truly indigenous music the United States possessed. Edward MacDowell's curt riposte to Dvořák typified the response of many European-trained composers: "Masquerading in the so-called nationalism of Negro clothes cut in Bohemia [that is, the *New World Symphony*] will not help us. . . . So-called Russian, Bohemian, or any other purely national music has no place in art. . . . The vital element of music—personality—stands alone."[7]

Dvořák sailed back to Europe in 1895, leaving a highly productive turbulence in his wake. MacDowell and Parker said good riddance, but the debate over American music had heated up and would not subside. We do not know how Charles Ives perceived the debate during his Yale years, but it was in the air, it touched him as it did everyone else. Maybe he discussed nationalism with Griggs, read Griggs's dissertation. In any case, Ives ultimately found his own solution. Before he could do that, he in effect recapitulated most of the strategies that had already been tried in addressing the problem of an American art music.

With the *"America" Variations,* written at age seventeen, Ives contributed to one kind of genre aimed in the general direction of nationalism: variations or fantasias on familiar airs, essentially European in technique and style. Other examples include Louis Moreau Gottschalk's piano fantasies on Civil War tunes and Dudley Buck's organ variations on "Home, Sweet Home." Composers produced reams of such patriotic music in the nineteenth century, their Americanism lying largely in the provenance of the melodies.

Another genre of Gottschalk's, fresher and more original, involved pieces derived from the folk music of his native Louisiana, most famously *Le Banjo* and *La Bamboula*. Similarly Ives, from as early as his "New Year's Dance" written at around age twelve, echoed the folk and popular music of his community. This was potentially a fruitful direction, but to make a folk tradition part of an art music, it needed to be transformed in ways that Gottschalk—and for some years Ives—could not manage.

In a curious way, Ives touched on an older native tradition in some of his *Psalms*. With its chanted outer sections and rhythmic, imitative center, *Psalm 67* resembles nothing so much as the "fuging tunes" of William Billings and his fellows. As noted before, colonial hymnody, displaced by the more learned work of Lowell Mason and other nineteenth-century hymnodists, survived underground in New England. Ives may have heard fuging tunes and, consciously or not, modeled some of his experimental *Psalms* on them. (Or it may have been coincidence, or some innate Yankee spirit.)

In most of his classroom music at Yale, Ives submitted to the attitude that predominated in the academy: forswear self-conscious nationalism, write in the European tradition, let the growing presence of that tradition build up American musical life in the image of that in the Old World. American music would simply continue in the European vein, with whatever native elements it may have picked up in the natural course of things.

By the time he finished his First Symphony, Ives had recapitulated those strategies of the past and begun to find solutions that incorporated them. In the long run he could not really choose sides in pursuit of a native musical tradition. His method would of necessity involve synthesizing American traditions with elements of nineteenth-century European art music.[8]

His means of doing that proved to be complex. The process began relatively simply, however, with the First String Quartet. This work is more than a matter of stirring American tunes into an otherwise Old World recipe, as he did in the *"America" Variations*. For the first time in the quartet, there is a consistent *mediation* between native and imported elements. Previously, Ives had kept his genres distinct—here a fiddle tune, there a march, here a symphony, there a church anthem (the latter sometimes unconventional, yet still recognizably service music). For some time he would tend to maintain stylistic and genre distinctions from work to work. But in the First Quartet the borders begin to blur. The First Quartet's second (later first) movement begins with a robust melody that is clearly string-quartet music as it had been heard since Haydn. Still, aspects of the sound—the melodic shape, the gospel rhythm, the spare texture—are audibly American as well. Even more revealing is the middle section of the movement, an elegant three-beat cantilena recalling, say, the famous one in Beethoven's late A-minor quartet. At the same time, Ives's cantilena subtly recalls the revival tune it is derived from—*Shining Shore*.

If such a mediation between American and European elements was going to be the essence of Charles Ives's solution to the problem of an American art music, the quartet's way of doing that set him on the path toward his maturity. Appropriately, the ending of the second movement is the first true Ivesian ending—an as-if midphrase chromatic fillip that paradoxially seems to wind up the piece while suggesting a new beginning. Many of his most memorable and innovative endings would be, in effect, non-endings.

Ives inherited as birthright a solution to another dilemma, that of which American tradition to embrace. Some American composers took Dvořák's suggestions literally and shoehorned African-American and Native American elements into their concert music. Arthur Farwell spent years studying Indian music and wrote his own copies of it, *hiyiyi*'s and all. Charles Wakefield Cadman concertized with an Indian princess who sang both traditional tunes and songs of Cadman's such as "Tell Her My Lodge is Warm." In the once-notorious *Dance in Place Congo* Henry F. Gilbert grafted "Negro" touches into a basically European musical framework. The results of such attempts were little more than earnest and quaint, Tiffany-window portraits of noble savages and happy Negroes. Aaron Copland, a Russian-Jewish composer from Brooklyn who studied mainly in Paris, would later write symphonic cowboy music with inexplicable effectiveness. None of these approaches, the failed or the successful, addressed the question of authenticity, the kind of bone-deep, living tradition absorbed from the cradle that gives much European music, nationalistic or otherwise, an integrity that cannot be taught or learned.

The problem in America has always been *which tradition*. One answer seems to be: any tradition, as long as it is your own or you can make it your own. In the melting pot, an important part of an artist's voice is a cultural identity, which belongs by birthright to European artists. Most significant American composers in the first half of this century—notably Ives, Copland, Ellington, and Gershwin—created primarily within the orbit of one tradition or another that acted as an anchor and catalyst. (Sometimes, as with Copland, the anchor changed from work to work.) So anchored, a number of composers would help create an American art music tradition on the public stage (while Ives remained offstage). Others, including Roger Sessions, would defiantly maintain a European orientation.

Ives was born into a limited and parochial but nonetheless vital tradition, call it *Danburian*, a subdivision of the New England Yankee heritage. He resonated with this tradition as strongly as Dvořák did with Bohemian folk music, Bartók with Hungarian, Ellington with African-American. Like those composers, Ives remained true to his roots. In doing so he would, single-handedly and privately, forge the first authentically native art music on the continent, and thereby become the American equivalent of the other nationalists of roughly his era, among them Musorgsky, Smetana, Dvořák, Bartók, Vaughan Williams, and the Italian opera composers.

In the end, though, as did Bartók, Ives disavowed nationalism. His goal was to reach the universal through the particular: "If local color, national color, any color, is a true pigment of the universal color, it is a divine quality, it is a part of substance in art—not of manner."[9]

So at Yale Ives began to address (whether or not he perceived it that way) aesthetic and stylistic problems that had afflicted generations of American composers before him. Lacking an audience for decades, he would not solve anything for anyone else of his generation. His solution was too personal, too radical. All the same, Ives continued to think in terms of the context available to him: his artistic and spiritual ambitions could only be played out in the concert hall. Yet after his childhood experience with cultivated music in Danbury, he felt alienated from that world. Under Horatio Parker he had been further subjected to the decorous and effete musical attitudes he had seen push aside George Ives's music-making in Danbury. To go wholly over to the cultivated world seemed to Ives not only a threat to his masculinity, but a betrayal of his father's memory.[10]

Ives had always functioned in one more or less "high" musical context that was familiar and congenial to him. This was the domain of church music, whose repertoire in those days stretched from Bach and Handel to Franck to hymns mainstream and gospel, with many styles and composers in between. The church and revival setting also involved public participation, including the "great waves of sound" from thousands of "let-out" souls that thrilled Ives in the camp meetings of his youth. Contrary to his later public image, Ives was a highly capable and experienced professional musician; but that experience lay mostly in church services, somewhat in the theater orchestra pit, and relatively little in the concert or recital hall (except as a listener). Ives's advanced training at Yale and his musical ambitions, meanwhile, left him unfulfilled simply being a church musician. Instead, his training and ambitions led him, always kicking, to the concert hall.

These inner pressures pulled Ives in contradictory ways. He loved cultivated music but hated the rules and the orthodoxy, hated the economics, the sissified posturing of conductors and virtuosos, the cash prizes given to mediocre works (including Parker's), the inevitable connection of the whole business to Gilded Age trappings and cultivated effeteness: "I personally . . . think that many or most the celebrities of world fame are the greatest enemies of music . . . degenerating down to one function and purpose only—that is, to massage the mind and ear, bring bodily ease to the soft, and please the ladies and get their money."[11] His distaste for the connection of serious music to high society and commerce mirrored in reverse Horatio Parker's hatred for the music hall and the camp meeting—in both cases, an idealistic Victorian squeamishness before the specter of vulgarity and corruption. To Ives "an honest mushy ballad" from the music hall had at least a kind of authenticity, a connection to the heartstrings of ordinary people that too often he missed in cultivated settings.

This complex of feelings left Ives with a potentially fatal dilemma as he moved into adulthood. He was composing for an urban musical world that, as it was constituted, his experience, ideals, and predispositions made uncongenial to him. He thereby became an anomaly in the history of his art: a composer without a milieu.

A situation like that would have been unimaginable in the past. Musical media are expensive; orchestras and operas call for dozens of artists and floods of material; they need money, organizations, partisans: a milieu. Composing like all the arts had long been a trade, a craft, a means of making a living. One wrote for church or court or concert hall, using the common skills of players and existing ensembles and organizations. Composing was rule-bound because it was geared for speed, because it was a job, so the more wares one had to offer the better. The most gifted creators leapt beyond mere craft and often broke the rules, but they still worked for a living within an existing milieu.

Of course, Ives was hardly the first artist to have troubled relations with the public. A gulf between artists and their audience had been widening throughout the nineteenth century, when for the first time composers began to see themselves, in the context of the new science of music history, as prophets fighting the Philistines of the status quo. Their true audience, declared Schumann and Berlioz and Wagner, lay in the future; though in their time they commanded audiences of thousands, they dreamed of millions, and posthumously they got their millions. Wagner built his own theater and gathered disciples and thereby shaped a new milieu, to which he expected the world to journey as pilgrims. Eventually, mostly posthumously, the pilgrims came, and so Wagner's "Music of the Future" agenda, and his concomitant megalomania, became part of the spirit of late Romanticism and thereafter of Modernism. The faith of most twentieth-century artists lay almost perversely in the posthumous, but the relation to milieu remained.

Still, Ives's eventual distance from any musical establishment was unprecedented for a composer. Danbury was the wellspring of his mature music and the mythical setting of much of it, but in its strangeness his music related no more to actual Danbury than to the Gilded Age concert halls of New York and Boston. Ives developed his own artistic and social vision and created a music that rejected, subverted, ignored much of concert life as it existed in Danbury or anywhere else. His music was in great part about the spirit of community, yet it seemed to participate in no community anywhere. This paradox led finally to the impossible dream of the *Universe Symphony,* whose setting is the mountains and the valleys. There, in his dreams at least, Ives escaped from the concert hall and let out his music into a kind of cosmic camp meeting. But he lacked the necessary variety of megalomania, or the sheer time, to create an edifice around himself as Wagner had and others (say, Scriabin and Schoenberg) after him. Gathering disciples, creating a milieu, was not Ives's style— partly due to temperament and circumstances, partly to his democratic ideals.

Prophets and visionaries are not ordinarily shy, but that *was* Ives's style. Whenever he would be asked to serve as some sort of leader or guru, his response would be to run away. In that lies a good deal of his consistency, his integrity, and his message. His dreams reached for the eternal and he entreated the world to follow that quest—but each woman and man on her or his own path, not following him or anyone else.

Given his personality and circumstances, after college Ives had to force his ideas into the only mold available. Resisting the institution of the concert hall, he wrote music for the concert hall. That self-defeating paradox would burden his work from his own time to the present, but it would not drag down his best music.

Charles Ives had a musical and creative mind of the highest order, and he was perhaps more divided against himself, and at odds with the musical world, than any comparable figure before him. For a few years he succeeded in making those dilemmas work for his music rather than against it. Like his psyche, his art became a wild, exhilarating, profound dialectic among centrifugal elements. What mainly seems to have held it all together in himself and in his music was force of will and force of genius. It is not surprising that in his bountiful output Ives produced something less than a double handful of first-rate large works. It is surprising rather that his greatest music shrugs off so many of his dilemmas and transcends so many of his paradoxes. Exactly that transcendence is close to the meaning of his art, his irreplaceable clarion call to the world.

Renunciations and Apprenticeships

CHARLES IVES CONFESSED THAT having gone through Yale he did not intend for his future family to suffer for his art: "If he has a nice wife and some nice children, how can he let the children starve on his dissonances"?[1] Accordingly, he started two careers in New York in the autumn of 1898, when the city and the country were awaiting the last turn of century before the millennium.

After moving into a communal bachelor apartment dubbed "Poverty Flat," on West 58th Street near Central Park, Ives started as a five-dollar-a-week clerk with the Mutual Life Insurance Company.[2] The new digs amounted to an extension of Yale into adulthood. Poverty Flat inmates maintained their post-adolescent style through their graduate studies, moving away as they succumbed to marriage and growing up. For some years Charlie, like the rest of them, kept in touch with the old school, taking the train up to New Haven for Tap Day, reunions, football games. Once roommate Ned Park asked Charlie where he would be staying during reunion and got the reply, "I shall be out all night, and daytimes will sleep under a tree."[3]

The Mutual Life home office where Ives went to work in 1898 was a stone fortress on the corner of Nassau and Liberty, near Wall Street. Employees, who tended to stay on with the company, called the building "the Marble Mother."[4] Mutual doctor Granville White, one of the Danbury Whites related to the Iveses, had helped get Charlie the job.[5] It was understood that this Yale man was executive material and should learn the business from the green eyeshades on. Ives would spend his first months as an assistant in the actuarial department, amidst the mortality tables, learning to calculate the dollar value of human life, hope, and charity.

Sundays he commuted to First Presbyterian Church in Bloomfield, New Jersey, where he served as organist and choirmaster—the first time he had a choir of his own. After nearly two years in Bloomfield Ives moved to Manhattan's Central Presbyterian, on Seventh Avenue at 57th. There he kept his musical efforts mostly polite, so as not to trouble the wealthy ladies and gentlemen of the congregation.[6] He was working his way into the insurance industry, but for the time being did not want to burn bridges in the direction of professional music. Besides, he had spent most Sundays for the last decade in the choir loft; it was a familiar routine.

During his first four years in New York Ives composed quite a bit for his churches, some of it risky but most of it proper. Soon after arriving in town he also took some law classes in night school, to keep ahead of managers' legal qualms.[7] Though it is hard to conceive that he had any spare time, in his spare time he pitched for company baseball teams. And despite polyphonic daily grinds and amusements, a stack of new, unplayed, sometimes nearly unplayable pieces accumulated on the piano he installed in Poverty Flat.

For Ives and the other ambitious men with whom he would live for the next ten years, there was more to existence than the usual excitement of being young and footloose and finding their way in the city. They seemed to breathe a grander air than the generations before them. At the turn of the century, Senator (and Yale man) Chauncey Depew wrote:

There is not a man here who does not feel 400 percent bigger in 1900 than he did in 1896, bigger intellectually, bigger hopefully, bigger patriotically, bigger in the breast from the fact that he is a citizen of a country that has become a world power for peace, for civilization and for the expansion of its industries and the products of its labor.[8]

The senator's hyperbole, his fuzziness of concept, and his unquestioning embrace of America's new imperial status were symptomatic of the period. Citizens would greet the new century with an orgy of optimism and self-congratulation. The world seemed remade. Charles Ives's generation had witnessed the most wondrous acceleration of science and technology in history. Electric light and power were still relatively new and incredible, likewise the telephone and X-ray. The motorcar, motion picture, airplane, gramophone, player piano, and radio were about to take a place in everyday life. Recent victory in the Spanish-American War had made the country a leading player on the international stage. The first twenty years of the century would be an age of "news": the New Woman, New Theology, New University, New Journalism, New Literature, Woodrow Wilson's New Freedom, Theodore Roosevelt's New Nationalism. Everywhere one found a sense of triumphs achieved or in the offing, a confidence overriding the poverty and exploitation simmering beneath the buoyant surface of the age. "Whatever the trouble, people were sure they could fix it," writes historian Walter Lord. "Everyone at least had a bold plan and could hardly wait to try it."[9] Surely the millennium was imminent in every dimension—scientifically, economically, and socially. Surely the United States was destined to lead the way to some brave new world.

With industry booming, citizens by the tens of thousands fled family farms and crowded into cities, looking for good jobs and good times. The

New York City of that era, its population pushing two million, was a money and idea machine that drove a substantial part of the country's economy. Soon the area around Wall Street would be the world's financial capital. At the turn of the century the port of New York took in two-thirds of U.S. imports and shipped out two-fifths of exports. Of the 185 largest trusts in the country, 69 were based in the city, and likewise the four biggest life insurance companies, Mutual among them.[10]

The bulk of the polyglot immigrants pouring onto the American shore, now largely from southern and eastern Europe, came through Ellis Island. In 1898, half of New York was foreign-born. Working conditions were virtually unregulated; immigrants percolated into ghettos and squalid sweatshops, where both sexes and all ages sat eighty or more hours a week making clothing and cigars and other small goods. Their starvation wages helped keep cigars cheap and life sweet for those who had money. At the turn of the century, 1 percent of the country's population held seven-eighths of the wealth.

New York's dynamism and prosperity both reflected and enhanced the country's. The castles of "Millionaire's Row" competed for glory along thirty blocks of Fifth Avenue. Skyscrapers pushed up from Manhattan seemingly overnight, like gigantic asparagus. Every day Charles Ives arrived to work on narrow Liberty Street, one speck among the derby-hatted hordes (though Ives's Danbury fedora tended to spotlight him in any crowd). Wrote the visiting H. G. Wells, "individuals count for nothing . . . the distinctive effect is the mass, the unprecedented multitudinousness." By the 1920s, the peak of Ives's business career, half the U.S. population was living in cities, and the life insurance industry was cashing in on those urban swarms.

Manhattan led the country in amusements during the Gay Nineties and after. Restaurants flourished, many of them entertainment centers with players and singers, where customers danced to the blithe syncopations of ragtime.[11] On Broadway the musical *Floradora* opened, with its chorus line of Gibson Girls queried by a line of handsome bachelors: "Are there any more at home like you?" Within a year all the original Floradora Girls were married to millionaires.[12] Gibson Girls—poised, athletic, shirtwaisted Anglo-Saxon goddesses, their long hair pinned up—bicycled through Central Park in summer, ice-skated at St. Nicholas Rink in winter. Before the Diamond Horseshoe of the Metropolitan Opera, Enrico Caruso made his debut in 1903. Two major orchestras, the Symphony and the Philharmonic, played at Carnegie Hall largely for the same wealthy movers and shakers who had built the Metropolitan Opera and the Metropolitan Museum of Art. In 1901 Andrew Carnegie, the richest industrialist in the country, became president of the Philharmonic. Even priggish Henry James was dazzled at the sights; the city, he wrote, is "so nocturnal, so bacchanal, so hugely hatted and feathered and flounced." Henry Adams saw both sides of the city, the dynamism and the unprecedented tension of modern industrial life:

The city had the air and movement of hysteria, and the citizens were crying, in every accent of anger and alarm, that new forces must at any cost be brought under control. Prosperity never before imagined, power never yet wielded by man, speed never reached by anything but a meteor, had made the world irritable, nervous, querulous. . . . All New York was demanding new men, and all the new forces, condensed into corporations, were demanding a man with ten times the endurance, energy, will and mind of the old type.[13]

All this Gilded Age flamboyance and hysteria were not Charles Ives's style, but in his bachelor years he would rein in his small-town Yankee instincts and allow himself a bit of fun. One finds the record of his New York bachelor-hood in memos and diaristic entries on scores, and in the music itself: *Over the Pavements, Central Park in the Dark,* and above all his ragtimes. Later, New York was to show up as Vanity Fair in the *Comedy* of his Fourth Symphony; but even there the city's high spirits compete with Ives's Puritan portrait of urban life.

At the turn of the century the other side of the story began to emerge. In 1890 police reporter Jacob Riis published his epochal book of slum photographs, *How the Other Half Lives.* From that point pressure for reform gathered. Alongside the imperialistic ambitions, laissez-faire economics, and coldhearted social Darwinism that dominated national policy, a complementary set of ideals was taking hold of the country with its own agenda for the millennium: a movement toward greater social responsibility that went under the name of Progressivism. Nurtured by a wide spectrum of liberal Republicans and Democrats, much of the Progressive agenda would make its way into law during the next two decades—women's suffrage, urban reform, ballot referendum and recall, tax reform, direct election of senators, increased regulation of big-time capitalists and their business trusts, and the beginning of a welfare state.

Progressivism would be the most ambitious and idealistic movement in American history that proposed to broaden democracy and spread its blessings. As with laissez-faire capitalism and its absolute faith in the market, Progressivism had its own absolutes: the majority, declared Great Commoner William Jennings Bryan, is infallible. Ives would echo that sentiment. Social science, art, and philosophy joined the liberal tide. Psychologist and Pragmatist philosopher William James declared truth not absolute but relative, a dynamic response to evolving reality. The most vital literary mode of the day was Realism; its exponents included Mark Twain, William Dean Howells, Frank Norris, and Theodore Dreiser, and their settings were often the mean streets of the new city. Rejecting social Darwinism and its survival-of-the-fittest dogmas applied to human society, a new generation of activists declared that society, rather than submit to inexorable evolution, must direct its own evolution in a just and humanistic direction. In 1889 Jane Addams founded Hull House in Chicago, galvanizing the settlement-house movement that tried to heal the festering urban slums of the country, serving the poor while providing a forum for debate of social theory. The powerless *could* be uplifted and empowered, and Progressives were sure they knew how to do it.

All these currents of the coming century would influence Charles Ives. Some currents he would pull with, some against. *New Music,* after all, was not in the era's lexicon of new ideas. The American sense of the arts, tied to the Gilded Age lifestyle, remained conservative. The "high" arts were preserved as in a museum, behind glass, supported and attended mainly by women and the rich. High art was a matter of European paintings, European statues, European singers, European music, all imported to this country with great expense and ballyhoo. A newspaper observed in 1915, "Music is not generally regarded as a profession for men. Men go into business; they become brokers, lawyers or politicians . . . but not musicians. Music is still par excellence, the avocation of long-haired libidinous foreigners."[14] Deviations from these norms were all but incomprehensible. In 1900, Brahms was still a difficult modern, Wagner a radical. Innovation was prized mainly in technology; in business it was countenanced, grudgingly, here and there. In the United States the better mousetrap catches the gold; the innovative sonata does not, and so verges on meaninglessness. "We are a commercial people," writes Harvey Swados. "We cannot boast of our arts, our crafts, our cultivation; our boast is in the wealth we produce."[15] The point of Progressive social theory was to spread wealth and power, not fresh creative ideas.

Nonetheless, Progressive ideals helped shape Charles Ives, his philosophy of art, and his philosophy of business. He came of age when the country saw itself as undergoing a second youth, when in the lights of bright inventions and good intentions problems old and new were being solved and every problem seemed solvable. Ives embraced that spirit—in his own fashion, as always. The trajectory of Progressive optimism would soar for less than twenty years before it crashed into the war, and the country would never quite regain that millennial optimism. It is no coincidence that those two decades of grand idealism also saw the creation of Charles Ives's most visionary music. Also not coincidentally, they saw his last years of health and creative energy.

In New York Ives juggled the conflicting claims of art and daily life as he always had, but now the demands on his time were less forgiving than ever. The former class-cutter had to show up at the office every weekday and sometimes on Saturday mornings. After several months at the actuarial tables, in April 1899 Ives was transferred to one of the Mutual flagship agencies, Charles H. Raymond & Company on Liberty Street.[16] Until its collapse in 1906, Ives stayed with this firm, learning the workings of the richest agency of its day. Then he would start his own company with a partner he got to know in his first days at Raymond—Julian Myrick, generally called Mike. They met when Colonel Raymond put new-boy Ives on Myrick's job: Mike had turned out to be not such a good applications clerk. After a few months struggling to make out Ives's handwriting, Raymond returned Myrick to applications and set Ives to working with agents.[17] There Ives caught fire. It was to be mainly at that task, training and motivating salesmen, that he made his name in the industry.

It was a strange partnership, very much a friendship too, between old Yankee Charles Ives and southerner Mike Myrick: the driven artist and the conventional businessman, the introvert and the extrovert, the man indifferent to social amenities and the snappy dresser and inveterate joiner. Charlie would be best man at Mike's wedding. John Kirkpatrick summed up Myrick as "the glad-hander well met."[18] Tennis, one of the most sociable of sports, would be his consuming pursuit outside making money. He applied his glad hand to developing the Davis Cup tournament and held nearly every office in the U.S. Lawn Tennis Association. Myrick ended up in two Halls of Fame, life insurance and tennis. In his legendary later years he was dubbed "Mr. Life Insurance."[19]

Myrick was not a Yale man or even a college graduate, but he was the type that Ives had known and charmed in college. From early on the two felt like a team: Mike at the desk doing the numbers, pressing what flesh needed

Julian W. "Mike" Myrick, Ives's longtime partner and friend.

pressing, running the office; Charlie coming up with new angles and turning recruits into relentless salesmen. Ives himself, of course, never in his life went into someone's kitchen and convinced them to buy an insurance policy. He was too bashful to try to sell anybody anything in person. From a distance, he proved to be splendid at coming up with ideas and writing sales pitches and advertising copy, just as he was splendid sitting at an organ, facing away from his audience. Later, when the partners made it into clover with their own agency, they placed Myrick's office behind a glass partition in the middle of things; Ives's office was out of the way, with the door shut.[20] They were the only successful long-term partnership Mutual Life ever had.[21]

May 1899. Charlie walks home from work up Broadway, stopping in for a beer at Healy's. The pianist notices him at the bar and waves him over. Charlie slides onto the bench, parks his beer on the piano, and launches into a rag while the regular man hoists one, jawing with the after-work crowd at the bar. A half hour later Charlie is strolling over to Central Park to have a look at the budding trees, the ladies strolling and bicycling. The smell of Healy's beer and cigars and chops follows him, giving way to flowers and leaves. He stops to watch a scratch game at the ball field. His fingers itch to massage the ball and send it over the plate; he's better than this guy. He half-hears the carriages jingling and clopping up and down Eighth Avenue. Newsboys shout the late-edition news, the Elevated roars in and out of hearing. From across the street come the sounds of a tinkly piano, a violin, a banjo; they are playing rags, "Ta-ra-ra Boom-de-ay," "Hello Ma Baby," songs from Floradora. Music, crowds, shouts, smells, the liquid spring air under the trees. He thinks of going over to the zoo, but he's got an agency ball game after work tomorrow and law class the night after, and he's trying to get some new pieces off the ground—to be a composer again after a year of mostly business, getting his bearings. Here comes Ned Park, finished with medical classes for the day. They stroll back to Poverty Flat. Mrs. Chen will have dinner ready, and after that the piano awaits. He'll get out of the vest and collar and look for some ideas. It's spring. He feels music budding like the leaves.

When Ives moved to New York in 1898, his social life fell into the pattern he would maintain for a decade. When he moved in, Poverty Flat had been a going concern, founded by Yale graduates studying medicine at Columbia. Like its successors at other locations in the city, the place on West 58th belied its name. It consisted of two comfortable apartments flanking a staircase on the fourth floor; a maid took care of cooking and housekeeping for eight or so residents. During Ives's tenure, aspiring lawyers made a strong showing among the changing assortment, but most continued to be Yale men.[22] Forty years later, old roommate Michael Gavin would write Ives a reminiscence:

Our clothes hung together on the line as a sort of "community chest" from which any of us who wanted to make a big splurge was allowed to pick the best pair of pants and coat, which was perfectly satisfactory to all of us, because we wanted to make a good showing as a group. . . . Them were the days! and I shall never forget them.[23]

Ives was close to several roommates, some of them college friends and others newer. Dave Twichell, just out of the army, stayed over in October 1899 as he got ready to start medical studies at Columbia. Thoughtful, melancholic Bart Yung became a long-remembered Ives friend. Dave's father,

Reverend Twichell, was a friend of the elder Yung, a revolutionary who had fled China and ended up in Hartford. Ives would recall Bart as "one of the most perfect personal characters (intellectually, morally, spiritually) I have ever known."[24] Other Poverty Flat alumni who showed up in cameos during Ives's lifetime—memos on manuscripts, nostalgic letters—included Harry Keator, George Lewis, Keyes (rhymes with *skies*) Winter, and Ned Park. Housemates were recruited once in a while to fill out Charlie's church choirs; Yale roommate Mull Mullally was a chorister.[25]

In that cheerful company Charlie enjoyed the pleasures of the city he would later, in his reclusive years, call "Babylon" and "Hell Hole."[26] Enjoying the city and hating it, he would spend his career working in the heart of the financial district. Around the turn of the century he fit in fine with the bright-eyed bachelors of Poverty Flat, who had a leg up on success and knew it. Their diversions included Healy's restaurant on 66th Street for food, drink, and tunes, nearby Central Park and its zoo and ball field, the Giants-Dodgers rivalry at the Polo Grounds, the beaches and amusements of Coney Island, and the other pleasant sounds and furies of the city. College friends came to visit. David Stanley Smith, the classmate destined to follow Horatio Parker as dean of Yale music, dropped by to see Ned Park one day and deplored Ives's polytonal version of "Abide With Me."[27] The house Thanksgiving in 1902 was enlivened by John Griggs, the Center Church choirmaster, singing some songs including one of Charlie's.[28]

On weekends for many years Ives escaped the city to Pine Mountain near Danbury, where his family owned property. Even before 1903, when he and brother Moss built a plank cabin at the top, he climbed up to write music within the hickories and the silence, looking out from the summit to the rolling countryside of his youth and the sunset over West Mountain.[29] A number of pieces have "Pine Mt" jotted on the manuscript. For August vacations he sometimes returned to the Adirondacks, visiting the Twichells or other friends summering there. In Adirondack hospitals Dave Twichell began his career as a tuberculosis specialist.

Memos on Ives's manuscripts echo a turn-of-the-century bachelorhood. On the 1902 sketch of a musical skit for the Danbury Fair we find, "Davey Allen beats up Keyes—smiles, scolds smirks—then over to Healys."[30] Restaurants and popular romance of the day are lampooned in the song "Morceau du Coeur [or] . . . Romanzo di Central Park or Intermezzo table d'hote," whose expressive indication is "andante dulce con grazia, con expressione, con amour, con plat de jour." (The text is entirely one-word clichés: "Grove, Rove, Night, Delight, Heart, Impart. . . .") Everybody in the place could hear Charlie's piano racketing around at night and he expected them to listen in and comment. On the sketch of *Rube Trying to Walk 2 to 3!*[31] we find: "written as a joke, and sounds like one! Watty McCormick only one to see it! and Harry Farrar! at 2:45 A.M." On *Country Band March:* "Geo., Bart, Tony M—three quite right critics!!—say I haven't got the tune right, and the chords are wrong—Thanksgiving 1905 . . . Keyes says these notes are O.K.—he is the best critic, for he doesn't know one note from another." (Failing to find the approval of the sophisticated, Ives settled for that of the tone-deaf. So far, he seemed to find it funny.)

Most days Ives got home from work on the run, threw off his coat and collar and vest, and composed until the cook announced dinner. After the meal he went back at it, pounding at the piano and singing into the night, his pen racing over the paper.[32] The more or less good-natured term for his labors, and his harmonies, was "Resident Disturbances." He was still young and unbruised enough to brush aside complaints. On an early sketch for the song "On the Antipodes" we find: "Bill Maloney mad at this—65 C.P.W. St. Pat[rick's] Day '04—says just hammers—can't sleep." (Poverty Flat moved a few blocks to Central Park West in 1901, then to elegant digs at 34 Gramercy Park in 1907.) Roommates complained, but they also contributed. The seminal song "In the Cage," with its meterless rhythms and symmetrical harmonies, came from a visit to Central Park Zoo with Bart Yung and George Lewis. As they watched a leopard pacing endlessly around his cage, Bart speculated, "Is life anything like that?"[33] His existential quip became the end of the song. House altercations practical and political seem to have contributed to the symbolic debates in Ives's Second String Quartet, the movements called "Discussions" and "Arguments": a memo on the score says, "Keyes takes exception—'on that point'—So do the others, each has his say."[34]

Ives was still Dasher, a wiry bundle of energies, his eyes electric and amused, always going explosively *at* something: going at the piano, going at the page, going at you with his wild jabber. His demons seemed puckish rather than neurotic, but they lashed him all the time. The boys had their little adventures—in Charlie's case, apparently, chaste ones. The occasional night with friends he would get sloshed in one of the city's clamorous smoky saloons and contribute some rags at the house piano. Sometimes after a Saturday night out he barely had time to jump into his church clothes and head for choir practice.[35]

Thus went Ives's external life social, professional, and musical for his first years in New York. These years saw the last of his socializing, his public musical life, his bachelorhood, his living in the Yale style. He would leave it all with hardly a look back when he found another life that suited him better and taught him more. His friends enjoyed his wit and energy and largely ignored him as an artist. It was roommate Ned Park who wrote, probably speaking for the whole crowd, "I had not the slightest intimation that Charley was a musical genius. . . . I regarded him as a most delightful man and companion, completely unpredictable . . . one never knew what to expect next."[36]

Ives was a regular concertgoer in those days—another pattern he would later break. New York was, in the natural course of things, the musical mecca of the country. Ives had been going to Carnegie Hall concerts since his father took him in his teens. The venerable New York Philharmonic had been under the baton of Wagner disciple Anton Seidl for over a dozen years before his death in 1898. Emil Pauer, whom Ives had probably heard conduct the Boston Symphony in New Haven, took over. Walter Damrosch conducted the New York Symphony, having inherited the orchestra from its founder, his father Leopold.[37] Each year the Boston Symphony visited Carnegie Hall for a few concerts, which Ives frequented all the way into the 1930s. These orchestras dispensed a repertoire heavy in Beethoven, Brahms, Dvořák, Wagner, and Tchaikovsky; but more exotic composers were beginning to make their way into programs, among them Strauss, Rimsky-Korsakov, and eventually Debussy. Among the best-known American composers in those days were Edward MacDowell, George Chadwick, Henry Hadley, Frederick Converse, and Horatio Parker. By midcentury the latter four would mostly be forgotten; even at the peak of their fame, little of their orchestral music made it to mainstream concerts.[38]

One finds American musical life of the time mirrored in the weekly *Musical Courier*. In 1897 the paper made so bold as to champion Richard Strauss; this is the way it championed him in reviewing a 1903 performance of *Also sprach Zarathustra:* "[Strauss's] themes, with few exceptions, are ugly, but the infernal skill of the man holds you in a vise. . . . He may be a degenerate, but he is terribly in earnest."[39] Five years later the *Courier* was calling Strauss "a genius of the first rank, the greatest of living composers."[40] By 1909 the paper had advanced so far as to embrace the French: "We are on the eve of new things through the Straus [*sic*], Reger, Debussy, Ravel innovations. Where are our English and American composers? Wake up! Wake up!" By that year Charles Ives, fully awake, had finished a series of revolutionary new works including the *Ragtime Dances, The Unanswered Question,* and the First Piano Sonata.

In his early New York years Ives heard a good deal of chamber music, especially from the city's favorite string quartets the Dannreuther, Kaltenborn, and Kneisel.[41] Making it his business to get to know musicians in town, he became friendly with the Kaltenborn Quartet, who in 1902 played in the premiere of his *Celestial Country*. The following February the Kaltenborns visited Poverty Flat to take a stab (probably a desperate one) at Ives's polytonal/polymetric study *Holding Your Own*.[42]

In the 1930s Ives gave Lucille Fletcher, who was trying to write a *New Yorker* article on him, this third-person account: "If he went out at all, it was usually to a concert of Beethoven or Bach, where he would sit high up in the topmost gallery, crouched behind the last row of seats, with his back to the audience."[43] Certainly Ives heard a good deal more than Beethoven and Bach (though they would always be his favorites), but sitting behind seats in the gallery sounds right for him: facing away from the show onstage and in the audience, alone with the music and not giving a damn about the rest of it. So many concertgoers were there to kibitz and gossip, to show off, to see who was there, to pursue the Gilded Age lifestyle or to affect it. Ives was there for the music, and he accepted no other justification for the great hall and the grand orchestra. The plain Danbury Baptist Church and Opera House had been good enough for him.

In his organist/choirmaster jobs from 1898 to 1902, Ives remained the well-rounded church musician, playing services and recitals and composing practical pieces. Though he mentions giving a number of organ recitals in this period, the only ones that have come to light were at Central Presbyterian in early 1902, the first jointly with famous organist William C. Carl, head of the Guilmant Organ School; the second recital included the premiere of *The Celestial Country*. Ives's repertoire for these programs, some of the pieces under his fingers since Danbury, included organ works and arrangements of Bach, Mozart, Handel, and Brahms, and usually music of his own.[44]

In New Haven he had composed "about 20–25 Anthems, responses, and hymn anthems (alla Harry Rowe Shelley and Dudley Buck)."[45] He reused these conventional Victorian pieces in his New Jersey and Manhattan churches. Besides the choral music, at Yale and in New York he produced a number of relatively mild organ pieces for recitals and services—preludes, postludes, and the like—which formed a body of material he would draw on for the rest of his creative life. Sometimes heavily recomposed, the organ pieces would become movements of symphonies, string quartets, and violin sonatas, become songs, metamorphose into whatever other genres Ives was pursuing. From about 1902 on, new works most often fed on old ones. For a given work or movement, he could reach into his older music as into a scrap-lumber heap, sometimes refashioning material in directions more ambitious and radical than the original form would imply: years later, the lost 1901 organ work *Memorial Slow March* became the core of the Fourth Symphony's mystical finale; the teeming *Fourth of July* grew from the harmonies of the little song "In the Cage."

Another piece of material for future reference turned up when Ives discovered that two pianos in a Central Presbyterian Sunday School room were tuned a quarter tone apart. He probably spent hours sitting between those pianos, finding harmonies never heard on this earth, but hinted at in George Ives's quarter-tone experiments. Before Charlie could quite get the harmonies into his ears, though, one of the pianos was moved.[46] It would be some time before he would seriously try composing for these intervals in the cracks of Western tuning.

When he left Central Presbyterian, Ives deposited most of his organ and choir/organ works in the music library. Presumably he thought successors might find the pieces useful. All those works disappeared from the library, probably thrown out when the church moved to Madison Avenue or later to Park Avenue.[47] John Kirkpatrick calls this loss tragic,[48] but Ives might disagree. He left that music there because it did not mean much to him. What he needed of it, the seeds that might sprout into something else, stayed in his compendious memory.

Similarly to his style at Yale, Ives's production in these years ran in two streams—the public and usually conservative, the private and sometimes radical. To a degree the two streams overlapped: at a Bloomfield Christmas service in 1898 Ives played his organ prelude on "Adeste Fideles," in which mirrored versions of the melody are combined into interweaving polytonal lines. It was on that manuscript that Ives jotted the laconic note, "Rev J. B. Lee, others & Mrs Uhler said it was awful." That work is actually fairly tractable by his standards. It is more surprising that with his choir at Central Presbyterian Ives may have done *Processional: Let There Be Light,* in which pungent harmonies conjure up a spiritual radiance: "Let there be light today!" the chorus declaims in pealing dissonances. The piece is dated December 1901 and dedicated "To the Choir of the Central Presbyt. Church, New York"—perhaps in gratitude for their performing it, or at least having the moxie to try it over in rehearsal. Some of his larger and more orthodox works, on the other hand, were too big to find a performance. No orchestra was waiting to play his symphonies.

Ives's usual composing method was already settled. For longer and more elaborate works, most of the time he began with rough sketches of key portions, often building on older ideas or pieces. Then came a score-sketch (sometimes more than one) of the new piece on the fewest staff lines that would hold the notes—usually two for a string quartet, four or more for an orchestra piece. Often the score-sketches were quite cleanly notated, but Ives tended to obscure them with added layers of material. Then he would make a pencil full score, revision patches for that, then an ink fair copy and more patches. Finally that ink score, with its own revisions and additions and patches, went to a copyist. The copyist's score in turn tended to accumulate further revisions and patches. There were of course many variations on this pattern, and pieces could stop at any stage if Ives did not care to finish them. Some of the laboratory works seem to have been done in one draft. But the big scores, the ones he cared about, usually got the full treatment.

In the summer of 1898, before he moved to New York, Ives probably added to his set of *Psalms.* But during his first year or so in the city he composed relatively little—a few songs, some of the early ragtime sketches, some psalms. At that point he was getting adjusted to his job, taking law courses, and clearing the decks creatively. When he geared up again around 1900, as usual taking off from older pieces, he directed his main effort to the kind of work Horatio Parker and the mainstream would expect him to write—another symphony, his second. It was his primary project for two years.

Material for the Second Symphony goes back to his teens. In a preface to the score Ives writes, "The second theme of the last movement is partly from an early short piece called *The American Woods.* . . . The part suggesting a Steve Foster tune . . . was played in Danbury on the Old Wooster House Bandstand in 1889." The third movement was apparently a Center Church organ prelude that became a slow movement for the First Symphony. Horatio Parker forced Ives not only to remove this movement from the First (as "not dignified [enough] for a real symphony"[49]), but to bowdlerize it: a memo on the manuscript, probably from the aged and cranky Ives, reads, "This was the one played in Center Ch. When scored later, it was made better and spoiled (by advice HWP). . . . P said—a movement in Key of F should start in key of F. so change and weaken it!!!!!!!!!"[50] (The movement originally began in G♭ before getting around to the main key.)

Given its scattered pedigree, the Second Symphony holds together well, though like the First it has its aimless stretches, and it contains some deliberate stylistic incongruities. Maybe because it developed out of band and organ pieces, the scoring is simpler than that of the First, which was orchestrally conceived from the beginning. But the difference is also aesthetic. Ives turned away from the lush Romantic scoring of the First Symphony in favor of a lucid simplicity that matches the folklike material. The quiet opening movement of the Second is mostly for strings, fuguelike and brooding in effect, part Renaissance-style polyphony, part echoes of Brahms and Dvořák. It works in some Americanisms, a hint of Foster's "Massa's in de Cold, Cold Ground" and a few measures of "Columbia, the Gem of the Ocean." The second movement takes off with a spry tune unmistakably "Americana" in feel—or rather what would be so called thirty years later, when composers including Virgil Thomson and Aaron Copland were writing similar music. This movement is full of dotted rhythms and entirely based on old tunes, among them a robust (and at first minor-key) version of the hymn "Bringing in the Sheaves" and languid and beautiful interludes based on the college ditty "Where O Where are the Pea-Green Freshmen?"

After the hymnlike and sentimental slow movement, the fourth movement starts maestoso in the horns, with a transformation of the symphony's opening: here most noticeably, but in fact throughout, Ives is thinking in terms of the Romantic cyclic symphony, with themes recurring from movement to movement. The finale is mostly a skittering fiddle tune, quoting or suggesting Stephen Foster songs including "Camptown Races" and "Turkey in the Straw." (It has some striking whirlwind transitions resembling the yet-to-be-invented cinematic "wipe.")

The Second ends with another of Ives's climactic quodlibets where, as in the First Symphony and First Quartet, he piles up themes from throughout the work. He had trouble, though, getting the end to settle. The sketches and fair copy have several versions of a final cadence, none of them quite right: a bland F-major chord, a couple of more elaborate sketches working in "Columbia" awkwardly. Ives had one of his copyists do an ink score in 1909 (by then he was using the Tams Copying Service, on Tin Pan Alley). Since this copy was lost, there is no record of what sort of ending the symphony had at that point. Finally some forty years later, Ives added the present ending, the eruption of "Columbia" and famous final blat—an eleven-note cluster that finishes the piece, Ives wrote, "like a traditional evening of square dances, with a resounding discord."[51]

Peter Burkholder has shown that even the "original" themes in the Second are constructed on old songs, mainly Foster's. The skeleton of the last movement's main fiddle tune, for example, is "Camptown Races," which also shows up as an overt quote.[52] This is the technique of building new themes from borrowed vernacular material that Ives had explored in the First Quartet. In the Second Symphony borrowed tunes permeate the texture both as foreground quotes and as background superstructure. Once again, the kinds of motivic relationships Ives learned from Horatio Parker shape and hold together a long work derived from disparate sources.

But even when writing his teacher's kind of piece, Ives was no longer doing it at all Parker's way, with Parker's ends. This is shown as much as anything by the strangest aspect of the Second Symphony, its habit of suddenly lurching into quotes from European music—bits of Brahms symphonies pop up in several movements, and references to Wagner's *Tristan* and to Bach. Some of these episodes are more discernible than others, but most are intrusions of dense, European symphonic texture and harmony into the Yankee plainspokenness of most of the music. Why did Ives throw Old World ingredients into what is, essentially, the first symphony unmistakably American in voice? After all, here Ives laid the foundation, if anybody had known it, for the American symphonic music of which musicians including Dvořák and Griggs had dreamed. Ives's Second might have inaugurated the Americana school thirty years earlier, had it managed to get heard.[53]

In later life, tending to be intolerant of his "soft" pieces, Ives called this hybrid of American tunes and European symphonic music "sort of a bad joke."[54] But there is a logic to the Second's stylistic meandering. Ives was continuing the process he began with the First Quartet, mediating between Europe and America. Here he is still writing a large, cyclic tonal symphony as the Europeans understood it, but filling it with material both American and European. At this stage of his symphonic music, the mixture is still undigested, a "bad joke." All the same, this strange confabulation produces a symphony of considerable coherence and charm; for most of its course, the Second is actually more consistent in style than much of his music.[55]

Ives pulled together the smaller-scale Third Symphony in 1904 from three 1901 church-organ pieces later lost. Subtitled "The Camp Meeting," the Third is another echo of his youth, and like the First Quartet a fantasia on gospel tunes. The three movements follow the progress of a camp meeting. "Old Folks Gatherin' " features a fugue on *Azmon* ("O For a Thousand

Tongues"); the second movement is a playful "Children's Day"; the third is an intense, chromatic piece called "Communion." In each movement cyclically recurs one of the most sentimental of revival hymns, "Just As I Am, Without One Plea."

Ives would call the Third Symphony "a kind of crossway between the older ways and the newer ways."[56] It is that for several reasons. The Third was the most controlled and succinct of his larger works to date, the most consistently related to his childhood, and it is as nationalistic as the Second. Technically, it is mostly routine in the first two movements. The first, for example, has a standard introduction and fugal first theme, and roughly follows the traditional first-movement sonata form. The finale is the strongest of the three, probably the most complex and sustained polyphonic movement Ives had written by then.[57] Unusually passionate for him (though the passion is entirely religious), the finale is a prototype of an innovative formal device of Ives's, an organic way of putting pieces together that would mark a good deal of his mature music. Burkholder calls it *cumulative form:* A movement or an entire piece grows from the motivic (and sometimes phrasing and harmonic) elements of a single melody. This melody gradually makes its way from background to foreground until it is proclaimed straightforwardly at the end.[58] There is a symbolic dimension to cumulative form too, in the idea of an underlying generative force slowly making its way to the surface. This would be the technique, and ultimately the meaning, of the Fourth Symphony.[59]

Cumulative form reverses the procedure of traditional sonata form, in which a movement's themes are stated in the exposition, pulled apart and reworked in the development, then restated in the recapitulation. Still, Ives stood traditional procedure on its head in the same spirit of handling motivic relationships and thematic development that he had learned composing more conventional sonata forms. His technique also grows logically from late-century thematic practice, notably Brahms's: more thematic transformation than fragmentation, with developmental processes tending to pervade the whole movement.

Cumulative form is central to all four of Ives's violin sonatas, which, as with the Third Symphony, he largely derived from his turn-of-the-century church pieces.[60] Some of Ives's most moving conclusions derive their sense of meaning and inevitability from this device. In the Third Symphony finale, the cellos gently conclude the long, complex meditation on motives from "Just As I Am" by playing the hymn through plainly at the end. The piece finishes with an exquisitely drawn-out version of the conclusion of the hymn, wordless but with the words resounding in the music: "O Lamb of God, I come, I come," accompanied by an effect of distant churchbells. That hymn is most often heard at the conclusion of Sunday services and camp meetings, urging worshippers to come forward and be reborn.

With these two symphonies Ives created, single-handedly, the nationalistic art music for which Dvořák had called and a good many American composers attempted without success. Rather than trying to cash in on that accomplishment, Ives moved on. Though the American voice would be a constant, he never wrote another piece in the style of the Second or the Third Symphony. His goal was never in the direction of what he would denounce as "the old medieval idea of nationalism."[61] Local color to him was a means, not an end. Moreover, after these two works Ives abandoned the symphony, so called, for years. He knew the Second and Third succeeded in their way, but neither seemed satisfactory. The whole idea of the symphony had begun to oppress him. Even if American in material, the genre was too redolent of the past, of rules and regulations, of Horatio Parker and all he represented:

I was getting somewhat tired of hearing the lily boys say, "This is a symphony?— Mercy!—Where is the first theme of 12 measures in C major?—Where are the next 48 measures of nice . . . development leading nicely into the second theme in G? . . . the nice German recipe . . . to hell with it![62]

It was time for Ives to grow beyond his apprenticeship and its constrictions. Now he developed his own kind of multi-movement instrumental work, which he usually called *set*. The name implies an assemblage of pieces from here and there, and that is what his sets amount to. In a way, of course, so do most of his large works. Certainly he was capable of following a unified development of ideas through a multi-movement piece; he would do that in a series of pieces before 1910, most of them called by, and related to, the traditional genre designation of *sonata*. He could, in other words, put together a well-unified, even cyclical work from pieces originally conceived independently.[63] In his *sets,* however, Ives tended to assemble a grouping of more or less self-contained pieces without worrying overmuch about the details of their connection. They relate more in terms of medium, contrast (often slow–fast–slow), and sometimes through the program. Ives thereby executed an end run around the nice German recipe. His loose assemblages would include some of his finest works—the First Orchestral Set called *Three Places in New England,* the Second Orchestral Set, the Set for Theatre Orchestra. *Holidays,* called a symphony, is a set in practice, an assemblage of four independent orchestral works related mainly by their programmatic subject and their more or less cumulative form. After 1909, when Ives was worrying less what the lily boys would say (though he never completely lost that anxiety), he returned to the Romantic symphonic tradition with the Fourth, having gained the confidence that he could produce a unified work worthy of the genre, entirely in his own voice.

After the Third Symphony, then, Ives set aside for a while the sort of large orchestral pieces that Horatio Parker and the cultivated musical world

expected him to write. By that point he had also given up another of his efforts
to play Parker's game: being a respectable church organist.

The occasional strange chord and polytonal anthem aside, Ives had done
a perfectly good job at the organ in all his churches. Roommate Ned Park
recalled, "I am sure that various members of the congregation were in a state
of continual quandary whether Charlie was committing sacrilegious sins by
introducing popular and perhaps ribald melodies into the offertory . . . but
the melodies were so disguised that the suspicious members of the congregation could never be sure enough to take action."[64] This is in the vicinity of half
right. If Charlie were continually under suspicion of clandestine ribaldry, and
threw too many funny chords into the hymns, he would not have lasted long
at any church. So even if his fingers sought out more distant harmonies now
and then, he mostly behaved himself. And in 1902 he premiered a work that
seemed calculated to convince Central Presbyterian once and for all that he
was the proper sort of organist/composer for their distinguished downtown
church.

Ives had begun the seven-movement cantata *Celestial Country* at Yale. The
manuscripts suggest it was mostly a one-draft job. Figuratively speaking, he
could write these kinds of pieces with his left hand during the sermon. The
cantata is modeled, all too evidently, on Parker's *Hora novissima*. In fact, because of a confusion of names, Ives believed that his text was translated from
the same St. Bernard Latin verses that Parker excerpted for his oratorio. Actually Ives's English text is from Henry Alford's processional hymn *Forward! Be
Our Watchword*. The treacly religiosity of Alford's title is an indication of the
style. He exhorts the Pilgrim to Climb the Path Ever Forward and Faint Not
in His Journey Toward the Light, "thither, onward, thither/In the spirit's
might," and so on.

Ives set these verses as they deserve, following their pious maunderings
hither and thither. There is even a concluding fugue of the most drearily
uplifting variety. The music steals one idea after another from *Hora novissima*,[65] but in the end barely rises above stale Victorian claptrap. Ives didn't
even approach Parker's somber nobility—stale in its own way, but from a
high-church bakery. Certainly one can detect Ivesian moments in *The Celestial
Country*, mainly the quiet, novel harmonies of the organ preludes, which create
a nicely mysterious effect.[66] Other touches of innovation backfire, such as
the ragtimey syncopations in the first and last numbers. Setting the words
"Pilgrims!" and "Angels!," the syncopations have a coincidental but comical
affinity to a familiar rhythm of the 1920s: these Pilgrims and Angels seem to
be doing the Charleston.

Ives pulled out all the stops for the Central Presbyterian premiere of *The
Celestial Country* on April 18, 1902. It is scored for two solo quartets and

choir, string quartet, brass, timpani, and organ. Ives's sanctuary choir and
soloists handled the vocals, and he recruited the Kaltenborn Quartet for the
string parts.[67] The concert, an ambitious one for the church, began with some
organ pieces from Ives. Then came his cantata, diligently rendered. Soon after
the performance it was reviewed in prestigious columns. Said the *New York
Times:* "It has the elementary merit of being scholarly and well made. But it is
also spirited and melodious." Said the *Musical Courier:* "The work shows
undoubted earnestness in study and talent for composition, and was fairly
creditably done."

As far as that critical response went, the cantata could not be called a
failure. The biggest performance of his career got polite critical reviews and
presumably polite responses from the church music committee. Ives had spent
fourteen years before the public as a church musician and this is what he had
earned for it: he was earnest, he was scholarly. He had creditably done what
was expected of an aspiring composer—he had made himself a first-rate organist and written the sorts of things professional composers were supposed to
write. He could build on that foundation and likely make a name for himself.

Two weeks after the premiere of *The Celestial Country,* Ives took what he
decided was the appropriate next step in his artistic career. He quit. He resigned from his position at Central Presbyterian, effective at the beginning of
June 1902. Abandoning the path of a conventional composer as he had earlier
abandoned the path of a writer of marches and glees, he would write no more
church music. He had discovered that making music people wanted to hear
put his creative soul at risk. He would never apply for another musical position.[68] The cantata was the last work of his to be heard in a public concert for
twenty years.

Why did he "quit music," as he would put it—meaning quit it professionally? His own explanations make sense, as far as they go:

I seemed to have worked with more natural freedom, when I knew that the music was
not going to be played before the public, or rather before people who couldn't get out
from under, as is the case in a church congregation. . . . To a body of people who come
together to worship—how far has a man a right to do what he wants, if he knows that
by so doing he is interfering with the state of mind of the listeners, who have to listen
regardless. . . . A congregation has some rights.[69]

A congregation has the right, in other words, not to listen to what he
wanted to compose. "I felt I either had to stop music or stop this"—meaning
the compromises.[70] "The way I'm constituted, writing soft stuff makes me
sore—I sort of hate all music."[71] He therefore made a decision utterly unprecedented for a composer: to preserve himself, to find freedom for his music, he
had to quit music. This is when he became a composer without a milieu—the
profession was too narrow to contain what he felt compelled to do. Besides,

he had been slapped down a lot now and the scars were accumulating. He was weary of inflicting pain on captive audiences, weary of the rows of scowling ladies every time his fingers strayed into a fresh harmony.

Speculation must fill in the unspoken part of why he quit. It may not have been coincidence that just after the premiere, Yale appointed Ives's old acquaintance William Edward Haesche to a teaching job. (Haesche would work there until 1923, alongside Ives's classmate David Stanley Smith.) Did Ives have pipe dreams of securing a teaching position himself, maybe at his alma mater? Was that part of the reason he had kept his church jobs and written *The Celestial Country*? He had, after all, begun a musical career in New York in the same way Horatio Parker had. Was he trying to catch his old teacher's attention with an act of homage?

If Ives had allowed himself fantasies about a teaching career, he had failed in earnest. Surely he knew what his cantata amounted to: an exercise in sentimental religiosity without even the authenticity of "an honest mushy ballad," written largely for self-serving rather than spiritual purposes. The reviews, polite but tepid, left the cantata's essential dishonesty in high relief. It is conceivable that Ives quit music as much as anything because he was disgusted at what he had done. He had betrayed his musical convictions, had proposed to sell out, and nobody had bought.[72] Across his clip of the *Musical Courier* review, the one citing his "undoubted earnestness," one finds his livid scrawl: *"Damn rot and worse!"*[73]

Now Ives was free of the demands of audiences, but not entirely free of his inner constraints. He also had a backlog of relatively conservative pieces that deserved better than to be abandoned. Though leaving the church job was an epochal step for him, the line of demarcation in his music is not all that bold. His compromises were hardly finished; time and again throughout his career Ives would pull his punches in one way or another. For years he spent some of his time reworking the church pieces, turning them into longer works. Some of those, notably the violin sonatas, he conceived as easier, more or less repertoire pieces (which he eventually held against them[74]).

Nor had his experimental side entirely gone by the board during his New York years as a public composer.[75] Sometime around 1901 Ives seems to have started his revolutionary and magnificent *Harvest Home Chorales* with No. 2, "Lord of the Harvest."[76]This movement begins with a somber chord cycle in brass, schematic in construction but still evocative of New England late autumn: the lowering leafless landscape beautiful in its bleakness. Then over this chord cycle he proclaims the text in a muscular and elegant tenor line, one of his most striking original melodies. To that line he adds, one at a time, two more melodic and rhythmic planes, until he has constructed a massive contrapuntal texture going in three speeds at once.

By now he was confidently working with an unprecedented vocabulary of "bracketed" rhythms—triplets, quintuplets, septuplets, nontuplets, and the like—to create polyrhythm, polytempo, polymeter. In the next years he added two other pieces to the first. The *Harvest Home Chorales* amount to his finest choral work, possessing a harsh, primeval majesty to which he never quite returned. Like many of his works in those days, this one would remain unique. Still, with "Lord of the Harvest" Ives shaped a form involving thoroughgoing polyrhythm, and that new kind of integrity in contrapuntal lines stayed with him, steadily becoming more complex and subtle.

From around the same time as "Lord of the Harvest," perhaps started at the end of 1901,[77] dates a laboratory piece as wild if not as expressive as the chorales: *From the Steeples and Mountains,* for bells, trumpet, and trombone. The fanfarish and more or less atonal brass parts involve shifting canons—changing intervals of imitation, inexact mirrors, then a routine of working backward measure by measure. Meanwhile the four sets of bells run through scales in three different keys, in a rhythmic canon of condensing, then expanding, note lengths. These schematic pitch and rhythmic patterns climax with what David Nicholls calls "an early example of Ivesian pandemonium."[78] As usual, however, the formalistic calculations underlie a programmatic idea. A manuscript memo, part technical and part metaphorical, says: "The bells start together and get more and more off, i.e. independent—till final jangle . . . and the high rocks or 1st bell and the low rocks on the mountains begin to shout!" The piece takes memories of Danbury churchbells—perhaps from the night he watched his father standing in the rain, listening to them peal—into an ecstatic vision of nature.

So when Ives resigned from Central Presbyterian in April 1902, his laboratory had been going strong, and for years after he would continue to work through his stockpile of more domesticated church-originated pieces (mainly in the Third Symphony and violin sonatas). Most of his songs from this period are conventional too, sometimes beautifully so—Victorian parlor songs ("There Is a Lane," "The Light that Is Felt"), German and French songs of the kind he wrote for Parker ("Weil' auf mir," "Ilmenau," "Elégie"). The time before his resignation also produced one of his most original and brilliant songs, the little "Walking," with its supple melody and sparkling harmonies—often Debussyan in gist, but applied to an American's exuberant gait.

Still, even though the before and after overlap, his resignation was a watershed. Ives had not only resigned from a church job; he had cast off his mooring, forsworn the connection with an audience and profession—the milieu—that had nourished him as a setting nourishes all composers. The dilemma was that it also stifled him more than most composers. Did he have any idea how long and lonely the rest of his creative journey was going to be? Could he have survived two decades of creative isolation if he had seen it coming? Aaron Copland would write that Charles Ives had the courage of a lion. In reality Ives had the unsteady courage of a human being, who knows what is happening to him, who wonders if he is fighting a lost cause, who sometimes cannot help but fear that the problem is with his own ears and not his listeners'.

After his resignation in 1902, Ives took decisive steps toward finding his mature voice. A good deal of that progress would come from his researches in ragtime, carried on in a series of pieces dating back to 1899, when one of his rags was tried over at the Hyperion Theater in New Haven.[79] That led to the related *Skit for Danbury Fair* of 1902, played informally at the Fair in September.[80] Also that year he more or less finished (all are lost in their original form) nine or so additional rags. These in turn fed into a number of works including the four *Ragtime Dances,* which Ives dated as finished on July 14, 1902.[81]

These "dances" were a response to long experience with ragtime: "I had even heard [blackfaced comedians ragging their songs] at the Danbury Fair before coming to New Haven."[82] Ives probably heard more fully developed rags in his visit to the Chicago Exposition. After that, ragtime was a fixture of the New Haven theaters and parties of his college years, then in the restaurants and saloons of New York. In his *Essays* Ives writes,

[Ragtime] is an idiom . . . similar to those that have added through centuries and through natural means some beauty to all languages. . . . Ragtime, as we hear it, is, of course, more . . . than a natural dogma of shifted accents, or a mixture of shifted and minus accents. . . . Ragtime has its possibilities. . . . Perhaps we know it now as an ore before it has been refined into a product. It may be one of nature's ways of giving art raw material.[83]

What did Ives see in this raw material, and why did he spend so much time exploring it? The dancing polyrhythms of ragtime gave him a fresh way of writing fast music, helped him break out of the stiff dotted rhythms of the march. We see his new kind of raggy allegro in works of 1902–10: the "In the Barn" movement of the Second Violin Sonata; some of the *Country Band March;* parts of the *Three-Page Sonata* for piano; the *In the Inn* movement of the Set for Theatre or Chamber Orchestra (which went into the First Piano Sonata along with material from other rags); *The Rockstrewn Hills* from the Second Orchestral Set.[84] After 1902 the music that sounds most essentially "Ivesian" to us would often involve ragtime, the ore he refined into an integral element of his voice. In that he followed, perhaps without realizing it, another aspect of Dvořák's call—creating an American native music using Negro elements. For Ives and for composers to come, ragtime, blues, and jazz—African-American idioms bred on these shores—would be touchstones for the creation of a native art music uniting European and American traditions.[85] As with so many other things, Ives pioneered that process, in secret.

Ragtime was a folk music with a natural daring, freshness, and freedom that fit seamlessly into his experimental vein. When writing sacred music, from which most of his large works developed around the turn of the century, Ives felt constrained:

Not until I got to work on the *Fourth Symphony* did I feel justified in writing quite as I wanted to, when the subject matter was religious. . . . The early ragtime pieces and marches, most of the *First Piano Sonata* most of the *Theater Orchestra Set* etc [only the secular pieces] seemed to get going "good and free"—and the hymn-tune sonatas and symphonies less so—until . . . the [religious] *Fourth Symphony* and the last movement of the *Second Orchestral Set* were reached.[86]

Many people in those days, Horatio Parker probably included, considered ragtime wicked Negro music, but it helped get Yankee-Puritan Ives going good and free. You can sense his enthusiasm in the *Ragtime Dances.* Ives wrote of them, "some have the same themes, strains, etc. but used somewhat differently. Thus they do not all stand as different pieces."[87] The four surviving are similar, as he notes; all are based on the same hymns, mainly a syncopated "Bringing in the Sheaves." Such mixtures of sacred and secular were characteristic of Ives from at least the First String Quartet, and from his habit of working popular songs into church improvisations. The point was not to sully the sacred, but the other way around: to infuse the secular with spiritual joy. (In fact, in the *Dances* Ives tends to amalgamate "Bringing in the Sheaves" with the similar hymn "Happy Day"—which happens to be the same tune as "How Dry I Am.") The fourth and most satisfying ragtime of the set stands as an example of how a first-rate creative mind can recast and personalize a borrowed style. This is music evocative of turn-of-the-century vaudeville and saloons, but it is also an Ivesian rhythmic phantasmagoria full of startling cuts and stumbles and shifts of perspective, eventually gathering into a romping, stomping finish. The *Dances* are cubistic ragtime, enlivened with slapstick.[88] Nobody else ever wrote pieces quite like these, at once so authentic and so original.

Ives kept trying to get his rags performed. He wanted to hear how they sounded in their implied setting, a theater orchestra pit. One he showed to Franz Kaltenborn, but the violinist handed it back, probably with a smirk, saying it was too hard to play. "Professor" Fichtl aired a couple, arranged for piano, at the Hyperion in May 1904 (Ives was probably visiting New Haven for Tap Day).[89] The following year, during a matinee in New York at Keith's Theater, Ives got a pit orchestra to run through some, but on the second performance the manager emerged and put an end to the "disturbance."[90] The Keith Theater players were probably bribed. In the next decade or so New York theater musicians would get to be familiar with Ives. He was the guy who appeared at the edge of the pit after the show and handed you cash on the spot to read through his crazy music.[91] No doubt they considered him another fruitcake among many, but his money was real enough.

So after his resignation from Central Presbyterian in the spring of 1902, Ives got going as a private composer, even if he did not yet know exactly where he was going. Among pieces begun in that period was what would become, after many years and much struggle, the monumental First Piano Sonata. For this, his first attempt to write a big work in his most radical mode, he stuck to his own instrument and to a familiar genre, which he would recast but still maintain as a formal reference. He began sketching most of the First Sonata's five movements in 1901–2 and on the manuscript dated its completion as 1909. The voluminous sketches and drafts show dead ends, pages of rejected material, dozens of revision patches. In a memo he mentions a rejected movement.[92]

These pages look as painstaking unto painful as any he ever wrote—not surprising, for other than the general Germanic idea of a sonata he had no model at all for shaping a work like this, whose harmonies and rhythms are largely of his own invention. What could the terms of the shaping be, if he had discarded the harmonic and tonal language around which genres like symphony and sonata had been created? No one had ever imagined anything like that before. As he had in the earlier *Psalms,* Ives faced again, but now in large scale, the question that would bedevil European Modernists: How does one organize highly chromatic, dissonant, sometimes atonal extended works? This question (among others) led Schoenberg and his school to create the twelve-tone system, Stravinsky and his school to a neoclassic retreat to the past.

In the First Sonata, much of Ives's answer to the problem was: *symmetry of form and continual melodic development*. As H. Wiley Hitchcock describes the overall form: "rhapsodic first movement balanced by heroic finale, complementary ragtime scherzos in movements 2 and 4, and a central movement itself quite symmetrical (Largo, Allegro, Largo)." Ives created cyclic thematic relationships among the movements; Hitchcock notes, "First, third, and fifth movement work with the hymn tune *Lebanon* . . . second and fourth movement with the three hymn tunes 'Happy Day,' 'Bringing in the Sheaves,' and 'I Hear Thy Welcome Voice' (which are themselves inter-related); and a descending three-note motif—semitone, minor third—increasingly informs the whole work . . . until it saturates the texture of the finale."[93]

In relying on a fabric of *motives* (or *motifs*—short, germinal melodic ideas) and methodical pitch structures to unify a large work lacking traditional diatonic-tonal relationships, Ives first broke the future trail of many European Modernists. In his laboratory pieces from early on, he discovered for himself some of the organizing devices Schoenberg would apply to chromatic music: "liberation of the dissonance," inversions and retrogrades of melodies and whole sections, elaborate motivic structures, melodic motives turned on end to form harmonies, even proto–twelve-tone rows (there are rowlike patterns in the 1907 *Three-Page Sonata*). Like Schoenberg during his free-atonal period, Ives lets the melodic/contrapuntal development create the harmony rather than submitting to conventional rules, in which counterpoint is shackled by harmony. As did the European Modernists, Ives got his cue for these techniques from the motivic structures of late-Romantic music, including Brahms's way of saturating a texture with motives that meanwhile evolve and transform.

While the First Piano Sonata ended up one of Ives's most ambitious and important works, he would leave it an orphan. He had a fair copy made at Tams and mailed it to his old choirmaster John Griggs, for comment. Griggs never commented and lost the score. Thereafter, Ives wrote, as in other cases, "I got started on something else, and I kept putting it off . . . for so long a time, that, when I did look back at it, I had lost interest."[94] Not until the 1940s would Lou Harrison copy out the piece from a pre-final score.[95]

Perhaps a big reason Ives lost interest was that the programmatic underpinning of the First Sonata was not grand enough for him. In a manuscript memo he wrote out a detailed but mundane program: "What is it all about?—Dan S. asks. Mostly about the outdoor life in Conn. villages in the '80s & '90s—impressions, remembrances, & reflections of country farmers in Conn.

farmland. On page 14 back, Fred's Daddy got so excited that he shouted when Fred hit a home run & the school won the baseball game. But Aunt Sarah was always humming <u>Where is My Wandering Boy</u> after Fred an' John left for a job in Bridgeport. . . ."

And so on in nostalgic mode. (Recall the words of an observer of Ives's college: "Ask a Yale man the reason for anything and he will give you its origin; and he thinks he has answered your question.") To John Kirkpatrick, Ives suggested a different program for the sonata, also implied by the tune "Wandering Boy" quoted in the piece: "the family together in the first and last movement, the boy away sowing his oats in the ragtimes, and the parental anxiety in the middle movement."[96] Perhaps the problem was that neither of these programs turns on the lofty conceptions that were inspiring Ives in the teens: the apotheosis of American writers in the *Concord Sonata,* the spiritual journey of the Fourth Symphony, the cosmic drama of the *Universe Symphony.* The First Piano Sonata is large in expressive effect, but as Ives became more ambitious, maybe it became too small in concept for him. He refused to recognize notes in themselves as an ultimate value in music. So he left one of his finest works in limbo. Later, for different reasons, he would do the same with *Robert Browning Overture.*

Two slighter pieces from 1903–4 stayed with him—*Country Band March* and the Overture "1776."[97] Eventually Ives spliced them together to form *Putnam's Camp,* the uproarious second of the *Three Places in New England. Country Band March* parodies the amateur bands Ives grew up with. In his music players fall off the beat, toss in off-the-cuff countermelodies in the wrong key, and a saxophonist plays two extra beats after everybody else has finished. The melange of tunes includes a deliberately bordering-on-banal one of Ives's (it would turn up again in *Three Places,* the *Concord Sonata,* and the Fourth Symphony), "Marching Through Georgia," "The Battle Cry of Freedom," "Arkansas Traveller," "Yankee Doodle," and Sousa's *Semper Fidelis.* It also uses "piano-drumming" effects of the sort Ives invented in childhood— thick handfuls of chords on drum patterns. The manuscript is full of descriptions of the intended effect: "count as if practicing the beginning & getting it wrong," "miss whole beat," "miss step." (There is also a cryptic reference to "Adam Forepaugh's Steam Piano.")

The Overture "1776" possesses a more elaborate pedigree, having been intended for an opera on the play *Major John Andre* by Ives uncle and amateur poet Lyman Brewster. The manuscript of the Overture dates its beginning in Danbury, Christmas 1903, its end on Pine Mountain the following July. Lyman's death in February 1904[98] may have scotched the project, but it hardly seems promising anyway. It is hard to imagine Charles Ives setting to music Lyman's pseudo-eighteenth-century lingo: "O ho! So runs the rede! I thought as much. / He has at times a far off dreamy look / That seems to reach almost a thousand leagues."[99]

In the Overture Ives plays intricate games with polyrhythm, polymeter, and polyphrasing, at one point creating the effect of the same march rhythms going on simultaneously at different speeds—a memory of bands passing on the march. This would survive as the most famous effect in *Putnam's Camp*. Both "1776" and *Country Band March* also feature a characteristically Ivesian formal pattern: they move from areas of relative simplicity through accumulating complexity to a climactic bedlam.[100] Perhaps more often Ives would create the opposite effect, starting with complexity and moving toward integration and simplicity—as with the end of the Third Symphony. Also characteristic, however, is that Ivesian bedlam can create effects ranging from comic, as in *Country Band March,* to mystical, as in *The Housatonic at Stockbridge.*

An Ives note on the fair copy of the orchestral *Thanksgiving,* developed from Yale organ pieces, says "finished and all scored on Pine Mt Aug 14 1904." One of the most sheerly beautiful of his works, *Thanksgiving* would eventually serve as the finale for the set / symphony *Holidays.* The middle section has a folklike simplicity and grace that Ives rarely allowed himself in orchestral music (the simplicity did not come easy—there are many sketches). The concluding choral entrance on "God, Beneath Thy Guiding Hand" is one of his most exalted moments. In this work Ives is perhaps for the first time, in substance if not always in manner, an innovative orchestral composer and a splendid one.

But he is still not quite himself, not entirely the artist he would become and which we call *Ivesian.* Most of the elements that would help him realize that self were in his possession by 1904: the disparate but fundamental lessons he had learned in Danbury and at Yale, the sophisticated control of complex rhythms and chromatic pitch relations that he taught himself after the turn of the century, the fresh rhythmic effects of ragtime. In 1904, though, Ives could not tell where to take all this, what to do next. After he finished *Thanksgiving* there is a lull in his output for nearly a year. Likely he was working on things, songs, maybe the First Piano Sonata, which perhaps was not pulling together.[101] The insurance business, caught up in a hullabaloo over corruption, may have drained his energy. His health was deserting him; that would come to a crisis in late 1906. But at other times Ives kept composing no matter how demanding business got. His main problem may have been one of direction.

As of 1905 and age thirty, Charles Ives appeared to be no more than a workaday insurance man and a composer of music hardly anybody heard or asked to play. His experiments had gone far, but in no particular direction. He had composed a pile of pieces in a Babel of styles. In those pieces he crafted a number of unique voices, but he had yet to mold his ideas into a harmonious vision. By 1905 he had laid the foundation of a mature art but was still unsure what to build on it; he had learned much of the how, but did not yet know the what and the why. The rough, vital expression of everyday human life and spirituality, the music of the ages, eluded him. His mature works, from 1909 onward, encompass a diversity of voices which he somehow made his own. He

would find that music not so much through further technical experiments—
though there would be many—as through a renewal of his confidence and
inspiration by the workings of a transcendent quality he had not yet experienced: the power of love.

Ives had kept up with Dave Twichell over the years as he had kept up
with other college friends. A September 1903 letter to Dave, then working at
Dr. Trudeau's tuberculosis sanitarium on Saranac Lake,[102] is a specimen of
the Yalie banter they still indulged in:

Dear Dave, / Why dont you occasionally write (<u>damn</u> you any way I hear <u>good</u> reports
from time to time). Willis Wood spent a day with us recently, tells us you're in good
form, and an able foreman in the "wheez factory." Del Wood took me to Keene Valley
over Labor Day. We didn't seize any panthers, but had an enjoyable time, though am
afraid I was a disturbing element being full of malaria . . . quinine and <u>whiskey</u> at the
time. . . . We finally succeeded in placing that shanty on the mountain in Ridgefield,
but did it unbenowed to Aunt Amelia fearing adverse suggestions. It makes a good
young camp. Geo Lewis went up with me last month taking <u>Sat. afternoon off</u>—what!
We spent the night on the mountain. Having no curtains on the window, it took 2
hours of kind words to get the old scrunch to disrobe. He being afraid that some of the
farmers' wives in the next house (about 3 miles down in the valley) would peek at him.
He walked all day long in a circle among the woods and discovered an egg—that
Benedict Arnold laid in the battle of Ridgefield. Remember me to Deac. [Deac was
Dave's eccentric brother, of whom Ives was fond.][103]

At the end of July 1905, Ives traveled to Hartford to join the Twichells in
preparation for another Adirondack vacation. He had spent several summer
months with the minister's family since 1896. Two years before that, in the
last letter he had written his father, he had mentioned his intention to hear the
famous Reverend Joseph Twichell preach. The last word he ever wrote to his
father (about a textbook) had been the word *Harmony*. Charlie had known
Dave's sister Harmony Twichell going on ten years now. She had heard Charlie play at Center Church, had been on his arm at the Yale Junior Prom.
Beyond that they seemed to have had little connection, compared to Ives's
friendship with Dave or even with his brother Deac. Charlie was still mainly
Dave's friend, a passing acquaintance to his sister, who always had a lot of
men around.

On this visit something happened. On July 30, 1905, Ives and Harmony
Twichell went together to a concert in Hartford.[104] Two years later, when the
passionate part of their courtship began, they backdated the diary of their
relationship to that concert, where they heard Dvořák's *New World Symphony*.
In the diary they named "Our Book," they called that night the beginning of
"La Vita Nuova," the new life.

NINE

La Vita Nuova

IN AUGUST 1899, the month Charles Ives composed his song "Omens and Oracles," Reverend Joseph Hopkins Twichell wrote a letter to his daughter Harmony, who would be light and muse of Charles Ives's maturity. Harmony was then a student at the Hartford Hospital Training School for Nurses. Reverend Twichell called this daughter Meg, partly to distinguish her from her namesake mother. Writing from Scotland in prose characteristically labored but affectionate, he compares the burdens of his daughter's calling to what she had experienced at the family vacation spot in the Adirondacks:

But oh my, Meg. *What* a contrast between your story of the pleasures you found at Pel Jones' and the work to which you have returned! We . . . soldiers must take what comes, and so must nurses. I often wonder, Meg, how, from your present standpoint, Humanity and the Human Problem look to you. To me, I confess, as I grow older, they grow more and more inscrutable, though I also . . . grow more and more certain that the mind of Christ is the only glass through which to contemplate them.[1]

Joe Twichell's words ring not with theological dogma but with a devotion to religious mystery and human service. His ideals would resonate more with his children than they ever would with his friend Mark Twain, whose zestful cynicism the Reverend would occasionally attempt, vainly, to crack.

Partly because of that friendship, which had been commemorated in print, and because of his warmth and wit, and because he was a cherished pastor of a prosperous church, Joe Twichell was an eminence in the territory between Hartford and New Haven. He first had laid eyes on Sam Clemens at a New York birthday dinner for the writer in 1876, during which Twain christened Joe's pulpit, Asylum Hill, "The Church of the Holy Speculators." Characteristically, the Reverend found that pretty funny, and struck up a friendship with the perpetrator that lasted over thirty years.[2] Joe Twichell helped marry Sam Clemens to his beloved Livy, married their daughter Clara to the pianist Ossip Gabrilowitsch, and pronounced the benediction over his friend's grave. As few men manage to do, this handsome, unassuming, boyish Hartford minister would go through much of his life in something like a state of grace both worldly and spiritual. Like his composer son-in-law, Joe Twichell would never recognize much of a distinction between those domains.

Twichell's Yale career foretold neither eminence nor grace. An average student, though socially adroit, he was tapped for Scroll and Key. Finally he came to the attention of the faculty in the worst way: he was whooping it up at a spring riot when a friend of his shot and killed a town fireman. Joe never revealed the name of the culprit and his college years ended under a cloud.[3] Maybe the event sobered him up; after Yale Joe entered Union Theological Seminary. When the Civil War broke out, he signed up as chaplain of a New York Zouave regiment largely made up of Irish rowdies, part of the Army of the Potomac.[4] During his soldier years Joe Twichell saw every major engagement of the biggest Union army, at the Peninsula, Fredericksburg, Chancellorsville, Gettysburg.[5] He watched deserters getting shot, the condemned men standing erect and looking gallantly into the barrels of the firing squad, who were white-faced and shaking.[6] He heard Abraham Lincoln give his little address a year after the battle at Gettysburg.[7] Probably he heard, now and again at parades or concerts or on the battlefield, the brassy clamor of the best band in the army, led by teenaged George Ives.

Joe Twichell would say he entered the army a narrow Puritan and came out with a more humanistic view of life and religion, nearly indifferent to sect and theology: God had to do with your and your neighbors' lives, here and now. Besides his experience of the grand and terrible panoply of war, the change in him also came from a friendship he found in the army with Jesuit Father Joseph B. O'Hagen.[8] And Twichell came to love the profane exuberance and courage of his Irish regiment, who led him to understand that goodness was more than superficial niceties,[9] manliness a matter of courage and grit.[10]

As the Civil War shaped George Ives and the children he reared, so it went with Joe Twichell. After being mustered out in the summer of 1864,[11] he found his first and final pulpit. During the war he had met the man whose disciple he was destined to be, Horace Bushnell. The Congregationalist iconoclast was impressed by the young chaplain and recommended him to the new Asylum Hill Church in Hartford.[12] The deacons never considered anyone else. Joe accepted their offer and two weeks later Julia Harmony Cushman accepted his proposal.[13] They would rear nine children.

Reverend Joseph Twichell began his pastoral and domestic life at the end of 1864 and stayed with both for nearly half a century. He became the personification of that lofty stone church built by and for Hartford's loftiest businessmen. (Soon after Joe began there, he sneaked Father O'Hagen into the building for an unofficial Catholic consecration.[14]) Among a profusion of community endeavors, Twichell for thirty years was a member of the Yale Corporation.[15]

That Joe Twichell was almost universally liked testifies to his kindly and gregarious disposition, despite his mentor Bushnell being a howling heretic to many Protestants. The name of Joe's second son, Burton Parker Twichell, joined the names of three ministers who were Bushnellian mainstays in Hartford.[16] Bushnell, called "the father of American religious liberalism," put forward a theology in many ways still progressive a century later; in his time it was breathtaking. He rejected the idea of original sin, declared the Trinity symbol of an integral divinity, denied the arch-Puritan doctrine that Christ was sacrificed as literal atonement for man's sins.[17] Like the Gnostic heretics, Bushnell felt the divine as imminent, as existing within humanity and nature rather than out there in the sky. He said early religious training for children was better than campground conversions later; religion should be a habit of life rather than a product of fear and trembling. God was beyond language or comprehension, religion above all a force to spread love and goodness in the world. Christ came not as an unforgiving judge, but as the earthly exemplar of divine love and compassion.[18] At the same time, Bushnell also had an anti-feminist streak: women were to be the angel in the house, a tempering influence, more spiritual because less thoughtful than men.

Neither Joe Twichell nor his daughter Harmony would care for theology as such, but Bushnell's vision of the divine would govern their lives and, through them, help shape Charles Ives's music. One of Twichell's sermons, "The Coming Man," predicated on natural and spiritual evolution, anticipates the ideals of his future son-in-law:

It is the testimony of revelations and of science alike that the crowning product of the creative energy is man. . . . Both agree, also, that though created he is still incomplete; still the forethought of the universal world process. . . . And his perfection is to be wrought out along the lines of his spiritual nature . . . whereas the soul has long been an appendage of the body, the body will become the vehicle and appendage of the soul.[19]

Besides many of Hartford's wealthiest businessmen, the parishioners of "The Church of the Holy Speculators" included notables of the Nook Farm literary community on which the church bordered—Charles Dudley Warner, Harriet Beecher Stowe, and, belting out hymns beside his wife every Sunday, Mark Twain. Other family friends included novelist William Dean Howells and poet John Greenleaf Whittier.[20] The Twichell children had a lot of honorary uncles and aunts coming and going in the parish house, but their favorite was Uncle Mark. Harmony Twichell grew up knowing a genius when she saw one.

Besides being an ideal minister, Joe Twichell was an ideal sidekick, a jolly, agreeable Watson to Twain's trenchant Holmes. It was Joe who suggested to Mark, during a dry spell, that he turn his old Mississippi yarns into stories.[21] When Twain required company on a walking trip around Boston or a six-week tour of Europe, he naturally called on Joe, and Joe jumped. The European trip, in 1878, became *A Tramp Abroad*. Joe is called "Harris" in the book, but everybody knew who it was. When Joe toured England in 1908, he was hailed and regaled as Mark Twain's minister.[22]

There was a "Twichell atmosphere" around this family, which flowed above all from the patriarch and the famous friends who visited the parish house at 125 Woodland Street. Chronically generous, the Twichells were never well-off, but they got by. Joe and his wife loved poetry and music, and defended novels against Puritan prejudices.[23] Every August the family headed for the mountains and lakes of the Adirondacks. In the Twichell atmosphere Joe and Harmony Cushman Twichell raised their children—a doctor, a teacher, a minister, several good wives, a nurse and good wife to a genius, and a couple of wandering souls. Joe and his wife would do their best to preserve Mark Twain's soul after Livy died. Some of the Twichells eventually lost their way as well. No family is too good to be true. Joe himself lost his ebullience at last, but never lost the affection of nearly everyone who knew him.

Charles Ives would write, "I heard Mark Twain say through his own mouth, nose and cigar as he pointed across the room . . . to Mr. and Mrs. Twichell: 'Those two blessed people—how greatly indebted I am to them.' "[24] Twain the cynic honored goodness and friendship when he found it. But he was an exception in an age when exalting the best in life—love, friendship, compassion—often meant refusing to recognize tragedy, even to grant that darkness existed. This was a splendid quality of the age and a narrowing one, as Mark Twain knew too well for him ever to be really happy.

Born on June 4, 1876, and given her mother's middle name, Harmony Twichell was the third daughter in the family. In his diary that night, her father wrote, "On learning that a stork had been heard around the house during the night . . . Eddie and Julia . . . went out to look for the stork's tracks and found them!"[25] Harmony was the daughter of two handsome parents; she had her mother's rounded face and features, her father's luminous eyes. In her Gibson Girl twenties she would be called the most beautiful girl in Hartford. For the rest of her life that beauty would usually be the first thing people noticed about Harmony, and after that her extraordinary poise and serenity. Time and again people would say that Harmony embodied her name.

She was schooled first at home, then at Hartford High with her brother Dave, with whom she would always be closest. During 1893–96 a family friend paid for her (Joe couldn't afford it) to attend Miss Porter's School at Farmington, which existed as much as anything to give final polish to future Yale wives. Her roommate at Farmington was Sally Whitney, Eli's grand-daughter. After school Harmony returned home and spent two aimless years pursuing the womanly arts—writing poetry, ghostwriting a newspaper column, studying a little painting and piano and singing, accompanying her father on speaking trips,[26] and holding off the swarm of boys that perennially gathered around her. Charlie Ives was not really one of them, though she had met him during the 1896 Adirondack vacation and was his prom date the next year. Harmony had been reared to be a perfect wife and probably a minister's wife at that, but something held her back. By 1898 she had decided what she wanted to do. She entered nursing school in Hartford and spent two years living and studying in the city hospital.

Harmony Twichell in her nurse's uniform.

In deciding to put off marriage and take up a career, Harmony was not pursuing a conventional route, but neither was she being rebellious. Ann Douglas notes that in those days many well-educated, middle-class women went into professions rather than taking a husband.[27] There were few seemly careers available to middle-class women at all, and the ministry was generally closed to them.[28] None of the available careers appealed to Victorian and Progressive ideals of feminine service more than nursing to the poor. Women, wrote settlement-house pioneer Jane Addams, should work not only in the home but in the community, for the whole human family. Harmony's view of it is shown in her nursing school graduation speech, "The Nurses' Gain":

The fullest development individually comes from altruistic effort, and fullest development means in the end the greatest usefulness and happiness. . . .

We find how people live, of whose lives we were before in perfect ignorance. Almost unconsciously we are introduced to some of the great sociological questions so widely discussed.

The people of the slums become our acquaintances. We come near the grim affairs of living, poverty and pain—and what food for reflection is offered! See what an immense gain in the *furnishing of our minds!* We come into a sort of humble fellowship with some of the noblest women that ever lived. Florence Nightingale and Sister Dora and Alice Fisher. . . .

There is another matter that possesses the public mind greatly—that a nurse must of necessity have her finer feelings and perceptions blunted. In what work, I would ask, could a woman's gentleness and care be *more* appealed to or exercised?[29]

Here Harmony already seems to have decided that she was going to be a nurse to the poor, living in slums as a worker in the urban renewal and reform movement. Improving public health, especially fighting tuberculosis, would be a large part of the settlement-house agenda.[30] Harmony would spend much of the next years doing that, but always with interruptions. The first was just after graduation in 1900, when she took a two-month vacation to Italy with her father. They toured some of the cities and museums to which she later led her husband—Milan, Venice, Florence, Rome, Naples. In 1901 she took a position with the Visiting Nurse's Association of Chicago. It was a rough job, she would recall, a year and a half of running "from slum house to slum house."[31]

Soon after she started, her father wrote that he had ministered to Harmony's best friend as she died in childbirth. Harmony's diary entry on hearing the news reveals much of her warmth, unstinting love, and Victorian religiosity.

Sally Whitney Sanford died today. My dearest friend. . . . This has been a sad and lonesome week. I have constantly thought of Sally and the beauty of the passing of her soul. The sweet peace & kindness of her last hours have been comforting & inspiring to dwell upon. I am exalted by having such a friend & have a new & dear incentive to go on living. But she is now laid away. She is no longer of this world & life & to me it cannot be the same—much joyousness has gone & a sad though inexpressibly sweet & blessed memory has begun. . . . Yesterday as we sang the Doxology, I thought as I sang "Praise Him above, Ye heavenly Host" that Sally was this Sabbath one of that glorious host. . . . Dear brave Sally—my girlhood closes with her life & with her are its sweetest merriest & happiest memories.[32]

This shows Harmony as a Bushnellian woman, whose religion was ingrained and habitual and sentimental. She had grown up hardly ordinary or conventional, but in her religious sentiments she toed the line. Reflecting on her friend's death, though, she could not quite succeed in turning her anguish into the proper inspiration and uplift.

Harmony returned home from Chicago in October 1902. For a month of the next year she went with brother Dave for a rest in South Carolina; his medical studies had used him up.[33] That summer Harmony spent as companion to a family friend, "Aunt Sally" Dunham. From September 1903, after the family's annual Adirondack vacation, she stayed on for a year with Dave at Lake Saranac, as a visiting nurse in the tuberculosis sanitarium where he began his specialist's career.

By the time she left Saranac, Harmony was losing her dedication to her career. Maybe as a result, she gave in to what seemed her fate: she became engaged to Reverend Walter Lowrie, whose family had long been close to the Twichells,[34] whom she undoubtedly admired, whom she did not love. Despite all the men around her, Harmony had yet to find anyone to love as she did her parents and Dave and Sally Whitney. So she considered taking the role of helpmeet to a minister and ornament of the parish house, like her mother. After a few months she realized, consciously or not, that she needed more than that, and broke off with Reverend Lowrie. Now Harmony was approaching thirty and spinsterhood. She seems not yet to have discovered her capacity for romantic love. When she found someone with the key to unlock those feelings, she would drop everything else. She was lucky enough to find someone who felt the same about her, and who needed everything she could give him, in her immense capacity for giving.

Harmony may have run into Charlie Ives in the first part of 1905, having perhaps not seen him for years.[35] If so, the occasion produced no revelation. That March she served as companion to Mrs. Sage, another family friend, for a spring tour of Europe and England. She was back by July. On the last Sunday of that month Charlie took her to hear the *New World Symphony* in Hartford. That was the night they called "La Vita Nuova," when their lives turned a corner they had long waited for, whether or not they had realized it.

Besides the usual rambling course of love, Victorian mores made the mating dance so discreet in its early stages as to be almost imperceptible. Harmony observed later, "we were very *formal* then."[36] It is as if romance were something unseemly, to be approached with the most studied obliqueness. There were other problems too, specific to Harmony and Charlie. At the end of 1905 there was the matter, still fresh, of Reverend Lowrie. More immediately, at some point Bart Yung innocently told Harmony that Charlie had a girlfriend. Later she would write Charlie, "I think now I loved you then, dear, tho' I <u>didn't</u> because I knew I mustn't . . . when Bart told me about your girl. . . . I really didn't harbor the thought [of loving you]—I <u>couldn't</u> in self defense." But she added, "that day we went up to Saranac seems almost a miracle—I remember saying then, as we looked across the lake to the mountains at the sunset, that I didn't think Paradise could be any more beautiful."[37] They were falling in love, then, when in August 1905 Charlie went to Lake

Saranac to spend six weeks with the Twichells. Harmony spent that August working at the Henry Street settlement house in New York, then joined Charlie and the family at Saranac. Maybe her arrival there was the day of the sunset, when she began to accept her feelings and suspect his.

Ives had decided to spend that vacation with the Twichells, after a hiatus of several years, because he was in bad shape. He had been burning his reserves too fast; he felt overworked and depressed, enough to convince Aunt Amelia that he was verging on nervous collapse.[38] Along with or partly because of that depression, composing and business had stagnated. Ives went to the Adirondacks in search of healing and renewal. He got a new life.

It would be another two years before he found the courage to speak his love to Harmony. All the same, from the beginning of their courtship love's electricity spilled into his music. Working away during the 1905 vacation with the Twichells, he produced two hymn settings, one for cornet and strings of "Beautiful River" (later put into the Fourth Violin Sonata) and, on Dave's suggestion, one for horn and strings of *Watchman* (later expanded for the Fourth Symphony). Most significantly, in a burst of inspiration that August he set down three pages of dissonant, densely polyphonic, highly structured music for piano. At the end, noting the length, he gave the generally free-form, one-movement piece the ironic title *Three-Page Sonata*.[39] It would be the first of several pieces in the next months that together formed the staging platform of his full maturity.

The *Three-Page Sonata* is one of his laboratory pieces. Nicholls calls it "a kind of preliminary squall to Ives's experimental storm."[40] Here Ives explored, more systematically than ever before, the chromatic motivic / harmonic devices later "discovered" by Schoenberg and his disciples. Ives began this piece, for a change, with neither an old piece nor a program, but rather with a pregnant set of four notes. Musicians call it the "BACH motive," because it can be spelled with the letters of Bach's name: B♭–A–C–B♮ (the first note is called B and the last note H in German notation).[41] The first section of the *Sonata*, through changes of texture, rhythm, and mood, maintains the BACH motive, subjecting it to the "Schoenbergian" devices of transposition, inversion, and so on. The set of notes turns up later in the piece as well. During its course Ives experiments with twelve-tone lines, various sorts of rhythmic series, and polyrhythmic and polymetric layerings complex beyond anything in other composers' piano music for years to come.[42]

Ultimately, maybe the *Three-Page Sonata* is the sort of piece more likely to entertain theorists than listeners. Ives showed no particular signs of liking it himself, and its lack of a program suggests he did not take it too seriously. Certainly it is not without its pleasures; for example, the serene, dreamlike middle section—Ivesian "night music." Did falling in love inspire him mainly to a new level of dissonance and formal abstraction? Only for the moment. Love, which inflames mind and body, gave him courage to plunge deeper into the personal, experimental stratum that would produce not only his most revolutionary but his most profound and heartfelt music.

The next year, 1906, was a watershed for Ives even more significant than 1902, but emotionally it was a stretch of rapids. Charlie and Harmony were still in the early stages of the Victorian mating pavane, wary of too-impetuous steps, each unsure of the other's feelings, each fearful of disappointment. In February Harmony went off to California with Mrs. Sage. At least that kept her out of circulation. Ives knew excruciatingly well, as Mike Myrick would put it, that "he had a lot of competition . . . a lot of men were chasing her." During this period lovesick Charlie began to get on the nerves of his Poverty Flat roommates. Said Mike: "When he'd concentrate [on a woman], he became very intense."[43] Harmony was not his first girlfriend, but she was the one he was ready to stake everything on.

In May, June, and July of 1906 Ives started, and mostly finished, five seminal works. For a few months, Poverty Flat thundered with some of the most startling "Resident Disturbances" yet. The rush of revolutionary pieces was prefaced by one of the shortest but most beautiful, gentle, and significant of his songs, "The Pond" (called "Remembrance" in its 1921 piano-vocal version). Over a gently babbling instrumental texture, the voice proclaims Ives's haiku-like text:

> A sound of a distant horn,
> O'er shadowed lake is borne,
> My father's song.

It is an evocation of George Ives playing from across the water and across the years. As Ives reached the decade of his greatest work, he evoked like a talisman the image of his father playing from the shadows.

That same month, apparently, Ives did the little sketch *Take-off #3: Rube Trying to Walk 2 to 3!*, which over the next half dozen years he extended into one of his most innovative chamber works, *Over the Pavements*. That piece takes its tone from the opening "Rube" music, a jaunty and ironic clarinet tune in $\frac{3}{8}$ over a $\frac{2}{8}$ bassoon accompaniment, with raggy interjections by the piano. It began, Ives wrote,

one morning when George Lewis and I had the front bedroom in Poverty Flat, 65 Central Park West. In the early morning, the sounds of people going to and fro, all different steps, and sometimes all the same—the horses, fast trot, canter, sometimes slowing up into a walk (few if any autos in those days)—an occasional trolley throwing all rhythm out . . . then back again. I was struck with how many different and changing kinds of beats, time, rhythms, etc. went on together—but quite naturally. . . . This piece . . . is also a kind of take-off of street dancing. . . . The cadenza is principally a "little practice" that I did with Father, of playing the nice chromatic scale not in one octave but in all octaves—that is, 7th, 9ths, etc.[44]

In other words, in its technical dimension *Over the Pavements* is primarily a rhythmic study, one of Ives's most far-reaching. As he had before and would many times again, he began with an aural experience: the sounds of the city, "street dancing." This idea was expressed as a technical study: polyrhythm, with a strong ragtime component. Then he developed the programmatic / impressionistic and technical dimensions together. Here the complexity gradually accumulates from the simple beginning (the streets getting crowded) until he is stacking up six levels of polyrhythm and polyphrasing. Ives manages not only to keep all this clear, but to make it swing—few pieces of this complexity maintain as much forward drive as this one, and few are as rambunctious and entertaining.[45] The ending, or rather non-ending, is one of Ives's most startling, peculiarly apt, and funniest: after all the wild rhythmic counterpoint, free harmonies, and piano drumming, it suddenly winds up with two bars of old-time oompah accompaniment, in plain C major.

(In Ivesian works where the program predominates with little technical focus, we get his sketchier "cartoons" and "takeoffs" such as *"Gyp the Blood" or Hearst!? Which is Worst?!* [1912]—a semi-musical excoriation of the yellow press. When the technical experiment predominates over the program and the "music," we get pieces such as the ferociously difficult, near-serial rhythmic etude for piano quintet. *In Re Con Moto Et Al* [1913]. As Ives wrote of the latter: "Some of these shorter pieces . . . were in part made to strengthen the ear muscles, the mind muscles, and perhaps the Soul muscles."[46] Which is to say, he expected them to teach him and his [mostly imaginary] listeners something, but not to *express* much. Like others after him, Ives first resorted to mechanical patterns to explore uncommon sonorities; these patterns were an anchor under unmapped stars. Ives was quick to understand the uses of this sort of formalism, and also to understand its limitations—thus his term "wall paper design music." Formalistic experiments were a vital part of his overall development, the shape of his work, but they were never the essence of it. Mechanical patterns were a way to find new sounds and means of organizing them. They were no path to the heart.)

Also in 1906 Ives began the three-movement Set for Theatre Orchestra. The first, *In the Cage*, comes from the afternoon at the zoo when the roommates watched a leopard's endless pacing and Bart Yung wondered, "Is life anything like that?" We hear a wordless whole-tone tune in the English horn (Ives added the text in the later piano reduction), as accompaniment a series of apparently independent and meterless fourth chords (the instrumental introduction is an accelerating rhythmic series, in sixteenths: 8, 6, 4, 3, 2, and 1), and a hypnotically repeated timpani figure (the leopard), which also goes its own way. These independent layers add up to a single effect; the relationships holding them together are subtle, but they work. The set's second movement, *In the Inn*, is a rhythmic vaudeville based on some of his earlier ragtime dances. (This music makes another appearance in the First Piano Sonata.)

The dreamlike final movement, *In the Night,* is one of Ives's first many-layered phantasmagorias, supporting another wordless song in French horn or clarinet. Its program: "The heart of an old man, dying alone in the night, sad, low in heart—then God comes to help him—bring him to his own loved ones. This is the main [melody], the substance. All around, the rest of the music is but the silence and sounds of the night—bells tolling in the far distance, etc."[47] Hitchcock describes the sound: "The melody is projected against a vibrant, palpitating background—a line of warmly luminous color against a dark wash—in a paradigm of an orchestral texture Ives was particularly fond of. The background 'vibrates' through the interplay of five planes of rhythmic ostinatos and near-ostinatos so planned as hardly ever to coincide."[48] *In the Night* presages later and more elaborate Ivesian meditations, from *The Housatonic at Stockbridge* to the first and last movements of the Second Orchestral Set to the last pages of the Fourth Symphony. Like them it does not really end but rather seems to fade out of hearing.

In the midst of working on these pieces, in July 1906, Ives jotted down on one crowded page a sketch he called *The Unanswered Question*. Here is music utterly unlike anything before Ives, made of three planes that have little audibly to do with one another. Each layer has its own texture and instrumentation and style, their juxtaposition only loosely controlled: A background of strings playing almost inaudibly a slow-cycling, mysterious sequence made up of traditional chords but elusive in tonality; periodically, six times over this background, a solo trumpet intones the same cryptic, unmistakably questioning phrase.

After each of these questions a group of flutes lurches into a response, each time getting more frenzied, dissonant, and apparently desperate. Finally the trumpet poses the Question once more and evokes only the strings fading into silence. This "cosmic drama," as Ives called it, lasts under five minutes.

In the 1930s, when he was rummaging for new pieces to put before the public, Ives picked up *The Unanswered Question,* carefully revised it, and attached a program something like what must have been in his mind in 1906. The strings are "the silences of the Druids, who know, see, and hear nothing"; over this indifferent universal background the trumpet repeatedly poses "the perennial question of existence"; the winds are the "fighting answerers" who, for all their sound and fury, get nowhere. His later revisions affected nothing of the essential and astounding radicalism of the original concept—three essentially separate pieces of music juxtaposed—or the highly dissonant music of the winds. Ives simply touched up the wind parts and, most important, varied the last note of the trumpet Question to make it less static, more ambiguous. It would become his most famous piece.[49] Certainly it is striking, the program easy and entertaining for audiences to follow. And certainly each of the three elements expresses its role; the string part alone is of a marvelous, ethereal beauty. The program also encompasses a philosophical idea that Ives would address incomparably in his music and in his writing: in contemplating the sublime mystery of creation, a question can be better than an answer. But *The Unanswered Question* is not up to its concept in the way Ives's later pieces are. The planes are too discrete; they seem a static tableau, slaves to the program, in contrast to the more integrated layered music that Ives was soon to create.

This work is part of a two-piece set from that summer, whose complete moniker runs approximately: "*Two Contemplations:* 'A Contemplation of a Serious Matter' or 'The Unanswered Perennial Question' and 'A Contemplation of Nothing Serious' or 'Central Park in the Dark in The Good Old Summertime.' " The second of the *Two Contemplations, Central Park in the Dark*, written in July–December 1906,[50] has some of the static quality of its partner, but it works better. The piece is an aural souvenir of Ives's bachelor years in New York—summer nights in the park and the sounds of the city. The background is another quiet sequence of chords in muted strings, but this time made of complex, atonal, schematically structured harmonies.[51] One could associate this texture with all sorts of programs, but once attached to Central Park it becomes inescapably that, a haunting evocation of a humid summer night in the city.[52]

The effect of this string part is something quite new in music, a function of its drifting rhythms and unique close harmonies moving in parallel, unpredictable but with a subtle logic. Over this whispering background, through the trees, the sounds of the city begin to intrude. The "silent darkness," Ives wrote, "is interrupted by sounds from the Casino over the pond . . . street singers coming up from the Circle singing . . . the tunes of those days [including 'Hello, Ma Baby']—of some 'night owls' from Healy's whistling the latest . . . the 'occasional elevated' . . . of pianolas having a ragtime war in the apartment house . . . a cab horse runs away, lands 'over the fence and out', the wayfarers shout—again the darkness is heard—an echo over the pond—and we walk home."[53]

Ives had thrown tunes together since college, both off-the-cuff and in rough written-out improvisations like *Calcium Light Night*. In *The Unanswered Question* and *Central Park in the Dark* he notated such effects more concisely, using what he had taught himself about an extraordinary range of new harmonic, rhythmic, and polyphonic devices. He had learned, among other things, to notate unprecedentedly complex polyrhythms. (Brahms had not been in his grave ten years when these pieces were written.) In the *Two Contemplations* revolutionary technique, impressionistic description, and sheer musicality worked together for him as they never had before. Ives had a way to go in that direction, but not such a long way now. He had taken the final step in a process that began with polytonality, extended to polyrhythm and polymeter, and now came to rest in a *polyphony of groups*—juxtaposed planes of music each with its own character, style, integrity, and even space: quasi-independent pieces of music juxtaposed as in a collage. In terms of music arranged in space, here was the outcome of a train of logic that began when George Ives's band performed his son's variations on "Jerusalem the Golden" with detachments spread around the village square, playing theme and assorted variations at the same time. After the *Two Contemplations* Ives began to think in earnest about planes and layers, about arranging smaller performing groups at varying distances. Like planets circulating around the main ensemble, each group can play its own music in its own implied space, in a kind of super-contrapuntal democracy. In contrast to his earlier attempts, Ives now possessed the technique and the ear to keep unprecedented contrapuntal layering under control.

If the music of that year hints at Ives's response to Harmony Twichell, her side is told in letters, preserved while he destroyed most of what he wrote to her. Her first extant letter to Charlie is dated August 16, 1906. That summer they had gotten together here and there, took a romantic walk in Hartford on Midsummer Eve,[54] and he set a Monica Turnbull poem she sent him. (He would compose regularly during visits to the Twichell house.) But Harmony's first letter to him is polite, guarded. She was going to Pell Jones's cabin in the Adirondacks, the family's favorite spot.

Dear Charlie, Sort of a vague remembrance came into my mind this morning that I'd said I'd write you when I was going over to Pell's. . . . I feel rather afraid, we shant see you but you know we'd like to. . . . With best wishes I am Yours sincerely, Harmony Twichell.[55]

They had a long way to go. Given his shyness, it probably seemed incredible to Charlie that a woman like Harmony would pick him out of the crowd, which included the cream of any imaginable crop of suitors. Yet she kept writing him little letters, reserved but clearly friendly, and kept agreeing to see him. Around the beginning of December they went to Williamsburg, Virginia, to visit Bart Yung and his business, the Rotary File Machine Company. Afterward Harmony cheerily wrote Charlie how much she enjoyed the trip.[56] For him, though, the trip failed to crack the long stretch of bad health and depression. Later he admitted it to her: "It rained constantly and I took you back to the Holland House and bid you goodbye for sometime and felt very very badly and felt as if I'd lost and left behind all that meant anything real to me."[57]

Harmony was to recall that their intimacy began this year, probably around this time.[58] Intimacy can mean heart-filling joy, and no less anxiety and fear. Two or three weeks after leaving Harmony at Williamsburg, Ives collapsed.

It was a heart attack, or something like it. Mutual Life doctors had been expecting some such crisis[59]; so had Aunt Amelia. When it came, the doctors suggested he take a vacation over Christmas. With Myrick, Ives headed for

Old Point Comfort, a Virginia health spa. It would be a characteristic Ivesian rest cure; he spent it not only working on music *(Central Park)*, but also with Myrick planned a new insurance agency of their own. As Ives & Co., it opened at 51 Liberty in New York, on the first day of 1907,[60] selling for the Washington Life company. The effort that entailed, and his continuing anxiety over Harmony, did not allow Ives much room for recovery in the next year.

By the end of that January 1907, Harmony had begun to reveal herself to him, bit by cautious bit, especially her weariness with the gypsy life of a settlement-house nurse: "I don't wonder it was hard to say good by to the [office] & people you'd been in and among for eight years. . . . Think of the way I have wandered around in those same eight years. It makes me feel rather ashamed."[61] That spring some of Charlie's bachelor friends succumbed to the yen for settling down; Ives was best man at Keyes Winter's wedding,[62] and Dave Twichell made what would prove a fateful marriage to Ella Fitch, one of his tuberculosis patients.[63] (Moss Ives had married Minnie Goodman in 1900.)

Inevitably, as part of his courtship, Charlie tried to involve Harmony in his work—set some of her poetry, get her into some sort of project involving the two of them bending close over a sheet of paper. Sometime in 1906 Harmony had, with trepidation, sent Charlie a new poem of hers called "The World's Highway." He set it to music immediately. This would be the only song of his she tried, even privately, to sing.[64] As Ives worked on it, making the song into a miniature tone poem, worrying every turn of feeling (the song is not a creative high point for either of them), how could a composer sensitive to poetic nuance have missed that it was addressed to him personally, that behind the veil of conventional lady's poeticizing lies an unequivocal message? The poem practically shouts, I'm tired of this life, of being a saint to the sick! I have made up my mind among all these men. You're the one I want

> For long I wandered happily
> Far out on the world's highway.
> My heart was brave for each new thing
> And I loved the far away.
>
> I watched the gay bright people dance,
> We laughed, for the road was good
> But oh! I passed where the way was rough
> And I saw it stained with blood.
>
> I wandered on 'till I tired grew
> Far on the world's highway
> My heart was sad for what I saw
> And I feared the far away.
>
> So when one day, O sweetest day!
> I came to a garden small.
> And a voice my heart knew called me in
> I answered its blessed call.

> I left my wandering far & wide
> The freedom and far away,
> But my garden blooms with sweet content
> That's not on the world's highway.

That summer of 1907 Harmony saw a lot of Charlie and no one else. His rivals had fallen by the highway. Together they went to the Kaltenborn Quartet's concerts at St. Nicholas Rink, heard *Parsifal*,[65] saw *Twelfth Night*. During June and July Harmony worked at the Henry Street settlement house in New York. Its founder Lillian Wald was a socialist like many in the movement, and had set up a visiting nurse service.[66] Harmony had no longer any intention of staying in that kind of job.

At some point, probably that year, Ives took a deep breath and showed her some of his experimental music. "The World's Highway" has its touches of boldness, but the dominant tone is Victorian parlor song. Now, with what must have been agonizing apprehension, he sat her down next to the piano and played *The Unanswered Question* and *Central Park in the Dark*. This was not his decorous side now, the kind of music well-brought-up ladies were brought up to appreciate. This was his heart and soul. His pictures in clashing layers of sound did not drive her away from him, but the contrary.

Who knows what Harmony thought, what she really understood about his music, then or later. "He fixed it," she would say, "so I could understand it somehow."[67] She understood, at least, what was most important about him as a person and an artist, and that made her want to fill her life with him. His music reminded her of him, so she loved them together. At the end of that year, when all the veils were ripped aside, he would write her: "<u>You</u> are always absolutely loyal and loving and gentle and <u>always</u> have understood me, from the beginning. I always <u>felt</u> that intuitively as you always seemed to understand intuitively. That was one of the most wonderful things about it all."[68]

The pressure to speak their piece was building on both of them now, and probably on her family too. He spent most weekends with the Twichells in Hartford. Yet the lovers put off speaking their hearts for the entire summer of 1907. He set her poem "Spring Song" and she gave it to friends to try over. She worked desultorily on a story by Sir Gilbert Parker he had given her, which they called *The Kimash Hills,* trying to make an opera libretto out of it.[69] The project was unlikely from the beginning, but this tale of the frozen north and Pierre the outlaw and his encounter with a missionary at least helped bring them closer. Harmony outlined to Charlie her idea for the libretto as a tidy morality tale in which "they show [Pierre] how mistaken he is . . . and it can all end happily." Her next letter shows his reply and her uneasiness: "I like your idea about Pierre's & the other man's getting something out of each other's point of view and think it would be far more interesting to work that in tho' rather harder."[70] They would talk about it for a while yet, but that more or less put the kibosh on *The Kimash Hills*. "The part that I can't get at yet," she wrote him, "is Pierre."[71] Even if Harmony could accept, in theory,

Charlie's idea of a man of God being enlightened by an outlaw, that was not her cup of tea. He encouraged her to write and they did a few more songs together, but they were not destined to collaborate much. Poetry had always been a pastime for Harmony; she was happier reading than writing. Now she was thinking mainly about getting off the world's highway and into that garden.

And so the pressure built on into autumn until neither of them could stand it any more. Charlie was not able to join Harmony for the family vacation at Pell's until September, though at the beginning of August they spent a week at Mrs. Sage's in the Adirondacks.[72] That took their intimacy up a degree. Harmony wrote him afterward, "I dont feel badly Charlie to have you say you care and there is just one reason why I dont & that I shant tell you until you ask me."[73] In other words, after nearly two years of courting and ardent yearning he had summoned the fortitude to announce that *he cared for her,* and then apologized for his impetuousness. She sent him another poem: "As I walked lonely in the throng." When was he going to get the message?

At the end of August brother Deac drove Harmony to Saranac Lake, where she filled in for Dave's vacationing nurse at the sanitarium. Dave asked her to stay with him, but that was not for her any more. "The tragedy of this place," she wrote Charlie, "strikes you all over again when you've been away as long as I have."[74] She was through with the everyday tragedies of hospitals; she wanted joy now. At the end of September she wrote, "I'm sitting right where you & I sat so many hours—on the ground looking at the marsh where the sun sets up at the Roberts camp—do you remember? . . . It doesn't seem right to be here without you."[75] Then she went home to Hartford and waited for him.

Unable any longer to put off the terrifying moment of laying his feelings before her, Ives announced he was coming. Then he got sick again. Her letters became desperate:

I'm so sorry, Charlie, that being sick is what kept you yesterday—I thought it was lots to do perhaps . . . I'm awfully disappointed—these days are so heavenly. I've always called this time of year the peace of God . . . the earth has done her year's work and seems to be resting and these days seem to be a smile of approval. But I shant enjoy them now until I know about you.

[Next day:] I hope you are better and that you are writing me. . . . I am going to telephone the flat if you dont. . . . I feel very badly that you aren't here. . . . I hope I don't bother you but I wish I had you where I could bother you a lot more. [Signed: "Yours as ever."][76]

On October 21, 1907, recovered for the moment, Charles Ives set out from New York to Hartford, his head spinning with speeches and avowals and love and awe and dread, in the season his beloved called the peace of God.

Next day, Tuesday, they walked together on the Wood Road to Farmington and said at last what they had to say. Probably each was astonished at the ardor of the other, after all the bottling up. With their first kiss it was first love and first grand passion, all flowering in the same moment. "When you said there what you did," she was to write him, "I was swept into a flood & can't remember much else. . . . that moment can never be changed or lost—It is one of the supreme moments of existence."[77] At dinnertime they floated back into the Twichell house, hardly seeing anything but each other. Many years later, her brother Joe remembered "with a lump in my throat . . . the meal to which you and Meg and I sat down . . . after you two had returned from an afternoon's walk out around the West Hartford reservoir, . . . both of you surrounded by an impenetrable halo of complete absorption in each other."[78] From then on, they would lose very little of that absorption.

Victorian proprieties were maintained. Everybody knew, nobody said anything. But now Harmony spoke to Charlie words that she had never spoken before. As soon as he left she wrote him, her pen flying over the page:

Dear—I never wrote a love letter & I don't know how. If I don't mail this today you wont get mail until Monday and I can't wait that long to have you see in my writing what you've seen these perfect days in my face—that I love you I love you I love you and no numbers of times of saying it can ever tell it. But believe it that I am yours always & utterly—every bit of me—Harmony.[79]

In that first flush of revealed love (it would last for months if not years, if not for the rest of their lives) Harmony took a few phrases she had written him and made them into her finest poem. "Do you think it seems like last Tuesday at all?" she wrote in sending it.[80] In it there seems an analogy, perhaps intended, between the face of the sun and the face of her lover, the earth and Harmony herself, redeemed from loneliness and labor and encroaching age. Recycling an older song, Ives made it into the exquisite "Autumn."

> Earth rests! Her work is done,
> her fields lie bare.
> And ere the night of winter comes
> to hush her song and close her tired eyes,
> She turns her face for the sun to smile upon
> and radiantly, thro' Fall's bright glow, he smiles,
> and brings the Peace of God![81]

At the end of October Charlie was still ailing; Harmony coos over his "poor sore heels." But more to the point,

Do you know how I love you and how perfectly adorable you are altogether to me? I can never tell you how I feel when I kiss you—you are a man and child and my best Beloved all together.

[Next day:] In church I thought all of a sudden of your father so intensely that the tears came into my eyes . . . actually as if I'd known him. I almost felt him and I am sure he knows all about this and how dearly I love you.[82]

In Harmony, Ives found the second great figure in his life, but so different from the first one—his father, brilliant and inspiring but also demanding and admonishing; now the lover who unconditionally accepted and admired and understood him as an artist and person, and allowed him finally to accept and understand it himself:

One thing I am certain of is that, if I have done anything good in music, it was, first, because of my father, and second, because of my wife. . . . *She* urged me on my way— to be myself! *She* gave me not only help but a confidence that no one else since father had given me.[83]

After the first declaration they believed they were keeping things discreet. The Twichells, of course, had been waiting months for him to speak up, and now they had to wait another month for the cat to escape the bag. On November 12 Harmony wrote with genuine shock, "I saw Aunt Sally just for a moment and Charlie, she <u>knows</u>. In fact she asked me a good many days ago and I told her yes, I was engaged. . . . I cant bear to tell anyone else but we must tell mother." In response, her mother told Harmony that she had once gone to visit legendary matriarch Sarah Ives in Danbury.[84] Finally, the day after they all watched a Yale-Princeton football game in New Haven, Ives asked father Joe for his blessing. "It was not much of a surprise," he noted in his diary. "He is a classmate of Dave's who has loved him fondly."[85] A few days after that, Charlie sent the Reverend a letter he immediately regretted. To Harmony: "I wrote your father yesterday, not much of a letter . . . as I express myself so poorly."[86] He was, as usual, an astute judge of his work. He had written Joe Twichell,

It is impossible and futile for me to try to <u>write down</u> or say what Harmony means to me. . . . She is not only my idol but the reason for all highest and best things that man could live for. / I have always felt unworthy of her but don't think it best for her to let myself think much about that. I can only keep pounding away at myself until I do know that I deserve all that she has given and done for me. . . . / But what I wanted to ask and wanted to write you especially for . . . [is] to ask if you will let me come to you, as Dave does when he wants to talk things over and get your advice and encouragement.

Father died just at the time I needed him most. It's been years since I've had an older man that I felt like going to when things seem to go wrong or a something comes up when it's hard to figure out which is the best or right thing to do. . . . / I hope you'll let me—<u>Please do.</u> Whenever you come to New York, if you can conveniently, I hope you'll let me see you if only for lunch or something like that.

He ends this letter with a P.S.: "Received copies this morning from Dave, of his and Dr. Kinghorn's 'sputum' thesis and researches."[87]

Thus bashfully and mawkishly did Ives try for the last time to find a replacement for his father. It had not worked with Horatio Parker or Billy Phelps or even John Griggs, and it would not work with Joe Twichell. The Reverend expressed his appreciation of the letter, but he was getting old and tired. He had a lot of children and more in-laws and many more parishioners and friends on his mind, and only so much energy to give this new son-in-law. Daughter Sally's mental illness was further wearing him down. Besides, Ives would discover he did not need a substitute father any more. Harmony would be all he needed, as he was for her.

After the announcement, things settled into a pattern. Charlie was still not healthy and Harmony came down with a case of peritonitis that kept her for weeks sitting in the family home dreaming, reading, thinking, and writing to Charlie. Soon after the parents gave their blessing, other members of the family added their own. Sister Sally wrote Harmony, "Louise and I have always agreed that Charlie was wonderfully attractive. . . . His music is so a part of him that he affects you the same way it does." Newly married Dave wrote his closest sister a strangely fervent letter:

You both are knowing the very heart of the matter. In its power and blessedness it is a weird phenomenon, and how barren a life that does not know it. I know how real love grows more binding every day. . . . You know how I have always loved Charlie. He is real and has a character of solid gold.

Puckish Deac, whom Charlie had long enjoyed, wrote congratulations in his mode:

What ain't you up to old man, you must be growing young again, bully for you I say. You wanto treat em pretty, as dear Meg has a very warm place in my heart boy. I am proud of each of you, and I know you two will match up "O.K." . . . Well I can't say much more now, as I have to go over to Dr. K's and open some Prince Island oysters for him.[88]

After suitable hair-pulling and strain and compromise, the wedding was set for June 1908.

A new life had begun, and a dialogue. The story of that dialogue contains more than the usual lover's colloquy, the idyllic and practical part. For these two it had to be more. They were earnest and intelligent and religious people, and even if Harmony Twichell had fallen in love mainly with Charles Ives the man, his music still stood within the inner circle of their relationship. Their dialogue about the place and meaning of his music in their lives would develop in conversations and letters over the next months, amidst the sweet words. The surviving words are almost all hers. He destroyed his letters, probably because their awkwardness embarrassed him in comparison to her guileless and beautiful ones. Ives's real love letters are in his music.

During their courtship Harmony, hearing that brother Joe was going to become a preacher, had written Charlie, "think of Joe becoming one of those awful theologues we girls always avoided."[89] Neither she nor her father had been interested in fancy theories about religion and divinity. But now she and

Charlie began to formulate a kind of theology around themselves and his music. Only her half of the dialogue survives on paper, but it belongs to both of them. In those months Harmony, bedridden much of the time, seems under the influence of illness and love and her sense of the divine to have been in a kind of sustained ecstasy, to which Ives, stuck most of the time in his office in New York, contributed as best he could.

The first element in their theology was the revelation of love itself:

Charlie what you see in me that is admirable to you is only what the power of loving has done. . . . This flame of love—and I see now why it's been called that so much—is the most purifying and illuminating thing in this world—or any world.[90]

You don't know Charlie, how changed I am—I was really a wanderer before and now, darling, I'm home. You've given me my life.[91]

Then came another element: they began to see their love as an adumbration of divine love, and it was their duty and joy to reflect it into the world:

Darling—I feel so strongly what you say about our love . . . bringing happiness into other lives besides our own—I know the joy & beauty of it can be communicated to others and that is what I long to do with it—to give out of my abundance that the world may be a little happier.[92]

Charlie dear, your love is the greatest help & dearest possession I have . . . take mine & use it dear, & dont be afraid ever to ask things of it. . . . if at the end of my life I could know it had been to you what you ask a woman's love to be I'd feel that my life had fulfilled itself—Demand everything of it.[93]

May I live to guard & grow more worthy of the love you give me . . . always, darling, we will give God thanks & praise for revealing Himself as much as he has in each of us to the other—I care to love you so fully, so utterly because it is all just God & religion . . . in fact I feel as if I'd just really begun to experience the meaning of religion in my life . . . no one ever had a clearer call to their life's fulfillment & duty than I have had thru my love . . . my dear, dear love.[94]

And finally, as the wedding approached, after they had visited Danbury and spent days with his family, walked the streets and fields of his childhood, stayed in the old Ives House, they put the last element into their private theology.

I think, as you say, that living our lives for each other & for those with whom we come in contact generously & with sympathy & compassion & love, is the best & most beautiful way of expressing our love . . . but to put it too into a concrete form of music or words would be a wonderful happiness, wouldn't it? I think you will & that will be doing it for both of us, my darling, my blessed lamb.[95]

My darling, nearer & dearer to me than anything in all life—your letter this morning was so welcome & so wonderful—Beloved I feel your love so gloriously it is around me and the crown of my life. . . . I too long to do one perfect thing to show my perfect love. . . . What it is entire that is stronger & greater than love that it and you are the revelation of God to me [and what] it can do & <u>will</u> do is to make our lives good & helpful. . . . The comfort of a beautiful expression of our love in music or words is that it would let people see in a concrete form the beauty of it and share, if but for a moment the heaven we know.[96]

This was the meaning, finally revealed to him, of what Ives had been aiming for in all those years of scribbling on paper, all that fascinating, incomparably bold, sometimes moving, but never quite focused music. Here was a key to the music of the ages. Their love was a reflection of God's love; his music would be their way of spreading that love into the world. The trajectory of that shared faith would rise over the next decade in his work and reach its zenith in the Fourth Symphony. When Charles Ives died after a half century of mingling their lives, Harmony would quote to friends a poem she had just read: "We knew joy unchanging and thro' this unchanging joy I apprehend the joy unchangeable."[97]

As the wedding neared in 1908, the problems of arranging the ceremony and finding an apartment in New York forced themselves onto center stage, at the same time as Charlie and Harmony speculated about how they wanted to live. Most of Ives's surviving letters to his fiancée have more to do with business than affection. He wrote her in May 1908:

My Best Beloved / Am just back from Jersey—Newark and had one devil of a day. The former manager whose place we took came in with his lawyer—who by the way is suing the Co.—on what grounds I can't figure—although they took about 2 hours— trying to explain—Hoffman who's out for Hoffman—listened as long as he could and then started writing letters—the lawyer after a long Micawber speech would wind up at the end of each effort—am I not right? and look at Hoffman—Harry usually answered—no—then seeing his error—prima facei—would jump around making 10 blots on his letter and shout "yes"—and then lose all interest until the next crisis came.[98]

Increasingly their families entered into the story. In March 1908 Harmony, her peritonitis lingering, accompanied Charlie's Aunt Amelia to a sanitarium in New Jersey and then to Atlantic City.[99] Next month Amelia tried to wheedle the couple into living with her in the old house: "If you knew how lonely I get at times . . . you could begin to realize what your being here would mean to me."[100] Her request was politely ignored. Amelia contented herself with dispensing advice about the wedding. Joe Twichell was sinking into a funk from which he would never really emerge: "It almost <u>kills</u> me to see Dad so solemn," she wrote Charlie. "I think he's tired, but Mother says he feels having a daughter get married a good deal." They made a ceremonial visit to Uncle Mark, to exhibit the bridegroom. "Well," growled the grizzled Twain, "the fore seems all right; turn him around and let's see about the aft."[101] To Harmony's sister Sue, who told him about Ives's music, Twain said, "Now that the young man has joined the Twichell family, he will get the same inspiration from his Harmony that I did from Joe and his Harmony."[102] The younger Harmony's embrace of the Victorian role of artist's wife, to lose herself in her husband as supporter and muse, probably had much to do with her experience of Twain and his irreplaceable Livy.

By May, Charlie's mother Mollie—actively entering the scene for a change—had helped them find an apartment in New York, at 70 West 11th, where some friends of hers had been living.[103] As wedding day neared, the tone of Harmony's letters shifted from romance toward questions practical and religious. In February, Harmony laid out an accurate prophecy of the life they would lead, very different from the way they had lived before, which their socially prominent families lived, which people like them were supposed to live:

I've been thinking of ways and longing to make and keep my heart and life what our love would have it. For one thing, we must plan to have times for leisure of thought and we must try and read a lot, the best books—we can live with the noblest people that have lived that way—and we will have your music. . . . I have a horror of fitting into things in N.Y. . . . and of having no quiet hours and solitude—I think I never shall, for I hate it. . . . And then, dearest, we must grow in our perception of the spiritual and unseen things thro our religion—and we can only do that by exercise in religion—by observance.

So it would be. Many couples have begun by declaring they will live only for each other and care little for the outside world. Few stick to that declaration to the extent Charles and Harmony Ives would. In nearly every photo of them, they are pressed as close as they can get. They would live a great deal of the rest of their lives in sight of each other, often within arm's reach. Most of their evenings would be spent with Harmony reading aloud their favorite authors—Dickens, Trollope, Browning, among others. And they would be regular churchgoers. They were believers, Harmony more conventionally than her husband, but they had also grown up in churches; they were comfortable amidst the old hymns and inspiring words. Whatever meaning they would find in life and love and music, for them it naturally grew from a foundation in religion.

On June 9, 1908, Charles Ives and Harmony Twichell were married by her father at his Asylum Hill Church in Hartford. About fifty friends and family came, including Dave and the other Twichell siblings and spouses, college friends of Charlie's, Mike Myrick, Aunt Amelia, Uncles Ike and Joe, and Mollie Ives somewhere out of the way. They returned to the parish house for the reception. The couple had come to marriage late: the groom was almost thirty-four, the bride had turned thirty-two five days before. Charlie was, by his standards, a touch fleshy in those days, clean-shaven, just beginning to go bald. In his wedding suit he looked, in fact, quite like a prosperous business executive. Harmony had matured from her Gibson Girl years to become a strong-featured woman; her name reflected her face as well as her personality. In wedding snapshots she appears serene and happy, while Charlie looks mortified in the middle of all the white satin. The formal wedding photo, everyone posing on the elegant lawn of the parish house, is all Twichells and their spouses except for Charlie: Joe looking stolid and his wife prematurely aged, Dave still handsome but a little haggard, Deac tanned and gawky like a farmer who had strayed into some distinguished family's picture.

Charles and Harmony Ives's wedding—the new couple in middle rear, Deac in left rear, Dave in right rear, Reverend Twichell and his wife Harmony seated in the middle.

Then the newlyweds headed out by motorcar for the honeymoon. In the next two weeks, rather than having a languid and romantic interlude, they seemed to be infected by an insatiable desire to stay in motion. After a night in Middletown, Connecticut, at Aunt Sally Dunham's, they went on to an inn in Salisbury (preserving the receipt for that first night alone), and on the 11th walked to Lakeville, where Charlie bought a hat, pipe, and razor strap. Next day they climbed Mount Riga, the day after that watched a baseball game, toured a cemetery, and took a train for Great Barrington, in western Massachusetts. A couple of days later they hiked nine miles in a downpour. And so on, in various picturesque Berkshire locales. On the 20th they took a train to Connecticut, where Aunt Amelia and Aunt Nell Parmelee met them with a buggy and the family horse Rocket, and dropped them off at the Wayside Inn in New Milford. After several days bustling around the Connecticut country-side, Charlie and Harmony arrived in New York, to 70 West 11th Street, on June 25. "Our Book" notes of the 30th, "1st meal at our own table—break-fast." A week later, Mollie Ives and brother Moss visited, and soon after that Bart Yung and George Lewis.[104]

There was a sort of second honeymoon to the Berkshires a month after the wedding. On July 28, "Our Book" notes "Sunday morning walk . . . near Stockbridge." As they walked along the Housatonic, still in the reverie of new marriage, the sound of a hymn, *Dorrnance,* floated over the water. "We walked in the meadows along the river," Ives recalled, "and heard the distant singing from the church across the river. The mist had not entirely left the river bed, and the colors, the running water, the banks and elm trees were something that one would always remember."[105] When they got back to New York, Harmony saw Charlie writing something down.[106] He was trying to get that scene into music: the murmuring water and the trees, the hymn drifting through them, and the revelation of human and divine love penetrating all of it. He was writing the first sketch for *The Housatonic at Stockbridge.* His matu-rity had begun.

Measuring the Prospect

THE PROSPERITY OF Charles Ives and Julian Myrick in the life insurance industry would follow from a lucky alignment of talents, ambition, and understanding of the historical moment. The partners floated to the top of the business after the turn of the century, when the economy was burgeoning and insurance becoming less a luxury than a safety net for people across the economic spectrum. Millions were crowding into cities, leaving behind the farms and small towns that had kept families close and sustaining; other citydwellers had left families in the Old World. As a result, Ma and Pa were no longer sure the children would be around to take care of them, and widows and orphans could no longer depend on Granddad and Uncle to put a roof over their heads. In the absence of government commitment to treating the new maladies of capitalism and urbanization, it was left mainly to charity and commerce to look after the ones who fell between the cracks.

So it was that the insurance industry found itself in one of the most agreeable of business situations: selling a product most families actually needed. All that was necessary was to convince them of the fact. Charles Ives would address that challenge earnestly during his career in business. A former employee remembered Ives telling him, "There was not a service that I could render to my fellow man that was more important than the business of life insurance, because it instilled in the soul and mind of my fellow man the responsibility of meeting his obligations."[1]

History and demographics cooperated with Charles Ives and Mike Myrick not only in the broader social respects but in a more direct way, beginning one evening at the end of January 1905 when James Hazen Hyde threw a party at Sherry's ballroom in New York.

The host was the son of Henry B. Hyde, founder of the Equitable Life Insurance Company and Gilded Age tycoon. Son James, accordingly, was about as well set up as a young man can get. The routine nepotism of the era, plus the cozy cohabitation between life insurance and other big business and finance, had already provided James director's seats at the Equitable and forty-six other companies.[2] The next year he was slated, at thirty, to take over his father's company. The younger Hyde's primary interest, however, was in having a grand time on a splendid scale.[3] He had a passion for everything French; his party preparations involved a Beaux-Arts-trained architect remaking Sherry's ballroom, already the most sumptuous in the country, into a replica of the court of Louis XV, down to the costumes of the entertainers. The entertainers consisted of forty members of the Metropolitan Opera Orchestra, the full Met corps de ballet, and celebrated actress Madame Réjane, who had been imported from France to star in a racy little farce written for the occasion. The flower of New York society showed up for the ball, each nabob doing her and his best to outdo the rest in eighteenth-centuryish profligacy. The dancing and singing and playacting and feasting went off handsomely. Eager to show the world what high society looked like in its native habitat, Hyde hired photographers to shoot every breathtaking detail.

The photos proved not only the last straw and James Hazen Hyde's downfall, they nearly wrecked the life insurance industry. The tab for the party came to something over a quarter million (1991) dollars, rumored to be charged to the account of Equitable Life. Muckrakers began working overtime to find out why the company had that kind of money to burn. They discovered quite a number of interesting things. Over the next months the public rocked from titillation to outrage as a series of revelations detailed what had filled the coffers of these "robber barons" and "bloodsuckers."

By 1905 the American life insurance industry, less than a century old, had become one of the giants of American business. Mutual, first of the big insurance companies to put life insurance on its books, issued its first policy in 1843.[4] The amount of insurance in force in the United States had been climbing faster than the population for some two decades when Charles Ives began working as an actuary's assistant. Boom led to abuse; government regulation, still finding its footing in a laissez-faire age, was slow to catch up. In 1905–6 the American public learned that the corruption of the insurance industry went considerably deeper than fancy balls and French actresses and nepotism. Insurance profits were funneled into all sorts of covert speculation in banks and railroads, in the houses of Morgan and Rockefeller et al. The Big Three companies—Mutual, Equitable, and New York Life—controlled some of their own trusts and banks, whose investors unknowingly assumed risks from the insurance business. Companies gave managers of individual agencies, notably Ives's boss Colonel Raymond, freedom to engage in their own speculations. There was plenty of cash available to keep government away, the largesse including a Mutual-maintained "House of Mirth" near Albany, dedicated to making New York legislators happy.[5]

The public was further enlightened during committee hearings set up by the New York State legislature, chaired by Senator William W. Armstrong. From that day to this, for the insurance industry the Armstrong Committee has been *the Investigation*. Chief counsel Charles Evans Hughes, with a courtly relentlessness that paved his way to the New York governorship and the U.S. Supreme Court, sat the principals down before the public and defrocked them. When, for example, imperious Mutual president Richard McCurdy proclaimed that life insurance was "a great beneficent missionary institution," Hughes politely responded, "The question comes back to the salaries of the missionaries." Fifteen million dollars of those tithes, it turned out, had gone to McCurdy's family.[6]

As a result of the Investigation, by the end of 1906 New York State possessed the toughest insurance regulations in the country; they became a model for all the states. The more immediate result was a spasm of disillusion, discouragement, and scapegoating in the industry. The dozens of executives forcibly rusticated included McCurdy, James Hazen Hyde (he departed for France), and Ives's employer Colonel Raymond, whose giant agency was dismantled by Mutual. In the longer run, though, the new laws reduced corruption and increased public confidence. The graph of life insurance growth, which climbed steadily from about 1880 until the Great Depression, shows the aftermath of the Investigation as only a brief hesitation. At Mutual, between 1907 and 1917 the amount of ordinary life insurance in force doubled. In the boom times between 1914 and the Wall Street crash in 1929, the overall amount of new Mutual business nearly quadrupled.[7] Charles Ives and Mike Myrick found themselves standing in a historic sweet spot, with the ideas and talents to make a fortune.

Ives never wrote about how he viewed the Investigation and the corruption that precipitated it. His writings on life insurance would never vary from practical and idealistic. Moral ambiguity was not his style, and he was generously endowed with the American propensity for refusing to see what one does not want to see. Ives himself had a consistent honesty and integrity of intention, even when things did not play out strictly that way in practice. And he had never been part of the genteel lifestyle or sympathetic to it. Maybe he felt the tycoons got what they deserved in the Investigation. Besides, idealism would prove a useful selling tool in a business that had spectacularly compromised itself.

In any case, the effect of the Investigation on Ives and Myrick was dramatic. The departure of so many executives left a power vacuum that the two bright young men stepped into. The possibilities must have been on their minds during their Old Point Comfort vacation of Christmas 1906, when Ives was recovering from his breakdown, when they planned out the enterprise that opened as Ives & Co., at 51 Liberty Street, on January 1, 1907. Within five years they would have one of the biggest agencies in the country.

Ives & Co. operated in New York, Hartford, and Newark for the relatively small Washington Life Insurance Company. Over the next year and a half Ives developed his organizational skills and built up business nicely. In the same period he sketched some revolutionary musical works and courted the woman with whom he hoped to start his family. Ives & Co. had a branch office in Harmony Twichell's hometown; there were lots of trips to Hartford to take care of business and romance. When Charlie and Harmony married in June 1908, he was the rising executive with his own little agency.

In 1907–8, while Ives's composing amounted mainly to laboratory pieces, in his business he began searching for better ways to sell his wares. Now that he had his own company the Ives business instincts, the blood heritage of both Isaacs and George White Ives and the Whites and the Merritts, emerged as they never had with Charlie's father or his brother. They emerged, though, like everything else concerning Charles Ives, singularly.

His most productive business innovation, as it turned out, was one of his first: Ives and Myrick began recruiting general insurance brokers from around the industry to sell policies part-time for their agency. Gregarious Mike was central to this process of enlisting salesmen; shy Charlie could never have done it so well alone. Over the years, the network of salesmen they developed— eventually hundreds of them—brought in torrents of customers. Beyond Ives's more celebrated innovations, this simple idea was the real foundation of the partner's prosperity.[8] An employee remembered them recruiting at the Mutual actuarial department: "[There were] about sixty people at two long rows of desks. Mr. Myrick went down one aisle and Mr. Ives down the other and they passed out cards, saying they would like to have us contract with Ives & Myrick to handle any business we got."[9] For their second agency, a pithy ad in the *Times* attracted agents for years: "$100,000 [sold]—$1500 [commission], $200,000—$3000. Interested? Call Ives & Myrick."

Ives was one of the first to develop standard letters to send prospects.[10] "There isn't a young married man in New York," began one year's Letter No. 1, "that doesn't need some kind of life insurance. What is the right kind?" Letter No. 2 was for people whose business had grown, No. 3 for new businesses, No. 4 for soldiers. All were carefully calculated pitches. Rather than writing his own off-the-cuff solicitations, an agent now had only to tell a secretary, "Send No. 3."

An Ives paper on general suggestions for selling business insurance, written during the Ives & Co. period, is extravagantly detailed given that its writer had personally probably never sold a policy:

Don't try to make TOO MANY points—no matter how good your arguments may be. Always be on the lookout for a chance to close in, get the application or arrange a medical examination. In this connection, put what you have to say in the form of a statement, not a question. There comes a time . . . when he must chance offending the prospect and losing out altogether, by "taking the bull by the horns" and "by going to the mat hard". . . . [After several other tactics practical and psychological:] If you cannot interest the prospect . . . try not to leave his office without getting some information for future reference. At least get the date of birth. . . . If you cannot interest the head man, make him at least admit that your plan in principle is valuable. . . . It is not a bad plan to carry a specimen-bottle with you. [Ives does not suggest how the agent should bring up the last.][11]

Ives already showed the incisive, straightforward prose style that would distinguish his business writing. This was a different game than art. Most of this prose—including the companies' advertising—would have little "Ivesian" in it. Only later, mainly in the 1920s, would his office prose take on Transcendental overtones. More characteristic copy is shown in a 1907 Ives & Co. ad:

It is important to know that a life insurance company is legally liable only for that which it GUARANTEES. The Washington Life has met its guarantees promptly since its organization in 1860, $48,000,000 having been paid to its policyholders. . . . Since [the new president's] occupancy the company has shown PHENOMENAL advancement. . . . This company is a "COMER."[12]

In fact, this company was a goner: In 1908 Pittsburgh Life bought out Washington Life. Since the new owners did not sell in New York, Ives & Co. evaporated and Ives had to go home and tell his bride of four months that he was out of a job. He got little chance, however, to brood about the future. His short-lived but industrious agency had been noticed; Ives and Myrick received feelers from several companies. After an appealing offer from Mutual they returned to their old company with an agency based in New York but with unlimited territory.[13]

The new agency, this time named Ives & Myrick, opened at 37 Liberty Street on January 1, 1909. Their only employee at first was William Verplanck, who as associate manager, Ives protégé, and office whipcracker would be with the company for the rest of his life.[14] In their first year the partners collected $1,600,000 in premiums (over 18 million in 1991 dollars). In 1914, it was $7,700,000; in 1919, $22,500,000. Their advertising of the 1920s would proclaim the company "THE LARGEST AGENCY without exclusive territory IN THE COUNTRY." In 1929, the last year Ives was in business, the company made $48,000,000.[15] In their twenty-one years in business for Mutual, the partners would take in the unprecedented sum, for an agency, of $450,000,000. Of that, apparently, Ives in his first dozen or so years may have made $1.8 million for himself. In 1991 dollars, that amounts to nearly 20.5 million during the first, and less prosperous, half of his career.[16]

In 1909 Ives got a physical from an agency doctor. At age thirty-four he was five feet, nine and three-quarters inches tall. As always he was wiry—waist 30 inches, chest 38, weight 152. He guessed he consumed one or two beers a day. The report mentions no pressing health problems.[17] His marriage seems to have ended a long period of shaky health.

Ives cut a singular figure walking to and from work in the financial heart of New York. A nephew said: "Willie Verplanck . . . used to tell me that Uncle

Charlie could be spotted a mile away and that there wasn't a single man in Wall Street who didn't know him. They could see him coming because of the crazy hat he'd wear, and they all were fascinated with him, because he was a real old-fashioned Connecticut Yankee with a sense of humor and eccentric ways."[18] Working out music in his head as he walked, composing during his train commutes, Ives was probably oblivious to the audience for his exotic figure, his hustling gait, his startling and ironic features.

The Ives and Myrick office around 1914. Myrick is on the left, Ives as usual out of the picture.

Much of his active life would be spent amidst the quotidian monotony of offices: the chatter of typewriters, the smells of oiled wooden desks and dusty files, the shuffle and murmur of fifty or sixty people chasing business. Ives generally stayed out of sight, writing and thinking and consulting. An employee remembered him as so shy he "almost would pull back when you spoke to him."[19] He all but apologized for asking a secretary to take dictation.[20] At the same time he was intense, volatile, full of restless energy even behind his desk. He talked fast, moved fast, worked fast, holding to the same kind of relentless schedule he had set himself as a teenage organist and ballplayer. Later, when Myrick wrote his testimonial on his partner's retirement, he would characterize Ives as a philosopher and a loner: "This remarkable student, seated . . . with pen in hand, has loved to concentrate upon and to analyze the problems of insurance and of finance, and to solve or readjust those problems with a master mind."[21] Myrick ran day-to-day operations, smoothed communications with the home office, reviewed rejected cases, put Ives's ideas in motion, spent nights and weekends (when Ives was composing) networking around the industry.[22] Behind Mike's back—they had vowed not to do it— Ives constantly slipped cash to employees down on their luck.[23] During their years together the record shows only one set-to; it was the more or less inevitable one about who did more for the company. They resolved never to bring up the subject again.[24]

Employees remembered Myrick as generally soft-spoken, agreeable, a dandy. Ives they tended to recall as a remarkable presence:

Mr. Ives was a very shy, retiring man. His office was on the courtyard, way around the corner, completely out of sight from everyone. Mr. Myrick, on the other hand, was in a glass enclosed office where he could see and be seen by everyone. . . . When [Ives] talked with someone, he elevated them. He had that—it's very hard to describe but he made everyone feel important. . . . I believe that 90% of the success of the agency was due to Mr. Ives, not only his genius, his planning, his aid to the salesmen, his teaching, but also the kind, gentle soul that he was. I never saw him angry. I never heard him speak harshly to anyone.[25]

A secretary recalled an occasion when Ives did blow up, in the 1920s, over a slight to her. During a dispute, office manager Verplanck called this secretary "Mussolini," a slur on her Italian background. She tearfully reported that to Ives, who sat her down and extolled the culture of Italy and told her she should never let anyone belittle her. Next day Ives called Verplanck into his office and employees heard him shouting from behind the door: "You treat her like a lady! She's got nothing more to do with you! She's my secretary now." Grabbing his hat and coat, Ives stormed out of the office. Everyone knew that his health was bad then, and excitement could be deadly.[26]

More often, employees would hear laughter coming from conferences in Ives's office.[27] It was cluttered in there, with papers all over the place, but like some of his music it was a clutter in which he moved decisively. Secretaries were told not to clean up; the mess was orderly in his mind.[28] Recalled employee Fred Wenzel, "I was in Mr. Ives's office one day looking for [an agent record] card . . . when Mr. Ives came in and asked what I was looking for, [and] after telling him he picked it out for me and, not to exaggerate, there must have been at least two or three thousand cards on his desk at the time. I will never forget how he knew just where to find the one I wanted."[29] Others reported similar feats of near-photographic memory. In both music and business Ives depended on that memory, though it was less reliable than he believed—with results ranging from mistaken dates to lost scores. Some employees knew Ives was involved in music, but he said little about it and nobody asked. The ones closest to him understood that he was always surrounded by music. Said a secretary, "At work sometimes Mr. Ives would be dictating a letter, and all of a sudden something in the music line would come up in his head, and he'd cut off the letter and go into the music. I think that music was on his mind all the time."[30]

As Ives & Myrick developed during the early years, Ives steadily broadened his thinking about the business, figuring the odds and angles. In 1909 he established Mutual Life's first classes for agents; the success of the idea at Ives & Myrick would help spread schools around the industry.[31] The classes were aimed at producing more systematic and professional agents, who with luck would gain more respect from the public. Besides, among other reforms the Investigation had drastically lowered agents' commissions, so salesmen had to be more efficient to get ahead.[32] Ives gave a great deal of time to the classes. A draft paper, probably from the later teens, shows some of his thinking:

In training new agents and in the office classes of instruction we have found that the most difficult thing to do in the limited time we have is to avoid a confusion of mind. In this connection we have found that if the fundamentals can be kept to their true proportion the student won't be drawn either by himself or by the enthusiasms of the instructor into the "secondary" until it is time for the "secondary." In this way details will straighten out themselves. For a student that has a clear idea of the fundamentals will appreciate the all-powerful part that the law of average plays in our business. For instance, in taking up the actuarial principles, a picture of a hypothetical company is drawn without using any technical expressions. He sees the laws that have to do with a great number of units are constant . . . . Thus he sees that unless the averages run unevenly, which they don't, that participating is a more natural way of issuing insurance than non-participating.[33]

By 1929 Ives & Myrick had an ongoing series of ten classes, with a reading list.[34] Ives apparently taught no classes himself; he trained the instructors and met privately with students to go over the material. Always he stressed motivation, altruism, spreading the gospel. One of his instructors said, "My basic premise, approved by Mr. Ives, was that in entering the business of life insurance, you would have to consider yourself as responsible as a theologian, a physician, a lawyer, and a financial adviser. I stressed to the new agents that insurance encompassed all of these fields."[35]

Even though the public was coming around to the idea that families need life insurance, they had always been suspicious of the whole affair. To many people it seemed a perverse gamble, the company betting that you will live and you betting that you will die. In his essay "Civil Disobedience," bachelor

Henry Thoreau scorned the sort of public-spiritedness Ives was trying to foster in Mutual customers:

The American has dwindled into an Odd Fellow—one who may be known by the development of his organ of gregariousness, and a manifest lack of intellect and cheerful self-reliance; whose first and chief concern . . . is to see that the almshouses are in good repair; and . . . to collect a fund for the support of the widows and orphans . . . [who] ventures to live only by the aid of the Mutual Insurance company, which has promised to bury him decently.[36]

The participation of big business in a supposedly humanitarian enterprise further sullied the picture. Wrote one turn-of-the-century insurance executive, "We have then in this business . . . an unprecedented combination of the moral and the material, of conviction and reason, of preaching and mathematics, of the zeal of the fanatic and the dispassion of a business contract." There was more to it. Viviana Zelizer writes of the "unresolved dilemma . . . the uncomfortable blend of business and altruism" that dogged the industry.[37] With no apparent discomfort, Charles Ives downplayed profit while teaching his agents some of the most tenacious foot-in-the-door tactics ever devised. This was in part symptomatic of the times. Zelizer notes that the moral appeal "yielded to the capitalist ethos, but not without compelling the latter to disguise the materialist mission in spiritual garb."[38] For Ives, the spiritual garb was capacious and sincere.

There was a related public distaste for insurance selling, which had always involved go-for-the-jugular pitches by fast-talking salesmen on commission: Your widow and children are going to the poorhouse if you don't sign.[39] The salesman pounding the streets and knocking on doors, nickel-and-diming prospects, was widely despised (which is why Yale men did not tend to be assigned the salesman's dirty work). Among the main practical problems facing Ives was how to make the public appreciate the industry more. Conversely, he knew the industry had to become more receptive to changing needs, and to make salesmen more professional and scientific in their methods. The word *scientific* was one of the great shibboleths of an era in which technology seemed to be advancing comfort and happiness year by year. It would be some time before anyone seriously questioned the benefits of progress, of applied science. This was the age of Edison and the Wright brothers, of the inventor as hero; science, or the appearance of it, was a marketing gimmick that suited the times.

"The 'peddling' of life insurance policies," Ives wrote, "is fast giving way to 'programming' the insurance needs of the public. . . . As [life insurance] functions become more and more a matter of common knowledge, the need for emotional processes, which constituted the chief stock in trade of the life insurance agent of the past, become[s] less and less."[40] Maybe, but Ives & Myrick hardly stinted old-fashioned melodrama. A 1927 issue of the agency magazine *Estate-o-Graph,* some of it perhaps written by Ives, is an illustrated compendium of the calamities that result from failure to buy life insurance. Among its parables: "From Affluence to Poverty," "Stocks Drop, Commits Suicide" (the victim shown holding a polo pony in his salad days), "Loses Fortune, Wife, Children," "Richard G. Peters dies in 1927 at age 95, blind and practically penniless."[41]

In 1910 Ives printed for his agents the first version of a how-to-sell pamphlet[42]; by 1920 it had grown into an elaborate and historic publication called *The Amount to Carry—Measuring the Prospect*. It is still read in the industry as one of the first studies of what came to be called "programming" or "estate planning," a mathematically based system of calculating the amount of insurance a given person should buy, keyed to income and expenses. The concept of estate planning would become basic to the insurance industry, and Ives's pamphlet was the most systematic analysis of the day.

In contrast to Ives's prewar insurance writings, which were mostly practical, *The Amount to Carry* begins with some ruminations on ultimate goals and purposes. For readers not interested in sociology and metaphysics but just in how to sell the stuff, Ives thoughtfully advises at the outset, "The subject matter relating to practical agency work begins in Section IV." A blurb on the back solicits criticism, declaring that "a free exchange of ideas and experiences is one of the ways by which life insurance salesmanship can be raised to higher professional standards." Thus he encourages the referendum among salesmen as a means of progress. In his business as in his musical writings of that period, his favorite words are "progress," "scientific," "natural." *The Amount to Carry* begins,

There is an innate quality in human nature which gives man the power to sense the deeper causes, or at least to be conscious that there are organic and primal laws (or whatever you care to call the fundamental values of existence) underlying all progress. Especially is this so in the social, economic, and other essential relations between men.

After this introduction, reminiscent of the Declaration of Independence and the Constitution, Ives touches on ideas that obsessed him after the war:

From evidence in all civilizations, the instinctive reasoning of the masses has been the impelling influence on social progress. . . . The influence of science will continue to help mankind realize more fully, the greater moral and spiritual values. As Voltaire suggests, "a little science takes us away from religion, and a great deal brings us back to it". . . . Perhaps we can expect little progress politically until some practical plan can be worked out to encourage people to think, and then to act, in terms of principles and convictions rather than of persons and parties. Perhaps we will have to get rid of all parties, or at least the prejudices which they thrive on, before political progress will be more secure.

Gradually he works his way down from "the foregoing, which will probably bore more readers than it will interest," to the subject at hand: "Life insurance is doing its part in the progress of the greater life values. . . . The manner of selling is becoming more and more scientific." What interests the agent is "to know how he can do his duty as it ought to be done. In answering this 'How' more accurately, the agent has many chances of effectively pressing home the perennial 'Now!' "

Finally he gets to the "How"—estate planning in action. The process is as natural as "transmitting the molecular force." It is a matter of convincing the prospect by means of simple mathematics that he performs himself: here is what you earn, here are your expenses, here are your future earnings and expenses, here is how much your family would need to sustain them if you were to die, and so here is the precise amount of life insurance you require. Through sundry circumstances and formulas, the prospect is invited to work out the corollaries for himself: "Measuring Insurance Needs," "Inadequate Conception of Insurance Amounts," "Productive Periods," "When There Are Two Children or More." In theory, somewhere in all this the prospect sells himself the policy.

Ives provides some cues for agents in how to go for the sale. A list of "Twenty Opening Suggestions" includes:

I want to talk life insurance to you for four minutes. I will tell you something no agent has ever told you. I can answer scientifically the one essential question. Do you know what that is?

My company has recently worked out an answer to a question that has been asked for forty years and never answered. Do you want to know what it is?

The Mutual Life has asked me to get your opinion about a new formula which scientifically answers an important question which all men ask.

Do you believe in natural laws or laws of chance (gambling chances)?

If I ask you a rather personal question, I hope you won't take offense. I can be of help to you in a vital matter. Is your wife spending too little or too much for clothes?

If the prospect makes one sort of objection, you answer like so. If he makes another sort of objection, here is your rejoinder. "If He Debates," runs another heading, "Your Hold On Him Is Growing." Keep him doing the figures with pad and pencil. Then, when you see him cracking, "Go to it hard now, with all the persuasive power you have—(In some cases it is well to use, at this point, the usual moral and emotional appeals [Your widow! Your orphans!].) . . . When he admits the reasonableness of it all, urge him to act, to settle the matter now; the way to his duty is self-evident." If he asks about costs at this point, "tell him quickly . . . without giving him a chance to dwell on it." As you hand him the pen, does he worry about how to make the premiums? Give him this complete monthly budget covering all necessities including, of course, life insurance premiums.

The principles of estate planning that Ives articulated in *The Amount to Carry* became essential to the industry because they worked. His plan assembled an unprecedented combination of mathematics, reasoning, and wolfish salesmanship, all at the service of an idealistic social and philosophical agenda. It was compelling on both sides of the sale. More prospects than ever did their duty and signed up. These writings were not the main reason for Ives & Myrick's success—recruiting outside brokers was—but they are the main reason for Ives's place (a middling place) in the history of the modern life insurance industry.

Schooling and estate planning were not the only ideas Ives helped pioneer. He had realized, in another happy conjunction of ideals and business evolution, that small policies for working people were going to be the meat and potatoes of the industry. He could thereby serve the little man and Mammon at the same time. "Sell to the masses!" he proclaimed: "Get into the lives of the people." Even in his 1919 article "Selling Big Policies of Life Insurance," Ives cautions near the beginning, "In the development of life insurance, as in the history of most institutions, the small unit is the crusader and the large then follows in its train."[43] This article reflects as well that as income and inheritance taxes were imposed in the teens, Ives pioneered in developing policies for business executives as a way of deferring taxes. (A policyholder can cash in a certain percentage of his premiums on retirement, so the policy serves as a kind of savings.) When Ives got married, he developed policies for young couples; when their child Edith arrived, he introduced plans to provide for children's education.[44] He also recruited foreign-born salesmen to specialize in immigrant customers; some Ives & Myrick agent solicitations are in Yiddish.

Early on, Ives seems to have discovered a theoretical foundation that would eventually be articulated for the industry by economist Solomon Heubner: your life and labor add up to a certain economic value; this value can be calculated as your insurable value, beyond which you should not go; and this life value is destroyed by your death unless you have life insurance.[45] When a bank forbade its officers to carry insurance, Ives wrote a letter for the *Eastern Underwriter* magazine declaring, "A bank cannot disregard human life values, the practical use of business insurance . . . any more than any other business can disregard them without subjecting itself to losses that will be felt in the future."[46] "Human life values" seems to have meant two things to him—the economic value of a person's life à la Heubner, and also the fundamental values necessary to social evolution: *"Life insurance is doing its part in the progress of the greater life values."*[47]

Ives's ideas and innovations ranged thus broadly from practical minutiae to philosophy and sociology. Myrick was to recall of his partner's style, "He would prepare any plan of insurance operation with the greatest, detailed accuracy backed up by tremendous imagination, would put the plan on paper for minute discussion, change and consult until the whole thing was finally set up in complete form which would interest the people purchasing insurance as well as the Agents who sold it."[48] The approach Myrick is talking about can be observed in an Ives memo of 1922, in which he throws ideology aside and goes after wealthy prospects:

Dear Mike: Business, generally speaking, is unsatisfactory. The number of applications show normal activity and there is a gain during the first six months both in applications and amount applied for (see attached memorandum). As I see it, the principle trouble at present is the small number of large applications and that so many that we do get are on a quarterly- semi-annual or term basis.

In order to get more large policies and in the quickest time, I told Bill [Verplanck] to have someone go through the cards and pick out as many cases as possible of policies of $25,000 and over. These are to be distributed among the men and arranged according to agents, the agents be seen immediately and an individual proposition worked out for writing new insurance under each case. . . .

As soon as possible, have these 20,000 names arranged according to dates of birth. This on the average, will give about 1600 prospective cases each month. First, select the policies which were written by agents who have died, left business etc. . . . Then take the rest up in order, the larger ones first. Work out the definite propositions for each case and <u>make</u> the agent present it to the man.[49]

The memo continues chapter and verse, working out an intricate, agencywide plan for developing large policies. The following year, 1923, saw a surge in Ives & Myrick profits—probably due in part to this plan, which is why Ives proudly pasted it in his scrapbook.

The two partners, different as they were, genuinely liked each other beyond their economic relations. Mike of course knew about Charlie's music, and he would be enthusiastic to have *The Fourth of July* dedicated to him. Long after Charlie died, Mike would be in the audience for the 1965 premiere of the Fourth Symphony. All along, Mike felt solicitous toward his old partner's music, in theory, anyway. In practice, the stuff was incomprehensible to him— he was a Duke Ellington man. Introducing Ives's music to a business acquaintance one day, Myrick admitted, "I never understood a damned thing he wrote."[50]

In the 1920s Ives put down some paragraphs about business that would become famous. They include a distillation of what he had been preaching at the office all along, and what he had experienced in the insurance industry:

My business experience revealed life to me in many aspects that I might otherwise have missed. In it one sees tragedy, nobility, meanness, high aims, low aims, brave hopes, faint hopes, great ideals, no ideals, and one is able to watch these work inevitable destiny. And it has seemed to me that the finer sides of these traits were not only in the majority but in the ascendancy. I have seen men fight honorably and to a finish, solely for a matter of conviction or a principle—and where expediency, probable loss of business, prestige, or position had no part and threats no effect. It is my impression that there is more open-mindedness and willingness to examine carefully the premises underlying a new or unfamiliar thing, in the world of business than in the world of music.

It is not even uncommon in business intercourse to sense a reflection of a philosophy . . . akin to a strong sense of beauty in art. To assume that business is a material
process, and only that, is to undervalue the average mind and heart. To an insurance
man there *is* an "average man" and he is humanity.

I have experienced a great fulness of life in business. The fabric of existence weaves
itself whole. You cannot set an art off in the corner and hope for it to have vitality,
reality and substance. There can be nothing *exclusive* about a substantial art. It comes
directly out of the heart of experience of life and thinking about life and living life. My
work in music helped my business and work in business helped my music.[51]

Ives is being earnest and in some ways accurate here, but characteristically
he is more ideal than real. His justification of his business career is after the
fact: if he could have supported a family and remained a professional musician,
he might have done it. Moreover, shortly before writing these paragraphs he
had raged in an office memo about the "stupid, reactionary ideas" of the
home office,[52] and had written a fifteen-page memorandum to Mutual officers
detailing current problems of direction and procedure, with suggestions on
how to deal with them.[53] The home office brushed them off. Business life
probably was, as Ives wrote, less conservative than musical life in those days;
but business did not progress as he wanted it to. Of all the pictures of everyday
life Ives painted in his music, not one of them would take place in an insurance office.

That Ives found immense success in business as an iconoclast shows that
he was capable of seeing and responding to reality in some respects better than
his competitors. One cannot paint Ives, in his prime at least, as someone
separate from the world, as a naive idealist. His words ring true about the
sense of living and breathing life his business experience gave him. At the
same time, there was always a strain of self-deception in Ives's approach. His
downplaying of the profit motive shows that self-deception, and so does his
ignoring the corruption that led to the Investigation. So does his refusal to
face his own ambitious streak, which was as strong in him as in flamboyant
Uncle Ike. Complimented on his organ playing in childhood, Charlie declared
himself a shortstop. As a grown-up, when it came time to face his own character and achievements, there was always a boyish part of him that emerged as if
kicking the dust and saying, "Shucks, it weren't nothin'." It was an authentic
response in a way, characteristically American, Yankee, even Yalie. It was
deceptive all the same. Just as he ended up composing a few works of the
highest importance partly because he had determined to do just that, the riches
he earned in life insurance resulted partly from the same kind of determination.
Ives was capable of sober self-criticism and, for that matter, of exaggerated
self-abnegation. But ambition was a sin he would never confess to.

Moreover, in business and in music, Ives's tendency to stay behind the
scenes, apart from the dusty world of pounding the streets or jockeying for

attention in the musical world, steadily drew him away from the very course
of everyday life he claimed his business experience kept close. Illness would
deepen that withdrawal. Up to a point, in business and in music, his isolation
worked for him; it kept his view on the ideal and on the big perspective. Being
a lone wolf was, up to a point, a factor in his triumph in two endeavors.
Beyond that point, though, it was a factor in his collapse both as an artist and
as a businessman.

Again, none of this is to say that Ives talked through his hat when he said
his life in business helped his music. Some of his most significant ideas seem
to have developed first in the office, then been applied to art and life. Many
fundamentals of the Ivesian business and artistic creed clearly came from the
Progressive zeitgeist—always filtered through the singular consciousness of
Charles Ives. In background, he fits historian Richard Hofstadter's profile of
the Progressive man: Yankee Protestant, liberal Republican / Mugwump. Ives
proclaimed what Hofstadter calls the "agrarian myth"—the moral and democratic superiority of the country life, the "lost agrarian Eden [before the Civil
War] when there were few millionaires and, as they saw it, no beggars, when
the laborer had excellent prospects and the farmer had abundance, when states-
men still responded to the mood of the people and there was no such thing as
the money power."[54] That is what Ives's memory made of postwar Danbury—
a place in reality more industrialized, polluted, profit-driven, hard-drinking,
and dangerous than most small towns. Ives painted Danbury as the idyllic
country village it had not been since his father's boyhood, if then. (Even so,
his Danbury was truly a more human-sized place than the cities, and nature
closer at hand.) "Debussy's content," Ives wrote, "would have been worthier
his manner if he had hoed corn or sold newspapers for a living, for in this way
he might have gained a deeper vitality and a truer theme to sing at night and
of a Sunday."[55] This is the agrarian myth applied to aesthetics: the farmer with
his hoe is a healthier model for the artist than the Bohemian city slicker.[56]

Progressives everywhere rebelled against urban political bosses and their
corrupt party machines. Ives took up that theme with a vengeance. "Perhaps
we will have to get rid of all parties," he wrote in *The Amount to Carry*.
His Twentieth Amendment proposed to bypass not only political parties but
representative democracy: "The need of leaders in the old sense is fast going."[57] His amendment gives all lawmaking power to the voters, in a radical
conflation of New England town meeting and the Progressive ballot referendum. Few in Ives's day or since have proposed to carry direct democracy as far
as he wanted to.

Hofstadter writes, "The central theme in Progressivism was [a] revolt
against the industrial discipline. . . . The Progressives . . . did not seriously
propose to dismantle [industrial] society [but] . . . to keep the benefits of the
emerging organization of life and yet to retain the scheme of individualistic
values that this organization was destroying."[58] Compare Ives, who appealed
regularly to science but also looked back to the agrarian Eden. In a 1929

newspaper ad he begins with a quote from Emerson ("I appeal from your customs. I must be myself") and goes on to formulate his pitch to potential salesmen in terms of resisting the conformity of modern life:

There is a tendency, today, to minimize the individual and to exaggerate the machine-like customs of business, and of life. Some men . . . are becoming "cogs" and they don't want to be "cogs." Work in the life insurance field, certainly doesn't cramp individuality, ingenuity, or initiative.[59]

But Ives's thinking went beyond a reflection and exaggeration of the Progressive agenda. He also forged highly personal connections among his business and artistic lives and his vision of the millennium. At least in part, his ideas and his practice lived up to his stated ideal: "The fabric of existence weaves itself whole. You cannot set an art off in the corner and hope for it to have vitality, reality and substance."

Behind Ives's practical work in life insurance lay a core of ideas and values that eventually took in the whole human community—or at least attempted to. Ives began his insurance career learning the foundation of the business, actuarial science. An actuary works with the always-evolving mortality tables, figuring death curves for various groups, calculating risks, generating the premium schedules that must prophesy mortality probabilities for years into the future. Learning the process of turning people into statistics, into graphs from cradle to grave, gave Ives a perspective broader than most people achieve in their younger years. He saw human life and hope and history take shape on a page, in the law of averages. So from early on he saw life as a unity, from the individual to the mass: *the fabric of existence weaves itself whole.* He knew the limitations of statistics—his private memos would be full of lampoons of them—but the numbers impressed him all the same. It is no accident that his phrase "human life values" means at once the cash value of a person's life and labor, and the humanistic and spiritual values people live by.

Both as artist and businessman Ives began early on to think about the progress of life, individually and en masse. What are the fundamental values and requirements? What do you need at this age, at that age? A man "wants to have his boy go to college, he wants to ease up in business when he gets old, he wants to establish a future fund for this purpose or an income for that. . . . He wants to feels that the structure he has built—the fruit of his heart and mind—will live after him and do their work."[60] What do a working man and his wife need, and their children? What does a businessman need, for his family and for his business? What does modern civilization need, and how can business help meet, and profit from, those needs, and thereby advance business and society together? What faculties and emotions do insurance men need to arouse, to make customers aware of their obligations to family and the future? *How can music help advance civilization?* In its philosophical dimension, the story of Ives's parallel careers would turn around these fundamental questions. "To an insurance man," he wrote, "there *is* an 'average man' and he is humanity." That conviction lies at the intersection of his business, his music, and his politics. It developed first in business.

What Ives saw around him in the United States of the century's first decade was this: a dissolution of agrarian communities and family ties, and a desperate need for something to replace them in the brutal struggle of modern industrial capitalism. Himself a product of a changing and dissolving small-town community, Ives began to define his task as extending traditional small-town values into larger and larger communities—the city, the country, ultimately the People's World Union. Policyholders were themselves a kind of community. Life insurance was a way of binding people together for mutual benefit. *Music was another way*. Jane Addams had proclaimed that humanity must no longer submit to the indifferent forces of natural evolution or unbridled capitalism, but must direct its own evolution. Ives saw that the fundamental needs and responsibilities of life, which used to be addressed by family and neighbors, must now be taken over by a larger community. Someday, he prophesied, all humanity would become an extension of the primal village: an extension not of the real, but of the mythical Danbury.

Ives's writings from the workplace build up piecemeal a picture of his millennial philosophy. Later it would be pursued, less piecemeal if never entirely coherently, in his aesthetic and social essays. "The idea that made [my business success] possible was called not only visionary but that it would ruin us within a year," he writes in a sketch for his 1919 story/essay "George's Adventure." "I assumed that the law of averages was divine, and that . . . *most* men were honest and most men were intelligent."[61] Given that faith, the process of helping people make the right decisions—about life insurance or about how to run the country—was a matter of providing them with clear and accurate information and letting them make the decision. Thus *The Amount to Carry,* thus his Twentieth Amendment proposal, thus his dream of the People's World Union. The divine law of averages would ensure that the majority would tend to make the right decisions. Society, evolving along with nature, moves always toward greater democracy, greater cooperation, greater unity within its inevitable diversity. "Darwin told but another of God's parables," Ives wrote in another sketch for "George's Adventure."[62] He extended this point in one of the speeches he wrote for Mike Myrick to deliver at a business conference:

Because the world has been able to get along without life insurance until comparatively recently, it has been looked upon to some extent as a luxury, necessary perhaps to those with a deeper sense of responsibility, but not a first essential. . . . Before insurance existed as an institution the family paid the loss; now the company pays it. The need for a better distribution of man's efforts in producing economic goods, and for something that would equalize the waste after [retirement,] was felt long before the mortality tables were compiled. Social evolution is a closer forbear of life insurance than the actuary.[63]

Time and again, Ives preached his essential points. Life insurance is a natural step in social evolution, a humanistic and scientific response to fundamental needs. Buying insurance has become a basic responsibility of the head of a family. Teaching men, most of them innately good and reasonable, to fulfill that responsibility is a matter of presenting them with a few easily comprehensible facts. Spreading that responsibility in society is an indispensable part of progress toward a better and more prosperous community. Insurance "is an integral part of social evolution, an organism that has not been thrown on society, but which society has evolved."[64] In another paper: "Without going far in the field of metaphysics, an insurance idealist might hold that life insurance is altruism scientifically organized, or perhaps commercialized, accepting the term as more of a paradox than a contradiction. A practical insurance man will say that life insurance has a certain influence on the moral and economic development of a country."[65] If life insurance were abolished, "Mankind in general would be thrown backward into a state of mind that would not be far from . . . the middle ages. Civilization . . . would have to adjust itself to many medieval standards, for Life Insurance has become not only a vital part of civilization but a civilizer itself."[66]

So it was more than a sales pitch when Ives took new employees aside and told them, "There was not a service I could render to my fellow man that was more important than the business of life insurance." It was entirely honest; it happened also to be a *good* pitch, one that helped take Ives and Myrick to the top of their industry. For all the anti-commercialism of his musical ideals, Ives had no qualms about assessing the value of his business philosophy in cash terms: "Our business grew from a few thousands to 15,000,000 in twelve years. . . . The largest [competitor], who did 2,000,000 when he told us what failures we would be, has made an increase to 4,000,000 (with the same goods to sell)."[67] To Ives, dollars validated his ideals in ways music could not.

If his business life demonstrated that a few fundamental, mostly Progressive ideals could pay off in dollars and cents, it would follow logically, to him, that they could pay off in art and politics as well. When the First World War broke out and threw incalculable amounts of blood and money against the Progressives' faith, Ives's response would be not a breakdown of conviction, but a physical breakdown. He may have been fated to that from birth, but the war would pull the trigger. For him it would be the end not of idealism, but rather of realism in his ideals.

A unifying theme in all Ives's work, in and out of music, was the dream of a universal community. Music, he wrote near the end of his creative life, "will develop possibilities inconceivable now—a language so transcendent that its heights and depths will be common to all mankind."[68] "Build a People's World Union," he would write still later, in his dotage, "where every honest man and every honest country has a fair chance to work out their own problems in their own way and live their own natural life—a life that God Almighty will be proud of."[69] That his music largely existed outside the social and artistic milieus of its time galled and outraged him now and then, but did not ultimately discourage him. His situation, he might have said, was "more of a paradox than a contradiction." One must remember that paradox, for Charles Ives, was a high road to truth. It would be the high road of his music as well. Like all Progressives, he dreamed of a higher, more democratic, more spiritual humanity, a transcendent new community.[70] He saw everything he did as a signpost pointing in that direction. In his life and art, the fabric of existence wove itself whole.

Ives moved his business once and his home several times during 1907–17, when he was settling into marriage, acquiring a child, building his agency, and writing his most revolutionary music. Ives & Myrick moved in February 1914 from 37 Liberty to 38 Nassau, on the second floor of the Mutual Life home office building. By then the partners had built the second largest Mutual agency.[71] In the new place Ives occupied a corner office with big windows facing Nassau and Liberty Streets. Myrick's domain was the long, hall-like room with its imposing rows of desks, its agents and secretaries.[72]

In a series of private memos Ives wrote that month, during a period of galloping business and incredible creative activity, he meditated on his life. It was then that his thoughts returned to the make-believe trains of his childhood, recalled while "Travelling down & back to Redding now every day" on a grown-up train. Other jottings hint at rankling dissatisfaction, uncertainty, perhaps depression. They also reveal that when writing his paeans to the virtues of business he fudged considerably.

Feb 16—[19]14 1st day of business in new offices. There isn't anything humble or homely about [them] as with the old quarters. Too much mahogany—all costs too much no matter how much business we do—But it all makes an impression on some agents usually those that give us the least business

Feb 17—14 There is too much shine & make believe about these large offices—like a man digging potatoes in a dress suit. Everybody ought to dig potatoes but no one ought to wear a dress suit. Some men only tell the truth when they exaggerate (I feel that way myself most of the time)

Feb 20 A bad day underfoot misunderstood as usual—if I could arrange my thoughts through my mouth as well as those that don't reach the mouth—it would be much more comfortable for me—my mind & tongue find it hard to work in junction I said something today to a man which gave him . . . entirely the wrong impression. I knew when I was saying it, that it was almost opposite to what I had in my mind—yet I couldn't say it any differently.

Feb 25 Mike has just been elected Pres of the underwriters for 1914 He is a different kind than most of them. He says what he means at least—most associations of business-men have the same fault as the underwriters—They don't practice what they preach. Thoreau is inaccurate, exaggerates, wild in statement—but he practices what he teaches—Wagner is one of the best examples of make believe—His music is full of make believe bravery, make believe love, make believe nobility

Mch 2—14 Big snow storm. Reached office at 1^{00} came down on the crust to the station 10.6 [inches] A storm like this makes people seem more sympathetic toward each other, as they do on days before holidays or any public catastrophe. An exceptional condition relieves the routines lines in the business mind & makes them almost human.[73]

In the latter entries Ives is involved in processes of thought leading toward the *Essays Before a Sonata*. In the last one, he prophesies the day on a crowded railway platform two months later, when he would hear New Yorkers erupt into an old hymn in response to a disaster, and conceive one of his last master-pieces.

Between the lines of these jottings there seems a weariness—physical, but more than that. Ives was working superhumanly hard in 1914 and it was wearing him down. War loomed in Europe. One of his signs of frustration and exhaustion, then and later, was explosions of rage. There are signs of strain even in his marriage. From Hartford, where she was nursing her ailing father, Harmony wrote Charlie at the end of that April, soothingly but with obvious anxiety: "We must try and take life as easy as we can—lately we have been sort of complicated. It is silly to let the things one has get in the way of pure enjoyment—of course we are in a transition now & must be upset."[74] It was around that time that Ives dejectedly wrote, "A bad day underfoot misunderstood as usual." Around then he played sections of the *Concord Sonata* at an impromptu concert at First Presbyterian in New York.[75] That too was certainly misunderstood.

The strains on Charlie and Harmony, the disappointments and tragedies that would mark their life together, went back several years before that, to their first year of marriage. Harmony had become pregnant in their first weeks together. Both of them were overjoyed to anticipate the children they had long wanted, that seal of their love. Then in April 1909 Harmony was raced to the hospital where she lost the baby and was given an emergency hysterectomy. She spent nearly a month in the hospital.[76] Sister Sally came to take care of the housekeeping at 70 West 11th. Ives was devastated. On the manuscript of the moaning, painful 1913 song "Like a Sick Eagle," Ives jotted its tone and genesis: "(Draggingly) (Voice intones word with [English horn]) (not like singing) H.T.I. in Hospital Sally singing."[77] The words are from Keats:

> The spirit is too weak;
> mortality weighs heavily on me
> like unwilling sleep,
> and each imagined pinnacle and steep
> of Godlike hardship
> tells me I must die,
> like a sick eagle looking towards the sky.

Harmony's mother would write her daughter of how struck she and Sally had been with Charlie's anguish and empathy. Nobody had seen him like that before. Mother Twichell wrote,

My heart is full of joy and gratitude over you, over Sally, and I must say over dear Charley with his great loving heart. I thought myself so happy in my trust in him, but now, after the revelations of tenderness in him through the great trial that has come to you, I feel that I did not appreciate half of what was in him. With him to protect you, life cannot bring you anything you cannot bear—and still have in your heart abiding happiness.[78]

From the buoyancy of her mother's letter one might assume Harmony had experienced an uplifting case of the flu rather than a brush with death that left her childless forever. Sister Sally meanwhile was slowly being overcome by mental illness. The mother's letter shows the style of the day: do not dwell on tragedy, turn darkness into light.

During late August through mid-September 1909 much of the family were vacationing again at Pell Jones's, on Elk Lake in the Adirondacks. In her diary Harmony calls it "A perfect vacation. Charlie working on the Symphony." He was reworking the Third. On the same vacation he also sketched— using old ragtime material—what became the second movement of the Second Orchestral Set, and began orchestrating the Fugue from the First String Quartet toward the Fourth Symphony (though he did not realize that yet). Photos from the vacation look sunny and pleasant. Charlie sits beside Harmony with a board on his lap, working on the Third Symphony score; she knits, he sports sunglasses, pipe, a little Swiss cap with feather, and high leather hiking boots. (He looks, for once in a photo, almost *artistic,* even self-consciously so.) In most of the pictures Charlie is dressed the same, with feather and pipe, contriving as usual to keep his face hidden from the lens. Other pictures show the rugged logs of Pell's cabin, a covered porch with couch and chairs, a stone fireplace in the yard that slopes down to the water, the rhythmic frieze of Adirondack hills beyond. More photos: A sunny day, Dad, Mother knitting, Deac and Harmony reading in chairs in the front yard next to the fire, Charlie reclining in a hammock on the porch. The family sitting around the fire, Harmony grimacing from the smoke. Charlie, Harmony, and Sally boating, he with pipe, Harmony with parasol. They had a wonderful time. They were ready to embrace a perfect vacation in an imperfect world.[79]

In November 1909, back in Hartford, Harmony wrote Charlie in New York, "My blessed blessed Bunny, I am so glad that tomorrow at this time you will be here. . . . I miss you and I dread this evening & tonight without you— my living is all with you."[80] "Our Book" notes they spent that Christmas in Danbury, with Aunt Amelia in the old house, and next day went sleigh-riding in a snowstorm. No mention of Mollie Ives, who was surely present.[81]

The next April 21, 1910, Mark Twain died at seventy-four—near Danbury as it happened, in Redding, Connecticut. Joe Twichell rushed to officiate at his old friend's funeral. There Joe got word that his wife had fallen ill. Harmony Cushman Twichell passed away the night her husband arrived back in Hartford. Joe's own decline would accelerate from that point. A few weeks later, the family insisting, he resigned, at seventy-three, from the pulpit at Asylum Hill he had occupied for forty-five years.[82] An era passed. Harmony would spend much of her time over the next years watching over her father as he slipped into melancholy silence.

Still, four months after the death of the Twichell matriarch, they were all

Charlie and Harmony at Pell Jones's in the Adirondacks, 1909. She is recovering from an operation, he scoring the Third Symphony.

back at Pell's again. "Beautiful vacation," writes Harmony in "Our Book." There Ives began the first movement of the Fourth Symphony, reworking his setting of the hymn "Watchman" done, on Dave's suggestion, at Pell's five years before. On the way home Charlie and Harmony stayed over at the Spragues, old friends of the Twichells' whose daughter Elizabeth would figure importantly in the story of twentieth-century music and, less constructively, in Ives's story. Ives finished a draft of the Fourth Symphony movement with "Watchman" the next October. From New York he wrote Harmony in Hartford,

I have finished the score of the 1st movement and I feel fairly satisfied with it. Its free from extraneous substances & closely woven & the product of our summer at "Pells." Outside of that its value I believe is doubtful . . . how much I love to work when you're by me & how hard it is to without you.[83]

In May 1911, Harmony and Charlie moved for seven months to a small rented house in the suburbs, at Hartsdale, New York. From that point they would move six times in the next six years. Ives's life by then consisted of music, Harmony, the office, and moving—house to house, commuting from Hartsdale the nearly two years they lived there, long Adirondack vacations in 1911, 1912, and 1915. This gypsy life increased the pressure on him; so did the longing to have a retreat from the city. Besides that, the need for space was growing, along with the sheets of manuscript that tended to drift around the house like leaves in autumn.

In New York they had little social life and wanted little. Harmony would tell John Kirkpatrick that shortly after their marriage they went to dinner at some friends' house and Charlie's behavior (she did not elaborate) was so alarming that she vowed never to do it again.[84] The volatile Ives personality, familiar to generations of Danburians, would not do for genteel social occasions in Manhattan. Over the years Charlie and Harmony developed a circle of acquaintances, but on Charlie's terms. His friends during the teens were mostly musicians willing to play over his pieces now and then, or who—with more enthusiasm—played chamber music with him. (Even in later years Ives would astonish visitors with the strength of his playing.)

It was clear early on that Ives was going to prosper with his agency. His income in 1913, Ives & Myrick's fourth year and the first year of income tax, was over $10,000 (some $110,000 in 1991). So he and Harmony felt ready to buy their retreat, their Eden. An entry in "Our Book" for August 1912 notes: "Bought 14¾ acres in Redding, Conn—6 in meadow & 7 in woodland. No buildings—C.&H. joint-owners."[85] It was West Redding actually, with a view across rolling hills toward Danbury. There during the next year they designed and built a house and barn (with a stall for the horse Rocket) and a rustic cottage by the driveway where Deac would often stay, so-called "Deac's house." Ives liked having this brother-in-law around as a sort of petite Thoreau in residence; Deac had his own eccentric humor, and he laughed at Charlie's jokes. Despite family prodding, this oldest of the Twichell brothers never settled into a job or family. Charlie and Harmony spent May 1913 in Redding supervising final touches on the building, staying nights with Aunt Amelia in Danbury. That month Charlie and Deac put in nearly an acre of potatoes next to the barn. Apple trees were planted along the driveway.[86] Later there would be a tennis court and chickens. In September 1913 the Iveses spent their first month at the house.[87]

Pine Mountain and the Adirondacks had provided years of inspiration for Ives, but those were vacation spots. Now he had a room of his own where from late spring into autumn he could compose with a view of trees and hills. The house was never winterized; most years after 1913 the Iveses left Manhattan for Redding around May, and returned to the city, invariably with heavy hearts, around November. They eventually had a maid / cook or two, who went with them from city to country. West Redding was six miles from Danbury, far enough to keep Aunt Amelia at a distance and to keep out of sight what Danbury was becoming—a grimy, forgettable town full of empty factories.[88] In the Redding landscape like that of his childhood, Ives could preserve his memories of Danbury like pressed flowers.

In 1921 they expanded the house, adding a porch upstairs and under it Charlie's narrow studio, the upright piano at one end, desk with pigeonholes at the other, bookshelves along the wall full of volumes and memorabilia: his father's cornet, the old sign saying "BALL FIELD." At the same time they added the pond at the bottom of the field, for children to swim in.[89] As they designed it the Redding house is shingled and unassuming, comfortable, planned from inside out, entirely Ivesian. There is no facade and no front door; every door is the front. On the first floor most of the rooms flow into one another without doors. The second-floor hallway opens into the high-ceilinged living room below, its big window overlooking the hills. Ives's studio addition has double doors next to the piano, opening into the dining room. With them closed he had his privacy; with them open, he could play and sing out into the house. Over the years those doors would accumulate a collection of tacked-up pictures and programs and business memorabilia: the collage of his life, so much like the collages in his music.[90]

In Redding close to his Danbury wellspring Ives would do much of the work on the *Concord Sonata,* the *Three Places,* the Second Orchestral Set, the *Holidays,* the Fourth Symphony, and the other works of his maturity. Here he dug his potatoes and walked in his woods. Here his spirit and imagination spread to their broadest and boldest compass. Harmony and Charlie spent their winters in New York, but West Redding would be the only place they ever again called home.

By the time the house was finished in 1913, Ives may already have evolved a long-term plan that, given his prospects, was entirely reasonable: to make enough of a pile to provide for himself and his family, then retire to Redding and devote his time to music and his garden.[91] He may have felt himself within, say, fifteen years of that pleasant prospect, leaving the office in his prime at fifty or so with a good many years left for composing. He had done his part toward realizing that goal. It was up to the fates to cooperate.

ELEVEN

Entelechy

THROUGH LATE SUMMER OF 1911, Charles Ives spent his evenings and weekends sitting at the piano of a rented cottage, much of the time working over pages of dense harmonies topped by a drifting, blues-tinted melody. The Iveses, along with beloved and broken-down family horse Rocket, had settled for the summer in the rural suburb of Hartsdale, New York. After spending the next winter in Manhattan, they would return for nearly two years to a larger place nearby, a pretty house with makeshift plumbing, no hot water, views of open fields and a chicken farm. Family and steed thrived on the property. Friends found Ives notably less nervous in the country than in the city.[1] When Rocket was up to it, Charlie rode him through the fields and woods. In Hartsdale he composed with a freedom and fertility that would continue at his own country house in West Redding.

Ives called this summer's piece the "Black March."[2] Unlike the majority of his works by 1911, it was not based on things written earlier but created from whole cloth, even if growing out of ideas and textures going back some time.[3] Though the "Black March" was intended for orchestra, Ives worked it out in two-line score-sketches. The carefully notated pages echo his hours at the keyboard, playing over and over these free but exquisitely shaped harmonies, their quiet dissonances forming a slow march in the imagination. The piece is a meditation on the Civil War and on the heart of the American racial dilemma, and a stream of consciousness no other composer had attempted before.

At some point Ives had seen Augustus Saint-Gaudens's bas-relief on Boston Common, depicting the march to war of the 54th Massachusetts Volunteer Infantry: the Civil War's legendary black regiment and, on horseback, their white colonel Robert Gould Shaw, who would fall and be buried with his men in the attack on Fort Wagner. Ives's artistic response is one of many to the story of the 54th, by writers including Emerson, James Russell Lowell, Robert Underwood Johnson, Henry James, John Berryman, and Robert Lowell, as well as Augustus Saint-Gaudens.[4]

How unexpected this music is, as a response to that sculpture. Ives grasped its most striking features: the faces of the black soldiers modeled from life; the realism so vivid one nearly hears the squeak of leather and the rattle of canteens; and the frozen marching rhythm of the legs, rank on rank. As the bending, weary legs of the soldiers approach music in bronze, Ives's music approaches poetry. Instead of a heroic piece this is a dream-march, a music of rhythmic and tonal freedom no one had heard before Ives, yet which seems timeless and inevitable. The leading string line sounds almost like blues, though Ives had never heard that music: he invented for himself the effect of a slow blues from its elements, from spirituals and work songs and minstrel music. Here and there in the wandering stream of melody we catch distant reverberations of Stephen Foster and of Civil War marching songs. *I'm comin'*, *I'm comin', for my head is bending low,* the music breathes; *The Union forever! Hurrah, boys, Hurrah!* The plangent minor thirds of *I'm comin'* and *The Union forever* melt into an echo of "Marching Through Georgia": *Hurrah! Hurrah! We bring the Jubilee!*[5]

Ives would call it *The "Saint-Gaudens" in Boston Common (Col. Shaw and His Colored Regiment)* and after various experiments place it first in the set *Three Places in New England.*[6] By the end of August 1911 he had completed the final score-sketch. Perhaps around the same time he wrote the poem that would preface the movement. Ives was an occasional and indifferent versifier, but in contemplating this subject he produced the most moving poem of his life. In his lines a vision of marching black soldiers becomes an evocation of the world spirit, and of universal emancipation.

> Moving,—Marching—Faces of Souls!
> Marked with generations of pain,
> Part-freers of a Destiny,
> Slowly, restlessly—swaying us on with you
> Towards other Freedom . . .
>
> You images of a Divine Law
> Carved in the shadow of a saddened heart—
> Never light abandoned—
> Of an age and of a nation.
>
> Above and beyond that compelling mass
> Rises the drum-beat of the common-heart
> In the silence of a strange and
> Sounding afterglow
> Moving—Marching—Faces of Souls!

Probably it was that autumn when Ives tried to play the draft of the *"Saint-Gaudens"* for New York violinist and conductor Edgar Stowell during a session of chamber music. It was a brutal awakening from the poignant dream of the subject and the music, and a pattern often repeated: after the inspiration, the humiliation. Stowell would not let Ives finish; apparently the word "awful" was spoken. Ives had heard it many times. He sighed and showed Stowell something from the Second Symphony, which was better received.[7] On another visit around 1912, Stowell glanced at the sketch of *The Fourth of July* and snapped, as Ives recalled it, "This is the best joke I have seen for a long time! Do you really think anybody would be fool enough to play a thing like that?" That day they played from a couple of the violin sonatas. Stowell was less perturbed by these, but felt obliged to point out that they weren't up to the sonata of Daniel Gregory Mason (hymn-writer Lowell Mason's grandson, who taught at Columbia). Mason's sonata is *Geigermusik,* Stowell said, real fiddle stuff.[8]

At Hartsdale another day, Ives played over the Third Symphony for visiting Yale friend Max Smith, then music critic of the New York *Press*. Responded Smith: "How did you get so modern?" This for the sweet, charming Third, in 1912. With masochistic tenacity Ives kept going. If the critic thought that was modern, Ives would show him modern. He launched into the *"Saint-Gaudens"* and parts of other in-progress pieces—*Putnam's Camp,* the *Concord,* the Fourth Symphony. As he played, Smith drifted out to the stoop and sat looking dejectedly across the fields. When Ives finished, Max intoned: "The first one was bad enough, but these were awful! The *Concord* makes me half sore, half cuckoo. How can you like horrible sounds like that?"[9]

A year or two later Ives tried the *"Saint-Gaudens"* and *Washington's Birthday* on visiting Elizabeth Sprague Coolidge. Daughter of Twichell family friends, the genteel Coolidge had some musical training and would go on to be a historic patroness of composers. That summer day in Redding around 1913, Mrs. Coolidge listened sourly, deplored the awful sounds, and finally walked out of the house. As she got in her motorcar she fired a parting shot: "Well, I must say your music makes no sense to me. It is not, to my mind, music. How is it that—studying as you have with Parker—you ever came to write like that? You ought to know the music of Daniel Gregory Mason. He has a real message."[10]

In the long chronicle of humiliations, none topped the October 1914 encounter with Franz Milcke, a German violinist who had once been New York Philharmonic concertmaster. Harmony had known Milcke in Hartford and coaxed him to come out to the house in Redding, where they were spending their second autumn. Ives was working on the Third Violin Sonata and, sensibly enough, wanted to play over the First and Second Sonatas with a good violinist before finalizing the new piece. (The sonatas went back over a decade to his organist days, but he took his time pulling them together.) Certainly it would be a bonus if the great man would get interested in the music, perhaps champion the sonatas. They were after all intended as repertoire pieces—communicative, warmly expressive, not overbold.

Milcke arrived in a buggy that autumn afternoon and dispensed a lot of grand talk. He had been a concertmaster under Anton Seidl, probably knew

Richard Strauss, and so on; weighty names dropped from his lips like talismans of the glittering world. Ives and Harmony were nervous and excited to have somebody like him in the house. Perhaps while rosining his bow and tuning up, Milcke glanced at some of the scores scattered around Ives's piano. At sight of *In Re Con Mote Et Al* and *From the Steeples and Mountains,* Ives recalled, "He jumped back, mad. Then I thought I shouldn't treat him so rude and gave him . . . the second movement of the First Symphony. He looked and felt better and smiled—'Now that's something like—etc. etc.'" But one of the experimental *Tone Roads* turned up in the symphony score, and Milcke curtly tossed it aside. They had a go at the First Violin Sonata.

Imagine Ives playing the introduction at the piano, autumn lying on the trees outside, the famous virtuoso waiting for his cue with that famous-virtuoso air. Milcke begins to play, swaying to the rhythm, the famous tone filling the house. He loses the beat, trips, stops, tries again, stops, tries again muttering this time. He is a celebrated violinist and there is not supposed to be any music in the civilized world he cannot understand and cannot play. He stops for the last time, declaring, "This is awful! It is not music, it makes no sense." Patiently, desperately, Ives plays over the page for him, several times. It only gets the violinist more agitated. Finally Milcke bolts from the room, hands clapped over his ears, moaning, "When you get awfully indigestible food in your stomach that distresses you, you can get rid of it, but I cannot get those horrible sounds out of my ears by a dose of oil!"[11] *He cannot vomit them out, he means, much as he would like to.*

An artist remembers a moment like that. Usually the immediate effect is depression, a creative stumble. Two decades later Ives wrote,

After he went, I had a kind of a feeling which I've had off and on when other more or less celebrated . . . musicians have seen or played (or tried to play) some of my music. I felt . . . that perhaps there must be something wrong with me. Said I to myself, "I'm the only one, with the exception of Mrs. Ives (and one or two other perhaps, [neighbor] Mr. Ryder, Dr. Griggs), who likes any of my music, except perhaps some of the older and more or less conventional things. (Why do I like these things?) Why do I like to work in this way and get all set up by it, while . . . it just makes everybody else mad?

The Third Violin Sonata, he goes on, "is a good sample of an occasional result of the above kind of experience. . . . The sonata on the whole is a weak sister. But these depressions didn't last long."[12] They did not last as such, but the scars accumulated Every artist needs a thick hide, but to protect his feelings and his very existence as an artist, Ives was forced to erect a wall of defenses between himself and the "experts" who told him time and again, year after year, that what he was doing was awful, crazy, not music.

The defensive wall arose from a simple formula: *If experts practically without exception tell me I am crazy and I am not, then there is something wrong with them, with their training, with the music they make their living dispensing.* There must be something terribly awry in the world of "classical" music if it so relentlessly rejected *his* music. Around 1913, the period of dismal hours with Stowell, Smith, Coolidge, Milcke, and any number of others, Ives went to an orchestral concert in New York and came home

> with a vague but strong feeling that even the best music we know, Beethoven, Bach, and Brahms (played at this concert) was too cooped up—more so than nature intended it should be . . . not only in its chord systems and relations, lines, etc., but in its . . . rhythms and spaces. . . . producing some sense of weakness, even in the great. And the conductor . . . what did he do but wear his nice permanent wave from I to IV—the ladies smiled nice, and renewed their subscriptions! Same old stuff! It came over me again . . . (as it had come over Father):—Is music an emasculated art? No, not all of it, but too much of it, even the best.[13]

In his younger years Ives had been able to shrug off the complaints of friends and congregations. But the bolder his music became and the more indignant the responses to it, the more he was forced to defend his creative consciousness, and his masculinity, by turning against the very setting for which he was writing—urban concert halls and the legions of women and wealthy men who were their main support. Ives the church musician had never been part of that world, and its orthodoxy was a genuine threat to his creative soul. The more brutal the rejections, the more bricks had to go into his defensive wall. That process left him more and more isolated inside his mental barricades, alone and stewing. In the end, his work could only be realized within the professional musical world that he rejected—and given the difficulty of his work, a highly expert level of that world.

Of all the paradoxes in Ives's inner and outer life, the dilemmas and cross-purposes, being a composer without a milieu was one of the most dangerous. The situation had existed to some extent since he and his father developed their private musical world in Danbury. By his thirties, the isolation was critical. That Ives and his music survived it must be counted an extraordinary personal and moral triumph. But inescapably, the situation tore at him in ways pervasive and accumulative.

It is not that he blindly condemned the past, or that his complaints about the profession lacked reason. He loved Bach and Beethoven and Brahms too much to repudiate them completely, and by the time of his maturity he had come to see himself as part of their heritage. His main grievance against the old masters was that they were cooped up in diatonic harmony and regular meter. Having stretched his ears with decades of tonal and rhythmic adventures, Ives sometimes heard familiar music with a yearning for fresh perspectives: "Beethoven [is] a great man," he wrote, "but Oh for just one big strong chord not tied to any key."[14] That sort of yearning is common among composers; now and then the giants of the past are apt to strike one as too stylized, too confined. That can also be a way of clearing space for oneself, by circumscribing the space allotted to the giants.

Much of what Ives held against professional music was understandable too—the sniffy conservatism, the theoretical dogmas, the arrogance and fakery of some of the renowned, the pompadoured virtuosos grandstanding the same pieces year after year, the Gilded Age trappings of the whole routine. Composer Bernard Herrmann remembered Ives, during the 1930s, pointing across the street to a violin lesson at the Mannes School and saying, "Look at that old guy across there teaching that lovely girl how to murder music. . . . They walk into that building and they walk out more ignorant than before."[15] He loved the fervor and authenticity of untutored amateurs, who play for love instead of money. In the long run, though, no one in a public, communicative art can remain whole when cut off from the practice of that art. Even though Ives periodically got musicians to play over things, the results of his isolation thwarted his music in some important practical ways, his mental and physical stability in others.

The practical part would be as much an impediment as any. Ives worked on everything at once, in a jumble. He wrote so fast, and his memory was so nearly photographic, that he had the habit of tossing sketches over his shoulder to the floor, from where he only occasionally needed to refer to them.[16] Since any blank staff was fair game, a given piece of paper might have on it music spanning twenty years or more. Final scores got mixed up with sketches. Unless something was going to a copyist, the dusty piles of paper rarely got sorted out. Manuscripts journeyed back and forth on commuter trains, drifted around two houses after the Redding place was built, went out to copyists, found their way into safes at Ives & Myrick. As in his piled-up office at work, Ives believed he knew where everything was. He had a remarkable memory but sometimes he was wrong, or a manuscript had disappeared when he looked for it. In an effort to forestall losses he put his address on nearly every page. That did not always work; besides, some pages accumulated two or three addresses as he reused paper. It is surprising more did not get lost. In 1914, when the partners were moving out of their old office, Myrick nearly threw out the draft of *The Fourth of July*, which had been sitting in his section of the safe. But he thought to ask. "Why Mike! My God!" Ives gasped when Myrick flourished the stack of music, "that's the best thing I've written!"[17]

Artists tend to see their work as part of themselves, almost part of their bodies, and they can be as careless of its well-being as they are of their health. Ives's isolation allowed him to let things ride, to leave scores incomplete or sitting around in safes, to leave even relatively finished works without enough editing and expression marks. There was no barrier to his habit of picking up old pieces, even printed ones, and adding new sketches at random, the sketches ranging from the meticulous and brilliant to the tentative and obfuscating. Ives was a compulsive reviser and that helped him up to a point; but having pieces in the public arena all along would have put some brakes on his always-burgeoning creativity. The practical result of all this would be vexation for players and editors in perpetuity. (There are few things players hate more than unclear scores and parts, or being asked to play something hard that can't be heard by the audience.)

By the time of his greatest music Ives was so far from the profession that he no longer much cared, at least in the heat of composing, what was practical to read or to play, or what could be reliably heard in an orchestral texture. By then he only cared about his dreams. The world of music has been enlarged by those dreams, but they cost him in all kinds of ways. Ives sometimes treated a symphony orchestra as if it were a theater orchestra, asking players to listen to a piano or a drum to get their tempo amidst a thick texture and competing tempi.[18] In some scores, turning his attention to performance, Ives added copious and sometimes astute performance notes, especially for the Fourth Symphony. Other scores (the *Robert Browning Overture,* the Second String Quartet) have long stretches with no markings at all. In fair copies his hand-writing was impeccable—far better, to name one, than Beethoven's. Then the additions and revisions would begin, sometimes burying clear copy under layers of scribble. Even in the relatively clean and annotated pages (including much of the Fourth Symphony), practical problems linger. Ives had grown up writing band arrangements and knew his way around several instruments; but just as Beethoven in his deafness forgot what sopranos sound like shrieking above the staff page after page, so Ives in his isolation forgot or ignored that trumpets cannot play nonstop for a whole movement without considerable stress, as they are asked to do in the Fourth Symphony finale. "The instrument!—there is the perennial difficulty—there is music's limitation," Ives wrote in the *Essays.* "Why can't music go out in the same way it comes in to a man, without having to crawl over a fence of sounds, thoraxes, catguts, wire, wood and brass?"[19] Why, in other words, can't music be entirely disembodied? By then his ideals and his music, as late as the Fourth Symphony still essentially realizable, were beginning to transcend reality once and for all.[20]

If the outer, practical effects of Ives's isolation would inhibit the public progress of his music, the inner effects were more insidious. He grappled with a terrible dilemma. His isolation made his maturity possible—secluded from an audience and, most of the time, from the carping of players, he expanded to the extraordinary fullness of his imagination. At the same time, his forced confinement within a wall of defenses could only amplify the centrifugal tensions within himself. In the heady years of his finest work, the tensions within and without were increasingly expressed as depression and fits of choking, profane rage. More and more his adolescent sexual anxieties, his old fears of music being innately unmanly, knotted his relationship with his art. These tensions were part of still another dilemma—they were inseparable from his creative ferment. The heat of creativity, the heat of passion, the heat of joy, the heat of wrath, all rose from the same sources.

Eventually and still more dangerously, the tensions and the anger emerged in the notes Ives put on the page. Around 1913, after hearing a symphony concert and grumbling that music was getting emasculated by matinee idols, "A wild idea came to me . . . to make a piece that no permanent-wave conductor (of those days) could conduct." What came out in that case was the virtuosic rhythmic etude *In Re Con Moto Et Al.* What did not come out, when all is said, was a particularly expressive piece. Another time,

After coming from some of those nice Kneisel Quartet concerts . . . [I felt] too much of what was easy and usual to play and to hear was called beautiful, etc.—the same old even-vibration, Sybaritic apron-strings, keeping music too much tied to the old ladies. The string quartet music got more and more weak, trite, and effeminate. After one of those Kneisel Quartet concerts in the old Mendelssohn Hall, I started a string quartet score, half mad, half in fun. and half to try out, practice, and have some fun with making those men fiddlers get up and do something like men.[21]

Thus the Second String Quartet. Here is arguably a watershed in Ives's music that contributed, not immediately but in the long run, to his collapse: he began to write music out of rage. So many components of his art—the love of experiment, dissonance, rhythmic vitality, happenstance, vernacular tunes—had been with him since his earliest creative years. These ideas and techniques, many derived from his beloved father, had led him toward a music of the highest imagination and idealism, of the religious spirit, of nostalgia, community, love. To whatever degree Ives began to write not for an audience but against them, not for musicians but against them, not for love but to shock the "old ladies of both sexes," not to uplift the spirit but to prove his manhood—at that point he began to lose the thread of his art, the meaning of what he was doing. When he wrote the Second Quartet in anger, much of his finest music lay ahead of him, some of it in that quartet. The real moments of self-betrayal would not begin until later, and his creative crash would be more physical than spiritual. Still, a shadow had invaded his work, and that would play its part in the story of his music.

It was above all Harmony his harmonious muse who preserved Ives from the ravages of isolation and rage, for as long as it was possible. Her indifference to upper-middle-class social life helped him to live for ten critical years largely for her, his composing. and his business. He abandoned the Yale social tradition and most of the attitudes that implied—the conservative politics, community service, and conventional accoutrements of success. They had friends, Harmony did church and charity work, she served for some years as president of the Mark Twain Society. As he would say in a late interview, though, "We never went anywhere, and she didn't mind."[22] Both had grown up in churches; in New York they belonged to First Presbyterian on Fifth Avenue and attended regularly. Harmony's religiosity—probably more conventional than her father's—reinforced Charlie's hereditary Yankee puritanism. (One of his

1914 commuting memos condemns the very idea of the nude in art: "The human anatomy can never be & has never been the inspiration for a great work of art. It's a medium to be used in Gods service and not stared at by Gods servants."[23])

Much of the tenor of Ives's mature music came directly or indirectly from Harmony. During their courtship and early in their marriage she encouraged him to return for subject matter to his roots—the churches and streets and fields of Danbury, the Transcendental writers he grew up hearing quoted in the family, the Romantics he read under Billy Phelps at Yale. Around the time of their engagement Ives began an *Emerson* piano concerto; it was intended for a "Men of Literature" series that never developed as such, but these literary ideas fed into his second piano sonata, the *Concord*.[24] Harmony may have read to her husband from Matthew Arnold and Robert Browning[25]; they spent many evening hours with her reading aloud. Harmony helped reconnect Charlie with his father as well. Following a visit to Danbury before they married, she wrote him, "Your Uncle Joe said how proud your father would be of you two boys if he were here now. . . . I feel sure that your father knows your lives & sees what his love & thought has meant to you."[26]

Beyond Harmony's encouragement to reclaim his past, Ives was inspired by their theology of love, their private variety of Romantic transcendence. "The comfort of a beautiful expression of our love in music or words," she had written, "is that it would let people see in a concrete form the beauty of it and share, if but for a moment the heaven we know." The call of Horace Bushnell and Joe Twichell for a life of Christ-like love and service reinforced the couple's own ideals. The river of *The Housatonic at Stockbridge* is a particular river, a particular scene, and the ecstatic rush at the end pictures the river's union with the sea; but it is also a spiritual climax linking divine love and these particular lovers.

Harmony wrote Charlie in 1912, four years into their marriage,

I love you so much—our love does seem better & fuller & more ideal all the time—you seem more and more me—my best & unselfish self somehow. Dearest—you know how I love you & yet you cant know all—I feel as if I didn't know all my love . . . I feel it there stretching beyond my realization—my blessed, blessed boy. . . . You are everything I long for. . . . Fred Van Beuren [an old friend] didn't sound very fruitful—aren't you bad to go on a Wagner tirade. I am afraid he will think your wild nature untamed.[27]

In 1914 Harmony wrote from Hartford (she was often there taking care of her father), "I dont mind an occasional appropriate expression—but frequent consecutive cursing such as you've indulged in lately is what I dont like to hear—poor old lamb—you do get so mad, don't you?"[28] Next year, in the authentic gentle and wise and loving Harmony tone: "My lamb—I wish you were here. The house is quiet & the piano needing exercise. I hope you got up in time this morning. If you cant go to heaven with me on account of your badness I'll go somewhere else with you."[29]

The rages persisted, and spilled here and there into his music. *There was no way out.* Either the experts were right and he was crazy, or he was right and they were narrow and timid, and he might be doomed to be unheard.[30] Ives's nature, the nature of his genius, and the nature of his inspiration conspired to make him, in a few works, a very great composer. At the same time they conspired to wreck him on shoals of isolation and wrath. And all the while his physical reserves were running out. Yet whatever the frustrations and depressions, Ives kept the love and respect of nearly everybody who knew him. Far more than explosive, he was a kind, generous, provoking, funny, fascinating spirit. That is the man with whom Harmony fell in love and stayed in love. His enthusiasm was as expansive as his anger. His tirades were always directed against ideas, forces, abstractions, never against individuals or countries or races.

Despite the rebuffs Ives never stopped girding his loins and approaching professional musicians. If he could not catch them with a tough piece he would try an easier one, and if that didn't work a still easier one. He responded to insults with good humor and dogged persistence—at least until he was alone with Harmony, when anger and doubt would overwhelm him and he would cry out, *Are my ears on wrong?*[31] Then, after a day or a week or a month, he would pick up his pen and go on.

Even his courage and integrity, though, were as inconsistent as everything else about him. Ives was composing with unprecedented boldness and freedom, but before showing his most radical scores around he would often compromise, pull his punches. He simplified the full score of the *Three Places,* took some of the bite out of the *Concord* and the songs for publication. Then he defiantly placed the pealing tone clusters of "Majority" on the first page of the *114 Songs,* to spook the "old gals."

Not until 1918 would the dilemmas overtake him. In the decade before that Ives was magnificent, virtually superhuman in his labors and his inspiration. Everything he had been building toward since childhood had become clear. Danbury had charged him like a battery with feelings and experiences, and now he possessed the means to express them. The exhilaration of that experience, the revelation of his full powers, swept aside his inner and outer dilemmas, held together the centrifugal forces of his nature and allowed those forces to enrich his music. He had begun his courtship of Harmony already a brilliant and innovative artist, but unsure where he was going or why. With her inspiration he was ready to take on Bach and Beethoven. He knew now he had the talent and imagination for the job, and if he could not reach the level of his heroes he could still explore potentials in music and spirit that had been closed to them.

During 1908–16 Ives experienced a mounting creative ecstasy. Music like no one ever heard was flowing from him in a strong and steady stream. His mind was on fire. The burgeoning ideas and rage and depression all boiled into music. His body kept up as best it could. It seemed for a while as if nothing could stop him, just as nothing could stop the upward progress of music and of humankind. There is a grainy photo of Ives taken in 1913 in Manhattan's Battery Park, probably on a workday. In the picture he stands straight and thin in his businessman's overcoat, old flatbrimmed Danbury hat high on his head, leaning a little as if barely catchable by lens and film in his implacable bustle. His strange eyes squint inquisitively at the camera, his mouth pursed as if on the brink of an Ivesian riposte. He looks as if he were giving off sparks, as if he were about to rocket off the planet.[32]

Charles Ives in Battery Park, New York City, around 1913—in the heart of his most creative years.

The "Saint-Gaudens" in Boston Common spoke with a new voice in the history of music, but Ives was not part of the history of music in 1911 and that voice was not new to him. Pieces including the *"Saint-Gaudens"* and the earlier *Washington's Birthday* show his personal variety of impressionism and stream of consciousness. These works trace back to the rough, improvisatory college takeoffs, to *Calcium Light Night* and the *Yale-Princeton Football Game,* and to later works such as *Central Park in the Dark*. Around the 1906

In the Night, Ives began to create distinctive layered pieces in which webs of overlapping ostinatos and dissonant counterpoint create a dreamlike atmosphere.

Certainly Ives was familiar with French impressionism. Debussy had begun to emerge into the American scene in the first decade of the century; Ives would have encountered his music in New York concerts and on the shelves of music stores.[33] Debussyan impressionism, however, is a matter of wind and waves observed from the outside, abstracted images of festivals and Spanish music and the like. Always the French looked for a polished and sensuous surface. Ivesian impressionism is intimate, interior, Puritan. He is close to his subjects; his scenes and quoted tunes are filtered through human consciousness, with the emotions added. He does not give a damn for sensuousness or polish. By Ives's maturity, roughness had become a virtue. As in the hoarse hymn singing of stonemason Bell, roughness was an emblem of sincerity and authenticity, of the supremacy of amateur over professional, of substance over superficial, sensuous manner.

The impressionistic *Washington's Birthday,* from 1909, would become the first movement of the *Holidays* symphony, a work straight out of Danbury and environs. "The first part of the piece," he wrote of *Washington's Birthday,* "is but to give the picture of the dismal, bleak, cold weather of a February night near New Fairfield."[34] It is a portrait of winter expressed as a soft web of dissonant harmony. The 1909 *An Elegy to Our Forefathers,* which later began the Second Orchestral Set, has a similar approach. Like the slow music in the other pieces, the *Elegy* unfolds as a single gesture, with no strong contrasts, its layered texture supporting a wordless, elusive, mournful song. (The same year Ives also assembled some of the ragtime ideas into a piece eventually titled *The Rockstrewn Hills Join in the People's Outdoor Meeting,* the second movement of the Second Orchestral Set.[35]) *Washington's Birthday* and *Elegy to Our Forefathers* led to *Decoration Day* and the *"Saint-Gaudens"*—all impressionistic pieces featuring complex harmony scored mostly for many-stranded strings. Each expresses its particular scene and feeling. Each uses the mingling of stylistic voices, the meta-style, that had become second nature to Ives.

Washington's Birthday, after gradually accumulating momentum and intensity, erupts into a Yankee barn dance complete with twanging Jew's harp. This is a single-movement pattern of splicing introverted slow music and extroverted fast music that recurs in the succeeding *Holidays: Decoration Day, The Fourth of July, Thanksgiving.* As in the older *Ragtime Dances,* the barn dance is traditional music cut-and-pasted into new configurations. The juxtapositions and polyrhythms, the dozen or so jigs and reels and waltzes quoted, re-create Ives's memories of what used to happen: "In some parts of the hall a group would be dancing a polka, while in another a waltz, with perhaps a quadrille or lancers going on in the middle. Some of the players in the band would, in an impromptu way, pick up with the polka, and some with the waltz or march. . . . Sometimes the change in tempo and mixed rhythms would be caused by a fiddler who . . . was getting a little sleepy." Ives, at age twelve inspired by country fiddlers like John Starr to write "New Year's Dance," returned to that genre a mature master with the 1909 barn dance. Now rather than just imitating a fiddle tune, he could suggest the whole scene: the barn packed with sweating happy townspeople dancing in lines, the callers, the musicians—often George Ives among them—fueled by their joy in playing and a steady infusion of whiskey, the lilting silver stream of melody sounding above a dusty uproar of laughter and flirting and clog dancing. *Washington's Birthday* ends with the sleepy players intoning "Good Night, Ladies," then the music seems to dissolve in the mind.

Ives got the piece played informally several times during the teens. He read through it with theater musicians at Tams Copying Service in 1913 or 1914, and it was played in the Globe Theater pit a couple of times in the next years. Around 1918 Ives's violinist friend Reber Johnson brought some of his fellow New York Symphony players over to Ives's house on East 22nd Street for four or five rehearsals of *Washington's Birthday,* some perhaps with guests invited. Reported Ives, "the old theater orchestra did as well, if not better. [The Symphony players] made an awful fuss about playing this, and before I got through, this had to be cut out, and that had to be cut out . . . and in the end the score was practically emasculated."[36] Nonetheless, from these attempts he got a feel for how one of his most imaginative scores sounded.

Well before the time of *Washington's Birthday,* Ives had gained control of a range of harmony broader than any past composer's, as rich and varied as anyone's since. When in the teens of the century Arnold Schoenberg decreed the liberation of the dissonance and an end of tonality, he banished all reference to conventional triadic harmonies and developed elaborate devices to suppress a sense of key. Many composers followed suit. In contrast, Ives was characteristically inclusive rather than exclusive: "Why tonality as such should be thrown out for good, I can't see. Why it should be always present, I can't see. It depends, it seems to me . . . on what one is trying to do, and on the state of mind, the time of day or other accidents of life."[37] Ives never let go of tonality and triads. Instead, he added to tonality the technical and expressive possibilities of polytonality and atonality, and interwove them as the state of mind and time of day demanded. He developed the ability to move fluidly from dissonant, atonal sonorities to old-fashioned harmony, sometimes in one breath, like the unexpected gospel cadence of the *"Saint-Gaudens."*

Mediating between harmonic worlds that Schoenberg would declare antithetical, Ives moves at times through intermediary stages by way of symmetrical chord forms (say, quartal or whole tone). In his harmonic techniques he thereby holds on to something like the traditional interplay of consonance and dissonance, smoothness and roughness, repose and activity—the old dialectic between passive and active forces in music. Palestrina and Mozart each had his characteristic poles of dissonance and consonance. Ives kept their diatonic harmonies, but extended the pole of dissonance nearly as far as it could go, to the tone cluster. (His invention of the tone cluster—a chord made from adjacent notes—goes back to the piano drumming of his youth.) Earlier composers excluded steady dissonance and tonal ambiguity in the same spirit as Schoenberg excluded consonance and tonal certainty—in both cases, to achieve consistency. Ives, raised by his father on the theoretical relativism of Helmholtz, indifferent to conventional notions of consistency, kept the full range of sonorities and showed he could make the results of a piece.[38]

Ives was the first composer to reveal that dissonant music can encompass as wide an expressive range as consonant. Composers in the past had occasionally used biting sonorities—Beethoven, for example, at the beginning of the Ninth Symphony finale. Strong dissonance, though, had tended to express unrest, alarm, anger, violence, and the like. And always in the past dissonance had eventually to resolve into consonance, harmonic tension into rest. Ives used the conventional associations of dissonance when he needed them; in the choral *Psalm 90* grinding chords express God's wrath and vengeance. But to the old associations (inclusively rather than exclusively) Ives added a range of other implications. He could use dissonance to express a pantheistic mysticism, as of many things whirling together, like the climax of the *Housatonic* and the Fourth Symphony finale. Dissonance amplifies the comic pandemonium of *The Fourth of July* and *Putnam's Camp*. The babbling harmonic webs of *Washington's Birthday* and similar pieces have a warm sense of dreaming consciousness, or the murmuring of nature. Often, from at least the time of the Third Symphony, one hears distant churchbells or stars suggested by soft bell sounds dissonant to the main harmonies. Ives's music is full of shadows, overtones, distant echoes, memories of Danbury bells; and the vibrant sonority of dissonance is part of those effects.

His grasp of consonance has a scope no less broad. Whole songs written in traditional styles may be warm and nostalgic, like the second of the "Memories," a heartfelt Victorian parlor song, and the late and beautiful setting of "In the Morning' "; or he may use convention for satire, as in the "Romanzo di Central Park." In a generally dissonant framework the sudden interjection of conventional harmony can have a similar variety of effect, from the eloquent gospel cadence of *General William Booth* to the chiding, clichéd harmonies on "that's the easy way" in the election song "November 2, 1920." The late-Romantic harmony of his German song "Feldeinsamkeit" creates, in its style, as impressionistic an effect as the ecstatic dissonances of *The Housatonic at Stockbridge*. In this dimension too, Ives declined to throw out the old in pursuit of the new. A master of the expressive effects of diatonic harmony, he added to that tradition the equally broad expressive possibilities of dissonance and atonality. And despite the emotional vagueness of instrumental music, his implications are usually clear. Ives can make similar gestures, from tonal to atonal, serve dissimilar purposes, and we still sense (usually) what he's getting at.

Ives did not feel obliged to resolve his dissonances, to cadence at the end of a phrase or a movement whatever its style, to settle all the searching into rest. Some of his pieces cadence conventionally (the First Symphony), some cadence conventionally but on an upbeat (the First Quartet second movement), some satirize a standard cadence (*Over the Pavements*). But many of his characteristic works do not cadence in the traditional sense at all. They evanesce, still seemingly in motion, or like the *Housatonic* fade out on a somehow final but still-unresolved harmony. The latter piece also features the Ivesian bell cadence: the texture builds to a full-orchestra roar that cuts off to reveal a quiet, hanging, cryptic chord sequence that recedes into an afterglow.

The most characteristic endings of Ives's maturity, and some of his beginnings as well, fade in or out, as if what we hear were only a fragment of some universal music that comes from and returns to someplace beyond hearing.[39] Horace Bushnell and Joe Twichell preached that the divine is imminent, here among us, reachable, if only we can learn how to hearken to it. Ives's quiet harmonies emerging from a roar imply the presence of an abiding spirit beneath the tumult of nature and of human life. His open-endedness suggests that the music cannot yet be completed, that more is to be said. In his setting of the revival hymn "Shall We Gather at the River?" Ives ends with those words on an open harmony, leaving the question to resonate in our minds: *Shall* we gather at the river? He invites us to complete the question, to seek further, to listen for the yet-unheard.[40]

Paradoxically, though, even in his open endings Ives seems rarely to negate the idea of a cadence, of conclusion and rest. In harmony with his philosophy of life as questioning, seeking, becoming, but always on the way to finding and answering, even his non-endings imply the possibility of cadence and fulfillment somewhere at the end of some road, whose way is long and arduous, but which exists, which we Pilgrims can find if only we believe enough in the road and in ourselves.

These conceptions of a heroic journey through life's mysteries lie behind the twenty-minute *Robert Browning Overture*. Ives worked at it between 1908 and 1912, prompted in part by memories of Billy Phelps's classes and by Harmony's love of Romantic poets. (This was the only one of the "Men of Literature" series he would finish as such. The sketches include a Matthew Arnold, an Emerson, an Alcotts, a Hawthorne.) Ives's *Browning* is based on the poet's epic of the alchemist and metaphysician Paracelsus, a Faustian figure who finally concludes "the power I sought for man seemed God's," that love must precede power, "and with much power, always much more love." Here is Browning's picture of the denouement of Romanticism and its grand designs, in frustration and despair—and an answer to that despair in an evocation of divine and human love. If the demonic aspect of Faustian figures was not Ives's style, that resolution was. His copy of Browning's *Paracelsus* has the inscription, "to Charlie. with love, Oct 20 1908," from Harmony.

The slow introduction to the *Browning Overture* has a brooding, mystical quality unlike anything else in Ives, including his other mystical pieces. Then it erupts into a ferocious, atonal, polyrhythmic, and completely un-Yankee march that surges on and on, working through complex polyphonic devices in wildly leaping themes. The first breathing space is the sudden appearance of the Adagio, a series of variations recalling the introduction. Then the Allegro breaks out again and drives into a fugal coda and finale.[41]

Even more decisively than with the First Piano Sonata, Ives would leave *Browning* an orphan. This is the piece that in later years he threw across the room to shock Carl Ruggles, who rescued it. Ives decided the piece had too much game-playing and manner, not enough substance and story. Certainly it has its shortcomings; the Allegro, for one, shouts on and on at the top of its voice, and Ives never added dynamic and phrasing nuances. Some twenty years after dropping *Browning* at the pencil-draft stage, he wrote in the *Memos:*

It is a kind of transition piece, keeping perhaps too much (it seemed to me) to the academic, classroom habits of inversion, augmentation, etc., etc., in the development of the first theme and related themes. But the themes themselves . . . were trying to catch the Browning surge into the baffling unknowables, not afraid of unknown fields, not sticking to the nice main roads, and so not exactly . . . limited to one key or keys (or any tonality for that matter) all the time. But it seemed (I remember when finishing it) somewhat too carefully made, technically.

It is startling to find a composer calling his own work "too carefully made." He meant too schematically made, in its fugues and mirrors and serial canons. For him, *Browning* stepped over the line into "wall paper design music"—even though its contrapuntal formulas are there to suggest (by Ivesian programmatic logic) the alchemical formulas of Paracelsus.[42] Metaphorical or not, few of Ives's largest, most ambitious, and most earnest pieces would contain that sort of formalism (*The Fourth of July* being the main exception). Besides, *Browning* has practically no quotes—mainly a bit of "Adeste Fideles" toward the end. It did not tell the stories Ives had come to demand, the ones from his childhood or his country's history. It did not capture his accent, his particular niche in the world as distinct from Browning's and the Romantics'.

His subject was a high-Romantic poet and in the slow music of *Browning* Ives is closer than usual to the sound and expression of nineteenth-century music. At heart he is a Romantic, but one usually has to look below the surface to find that essence. Peter Burkholder summarizes the Romantic sense of music as

1) an authentic statement of the composer as an individual and as a product of his age and nation, and yet 2) able to speak to all people of any age or nation; 3) original, yet 4) capable of enduring for all time; 5) innovative and forward looking, yet 6) well crafted, with deep knowledge of tradition. This is how Beethoven's music was viewed, and it describes the aspirations of countless followers of Beethoven, including Ives.[43]

Ives was characteristically Romantic too in his sense of the unfinished, unreachable, and unknowable. One could argue that he carried these intuitions to their most profound projection in music. These intuitions are allied to his vision of music as contributing to human progress and salvation.

Some listeners' problem with Ives all along may be that he does not usually sound like the Romantic he actually is. Here and there he sounds it, but then (sometimes in the same breath) he appears the Modernist. He is Romantic in his own way, and the echoes and prophecies of other styles become Ivesian in the mix. We rarely hear in him the Romantic tone Walter Pater described as "the addition of strangeness of beauty." Ives may be strange in his way, but not in the demonic or hyperbolic way of Berlioz, or the elfin way of Mendelssohn. Ives came to hate the voluptuous heroics of Wagner that so influenced the later nineteenth century. He usually lacks the ponderous passion of Brahms, the sweetness of Brahms and Schumann and Schubert, the eeriness of Schubert's late songs and some of Schumann's.[44]

Nor was Ives ever headed remotely in the direction of the archetypal Romantic hero, Goethe's suicidal Young Werther, whom Brahms cited as inspiration for his C-Minor Piano Quartet. In his tone Ives rarely suggests suffering or tragedy.[45] His music is an almost unbroken outpouring of optimism—among its greatest values and at the same time one of its limitations. Suffering and tragedy approached meat and potatoes for the Romantics; Ives seems nearly oblivious to those qualities, despite having more than a fair measure of suffering in his own life. Even less than tragedy did he seem to recognize evil. His view of humanity was too optimistic to encompass something unredeemable. (Later, when he was presented with facts about Hitler that were inescapably evil, his response would be helpless and sometimes crazy rages. In his dotage he simply could not bear the reality of mass murder.) This was characteristic of his time and his culture and of the Emersonian ideals that helped shape his time. Ives's optimism was Transcendental and Progressive. To him evil was an illusion; like everything else it was fixable, sooner or later.

If Ives was admirably free of despair and self-pity, then, he was also bereft of a tragic vision of life that might have broadened his art. One of the things that makes the *Robert Browning Overture* so striking is that in its tone the slow music does sound Romantic and tragic. Hitchcock calls it "somewhat

Mahleresque," which describes nothing else in Ives.[46] In rejecting the *Browning,* Ives may have been rejecting a tone and a philosophy he recognized as not his own. Besides, by the time he was finishing *Browning* Ives had taken up Emerson, a seeker in the "baffling unknowables" closer to home.

Shy and battle-scarred as he was, through the teens Ives doggedly continued his search for a forum to get his music heard. If somebody took an interest, that would be fine (for many years hardly anyone did); if not, at least he hoped to hear something in the vicinity of what he wrote. He coaxed musicians into his study, hired players for run-throughs in his home or at the Tams Copying Service, paid theater musicians to read over things after the show, sent out scores when there was a call.

In 1910 the renowned Walter Damrosch responded to Ives's submission of the First Symphony for an informal reading session with the New York Symphony Orchestra. On March 19 the Iveses showed up at the orchestra's Saturday-morning rehearsal with the dozen-year-old, unheard score, for which its composer no longer much cared; he was in the middle of a different musical journey now. A hearing, though, was a hearing. Ives did not give the first movement to Damrosch because Parker had declared its modulations excessive.[47] Ives knew his man. Damrosch called performing American composers a "solemn duty," but stuck safely to Chadwick, Mason. and other European-oriented conservatives.[48] At the reading Damrosch earned himself an enduring place on Ives's little list. "Everything Wally said, and the way he said it—his looks, his manner, his motions, the stream of his voice, comment, and reply . . . remind me of everybody of that breed (I mean mentally, not racially) that I had run into."[49] This conductor had made his career more on society connections and money than on musical endowments.[50] In Ives's lexicon of invective Damrosch would become a model of the permanent-wave matinee idol out to please the ladybirds of both sexes. (Pianist/conductor Ossip Gabrilowitsch, who married Mark Twain's daughter and had a celebrated hairdo, shared honors in that category.[51])

After Ives had hurriedly yanked a page of more unruly music that had wandered into the First Symphony score, Damrosch launched into the second movement. He chirped "Charming!" at a felicitous passage, then got himself lost at the first sign of complexity (the mildest sort of complexity, in this Parker-approved music). "He acted somewhat put out, and said it could[n't] be played without a great deal of rehearsing." The problem, Ives recognized, was not with the score but with the man behind the baton. At the end, playing the benevolent maestro, Damrosch declared to Harmony, "This instrumentation is remarkable, and the workmanship is admirable." The kind words only made Ives madder; his real music never got praise like that.[52] In memos of twenty years later, Ives would spend many words sending Damrosch, his "workmanship," and his ilk, to the same hell: of *In Re Con Moto Et Al,* "No mollycoddle mind (like O.G., A.S., W.M.G.D.) could like it, play it, or make any sense of it."[53] (The cryptical listees are Ossip Gabrilowitsch, Albert Stoessel of Juilliard, and—presumably—"Walter Mollycoddle God-Damrosch.")

The First Symphony reading got him nowhere. Next year, 1911, Ives wrote Damrosch asking him to read the Third Symphony; he was having a professional copy made for the purpose. He sent the copy and got no response. Later Ives sent the maestro the Second Symphony. Neither score was ever seen again.[54] The Third Symphony would receive its premiere in 1946, the Second in 1951, the First in 1953.

Another copyist score of the Third Symphony was lost too, and the reason makes for an intriguing sideshow in the Ivesian chronicle. In early 1911 Gustav Mahler, finishing his unhappy tenure with the New York Philharmonic, visited the Tams office and noticed the score. After looking it over he took the piece back to Europe, apparently intending to perform it.[55] Mahler had glanced at a symphony by an unknown and apparently amateurish American and recognized a kindred spirit. He saw a composer placing, as he did, the commonplace, the humble, the shopworn in a symphonic context, and in the process renewing both the material and the symphonic genre. Mahler also saw a deliberate and touching musical naïveté close, in its Yankee voice, to his own way of evoking Austrian folk songs and ländlers.

Musicologist Robert P. Morgan has explored the affinity of the two men, which went beyond anything Mahler could have grasped from the Third Symphony, but might have understood if he had known the later works. While the two generally sound quite different, in their eclectic mixture of folk and classical sources, Morgan writes, "the sense of intrusion from a foreign musical realm becomes an essential component . . . and reflects a radically new conception of the nature and limits of serious musical language." Because they used familiar material, both have been accused of banality and lack of invention; in fact, they were fashioning "a new type of music based on older and simpler models largely neglected by the main tradition. They thus set about renewing musical prototypes."[56] If Mahler had lived to perform Ives's Third, had gone on to champion the more advanced scores (as he had Schoenberg's), how different would have been the career of Charles Ives and how different might have been the story of twentieth-century music. But Mahler died that May in Vienna, and Ives would remain unknown for another ten years.

During 1911, the year Mahler almost discovered him, Ives began, finished, had in the pipeline, or copied out pieces including *Calcium Light Night,* the *"Saint-Gaudens," The Housatonic at Stockbridge,* the *Ragtime Dances,* the *Browning Overture,* the Third Violin Sonata, the songs "Last Reader," "New River," and "Requiem,"[57] *The Fourth of July, Tone Roads No. 1,* the Fourth Symphony, the Second String Quartet, the *Waltz-Rondo* for piano, and three movements of the *Concord Sonata.* Most of the large works would be finished by 1914, all but one—the Fourth Symphony—by the end of 1916. He worked on them in New York, in Hartsdale, and finally in Redding. (After three years at 70 West 11th Street, the Iveses would spend the winters at four different Manhattan addresses during 1911–17—two of those years in Hartsdale— then settle at 120 East 22nd until spring 1926.[58]) Business rolled into Ives & Myrick in mounting waves. With Ives grumbling, the agency moved to the opulent new quarters at 38 Nassau in February 1914. Also in that period, Charlie and Harmony bought the property for their summer place in West Redding, designed the house and oversaw construction, and in the summer of 1913 planted the garden and began to move in. Thus the word for Ives in that period: *superhuman.*

Ives started pulling together the Second String Quartet in 1911, after the Kneisel Quartet concert had set off his tantrum about emasculated music. (That shows his increasing frustration—he had been attending Kneisel concerts since his freshman year at Yale.) On a sketch he describes the Second Quartet's program as "four men—who converse, discuss, argue (in re 'Politick'), fight, shake hands, shut up—then walk up the mountainside to view the firmament!"[59] Its three movements are called "Discussions," "Arguments," and "The Call of the Mountains." "Arguments" went back to 1907 and the spats, often "in re 'Politick,' " that enlivened Poverty Flat. Says a memo on a sketch, "Keyes [Winter] takes exception—'on that point' So do the others each has his say. . . . But on this—they all say Eyah! Everybody can see that!"

No Ives work would be more thoroughly shaped by its program than the Second Quartet. In his best music, however, Ives composed not simply according to a program, but also looked to his programs and borrowed themes for intrinsically musical ideas. Many innovations developed from his way of shaping musical form and technique from the character and shape of events. *Over the Pavements* began with the sound of people walking on the street, and that observation became a study of polyrhythm. Likewise the literal image of a summer evening in the city became the layered spatial effects—the collage— of *Central Park in the Dark.*

Ives never embraced Horatio Parker's idea of abstraction in music. He did accept, of course, that music *contains* abstractions, and he inherited from his father a penchant for technical experimentation: How can you harmonize a whole-tone melody? How would it work to have chords moving apart in a chromatic wedge? At Yale, Ives absorbed the European abstract genres and continued to use them, occasionally and in his fashion, throughout his career. They include sonata form, the king of abstract procedures, as well as fugue, canon, and the devices associated with them—thematic relationships and development, augmentation and diminution and inversion of themes. In 1911 Ives wrote Harmony, "finished quite a bit of the Free Fantasia of the last movement last evening; it's only ½ satisfactory."[60] (Probably he is referring to the Third Violin Sonata.) Here Ives is thinking in something like Parker's terms: the free fantasia or "development section" of a sonata movement. When he came to write program notes for the Fourth Violin Sonata, he wrote of it as an inversion of sonata form, the free fantasia coming first. In like ways he continued his mediation with European tradition and its abstract forms.

While acknowledging that music contains abstractions and dealing with them as such, Ives still refused to concede that music in its essence *is* an abstraction. Music that proposed to be that, anything smacking of art for art's sake, he denounced as "an emasculated piece of nice embroidery."[61] Music to him was something people did for and about people: "The fabric of existence weaves itself whole. You cannot set an art off in the corner and hope for it to have vitality, reality and substance. . . . It comes directly out of the heart of experience of life and thinking about life and living life."[62] *Music*, he wrote Harmony in 1918, *is life*.[63] For him music attained the spiritual by expressing the highest vision of the human.

So in Ives the program, the concrete and humanistic inspiration, is trans-muted into abstract gesture, technique, and form. Thus the Second String Quartet. He began with the old sketch "Arguments," which would become the central movement. His 1907 sketch was based on the idea of four people arguing.[64] How, he considered, could you make music out of that? Well, a piece about an argument would naturally involve fractious harmonies and violent gestures. Phrase joinings should be curt, fragmentary, digressive. So far, simple enough. More subtly, Ives made the instruments of the quartet represent four individuals with more or less distinct musical "personalities"—melodically, gesturally, sometimes rhythmically and metrically. Here he mar-shals techniques developed through years of experimentation, taking his heightened integrity of lines in a new but entirely logical direction. The collage effect of pieces such as *Central Park in the Dark* and *The Unanswered Question*, where each layer has its own style and implied space, becomes in the Second Quartet a musical fabric made up of four characters inhabiting, however frac-tiously, the same space. "Arguments" proceeds realistically in a chain of playful or peevish or grandiose assertions, clichés, outraged dissonances, and so on. (Ives represents the clichés by sudden intrusions of familiar material ranging from "Hail, Columbia" to fragments of Tchaikovsky, Brahms, and Beethoven. This is symbolically a *musical* argument.) The four characters are not always in evidence as such, but each has his say. Most egregious of them is the delicate, refined second violin, whose sections are marked "Andante Emasculata" and "Largo sweetota."

This violin part has a name, "Rollo," written on the manuscript but not in the printed score. This may be the first appearance of that *bête noire* in the Ives pantheon—sissy, orthodox, lily-eared Rollo. His name comes from a nineteenth-century series of children's books by Reverend Jacob Abbott, whose hero Rollo is always a good, earnest, honest, thrifty, inquiring yet obedient, literal-minded, *nice* boy. Rollo's contribution to the "Arguments" seems to be an earnest insistence on sweetness and light. In his little cadenzas he is given to sentimental chromaticism and dainty grace notes. Obviously an aesthete, Rollo loves the great European masterpieces, and doubtless Ethelbert Nevin and Horatio Parker too. One may presume he is devoted to Walter Damrosch and the Kneisel Quartet. Near the end of the second movement, with everybody shouting at once, Rollo saws away determinedly on Beethoven's *Ode to Joy*. Ivesian notes on the manuscript (perhaps from his later years) jeer at him like a Danbury teenager: "Hard Rollo This is music for men to play—not the Lady-bird K[neisel] Q[uartet]. . . . All in key of C. You can do that Nice and pretty, Rollo."

The quartet's opening movement, "Discussions," composed in Ives's full maturity four years after "Arguments," is more serious and integrated.[65] In this movement the programmatic idea of a heated conversation is rendered by complex, chromatic, dissonant counterpoint. The lines, modeled on speech, tend to sound like conversation. Periodically the instruments join in rhythmic unison, representing points of agreement in the discussion. Otherwise the four voices are distinct in a more traditionally contrapuntal way, the mostly atonal harmonies producing a sonority close to what Schoenberg was developing during the same period, a continent away.

Program becomes abstraction; devices both realistic and formal hold the first movement together. The pace and intensity gradually build, the simmering tension periodically erupting into anger. The occasional monorhythmic comings-together form a pattern, as do the sudden jumps from style to style, from chromatic/atonal/jagged to diatonic or fractured-diatonic. (The discussion is thus a mixture of the clichéd and the original.) Motivic relationships and subtle tonal references to the central note C help unify the movement, and it ends with a variant of its quiet beginning.

However revolutionary its sound and technique, this is also a "heroic" first movement in the European mode, with the traditional contrasting lyrical sections; and the "Arguments" movement is a sort of scherzo. European genre traditions may not lie in the foreground in the Second Quartet, but they are part of its inspiration and infrastructure. The piece nonetheless remains an Ivesian form, self-creating, a personal mediation with older genres. In contrast to the standard patterns of repetition in sonata form and scherzo, Ives avoids literal repetition in this and many other works of his maturity. Instead of repeats and recapitulations there is continual protean development and transformation of material.[66] It has much of the feel and function of tradition, without many of the specifics.

The last movement, "Call of the Mountains," begins with reference to the beginning (and end) of the first movement. Once again Ives uses cyclic form, creating myriad interconnections—of motive, theme, harmony, texture, rhythm, gesture—among the movements. In tone the finale is meditative and mystical. Now the four characters are climbing a mountain to look at the stars, as Ives had done with friends and loved ones in Connecticut and the Adirondacks. As in the first movement there is a gradual picking up of motion, this time with a sense of expectation rather than tension. With a sudden cut, an electrifying conclusion breaks out. Over a downstriding whole-tone scale in the cello, the violins and viola chime like great bells in the heavens, in patterns like bell ringing.[67] The struggle and the arguments have prepared the way for a revelation. Singing in the bells, we hear "Nearer, My God, to Thee."[68]

Ives finished the Second Quartet, along with the fair copy of *The Fourth of July,* during his first month's vacation in the new house at Redding, in September 1913.[69] By the time he wrote the conclusion of the quartet, he may already have imagined its expansion into the ecstatic peroration of the Fourth Symphony finale. Now he knew his way around the artistic and spiritual territory that, as he would put it, "came not only from folk music he was brought up with but to a very great extent from the life 'around & in him'. . . something reflecting a kind of 'inheritance' from his forbears & father— a natural interest in wanting to make his own paths around the hills & mountains."[70]

"Fourth Symphony," Ives wrote. "This was started, with some of the Hawthorne movement of the Second Piano Sonata, around 1910–11 (though partly from themes in the unfinished Alcott overture, 1904). It was all finished around the end of 1916."[71] Thus in the 1930s he skimpily outlined the genesis of the Fourth. Skimpily and misleadingly, whether deliberately so or not. The Fourth Symphony had a complicated genesis and it was not finished by 1916.

Ives would always be reticent about this work, even to having a friend write the program note (from Ives's suggestions). Part of the reason for the reticence may have been that this music lay close to his holy of holies; he did not and maybe could not put its aspirations into words. Source material for the Fourth goes back to the fugue on "Greenland's Icy Mountains" that Ives wrote at Yale in the mid-1890s and grafted onto the First String Quartet. (In the *Memos* he claims the fugue was written in 1916.) The Fourth Symphony would draw on other pieces large and small through the course of his life. The immediate event that inspired something so unexpected for Ives, by then, as a true symphony may have been the appearance of Halley's Comet in May 1910.[72] Watching the apparition blazing through the sky, Ives may have found an old hymn sounding in his mind:

Watchman, tell us of the night,
What its signs of promise are.
Trav'ler, o'er yon mountain's height,
See that glory-beaming star.

He had already set *Watchman* twice, in 1901 for organ and soprano, in 1905 for organ and strings. The latter was done at Dave Twichell's suggestion, during the Adirondack vacation that united Ives and Harmony.[73] Another element of the Fourth Symphony was foretold at Pell Jones's cabin on Elk Lake in 1909, when Ives began reworking the old string quartet Fugue for orchestra. By August vacation a year later, Ives had watched the passage of Halley's Comet and conceived the symphony. During that Elk Lake sojourn he worked on the first movement, which is primarily a choral version of *Watchman* developed from his old settings. The Fourth would come to embody his highest hopes for music and its future, for humanity and its future. For himself, though, its meaning would always have intimately to do with the spirit of the

Adirondacks, and with Harmony. As he wrote her in Hartford that October 1910, "It's free from extraneous substances & closely woven & the product of our summer at Pell's."[74]

The Fourth Symphony would be much on his mind in the next years, but other pieces pushed it aside. The period 1911–14 seems to have been dominated by work completing the Second String Quartet, *Holidays (The Fourth of July,* then *Decoration Day), and the *Three Places,* and by composing most of the *Concord Sonata.* There were smaller pieces in this period too, including songs (among them *General William Booth*), piano studies, and the first two *Tone Roads.* Some of the instrumental miniatures are takeoffs (such as *The Anti-Abolitionist Riots* for piano), some are further autodidactic explorations of what a later age would call serialism. Ives called them "hardly more than memos in notes . . . [they] strengthened the ear muscles, and opened up things naturally that later were used naturally and spontaneously."[75]

The first two chamber pieces called *Tone Roads* date from 1911. Ives finished the first that year and the second later, and added a third in 1915. *No. 2* eventually got lost in his shuffles of homes and papers. In sound and effect, *Tone Roads Nos. 1 and 3* are further sports in Ives's work. Both use chamber ensembles. In the *Memos* Ives describes their leading idea this way: "If horses and wagons can go sometimes on different roads . . . at the same time, and get to Main Street eventually—why can't different instruments on different staffs?"[76] The several roads are symbolized in *No. 1* by semi-serial arrangements and juxtapositions of rhythmic patterns and harmonic and melodic interval patterns that cycle through the piece not entirely systematically, but generally audibly. *No. 3* uses what Schoenberg would call a twelve-tone row. The effect of both pieces is of contrapuntal lines clipping along each on its own track, but trading material and occasionally coming together in a climactic rhythmic unison—the arrival at "Main Street" or "Town meetin'."[77]

What became *Three Places in New England* began its course in summer 1908, when after the newlyweds returned from their romantic walk in Stockbridge, Ives jotted down a single measure trying to capture the scene along the Housatonic River, and the hymn they heard coming from a distant church.[78] With a characteristic mixture of programmatic and technical notions, he wrote on the sketch: "Housatonic Church across River sound like Dorrnance . . . River Mists, leaves in slight breeze river bed—all notes & phrases in upper accompaniment . . . should interweave in uneven way, riversides colors, leaves & sounds—not come down on main beat. . . ." Soon he fleshed out the idea in a longer sketch, shaping a complex, multi-layered texture. That petered out after a page or so and Ives apparently put it aside for some three years. Perhaps he did not yet know how to find his way through this extraordinary thicket of sound. Then in 1911 he returned to the idea and sketched the whole movement in ink; only a page of that survives. When he composed the "Black

March" / "*Saint-Gaudens*" at Hartsdale in the same year, he did not yet have the idea of joining it in a set with the *Housatonic* material. (He finished the full "*Saint-Gaudens*" score in September 1912, on vacation in the Adirondacks.)

That autumn another element of the eventual *Three Places* took shape when Ives spliced together two pieces from around 1903—*Country Band March* and "1776." The result of the joining was *Putnam's Camp*, eventually the rambunctious second movement. (Inverting the usual tempo pattern of three-movement pieces, Ives liked the arrangement slow–fast–slow.) *Putnam's Camp* is prefaced by a story, whose setting is the Revolutionary War Camp of General Israel Putnam, near Danbury: A child, visiting the camp on a Fourth of July picnic, wanders away from the music and festivities. Then, Ives writes, "He rests on the hillside of laurel and hickories . . . when—'mirabile dictu'— over the trees on the crest of the hill he sees a tall woman standing. She reminds him of a picture he has of the Goddess of Liberty . . . she is pleading with the soldiers not to forget their 'cause' and the great sacrifices they have made for it. But they march out of camp with fife and drum to a popular tune of the day." In the boy's dream, General Putnam returns from town and the deserting soldiers turn back with a cheer. Awakening, the boy runs back to his family to listen to the bands and join the fun.

Ives's program describes the music down to the magical chord that signifies the beginning of the dream.[79] But the program is not the whole story of the piece. The "mirabile dictu" chord not only pictures the moment the dream begins, but also has an abstract function—it creates a transition between *Country Band* and "1776" material. And while the overall form of *Putnam's Camp* outlines the program, it is also a march more or less in march form, rich with Ives's understanding of that genre.

What are the genres that we give names to—march, symphony, string quartet, opera, ballad, blues, show tune, and dozens of others? Except in some of this century's avant-garde, most music everywhere is composed in familiar patterns and modes, each with its characteristic elements, its traditions. Composers respond to genres freely and bend them to their purposes, but still respect them as bearers of coherence and tradition. Ives grew up with a number of traditional musical genres still vital and developing, among them the classical ones of symphony, string quartet, keyboard sonata, and the like, and the vernacular ones of march, hymn, household song, and the like—kinds of pieces that seemed tired to moribund by the mid-twentieth century.

Genres often originate as social, functional music—for dancing, for the theater, for worship. The minuet, for example, began as a three-beat French folk dance, was taken up by the court of Louis XIV, became standardized into a particular outline of sections and repeats, attached itself to the classical symphony as an "abstract" movement, was transformed by Beethoven and later composers into the faster scherzo movement of various large genres, and was further transformed by Brahms, Mahler, and Ives. When the minuet movement was grafted onto the symphony, it became a kind of subgenre, with its own distinct tradition, and its history continued to evolve.

The march developed in Europe around the sixteenth century from the drum and trumpet signals used to coordinate troop movements. When Charles Ives was playing and composing marches in his youth, this music was still associated with uniformed men on the march. By then, American marches had developed their own characteristic accent. One hears that accent as well as anywhere in Ives's 1894 march "The Circus Band." "Ain't it a grand and a glorious noise?" his words proclaim, and surely it is.[80]

Most musical genres have distinctive formal outlines and loose rules of various sorts—say, the walking tempo and two- or four-beat pattern of the march, the dance-tempo three-beat of the minuet. Once evolved, a genre becomes an archetype moving through history, a broad, complex, highly variable, but still distinct vocabulary of typical forms, rhythms, texture, harmonic style, gestures, meter, tempo, and so on. Composers draw on these elements partly in conscious conformity to the genre, partly intuitively. Beyond the general outlines, to a large extent a composer simply *knows how it goes*. Both minuet and waltz have three beats, for example, but they sound quite different; a composer may be hard put to explain some of the differences, but understands them instinctively. In the same way, the first and last movements of a classical symphony are usually both fast, sometimes both in the same sonata form; but any symphonic composer worth his salt knows which kinds of gestures suit a first movement and which a finale.

Ives was of the last generation of composers to work when a number of venerable genres, cultivated and vernacular, were still alive in something like their original shape, not yet fossilized in history. When he began his First Symphony Tchaikovsky had just died, Brahms and Dvořák were still alive. And as much as any kind of piece, Charles Ives knew how a march went. He wrote half a dozen or so conventional ones himself, contemporary with Sousa's. A common formal model for a nineteenth-century march worked like this: a brassy introduction; then a first strain with a lilting tune, which is repeated; a second strain with a bit of contrast to the first, repeated; some kind of transition into a *trio* in two repeated strains, the trio material usually a little lighter, though it may have a brassy break between the strains; then a da capo back to the first strain; and finally, perhaps a coda after the return of the opening two strains.[81] Erratically, but still discernibly, *Putnam's Camp* follows that outline, and the "mirabile dictu" chord introduces the trio.

There is much more to a genre than formal outlines, meters, and the like. There is a *feel*. You have to know how it goes. In the case of the march, the feeling has to do with certain kinds of tunes and rhythms, with drums and brass, men in uniform striding down a dusty street, crowds cheering, memories of battlefields, bandsmen drunk and sober, expert and dilettante: "Band

Stuff," Ives called it. These intangibles are as important as the meter and tempo and formal outline. Many of them cannot readily be explained, any more than a bluesman can explain precisely, technically, what the blues is. But every true bluesman or composer of marches understands, intuitively, what's right for the thing and what isn't. The blues is a feeling, an evolving archetype, and so are a march and a symphony.[82] Meanwhile each of those genres has its familiar milieu—a saloon, a parade, a concert hall. The setting is somehow conveyed in the music even if the bluesman is singing in Carnegie Hall.

It is that kind of understanding that informs *Putnam's Camp*—the brash brassiness of the introduction, the stalwart melody of the first strain, the deliberately banal second strain (which emerges with an almost audible sigh of relief after the bandsmen have lost track of the beat for a while), the fanfares with a couple of horn players tripping over the rhythm, and the dream-trio with ghostly images of two bands playing the same drumbeat in two different tempos. After the da capo the piece ends with a boisterous Ivesian racket, band and crowd roaring together, the basses winding up with the beginning of "The Star-Spangled Banner" while a trumpet adds a touch of *Reveille*. This beginning-as-ending is one of many jokes in the movement, some subtle and some flamboyant. *Putnam's Camp* is among the most scrupulously comic excursions in music, but it is not only that. The difference between a joke and a comic masterpiece is the difference between *Country Band March* and *Putnam's Camp*. The latter may be three-quarters the same as its source in *Country Band* and *1776,* but the quarter's difference contains what Ives had learned about continuity and logic and substance in the nine years between. The mature piece is fleshed it out with affection, nostalgia, and a joyousness that, for all the similarity, can't be found in *Country Band March* or in *1776.*

The Housatonic at Stockbridge, which would end *Three Places,* is the summit of Ivesian impressionism, permeated by the romantic and spiritual glow of his first weeks of marriage and the honeymoon walk in Stockbridge. Like all great works, it transcends individuals and particulars. The orchestral texture that Ives spent years thinking about, advancing and backtracking and restoring, is one of his finest imaginings. In the 1940s he would draft a letter about it (in third person) to Alfred Frankenstein: "The grand old River is one [of] natures masterpieces, and has been an inspiring friend of Mr. I from his boyhood days, and the music could reflect . . . the moving River, its landscapes & Elm Trees on its way to the adventurous Sea. From the beginning of the score until the sea is near, it was, in a way, intended that the upper strings, muted be heard rather subconsciously as a kind of distant background of an autumn sky and mists seen through the trees and over a river valley."[83] At the beginning there are five distinct layers in the strings—slow-changing harmonies over a drone, a viola line flowing chromatically, two faster-flowing lines above that (one in a complex polyrhythm that blurs the meter), and on top lines in thirds, tremolo, quietly soaring in even eighths but grouped mostly in threes.

The exquisite melody, like a folk tune that grows throughout the movement within the gently babbling texture, is a song without words built from *Dorrnance,* the hymn the Iveses heard during their walk.[84] Ives put the unspoken text of his melody, a poem by Robert Underwood Johnson, at the beginning of the score: "Contented river! in thy dreamy realm—/The cloudy willow and the plumy elm . . . ," and at the conclusion, "Wouldst thou away, dear stream?/Come, whisper near!/I also of much resting have a fear;/Let me tomorrow thy companion be/By fall and shallow to the adventurous sea!" The music builds seaward to its ecstasy, and its unforgettable afterglow (see the final two pages of the score, on the following pages).

So *Three Places in New England* began in 1908 with a one-bar sketch toward the *Housatonic,* picked up the *"Saint-Gaudens"* from 1911, and ended with the full score of *Putnam's Camp* (only in the last three years had Ives decided to put these particular pieces into a set together).[85] As it turned out, though, the 1914 full-orchestra score of the "completed" set stands as one of Ives's most perplexing episodes of punch-pulling. Apparently in hopes of making it more presentable, he watered down a good deal of *Three Places* from the sketches. His arrangement/reworking of 1929, the version the world knows, is not quite the same as the "final" score of 1913–14.

The main compromises were in the *Housatonic.* Ives's original 1908 sketch is one rough measure of texture. The more elaborate sketch, made soon after, has three more lines in the texture than the eventual published score of twenty years later. Besides that, in the earliest sketches the French horn/English horn melody was harmonized in two parts and in a different key than the accompaniment—E major over D♭. (Finally both melody and drone would be in C♯/D♭.) The 1908 sketches, in other words, are *more* complicated and dissonant (and probably less effective) than the eventual published version.[86] When Ives made his first "final" score of the movement he pruned back the textural lines dramatically. Which is to say: the 1913 score of the *Housatonic,* the only full-orchestra one that survives, dilutes one of the chief glories of the piece. Apparently Ives immediately regretted that and paid a copyist to make another score, restoring some of the original ideas. That score got lost.[87] Finally, Ives's 1929 chamber-orchestra version replaced some of the lines, but the texture is still not as complex as the original 1908 sketch.[88]

So it went for Ives during the teens—gigantic steps forward, then sometimes (only sometimes) compromise, an attempt at accommodation to reality. Maybe, he thought, a conductor who would reject the original *Housatonic* might countenance something a little simpler. After all, in its essence the movement has a beautiful tune, harmonized normally. Maybe if he could do without some of the complexity and dissonance, somebody would play the thing. (He did not do the same with, say, *The Fourth of July,* because he figured that piece was unlikely ever to be played anyway.) Ives had immense courage and vision and integrity, arguably as much as any composer who ever lived. But he was also farther out on a limb than most artists have ever been, had endured countless rejections, and his courage and integrity were not unlimited. Occasionally, they failed him. Yet the *Housatonic,* like most of his "finished" works, would eventually come out as he wanted, as he had imagined it.

In 1912 Ives added the two final *Holidays* to his four-season symphony.[89] In an Ivesian collection of holidays there would naturally need to be a Fourth of July. He got to it late, probably because it required most of what he had learned through years of experimenting with the materials of music as well as the control of form and development Horatio Parker had given him. For Ives *The Fourth of July* would be a joyous eruption of creative energy, emancipation, and autonomy: "I remember distinctly, when I was scoring this, that there was a feeling of freedom as a boy has, on the Fourth of July, who wants to do anything he wants to do. . . . And I wrote this, feeling free to remember local things, etc, and to put [in] as many feelings and rhythms as I wanted to put together. And I did what I wanted to, quite sure that the thing would never be played, and perhaps *could* never be played."

The score-sketch of the *Fourth* notes: "In Whitmans little house Hartsdale—Sally [Twichell] came out hot 4th of July—Rocket sick." He started the work with three older pieces of material. One was part of the "1776" Overture,

a setting of the tune "Red, White and Blue" (better known as "Columbia, the Gem of the Ocean"). Ives had been using this lusty patriotic song since at least the Second Symphony; he would end up quoting it in over fifteen works.[90] The other sources are the chords from the little song "In the Cage" and a schematic explosion effect from a sketch called *The General Slocum,* after the infamous 1904 steamboat disaster. Thus new pieces grew from old: Ives would begin with a core idea, say, the settings of "Watchman" that grew into the first movement of the Fourth Symphony, the organ *Memorial Slow March* that evolved into the finales of both Second Quartet and Fourth Symphony; around the core he would improvise, preface, interpolate, extend, and layer, all of it an expansion of the central expressive and/or technical ideas of the source piece. At times, as with the "Cage" material in *The Fourth of July,* the source was swallowed up. (Sometimes he reversed the process by reducing a big piece—such as the song "Paracelsus" derived from the *Browning Overture,* and his arrangement of the *Housatonic* for voice and piano.)

The explosion from the *Slocum* sketch certainly suits the *Fourth of July*'s program, and the connection between the other two sources—*1776* and "In the Cage"—is not arbitrary. The main feature of the "Cage" harmony is chords made of stacked fourths, and "Columbia, the Gem of the Ocean" is full of melodic fourths. Ives would end up using about fifteen tunes likely to be heard around Danbury on the Fourth of July, including "Columbia," "Battle Cry of Freedom," "Marching Through Georgia," "Battle Hymn of the Republic," "Yankee Doodle," "Dixie," and traditional fiddle tunes. All relate melodically to "Columbia," which is implied, distantly, from the first measure.[91] Through a carefully shaped yet apparently serendipitous musical journey it grows steadily in definition (cumulative form) until it is blared out by the brasses at the center of the swarming and riotous climax. Ives ironically and accurately described the piece this way: "This is pure program music—it is also pure abstract music—'You pays your money, and you takes your choice.' "[92]

He would stint neither story nor form. He insisted on getting into music the event as he remembered it from Danbury—clamorous hoards of revelers in the streets, parades, musicians playing drunkenly all over town, runaway horses, churchbells, boys with firecrackers, the climactic pyrotechnics. In this piece (the scherzo of the loose *Holidays Symphony*) Ives stayed away from the ostensible seriousness of the day: "It's a boy's 4th—no historical orations—no patriotic grandiloquences by 'grownups' . . . festivities start in the quiet of the midnight before, and grow raucous with the sun."[93] Likewise the music, beginning as a quiet nocturne mostly in strings, the texture and intensity building bit by bit. Like a cinematic cut, a fife-and-drum corps appears on its own rhythmic plane (accompanied by piano-drum chords from young Charlie Ives). The music develops like a cinematic montage, panning and cutting from one scene to another: crowds, bands, drums, distant tumult, the explosion of the first rocket, which falls in a shower of sparks.[94] After a pause the camera moves through the throng again while a band marches closer. Now we're at the parade, the passing band roaring out "Columbia, the Gem of the Ocean" while the crowd cheers; at the same time, other bands play their own tunes somewhere down the line. If the trumpet players are a little drunk and miss some notes, if somebody gets a tuning shank mixed up and plays in the wrong key, if a few bandsmen fall off the beat—why, that's what it's supposed to sound like on the Fourth of July. "Band Stuff," Ives wrote on the score; "they didn't always play right & together & it was as good either way."[95]

Finally a breathless silence before the grand finale. The last skyrocket ascends in string glissandi and hugely explodes, tutti *fff*. Like the whole piece, the explosion is pure program and pure abstraction: "I worked out combinations of tones and rhythms very carefully by kind of prescriptions, in the way a chemical compound which makes explosions would be made." While a cloud of strings swirls up and down in glissando clusters (the smoke), the explosion proceeds through a series of micro-stages from homogeneity (held cluster) through disorder and back to homogeneity, with patterns forming and dissolving, instruments coming into agreement and breaking apart. In the fourth measure of the explosion, bracketed rhythmic values mathematically / chemically divide the bar into 2, 3, 4, 5, 6, 9, 10, 11, 12, 14, 15, 16, and $21\frac{1}{3}$ equal parts.[96] Once Ives has set up rhythmic and pitch patterns, however, he breaks up some of them with small changes, so things don't get mechanical.[97] After the explosion the strings trickle down like the last sparks, and the boy's Fourth is over.

In the *Essays* Ives writes the cryptic aphorism, "not something that happens, but the way something happens." As Henry and Sidney Cowell gloss, "For Ives the meaning of an event seems to lie in the behavior of the elements that create it, and when he wants to convey an emotion about something, he reproduces the behavior of the sounds that are associated with it, their approach and departure, their pace and drive, interweaving and crossing."[98] Thus in *The Fourth of July* and much other Ives, the meaning is in *how* something happens (say, the passing of a parade, the joy and even the strong drink affecting the playing of amateurs) not in the *what* (the old tunes so stale on the page). For most of the years since his childhood there had been a barrier between Ives and his formative experiences in Danbury. He did not yet possess the language and technique to transform and stylize massive public events into the terms of concerted music. The language he eventually taught himself through his long apprenticeship was less a matter of imitation than of equivalence: the behavior of events is transmuted into equivalent musical behavior. With that language and technique Ives reclaimed his past in vital forms, and, more important to him and to us his audience, the larger human resonances of that past.

After sketching out *The Fourth of July* in 1912, Ives went on to *Decoration*

Day. It recalls the ceremonies of commemoration for the Civil War dead (which became Veteran's Day). On those holidays his father's band would march, to a somber dirge, from the Soldiers' Monument at the center of Danbury to Wooster Cemetery on the outskirts, where veterans' graves would be decorated and George Ives would intone *Taps*. After the ceremonies the band marched back to town playing a sprightly tune, often Reeves's *Second Regiment Connecticut National Guard.*

Decoration Day begins, like *Washington's Birthday* and *The Fourth of July,* with an extended meditative section, mostly for strings, at first barely audible. It is an evocation of early morning and the awakening of memory. As with many of his pieces in those days, Ives adds what he called "shadow lines"—a player or two, sometimes offstage or to the side, plays as if to himself, like somebody in the next room or down the street. At times the shadow lines suggest other realities, parallel memories, the subconscious. They murmur sometimes inaudibly in the texture, but float up now and then like a phantom presence within the music. Always they suggest something beneath the surface, beyond the immediate time and place.

Like the morning, the music of *Decoration Day* slowly awakes, rising and sinking, with an occasional eloquent silence like a held breath. Periodically one motive slips to the surface, a poignant blend of major and minor (with a suggestion of *Taps*).[99] Traces of "Marching Through Georgia" drift through the music. A series of quiet sighs is heard in the strings—tone clusters falling a half step in glissandi.[100] "The march to Wooster Cemetery," Ives wrote, "is a thing a boy never forgets. The roll of muffled drums and 'Adeste Fidelis' [*sic*] answer for the dirge." So in his memory "Adeste Fideles" begins, transforming into a suggestion of the Civil War's mournful "Tenting on the Old Campground."

The dirge dissolves and we are in Wooster Cemetery: townspeople hatless in honor of the dead, aged veterans standing at attention stolid or weeping, George Ives's trumpet sending *Taps* floating over the hills and trees and graves, the strings whispering "Nearer, My God, to Thee." On the last note of *Taps* the music begins to surge into a drumbeat that crescendos until with a sudden cut we are in the middle of the march back to town, and the pealing melody of Reeves's *Second Regiment*. Or rather we are in a super-march made of memories of drums and trumpets resounding in the mind, the sounds of music and crowds mingling and echoing off buildings. After a few strains of an intoxicating joy and youthfulness the memory vanishes, and we hear as an afterglow the gentle music of the beginning, the poignant major-minor motive, a distant *Amen.*

Years later, when Stravinsky was asked to define a masterpiece, he defined it with *Decoration Day*. Despite his insistence on music as pure abstraction, Stravinsky called the ending "the loneliest and one of the most touching I know of."[101] Neither the program nor any description of *Decoration Day* can capture its heartfelt quality, though Stravinsky came close for the ending. In form and style the piece is much like its neighboring movements in *Holidays,* but its exquisite, succinct expressiveness goes beyond them, perhaps in those respects beyond anything else in Ives's major works. So much of his most essential life and memory inhabit this music. George Ives and his Civil War are there throughout, resurrected in the gently flowing violin of the shadow lines perhaps, certainly in "Adeste Fideles" and *Taps,* and in the march. The boy Charlie Ives is there too, in the brash playing of the percussion battery. Here in memory, George Ives intones *Taps* over his own grave, and over the hill topped by the monument to George White Ives, where Charles Ives knew he would lie someday. The Danbury of the 1880s is alive again, and for this *Holiday* Ives drew on his own music going back to *Holiday Quickstep* from 1887, which paraphrased the same Reeves march.

Perhaps most important for Ives's personal relation to the work is its connection to that exalted moment of his boyhood when (as he wrote in the *Essays*) "a village band is marching down the street—and as the strains of Reeves' majestic [*Second*] *Regiment March* come nearer and nearer—he seems of a sudden translated—a moment of vivid power comes, a consciousness of material nobility—an exultant something gleaming with the possibilities of this life—an assurance that nothing is impossible, and that the whole world lies at his feet." With that radiant image of his father transformed into an epiphany of the infinite possibilities of human existence, Ives's journey as a composer may have begun. The joyousness of the march in *Decoration Day* may recall that second birth, into creative life. The loneliness of the end, if Stravinsky is right, may be the inevitability of death and loss dissolving the exalted moment: "the boy's vision slowly vanishes—his 'world' becomes less and less probable—but the experience ever lies within him in its reality."[102] So his creative life was to ebb, leaving behind the echo. With *Decoration Day* Ives touched the essence of his own past and future and the reality of his community, and transmuted them into universal music.

The *Holidays Symphony* was done: *Washington's Birthday, Decoration Day, The Fourth of July,* and the *Thanksgiving* finished in 1904. In these movements Ives captured much more than four seasons or holidays or a set of memories. He would write of the piece:

The three holiday movements (perhaps less in *Thanksgiving,* which has some religious significance) are but attempts to make pictures in music of common events in the lives of common people (that is, of fine people), mostly of the rural communities. . . . The more inartistic and unmusical they seem to Rollo, probably the better pictures they are. They could be played as abstract music (giving no titles [or] program), and then they would be just like all of "abstract" things in art—one of two things: a covering up, or ignorance of . . . the human something at the source—or just an emasculated piece of nice embroidery![103]

In these pieces Ives memorialized not just Danbury but rather the boundless human territory he would write of in his 1917 song lyric, "The Things Our Fathers Loved":

> I think there must be a place in the soul
> all made of tunes of long ago;
> I hear the organ on the Main Street corner,
> Aunt Sarah humming Gospels;
> Summer evenings, The village cornet band playing in the square . . .
> Now! Hear the songs! I know not what are the words.
> But they sing in my soul of the things our Fathers loved.

In *Holidays* more directly than in any other work, Ives took for his theme the life of communities in the streets and fields and churches, in festivals and worship services, each with its appropriate music. Here are melodies like icons, resonating with memory and history, with war, childhood, community, and nation. Here Ives united his soul's song with what his own father loved, and touched the music of the ages that George Ives taught him to hear in a stonemason's bellowing of hymns. *Music is life*. As Ives transforms his own experience in these pieces, he transforms Danbury and its people into a myth of the primal community. Danbury is anyplace and everyplace that people do what people do: gather to worship and celebrate and memorialize the dead, all of it accompanied by music. It is that kind of transformation he writes of in the *Essays:* "If local color, national color, any color, is a true pigment of the universal color, it is a divine quality, it is a part of substance in art."[104]

Ives completed *Holidays* in September 1913. By then every other major work he had left in him was under way. He had three relatively unfettered years to finish them.

TWELVE

That Beautiful Shore

IN THE TEENS OF THE CENTURY a second transforming calamity began to stalk Charles Ives. Like the death of his father in 1894, the second event would be interwoven with the fate of George Ives. While the world and Ives's creative life moved imperceptibly toward parallel crises, his days circled around music, family, business, and increasingly around politics. Fate circled them all. Ives was then in the white-hot prime of his creative life and his wife a wise and loving muse. Nonetheless music, family, and politics all burdened him in one way or another. The humiliating scenes with musicians continued, nearly every time he showed anyone his music—and he never stopped showing it. Ives's father-in-law Joe Twichell was sinking into senility and despair after the death of his wife; Harmony Ives spent many weeks away taking care of him. Dave Twichell, Harmony's beloved brother and Charlie's old friend, was drawn away from them by his ailing wife.[1] "Lately we have been sort of complicated," Harmony wrote Charlie in April 1914. "Of course we are in a transition now & must be upset."[2]

Part of the transition may have been embroilments around their new country home in West Redding, but Harmony also meant the passing of the older generation. Joe spent February 1913 in a sanitarium in Brattleboro, Vermont; Harmony stayed with her father, Charlie visited. That July the old minister was well enough to attend with them the ceremonies at Gettysburg, on the fiftieth anniversary of the battle. Joe spoke with survivors of his regiment, soldiers with whom he had prayed before that and many another fight. On the last day of the ceremonies the ancient Confederates struggled up Cemetery Ridge as they had during Pickett's Charge, this time to be met at the top not by cannons but by cheers and embraces from the Yankee veterans. Ives had spoken with an old Rebel who had concluded the Civil War was a sham, "a rich man's war. We were just handed out bunk by the newspapers, and by the politicians."[3] Ives remembered those words. With their party was General Dan Sickles, whose life Joe Twichell helped save during the battle. Ives wrote Mike Myrick, "So far more Yankees than Johnies are drunk—isn't that running a little out of form? Apparently I've been appointed body guard to Gen. Sickles as his cussin' keeps the ladies away."[4]

That September was the first sojourn in Redding; in residence with Charlie and Harmony were father Joe and brothers Deac and Burt.[5] On visits to
Redding old Joe would lead prayers every morning, his voice swelling over the
family as it had over worshippers for forty-five years at Asylum Hill Church.[6]
Harmony's happily desultory brother Deac would live much of the time in
the cottage at the head of the driveway, "Deac's house." The Iveses spent
Thanksgiving 1913 at the parsonage in Hartford—the grateful congregation
let Joe stay on there when he retired—and that Christmas in Danbury.

In the presidential election of 1912 Ives had been disgusted with American prospects. On a sketch for *The Housatonic at Stockbridge* he jotted over
three identical chords, "this, this, or this??? A Sad chord—a hopeless chord—
a chord of futility—Same 3. . . . After leaving the [Hartsdale] polls on Nat'l
election Day of 1912 walking back over Healey Chicken Farm." The sad chord
was Teddy Roosevelt in his attempted comeback, the hopeless chord President
Taft, the chord of futility the idealistic Princeton professor Woodrow Wilson,
who won by a landslide. All three were Progressives, but that year Ives did
not like the country's agenda or that of any candidate—not Wilson's "New
Freedom" or Roosevelt's "New Nationalism" or Taft's business as usual.
Around the time of the election Ives wrote his bitter political song "Vote
for Names." Notes on the manuscript say, "same chord hit hard over & over
Hot Air Election Slogan. . . . After trying hard to think what's the best
way to vote—I say—just walk right in & grab a ballot with eyes shut."
For Ives, caught up in the transcendent dreams of his greatest works,
nothing was progressing fast enough. Apparently it would be the coming of
war in Europe, and President Wilson's lofty words about American ideals
relating to the war, that would transform Ives into a Wilsonian and a maverick
political philosopher.

Before the onset of politics and philosophy, music claimed most of Ives's
time and thought. During a twelve-day Elk Lake vacation of September 1911,
staying in Pell Jones's cabin with Joe and assorted Twichells, he worked on the
Browning Overture and again restructured the old First String Quartet Fugue,
this time toward the Fourth Symphony. The most significant item, though, is
shown in a diary note: "Idea of Concord Sonata." On this vacation a collection
of older ideas (the 1904 sketch of an *Alcotts* Overture, the 1907 sketch of an
Emerson Overture / Piano Concerto, some ideas from around 1909 based on
Hawthorne's short story "The Celestial Railroad," and the "Men of Literature" idea in general) became his Piano Sonata No. 2, a piece evoking the
sages of nineteenth-century Concord: Emerson, Hawthorne, the Alcotts, and
Thoreau.[7]

Soon the musical ideas based on Hawthorne developed into a closely
related pair of pieces: a piano concerto, and a movement for solo piano intended for the *Concord*. Ives completed an ink draft of the solo *Hawthorne*

dated October 12, 1911. *Emerson* would be noted as finished the next summer. Sometime that year Ives played through much of the sonata for Max Smith, improvising parts not yet completed. In an impromptu concert at First Presbyterian in spring 1914, he played *Emerson* and parts of *Hawthorne* in front of an audience. The listeners' feelings presumably ranged from shock to outrage.[8] *The Alcotts* would be dated November 28, 1914, *Thoreau* May 30, 1915. This sonata so involved with nature was composed mostly in the country, the first two movements at Hartsdale, the second two at Redding. Soon after he finished the *Concord,* Ives began collecting ideas for essays to go with the score.[9] Under the guise of meditations on the authors, *Essays Before a Sonata* would lay out the program, aesthetics, and some of the technique of the music.

From the beginning Ives called the *Concord* quite particularly a *sonata,* not a *set,* not a *study,* not one of his nostalgic titles placed on an ad hoc form. In contrast to his loose definition of *Holidays* as "symphony = my symphony," this time by the term "sonata" he meant something resembling what musicians perceive it to be. For the first time since his years of wrestling with the First Piano Sonata, he was ready to take on the genre again.

Late-Romantic tradition and Horatio Parker had taught Ives the norms of large-scale instrumental works such as symphony and sonata: first movement medium to fast in tempo, often "heroic" in tone with gentler contrasting material, the effect sometimes described (in those days) as a contrast of "masculine" and "feminine" themes; next two movements usually a slow one followed by a fast scherzo, or vice versa; scherzo usually light, racing, airy, or vivacious in tone; slow movement mostly soft and introspective, lyrical, often with contrasting large sections; finale variable in approach—medium to fast, perhaps heroic again, or light and breezy.

Most of these characteristics apply to the *Concord Sonata.* More systematically than ever before, Ives also modeled the work on the Romantic cyclic form, sharing themes among the movements. The *Concord* is unified by a steadily developing thematic design that culminates in the finale. The main exception to the usual arrangement is that the finale, *Thoreau,* is the slowest and most introspective of the four.[10] There are other features of conventional multimovement form that Ives neglects in the *Concord:* characteristic key structures (much of it is atonal or polytonal); patterns of repetition (there are few literal repetitions even of phrases, none of sections); characteristic formal outlines for each movement (no sonata or scherzo form, no ABA or the like).

For all the Ivesian variations on tradition, the *Concord* and the Fourth Symphony stand as his decisive return to European Romanticism and its genres, if not particularly to the *sound* of those genres. Again Ives mediates between European tradition and the tradition of the Yankee tinker, iconoclast—and church organist. Even though for much of his career he avoided the traditional genres and patterns ("the nice German recipe . . . to hell with it!"), all along he had played with ideas from traditional genres. If the *Concord*

is a Yankee sonata, it is still laid out in the four movements Beethoven had
used a century earlier and in much the same spirit as Beethoven's epic later
sonatas such as the *Hammerklavier*.[11] Partly by way of a nod to that connection, the *Concord*'s most striking melodic motive—recurring in every movement, one of the comparatively few quotes—is the four-note tattoo from
Beethoven's Fifth Symphony.

First movement, *Emerson:* Much of Ives's feeling for this movement, a
fixation that never ended, had to do with the subject's intimate connection to
his past. The philosopher was the most powerful of the Ives and Twichell
families' links to epic American figures, others including Lincoln, Grant, and
Twain. Emerson had slept in the house Ives was born in. Ives grew up hearing
Emerson's words through grandmother Sarah and his Uncle Joe, who knew
the man personally. Uniting his sense of the philosopher with his most admired composer, Ives saw Emerson as a Beethovenian figure. He finished his
preface for the movement in the *Essays Before a Sonata* this way:

There is an "oracle" at the beginning of the Fifth Symphony—in those four notes
lies one of Beethoven's greatest messages. We would place its translation above the
relentlessness of fate knocking at the door . . . and strive to bring it toward the spiritual
message of Emerson's revelations—even to the "common heart" of Concord—the Soul
of humanity knocking at the door of the Divine mysteries, radiant in the faith that it
will be opened—and that the human will become the Divine![12]

Emerson opens with a great wedge of sound, the left hand striding downward in heroic octaves, the right hand striving upward into pealing dissonant
handfuls of notes—the two most characteristic gestures of the movement.

Germinal melodic motives for the sonata are suggested in the first seconds.
The piece alternates between sections Ives called *prose* and *verse*, corresponding

to the contrasting theme-sections of sonata form: the prose tending to craggy, searching, heroic; the verse to placid and lyrical.[13] There are a few bar lines, but they only indicate phrasing; the music refuses to be contained by the regular beat patterns of meter.

Ives had learned mainly from Brahms, perhaps, to saturate a texture with melodic motives, sometimes highlighting them, sometimes submerging. But throughout the sonata and especially in *Emerson,* the motives and themes remain protean, kaleidoscopic. Future analysts would disagree on exactly what the leading motives are, and on their "normal" form.[14] There *are* no normal forms of the themes, nor is there the kind of literal repetition that would settle a definitive theme. Still, two primal motives stand out: the Beethoven's Fifth tattoo, which by Ivesian musical punning is also the beginning of the hymns *Missionary Chant* ("Ye Christian heralds") and *Martyn* ("Jesus, lover of my soul"); and the other a usually-lyrical, sometimes-extended line Ives called the "human-faith melody," which finds its apotheosis in *Thoreau.*

Other themes turn up in the course of the first movement, sometimes clearly related to the Beethoven and human-faith themes, sometimes not.[15] In *Emerson* motives switch character, blend into one another, continually appear and dissolve in myriad forms and intimations.

Emerson is the heart of the *Concord,* as *Thoreau* is the soul. Densely and dissonantly polyphonic, the first is the most radical movement, the most searching, hardest to understand, most problematic. Its idiosyncrasies arise from Ives's conception of the philosopher himself. In *Essays Before a Sonata* Ives hints at the formal and aesthetic foundations of the *Emerson* music, in some ways the most revolutionary of all his "completed" works:

Emerson is . . . America's deepest explorer of the spiritual immensities—a seer painting his discoveries in masses and with any color that may lie at hand—cosmic, religious, human, even sensuous; a recorder freely describing the inevitable struggle in the soul's uprise, perceiving from this inward source alone that "every ultimate fact is only the first of a new series" . . . who would then discover, if he can, that "wondrous chain which links the heavens with earth—the world of beings subject to one law". . . . We see him—standing on a summit at the door of the infinite. . ., peering into the mysteries of life, contemplating the eternities. . . . We see him—a mountain-guide so intensely on the lookout for the trail of his star that he has no time to stop and retrace his footprints.[16]

Every ultimate fact is only the first of a new series. Emerson has no clear-cut "themes" as in conventional sonata movements, but rather a protean progression of motives and themes always in evolution.[17] The philosopher *has no time to stop and retrace his footprints*. Neither will there be in the music the kinds of repetition that were considered necessary for coherence. Instead, *Emerson* is a vortex of a few motives transforming and combining and recombining, symbolically breaking trail toward a new frontier. *The world of beings subject to one law:* That law in life as Ives saw it, and expressed it in his most far-reaching music, is both manifest and secret, unsearchable and generative, like the motivic and formal designs that hold together the teeming worlds of the *Concord* and the Fourth Symphony. The law is the wondrous chain linking humanity to nature and the heavens. It is available to the child and the sage, each in their own way. The law unites the myriad world of beings that are Ives's mature works; it keeps everyone, however solitary the path, moving toward the same horizon, the great someday when the human becomes the divine.

In fragments scattered through the "Emerson" essay, Ives suggests the background of the technique, the spirit, the baffling formal digressiveness of this music.

The activity of permanence is what Emerson will not permit. He will not accept repose against the activity of truth"[18]. . . . These struggles toward the absolute . . . do not these in themselves impart something . . . of their own unity and coherence which is not received as such at first, nor is foremost in their expression?[19] . . . His underlying plan of work seems based on the large unity of a series of particular aspects of a subject rather than on the continuity of its expression. . . . Nature loves analogy and hates repetition. Botany reveals evolution, not permanence. An apparent confusion, if lived with long enough, may become orderly.[20] . . . Initial coherence today may be dullness tomorrow, probably because formal or outward unity depends so much on repetition, sequences, antitheses, paragraphs. . . . Perhaps there are flashes of light, still in cipher, kept there by unity, the code of which the world has not yet discovered. The unity of one sentence inspires the unity of the whole.[21]

Then in the Epilogue Ives summarizes the conception of form that rules the *Concord:*

Unity is too generally conceived of, or too easily accepted as analogous to form; and form as analogous to custom; and custom to habit. And habit may be one of the parents of custom and form, but there are all kinds of parents. Perhaps all unity in art, at its inception, is half-natural and half-artificial, but time insists . . . that it is all natural. The "unity of dress" for a man at a ball requires a collar; yet he could dance better without it. . . . The unity of a sonata movement has long been associated with its form . . . a first theme, a development, a second in a related key and its development, the free fantasia, the recapitulation. . . . Some claim for Tchaikowsky that his clarity and coherence of design is unparalleled. . . . That depends, it seems to us, on how far repetition is an essential part of clarity and coherence. . . . If nature is not enthusiastic about explanation, why should Tchaikowsky be? . . . To Emerson, unity and the over-soul, or the common-heart, are synonymous. Unity is at least nearer to these than to solid geometry, though geometry may be all unity.[22]

Yet the singular approach to form in *Emerson* is not its most radical element. In keeping with his vision of the great searcher, the spiritual pioneer in untraveled territory, Ives *extended the act of composition into time.* Going beyond the fade-ins and fade-outs of other works, which suggest a fragment of a greater music, Ives made *Emerson* a literally uncompletable piece. He wrote,

This is, as far as I know, the only piece which, every time I play it or turn to it, seems unfinished. Even the *[Four Transcriptions from Emerson]* are not exactly as I play them now. . . . It is a peculiar experience and, I must admit, a stimulating and agreeable one that I've had with this Emerson music. It may have something to do with the feeling I have about Emerson, for every time I read him I seem to get a new angle of thought and feeling and experience from him. . . . I find that I don't play or feel like playing this music even now in the same way each time. Some of the passages now played haven't been written out . . . and I don't know as I ever shall write them out, as it may take away the daily pleasure of playing this music and seeing it grow and feeling that it is not finished (I may always have the pleasure of not finishing it).[23]

That is the ultimate radicalism of *Emerson:* the expression of the program, the leading idea, becomes an endless process of composition. The music is an analogue of Emerson's endless quest. As such it will go on (to the satisfaction of those who appreciate the idea, to the despair of editors), because Ives left no "final" form of *Emerson.* In the 1920 vanity-press publication he would water it down, simplify the harmonies, remove some of the dissonances. In 1917, though, Ives may already have written one of the eventual *Four Transcriptions from Emerson,* which restore some of the earlier sketches' complexities and take the ideas in new directions.[24] Then in the 1940s, editing the sonata for a new edition, he restored some of the original complexity and dissonance and added more—mainly in *Emerson,* but somewhat in all the movements.

All these versions are *Emerson,* not any one of them. In all its avatars the music still speaks with the same voice. A given performance of the *Concord* may simply use one of the two published editions, or some amalgam of sources chosen by the performer. Different performances and recordings of *Emerson* will have different notes. In this way, perhaps without having planned it as such, but thoroughly from within his nature, Ives made each performer, each editor, and ultimately each listener his co-creators.[25]

Second movement, *Hawthorne:* "Any comprehensive conception of Hawthorne," Ives wrote, "either in words or music, must have for its basic theme something that has to do with the influence of sin upon the conscience— something more than the Puritan conscience, but something which is permeated by it." Having made that point, Ives declines to be comprehensive. Puritan guilt is not his style. Besides, this is supposed to be a scherzo. Ives bases his impression on the charming and magical Hawthorne, not the dark one:

This fundamental part of Hawthorne is not attempted in our music . . . which is but an "extended fragment" trying to suggest some of his wilder, fantastical adventures into the half-childlike, half-fairylike phantasmal realms. It may have something to do with the children's excitement on the "frosty Berkshire morning" . . . or something to do with "Feathertop," the scarecrow . . . and "the little demons dancing around his pipe bowl"; or something to do with the old hymn-tune that haunts the church and sings only to those in the churchyard to protect them from secular noises, as when the circus parade comes down Main Street . . . or something else in the *Wonder-Book*—not something that happens, but the way something happens . . . or something to do with "The Celestial Railroad"; or something personal, which tries to be "national" suddenly at twilight, and universal suddenly at midnight; or something about the ghost of a man who never lived, or about something that never will happen, or something else that is not.[26]

The program proceeds along those lines, evoking a child's winter morning in Concord, a churchyard and passing parade, the "Celestial Railroad" story. If *Emerson* is quasi-orchestral in effect, *Hawthorne* is an entirely pianistic race over the keyboard, a kaleidoscopic dream-scherzo, a mostly atonal ragtimey toccata interspersed with hymns. The spectral hymns are rudely interrupted by secular noises, the last interruption being a circus band on Main Street playing Ives's old *Country Band March*. The organization is programmatic and abstract at once. Though *Hawthorne* evolves constantly, never retracing its steps, John Kirkpatrick saw it as a symmetrical form: phantasmagoria / nocturne / ragtime / alternation of "chaos," "hymn," and "march" / ragtime / nocturne / phantasmagoria.[27] On the whole the movement sticks to its own themes (prominently *Country Band March* and "Columbia, the Gem"), but touches of the Beethoven and human-faith melodies turn up, and it is pervaded by intimations of the other movements—two or three notes, a gesture, a texture, a shape. The first nocturne presents an innovation that in the sonata's early public career would elicit much wit at Ives's expense: the pianist picks up a length of board to play a series of gentle tone clusters. "It gives a kind of sound," Ives wrote, "of distant reverberations that one may hear in the woods."[28] There are loud clusters too, later, in violent flurries. *Hawthorne* ends with a swooping upbeat, an end more like a beginning.[29]

Third movement, *The Alcotts:*

> We dare not attempt to follow the philosophic raptures of Bronson Alcott. . . . And so we won't try to reconcile the music sketch of the Alcotts with much besides the memory of that home under the elms—the Scotch songs and the family hymns . . . though there may be an attempt to catch something of that common sentiment . . . a strength of hope that never gives way to despair—a conviction in the power of the common soul which, when all is said and done, may be as typical as any theme of Concord and its Transcendentalists.[30]

This movement, then, has less of the garrulous philosopher Bronson than the sentimental and domestic Louisa May Alcott, author of *Little Women*. It is the sonata's slow movement. The tone is mostly simple, gentle, lyrical, diatonic or mildly bitonal. Near the beginning we hear the most extended version yet of the human-faith melody, which returns later. There are suggestions of Beth Alcott playing an old Scotch air on the parlor piano, attempting Beethoven's Fifth. The music is lucid and intimate, appropriate to the little parlor of the

Alcott's Concord home. The melodies return to themes and motives introduced in *Emerson,* now domesticated by the setting. While *Emerson* is heroic and "masculine" with gentler intervals, *The Alcotts* is gentle and "feminine" with heroic interludes. It builds to a pealing climax on the Beethoven theme: "the soul of humanity," Ives wrote, "knocking at the door of the divine mysteries, radiant in the faith that it *will* be opened—and the human become the divine!" That attempt, Ives implies, may be made as well in a parlor as on an Emersonian mountaintop. The Beethoven motive, in fact, tends to have a different disposition in each movement—call it striving and monumental in *Emerson,* rushed and marchlike in *Hawthorne,* gently lyrical at the beginning of *The Alcotts* (though heroic at the end), meditative in *Thoreau.* The motive evolves during the course of each movement as well.

The whole of the *Concord,* with its pervasive sense of the actual presence of the unspoken and unseen, gathers together in the finale. And for that who better than Thoreau, who loved music and the sounds and silences of nature— to him there was no difference—and who was a great poet of the ineffable:

> I hearing get who had but ears,
> And sight, who had but eyes before,
> I moments live who lived but years,
> And truth discern who knew but learning's lore.

Ives wrote of *Thoreau,* his finale: "If there shall be a program for our music, let it follow his thought on an autumn day of Indian summer at Walden—the shadow of a thought at first, colored by the mist and haze over the pond."[31] This image of the writer merged with Ives's recollection of the autumn day his father died, and Thoreau became "that reassuring and true friend, who stood by me one 'low' day, when the sun had gone down, long, long before sunset."[32] The music, among many things, is an homage to the friend who once consoled him with the assurance of self-reliance, and gave him a vision of a musical journey through life. Thoreau wrote:

A man's life should be a stately march to a sweet but unheard music, and when to his fellows it shall seem irregular and inharmonious, he will only be stepping to a livelier measure, or his nicer ear hurry him into a thousand symphonies and concordant variations. There will be no halt ever, but at most a marching on his post, on such a pause as is richer than any sound, when the melody runs into such depth and wildness as to be no longer heard, but implicitly consented to with the whole life and being.[33]

In the years of Ives's apprenticeship two mentors had expanded his conception of music. When Ives wrote *music is life,* he wrote what Thoreau and his father had taught him. Thoreau taught him as well to see silence and the sounds of nature as a higher, eternal music: "Music is the sound of the circulation in nature's veins. It is the flux which melts nature. . . . The healthy ear always hears it, nearer or more remote."[34] When Ives wrote of music as a primal human activity and symbol, he echoed Thoreau:

The brave man [wrote Thoreau] is the sole patron of music; he recognizes it for his mother-tongue—a more mellifluous and articulate language than words, in comparison with which speech is recent and temporary. It is his voice. His language must have the same majestic movement and cadence that philosophy assigns to the heavenly bodies. The universe falls in and keeps pace with it, which before proceeded singly and discordant. Hence are poetry and song. . . . All sounds, and more than all, silence, do fife and drum for us. The least creaking doth whet all our senses and emit a tremulous light, like the aurora borealis, over things. As polishing expresses the vein in marble and the grain in wood, so music brings out what of heroic lurks anywhere.[35]

When George Ives played his cornet to Charlie from across a pond, he was exploring effects of space Thoreau knew well, and saw as a spiritualization of sound:

Heard at a distance, the sound of a bell acquires a certain vibratory hum. . . . All sound heard at a great distance thus tends to produce the same music, vibrating the strings of the universal lyre. There comes to me a melody which the air has strained, which has conversed with every leaf and needle of the woods.[36]

Wrote Thoreau as well, "Music is perpetual, and only hearing is intermittent." Likewise Charles Ives's vision of a greater, more eternal music, of which his music was only sketches, suggestions, fragments.

In Ives's relationship to the *Thoreau* music there was another personal connection, to another central figure of his life. On the ink copy of the movement an Ives memo notes, "from some ideas—'Walden Sounds—Ch Bells, flute Harp (Aeolian) to go with Harmony's Mist . . . Elk Lake 1910." At the end of that vacation at Pell Jones's they had watched the last mist over the lake, and afterward Harmony had written a poem called "Mists," about loss and renewal:

> Low lie the mists; they hide each hill and dell;
> The grey skies weep with us who bid farewell.
> But happier days through memory weaves a spell,
> And brings new hope to hearts who bid farewell.

Ives set it to a simple melodic line, while the piano weaves around it a haunting atmosphere made of whole-tone chords.[37] With this song they bade farewell to Harmony's mother, to Uncle Mark Twain, to their own lost child. That particular mist and those farewells touch *Thoreau* as well.[38]

The finale encompasses so many things personal, musical, natural, mystical. Like the other movements of the *Concord*, *Thoreau* has its own sound, texture, rhythm, atmosphere; like each of the others, it is interwoven with the whole. Most of the sonata's motivic material circulates through it, present in every phrase, but transformed into an atmosphere of quiet reflection, "the slow, almost monotonous swaying beat of this autumnal day and the gently lapping waters of Walden Pond."[39] Ives's programmatic description cites Thoreau's "Aeolian harp" of telegraph wires humming in the wind, and paraphrases the passage of the bell acquiring "a certain vibratory hum, as if the pine needles in the horizon were the strings of a harp which is swept . . . a vibration of the universal lyre." The music is full of secret sounds, echoes, murmurs, flurries, ripples. The tempo fluctuates constantly, moving ahead, slowing, pausing. The harmonies are steadily chromatic and elusive, with a touch of whole-tone haze. The form is rondo-like,[40] marked by the periodic return of a gently striding ostinato bass line, the "monotonous swaying beat" of the day, moving upward while above it mystical chord sequences descend like a sigh.

In these figures the opening wedge of *Emerson* is matched by a condensing wedge that moves the music toward its whispered conclusion.

Program becomes form, the literal becomes abstract: "the poet's flute is heard out over the pond."[41] A literal flute enters near the end of a piano sonata. The whole of the striving, heroic, songful, wistful, magical, comical, paradoxical, protean, and dynamic *Concord* comes down to the image of Thoreau playing his flute over Walden Pond.

In its beautiful, yearning melody the significant thematic ideas of the work— mainly the human-faith and Beethoven motives—find their apotheosis. But not rest, not finality. In the sonata paradox and diversity condense *toward* unity, not yet all the way. Though the flute's melody is mostly in B♭ and the effect gentle, the piano accompaniment remains chromatic and searching, and the last notes of the flute are the three that begin the Beethoven motive, but without their resolving descent. At the end, with an evocation of the distant Concord bell floating over Walden, the tonal course settles on D. But the last note heard, barely audibly, is the unresolved leading tone C♯. Rather than a traditional resolution into stability, this is a dynamic conclusion for all its quietness. Ives describes the end of the music and the program, "He goes up the 'pleasant hillside of pine, hickories' and moonlight to his cabin, 'with a strange liberty in Nature, a part of herself.' "[42]

The outer movements of the *Concord* are set in nature—the Emersonian mountaintops of the beginning, Thoreau's intimate woodlands at the end— and so America's two greatest visionaries of nature frame this work of strange liberties and deep import. In between we find in *Hawthorne* a phantasmagoria on the life of towns, of human societies, and in *The Alcotts* the society of home and family. The image of Concord, like Danbury a town both real and mythical, a symbol of eternal community and human aspiration, enfolds the four movements. Rarely in music have the unseen and unspoken mysteries of life seemed so imminent—from Emerson's heroic journey, to Hawthorne's "ghost of a man who never lived," to the Alcotts' "conviction in the power of the common soul," to Thoreau's melody that "runs into such depth and wildness as to be no longer heard." Ives wrote at the end of the *Essays Before a Sonata,* "The strains of one man may fall far below the course of those Phaetons of Concord . . . but the greater the distance his music falls away, the more reason that some greater man shall bring his nearer those higher spheres." The *Concord Sonata* is another Ivesian signpost pointed toward the ultimate millennium.

In March 1914, with the *Concord* and Third Violin Sonata and Fourth Symphony in the oven with other things, Charlie and Harmony prepared for their first full season in Redding. He was waxing grouchy over the frustrations involved in building the place. Harmony wrote him from Hartford, "I do hope you will get up tomorrow night & then we can go to Redding Sat. I have a perfectly mad desire to see the house again. I <u>love</u> that house—I dont care what <u>you</u> say!" He would come to love it as much as she did. But the Iveses did not get to Redding that March. At the beginning of May Charlie wrote Aunt Amelia,

We expect now to be settled in Redding on June 3rd or 4th. . . . Harmony will have her hands full with housecleaning and moving. Rocket has been so lame during the last six weeks that we are afraid that he cannot be driven to Redding. We have a small automobile which will be a necessity in Redding, as I am to commute all summer. It is quite easy to run. We are getting to be quite experts with it.(Harmony especially). . . . Neither of us enjoy riding in it—per se—we use it as a matter of business.[43]

He was ritually reassuring Aunt Amelia, as he had been doing all his life. He was hardly expert with the car. One of the nephews, Moss's son Bigelow, would remember the Model T Ford Ives used mainly to drive to the train station: "He was really one of the world's wildest drivers. . . . On one occasion he tried to go up to Bethel with it. This was quite an extensive drive of six miles or more, and farther than he usually went. I remember going though a very narrow, twisting tunnel under the railroad tracks. . . . He said, 'I was killed here once, and that was enough for me.' "[44]

Soon after arriving that June 1914, Ives wrote Moss, "We're getting settled in R. It's great down there now. The planting is about done. Four kittens joined the household yesterday. We expect Mother tomorrow."[45] Mollie Ives was sixty-five. It may have been during this visit that her son told her, for the first time, the kind of money he was making. In his first income tax report for 1913, Ives had put down $10,342.32 in gross income—over $111,000 in 1991 dollars.[46] Mollie reported the news back to the family in Danbury, declaring herself flabbergasted.[47] Probably it was also during that summer's vacation that Ives wrote in "Our Book" a Redding schedule for himself:

6:30 up & at them. / 6.45–7.30 chores (fire, coal, pump, spring water, etc) / 7.30–7.45 [play] Bach / 7.45–8.15 Breakfast / 8.15–11.00 Hard work [presumably composing] / 11–12.30 Farm work / 12 30–1 loaf / 1–1.30 lunch / 1.30–2 read / 2–6 Farm work & water trees & wood / 6.30–7.30 dinner (big) / 7.30–8 smoke and talk / 8–9 read . . . / 9

The house in West Redding—it has no front or back, and every door is the front door.

to bed. D.C. at coda. [Below:] Farm work = potatoes, husk corn, dry beans, burn weeds, dig around not up apple trees . . . (Oct 15 screen off) Cut weeds around spring.[48]

At the end of June, as Ives agreeably busied himself with commuting and composing and digging in his garden, Archduke Francis Ferdinand was assassinated in Sarajevo and sleeping monsters awoke all over Europe.

In Redding on September 26, 1914, two weeks after the first Battle of the Marne, perhaps a week before the disastrous visit of violinist Franz Milcke, Ives finished and dated the ink score of his finest song. If the *Concord* is one of the essential Ivesian works on a grand scale, *General William Booth Enters into Heaven* is an essential one on a small scale. With Vachel Lindsay's folk-poetic memorial to the founder of the Salvation Army, Ives found a theme at the heart and soul of his art.[49]

Vachel Lindsay used to make a wild music out of this poem, chanting and braying and clapping like a hot gospel preacher.[50] Its scene is a march into heaven by a crowd of drunks and floozies and drug fiends, with General Booth at the head, pounding out the march time on his bass drum. The verses include musical cues: "Bass drum beaten loudly," banjos, "sweet flute music." Ives called his setting a "Glory trance."[51] He picked up Lindsay's cues, caught every line and image, and built a temple of sound and imagery with all the shabby ecstasy of a sawdust revival. *Booth led boldly with his big bass drum. (Are you washed in the blood of the lamb?)*[52] The beat here is Ivesian piano drumming, in a steady march time. *Hallelujah!* the marchers bawl. *Walking lepers followed rank on rank, Lurching bravos from the ditches dank / Drabs from the alleyways and drug fiends pale . . . Vermin-eaten saints with mouldy breath / Unwashed legions with the ways of Death. (Are you washed in the blood of the Lamb?)* Now the parade to glory is in full cry, marching in tattered array past the bewildered hosts of heaven. The piano becomes fiddles and banjos: *Big-voiced lassies made their banjos bang, bang, bang / Tranced, fanatical they shrieked and sang: Are you? Are you washed in the blood of the lamb?* Music and words together rise to a rapture. *Hallelujah! Hallelujah, Lord! Bull-necked convicts blowed a blare, on, on, upward thro' the golden air!* The piano blares out tinny but triumphant bugle calls. Like the revivals it evokes, the scene is strange and comical as it reaches its peak of delirium. Then suddenly, everything changes. *Jesus came from the courthouse door, / Stretched his hands above the passing poor. / Booth saw not, but led his queer ones / / Round and round and round and round. . .* The music rocks gently into silence. Even if Booth saw not, the miracle happens anyway. The march begins again, transfigured: *All that blear review marched on spotless, clad in raiment new. / The lame were straightened, withered limbs uncurled, / And blind eyes opened on a new sweet world.*

At the end Ives creates one of his most indelible moments, with the simplest of means. *Are you washed in the blood of the lamb?* the singer asks once more, to rolled chords. He poses the question a last time, now accompanied by plain gospel harmony. With that simple, eloquent gesture, Ives captures the miracle: these freaks and floozies, this rabble every one, these preposterous angels, *are* washed in the blood of the lamb. As the parade fades into the distance a question hangs in the golden air: *Are you?* It is a microcosm of so much of what Ives was about—the mundane transformed into the spiritual, the comic into the sublime, paradoxes transcended before our eyes, and a final question awaiting answer.

Wrote musicologist Wilfrid Mellers, "The art of this marvelous song is thus inseparable from its literalism. It renders incarnate the heart of the gospeller's experience, without destroying its grotesque comedy. . . . We become the gospeller, share in his vision."[53] The wondrous simplicity of the end pays off the complexity and comedy of the beginning. Ives's mediation and modulation among apparently incompatible styles have been wedded to expression, illustration, and meaning. He has created a *technique of paradox*. In 1914 he was already carrying that technique to its highest finesse and significance in the Fourth Symphony.

In November 1914 the Iveses were back in the city, where he took some Globe Theater musicians through *Washington's Birthday* with fair results. The band would play it again the following spring.[54] The Iveses spent the winter in Manhattan at 27 West 11th Street. There Charlie finished *The Alcotts* at the end of November, the Third Violin Sonata on December 20. In March 1915, taking care of her father in Hartford, Harmony wrote,

I had the nicest dream about you, my lamb, just before I waked up—that I'd just kissed you for the first time & I felt just as I did in the woods near Farmington. It was so sweet my darling darling love. I loved you then as hard as I could & harder but I love you more & more & more all the time for loving makes loving. I love you so much more than this mind & body is capable of loving.[55]

The world would not leave Ives alone with love and music. On Friday May 7, as the Iveses prepared to leave for Redding, a German submarine sank the British liner *Lusitania;* 1,198 people died, 114 Americans among them. From President Wilson down, the country was shaken and apprehensive. On the way to work and all day in the office, Ives saw the news in everyone's faces. After work he walked to the Hanover Square station to take the Elevated home. The train was delayed and a big crowd gathered on the platform. Below on the street a hurdy-gurdy man cranked out an old hymn. Someone began to whistle along, others joined in, humming and singing. Ives described the moment when the crowd broke into full song:

A workman with a shovel over his shoulder came on the platform and joined in the chorus, and the next man, a Wall Street banker with white spats and a cane, joined in it, and finally it seemed to me that everybody was singing this tune . . . as a natural outlet for what their feelings had been going through all day long. There was a feeling of dignity all through this. The hand-organ man seemed to sense this and wheeled the organ nearer the platform and kept it up fortissimo (and the chorus sounded out as though every man in New York must be joining in it). Then the first train came in and everybody crowded in, and the song gradually died out, but the effect on the crowd still showed. Almost nobody talked—the people acted as though they might be coming out of a church service. In going uptown, occasionally little groups would start singing or humming the tune.

What they sang "wasn't a Broadway hit, it wasn't a musical comedy air, it wasn't a waltz tune or a dance tune or an opera tune or a classical tune. . . . It wasn't a tune written to be sold, or written by a professor of music—but by a man who was but giving out an experience."[56] The tune was "In the Sweet By and By," and it had been one of George Ives's trademarks. Through his youth Charlie had heard his father play that hymn at church and concerts and camp meetings, sometimes using his echo attachment to make it seem to come from far away. On the Hanover Square platform Ives was moved as he perhaps had been by no musical experience since his youth. Here was an outpouring that transcended all barriers, a moment when the humblest melody became the voice of a people in their hour of anguish. Surely it was unforgettable for everyone there. For Charles Ives, the combination of that scene with that particular music rang his most cherished memories and convictions. Inevitably he would make a piece of it, and he was then at the height of his powers. He would call the work *From Hanover Square North, at the End of a Tragic Day, the Voice of the People Again Arose.*

He composed it in Redding during the months following the scene on the train platform. In it we hear late Ives at his most seasoned and most subtle. In technique the piece draws on his phantasmagorias going back a decade; it sounds similar, for one, to *An Elegy to Our Forefathers.* (He would join that, *The Rockstrewn Hills,* and *Hanover Square* to make up the Second Orchestral Set.) *Hanover Square* also owes much to the contemporaneous finale of the Fourth Symphony—especially in the offstage group of instruments and the continuous patter of the percussion battery. The expressive feel, though, is different from the Fourth Symphony; for all its tangle of individual voices, *Hanover Square* seems more concrete, a specific remembered scene rather than the ethereal music of the symphony finale.

Hanover Square begins with the distant group, the voices chanting the liturgical Te Deum: *We praise Thee, O God. We acknowledge Thee to be the Lord. All the Earth doth worship Thee.* One offstage instrument after another joins a babbling web of sound. It is the vibrations of the city, made up of myriad individual strands each seemingly in its own world, each contributing to the progress of the whole. The piece accumulates line by line, evoking the gathering of the crowd. The cellos of the main orchestra enter on a theme hinting at "The Sweet By and By." The onstage group begins to accumulate as well; meanwhile the offstage instruments, continuing, give the sonority a remarkable three-dimensional quality—more lucidly than the *Comedy* of the Fourth

Symphony, *Hanover Square* sounds like it extends into the distance. The phrases in the music succeed one another like changes of perspective, the eyes / ears moving from one part of the crowded panoply to another. It unfolds in cumulative form; the hymn slowly gathers definition, its words more and more present though unspoken: *There's a land . . . that beautiful shore . . .*

When everyone in the orchestra has entered we are carried to the climax. More than thirty separate parts—some of them variants of one another, some harmonizing another, most on their own tack—join in the exalted commotion. Over it all the trumpets and horns peal out the chorus of the old gospel hymn that unites all those individuals: *In the sweet by and by / We shall meet on that beautiful shore.* It is a climax in the earnest and profound voice of ordinary "unmusical" people, the music of the ages. Some of the trumpets add off-key attempts at harmonies and counterpoints, as the trumpets did in *The Fourth of July.* There, though—and in each piece the sense is unmistakable—the trumpets were drunk; in *Hanover Square* they are singing through tears. The refrain over, the crowd begins to break up. Echoes of the tune recede into the distance, into inaudibility.

The subtlety of this work lies not only in its unique sonority but in its expressive and programmatic depth. In effect, the opening Te Deum chant is gradually transformed into "The Sweet By and By," the transformation symbolic as well as musical. The formal liturgy of the church sanctuary becomes the spontaneous testament of the man in the street, but they are the same in spirit: *We acknowledge thee to be the Lord.* Surely this is the ultimate meaning of *Hanover Square,* which Ives's prose writings would proclaim time and again: the spirit of the people is the answer to tragic days like that one. When myriad individuals unite they speak in a whirlwind, however roughly, with something like a divine voice. Thus the text Ives wrote for his song of the same era, "Majority" or "The Masses," whose thundering tone clusters would begin his book of songs:

> The Masses!
> The Masses have toiled,
> Behold the works of the World!
> The Masses are thinking,
> Whence comes the thought of the World!
> The Masses are singing,
> Whence comes the Art of the World!
> The Masses are yearning,
> Whence comes the hope of the World!
> The Masses are dreaming,
> Whence comes the visions of God![57]

It is this impossible, doomed, and magnificent vision of humanity that is proclaimed in the climax of *From Hanover Square North, at the End of a Tragic Day, the Voice of the People Again Arose.* In the world since then, there has rarely appeared anything like that climax, or that faith.

Tom Sails Away

As the complexities of texture and conception accumulated in Charles Ives's last works, so did the complexities of his external life. Ives & Myrick, every year bigger and more profitable, kept its claim on him, though he always managed to contain business within the bounds of his rigid schedule. Much of his composing was done in his head while walking to work, commuting on the train to and from Redding, in odd moments at the office. The war was another claim on his energy and attention. Ives spent the first years of the war bitterly resisting it and the last year, when America entered, exhaustively embracing it.

Another claim, the most satisfying one despite the stresses, was his family. He and Harmony had lost their chance at having children with her hysterectomy, so their parental yearnings fell at first on the nephews. Since George Ives died, it had always seemed inevitable that Charlie would be head of the family—or at least, co-director with Aunt Amelia. From the teens into the twenties, one or two of Moss's six children would be living with Charlie and Harmony much of the time, especially during the summers at Redding. Ives knew children well; he was so close to his own childhood. He knew how to amuse and challenge and provoke them in their own spirit. The nephews found him more like a playmate than an uncle. Charlie and Uncle Deac would clog-dance while the children laughed and clapped time.[1] At Redding Ives had a pond dug for swimming and built a tennis court next to the barn. Though he had long stopped playing tennis he liked to watch young people on the court.

His brother's son Moss White was physically and mentally handicapped; for just that reason, Ives was most devoted to this nephew. During the teens Ives gave Moss White violin lessons, apparently to good effect. On a page of the *Browning Overture,* which evokes the sounds and rhythms of nature, Ives notes, "after a walk with Moss White Hartsdale July 1912."[2] (In "Our Book" Ives wrote down some of this nephew's quixotic sayings: "Moss which is greatest masterpiece—'Bleak House' or B' 5th Sym'—M—'Bleak H—because it sounds better.' . . . 'Do you brush your teeth every day'.—Moss—quick strong voice 'Yes—once in a while.' "[3]) With all the nephews Uncle Charlie discussed art and politics, suggested readings and listenings, kept track of their schooling (and helped finance it), took them for walks in city and country, brought them to work with him. He came to resemble Uncle Lyman, who because he and Amelia could not have children informally adopted Charlie and Moss. Besides, sharing out children was an old family tradition, and Moss's pay as a judge was barely up to a family of eight.[4]

Nephew Brewster remembered being in his uncle's study in New York, Ives composing the *Concord* and stopping to explain the music. In later years, when the elevated train roared by Brewster's Manhattan apartment while Uncle Charlie was visiting, the old man would race over to the window and stick his head out to listen.[5] (For all his technophobia—Ives never owned a radio, disliked autos, hated movies, and rarely touched a telephone—he had the authentic American love of trains.) It is perhaps surprising to hear Brewster recall, "I know that he was interested in Picasso, John Marin, and many other artists."[6] Mostly the nephews remembered games with their uncle—baseball and touch football with Charlie leading one side and Moss the other. Said Chester Ives, "He'd wind up [to pitch]—he really had a classic way of the windup, just as any professional player. My poor father was always catching for him. Father used to lose his interest in catching the ball for him, and Uncle Charlie would get mad and say, 'Come on, Moss. Pay attention when I'm throwing.'."[7] The nephews, though, could not appease Charlie and Harmony's yearning for children of their own. So in a roundabout and painful way they got themselves a child.

Harmony had been involved in the Fresh Air Program from its inception, and during the summer the Iveses opened Deac's house, their cottage, to poor urban families.[8] The first family arrived in mid-July 1915. They were succeeded by the Osbornes, a mother and five children; another child or two stayed in New York with their father.[9] One of the Osborne children was a sickly girl of fourteen months named Edith. The Ives family had taken in the needy for generations and Harmony had been a nurse to the poor. When the Osbornes left in August the Iveses naturally offered to take care of Edith until she was well again. They soon began to feel they could not give her up.

They spent that Thanksgiving at Aunt Amelia's, then Harmony took the baby to Hartford while Charlie moved into another Manhattan place, at 144 East 40th Street. Harmony, with Edie, would be in Hartford taking care of her father for much of the next year. She wrote Charlie, "Margaret took her out in a baby-carriage this afternoon & said she called 'ma-ma' and 'Charlie' several times. . . . The baby has a new dollie that she is crazy about. I feel as if I couldn't let her go from us. . . . I'm afraid we made a mistake from our point of view ever to keep her."[10] It was a plea. At the Christmas table in Hartford were old Joe, sister Sue, and the Iveses who now seemed to be three; they made a tiny Christmas tree for Edie.[11] In February Harmony wrote, "The baby was very sober after you left her—us—for sometime & asked, 'Where's

Slolie?'—ever so many times. . . . I am afraid I am getting too fond of her."[12]

Finally they decided to adopt, a delicate proposition when both parents are alive. Certainly Charlie had fallen for the baby as well, and adoption might save Edie's life. The Osbornes were a destitute family with too many mouths to feed; Edie never had been healthy (nor ever would be). In practice the Iveses bought the baby from her family. Securing her was inevitably going to be messy, risky, and expensive, made more so by Ives's compulsive generosity.

On October 18, 1916, Ives wrote in "Our Book," "Edith now our own. Edith Osborne Ives." By the time the adoption was legalized, a considerable amount of money had probably changed hands. Charles Osborne, Jr., the father, kept demanding more. In a legal document sworn out a year or so after the adoption, Harmony wrote, "The family were perfect strangers to us and while we have desired to help them until they got on a self-supporting basis, there is no obligation and we deem it wisest and best that communication with them be carried on thro' a third person."[13] (On the back, Ives has added 36,500 and 3,500 to get 40,000. If that was in fact money going or gone to the Osbornes, it is nearly half a million 1991 dollars.) In March 1917 Ives wrote Edie's father,

I telephoned [lawyer?] Mr. Clark and found that he is still out of town . . . so I thought it better instead of going over the matter with some one else to wait until he returns . . . and the new arrangement can start a week from Saturday instead of tomorrow. [Keyes] Winter also has been delayed . . . and will be here Monday or Tuesday, and I will then have him straighten things out for us. I hope you feel better and everything is going well.[14]

Two lawyers, "new arrangement," and this months after the supposedly final adoption. Ives was supporting the Osbornes now and there was no telling how long it might go on. The situation remained fraught for years. Willie Verplanck's wife Katherine, who worked at Ives & Myrick, recalled, "I knew what was going on between Mr. Ives and Edith's family. Mr. Ives was so generous to them. . . . After the Iveses took Edith, her family bothered him to death for more money, and he kept giving to them."[15] As late as 1921, five years after the adoption, Ives would warn a new secretary not to respond to inquiries about Edith.[16] At length the Osbornes faded from the picture.[17] Edith grew up knowing little about them. "I don't know how," Katherine Verplanck said, "but Mr. Ives settled the thing. I know that later he felt free and clear about having Edith as his child." It probably cost him a great deal in cash, more in worry and time. He had the money, but he was running out of energy and time.

Edith became a kind of enchanted woodsprite, blond and elfin, ailing a good deal of the time. Visitors often found her sick in bed, a book in hand. John Kirkpatrick described Edie as "like one of Hawthorne's characters, a little unreal; but there was a lot to her."[18] Later she played piano a little, but was more interested in reading and writing and drawing. Following her father's lead, she made up stories about animals and magical places in the woods. She loved Redding more than anywhere.

As Horace Bushnell had counseled, Harmony filled her daughter with religion, sending her to classes at First Presbyterian. Edie talked about God all

Harmony and Edith Ives, 1915.

the time, her father jotting down her cute notions in "Our Book": "She wished when God made her, he'd made her head first & then she could have seen Heaven." When being kissed goodnight by her mother, "I love you just as much as I do God." Walking over snow, "I'm just like Peter walking on the water." As a teenager, a sickly daughter of reclusive parents, Edie would feel lonely and resentful, but before and after that she was girlishly affectionate and loyal to her parents (they told her she was adopted, to some of their friends' dismay[19]). What rebellions she felt she apparently did not express, at least not to Charlie and Harmony. From the time she arrived on the scene, much of Ives's composing was done with the little blond child under the piano, playing with her dolls.[20] She was the angel of the house and played the role instinctively. Ives would write to his mentor John Griggs of Edie, "She reads and writes and sings and draws all day contentedly. . . . No child has ever given her family more than she has us." Music and his wife and daughter would be the main forces that preserved Charles Ives's life longer than anyone could have expected.

One of the things husband and father would have to be preserved from was the war. When the Germans sank the *Lusitania* in May 1915, President Wilson declared, "There is such a thing as a man being too proud to fight. There is such a thing as a nation being so right that it does not need to convince others that it is right." The rhetoric sounds almost Ivesian. For Ives around that time, Wilson modulated from a "chord of futility" into a hero.

Ives was then in the midst of his greatest works, but getting toward the end. By 1916, when the great wave of his creativity crested, *Holidays, Three Places,* the *Concord,* and the Second Orchestral Set were essentially done. Ives seems to have been working during later 1915–16 mainly on the Fourth Symphony; his fair copy of the last movement, maybe his most profound achievement, dates from the latter year. As of then he considered the Fourth finished in draft, but he would turn out to have a considerable second thought about that. Meanwhile a grander project had begun to grow in his mind.

During an October 1915 Adirondack vacation—his last in those mountains—Ives looked over the splendid prospect of the Keene Valley plateau. The area is rich with beauty and with historical resonances. Theodore Roosevelt came there as McKinley lay dying and learned he was president during an ascent of Mount Marcy. In Keene Valley the philosopher William James experienced a transforming spiritual awakening after a day of hiking in the mountains. Ives wrote of his own moment of inspiration there:

When we were in Keene Valley, on the plateau, staying in the fall of 1915 with [Harmony's sister] Sue and Grossie [Edie's name for old Joe]—and with Edie . . . I started something that I'd had in mind for some time (and [of] which some sketches were made a few years before) . . . trying out a parallel way of listening to music, suggested by looking at a view (1) with the eyes toward the sky or tops of the trees, taking in the earth or foreground subjectively . . . (2) then looking at the earth and land, and seeing the sky and the top of the foreground subjectively. In other words, giving a musical piece in two parts, but played at the same time—the lower parts . . . working out something representing the earth, and listening to that primarily—and then the upper . . . reflecting the skies and the Heavens. . . . This was suggested by a few pages of a sketch or general plan for a *Universe Symphony* or "The Universe, Past, Present, and Future" in tones . . .

   I. [Section A] (Past) Formation of the waters and the mountains.
   II. [Section B] (Present) Earth, evolution in nature and humanity.
   III. [Section C] (Future) Heaven, the rise of all to the spiritual.[21]

So the *Universe Symphony* began. In the memo of 1932 Ives added, "I had this fairly well sketched out, but not completed—in fact I haven't worked on this since that time, but hope to finish it out completely this summer." The reality was that by 1932 he was past being able to compose anything. Over the years, the less able he was actually to work on it, the grander the *Universe* became in his imagination. Meanwhile its ideas of perspective effects in sound percolated into the Fourth Symphony.

When the war broke out in Europe, Ives despised it and everything to do with it. He wrote in some of his jottings on the train,

"I'm for my country right or wrong" may have had its uses in centuries past—but it hasn't now, unless our civilization is imaginary. The biggest coward is the man who does most of the fighting & carries the biggest gun. There is enough physical bravery in the world what we need is more of the other kind. A widow who washes for a living & brings up her 10 children in the fear of God so that they can believe in things they can't see—is doing more for posterity than Gen Grant ever did. . . . For about the 179th time, during the last 179 days I have to listen to this remark, "These are interesting times, do you realize history is being made now" etc. etc. . . . If watching a boy grind an axe all day so he can try it on his foot at night, is interesting, then this war is interesting—this war started by rich degenerates fought for rich degenerates but fought by the people against the people—people who the stupider they act the braver they are called. . . . When a man says he hates war, but believes it's got to come, He's a coward . . . the kind that makes war possible. He says you must be practical—you haven't—as soon as you are practical you're a coward. . . . I heard a man say in theory [he supported] woman suffrage but it wasn't expedient—Expediency is cowardice with a tinge of sordidness to it. . . . The stupidity of politicians . . . is the only cause of war.[22]

In the 1916 election Woodrow Wilson beat Republican Charles Evans Hughes with the slogan "He Kept Us Out of War," but within months German predations on the seas forced America's hand. On April 2, 1917, the president asked Congress for a declaration of war. Proclaiming that "the world must be made safe for democracy," Wilson made America's entry a Progressive crusade on a global scale. That foredoomed dream of American ideals entering the world stage jolted Ives practically overnight from antiwar zealot into a crusader for the war. He responded to a call for "Yale Units" of ambulance drivers in France, donating money for an ambulance and volunteering to drive it for six months.[23] There was only the formality of passing a physical and he could be on his way to battlefields in France. The idea of going over to do his bit became an obsession in the next months—one of several obsessions.

He involved himself in all sorts of questions about mobilization. A few days after Wilson's declaration, when the War Industries Board was established to control production, Ives wrote a tract he called "Stand By the President and the People."[24] The Board seemed to him simply another case of the rich grabbing power. He begins his paper trumpeting one of his main themes:

Property, in the name of efficiency, is trying to get control of the war machinery, and so more effectively establish itself in control of this country.

This is a war for democracy. It must be fought by democracy. It can be won only by democracy. President Wilson has done more than any other President to voice the sentiments of the people rather than of politicians. He has been quick to sense the great change that is going on throughout the world, the resentment and the growing social consciousness among the proletariat the world over against the medieval idea of government by property, carried to its most brutal extreme by the Hohenzollerns, but still hung to by some of the reactionaries of this country. There are a great number of these men in the United States Senate and some in Congress. . . . They point to the fact that this government is a representative government. It is only in theory.[25]

He goes on to propose a direct democracy: "Fundamental questions can be put before the whole people, and the whole people can be trusted to act intelligently" about war, peace, trade, prohibition, and everything else. He lists, in specific millions of dollars, the assets of a group of political leaders, "a few samples of the men who have a great deal too much to say regarding the people's government." He prefaces the list, "The time has almost come when no man who has personal property to the amount of, say, $100,000 should have any active part in a government by the people." The paper concludes, "It is time the people had something to say about war, about peace, and about property." He would himself have much to say on these matters, including a proposal for limiting personal property, an essay called "The Majority," and a plan for a Twentieth Amendment to the U.S. Constitution.

He was winding down as a composer. "In 1917 the War came on, and I did but little in music. I didn't seem to feel like it. We were very busy at the office at this time with the extra Red Cross and Liberty Loan drives and all the problems that the War brought on."[26] The possible outcomes of the war formed another obsession. In January 1917, with America still poised on the brink of the fighting, Woodrow Wilson made his idealistic and absurd call for "peace without victory." In the same speech he proposed a world organization, a league of peace. The idea electrified Ives.

More and more he wrote words in place of music. Still, he got a few pieces done and done well. In 1917 he may have written the first of the *Emerson Transcriptions* for piano, more reworkings of that material. Otherwise he composed four songs, three of them on his own texts, three of them war songs, each unique, each effective in its way. In April, just after the declaration of war, Mike Myrick suggested that Ives make a song from the poem "In Flanders Fields." It was written by John McCrae, a Canadian army doctor and Mutual associate.[27] Wouldn't it be nice, Mike said, if this famous patriotic lyric by a company man could be set by another company man? It could be featured at an April managers' luncheon at the Waldorf-Astoria. Ives agreed to do it. He composed the music carefully but tentatively, putting in dissonances and taking them out. The result, a song of about two minutes but large in effect, was perhaps compromised by his anxieties over this his first full-scale semi-public performance in some fifteen years. A patch of pedestrian "inspirational" rhetoric projects the ringing peroration:

Take up our quarrel with the foe!
To you from falling hands we throw
The torch. Be yours to hold it high.
If ye break faith with us who die
We shall not sleep though the poppies grow
In Flanders fields.

The distinction of the song is how at the end Ives suddenly turns it not into a heroic direction, but an ambiguous one.[28] The last words are sung decrescendo, accompanied by a fading drumbeat on a foreboding harmony. It seems to tear us from heroic homilies into a silent field of gravestones. Expressive subtleties, though, were lost at the Waldorf-Astoria managers' luncheon of April 15, 1917. In retrospect it was a historic occasion—Charles Ives's return as composer to something like the public arena. In the event, it was nothing or less than nothing. The music was tame for Ives but nonetheless challenging for the ears of the time, and despite his coaching neither singer nor pianist was up to it. Likely an embarrassed time was had by all.

Just one week later came another milestone when David Talmadge— nephew Moss White Ives's teacher—played the Third Violin Sonata at Carnegie Chamber Music Hall, accompanied by pianist Stuart Ross. It was an invitation recital for friends and students of the soloist. Talmadge had been practicing Ives's first three sonatas, apparently seriously. Wrote Ives, "in his nice way, [he] liked to kid me more or less about those funny sounds, but he said that, the more he learned and studied the music, the more he thought there was something in it." This was an unprecedented response to these pieces by that date. So in Carnegie Chamber Music Hall on April 22, another secretly momentous occasion took place: a private premiere of a major chamber work by an unknown genius. The Third Sonata made scarcely an impression on anybody, unless a negative one. Ives recalled, "Talmadge played remarkably well, and Ross fairly well. Ross told me at the time that it was the hardest music he had ever played. To look at it now . . . that anybody could have felt that way seems incredible."[29] He was still frustrated in his hopes for the violin sonatas to be relatively approachable repertoire pieces. It would be five years before another performance of anything turned up.

Talmadge was more receptive than Ives's other violinist friend Reber Johnson, assistant concertmaster of the New York Symphony and a first-rate musician. After reading through the Second Violin Sonata Johnson complained to Ives, "After stuff like that, if you consider that music and *like* it, how can you like Brahms or any good music?" Despite those feelings, Johnson arranged the rehearsals at Ives's house—with invited guests—of *Washington's Birthday* in 1918 or 1919. This was the time when Ives discovered that these New York Symphony players had considerably more trouble with the music than the boys in the pit at the Globe Theater. Episodes like that did not increase his regard for orchestral musicians. Still, one of the players went so far as to suggest they perform part of the piece (probably the barn dance) in public. Quoth Reber Johnson: "No—we must think of the audience." The violinist still liked Ives as an accompanist and they played together for pleasure. Ives recalled with customary generosity, "He had a beautiful tone on the strings, and played Mozart perfectly. I'll have to admit I enjoyed playing Mozart with him, but a whole afternoon of Mozart is a whole afternoon of Mozart."[30] In January 1918 Harmony's brother Burt, stationed at Camp Upton at Yaphank, Long Island, brought Johnson and Ives out to play a recital for the soldiers.[31]

In May 1917, a month before the first American forces landed in France, Ives wrote the song "He Is There!" on his own text, an exercise in patriotic nostalgia:

> Fifteen years ago today
> A little Yankee boy
> Marched beside his granddaddy
> In the decoration day parade.
> The village band would play those old war tunes,
> And the G.A.R. would shout,
> "Hip Hip Hooray!" in the same old way
> As it sounded on the old camp ground.
>
> That boy has sailed o'er the ocean,
> He is there.
> He's fighting for the right, but when it comes to might,
> He is there;
> As the Allies beat up all the warlords!
> He'll be there, and then the world will shout the Battle cry of Freedom
> Tenting on a new camp ground.

He draws an analogy between the Civil War and the Great War, seeing both as a struggle toward a new campground, a new freedom. Probably he hoped the song would be taken up by Yankee soldiers in Europe. Sure enough, it is a sprightly and syncopated little number, if too convoluted and wide in range for most soldiers to manage. Given that it is in the tradition of Civil War fighting tunes, Ives works in quotes from some fourteen songs, most of them his favorites, including "Marching Through Georgia," "Columbia, the Gem," "Tenting on the Old Camp Ground," and "The Battle Cry of Freedom." He also tosses in a hint of George M. Cohan's brand-new "Over There"—which Yanks in Europe *did* enthusiastically take up. Ives's own title and tag line are probably based on Cohan's. For all the borrowings, no one else could have written the song. Ives tried to get nephew Bigelow to sing "He Is There!" but as the victim reported later, "If I didn't sing with enough spirit or gusto, he would land both fists on the piano. 'You've got to put more life into it,' he'd say. . . . 'Can't you shout better than that? That's the trouble with this country—people are afraid to shout!' "[32]

So far that year Ives had produced the ambiguously patriotic "In Flanders Fields" and the rabidly patriotic "He Is There!" The two other songs of 1917, on his texts, are gentle, sentimental, relatively straightforward evocations of childhood. In the midst of war, plunged over his head in family and business and volunteer responsibilities, Ives's thoughts returned to Danbury. In "The Things Our Fathers Loved" he employed his gift, never lost, for writing an old-fashioned tune in the tradition of Stephen Foster. Though the harmony is chromatic, simplicity and sentiment predominate, warmly expressing his lyric: *I think there must be a place in the soul all made of tunes of long ago. . . .*

The other song of that year, "Tom Sails Away," is one of his impressionistic moments, his nostalgic lyric expressed through a mist of memory. "Tom" and the occasion are invented, but the memories are mostly Ives's—the family, the old house, his mother's vegetable garden, his father coming home:

> Scenes from my childhood are with me,
> I'm in the lot behind our house upon the hill,
> a spring day's sun is setting,
> mother with Tom in her arms is coming towards the garden;
> the lettuce rows are showing green. . . .
>
> Daddy is coming up the hill from the mill,
> We run down the lane to meet him.
> But today! In freedom's cause
> Tom sailed away for over there!
>
> Scenes from my childhood are floating before my eyes.

The song builds from the opening *ppp* to a climactic fortissimo on "In freedom's cause Tom sailed away." Then what might be the expected heroic peroration on "Over there, over there, over there . . ." instead fades, on George M. Cohan's tune, like a dying bugle call. The song is nostalgic, moving, and in tone strangely valedictory for the production of a busy businessman and war volunteer about to turn forty-three.

Ives hardly seemed to acknowledge that he was still involved in music in 1917–18: "I did but little." He was more preoccupied with trying to get to France to drive his ambulance, and his other war-related efforts. During the Liberty Loan Bond drive his agency promoted, he would go down with one of his men, who remembered, "They had girls there selling them, and if you bought a bond, you got a kiss. Ives and I would go down together, and he would buy a hundred-dollar bond, and then push me over and I'd get two kisses."[33] Ives wrote and probably paid for a broadside issued by Ives & Myrick with suggestions for ways civilians could contribute to the war effort. The big yellow broadsides were posted around Manhattan. Buy bonds, they exhorted, but also change your life:

A pleasure car is worse than a non-essential—it is a contra-essential. Put your car to some useful purpose or put it in storage. . . . If you must have a chauffeur, get one over forty or fifty. . . . The theatre twice a month is enough for anyone. Too many moving pictures dull the mind. . . . Two square meals a day are enough for office workers. . . . HOUSEWIVES!—Learn to do your own work. . . . TRAVEL: Don't take long vacation trips. THE SOLDIER GIVES UP EVERYTHING! Except the fight. WHAT ARE YOU GIVING UP![34]

By 1918 Ives was carrying on a killing pace, racing in half a dozen directions. He still made gestures toward music, but most of the time he seemed to be trying to save the world. There were the *Washington's Birthday* readings, playing and performing with Reber Johnson, bond drives, work and writing at the office, caring for Edie and keeping her parents at bay. In February 1918 Myrick delivered an Ives-written speech to the Connecticut Life Underwriters, its points including: "In our opinion a man who makes a transfer of property . . . with the direct idea . . . of escaping the inheritance tax is—to put it mildly—a 'drag' on society and a hindrance of every endeavor towards the economic, social and moral progress of a community. In times like these this recourse is almost an act of treason."[35] (That said, life insurance continued to help the wealthy avoid inheritance taxes.) In March, Ives loaned $200 to an Isaac Bleier, probably an employee. The IOU has an attached note to his secretary: "This loan was made to . . . help him get to Los Angeles Cal with his family. He had tuberculosis & had to move to a better climate. Don't call this note unless Bleier is perfectly able to pay."[36] He sent $730 to "The Fatherless Children of France," who thanked him for "his continued interest and support."[37] In May he produced a paper, "The Need of the Production and Conservation of Legal Reserve Life Insurance in Relation to War-time Economics."[38] In June he went to Redding for three weeks to plant his potatoes.[39] (Harmony wrote him there from Hartford, "Dad seems to know me—called me by name a few minutes ago & asked when you were coming."[40]) Back in Manhattan in July, he sent $250 to the Red Cross.[41] At some point he began promoting the idea of a $50 "baby bond," to give working people a chance to make a contribution to the war.

President Wilson issued his historic "Fourteen Points" for a peace settlement in January 1918. The final one envisioned a "general association of nations . . . for the purpose of affording guarantees of political independence and territorial integrity to great and small states alike." By April, after talking over the matter with dozens of citizens from all walks of life, Ives had developed his own proposal for a world organization that he would come to call the People's World Union (or Nation). His points included total disarmament, an international police force and Court of Arbitration, free trade, and support of Wilson's Fourteen Points. As he usually would, at the end Ives solicited comment from all and sundry.[42] He sent the proposal to newspapers (there is no indication any published it) and read it before a Mutual managers' meeting in

June.[43] Soon other initiatives took precedence over the People's World Union, but it would be an abiding concern. Drafts and sketches relating to it stretch from 1918 into World War Two. Ives saw the creation of a world government as an inescapable step toward peace, justice, the millennium. (His fixation on the idea would end only with the establishment of the United Nations, for Ives perhaps the most gratifying political development of his life.)

Amidst all this he went to a Mutual doctor for the physical required for clearance to drive his ambulance in France. After looking him over the doctor brutally announced, as Ives recalled it, "If you have a heart attack, which you probably will . . . you will most likely send yourself to the next world, and also the wounded soldiers in your ambulance."[44] As far as Ives was concerned this medical opinionating was just another obstacle to overcome. He wrote to the Yale Ambulance Unit,

I have your letter of August 30 asking for my medical certificate. Shortly after making application to the Y.M.C.A. I was examined by . . . one of the staff here. He seems to think that there are a couple of medical points to be cleared up before approval. I know that there is nothing whatever the matter with me except that I have been at business steadily for some time with no let up. I have decided to take a two or three week's vacation, and am sure that I can give a clean bill of health before the end of the month. . . . I have enlisted for six months service in France.[45]

That was September 4, 1918. The war, as it turned out, was nearly over. On the 20th Aunt Amelia Brewster passed away and an Ives family era came to a close. Now Charlie was head of the family.

About that time he wrote in "Our Book" one of Edie's cute sayings. Only hindsight can catch the prophecy in those words of a four-year-old child, which went more to the point than the doctor's prophecy. Harmony had heard Edie playing out on the porch in Redding. The little blond sprite was picking up her doll and chanting, *Come right up, Dollie, come right up into heav'n. I'm an angel—I'm the only angel here—come right in & see me. For God's dead and I'm lonesome.*[46]

A Fall and a Credo

SINCE CHILDHOOD, Charles Ives had lived the life his energy and intelligence and talent allowed him. At length he had decided not to become a professional musician, but beyond that he declined to choose one thing or the other. He was too ambitious to be only a Sunday composer. Neither was he cut out to be a workaday wage earner, but aimed for the highest level in business too. As in childhood when he was organist and ballplayer, he crowded everything in and played full-out.

By autumn of 1918 Ives was trying to live beyond a double life. New elements had entered the equation—his adopted daughter and the interminable troubles with her family, and the war. Music receded as his social concerns became obsessive. He wanted to drive his ambulance in France; he had political schemes in several directions; he wanted to remake the country and perhaps the world, to address the fundamental concerns of humanity in the same way he had addressed, so brilliantly, the concerns of the insurance business. Meanwhile he had been cautioned by doctors and by his own body that he could not survive the pace he had set himself. He ignored the inner and outer warnings.

Among other initiatives Ives had developed a plan for a $50 bond designed to give working people more participation in the war effort. The conception was allied to his promotion of small insurance policies; in both cases he wanted to broaden the benefits of democracy and involve more people in the process. Ives exhausted himself promoting the plan as a member of the Liberty Bond Committee. On October 1, three weeks before his forty-fourth birthday, he confronted the committee during a public hearing at the Manhattan Hotel. Chairman Franklin D. Roosevelt, who had rejected the bond idea out of hand, was ill and absent that day. Eventually Ives won his point and "baby bonds" were the result. But the hearing was rancorous, a shouting match for a while, as could happen when Ives got worked up.[1] After the meeting he would still have been boiling along, cursing the damned mollycoddle politicians, and Harmony trying to calm him down. That night they stayed over at the hotel. Probably they planned to go back to Redding the next day, after a new physical examination Ives had scheduled when he failed the last one.[2]

In the middle of the night all the labor and frustration of the last years seemed finally to come down on his heart. As he gasped and rolled in pain, Harmony frantically called in the hotel doctor; Charlie's condition was so precarious he could not be moved from the room for a week. Finally they brought him to the house at East 22nd Street, where Harmony's brother Burt came to help out.[3] After Charlie had recovered for several weeks in the city, Cousin Amelia Van Wyck and her husband drove them to West Redding.[4] They set out with Charlie and Harmony in the back and Edie between, to be dropped off with an aunt in Scarsdale. Amelia recalled of that melancholy journey, "I had a bottle of spirits of ammonia in one pocket and a bottle of brandy in the other, and I'd look around every once in a while to see if either were needed, because they were both so frail."[5]

On December 20, Reverend Joseph Twichell died after a decade of decline. It must have been a bleak Christmas for the Iveses. Even the armistice, signed in November, probably did not cheer them up. If anything it made Charlie's disastrous efforts to support the war seem even more futile. As 1919 arrived he was lucky only in not knowing the future. Everything was changed after the heart attack. He would never recover his health. His interior life would not transform utterly, all at once; the mind keeps going when the body falters. But the decline of the body tends eventually to bring the mind along, and so it would be with Ives.

In the middle of January the family left Pennsylvania Station for a rest cure in Asheville, North Carolina. Charlie and Harmony both needed it. Asheville is a beautiful spot in the mountains, but the reason they picked it was probably that Harmony's sister—unfortunate, unbalanced Sally—was living there under a nurse's care. Harmony wrote in "Our Book," "were there two months, most of the time at Sally's little house. Charlie had sort of a relapse & we didn't have a very cheerful time." She was near collapse herself. Convalescence or no, Charlie brought a pile of work to do and did it.

The gods' great joke on Charles Ives was that while granting him the energy and intelligence and talent to carry on a double life, they bequeathed him a constitution that could only stand that pace for a little over half his life. He would not be allowed his dream of retiring full-time to music. His ruin was born into him along with his gifts.

As Ives would tell it and most writers after him, with the heart attack of 1918 his health broke and sent him into a declining spiral of ailments. That is probably the reverse of what happened. There had been a silent player all along: diabetes. That disease, probably inherited from his father, did not follow his breakdown but rather precipitated it. The devastating attack was only the most dramatic symptom of a physical condition that had already afflicted him on and off for at least fifteen years. The situation was likely the same with George Ives, and possibly with his other son Moss. Both had cardiovascular disease that suggests they may have been undiagnosed diabetics—George suffered a sudden stroke at forty-nine and Moss the same at sixty-three. Charlie probably had a coronary occlusion. He was the only one to survive an attack, but he did not survive whole.

Diabetes is a complex and devious disease.[6] There seems always to be a hereditary predisposition. An adult onset is often triggered by stress and sometimes announces itself with a heart attack, by which time considerable damage may already have been done to the cardiovascular and nervous systems. Among diabetic symptoms: exhaustion, breathlessness, palpitations, heart and circulatory diseases. Long-term complications can include cataracts and other vision disturbances, sensitive skin and various nervous symptoms, hardening of the arteries. Ives suffered all those complications, including a string of smaller heart attacks and strokes that punctuated the rest of his life. Another symptom, appearing in 50 percent or more of men, is impotence.[7]

At this distance one cannot say whether Ives's doctors suspected diabetes at the time of his attack. In 1918 diabetes could be diagnosed, but not effectively treated. Before the discovery of insulin three years later, a severe case was practically a death sentence; only after that did medical science begin to get a handle on the disease. What doctors could understand more easily in the first two decades of the century were the heart complications, and Ives had been coping with those for a long time. A 1931 Joslin Clinic report notes: "In 1906 had heart attack & marked tachycardia and palpitation. Has had several other attacks since." (Heart attacks? Or only tachycardia?)

Ives was seeing doctors even before his previous health breakdown in 1906.[8] Charlie and Harmony began courting in earnest that year, and her letters show him ailing off and on at least two years more. In 1907: "I'm so sorry, Charlie, that being sick is what kept you yesterday," and later that year she coos over his "poor sore heels" (diabetics can have foot problems because of soft-tissue deterioration). In 1908: "How hard it is to have you go and not feeling quite well—Be careful darling."[9] Aunt Amelia—probably with her brother George in mind—warned Harmony about Charlie's health. Harmony did not have to be warned. She was a nurse; she understood what both of them could be in for if he already had heart trouble at thirty-two. It made no difference to her.

Diabetes and heart disease may not have been everything afflicting Ives. There may have been a rift in his psyche too. There is evidence for some degree of manic-depressive disease that built up over the years and accelerated after his heart attack. This hereditary mental vagary can send its victims on a nonstop emotional rollercoaster: the manic intervals fill you with hyperbolic energy and enthusiasm; you throw yourself into projects and go without sleep; you feel your imagination and creativity and insight magnified (or convince yourself they are). The disease is found more often in creative people than in other groups. Those afflicted are often enjoyed and much loved; in an up phase they can be great talkers, effusive and full of life. At the same time they are emotionally brittle, prone to crashes and down periods, liable to fall into nervous agitation or blustering rage. Like diabetes, this illness runs in families. Here could be a clue to the legendary eruptiveness of the Iveses that convinced some Danburians there was a streak of madness in all of them. Here may also be a prime reason for Ives's decreasing grasp of reality after 1918— the grandiosity of his political writings, the superhuman scope of the *Universe Symphony*.[10]

Charlie seems to have been rejuvenated by Harmony in every way, creatively, mentally, physically. There is no report of bad health for ten years after they married, and his life was extraordinarily active. On the other hand there are no regular letters, as in their courtship, to tell us about his condition. Besides, diabetes can have a "honeymoon" period after an outbreak. As for manic-depressive signs, his rages were enough to alarm Harmony. She wrote him in 1914, "frequent consecutive cursing such as you've indulged in lately is what I dont like to hear—poor old lamb—you do get so mad, don't you."[11] Ives declared himself a healthy man until 1918, but he may have been deceiving himself. In any case his diabetes was with him, corroding his nervous system and arteries and heart. He may have had episodes of tachycardia and minor heart attacks. His memos hint at down periods, mental weariness amidst the whirlwind activity of those years. There were rages characteristic of manic-depressive illness, inexplicable eruptions over small things, periods of euphoria and depression.

One enters a shrouded area here, a realm part speculation and part poetry. Diabetes, heart disease, and emotional instability were Charles Ives's dark companions, a blood legacy from his family just like his talent. His greatness and his ruin came from the same source. If these afflictions were involved in Ives's physical and creative ruin, however, they may also have had a share in his triumph. With artists, small increments can mean everything. Besides the depression of bipolar disorder there is the euphoria, besides the fatigue the hyperbolic energy. Ives was temperamentally vigorous, curious, enthusiastic, and sometimes depressed. Harmony was his muse, the main inspiration of his maturity. But illness could also have played a part by exaggerating his personality, helping to push him over the line from a talent to a genius, and then pushing him further to a crank with delusions of grandeur. To the degree that this poetry and speculation is tangibly and medically true, Ives's doom helped create him, his genius consumed him.

As diabetes settled in, he would have to live with the kind of steady physical and mental pain that tolls like a bell through one's days and nights. As it is perceived, one's body is betraying one's self. There is a sense of helplessness and—for men—of impotence, which with diabetes is often literal but always figurative. Either you give in to powerlessness and despair or you compensate, and sometimes overcompensate. If your body betrays you, you may despise the body. If your nervous system distorts your senses, you may flay the sensuous. If you feel unmanned, emasculation is the great enemy and you see it everywhere and fight it with everything you've got. Ives was heroic in standing up to his illnesses, but courage comes at a price. The weapons he possessed to fight emasculation, within and without, would be words and paper and rage and music. At times, his music would come close to being a casualty of his rage.

The failure of his health brought a more direct and pragmatic conse- quence in its wake: a change in priorities. Before, the priorities had been to support his family and to get the music written. After this second major breakdown of his life, sooner or later but probably sooner, Ives realized he was living on borrowed time. Three strikes and you're out. (Who could have predicted how much time he would have left—another joke of the gods, because much of it would be spent in misery.)

From the perspective of 1919 Ives had to make new priorities, mainly two: one, to build up his income to provide for his family in case he died (his earnings would skyrocket in the 1920s); two, to get his music before the public while he still could see to it himself.[12] His doings from 1919 onward, especially during the next decade, must be seen in the content of those two priorities and their corollaries. Now getting out what he had written had to take precedence over producing new work. He had to rethink how to promote himself. His attempts to show his music to professionals had gained him nothing; besides, he was too delicate now to be always trolling for performers, running around hiring players for makeshift readings. He had to find some- thing new. He decided to print the *Concord Sonata,* the *Essays,* and a book of songs, and mail them to hundreds of strangers in hopes that somewhere they would take root.[13]

On top of these repercussions of his health, in 1919 Ives faced an artistic dilemma that was only amplified by his physical breakdown. He had arrived in the vicinity of a creative impasse. He could only see music, only see history as a steady upward progression. For that reason, after the gigantic imaginative achievement of the Fourth Symphony (not finished in fact by 1916, but done in concept), he left himself little option creatively other than to go on to the colossal design of the *Universe Symphony.*[14] That work reached for the stars partly because that was the only place Ives had left himself to go. Certainly he never saw it this way, but even before illness hamstrung him and his inspiration began to close up shop, he had ridden his train of thought nearly to the end of the line. With the unconscious logic of fate, by the time his health broke Ives had nearly rounded off his art with the Fourth Symphony, a masterpiece that in scope and complexity went about as far as he could go, on this particular planet.

The Iveses journeyed to Asheville in January 1919 for rest and recovery, but Charlie did little of either. He worked at nearly his usual pace, with admirable results creatively and predictable ones physically. He had a relapse;

it is a wonder he did not finally drive himself to his grave. Harmony watched over him quietly but relentlessly. She had married her love in part to get away from nursing; now she was a nurse twenty-four hours a day. In coming years she would have more than one breakdown from the strain.[15] But there was only so much she could do to slow him down.

In Asheville Ives made an ink score of the *Concord Sonata* for publication. As he copied, he simplified some of its thornier passages and tamed some of the dissonance, especially in *Emerson*. At the same time, he wrote *Essays Before a Sonata* from sketches going back several years, with the idea of prefacing each movement of the score with its essay. Given the length the essays got to, he would finally issue them in a separate book; in the published score, excerpts preface the movements. Their diary notes at the end of January, in Harmony's hand, "Charlie finishing up copy of Sonata 'Prologue.' " A few days later, in Charlie's hand: "Harmony sick—all right now. C. worked at Thoreau—trying to make people think Thoreau movement sounds like Thoreau." But a few days after that: "H. stays in bed most of day, resting after 3 mos. work in a boiler factory." By boiler factory he means taking care of him. Ives knew the toll his illness exacted on his wife; that would be part of his own burden from then on.

He had not accepted yet what happened to him. In response to a reunion notice, at the end of January he wrote a Wolf's Head friend in the old Yale tone:

I had enlisted for 6 mos. service with that damned old Y.M.C.A. of yours [the Yale ambulance outfit] and after standing in line (for a good part of the 17th century) . . . everything had straightened out, except the medical side. So . . . to fulfill all the doctors hopes, I had a few attacks—the nature of which apparently were as different as the nature of true doctors are different . . . anyway we have been down here, most of the winter trying to get well. Personally . . . I think I have had the "flu"—for that is the one thing that all the doctors have eliminated. But now . . . Mrs Ives has decided to take charge—and I am almost well again—how could it be otherwise?

If that God-like institution had turned me down for super-abundant morality or a subnormal mentality, I might have borne it without surprise, but to be found so physically sub-standard that I cannot be even entrusted to pass around cigarettes . . . is humiliating to say the worst. But on the other hand (most men have other hands)—it has given me opportunities of proving various (subconscious) hypotheses . . . one of which is that vagueness is as much the true source of medical inspiration, as it is of modern Russian music, or even modern Egyptology. . . .

In closing, Tommy, let me say that in imposing all this on you, does not cancel any of the indignities that you inflicted upon us of a Thursday evening. —but when one has been on his back long enough, he takes desperate chances to amuse himself—; and the outbursts of his mind become as heedless as those of his pancreas or any other hidden Muse!

Our little 5-year old has just come in to entertain me. . . . She tells me that "She doesn't mind not going from Sunday School very well but she feels so sorry for the little rain drops, to have to leave God, up there all alone on Sunday."[16]

Sister Sally saw to Edie when she could in Asheville.[17] One day, sitting on the porch, Harmony wrote down how Edie's face, flushed and happy at play, looked like a flower. From that came her poem "To Edith" ("So like a flower, thy little four year face"), for which Charlie adapted a sentimental old tune of his. Later, the same idea applied to Edie and her friend Susanna would become the exquisite song "Two Little Flowers."

Illness had not crushed his wit. They had stayed the first ten days in the Battery Park Hotel and Ives recounted a scene there in "Our Book": "In the drawing room of the 1st hotel of magnificence erected for wealthy people of refined tastes in Asheville a lady with diamond rings and 2 Peirce Arrows was heard to say 'I kin remember agoin' up the Statute of Liberty when they warn't no elevator but they was some stairs believe me.' Pure U.S. is better than pure English." The diary also shows that between them Harmony and Charlie consumed a pile of books, his ranging from *Walden* and Emerson's essays and Bushnell's sermons (all toward his *Essays*) to Jane Austin, George Eliot, and Anthony Trollope. The diary notes that he finished the "Thoreau" essay on February 5 and gave it to a hotel stenographer to type up. By the 15th he was not feeling like working; this may have been the relapse. Then on the 20th: "Emerson, Alcotts & Thoreau [the music] all finished & copied 3 movements." In Asheville he began sketching a Third Orchestral Set. He would finally give up on that work in 1925, with three movements partly drafted. (On the title page he has carefully noted by each movement "NG"—No Good. As the notes trickled to a halt he wrote on the last page: "This was to be the crisis before the Benediction.")

They returned to New York in mid-March not much refreshed in body or in spirit. Recovered or not, Ives had no intention of wasting time. At Asheville or soon after, he made one of his lists of things to do:

1 Article for Eastern Underwriter (by Aug 1) [presumably "Writing Big Policies of Life Insurance," which came out in October]; 2. Prefaces for Sonata for Schirmer (by July 25); 3. Finish & copy "Circus Band" (as soon as possible); 4. After 1 & 2 are finished work daily on "Majority"; 5. Score #3. NE Holidays, "4th of July" (any time before Oct 1); 6. (correct) Presentation, Torts (Insurance). 7. Send "20 amendment" paper to magazines (any time); 8. Address list from "Musical Courier" of names to send Sonata (after Oct or Nov); 9. Select & correct 25 or 30 songs for printing [they would finally total 114], also get English words for some of the German (Oct or Nov)[18]

Meanwhile he tried to get back to work at Ives & Myrick, but after three months his doctors advised him to go home to Redding instead, and stay there a while.[19] Presumably he spent much of that time taking care of items on the list. His musical activities would match his usual pace for a few more years, but more of it practical and less of it creative than before.

On September 25, 1919, just after Ives got back to the insurance office to stay, Woodrow Wilson had a crippling stroke and, without his leadership, the

League of Nations was doomed. Americans were tired of Wilson and tired of idealism. The country entered an era of conservative backlash that would leave Progressives like Charles Ives in limbo. Meanwhile he entered another sort of limbo, his ambitions undimmed but his physical and mental capacities flickering and uncertain. His music, at least, was about to begin a long process of emerging from oblivior. That would be immensely gratifying to him, despite the frustrations it brought. But it would come too late to save him.

Though Ives produced a good deal of prose from 1919 into the twenties, *Essays Before a Sonata* would be the most substantial. Despite a measure of rambling and rant and confusion, in those pages lie not only the rationale of the *Concord Sonata,* but an unprecedented philosophical and spiritual credo by a composer of major importance.

For a composer, Ives could write and think articulately—sometimes. His business prose is concise and straightforward; his creative writing has considerable character and vitality, in much the same way as his music. As an example, the first sentence of his Postface for the *114 Songs* reels on garrulously like one of his musical phrases, an expanding wedge of free association that obscures the point and expresses it at the same time, and concludes with an Ivesian paradox: "Greek philosophers, ward-politicians, unmasked laymen, and others, have a saying that bad habits and bad gardens grow to the 'unintendedables'; whether these are a kind of 'daucus carota,' 'men,' 'jails,' or 'mechanistic theories of life' is not known—but the statement is probably or probably not true."

As that demonstrates, in his creative essays Ives was often more exuberant and provocative than precise. He tended to look more to the music of a sentence, the color and rhythm and electricity, than to the sense. (The sample, it should be noted, is excessive even for him.) To repeat with new emphasis: At his best, Ives was an articulate writer and thinker *for a composer*. Which is to say, by trade or experience he was no philosopher at all, or much of an essayist for that matter. Besides, the *Essays* seem to have been written in a rush, amidst illness and other labors during Ives's two-month convalescence in Asheville. Though he did work over them and get some rough editing before publication, he did not give the *Essays* the care he gave his best music.

To say Ives's philosophy lacked rigor is saying nothing against him.[20] Artists do not need to be philosophers, and good artists tend to have a very keen antennae for what they need, which is essentially to do their work and get it noticed and not starve. From nearly any question in life, an artist asks for something useful. Driving a cab, working in an insurance office—all activities are turned to the purpose. Sometimes this is as selfish as it sounds, but otherwise it is simply practical, life being short and art exigent. Likewise nearly everything artists say in public is in one way or another self-promoting; otherwise it would not be worth the effort. (Nearly everything an artist believes in is similarly pragmatic.) Ives was no more self-serving in his public endeavors than other artists; in fact, he was less so than most. Inevitably, though, he saw his essay subjects in light of what they could do for him. What is going to be the most useful idea? What will inspire the best work from me? What will help put my music across to people? In the guise of pieces on great American writers, *Essays Before a Sonata* is about Charles Ives and his music.

As is most often the case as well, neither did the *Essays* inspire the music, but the other way around. Because of the book, critics would perennially connect Ives's music to the Concord Transcendentalists from his early works on. Peter Burkholder has shown that notion to be rather backward as well. Ives knew Emerson and Thoreau from early on, but only in the latter part of his creative life, mainly while composing the *Concord,* did he seem to take them up as primary themes and mentors.[21] Burkholder concludes, "his enthusiasm for Emerson [was] a point of arrival rather than a point of departure." Ives turned to Emerson as he did to memories of Danbury, as another way of returning home.

For many reasons, then, *Essays Before a Sonata* is careless, erratic, self-contradictory, sometimes inchoate, and full of inaccurate or imaginary quotes. Moreover, the essays' main purpose is not their stated purpose, and they often fall into irrelevent polemics. Yet here is another Ivesian paradox: despite all that, the essays are also fascinating, wise, vital, and in the long run invaluable. They have rarely been perceived at their worth, or in the context of the zeitgeist, the rich culture of ideas that rejuvenated American thought at the beginning of the twentieth century. Their main purpose is to tell us about Ives in general and the *Concord* in particular, and they do that very well. Their second purpose is to tell us about art and life and spirituality, which here and there they do eloquently. Running a poor third, they tell us Ives's thoughts on Emerson, Hawthorne, the Alcotts, and Thoreau.

The most significant parts of the *Essays* are the Prologue, "Emerson," and the Epilogue. The Prologue begins with a high-Ivesian gesture, a fusillade of questions that would seem to contradict his actual point:

How far is anyone justified, be he an authority or a layman, in expressing . . . in terms of music . . . the value of anything, material, moral, intellectual, or spiritual, which is usually expressed in terms other than music? . . . Can a tune literally represent a stone wall with vines on it or even with nothing on it? . . . Does the success of program music depend more upon the program than upon the music? If it does, what is the use of the music? If it does not, what is the use of the program?

Having marshaled a number of arguments against program music, Ives stands the questions on their heads: "On the other hand is not all music program music?" In one of the more sustained stretches of lucid writing in the book, he makes a case that experience lies behind all music, that its content goes beyond notes and sounds regardless of whether the composer is aware of the inspiration. As usual, Ives declines to answer his questions definitively. Program music is problematical and he leaves it that way, for now. But in the future, he prophesies music "will develop possibilities inconceivable now—a language so transcendent that its heights and depths will be common to all mankind."[22] From this millennial conclusion to the Prologue a good deal of the ensuing ideas and images flow.

In the context of the sonata we have looked at "Emerson" the essay for what it says about the *Emerson* music. What does it say about Emerson himself, and about Charles Ives? In his essay "The Transcendentalist" Emerson defined his movement as belief in "a very important class of ideas, or imperative forms, which did not come by experience, but through which experience was acquired . . . intuitions of the mind itself."[23] These innate intuitions shape the input of the senses and are therefore called *transcendental*. Barbara MacKinnon summarizes three primary themes in the movement's writings: "the divinity of nature, the worth of the individual person, and the capacity of each person to know the truth directly."[24] Ives defined Transcendentalism for himself as belief in the innate goodness of humanity, and glossed in "Thoreau": "What are the great fundamentals? Freedom over slavery; the natural over the artificial; beauty over ugliness; the spiritual over the material; the goodness of man; the Godness of man; God; with all other kindred truths that have been growing in expression through the ages, eras, and civilizations—innate things which once seemed foreign to the soul of humankind."[25] He still believed, despite the contrary evidence of the war, that the Godness of humanity had never been so close to revelation.

Emerson called on humanity to remake itself by following its inner wisdom. He proclaims at the beginning of "Nature": "Why should not we also enjoy an *original relation to the universe?* . . . Why should we grope among the dry bones of the past? . . . I become a transparent eyeball; I am nothing, I see all; the currents of the Universal Being circulate though me; I am part or parcel of God." In his "Divinity School Address" Emerson denies the reality of evil: "Good is positive. Evil is merely privative, not absolute: it is like cold, which is the privation of heat. All evil is so much death of nonentity. Benevolence is absolute and real." In "Self-Reliance" he begins, "To believe your own thought, to believe what is true for you in your private heart is true for all men—that is genius. Speak your latent conviction, and it shall be the universal sense. . . . A foolish consistency is the hobgoblin of little minds. . . . Speak what you think now in hard words and to-morrow speak what to-morrow thinks in hard words again, though it contradict every thing you said to-day." For Ives these ideas became articles of faith that played out in his writings from the mid-teens on. And in Emerson's "American Scholar" we read, like a prophecy of Ives's music: "We have listened too long to the courtly muses of Europe. . . . We will walk on our own feet; we will work with our own hands; we will speak our own minds. . . . A nation of men will for the first time exist, because each believes himself inspired by the Divine Soul which also inspires all men."

Emerson was a personal hero for Charles Ives, and a role model. Ives wrote,

Though a great poet and prophet, he is greater, possibly, as an invader of the un-known—America's deepest explorer of the spiritual immensities—a seer painting his discoveries in masses and with any color that may lie at hand—cosmic, religious, human, even sensuous; a recorder freely describing the inevitable struggle in the soul's uprise, perceiving from this inward source alone that "every ultimate fact is only the first of a new series" . . . and who would then discover, if he can, that "wondrous chain which links the heavens with earth—the world of beings subject to one law."[26]

That is a reasonable description of Emerson the sage. It is a concise description of what Ives attempted in his last large works, especially in the *Concord,* Fourth Symphony, and *Universe Symphony*. Ives writes, "The inactivity of permanence is what Emerson will not permit. He will not accept repose against the activity of truth."[27] These phrases seem to resound throughout the finale of the Fourth Symphony. In his late works Ives became the musical embodiment of Transcendental thought.

In the *Essays* Ives's approach to his subjects is always selective and subjective. He takes pains, for example, to deny that the Transcendentalists were heirs of the European Romantics.[28] In contrast, the standard wisdom as seen in *The Encyclopedia of Philosophy* summarizes Transcendentalism as an adaptation of Romantic ideals:

a vague yet exalting conception of the godlike nature of the human spirit and an insistence on the authority of individual conscience; a related respect for the significance and autonomy of every facet of human experience within the organic totality of life; a consequent eschewal of all forms of metaphysical dualism, reductivism, and positivism; nature conceived not as a vast machine demanding impersonal manipulation but as an organism, a symbol and analogue of mind, and a moral educator . . . in general, the placing of imagination over reason, creativity above theory, action higher than contemplation, and a marked tendency to see the spontaneous activity of the creative artist as the ultimate achievement of civilization.[29]

Ives would reflect all those elements—except the rejection of dualism—while never defining or even admitting his or Emerson's connection to Romanticism. He had the American habit of seeing everyone as unique, standing virtually outside history. For himself and his heroes, he resisted labels of any kind. At one point he even tries to deny the categories: "there is no such thing as 'classicism or romanticism.' "[30]

Ives probably envied Emerson's position as an uncompromising seer who influenced the course of American culture. Nonetheless, if Ives identified with Emerson, learned from him, honored him, and envied him, he also embodied the spirit of Emersonian self-reliance enough to find his own way up the mountain. It is a mistake to see Ives as nothing more than an echo of Emerson or any of his other heroes. (George Ives admired Wagner, Charles Ives came to despise him.) While Emerson was aristocratic, more interested in the great souls,[31] Ives connected his sense of the masses and the majority to the Emersonian oversoul. That connection was his own. His attitudes about direct democracy and the divine law of averages came more from actuarial tables and the Progressive movement than from Emerson, and still less from the anarchistic Thoreau.

Nor could Ives let go, though he tried, of the kind of Puritan dualism that Emerson rejected. Ives writes, "The intellect is never a whole. It is where the soul finds things. . . . It can never discard the other part of its duality—the soul, or the void where the soul ought to be."[32] Ives could only see the body as distinct from and irrelevant to the activity of mind and soul.[33] He proclaimed an underlying substance in music partly because he could not accept the sensuous appeal of sound as part of its meaning. "Debussy's attitude toward Nature," Ives writes, "seems to have a kind of sensual sensuousness underlying it, while Thoreau's is a kind of spiritual sensuousness." Therefore Thoreau is closer to substance, Debussy to manner. (Hinted there and elsewhere in the *Essays* is Ives's Puritan conflation of the body and sin. He condemned, after all, the very idea of the nude in art.)

Instead of facing contradictions with his subjects (if in fact he realized them), Ives simply places his words in their mouths while taking off on his own hobbyhorses. Attributing his own ideas to his subjects is perhaps the most intellectually shabby aspect of the *Essays*. "[Emerson] might have said . . . that the cause of [the war] was as simple as that of any dog-fight—the 'hog-mind' of the minority against the universal mind, the majority."[34] The language and the ideas are entirely Ivesian. Later he gives Thoreau the same treatment, with even less congruence. "It is conceivable that Thoreau, to the consternation of the richest members of the Bolsheviki and Bourgeois, would propose a . . . policy of a limited personal property right. . . . This limit of property would be determined not by the *voice* of the majority but by the *brain* of the majority under a government limited to no national boundaries."[35] Here we are amidst Ives's own agenda, his constitutional amendment and limited property right and People's World Union.

After brief essays on Hawthorne and the Alcotts that end with hints of programs for those movements of the sonata, Ives arrives at his second Transcendentalist mentor, and that for good reason. He begins the essay,

Thoreau was a great musician, not because he played the flute but because he did not have to go to Boston to hear "the Symphony." The rhythm of his prose, were there nothing else, would determine his value as a composer. . . . In their greatest moments, the inspiration of both Beethoven and Thoreau express profound truths and deep sentiment. But the intimate passion of it, the storm and stress of it affected Beethoven in such a way that he could not but be ever showing it, and Thoreau, that he could not easily expose it.[36]

These are apt words about Thoreau and Beethoven—and about the meta-morphosis of the Beethoven motive in *Thoreau,* where it becomes introspective rather than heroic. Thoreau was passionate about music and had helped teach Ives that "music" encompassed silence as well as sound, and the course of life itself. Still, however much Ives understood and admired Thoreau, he resembled him little. Ives was never a true solitary; he was used to having a house full of family and his wife at his side. Thoreau could not have lived nearly half his life in Manhattan, as Ives did, nor would Thoreau have had much sympathy with Ives the businessman. While Ives tried to make government more democratic, the Concord anarchist's attitude was largely to ignore it, wish it gone: "That government is best which governs not at all." Ives spent his life looking for consensus and collaboration, even if he rarely found them.

Ives uses much of his "Thoreau" essay in rambling apologetics for his subject's personality and withdrawal from society. Near the end he returns to "my Thoreau—that reassuring and true friend, who stood by me one 'low' day, when the sun had gone down, long, long before sunset."[37] The conclusion of the essay is an interweaving of Ives and Thoreau that captures the atmosphere of the *Concord Sonata*'s finale about as well as it could be done in words: "The poet's flute is heard out over the pond and Walden hears the swan song of that 'Day'—and faintly echoes . . . 'Tis an evening when the 'whole body is one sense,' . . . and before ending his day he looks out over the clear, crystalline water of the pond and catches a glimpse of the 'shadow-thought' he saw in the morning's mist and haze."

Ives begins the Epilogue of the *Essays* like the cyclic symphonist he was: he returns to the themes of the Prologue, the question of the point and possibilities of program music. At length he sidesteps that matter with an observation that would appear to call his own defense of program music into question: "Maybe it is better to hope that music may always be a transcendental language in the most extravagant sense. Possibly the power of literally distinguishing [programs] is ever to be denied man for the same reason that the beginning and end of a circle are to be denied."[38] Abstract and representative, objective and subjective, can be seen as the sides of a circle; they melt into vagueness. For the moment Ives has escaped duality, but he soon submits to it again.

After an anti-Wagner detour and a paean to Bach and Beethoven, he picks up a theme hinted at throughout the *Essays*. He declares that art has a duality of values: "The higher and more important value of this dualism is composed of what may be called reality, quality, spirit, or substance against the lower value of form, quantity, or manner. Of these terms, 'substance' seems to us the most appropriate . . . for the higher, and 'manner' for the under-value." Here is the formulation of the famous Ivesian dichotomy, *substance* versus *manner.* He avoids precise definitions, but suggests the qualities by association and attribute: "Substance in a human-art-quality suggests the body of a conviction which has its birth in the spiritual consciousness, whose youth is nourished in the moral consciousness, and whose maturity . . . is then represented in a mental image." By that he implies what he hopes he achieved in some of his own works—say, *Decoration Day,* which began with the memory of an epiphany and was represented in a musical image. Substance "is appreciated by the intuition, and somehow translated into expression by 'manner'—a process always less important than it seems."[39] Manner is mere style, execution, intellect. Substance is vital, interior, of the soul and intuition. The difference, he says, is like that "between Dr. Bushnell's 'Knowing God' and knowing *about* God."[40] Always there is a moral dimension: "Substance has something to do with character. Manner has nothing to do with it. The substance of a tune comes from somewhere near the soul, and the manner comes from—God knows where."[41] The dichotomy is also comedy versus wit, genius versus talent, innate integrity versus self-conscious posing.

With the *Essays* Ives settled on "substance" to represent the underlying value and import of art, the fathomless mystery at its core. Substance is the passion of a stonemason shouting his hymns, the epiphany of a parade on Decoration Day, the spirit behind the notes of Bach and Beethoven and the Saint-Gaudens monument in Boston Common, the music of the ages that has nothing to do with catgut, brass, vibrations in air: "My God! What has sound got to do with music!" It is the unseen and unspoken spirit that animates everything seen and spoken.

After setting out his central duality, Ives makes another excursion, a well-integrated one this time. When his music got out he knew he was going to be labeled a nationalist, and he hoped to nip that in the bud. He had observed the decades-long search of American composers to establish a native tradition in concert music. As is clear in the *Essays,* he knew the efforts of Arthur Farwell and C. W. Cadman with their Indian tunes, of Henry F. Gilbert with his "Negro" orchestral music. Ives knew perfectly well that he had found his own answers, the most viable ones yet, to the question of an American art music. But he did not believe that the question went very far, on its own tack. Nationalism itself he considered the kind of "medieval" prejudice that leads to wars. Though few would notice in future years, Ives carefully distanced himself from artistic nationalism as it is usually conceived.

This lack of interest to preserve, or ability to perceive, the fundamental divisions [of substance and manner] . . . is evidenced in many ways . . .—overenthusiasm for local color—overinterest in the multiplicity of techniques, in the idiomatic, in the effect as shown by the appreciation of an audience rather than in the effect on the ideals of the inner conscience of the artist or the composer. . . . If local color is a natural part (that is, a part of substance), the art-effort cannot help but show its color—and it will be a true color, no matter how colored. . . . [But problems arise] if there is overinsistence upon the national in art. Substance tends to create affection; manner prejudice.

Ives is not counseling some kind of cultureless, accentless music, but saying instead that the accent cannot be forced or put on like a fashionable suit, and must be a means rather than an end. In the right spirit, why not an accent, even an acquired one: "If a man finds that the cadences of an Apache war-dance come nearest to his soul," he should learn that music until it becomes utterly a part of himself. Then, "his music will be true to itself and incidentally American, and it will be so even after it is proved that all our Indians came from Asia."[42]

As for a Yankee like himself, Ives writes that he "may find a deep appeal in the simple but acute Gospel hymns of the New England 'camp meetin' '" of a generation or so ago. He finds in them—some of them—a vigor, a depth of feeling, a natural-soil rhythm, a sincerity . . . which, in spite of a vociferous sentimentality, carries him nearer the 'Christ of the people' than does the *Te Deum* of the greatest cathedral." If he can be true to those roots, "if his music can but catch that spirit . . . it will come somewhere near his ideal—and it will be American, too. . . . In other words, if local color, national color, any color, is a true pigment of the universal color, it is a divine quality, it is a part of substance in art—not of manner."

Ives ends the *Essays* with speculations on form and the future of music, interspersed with asides tendentious here and shrewd there. He turns again to the moral aspect of art and of artists, quoting a definition of beauty as "an infinite source of good . . . the love of the beautiful . . . a constant anxiety for moral beauty."[43] He adds in a famous paragraph,

Beauty in music is too often confused with something that lets the ears lie back in an easy chair. Many sounds that we are used to do not bother us, and for that reason we are inclined to call them beautiful. . . . impersonal tests will show, we believe, that when a new or unfamiliar work is accepted as beautiful on its first hearing, its fundamental quality is one that tends to put the mind to sleep. A narcotic is not always unnecessary, but it is seldom a basis of progress.[44]

In the last section of the Epilogue he summarizes this way:

Art-activity can be transformed or led towards an eventual consecration by recognizing and using in their true relation. . . these higher and lower dual values [of substance and manner]. . . . The doing so is a part if not the whole of our old problem of paralleling or approving in art the highest attributes, moral and spiritual, one sees in life.

To help accomplish that, one can attach one's own creations to those of the great figures of the past, including the American past:

America is not too young to have its divinities, and its place-legends. Many of those "Transcendent Thoughts" and "Visions" which had their birth beneath our Concord elms—messages that have brought salvation to many listening souls throughout the world—are still growing day by day to greater and greater beauty—are still showing clearer and clearer man's way to God![45]

Note his terms: *consecration, moral and spiritual, salvation, man's way to God*. What does he mean by them?

To examine those terms and their relation to his music, it has to be understood that the ideas in *Essays Before a Sonata,* however singular their expression, are not exclusive to Ives or to the Transcendentalists. Many of them were intellectual common parlance at the beginning of the century. We can see Ives's connection to the zeitgeist by way of two roughly contemporary philosophers whom, as far as one can tell, Ives never read: C. S. Peirce and his sometimes disciple William James.[46]

Peirce was something of an Ivesian character, original, eccentric, and neglected. On many matters personal and philosophical the two differ, but there are still affinities. Peirce laid the groundwork for what became semiotics, the study of signs.[47] The things of this world, he said, are elusive, shrouded, and we can know them only through the mediation of signs and relations of signs. Ives saw music as symbol and sign of experience and unseen spirit. Peirce is most known for his development of *pragmatism,* a theory of meaning and belief which looks for truth not in stone engraved by gods, but rather in how things play out in practice. "A *conception,*" wrote Peirce in his definition of pragmatism, "lies exclusively in its conceivable bearing upon the conduct of life."[48] Truth is as truth does; the proof is in the pudding. Or as Ives poetically put it, "not something that happens, but the way something happens."

For Peirce *belief* plays a critical role in defining truth in a universe where ultimate reality is, at least for the present, an unanswered question. Since we cannot presently know ultimate truth, we have to test out things and believe in the results, until something better comes along. Having made truth a process of questioning and testing rather than a static revelation, Peirce adds his own belief in an almost Ivesian millennium. Louis Menand summarizes that imagining: "As the universe becomes more predictable, our beliefs about it become truer, less plastic, more 'fixed,' " until the entire universe reaches a state which "is perfectly lawlike and our beliefs perfectly rational and true." Truth itself "is what the community of inquirers, in the last analysis, agrees on."[49] Here is another variation on the Emersonian oversoul, similar to Ives's sense of community small and large, the divine law of averages with which the majority drives human progress. Like Peirce, Ives saw the masses ascending in insight and creativity until he imagines "the soul of humanity knocking at the door of the divine mysteries, radiant in the faith that it *will* be opened—and the human become the divine!"

Both men rode a wave of humanistic faith that drove the Progressive movement. Socially and spiritually, Progressives saw humanity evolving ever upward. Ives, Peirce, and William James predicated their ideas on the great scientific revelation of the nineteenth century, Darwin's theory of evolution, which Ives called "another of God's parables." The literal and metaphorical idea of evolution lay behind most American thought, both liberal and conservative, at the turn of the century. When species and landscapes and the cosmos are fixed, truth and society tend to be fixed. When Darwin and others set

species and continents and cosmology to shifting like a summer cloud, humanity tended to rethink society, economics, truth, God. Significant to that process, evolutionary theory in those days thought of species as always improving,
always moving toward greater sophistication and complexity. And if species
evolve thus physically, surely humankind will also evolve to a higher plane
intellectually, morally, socially, and spiritually. For Progressive-era scientists,
the Worm struggled to become Man, and Man marched inexorably toward
Superman.[50] Species and societies alike were part of a mighty stream flowing
to a future that surely had to be better, or could be steered to become better.

We find more Ivesian parallels in the way William James, the central
philosopher of the time, developed Peirce's concept of pragmatism. Wrote
James, "The truth of an idea is not a stagnant property inherent in it. Truth
happens to an idea. It *becomes* true, is *made* true by events. Its verity *is* in fact an
event, a process."[51] Compare Ives: "The meaning of 'God' may have a billion
interpretations if there be that many souls in the world"; his quoting of Emerson, "every ultimate fact is only the first of a new series"; his observation that
Emerson "will not accept repose against the activity of truth." For James as for
Ives, the search for truth is an endless human activity, and God is conceived in
terms of his meaning and value to humanity.

James first named and described the "stream of consciousness." Ives was
the first composer to create something like that stream in music, in works
including the *"Saint-Gaudens," Decoration Day,* and *Thoreau.* Ives carried the
idea into the mind of the performer and the stream of history. In memos about
performance of the *Concord* he wrote that the score must not be considered a
static artifact or be performed too literally: "Play it before breakfast like ——!
Play it after breakfast like——! Play it after digging potatoes like ——! In fact,
these notes, marks and near pictures of sounds etc. are in a kind of way a
platform for the player to make his own speeches on. . . . [*Emerson* and *Thoreau*
especially] change and grow, rise to this mountain, then to that, as the years
go on through time to the Eternities."[52] Compare James in "The Stream of
Consciousness": "We feel things differently accordingly as we are sleepy or
awake, hungry or full, fresh or tired; differently at night and in the morning,
differently in summer and winter."[53] With *Emerson* more than anywhere else,
Ives created a work conceived as evolving through time and feeling and performers and performances—the whole human stream of consciousness.

As Ives lambasted the literal-minded, the categorizers, those "over-partial
to the specific," James divided people into "tended-minded" literalists and the
"tough-minded," who can adapt to the pluralism and unpredictability of life
and truth. Ives, the archetypal tough-minded man, wrote approvingly that
Emerson "wrings the neck of any law that would become exclusive and arro-
gant, whether a definite one of metaphysics or an indefinite one of mechan-
ics."[54] As seen there, Ives like James fell at length, and of necessity, into
vagueness in contemplating reality. But Ives elevated that to a principle:

"Vagueness is at times an indication of nearness to a perfect truth."[55] The Fourth Symphony finale seems to melt into the stars, into a resounding silence, a universal vagueness.

That symphony, conceived in part amidst the mountains of the Adirondacks, permeated with the sublime mystery of that landscape and Harmony Ives's presence in it, parallels William James's ecstasy one day in 1898, while hiking in the same country. James wrote his wife that night,

It seemed as if the Gods of all the nature-mythologies were holding an indescribable meeting in my breast with the moral Gods of the inner life. . . . The intense significance of some sort, of the whole scene, if one could only *tell* the significance; the intense inhuman remoteness of its inner life, and yet the intense *appeal* of it; its everlasting freshness and its immemorial antiquity and decay; its utter Americanism, and every sort of patriotic suggestiveness, and you, and my relation to you . . . beaten up with it, so that memory and sensation all whirled inexplicably together. . . . I can't find a single word for all that significance, and don't know what it was significant of, so there it remains.[56]

Ives and James were devoted to mystery, to unanswered questions, and they were both optimists. They reveled in the Progressive sense of infinite potential in fresh, *American* conceptions of reality and truth and progress. At least James did not live to experience the misfortune Ives did, to see that optimism fall into the abyss of the First World War. Ives lived on into the backlash of the 1920s, the resurgence of conservative pessimism about human goodness, the return of dogmatic religion and survival-of-the-richest social Darwinism. He had to watch the dismantling of Progressivism presided over by the witless bluster of Warren G. Harding and the passivity of Calvin Coolidge. At the same time he found nothing in common with the rebelliousness of the period, the Jazz Age, the time of F. Scott Fitzgerald's beautiful and damned, when many artists fled to Europe, as Ezra Pound said, not in search of ideas but "in disgust." The catastrophe of the war belied everything Progressives believed in, and afterward mostly emptiness, greed, and jazz were left.

Having experienced for twenty years an ascending curve of artistic and business success and growing optimism, Ives would never really understand what hit him or the country during the 1920s. What happened to him would be symbol and paradigm of what happened to Progressives everywhere: politically, they became invisible; personally, they could only stew and curse, like a generation of invalids.

What sustained Ives through the long years after 1918 was faith in ideals that to him were all the more precious for being indefinable. On a sketch of the *Universe Symphony* he wrote, "The only hope of humanity is the unseen Spirit." The element of Ives's music and thought that has been most neglected, perhaps because it does not conform to critical categories of our age, is their foundation in religion. Ives's music is as essentially religious as Bach's, though his faith is very different from the fire-and-brimstone Lutheranism of the German composer. But as with Bach, nearly everything Ives wrote in his maturity was permeated by a religious spirit.

To the extent that Ives's religion has been noted, it has generally been misunderstood. Even John Kirkpatrick said, "His churchgoing self was conservative almost to the point of what's called Fundamentalist. He was almost in a state of 'Give me that old-time religion, it's good enough for me.' "[57] That does not capture the breadth of Ives's faith. The old-time Sunday service in the white-steepled church, yes; bringing up his child in the faith, yes. In the longer view, organized religion could not give Ives the perspective he reached for, "A conception unlimited by the narrow names of Christian, Pagan, Jew, or Angel!"[58] There is an echo in that of the old Yankee indifference to sect—any roof and rubric will do as long as God is addressed—but he goes beyond that into a pluralistic and Gnostic conception of religion. Which is all to say that while Ives expressed his religion conventionally, he believed by his own lights. Scattered through *Essays Before a Sonata* we find hints of Ives's religion and how music expressed and fulfilled it. In "Emerson" he begins his ruminations almost jokingly:

Picking up an essay on religion of a rather remarkable-minded boy—perhaps with a touch of genius [surely meaning himself, though the essay does not survive] . . . we read: "Every thinking man knows that the church is dead." But every thinking man knows that the church part of the church always has been dead—that part seen by candle-light, not Christ-light. . . . if the church holds itself as nothing but the symbol of the greater light, it is life itself; as a symbol of a symbol, it is dead. Many of the sincerest followers of Christ never heard of Him.[59]

Here, in the same way as Ives, following Thoreau, defined "music" as a principle beyond mere sound, Ives defines "Christ" not as a dogmatic icon but as a principle (say, of peace and compassion) that can be found anywhere. A few lines after that he does the same with the concept of "God": the critic of religion "forgets that 'being true to ourselves' *is* God, that the faintest thought of immortality *is* God, and that God is 'miracle'. . . . Is the Christian religion . . . anything but the revelation of God in a personality—a revelation so that the narrow mind could become opened?" Later he spells out his "great primal truths: that there is more good than evil, that God is on the side of the majority . . . that he had made the universal mind and the over-soul . . . a part of the individual mind and soul, that he has made the Divine a part of all."[60]

So the God of mainstream Judeo-Christianity, existing apart from His creation, was not Ives's kind of metaphor. He believed in an immanent divinity that inhabits and exalts nature and every human soul, like the Gnostic heretic who wrote, "Split the stick, and you will find Jesus." Transcendentalism earns its name not because God is transcendent but because humanity, inhabited by

God, has the potential to be. (Ives carried that conviction nearly as far as it could go, and well beyond how it could actually play out in the world.)

Ives does use one familiar metaphor, at the end of his passage describing the transforming epiphany of his boyhood, when his father's band came marching down the street and he experienced "an exultant something gleaming with the possibilities of this life—an assurance that nothing is impossible, and that the whole world lies at his feet." That experience fades, leaving its afterglow, and in adulthood is transformed into a faith institutionalized in practice, but vital in import:

Later in life, the same boy hears the Sabbath morning bell ringing out from the white steeple at the "Center," and as it draws him to it . . . a Gospel hymn of simple devotion comes out to him—"There's a wideness in God's mercy"—an instant suggestion of that Memorial Day morning comes—but the moment is of deeper import . . . a profound sense of a spiritual truth. . . . And as the hymn voices die away, there lies at his feet— not the world, but the figure of the Saviour—he sees an unfathomable courage—an immortality for the lowest—the vastness in humility, the kindness of the human heart, man's noblest strength—and he knows that God is nothing—nothing—but love![61]

That is what Ives found in the steepled church, in ritual, in old-time religion and gospel music. In "Thoreau" he calls the church and revealed religion "the path between God and man's spiritual part—a kind of formal causeway."[62] He never took the Christian church for the exclusive dwelling place of God, which is precisely what old-time religion does. "The soul," wrote Ives, "is each man's share of God."[63] The law of averages is divine because God dwells in each, and the majority properly informed speaks with something like a divine voice. That process of the people speaking both as individuals and en masse—and singing and playing—will lead to "the eventual triumph of the soul and its union with God!"[64] Ives's pluralistic conception of religion is the foundation of his personal variety of socialism, his millennialism, and eventually his conception of music.

In the Epilogue of the *Essays* Ives develops the idea of the stream of consciousness and of life, a conception at once Progressive, Darwinian, and spiritual. "This stream of change flows towards the eventual ocean of mankind's perfection."[65] Music is part of that stream, contributes to its progress, and in it is purified along with humanity. That is why, so far,

Music may be yet unborn. Perhaps no music has ever been written or heard. Perhaps the birth of art will take place at the moment in which the last man who is willing to make a living out of art is gone and gone forever. In the history of this youthful world, the best product that human beings can boast of is probably Beethoven; but, maybe, even his art is as nothing in comparison with the future product of some coal-miner's soul in the forty-first century.[66]

This is a visionary and touching eschatology, that music is unborn. Ives's conviction of the value of music and of composing is so strong that he cannot imagine it as anything but necessary to human evolution, cannot imagine anything more spiritual and democratic than that every man shall become a composer and his life a symphony. Only then will music truly be born. Ives arrives finally, by way of quoting poet Sidney Lanier, at a mystical view of music as the highest expression of the sacred.

Lanier . . . writes, "I have so many fair dreams and hopes about music in these days. It is gospel whereof the people are in great need. . . . I think the time will come when music, *rightly developed* to its now-little-foreseen *grandeur* [both italics Ives's] will be found to be a late revelation of all gospels in one." Could the art of music or the art of anything, have a more profound reason for being than this? A conception unlimited by the narrow names of Christian, Pagan, Jew, or Angel! A vision higher and deeper than art itself![67]

There, as much as Ives ever defined it, is his credo as a composer. It is in these terms that we may understand the Fourth Symphony as a work of universal religion. For Ives all spirituality was equivalent because each man and woman has within them the same parcel of the divine, the same potential for salvation. In the epic journey of the Fourth Symphony, after the introductory hymn and the urban uproar of the *Comedy,* the third movement is set in a New England church, the ritualistic causeway of conventional religion symbolized by the formal genre of the fugue. The significant thing is that Ives's fugue is only a waystation to the transcendent last movement, which is at once a symbol of the future of music and of a greater spiritual journey that goes far beyond old-time religion and beyond music as we have known it. Ives had written *music is life,* but prophesied a time when life became music.

There is another, more personal, unspoken part of his credo. The Fourth Symphony is also an autobiography. The unspoken part of Charles Ives's credo is love's part, the private theology between him and his wife. During their courtship they came to see their love as an image of divine love and his music their way of spreading it. Harmony wrote him in 1908, "You are the revelation of God to me [and what] it can do & will do is to make our lives good & helpful. . . . The comfort of a beautiful expression of our love in music or words is that it would let people see in a concrete form the beauty of it and share, if but for a moment the heaven we know." Ives never spoke of this dimension of his music; it was their most intimate secret. For Harmony especially, these feelings were holy and not to be shared. She forbade Charlie to write about her and their relationship. ("What she has done for me I won't put down, because she won't let me."[68]) She told the Cowells she never liked seeing their name in print.[69]

Some of this is the reticence of the Victorian wife, the role Harmony chose for herself. More than that, it is a reserving of something that lay at the core of their marriage and behind all his mature music, as a secret presence and revelation. When Ives wrote in the *Essays* "God is nothing, nothing but love," he was not voicing a commonplace but speaking from experience. That experience is manifest in his music, the spiritual radiance behind his greatest works. John Kirkpatrick wrote, "their own devotion to each other enlarged their perceptions into what amounted to a mystical vision of reality. The exalted peroration of the Second String Quartet and the Fourth Symphony are probably not more from transcendentalist sources than from this source."[70] Ives succeeded, in other words, in his private goal of spreading the news of divine love into the world. As with Bach, that love speaks wherever Ives's music is heard.

In *Essays Before a Sonata* we read what Ives thought about what he had done, looking back in 1919 over his life and, as it turned out and he perhaps already feared, a nearly completed body of work. These intimations of what he was doing and why, what music was doing and why, had accumulated over the years as he was preoccupied with getting the notes on paper. Finally, when most of the notes he had in him were set down, the ideas gushed out in the *Essays* something less than fully formed, but formed enough to say a great deal.

The *Essays* finished, Ives, still weak but working full-tilt again, turned his attention more than ever to the practical side of being a composer. At the end of 1919, as he returned to the office, music publisher G. Schirmer began engraving the *Concord Sonata*. *Essays Before a Sonata* would come out in 1920, in an edition by the Knickerbocker Press. At the beginning of 1921, 750 copies of the sonata would be mailed out. Both were issued under his own imprint, as vanity books. Meanwhile he was assembling a book of songs, for which during 1921 he arranged or composed some two dozen new ones. These publications were his last-ditch attempts to find an audience.

During the frustrating months of incomplete recovery in 1919, Ives composed one of his unforgettable songs, "Serenity." Over a quiet, slow-cycling chordal ostinato that seems to stop time in its course, the voice chants John Greenleaf Whittier's prayer for inner peace, which is surely Ives's prayer as well.

> O, Sabbath rest of Galilee!
> O, calm of hills above,
> Where Jesus knelt to share with Thee,
> the silence of eternity
> Interpreted by love.
> Drop Thy still dews of quietness,
> till all our strivings cease;
> Take from our souls the strain and stress,
> and let our ordered lives confess,
> the beauty of Thy peace.

Overtures

CHARLES IVES SPENT THE YEARS 1919–21 writing much prose and little music while he waited at the brink of public life as a composer. His new attempts to find an audience would be successful, in the sense of lighting a very slow fuse. But that effort alone was not enough for him. His writings of those years included *Essays Before a Sonata* and articles for insurance magazines. Even more than on those clearly relevant subjects, he would write obsessively on government, economics, and society. The old Yankee could not bear to see himself simply as an artist peddling his wares. Ives was all for art, but perennially uncomfortable with the mantle of artist. Besides, living on borrowed time, he felt driven not only to get his music into the world but to say everything he had to say, while he could.

His article "Writing Big Policies of Life Insurance" appeared in the trade magazine *Eastern Underwriter* in October 1919. Around the same time Schirmer began engraving the *Concord Sonata*. Charlie and Harmony spent a quiet Christmas with family that year at 120 East 22nd Street. Next year his historic article "The Amount to Carry" came out in the *Underwriter,* and *Essays Before a Sonata* was printed. Ives spent a good deal of 1920 struggling with proofs of the *Concord.* Like his copyists, the Schirmer engravers had a habit of "correcting" his notes.[1] He had already simplified the score against his better judgment, and would repent that as soon as it was out of his hands.

As of autumn 1919 he was officially back to work at Ives & Myrick. Now he kept a supply of pills for his heart, and installed a couch in his office where he could collapse when a fit of breathlessness or angina overcame him.[2] Over the next decade he would no longer always arrive at work first thing but sometimes at ten or so, if he showed up at all, and he might leave in midafternoon. Often he slipped into his office by a private entrance and nobody knew he was there until he called someone in.[3] He would stay home for a week at a time. Besides the drain of illness, he was still anxious about Edie's family trying to get at her. That had something to do with the secretiveness, but it was not the whole story. His new habits seemed peculiar to the employees; he didn't look that sick to them.

For the moment Ives's creative output had slowed dramatically. In 1920, amidst working over proofs, he composed only a few new songs toward his songbook, some complex (including "Grantchester"), some nostalgic and sentimental (including "The Collection"), and one satirical of the Gay Nineties— "On the Counter," which would appear with the note: "Though there is little danger of it, it is hoped that this song will not be taken seriously, or sung, at least, in public." Otherwise Ives tried with little success to get well, and wrote political screeds with a determination that swelled into something like hysteria.

First came an essay called "The Majority," for which his final handwritten draft, after earlier drafts and sketches, covers some one hundred legal sheets,[4] the longest stretch of prose he ever wrote. While he spent a good deal of time and energy on this political testament, there is no telling what he intended to do with it. He would produce two companion pieces to "The Majority," a sketch called "George's Adventure," and "Concerning a Twentieth Amendment." The latter he would attempt valiantly to place before politicians and voters.

The genesis of "The Majority" goes back some time before 1919. In the first fifteen years of the century Ives evolved from McKinley Republican (his family background, though not necessarily his father's) to Wilsonian Democrat, a rare species in New York business circles. Onetime settlement-house nurse Harmony may have had a part in liberalizing her husband's politics, though she would never be as outspoken or as radical. Ives's social concerns mounted to a state of alarm during the war. The larger his earnings grew, the more outraged he became at the distribution of wealth in the country. In part that probably revealed an antipathy for the wealthy capitalist class. They were not Ives's kind of people in general, and they were the sort who sat on symphony boards and applauded Walter Damrosch and thought music died with Brahms. Ives's opinion of money and power came also from the Puritan in him that saw riches as a sign of divine approval (or in his case, validation of his ideals), but at the same time recoiled from money as a worldly temptation.

More tangibly and bitterly, Ives blamed international moneyed interests for creating World War I—not an uncommon or unreasonable opinion. He remembered the old Rebel at the Gettysburg reunion, who had declared that conflagration "a rich man's war." In a letter to a newspaper around 1915, Ives wrote,

Has there been a war, during, say, the last two or three hundred years, where the primal cause has not been the desire of a small number of men of large property to conserve or increase their property, and where most of the fighting has not been done by a large number of men of little or no property? Would a limited property right be a natural . . . means of increasing the unit of energy and the resulting economic goods, and the power of man to utilize and enjoy them in such a way that, as his material benefits increase, his mental, moral, and spiritual life can develop proportionately? Further, can a man of average social consciousness feel that he has a moral right to all the property he can acquire legally and honestly?[5]

So far Ives was asking more or less sensible questions, and those questions were the foundation of his political thought. On that foundation, however, he erected shaky constructions. One of his ideas, appearing in writings from around 1915, was a government-enforced limited property right that he set sometimes at $50,000, sometimes at $100,000. His goal was twofold: to reach a more equitable distribution of wealth, and at the same time make it harder for the rich and powerful to foment wars. Certainly it is wonderful to find a millionaire proposing to limit property. (He insisted he would comply with his proposed maximum, if he weren't the only one to do it.[6]) It is more startling to find Ives, so suspicious of authority and its power, proposing to give the government ultimate power over everyone's pocketbook.

In 1919, ill and disgusted with the American leadership that had rejected the League of Nations, Ives began his long essay "The Majority" with a tone of outrage and apocalypse:

Who are going to run things in this country—in this world, for that matter? A few millionaires, a few anarchists, a few capitalists, a few party-leaders, a few labor-leaders, a few political-leaders, a few "hystericals," a few conservatives, a few agitators, a few cranks, a few this, a few that, or YOU!—the Majority—the People?

If some such question could be branded in the horizon, would it penetrate the hog-mind, the self-will of the Minority (the Non-People)?[7]

He rails on likewise for a while, finally speaking for God in proclaiming "the great primal truths: that there is more good than evil, that God is on the side of the Majority, that He is not particularly enthusiastic about the Minority, that He has made men greater than Man, that He has made the Common Heart . . . greater than the individual heart, mind, and soul, and the predominant part of each."

Here he created another of his dualities. To one side of the dichotomy he placed business interests, wealthy interests, the ruling oligarchy of all times and places. These he called *the Minority,* and added the suffixes "Non-People" and "hog-mind." He thereby distanced the moneyed class from the People and painted its members as inhuman swine. In his invective against the Minority Ives does not mean the term as it is understood today, but rather any interest group that gains inordinate influence or aspires to it: the greedy, the grasping, the hog-mind intoxicated with power. (That other kinds of minorities might exist under the thumb of unenlightened majorities was out of Ives's field of reference. He deplored racial prejudice, but "race" and "minority" did not fall into the same category in his mind. Nor did "poor" and "minority." Poverty to him was not a matter for governments but for private philanthropy like his ancestors' and his own.)

On the other side of his dichotomy lie *the Majority,* the People, that he glorified in his song called both "Majority" and "The Masses": *The Masses have toiled, / Behold the works of the World! / The Masses are thinking, / Whence comes the thought of the World! / The Masses are singing, / Whence comes the Art of the World!*

For Ives the Majority embodied the Emersonian oversoul, the spirit of the common man that was the prime wellspring of his music. In itself, this dichotomy of Minority and Majority is idealistic, populist, and Progressive, even if his expression of it could turn shrill and absolute. His tone would only get more so, the more his outrage with American politics and with his own inability to effect anything.

Eventually "The Majority" settles down to a calmer tone, to speculations and proposals. What is a state? Who runs it and to what purpose? What groups have proposed alternatives and what do they amount to? "The Communist," to name one minority group, "begins to shout [his solutions,] not the reasonable kind partial to government ownership of public utilities and general socialization of some industries, but the Communist in the essence, the furious but partial thinker."[8] Here and elsewhere Ives the fierce individualist reveals a touch of affinity for socialism and even communism, but he also distinguishes himself from them: "Any plan . . . that takes everything away from everybody . . . cannot stand up against the simplest laws of evolution and any progress in human nature."[9] Except, eventually, as a supporter of Modernist musical organizations, Ives was not about to join any movement. His socialism was personal and ad hoc, though no less millennial than the European variety: "The divinely inspired Majority influence will guide mankind, we believe, more and more completely, and . . . lead it to eventual perfection." In the essay he proposes a referendum questionnaire for governments to present to everybody in the world, the items including, "Do you or do you not agree to have . . . no army or navy now and forever if the Majority (the People) of all other countries agree to the same?" In the guise of objective referendum questions he promotes his limited personal income and raises the possibility of a world government and police force.

He goes into nuts and bolts. How would it work to hand the United States government over to the Majority? It would involve some kind of lawmaking by systematic countrywide referendum. The function of Congress would change as representative democracy gave way to direct democracy. And about time: "The leaders, for the most part, have been under-average men with skins-thick, hands-slick, and wits-quick with under-values . . . and so the day of leaders, as such, is gradually closing—the people are beginning to lead themselves." Congress would be reduced to "the clerical machine of the people,"[10] a body for analyzing popular proposals for laws, framing referendum questions, tabulating voting results. Ives says with satisfaction that Congress would eventually become "but a body of technical experts or specialists." He implies this kind of direct democracy could be a model for a People's World Union.

These are appealing ideas, maybe, but the devil is in the details. "All citizens should be *required* to give consideration to the issues as they appear, and to vote at both primary and final elections."[11] To support that requirement, Ives makes one of his trademark generalizations based on faith rather than facts: "There is no man or woman in the world today, provided that he or she is . . . normal, who cannot . . . give serious study of say thirty minutes a day for three or four months to the dozen or so questions with their classified facts and digests of the arguments from all important viewpoints." In pursuing his train of logic Ives dispenses with the oppression of leaders and replaces it with the law watching over citizens to make sure they study their issues, nightly, for the required months, and duly vote. Which any "normal" person would be happy to do. Does Ives really mean, "The Majority, right or wrong, are always right"?[12] Given a properly informed citizenry, that is exactly what he means. As for an enforced limitation on property, "normal" people, "good" people, don't do what they do to get rich anyway. In another extravagant generalization Ives argues, "No genius ever stopped creating because he knew he never could make a million dollars. . . . If Edison had known in advance that he could be worth in property no more than Beethoven, would he have stopped inventing any more than Beethoven would have stopped composing?"[13]

At the end of "The Majority" Ives arrives at the question of what the Minority man can do if he doesn't see the virtue in all this. He can lump it, or else: (1) "abide by the winner's terms, live up to the Majority law like a man," (2) "go to some other country whose laws are more congenial to him," (3) "begin to shriek, to get nasty . . . and then the Majority will strangle him— and treat him like a farmer treats a skunk who loses his self-respect."[14] His pages of practical suggestions and examinations of potential problems come down to that dark prophecy of violence. It would not be the last time.

Before that point, though, much of "The Majority" resembles the kind of practical planning Ives had been doing for years at the office creating agents' classes, selling schemes, and innovative programs. As Mike Myrick wrote, "He would prepare any plan of insurance operations with the greatest, detailed accuracy . . . put the plan on paper for minute discussion, change and consult until the whole thing was finally set up in complete form." "The Majority" is similar in style and approach to the contemporary insurance essay "The Amount to Carry." Likewise, the didactic dialogue of "George's Adventure" is similar to "Broadway," a how-to-sell story Ives wrote for agents in 1922. Those office plans had been brilliant and their playing out had helped bring Ives spectacular success. Why not, he reasoned, apply the same approach to the perennial problems of the world? The world might call him crazy, but so did the insurance industry until he showed them he was right.

The telling differences between the business essays and the political screeds are not so much in approach as in tone and general connection to reality, the comparative intimacy with how things work and can be made to work. As well as anybody, Ives knew the insurance business and how it related to society. The mechanisms and demands of politics he hardly knew at all, and hated them too much to seriously investigate how they worked. Besides, many of his fantasies about what he could accomplish politically followed from a willful misperception of his own success in business. Ives attributed his prosperity mainly to his ideals. In "George's Adventure" he writes his dollar justification of his ideals:

I assumed that the law of averages was divine, and that . . . *most* men were honest and most men were intelligent. Therefore, if your goods had as much good in them and truth in them as you knew how to put in them . . . the less . . . will be the force of dishonesty and unintelligence against you. . . . Our business grew from a few thousands to 15,000,000 in twelve years. . . . The largest [competitor], who did 2,000,000 when he told us what failures we would be, has made an increase to 4,000,000 (with the same goods to sell).[15]

In fact it was mainly agent recruitment that made Ives & Myrick rich, more than his other innovations, more than ideals. His surge in earnings during the 1920s would not be based on ideals either, but on financial machinations.

Beyond the personal obsessions, "The Majority" and all Ives's political writings must be seen in the context of the First World War and its aftermath. The war was a global catastrophe. Every thoughtful person wanted mechanisms to stop it from happening again. Progressives among others tried to invent those mechanisms. Some people understood, Ives among them, that the attempts fell disastrously short of ensuring a lasting peace. If Ives was an extreme Progressive, his response to the war and to the conservative backlash of the 1920s was inevitably going to be extreme. He tilted at windmills called Minority, hog-mind, Non-People, and over the years that would both feed on and exacerbate his deteriorating physical and mental health.

It is not that his feelings about government were unique. Progressives mistrusted party politics as a part of the general American suspicion of politicians. In that too, Ives was an extreme of common opinion. Americans tend to enjoy the game of politics but to despise the players. Writes Geoffrey Gorer in *The American People:*

The prized quality of Americans was and is dependent on the weakness of their government . . . to reject authority became a praiseworthy and specifically American act. . . . Authority is inherently bad and dangerous; the survival and growth of the state make it inevitable that some individuals must be endowed with authority, but this authority must be as circumscribed and limited as legal ingenuity can devise. . . .[16] Awe directed toward people is always painful and reprehensible; but awe directed toward things, or abstractions regarded as things, is tolerable and in some cases mandatory. The Flag, abstractions such as Freedom and Democracy, certain buildings and places . . . are all fit objects for awe and reverence.[17]

Charles Dickens, addressing in *American Notes* a people he both admired and regretted, put the national sentiment in a nutshell:

You no sooner set up an idol firmly than you are sure to pull it down . . . directly you reward a benefactor, or a public servant, you distrust him, merely because he is rewarded. . . . Any man who attains a high place among you, from the President downwards, may date his downfall from that moment; for any printed lie that any notorious villain pens . . . appeals at once to your distrust, and is believed.[18]

Once Ives had his own political heroes, among them Woodrow Wilson and New York governor Al Smith. Disillusioned with them, he set up sacred abstractions called the Majority, the People. And he decreed that God turns his face from leaders, "under-average men with skins-thick, hands-slick, and wits-quick with under-values."

Even though Ives took "The Majority" through several hand drafts and typescripts (done by secretaries at the office), he never sent it around. He may have decided to use it as a way to collect his thoughts. Its partly autobiographical partner, sketches in the form of a debate between a man and his wife called "George's Adventure," is more frankly steam-blowing.[19] In the story the fictional George mainly extolls the Ivesian plan for limiting income. His wife is skeptical and sardonic, as Harmony probably could be on these matters, though pleased that George believes in women's rights (he accepts that women marry for money only "until women have an equal chance with men to make money"). The debate ends peaceably, but the wife is not really convinced. At some point Ives noted on the manuscript of "George's Adventure": "This is just to show how a man should write who considers himself a nice author and whom everybody else considers crazy." He suggests there what one finds in his writings in the early 1920s and in his music a few years later—a deterioration of focus and coherence, a tendency to blow off steam rather than do his real work.

Ives's public effort to spread his plans for a new order came in the form of a six-page article, sent to eight New York papers in February 1920, called "Concerning a Twentieth Amendment." In the introduction he admits his attempt is "clumsy and far from adequate," but a step toward addressing "the effect of too much 'politics' in our representative democracy—we submit it for what it is worth."[20] None of the papers thought it worth printing at all.

His proposed amendment to the U.S. Constitution adds up to a call for more direct democracy and a reshaping of government only a little less sweeping than in "The Majority." Congress is not yet to be reduced to clerks. Nine months before each presidential election the public shall submit to Congress proposals for laws, which Congress shall reduce to no more than twenty issues for public consideration. All citizens are required to send responses to those issues. Congress digests and analyzes the millions of responses, every one of them, and then distributes ten referendum questions, attaching arguments pro and con based on the public comment. After studying the questions the public votes on them and a simple majority creates the law. Ives is proposing, in effect, a national version of the New England town meeting[21]: each person stands to have a say, and then everybody shows hands. That this would be inconceivable on a national scale seems not to have occurred to him. At one point he suggested that the populace could vote by telephone.[22]

When the New York papers rejected the amendment article, Ives sent it to the *Atlantic Monthly* and a collection of politicians, with no better results. Among politicians who politely brushed him off were Calvin Coolidge, William Jennings Bryan, and secretaries to President Wilson and Herbert Hoover.[23] Former president William Howard Taft wrote what may have been the only serious response Ives ever got: "I am very much opposed to approve such an amendment as that which you suggest. It is impracticable, and would much change the form of our Government. It would be introducing a principle of the referendum, which I think has already been demonstrated to be a failure in securing the real opinion of the people." Ives wrote back, still trying to convince the ex-president.

Meanwhile he got the idea of distributing the amendment at the Republican and Democratic National Conventions. For the purpose he had 5,000 copies printed up as a broadside, author unnamed. Ives needed to see himself not as a leader but rather as a humble, anonymous catalyst for change. All the same, in the broadside the relatively sober and considered tone of the original newspaper piece has become the language of hard sell. In the introduction and following matter of the amendment proper, much of it taken from "The Majority," Ives uses screaming capitals to highlight the essential ideas. It is the hyperbolic mode of an insurance ad, of the Ives & Myrick *Estate-O-Graph*, of his 1918 poster of wartime suggestions.

The following contains an attempt to suggest a "20TH AMENDMENT" to the Federal Constitution—AN ATTEMPT clumsy and far from adequate, we admit . . . but as its general purpose is TO REDUCE to a minimum, or possibly to eliminate, something which all our great political leaders talk about but never eliminate, to wit: THE EFFECTS OF TOO MUCH POLITICS IN OUR representative DEMOCRACY. . . . A dispassionate examination of social phenomena in this and other civilizations indicates that THE INTUITIVE REASONING OF THE MASSES IS MORE SCIENTIFICALLY TRUE AND so OF GREATER VALUE TO the wholesome PROGRESS of social evolution THAN the PERSONAL ADMONITIONS of the intellectual only.[24]

And so on in a harangue against party politics, which Ives proposed to have distributed at the biggest and most rabidly partisan political gatherings in the world, the Republican and Democratic National Conventions. Ives cries in a footnote, *There will be no plank in any party platform more important!* Thus he asks party platforms to call for party suicide and the end of representative government.

The thing was doomed from beginning to end. Ives wrote Darby Day, head of a Mutual agency in Chicago, asking him to find a distributor to hand out the amendment at the Republican Convention there in the middle of June. Despite Ives's best efforts and an anxious series of exchanges, the broadsides were mailed but did not arrive in time.[25] Ives wearily asked Day to have somebody hand them out on the streets.[26] At the convention, the lamentable Warren G. Harding was thrust on the delegates by a few kingmakers working out of the legendary smoke-filled room. Ives made a similar attempt to send his broadsides to the Democratic Convention in San Francisco; there is no record they got there. Meanwhile the *Atlantic* rejected the proposal and Ives sent it to *The Outlook,* which briskly returned it. Exhausted, frustrated, enraged, Ives scrawled on the *Outlook* rejection, "YOU WEAK SISTERS!" That autumn he tried again, sending two versions, a shorter and a longer, to New York and Brooklyn newspapers. No takers. Ives would have stacks of the broadsides sitting around the house for the rest of his life; he sent out copies to all and sundry, whether they asked or not (there is no indication anyone did).

So he never gave up on the amendment. It lay close to his essential faith, the beliefs that had animated his life and two careers. His essential reasoning about the Majority was perhaps most plainly stated in the cover letter he sent to newspapers with the first proposal:

If one will admit that God made man's brain as well as his stomach, one must then admit that the brain (that is the majority-brain!) if it has the normal amount of wholesome food—truth, in its outward manifestations, specific knowledge, facts, premises, etc., which universal education is fast bringing—will digest and will function, as normally as the stomach, when it has the right kind of food. If one won't admit that, he comes pretty near admitting that God is incapable.[27]

Here is the crux of Ives's political reasoning. He linked the idea that "the Majority, right or wrong, are always right" to his very faith in God. If he lost one side of the faith he lost the other, and then he lost everything he had served in his art and his life and his business.

The pattern of reasoning behind Ives's politics thus developed from a few simple, not entirely unreasonable premises, part based on observation and part on good-hearted faith and idealism. First, God made human beings innately intelligent and good—an article of faith, distinctively Bushnellian. Second, the law of averages is divine—partly derived from the actuarial tables (which *are* holy writ for an insurance man) and partly from the first premise. Third, evolution is the law not only of nature but of music and society, and evolution always progresses upward. Fourth, the United States, like most countries, is run by a wealthy oligarchy whose members include government and party leaders.

If 1, 2, and 3 are correct, then 4 is intolerable. The problem can be fixed by an application of Progressive models but aiming higher than mere referendum and recall. The solution is to kick out the elite of elected leaders and replace them with direct democracy, which will unleash the divine wisdom of the Majority, the Common Mind, the virtual will of God. The situation may be unsettled for a time, but in the long run it will work because surely God made our brains as well as He made our stomachs and our souls.

This is a splendid vision of humanity and a hopeless one. With it Ives painted himself into a very confining, very frustrating corner in his later years. It is one thing to hope for the perfection of humanity in a great someday, as did C. S. Peirce, as did *Essays Before a Sonata*. It is another to try and jump-start the millennium right now. Attempts like that can go hard on a man, especially one out of touch and out of tune with the popular will of his time, and whose strength is already waning. After the writings of 1919, Ives would begin to repeat himself, his grand ideas becoming ritualistic incantations: the Fundamental Problems, the hog-mind, the People, the People's World Union.

Harding's landslide presidential victory in 1920 was the final insult to Ives and his fantasy of touching off a groundswell for direct democracy. Once again party politics had danced to the tune of the oligarchy. Before Harding died and left the government to "Silent Cal" Coolidge in 1923, his administration would establish a record unequaled in the United States for bluster, incompetence, and corruption. In response to Harding's election Ives wrote words and music to a song called "November 2, 1920." It is a barely coherent blow-off set to deliberately chiding, banal music. With a sudden change of tone it ends memorably, though, on a summons to hope and renewal, the final words borrowed from Walt Whitman:

It strikes me that . . . Some men and women got tired of a big job; but, over there our men did not quit. They fought and died that better things might be! . . . The pocketbook and certain little things talked loud and "noble," and got in the way, Too many readers go by the headlines, party men will muddle up the facts. So a good many citizens voted as grandpa always did . . . "It's raining, let's throw out the weatherman" . . . Then the timid smiled and looked relieved. "We've got enough to eat, to hell with ideals!" Some old women, male and female, had their day today, and the "ole mole came out of his hole"; But he won't stay out long. God always drives him back! Oh Captain, my Captain! a heritage we've thrown away: But we'll find it again, my Captain, oh my Captain.

When he printed "November 2" in *114 Songs* Ives appended a calm note about the election, saying the writer would send any concerned parties a plan for a constitutional amendment. Like the amendment broadside, the song is not calm at all. It is a caustic requiem for the Progressive era and a hope for its resurrection in new and grander form. By the time something like that resurrection finally did come to pass, Ives would be too sick and too far from the world to comprehend it.

Disaffection from the will of American voters was hardly Ives's only dilemma. Again and again over the next years he would be reminded that the majority was hardly more interested in his music than in his politics. He had wanted to fashion a universal art by uniting the voice of the common people with the genres of the great European masters. He had hoped to create the ultimate democratic music, to embrace the world as Beethoven had proclaimed in the Ninth Symphony: "O ye millions, I embrace thee!" And the people pushed him away. A galling paradox, that one. Yet as "November 2, 1920" reveals, Ives had not lost hope for his country or for humanity. Nor had he lost faith that the masses would someday embrace the music he had written to exalt them. He never lost that faith.

Besides working on the *Concord* proofs and writing a few songs in 1920, Ives tried to stick with something like his usual round of music. He heard the New York Symphony play Ravel's *Daphnis and Chloe* in February. There was no way he could approve of the creamy eroticism of that work. As usual he scribbled his complaints in the margin of the program: "Listening hard, & carefully as I know how to & 'fair' as I tried to be, there was nothing big, new—the same old cloth boquets just changed around a little."[28] A week later he heard the Boston Symphony at Carnegie Hall, the program including the Schumann First Symphony and Mendelssohn's *Calm Sea and Prosperous Voyage*. No scribbles on that program.

He had responded to another call for scores and been notified that Paul Eisler, assistant conductor of the New Symphony, would read through *Decoration Day* with the orchestra at Carnegie Hall. The score may have been chosen by an orchestral committee. After Eisler had a look at it he sent Ives a letter reneging on the offer.[29] In reply Ives politely but firmly held the orchestra to the reading and offered to pay for extra rehearsal time. But he would not water down the piece, as he had a few years before with the *Washington's Birthday* readings at his apartment. "To change it to a more acceptable or practicable form would be possible," he wrote the conductor, "but I feel that as a matter of principle I cannot start in and work that way now. I'm afraid that I'll have to work things out in the way or ways which appeal to me, or not at all."[30] Eisler gave in. He came to the house and listened to Ives go through the music at the piano, exclaiming in surprise, "Why, you play like an artist!" From the score the conductor had apparently concluded, as musicians would be apt to for a long time, that Ives was an amateur if not a primitive, if not plain crazy.

Carnegie Hall is usually warm and intimate, but the day of the reading in spring 1920 it was chilly and hollow, with a sprinkling of audience. The New Symphony tuned up, the hall fell silent, and Eisler started off the ethereal daybreak that begins *Decoration Day*. By the end of the first section the only person left playing was a violinist in the back. The conductor stopped and got everybody started together again, with the same result. The reading proceeded in fits and starts, in each section the orchestra shriveling down to the same lone and intrepid violinist. Ives's heartfelt evocation of a childhood epiphany was being deconstructed before his ears, phrase by excruciating phrase. Watching in horror from the seats, where he was sitting behind principal conductor Artur Bodansky, who did not look pleased, Ives noted that as each player dropped out he would turn around to his fellows with a pained smile, "the same kind of a smile that a fat lady has when she runs for a trolley, half mad, half embarrassed, and half something else." He estimated that not a single measure made it up to half played. By the end "a bass drum and the fiddler were the two survivors." As the boom and squeak straggled into the rafters, the atmosphere in the hall was distinctly not cheerful. On occasions like that the players feel they have been swindled and made to look bad, and the composer enjoys a kind of despair that does unpleasant things to the stomach, the confidence, and the *joie de vivre*. A stony Eisler handed the score back to Ives saying, "There is a limit to musicianship."[31] Then Ives went home to his desk covered with proofs of the *Concord Sonata*.

Yet despite the indignities, debacles, calamities, and fiascos that would afflict his music to the end of his life, that year the story of Charles Ives turned a corner. He would never be entirely alone again. In 1920 copies of *Essays Before a Sonata* went out and responses began coming in. Among the first surviving ones, dated May 1920, is from the venerable Henry F. Gilbert, composer of *Dance in Place Congo, Negro Rhapsody, Indian Sketches,* and other works that attempted to follow, too literally for their own good, Dvořák's call for a national music based on native material. Gilbert expressed temperate enthusiasm for the *Essays*. Ives wrote back a thoughtful, respectful, revealing letter.

I had little or no idea of jumping into print much less a book when I started these prefaces—but Mrs. Ives was getting somewhat tired of having all her closet room piled up with unseen M.S.S. which I was always talking about showing to someone but never getting to it. . . . Your friend, the critic [who said if Ives was a good writer he could not be a good composer], is wrong again. I am not a bad composer—I'm a very good one though its inconvenient to have no one know that but myself!—and sometimes . . . our 6 yr. old daughter says she likes "to have the piano keys washed because it sounds like Daddy's music." . . .The first movement [of the *Concord*] is impossible from many standpoints. It's a long mass of experiments, which no one will ever play—a self-respecting pianola would hesitate at the 3rd chord. "The Alcotts" is short and playable—but I found myself getting pretty tired of it before the last note was dry. The Thoreau movement perhaps measures up the nearest to what I wanted—but it is below something it should be![32]

Here one meets, perhaps for the first time in his correspondence, the singular mixture of advance and retreat, elation and depression, charm and eccentricity, bravado and self-deprecation with which Ives would address the world as an artist. Soon he got a bubbly response from his old professor Billy Phelps: "I'm so proud of you! And this in the work of 'Ives '98' my pupil and friend!"[33] Phelps wrote a rhapsodic review of the *Essays* for the *Yale Alumni Weekly:* "A brilliant and provocative book, full of challenging ideas, and marked by chronic cerebration. I enjoyed every page of it, and I heartily recommend it to those who have minds, and wish to use them."[34] It was the first rave Ives ever got in print. (Of course, everybody knew Billy Phelps raved over everything Yale men did.)

In August 1921 Ives received a much-anticipated response to the *Essays* from John Griggs. After being denied tenure at Vassar, Griggs had gone to China to teach English at Canton Christian College. Over the decades since their time in New Haven, Ives's choirmaster and mentor had maintained his paternal role, exchanging work and ideas with Charlie, singing his songs, listening to his music and ideas and giving an honest response. It is unlikely this thoughtful musician enjoyed Ives's later music, but he kept his ears open. His response to the *Essays* is like most of his encounters with Ives, friendly if a little distant. After some personal catching-up Griggs gets to the point. "Your 'Emerson' and 'Thoreau' seem to me really fine.—the former one of the most satisfying treatments of the subject I have ever seen." But in the end he cannot accept one of the central tenets of Ives's art. Strangely for an admirer of Wagner and Debussy, Griggs rejects the idea of program music. "You seem faced in the direction of an ultimate 'translatableness,'—a direction in which I can see no light. . . . Music is preeminent (because of its aloofness from spoken word, material form or temporal thought). . . . Why insist on always turning it back to a review of . . . past experience?"[35] He winds up his long and scrupulous demurral gently: "Thus Spake Zarathustra without knowing much of what he was talking about."

Ives surely sent a reply, but it did not survive in Grigg's papers. (This was the man who lost the final draft of the First Piano Sonata.) After Griggs retired to California, Ives would write him the warm letter of appreciation talking about the "awful vacuum" of college, and Parker's coldness, and how Griggs "didn't try to superimpose any law on me . . . or boss me, or say very much— but there you were."[36] Ives owed this friend a great deal, too much to resent Griggs's failure to approve of something he believed, even something at the heart of his music.

The *Concord Sonata* was shipped in January 1921 to a collection of hundreds of critics, libraries, music lovers, and musicians. Apparently Ives picked most of the names from *Who's Who* and the subscription list of the *Musical Courier*. He deliberately omitted copyrighting the score.[37] For years he would shock publishers by insisting that his music was not a commercial proposition and anyone could do with it as they liked. In return, as with the *Concord* and the songs, he always paid the expenses of publication.

Throwing this particular music to the wind was a very different matter from the *Essays*, which at least were in the English language. The *Concord* spoke a tonal language hardly anyone but the Ives family and a few protesting victims had ever heard. From that point the responses Ives received changed dramatically, in two directions—most puzzled or angry, a few enthusiastic.

Henry F. Gilbert acknowledged receipt of the sonata but made no comment. An elegantly vicious letter arrived from Charles Wakefield Cadman, composer of "Tell Her My Lodge is Warm" and other Indianisms: "As for the 'music', I confess . . . that it is incomprehensible to me. I do not ridicule you, I do not criticize you . . . because it would do no good anyway." Ives wanly thanked Cadman for his "interesting" letter.[38] A Walter Goldstein wrote to say, "To me the Sonata seems to be expressed in the Schoenberg-Scriabin-

Ornstein idiom, the musicality of which is not yet comprehensible to me." Those were fighting words. Ives sketched a reply he had no intention of mailing: "Dear Goldy: Ain't never heard nor seen any of the music—not even a god damn note—of Schoenberg-Scriabin—Or Ornstein—Just because I swear & use cuss-words, aint no sign my name is Murphy."[39]

Naturally among the recipients was family friend Elizabeth Sprague Coolidge. By then she had founded the Berkshire Festival of Chamber Music and settled into her career as a patroness of players and composers.[40] Coolidge wrote to Harmony in March 1921 that she had sent Charlie's music to a composer friend in Boston who was interested in new ideas. "I must confess that I found nothing in it which I like. . . . I have today a response from this gentleman and it is not encouraging to Charlie's work. I do not want to quote him because I think it would hurt you."[41] Coolidge may have been a new-music benefactor, but to Ives she was of the breed of arty, narrow-minded ladybirds who had been giving him grief since childhood. His unsent reply to her included: "If it isn't asking too much I would like to have all your Boston friend has to say about my music (I still call it that). He can't hurt my feelings— I've been called all the names in the criminal code."[42]

But that year three enthusiasts stepped forward, all of them strangers to Ives. In a letter dated March 15, the same day as Mrs. Coolidge's letter, organist and composer T. Carl Whitmer wrote to say, "You could not have found a more ready listener than my-self to whom to send your very fine, original and altogether interesting Piano Sonata. . . . May I send you in return my latest book THE WAY OF MY HEART AND MIND?"[43] Ives replied in kind, "Your book holds a place of affection in our home. . . . You carry one high— and keep him there." A long friendship began.

At that time Whitmer was a church organist in Pittsburgh, writer on music, and composer of modest reputation but enormous ambition. He had created a series of six "Spiritual Music Dramas" or *Mysteries*. When the *Concord* arrived on his doorstep he was preparing to buy a Hudson River farm he would christen "Dramamount," where he intended to produce the *Mysteries* in an outdoor amphitheater through the course of a week. The subject of the piece was biblical, the idea post-Wagnerian in the apocalyptic and *Gesamtkunstwerk*ish line of *The Ring of the Nibelung,* but going Wagner two days better. Whitmer's *Mysteries* also appear indebted to the work of someone the object, in those days, of a flourishing cult among Ultra-Modernists: the Russian composer/theosophist Alexander Scriabin, composer of *Poem of Ecstasy* and *Poem of Fire*. Scriabin died in 1915 in the midst of writing a *Mysterium* intended to be performed in the Himalayas for a convocation of pilgrims, and thereby to bring on the apocalypse. Whitmer seems to have envisioned his *Mysteries* as some intersection of Scriabin's *Mysterium*, Wagner's *Ring*, Greek drama, and the Oberammergau Passion Play.

Part of Whitmer's idea of Dramamount was to make it available to other composers for out-of-doors productions.[44] Ives visited the farm in 1923, having a similar project in mind—or a project that became similar through the contact. Ives wrote Whitmer after that visit, "The outdoor side of music, and the outdoor side of people, is something that can be brought together and helped . . . in what you are doing in Dramamount." The *Mysteries* would be produced in some form, but went nowhere; eventually Whitmer started a music festival at his farm.[45] Ives's plans for that setting would likewise never be realized: the *Universe Symphony*.

A month after Whitmer's introductory letter came one from Henry Bellamann in Columbia, South Carolina: "Recently I received a copy of your second piano sonata. . . . I have just recently had time to go over it . . . and I want to tell you how remarkable a piece of work it is." He and pianist Lenore Purcell had been giving lectures on modern composers and he planned to add a lecture-recital on the *Concord*. The letter concludes, "One feels very happy to know that a creation of such calibre on an American subject may be done in America—tho I must say truthfully that I am not much interested in the geography of any work of art."[46] Bellamann would be a pioneer advocate for Ives and, for a decade or so, a good friend. Trained in piano, organ, and composition, he was then dean of the School of Fine Arts at Chicora College for Women. He moved to New York in 1924 to work at Juilliard, then became dean of the Curtis Institute of Music in Philadelphia. Beyond a musician and occasional composer, Bellamann was a writer, baroquely Freudian as it turned out, as in his best-selling 1940 novel *King's Row*.

Ives wrote back to Bellamann after several weeks, pleading illness for the delay. Ailing or no, he was busy correcting proofs for his upcoming songbook and composing and arranging new items for it—he was continuing, that is, to push his luck. In the letter Ives commends Bellamann's courage in taking up the piece, apologizes in usual form ("there are some passages that were not exactly intended to be played literally—at least by two hands"), and makes suggestions for the presentation (go easy on *Emerson* and *Hawthorne*). He invites Bellamann and Miss Purcell to bring their lecture to New York, at his expense. Bellamann had inquired about the First Piano Sonata, but Ives, in a letter enclosing *Concord* revisions and biographical material, brushed that aside: the First "was written about 6 or 7 years ago. In some ways, it seemed satisfactory enough to keep—in other ways doubtful; so I thought it best to put it away." He did not send it, had no presentable score and no longer cared to make one. Bellamann's lecture-recitals on the *Concord* never got to New York, but were mounted the following winter in Columbia and other southern cities. In bits and pieces, if in fact she played the whole thing, the obscure Miss Purcell gave the unofficial world premiere of the *Concord*. For its official premiere the sonata had to wait another eighteen years.

In October 1921 Henry Bellamann wrote the first journalistic piece on Ives's music, for the New Orleans arts magazine *Double Dealer*. He begins by dismissing the issue of nationalism—"Music is always just music, neither

American music, nor French music, nor Spanish music . . . the universal voice of thought and feeling . . . Its national character is but a superficial difference in idiom." He generally agrees, in other words, with what Ives wrote in the *Essays*. Bellamann was not picking up ideas from his subject, though; he thought for himself, and he was mainly concerned to place the sonata in the context of international Modernism. He generally describes the music, comparing *Emerson* in passing to the Italians Casella and Malpiero, even to Richard Strauss. He mentions the "Ornstein-like fury" of *Hawthorne,* but adds that it is "used to finer purpose." (American pianist and composer Leo Ornstein was then a leading Ultra-Modernist wild man. He eventually dropped out of sight.) Bellamann is careful not to make excessive claims for music he has heard incompletely. He ends with questions. Is this great music? Well, "Mr. Ives' sonata is a piece of work sincerely done, and if a failure, a rather splendid one. . . . Its loftiness of purpose is evident; its moments of achievement elevating and greatly beautiful."

Ives thanked Bellamann, holding back his emotions as best he could.

It is hard for me to tell you how I felt upon reading the article, or to thank you as I want for the interest and care you have given. I'm by no means certain that all of what you say—the favorable part of the impression is justified; but I am certain of this,— that you have strengthened and deepened in me the sense of responsibility towards future work.[47]

Ives generally did more than thank people. He invited Bellamann and his wife to visit and sent some of his poems to Billy Phelps and to a publisher. Bellamann soon moved to New York, where he spent a good deal of time with Ives. Their first meeting was at the insurance office on 38 Nassau Street. After some difficulty persuading a secretary that he actually had an appointment with the boss—not a normal thing apparently—Bellamann was shown into the large and legendary sanctum of the phantom of Ives & Myrick. He decided he had to have come to the wrong place. Composers did not sit behind desks like that, in offices like that. Then they started talking music; some time passed before Bellamann emerged, in a daze. That afternoon he mentioned to a Wall Street banker that they had spent three hours together. The banker declared him a liar: "Nobody gets three hours of Charles Ives's time."[48]

In August 1921 came the first letter from another convert, and Scriabin-ist, Clifton Joseph Furness. After studies at Northwestern and Harvard, Furness was to shape up a polymath and lifelong bachelor. Then twenty-three, teaching and finishing an A.B. at Northwestern, he would spend his career lecturing and writing in various musical fields (he played piano and composed a little), also in German and fine arts. He was moreover a Whitman scholar with biographical ambitions. Besides that, he studied in Germany with Dr. Rudolph Steiner, founder of an occult program called "anthroposophy." Furness's article "Mysticism in Modern Music" appeared in the anthroposophical journal *Threefold Commonwealth* in 1926.[49] In it he declares Ives a "musical Emerson," but most of the article is given to esoteric patois: "This music of the soul, inwardly apprehended, brings into conscious action the Will nature, the highest of the three-fold activity of the human spirit," and so on.

In his first letter to Ives Furness says that he has already presented a lecture-recital on the *Concord:* "I took great pleasure in presenting it, both to classes in modern harmony, and in esthetics and criticism. . . . For my part, I must confess that I was completely non-plussed by it for some time—altho I am an ardent devotee of Schoenberg, and keenly alive to all new phases of the great fundamental problem of art-expression." Ives drafted a painstaking reply. As with Bellamann, he commends Furness for his courage—"a man takes unpleasant chances, when he puts my music in front of an audience." Explaining and apologizing, Ives continues that the *Concord* "is more or less of an experiment and one which goes too far in some ways—the first two movements particularly so. It is but an attempt at piano-transcendentalism."[50] Ives sent Furness a copy of *Essays Before a Sonata.* After perusing the music and words, Furness was hooked. In turn, he sent Ives some autobiographical and other writings. Ives's response was surprisingly forthright given their fresh acquaintance, but that was how these two men would treat each other. Ives grudgingly commends Furness's "strong kind of frankness" in writing about himself, but implies a dose of reticence might have improved it. He continues,

The "Brahms" [prose piece] is fine—it has a buoyant stride and reminds me of the way he first "got me." I enjoy him now more than ever, he stirs me but in a different way perhaps—more as a personal friend; I sit back and let him carry me high but with less exertion on my part. I'm not inclined to parallel Whitman and Brahms altogether in the way you do. Both, as you say, are swept by the great universal impulse, but Brahms doesn't let his personality get in the way of his expression. Whitman, it seems to me, tells us with wonderful power of the great life values of everything in life and out of it, of the way he enjoys roast beef, but he likes to squeeze all the blood out of it himself; he doesn't let us have enough of a hand in it. Whenever he wants us to know how human he is . . . he becomes somewhat of a "loud talker,"—I'd take his word for it with less effort on his part. . . . I have read Whitman very little lately, and I'm probably prejudiced; Mrs Ives says she doesn't like the over-human leer in his face.[51]

Thereby Harmony Ives helped estrange her husband from a writer who might have been a soulmate. Ives had set to music only one fragment of Whitman, when he could have set so many of those poems maybe better than anyone else. Furness didn't hold Ives's puritanism against him. Soon Ives would help Furness find a job in New York and begin accompanying him to Scriabin concerts and soirées. For all their differences, Furness would become one of the closest artistic friends Ives ever had.

Whitmer, Bellamann, and Furness would be the heralds of Ives's triumph in the world, even though that triumph came when all three, along with Ives, had passed on. It is indicative that his first champions turned out to be trained musicians but not entirely specialists, either as composers or as performers. They were men of broad interests who wrote words as well as music—especially Bellamann and Furness, with whom Ives would be closest. Those two would spend much time with him during their New York years, and Ives and Whitmer exchanged visits. More so than performing musicians, these men could trace Ives's ideas in the *Essays* and follow the larger implications of his music. They responded, that is, to his words and his spirit as well as his notes. That remains, to this day, useful if not essential in dealing with Ives.

It is also significant that two of them, Whitmer and especially Furness, were Scriabinists. Many early Ivesians would be the same, and many of those followed theosophy or anthroposophy or one of the other esoteric systems fashionable among artists on both sides of the Atlantic. (Yeats, for one, was involved with the theosophists.) With the connection of Charles Ives to Whitmer and Furness began one of the most surprising and least examined sideshows in the Ivesian chronicle: the suggestive affinity of Ives, his admirers, Alexander Scriabin, and the *Universe Symphony*.

The reasons for the Ives / Scriabin connection must be speculative, but besides the inclination of Modernist musicians toward chromatic mysticism, it may have resulted from something else almost absurdly simple that worked as follows. One day out of the blue you receive in the mail an extraordinary musical score, handsomely printed, by an unknown composer. You open it to *Emerson*. After a quick and incredulous perusal you either slam the book shut or page though, passing the impossible *Hawthorne,* until you find *The Alcotts*. If you are a pianist you play through that movement, perhaps finding it fresh and attractive but nothing earthshaking. Then you try *Thoreau*—harder, but still relatively slow and playable. This music is not simply pleasant: it is magical, extraordinary, esoteric in some way. How do you classify it? A musician rarely hears music as something unique. Rightly or wrongly, one generally tries to grasp it by comparison to something else (a process that drove Ives to distraction).

To an Ives neophyte in 1921, what does *Thoreau* most sound like? It sounds, not all that much like, but *most* like, the piano sonatas of Alexander Scriabin, especially the visionary last four. In slight but detectable ways *Thoreau* resembles Scriabin in harmony, texture, piano writing, and expressive tone. Like Ives, Scriabin liked soft endings; the conclusion of his Tenth Sonata is similar to the distant bells and whispers that end the *Concord*. Scriabin even had a penchant for a three-note motive that sounds rather like Ives's handling of Beethoven's Fifth. If you meanwhile read the *Essays,* you find in them a composer of manifest spiritual alignment and something like cosmic consciousness. If you are already a Scriabin devotee, you are likely to stick Ives in the same category. Thus, perhaps, a Scriabin / occult faction formed among the early associates of Charles Ives. They would include Katherine Heyman,

John Kirkpatrick, Elliott Carter, Henry Cowell, and Dane Rudhyar, who had yet to know about Ives in 1921 but would before the decade was out.

Those and earlier friends Furness, Bellamann, and Whitmer characterized Ivesians for a long time. He was lucky to find them because they admired his music, believed in artistic innovation, and had forums for saying so publicly. They were no sycophants but well-educated, strong-minded people with ideas and careers of their own. Ives's first supporters tended to resemble, in fact, John Griggs—musicians open-eared, independent, with wide interests and a literary or at least sermonizing streak. Ives could not have borne disciples and hangers-on. Influences would flow in both directions. Up to a point, he liked having musical friends different from him, not afraid to disagree and criticize his work. Believing in consensus as he did, he yearned for collaborators (at least in theory, if not necessarily in practice). In the long run, though, his illness, biases, and anxieties would work to keep Ives at a remove from even his most dedicated partisans.

A small circle would gather around Ives's music in the 1920s and into the next decade. Mostly they were a varied lot of Scriabinists, mystics, Marxists, and related genera. A number were homosexual or bisexual, many of them Bohemians. Besides their talent, energy, and far-sightedness, a significant thing about most of these Ivesians was that *aside from his own music, Ives had little in common with them.* What of their beliefs and lifestyles he did not deplore (including sexual looseness of any kind) or find absurd (fashionable occultism), he was more or less indifferent to (such as most living European composers).

Among the other things, Ives's friends often declared themselves "Ultra-Modernists," the preferred term of the time, and saw themselves in the image of the European artistic revolutionaries of the day. For his part, Ives was nearly finished as a composer before he heard any Stravinsky, and heard Schoenberg only later if at all. Though he would pick up ideas from his Modernist friends, that was not really his style either. Yet musically speaking, people involved in such things were the only friends he had. Ives was glad to have them and needed them at least as much as they needed him, because in the long run he would prove too ill to take on everything that had to be done to promote his work.

In the story of the dissemination of his music, the gulf between Ives and the Ivesians would impede and obscure matters in all sorts of ways, despite the goodwill, sympathy, and best efforts of all concerned. Ives was lucky in his friends, and in some critical ways unlucky too. Nothing could entirely bridge the divide between them. Yet the world would come to know Ives largely filtered through those friends, with whom he had so little in common. That too would play a part in the career of his music.

The Work of Our Hands

IN FEBRUARY 1922 music publisher G. Schirmer sent Ives revised proofs of numbers 2–97 of his vanity publication *114 Songs,* and in May galley proofs of the prose Postface. It was around then that Ives decided to begin the book not with the mild "Evening" but with the crashing tone clusters of "Majority," or "The Masses." Ten years later Ives would write in his *Memos* that he felt "mean enough to want to give all the 'old girls' another ride . . . it would keep them from turning any more pages."[1] The song was in that sense a testament of musical principles. In 1922, probably as important to him as shocking the fainthearted was the political manifesto of his text. So both dimensions of the song on page one tend to represent Ives as a radical and a crank. His obsessions were beginning to work against him, as they would periodically from then on.

In June he ordered a printing of 1,500 copies, 1,000 in cloth and 500 in paper,[2] of his songbook. They include most of the songs he had written by that time, good, bad, indifferent, and magnificent.[3] That summer Ives mailed the book to a similar and overlapping list of musicians, critics, and libraries as had received the *Concord* and the *Essays.* In the fall and following spring the bills arrived from Schirmer. Engraving, printing, binding, and mailing the *114* came to around $3,200 (over $36,000 in 1991), and that was probably not the whole story. To that can be added the bills for the *Concord Sonata* and *Essays Before a Sonata,* which surely totaled at least another $2,000. So between 1919 and 1923 Charles Ives, whose later legend said he hardly cared if his music was heard, spent some 60,000 late-century dollars printing and distributing his music and words.[4]

He had begun writing songs in his early teens. In recognition of that he included in his songbook the "Slow March," quoting Handel's "Dead March" that he wrote for a departed pet around 1887. Since then he had written more songs in some periods than others, but they amounted to a regular outlet, recreation, steam-blowing device, and diary (probably the same as for most song composers).[5] Ives had a good supply of a songwriter's gifts. He could write a handsome and even sensuous melody when he needed one, and he knew—superbly, much of the time—how to make an accompaniment support the voice and conjure the mood of the text.

The *114 Songs* reveals what tends to slip the world's notice, that Ives wrote as much conventional music as radical, and every degree in between. Hitchcock notes that Ives's single most common type is the "household song,"[6] which is to say the sort of sentimental Victorian expression suitable for amateurs to sing in the family parlor. The rest can roughly be divided into popular songs of one genre or another, art song as the Europeans understood it (sometimes in German or French), and experiments.[7] These categories hardly convey the mélange of styles, tones, expressions, harmonies, textures, rhythms, melodies, and subjects found in the *114*. There are childhood songs, love songs, war songs, songs of birth and death, of times of day and seasons of the year, songs nostalgic, religious, and sentimental, songs reminiscent of German Romantic reverie and French boulevards, songs of personal joy and fury, miniature tone poems, sociopolitical tracts, larks and satires, mystical visions, and dance-hall ditties. No two are alike enough to be confused. Like its author, *114 Songs* contains antithetical worlds while always being itself. Even though there is little of the tragic and none of the erotic, the range of styles and feelings and approaches may never have been equaled in anyone else's portfolio of songs. (Which is not to say that the quality has never been equaled, or excelled.)

We are constantly reminded in *114 Songs* that Ives is the first composer in the long history of music to have in his ears, under his fingers, at his command, virtually every conceivable harmony from the naively conventional idiom of "Slow March" to the tone clusters of "Majority," and something approaching 112 steps in between. Ives knew how to modulate not only from key to key in the old sense of "modulation," but could modulate from harmonic style to style with singular virtuosity. (He could also fumble the attempt—as in, say, "On the Antipodes.") Ives's stylistic virtuosity has something to do with genius, certainly; another reason may have been that he always knew where he was stylistically. The old diatonic song genres were not learned, fossilized idioms to him but living species that he heard and composed from his earliest years. On a foundation of traditions cultivated and vernacular Ives erected his own explorations, and could move from settled territory to fresh in a second and without ever losing his way (well, hardly ever).

In other words, Ives's ingrained sense of genre is the foundation of his songwriting.[8] His cornball college tune "In the Alley," words and music written at Yale, whose subject naturally is Sally, makes us laugh because it is dead-on—not a satire (Ives wrote few deliberate satires) but the real thing, funny only in retrospect. (Ives knew that; in the book he added a note: "This song . . . is inserted for association's sake—on the ground that that will excuse anything; also, to help clear up a long disputed point, namely: —which is worse? the music or the words?") The German lied "Feldeinsamkeit" evokes the Schubert-Schumann-Brahms heritage while hanging on to a touch of independence. Hardly less effective is the French song from the Yale years, "Chanson de Florian," which might pass for early Debussy not only in style but in its silken sophistication. Yet Ives generally went beyond imitation and added something of himself. The delicious march "Circus Band" has rhythmic shifts that would never have occurred to Sousa; the otherwise *echt*-1890s "Side-Show" changes meters constantly; and time and again Ives sets a familiar hymn in a way that subtly reveals and renews its essential meaning. Whether or not the melody is overtly a hymn, many of the songs sustain a tone of quiet, timeless meditation, none more beautifully than "Serenity."

As there are modulations of harmonic style, and always the possibility of meta-stylistic excursions, there are also meta-genres that evoke one thing while being something more. "The Things Our Fathers Loved" has the words and tone of a sentimental household song ("I think there must be a place in the soul all made of tunes of long ago"), but the harmony drifts effortlessly from orthodox to chromatic and complex. In his meta-genres Ives conjures the atmosphere and some of the elements of a musical archetype but expresses them with new means. And often, even in some of the most conservative ones, we arrive at the exquisitely ambiguous Ivesian conclusion that seems to end on a question, an anticipation, a summons: "Shall we gather at the river. . . ?"

Of the songs omitted from the book, some had to be left out because of copyright problems, notably *General Booth;* some Ives simply lost track of; and he still had a few more to write when the *114* were published. It is not that he put in only the best ones; there are several self-deprecating footnotes, and at the end he cites a number of songs that have "little or no musical value. . . . It is asked . . . that they be not sung, at least in public, or given to students except as examples of what not to sing." Including these items—the music and the footnotes—was one of Ives's continuing disservices to his reputation. But in perspective his body of songs, 151 when he was done, adds up to one of the great collections in the history of art song, and incomparably the finest from an American.[9]

In person, Ives could never have taken a compliment like that without immediately running the stuff down. His extraordinary note that some of them are too wretched to sing is followed in the book by the equally peculiar Postface, the one beginning "Greek philosophers, ward-politicians, unmasked laymen, and others, have a saying that bad habits and bad gardens grow to the 'unintendedables.' " The Postface appears to be a *mea culpa* for printing the thing in the first place. In fact, Ives ends up declaring that he has not even produced a book:

Some have written a book for money; I have not. Some for fame; I have not. Some for love; I have not. Some for kindlings: I have not. . . . In fact, gentle borrower, I have not written a book at all . . . I have merely cleaned house. All that is left is out on the clothes line; but it's good for a man's vanity to have the neighbors see *him*—on the clothes line.[10]

Laying aside that there are two or three fibs in those lines, why would any composer apologize for putting his songs before the public? Given the nature of the book and the nature of the composer, the answers are not hard to find. There is a modicum of truth in his claim that the songs were scattered all over the house and getting in his wife's way and not doing anybody any good. More to the point, Ives had some idea of the anger and ridicule that were going to come his way (with luck, a little interest too). In that regard he was already running for cover in the Postface. The main reason for the tone of the Postface to *114 Songs*, however, must be understood in comparison to the more confident and thoughtful *Essays Before a Sonata*.

In part the difference shows that Ives took the *Concord* more seriously than the songs. But the difference has most to do with his anxieties about standing before the public as an artist. The *Essays* dissemble about their main subject: Charles Ives and his music. He was comfortable talking about his work only through the screen of a book purporting to be about great American writers rather than about himself. (In the same spirit, in later years Ives would sometimes send his good reviews around with the note that they were a testimonial to the critic's writing and wisdom.) With *114 Songs* he could not evade that he was presenting himself as a composer. So his innate bashfulness, his Yankee-businessman heritage, plus all the wounds from over the years drove him to squirm and apologize and obfuscate his way through the Postface. He ends, at least, with a touch of bravado:

Some of the songs in this book . . . cannot be sung, and if they could, perhaps might prefer, if they had a say, to remain as they are; that is, "in the leaf". . . . A song has a *few* rights, the same as other ordinary citizens. If it feels like walking along the left-hand side of the street, passing the door of physiology or sitting on the curb, why not let it? . . . Should it not be free at times from the dominion of the thorax, the diaphragm, the ear, and other points of interest? If it wants to beat around in the valley, to throw stones up the pyramids, or to sleep in the park, should it not have some immunity from a Nemesis, a Rameses, or a policeman? Should it not have a chance to sing to itself, if it can sing. . . ? If it happens to feel like trying to fly where humans cannot fly, to sing what cannot be sung, to walk in a cave on all fours, or to tighten up its girth in blind hope and faith and try to scale mountains that are not, who shall stop it?

-In short, must a song
always be a song![11]

Ives has some points there, however belabored. But most of all he is trying to get the jump on his critics, to assert that some of the wilder songs don't ask to be sung at all. As far as audience and critics went, of course, his attempt to get the jump would fail. His own words, of course, would be used against him.

Ives launched his essays, sonata, and songs into an American musical scene evolving in unprecedented directions. On the whole, and with some unwelcome side effects, he would benefit from those directions for a decade or so. If his music had been offered to the public ten years earlier there would have been few if any prepared to deal with it. In the 1920s some ears proved ready to hear him—relatively few, but enough.

Alongside the postwar conservative retrenchment in U.S. politics came a surprising flowering of the arts, most of it taking cues from European Modernism. After Joyce and Proust remade the novel in Europe, the ground was broken for Faulkner and Hemingway to do likewise. Picasso and Matisse had made their American debut in New York's Armory Show of 1913, to considerable effect on American painting in the next decade. In 1923 Wallace Stevens published *Harmonium,* his revolutionary first book of poems. During the Roaring Twenties American jazz conquered the world, as much as anything by means of the new media of records and radio. In that decade the movies, having charmed the millions with images accompanied by a tinkling piano, started talking and singing.

During the teens and twenties the first generation of musical Modernists set off shock waves across Europe. Schoenberg and Stravinsky sealed their reputations with a string of scandals and triumphs in Paris, Berlin, and Vienna—usually a scandal and a triumph at the same time. An annual festival of contemporary music got under way in Donaueschingen, Germany, in 1921; the International Society for Contemporary Music held its first festival two years later. From that point avant-garde music, more so than with painting or literature, would tend increasingly to be consigned to special forums and organizations, with specialized audiences. Nothing like that had ever happened. Until at least the mid-nineteenth century, most mainstream music played everywhere in the West had been contemporary music.

By 1920, when Charles Ives was preparing his publications, Modernism musical and otherwise was gearing up in the United States, especially in New York. Ultra-Modernists, leftists, theosophists et al. would create a wide-open atmosphere through the decade, despite sniping from critics and the continuing orthodoxy of most musical organizations. For some years, Leopold Stokowski in Philadelphia was the only conductor of a major orchestra who had the courage and clout regularly to play composers like Varèse and Schoenberg. (Stokowski would eventually be fired, at the peak of his popularity, for playing the Schoenberg Violin Concerto.[12]) Serge Koussevitzky championed American composers after he took over the Boston Symphony in 1924, but he generally favored milder moderns such as Aaron Copland, Walter Piston, and Roy Harris. One European composer after another sailed to America to test the waters. Most soon went home, a few stayed, but many made an impression. Prokofiev, for one, had several important American performances around 1920, but brutal critical outcry sent him fleeing for Paris. Ives would have little directly to do with any of this, but he followed the scene in papers and journals and made his own contribution, always from behind the scenes.

In the United States one can map the changes in *The Musical Courier*. By the mid-teens the name Schoenberg was beginning to show up in the journal, mostly as a bogeyman or a joke. By 1921 the paper was declaring Stokowski's performance of Schoenberg's early, post-Wagnerian *Pelleas und Melisande* "tremendously effective."[13] Most listeners knew by then that there were things out there called "atonality," "Ultra-Modernism," "barbarism," and such, and that these were new and European and probably a threat to art if not to morals; but relatively few listeners had heard examples of them. That would change. During the mid-twenties the *Courier* reported regularly, often enthusiastically, on the activities of progressive European composers and organizations. In 1927 the paper had a feature on the Baden-Baden Festival saying "Paul Hindemith is the life of the party" with the absurdist opera *Hin und Zurück,* Kurt Weill had "an overwhelming success" with *Little Mahagonny,* and Berg's *Lyric Suite* was a remarkable if difficult work. Elsewhere in the same issue there is a story on the International Festival of Contemporary Music in Frankfurt, playing Bartók, Copland, and Henry F. Gilbert *(Dance in Place Congo)*. The London premiere of *L'histoire du soldat* received "the regulation Stravinsky applause."[14]

It was an astonishing development for a periodical that a few years before had been patting itself on the back for supporting Richard Strauss, and spending most of its pages celebrating sopranos, tenors, and virtuosos. The change in the *Musical Courier* reflected a shift in the artistic climate. The teens and twenties saw what may have been history's most concentrated outpouring of innovation by genuinely first-rate artists. For all the clinging orthodoxy of the mainstream, that fact sunk in enough to set off a revolution in Western arts and to a degree in the whole culture. The avant-garde explosion began before the war, but afterward many more people were ready to embrace or at least tolerate Modernism—as much as anything out of disgust with a past that the war had discredited.

In autumn 1916 California composer and pianist Henry Cowell, then nineteen and already writer of dozens of determinedly revolutionary pieces, came to New York and met fellow young firebrand Carl Ruggles.[15] These two, along with Cowell's occultist friend Dane Rudhyar, became prime founders of the musical avant-garde movement in the United States—"Ultra-Modernism" as it called itself, proudly. Cowell made a sensational European tour in 1923; his tone clusters and strumming and drumming inside the piano fascinated Bartók, Schoenberg, Berg, and Webern.[16]

It is notable, though, that in the States some of the first steps to put new music on the map were taken by transplanted Europeans. Among the new generation of new-music promoters was composer Edgard Varèse, who emigrated to New York from France in the teens. In 1921 Varèse founded the

International Composers' Guild, one of the first of its kind in the country, and announced a concert slate of works by composers including Bartók, Berg, Casella, Honegger, Milhaud, Poulenc, Prokofiev, Rudhyar, Salzedo, Satie, Schoenberg, Stravinsky, Webern, and Varèse. It was an age of manifestos. In the one Varèse issued with the group's founding, he proclaimed, "Dying is the privilege of the weary. The present-day composer refuses to die." The Guild "disapproves of all 'isms, denies the existence of schools, recognizes only the individual." His group would live up to its manifesto, presenting a broad spectrum of new American and European music in American concert halls. It would also sponsor performances of Varèse's own seminal Modernist works—*Hyperprism, Octandre, Intégrales.* Due mainly to the founder's imperious personality, however, a group called the League of Composers splintered from the Guild in 1924 (presaging the Guild's demise three years later). With Aaron Copland as one of its prime movers and more of a commitment to native composers, the League would come to be associated mainly with the immensely successful "Americana" school that arose in the 1930s. But in the 1920s, critics and audiences tended to group all progressives in the camp of wild men.

Camping alongside them would be Charles Ives. He may have been irrelevant to the Jazz Age and the Lost Generation and on a side path to Modernism, but his message could not have been more relevant to composers trying to create a nationalist tradition of art music. By and large, though, those who needed Ives most would never get the chance to hear him, or hear enough to understand him. Always a special case, always peripheral, Ives would inhabit the Ultra-Modernist camp mainly because there was nowhere else to go.

All the same, that alliance went beyond expediency. Ives was in the same camp as all the American radicals in another sense: *He could not began to be taken seriously by American musicians and the listening public until European Modernism had prepared the way.* The establishment, however tenuous, of Ultra-Modernism in the country followed the same pattern as the establishment of cultivated music in the first place; it was introduced as something imported from abroad and pursued mainly by Europeans. When American ears had been educated by the new harmonies and tonalities of Stravinsky and Schoenberg and their fellows, those ears began to countenance Charles Ives and his fellows. Inevitably, then, everyone tended to think of Ives as one more Modernist. As one of the early *Concord* recipients saw it, he was part of the "Schoenberg-Scriabin-Ornstein idiom."

That kind of thing always enraged Ives. Even though in the 1930s his first European reviews would be remarkably generous, he exploded when French critics said he knew his Schoenberg or Hindemith or Stravinsky Composers never like to have their own ideas attributed to others, but most take it in stride. Ives, increasingly ill and reclusive and with his defenses down, could not endure it. In his anger he would eventually go beyond the claim, which was perfectly true, that his innovations were essentially his father's and his own, and declare that the sole influence on his music came from his father, which was perfectly untrue.[17] Besides, his exposure to Modernism and its milieu helped give Ives the courage, and the sympathetic atmosphere, to go back and restore the original versions of ideas he had once watered down. The trouble is, the same train of thought also encouraged him to go further, to punch up the dissonance and complexity even if at times that muddied the music.

Ives's vicissitudes and disappointments and truth-stretching as a public composer come later in the story, but the foundation of it all was laid in his first steps toward disseminating his work. He had little in common with his friends, and he was lumped by default with Modernists American and European. Meanwhile his Modernist friends' obsession with his innovations—and his nationalism—only obscured the deeper ambitions of his music. This situation made it harder for anyone to discern what he was up to, how special he really was. Charles Ives was not really a Modernist but a seeker on a parallel path, with his own baggage and his own destinations. It would take the better part of the century for his uniqueness to sink in.

He sent out his printings and waited. Responses arrived blandly polite, outraged, excited. From a few letters grew friendships, from others performances, a circle, an audience, the beginning of a reputation. Clifton Furness, Henry Bellamann, and T. Carl Whitmer became regular correspondents. In January 1922, before they had met face-to-face, Furness sent an agitated note asking Ives to help him find teaching work in New York. Ives tried several leads, wrote a letter of recommendation, and finally connected Furness to a teacher's agency that got him a job at the Horace Mann School for Boys.[18]

One of Furness's first students at Horace Mann was a talented youth named Elliott Carter, whose mature music would owe a great deal to Ives, and who would pay back his mentor with a baffling mixture of admiration, advocacy, and cold repudiation. As Carter recalled, it was around 1924 when Furness first took him to meet Ives on a rainy Sunday afternoon. The Iveses were living then at the place on 120 East 22nd Street, just off Gramercy Park, a house owned by author Henry Dwight Sedgwick. Wrote Carter, "We stepped into a cheery, old-fashioned interior, discussing excitedly modern music all afternoon." To the boy it seemed like something out of Henry James. For several years afterward Carter would accompany Furness on visits and join the two men at concerts and recitals in New York.[19]

Carter discovered a character unlike any he would ever know. Ives had an amazing ability to sit down at the piano and mimic things they had just heard in concert—long stretches of Ravel or Stravinsky orchestra pieces played (and expertly faked) from memory after one hearing, with a continuous overlay of jokes and sarcasm at the expense of the composers. After playing a Stravinskyan polychord Ives might growl, "Anybody can do that," and rip off "My Country 'tis of Thee" with each hand in a different key. The main things Ives liked to play, Carter discovered, were Bach, Brahms, and Franck, and he began every day with a fugue from *The Well-Tempered Clavier*. When Ives played his own music, though, "the respectable, quiet, Puritan atmosphere was oddly disturbed, a gleam would come into his eyes as fiery excitement seized him, and he would smash out a fragment of *Emerson,* singing loudly and exclaiming with burning enthusiasm. . . . It was a dynamic, staggering experience which is hard even now to think of clearly. . . . We always came away from Ives full of life's glad new wine and a thousand projects for the future."[20] Carter got into Harvard in 1926, his admission partly due to Ives's recommendation: "Carter strikes me as rather an exceptional boy. . . . I am sure his reliability, industry and sense of honor are what they should be—also his sense of humor which you do not ask me about."[21]

Henry Bellamann and his wife first visited the Iveses at Redding in August 1922. Katherine Bellamann nearly refused to go because she considered her wardrobe insufficient to be entertained by a Wall Street businessman. She finally came along and Ives met them at the door in battered hat and grizzled corduroy jacket. (He often wore coveralls around Redding.) For his part Ives would be delighted to find Katherine Bellamann a first-rate lieder singer who could handle some of the songs he had assumed "passed the door of physiology." Listening to her sing them he would declare over and over, with evident surprise, "Why, they sound just like I thought they would!"[22] The following year Ives set, beautifully, Bellamann's poems "Yellow Leaves" and "Peaks." All the same, this friend's literary productions proved too darkly modern to suit Ives. Even though he was setting Bellamann to music and showing the poems around, he wrote complaints to Furness, who replied placatingly, "I am sure [Bellamann] gives evidence of a very penetrating and aggressive masculine perception, even tho he may run, as you suggest, toward the effeminate in his own work." (In the same letter, brashly but honestly, Furness declares his "sneaking prejudice against hymn-tunes.")

Meanwhile Ives's music was out in the world and a few felt moved to do more than ignore it. Responses trickled in from friends and strangers.

From the well-bred Mrs. Dossert in Carnegie Hall: "It is to be regretted that with your evident knowledge, your sense of humour, a certain vein of sympathy, and a fine appreciation of the best in literature, you do not really express <u>yourself</u>, but have striven to over-emphasize your technical ability. You have been clever, but not sincere. . . . The volume of songs will find a place . . . if only for the amusement it has afforded us."[23]

From Furness when he first received the *114:* "Your song-offerings which recently came to me here were a welcome reminder of my pleasant chat with you last spring." He commends Harmony's verse, her "Victorian touches [with] up-to-the-minute diction." He compares "Mists" to Scriabin, but "I fail to swallow 'Majority'—the words are so direct and powerful that I'm sure there must be some explanation for the apparent 'wordiness" of the music. I anxiously await an alibi for this."[24]

Rudyard Kipling's secretary sent a routine acknowledgement.[25] (There are several settings of Kipling.)

French composer Albert Roussel thanks Ives "pour l'envoi du son curieux et interessant recueil de melodies."[26]

From Whitmer: "In with the 'ultras' [that is, ultra-modern songs] I find completely assimilated grasp of the difficult art of repeating figures without monotony, like the charming Serenity. And you have 'Bela Bartok's' a dozen or so and have outrun him. Perhaps the technical point that interests me most is . . . your variety of rythms [sic]."[27]

From composer Percy Goetschius: "I say, frankly, that I do not like this manner of sound-associations. For I am too fully grounded in the habits . . . of the classic methods . . . confirming the eternal physical laws which govern tone as well as stone. . . . I am absolutely convinced of your sincerity. . . . I hesitate to call it 'Music,' for I believe in accurate definition." (Next to Goetschius's line, "The classic methods are correct ones," Ives scrawled, "for soft eared cissies and aural cowards!"[28])

From British composer and pianist Arnold Capleton, writing from Prague: "The close of 'Thoreau' is for me one of the most wonderful things in music which I know. In it you reach the mystical Borderland of the Occult . . . that supernal close of yours to Thoreau has a strange almost physical effect upon me. . . . It has often run though my head for hours, and yet I feel it to be dangerous for me. . . . The effect upon me can be such an one as that produced by, say, some occultistic science!" Capleton requested a photograph so he could study Ives's forehead.[29]

From John Philip Sousa: "Permit me to thank you for your kindness in sending me your volume. . . . Some of the songs are most startling to a man educated by the harmonic methods of our forefathers."[30]

In a diary entry of April 1923 Ives wrote, "Sent some copies out of <u>114 Songs</u>—gives offense to several musical pussies."[31]

It was not only the private complaints that rankled. Ives stood before the public now and some of the objections were going to be public. The *Musical Courier* handled him roughly. In a series called "The Perfect Modernist" detailing the sins of contemporary composers, chords from the *Concord* were printed with the observation, "The inevitable result of all such insincere experiments is so to confuse the basic harmonies (if there are any) that the listener is unable to understand the music at all."[32] When the songbook came to hand the editors cited Ives's own jokes and repudiations in the Postface and chortled, "Who is Ives? We have not the least idea. We only know that he sends us music from time to time. . . . Ives is the American Satie, joker par excellence."[33]

The New York *Sun* put in a wry little notice headed, "Here's a Chance to

Get a Nice Song Book Free," assuming Ives was prepared to send it to anybody. Hundreds of requests came in. Ives sent a furious letter to the paper
saying they should have asked him, and concluding, disingenuously, "I'm not
looking for publicity."[34] To keep faith, though, he decided to print 500 copies
of a selection, *50 Songs,* which he sent out to the requesters—certainly to the
chagrin of most of them, when they saw what it was they had asked for. An
adolescent joke began going around about this crank composer who issued
books that were good for nothing but raising the height of a piano bench. It
would be in that regard that Henry Cowell first heard the name Charles Ives.[35]

The first response of the kind Ives was above all waiting for came in mid-
August 1922. Within a week or so of receiving the *114 Songs,* baritone George
Madden wrote that he would sing two in a forthcoming recital at New York's
Town Hall. Ives's excitement at the prospect of his first mainstream performance since *The Celestial Country,* twenty years before, was muted by Madden's timid choices—"A Night Thought" and "The Old Mother," both from
the 1890s. Ives replied, "The thing that surprises me is to find that singers are
inclined to select the songs, which in my opinion, have the least musical
value—however a composer may not be the best judge of his work from all
aspects."[36] He would hardly decline the performance, though. On November
28, 1922, Ives shared Madden's program with music by Edward MacDowell,
Stephen Foster, Chopin, and Mendelssohn. Critics did not mention his songs
in their reviews and in general did not much care for the recital.[37] Thus passed
absolutely unnoticed another piece of history.

By the evening of Madden's recital Ives had already received another
inquiry, from which he could hope for better. Violinist Jerome Goldstein, a
champion of Ultra-Modernist composers, wrote Ives asking for the *Concord*
and "any personal aesthetic-philosophic writings developing your views."
From the *Essays* Goldstein would get an earful of the latter, and liked what he
heard. Ives wrote Goldstein,

How prejudiced many musicians seem to be against accepting anything that has not
been officially recognized . . . by a kind of professional-rubberstamping. . . . They seem
held up by a kind of fear that their ears may be hurt, a kind of emasculation, a dread
that the ladies may scowl, that some marketable value may be lost. There is a remark in
a symphony prospectus this year—"No music will be played that hasn't passed the
experimental stage." Wherever music passes that stage, it has started on its way down.
It has become but a sterile, withered old woman,—It is dying; every great inspiration
is but an experiment—though every experiment we know, is not a great inspiration.[38]

Ives was moving toward a frame of mind in which he would disown much
of his more conventional music and rework pieces not always to their benefit.
He was beginning to associate the value of music with its novelty, even with
its sheer dissonance. It was an attitude that would take him closer to his
friends and to Modernism. But if a twentieth-century platitude summarizes

the revolutionary aesthetic—"Make it good or make it bad, but make it *new*"—then that essential aspect of Modernism was contrary to the ideals of Charles Ives. Innovation and experiment had been a central part of his creative process, as progress was central to his thinking about art, life, and business. But in his finest works writing meaningful, powerful, *good* music had always been the priority.

In October, violinist Goldstein replied enthusiastically if fuzzily to Ives's material: "When real individual consciousness is aroused the natural faith in the truth and beauty of the individual subjectivity and a glowing faith in its reality and its connections with the grosser world of materiality will be born. . . . Your essays are truly inspired!"[39] Soon after, Ives received an inquiry from Swiss-born pianist Oscar Ziegler, who had something of a reputation as a recitalist. Ives sent Goldstein copies of the violin sonatas and the *Concord* to Ziegler. Meanwhile he discovered someone had forwarded *Three Places in New England* to the New York Philharmonic, and wrote a letter to the manager prodding him to show the score to conductor Willem Mengelberg.[40] That got nowhere.

What with the demands of illness, promoting himself, and exchanging ideas and visiting new friends, Ives's life had changed remarkably in three years. He had spent a lot of money publishing his three books. The time they and their results consumed was time out of composing and business, energy out of a depleted reservoir. But those three books made all the difference.

During 1923 the Danbury National Bank acquired the plot on Main Street where the Ives House had sat for nearly 150 years. When Aunt Amelia died in 1918 she bequeathed the family seat not to Mollie Ives but to Charlie and Moss. Mollie's spinster sister Lucy Parmelee, called Aunt Nell, had been living there with Amelia. Soon after Amelia died Mollie moved back to the house where her children had been born, living there with Aunt Nell and "Cousin Suzy," widow of Colonel Nelson White (a relative, the man who had officiated at George Ives's court-martial during the war). When the bank took over the property it was assumed that the old house would be torn down, like nearly every other landmark in Danbury. Though he rarely visited any more and the house was now a lonely home to three old women, Charlie could not bear to lose the place. He paid to have it moved up the hill lock, stock, and Mother: Mollie would not budge from the house while it traveled up Chapel Place.[41]

In autumn of that year Ives happened on another musical acquaintance, the best prepared of anyone yet to bring works of challenging composers before the public. As the story goes (it may be apocryphal), French pianist E. Robert Schmitz showed up at Ives & Myrick looking for an insurance policy and found himself in Charles Ives's new and yet more imposing office at 46 Cedar Street (the agency had again moved to bigger quarters). At some point the conversation turned to music and Schmitz was startled to find this insurance executive a composer of apparently unconventional cast. They sat talking for hours.[42] Before or soon after their meeting, Schmitz received a copy of the *Concord*.[43]

This time in his serendipitous musical encounters Ives had hit something close to the jackpot. Schmitz had been a superb pianist since his prize-winning years at the Paris Conservatoire. He became a protégé of Debussy and a teacher with scientific ideas about keyboard training. Equally talented and tireless as a concert promoter, his main interest outside Debussy was contemporary music. In Paris he founded the Association des Concerts Schmitz, assembling a full orchestra and chorus to perform French works. The war put an end to that, but in 1918 Schmitz emigrated to the United States and cobbled together a second career of playing, teaching, and promoting living composers. During his first years in America he soloed with the Boston Symphony and New York Philharmonic, and played moderns regularly in recital. Interested in new instruments as well as composers, Schmitz consulted with Thomas Edison on the idea of an electric piano.[44]

In 1920 Schmitz and his wife Germaine founded the Franco-American Musical Society, capitalizing on their French contacts to exchange composers between the two countries. Edison signed on as a sponsor. In 1923, wanting a more international perspective, they changed the name of the organization to Pro Musica. They developed chapters around the world. By 1930, when the depression began to erode their resources, Pro Musica had more than forty affiliates ranging from Salt Lake City, Los Angeles, and Honolulu to Paris, London, Tokyo, and Moscow. Schmitz traveled from chapter to chapter, planning, playing, and teaching. During the twenties the organization sponsored American tours by Prokofiev, Bartók, Milhaud, and Ravel.[45] Schmitz's daughter Monique recalled her father sitting around the living room with those composers speculating which of their pieces would go over best in Kansas City, Seattle, and Dubuque.[46]

Schmitz began his long correspondence with Ives in October 1923, inviting him to join the Society and inquiring after the First Piano Sonata. Ives readily agreed to join, but once again put off questions about that piece: "The earlier piano sonata is in lead pencil—I looked it over yesterday. Two movements wont have to be changed at all . . . the 1st movement will have to be compressed & revised. The 3rd movement cut out altogether. . . . It may take a month or two to get it in shape. . . . Most of it is a rough-hewn kind of a thing—but I am not going to soften it up." Then, once again, he dropped the subject of the First Sonata. Pro Musica would elect Ives a director in 1925, and he sat on the executive committee.[47] For some time Ives's office manager William Verplanck served as treasurer of the group; a good deal of the money he handled came from Ives.

Certainly at the outset Ives and Schmitz sized up each other as of potentially gratifying benefit. Ives had encountered a brilliant pianist and promoter, Schmitz a fascinating and undiscovered talent who happened to be rich. What could be better? The two admired each other as musicians and spent hours swapping off at the piano bench or playing through scores four hands.[48] The first project they developed together turned on an overlapping interest— Schmitz in new instruments, Ives in quarter tones. Ives set to writing an essay on the subject for the group's magazine and to composing and arranging quarter-tone pieces for an upcoming concert.

Ives's article "Some Quarter-Tone Impressions" came out in the Franco-American Society *Bulletin* in March 1925.[49] This examination of the intervals falling between the cracks of the piano keyboard is Ives's only theoretical essay. In style it is straightforward, but with autobiographical details ("my father had a weakness for quarter-tones"[50]) and Ivesian epigrams ("Why tonality as such should be thrown out for good, I can't see. Why it should be always present, I can't see"[51]). The article reveals a good deal of how he thought about technique. Much of it is given to speculations on quarter-tone harmonic theory as an extension of traditional harmony. What sort of chord could serve as a basic unit? What would be the secondary chords? What other kinds of harmonies seem to work? The discussion ranges from matters mathematical to personal to practical, the latter always with reference to the ear: "It seems to me that parallel motion [in voice leading] . . . is just as agreeable as opposite motion, and that the need of passing notes is felt less. This may be because the ear, as it gradually identifies the character of a chord to which it is more or less unaccustomed, feels disturbed in having that character changed."[52] He ends with descriptions of, and apologies for, his pieces for quarter-tone keyboards.

These micro-intervals were enjoying a modest vogue in the 1920s. Ives's experience with them went all the way back to his father's quarter-tone gadgets, to the two pianos in his old New York church that happened to be tuned a quarter tone apart, and to pianos tuned likewise in the Redding house.[53] Of the *Three Quarter-Tone Pieces* Ives wrote for Schmitz, all for two pianos tuned apart, only the first was newly composed. The final one, "Chorale," he based on a lost piece for strings from perhaps 1914. In the *Memos* Ives describes them as "simply studies within the limited means we had with which to study quarter tones."[54] They do sound entirely Ivesian, only expressed in clanging quarter-tone harmony and with hallucinatory moments including a micro-tonal "Battle Cry of Freedom." There are some highly funny spots, and deliberately so. For the last piece, in honor of the French-American connection, Ives worked in quotes of "America" and "The Marseillaise."

The "Chorale" of the *Three Quarter-Tone Pieces* was premiered on February 8, 1925, during a Schmitz lecture-demonstration on microtones at Chickering Hall in New York. Playing the Chickering pianos were Hans Barth and Sigmund Klein. On the 14th the same players would do numbers two and three for a Pro Musica "International Referendum Concert" at Aeolian Hall. Those performances were part of a busy season for Ives and for American music. His cowboy song "Charlie Rutlage" was sung at Tulane University in January 1924, and next month George Madden included "The White Gulls" and "The Greatest Man" in another Town Hall recital (the selection certainly pleased Ives better than Madden's last).

Meanwhile the New York press and public were transfixed by the February 1924 premiere of George Gershwin's *Rhapsody in Blue*. This was not the world's first attempt to "make a lady out of jazz" by fusing popular and classical music—Milhaud had already done it in Paris, with his ballet *Création du monde*—but it would be then and forever the most famous. Soon Gershwin would begin a piano concerto for Walter Damrosch; Ives's least favorite conductor would also premiere *An American in Paris* in 1928. As far as many critics and listeners were concerned, Gershwin's orchestral pieces placed jazz in the company of American concert music once and for all. Some considered that keeping disreputable company, but the idea spread. The dream of an American art music seemed finally to have borne fruit. Other European composers including Stravinsky and Ravel produced jazz-inspired pieces. Ives never commented about jazz as such. He was dubious about it like many things outside his experience—but he tracked its development.

On March 18, 1924, violinist Jerome Goldstein and pianist Rex Tillson premiered the Second Violin Sonata at Aeolian Hall, as part of Goldstein's "Modernists" recital series. It was Ives's most visible performance yet in the same hall as the *Rhapsody in Blue* premiere a few weeks before. Critical comment would turn out respectful, if odd. The *Herald Tribune* saw in Ives's sonata "program music, of what might be called an advanced French postromantic type, but with a certain American flavor." The critic of the *Christian Science Monitor* envisioned the composer as no garret Bohemian but rather "one of those who write comfortably in a library, with flowers, if they wish, in a vase on the table."[55] There is no record of what Ives made of these critical caprices, but his reaction must have been entertaining.

Goldstein's recital had hardly been as jolly as the critics implied. Ives brought his teenaged nephew Brewster, who sat with him in the back of the hall. Harmony may have come, but they never stayed together. "It was such a harrowing experience every time," she would say, "that we wanted to endure it alone."[56] When came that agonizing silence before the first downbeat, for composers often a moment of vertigo and cold sweat, Ives sat staring at the score on his lap. As Brewster recalled, there were protests as soon as the music began. Some of the audience shouted "No! No!" and stalked noisily out the door while boos and catcalls rippled around the hall. Finally Ives closed the score, tapped his nephew on the knee, and said quietly, "I think we'd better go home." They stole out before the piece was finished. Recalled Brewster, "He was right back at it the next day. But I think it did shake him."[57]

Perhaps it cheered Ives a little shortly after when Carl Engel, of the Library of Congress, asked him to send scores. Ives had been admiring Engel's puckish writings in the journal *Musical Quarterly,* and Engel had mentioned Ives in his column. In his response Ives wrote, "Can't you induce [editor] Mr. Sonneck to put the 'Musical Quarterly' on a monthly basis? In three evenings we have read it through and most of it re-read. Then you keep us waiting for three months."[58]

From journals and newspapers Ives kept tabs on the musical world he only occasionally saw in person. In the *Musical Quarterly* of that decade he read Dane Rudhyar on "The Relativity of Our Musical Conceptions," Herbert Antcliffe on "The Significance of Scriabin," Henry Bellamann on Alkan's piano music, Charles Seeger's "On Style and Manner in Modern Composition," Carl Engel's defense of jazz, and critic Paul Rosenfeld's weird description of Schoenberg's *Pierrot Lunaire:* "the thing without arms, without legs, without organs of communication, without a phallus." Ives also subscribed to and devoured *Modern Music,* the journal of the League of Composers. There he read Gilbert Seldes on jazz, read about Berg's *Wozzeck,* regular articles on Schoenberg and Stravinsky and Bartók, one on Janáček's *Cunning Little Vixen,* Aaron Copland's "Jazz Structure and Influence," critic Pitts Sanborn on Ruggles, Varèse, and Cowell, reviews of European new-music festivals, and a pan of the American premiere, in Carnegie Hall, of George Antheil's futuristic noise-piece *Ballet Mécanique.* From newspapers Ives clipped and saved dozens of articles about Schoenberg and Ravel and Stravinsky and Bartók. Quietly, from a distance, he stalked the competition.

In April 1924 Clifton Furness took Ives to hear Walter Damrosch conduct the New York Symphony in Stravinsky's *Chant du Rossignol,* the Brahms Double Concerto, and Scriabin's *Poem of Ecstasy.*[59] It was mainly the last they wanted to hear. Around the same time Furness invited Ives to pianist Katherine Heyman's all-Scriabin concert at Aeolian Hall. She was to play, Furness wrote, "several of the late works, including the VIII Sonata and the last set of preludes that you like. . . . Will you and Mrs. Ives join me?"[60] Ives accompanied Furness, and often Elliott Carter, to some of the private salons Heyman held in her New York loft.[61] This pianist was interested in Ultra-Modern composers and in the *Concord;* though she lacked the technique to manage the thornier parts of Ives's score, she still played at it in the salons.[62] (Heyman's main passion would always be Scriabin. In her Paris years, partly Ives-financed, she would receive daily spirit messages from the late Russian, which she shared with her Scriabin circle.[63])

Furness visited Redding in June 1924. About that time, as Edie noted in her diary, "we got a wonderful beautiful grand piano."[64] It would reside in the living room at Redding, while her father kept his excellent upright in the studio. Ives and Furness returned to New York together, Charlie to prepare for a six-week vacation to England that he and Harmony had planned. Furness was to meet them there.

On July 27, just before the Iveses sailed, Harmony's brother Dave Twichell wrote a sad letter from Asheville, where he was visiting sister Sally. "Dear Meg, As Sunday afternoon comes around I want my little chat with you so I will send this line to the London address you gave. It may be there to meet you. . . . I have been trying to get around a little more and take some interest in things. . . . Love to you and your dear ones all the time and wherever you are."[65] Dave, Harmony's closest sibling, one of Charlie's oldest friends, who had gotten them together in the first place, had been in a bad way. His beloved wife Ella, beautiful and wealthy and high-strung, had died three years before. She had been a tuberculosis patient of his and never recovered her health. Dave, always delicate and prone to overwork, wore himself down trying to save her. Finally he caught the disease he had spent his medical career fighting. Ella, convinced that his family were against him, had gotten Dave to move to Quebec to get away from the Twichells and the Iveses.[66] Since Ella died Dave had been wandering aimlessly from place to place.

On July 30 the Iveses sailed on the S.S. *Empress of Scotland,* Quebec to Southampton. While they were gone, George Gershwin phoned Ives & Myrick and asked to speak to Charles Ives. He told Verplanck he wanted to meet

Passport photo of Charles Ives and daughter Edie, 1921.

the composer of the songs and the *Concord,* that they had been an inspiration to him.[67] Ives learned of Gershwin's call when he got back but never returned it, maybe because he had more pressing matters on his mind.

The 1924 British vacation was a first trip overseas for both Charlie and Edie. For Harmony it was a return to scenes of her youth, when she traveled there with her parents. In the first week they bustled around seeing touristy things—Stonehenge, Carlyle's house, St. Dunstan's. At the Tate Gallery Charlie could steep himself in his favorite painter, J. M. W. Turner, whose epic landscapes and storms wildly painted are so much like Ives's music. They took in Shaw's *Saint Joan,* noting in the travel diary, "a great play. Edie sat on the edge of her chair most of the time."[68] As had become his habit, Charlie struck up dozens of conversations on the streets, querying citizens on their opinions of politics and the last war.[69] Harmony recalled how happy her mother had been in London. So were the Iveses, until the middle of August when the cable arrived from brother Burt.

Not Dave's medicine, success, good looks, popularity, religion, or family had been enough to save him. He had gone to stay with Burt in Keene Valley, in the Adirondack mountains where the Twichells had spent their summers, and the day he arrived walked into the woods and killed himself.[70] On August 20 Charlie and Harmony went to Cumnor, where she wrote in their diary,

Walked 2 miles to this pretty village—wanted to be by ourselves. Went into a field & sat on the grass. The following from a notice in Old Cumnor Church (1200 abt.) "So far. The future is not yet. It is in the Hands of Him who alone knows the End from the beginning, and whom all things, both good and Evil, serve." Have felt much lightened of the load in thinking of Dave today—a strange assurance that all is well with him.[71]

All they could do was hope Dave had found salvation somehow. They returned home in mid-September to a life once more indelibly diminished.

It may be that Ives took his first overseas vacation during 1924 in part to celebrate finishing a big project. If so, he never shared that celebration with anyone but the family. To look at his lists of compositions and their dates, and those of later scholars, we find only a little to contradict Ives's statement that "I did almost no composing after the beginning of 1918."[72] With that he manifestly ignores a fair amount of music, especially all the songs he produced in 1920–21—though the majority of those are arrangements of earlier pieces. His stated reason for the long-term decline in output was his illness. During the early 1920s he would often plead bad health at the office, and he was genuinely in shaky condition. But during that period Ives clearly was more active than was good for him, more social than usual, and in 1924 he took the demanding trip to England with no apparent ill effects. During this period office scuttlebutt at Ives & Myrick had it that the boss was not as sick as he claimed to be.[73] What was he doing with all those days he called in sick, or slipped out early by the back staircase?

Contrary to his own testimony and the guesses of later historians, what Ives mainly seems to have been doing in roughly 1921–23 was composing the *Comedy,* the second movement of the Fourth Symphony.[74] In the time when by his own account his store of inspiration was nearly empty, he produced a work that for audacity, extravagance of invention, and revolutionary imagination is perhaps challenged by only one other achievement in his life—the final movement of the Fourth Symphony. The *Comedy,* in other words, was Ives's last major outpouring of creativity, an extraordinary climax to his life's work.

It was also one about which he would consistently fib. In the few paragraphs he devotes to the Fourth in the *Memos,* Ives writes that the symphony was completed about 1916, the Fugue just at the end of the process.[75] He is patently equivocating there—the Fugue was written some *twenty years before* that, put into the First Quartet and later taken out. The reason for this fib may be that Ives wanted to make sure the Fugue would be seen as part of the symphony and no longer of the quartet. Meanwhile the first and fourth movements of the symphony likely date from when he said they did, roughly 1910–16. What was going on with the *Comedy,* then, and why did he claim to have composed almost nothing after 1918?

To examine that question we must turn to what is nominally a distinct piece, called *The Celestial Railroad.* Ives writes in the *Memos* that this was "an arrangement . . . for piano from parts of the Hawthorne movement of the [*Concord*], but mostly from the second movement of the Fourth Symphony."[76] So Ives said the sequence was *Hawthorne → Comedy → Celestial Railroad.* In 1991 Thomas Brodhead, examining the latter piece toward a new edition, discovered that the reality is the other way around: the draft called *Celestial Railroad* is neither an arrangement of the *Comedy* nor exactly a piano piece at all—it has too many notes for two hands. What the *Railroad* turns out to be is a draft for the Fourth Symphony's *Comedy.* The actual sequence is *Hawthorne → Celestial Railroad → Comedy.* Given that fact, the *Comedy* could not have been composed by 1916 as Ives said, because the *Railroad* draft incorporates *printed* material from *Hawthorne,* which did not exist until the *Concord* was published in 1920.[77] The manuscript of the *Railroad* is built up in layers, patches pinned on patches, on an underlying framework of measures cut out of the printed *Hawthorne* and pasted onto music paper. Ives linked the printed sections with handwritten material and added new layers with the patches.

Why did Ives so determinedly lie about the provenance of the *Comedy?* As Brodhead points out, it was not a pure lie. Apparently Ives really considered the Fourth to be finished in 1916. Both *Hawthorne* and the *Comedy* are related to the *Hawthorne* Piano Concerto, a sketch Ives says was done in 1913.[78] As far as Ives was concerned during the mid-teens, the concerto *was* the second movement of the Fourth Symphony. Then, Brodhead speculates, in the 1920s Ives began working on a piano piece from the same material and that snowballed into the *Comedy,* which replaced the original concerto as second movement. So the genesis seems to run approximately like so: the *Concord*'s *Hawthorne* and the closely related (lost) *Hawthorne* Piano Concerto from 1913 (or 1911, or 1911–13), then the draft called *Celestial Railroad,* then the orchestral *Comedy* done during 1922–23, after Ives had finished work on the songbook.[79] If that indeed is the genesis of the *Comedy,* why didn't Ives say so? There is nothing unusual for him in any of this; one piece grew into another all the time. Moreover, he had no need to lie to make himself look prophetic; his work had been unequivocally prophetic for decades.

To find reasons for the smoke and mirrors, one has to remember Ives's situation in the 1920s. After his heart attack he had two fundamental priorities—to provide for his family in case he died, and to put his music before the public. The effort to get his music out began with his publications of 1920–22, and during the rest of the decade he devoted a good deal of time to developing musical contacts.

That left the other priority of providing for his family. To that end Ives would concentrate in the 1920s on building up his savings and investments. As best one can tell, the main way he did that was to buy renewal commissions from perhaps hundreds of agents associated with Ives & Myrick. Each time a customer renewed a policy already in force, the agent who originally sold it was due a small commission. For an individual agent with rent to pay, these commissions trickled in too slowly over the years. Executives like Ives who had the capital could pay agents a percentage of those prospective renewal commissions in a lump sum, which many agents were glad to have. Ives could then collect on the many small commissions he had bought.[80]

This little financial maneuver (later made illegal) worked quite nicely. In 1991 dollars, Ives made around one and a half million between 1913 (the first year of tax records) and 1919. Then in the 1920s he made nearly six million. In 1923 he established a trust fund for Harmony. By 1930 he could be sure, between his savings and life insurance, that his extended family and his music were provided for.[81] During his retirement Ives would finance not only his own performances and publications but a good percentage of the avant-garde music that appeared all over the United States. Maybe something like that was part of the plan all along. He had intended, in any case, to make his pile and retire to music full time.

Here we come to the crux, it appears, of why Ives lied about the *Comedy* and how much he composed during the early 1920s. He lied because of a conflict between his two priorities, his family and his music. In order to address the first priority, which involved making a lot of money, he needed to appear as committed to Ives & Myrick as he had always been, not a slacker because he was doing more on the musical side. In reality he *was* slacking off, by his standards. He was staying home and pleading bad health because he needed time for developing musical contacts, going over proofs, and composing—most of that to create the *Comedy,* a gigantic, complex piece that required an enormous commitment of time.

In short, the main reason Ives lied about when he composed the *Comedy* was because he did not want the office to know how much time he was giving to writing and promoting his music after 1918, because he did a lot of it on company time. Certainly he continued to do useful work at the agency, including planning a successful selling initiative in 1922 that boosted profits by going after wealthy clients. But he tried to hide from the agency that he was no longer a hundred percent on the job. Exactly that rumor was going around the office. Ives was especially concerned not to let Mike Myrick think he wasn't holding up his end of the partnership. (Ives's misrepresentations of the *Comedy* dates are in the *Memos,* written when he was only recently out of the office and still consulting regularly with Mike.)

Beyond those matters, it may be that Ives never wanted to admit even to himself what he had done. He had vowed from the beginning never to sacrifice his family's security to his art, and he never did. But neither had he compromised business with art, until the 1920s. Maybe he felt troubled as well by his burgeoning profits of that decade, which not only spectacularly exceeded his own proposed income limit but were gained by methods dubious by his own precepts—selling more insurance to the rich and siphoning commissions from agents.[82] So with the best of intentions Ives fibbed for the benefit of family and associates and posterity, and maybe his own conscience. He did not entirely lie, however, about his health. In spite of a deceptive vitality, his condition was bad and getting worse through the 1920s. He ignored that, and he paid the price.

In July 1925 Ives wrote from New York to "Raggedy Ann Ives" in Redding—that is, a letter to Edie's doll:

Please tell your Mamma to tell her Mamma that it is very cool & pleasant in New York today, that Gramercy Park hasn't grown an inch since you saw it, & I will see you all at Wilton [Station] 4.56 Thurs July 2—1925 A.D. Do you know what A.D. stands for. It doesn't mean "Advertise Daily" or "Ask Daddy", but it is from the latin "Anno Domini." Your Grandmother will tell your Mother, and she will tell you what that latin means. . . . I expect to call on the Bellamanns tomorrow night.[83]

His family was still the main thing that sustained him. Redding remained his retreat away from the external world and into his own setting of music and loved ones. There he and Deac—formally speaking, Edward Carrington Twichell—could spend time giggling together, Charlie reciting doggerel composed for the amusement of his simplehearted brother-in-law:

> E.C.T. is the man for us!
> He certainly is a nice old Cuss
> He's steppin' fleet & neat
> Right down old Center Street
> 'a makin' for the Danbury Bus.[84]

Ives's own cheerfulness and charm remained intact, but after the exertion of composing the *Comedy* his reserves of physical and creative energy were running toward empty. He had spent five years refusing to give in to illness.

After the *Comedy* was done he came up with a few songs including the wild formalistic experiment "On the Antipodes," based on sketches from years before.[85] He tinkered with the Third Orchestral Set, but that was never very promising and he finally gave up on it. The *Three Quarter-Tone Pieces* were trifles. He worked gamely at the *Universe Symphony*, but that superhuman concept was exhausting even to contemplate.

At some point Ives started to think about one of his old choral psalms, part of the batch Central Presbyterian threw out after he left. In 1923 or 1924 he decided to recompose *Psalm 90* based on what he remembered of the original. The result unites the artless sincerity of his youth with the wisdom and skill of his maturity. That despite his exhaustion he chose this project and finished it, and brought it off beautifully, has much to do with the text and associations of the music, and its resonance as a work from his youth. Fate again showed its talent for drama and pathos. With the new *Psalm 90* Ives came full circle. His last significant work is valedictory in every dimension.[86]

Tradition says that these verses were written by Moses himself.[87] Their theme is human life and death. *Lord, thou hast been our dwelling place from one generation to another. Before the mountains were brought forth, or ever thou hadst formed the earth and the world, even from everlasting to everlasting, thou art God.* Ives's setting, with its contrasting sections from verse to verse, is composed over a low C drone in the organ pedal, symbolic of unity within diversity. He begins with an organ introduction, each of the first four measures a distinct harmonic flavor, each harmony specifically labeled: "The Eternities. Creation. God's wrath against sin. Prayer and Humility. Rejoicing in Beauty and Work." Behind the last chord, three sets of bells and a gong sound briefly from the distance. These are the essential materials. Then the chorus begins, softly as if in prayer, and the piece unfolds with each verse flavored and expressed by one of the opening harmonies.

The first verses voice praise and reverence and awe. *For a thousand years in thy sight are but as yesterday when it is past, and as a watch in the night.* As for us on earth, *We spend our years as a tale that is told.* Then come the verses of supplication. *Teach us to number our days, that we may apply our hearts unto wisdom.* To convey these words Ives recalls the haunting chordal sequence from the opening movement of his First Symphony. He had composed that music at Yale thirty years before, in the months after George Ives died, and it may have been his memorial for his father.[88] Now, suggesting those chords and mindful of the words, Charles Ives becomes the psalmist. *Teach us to number our days.* He addresses his heavenly and earthly fathers together, uniting his father's death with his own looming mortality, finding in that act a wisdom and a reconciliation.

After music of great contrast and recurrent unrest, involving practically every harmonic color Ives had in his palette, the end settles into a gentle and moving prayer in C major. Behind the choir, bells sound in the distance like reverberations from another world. *Let the beauty of the Lord our God be upon us; and establish thou the work of our hands upon us; yea, the work of our hands establish thou it.* With the final *Amen* the work of Charles Ives's hands became in essence a tale that was told. Surely in some part of his mind he recognized that, and the recognition gives the ending its eloquence. He said to Harmony that *Psalm 90* was the only work of his that satisfied him.[89]

Ives did attempt at least two more pieces, the first a song called "Sunrise" that he sketched out at Redding. The text, a plea for renewal, for new light, is his own. It recalls the mornings of his childhood, when he and Moss would awake and plan the day's games, and the anticipation seemed the best part: "We felt then sub-consciously the fun was when the sunrise would . . . start to throw its color & hope into our bedroom, we would lie a while & live the day to come." Now he could no longer trust what the day would bring, and could only hope for hope.

> A light low in the East,
> as I lie there, it shows but does not move,
> a light, a light as a thought forgotten comes again. . .
>
> Later on, as I rise,
> it shows through the trees
> and lights the dark grey rock
> and something in the mind,
> and brings the quiet day.
>
> And tomorrow, tomorrow
> the light as a thought forgotten comes again, again,
> and with it ever the hope of the New Day.

Set for voice, violin, and soprano, hushed for most of its course, "Sunrise" sounds like nothing else in Ives's music. It is unsettling in some indefinable way. The strangeness of its effect is not exactly that the music contradicts the text, and certainly it conveys a sense of early morning and awakening. But everything seems rapt in emptiness and loneliness and unspoken sorrow. The same keening motives keep turning up, as if the singer were immobile or paralyzed.

Ives wrote off the first page of the song clearly, but the second is violently scribbled out and beside it is written "N[o] G[ood] here! Arthur!"[90] The sketch straggles through to the end, where Ives notes, "Taken from chords & parts of a II S[tring] Q[uartet] & put into this song Aug. 1926—but not a good job—the words are NG, but better than the music." So he says. Some would call "Sunrise" one of his most striking songs. But whether it was objectively any good or not was no longer the question. What mattered was whether he believed he could do it any more.

In November 1926, two months after his struggle with a simple song that somehow defeated him, the Iveses moved to 164 East 74th Street. The elegant old brownstone was the first house they had owned in Manhattan. It would be their city home for the rest of their lives together. Charlie had begun a one-movement piano sonata.[91] (He may have finished a draft, but later lost or destroyed it.) On the face of it this was a good time for them. They had a beautiful and spacious house with a studio for Charlie on the top floor. Interest in his music had been gathering. Schmitz and Pro Musica had settled plans for a January Town Hall performance of the Fourth Symphony. For Ives that airing of one of his most ambitious scores could be a decisive turning point in his reputation. Physically he was not his old self, but still he had strength enough to carry on at the office and make time for writing, and he could retire from business in a few years with enough in the bank for his family's security. His musical career had never been so promising. It was at that point that everything fell apart.

In the living room at 74th Street Harmony sits knitting while she waits for Charlie to finish and come down for her to read to him. She has been scared for eight years. How long can somebody live with what he's going through? The fear seems to catch every breath, every step alongside him. She strains to hear the piano upstairs. Now she has to listen as intensely as Charlie has always listened to things, but for such a terribly different reason.

It seems to be all right. He has been upstairs for hours, the piano going in its fits and starts: an eruption of sound, spinning out or repeating, homing in on something, a chord, those strange chords of his, crashing ones, mystical ones, over and over as he makes some incomprehensible adjustment. When the piano stops for a moment she knows he is leaning over the keyboard scribbling impatiently, muttering and cursing, getting it down before he loses it.

She bends to her work. Then at some point she realizes something has changed. He is still playing but it is different, she can't think how. His music has always been a mystery to her, the same magnetic mystery as Charlie himself. But there is some-thing wrong now. Something she can't place has crept into those rising and falling waves of sound.

The piano stops. Staring hard into the ceiling she waits for him to start again. The silence stretches on. Why doesn't he start, or come down? Should she run up and check? He hates it when she does that, dashing breathless into his room to see if— what? To see if he's still alive.

Silence. No, she has to go see. As Harmony leaps up she hears his footsteps coming down the stairs. When he appears at the door she is so relieved that at first she does not notice the tears shining on his face.

"I can't seem to compose any more," he says, his voice catching. "I try and try and nothing comes out right."[92]

All his life, Charles Ives had reined in the warring paradoxes within and without, and the energy of their dissonance helped create and fuel his art. Now the centrifugal elements of his self had escaped his grasp, leaving him fragmented and exhausted. At fifty-two, he was finished as a composer.

Entr'acte Three:
Watchman, Tell Us of the Night

UNLIKE ANY OTHER OF HIS large orchestral works, Charles Ives's climactic masterpiece the Fourth Symphony begins commandingly rather than meditatively, with a portentous bass line answered by searing string harmonies and a pealing bugle call.

After avoiding the symphonic genre for over a decade, Ives returned to it in his full maturity with a work that subsumes ideas from his entire life and music. Henry Bellamann, writing from Ives's cues, described the Fourth as a question and three responses: "The aesthetic program of the work is . . . the searching questions of What? and Why? which the spirit of man asks of life. This is particularly the sense of the prelude. The three succeeding movements are the diverse answers in which existence replies." Thus Ives also returned to the kind of program posed in *The Unanswered Question,* but now with the command he had acquired since that miniature of 1906. In tone and scope the Fourth Symphony is made in the mold of *Emerson*—a heroic quest into the immensities.

In keeping with that scope, the symphony stretches the sounding space beyond the proscenium. In the quiet after the opening string declamations, a distant choir of strings and harp whispers fragments of *Bethany*—"Nearer, My God, to Thee."

This ensemble continues independently through the first movement, like a spiritual presence behind the music, revealed only during windows of silence from the onstage orchestra. The effect is a development of the polyphony of groups Ives had begun writing down with *The Unanswered Question,* that work in turn based on his college experiments with throwing tunes together, and on the "Jerusalem the Golden" variations that his father's band once played in detachments spread around a Danbury square. By the Fourth Symphony, space has become part of the music's meaning and drama.

Already in the opening measures Ives presents contrasting themes as in traditional sonata form: the bass line, the element striding and heroic and sometimes atonal ("masculine" first theme, as Horatio Parker taught); the distant choir, the element lyrical and meditative, often tonal ("feminine" second theme). Here is the essential polarity. The idea is hardly new; symphonies had always involved presenting and reconciling contrasts. But by including so many expressions of these basic elements, by excluding so little, Ives enormously amplified the scale of contrast, the scope of what needs to be reconciled during the course of the work. Much of the structure, technique, and meaning of the Fourth Symphony are found in its mediation among centrifugal forces. These polarities are found in every dimension: atonal and tonal, loud and soft, march time and free rhythm, masculine and feminine; styles old and new, traditions vernacular and cultivated, American and European, rhythms duple and triple, textures complex and simple. The music unfolds as a quest for wholeness within a musical diversity unimaginable before Ives. His means of approaching that reconciliation is a systematic *technique of ambiguity:* a pattern of setting up and exploiting ambiguities, especially in the harmony and rhythm.[1]

Once again Ives turns program into form and technique. The essential polarity of the music will be expressed by two fundamental melodic motives and their associated rhythms. The first note of the symphony, the basses' D, defines the central tonality to which the symphony will return only at the end of the last movement. The first three notes of the opening bass line, a half step and minor third, form a motive on which Ives had built much of the First Piano Sonata. In the Fourth Symphony this motive is, in its main garb, the Hero, the Pilgrim, the "masculine" striver and strider, characteristically in duple time:　　　. In German this melodic cell might be called the *Urmotiv,* "ur-" conveying origin, source, primeval energy.

The other primary motive is heard first in the distant choir's fragment of *Bethany,* a violin line of descending whole steps—the *lyric motive:*　　　. In its main guise it is a hymn or something like it—spiritual, lyric, "feminine," triple. (The motive is as likely to go up as down; it begins both *Bethany* and *Watchman.*) These primary cells exchange elements throughout the work; their personalities are clear in the large view, changeable in the details. The two simple three-note motives, being contained in the fifty or more tunes quoted in the symphony, convey the underlying unity within a babel of voices and styles. Moreover they are subtly linked from the outset: both Urmotiv and lyric motive derive from *Bethany,* the central melodic and symbolic theme of the work, which will not be heard plainly until the last pages of the symphony.[2]

Many other tunes put in appearances, much of Ives's familiar songbag sacred, patriotic, and popular. The hymns remain central. As much as anything, the Fourth Symphony is an apotheosis of American hymnody in general and *Bethany* in particular. One other hymn tune pervades the texture—"Sweet By and By."[3] This was the theme of *Hanover Square,* another iconic melody Ives heard from his father's cornet and from thousands of "let-out souls" in camp meetings. The words of both the central hymns resonate throughout the symphony, both of them beginning with the lyric motive. *Bethany:*

> Nearer, my God, to thee, Nearer to thee!
> E'en though it be a cross that raiseth me;
> Still all my song shall be,
> Nearer, my God, to thee.

> Though like the wanderer, the sun gone down,
> Darkness be over me, my rest a stone;
> Yet in my dreams I'd be
> Nearer, my God, to thee. . . .
>
> Or if, on joyful wing cleaving the sky,
> Sun, moon, and stars forgot, upward I fly,
> Still all my song shall be,
> Nearer, my God, to thee.

And likwise "Sweet By and By," which once again rang deep chords connecting Ives with his father:

> There's a land that is fairer than day,
> And by faith we can see it afar;
> For the Father waits over the way
> To prepare us a dwelling place there.
>
> In the sweet by and by
> We shall meet on that beautiful shore.

Epic journey and apotheosis of hymnody, the Fourth Symphony is an autobiography as well. It contains over a dozen of Ives's own works in part or nearly in whole. The first movement goes back to his settings of the hymn *Watchman,* one of them done at Dave Twichell's suggestion during a Saranac Lake vacation of 1905, another contained in the finale of the First Violin Sonata. The third movement is a reworked version of the Yale-period First String Quartet Fugue. The core of the last movement is the *Memorial Slow March* Ives wrote on the death of President McKinley in 1901, and used again at the visionary climax of the Second String Quartet. The *Comedy* is based on the earlier *Hawthorne* pieces and quotes his own *Country Band March.*[4] The trajectory of his lifework reaches its zenith in an encyclopedic symphony.

Journey, apotheosis, autobiography, the Fourth is no less another mediation, the most far-reaching of all in Ives, between art "low" and "high," vernacular tunes and cultivated genres, the voice of the American people joined with the monumental European tradition. A cyclic symphony in outline, with themes recurring from movement to movement, during its course the Fourth subsumes episodes of chamber and parlor music, sonata (elements of the *Concord*), fugue, march, chorale prelude, song, hymn, piano concerto. Above all it is one of the last examples of what late-Romantic composers conceived a *symphony* to be: loose in form but still in the standard four movements, with something resembling their familiar tempos and tones, and with the intention of evoking the highest mysteries of life in a unique and transforming way.

After the opening and its dramatic juxtaposition of heroic Urmotiv and ethereal lyric motive, the Prelude settles for a moment into a quiet passage. In the foreground a solo cello intones a melody based on "Sweet By and By," but drawn out, divorced from the vigorous rhythms of the gospel hymn.[5] It is George Ives playing his trademark tune across the years, a phantom presence in the music. For Charles Ives, the Father who "waits over the way" seems to mean both heavenly and earthly Fathers. The symphony is a pilgrimage universal and personal, abstract and autobiographical, and those conjoined Fathers encompass both dimensions.

Besides a question posed of life and a truncated sonata form presenting two contrasting themes, and besides an introduction to the succeeding movements, the Prelude is shaped as an introduction and hymn. So after the introduction a choir enters with the Epiphany hymn *Watchman:*

> Watchman, tell us of the night,
> What the signs of promise are:
> Traveller, o'er yon mountain's height,
> See that Glory-beaming star!
>
> Watchman, aught of joy or hope?
> Traveller, yes, it brings the day,
> Promised day of Israel.
> Dost thou see its beauteous ray?

Even the words of the hymn Ives would prefer to make more ethereal, more interior. Under the trumpet part he writes "preferably without voices." It is an evocation of his father's hymn performances, when George Ives asked the congregation to imagine the words as he played, that inner voice closer to the spirit than the singing voice.[6] Spoken or unspoken, the great question of life is posed to the Watchman, *What of the night?,* and the symphony proper is under way. At "beauteous ray" the foreground music pauses and we hear again the distant choir of strings and harp. Now we know who they are: an avatar of the glory-beaming star and its promise that draws the Traveler, the Pilgrim, over the mountain's height. It is the star of Bethlehem, the omen of Halley's Comet, the Celestial City of *Pilgrim's Progress,* the star of joy or hope or love. ("The product of our summer at 'Pells' " Ives wrote Harmony when he sketched the movement.) All these, the stars of all Pilgrims, are suggested in the distant choir. It is the promise that draws us through the wilderness of this world toward the mountain's height.

The chorus sings *Watchman* within a rich fabric of orchestral sound mostly made from fragments of other hymns including *Bethany* and *Proprior Deo* (there is a Wanderer in the words of *Bethany* too). During the hymn meters are stacked up—$\frac{6}{8}, \frac{3}{4}, \frac{4}{4}$ sounding together, and more arcane polyrhythms. While *Watchman* is in D, the harmony increasingly undercuts that key with an added B, creating an ambiguity between D major and B minor.[7] As soon as B minor seems established, Ives undercuts it by adding G to the harmony. The end of the movement seems to settle in G major, but that chord is blurred with an added E. Even amidst this gentle hymn setting Ives suggests

the technique of ambiguity that in the second movement will be expressed as
a comic battle of rhythms and meters, and in the third movement as systematic
harmonic equivocation.

    Like the other movements, the first does not end but rather evaporates,
the chorus chanting its question of the Pilgrim: *Dost thou see its beauteous ray?*
. . . At the end the piano and celesta turn the Urmotiv into a rising form like
a question:

Sound in strings dies away and
stops just after harp is struck.

Then, barely audibly, the distant choir of strings and harp glimmers once more: *Nearer, my God . .*

Hawthorne began his story "The Celestial Railroad": "Not a great while ago, passing through the gate of dreams, I visited that region of the earth in which lies the famous City of Destruction. It interested me much to learn that by the public spirit of some of the inhabitants a railroad has recently been established between this popular and flourishing town and the Celestial City." What Hawthorne is mainly satirizing, picking up settings and characters from John Bunyan's Puritan epic *Pilgrim's Progress,* is American faith in material progress. Yankee know-how has replaced the grueling journey of Bunyan's Pilgrims with a comfortable railroad line to paradise, with a pleasant stopover in Vanity Fair. From the windows of the train, passengers observe old-fashioned Pilgrims struggling through the swamp on foot, and greet the sight with laughter. Unfortunately, as the narrator learns in the final scene, modern travelers are fated to miss their connection over the river of death. As the cold waters close around him, the narrator awakes "with a shiver and a heartquake," and realizes it was a dream.

Ives did not propose to illustrate Hawthorne's story point by point. Bella-mann wrote,

It is a comedy in the sense that Hawthorne's Celestial Railroad is comedy. Indeed this work of Hawthorne's may be considered as a sort of incidental program in which an exciting, easy, and worldly progress through life is contrasted with the trials of the Pilgrims in their journey through the swamp. The occasional slow episodes—Pilgrims' hymns—are constantly crowded out and overwhelmed by the former. The cream, or fantasy, ends with an interruption of reality—the Fourth of July in Concord—brass bands, drum corps, etc.[8]

Years before, the story had helped inspire *Hawthorne* in the *Concord So-nata* and the companion *Hawthorne* Concerto. If Vanity Fair wanted a literal analogue on earth, New York City would do fine. Charles Ives deplored materialism but didn't mind becoming rich, avoided modern technology but loved trains, and both enjoyed and despised the city he called "Babylon" and "hell hole."[9] So his *Comedy* is a Puritan critique of urban life and materialism mixed with affection and nostalgia. In Hawthorne's story Vanity Fair is, like New York, a high-spirited, profitable, progressively minded sort of town where virtue itself has been perfected by technology:

There is another species of machine for the wholesale manufacture of individual morality. This excellent result is effected by societies for all manner of virtuous purposes, with which a man has merely to connect himself, throwing, as it were, his quota of virtue into the common stock. . . . All these, and other wonderful improvements in ethics, religion, and literature, being made plain to my comprehension by the ingenious [tour guide] Mr. Smooth-it-away.[10]

The musical substance of the *Comedy* concentrates on *melody*—some thirty related tunes, including hymns often stripped of their sacredness and ragged up; *rhythm*—the most elaborate extension of polyrhythm in Ives's career, or in the career of Western music for years to come; and *texture*—the shaping and clashing of sound masses, the closest Ives ever came to the sheer sonic turmoil and weight of public events, the summit of his unique musical realism (see the following sample page of the score).

The basic gesture of the *Comedy* is a quiet Pilgrims' hymn (or a salon interlude) flattened by a roaring march. The battle of hymn and march is another avatar of the two theme groups presented in the symphony's opening—the striding and marchlike, and the meditative: Urmotiv and lyric motive.[11] Most of the quoted tunes are tonal and familiar—"Massa's in de Cold, Cold Ground," "Sweet By and By," "Marching Through Georgia," *Beulah Land,* "Camptown Races," "Columbia, the Gem," "Yankee Doodle," and so on. In busier passages the maelstrom of competing keys often makes the overall effect atonal. Outside the occasional tonal episode, rationalized harmony is lost in the storm.[12] Counterpoint is expressed as a polyphony of groups: everybody is out for himself. Here is the ultimate integrity of contrapuntal lines toward which Ives had been moving since he discovered polytonality and polyrhythm in his teens. Now keys, rhythms, styles can be juxtaposed in a collage of individual voices. All the same, the violent contrasts that rock the movement keep its phrase structure concise; we hear themes and rhythms evolving in clear stages.[13]

The instrumental selection in the *Comedy* is particular, as in each of the movements. Ives omits oboes and French horns and adds a large percussion section. Brass and drums predominate, giving much of the movement a brass-band sound. The movement's origin in the *Hawthorne* Piano Concerto is reflected in a virtuosic solo piano part (there are two other pianos, one of them quarter tone). While the first movement concerned itself with literal space, adding a distant group to the onstage orchestra, in the *Comedy* everything originates from within the proscenium. Still, Ives imagined the music in layered perspective. In the "Conductor's Note" published with the score he writes,

It is difficult to reproduce the sounds and feeling that distance gives to sound. . . . A brass band playing *pianissimo* across the street is a different sounding thing than the same band playing the same piece *forte,* a block or so away. . . . A horn over a lake gives a quality of sound and feeling that is hard to produce in any other way [he is remembering George Ives's experiments with space]. . . . As the eye, in looking at a view, may focus on the sky, clouds or distant outlines, yet sense the color and form of the foreground, and then, by bringing the eye to the foreground, sense the distant outlines and color, so, in some similar way can the listener choose to arrange in his mind the relation of the rhythmic, harmonic, and other material. . . . The general aim . . . is to bring various parts of the music to the ear in their relation, as the perspective of a picture brings to the eye. As the distant hills, in a landscape, row upon row, grow gradually into the horizon, so there may be something like this in the presentation of music. Music seems too often all foreground even if played by a master of dynamics.[14]

This description of perspective in the *Comedy* resembles Ives's conception of the *Universe Symphony* as he describes it in the *Memos:*

In the fall of 1915 . . . I started something that I'd had in mind for some time . . . trying out a parallel way of listening to music, suggested by looking at a view (1) with the eyes toward the sky or tops of the trees, taking in the earth or foreground subjectively . . . (2) then looking at the earth and land, and seeing the sky and the top of the foreground subjectively.[15]

We find here the intimate connection of the Fourth Symphony and *Universe Symphony*. Some of the perspective ideas belonging to the *Universe* appear to have percolated into the *Comedy* and into the finale. Which is to say, as the conception of the Fourth Symphony expanded, it picked up ideas from the more ambitious piece, and freed the *Universe* to soar beyond the concert hall and beyond human fingers and ears.[16] The Fourth was the climax of Ives's music not only roughly in time, but in how far his ideas could reach and remain achievable.[17]

After posing the questions of *What* and *Why* in the Prelude, in the *Comedy* Ives intended to leave out as little as possible of the reply of modern urban life: all the ears could hold, and more, of the great throbbing, marching, dancing, hymning, ragtiming, holidaying, incorrigibly secular city he knew from his bachelor years in New York.[18] He begins the movement with a passage of uncoordinated rustling, each layer a solo, like an awakening cityscape. There comes a Pilgrims' hymn, harmonized in dreamlike quarter tones. Then the train gathers steam. Ives knew his railroads, the imaginary childhood ones, the adult locals and expresses (he was a commuting man) and the celestial ones too. He made his *Comedy*'s train crank up graphically, mostly in the strings, like George Ives playing violin sound effects for the Ives Bros RR. The locomotive rhythms catch on and begin to syncopate, to rag in antiphonal accents, and with a shriek of the whistle we are on our way to Vanity Fair.

The trombones blare out "Tramp, Tramp, Tramp," then with a cinematic wipe we are back in the Pilgrims' journey, the strings playing "Sweet By and By." With a roar the brass reappears in lurching rhythms like iron smashing on iron. That collapses to reveal again the hymn, which has been continuing on its own, as undaunted as Hawthorne's Pilgrims by the tumult around them. Once more rhythmic machinery intrudes into the foreground, the trombones back at "Tramp, Tramp, Tramp," which transforms into a howled-out fragment of "Sweet By and By." (Hawthorne's Vanity Fair is, after all, well supplied with churches.) From a bustling texture with a syncopated version of "Camptown Races" the sound gathers to an incipient march in the brasses.[19] That dissolves, depositing us apparently in a Vanity Fair salon. A piano tinkles

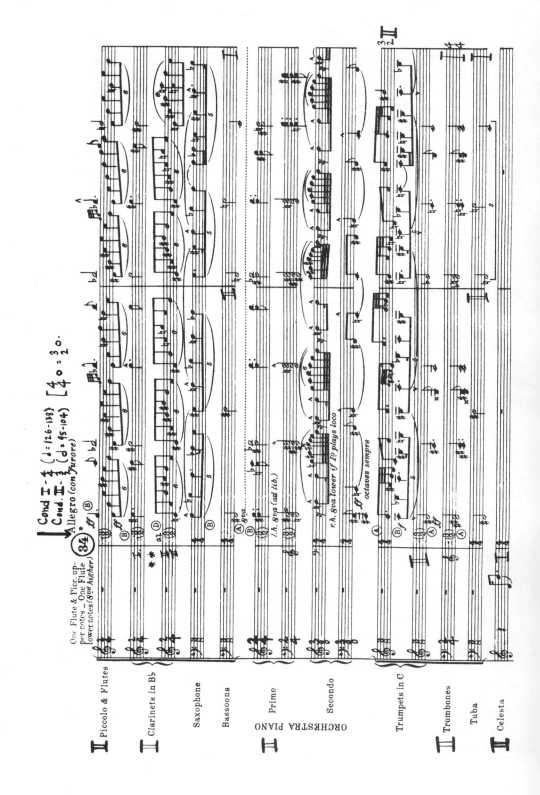

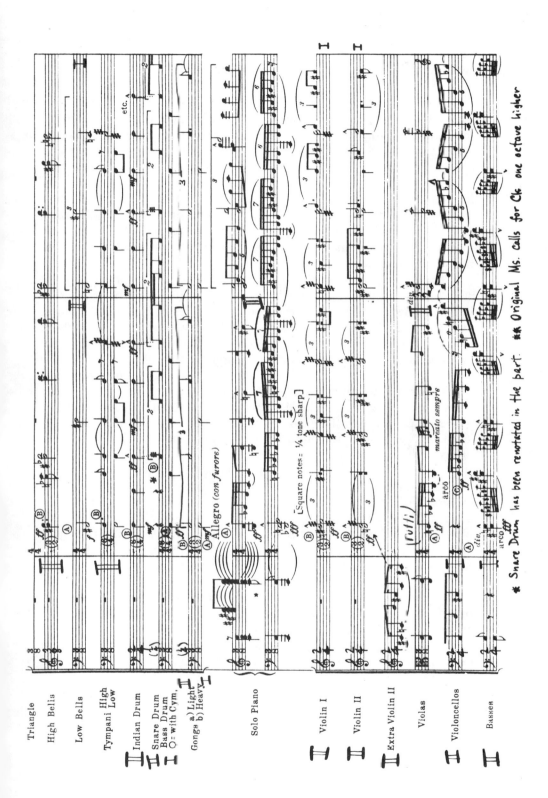

sweetly amidst a buzz of conversation. It is the elegant milieu of Mr. Smooth-it-away.[20]

Then the major factions of the battle—Pilgrims' hymns and street marches—move toward their respective climaxes. Syncopation breaks into the salon music, Charlie Ives ragging at the piano, and the music builds to another vertiginous, polyrhythmic march, the brass screaming above the fray. In response the strings break into a raggy combination of *Bethany* and "Throw Out the Lifeline," secularizing the sacred as Ives did in his *Ragtime Dances*. A brief interruption of hymn is thrust aside by the wildest vortex of sound yet.[21] With another dissolve we arrive at a calm within the storm. A solo violin sings *Beulah Land,* seeming frail and sentimental but undaunted, full of the lyric motive, accompanied mainly by somber chords and strange noodlings from the quarter-tone piano.[22]

Throughout the violin's solo we are waiting for the inevitable crash. It arrives as the hymn is about to cadence, an explosion Ives maybe intended to be the damnedest racket ever to come out of an orchestra. Just as in the climax of *Hawthorne,* the ruckus gradually condenses into "the Fourth of July in Concord," by way of *Country Band March*. Here is what the brassy material has been aiming for: an old-fashioned George Ives march tune, with nearly everybody on the same beat and even in the same key. But soon rhythms and tunes break up, wander off beat and off key, until we come to the entire orchestra yawping out "Yankee Doodle" in a half dozen keys at once, like a grotesque parody of the lyric motive, which indeed begins "Yankee Doodle." Then the Pilgrim's journey through modern life vanishes, as does Hawthorne's dream of the Celestial Railroad.

Of the third movement Fugue, Ives's program says only that it is "an expression of the reaction of life into formalism and ritualism." To the question of the Prelude, this is the response of conventional religion. Its setting is a New England church, the Fugue the kind of piece Ives used to play Sunday after Sunday at the organ.[23] This particular one, transferred from the First String Quartet to the Fourth Symphony, is in a way the most revolutionary movement of all. To follow the wild outburst of the *Comedy* with the apparently traditional harmony and counterpoint of the Fugue belies every concept of stylistic integrity traditional or Modernistic. Even for Ives the contrast is extreme. Yet he probably did not give the matter two thoughts. By then a meta-stylistic approach was so ingrained that he considered every kind of music in the same terms, and everything came out sounding like Ives. The Fourth Symphony is his attempt to say all he knew how to say, to fit in as much life, secular and spiritual, high and low, as he conceivably could. *Music is life*. Human experience contains Bach and New York and everything in between, and so should his symphony. In a way it was that simple. As Mahler proclaimed at the end of the Romantic era, and Ives here approached closer than anyone else: *a symphony should be a world.*

Besides, the Fugue is not so conventional as it appears. Here as in the other movements, the technique of ambiguity works to undercut conventional expectations and resolutions. There are maybe two firm harmonic cadences in the piece—at the stretto and just before, but not at, the end.[24] The conventional key structure of a fugue is carefully sidestepped. Even though the piece ends on the right chord, that chord falls on the wrong beat; the ending of this tonal Fugue is nearly as open as the atonal second movement. (The harmonic idiosyncrasies of the old Fugue may have, in fact, suggested to Ives the ambiguity he pursued throughout the symphony.[25])

The fugal theme is the missionary hymn "From Greenland's Icy Mountains," generally in the orbit of the lyric motive but containing elements of both that and the Urmotiv.[26] In the Fugue the lyric, hymnlike side of the symphony, beleaguered in the *Comedy,* finds its voice. The Fugue precedes in much the same gentle, beautiful way it did in the Quartet, now fleshed out in color with basses, flute, and clarinet, and with horns entering periodically in the manner of a Bach chorale prelude.[27] Finally the *stretto* arrives, the traditional place where entries of the fugue theme appear almost on top of one another. Instead of the main theme, which is the verse of "Greenland," Ives bases the stretto on the spacious refrain of the hymn.

That was the climax of the old Fugue. Now Ives adds a new section. The lines become chromatic and turbulent. The horns enter on pealing dissonances, their lines an upturned, questioning, questing version of the Urmotiv—the version that was heard, softly, at the end of the first movement. This new, dissonant, second climax integrates the Fugue into the harmonic and programmatic worlds of the other movements. In a way this passage is the fulcrum of the Fourth Symphony, where the Hero reappears to hurl his question at the immensities. It is that gesture that calls into being the mystical journey of the finale.

With a beautiful retransition the music sweeps back into the old Fugue.[28] It ends nearly as did the original, but with the addition of a delicate shadow line in clarinet, and a trombone playing a fragment of "Joy to the World": *And heav'n and nature sing . . . repeat the sounding joy.* Ives found that joy in a New England church, in the revealed religion he called in the *Essays* "the path between God and man's spiritual part—a kind of formal causeway."[29] Here that causeway is symbolized by the formal tradition of the fugue. The country church is not the end of the Pilgrim's journey, but for Ives it is a critical stopping place. The Fugue links the earthly and transcendent domains, the *Comedy* and the finale. Set in a steepled church, it represents a ritualization dead in itself but living as it shares the light of the spirit. Beyond the Christian specifics, the Fugue represents the place from where man looks upward to the glory-beaming star, the point of reciprocation between humanity and the divine.

Ives also writes in the *Essays,* "There comes from Concord an offer to every mind—the choice between repose and truth—and God makes the offer."[30] There is no repose in the Fugue, no unequivocal final cadence. Ives is after truth, not only ritual, and certainly not repose. Thus the finale.

Ives said, "The last movement is an apotheosis of the preceding content, in terms that have something to do with the reality of existence and its religious experience." If the *Comedy* is modern secular life, *the present;* and the Fugue the voice of formalized music and ritual, *the past;* then the finale is *the future*— at once evoking the transcendent future of music and of the religious spirit as Ives prophesied it.

It begins with sparse strokes on a group of percussion instruments he calls the "Battery Unit." They accumulate to form polyrhythmic patterns that continue quietly, independently, throughout the movement. The Battery Unit represents something like the pulse of the universe, the rhythms of the spheres.[31] As the percussion settles in, the orchestral basses murmur a line based on the refrain of *Bethany,* which in many hinted forms will be a penumbra around the music: *Still all my song shall be. . . .* The basses rise into a theme, the opening bass line from the Prelude, coming around again transformed. The beginning of the symphony is recomposed into a tone of meditation and enigma. Before, the basses' gesture was heroic, demanding, and based on D. In the finale it is a mysterious sigh, implying a tonal base on B.[32] It was B minor that blurred the D major of the Prelude, and that ambiguity emerges again in the finale, which drifts between tonality and atonality. The distant choir of strings and harp reappears, the glory-beaming star of the beginning. That group continues through much of the finale as it did in the Prelude.

In the orchestra melody begins to accumulate within an aura of foreground and background murmurs. It gathers to what would be called in German *unendliche Melodie,* endless melody, turning up the Urmotiv and lyric motive in continually new forms and contexts, suggesting now one hymn tune and now another, in rhythms sometimes moving forward, sometimes drifting. This endless line is an abstraction of hymn tunes. Below it the basses move from wandering rhythms to a quietly striding pulse and then are reabsorbed into the atmosphere. The ambiguities of the earlier movements—the harmonic equivocation of the Prelude, the rhythmic games of the *Comedy,* the tonal ambivalence of the Fugue—have found a kind of reconciliation: they melt into the vagueness Ives called, in the *Essays,* "an indication of nearness to a perfect truth." The texture accumulates with an extraordinary radiance of sound; its strands drift with an elusive but inexorable sense of movement forward. "Each sentence seems not to point to the next but to the undercurrent of all," Ives wrote of Emerson, and he quoted "every ultimate fact is only the first of a new series." Behind the foreground of the finale lies the penumbra, repeated over and over, *Nearer, my God*. . . . "Music may be yet unborn," Ives wrote. *Music* in the finale seems melted into primal sound, drifting toward new forms, melodies never heard before. In the *Essays* Ives quoted Sidney Lanier: "I think the time will come when music, rightly developed, to its now-little-foreseen grandeur will be found to be a late revelation of all gospels in one." Music will attain, Ives appended, "A conception unlimited by the narrow names of Christian, Pagan, Jew or Angel! A vision higher and deeper than art itself!" That time has not come and will not for many ages. But Ives wants to see how far he can get in the direction of that vision, toward a universal religion expressed in music, "a language so transcendent that its heights and depths will be common to all mankind."

A kind of abstract slow march takes shape. Above an inexorably down-striding bass the trumpets and horns spin out a line part *Bethany*, part *Dorr-nance*, part *Missionary Chant*.[33] The lines gather impetus and weight. Finally the trumpets are pealing out wild, free, ecstatic harmonies like flashing rays of light over the pounding strides of trombones and basses. (Here in the climax is the other part of the reconciliation of conflicting forces: rhythm boiled down to free rhythm in the upper parts, meterless pulse in the lower.) After this climax the music subsides into quietness and birdcalls, then into an echo of the march, slowing and dissolving in a many-stranded quodlibet of hymns (but also a touch of "As Freshmen First We Came to Yale"). From that texture magically emerges, as if by chance coalescing of natural forces, an old harmonic formula written a million times, but sounding as if it were discovered for the first time. It is a formula that prepares the arrival of the main chord in a key.[34] Here it leads to the coda of the finale, and the great cadence of the Fourth Symphony—back to the D major that was suggested, never resolved, in the beginning of the work.

With the cadence comes an ethereal chorus of voices, wordlessly singing the refrain of *Bethany* more plainly than it has been heard anywhere in the symphony. *Still all my prayer shall be*. . . . It is Ives's most profound consummation in cumulative form, a pervasive undercurrent rising to the surface like a revelation. In that mystical weaving of voices the Urmotiv and lyric motive are reconciled as they were destined to be all along. As the once-battling motives intertwine amidst the sounds of distant bells, they form in our mind the words that have permeated the music but were never so directly intimated before: *Nearer, my God, to Thee*. Here is the Pilgrim's destination, the answer to the first movement's question, *Watchman, tell us of the night*.[35] And then chorus and orchestra evanesce into the universal obscurity, as if the music were searching into the stars: *On joyful wing, / Cleaving the sky, / Sun, moon, and stars forgot, / Upward I fly*. The last notes we hear are a distant violin playing over and over B–F♯, B–F♯, blurring the fading D-major chord just as an added B blurred the Prelude's tonality. We have come full cycle, to a new beginning from a new place. The last sounds are soft strokes of percussion, the cosmic rhythm fading from our ears but not concluding. The music has not found its full cadence yet, but it has accomplished a long journey and brought us Pilgrims perhaps a little Nearer.

The finale's extraordinary effect of many strands united in a sounding radiance, its unmistakable sense of motion toward some end even if that end is unimaginable and never reached, its sense of the journey itself as an ecstasy and a vision, unites the Fourth Symphony with Ives's fondest imaginings for the human race.[36] He saw humanity moving forward as myriad individuals toward the millennium, perhaps not to be achieved for thousands of generations, but inevitable in its promise. He wrote of "a kind of glorified or transcendent democracy . . . willing to be leveled towards the infinite," of the "wondrous chain which links the heavens with the earth—the world of beings subject to one law."[37] He saw that mystery as a kind of answer, for the present. His music became an embodiment of his politics and his philosophy, a great chorus of individuals moving each on his and her own path toward the radiant future, following the law of the Majority that links humanity to the ethereal rhythms of earth and heavens.

Ives ended his preface for the publication of the *Comedy* with words that seal his superb vision of music and society, which all his music serves:

The future of music may not lie entirely with music itself, but rather in the way it makes itself a part with—in the way it encourages and extends, rather than limits, the aspirations and ideals of the people—the finer things that humanity does and dreams of.

Ives himself, of course, did not stop with the exalted vision of the Fourth Symphony. Inevitably he aspired to higher philosophies, a more unbounded canvas. But the vehicle of his greatest hopes, the *Universe Symphony,* escaped his grasp. Mainly in his imagination would resound its orchestras and choruses in mountains and valleys, its super-scales without octaves, its gigantic rhythmic cycles.[38] On a sketch page he wrote,

The "Universe in tones" or a Universe Symphony. A striving to present—to contemplate in tones rather than in music as such, that is—not exactly within the general term or meaning as it is so understood—to paint the creation the mysterious beginning of all things, known through God to man, to trace with tonal imprints the vastness, the evolution of all life, in nature of humanity from the great roots of life to the spiritual eternities from the great inknown to the great unknown.

He covered page after page with charts and graphs and plans and program notes. He made sketches (most have disappeared[39]), but eventually words and diagrams superseded notes. The tangible musical ideas fell into sporadic fragments, as finally did nearly everything else with Ives. He would add notes to the *Universe,* here and there, for the rest of his life. Eventually, turning his defeat into an entirely characteristic ideal, he declared he was leaving it for someone else to finish.[40]

In his greatest music Ives created, for the first time in Western history, a masterful art of suggestion, of ambiguity, of incompleteness.[41] He created forms open, in process, incomplete and incompletable in the world he lived in. Rather than a circle, a closed system, he built arcs that imply the possibility of completion. He had not fallen as far as many in this age, who know humankind does not have the answers and no longer believe we ever will. (The fragmentation of our art is not an implied wholeness. We can no longer conceive of wholeness.) Ives believed we would ask the questions long enough to find the answers, to accomplish on earth the triumph of the spirit, to make the human divine. He believed music to be central to that journey. So he left the *Universe Symphony* to be finished by others in the purifying flux of the ages, to be made complete at last.

Advances and Retreats

BY THE END OF 1926 Charles Ives was finished as a composer, in the sense that he could no longer conceive and pull together a piece. It would be some time before he confronted that, if he ever entirely did. For the rest of his days, captive to an inexorable rhythm of up and down swings in health, he would keep sitting down to the piano when he had the energy to sit at all. He added notes to the *Universe Symphony,* copied and arranged and edited works, restored ideas he had watered down, and penciled new ideas around and on top of old notes—often adding more complexity, more dissonance. He did that because his creative mind had not stopped even if his ability to command it had. He did it because he had decided the Rollos and sissies and old ladies of the world needed to be rebuked, even by the music itself. And he did it to convince himself that he was still a composer and still alive: for Charles Ives, those amounted to the same thing.

The central story of his last twenty-five years is the voyage of his music into the world. By and large in this century, an artist's reputation is spread by relentless promotion. Ives would aid that process as best he could, when he could; his friends and admirers did the legwork (sometimes with Ives obstructing them). His champions would keep at the public until the force of the music could make its own case. That process was still proceeding when Ives died, though by then it was clear his music had found a niche. All the same, in his lifetime his work never reached the place it deserved, among the artists with whom he belongs. If Ives is not the peer of his musical heroes Bach, Beethoven, and Brahms, he belongs in their company. A few people, very few, understood that from early on. For all his modesty, Ives understood it too.

In January 1927, shortly after Ives had told Harmony he couldn't compose any more, an event occurred that would have seemed impossible a few years before, given the practical hurdles and the composer's lack of recognition: the first two movements of the Fourth Symphony were to be played at Town Hall in New York, by fifty Philharmonic musicians under the baton of

Eugene Goossens. The occasion was a Pro Musica International Referendum Concert, one of the most ambitious E. Robert Schmitz's group had attempted. Schmitz assigned himself the intimidating solo piano part in the *Comedy*. The original intention was to do the whole symphony, but that idea was soon abandoned; Ives would share the program with music by Debussy and Darius Milhaud. Ives helped out behind the scenes, among other things inviting the percussionists to the house on 74th Street to pound out their parts for them on the kitchen table. He had Milhaud to lunch.[1]

Eugene Goossens put in an appearance at the house to go over the score. Belgian-born and British-trained, he was then a rising conductor and prolific composer of post-Debussy orientalisms, and the *Comedy* was not his cup of tea.[2] Besides, Goossens knew his players would be lucky to get from one end of it to the other. He had been sitting up night after night trying to make sense of the *Comedy* and find some way of faking through it. When he came to the house, Goossens was as impressed and bemused as most people by the singular spectacle of Charles Ives. During their talk Ives pulled out a chamber piece that included a basset horn, an instrument mostly forgotten by then. When the conductor suggested substituting a modern bass clarinet or bassoon, Ives lectured for ten minutes on the excellence of the instrument (his father had played it), then sat down at the piano and performed an imitation of a basset horn so realistic that Goossens's assistant, who had come with him, peeked around the door to see if a player was hiding in the hall. It was a moment so weird, so unexpected, that Goossens never forgot it.

Charlie and Harmony came to the rehearsals at Town Hall but invariably stayed hidden in the green room backstage, where they could hardly hear anything. Goossens would come back to consult and Harmony would slip out while "the men" talked. Nothing could entice Charlie to come into the hall and face the players. They thought he was a snob. He was simply too scared.[3]

It is hard to imagine the temper of the audience at Town Hall on January 29, 1927, hearing two movements of the Fourth Symphony—the Prelude dominated by a heartfelt setting of a simple hymn tune, then the rampaging *Comedy*. At the best of times it is hard to tell when a genuinely new voice is speaking. Among the audience was a young pianist named John Kirkpatrick. Though he was destined to become Ives's leading champion, the main thing Kirkpatrick remembered was Schmitz working heroically at one piano while two players belabored another, "and everybody producing general pandemonium, which to my ears at that time was completely opaque."[4] When somebody asked Goossens about it later he replied, "My dear boy, I didn't know what happened after the downbeat."[5] As Ives left the hall he caught this exchange between two listeners: "Is Debussy dead?" "Yes." "Is Ives dead?" "No, but he ought to be."[6]

All of which makes the reviews the more astonishing. Some critics recognized, or at least suspected, that something significant had happened. Contrary to later legend, from that early point Ives would receive, once in a while, critical admiration of a kind many artists never get in a lifetime. In a long review for the *New York Times,* the celebrated Olin Downes wrote an appreciation that for enthusiasm and insight has only occasionally been bettered (though he got the composer's name wrong):

At the risk of appearing provincial, chauvinistic, this writer records that his preference among the new works of the afternoon was for the music of Mr. St. Ives. This music is not nearly as compact, as finished in workmanship, as smart in tone, as that of Mr. Milhaud, but it rings truer. . . . The thing is an extraordinary hodge-podge, but something that lives and that vibrates with conviction is there . . . a "gumption," as the New Englander would say, not derived from some "Sacre du printemps," or from anything but the conviction of a composer who has not the slightest idea of self-ridicule and who dares to jump with feet and hands and a reckless somersault or two on his way. . . . It is genuine, if it is not a masterpiece, and that is the important thing.[7]

On the other hand Pitts Sanborn, whose tolerance for Modernist manifestations was limited, headlined his review of the Pro Musica Referendum Concert "Pro-Musica or Anti?" and ended, *"Initiative, referendum; why not recall?"*[8] The *New Yorker* elegantly scratched its chin: "There was one hilarious weekend of new music not so long ago. . . . Mr. Ives is a strange figure in music. Several years ago he distributed a volume of . . . songs, all of them slightly queer, and some of them entirely so. The same quality of madness was evident in the symphonic movements. . . . However, we should like to hear more of Mr. Ives' output. He seems to be thumbing his nose most of the time, but, after all, it is his own nose." Lawrence Gilman, who a dozen years later would write historic words about Ives, wrote on his first encounter: "This music is as indubitably American in impulse and spiritual texture as the prose of Jonathan Edwards . . . it has at times an irresistible veracity and strength, an uncorrupted sincerity. This symphony of Mr. Ives is evidently built upon a far-reaching spiritual plan. . . . [We] should like to hear the entire score."[9]

Gilman would be long dead and so would Ives when Leopold Stokowski finally played the entire symphony in 1965. Ten years after the *Comedy* premiere, Olin Downes had to be reminded that he had ever heard anything by Charles Ives. In other words, little happened in the wake of the concert. As would often be the case, though, in the long run that little counted for a lot.

In July of 1927 Ives received a letter from composer, pianist, and promoter Henry Cowell. He invited Ives to subscribe to his new publication called *New Music Quarterly,* to submit scores for consideration, and to join the New Music Society of California advisory board.[10] Ives did as requested, writing Cowell, "Your idea of a circulating music library via a magazine of unsaleable scores is admirable."[11] The first score published in *New Music Quarterly* was Carl Ruggles's *Men and Mountains.* Immediately half the subscribers canceled. After having a look at Ruggles's music, Ives ordered twenty-five more subscriptions for himself.[12] Ives, Cowell, and Ruggles were about to become a team that would endure, with one near-tragic interruption for the rest of their lives.

In 1914 Henry Cowell arrived for his first composition lesson with Charles Seeger at the University of California, Berkeley. On Seeger's piano rack the seventeen-year-old composer placed his Opus 108.[13] Those pieces included *The Tides of Manaunaun,* in which the pianist uses elbows and fore-arms to produce roaring tone clusters. Cowell had been born near San Francisco in 1897, the son of two Bohemian would-be poets. The parents divorced and he often had to support his improvident mother. At one point, sick and marooned in New York, Cowell and his mother nearly starved before a friend gave them money to buy a sack of cornmeal, on which they survived for weeks.[14] For all the poverty Henry was brilliant and precocious. He studied piano and taught himself composition, turning out pieces in a welter of styles. Like Charles Ives, Cowell discovered tone clusters in his youth, and like Ives he came to see clashing harmonies—dissonance—as a kind of holy cause.

Cowell's perception of new harmonies and rhythms as revolutionary musical resources arrived early. The teenaged Charles Ives did not set out to be a rebel; Henry Cowell did. Even though Ives finally picked up some of Cowell's attitude (in his fashion), that difference would remain between them and their respective musics: Ives's innovations developed largely from imitative, humanistic, spiritual, and innately musical concerns, while Cowell aspired to be an inventor of artistic technologies, a kind of musical Thomas Edison. What success Cowell found would reflect that presentation of himself as inventor, as self-proclaimed Ultra-Modernist in an age obsessed with invention. Aaron Copland once called Cowell more inventor than composer.

As a youth impoverished, ambitious, resourceful, and personable, Henry developed a fine skill at acquiring friends and patrons, some of them from a theosophical community at Halcyon, on the California coast. Cowell showed up at a meeting there, listened to the group's hymns, and announced that they should not be singing that stuff but his music instead. They did. (Naturally, Scriabin was a favorite there too.) At Halcyon in the early 1920s Cowell became friends with Dane Rudhyar, whose piano music would be in vogue for a while, but whose main career would be as an occultist and astrologer.[15] Rudhyar's titles reflected his preoccupations: *The Surge of Fire, Threshold of Light, Prophetic Rite,* and so on—the music ecstatic, visionary, and fiercely dissonant.

Cowell met Carl Ruggles during his first stay in Greenwich Village. Those two and Rudhyar formed the leading edge of avant-garde music in the United States in the early twenties. Of the three, Henry had the best promotional skills, plus the fundamental generosity to help get other composers' works into circulation. Cowell's first, triumphant concert tour of Europe came in 1923. He returned to the States to make a spectacular Carnegie Hall debut. Around then he first heard the name Charles Ives, something about these bizarre self-published books floating around. Ruggles and Seeger advised Cowell not to bother with this crank.[16]

Henry Cowell.

With an October 1925 Los Angeles concert of Rudhyar, Varèse, Schoenberg, and Ornstein, Cowell launched the New Music Society, finally based in San Francisco. His intention was to make the Society a forum for Ultra-Modernist composers on the West Coast. He founded *New Music Quarterly* in 1927, to publish the same composers' scores.[17] That year as well, he joined Edgard Varèse and others to form the Pan-American Association of Composers, based in New York. With the presence of these two groups on opposite coasts and Cowell's periodical, plus Schmitz's Pro Musica and the League of Composers, a spectrum of new music from conservative to avant-garde thrived about as well as it ever would in the United States—always precariously, mostly outside the mainstream, but with a small and loyal audience. The later twenties were an exhilarating time to be a revolutionary composer in America. Much was happening, everything seemed possible, and everybody knew everybody else at least by reputation.

Though Cowell had been warned off Ives, the *Comedy* performance—and probably grapevine reports of this businessman's money—led Cowell to make his invitation. When Ives ordered twenty-five extra subscriptions of *New Music,* Cowell realized, if he hadn't before, that he had a prize fish on the line. He wrote Ives, "You asked me some time ago whether you could do anything for the Pan American—if you feel like donating something to it financially, it would be of great aid."[18] Ives responded with an offer of regular support for both the Pan-American Association and *New Music Quarterly*. (As it would turn out, one-third of *New Music*'s support during its thirty-year history flowed, anonymously, from Ives.[19] When he died, *New Music* soon followed.)

Cowell was quick to realize there was more to Ives than a bank account. On September 19, 1928, pianist Arthur Hardcastle premiered one of the *Emerson Transcriptions* at a New Music Society concert in San Francisco. It was the first of many Ives performances sponsored by the group. Moreover, Cowell decided to publish the *Comedy* from the Fourth Symphony.

The course of that bold venture foreshadowed much Ives publication in the next decades. The combined effects of his health interrupting his ability to work, the scruffy state of some manuscripts, his compulsive tinkering with the music, the unprecedented complexity of some of it, and his insistence on paying for publication while forbidding royalties or even copyright, would make publishing Ives a tough proposition.

At their first meeting in New York, Ives and Cowell agreed to set publication of the *Comedy* for the October 1928 issue of *New Music Quarterly* Meanwhile the second issue, Dane Rudhyar's *Paeans,* had further decimated subscribers. At that point the journal had less than a hundred dollars in the bank.[20] Even though Ives was ready to pay all expenses for his engraving, it was unlikely to boost sales. Moreover Cowell's San Francisco engravers refused to deal with the score, as did others in Chicago and Philadelphia, and Schirmer in New York.[21] The *Comedy* finally landed in the hands of engraver Herman Langinger, who was up to the job. During the eight months of work on the score, Ives visited him regularly to give advice, answer questions, and provide largesse. Langinger's extraordinary score came out in *New Music,* only a few months late, in January 1929.

Few Ives publications would go so smoothly again. Even then, potential disaster struck when he discovered *New Music* had copyrighted the piece against his wishes. At a meeting Ives strode up and down the room brandishing a cane, his face bright red, proclaiming, "EVERYBODY who wants a copy is to have one! If anyone wants to copy or reprint these pieces, that's FINE! This music is not to make money but to be known and heard. Why should I interfere with its life by hanging on to some sort of personal legal right in it?"[22] Cowell de-copyrighted it in a hurry.

As with the American avant-garde generally, the later twenties would be exhilarating years for Ives's music. Performances, mostly of songs and piano works, spread around the country and made inroads into Europe. Five pianists (none of them Schmitz) took up Ives. In March 1928 Katherine Heyman played *Emerson* and lectured on it for the radio in Paris; Oscar Ziegler played *Alcotts* in New York in May 1928 and two months later at the Mozarthaus during the Salzburg Festival; Arthur Hardcastle's *Emerson Transcriptions* performance came that September in San Francisco; Anton Rovinsky played *The*

Celestial Railroad at Town Hall in November; and in December young Keith Corelli began a series of *Emerson* performances with one in Santa Barbara, California.

Of those, Ziegler seems to have been the only first-rate pianist fully on top of the music. Katherine Heyman would never be much of an Ivesian and was a cryptic figure on the whole. (One of her radio lectures ended, "It is natural then—that evolution should give us a Scriabin and a Charles Ives, whose emotions in music are beyond the Human Emotions—that pass like a white cloud—before the moon!") She was then living in Paris partly on Ives's manna, specializing in modern composers generally and Scriabin particularly. Keith Corelli, for another example, would play *Emerson* on a Modernist program through an extensive concert tour. Clifton Furness wrote Ives in April 1929, "Keith descends on Boston this week. He wrote appreciatively of his visit with you."[23] Reviews of the tour mostly ranged from bewildered to savage. From Germany, Cowell wrote in June, "I am glad to hear that Corelli is a normal young fellow. . . . I still hear occasional strange things about how he quotes critics who never have written about him."[24] Finally Corelli took his Modernists to Europe, but was called back by the death of his mother and disappeared from the chronicle.[25]

Ives performances became almost regular in the 1928–29 concert season. The First Violin Sonata and the *Emerson Transcriptions* were played at New Music Society concerts in San Francisco; soprano Mary Bell sang "Serenity" and "The Things Our Fathers Loved" at Carnegie Hall; *Thoreau* was part of a wild concert by Elliott Carter and Furness for a group called "Friends and Enemies of Modern Music" in Hartford. On the latter program they also played Stravinsky's *Sacre du printemps* in the piano-four-hands arrangement, plus works by Schoenberg, Milhaud, Poulenc, Casella, Malpiero, Satie, Hindemith, and Antheil. Afterward, Furness reported to Ives, there was "general interest, even enthusiasm . . . but [few went] so far as to say they really liked it." Furness added, "Many people came up afterwards to speak about you, and the warm affection for the Twichells which is a permanent Hartford tradition. Several said, 'I remembered Charley Ives but it never occurred to me that he was that Ives who writes all this modern music.' "[26]

So Ives was known now, even if the kind of known figure whom most people have never actually encountered. Generally he was mentioned in the same breath as the notorious Modernists: Schoenberg, Stravinsky, Hindemith, Cowell, Ornstein et al. A reputation, however distorted, was forming and the curious gathered. In June 1927 Katherine Heyman wrote, in a note to Ives, "Introducing Mr. John Kirkpatrick Jr. who likes your music."[27] Soon a letter arrived from that young man:

Would I be troubling you too much to ask you how I could obtain a copy of your "Concord, Mass." Sonata? Miss Heyman showed it to me in Paris. . . . I must admit that I feel as yet only the more diatonic Alcotts, but I would love to study the work further. I am an amateur musician on the brink of becoming a professional, and very much interested in almost anything concerning American music.[28]

By his own later description John Kirkpatrick at that point, age twenty-two, was a spoiled and lazy rich kid.[29] Handsome and dandyish, he was part of Heyman's circle and so ran with an arty, polysexual Parisian crowd amidst the intoxicating atmosphere of Joyce and Pound and Hemingway, Janet Flanner and Djuna Barnes and George Antheil, Picasso and Stravinsky. In that period Kirkpatrick kept a mistress financed by his brother and flirted with the occult. He had dropped out of Princeton and hated to practice, but was nonetheless serious about music. For a while he studied with Nadia Boulanger, the French pedagogue whose American pupils included Copland, Virgil Thomson, and Samuel Barber. Boulanger believed the United States was about to lead the world in music. By the time Kirkpatrick wrote Ives, he was playing the recitals of American works he would pursue for the rest of his career. Kirkpatrick became an advocate not only of Ives but of MacDowell, Griffes, Gottschalk, Rudhyar, Ruggles, Harris, Copland, and many others. It would be years, though, before he brought his technique up to playing the entire *Concord*.

Now strangers were writing Ives, intrigued by what they had seen and heard. He had friends, admirers, a growing collection of kind words from critics (along with the protests), something like a milieu (Ultra-Modernists and their circle), regular performances, exciting possibilities for the future, maybe the realization of his most extravagant dreams. Despite that satisfaction his health was deteriorating, and with it his state of mind.

Ives's letters of the later twenties trace periods when he could not make it to work at Ives & Myrick or see to his musical correspondence because he was bedridden. In mid-October 1928 he wrote Cowell (they were trading letters regularly): "I should have written sooner but about the middle of last month I got laid up just as I was planning to get 2 weeks vacation."[30] To T. Carl Whitmer in July of the next year, "About the middle of April I ran into one of those bad spells . . . and haven't been able to do anything—business, music, or correspondence. Am getting around now though the doctors say I'll have to go slow all summer."[31] When he could, he got out to concerts. He heard Ravel play during a tour in January 1928, perhaps heard Bartók and violinist Joseph Szigeti at a Pro Musica concert the next month, and heard Rovinsky play *The Celestial Railroad* at Town Hall in November. Just as often, Ives could not make it out the door to hear or see anybody.

On top of the spells of physical debility came depression. Ives spoke less of that, but as had been the case earlier in the teens, dejection and discouragement show up between the lines of letters and memos. In a draft of a 1927 letter to Whitmer (noted "not sent/cut down") Ives all but dismisses his own work:

You ask about my violin sonatas. . . . I don't know exactly what to say about them. They were written one after another some time ago and they look it. . . . I should say that the principle [sic] trouble with the sonatas is that they were not first thought of in terms of the piano and violin but shoved on them as the handiest things around. I am afraid that in "thinking up" music I usually have some kind of a brass band with wings on it in back of my mind and when it comes to putting it down on paper it turns the nearest corner. Now you know that's not the way to do it. One was played a few years ago here at a sonata recital with two others by Pizzetti and Milhaud. I learned from the newspapers that Pizzetti's was so bad that none could be worse and that Milhaud's and mine were worse.[32]

Ives & Myrick continued to prosper. In 1928 the *Herald Tribune* wrote: "The Ives & Myrick agency has shown a steady growth since its organization in 1909. This is simply the result of hard work, progressive ideas and sound principles. . . . It is one of the great agencies of the country." By then the agency was fattening more on its list of clients than on new ideas. Ives was no longer producing grand visions like *The Amount to Carry*. His advertising copy that had once been to the point ("Loses Fortune, Wife, Children") took on grandiose overtones that probably befuddled readers. In a 1929 ad, perhaps his last one, Ives headlines Emerson—*I appeal from your customs; I must be myself!*—and solicits agents with a paean to individualism.

Mollie Ives died at seventy-nine on January 25, 1929, in the old house now moved up the hill from Main Street. Charlie and Moss had seen to her needs over the years and visited, but she remained as nearly invisible as ever. No extant letter from Ives mentions his mother's death. In the middle of that year he suffered a bout of neuritis in his arms and couldn't touch the piano for months. It was around then that he grew his beard; his skin had gotten too sensitive to shave. The neuritis left behind a palsy that made his handwriting in ink shake uncontrollably; the effect would come and go, but he never entirely lost what he called his "snake tracks." Increasingly he would write out drafts of letters in pencil and in third person, for Harmony or Edie to recopy as if the letter were from them. Embarrassed by his frailty as by his handwriting, he became less willing to have anybody but friends see him. (Asking family to write out letters also kept him at a remove from the world, a position he had always preferred anyway.)

Diabetes was kicking in hard by 1929. Among its chain of torments, if there was impotence involved it may have appeared around then. Ives began to rave even more than before about pansies and pussies and emasculation. A memo from this period shows his habit of grabbing a piece of paper and blowing off steam:

Emasculating America, for Money! Has the seed of "1776" gone soft? Is the Anglo-Saxon going "pussy"[?] The nice Lizzies, the ta ta boys, of today, the . . . "play it pretty" minds, the "old gals" running the Broadcasting Co's, the great national brain softeners the movies, the mind-dulling Tabloids, the easy concert-hall parlor, entertainment . . . they all get theirs & America is gradually losing her "manhood." The Puritans may have been . . . hard-minded "rock eaters" but they were not "effeminates."[33]

To a similar memo he attached a footnote that shows his tirades were not simple misogyny: "Emasculated is used not as a reflection on the ladies—that is all the ladies—or because Prof. Ladd finds according to his examination of the premises . . . that ladies are inherently incapable of composing music— that men . . . *can*."[34] In practice if not in rhetoric, Ives was as progressive on women's matters as on most things. His egalitarian impulses drove him to believe in votes, careers, equal pay, equal creative potential for women. Like his philosophy and politics his language was an exaggeration of his time. With Theodore Roosevelt and many of that generation, "manly," "emasculated," "mollycoddle," and so on were common shibboleths. Homophobia (a word not yet invented) went along with all that in a characteristically American complex. In *The American People* Geoffrey Gorer writes,

[The] concept of being a sissy is a key concept for the understanding of American character; it has no exact parallel in any other society. It . . . can be applied to anyone, regardless of age or sex. . . . Schematically, it means showing more dependence or fear or lack of initiative or passivity than is suitable for the occasion. . . . Among the generality of Americans homosexuality is regarded not with distaste, disgust, or abhorrence but with panic; it is seen as an immediate and personal threat. . . . Because every American man has a feminine component in his personality, there is always a deeply hidden doubt concerning his own masculinity, and any person or situation which might bring this into question is seen as a drastic threat to a man's integrity and reacted to with violence and panic.[35]

Violence and panic exactly describe Ives's response to the specter of homosexuality, which was part of a fear of feminization even more threatening to him than to most artists of his time. From childhood on, when he was "partly ashamed" of music and feared friends would call him sissy for playing the organ, when in church and in recitals women led the charge against his experiments, it had eaten at him: the clubs full of genteel ladies who aspired to the refined and sublime, who inhabited the Literary Circles and the Afternoon Music Societies and the Symphony Dames and the church choirs, who implacably aspired to elevate the spirit and mind of their communities and to redeem rough randy Man. These ladies came to symbolize to Charles Ives the enemy, the immovable obstruction between him and his dreams, the reactionary force that kept his most daring and heartfelt music bottled up in his study like a tempest in a teapot, boiling and boiling. Those carping church ladies: "Mr. Ives, it was awful!" The aristocratic ones like Elizabeth Sprague Coolidge: "It is not, to my mind, music." Those he branded critics with skirts, who wanted to feminize art, to keep it polite and uplifting and *pretty*. Charles Ives was not fair toward these women, he was not reasonable, and through the long years of physical and mental decline his hatred for what they symbolized branded his spirit. But at its inception, his fury was founded on experience as a shy composer of shocking music. In response Ives could only rant in private, and the most damning word in his blistering vocabulary of invective was the word *nice*.

If Ives's diatribes against the "old ladies of both sexes" were irrational, unfair, neurotic, they were not crazy and not ultimately misogynistic. Nor did he originally use dissonance as a way of proclaiming his manhood and shocking the ladies. Dissonance was part of his musical language from the beginning, from childhood when he practiced drum parts on the piano with his fists. Later, when physical debility and rage and maybe impotence settled in, dissonance would indeed become his way of striking back at the lilypads—the main way he had left to strike back.

In the 1920s and 1930s Ives began to go over some of his pages and change consonances to dissonances. Little of that process would arise from his natural musicality and spirituality, but rather from his rage and frustration. It was a kind of self-betrayal. And in that period he began to write (not for public consumption) those juvenile notes about the old composers: "One just naturally thinks of Chopin with a skirt on." His rage was one of the bricks in his wall of defenses, but his failing health, and that wall itself, conspired to cut him off from the musical mainstream and from the greater world. His gateway to the outside had to be through others, mainly by way of the sympathetic generosity of Henry Cowell. Henry, as Ives would admiringly have put it, was a *man*.

Finally it became too much for Ives to pretend he could live as he had. In July 1929 he wrote Mike Myrick,

It's an uncomfortable enough feeling to be drawing full profits and not be able to be on the job. . . . I realize fully now that I could not keep going for another year—though I always want to do anything I can to help you & the office. . . . My main regret is entirely one of sentiment—for you. . . . If I'd had as much sense as [Mrs. Ives] I would have resigned some time ago. . . . The reasons partly that I didn't "come to this sooner" was that for certain periods I seemed quite all right, & felt I could go on forever. But lately these times have been shorter & farther apart. This last bad spell hasn't been so much due altogether to the physical condition—it's been more of a general running down—and there's been a kind of depression that I can't account for.[36]

His official retirement date would be January 1, 1930. Throwing in the towel at work was in a way the most profound letting go and giving in Ives could do. His inspiration had deserted him, but he still had hopes it would return. (Letters of that period dealing with his financing a quarter-tone piano mention his desire to compose on it.) Even though he had always been more devoted to music than to insurance, even though he had been sacrificing business to music for some time, and even though he had planned to retire to music entirely, still Ives & Myrick had been part of Ives's identity. He had not chosen to leave at his own time and on his own terms but had it forced on him. Never in his life had he quit anything that way, not even when he chose to leave his last church job

With this forced retirement his energy and confidence slipped another notch.[37] All the same, Ives did not entirely leave the business he loved. For years Myrick would come over on Sundays when the Iveses were in New York and the partners would talk shop for the afternoon. Every Christmas for years after he left, Ives sent checks to everyone in the office.

Around the time he decided to retire, Ives produced what amounted to his last song. From the singing of a Miss Evelyn Stiles he took down the black spiritual "In the Mornin'." A note on the score says, "Miss Stiles remembers from her father, Major Robert Stiles, of Richmond, Va., who heard it when a boy." With the simple but profound affirmation of the text and the music, Ives in the ashes of his creative life turned back to religion and to his father's Civil War, and made one of his most beautiful settings of an old tune:

> In the mornin' when I rise,
> Give me Jesus!
> You can have all the world, but
> Give me Jesus!

Around the time he gave up on business, Ives received a letter of inquiry from Nicolas Slonimsky, whom he had met through Henry. This young, ambitious, and extravagant Russian émigré played piano, composed a little, and had literary and linguistic inclinations, but at that point mainly wanted to establish himself as a conductor. He had fled the Revolution and in Paris became secretary to conductor Serge Koussevitzky. Following Koussevitzky to Boston, Slonimsky served for a couple years as a musical crutch for a conductor with shaky technical skills before he was fired for (so he claimed) showing off too much.

In 1927 Slonimsky established the Chamber Orchestra of Boston, partly with the intention of disseminating Ultra-Modern music.[38] The orchestra and its conductor naturally attracted the attention of Henry Cowell. Soon Slonimsky's piano studies appeared in *New Music;* Cowell included the younger man in his article "Four Little Known Modern Composers" (the others being Ives, Carlos Chávez, and Adolph Weiss); and in 1929 Slonimsky conducted in Boston a Cowell piece for piano and chamber orchestra that included *The Banshee,* its ululations created by scraping the piano strings.[39] (After soloing in that performance Cowell headed for the Soviet Union, where he was the first American to concertize since the Revolution.[40])

Cowell regularly preached Ives to Slonimsky, and in 1928 the two were invited to lunch at the Iveses' in New York. Slonimsky recalled of their meeting, "There was something endearingly old-fashioned in his way of life; he spoke in trenchant aphorisms, akin to the language of Thoreau and Emerson."[41] In due time Ives made a proposal:

Henry Cowell told me that you had been kind enough to ask for a score of mine which your orchestra might play. I should have written before but have been laid up for some months. . . . I have one which I got out the other day and played for Henry Cowell who liked it and thought it should be played, and could be, with some revisions reducing it to the chamber group. The 1st and last movement lend themselves quite readily, but the 2nd which has some old "brass-band and town-tune" things in it, has a considerable brass part. But, I remember, this (in part) was first played by a theater orchestra. . . . They made it go quite well with only a cornet and trombone,—a piano taking off the rest of the brass. So, I think, it can be brought down with the help of a piano part. At any rate I'm going ahead with it on this basis.[42]

Rather than picking a safe piece like the Third Symphony, Ives had decided to propose *Three Places in New England,* trimming that work for large orchestra to the twenty-four players Slonimsky commanded. In the process Ives first went back to the original sketches, adding new layers and ideas and often more dissonance and rhythmic complexity.[43] Some of the revisions restored things he had watered down in the original full-orchestra score. The changes also reflect Ives's creative evolution since that score, the experience of composing the Fourth Symphony and working at the *Universe.* His music had grown steadily more complex, richer in texture, bolder. The fact that he had been welcomed into a community of avant-garde composers encouraged him to be bolder still. The less clearheaded of his revisions came again from rage against the "old ladies of both sexes." Ives had placed "Majority" at the beginning of *114 Songs* to shock the sissies, and in his dotage that motive would periodically sully his thinking and his ideals.

All the same, in the end Ives made a fine job of his 1929 arrangement of *Three Places.* From his experience with theater orchestras he was resourceful in giving the piano some of the wind and brass parts he had to cut back. Slonimsky recalled that when he looked over the result for the first time, "I experienced a strange, but unmistakable, feeling that I was looking at a work of genius."[44] He agreed to play it.

In February 1930, a year before the official premiere, Slonimsky conducted the *Three Places* for a committee of the International Society of Contemporary Music, as a prospect for one of the organization's international concerts. As would become his habit, Slonimsky stayed with the Iveses during the rehearsals. (Cowell was around too.) Always there was great excitement in the household when Slonimsky arrived. As soon as the little Russian would walk in from 74th Street there would be shouting from Ives in the studio four floors up, and the piano rang all day as the two of them swapped off at the keyboard.[45]

The national ISCM committee recommended *Three Places* for performance but the international committee turned it down. It was one of the most bitter rejections Ives ever received. He was getting older and sicker and needed all the assurance he could get that his work would not turn to dust. His letter to Slonimsky on hearing the news, written from Richmond where he and Harmony were vacationing, is almost incoherent with anger:

The action of the "Non-contemporary Society of Music & Commercial Travelers" is a good one—for our vanity. . . . We can be good sports, as the man said when the undertaker came in— and when they ask for more American beauties we can say "nix on that stuff—you know me Al!"—and Johny Spiel Auf [Austrian Ernst Krenek's jazz opera] will put it to American Music. In a new country like ours, children should be obscene & not heard—but the real cause of the situation is the Republican Party, they kept us [out of the] L[eague] of N[ations] Chorus & we are still out.[45]

Back from vacation, Ives learned that the premiere had been set for the following January, 1931. Feeling placated and well enough, he went to hear Henry Cowell solo in his Piano Concerto with the Conductorless Orchestra. Cowell had begun directing music at the New School for Social Research in New York, a hub for leftists political and artistic, who indeed tended to travel together in those days.[47] (Most of the leading American composers of that era were Marxist in some degree, Cowell among the Reddest.) Henry's presence in New York brought the two men closer. Ives paid Leon Theremin, inventor of the eponymous electronic instrument, to build a "Rhythmicon" to Henry's specifications. (It would be built, but results were disappointing.) Cowell had come to see Ives as a musical and spiritual father, and Ives felt paternal toward this young man who was devoting himself to the cause of progressive American music and maybe doing more for it than anyone else. In 1930, as part of his endless drumming, Cowell included Ives in his article "Three Composers" for *The New Freeman*. His historic book *American Composers on American Music* would come out in 1933, with his essay on Ives and a short one by Ives.

In September 1930 Mike Myrick, part of a world far from Ives's new crowd, made his testimonial to his retired partner with a page in the *Eastern Underwriter*. Headed "What the Business Owes to Charles E. Ives," it was the final cadence of a brilliant career in life insurance. "His creative mind," Myrick wrote, "great breadth of culture, intensive sympathies and keen understanding of the economic as well as of the material needs of the community made it possible for him to evolve literature which paved the way for additional sales of life insurance and helped straighten out complications which confront the underwriter. . . . The passing years will demonstrate that his philosophy will ever hold good."[48]

Both Iveses wrote thanks. Said Charlie: "The page . . . with your fine thoughts of me was unexpected—and also a good deal undeserved. . . . Harmony says it is typical of you—of your friendship, fine mind and heart—that you've always seemed more like a member of the family, than a business partner. . . . Reading it made me feel less low in mind than I do sometimes." Said Harmony: "He is an extraordinary man and what he has done in the two fields of business & music shows unusual brain power doesn't it? He is so modest he thinks little of himself and I am most glad to have you say in public what you think. . . . Charlie has had a good summer on the whole but he hasn't the grip on things that I hope to see him have again. We are going off next week for a short vacation for me—I want to shake housekeeping for a week or two!"

The month before, they had fled to Quebec, from where Ives wrote Slonimsky, "We didn't intend as much of a trip as this but Mrs. Ives seemed pretty much tired out with the long job of housekeeper, chauffeur, nurse and general caretaker—and needed a rest. . . . We went to the old English church this morning, the 'Plain Chant' and canticles, sung by everybody in unison, each one making a little music of his own to Mr. Tallis—may stand as a point of departure into collective composing—and the universal 'Lyre.' "[49] Harmony's exhaustion and frustration, which at times boiled into breakdown, would drive them on several vacations during the decade. They were trying to outrun their suffering.

The premiere of *Three Places in New England* by Nicolas Slonimsky and his Chamber Orchestra of Boston was set for New York's Town Hall. Ives laid out some $15,000 (1991) to bankroll the concert.[50] Sharing the program would be Mozart's First Symphony and *Musical Joke,* a piece by British composer Robin Milford, Cowell's *Marked Passages,* and Ruggles's *Men and Mountains.* It had been the publication of the latter that might have sunk *New Music Quarterly* had Ives not come to the rescue. (Ives and Ruggles had met by then, perhaps in 1929, and each had come to see the other as his favorite composer.)

Ives was terrifically excited. He wrote Slonimsky, "You're the only conductor that ever asked me to do anything. This score would never have gotten off the shelf, if it hadn't been for you—come down soon."[51] The conductor had tried to get radio and recording companies interested in the concert, but no go. To that Ives wrote Slonimsky, "Radio: Art and business all hitched up together. 91³/₈% (I like to be precise) of all radio and phonograph records— are 'sebaceous cysts,' and soft ones at that—and they sell—though if a 3-year old is always fed candy for breakfast he will always be a 3-year-old."[52]

At the premiere on January 10, 1931, Slonimsky played *Three Places* twice. The performance he recalled as "somewhat scrambling."[53] As they finished each movement the concertmaster sighed, "So far, so good."[54] After the second time through there was more applause.[55] Putting his hand to his brow,

Slonimsky peered around the darkened hall, trying to get Ives to respond. Ives sat tight. Ruggles's *Men and Mountains* evoked some boos and hisses; Ives would later write what he wished he'd jumped up and shouted at that point, but almost certainly didn't: "Don't be such a god-damned sissy! When you hear strong music like this, get up and use your ears like a man!"[56]

Afterward Ives said judiciously to Slonimsky, "This was just like a town meeting, everyone for himself. Wonderful how it came out!" Rather than the compliment posterity would take it for, that was Ives's typically tactful way of saying that the performance was something of a mess. He wrote a more straightforward opinion to friend T. Carl Whitmer: "It went fairly well— Slonimsky is a remarkable man—but a few of the players, especially the older, first-chair men, are soft-eared, soft-headed, dumb & lazy. . . However, the younger men played well & were interested. Moral—beware of old men!"[57]

Just after the premiere Ives headed for Boston and the Joslin Clinic, a pioneering diabetes institution. The doctors had finally settled on that disease as his root problem and Mike Myrick encouraged his debilitated friend to go to Boston. At the clinic Ives was poked and prodded and pinched. The doctors decreed a strict diet and detailed Harmony to give him three insulin shots a day. For a few years this treatment provided some relief.

While at the clinic Ives went, incognito, to hear Slonimsky's Boston performance of *Three Places*. Next day a *Herald* reviewer described the audience as "extremely cordial." In the *Post* Warren Story Smith snarled, "Mr. Slonimsky's programme might be described as food for jaded musical palates . . . nor does he ignore . . . what might be called the lunatic fringe of modern music." Venerable Boston critic Philip Hale seems to have ignored the event, but he would get around to Ives in due time. Slonimsky took *Three Places* to Havana, where composer Amadeo Roldán became an enthusiast.[58] Roldán premiered *Decoration Day* with the Havana Philharmonic in December 1931.

Soon after the *Three Places* premiere, Ives, Cowell, and Slonimsky met in New York to talk over the next step for the Pan-American Association of Composers. Ives suggested producing concerts of American music in Europe under the Pan-American banner and with his financing.[59] Varèse had moved to Paris and could help arrange things there. Nothing like that had been done before; Europe was generally oblivious to American music. In April 1931 Slonimsky sailed for Paris with Ives's $1500 letter of credit in his pocket.[60] In those days that could buy a lot of music.

On Varèse's suggestion they settled on two concerts, four rehearsals for each, a full orchestra the first time and chamber the second. Posters went up all over Paris announcing music "américaine, mexicaine et cubaine." Slonimsky saved Ives one of the big red-lettered posters; it went onto the studio wall in Redding. Ives cheerfully wrote Slonimsky, who had just become a U.S. citizen, "Now that you are a reg. Yankee—you will spit through your teeth, talk through your nose, cuss between syllables and let 'em 'learn you' in Paris how to compose real Amer. stuff."[61] He dispensed money over the wire and also inspiration (mixed with subtle caveats): "Just kick into the music as you did in Town Hall—never mind the exact notes or the right notes, they're always a nuisance. Just let the spirit of the stuff sail up to the Eiffel Tower and on to heaven. Never mind the ladybirds, male and female, in the audience—they're dear and nice."

On June 6, 1931, Paris heard *Trois Coins de la Nouvelle-Angleterre* in the Maison Gaveau, and it sailed. Also on Slonimsky's program were Ruggles's *Men and Mountains* and pieces by Cowell, Roldán, and Weiss. The chamber orchestra program five days later included Varèse's steely *Intégrales*.[62] In attendance was a crowd of journalists, the curious, pale-faced *artistes* demanding to be amazed. Critics most smiled on their countryman Varèse, but despite the strangeness of Ives's music and its high-American material, audience and critics responded warmly. Prominent critic Boris de Schloezer called Ives "a real forerunner, a bold talent . . . despite his awkwardness, or rather just because of his awkwardness, this modernism acquires a flavor all its own." Ives, wrote Paul le Flem in *Comoedia*, proved himself "the most spontaneously gifted musician, whose truculent boldness, although occasionally awkward, is not inconsistent with the feelings that he is trying to express. . . . he knows how to temper his science with something sensitive, fresh, and lively." In *Excelsior* Émile Vuillermoz called the music an "astonishing revelation."[63] The conductor received raves from all quarters. Ives, Slonimsky, and American Ultra-Modernism had gained a foothold in Europe. Or so it appeared.

Ives was thrilled at the good words but could not restrain his outrage at the sour ones. *New York Times* correspondent Henry Prunières wrote as part of a long article, "I cannot say that these concerts had a very great success. The first left a terrible impression of emptiness. . . . If it be true that Charles Ives composed his *Three New England Scenes* before acquaintance with Stravinsky's *Le Sacre du Printemps,* he ought to be recognized as an originator. There is no doubt that he knows his Schoenberg, yet gives the impression that he has not always assimilated the lessons of the Viennese master as well as he might have."[64] That sent Ives swinging into the ring. He wrote E. Robert Schmitz,

Prunières says that I "know my Schoenberg," interesting information to me as I have never heard nor seen a note of Schoenberg's music. He says that I haven't applied the lessons as well as I might. This statement shows almost human intelligence. It's funny how many men, when they see another man put the breechin' under a horse's tail . . . think that he must be influenced by someone in Siberia or Neurasthenia. No one man invented the barber's itch. But one thing about the concert that everyone felt was that Slonimsky was a great conductor.[65]

Ives was hedging there. He had not seen Schoenberg's music when he wrote *Three Places,* but since then as an avid reader of the journals *Musical Quarterly* and *Modern Music* he had at least seen excerpts and read a good many analytical words on Schoenberg. And while there is probably no direct Schoenberg—or Stravinsky—influence on his later revisions to *Three Places*, knowing about those composers may have helped embolden Ives to toughen up his work. He had compromised for years, however inconsistently, and maybe now he did not want to be out-uncompromised by anybody, did not want anyone to *epatér le bourgeoisie* more than he did. Entirely on his own he had discovered much new territory for music, perhaps more than anyone else in history. Even if innovation was an incidental matter to him (and it always had been), if innovation were going to be the coin of acclaim he wanted his due as the original he certainly was.

He was even more incensed, though, by a Boston *Herald* screed from the venerable Philp Hale, who in Ivesian terms was the very model of a Rollo and a ladybird. Wrote Hale,

Nicolas Slonimsky of Boston, indefatigable in furthering the cause of the extreme radical composers, has brought out in Paris orchestral compositions by Americans who are looked on by our conservatives as wild-eyed anarchists. He thus purposed to acquaint Parisians with contemporaneous American music. But the composers represented were not those who are regarded by their fellow-countrymen as leaders in the art. . . . If Mr. Slonimsky had chosen a composition by Loeffler, Hill, one of Deems Taylor's suites, [or] Foote's suite . . . his audience in Paris would now have a fairer idea of what Americans are doing.

Having with dazzling consistency picked, as David Wooldridge observes, a solid slate of historical losers at the expense of Slonimsky's winners, Hale continued in kind. His choice of terms, classically conservative, ran to "restless experiments," "no melodic gift," "tiresome repetition," and ended with a grand paean to the great composers whose "harmonic and orchestral invention [brought] strength and beauty" rather than mere anarchy.[66] In a letter to Slonimsky's Boston manager Ives howled in response:

Thank you for [your] note and the enclosed pretty lines from a nice old lady. Mr. Hale has quite the philosophy of Aunt Maria—"When you don't understand some'n, scold some'n." . . . Where does he find the authority for all his sweeping statements? . . . Does Mr. Hale actually know all this music he knows so much about? . . . What Mr. Hale [says] is partially true—in every movement in art, in politics, in every kind of evolution, there is a struggle for a changing bad, good, and towards perfection. But it sounds to me that he wants everybody to think that there is only one kind of good music and he knows exactly what it is—which is what he had been brought up on— what he has been told—what he has limited his mind and ears to—habit forming thoughts and sounds—which go on in the cosmic process of degeneration, whether in art, business, religion, or any part of humanity. If men like that were the only influence in music or any art—it would die out of the world.[67]

Hale's complaints could not much dampen the excitement of the concerts. Slonimsky returned to America the Ultra-Modernists' conquering hero. On

September 3, 1931, he premiered *Washington's Birthday* in a San Francisco New Music Society concert. Reviews of the piece were mixed to bad, but the conductor acquired powerful friends in California. Meanwhile in Germany, Cowell arranged a concert of American pieces at the Bauhaus, the composers including Ives, Rudhyar, and Cowell. Six days later John J. Becker premiered Ives's *In the Night* (from the Set for Theater Orchestra) at a historic concert in St. Paul, the first midwestern showcase for avant-garde composers. The following February Becker premiered the entire set at the New School, with the Pan-American Chamber Orchestra (*New Music* was about to publish the score). Becker stayed with Ives in New York during the rehearsals for that performance and the two became friends.

By the time John Becker contacted him about the set, Ives had seen and liked the younger composer's *Symfonia Brevis,* published in *New Music Quarterly*. Conservatively trained, Becker had been reborn under the influence of *New Music* and a friendship with Henry Cowell. Like most of the Ultra-Modernist circle, Becker came to view dissonance as a holy cause and himself as a missionary. "Dissonance and discord do not actually exist," he wrote. "They only exist because of our habit of thinking."[68] Catholic, with a large family, then teaching at St. Thomas's College in St. Paul, Becker was determined to establish progressive composers in the Midwest. To that task he brought a fiery energy and imagination; he was also blunt, bearish, and not the towering composer he imagined himself to be. Lacking Cowell's charm or Ives's nobility and endearing eccentricity, Becker would have a hard time realizing his goals as composer or promoter. Eventually, reaching for coattails perhaps, he would embrace the idea of an "American Five" group of composers, to match the Russian Five and *Les Six* in France: Ives, Ruggles, Cowell, Wallingford Riegger, and Becker.

Soon after premiering *Washington's Birthday,* Nicolas Slonimsky was dispatched back to Europe for more playing and proselytizing, again financed by Ives. Cowell was still plying the European angle as well. In Berlin Cowell made an arrangement with Edition Adler to engrave and distribute *New Music* scores in Europe, including Ives's *Fourth of July* and Ruggles's craggy, ecstatic *Sun-Treader*. In February 1932, a Pan-American concert in Vienna featured Ives songs, Ruggles's *Portals* conducted by Anton Webern, and pieces by Copland, Cowell, Riegger, Chávez and others. Willi Reich sounded a jingoistic note in the program: "Ives . . . stands as the leader and inspiration of the younger generation of American composers, which has fixed for its aim the creation of a pure, national art in music."[69] These were ominous words in those times, in Austria.

The same day in Paris, Slonimsky conducted the Orchestra Symphonique de Paris in an ad hoc suite of Ives pieces—*In the Night, In the Cage,* and the world premiere of *The Fourth of July*. Besides the American works, on the program was the Paris premiere of Bartók's First Piano Concerto, with the composer at the piano.[70] During the rehearsals Slonimsky wrangled with Bartók and nearly canceled the concert; Ives cabled money for more rehearsal time.[71] At a second concert four days later, Arthur Rubinstein played Brahms's Second Piano Concerto. Slonimsky premiered Ruggles's *Sun-Treader*, and for a conclusion unleashed Varèse's screaming *Arcana*. Ives's first surviving communication to Ruggles is a telegram of congratulations for the premiere: "We are all elated that Paris is up with you treading the sun." From home—he could not afford to go to Paris—Ruggles replied in his bold calligraphy, "You wouldn't let me express to you how deeply I felt regarding all you have done for the 'Sun-treader' and for me. So I'm taking this occasion to tell you that if it hadn't been for your high-minded attitude, and your fine generosity there would have been no performance, and consequently no success."[72]

Different as they were (Ruggles for example was conservative, racist, and chronically poor) the two men had become inordinately fond of each other. Their relationship began with shared respect as artists but went far beyond that. They visited whenever possible, though Ruggles often lacked the wherewithal to travel far from his home in Arlington, Vermont. Unlike most of the Ultra-Modern crowd Carl was no Bohemian but an old Yankee like Charlie, with a wide Romantic streak (the name *Sun-Treader* comes from Browning). Like Ives too, Ruggles lived in his own unique atmosphere and charged people with it. He'd play one of his soaring melodies on piano and roar through his cigar to friends, *"Doesn't that twist yer guts!"* He kept a sign on his wall that read, "Dissonant chords have talismanic ecstasy." As Charlie wrote prose and poetry on the side, Carl painted remarkably well for a Sunday painter.

Ruggles's atmosphere was made of cigar smoke, dirty jokes, profane bluster mixed with puckish charm, burning intensity at whatever he did from composing to umpiring baseball games, fierce belief in the power of music, and pugnacious self-assertion mixed with a fine sense of his own outrageousness. Carl Ruggles was in large degree a parody of Carl Ruggles. As it was with Harmony Ives, Carl's wife Charlotte was his muse and greatest pal. Even if Charlie didn't care for the jokes, Carl tickled Ives no end. They loved to sit and cuss together, to celebrate each other and skin the competition. Probably Ives felt that if there were an "American Five," then Ruggles was the only one of them in his league. For Ruggles's part, Ives was the only composer alive he rated his peer.[73]

From Paris Slonimsky headed for an engagement with the Berlin Philharmonic at the Beethovensaal. His program included the same Ives set, *Sun-Treader*, *Arcana*, and Cowell's *Synchrony*. A Boston *Herald* correspondent reported that the nearly full house responded with "wild applause mingled with catcalls and hisses."[74] During the Varèse, some audience members took to whistling through their housekeys; combined with the music, the effect rattled the walls of the old hall. This was an age of demonstrations, riots, and violent partisanship in Modernist productions.[75] Some critics raved over Slonimsky's program, others snarled, some took a more malevolent tack. In a review Slonimsky would make famous in his *Lexicon of Musical Invective,* one critic said Ruggles's *Sun-Treader* "should have been surely renamed 'Latrine-Treader' . . . I had only the impression of bowel constrictions in an atonal Tristanesque ecstasy."[76] Another in *Germania* showed how Nazi ideas were invading aesthetics: "The leader of this impudent exhibition was naturally a Jew. Slonimsky can call himself a hundred times an American, but one has only to watch his shoulder movement to recognize at once that he is a 100% Polish Jew."[77]

Still, other reviewers cheered. Slonimsky had scored a triumph with some of the most difficult music ever written. From Berlin he went on to Budapest to conduct much of the same, including the Ives, with the Hungarian Symphony Orchestra. Back in the United States after his tour, Slonimsky would, for a while, find something like the same success. His ascent in a few years had been dizzying. The Pan-American concerts in Europe had received far more attention and acclaim than anything the group had experienced in the States— or ever would. As for Slonimsky's contribution to Ives's cause, *The Fourth of July* was the fifth major premiere since *Three Places* a year before, three of them conducted by Slonimsky and one—*Decoration Day* in Havana—inspired by him. Ives, Cowell, and the Ultra-Modernist camp saw Nicolas Slonimsky as their shining hope, the man who would bring their music into the orchestral mainstream.

Amidst the exhilarating news from Europe in spring 1932, Ives received an unexpected letter from Aaron Copland: "I have programmed a group of 5 or 6 songs, from your volume of '114 Songs' for performance at a Festival of Contemporary American Music at Saratoga Springs in May." Copland had just created the festival at Yaddo, a financier's mansion turned artists' colony next door to the Saratoga racetrack. During the thirties the festival would become one of the most important forums of its kind. That importance was established at the outset, as much as anything, by the Ives songs performed by Copland and Hubert Linscott on May 1, 1932. Copland chose astutely, not only to project Ives's brilliance as a songwriter but the variety of his music as well: "Evening," "The Indians," "Maple Leaves," "The Se'er," "Serenity," "Walking," and "Charlie Rutlage." The last, a surprisingly authentic cowboy song (with Ivesian touches), appealed to the new vogue for concert music drawing on American folk sources—a trend of which Copland was about to become the most famous exponent.

Critics responded delightedly. The Boston *Evening Transcript:* "Nothing heard at the festival showed higher imaginative powers than the song of Ives. The variety of expression . . . is little short of amazing." *Trend:* "Charles Ives, surely one of our significant musical figures, was represented by a group of songs. . . . One wonders just how long it will be before Mr. Ives' great gifts will receive the recognition that they deserve." *The Nation:* "Defying classification were the seven songs of Charles Ives—of startling imagination, vitality and humour. One of them—'Charley Rutlege' [*sic*] stopped the show and had to be repeated." Also present at the festival was imposing critic Paul Rosenfeld. He had hated the *Comedy* in 1927, but after hearing *Three Places* and the songs became a convert. That year and the next Rosenfeld published pieces on Ives in *The New Republic.*

Composer Wallingford Riegger wrote Ives, "Your beautiful songs . . . aroused not only enthusiasm and wide-spread interest on the part of the audience . . . but keen appreciation in the numerous composers present. . . . There was much curiosity about the facts of your life—musical and otherwise. . . . Will you not consider seriously the recording of rather copious biographical matter concerning yourself, that you could from time to time dictate to a stenographer?"[78] Ives was already doing just what Riegger proposed, dictating a collection of biographical memos.

Many felt that at the Yaddo Festival Ives had finally been discovered. In fact he had been discovered once or twice already. For the rest of his life he would continue being discovered and discovered and nearly forgotten in the interims, and never quite get his due. The reasons for that are various—his health a major one—but another reason can be observed at Yaddo, which amounted to a showcase for composers of the younger generation. During the festival Oscar Levant played his Sonatina, John Kirkpatrick a Roy Harris sonata, and George Antheil several of his pieces. Also attending, some of them to hear their work, were Marc Blitzstein, Virgil Thomson, Paul Bowles, Walter Piston, Roger Sessions, and Henry Brant. By 1932 some of the older composers' groups had declined. Schmitz's Pro Musica was succumbing to the depression and the Pan-American Association did not have long to live (its European successes came to nothing). Copland and other younger artists at the Yaddo Festival would be leaders of American music in the thirties, shapers of its trends. The main thrust of those trends—simplicity of style, nationalistic folksiness, a turn from dissonance and atonality—would lead away from the Ultra-Modernists, and so away from Charles Ives.

At the end of March 1932, in response to the mounting performances and mounting curiosity about him and his music, Ives began dictating a series of memos to secretary Florence Martin. To prepare for the project he went through his manuscripts jotting ideas and reminiscences in the margins. (That is when the pages acquired many of the famous, often embarrassing or confusing marginalia, which scholars long assumed were all done at the time the pages were composed.) Forty years later John Kirkpatrick would shape Ives's rambling dictations to Miss Martin into the book *Memos,* at once some of the most valuable, illuminating, misleading, and self-damaging prose Ives ever produced. Often these memos were hardly gone over, never polished. Ives did not intend them to be published as such but rather to be a private store of information for the use of people writing about him.[79] If they *had* been intended for publication he would have worked them over, tempered what he knew perfectly well to be their excesses. Ives usually knew better than to pop off in print.

In other words the *Memos* are Ives's private, top-of-the-head tour of his life and work, the musical part of the tour done piece by piece in a jumble of technical notes, programs, asides, stories, recounting of humiliations, and potshots at performers, critics, and composers. The tone of the sniping, and the adolescent tenor of some patches, can be illustrated by Ives's justification for the complaints: "This and similar remarks have a right to be—for the same reason it is right to throw a bottle at the umpire who closes his eyes and yells 'foul!' And then they all [have] a double use, in getting something off the chest and over the garden wall, where it may disturb a pansy."[80] The style may be seen too in this portrayal of the three composers, perhaps the three human beings, whom Ives most admired:

Music has always been an emasculated art—at least too much—say 88⅔%. Even those considered the greats (Bach, Beethoven, Brahms, etc.) have too much of it, though less [than] the other rubber-stamp great men. They couldn't exactly help it—life with them was such that they had to live at least part of the time by the ladies' smiles. . . . This is not [so much] criticising or running down or under-appreciating Beethoven, Bach, et al, as it [is] a respect and wonder that they didn't do worse under the circumstances. Music is a nice little art just born, and they ask "is it a boy or a girl?"—and one voice in the back row says "It's going to be a boy—some time!"[81]

On another page he lumps together a collection of sissies and waves them all away:

When I think of some music that I liked to hear and play 35 or 40 years ago . . . I feel like saying, "Rollo, how did you fall for that sop, those 'ta tas' and greasy ringlets?" In this I would include [Wagner's] *Preislied,* [Nevin's] *The Rosary,* a certain amount of Mozart, Mendelssohn, a small amount of early Beethoven, with the easy-made Haydn, a large amount of Massenet, Sibelius, Tchaikovsky, etc. (to say nothing of Gounod), most Italian operas. . . , some of Chopin (pretty soft, but you don't mind it in him so much, because one just naturally thinks of him with a skirt on, but one which he made himself).

Eventually his better angels step in, reminding Ives of his actual respect for the past, but then he slides back into complaints:

Notwithstanding the above slants, which many would say are insults, it seems to me . . . that still today Bach, Beethoven, and Brahms (No) are among the strongest and greatest in all art . . . not quite as strong and great as Carl Ruggles, because B., B., and B. have too much of the sugar-plum for the soft-ears.[82]

Here is what had become of Ives's humanistic vision by 1932: the grandeur of the *Essays'* assertion that music was unborn has been laced with resentment, homophobia, depression fueled by bad health, and attacks on his own musical heroes and ancestors. Peter Burkholder writes, "In the *Memos,* Ives set out to disinherit himself from European music, calling all sorts of composers names." In the process, Ives attempted "to have everyone perceive him as a great original, coming out of nowhere, with no one but George at his back."[83] Or rather, two people at his back: "One thing I am certain of," Ives said to Miss Martin, "is that, if I have done anything good in music, it was, first, because of my father, and second, because of my wife."[84]

The most immediate of the ancestors from whom Ives distanced himself was his Yale teacher Horatio Parker: "Parker was a composer and widely known, and Father was not a composer and little known—but from every other standpoint I should say that Father was by far the greater man."[85] So he got his revenge on his teacher, who gave young Charlie the connection to European tradition without which he could never have accomplished so much, but failed to live up to this student's longing for a replacement father.

By the 1930s Ives, like Cowell and other Ultra-Modernist friends, had taken on the holy cause of dissonance, had come to view strong harmony as the only masculine kind, had muddled the value of music with its dissonance and novelty. He included in the *Memos* a long series of quotes from a 1931 Henry Bellamann *Musical Quarterly* article that focuses exclusively on his innovations—a stress on technical originality beyond anything in Ives's own writing, and less informative than most of his writing. In those moments (only some moments) when Ives gave in to the idea that novelty equals quality, he became by his own definition the greatest composer of all:

My brother says, "That's rather conceited of you, isn't it, to criticize the great men. . . . Some might say that you imply that your music is greater, less emasculated, and more to the point than any of the so-called great masters!" I don't imply any such thing—I don't have to—I state [that] it is better! Ask any good musician—those who don't agree with me are not good musicians—but if some of the poor musicians . . . should agree with me, then I'd begin to think I was wrong.

Many have noted what appears to be Ives's shocking assertion of superiority in those lines; few have noticed the oblique irony with which he retracts it. Ives had a very good sense of his own value and the value of his innovations. He believed that he had found potentials in music that had been waiting to be discovered since the invention of polyphony. He once wrote Carl Ruggles, "I don't know anything about modern music—ours is just 15 century stuff—that is, it was to have been made then—but they forgot to."[86] He also knew perfectly well, with the better angels of his nature, that Beethoven and Bach carried one higher (to use his own term of approval). For Brahms he felt less awe maybe but loved him as much as anyone. (There are three biographies and three pictures of Brahms in Ives's study, and one picture hangs on Ives's piano.)

If that passage in which he proclaims, however ironically, his superiority to the great masters exemplifies the dismal side of the *Memos,* in which Ives did himself an injury he may never live down, many pages tell us a great deal and show Ives at his best. Here we learn much about George Ives and the composer's youth. Of course, everything is dressed up to make a better story—as everybody does but artists do more because they are artists, myth-makers. (If Ives mythologizes himself a little in the *Memos,* he does it no more than any artist would, and with less eye to the grandstand than most.[87])

He speaks of his works with a characteristic interweaving of reminiscence, technical details, and program. In his description of *In the Night* we find the Charles Ives for whom the fabric of existence weaves itself whole:

The last part . . . was played in an evening service (and at an organ recital) at the Central Presbyterian Church. . . . When a man has played at church services for ten or fifteen years steadily, he gets slightly used to the three fundamental triads. . . . In this little piece I tried to find three chords that might be used in a similar or parallel sense to the usual tonic, dominant, and subdominant—a combination of chords that would not be undignified, that would have some musical sense and relation, and about which melodies or counterpoints could be used as a natural outcome from these combinations. In this movement, D♭ was taken as the main chord (or the tonic), and B♭ . . . was used as the dominant, and the chord of E major . . . was used as the subdominant. These chords have a note in common with the tonic, and B♭ used as the dominant seems to have a stronger resolving value than the subdominant, E major. Then the tune, *Abide With Me,* as a kind of cantus firmus, was sung by the male voices. . . . Of course what I have in mind was a general tonal effect, and the technical plan . . . as but a ways and means. Behind the music is a simpler picture—the heart of an old man, dying alone in the night, sad, low in heart—then God comes to help him—bring him to his own loved ones.[88]

In these *Memos* taken from dictation we hear the voice of Charles Ives, Connecticut Yankee and singular character, with his inextricable mixture of the feisty and witty and brilliant and noble and puerile. For an example of the wit, in the midst of an aside on modern music and poetry we find a lampoon of Dane Rudhyar's occultistic tracts: "the mystico interconnection from the self-experienco to the latent self and experienco-suo, [im]plying [that] the association of pre-imagos [is] but the association-self."[89] Or his slant on mechanical time-beating conductors (Toscanini had gone onto his list alongside Damrosch) who prattle about craftsmanship: "So, ladies, you see whenever now a properly dressed adding machine walks down the middle isle and gets off at Western Union Platitude #22, 'good workmanship'—I know there's something soft in that job."[90]

Here too Ives distances himself not only from past influences, but—more accurately—from Modernism:

There has to be a tag on a bushel of potatoes to be shipped, and probably a label on a manner of talking, but the latter is harder to label. . . . Personally I feel like cussing . . . the inevitable tag "modern," "ultra-modern," etc. It has to be used till something else better is found, but just the same the necessity for its existence is too much like that of a nice tombstone (with the wrong dead man). . . . The trouble with modern music is that [it's] somewhat too intellectual—the brain has [been] working a little more than that bigger muscle underneath."[91]

Ives was different from his Modernist friends in many ways, among them that he was not a Modernist. Certainly Ives shared with his era an exploratory path, a penchant for experimenting with technique, for creating new languages; his friends largely advertised him in those terms. But Ives was indifferent or hostile to neoclassicism, futurism, primitivism, *Gebrauchsmusik*, Eastern influences, twelve-tone composition, and most other subdivisions of musical Modernism. He concurred with Modernism (even more with late-century Postmodernism) in his integration of "high" and "low" art, but he was generally uninterested in popular developments after the turn of the century, after ragtime. He had none of the darkness of the Modernist type, or the characteristic Modernist poses of the despairing and neurotic, or the absurd and surreal. Modernism was shaped by the violence of this century; Ives never really grasped that violence. The century has also been shaped by technology and media. Though Ives put the electronic Theremin into the Fourth Symphony, helped build the Rhythmicon, and sought recordings and broadcasts of his work, he was essentially technophobic and hated modern mass media.

Expressionism in art and music is one of the founding elements of Modernism, from the metaphysical anguish of Munch's *The Scream* to the tortured paintings of the Fauves and the Blue Rider group, to the music of Schoenberg and Webern. Expressionism grew in part from a Freudian sense of the unconscious as a dark, irresistible swamp within, all of it tangled up with sex and the id. Ives was prudish and pre-Freudian—yet with his own highly developed sense of the unconscious, closer to the more affirmative vision of William James. Ives may have been personally neurotic, but his art was characteristically healthy and optimistic, nearer the Romantic than the Modern.

Modernism usually exalts the artist as superior to the philistine rabble, the lonely genius as the crown of society. Ives proclaimed the individual functioning *within* the community, everyone traveling a unique path but all drawn in the same direction, the artist one with the Masses in fulfilling the divine scheme of evolution. In a 1930 letter to musicologist John Tasker Howard, Ives sets out his own idea of the modern: "The various groups who set store only by the 'old' or only by the 'new' (or only by something else, for that matter) tie themselves all up. . . . What I had in mind rather by 'new' was something that gives one a sense, whether remote or vivid, of that constant organic flow going on in all life, the outward form of which may appear quite different to different men."[92] He was no Modernist but on a parallel path, with lighter and lighter-hearted baggage.

Thus the Ives of the *Memos* years in his wisdom and his pettiness, his illuminations and his evasions. As always, he took care never to show too overtly his intelligence or ambition or sophistication, and thus helped history paint him as a primitive. Ives loved to talk about himself and his music, but his underlying temperament was intensely private; he might have been dismayed to find the *Memos* had escaped unfiltered into the public eye. It never quite sank in to him that as a concomitant of getting the attention he wanted, everything would eventually come out.

The offhand and fragmentary *Memos* show one more thing about Charles Ives. In the old days, in music and in prose he had done rough sketches like most artists, then fleshed out and connected and shaped them. By 1932 he had lost the energy or ability to connect and shape, to follow through. His writings of later years are letters, memos, isolated pages of poetry or rant. That is why though he still had musical ideas he could no longer compose: nothing pulled together any more. The centrifugal elements of his nature had lost their coherence, his pen its directing consciousness. Paradox was no longer part of his message but part of his problem. As the *Memos* reveal, Ives had fallen into dissenting fragments.

Distant Bells

IN MAY 1932, Charlie, Harmony, and Edie Ives escaped for England on the S.S. *New York*. It would be the family's Grand Tour; for fourteen months they traveled and sojourned in England and the Continent.[1] The Joslin Clinic regime paid off; Ives was in relatively good health and spirits for the duration. From Interlaken, Switzerland, Harmony wrote Nicolas Slonimsky in November, "Mr. Ives is ever so much better—you would be delighted to see him."[2] For his music and for the family as a whole, these fourteen months would be perhaps the last thoroughly good, promising period they ever had. For some time afterward the story of Ives's music would be like the history of his health: spotty, unpredictable, brief advances interspersed with long periods of stasis or decline. His last decades also contain the story of the ebbing of a great mind under the assaults of diabetes, heart disease, stroke, depression, and isolation. Ives's great spirit, meanwhile, blazed to the end.

For the first two months they toured England then sailed to Germany, staying for a month at Pension Schmolke in Berlin where Henry Cowell and soprano Mary Bell were also in attendance. Henry and Frau Schmolke were old friends and the little pension had a clientele running to artists and psychiatrists. Ives played through songs with Bell, who had sung Ives in Dresden and was preparing more songs for Hamburg in December. While Edie flirted with a fashionable young baron,[3] the friends had a fine old time laughing and drinking at the Tiergarten, listening to the oompah band, and enjoying Ives's anti-Wagnerian blasts.[4] After touring medieval German towns and boating down the Rhine, the family headed for France. In Paris at the end of August, Harmony approvingly cited in their travel diary paintings by Derain, Braque, Leger, Picasso, Matisse, Pissarro, Sisley, and Rousseau.[5] Also in Paris they visited with Nicolas Slonimsky's mother, who wrote her son, "Mrs. Ives spoke of your talent, and Mr. Ives showed how you produce various criticism out of your pocket. . . . She is so beautiful, her stature, profile, her eyes, her smile. But he with his delightful way to laugh so joyfully simply enchanted me."[6]

Then to Switzerland, in Interlaken for several weeks. Back in the States during that time an article appeared in *Trend* by Bernard Herrmann, one of a group of young New York composers for whom the *New Music Quarterly* printing of the *Comedy* had become something of a bible.[7] Herrmann wrote, "The Fourth Symphony . . . is one of the greatest symphonies ever penned. It is the great American symphony that our critics and conductors have cried out for, and yet the symphony has remained unperformed except for an excerpt." His ambition to conduct the entire Fourth would never be realized, but next year he premiered the Fugue at the New School for Social Research—in his own lush arrangement—and performed it many times after.

At Interlaken Ives received a letter from Deac, who knew what his brother-in-law had been through: "I don't say all I think, but dear Charlie I feel for you, and am sorry you had to give up your business. You are a good sport the way you have acted in it all. . . . I'm proud of you."[8] Deac was sixty-five and living in a rest home, with Ives paying the bills. They shared a Danbury barber, who once told Ives he had come upon old Deac dancing around a blaring phonograph, wearing jingle bells and roller skates. "I believe every word of it," Ives said; but this time he said it sadly. In February 1934 Ives would write Slonimsky, "Uncle Deac died—quite suddenly after a stroke. You remember him living with us in Redding—the oldest of our generation—and one of the last of the old type, now quite vanishing—and the world loses something undefinable."[9]

During their stay at the Hotel du Lac, Ives wrote Cowell thanks for sending the engraved *Fourth of July,* about to be published in *New Music.* (Slonimsky had just played the piece in New York with the Pan-American Orchestra; the *Musical Courier* reported that it "was rewarded with laughter and applause."[10]) Ives complained to Cowell about mistakes in the score—mainly the missing dedication to Mike Myrick. The score had been engraved by Cowell's Berlin affiliate Edition Adler, who was also doing Carl Ruggles's *Sun-Treader.* Besides supporting *New Music* financially, Ives had become its star attraction. In 1932 the journal issued his *Lincoln, the Great Commoner* and Orchestra Set for Theater; *Thirty-four Songs* would come out next year, *Eighteen Songs* in 1935.

The family settled for the winter in Taormina, Sicily. Ives wrote Mary Bell in January 1933, "We are now living under an olive tree in a little stone cabin—(Italians are polite & call it 'villa') on a side hill, overlooking the 'Ionian' & we see (sometimes) the sun rise over Greece!"[11] In Taormina he made a fair copy of *Thanksgiving* from the rough score finished in 1904, its title page scrawled with asides to its dedicatee Edward Carrington Twichell, Deac: "This is a nice piece of turkey, Eddy! Put it there! Very Good Eddy! Yes we have no turkeys today. E. C. T. American!" and a drawing of a rampant eagle. The final *Thanksgiving* score may have been the last Ives made with his own hand.

April 1933 found the Iveses in a Florence pension frequented by artists. Edie, then nineteen, had been attending Harmony's old finishing school at Farmington, but had not thrived there as her mother had.[12] In Florence Edie struck up a friendship, maybe a mild romance, with writer Thomas Flexner. The young man found her charming, gentle, intelligent, and at that point unhappy with her aged and ailing parents. As her father had in his teens, she generally kept her defiance to herself. Among other things, Edie told Flexner that when her first period arrived, her mother explained that the blood was a piece of Eve's apple. The indoctrination had never stopped. For a while Flexner remained a friend of both Edie and her parents, and visited them in New York and Redding.[13]

In the States Ives's apostles had been busy. Becker wrote an article for the *Northwest Musical Herald* called "Charles Ives: Musical Philosopher." Cowell wrote on Ives for *Modern Music* and arranged for critic Paul Rosenfeld to lecture on Ives and Copland at the New School. ("Bad company for Ives!" Henry observed cattily in his report to Charlie.[14])

In California, supporters including composer Roy Harris had been pulling strings for Nicolas Slonimsky. In December 1932, Slonimsky conducted the Los Angeles Philharmonic in a program that included two of the *Three Places in New England*. Reviews tended to the ecstatic. Said *Rob Wagner's Script*: "He made the Philharmonic go through tricks . . . that most of us did not believe were still in the old horse. We need more conductors like Slonimsky. More men of his imagination, his suppleness, his vivacity, his musicianship, and what is even more important, his courage."[15] Following this success Slonimsky was engaged to conduct the orchestra's eight-week Hollywood Bowl season. The real hope was to install him with the orchestra permanently.[16] But Slonimsky's partisans included a group of California socialists, which hardly pleased the Symphony Dames and the businessmen who helped support the orchestra. These factions were determined to keep this conductor, his radical music, and his radical friends at bay.

The Hollywood Bowl concerts had traditionally been relatively light in repertoire. In the summer of 1933 Slonimsky subjected audiences to Ives, Varèse, and Schoenberg. Listeners fled in hundreds. Protests from players and the ladies' committee mounted. Slonimsky's Pan-American friends, Ives included, had entreated him to court the ladies and lay off the Modernists, but he felt himself part of a vanguard that could not be stopped, and so he persisted. Finally came the fiasco: Slonimsky was removed from the podium in mid-contract, paid off, and informed that his services would not be required again.[17]

Word got around. Though he would pick up a baton here and there afterward, Slonimsky's conducting career was destroyed. He never got over it, nor did his friends. With the fiasco in Hollywood Bowl the American musical vanguard lost its shining hope for a foothold in the orchestral mainstream. A musically more conservative generation was about to take over the lead, and the audiences. Ives would not have another major orchestral premiere until 1946, and few big performances at all.

The family finished their European tour with a return to England, where Ives made some private recordings. His increasing awareness of media had given him the idea of recording as a way to disseminate his music and supply a model for performers. Characteristically, he resisted modern media ("There's so much of the music that doesn't get recorded"[18]) but didn't want to be left out as their influence grew. He had experimented with aluminum disks at home in 1930. Now at the end of his European trip he recorded four sides (two later lost) at Columbia's Abbey Road studios in London. He would make more in coming years, all amounting to over an hour of piano music and one unforgettable vocal rendition.

On July 7, 1933, the Iveses were back in Redding, in good spirits from the trip. They returned to Manhattan on schedule in late autumn.[19] Ives's musical situation had changed since they left the country—mostly for the worse. Probably neither he nor Slonimsky yet realized how thoroughly the conductor's career had been curtailed, and how that would affect the progress of the orchestral music. On the other hand something of an Ives cult, small and short-lived as it was, had emerged in New York among the circle of friends now calling themselves the Young Composers Group.

With Aaron Copland as their immediate patron, Cowell as their sponsor at the New School, and Ives as patron saint, the Young Composers mounted a debut concert at the school in January 1933. The group included Bernard Herrmann, Elie Siegmeister, Arthur Berger, Henry Brant, Jerome Moross, Vivian Fine, Lehman Engel, and Irwin Heilner. Berger wrote that for the group Ives "stands in a relationship parallel to that of [Erik] Satie and the Six."[20] The Young Composers were all urban and Jewish, in experience far from the small-town Protestant and old-Yankee sources of Ives's music; little of their work would show a direct influence. Then as later, for his admirers Ives was unique and nearly inimitable, more a spiritual than a stylistic inspiration. Engel, Moross, and Herrmann became regular visitors in the Ives household. Moross remembered the old man (not really so old then, but looking it) showing up with Harmony at a concert where his music was being played, with a shawl draped around his shoulders.[21] The group gathered around him excitedly and he did his Ivesian act for them: the small rewards of small fame. Something of what Ives meant to the Young Composers is summarized by Elie Siegmeister:

Up to that point [when they became aware of Ives] the leader and "role model" . . . was, of course, Aaron. . . . But Aaron, Jewish Brooklyn boy that he was, still had a slight Frenchy . . . tinge to him . . . that made him a little precious. . . . When Ives burst upon me, mainly through Henry Cowell, Benny Herrmann, Jerry Moross, Nicky Slonimsky, ca. 1931, it was like the real path for an American composer suddenly opened up, and one that's been with me ever since. . . . [While] I'm a very different composer than Ives . . . we share so much in common—identity with common things, even commonplace things, and derive much of our thought and feeling from everyday American life, and are not afraid to use "found objects" as the themes for our stuff; and also (very important) are deeply anti-academic, anti-German, anti-theory as the source of music.[22]

The direction of Siegmeister and the rest of his generation would be different from the past, and Copland remained a major force in that direction. The reasons for the changes were partly the inevitable pendulum of the generations, but there was a compelling economic dimension as well. At first the new-music ferment of the twenties had seemed little affected by the stock market crash of 1929 and the depression that followed. But the arts are usually battered by economic decline, sooner or later. After a flurry of activity in the early 1930s, avant-gardists began having more trouble finding performances.

In response, American composers asked hard questions about their place and purpose. The questions were both philosophical, *What are we doing and why?*, and practical, *How can we make a living?* These were normal concerns, but the depression made them more urgent and shaped the answers. Oscar Levant (an active composer before his Hollywood years) observed the decline of new American music in orchestral programs in the 1930s and the near-total shutdown of private support. Previously dependent on wealthy patrons, composers now had to look to the broader public. So, wrote Levant, "Perhaps as a reflex of this there came a gradual recession in the excesses of the music that was being written, an attraction to simplicity, a reverence for clarity as opposed to the former adoration of complexity."[23] Wrote Aaron Copland of his metamorphosis from avant-gardist to populist: "During those years I began to feel an increasing dissatisfaction with the relations of the music-loving public and the living composer. . . . I felt that it was worth the effort to see if I couldn't say what I had to say in the simplest possible terms."[24]

If Grant Wood's severely plain painting of a farm couple called *American Gothic* embodies the spirit of the times, so did the "Americana" music that Copland, Roy Harris, Virgil Thomson, and many others began writing in the thirties. This music manifests a turn from art for art's sake, from the Romantic and Modernist image of the artist as high priest and crown of society. If Wagner set the model that society must serve art and the artist, many American composers who came of age in the thirties believed that art and the artist must serve society. They came to draw on folk sources, rejected steady dissonance and atonality, proclaimed simplicity and directness, and for the first time in Modernist music directly reached out to listeners.[25]

These trends intersected with the leftward drift of American artists. The depression would be the golden age of the Left in the United States. The socialist periodical *New Masses* appeared on coffee tables around the country. Still, while most of the intelligentsia were some shade of Red, plenty of discord persisted among the comrades. Musical circles debated which approach would best serve the People: internationalism and the creation of musical languages unsullied by the capitalistic past (generally the Ultra-Modernist view), or nationalism and an embrace of the people's voice in folk and popular music (basic principles of the Americana school). If the older Ultra-Modernists tended to works called *Soundpiece* (Becker), *Seven Paragraphs* (Cowell), and *Sun-Treader* (Ruggles), then Americanists tended to *Billy the Kid, Rodeo* (both Copland), *The Plow that Broke the Plains* (Thomson), and *When Johnny Comes Marching Home* (Harris). For the new generation this approach was both satisfyingly populist and anti-German, and pragmatically patriotic in an era when what money could be spared for the arts had to come mainly from the box office or the government.

Moreover, Copland and most of his circle had studied with Nadia Boulanger in Paris, and from her absorbed the gospel of Stravinskyan neoclassicism. This amounted to a conservative rebellion against Germanic ponderousness and pretention, dissonance and dodecaphony. In a way, neoclassicism returned to the spirit of Mozart through a Modernist prism: keep music light, elegantly simple, unpretentious, ironic, tonal (all of which harmonized with the politics of the new generation). As part of the reaching out to the public came a flowering of *Gebrauchsmusik,* music for use. Copland and others wrote pieces for schools, workers' songbooks, radio, and film. Having mined jazz in the twenties, Copland in the next decade looked for material in collections of Shaker melodies and cowboy songs; the Shaker song "Gift to be Simple" would be the centerpiece of his *Appalachian Spring.*

The League of Composers and its journal *Modern Music* became associated with the Americana school. As the thirties went on, competition heated up between the League and the Pan-American Association of Composers. This rivalry was not entirely hard-edged; organizations and ideologies overlapped. Henry Cowell not only helped found the New Music Society and the Pan-American Association, but also belonged to the League and turned to researching folk music, though he remained a radical at heart. Both composers' societies were predominantly leftist and both active in Cowell's music program at the New School. Cowell's *New Music* published Copland; the League put Pan-American artists on its programs. In other words, the two leading composers' groups competed, sniped, griped, and back-bit, but never fell into outright war and sometimes collaborated. Meanwhile, after a few years the leftist activity of all parties ebbed as many composers joined the WPA Federal Music Project, thus the New Deal mainstream.

History has decided that most of the significant North and South American composers of the thirties were the avant-gardists belonging to the Pan-American Association, the names including Ives, Varèse, Cowell, Ruggles, Riegger, Chávez, Salzedo, and Becker. Yet the Pan-American never commanded the prestige, backing, or audience of the League of Composers—partly because the League was more conservative, partly because it played well-known Europeans more than Americans, and published the important journal *Modern Music*. At the beginning of the thirties the Pan-American and the League had been roughly on a par (even if both were marginal in impact on the larger musical world). Despite the veneer of cooperation, by the end of the decade the League of Composers was thriving and the Pan-American Association was dead. The young (leftist) conservatives had won the battle for public regard over the old (leftist) radicals, whose godfather was Charles Ives. Led by Copland's immensely popular string of folk-based pieces, the Americana school and its French-honed air of down-home plainness would come to be perceived by the public as *the* American art music. So it would remain well into the fifties.

How did Ives relate to all this? Certainly he had written a good deal of folk-based music that nationalists could embrace—thus the success of his cowboy song "Charlie Rutlage." (The folksy Second Symphony never came out in a time ideal for it.) Ives also shared the leftward inclination of the new generation, though always in his own fashion. Yet the trends of the thirties marginalized him. A rejection of complexity and dissonance was a rejection not of all Ives's music, but much of his best. More generally, the eclipse of the Pan-American Association inevitably eclipsed him too, because those were his friends.

Ives saw it all happening. In the first meeting between Ives and John Kirkpatrick, the pianist happened to use the word "simplicity" in regard to notation, and was alarmed to find Ives launching into a tirade that wound up, "God *damn* simplicity!"[26] Kirkpatrick had innocently spoken the word by which the new generation condemned Ives's music, and Ives knew it. After the flurry of performances, publications, and interest between 1927 and 1932, his public career would stagnate for years—with periodic and short-lived episodes of "discovery." But if Ives was entering a frustrating phase by the mid-thirties, there was still Henry Cowell on his side, eclipsed but indefatigable.

By the mid-thirties the Iveses had settled into the life they maintained for the rest of their lives. His health swung up and down, more down than up. When he was able there was much to deal with—a constant flow of letters, practical matters to discuss with Henry and others, publications and copying. Ives and Cowell exchanged three or so letters a month on matters personal and organizational, and Henry often came to 74th Street and Redding on business and social visits.

Harmony tried to keep things calm. Her husband's life depended on it. They made their seasonal journeys from city to country—joyously up to Redding in the spring, sadly down to New York in the fall. A maid or two traveled with them, to take care of housekeeping and cooking. Nieces and nephews playing in the yard gave way to grandnieces and grandnephews and they got the same treatment, sometimes scary and sometimes fascinating. "If you'd ever get too serious," Chester Ives recalled, "Uncle Charlie would let you walk in front of him, then he'd trip you up!"[27] Recognizing a kindred spirit, the kids always came back for more. Sometimes Ives detailed Edie and the nephews to work on the scrapbooks of programs and reviews that he had begun in the twenties. Secretary Florence Martin typed up reviews, article excerpts, fan letters, and other publicity material. Harmony spent her days in volunteer work for church and such, but at night she was always home for Charlie. Several times a month she, or sometimes Edie, would copy out one of his letters dealing with musical business. He drafted and redrafted them in pencil, in third person as if from wife or daughter, because his hand did not shake with the pencil and because it kept the world a degree away. By then most of his letters were less "Ivesian" than businesslike, generally beginning with a standard formula: "I am writing for Mr. Ives because he has not been at all well lately." Years later, when John Kirkpatrick examined the papers, he was amazed to discover that for Harmony's first letter to him there were four pencil drafts in Ives's hand.[28]

In Redding Ives wandered like Thoreau in his woods, visiting favorite trees and views, resting on benches placed at intervals, coming back to the house with a leaf or feather in hand. If an airplane flew over the property he would leap up to shake his cane and curse at it. The Iveses visited often with the Ryders next door, from whom they had originally bought the property and who saw to the place in winter. In New York Ives walked the streets of his neighborhood in the evening. The house on 74th Street was a four-floor brownstone, his studio on top, everything plain but quietly elegant, with a backyard full of ivy and walkways. After dinner in city or country Harmony read aloud; at Redding she sat in front of the big window in the living room that looked west toward Danbury. She read Dickens and Thackeray and Browning and their other nineteenth-century favorites, and if they especially enjoyed a book she would turn back and read it over again. In later years when visitors came, Ives might take an old photo of Harmony from the mantel and intone, "Do you want to see a picture of the most beautiful girl in the world?" To Harmony he often exclaimed, year after year, "How I want to see Father again!"[29]

The maid could have a radio in her room but none was allowed elsewhere in the house. At some point Ives was persuaded to accept a wind-up phonograph, but it was little use to listen to his music on it. On the long European vacation he had first noticed a wavering of high pitches in his ears, and it got worse when he tried to listen to records or radio. It was part of the nerve deterioration of diabetes. His eyes were affected too, and on top of that he developed cataracts. For much of his remaining life Ives would hear and see badly. The "snake tracks" of his handwriting were like a graph of his nervous system. At the piano he still showed the old fervor, shouting and singing and stamping, and when he was up he jigged around on his cane with deceptive energy. But now his excesses of enthusiasm or rage usually ended in collapse, gasping and quivering. People often passed up seeing Ives because they were

Charlie and Harmony in the field below their house, West Redding.

afraid their visit might kill him. For days, weeks, sometimes months at a time he lay helpless in bed. Pain from the complications of diabetes could be terrible. After the frenetic schedule that had marked every day in the first half of his life, he spent the second half in a state of enforced tranquillity.

As the thirties wore on, the depression overlapping the approach of war, Ives's musical landmarks became smaller. Much of the activity amounted to investments in the future. In early 1934, seven years after John Kirkpatrick first saw the *Concord* on Katherine Heyman's piano in Paris, he wrote Ives, "I have decided quite resolutely to learn the whole sonata."[20] It would take five years more, painstakingly absorbing the music movement by movement, before he was ready to perform it complete. Ives's music was being published in a fairly steady stream, but most of it in *New Music Quarterly* with its tiny subscription list.

Ives and Slonimsky decided to approach other publishers about *Three Places*. Even though Ives proposed as usual to pay for everything, several turned it down before Boston's C. C. Birchard and Co. took it on. Ives hired Slonimsky to supervise the engraving and during 1933 they had detailed exchanges about it. By then Ives's eyesight was so bad he could only work in short bursts. He complained to Slonimsky of the white notes on green proofs that after "about 10 minutes they all start to move around—like rice in green soup to my eyes."[31] The Birchard score published in 1935 was beautifully engraved. The orchestral parts, meanwhile, were bad enough to obstruct performances for the next fifty years.

Mostly it would be the songs that were heard in the later thirties. At one of Cowell's New Music Society concerts, in San Francisco on September 26, 1933, mezzo-soprano Radiana Pazmor premiered *General William Booth Enters into Heaven*.[32] Long a standby performer for Ultra-Modernists, Pazmor was dark-voiced, over six feet tall, a striking presence onstage and off.[33] In 1934 she recorded *Booth* for New Music Quarterly Recordings, an Ives performance as fine as ever done.

The working relationship of Ives and Cowell, and their collaboration in *New Music Quarterly* business, can be seen in their exchanges over Henry's idea for that recording series. Since his money was going into it, Ives wanted hard figures for the project, and he was suspicious of the whole thing. "All I've tried to say," he wrote Henry at the end of a convoluted letter (he was confined to bed), "is that I don't know what to say—right now—except its safe to figure on $350 [from him] in January. . . . This with the $125 Dec 1 may leave a balance . . . for a record. After the first of next month I'll know better what we can do about the recording plans."[34] After his retirement Ives's income had shrunk year by year, from about half a million (1991 dollars) in 1930 to $130,000 (1991) from 1935 on. His uncertainty about the recording project probably came from his resentment of recordings, but also from a concern that he was no longer able to dole out unlimited funds.[35]

But Henry insisted on the project and in January 1934 New Music Quarterly Recordings announced plans to put out music by a number of composers. The original idea was to record Ives's *In the Night* and Ruggles's *Portals* in March 1934, at one of two ambitious Pan-American Society concerts Slonimsky was conducting at New York's Town Hall. The concerts turned out to be the death blow to the Society. Ives felt too sick to attend his rehearsals or performance and everything was underrehearsed.[36] On the podium Slonimsky was careless to the point of never noticing that Ives's French horn part was copied, and played, in the wrong key.[37] And there was no recording. These concerts had gone off like too many others with the Pan-American Society:

small audience, shaky performances, scarce critical attention, and Ives having to make up the deficit. Ives was disappointed but got to work arranging for a recording session. Ruggles, though, declared Slonimsky's performance of his piece a "massacre" and demanded a different conductor for it.[38]

Once again, probably with a sigh or a curse, Ives pulled out his checkbook and tried to make everybody happy. He would pay for another conductor for Ruggles but insisted on Slonimsky for his own pieces, and he would pay Nicolas the same as if he had done both sides. The record, the third release for New Music Quarterly Recordings, consisted of Ives's Barn Dance from *Washington's Birthday* and *In the Night,* and Ruggles's *Lilacs* and *Toys.* It was the first recording of either man's music, and thus beautifully appropriate for those two friends—but Ives was not beautifully played.

The disarray of the original concert reflected the state of the Pan-American Association of Composers. Cowell had been running it while Edgard Varèse was in Europe, but in late 1933 Varèse returned to the United States and applied his heavy hand to the organization. He insisted on playing his own music more than the market could bear, and wrote an article for *Trend* that implied things had been slacking under Cowell and he was whipping them back in shape.[39] Ives had never much liked Varèse or his music, and the treatment of Henry infuriated him. Ives wrote Cowell in summer 1934, "The thing about Varese that makes us the sorest is the stupid and unfair way he treats you. . . . I saw him only twice last winter and tried to tell him that 'an Association' in this country means a comprehensive group in which all members have a say. I thought he agreed."[40] By the end of 1934 the Pan-American Association, with its remarkable roster of composers and its fair hopes for American Ultra-Modernism on both continents, was finished.[41]

In the same 1934 letter in which he complained about Varèse, Ives told Cowell that they were going to England for a couple of months "I'll have to admit that I haven't been getting any better to say the least, for some time; and the trip before seemed to do us all good." And also, "I told Becker I would help him up to $200 if needed, on his Chicago concert. . . . Becker is a remarkably good conductor & more than that a good man but in a bad position just now." The year before, John Becker had lost his job at St. Thomas College and had not found anything since. Ives hired his friend to make a fair copy of the *Harvest Home Chorales* and to arrange *General Booth* for solo, chorus, and chamber orchestra. The planned Chicago concert collapsed along with Becker's health in September. His activities as composer, conductor, and teacher were all in decline. Copying work and donations from Ives would provide a good deal of the Becker family's support for years.

Shortly before the Iveses sailed for England on August 10, 1934, a hopeful sign appeared. John Kirkpatrick reported that he had *Emerson* under his fingers: "I can't tell you what satisfaction this beginning of an accomplishment gives me. My regard and admiration for the work has grown immeasurably with each degree of penetration and it is a great joy to be on the brink of being able to make it manifest to others."[42]

On this vacation the Iveses mostly stayed in London and returned home in early October, this time the worse for wear. It began to sink in that his health was not likely to get better. In fact it would continue to sink, though there would always be periods when he was up and about. This siege apparently lasted over a year. The next autumn, 1935, Ives wrote in despair to Henry, "Am just getting out of one of those g— d— slumps. . . . I guess music and I are parting company—can't see it—can't hear it most of the time—eyes & ears blur—It makes me—wild—it's the Creator's fault—not mine!"[43] But if he was going to be a wreck, he would at least go down fighting, and working.[44]

Cataracts and debility notwithstanding, the practical work that Ives had put off for so many years had caught up with him. He had his manuscripts photocopied and kept on file at Quality Photoprint in New York, to be dispensed (in that often unreadable form) to inquirers. After *Eighteen Songs* came out in *New Music* in 1935, Ives and Cowell turned to *Washington's Birthday*. Besides going over a steady flow of publication proofs, an enormous backlog of pieces needed to be gotten into fair copy if he hoped for publication, and Henry could provide only so much help. Ives began having his most devoted copyist, George F. Roberts, stay over in Redding and in New York, helping prepare new scores. Ives had some of the manuscript photostats enlarged so he could see them better. Roberts recalled their meetings in New York:

We'd go to the top floor, Ives creeping up on all fours [as his doctor had advised]. . . . Once there, he'd always offer me a cigar. He had them there for Carl Ruggles, and I don't know how many years he had them, but they were dust. . . . He'd play, sometimes for a couple of hours, if he got started on something. . . . He'd go over that piano with tremendous speed.[45]

In January 1936 John Kirkpatrick played *Emerson* in a Town Hall recital. That March a first letter arrived from teenager Lou Harrison, then a college student in San Francisco. "I am very sorry about your health," Harrison wrote, "of which Henry Cowell has told me. . . . Perhaps it may give you some consolation to know that you have the love and admiration of hundreds of the younger America, whom you touch in some wonderful but vicarious way thru your music."[46] Harrison had an exaggerated view of Ives's reputation, but the composer was happy to believe it. Immediately Harrison began receiving scores in print and photostat, then a wooden crate containing photostats of all the chamber music. "I simply went through it all," he recalled, "at the piano and studying it silently—for year after year."[47]

Like Lou Harrison, most new converts to the cause came directly or indirectly from Henry Cowell, constantly on the lookout for chances to promote Ives. The two men were an old team now—Henry the doting son, Ives the generous father. In April 1936 Cowell sent his version of *Calcium Light*

Night for Ives's approval. The original had been a rough sketch from a Yale-period piano stunt. Henry, from his composer's skill and understanding of the music, fleshed out the score. After years of association with Ives, who despite everything retained a certain Victorian formality, Henry had finally started addressing his letters "Dear Charlie."

In early July 1936, Harmony received a letter from John Becker saying Henry had been arrested. Becker knew he'd better write Harmony about this rather than Charlie. The charges against Henry amounted to sodomy and corrupting the morals of a minor.

Harmony read Becker's letter with horror and immediately wrote Charlotte Ruggles:

Have you heard this hideous thing about Henry Cowell—that he has been guilty of Oscar Wilde practices—a crime in California, must stand trial & probably receive a long sentence? Mr. Becker wrote me—fearing to write Charlie whom I shall not tell until I have confirmation. . . . If true I think it is the saddest thing in our experience. I had no inkling of this defect, had you? . . . of course it is a disease—"a quirk of nature", as Mr. Becker said . . . I am dreading this disclosure to Charlie—it is the only secret I've ever had from him.

At that moment Harmony was ready to accept Becker's characterization. Henry's proclivities were a quirk of nature: to see it that way was in the direction of forgiveness, of tolerance. But the attempt to forgive and tolerate lasted only until Henry's letters arrived. After that Harmony wrote Charlotte again:

In the mail with your letter was one from Henry addressed to me which contained a letter to be given to Charlie if I saw fit. It was a strange letter—admitting his commission of the offense but with no suggestion of contrition—there was in fact, a spirit of bravado it seemed to me—his "spirit was undaunted" (stock phrase) & he is "absolutely contented." Is he contented with himself do you suppose? Anyway, I told Charlie & he & I feel just as you do. A thing more abhorrent to Charlie's nature couldn't be found. We think these things are too much condoned. He will never willingly, see Henry again—he can't. . . . The shock used him up & he hasn't had a long breath since I told him but he will get used to it. . . . He said characteristically "I thought he was a man he's nothing but a g— d— sap!" I cant write any more—the letter from Henry was largely about the carrying on of New Music—He has planned it all out as you of course know. . . . We want to see New Music go on.[48]

It was the lack of contrition they found intolerable, that turned them against Henry. For the Iveses, sin was Sin in the conventional and Victorian sense of the word. From that point they would try to pretend Henry Cowell never existed.

To the authorities Henry had confessed to having relations, over a period of three years, with a group of teenagers he had given the run of his property in Menlo Park, California. Though claiming the boys had played on his weakness, he admitted his homosexuality, and that earlier encounters had included a number of boys. Cowell pled for leniency on the grounds that he had been as much seduced as seducer, and that he was not exclusively homosexual; he even claimed plans to marry a German woman. (Probably that was the gist of his letter to Ives.) At the same time as Cowell tried to shift some of the blame, though, he did not want the boys subjected to taking the stand in a trial. To protect them he pled guilty, hoping to get off with probation.[49] He got fifteen years at San Quentin prison. William Randolph Hearst's *San Francisco Examiner* ran a front-page picture of Cowell behind bars with the headline "California Oscar Wilde Jailed!"

Immediately Cowell's friends rallied to work for his parole—nearly all his friends except, for the moment, Ives. Helping Henry would not be easy in any case. The prosecutor and the papers had portrayed him as a dangerous deviant, an Oscar Wilde with all the connotations of artistic decadence; his outspoken leftist politics only made things worse. And he admitted the charge. It was an era when inclinations toward boys were perhaps romanticized in homosexual circles, which even then were active and relatively open in San Francisco.[50] Anyway, Cowell seems more innocent romantic than sexual predator.

Until the arrest Cowell and Ives had both been innocents in a way. Did Ives totally fail to perceive that Henry and much of his circle, and other Ivesians as well, were homosexual? Maybe he knew and didn't want to know, with his always robust capacity for self-deception. How could Cowell have been close to Ives for nearly a decade without understanding his fear of effeminacy? How could Henry not have understood that in Charlie's eyes he could only be a sap, a pussy, a pansy? He seduced boys. He was not a *man*. Maybe Henry hadn't wanted to know either. On both sides an innocence all along, and both of them self-crucified by it. So Henry wrote the letters to Charlie and Harmony that forced them to shut him out.

When Harmony finally told Charlie, his adolescent insecurities and anxieties rose up like bogeymen around him. But this was more than a kick in the center of his neuroses. It was a tragedy almost like losing his father or Dave Twichell. Henry seemed at that point practically Ives's last, best hope. For years, in nearly everything significant that had happened to Ives's music, Henry had been involved somewhere. More than the practical part, Henry was as close to a son as the Iveses ever had, and a devoted, generous, and tireless one. Together they had shared ideals, plans, dreams, and a great deal of laughter.[51]

As Harmony had written, nothing could have been more abhorrent to Charlie's nature. Now that nature nearly killed him. His health took a prolonged dive. In the middle of June 1937 he wrote Slonimsky, "haven't been able to do anything, play or see any music for a long time." And then in the (unsent) draft of the letter he slipped into a diatribe, probably with Henry tearing at his mind: "Emasculating America for money—that's the root of the snake. . . . A Nation Molly coddled by commercialized papp—America losing her manhood."[52]

If the Iveses never faced Henry's proclivities but instead tried to wipe him out of existence, Henry never during his years in prison faced the fact that Ives had deserted him. In letters we find him anguishing over the cutoff, but grasping for rationalizations. In December 1936 he wrote Slonimsky from San Quentin,

Do you hear from Ives? I have not had a word from him. I naturally feel very badly. I wrote the whole thing to Mrs Ives, with a letter to give Mr Ives if she felt it would not be too much of a shock for his health. . . . I asked them to please not form judgement until I have had a chance to tell them of the matter myself. It is very unlike Ives to suddenly cut me off from all communication. I can't conceive of it at all. I know that his eyes are very bad and probably he cannot write or read the letters himself. . . . Not hearing anything at all is really torturing, because as you know, I regard Ives the same as a father; no one who had ever known him—could fail to be attached.[53]

It was torturing on both sides. Yet Cowell, rather than giving in to despair, approached prison with his customary vigor. At San Quentin he showed himself a more than model prisoner, performing and composing and conducting, and running what amounted to a music school for the inmates.[54] He kept track of *New Music* affairs with Gerald Strang, who had taken over as director. Harmony had written that despite Henry's situation they wanted to keep the journal going, and they meant it. For the present Ives's yearly $1,500 contribution continued, and he financed the work on his *Washington's Birthday* score. Then in 1939 Ives announced he was reducing his yearly contribution to $600.[55] By that point his income was down to about $13,500 a year, steadily eroded by inflation. Even after the cut, though, it would mainly be Ives's money that kept *New Music* going. (In 1939, the journal made all of $371.09 in sales.)

By then the old generation of Ives disciples had largely run aground for one reason or another. Clifton Furness had turned his focus to his teaching and Whitman studies, Henry Bellamann to his fiction. Cowell was in jail. Slonimsky's conducting career lay in ruins. After years of struggle E. Robert Schmitz gave up on Pro Musica in 1938.[56] John Becker was often ill, depressed, and unable to organize concerts as he once had,[57] and Edgard Varèse about the same.

However, a new generation of partisans was taking shape. Bernard Herrmann continued to promote his version of the Fourth Symphony Fugue, arranging for a CBS Radio performance in September 1936 by Howard Barlow and the Columbia Symphony.[58] (In 1940 Herrmann launched a historic film career with his score for *Citizen Kane,* which left him less time for Ives.) In early 1938 baritone Mordecai Baumann did six songs for New Music Recordings; these and Radiana Pazmor's *Booth* stand as landmarks in Ives performance, and both singers kept performing the songs. Lehman Engel, formerly of the Young Composers, premiered *Psalm 67* with his WPA Madrigal Singers in May 1937, some forty years after it was sketched by a teenager mastering polytonality.[59] The performance was Ives's first significant premiere since 1932. As head of the new Arrow Press, Lehman Engel became Ives's main publisher outside *New Music.* (Ives naturally gravitated to that nonprofit company largely run by and for composers.)

Most significant of the new partisans would be John Kirkpatrick. He kept working at the *Concord* with his characteristic dogged desultoriness, learning it a movement at a time and playing each publicly. Composer and performer first met in May 1937, when Harmony phoned Kirkpatrick and invited him for lunch. After that they got together several times a year, a rare privilege for a late acquaintance.[60] Kirkpatrick naturally hoped for some coaching on the *Concord.* But the only thing he ever got to play for Ives, in one of their first visits, was a page of *Emerson,* after which Ives brushed him off the bench and launched into various pieces related to the *Concord.*[61] Maybe the reason Ives kept Kirkpatrick away from the piano was that this music was too personal, too interior, for him any longer to enjoy it coming from anyone else. Pleading ill health, Ives would not attend the *Concord* premiere. For that matter, after the mid-thirties he may never have heard anything played live again. He only heard his music, usually chafing and muttering as he listened, on radio or phonograph.

If Ives would not try to influence John Kirkpatrick's interpretation of the *Concord,* he did press on the pianist a copy of the Twentieth Amendment— one of the old broadsides still lying in stacks around the house. Among others who received the amendment in that decade was President Franklin Delano Roosevelt. Despite a record of brush-offs as consistent as those of his music for many years, Ives had not given up on his political fantasies.

The pretext for his 1938 letter to FDR was to support the Ludlow Bill, which would mandate a popular referendum for any declaration of war. (The bill had enormous popular support but, as would any president, FDR saw that it was killed.) Ives's cover letter to the president is brief and relatively sensible, sounding the familiar themes: "Let all the people stand up and say what they think about WAR," both within nations and among them. Attached to the letter was a long memorandum and the amendment.

Ives had taken his memorandum through draft after draft, but in restating his hyper-Progressive agenda these pages mainly reveal that he had slipped several notches in his connection to reality since writing the amendment in 1920. He and Roosevelt had met when FDR was head of the committee that first had rejected Ives's "baby bond." In 1938 Ives was still lecturing FDR in his personal perspective on history and humanity. Now he fell into his private language to make his pitch. This is how Ives wrote the president of the United States:

A fundamental reason for nationalism was fear, and it still is. . . . People grouped themselves together to protect themselves from other groups. . . . A few soft-headed, thick-skinned political parties may try to get "theirs" this way, but nowadays most people in most countries live without chronic fear of their neighbors. . . . [People] give more of their spare thought than is necessary to the easy unessentials, which include . . . the radio sap, the movie mush, the tabloid lolly pop. . . . But give these millions a fair chance to get their teeth into stronger food, and then . . . it will not be many generations before all these various political groups throughout the world—with their medieval stuff well organized, fancy labels, and strutting leaders—will be recognized as being as useless to humanity as a policeman in Heaven.

He proceeds likewise, page after page, with Rollo and the Old Ladies putting in appearances, and concludes with one of his uppercase perorations: "Who gets it in the neck? The Politicians? NO, THE PEOPLE. Who has the whole say in all countries? The People? NO, THE POLITICIANS." If the amendment seemed the work of an eccentric with grandiose ambitions, the memorandum slips into crankdom.

Well, what else could he do? War was coming around again: the "strutting leaders" he had in mind were Mussolini and Hitler. Ives did all he knew how, forlorn as it was, to keep disaster at bay. Sketches for the FDR memorandum include pages of anguished rant: "The Peoples World Union will get these dark age softies—make men of them—or kill them so they can't breed any more cowardly slaves—the people except the Nazis . . . of the lowest & weakest type, could be given a chance to prove they have some manhood left—but every politician in charge of these backward animal minds . . . will be Killed— not too quickly." The tactic of bombing civilians, so matter-of-fact to later generations, filled Ives with horror. He returned to the subject again and again in memos, one of them appended to the FDR memorandum: "If a coward flies over and drops a bomb on a sleeping child's head, the only thing for a man to do is to rise up and get that dehumanized pigeon whether it brings us to war, hell, or Heaven."[62]

Unlike most Americans by then, Ives had not spent years watching war in the movies; he never romanticized it, not even his father's Civil War. Though Harmony and everyone else tried to protect him from the daily news, the Nazis and the havoc of modern warfare reached a sensibility unhardened by the brutal media images of modern life. As with his response to Henry's disaster, innocence was afflicting him again, innocence one of the catalysts of his optimism and his depression, his triumph and his undoing. The dark violence and moral dilemmas of this century that Ives had always refused to countenance could now, in his infirmity and helplessness, only drive him nearly crazy. As it was said of Beethoven: *He lacked the weapons to resist the world.*

At the end of 1937 Harmony wrote to Charlotte Ruggles, "Charlie is frightfully used up—he tried seeing a few people & it just doesn't work. We are sailing for Glasgow [next May] 18th."[63] Harmony was herself close to another collapse. Still, at that time Ives was functional enough to write his memorandum to FDR and, in April, to record six sides at Melotone Studios in New York.[64] Then the family, Edie with them again, departed on schedule. Ives wrote Becker at the end of June 1938:

We sailed rather unexpectedly . . . I had one of those usual chronic low swings, am used to them, but this lasted longer than usual—but Mrs. Ives has been in quite a serious condition—it worried me—the doctors were afraid of a bad nervous break down. She has been under a constant strain with my condition for the last ten years or so.[65]

As with most of the European vacations, this trip revived them for a while. In their travel diary Harmony wrote of one adventure:

C. went out walking one evening . . . met a man playing an accordion—talked with him—The man asked him what he could play for him—"Shall I play Cavalleria Rusticana" . . . "No!—none of that Italian stuff—play an American air." The man played "My Old Kentucky Home." A policeman came up said "Nine thirty—time to stop"— CEI (taking conductor attitude) to policeman "No, no, not yet—not time till he has played that last chord!" The policeman laughed & seemed to enjoy it.[66]

Another night in a London hotel Ives began playing with a kitten, following it down the hall into a drawing room, where hotel guests were shocked to find an aged American crawling after a kitten shouting "Little Willie Pickleface!"[67] Another day he browsed the sheet music in a store and declared to the clerk, "That isn't music, that's mush." To his amazement the clerk replied that there were some very good British composers at work, but "of course we haven't men doing things like Ives and Copland."

They returned to the States in July. John Kirkpatrick wrote that in June he had played the entire *Concord* in public for the first time, at a private recital in Stamford, Connecticut.[68] In September Edie wrote to Becker: "We had a very pleasant summer in Scotland and England. . . . Mother is much better from the trip, and so was Daddy until three weeks ago, when he had quite a bad heart attack, and has had to be quiet ever since."[69] By the end of November Ives was well enough to have Kirkpatrick over for lunch. The pianist was near the end of his ten-year odyssey with the *Concord*. On November 28, he played it from memory—an extraordinary feat—for a small audience in Cos Cob, Connecticut. The official premiere was set for New York in January 1939. Every Ivesian in the country held his breath. This, finally, might be the breakthrough.

In better times Henry Cowell would have been working behind the scenes pulling strings, spreading the word, priming critics. Just before the official *Concord* premiere in New York, Henry sadly wrote soprano Mary Bell from San Quentin,

I often think of him; I do not hear from him, as I know he cannot write himself, but had a very fine note from him last year here. I wish that you would tell him that I think of him very often, if you do see him. And give him my staunchest greetings. . . . It has been with the greatest delight that I see the march forward of understanding of his work . . . and it gives me a tremendous satisfaction to feel that I have played a part.

Shortly afterward Bell asked to see Ives and sent a letter from Henry. Harmony wrote back that he was "too used up" to see her and "I return Henry's letter. That matter has been such a blow to Mr. Ives that we never speak of it."[70] (Had Ives actually written the note that Henry mentioned, or had the prodigal son imagined it?)

Lawrence Gilman, assigned to cover the *Concord* premiere for the *Herald Tribune,* was something of a Renaissance critic. Self-taught in music, Gilman had studied painting and also reviewed drama and literature. He wrote program notes for the New York Philharmonic and Philadelphia Orchestra, and was un-Ivesian enough to be a Toscanini champion and fervent Wagnerite.[71] The 1927 *Comedy* performance had intrigued him but he had heard nothing of Ives since. To prepare for the *Concord* Gilman wrote Ives asking for score and information. Gilman was stunned to read a reply from Harmony; in his Hartford youth he had been one of the boys smitten with her. Gilman wrote back, "Naturally I remembered you as Harmony Twitchell *[sic]*—you represented to me in those days a number of ideals!"[72]

For John Kirkpatrick's premiere of the *Concord Sonata,* at Town Hall on January 20, 1939, only a small group of enthusiasts turned out. The composer was represented by friends and family including his pianist niece Sarane; he stayed home in bed, Harmony with him. Ives could only imagine Kirkpatrick sitting down to the piano, the silence in the hall broken by the pealing octaves of *Emerson.* The sonata unfolded, a musical world perplexing here and ingenuous there, singular from beginning to end. After the barely audible evocation of Concord bells that ends *Thoreau,* the little crowd erupted in cheers. They brought Kirkpatrick back for seven encores.[73]

Most of the reviews, with one historic exception, were noncommittal to bad. Lawrence Gilman's review made a landmark of what otherwise would have been one more obscure Ultra-Modernist event preaching to the converted. Gilman had studied the music and the *Essays* and had used his ears and his heart. His words ring as fine and true as ever written about Charles Ives:

This sonata is exceptionally great music—it is, indeed, the greatest music composed by an American, and the most deeply and essentially American in impulse and implication. It is wide-ranging and capacious. It has passion, tenderness, humour, simplicity, homeliness. It has imaginative and spiritual vastness. It has wisdom and beauty and profundity, and a sense of the encompassing terror and splendor of human life and human destiny—a sense of those mysteries that are both human and divine. . . . [Kirkpatrick's] performance was that of a poet and a master, an unobtrusive minister of genius.[74]

Afterward, most of the story of Charles Ives's career in the world flows in some degree from those words. Resistance to Ives, some of it bitter, would

MUSIC

By LAWRENCE GILMAN

A Masterpiece of American Music Heard Here for the First Time

John Kirkpatrick

Piano recital by John Kirkpatrick, at Town Hall, Friday evening, January 20.

PROGRAM

1. Sonata in C major, Op. 53...Beethoven
   I. Allegro con brio
   II. Introduzione, adagio molto
      Rondo, allegretto moderato—prestissimo
2. "Concord, Mass., 1840-'60"
      Charles E. Ives
(First complete performance in New York City)

Player of Charles E. Ives's "Concord Sonata"

MUSIC by an unexampled creative artist of our day, probably the most original and extraordinary of American composers, yielded the outstanding experience of Mr. John Kirkpatrick's piano recital last evening at Town Hall.

The music in question was written by Charles E. Ives, a New Englander, now dwelling in New York, whose name means nothing whatever to most music-lovers and musicians—although that fact is almost certainly of small interest to the individual in question. For Mr. Ives is one of those exceptional artists whose indifference to réclame is as genuine as it is fantastic and unbelievable.

* * *

Charles Ives is sixty-four years old, and for nearly half a century he has been experimenting with musical sounds, and writing them down on paper, working quietly and obscurely (as revolutionary spirits in the regions of the mind so often work), known only to a few inquisitive students and observers who at first Shuffle'; or something else in the Wonderbook—not something that happens, but the way something happens; or something about the ghost of a man who never lived, or about something that never will happen, or something else that is not."

* * *

The review of Kirkpatrick's performance by Lawrence Gilman, January 21, 1939.

not stop and has never stopped since that night in 1939. The breakthrough was only partial, but it was permanent. There was no more respected critic in America than Lawrence Gilman. Even if few agreed with him that the *Concord* was "the greatest music composed by an American," Ives could never be ignored again.[75]

In the wake of the premiere, tributes, inquiries, and reminiscences poured in around bedridden Charlie. He could hardly keep up with them; the last heart attack had left him weak in body and mind, and each recovery regained less ground.[76] A long Olin Downes article in the *Times* declared the concert an event in American musical history. Clifton Furness wrote, "heartiest hand-clasps from mother and from me for this signal performance." *Time* magazine ran an article tentative on the sonata but generally positive: "little by little the few music-lovers who did hear [his music] began to realize that Ives was neither a trickster nor a crackpot, but a writer of real, live music."[77] Violinist Jascha Heifetz wrote to inquire after Ives's violin music (he received photostats, and gave up).[78] Around the country Ives performances heated up again, to a point where they had not been since the early thirties. In Los Angeles, pianist Frances Mullen began playing the *Concord* for the "Evenings on the Roof" concert series she ran with her husband, writer Peter Yates. In the forties Ives performances and all-Ives concerts would become a staple of Evenings on the Roof, and Yates one of Ives's most vigorous advocates.

A month after the premiere Kirkpatrick played an all-Ives program at Town Hall, repeating the *Concord* "by popular request." That was a joke; the request came from Lawrence Gilman. This time the hall was packed and no less enthusiastic. On the program soprano Mina Hager presented a collection of songs including *General Booth*, "Walking," "At the River," and Charlie's old courtship tune on Harmony's poem, "Autumn." Critics mostly harrumphed. In those conservative years, when Aaron Copland had become the most powerful composer in the country, Gilman's was one of the few completely sympathetic reviews Ives received.

In the League of Composers magazine *Modern Music,* Elliott Carter, Ives's protégé from the twenties, gave the *Concord* the back of his hand. In "The Case of Mr. Ives" he concluded, "there is a lack of logic which repeated hearings can never clarify. . . . The much touted dissonant harmonies are helter-skelter. . . . The esthetic is naive, often too naive to express serious thoughts. . . . possibly charming, but certainly trivial." He even questioned Ives's originality: "The fuss that critics make about Ives's innovations is, I think, greatly exaggerated, for he has rewritten his works so many times, adding dissonances and polyrhythms, that it is probably impossible to tell just at what date the works assumed the surprising form we now know."[79] It hurt his mentor deeply and Carter knew it.[80] He felt he had publicly disowned something like a father; he would call the effect on himself "disastrously traumatic."[81] Though Carter jumped on and off the Ives bandwagon several times afterward, and changed his mind about the *Concord,* he never had the heart to visit Ives again.

Kirkpatrick continued playing the *Concord* in various venues, one of them a New York Yale Club dinner honoring Ives. The honoree was too sick to attend, but his confederates from the class of '98 had a jolly time. Old room-mate Mull Mullally sent his approval of the music, and Poverty Flat roommate Charlie Farr, with a few drinks in him, declared he had seen God.[82] In January 1940 Kirkpatrick played *Alcotts* and *Thoreau* at a Danbury all-Ives concert in which niece Sarane accompanied some songs. Ives relatives and friends showed up for that celebration of the native son who was shaping up to be the most eminent Danburian of all. (No doubt the concert also satisfied a number of citizens that the Iveses were as crazy as they'd always maintained.)

Another upshot of the *Concord* premiere was that the *New Yorker* asked writer Lucille Fletcher, then Bernard Herrmann's fiancée, to write a profile of Ives.[83] She recalled their first meeting at 74th Street, shortly after the premiere:

I went with Benny. Ives met us at the head of the stairs, and he seemed very flushed, very tense and friendly and excited—shaking with excitement. We went into the front parlor, which was all sunlight and old-fashioned furniture, and there was a cat curled up in the chair. Ives talked very feverishly. He would get himself terribly worked up to an extent that he would suddenly gasp for breath and then have to lie down.[84]

Fletcher labored for months on her article, "A Connecticut Yankee in Music." Her subject cooperated at first, then attempted to take over. When Ives read a draft he would edit Fletcher's prose and write in phrases and stories (among them the one about shouting "God damn sissies" at the performance of Ruggles's *Men and Mountains*). At first Fletcher accepted the changes, but they only grew more elaborate. Finally Ives was writing, *in Fletcher's style,* long stretches of prose about himself and his ideas. He also insisted on voluminous quotes of his reviews and political writings and tried to suppress everything to do with his life and person—especially about his rages.[85] Fletcher balked, argued, finally gave up: "He was too old, he was too fine a person, and he was too sick to push it. I couldn't please him, and what I would have left would be nothing."

Ives turned out to be delighted when Fletcher killed the article, and sent her a nice check. "He really did not want any publicity," she said; "his music spoke for him."[86] She mistook that. It was more that his shyness contended with his desire to get the music out, and partly for that reason he preferred to do the speaking for his music himself, failing that to have as close control as he could over what got written. Mistakes and distortions in print plague all artists, Ives with his hair-trigger sensitivity all the more. He was hostage to a nervous system that could stand good news only a little better than bad, attention only a little more than neglect. And he was still encased in the self-protective wall he had built through decades of disappointment.

In later 1939, working with Fletcher, Ives was probably feeling lower and more vulnerable than usual. His brother Moss had died in April, at sixty-three. Shortly afterward his mother's sister Lucy Parmelee, the last of his parents' generation to live in the Ives House, also passed away. Maybe it cheered Ives a little when in July Edie married lawyer George Grayson Tyler, in a small wedding of family and friends on the front lawn at Redding.[87]

After Moss died, Ives made a last pilgrimage over the hill to Danbury, a kind of recapitulation of his beginnings as his life's coda approached. He had not traveled the few miles back to his hometown for over a decade. He wanted to see again the old house resonant with the history of the Iveses, of boyhood with Moss, of Father and Grandmother Sarah and Uncles Ike and Joe and Lyman, of Aunt Amelia and Mother. Now his brother lay among them in Wooster Cemetery. Remembering the family, Ives remembered Danbury itself like one of them: the parades and holidays he had captured in his music, his father's concerts in the park, the town he had exalted into an archetype of community that would sing through the media that were eroding the very kind of community that created him, and most Americans before him.

If Ives exalted his past, the town had not. The Ives House sat up on Chapel Place, moved from Main Street to make way for business. Ives wandered around the empty place with his nephews recalling the people, the stories. After dark he and Bigelow set out for the Soldiers' Monument. When he got to the middle of town and saw what had become of the square he groaned aloud. The Opera House was long gone, and the elm trees, the Wooster House and First Congregational Church, and most of the other landmarks of his childhood. Ives saw a run-down, featureless, ordinary town. He leaned on a streetside sandbox with his hands over his eyes and moaned to his nephew, "I'm going back. You can't recall the past."[88]

Even before the *Concord* hullabaloo Lehman Engel had agreed to a new edition of the sonata for Arrow Press. After the premiere Engel wanted to get the edition out right away, to capitalize on the publicity. Ives decided he would edit *Emerson* and John Kirkpatrick the rest. At first things seemed to go nicely; in autumn 1939 Ives wrote Engel that Kirkpatrick would send the last three movements soon and he was nearly done with *Emerson*. Then Kirkpatrick mysteriously stopped communicating.[89] Once again Ives had begun tinkering, and Kirkpatrick dug in his heels: "I wanted it more like the first edition. I wanted to fight shy of modernities and go for the logicalities, so I procrastinated."[90] Finally the pianist tacitly washed his hands of the project, and in the process damaged his relations with Ives for some time. (He kept up the performances though, touring at one point with soprano Hope Miller, who soon became Hope Kirkpatrick.)

With no other choice, Ives took on the whole job of editing the *Concord* with the help of copyist George Roberts. It was really beyond him; diabetes flare-ups and heart troubles were relentless, his eyesight and hearing worse than ever. He could rarely work directly on the page more than a few minutes a day, and that only on good days. In 1940 there were problems with engravers and a lost set of proofs, and his revisions delayed everything still more. "Every time I went there it was new," Roberts recalled. "The printers were on his neck all the time. He used to laugh about it."[91] The second edition would not come out until 1947, eight years after work began on it.

In 1940 violinist Sol Babitz and pianist Ingolf Dahl started playing the Third Violin Sonata in recitals and editing it for publication by Arrow. Soon they would find themselves in a morass similar to what was happening with the *Concord*. After endless difficulties getting a workable copy, they sent the engraved proof to Ives; he threw it back at them because they had changed his accidentals. That score would not see print until 1951.[92] The difficulty of some works and erratic condition of scores and parts, Ives's obstructions at unpredictable moments, the fact that much of the editing and copying were done, sometimes inexpertly, by others—all his habitual unprofessionalism combined with his health to impede the spread of his music. The coming of World War II added to the likelihood that stagnation would set in again.

But a driving energy for Ives reappeared when in June 1940 Henry Cowell was paroled from prison after four years, thanks to both his and his friends' exertions—the friends including Ives, who had written a letter of support to the parole board.[93] Cowell picked up where he left off with *New Music* (moving its base to New York), took executive positions on several other musical organizations, got to work on a row of commissions, and opened the 1941 New York Philharmonic season as soloist and composer.[94]

Having never admitted that his spiritual father had turned away from him, Cowell simply wrote the Iveses about *New Music* business. In August 1940 Harmony wrote a chilly reply: "I think you do not realize Mr. Ives's condition—He has to keep quiet—the doctor says this is very important to lessen the heart attacks. . . . He will be glad to continue the present monthly contribution. . . . He hopes you are well & that things will go well with you." By the end of the year they had thawed enough to send Henry Christmas greetings, with check. Henry replied, "I am greatly saddened that Mr. Ives' health is so poor, saddened to see the shakiness of his signature, but happy indeed that there is such a man in this world!"[95]

Then in September 1941 Cowell wrote astonishing news to Harmony: "I wish to tell you and Mr. Ives of my forthcoming marriage to Sidney Robertson." His fiancée was an ethnomusicologist.[96] The Iveses exploded with relief and warmth. Henry was getting married, all was forgiven, the prodigal son was redeemed. "It was great to hear your good news," Ives wrote through Harmony. "Our kindest wishes to you both—May the marriage bring a happiness which will last thro' to the end of Eternity and then on." And of course a big check. Henry returned to another job he loved, promoting Ives. In September he wrote that Columbia Records was interested in the *Concord,* in November that he had showed the Fourth Violin Sonata to Joseph Szigeti. In April 1942, Cowell and Ives met for the first time in six years. It was, almost, like old times. But never again would Henry presume, as he had just before the disaster, to begin his letters "Dear Charlie."

Cowell's initiatives played out well. Joseph Szigeti and Andre Foldes recorded the Fourth Violin Sonata for New Music Quarterly Recordings, then featured it at a Carnegie Hall recital on February 25, 1942, and continued playing it in recitals and broadcasts.[97] The Hungarian violinist, who had a long association with Béla Bartók, was the most celebrated soloist to take up Ives yet. Even if his interpretation of the sonata was largely oblivious to the American and Ivesian nuances, his advocacy could only help.[98]

Also during early 1942 Cowell began trying to get the *Browning Overture* into publishable shape. The process would drag on for years, Lou Harrison getting involved, and the score would not see print until 1959. Once again the

Henry Cowell and Ives after their reconciliation. Ives seems to be conducting something.

problem was Ives's frailty, in this case complicated by his ambiguous feelings about the overture and by a new project that obsessed him. During World War II, Ives mounted his last crusade.

As America sank into the war Ives picked up his World War I marching tune "He Is There!" and reworked it—the text rather than the music—into a song he called "They Are There!" or "War Song March." In the new version the little Yankee boy going off to fight has given way to a grander, more apocalyptic lyric that hardly stops to notice the new war. "They Are There!" ended up a distillation of ideas from *The Amount to Carry* through the Twentieth Amendment and "The Majority" to the People's World Union—all the social and political dreams to which Ives finally dedicated his life and work. The result is moving to contemplate in its shining futility:

> There's a time in many a life,
> When it's do though facing death,
> and our soldier boys will do their part
> that people can live in a world where all will have a say.
>
> They're conscious always of their country's aim,
> which is Liberty for all.
> Hip hip hooray you'll hear them say
> as they go to the fighting front.
>
> > Brave boys are now in action,
> > They are there, they will help to free the world.
> > They are fighting for the right
> > But when it comes to might
> > They are there! . . .
>
> When we're through this cursed war,
> All started by a sneaking gouger, making slaves of men,
> Then let all the people rise
> and stand together in brave, kind Humanity.
> Most wars are made by small stupid selfish bossing groups
> while the people have no say.
> But there'll come a day—Hip hip Hooray!—
> When they'll smash all dictators to the wall.
>
> > Then it's build a People's World Nation, Hooray!
> > Ev'ry honest country free to live its own native life . . .
> > Then the people, not just politicians,
> > will rule their own lands and lives.
> > Then you'll hear the whole universe
> > shouting the battle cry of Freedom,
> > Tenting on a new camp ground!

The song may have been the galvanizing reason why, around April 1943, Ives visited Mary Howard Recordings in New York, where he made the last and most ambitious of his private recordings. Mary Howard had worked with Toscanini and plenty of the celebrated, but she remembered this character vividly:

Ives was absolutely full of beans and it wasn't bad temper. It was just excitement. I remember that he sang one phrase from the *Concord Sonata* over and over. "Now do you get that?"—and he'd pound and pound and Mrs. Ives would say, "Now, please take a rest." He drank quantities of iced tea, and he'd calm down and then go back at it again, saying, "I've got to make them understand". . . . [Harmony] sat and read a book, but her whole interest was on the recording and on the music and once in a while she would correct him. She'd say [when he was choosing takes], "That's not what you said this morning."[99]

Among the recordings of those sessions, mostly excerpts and improvisations, was Ives's performance of *The Alcotts,* which in recordings since has been bettered in elegance of sound but never in spirit. And in those sessions Ives roared out "They Are There!" for posterity, with asides under his breath *(Goddamn thief!),* the recording as close as we will ever hear to the raw, unedited, cranky, magnificent Charlie that so many people loved, and who never lost the echo of his old volcanic energy.[100]

Rip-snorting as it is coming from his mouth, "They Are There!" is anything but a joke. Steeped since childhood in the emotional and patriotic potency of Civil War songs, Ives convinced himself that "They Are There!" could help win the war, change the world. His chance came when the League of Composers commissioned, from him and other American composers, a series of orchestral works with patriotic themes.[101] He may have been working on the song before, but the commission gave him an opening he had long dreamed of. He hired Lou Harrison to flesh out and arrange the draft for chorus and orchestra, meanwhile filling pages with sketches for program notes and cover letters:

The War Song March . . . suggests something that . . . 99% of all the people now living on our old Planet are strongly for or would be as soon as it is presented. . . . We have been told that this song especially in the last verse gives soldier boys—in a few words—& shouts—a clear or simple digest—the aim of what they are all fighting for—a new Free World! . . . It ought to be shouted out all around the world until all the governments of the world get together and build a Peoples Free World Nation.[102]

Once again, as in his old crusades, Ives appealed to the famous, asked for a hearing. To Serge Koussevitzky he proposed a ramshackle patriotic assemblage of *Putnam's Camp,* the Second Symphony finale, *Decoration Day,* and "War Song March."[103] (Aaron Copland had already tried Ives on the Boston Symphony conductor, and neither that nor this initiative convinced Koussevitzky to play any of it.) At length the march was scheduled for performance with the New York Philharmonic under Artur Rodzinski. The Office of War Information wrote Ives for permission to record it "for broadcast abroad for the purposes of troop entertainment and propaganda."[104] It was an incredible chance for his music and ideas actually to reach the soldiers, the politicians.

Then in June 1944 Rodzinski's secretary returned the score, with the excuse that the chorus made it impractical. Besides, the war was winding down. Probably devastated but not defeated, Ives immediately drafted a letter to Rodzinski saying the march "will be needed probably as much after the war as before."[105] Meanwhile Ives got Cowell to show "They Are There!" to Leopold Stokowski, with no more luck. Eventually he promoted it as a "United Nations Marching Song."[106] In the end nobody played the choral version of "They Are There!" in his lifetime.[107]

In 1941 Cowell reported that Columbia Records was interested in the *Concord Sonata*. From Los Angeles Peter Yates began pressing Ives to let his wife, Frances Mullen, do the recording—she had been playing the sonata at Evenings on the Roof. Ives may have gotten wind that this pianist was not entirely up to the piece; besides, despite John Kirkpatrick's recalcitrance over the editing, Ives still preferred him for the recording. So all through the war Ives cordially stonewalled Yates. Kirkpatrick for his part covertly maneuvered to keep Mullen out of the running, but at the same time dawdled as usual.[108] Kirkpatrick finally recorded the *Concord* on April 9, 1945. Then Columbia dithered three years before releasing it. (When they finally did, to their amazement it had a run as a classical best-seller.[109])

Events accelerated as the war ended. One attempt to get things to a new level came from Elliott Carter, trying to expiate his guilt over panning the *Concord*. In 1944 Carter wrote a seventieth-birthday tribute for *Modern Music* called "Ives: His Vision and Challenge." Soon after the article appeared, Carter wrote Ives about the idea of an "informal committee" to promote the music.[110] Ives was agreeable, but when Carter wrote him official notice of the formation of a Charles Ives Society, its subject panicked. He wrote Carter, as if from Harmony,

Your letter affected Mr. I so deeply that he says he was almost knocked over the ropes. . . . [He] says he cannot find words to express his great appreciation of all you Henry other kind friends are doing in his behalf—he feels that he doesn't deserve it all—and to have a society named after him is not fair to many other American composers—and also that it will bring you all too much trouble and take too much time. . . . There are other composers he says who need your help too—among them Carl Ruggles, and in the next generation Henry Cowell and a younger friend of his Elliott Carter, whom you may have met. . . . He doesn't feel quite right about having a society named after him (he says it makes him feel . . . "sort of like a Hog").[111]

The Society straggled on for a few years, hamstrung by his refusal to countenance it.[112] So much for an idea that might have done immeasurable good for the music—and did, after the Ives Society was reactivated in 1973.

Ives's response to Carter ensured that for decades the efforts of Ivesians would continue to be as erratic and disorganized as they had always been.

In due course honors began to turn up for Ives, of the sort bestowed on people as a pat on the back before they leave the scene. In December 1944 he was invited to join the National Institute of Arts and Letters. one of the highest honors available for an American artist. Despite what he called his "a-association" instincts, Ives accepted (and immediately started a campaign to get Carl Ruggles into the Institute).[113]

Eventually there would follow an honor more likely to get on the front pages of newspapers. The process began with Lou Harrison, who had been studying the manuscripts since Ives sent him piles of music in the mid-thirties. Offered a guest conducting job with the New York Little Symphony, Harrison thought of the Third. In summer 1945 he wrote Ives of his determination to play it and set to work copying the parts.[114]

Harrison premiered the Third Symphony at Carnegie Chamber Music Hall on March 5, 1946, the Little Symphony program including a motet of his own and Ruggles's *Portals*. Harmony came to represent her husband. Harrison repeated the symphony at the end of the program, as if it were the sort of difficult work that it certainly is not. In its gentle, hymn-suffused course the Third exactly fit the Americana aesthetic of the day. Critics gave it some of the best notices Ives had received in years. Said the *New Yorker*, it "manages to suggest a rural background without any self-conscious musical by-heckery." Said the *New York Times*, "It was music close to the soil and deeply felt."[115]

Among the repercussions was that publisher G. Schirmer, who had engraved the original *Concord* and *114 Songs* but kept the firm's name off them, wrote Ives asking to have the Third Symphony. His draft reply begins: "Go to HELL! No—Not a dam note will be sent to you—publisher of mushy cissy weak sister sugar plum musick."[116] (The sent letter was certainly more decorous.) Ives gave the symphony to Arrow Press and Lou Harrison became the well-paid (by Ives) editor. Meanwhile Harrison had turned to resurrecting the First Piano Sonata; he would continue working on it through a crack-up that landed him for a time in a psychiatric hospital.[117]

A month after the symphony premiere Elliott Carter helped produce an all-Ives program at Columbia University. A large and rapt audience heard the premiere of *The Unanswered Question* and *Central Park in the Dark*, plus songs, part of the Second Quartet, the Third Symphony, and the Second Violin Sonata. Among the audience were Serge Koussevitzky and Dimitri Mitropoulos, reportedly enthusiastic. A review by Paul Henry Lang in *Saturday Review* was neither the first nor last to call Ives a "legend."[118] For years that would be a familiar tag, and accurate enough: more known in legend than experience, more in reputation than performance. The ridicule continued. When in 1948 the Boston Symphony played *Three Places* in New Haven—under concertmaster Richard Burgin, not Koussevitzky—at the end the audience simply stood up and laughed, to the distress of Ives relatives and friends in attendance.[119] (Burgin's performances fared better in Boston and New York.)

Still, kind words were not lacking now. In September 1946 the Walden Quartet premiered the Second String Quartet, which Harrison had edited and here and there filled in. Echoing Lawrence Gilman's review of the *Concord*, *Modern Music* called it "the high point of American chamber music so far." The Walden recorded the quartet the next year. The November 1946 issue of *Listen* had two articles, a rather noncommittal one by Carter and one by Harrison that ended with some of the most poetic and sadly prophetic lines ever to appear about Ives:

I suspect that the works of Ives are a great city, with public and private places for all, and myriad sights in all directions. . . . In the not-too-distant future it may be that we will enter this city and find each in his own way his proper home address, letters from the neighbors, and indeed all of a life, for who else has built a place big enough for us, or seen to it that all were equally and justly represented?

Such is the work of Ives. And if we here, in the United States, are still really homeless of the mind, it is not because men have not spent their hearts and spirit building that home . . . but simply because we refuse to move in.[120]

A modest Ives vogue moved forward. Columbia student Curtis Davis had been so enthusiastic about the Third Symphony premiere that he had it recorded off the radio. Douglas Moore, later composer of *The Ballad of Baby Doe* and other high-Americana works, began using the record in his classes at Columbia.[121] Eventually Moore took it to the appropriate committee, who voted to give the symphony the 1947 Pulitzer Prize.

In the United States, a Pulitzer is the award above all others that takes a composer to the front pages, at least to a fingerhold in the mainstream. The telegram arrived at the Ives house on April 5. Ives proceeded to be thrilled and abashed and full of beans about the whole affair. In the one interview he agreed to, for the small Bridgeport *Herald*, he declared, famously: "Prizes are badges of mediocrity."[122] In private he hung the certificate proudly on the wall. Ruggles sent congratulations, to which Ives replied, "Just a few snake tracks from 'an ole feller's shaky paw', to tell you that <u>you</u> are the <u>best</u> composer in Europe, Asia, Africa, and America—but if you should ever have a Pulitzer prize swished on you, then that will mean that 'you ain't.' "[123] That letter went on Ruggles's wall. The prize money Ives divided between John Becker and Lou Harrison, the latter then in the hospital.[124] (When Harrison emerged from his breakdown in 1947 he met Ives for the first and only time. He entered the house on 74th Street to find Ives wildly swinging his cane and shouting "My old friend! My old friend!"[125])

The Pulitzer Prize set off one more period of discovery. Ives was all for attention to the music but steadily fought off publicity about his person. A press photographer practically broke into the Redding house, but was kept at bay by a fresh-painted floor and ejected. Letters of inquiry arrived and forms to fill out, most of them ignored. Requests came from doctoral candidates, psychologists, a phrenologist who wanted to palpate Ives's head.[126]

However unpredictable his mind was getting to be, however separated from the world and his time he had become, Ives appreciated that his work had an audience now, and that some of them understood it. Despite the pain and debility and fogginess of his old age, that gave him immense satisfaction. In the forties poet Louis Untermeyer visited, to have a look at the man who set to music his "Swimmers." Untermeyer recalled, "His presence impressed me. There are a few people who have presence per se . . . because they have a quiet dignity, a kind of self-assurance. He knew what he had done. He knew what he was, and that was that." When Ives's name appeared in print now, besides the "discovery" and "legend" themes, more and more the question was raised: Is this the Great American Composer? The question would lie disputed for many years, but after the Pulitzer Prize it would be regularly posed.

Part of the effect of new fame, of course, was that everybody wanted a look at his face. For years Ives had been sending people an old snapshot that he prized for its blurriness. Now friends and family and publications wanted more, and occasionally he was persuaded. Around 1947 Mike Myrick showed up at 74th Street with *Life* magazine photographer W. Eugene Smith. Ives had agreed to a portrait, but in the event he put up a hell of a fight. Recalled Smith, "In all of my years and experience of making photographs I have never seen anyone more terrified of the camera than Charles Ives. The only comparable reaction I have seen is that of the so-called uncivilized native who feels that the camera takes away something of his soul." Whenever a camera pointed his way Ives tended to stick out his tongue, sit on his hands, recite little poems, wheeze and sputter and gibber like some bizarre goblin. Smith was afraid his subject would drop dead before he got the picture. Probably this time as usual, Harmony sat knitting on the periphery quietly watching, calming him down when he got out of hand: "Well, Charlie, if you're going to carry on that way, you know this is going to happen."

Finally Smith got Ives sitting still on a wicker chair, grasping his cane like a rifle and looking up at the camera, being a good boy through a long exposure.[127] This is the main picture of Ives the world would know, the closest one to catching his spirit in two dimensions. His grandson said, "That was the way he used to look when he was getting ready to play a joke on somebody."[128] Smith's photo session put Ives in bed for three weeks.[129]

Around the family Ives was still foxy Grandpa and Granduncle, a fascinating presence to children. For his grandson Charles Ives Tyler (Edie and George's son, born in 1946) and the others, he had his weird nicknames: "Ratneck," "Little Willie Pickleface." He would sit down at the piano and roar out a hymn for a wide-eyed toddler, or pound out his surreal marches like

Above: *Charles Ives in terror of Eugene Smith's camera, jabbering at Mike Myrick at West Redding—1942.* Left: *The photo Eugene Smith finally got out of Ives, the main image the world knows. Grandson Charles Ives Tyler said, "That's the way he looked when he was getting ready to play a joke on somebody."*

"The Royal Star Bazoonya," with its refrain of "fishcakes in the sky." "I almost always think of him telling a joke," his grandson said, remembering his puns and fractured aphorisms: "A poor joke is better than a good one." There was a good deal of physical pain that the children didn't know about, but grown-ups saw it pass over his face, stop him in mid-sentence. Yet few people who knew Ives thought of him as a tragic man, but rather as an energetic and delightful and fascinating figure, a mythical creature in the flesh, a perpetual event.

Ives visited friends when he could, in Redding especially with the Ryder family next door. Besides seeing to the house, in later years the Ryders did much caretaking of the frail Iveses too. It was Will Ryder who in 1945 built the filing cabinets into the barn, in one of Rocket's old stalls, where Ives finally consolidated his manuscripts in ten drawers. For decades the scores and sketches had been scattered around drawers and shelves in two houses; now they were in one place—albeit an unlocked, unheated outbuilding.[130] (Thus the fable of Ives manuscripts sitting in a barn for fifty years.) Looking for something, Ives would go out and shuffle through the drawers, each time leaving the pages more muddled. Eventually it would take John Kirkpatrick and several others years to straighten out the mess.

In 1948 organist E. Power Biggs played *Variations on "America"* for a CBS Radio broadcast. The premiere had been given by the teenaged composer soon after he wrote it; Biggs's was the first performance in over fifty years. That March in New York, Robert Shaw's Collegiate Chorale memorably sang *Psalm 67* and premiered the *Harvest Home Chorales*. In New York the following February William Masselos premiered Ives's great orphan the First Piano Sonata, re-created by Lou Harrison from a yellowed draft (most of it clear, but some of the ragtime sections little more than sketches).

At the Masselos premiere Harmony and a collection of friends and relatives heard the audience cheer robustly at the end. As usual with the harder pieces, reviews were mixed. Composer Wallingford Riegger wrote Ives an unqualified testimonial: "It was one of the few high spots in my whole musical career to have heard it. . . . I suppose I'm gushing like a school girl [Ives struck out that line—too sissy] but I still can't get over the indescribable grandeur of your work [Ives left that part]."[131] Redding friend Gertrude Sanford wrote Harmony, "I've been sitting here thinking about Mr. Ives' 1st Sonata . . . and have been wondering if all composers reflect so much of their own character and personality in their music. . . . during that concert, I could hear and see Mr. Ives so plainly that it was positively uncanny."[132] To many relatives and friends, Charlie simply was his music and his music was him.

Henry Cowell and his wife Sidney began working on a biography in 1947. It would take them eight years to finish, with Charlie and Harmony helping out as best they could. Harmony wrote the Cowells at the beginning, "We are getting answers to Henry's questions. How he is going to get Charlie into a book I don't know—his outward life has been uneventful—so wide ranging inwardly—and he is so inexpressibly funny! I laugh and laugh in solitude at things he has said and looked."[133]

His jokes and their bantering had helped them survive more than their share of losses over the years. So many friends and family were dead now, among them Henry Bellamann in 1945, Clifton Furness the next year. Others had faded from the scene. Luckless John Becker wrote from Chicago in 1947, "Do you ever hear from the old crowd. I seem to be the forgotten composer as far as the New York crowd is concerned. Haven't had a performance for a long long time. Never a word from Riegger, Varese, Weiss, and rarely from Henry."[134] Around then Ives showed up in Lehman Engel's office at Arrow

Ives and Harmony at Redding in the last years, as usual sitting close together. She told the Cowells, "I laugh and laugh at the things he says."

Press to ask that they publish a work of Becker's. Engel flatly refused and waited for the explosion. Instead Ives burst into tears.[135]

Critic Howard Taubman cornered the legend for an interview in 1949, for a *New York Times Magazine* feature titled "Posterity Catches up with Charles Ives." It was another "Discovered at Last" piece, and not the last one. Harmony brought Taubman to the living room in Redding, where Ives stood up straight in his old country clothes, his eyes bright and alert, and said, "It's good of you to come and see this old broom." They sat down before the big window. On the table Taubman noticed a pile of current periodicals. Ives pointed across the hills where the sun was setting and said, "That's Danbury on the other side of that mountain. That's where I was born and grew up and learned a little about music. Pa taught me what I know." He said of Harmony, "We never went anywhere, and she didn't mind." When Taubman mentioned the innovations Ives waved his hand and said, "That's not my fault." (That was not the kind of prophet he had intended to be; he did not need it any more.) In his article Taubman ended, "As you go down the walk he stands there waving at you. You look back at this proud and humble man, knowing that time is working steadily to raise him to his deserved place among the great creative figures of American musical history."[136] Time still had some work to do.

By then Ives's diabetes had abated to the point that he was able to go off insulin, and his heart troubled him less.[137] That recovery was a tribute to Harmony's two decades of nursing. Still he was fading, physically and mentally. When Cowell dedicated a piece to him in 1949 Ives wrote, "When a ole guy is stumbling into his 76th year—he has a right to make a fool of himself! Good music like yours, should not be dedicated to a useless ole bum—but he (the old feller) is glad to have it dedicated to him and thanks you 1489699 times."[138] There were many letters with formulas like that, jokes repeated like an old record, scratchier every time. Now and then the old man would erupt from reverie into a hoarse bray resembling "Columbia, the Gem of the Ocean." Harmony would say, when he was gone: "Mr. Ives got a little *silly* in his last years."

One day in Redding a secretary came upon him pacing back and forth in front of the picture window, humming and singing. "If only I could have done it," he said to her, pointing out the window. "It's all there—the mountains and the fields." She asked him what he meant. "The *Universe Symphony*," he said. "If only I could have done it."[139]

Harmony wrote the Ruggleses in late 1950, "Charlie did have to go to the hospital . . . but nothing had to be done as the doctor manipulated the hernia which was giving the trouble, back in place. . . . I have been the really sick one as I had a sharp gall bladder attack three weeks ago. . . . Of course you know the Philharmonic here is to do Charlie's 2nd Symphony in Feb.— Bernstein conducting. I suppose we shall be in misery."[140] Leonard Bernstein was the golden boy of the podium then, determined to match his mentor Koussevitzky in championing American music. Like Koussevitzky he preferred the milder moderns. Besides his passion for Copland, Bernstein naturally turned to Ives, looking for something unperformed but not too wild. The Second Symphony suited his style and times: a winsome piece that had secretly started American art music, and which sounded uncannily like Americana pieces of thirty years later.

The Iveses entered the familiar period of misery before a big concert. The Cowells noted in their biography, "He seems to be unable to feel any confidence in a prospective performance; it is as if he were still bracing himself in the old way against disappointment, unable to realize that such necessity is past."[141] Charlie had long ago declared that if the Second were ever performed by the New York Philharmonic in Carnegie Hall, he would go.[142] That was *his* concert hall, where he had heard music since he and his father sat together listening to the Philharmonic and the Boston Symphony and Paderewski, when teenaged Charlie was writing the brass-band pieces that grew into the Second Symphony. Now that the fantasy was coming true, Ives dithered for weeks in the clutches of his anxieties, his self-protective shell. Bernstein offered to conduct a special rehearsal for him to hear the symphony alone. Finally Ives could not bring himself to endure any of it.

So at the premiere on February 22, 1951, Harmony sat in a box at Carnegie Hall with Edie and George Tyler, with brother Joe Twichell and his wife and Henry and Sidney Cowell. Below in the hall were the Ryders and many other friends and relatives. After the startling yawp of the end came a roar of laughter and shouts and applause. Harmony looked down into the audience and said in disbelief, "Why, they *like* it, don't they?"[143]

The performance was broadcast nationally. Among the ensuing letters and telegrams to the Ives house, some of the most satisfying came from people back in Danbury. The Second was something they could understand. Nephew Bigelow wrote, "One fellow told me that his whole family . . . gathered around the radio which was placed on the kitchen table. . . . Before the symphony was half way through—grandfather had jumped to his feet to pound his fists on the table and shout with joy, 'By God, that's the kind of music I always knew there was in America!' "[144] The following year the Danbury Orchestral Society gave the symphony its New England premiere.

For Bernstein the Second would become a signature piece. He recorded it twice, near the beginning of his full-time tenure with the Philharmonic, again with them just before he died. The conductor would be a double-edged advocate. On the one hand he famously called Ives "Our first really great composer, our Washington, Lincoln, and Jefferson of music." He thereby declared Ives the founding father of American art music. That label would stick and rightfully so, but so would Bernstein's less fortunate ones: Ives the "primitive," the "Grandma Moses of music." Though in the fifties some critics already knew better and took Bernstein to task for it, Ives would not escape those terms for decades, if ever.

Back in West Redding, how did Ives receive the Second Symphony premiere? In legend he heard it on the maid's radio and did a little dance of joy afterward. In reality he was dragged next door to the Ryders' to hear the broadcast and, unlike similar occasions, sat quietly through the whole thing. It was one of his *soft* pieces, as he called them; it was also perhaps the warmest audience reception of his life. As the cheers broke out at the end everybody in the room looked his way. Ives got up, spat in the fireplace, and walked into the kitchen without a word.[145] Nobody could figure out whether he was too disgusted or too moved to talk. Likely it was the latter.

As his music rose, Ives sank. Shortly after the premiere Harmony had a dangerous and long-delayed operation for gallstones. "I must live to take care of Charlie," she told friends.[146] Edie wrote Peter Yates about the operation's effect on him: "It brought father so low in body & mind that he was in serious condition."[147] Soon after, viral pneumonia put Ives to bed for a month. Everybody feared that was the end, but he recovered. In March 1952 he had a reunion in New York with Slonimsky, whom he hadn't seen for years. Slonimsky asked how he was doing. "Oh, how am I?" Ives rasped. "I can't even spit into the fireplace."[148] He was not too sick that year to write his annual letter recommending Carl Ruggles to the National Institute: "His music is not imitative but rather an expression of a deep sense of thought from his own soul and life and sense of freedom." Ruggles finally got accepted in 1954.

At Town Hall that year, Harmony and Edie listened to John Kirkpatrick play the *Concord* once again. Edie was just out of the hospital from a bout with cancer. Harmony wrote Kirkpatrick afterward, "The 'Thoreau' is my favorite movement—its lovely serenity always moves me & your playing left me at the end . . . in the quiet peace & silence of the pines & hickories of Walden."[149] She was thinking of Charlie, and the distant bells of the end. Ruggles, who had been at the recital with Varèse, wrote Charlie, "Concord still haunting me."[150] All of them, family and friends, waited for the clock to run down. On April 9 Antal Dorati and the Minneapolis Symphony premiered the complete *Holidays;* the *Star* review was headlined "Dorati Rears Another Symphonic Landmark."[151] That month as the Cowells were trying to finish their biography, Harmony wrote Sidney, "Mr Ives says ['TSIAJ" in the Piano Trio] is a poor joke anyway & of no importance—I wish he felt like even poor jokes these days."[152] When his wit failed, he was near his time.

In the spring of 1954 Ives's double hernia finally demanded an operation. For an invalid near eighty he was recovering surprisingly well at Roosevelt Hospital in New York, chafing in fine form to get home, when a stroke hit him. On May 19 Harmony and Edie sat holding his hands as he slipped away, like so many of his works, into an eloquent silence.

John Kirkpatrick wrote a report of the funeral to Carl and Charlotte Ruggles. Harmony's brother Reverend Joseph Hooker Twichell presided at the services in West Redding. During the service Mrs. Ryder played *Abide with Me* at the piano. Most of the time Harmony sat numbly beside the open coffin. Edie told Kirkpatrick that at the hospital, when she and her mother held his hands at the end, "he seemed as if transfigured—that it was a kind of intimate communion of unspoken awareness she could never have imagined . . . a kind of serenity resolving all the tensions of his life, that somehow persisted intact quite a bit after he had quietly stopped breathing."[153] At the end all his paradoxes seemed to resolve into the wholeness at their center. From Redding the funeral party headed for Danbury. It was raining in Wooster Cemetery as they laid him to rest beside his father and the generations of Iveses.

To their closest friends Harmony wrote, over and over, variations of her lines to Lehman Engel: "I am lost without him. He has been my care & my joy for so long that my life seems emptied of its contents and I do not know how I shall fill it—But our life together was one of joy unchanging & 'through this joy unchanging I apprehend the joy unchangeable.' "[154] Their love had taught them God's love, and from that inspiration grew his greatest music and her greatest happiness.

Slowly Harmony recovered and took over the duties of composer's widow. First Cowell, then John Kirkpatrick and others went to work on the papers, and they came to rest at Yale. In 1968 Kirkpatrick became curator of the Ives Collection there and would be a selfless keeper of the flame for twenty years. In a 1955 broadcast Harmony heard Bernstein conduct the Second again and wrote Sidney Cowell, "It was as Mr. Ives's very self—I was greatly moved."[155] Two years after Harmony buried Charlie she had to endure Edie's death from cancer. Harmony lived to know of Leopold Stokowski's triumphant premiere of the Fourth Symphony in 1965. At the concert, as Stokowski began his introduction to the piece he was interrupted by an explosive sneeze from the audience. "That's not in the score," the conductor quipped, and everybody roared because they knew nearly everything else would be. The sneeze came from Mike Myrick, for whom Charlie's music was still incomprehensible, but who wouldn't have missed it for the world. Over and over in the press, the symphony was called a masterpiece.

In the spring of 1969 Harmony joined her husband under the trees on the heights of Wooster Cemetery, the single tombstone with two tablets, his side engraved with the psalm Harmony had chosen for him with her poet's instinct: *Awake psaltery and harp: I myself will awake right early.* Maybe she imagined Charlie marching into heaven with a big bass drum like General Booth, waking up the place, his father there to welcome him. Maybe he would teach the angels a new song, the language he had prophesied, higher and deeper than art itself. Harmony found in Psalm 108 an epitaph incomparably apt for a man who rose early and remade his art: the last Transcendentalist, whose clarion Reveille calls each of us to believe and rise up, to remake humanity and give birth to the true music. *Awake psaltery and harp!*

Postlude

ON JULY 4, 1974, the Charles Ives Centennial Concert at the Danbury Fair Grounds kicked off a year of events to commemorate Ives's birth a couple of miles away, a hundred years before. The old wooden bleachers were packed and the crowd was primed. On the grounds where once George Ives's band played his son's music, Leonard Bernstein and Michael Tilson Thomas conducted an orchestra and chorus in works ranging from the Second Symphony to "The Circus Band" and "They Are There!," the latter prefaced through loudspeakers by Ives's own unsurpassable rendition of the song. When Tilson Thomas conducted it afterward, everybody sang along: *The people, not just politicians, will rule their own lands and lives, and we'll hear the whole universe shouting the battle cry of freedom!*

Ives would have loved it. The concert embodied the frame of mind his music demands—a frame of mind standing in for the hills and valleys he imagined as setting for his music. Among the audience, a grab bag of community people and visitors, were hippies whose T-shirts proclaimed Ives a countercultural hero. And among that crowd was I, about to study composition at the Yale School of Music. On that trip to Connecticut I met John Kirkpatrick, to whom I had sent my undergraduate thesis on the Fourth Symphony. He took me to the Ives Room at Yale and showed me the manuscript. I remember the chills down my spine as he turned those surprisingly meticulous pages.

During the course of that year the Ives Centennial Festival-Conference mounted a series of concerts and symposia in New York and New Haven. There were commemorative doings in south Florida, Buenos Aires, and Bangkok. In New York Pierre Boulez, as un-Ivesian a musician as one could imagine, mounted a "Mini-Festival Around Ives" with the Philharmonic. Columbia Records released a centennial album with two sides of Ives playing and singing. Still, time and again, critics prophesied that after the hullabaloo of the centennial, Ives's music would sink back into the obscurity that belonged to it. Eight years after the concert at the fairgrounds, one of the nodal points of the community's history, Danbury tore the place down and put up a shopping mall.

Though Ives appeared to be falling into eclipse when I began this book eight years ago, the critics' prophecies have not come to pass. Now in 1995, twenty-one years after the centennial and five before the millennium, Ives is more visible than ever. At the moment five recordings of the Fourth Symphony are out and a half dozen of the *Concord Sonata*—the very pieces hardest to grasp. Stokowski's 1965 recording of the Fourth is still in print. Nicolas Slonimsky told me that when a Russian book on Ives came out in the 1980s, it sold in tens of thousands. Beyond the volume of music coming out month after month in recordings, critical response to Ives seems warmer than ever. All this is astounding and gratifying. I remember in 1962 playing Ives for smirking friends, in 1967 proposing my thesis to smirking Harvard faculty.

Some of the reason for the change is simple: the Charles Ives Society has generated editions and playing material that for the first time, for a lot of the music, are up to professional standards. Now players can put the music on the stand and play it without undue fuss. For that reason alone performances tend to sound better, more enthusiastic. Some of the reasons come from the fact that, as Lou Harrison wrote, the works of Ives are a great city and the boundaries of that city—somewhere, say, between "The Circus Band" and the *Universe Symphony*—could not begin properly to be discerned until Stokowski premiered and recorded the Fourth Symphony. And some of the reasons reside in the thickets of sociology, which lie beyond this study.

Certainly Ives has not unequivocally triumphed. His work sounds peculiar to many people, and that is all right. He probably always will sound that way to listeners and musicians who ask for elegance and clarity of sound, because Ives did not much care about those things. Ives may never be a full-fledged standard composer, his work in the standard repertoire and among its certified masterpieces. The fact is, I would hate to see him subjected to that fate and am sure he would hate it too. Ives flayed the settled, the standard, the predictable. He will forever be the maverick, the great exception. More than any other artist on his level, he reminds us that greatness is not merely a matter of polish but of spirit, of substance rather than manner. He will remain a challenge to all of us and a threat to some. That is all right.

I am most concerned here with the spirit of Ives's music, and the yearnings that bring people to him. I can only believe that he has finally defined a space for himself, that some of his one-man milieu is coming through after the end of Modernism, at the brink of the millennium. His music has begun to free itself of obfuscating commentaries, including his own, and make a case for itself. Richard Wagner, another revolutionary, built a milieu of wood and stone and theory and ideology, all of it assembled around a pedestal with himself installed on it. It was Ives's genius to build a milieu of spirit, of material at once singular and familiar, new and shopworn, found and invented, Romantic, modern, collaborative, and individual. When he wrote of his ideas he argued less with theories than with parables and aphorisms. (One of his friends observed: "It's hard to quote Ives because he always meant more than what he said.") Rather than erecting a pedestal for himself, Ives pointed to us and said: Put yourselves on the pedestal, and see what you can make of it.

Ives and the other Progressives of his era greeted the turn of the twentieth century with joyous optimism at the approach of the millennium. Nearly a hundred imminent years later, the world seems to regard that approach more with dread than anything else. William Faulkner said in his Nobel Prize speech: "There are no longer problems of the spirit. There is only the question: When will I be blown up?" That was halfway through this century and the fear has only intensified, even in an era of decreasing nuclear peril. The questions have changed *(When will I get shot, lose my job, lose my family, lose my sense of meaning and direction)* but the dread has not.

Here is a guess for much of the reason: not art or religion or reason or science or progress or heroes have seemed to stave off any measure of the suffering and uncertainty that afflict human life. Humanity's shining dreams of salvation have toppled, one by one, and left us alone with our troubled and troubling selves.

What brings listeners to Ives I call yearning rather than certainty because he remains a man and artist of an optimistic era, of a country (and a music) more human-sized and a technology more apparently benevolent. He speaks from a time when Romantic hopes for music and art, the vision of new languages and higher peaks, were in the process of creating Modernism. For Ives and his time, *progress* was still the magic wand, in art no less than in business and science. It was a marvelous time, but like all times its grandest dreams fell short, and no comparable dreams have turned up to replace them. For the present at least we can only yearn for such a spirit; we can't participate in it.

Ives was so different from us. Some of those differences I take for his limitations, many for ours. Ives *believed*. He believed in love, he believed in wisdom, he believed in spiritual and moral progress, he believed in God (not conventionally, but expressed through convention), and he believed in *music*. Only someone who believed in those things and experienced their power could write the exalted conclusions of *Hanover Square* and the Fourth Symphony.

How distant this kind of faith seems now. For our salvation we've tried the big things and the small, and none has either saved us or provided any answers. Even the questions have become progressively smaller and more tired. Snared in the congestion of technology and material progress we've run out of things to believe in. Ives saw that coming and feared it. He was right to.

Ives's way of expressing his faith has led some to call him naive, pathetic, even dishonest. He was none of those things. He was earnest, exceptionally generous, boundlessly optimistic, a born genius, a great man. Nearly everybody who knew him soon figured those things out, for all the peculiarity of his temper. Much of his greatness was self-made too, except that he was lucky enough to have the help of an extraordinary father and wife.

For our part, too many of us don't believe in great men any more. The attempt to celebrate great women hasn't helped matters because it's greatness itself we've lost touch of. Anthony Lane wrote recently in the *New Yorker* of "the dismal prospect that our age has become offended by genius." Many of us, including some of the more thoughtful, don't believe in progress, don't believe in quality, don't believe in wisdom, don't believe in Mozart, don't believe in love human or divine, and are suspicious of any attempt at moral uplift. Those of us branded liberals, who should be on the same Progressive line as Ives, are on the verge of believing in nothing at all, except in our complaints and a vague foundationless aspiration toward peace and goodwill.

From the sophisticated academic to the woman and man on the street, the pop culture fan to the audience in the concert hall, from top to bottom, Ives is distant from us. Yet paradoxically, he has never been more relevant, and perhaps there's more to it than nostalgia for simpler times. In the West, Modernism has run its glorious and wrenching, creative and destructive course, and appears to have ended in a wave of rage and paralysis of imagination that afflicts all the arts. Ives was on the periphery of Modernism's course, finally perhaps made some contribution to it. Ultimately, however, he was on another path.

It is that path that makes him relevant, in ways political, aesthetic, and spiritual. If in his politics he failed to find a workable vision for a perfected democracy, in his music and his life he embodied a genuine pluralism, a wholeness beneath diversity, that in itself is a beacon for democracy and its art. Aesthetically he is an alternative to Modernism, an exploratory road without the darkness and despair of the twentieth century. In spirit he handed us a baton and calls on us to carry it further. He suggests a way out of despair, but leaves it to us to find the route for ourselves. If we are alone with ourselves today, Ives speaks incomparably to that condition.

Whenever we reach beyond the trivial and ominous present, whenever we attempt to go beyond ourselves, Ives is there cheering us on, pointing upward and beyond. His vision stretched further than even his great gifts could express, beyond anything plausible, surely beyond what we deserve. Thus the *Universe Symphony,* which was unfinishable in this world. But to the degree that our culture can rediscover a little belief in ourselves and our potential, and in the potential of art and music, we should remember and honor Charles Ives.

More than anything Ives wanted his music to arouse the innate grandeur and spirituality of the human community. Soberly considered, his faith in progress and music and humanity was prodigal and unworkable. But who has believed more passionately in all of us? Who in this heartsick century has proclaimed a more magnificent delusion?

Editing Ives

WHEN MICHAEL TILSON THOMAS'S recording of the new Ives Society edition of the Fourth Symphony came out, a *Gramophone* reviewer expressed surprise that the music sounded very much like Stokowski's original recording, made just after the work's premiere in 1965. The reviewer thus revealed a common misperception that Ives's manuscripts are little more than rough sketches that must be assembled, and no doubt partly composed, by editors. For some time I had that impression myself. Rumor had it, for example, that Ives's score of the Fourth Symphony finale was near-gibberish and that a couple of pages were lost and had to be recomposed. I remember my surprise, sixteen years ago, when I first looked over Ives's draft of the finale and saw a fairly clear, complete manuscript—with scribbles and hazy spots here and there. For many pieces Ives hired copyists, quite expert ones, to make final scores.

As is so often the case with Ives, the legend is wrong but the situation is still uniquely complicated. *Some* pieces are indeed fragmentary and must be resurrected. An example is the late work *Chromâtimelôdtune,* in which Ives experimented more consistently than elsewhere with a twelve-tone theme. Different editions of that piece do sound quite different. The reason Ives didn't finish *Chromâtimelôdtune,* however, and other experimental pieces, is that he didn't think they were worth it. Most of the time the pieces that have to be reconstructed by editors are ones Ives abandoned after he had learned what he wanted to know technically and saw that the music wasn't up to par. Some of the editors' reconstructions seem to me to prove Ives right. As shown in the book, the pieces he really cared about were for the most part composed carefully and taken through draft after draft. (The main exceptions, what I have called his orphans, are the *Robert Browning Overture* and First Piano Sonata, though he labored long on both before giving up on them.)

That said, there remain some grueling problems with which editors have to contend. Most of the dilemmas result from two things: (1) Ives sometimes watered down final scores from the sketches, and (2) he tinkered with pieces in later years, adding new ideas, some deliberate and some tentative, restoring things he had watered down, sometimes randomly changing consonances to

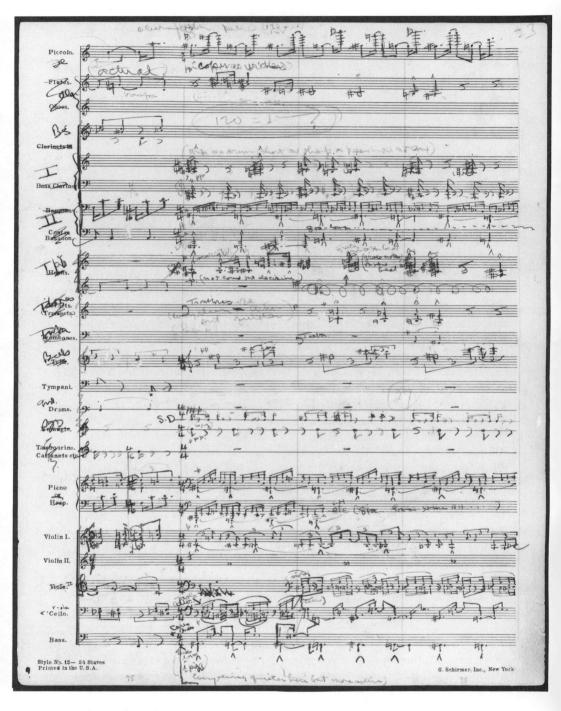

A page from the autograph score of Ives's Fourth Symphony, second movement.

dissonances (say, going through a song and changing every octave to a major seventh or minor ninth). Some of these changes were made on the hitherto immaculate copyists' scores. To complete the nuisance, Ives's later revisions range from effective through neutral to regrettable. As John Kirkpatrick put it: "Some of the [*Concord*] changes are strokes of genius, and others just muddy the waters." Who's to decide which is which? By default, editors and performers.

The Fourth Symphony, Ives's most elaborate and revolutionary work, is actually one of the easier challenges. The riotous second movement was engraved for publication, with Ives's minute involvement, soon after its final version was composed. The main problems with the finale are some sketches he jotted into the manuscript, which have to be decided case by case. For example, in one passage of the last movement he penciled in some birdcall-like figures that trail off into vague scribbles; editor Wayne Shirley included the more clearly written ones in his edition and left out the rest, which seems sensible. The "ether organ" (a.k.a. Theremin) jotted into the scores of the Fourth Symphony and orchestral sets is a later addition and thus ad lib.

These kinds of things can drive editors batty but have little effect on the outcome. Meanwhile, Ives's notational quirks can be smoothed out to make the music significantly easier to read and play, but there is ardent debate among editors over the ethics of doing so: is simplifying Ives's notation as unallowable as changing his harmonies?

Even if that question were to be resolved, there would remain some intractable problems. Using *Three Places in New England* and the *Concord Sonata* as examples, I'll outline briefly what sorts of problems Ives left posterity to wrestle with—or, to put it in Ivesian terms, matters on which he required our collaboration (whether we like it or not).

As noted in the text, *Emerson* was for Ives an unfinishable piece, the ultimate demonstration that motion and change are superior to fixed and final. This may be swell in concept, but on this planet as presently constituted it's hard enough to play the thing if the notes aren't changing on you. When Ives asked John Kirkpatrick to help edit the *Concord* in 1939, Kirkpatrick ran afoul of the dozens of changes, mostly in *Emerson,* that Ives had made since the 1920 edition, which Kirkpatrick had so painstakingly learned and premiered. At that point Kirkpatrick didn't like most of the revisions and bowed out of the editing. Later, after the new edition came out in 1947, he began to integrate more and more of the revisions into his performances. (Some of the changes, after all, restore earlier ideas Ives had taken out for the 1920 edition.) Kirkpatrick's 1969 recording of the *Concord* is an amalgam of both editions, plus things in the sketches that had caught his eye. When the pianist died he was working on a personal version of the sonata.

The fact is, as an editor John Kirkpatrick probably took Ives's invitation to collaboration too much to heart. By current standards some of his editions have too much of Kirkpatrick's filtering in them. (He changed Ruggles's notes too, and probably those of others.) The problem remains: What does a pianist do with the *Concord*? Like everything else, the answer must be judgment calls, case by case. To me it makes sense for a performer to compare the two published editions and try to make some consistent choices. Going back to sketches, other than to correct mistakes, seems over the line. And as said in the text: the later the revision, the more suspect. Even though Ives was capable of surprising feats nearly to the end, there are signs of mental decline by the later 1930s, if not earlier. One should keep in mind, though, that in all versions the *Concord* is the same piece.

As we saw also, Ives first sketched the fluid, dreamlike texture of *The Housatonic at Stockbridge* in 1908, directly after the honeymoon trip that inspired it. When he scored the work for full orchestra in 1912, he simplified the *Housatonic* texture. Then in 1929, making the chamber-orchestra reduction, he restored *some* of the complexity of the original sketches. When James Sinclair came to edit the Ives Society edition of *Three Places* he faced a dilemma: (1) the piece was originally for full orchestra, and the music clearly needs that; (2) the reduced 1929 version was a makeshift, but still Ives's last word on the piece; (3) the full texture of the *Housatonic* was missing from the only surviving full-orchestra score, that of 1912. So was Sinclair slavishly to copy the 1912 version, leaving out one of the chief glories of the piece? Fortunately, no: Sinclair made a hybrid version, putting the 1908/1929 *Housatonic* texture into the 1912 score (and made smaller but similar choices in the other movements). The *Housatonic* decision was a judgment call, but few people who know the piece would disagree with it. (Likewise, I would say, for keeping the tone cluster Ives grafted onto the end of the Second Symphony around 1942—but Peter Burkholder disagrees.)

In the direction of answering the unanswerable questions in the manuscripts, the Ives Society publishes editions including as many variants as feasible, from which performers can make decisions. Some performers' decisions—such as to include the "shadow lines" in the Third Symphony or to keep the Fugue in the First Quartet—will turn out dubious, but so be it. Ives's music challenges us at every turn, beginning with the notes on the page. It is the connection of all aspects of his world, from the inconclusiveness of some of his manuscripts through his political convictions to his aesthetics and metaphysics, that shows the ultimate unity in the vision of this paradoxical genius. If he overrated our abilities as collaborators, his heart was in the right place and his generosity as lavish in that as in everything else.

Notes

Prelude

1. Danbury *News* 10/28/1874.

O N E *At Home*

1. Draft of letter to Paul Rosenfeld in Ives Papers 31/9.
2. Devlin *We Crown* 9.
3. Durgy Prologue.
4. Bailey 26.
5. Devlin *We Crown* 9.
6. Devlin *We Crown* 11.
7. Devlin *We Crown* 12–13. Specifically, Reverend White flirted with the controversial ideas of Scottish preacher Robert Sandeman, who eventually founded a church in Danbury.
8. Devlin *We Crown* 11.
9. Devlin *We Crown* 13.
10. Devlin *We Crown* 13–17.
11. Brewster Ives in Perlis CIR 74.
12. Lee 6.
13. Bushman 188.
14. Bushman 287.
15. Brooks 66.
16. Cowell and Cowell 17.
17. Lee, chapter on "Artists" passim.
18. Bailey 558–59.
19. As Danbury historian William Devlin (*We Crown*) details in a note, this story about Zadoc Benedict and the origin of hatting in Danbury seems to have been transferred whole cloth from a legend about St. Clement.
20. Durgy 11–12.
21. Devlin *We Crown* 52.
22. Burpee entries on the family in vol. IV.
23. Devlin *We Crown* 49.
24. Bailey 551.
25. Devlin *We Crown* 51.
26. Bailey 183.
27. Ives *Memos* 245.
28. Perlis CIR 4.
29. From George White Ives's Danbury *News* obituary, quoted in Bailey 32.
30. Devlin *We Crown* 30–35.
31. Burkholder "Evolution" 68.
32. Perlis Oral History 1/2.
33. Ives *Memos* 201.
34. Bailey 432.
35. Bailey 462.
36. Perlis CIR 4–5.
37. Devlin *We Crown* 35–40.
38. Devlin *We Crown* 58–61.
39. Rossiter 4.
40. Bailey 433.
41. Perlis Oral History, unpublished transcripts of Amelia Van Wyck.
42. Feder *Ives* 85.
43. Ives *Memos* 246.
44. Bailey 472.
45. Isaac Ives entry in the Connecticut Commemorative Biographical Record.
46. Danbury *News* 12/12/1910.
47. Feder *Ives* 55.
48. Based on a Danbury *News* column of 2/7/1872 recounting the lecture and signed "Geo. Francis Train—*nee* I W. Ives." Presumably the column is based on his phony lecture, and this was the event mentioned in Ike's *News* obituary of 12/12/1910. (Train gave at least three lectures in Danbury in the 1870s, probably under Ike's sponsorship.) A contributory element to Ike's extravagant style may have been strong drink. In a public lecture reported in the Danbury *News* of 12/21/1892, he claims to have nearly died the previous year from alcohol. This confession has to be

taken with a grain of salt, however, because Ike was, as usual, trying to sell something—the Keeley Gold Cure, which he proclaimed "the only genuine emancipation from the curse" of alcohol.

49. Danbury *News* 9/24/1873.
50. Perlis CIR xii.
51. Perlis Oral History 1/7.
52. Dr. Charles Kaufman in Perlis Oral History 1/15.

T W O *The Music of War*

1. Wooldridge 23.
2. Perlis 5.
3. A cornet resembles a stocky trumpet and has a mellower sound.
4. Ives *Essays* 111, in the article "Some Quarter-Tone Impressions."
5. Chase 162–63.
6. Feder *Ives* 26.
7. Feder *Ives* 31.
8. Wallach 40.
9. Kirkpatrick in Ives *Memos* 246.
10. The story of Stephen Foster and George Ives may be apocryphal, but it was a mainstay of Charles Ives's conversation, as per Cowell and Cowell 216. Ives's wife told John Kirkpatrick that the two men may have nodded to each other in the street, but were hardly the friends her husband tended to make them.
11. Ives *Memos* 237.
12. Bailey 382.
13. Feder *Ives* 32–34.
14. Bailey 398.
15. Kirkpatrick in Ives *Memos* 246. This date of joining the army is based on George's note in one of his music copybooks. Feder, based on military records, says George was

actually sworn in the next summer, on June 16, 1863.
16. Feder *Ives* 37–38.
17. Hazen 22.
18. Hazen 22–23.
19. Wise 228–29.
20. Hazen 23.
21. Wise 170. The tradition of a mournful tune on the way to the grave and a lively one on the way back would survive in the Decoration Day celebrations of Charles Ives's youth, and to this day in New Orleans funerals.
22. Silber 7.
23. Wise 7.
24. Chattanooga *News-Free Press,* article of August 30, 1987, p. E11.
25. Ives *Essays* 42.
26. The story of George's court-martial is from regimental records, cited in Feder *Ives* 40–41.
27. Feder *Ives* 42.
28. Ives *Memos* 45–46.
29. Ives *Memos* 46.
30. Ives *Memos* 246.
31. Kirkpatrick Catalogue 213.

T H R E E *A Place in the Soul*

1. Bailey's paper was the *Times* until 1870, then the *News,* then the *Evening News.* Given that all were essentially the same paper and editor, all versions will be referred to as the *News.*
2. In 1870 the Danbury News Man was amused or bemused enough by a recently discovered Puritan-era letter to print it in his paper. In the same spirit, the letter is appended here: "There bee now at sea a shippe . . . called ye Welcome . . . which has aboard an hundred or more of ye heretics and malignants called Quakers, with W. Penne, who is chief scampe, at the hedde of them. Ye Court has accordingly given secret orders to . . . waylaye ye said Welcome . . . and make captive ye said Penne and his ungodly crew, so that the Lord may be glorified and not mocked. . . .

Much spoyle can be made by selling ye whole lotte to Barbadoes, where slaves fetch good prices in rumme and sugar, and we shall not only do ye Lord great service by punishing ye wicked, but shall make great gayne for his minister and people. . . . Yours in ye bowells of Christ, COTTEN MATHER."
3. Bailey 523.
4. Bailey 560.
5. Bailey 522–23.
6. Danbury *News* April 1870.
7. Derived from the Danbury *News* 1870–88.
8. Ives *Memos* 104n.
9. Ives *Memos* 101–2n.
10. Resolution by the directors of the Danbury Savings Bank, Danbury *News* 11/1894.
11. From interviews with Amelia Van Wyck (née Amelia Merritt Ives, Howdie's daugh-

ter), some published in Perlis *Charles Ives Remembered* and some not, in Perlis Oral History 1/2.

12. Perlis 7.
13. Danbury *News* 7/1/1869
14. Program in Ives Papers 50.
15. Danbury *News* 7/8/1869
16. Danbury *News* 6/1867.
17. Danbury *News* 2/10/1870.
18. Feder *Ives* 58.
19. As per that year's Danbury Town Directory.
20. Wallach 53.
21. Quoted in Hazen 44.
22. Quoted in Hazen 12.
23. Elkus 14.
24. Danbury *News* 6/26/1878.
25. From a *News* report, n.d., cited in Feder *Ives* 59.
26. Schwartz 82.
27. Perlis CIR 16.
28. Band people treasure a good, honest, fortissimo blunder. Alumni of the Chattanooga High School band still talk about the football game in the 1960s when the director hastily cued the students to play "The Star-Spangled Banner" but forgot to say which key—they knew it in B♭ and A♭. The best part came when they realized they were playing in both keys and everybody switched at the same time, with identical and hilarious results. They finished more or less in B♭, but as I discovered at the time, it's hard to play while doubled up laughing. It was a true Ivesian moment.
29. Feder *Ives* 70.
30. Rossiter 40.
31. Danbury *News* for that month.
32. As per various Danbury *News* items in the 1870s.
33. Amelia Ives Van Wyck in Perlis 6.
34. Danbury *News* 6/9/1870.
35. Danbury *News* 3/27/1872.
36. Danbury *News* 5/13/1873.
37. Danbury *News* 2/13/1878.
38. Ives *Memos* 47.
39. Perlis 5–6.
40. Scrapbook newspaper obituary in Ives Papers 43.
41. CEI to T. Carl Whitmer in Ives Papers 32/13. We will return to this self-deprecating draft letter, which reveals Ives's depression at the time.
42. Danbury *News* 10/18/1870.
43. From a handwritten CEI memo (for the Cowells' use) in Ives Papers 26/6.
44. Cowell and Cowell 17.

45. Kirkpatrick notes from Harmony interviews in Ives Papers Microfilm Addendum.
46. Kirkpatrick in Ives *Memos* 247.
47. Van Wyck in Perlis Oral History 1/2.
48. Perlis 14–16.
49. Brewster Ives in Perlis 72.
50. Perlis Oral History 1/2.
51. Feder *Ives* 65–66.
52. Estimate from 1870 and 1880 figures in Bailey 560–61.
53. Perlis CEI 7.
54. Quoted in John Kirkpatrick, Ives Datebook.
55. Wallach 53, from items in the *News*. It is unclear exactly when George got out of the hardware business and whether he had his own building. He may have used space in brother Ike's lumberyard office.
56. Wallach 53.
57. Ives Papers 50.
58. Feder *Ives* 78.
59. Danbury *News* 7/23/1875.
60. Danbury *News* 6/2/1880. The saluting boy could have been either Charlie or Moss.
61. Durgy 94. In practice, the Danbury Soldiers' Monument is ordinary as such things go, and topped by the conventional resolute infantryman. For years it would be dwarfed by a spindly steel tower of remarkable ugliness that held up a carbide streetlamp.
62. The story of George and the churchbell and its aftermath is in Cowell and Cowell 18. William Devlin, in a note to me, speculates that this could have been a fire alarm, for which church bells served—on a town-wide electrical system that often did not work. It did ring successfully for a fire on April 23, 1880, which may be the date of five-year-old Charlie's memory. The effect of firebells ringing all over town was probably what Ives aimed for in *From the Steeples and Mountains*.
63. Amelia Van Wyck in Perlis 7–8. John Kirkpatrick's guess is used for the year (Catalogue).
64. Ives *Memos* 115.
65. Cowell and Cowell 24.
66. Cowell and Cowell 26.
67. Danbury *News* 11/29/1882.
68. Ives Papers 32/12, from a letter written to CEI in 1939 by a Mrs. Walsh, who sang in the chorus for George Ives's production. She also reminded CEI, "You were induced to join the choir in a picnic in Redding Glen. I was selected for your en-

tertainment. In your shy way you enjoyed a walk and was quite pleased to follow me in breaking windows in an abandoned barn." In his draft reply Ives noted, in third person, "He says he doesn't like going back on an old friend but it seems to him that it was W[illie] R[obinson] who broke the first window in that barn."
69. Cowell and Cowell 25.
70. Ives *Memos* 42–43.

71. Ives *Memos* 115.
72. Ives Papers Microfilm Addendum.
73. Moss Diary in Ives Papers 45/ D1.
74. Moss Diary in Ives Papers 45/D1.
75. Moss Diary in Ives Papers 45/D1.
76. Kirkpatrick transcript in Ives Papers 26.
77. Moss Diary in Ives Papers 45/D1.
78. Ives *Memos,* caption note in photo section.
79. Ives Papers Microfilm Addendum.

F O U R An Apprenticeship

1. Ives Papers, program in Scrapbook, box 43.
2. Osborne 58. Charlie was presumably studying organ with Hollister, since he was working with her and performing as an organist before one finds any other teachers.
3. Based on a quote from Harmony Ives in Ives *Memos* 103n.
4. Philip Sunderland in Perlis CIR 13.
5. Amelia Van Wyck in Perlis Oral History 1/2.
6. John Kirkpatrick in Ives *Memos* 248.
7. Van Wyck in Perlis CIR 8 and the original interview tape.
8. Osborne 58.
9. CEI diary in Ives Papers 45/D2.
10. Kirkpatrick Catalogue 130.
11. Ives Papers 43/Scrapbook 6.
12. Ives Papers 37/5.
13. Kirkpatrick Datebook.
14. Memo, Ives Papers 45/D4.
15. Draft of letter to Lucille Fletcher in Ives Papers 29/8.
16. Ives *Essays* 72–73.
17. Cowell and Cowell 27.
18. Ives *Memos* 147, 325 (Kirkpatrick Chronology).
19. Wallach 122.
20. Cowell and Cowell 27, in a section closely following Lucille Fletcher's unpublished article.
21. Besides Wagner, among George's other interests was Claudio Monteverdi, as Ives noted many years later in a letter subscribing to the first complete Monteverdi edition. (Ives eventually donated the volumes to the New York Public Library.) This is another testament to George's prescience; he lived long before the Monteverdi revival fully revealed the scope of the old Italian's work.
22. Feder "Decoration Day" 237.
23. Because it is not central to my purposes I have left between the lines a suspicion of

mine: the lack of sympathy that one sometimes finds in writings about Ives is in some degree a sign of our time's limitations— an ingrained cynicism and rootlessness that cannot comprehend Ives's ingrained sense of roots and community, his pre-Freudian veneration of his father, his optimism in spite of everything. Thus writers have tended to brand him naive and neurotic to a far greater degree than the facts support, at least during his productive years. (Feder's psychoanalytic study has been a corrective to that tendency, though he also does not take Ives's ideas very seriously.)
24. Ives *Memos* 46.
25. Ives *Memos* 44.
26. Ives quoting his father in *Memos* 47.
27. Based on Ives *Memos* 120. Ives wrote this description of working with his father much later in life, and it is probably enhanced in memory. But clearly a good deal of this sort of mutual exploration went on between them.
28. Ives *Memos* 130–31.
29. Perlis CIR 12.
30. This sexual anxiety among male artists probably persists in the United States. As to Ives's solutions, it is notable that there is one aspect of conventional "manliness" he apparently never resorted to—womanizing. He had neither the itch nor the time, and his morality was Victorian in theory and practice. "Manly" drinking he may have pursued at times, but hardly at the marathon pace of Hemingway et al.
31. Ives Papers 33/1.
32. Furnas 656–58.
33. Morison 784–85. Sports spread fitfully in the United States, however. President Theodore Roosevelt, despite his love for tennis, forbade pictures of himself in tennis togs because the game was considered sissy.
34. Ives Papers 40, Scrapbook #2.

35. Ives Papers 33/1.
36. Ives Papers 33/1.
37. Brewster Ives, one of Moss's sons who later lived with Charlie, in Perlis Oral History 1/16.
38. Ives Papers 45/D2, newspaper article pasted in diary. A note in the Kirkpatrick Datebook has Charlie playing tackle for New Street School the previous year.
39. Diary, Ives Papers 45/D2.
40. Ives Papers 45/D2.
41. Kirkpatrick Datebook.
42. A letter from Harmony Ives in Ives Papers Microfilm Addendum recalls visiting Aunt Amelia in a sanitarium, where she was getting electric shock treatments and drinking boiling water. Amelia Van Wyck, in Perlis Oral History 1/2, says when Amelia didn't get her way, "she turned on the tears." Harmony seems to have been one of the few members of the extended family ever to stand up to this formidable aunt. There are perhaps more extant letters from Amelia to Charles Ives than from anyone else in the family.
43. Devlin "Lyman Brewster." Danbury became a city in 1894.
44. Ives *Memos* 281.
45. Rossiter 47.
46. Article on J. Moss Ives in the *Dictionary of American Biography*.
47. Perlis Oral History 1/16.
48. Perlis CIR 72.
49. Rossiter 22.
50. Danbury *News* 3/7/1887.
51. Devlin *We Crown* 52.
52. Bailey 563.
53. Wallach (48) says that Thomas and his orchestra played in Norwalk in 1874 and George Ives served as ticket agent for that concert; perhaps he sold tickets again when the Thomas Orchestra played in Danbury in 1875 and 1885. At that point, Thomas was the most important conductor in the country. In short, Danbury was exposed, once in a while, to the highest level of music-making available in nineteenth-century America.
54. Bailey 561.
55. Danbury *News* 9/6/1882.
56. There is, in fact, a dip in Main Street close to where the Ives House used to stand.
57. New York *Herald* 1/5/1890, quoted in Wallach Appendix A.
58. Osborne 58.
59. Wallach 148.
60. Ives Papers 27/9, CEI addition to an introduction E. Power Biggs was to give before the radio premiere of the *Variations*.
61. Ives Papers 27/9, draft of a letter to Biggs.
62. Already in this early work Ives is using polytonality to enhance the integrity of contrapuntal voices—see Entr'acte One.
63. Kirkpatrick Catalogue 217. The memo about playing one of the "London Bridge" studies at church is on the manuscript.
64. Ives *Memos* 38.
65. Letter to E. Power Biggs in Ives Papers 27/9.
66. An extant letter of 1892 from publisher William Ashmall confirms receipt of the *Variations on "America."* After considering them for two years, Ashmall returned the manuscript.
67. Wallach 159.
68. There are a number of ingenious formal and thematic interconnections in the *"America" Variations*. For example, while the piece begins in F major, the Bb-minor chord of m. 3, borrowed from F minor in familiar Romantic fashion, neatly suggests the other keys in the piece—the Db major of Variation III and the F minor of the polonaise. The upper line in the second half of Variation I echoes the introduction, which itself uses motives from the theme. The chromatic left-hand 16ths of Variation III forecast similar figures in Variation V. The two polytonal interludes, besides joining the keys on either side, also run through the theme a half at a time.
69. The 1892 date for the Postlude in F is a John Kirkpatrick guess, cited in Wallach 165. Ives later dated the piece as 1890, but the manuscript says 1892 on the cover. As we will see, Ives's own dates for finishing his pieces can be dicey, not due to a wish on his part to deceive but rather because he quoted dates as he did Emerson, off the top of his head—and according to nebulous criteria of what constituted "finished" or a "piece."

F I V E **Farewell**

1. Devlin *We Crown* 36.
2. Bailey 497.
3. Article "Women's Organizations" in *The Encyclopedia of the Social Sciences*.

4. Wallach 70–71.
5. Slonimsky, in *Music Since 1900* 183–84, quotes Alma Mahler as claiming that the women of the New York Philharmonic board killed her husband with the pressures they had placed on him. (Of course, others claim that Alma finished him off.) The archetypal symphony lady is still thriving in the American musical world, as blessed and cursed as ever. Once at a musical benefit around 1982 an elderly, mink-coated, and tipsy lady sat down at our table and without introduction rattled off: "My brother —— is on the board of the —— Symphony and we don't like that new conductor. He's a brown man and brown men smell bad. We're going to get rid of him." Then she rose and tottered off, leaving us gaping. (The conductor, in fact, lasted another decade in his post.) Despite grievous examples here and there, the symphony ladies persist because many musical groups were largely created and shaped by them and, to date, often cannot survive without their contributions of time and money. At a composer's conference I attended in the 1980s, a publisher gave a talk that included this point: "You won't like this—but if you want to get published and you want to succeed, write what the blue-haired ladies want to hear." Ives's later diatribes must be understood in this context, which has changed perhaps in style and degree but not in character since his creative years.
6. Quoted in Douglas 100.
7. Douglas 141.
8. Quoted in Douglas 128.
9. Furnas 487. Beecher is quoted there as well. Ann Douglas writes of "the tragic dead end of Victorian American culture . . . the viciousness between the sexes" (253).
10. Commager 10.
11. Commager 23.
12. Rossiter and Feder (*Ives*) have discussed this situation, stressing Ives's irrational responses to threats to his masculinity. Without exactly quarreling with their conclusions, I am stressing the inevitability of his anxieties. Also, it is clear that in its inception, his obsession about women's response to his music was based on repeated and bitter experiences.
13. Danbury *News* 6/12/1890.
14. Kirkpatrick Catalogue 109.
15. This is on one of the sketches toward *The Rockstrewn Hills* in the Second Orchestral Set.

16. Perlis CIR 16.
17. Devlin *We Crown* 7.
18. Perlis CIR 16.
19. This according to George's obituary in the Danbury *News*. There is some ambiguity about when he began work at the bank: his obituary says 1891, the bank's Resolution after his death says 1892. Meanwhile, in a letter of August 1890 in Ives Papers 33/1, Moss writes to Aunt Amelia, "I guess Papa likes it pretty well in the bank." Perhaps George worked there part time until 1892. Moss was probably wrong about his father's liking it.
20. As per the Resolution on George's death in the *News*.
21. Wallach 61–62.
22. In an interview of 3/88, John Kirkpatrick agreed with my surmise that George was depressed in his last years. Feder also thinks so. One should note that we are all guessing, mainly based on George Ives's last photo and the tone of his letters.
23. Feder treats Ives's adolescence extensively in his psychoanalytic biography. Since Feder *is* a psychoanalyst, he goes beyond Rossiter's and Solomon's less convincing psychologizing concerning these questions. In conversation, Feder and I agreed that the strains between George and Charlie were not particularly unusual or excessive for late adolescence. Essentially, Charlie must have known that his father was right to be upset: he was playing too much ball and failing in his classes. Were it not for the tragedy that followed, all this would likely have been a temporary phase in their relationship. And once he got his sons through college, George might well have returned to a more active musical life.
24. Program in Ives Papers 44.
25. Ives *Memos* 326, Kirkpatrick Chronology.
26. Moore 21.
27. Davis passim.
28. Ives Papers Microfilm Addendum.
29. Letter CEI to GEI, Ives Papers 33/1.
30. Ives Papers 33/1.
31. Theodore Thomas was not conducting, however; he had already resigned.
32. At the Chicago fair Charlie missed by a few days a program of American colonial hymnody, including several works by William Billings, done by the Old Stoughton Musical Society (which Billings founded). (Wallach 324.)
33. Forma 24–26.
34. Chicago's Louis Sullivan, whose Transportation Building may have been the only au-

thentic masterpiece of the Columbian Exposition, was disgusted by the rest of the White City. In his 1922 *Autobiography* Sullivan called it a "slow-acting poison" on American architecture, not only derivative of French Beaux-Arts but a debasement of classical style. (Quoted in Furnas 766–67.)

35. Mazzola 413.
36. Mazzola 420.
37. "Ta-ra-ra Boom-de-ay!" appears in Ives's *In the Inn* and the *Mike Donlin–Johnny Evers* baseball piece. "Streets of Cairo" pops up mischievously in the scherzo *Holding Your Own*.
38. Ives in *Memos* 56 mentions hearing ragging syncopations earlier at the Danbury Fair and in New Haven. His memory indicates that black-influenced syncopation was working its way into popular music even before the ragtime craze.
39. Forma 26.
40. Mazzola 421.
41. Ives *Essays* 47.
42. Ives Papers Microfilm Addendum.
43. Ives Papers 33/1.
44. Kirkpatrick Datebook.
45. Ives Papers 33/1.
46. Nephew Chester Ives in Perlis CIR 88.
47. Letters home in Ives Papers 33/1.
48. Ives Papers Microfilm Addendum.
49. Quoted in Ives *Essays* 250n.
50. John Kirkpatrick article in *The New Grove*.
51. Kirkpatrick account of the Yale-Hopkins game in Perlis Oral History 2/32.
52. Ives Papers 33/1, letter of 5/20/1894.
53. Ives Papers 33/1. George's letter eliciting this reply, like most of his correspondence, does not survive.
54. Ives Papers 33/1.
55. Ives Papers 33/1.
56. Wallach 236–38 discusses the connection of Ives's *Psalms* to Episcopal chant, as suggested by Ives's own description of the *67th* as "a kind of enlarged plain chant."
57. The 1894 date given for this first collection of experimental psalms is the traditional John Kirkpatrick guess. In her Yale doctoral thesis, Gayle Sherwood is inclined to date these psalms, in their surviving form at least, around 1898. Contra Maynard Solomon's charges of Ives consistently dating his music early, Ives eventually dated *Psalm 67* as 1898 (and Sherwood agrees). But years after the piece was composed, Ives also said his father had tried *Psalm 67* in Danbury, which would have to have been before George died in 1894; thus that was John Kirkpatrick's best guess for the

date of this and some of the other psalms. (Ives added many of the dates and other memos on his manuscripts in later years, when his mind and memory were less reliable.) As Sherwood readily confesses, her researches (mainly based on dating the manuscript paper) are shot through with uncertainties and in general have not solved a number of dating mysteries. Her years of researches have, however, *not* significantly challenged the datings by Ives and/or John Kirkpatrick, and in several cases have confirmed those datings. The mysteries remain. To cite one example: there is a revision patch for the Yale-period, conventional First Symphony for which the paper cannot predate 1907. The moral of these researches is that we will never have more than in-the-ballpark dates for some Ives works. In regard to the early psalms, there is no reason to doubt Ives's statement in the *Memos* that his father and his Yale choir director tried over some of them. *What* they tried over may have been either completed or provisional versions.

58. Ives *Memos* 178.
59. As Hitchcock notes in *Ives* 29.
60. That Ives was familiar with the popular vocal style is shown in his circa-1890 choral work *Turn Ye, Turn Ye* which in spots suggests a novel genre: sacred barbershop.
61. As Nicholls points out (10) in his discussion of the pieces, after these four psalms "bitonality seldom dominates any work, but rather is used relatively sparingly at appropriate moments . . . once a new technique has been successfully tried out in a piece . . . then it becomes simply another available colour in his ever-widening palette of compositional resources."
62. In *Psalm 67* too, Ives also applies original theoretical concepts to his explorations. Though some of the characteristic chords could be analyzed as ninths, they result from a superimposition of a major chord on top and its minor dominant on the bottom; later, in a B section, this arrangement is inverted. The harmonic sequences in both planes sometimes match, but are expressed in different keys. Nicholls notes (10) that Ives deliberately shapes polychordal equivalents of imperfect and full cadences, using his opening polychord as a "tonic."
63. Stravinsky *Poetics* 66.
64. Stravinsky *Poetics* 66.
65. Quoted in Nicholls 7.
66. Again: In most of his large pieces, Ives

would avoid such rigidly imposed systems as in *Psalm 24*.

67. The 1890s probably also saw the first version, later lost, of *Psalm 90,* which Ives would rework in 1923 as more or less his valedictory piece.

68. Ives *Memos* 131.

69. Ives Papers 33/1.

70. Ives Papers 33/1. One yearns to know the nature of Mollie Ives's illness, physical or mental, and how long it lasted; but this is the only reference to her being ill and needing a nurse. She seems in any case to

have remained active and competent into old age—she traveled a few times to visit her son and looked after her grandchildren. She remains a mysterious figure, and there is no information as to why: Some dark secret? Or only that she wasn't interesting enough to rise, as did Aunt Amelia, above being taken for granted? Dull as it is, the latter seems the best guess.

71. Ives Papers 33/1.

72. From several letters in Ives Papers 33/1.

73. Ives Papers 33/1.

Entr'acte One · *The Music of the Ages*

1. Ives *Memos* 133.

2. Ives *Memos* 132. Maynard Solomon has questioned the overall veracity of Ives's memories of his father, surmising that the older Charles Ives made up the stories to account for his own musical proclivities. While Ives's memories certainly exhibit the usual retrospective romanticization and tidying-up of family stories—a familiar human foible—there is no evidence that leads one to doubt the gist of them.

3. Ives *Memos* 133.

4. Ives *Essays* 42.

5. Ives *Essays* 84. Wallace Stevens expresses the same idea: "Music is feeling, then, not sound." In the *Essays* Ives continues, "Why can't music go out in the same way it comes in to a man, without having to crawl over a fence of sounds, thoraxes, catguts, wire, wood, and brass?" Besides an aesthetic statement, this passage may also be seen as a riposte to the accusation, which Ives could not entirely escape, that some of his later music can be impractical, unidiomatic, perverse in notation, at times verging on impossible to play. As an example: Ives performer and scholar James Sinclair criticizes the Barn Dance in *Washington's Birthday,* which modulates in the middle from D major to A♭ major. As Sinclair points out, the latter is not a fiddle-tune key; they are always in one of the resonant open-string keys, especially G, D, or A. The end of the Barn Dance sounds rather colorless and anticlimactic as a result of being in four flats. Certainly Ives knew about fiddle-tune keys; he played violin himself. Why didn't he modulate to another of them? As often as such problems occur in his music, however, his best work rises beyond them. Ives spent his creative lifetime reminding us in

music and in words that the value of a work of art is not in its perfection but in its spirit, its *substance,* however unquantifiable that quality is.

6. Quoted in an uncatalogued letter of 2/5/1918 from Harmony Ives to her husband, responding to a lost letter of his, and to which we will return later.

7. In the Ives Room of the Music Library at Yale. This discussion is aided by Eiseman "George Ives as Theorist."

8. Ives *Memos* 140.

9. Helmholtz *On the Sensations of Tone* 358, quoted in Ives *Essays* 254n. Ives several times referred to or paraphrased Helmholtz in his writings, and the Cowells say (19) that one of Helmholtz's books was in George's library. The best guess is that it was the magnum opus *Sensations of Tone,* mainly because Ives echoes that book in his writings.

10. Ives *Essays* 98.

11. Ives *Memos* 38.

12. Schoenberg similarly declared, with his "liberation of the dissonance," that he had freed counterpoint from its limiting dual allegiance to both melody and harmony, the "horizontal" and "vertical" aspects of music.

13. Since bitonality and polytonality are academic distinctions concerning the same effect, *polytonality* will be used hereafter for music in more than one key at a time.

14. In *Memos* 115 CEI adds, "I don't think [Father] had the possibility of polytonality in composition in mind, as much as to encourage the use of the ears—and for them and the mind to think for themselves and be more independent." Ives was quite aware of his father's creative limitations.

15. Described in Kirkpatrick Catalogue 219;

Ives manuscript page F7440. Ives describes his early bitonal "London Bridge" studies in *Memos* 47, adding that in playing them he'd repeat the tune switching the key of the accompaniment and adding a rhythmic fillip: "throwing off the last [eighth note] of a phrase, and beginning the tune (on repeat) on that off-beat, making it a main beat! Beat that, Jamey boy!"

16. Ives *Memos* 125. The polyrhythmic exercise he describes is phenomenally difficult.

17. Ives, part of the lengthy "Conductor's Note" for the second movement of the Fourth Symphony, now found in the 1965 Associated Music Publishers score of the work.

18. This song, and the connection between father and son it symbolizes, led to Stuart Feder's apt subtitle for his psychological study of their relationship: *"My Father's Song"* (see the bibliography). As everyone from the Cowells on has agreed, Charles Ives came to see himself as writing his father's music.

19. Or so Cowell and Cowell describe the *Universe Symphony* (201). As we will note later, Ives's ideas about the work may have evolved in his mind from its conception around 1915.

20. Ives *Memos* 124n. The *Coney Island* show may have been George's swan song as a concert producer.

21. Ives *Essays* 4.

22. Ives *Essays* 8.

23. Perlis CIR 173.

24. George Ives's attempts to re-create the spectrum of a bell on piano may have been stimulated by Helmholtz's theories about the components of timbre.

25. Ives *Essays* 110, from the article "Some Quarter-Tone Impressions."

26. Ives *Memos* 45.

27. Ives *Memos* 142.

28. Cowell and Cowell 21. The "not often" explains why little of George's experimental streak got into the papers or was recalled by townsfolk. They didn't see much of that part of George Ives, and likewise his knowledge of European classical music. His two-band episodes *were* recalled, by Sunderland in Perlis's interview. Anyhow, the bands-passing effect happens now and then with all marching bands; it was not a unique experiment of George Ives's.

29. Wallach 68.

30. Feder *Ives* 83.

31. Ives *Memos* 240. This advice of George Ives to his son is essentially what Sherwood Anderson advised William Faulkner, and many other elders many young writers: Stick to what you know; reach for the universal through the local, the macrocosm by means of the microcosm. In a 1933 draft of a letter to John Lomax, in Ives Papers 30/15, Ives remarks, "Some music by known composers & written & published, which has been used in communities for a generation or so, has become local color It seems to me that some of the old hymns & religious tunes, are almost a part of this country's folk music . . . they have grown into the lives of many people."

32. Charlie began studying orchestration with his father, doing band scoring but also exercises for ensembles with strings. Surviving are a string quartet arrangement of a Beethoven piano sonata movement and two piano pieces by Schubert arranged for full orchestra. A note on one of the latter, an Impromptu, says "arranged for Standard Orchestra Danbury July 4, 1892" (which is probably the performance date). None of these exercises, however, approaches the sophistication of the orchestral music Ives wrote under Horatio Parker at Yale.

33. Ives *Memos* 52n.

34. Ives *Memos* 42.

35. Ives Papers 51; CEI notes for a Danbury performance of the Second Symphony in the 1950s. Ives apparently told the same story about the final chord to Henry Cowell, who mentioned it in an article. According to John Kirkpatrick, in a letter to me of 1973, the present ending of the Second Symphony was added around 1942, to replace the original conventional cadence. Another explanation, appearing in a local paper after the Danbury premiere of the Second, was that George Ives's rehearsals, which for a long time were once a week in the Wooster House Hotel, often ended with a blast of trumpet or trombone. The replacement ending has often been seen as a sort of aural nose-thumbing at conventional expectations and conventional listeners. There may be an element of that, but still the startling chord should be seen mainly as another example of Ivesian realism and/or autobiography. (To my ears the end has always sounded tacked on, the scoring sketchy and ineffective, and thus typical of Ives's later tinkerings with his scores. All the same, I can't imagine the

Second ending any other way. Peter Burkholder disagrees. In any event, as we will
see, Ives had had problems with the ending
all along.)
36. Hitchcock *Music in the United States* 104.
37. Ives *Memos* 132–33.
38. Ives *Essays* 30. Stuart Feder has also written
a psychological essay (see the bibliography) on Ives's memories of Decoration
Day and his father. Feder does not cite this
passage from the *Essays* but instead uses
Ives's Postface to the piece *Decoration Day,*
which is similar but less personal.
39. The terms "cultivated" and "vernacular"
are more apt today than "classical" and
"popular." There is much to be said about
this dichotomy, its history in music and the
other arts, its validity, and the interpenetra-
tion of the two in both Modernism and
Postmodernism (of which interpenetra-
tion Ives was a prophet). This question
probably deserves a book to itself. Here it

comes up only as it applies directly to Ives.
I have largely avoided the word *elite,* which
is applied with too broad a brush these
days, and tends to (probably is intended
to) besmirch everything it touches.
40. Quoted in Tischler 26–28.
41. Ives *Essays* 22. This sentence is in quotes in
the original, as if it were from Emerson,
but editor Howard Boatwright cannot lo-
cate it. It seems then to be another of Ives's
many top-of-the-head quotes, or rough
paraphrases, or things he made up and deliberately or unconsciously attributed to
somebody else (similar, of course, to what
he did with quotes in his music). Overuse
of quotation marks was a common foible
of the time. In any case, Ives was not a
scholar; nobody was forcing him to check
his quotes, and he didn't have time anyway.
He had a compendious memory, but one
manifestly fallible—and creative.

s i x   *A College*

1. From George Ives's death notice in the
Danbury *News* 11/6/1894.
2. Danbury *News* 11/7/1894.
3. Danbury *News* 11/7/1894.
4. Ives *Memos* 258.
5. Ives *Memos* 261. Feder writes (136) that
given the tensions between them and Charlie's growing independence, George Ives
could be said to have died when his son
actually needed him the least. That may be
objectively accurate, but Ives's words reflect his own feelings at the time and later.
6. Ives *Essays* 67. This passage does not mention his father's death specifically, but that
certainly is what he means.
7. Perlis CIR 112.
8. Anticipating what is here called Ives's pattern of percolating to the top without overt
ambition, Starr writes of Ives's musical
achievement: "Without having posited the
making of 'works of art' as an ultimate goal
[but rather as spurs to 'the activity of
truth'], he managed to make a number of
them anyway, and a number of very fine
('great'?) ones" (150). Another Ivesian
paradox.
9. From the Yale '98 Class Book and the '98
Decennial Record.
10. Pierson 42.
11. Yale man Buchanan Winthrop, quoted in
Pierson 3.

12. Edwin E. Slosson, quoted in Pierson 10.
13. Quoted in Pierson 8.
14. Johnson 79.
15. Moore 83.
16. Pierson notes (63–65) that Yale was nominally a university from 1872 and legally one
from 1887, but President Dwight had to
take circumspect steps toward realizing the
university ideal during his tenure from
1886 to 1899. Harvard led the way to a
broadly applied elective system; Yale held
out as long as possible against that innovation, which created the modern American
university.
17. Noss 23.
18. Smith 153. Smith's terms—"real man," "ladies' seminary"—are the same sort that Ives
tended to use, turned up several notches in
shrillness. They were common terms and
concerns—patronizing from present points
of view, at the time simply conventional.
19. Kirkpatrick in Ives *Memos* 182–83.
20. Quoted in Hamm 332.
21. Smith 155.
22. Kearns 8.
23. Kearns 16–18.
24. Kearns 40. As Kearns notes (71), an ailing
and disappointed Parker near the end of
his life seemed to depart from his earlier
dogmatism, welcoming the breaking down
of barriers between highbrow and low-

brow music: "Training the lowly to enjoy exalted music is known to be meritorious. I never heard anyone commend the reverse process of training the fastidious to recognize vulgar excellence. . . . Good and bad are relative terms in music as well in life." This conversion to pluralism, however, came after Ives's years with Parker.

25. From H. Wiley Hitchcock notes in his Introduction to the 1972 Da Capo score of *Hora novissima.*
26. Ives *Memos* 28.
27. Quoted in Kearns 20.
28. *Hora novissima* is an oddly touching piece, for one so constrained in technique and generally overbred. Parker would become more adventurous in his later work, notably in the prize-winning opera *Mona,* performed four times at the Metropolitan Opera in 1912 and then forgotten, but he returned in his last years to a more conservative style.
29. Ives *Memos* 49. Kirkpatrick notes that Ives apparently performed excerpts from *Hora novissima* at Center Church, and other Parker works appeared on programs there.
30. Feder *Ives* 138.
31. Ives *Memos* 116. The quotes are as Ives remembered them, probably as much his own words as Parker's and his father's.
32. Ives *Memos* 48–49. Ives adds that Parker "was seldom mean" in his responses to novel ideas. This description contrasts with John Tasker Howard's description of Parker in *Our American Music:* "His friends were fascinated by him; those who were not his friends feared him. His brusque manner frightened the timid, and he despised those who were afraid of him. In this he was something of the bully; he would often wilfully confuse his pupils in class, and then scoff at their confusion. But for those who stood on their two feet and talked back to him he had the profoundest admiration. His manner was a challenge which he expected would be met in kind" (316). Given his resentment of Parker, Ives might have been expected to mention Parker's bullying. Since he did not, Ives was

probably not treated that way—either because Parker was new at the school and less weary of teaching, or because Ives gained Parker's respect by his talent and/or by standing on his own two feet. To these speculations one must add the probably unanswerable question of how Parker perceived this pupil's gifts. In Ives *Memos* 115n, John Kirkpatrick writes, "the editor was surprised to hear an unconfirmed report that Parker had once mentioned Ives as one of the most talented young men he'd ever taught." This report came from Ives's wife, who heard it from a Yale acquaintance. One wishes for a confirmation of this thirdhand rumor that Parker indeed noticed a spectacular talent.

33. Ives Papers 32/2.
34. Ives *Memos* 258, from the draft of a 1930 letter to John C. Griggs.
35. Ives *Memos* 115.
36. Ives *Memos* 258.
37. Ives *Memos* 253–54.
38. Ives *Memos* 253–54.
39. Ives *Memos* 39.
40. Cowell and Cowell 35.
41. Cowell and Cowell 35.
42. Eiseman mentions (103) that Griggs was dubious about equal temperament, the standard system of tuning since Beethoven's time. This may have influenced Ives's later, often baffling, sometimes infuriating eccentricities in the spelling of chromatic lines and chords. Though A♯ and B♭ are the same key on the piano, for example, Ives argued that in some metaphysical but significant way they are not the same note even in atonal music. He also looked at sharps as innately stronger (because they tend tonally to lead upward), flats as weaker (because they tend to lead downward). These ideas about spelling make a modicum of sense in other instruments, especially strings, which do make adjustments between flats and sharps—a violinist will tend instinctively to play a sharp a little higher than the enharmonic flat. But none of that applies to piano.

s e v e n   *Dasher at Yale*

1. Johnson 97.
2. Pierson 12–13.
3. Canby 63.
4. Ives *Memos* 227. This is from the political

story/essay "George's Adventure," which is nominally fiction but full of autobiography—though not *all* autobiographical.
5. Kirkpatrick in Ives *Memos* 181–82.

6. Quoted in Moore 80.
7. Pierson 32.
8. Canby 38.
9. Dink Stover's acquaintance Brockhurst includes music in his denunciation of Yale men's cultural illiteracy: "You have a hazy knowledge of Wagner, and you know that Chopin wrote a funeral march. That is your foothold in music; there you balance, surrounded by howling waters of ignorance" (Johnson 327).
10. Wallach 245.
11. From a CEI letter in Ives Papers 27/4.
12. Rossiter 78.
13. From a 1921 CEI letter to the *New York Times* about Yale sports, the clip in Papers 37/3. He is probably exaggerating his college passion for sports, but not necessarily by much. By then his playing and composing were so ingrained that they went on undisturbed by whatever else was occupying him.
14. Moore 20.
15. Ives *Memos* 41.
16. From the Yale '98 Class Book.
17. A campus publication assessing juniors' senior society chances gave Ives a fair shot at Skull and Bones, the top society, though "he is not a big man in any way." Among his strong points cited were his organ playing and that "he always acts with a becoming independence" (quoted in Rossiter 78).
18. Ives *Memos* 61.
19. Classmate Edward "Ned" Park, quoted by John Kirkpatrick in Ives *Memos* 267.
20. From the '98 Class Book, hinting of Mullally's attachment to a Farmington girl; but "he wishes no more said on the matter."
21. Information on New Haven theaters comes from the Dana Collection at the New Haven Colony Historical Museum.
22. Ives Papers 50.
23. Moore 30.
24. Ives *Memos* 56. Felsburg later played silent film accompaniments—probably still reading the papers—at Poli's Bijou Theater, across the street. He is mentioned, though not by name, in *Stover at Yale,* from which we may conclude that Felsburg was a familiar fixture. The piano part of Ives's sentimental song "In the Alley," subtitled "After a session at Poli's," indicates over a right-hand rest: "Attention! George Felsberg! turn newspaper."
25. Ives Papers Microfilm Addendum.
26. Osborne (59) notes that when and where

Ives studied with Buck and Shelley are speculative. But he always said he did, and at the time wrote his mother about it, so the likeliest supposition is that he commuted to New York for lessons. Perhaps he took the train with the commuting Griggs.
27. Ives *Memos* 148. As we will see, most of his more conventional church works for organ and chorus were lost.
28. Perlis CIR 20–21. As per pp. 183–85, Madge Roberts, the contralto soloist at Center Church, was aunt to Ives's later copyist George Roberts. She apparently joined Griggs in encouraging young Ives's experiments.
29. The prestige and sophistication of Center Church and its music are shown by Ives's predecessors as organist—the famous Harry Rowe Shelley and Henry Jepson, who went on to teach and play at Yale. Ives's successor would be David Stanley Smith, who succeeded Parker as dean of the School of Music. Churchgoers recalled Ives as a better player than Smith.
30. Perlis CIR 20.
31. CEI service diary in Ives Papers 45/D2.
32. Ives *Memos* 120.
33. Kirkpatrick in Ives *Memos* 183.
34. To the side of the rough sketch toward the opening of the First Symphony are two complex chords (the first a superimposition of seventh chords on B, A♭, and A) labeled "Sunrise chord/over East Rock/ last time up[?] in 1896 / Amos sings / Bring . . . [then first notes of 'My Bonnie Lies Over the Ocean']." East Rock is a prominence rising above the town, and excursions up it to play or picnic were a tradition of Yale and New Haven life.
35. Among the exercises Ives did for Parker in freshman year is the orchestral version of his organ Postlude in F. It was probably read over by the New Haven Symphony, as Parker often did with student pieces. The scoring of the Postlude is competent enough, but notably less sophisticated than the more or less contemporaneous opening movement of the First Symphony. This probably indicates more Parker advice on the scoring of the symphony movement.
36. Ives *Memos* 51.
37. H. Wiley Hitchcock discussed these aspects of the First Symphony in a 1988 symposium in Miami. Ives did not make his acquaintance with the *New World* and *Pathétique* by way of the New Haven Symphony—Parker played no Tchaikovsky and

only one Dvořák work (Slavonic Dances) during Ives's time. Ives may have studied the pieces in score or may have heard them with visiting orchestras or in New York. In those days he was an active concertgoer.

38. In the First Symphony the harmonic sequence constitutes most of the "development section" in the first movement, which therefore has little real development at all. However, in late-Romantic fashion, the movement treats the themes developmentally throughout, and recapitulates the opening theme in a new texture of close-harmony strings.

39. Cowell and Cowell 31 say Ives lived with Griggs, which if true was probably in the summers, part time.

40. Block Appendix 2.

41. Susan Benedict Hill is best known for completing the Danbury News Man's history of the town after his death. A letter from her in Ives Papers 30/8, dated 8/20/1896, says, "Woodward & Sons NY will publish our song and give us 10 per cent royalty on retail sales if we will take 100 copies at $20. . . . If this should make a hit we'll try our hand at some other song—after election— and who knows but we may yet be a howling success." (It is their only known collaboration.) Not knowing when he was coming back from the Adirondacks, Hill sent the publisher's letter on—not to Mollie Ives, but to Aunt Amelia. The latter was handling Charlie's business rather than his mother.

42. Canby 27.

43. Block 22.

44. Ives Papers 34/6, a letter draft of 1946. In the same letter Ives says he wrote a technical analysis of the First Symphony around 1906. That article has not turned up.

45. Burkholder "Evolution" 305n.

46. Many years later, John Kirkpatrick took it upon himself to restore the fugue in his edition, even though Ives had tried to erase its connection with the First Quartet—including renumbering the last three movements I, II, III on the manuscript. Ives was probably right to remove the fugue—except in the general sense of being based on a revival hymn, it has no stylistic or thematic connection with the other movements, and it throws off the overall key scheme (the last three movements show the conventional relationship G–D–G, while the fugue is in C). And Kirkpatrick was wrong to put it back—as if Ives had no right to

revise, and improve, his own music. Performances of the quartet the way Ives intended it will reveal a tighter, more effective piece. The fugue, too spacious and sonorous for a string quartet anyway, belongs in the Fourth Symphony or arranged for its original medium, organ.

47. Ives *Memos* 132. Ives only identifies the second speaker as "one routine-minded professor," but Eva J. O'Meara, former music librarian at Yale, told Kirkpatrick it must have been Parker.

48. Parker quoted in Kearns 203. Parker, organist at Boston's grand Trinity Church, did not object to hymns as such, of course, only the simplicity and sentimentality of most American ones. He produced his own edition of the Episcopal Hymnal in 1903.

49. Parker quoted in Kearns 49. A further comparison of attitudes can be seen in an article Parker wrote for the *Yale Review:* "It is indeed stirring to hear a great mass of people, including a seven foot policeman, singing. . . . The policeman's eyes and attitude show sincerity and devotion. . . . He is moved by his vocal efforts and enjoys his emotion and singing. So do I, but I wish the music were such as I could swallow without gagging" (quoted in Levy *Musical Nationalism* 11). Compare that to George Ives's admiration for the off-key singing of stonemason Bell, which he called "the music of the ages." Simply put, in amateur music George Ives and his son saw a spiritual radiance and integrity that Parker vaguely recognized, but he could not help gagging over the sound. Ives's counterpoise to Parker's fastidious reaction can be seen in the *Essays:* "What does sound have to do with music?"

50. Quoted in Eiseman 90.

51. Kearns (241) compares Parker's cosmopolitan eclecticism to the classical-pastiche White City of the Columbian Exposition. Parker was certainly part of the cultivated milieu that gave birth to the White City, which we saw Louis Sullivan denouncing as ersatz. It is worth mentioning that most of the Yale campus, as it took shape in the first half of this century, is describable as ersatz Gothic.

52. Kearns 49–50. To state the obvious: Parker here allies his vision of music to what seems, to later sensibilities, a vulgar racism. His hatred for ragtime and other African-American genres, which he shared with "cultured" leaders of his time such as Co-

lumbia's Daniel Gregory Mason, is part of the same tendency. Mason wrote of white composer Henry F. Gilbert's "Negro" themes as "half-breeds . . . descended by some repellent miscegenation from Beethoven and Mendelssohn," as if Gilbert had soiled the racial purity of the European tradition. Ives's love of ragtime doubtless shocked Parker as well.

53. Burkholder lays out an illuminating examination of the First Quartet's thematic relationships in "Evolution" 279–305. He calls the general method, in which traditional tunes provide the framework for apparently new melodies, "thematic paraphrase." From Parker Ives learned the Romantic techniques of thematic development and metamorphosis that had evolved from Berlioz, Schumann, Wagner, and Liszt.

54. The tunes for hymns are often named independently of the texts, which are mutable. The melody for "Come, thou Fount," for example, is called *Nettleton*.

55. Eiseman 36.

56. In the fugue, Ives, deliberately or negligently (he was still a student), weakens the dominant key in favor of the subdominant, creating a large-scale tonal ambiguity that he would exploit in the Fourth Symphony. Adding to the ambiguity are the long chromatic episodes, in which a fugal/contrapuntal texture gives way to simple homophony (though he keeps the rhythm lively with chains of syncopations). Incidentally, not only the archaic 4/2 time signature (added after the first draft) but the texture, thematic material, and form of Ives's fugue recall the 4/2 fugue "Urbs Syon unica" in Parker's *Hora novissima*. The main way in which Ives's fugue differs from Parker's is in its lilting syncopations. Like much of *Hora novissima*, "Urbs Syon unica" is pedestrian in rhythm.

57. Eiseman 32.

58. Block Appendix 2.

59. Ives *Memos* 39–41. He concluded this memory of his music-hall experiments, "If more of this and other kinds of ear stretching had gone on, if the ears and minds had been used more and harder, there might have been less 'arrested development' among nice Yale graduates."

60. As Ives wrote of *"Gyp the Blood" or Hearst!? Which is Worst?!,* "I can make out the reason for this piece politically, or socialistically, better than musically." Quoted on p. 34 of the notes for the 1992 EMI recording

A Portrait of Charles Ives by Ensemble Modern.

61. Song lyrics in Feder *Ives* 162.

62. From Sinclair's notes for the Koch International recording *Orchestral Music of Charles Ives,* by James Sinclair and Orchestra New England.

63. Harmony made this observation to John Kirkpatrick, apparently in regard to her long courtship. Her "easy laugh" is Kirkpatrick's report to me in an interview of 3/1988. Testaments to her beauty, which only occasionally shows in photos, are legion. In a letter in Ives Papers 30/17, a Henry Perkins writes, "I used to know Harmony Twichell when she was a young girl, perhaps the most beautiful I ever met."

64. Brewster Ives in Burkholder *Ideas*.

65. The program is in Perlis CIR 22–23. Ives's addiction to wretched puns was probably confirmed at Yale as well. When John Kirkpatrick met Ives once with son David in tow, the old man stuck out his hand to the boy and roared, "HOW'S ARTHUR?" To their look of astonishment, Ives added, "Arthur mometer." (From Kirkpatrick interview 3/1988.)

66. Parker taught Music History in once-a-week survey lectures. Interestingly, he included several lectures on world music, including Indian and Asian. (Moore 113.)

67. Smith 158.

68. Ives *Memos* 181–82. Ives chafed at going through Jadassohn's harmony text again and starting over in counterpoint; he had done both with his father. Kirkpatrick, having examined Charlie's surviving exercises from Danbury and Yale (mostly fugues and canons), says that the ones for Parker are more sophisticated. (Ives *Memos* 49n.)

69. Skull and Bones, whose alumni include President George Bush and other leading politicians and diplomats, is the most obsessively secretive of all. It is said that, to his dying day, a Skull and Bones man is obliged to leave the room when the name of the society is uttered in his presence. It also appears that among Skull and Bones rituals is naked wrestling, and, even more curious, lying naked in a coffin and narrating a complete sexual history to the assembled group. Inevitably, for most of their histories the societies were exclusively white and male, and largely Yankee Protestant.

70. Based on Owen Johnson's descriptions of Tap Day in *Stover at Yale*.

71. We will follow Dave Twichell's career to its end because his life is interwoven with Ives's. Mullally ended up in banking in New York; entries in reunion class books show him as crankily conservative. Mullally and Ives stayed close for some time after college, but after his marriage Ives pulled away from most of his Yale friends, and from Yale attitudes.

72. Though Ives took more music than anything else at Yale and wrote a thesis, the college did not in those days recognize a "major." That was the sort of university idea against which the college was still fighting a rear-guard action.

73. The extant final score of the First Symphony is in the hand of a professional copyist, and some or all of it may have been done after Yale. Ives had piano arrangements made of both the First Symphony and First Quartet, to show to potential performers.

74. This surmise about Parker's contribution to the First Symphony's second movement comes from James Sinclair. The only extant sketch has the melody an octave higher, thus out of English horn range. Ironically, then, the main resemblance to Dvořák may have been created by Parker, who deplored Dvořák's nationalistic aesthetic. Parker certainly gave Charlie advice on the instrumentation throughout, but on the whole the First Symphony's scoring ended up more creative and colorful, to my ear, than Parker's in *Hora novissima*. CEI in *Memos* 51 says Parker also complained about the original second movement beginning in a foreign key—G♭, in a piece in F. So Ives wrote the now-established second movement (which he liked less) and apparently put the Parker-rejected slow movement into the Second Symphony.

75. The brass-band quality of much of the last movement is probably due to its being based on a lost Danbury piece. Ives wrote in 1946, "The march in the [First Symphony] last movement was composed and partly played in 1892"—presumably by George Ives's band. (Ives Papers 34/6.)

76. In the ensuing years Ives went up and down in his feelings about the First Symphony, as demonstrated in this comically divided description in the *Memos* (87): "This music, at least the last three movements, is, if not the worst (No), one of the worst (No), poorest, weakest things (No) I've ever written. (The last time I played it over . . . I felt more like it, I liked it well,

and didn't feel the way I did once.)" At some later date he drafted a response to a query, apparently on a day that he was feeling less forgiving: "The 1st is some forty years old & he thinks it feels like resting on the shelf for a few more years (1 is a nice Sym—one that all of the celebrated trite lady bird eared European arm waving prima donnas who run most of the orch in this country could read right off 'nice'." (Ives Papers 33/6.)

77. It has been suggested that Parker's history lectures in Renaissance music influenced Ives; the games with meters and phrasing in Ives's First Quartet resemble such effects in Renaissance polyphony. While the polymetric climax of the First Quartet is ingenious in concept and clever in execution, it is a bit murky in sound—an experiment that doesn't quite come off. See Ann Besser Scott, "Medieval and Renaissance Techniques in the Music of Charles Ives: Horatio at the Bridge?" *Musical Quarterly* 78/1, 1994.

78. Ives *Memos* 39.

79. In the *Memos* (39) Ives explained the polychords of the *Thanksgiving Prelude* programmatically, as representing "the sternness and strength and austerity of the Puritan character, and it seemed to me that any of the [conventional] chords used alone gave too much a feeling of bodily ease, which the Puritan did not give in to." In its later orchestral incarnation this music certainly is describable as austere—a plain-spokenness in spots prophetic of Copland's "Americana" style of some forty years later.

80. From a description of the Princeton game in the Yale '98 Class Book history and in Sinclair's notes for the recording *Orchestral Music of Charles Ives*.

81. The immense gain in sophistication between the circa-1898 college takeoff *Yale-Princeton Football Game* and a mature piece such as *The Fourth of July* from 1911–13 shows how far Ives journeyed in his ability to turn massive public events into music. Mentioning another (lost) college takeoff, Ives recalls that they did get some response from some of his classmates: "I had Hunt Mason's encouragement, even enthusiasm, when . . . the sun was beginning to show over East Rock. At least we amused ourselves. Hunt would declaim in blank verse. He quite agreed with me that music could 'proclaim' any part of the human experience" (Ives *Memos* 61).

82. Ives *Memos* 183–84. The pencil draft of

"Feldeinsamkeit," begun on the reverse of the double leaf containing the early sketches for the First Symphony, is a remarkable document. Unless there were lost earlier sketches, Ives appears to have written the song, one of the few things he ever produced arguably near-perfect, straight off with few changes. (Kirkpatrick in the Catalogue [175] says Ives's later ink copy has a longer recapitulation.) The pencil score is headed "for Dr Griggs recital in Center Ch Chapl Nov. 10, 1897." (As usual, Ives's top-of-the-head date, added later, is wrong. The indefatigable Kirkpatrick discovered that Griggs was singing in Simsbury that night. Feder notes [135] that Ives in later years even got the month of his father's death wrong.) The end of the "Feldeinsamkeit" draft has a couple of bars of something else jotted down with the fake-Italian expressive indication "andante quasi fartio," which appears to mean "like a slow fart."

83. Ives *Memos* 248.
84. From a Class Day speech printed in the New Haven *Register,* in Ives Papers 54/1.
85. Moore 30.
86. Kirkpatrick Datebook.
87. Ives *Memos* 182.
88. The Kirkpatrick Datebook has Ives in Danbury for the summer of 1898, while the Kirkpatrick Catalogue 267 has him at the Yale Club in New York. The best guess is that Ives commuted, since he began the Bloomfield organ job around the end of June. He vacationed in the Adirondacks in August with friend Ash Fitch.

Entr'acte Two · *Graduation*

1. In the partition of Ives's career in Burkholder's *Ideas* (43) and Hitchcock's *Music in the United States,* the period of apprenticeship is given as lasting until 1902, four years after Ives left Yale. The approach here is more a difference in definition of apprenticeship than disagreement with them. Certainly the years after Yale were a period of development and assimilation, but from my perspective one finishes an apprenticeship when one has explored a craft and leaves teachers behind. Ives arrived at Yale already a competent composer of short works both conventional and radical; in short forms, he may already have been as sophisticated (if not as good a tunesmith) as Stephen Foster. At Yale Ives completed most of his conventional apprenticeship, and in a sense he would never quite acquire a final polish. He never wrote an entirely mature, "correct" conventional piece in a large genre. Meanwhile, even before Yale he had already begun the long journey to form his mature style—which involved another kind of apprenticeship, overlapping the conventional one, which went on for a long time.
2. Ives certainly learned much about orchestration from Parker, but probably as much, and more to his taste, from the theater pit. The orchestration in his conventional pieces would be mostly competent, often imaginative and individual, as in the First Symphony. But after he cut himself free of everyday musical life his scoring would become steadily more personal and indifferent to practicality.
3. Quoted in Burkholder "Evolution" 112–13.
4. Burkholder, in "Evolution," represents Parker's influence along similar lines to these. He convincingly challenges Kearns's and Perry's theories that Parker inculcated Transcendental ideas into his pupils. In that dissertation and the later *Ideas Behind the Music,* Burkholder develops the thesis that the Transcendental aspect of Ives's thought was not so early or so pervasive as it might seem. Burkholder also disputes Perry's idea that Ives developed his later dichotomy of *substance* and *manner* from Parker's ideas of "form and substance." Burkholder points out that Parker was thereby declaring abstract music ("form") superior to program music. To the contrary, Ives's idea of substance would be inextricably involved with music conjuring specific scenes and stories. In the end, Ives denies that there is any distinction between pure music and program music: "Is not all music program music? Is not pure music, so called, representative in its essence?" In examining the process I call "mediation" between European and American elements, Burkholder inclines more to the European side, I more to the American.
5. Despite all the militancy about "pure music," one has to wonder to what degree, by the later nineteenth century anyway, it existed among significant composers.

Brahms, the paragon of abstractionists, certainly deplored program music Liszt style, but he did not entirely accept the ideas of the abstractionists led by Hanslick. In practice, program music and "abstract" genres such as the symphony were more often allied than adversarial by the late nineteenth century—witness composers as diverse as Mahler, Horatio Parker, and Charles Ives.

6. Ives quoted in Burkholder "Evolution" 137; this paragraph draws from pp. 134–40.
7. Quoted in Zuck 58, 61.
8. In analyzing these kinds of dynamics within traditions and how composers respond to them, one should not lose sight of the fact that, on the whole, composers do not sit around contemplating how to synthesize this and that tradition in order to accomplish this or that—least of all young American composers. Artistic cre-

ation is usually carried on in the heat of inspiration, with little thought other than the work at hand. A complex and integrated work cannot be cooked up like a cake by mixing dashes of one thing and another (though Postmodernists might disagree). Still, the zeitgeist is a potent factor in an artist's creative consciousness, and the individual's awareness of history and context has a significant, if mostly unconscious, impact on the work.

9. Ives *Essays* 81.
10. Naturally, psychoanalyst Stuart Feder goes into these issues at length in "*My Father's Song.*" Ives's psychological dilemmas are examined here in a more practical sense: What public outlets were open and congenial to him? For a long time, the answer was: None, except for what he called his "soft" music.
11. Ives *Memos* 41.

E I G H T *Renunciations and Apprenticeships*

1. Ives *Memos* 131.
2. Perlis CIR 31.
3. Ives *Memos* 263.
4. Interview with MONY archivist Charron Fullerton, 6/1991.
5. Ives *Memos* 269.
6. Ives's first Sunday in Bloomfield was apparently June 26, 1898. He moved to Manhattan's Central Presbyterian in April 1900.
7. Cowell and Cowell 45–46.
8. Quoted in Lord 1.
9. Lord ix.
10. Nevins and Kraut 125–26, 180.
11. Morris 318.
12. Morris 267.
13. Adams 499.
14. From the notes for a 1984–89 recording of Ives songs, Etcetera ETC 1020, 1068.
15. Swados 83.
16. Kirkpatrick Catalogue 268.
17. Myrick in Perlis CIR 34.
18. Kirkpatrick interview 11/1988.
19. *New York Times* Myrick obituary 1/1909.
20. Interview with former Ives & Myrick employee Charles Buesing in Perlis Oral History 1/21.
21. Interview with Charron Fullerton.
22. Ives *Memos* 262.
23. Ives *Memos* 262.
24. This is in Ives *Memos* 222, from the CEI political essay "George's Adventure." Bart Yung is not mentioned by name, but it is clear he is meant.

25. Ives *Memos* 263.
26. Rossiter 122. In some letters of later years, Ives notes his return from Redding to New York with "back in Babylon."
27. Ives *Memos* 119.
28. Kirkpatrick Catalogue 188.
29. From a Fletcher draft, p. 12.
30. Kirkpatrick Catalogue 39.
31. The "Rube" trying to walk 2 to 3 may refer not to a generalized bumpkin but rather to baseball pitcher Rube Marquard. That, at least, is the surmise of John Bowman, coauthor of *Diamonds in the Rough*.
32. Cowell and Cowell 40.
33. Ives *Memos* 55. Ives ascribes Bart Yung's query about the panther to "Oriental fatalism."
34. Ives *Memos* 266.
35. Cowell and Cowell 40.
36. Park quoted by Kirkpatrick in *Ives Memos* 267.
37. Eiseman 127–28. The New York Symphony merged with the Philharmonic in 1928. Walter's brother Frank Damrosch specialized in music education and organized young people's concerts. This was, in other words, the era of the "Damrosch Dynasty" in New York. Walter would become an Ives *bête noire*.
38. Eiseman 127–30.
39. *Musical Courier* 9/16/1903.
40. *Musical Courier* 8/19/1908.
41. Eiseman 136.

42. Ives *Memos* 264.
43. From a Fletcher draft, p. 12.
44. Osborne 60.
45. Ives *Memos* 148.
46. Ives *Memos* 108–9.
47. Osborne 60.
48. Ives *Memos* 148n.
49. Ives *Memos* 51–52.
50. Kirkpatrick Catalogue 5.
51. Ives Papers 51.
52. Burkholder "Evolution" 327–48.
53. In the collection of Ives manuscripts at Yale there survive—mostly with other music sketched on the empty staves—several pages of professionally copied parts for the Second Symphony. James Sinclair speculates that Ives may have hired some players to go over the piece, as he would do a number of times during the years when his music was not being played publicly.
54. Ives quoted in Block 221, from an *International Musician* article of 3/1951.
55. I find the Second Symphony attractive, youthful, and shall we say secretly epochal in its relationship to the search for an American art music—it was the foundation of the American tradition, but no one knew about it. In the end, though, I also find it thin, more or less light classical; it has appropriately ended up in Pops concerts and recordings—not that this is a fatal flaw, but it does explain why for some of us the Second wears out its welcome faster than other major Ives works.
56. Ives *Memos* 128.
57. In Ives *Memos* 128 he writes that the organ piece that became the last movement of the Third Symphony "was fuller and more freely made than it is now in the final score." Some of that fullness may have been "shadow lines," soft off-key parts shadowing the main lines, which occur in all the movements of the final orchestral score. Ives later cut the shadow lines in the Third; still later, he suggested they be restored. Recent recordings of the new Ives Society edition of the Third Symphony by Michael Tilson Thomas and by Leonard Slatkin include the shadow lines. The results suggest that Ives was right to cut them in this piece—they don't suit the style and they muck up the texture. In other pieces the shadow lines work beautifully. In concept if not always in practice, they are one of Ives's most striking innovations.
58. In the *Ideas* (139n) Burkholder notes that composers including Tchaikovsky, Mahler, and Sibelius also used cumulative form.

Ives may have gotten the idea from one or all of them, but it is more likely he evolved it on his own, and he certainly used it more systematically than anyone had before. Burkholder also points out that the technique may have evolved from Ives's improvisatory organ preluding in church services—organists commonly improvise on a hymn during the offering or communion and gradually work up to the hymn itself, which the congregation rises to sing. That is very close, in fact, to the feeling of most of the violin sonatas when the underlying hymn bursts forth at the end.
59. Ives's own description of what Burkholder calls "cumulative form" shows that he was thinking in terms of sonata form. In a program note for the 1917 private performance of the Third Violin Sonata, he writes: "The last movement is an experiment: The Free Fantasia is first. The working-out develops into the themes, rather than from them. The Coda consists of the themes for the first time in their entirety" (Ives Papers 45/7). He was being modest in calling this formal model an experiment—by then it was a familiar technique with him.
60. In the Fourth Violin Sonata Ives used a student piece of his father's. His draft for a program note mentions it this way: "In this movement there are some passages . . . from a fugue composed (1859) by the boy organist's father—though there be a few off notes, thrown in by the same bad boy."
61. Ives *Memos* 65.
62. Ives *Memos* 94. His complaint about the German rules for symphonic form occurs in the context of his explaining the loose, non-symphonic form of the *Holidays Symphony,* called such, he says, because "Symphony = 'with sounds' = my Symphony!" *Holidays* is really another of his "sets."
63. One of many tangential issues is whether Ives consciously wrote some of his church pieces with an eye toward their later combination into large works. Were the separate pieces that he put together for the First String Quartet planned in that direction from the beginning? Likewise the Second and Third Symphonies and the violin sonatas. Perhaps no one has examined this question because many of the source pieces do not survive.
64. Quoted by Kirkpatrick in Ives *Memos* 263.
65. Yellin cites (504–5) Ives's imitations of Parker's *Hora novissima;* they include the No. 5 Double Quartet based on Parker's

Double Chorus "Stant Syon Atria," and the meter changes and other details in Ives's No. 3 Quartet lifted from Parker's aria "Spe Modo Vivitur."

66. The *Celestial Country* score as it was eventually published contained these short organ preludes involving the kind of stack-of-thirds harmonies Ives had been using since his youth. Whether or not these preludes were actually played at the *Celestial Country* premiere has not been resolved. In any case, in modern performances they stick out egregiously in style from the rest of the piece. Their presence in the score, played or unplayed, may reflect Ives trying to settle his conscience about this piece by including some unorthodox harmonies.

67. As per Ives Papers 50, the Kaltenborns repeated the "Intermezzo" a few days later in New Haven, at a concert in the old Ives hangout the Hyperion Theater. Ives dedicated the piece to the quartet, but there is no record they ever played anything of his publicly again.

68. In *Memos* 128 Ives mentions that after resigning from Central Presbyterian "I substituted for an occasional Sunday service for several years after that at different churches," and would try out some of his more advanced pieces on these hit-and-run jobs. He must have developed into a good choirmaster, to get church groups through some of his pieces.

69. Ives *Memos* 128–29.

70. Ives *Memos* 126.

71. Ives *Memos* 131.

72. The speculation that Ives was angling for a normal teaching or composing career seems to have been first suggested in Yellin's review of *The Celestial Country*. Feder theorizes (*Ives* 171–72) similarly on the purpose of *The Celestial Country*.

73. If Ives indeed turned against *The Celestial Country*, it is surprising to find him afterward regularly referring to the piece and performance in his musical résumés, notes to Yale Class Books, etc. He even had the "damn rot" review typed up and sent out with other publicity material. But we must remember that for many years, this performance was the biggest thing Ives *had* on his musical résumé, and he was perfectly willing to exploit its publicity value even if he regretted the piece.

74. In the *Memos* Ives describes the First Violin Sonata as "kind of a retrogression" (68), the Third as a "weak sister" (71), the Fourth as "a slump back" (70). In fact, all

are attractive and sometimes moving pieces, innovative and extraordinary in their cumulative thematic development leading to a final proclamation of the underlying hymn tune. (See Gingerich "Processes.") Besides evoking the camp meetings of his youth—their basic setting—they also contain some of Ives's finest evocations of country fiddling (the player must change styles, and thus very much *bowing* styles, from phrase to phrase in some pages). By the 1930s, when Ives was writing most of his *Memos*, he had become intolerant of his "soft" music. The violin sonatas were surely aimed at being mainstream repertoire pieces all along, and thus suspect to him. All the same, he bridled when musicians declared them too dissonant, as we will find the violinist Milcke doing with the First Violin Sonata. One reason for Ives's dismay on that and similar occasions might be his anxiety that, if even these things were too strong for the mainstream, then he had wasted a lot of time on them.

75. Words including "experimental" and "strange" echo language Ives used himself. Some pieces were more deliberately experimental, others more ambitious and expressive in intent. Burkholder has divided Ives's work into "concert" and "research" pieces. Most of Ives's ideas, even ones coming from sheerly technical experiments, had programmatic titles, and usually in some degree expressed those titles: *Hallowe'en* may be a technical study, but it conjures up the event. He tended, in fact, to name nearly every sketch, even if it lasted just a few lines, and sometimes referred to such sketches as if they were pieces.

76. Gayle Sherwood accepts Ives's dating of "Lord of the Harvest" as "before 1902." The Ives dates for the first of the *Harvest Homes* were 1897 and 1902; Sherwood guesses it was written down, at least, in the latter year. The third piece Ives puts down as "before 1912"; Sherwood dates its reconstruction as 1914–19. As noted before, Sherwood's datings are largely based on a close examination of the manuscript paper—but this is complicated by the fact that Ives constantly reused paper, viewing any blank musical staves with a sort of *horrore vacui*. Thus one often finds pieces decades apart sharing manuscript pages—sometimes the sheets ripped apart, sometimes not. His own explanation for his constant reuse of music paper, including ones con-

taining his father's old exercises, was the cost of music paper in his childhood. The 1891 sketch of the lost *Communion Service* has on the reverse a draft of "The Bells of Yale." A later CEI memo on the manuscript says, "This shows that in those days music was a heavy expense—This song for Yale Glee club was written (on back of fathers copy) some 6 or 7 years later—to save buying new paper."

77. Kirkpatrick dating in *The New Grove*.
78. Nicholls 22–24.
79. Sinclair Preface to the *Ragtime Dances* score iii.
80. Kirkpatrick Catalogue 39.
81. Sinclair Preface to the *Ragtime Dances* score iii.
82. Ives *Memos* 56.
83. Quoted in Sinclair Preface to the *Ragtime Dances* score iii.
84. Sinclair Preface to the *Ragtime Dances* score iii.
85. Extreme claims aside, it seems clear that ragtime, blues, and jazz are eclectic idioms, an integration of African and Western elements—the blues inflection African but blues harmony descended from Western hymns, and so on. It may be that African-American music is more adaptable to the requirements of "classical" music because it already contains Western elements. "Purer" indigenous music—Native American, say—is more intractable, as several American symphonic dabblers in Indian tunes demonstrate. In his writings about black music Ives sometimes uses terms that sound racist or at least patronizing to modern ears: "the darkies used [syncopations] in their own native way" and the like (this from *Memos* 54). In that passage Ives may appear to us to be denigrating black spirituals and other styles, and proclaiming the superiority of white gospel music. What he is really doing, though, is defending his tradition from the implication that it is inferior to the black tradition, and asserting that white churches "already had somepin' also natural, spontaneous, beautiful, and artistic," which contributed to the creation of black spirituals. Making allowances for the language of his time, I do not find Ives making a racist statement anywhere, and he often condemns what a later age would term "racism."
86. Ives *Memos* 129–30.
87. Ives *Memos* 155–56.
88. My Harvard student Jenny Giering had an-

other apt metaphor for Ives's dances: "ragtime run through a blender." Ives's personal adaptations of borrowed idioms resemble parallel developments in the era's visual arts—say, Picasso's study of African masks that led to *Les Demoiselles d'Avignon* and his later Cubist style—which is why I dubbed Ives's pieces "cubistic ragtime." Similarly to that visual style, Ives fragments ragtime gestures and pastes them into novel juxtapositions and perspectives.

89. Kirkpatrick Catalogue 41.
90. Ives *Memos* 119.
91. This report comes from an older New York violinist, who told me that some of his still-older friends, theater veterans from the teens and twenties, remembered Ives as a character who would show up with strange music and fistfuls of cash. In this and similar casual forums Ives heard his advanced music played, or played *at,* far more than is generally recognized.
92. This handwritten memo toward a program note—one draft by CEI, then a shorter version in his wife's hand—is in the Ives Papers 37/1.
93. Hitchcock *Ives* 51. Also see Marshall, "Charles Ives' Quotations," for a good examination of the way quoted hymns in the First Sonata are related melodically. The question often arises of how much Ives was thinking of the *words* of quoted material. The answer is that sometimes he was thinking of the text (for example, the words of the tune "Where is My Wandering Boy" in the First Sonata relate to both Ives's programs), but more often he was thinking in terms of musical relationships among his materials.
94. Ives *Memos* 74.
95. In Hitchcock and Perlis 83, Lou Harrison points out that "the First Sonata [manuscript] was in quite good condition . . . there were only a few places in which I had to make choices." James Sinclair adds, however, that Harrison "had to do a large job of choosing in the scherzos," which are quite rough in the manuscript.
96. Both programs are in Ives *Memos* 75, John Kirkpatrick quoting Ives. Kirkpatrick dutifully spent who knows how long trying to identify the "Aunt Sarah" in the program, finally concluding that she is an archetypal rather than literal auntie.
97. Neither *Country Band March* nor "1776" is a "completed" work, though the latter is relatively more finished. Both survive

in score-sketches that have been reconstructed for performance. Editor James Sinclair, for example, used some of *Putnam's Camp* to flesh out *Country Band*. The same is true of a number of minor Ives works—they are experiments that he never bothered to finish, some of them ending up in later and more finished works, some not.

98. Kirkpatrick Chronology in Ives *Memos*. Another connection to the past, Ives's grandmother Sarah Hotchkiss Ives, widow of George White Ives, died at ninety in January 1899.

99. The text of Lyman Brewster's play is in Ives *Memos* Appendix 20.

100. See Nicholls 26–29.

101. Feder speculates (*Ives* 183) that "the 'slump' of 1905 was likely to have been frank depression." Feder the psychoanalyst looks for causes in Ives's psyche, I the composer look for them in his creative development. Specifically, in that period the manuscript implies that Ives was struggling with intractable technical difficulties in the First Piano Sonata as well as nagging physical problems, overwork, and a general lack of direction. Feder is correct in writing that dramatic mood swings were characteristic of Ives. We must keep in mind, though, that artists have mood swings for any number of reasons. A sense of aimlessness or lack of inspiration, worries about what it's all coming to, an attack on one's work, even a few discouraging words can send even a thick-skinned artist into a funk. We will find Ives writing frankly about his creative slumps following bitter encounters with performers, and it does not always require a psychoanalyst to account for them.

102. Jillisky 10.

103. Ives Papers 32/10.

104. From "Our Book" in Ives Papers 45/D7.

N I N E *La Vita Nuova*

1. Ives Papers 33/3.
2. Strong 65.
3. Strong 13–14. The friend who shot the fireman may have been Edward Carrington, who died in the Civil War. Joe would name his first son after this friend, but most of the family called him "Deac," short for "Deacon." This was an ironic reflection of his reticence and reserve, though as we will see he was also engagingly eccentric. Deac was probably a little off in the head, in some way or other.
4. Andrews 10.
5. Strong 30.
6. Twain vol. 2 225–26.
7. Feder *Ives* 206.
8. Strong 30. Father O'Hagen became president of Holy Cross College.
9. Strong 61.
10. Strong 149.
11. Strong 37.
12. Strong 47.
13. Andrews 15.
14. Strong 48.
15. Strong 161–62.
16. Strong 58.
17. Strong 54.
18. Ann Douglas does not care for "the New Bushnellian Christ, meeting men on mortal terrain, shaping himself to human needs, offering himself as a model not as a governor." This image of Christ is "feminized in image, defined as a lover of all the world's 'little ones' " (130). She examines (141–42) Bushnell's anti-feminist streak, set out in theological terms in his *Woman Suffrage: The Reform Against Nature*. Harmony Ives, in her own way and while remaining her own person, would adapt the Victorian wifely ideal to her life. Though she and her husband supported votes and careers for women, we will find her no feminist heroine in contemporary terms. One can't make her into a modern woman, which, for all her extraordinary character and strength, she clearly was not. One age's loving devotion is another's co-dependency. Harmony made up her mind what she wanted to do with her life, which was to minister to someone she understood better than anyone else to be a great man. In that she sought her own fulfillment and greatness, and achieved them. We should not sully that achievement by holding Harmony to ideals that were foreign to her.

19. Quoted in Strong 121.

20. Cowell and Cowell 46.

21. Kaplan 184.

22. Andrews 70–71.

23. Strong 123.

24. From a CEI letter to Billy Phelps in Ives Papers 31/6. Ives also quotes President Taft saying in a Hartford campaign speech, "We won't worry about Hartford, which—

ever way it goes—for it still has its Joe Twichell and [Reverend] Ned Parker." Taft probably knew Joe from the Yale Corporation.

25. JHT diary quoted in Ives *Memos* 274.

26. Ives *Memos* 274. At one point, Harmony and her father were received in Washington by President McKinley.

27. Douglas 94.

28. Trattner 164.

29. Harmony's speech quoted in Ives *Memos* 275–76.

30. Trattner 142–45. Some social Darwinists declared that tuberculosis was nature's way of culling society's unfit, much as some describe AIDS these days. In that era TB accounted for one-third of the deaths in the age group fifteen to forty-four; it was the world's main killer (145).

31. HTI quoted by John Kirkpatrick in Ives *Memos* 276.

32. From Harmony's diary in Uncollected Letters, ones she gave to John Kirkpatrick. They were found in his papers after his death.

33. In a letter of 3/2/1902, Joe Twichell wrote his daughter a whim that would gladden a Freudian's heart: "I'm of a good mind to wish [Harmony] wasn't a Twichell; for then Dave could marry her!"

34. John Kirkpatrick in Ives *Memos* 276.

35. Ives *Memos* 276.

36. Ives *Memos* 277.

37. Harmony to Charlie, Uncollected Letters, 2/24/1908.

38. Feder *Ives* 184.

39. Despite its generally free form, the *Three-Page Sonata* does have some relationship, however ironic, to European/academic sonata form—including a repeat of a more or less normal exposition section complete with first and second themes and codetta, and an implied three movements in one, fast–slow–fast. Like many of the formalistic piano studies of these years, this seems to be written right off—there are no extensive sketches and drafts like those for the piano sonatas. Ives later added on a sketch a downputting memo about the *Three-Page Sonata*, which from the memo's adolescent verbal style John Kirkpatrick dates from the early 1940s: "made mostly as a joke to knock the mollycoddles out of their boxes & to kick out their softy EARS." It was Ives's habit, in old age, to dismiss pieces of his own he didn't like, or didn't like that particular day, as just jokes. The Second Symphony, the "TSIAJ" scherzo

of the Piano Trio, and several other pieces received that treatment. In expression, there is nothing jokey about the *Sonata;* it is serious and sometimes severe in tone. Ives may have come to see the *Three-Page Sonata* as too formalistic and not expressive enough.

40. Nicholls 34.

41. One of John Kirkpatrick's unfinished projects was to identify every occurrence of the BACH motive in Ives. He found dozens of examples and left many for others to find. Among musicians this motive has a traditional symbolic reference to the most transcendent of all composers (in Schoenberg's *Moses und Aron* it is the God-motive), but it also happens to be one of the most useful of all chromatic sets, and nicely elusive in tonality. It is as if the sublime musicality of Bach's legacy extended even to the letters of his name, and that across centuries and styles.

42. See the analyses of the piece in Nicholls 34–40 and Hitchcock *Ives* 44–48, from both of which this discussion has drawn.

43. Perlis Oral History 1/1. Myrick also says in the interview that in the 1940s someone taped an interview with Ives. This unique and invaluable tape was lost.

44. Ives *Memos* 62–63.

45. *Over the Pavements* moves decisively in the direction of the rhythmic concepts—tempo (or metric) modulation, accelerating and decelerating rhythms more or less independent of the meter, and so on—that would preoccupy Ives's protégé Elliott Carter. As Nicholls notes of this work of Ives's and others of around the same period: "This experiment in accelerating and static musical layers clearly follows on from the accumulating and accelerating polyrhythms of *All the Way Around and Back,* the proportional and mensural canons of the two *Largo Risoluto* pieces, *Holding Your Own* and *From the Steeples and Mountains,* the polytemporal marches of *Overture: 1776* and, ultimately, Ives's experience of musical accidents and his father's experiments in his youth" (57).

46. Ives *Memos* 63. Of what we are calling "laboratory pieces" (and Burkholder calls "research" pieces), Ives cites the *Tone Roads,* the running-the-bases piece *All the Way Around and Back,* one of the *Largo Risoluto* pieces, and *In Re Con Moto Et Al.*

47. Ives *Memos* 59. Feder theorizes (*Ives* 191) that the old man dying alone in *In the Night* is George Ives.

48. Hitchcock *Ives* 76. Ives based *In the Night* on a novel harmonic plan: "I tried to find three chords that might be used in a similar or parallel sense to the usual tonic, dominant, and subdominant . . . that would have some musical sense and relation and about which melodies or counterpoints could be used as a natural outcome from these combinations." So a D♭ triad served as "tonic," A♭ as "dominant," E major as "subdominant" (*Memos* 57–58). He says he wrote a version of the piece in 1902 and played it in a recital and in a Central Presbyterian service. At the latter, "Dr. Merle Smith turned around and glowered at the choir." Ives had earlier experimented with I–IV–V substitutions and layering in *Eventide* (1899?) and its derivative *Hymn-Anthem* (1902).

49. Ives's late-thirties revisions to *The Unanswered Question* have become strangely controversial in the musicological literature, as if they were made for suspicious or narrowly ideological rather than *musical* reasons, that is, to make a better piece. All the changes clearly make for an improvement, and none alters the revolutionary concept and sound first put down in 1906. Comparing by ear the two versions (as heard on Michael Tilson Thomas's recording of them), there is an obvious reason Ives revised the first version: The trumpet's original unchanging last B♭ is a lame note, neither satisfactorily tonal nor convincingly ambiguous. Furthermore, to keep ending on the same B♭ is static. So Ives wisely decided to alternate the Question's ending between two notes, C and B, both of them better than the B♭. Hitchcock and Zahler imply (441) that Ives did it to make the piece more atonal, and thereby betrayed the programmatic idea of the unchanging Question. This change of *a single note* is thus treated as of a piece with Ives's general habit, as Elliott Carter put it, of "jacking up the level of dissonance" of pieces after they were finished, presumably under the influence of modernist music he had heard. This was an incidental point for Hitchcock and Zahler, but Maynard Solomon inflated that same *single note* into a devious Ivesian scheme to make himself look more prophetic. Need I say, I don't buy any of this. It was an aesthetic revision. The original 1906 version is a rough draft, and in the 1930s Ives spruced it up before letting it out of the house. It's what a composer ordinarily does. Ives needed the

trumpet line to be more cryptic and dynamic, so he remade the original lame ending of the Question into an exquisitely sphinxlike one, with an intriguing vacillation in the last note. The wind's original, too-pretty final chord became a high tone cluster, a scream of rage and frustration. And so forth through a number of improvements. (The title *The Unanswered Question* is taken from Emerson's poem "The Sphinx.") In general, musicologists try to explain every musical detail in historical terms, theorists in theoretical terms, psychoanalysts in psychoanalytic terms—and Ivesians in programmatic terms. One or more of those terms can be valid at a given point, but composers spend a good deal of time working and reworking ideas simply to get the things to *sound right,* which is a criterion highly personal and undefinable, but still of great importance. When we see Ives writing out, say, piano draft after draft of The *"Saint-Gaudens" in Boston Common,* we can see what he was doing: playing it over and over, refining the harmonies and melodic lines and formal shape. That gruelling process, which consumes much of one's time as a composer, has little to do with history, Freud, gender, or theory, but with ear and intuition and soul and stubborn patience, and all the other indefinable but irreplaceable qualities that make good art good. So it was with *The Unanswered Question.*

50. Kirkpatrick *Catalogue* 44.

51. The basic chordal idea of the background in *Central Park* is harmonies made of expanding symmetrical intervals—major thirds, then fourths, then augmented fourths/fifths, and finally fifth chords (which have a somewhat cadential effect). The rhythm wanders in what Burkholder calls a "wave-like" pattern ("Evolution" 497), repeating every ten bars. The other layers in the piece, representing environmental sounds, accumulate to a characteristically riotous, poly-everything Ivesian climax, then subside.

52. Ballantine summarizes (181) the musical and philosophical ideas that *Central Park in the Dark* manages to convey: "We think about . . . nature as the permanent ground of all human activities, utterly indifferent to such activities, but in a strange, paradoxical sense hospitable to them; we 'know' human life as rich, deeply felt, conflictual, but in search of happiness, transient and spo-

radic in relation to the 'empty' permanence of nature. We 'know' nature as unfeeling and unconscious—in philosophical language, *in itself*—and human life as feeling and conscious—*for itself*." For something that would seem to be as subjective as this interpretation, I feel the same way for the most part and suspect many people would. Ives was remarkable at conveying "nonmusical" ideas.

53. Ives Papers 24/14. After getting *Central Park* in shape, Ives had a theater orchestra run through it between the acts of a show: "The players had a hard time with it—the piano player got mad, stopped in the middle and kicked the bass drum" (from a 1946 letter to Elliott Carter in Ives Papers 27/10).

54. Kirkpatrick Datebook.

55. Harmony to Charlie, Uncollected Letters, 8/16/1906.

56. Harmony to Charlie, Uncollected Letters, 12/12/1906.

57. Charlie to Harmony, Uncollected Letters, 11/25/1907.

58. In an interview with John Kirkpatrick in Ives Papers Microfilm Addendum, Harmony says "Charlie's & my intimacy didn't begin til 1906." Maybe it is worth mentioning that "intimacy" did not mean the same thing in 1906 that it does in the 1990s.

59. Myrick in Perlis CIR 36. Feder (*Ives* 198) speculates that "it seems unlikely that there was any physical problem at the time"; that is, he believes that Ives's breakdown in 1906 was largely psychosomatic, a result of inner and outer stress. I believe it was physical as much as anything, though certainly aggravated by contrapuntal stresses creative, romantic, and professional. Sources including Harmony's letters show that Ives was ailing frequently if not constantly from around mid-1905 until around their wedding in summer 1908. As Myrick notes, doctors had been worried about Ives for some time before his 1906 attack. So was Aunt Amelia. We will return to this issue when his health problems return.

60. Kirkpatrick Catalogue 268.

61. Harmony to Charlie, Uncollected Letters, 1/27/1907.

62. Kirkpatrick chronology in Ives *Memos*.

63. Kirkpatrick interview with Harmony in Ives Papers Microfilm Addendum.

64. John Kirkpatrick in Ives *Memos* 277.

65. Harmony to Charlie, Uncollected Letters,

6/14/1907. Harmony mentions "the *Parsifal* music"; it was probably excerpts in an orchestral concert. Studies that remain to be written are the influence of Wagner on Ives, and likewise of Brahms.

66. Trattner 172.

67. John Kirkpatrick quoting HTI in Ives *Memos* 277.

68. Charlie to Harmony, Uncollected Letters, 11/25/1907.

69. Sir Gilbert Parker's story, which is printed in Ives *Memos,* is actually called *The Red Patrol.*

70. Harmony to Charlie, Uncollected Letters, 10/9/1907.

71. Harmony to Charlie, quoted in Ives *Memos* 324.

72. A Kirkpatrick interview with Harmony in Ives Papers Microfilm Addendum places them at Mrs. Sage's.

73. Harmony to Charlie, Uncollected Letters, 8/13/1907. Aunt Amelia figures prominently in Harmony's surviving letters, Mollie Ives not at all.

74. Harmony to Charlie, 9/9/1907, quoted in Feder *Ives* 205.

75. Harmony to Charlie, Uncollected Letters, 9/21/1907.

76. Harmony to Charlie, Uncollected Letters, 10/17/1907 and 10/18/1907.

77. Harmony to Charlie, Uncollected Letters, 12/12/1907.

78. Letter of Joseph Hooker Twichell (one of Harmony's brothers) in Ives Papers 32/10.

79. Harmony to Charlie, Uncollected Letters, 10/25/1907.

80. Harmony to Charlie, Uncollected Letters, 10/27–10/28/1907.

81. The original text of "Autumn" that Harmony sent Charlie was changed somewhat in the final song. Two of his courting songs to Harmony's texts, both the beautiful "Autumn" and the soggy-sentimental "Spring Song," Ives later included, with a cool disregard for sentiment, in his list of "slumps" (Cowell and Cowell 71).

82. Charlie to Harmony, Uncollected Letters, 10/27/1907 and 10/28/1907.

83. Ives *Memos* 114.

84. Harmony to Charlie, Uncollected Letters, two from 11/12/1907.

85. JHT diary quoted in Ives *Memos* 260.

86. Charlie to Harmony, Uncollected Letters, 11/24/1907.

87. CEI to JHT, 11/23/1907, in Ives Papers Microfilm Addendum.

88. Twichell family letters from 12/1907 in Ives Papers Microfilm Addendum.

89. Harmony to Charlie, Uncollected Letters, 9/29/1907.
90. Harmony to Charlie, Uncollected Letters, 11/11/1907.
91. Harmony to Charlie, 11/23/1907, Ives Papers Microfilm Addendum.
92. Harmony to Charlie, Uncollected Letters, 12/6/1907.
93. Harmony to Charlie, Uncollected Letters, 12/12/1907.
94. Harmony to Charlie, Uncollected Letters, 12/30/1907.
95. Harmony to Charlie, 2/25/1908, Ives Papers Microfilm Addendum.
96. Harmony to Charlie, Uncollected Letters, 3/10/1908. Some of Harmony's love letters have been recopied by their adopted daughter Edith.

97. Harmony to Ruggles in Ives Papers 31/12.
98. Charlie to Harmony, Uncollected Letters, 5/13/1908.
99. Ives Papers Microfilm Addendum.
100. Amelia letter quoted in Feder Ives 211.
101. Cowell and Cowell 46.
102. CEI letter of 1/4/1937 to Eilly Phelps, in Ives Papers 31/6.
103. Kirkpatrick interviews with Harmony in Ives Papers Microfilm Addendum.
104. Information on the honeymoon comes from "Our Book" (Ives Papers 45/D7) and John Kirkpatrick's Datebook.
105. Ives *Memos* 87.
106. Kirkpatrick interview notes in Ives Papers Microfilm Addendum.

T E N *Measuring the Prospect*

1. Perlis CIR 56.
2. Lord 107.
3. Much of this information on the Hyde party and its aftermath comes from Forma 115–19.
4. Clough 3.
5. Lord 114.
6. Forma 118.
7. Clough 241–45.
8. Onetime Ives & Myrick employee Peter Fraser, later chairman of the board at Connecticut Mutual, in Perlis Oral History 1/30. Given that I&M might have thirty-five or forty regular agents on the payroll in its prime, one can see how a network of hundreds of outside salesmen could increase sales. Fraser concludes, "If Ives and Myrick had been general agents instead of managers . . . both men would have become immensely rich . . . instead of being on a paid salary. . . . They would have had a great fortune in deferred commissions that they never got. . . . When Ives quit, he was through" (Perlis CIR 62). Fraser seems to have been unaware that, as we will come to later, Ives *did* make a great deal of money from deferred commissions in the 1920s, and presumably Myrick did as well. Ives would have a comfortable if not extravagant income from his business earnings for the rest of his life.
9. Perlis CIR 51.
10. Interview 6/1991 with Mutual archivist Charron Fullerton.
11. The form letters and "General Suggestions" are in the MONY Ives file.

12. MONY Ives file.
13. Myrick to the Cowells, Ives Papers 30/18.
14. In Perlis CIR 48, Verplanck's son notes, "Father and Myrick never did get along, and when Mr. Ives retired my father worried about it." Apparently Verplanck's support of Franklin Delano Roosevelt turned Myrick against Verplanck; the son implies he blames Myrick to some extent for his father's death in 1941. Ives and Verplanck were close for years, and Verplanck later served as treasurer of one of Ives's composer groups. Ives was godfather to Verplanck's son (Perlis CIR 49.) In Perlis Oral History 3/56 a former I&M secretary, the one Verplanck called "Mussolini," declares him rather mean and dictatorial, and wonders why the kindly Ives kept him on. In contrast, Ives wrote Myrick in 1929 that Verplanck "does things [so] capably that he is called on to undertake more than he should undertake." It seems clear, in any case, that it was Verplanck's job to do the hard-nosed office tasks that neither Ives nor Myrick liked to do.
15. Scrapbook in Ives Papers 43. All money amounts are of the time unless noted that they are in 1991 dollars.
16. Ives *Memos* 224, from Ives's unpublished social-economic story/essay "George's Adventure," which is autobiographical in many respects. The sum of $1.3 million could be invented for his fictional speaker's fortune, but it sounds possible for Ives. As we will see, his tax records show that his most profitable years were in the 1920s.

17. Medical report in MONY Ives file.
18. Brewster Ives in Perlis CIR 74.
19. Perlis Oral History 3/56.
20. Perlis CIR 63.
21. Myrick's notice "What the Business Owes to Charles E. Ives," in *The Eastern Underwriter* 9/19/1930.
22. George Hofmann in Perlis Oral History 1/23.
23. Myrick in Ives *Memos* 271.
24. Cowell and Cowell 49.
25. Charles Buesing in Perlis Oral History 1/21. An edited version of his interview is in Perlis CIR.
26. Perlis Oral History 3/56. Ives was jingoistic in some ways but remarkably free of national or racial prejudices. When he lambasted a country, especially Germany during the wars, he specifically criticized behavior, not national character. As noted before, while some of his words about black culture may seem insensitive by our standards (though hardly by his time's), one never finds him declaring a country, race, creed, or sex innately bad or inferior.
27. Perlis Oral History 3/56.
28. Perlis CIR 63.
29. Letter from Fred Wenzel in Ives Papers 32/12.
30. Former secretary Katherine Verplanck (Mrs. William) in Perlis CIR 50.
31. Clough 282. From this history of the Mutual company and other sources including MONY archivist Charron Fullerton, it is clear that Ives was not quite the prophetic giant of the modern insurance industry that some writers have painted. Ives earns only a couple of in-passing mentions in Clough's history of Mutual. One reason is that Ives was usually working in the office while Myrick was out pressing the flesh, with the result that Ives was not nearly so widely known as his partner around the industry, especially outside New York. For another thing, most of Ives's innovations were not unique to him but part of the general thrust of the time. He simply tended to do a more thoughtful and systematic job working with ideas that were in the air. Ives was part of a new wave in the industry, not the cause of the wave.
32. Clough 277, 279.
33. MONY Ives file.
34. Various I&M courses of instruction are in the MONY Ives file.
35. Hofmann in Perlis CIR 56.
36. *Portable Thoreau* 117.
37. Zelizer 113.
38. Zelizer 153.
39. Zelizer 113.
40. From a draft for *The Amount to Carry,* section II, MONY Ives file.
41. MONY Ives file.
42. Ives *Essays* 232.
43. CEI article in *The Eastern Underwriter* 9/26/1919.
44. Cowell and Cowell 51.
45. Based on a 1992 Daria Sommers interview with Dr. Davis Gregg, former president of the American College of Life Insurance and friend of Julian Myrick. Gregg notes that Myrick knew Heubner, and so Ives may have known him as well. A book of Heubner's is on Ives's reading list for the agent classes of the 1920s.
46. MONY Ives file.
47. Quoted in Cowell and Cowell 55–56.
48. Myrick writing to the Cowells, presumably for their book. Ives Papers 30/18.
49. Scrapbook in Ives Papers 44.
50. Barnes; "As I See It."
51. Quoted in Cowell and Cowell 96–97.
52. CEI draft memo, presumably to Myrick, in Ives Papers 30/18.
53. The CEI memo to the home office is excerpted in Cowell and Cowell 59–62. Rossiter notes (118) that this memorandum was part of a campaign by agency managers to push Mutual president Charles A. Peabody in bolder directions. Peabody had reacted to the Investigation by governing the company in a conservative way intended in part to limit growth. Typically, Ives wrote a considered memorandum from behind the scenes while Myrick jumped into the political fray. Neither had much effect.
54. Hofstadter 62. He is talking here about the "agrarian myth" that underlay the Populists, but the myth lasted into the Progressive era.
55. Ives *Essays* 82.
56. Rossiter writes (121), "Hofstadter's 'Progressive' was a man who brought his small-town values with him to the city, who tried 'to realize familiar and traditional ideals under novel circumstances.' " But Rossiter says Ives also had elements of Robert Wiebe's "new middle class," who "developed a bureaucratic approach to social order."
57. The Twentieth Amendment draft in Ives *Essays* 206.
58. Hofstadter 216–17.
59. Newspaper clip in MONY Ives file. This is

one of Ives's last pieces of advertising copy, and shows the philosophic style that marked his postwar business writing. One has to wonder how effective an ad like this was, in comparison to his earlier and more pertinent ones: "$200,000—$3000. Interested?"

60. From a CEI article "The Program—Its Uses and Possibilities," in *The Eastern Underwriter* 9/18/1925.

61. From "George's Adventure," Ives *Memos* 224–25.

62. Ives *Memos* 215.

63. From the 1918 CEI paper "The Need of the Production and Conservation of Legal Reserve Life Insurance in Relation to Wartime Economics," in MONY Ives file.

64. From a CEI draft for a paper in MONY Ives file.

65. From a 1917 CEI paper for *The Eastern Underwriter*, in MONY Ives file.

66. From a CEI letter in Ives Papers 26/3 responding to an article called "If Life Insurance Were Suddenly Abolished."

67. From "George's Adventure," Ives *Memos* 225.

68. Ives *Essays* 8.

69. Ives *Essays* 231.

70. Rossiter writes (177), "Ives's thought was not imbued with that desire for community which motivated many progressives." He refused to involve himself personally in the business or artistic community as a leader or active participant, and generally described himself as a lone wolf. (Rossiter ignores Ives's burst of volunteerism during the war, but he is generally right that Ives avoided leadership and societies—he called it his "a-associative" sense.) Comparing Ives to his community-leader brother Moss, Rossiter concludes that "neither the desire for social order nor the goal of brotherly love could awaken a comparable sense of community in his brother, Charles." But failing to join the Chamber of Commerce does not represent a rejection of community. (Later, Ives did join and help support several new-music organizations.) In *Ideas* (83) Burkholder presents an Ivesian Romantic/individualistic sense of music: "He retained the conception of music as a private rather than a community experience." My saying that the idea of community lies at the heart of Ives's concept of music and life is in part disagreeing with both of them, in part looking at Ives's ideas more as he intended them than in how they

played out in his external life. Burkholder is certainly correct in saying that Ives's mature music belonged neither to the urban cultivated world nor to the reality of musical life in towns like Danbury. This situation I have described as a lack of milieu. And certainly a private, individualistic communion with music is an Ivesian ideal, derived both from the Romantics and from his own experience in childhood (Ives and his father lived in a private musical world as well as a public one). But, as we will see in the next chapters, Ives was ultimately thinking in everything he did—in music, in prose, in business, in his charities—about issues of the larger human community and its future, as shown in his dreams of a People's World Union, his support of the League of Nations and later of the United Nations. Even if hardly anyone was listening to his music or able to understand it, Ives ultimately *intended* it as a public act and a reflection of communal experience. If that contradicted his lone-wolf personality—well, we can add one more contradiction to a long list of them. (Or perhaps this is another case of "more of a paradox than a contradiction.") Unlike many Romantics Ives saw music as meaning little outside a community (even if such a community no longer existed as he imagined it). That is part of the reason why most of his pieces are programmatic, have some moral and evolutionary background. His programs are not dramatic but rather represent meaningful scenes or qualities from the life of communities. As much as anything, Ives's music is *about* community.

71. From a Myer Agency (successor to Ives & Myrick) Golden Anniversary essay in MONY Ives file. The biggest Mutual agency in 1914 was that of Darby A. Day in Chicago. (We will find Day doing legwork for Ives later, in the effort to distribute the Twentieth Amendment proposal.)

72. Photo in Ives Papers 46. There are twenty-four people in this photo of the main office space, including an elegantly dressed and behatted Myrick standing next to the rotund Verplanck. Predictably, Ives is not in the picture.

73. Kirkpatrick transcriptions in Ives Papers Microfilm Addendum.

74. Harmony to Charlie, Ives Papers Microfilm Addendum.

75. Ives Papers Microfilm Addendum and John Kirkpatrick interview 6/1958.

76. John Kirkpatrick interview 3/1988. Proper-Victorian Harmony always fibbed about her hysterectomy, telling Kirkpatrick it was a gallbladder operation. He suspected the truth; it was confirmed after Harmony's death by Amelia Van Wyck.

77. In Kirkpatrick Catalogue 192, because of the manuscript memo about Harmony in the hospital, he guesses the date of "Like a Sick Eagle" as 1909. In *The New Grove,* Kirkpatrick has changed the date to ?1913, the song therefore being a memory rather than contemporary with the event. Ives's date in *114 Songs* is 1920, but this is presumably the year of the piano arrangement, taken from the original version with instruments. The memo on the score is the sort of thing that led Maynard Solomon to accuse Ives of trying to convince us pieces were written earlier, but there is no compelling reason for that assumption here, or indeed in other cases Solomon cites. (In the *114 Songs,* in fact, Ives dates the song *later* than it probably was written. Solomon ignores these kinds of inconsistencies.) Ives used his manuscripts almost as a diary, jotting memories on them going back to his childhood—and many of the memos come from his later, less mentally acute years. "Like a Sick Eagle" is unique in Ives's music and one of his most extraordinary songs, the voice singing a kind of continuous falling glissando something like Schoenberg's *Sprechstimme* in effect. (Ives wrote of the voice also in terms of projecting the quarter tones between the written intervals.) The feeling of the song is one of the few moments in Ives that seems to me genuinely tragic.

78. Quoted in Feder *Ives* 216.

79. Photos in the Ives Papers.

80. Kirkpatrick transcript in Ives Papers Microfilm Addendum.

81. "Our Book," Ives Papers 45/7.

82. Strong 163–65.

83. Ives Papers Microfilm Addendum.

84. Kirkpatrick in Perlis Oral History 2/32.

85. "Our Book," Ives Papers 45/7.

86. Perlis CIR 96.

87. "Our Book," Ives Papers 45/7.

88. In the mid-1970s I found the old Ives House, which had been moved several times, sitting in the middle of a school parking lot with a group of hippies living in—and tearing up—what was left of it. Later the house was moved to the side of a pond in town to be the first element of a planned historical park. The park never got beyond an idea. At last, over a decade or so, funds were collected to restore the house to what it looked like when Charles Ives was born.

89. Kirkpatrick Chronology in Ives *Memos* 332.

90. Ives's collage on his Redding studio door is still there, gradually falling apart.

91. Ives *Essays* 170, from his essay "The Majority": "For my own part, we hope some day to obtain our maximum [savings under his self-imposed limitation] and retire *to* business on ten acres and dig potatoes and write symphonies." (Note that this also implies Ives saw music as his true business.)

ELEVEN *Entelechy*

1. Perlis CIR 102, 104.

2. As usual, problems enter into the dating of *The "Saint-Gaudens."* Ives wrote in a memo that a page of the piece got into the First Symphony score when Walter Damrosch was about to read that work over in 1910. In his notes to the reconstructed full orchestra score of *Three Places,* James Sinclair speculates that it was probably a sketch for the *Housatonic,* not the *"Saint-Gaudens,"* that startled Damrosch—a *Housatonic* sketch survives written on the back of the First Symphony finale's title page. This is the kind of dating confusion that creeps in time and again from various combinations of Ives's erratic memory, his tendency to reuse old manuscripts for sketching, and his habit of writing addresses on most pages (partly for his copyists, partly in case something got lost). In any case 1911 remains the best guess for the main work on the *"Saint-Gaudens."* Ives scored the movement for full orchestra in 1912, during a vacation at Lake Kiwasa in the Adirondacks, and reworked it in 1929 for Nicolas Slonimsky's chamber orchestra.

3. Predecessors of the *"Saint-Gaudens"* include a *Hymn-Anthem* on "Abide With Me"; *In the Night;* and *Elegy to Our Forefathers.*

4. Hansen 251. The works inspired by Shaw and the 54th include Lowell's "For the

Union Dead," Johnson's "Saint-Gaudens: An Ode," and Berryman's "Boston Common." William James in his speech at the 1897 unveiling of the sculpture spoke of "the dark outcasts, so true to nature that one can almost hear them breathing as they march" (quoted in Hansen 267). Ives's poem and music echo that sentiment. Ives also echoed Johnson's description of the *"Saint-Gaudens"* as "that sculptured music, that immortal dirge . . . the anthem of a rescued race" (quoted in Hansen 266). The unveiling of the "Saint-Gaudens" was an unforgettable occasion for the thousands attending; ceremonies included speeches by William James and Booker T. Washington, and survivors of the 54th marched. (William and Henry James's younger brother Garth was adjutant of the 54th and was wounded at Fort Wagner.) Recent commemorations have included the film *Glory.*

5. In the 1929 revision of *Three Places,* Ives added a quote of "Yes, Jesus Loves Me" to the *"Saint-Gaudens."* This tune also involves minor thirds—the interval saturates the movement.

6. The *"Saint-Gaudens"* is a great piece, though in most performances a notably boring great piece. One hears attempts at it that dutifully observe every one of Ives's elaborate performance instructions and add up to a very murky stew. But in the occasional performance with what can only be described as soul, it is as moving as anything Ives wrote—and another of his rare intimations of tragedy.

7. Ives *Memos* 87. Ives says Stowell conducted a movement of the Second Symphony— probably the first movement—at a concert of the Mannes School, where Stowell directed the orchestra.

8. Ives *Memos* 123. This encounter with Stowell and the one described in *Memos* 87 probably took place on two different occasions.

9. Ives *Memos* 121, 186.

10. Ives *Memos* 99. The quotes are Ives's memories of what Mrs. Coolidge said, but they sound very much like her kind of phrasing rather than his. He may have written down her comments, or simply remembered them indelibly.

11. Ives *Memos* 70–71. Again, the quotes of Milcke are Ives's memories, but they sound right. It was probably the metrically am-

biguous rhythms of the piano part that confused the violinist; the solo part is easy at the beginning. The once-famous Milcke may find his main place in history as the "typical hard = boiled, narrow-minded, conceited, prima donna" that Ives describes in the *Memos*—a fate similar to Horatio Parker's.

12. Ives *Memos* 71. By the time of the *Memos* Ives was down on all his violin sonatas, not just the Third—which I call the finest of them, in fact.

13. Ives *Memos* 100–101.

14. Ives *Memos* 44.

15. Herrmann in Perlis CIR 162. Herrmann says that Ives's final New York residence at 164 East 74th Street was opposite the Mannes School of Music. Herrmann added, "Leopold Mannes . . . never knew that Ives lived across the street from him."

16. Cowell and Cowell 64.

17. Ives *Memos* 271.

18. James Sinclair alerted me to Ives's occasional tendency to treat symphony orchestras as if they were theater orchestras.

19. Ives *Essays* 84.

20. Noting Ives's impracticality with instrumentation is not to call him incompetent. He grew up arranging for instruments and played several, including trumpet and violin; much of his instrumental composing is highly attuned to the instruments. Listening to two orchestras—the New World and Chicago Symphony—rehearse and perform the Fourth Symphony under Michael Tilson Thomas, I concluded that after some re-notation here and there in the parts, pros can play the piece without inordinate fuss or confusion. Moreover, what comes out is powerful and effective from beginning to end. Even if some things are clumsy to play, even if lines get lost in the ruckus, the Fourth still makes the effect Ives wanted to, in the way he wanted it to. The live effect of the *Comedy* in full pandemonium, for example, is unforgettable to hear (and much muted in recording). By my definition, this is not incompetence.

21. Ives *Memos* 74.

22. CEI interview with Howard Taubman in the Sunday *New York Times Magazine,* 10/23/1949.

23. Kirkpatrick transcription in Ives Papers Microfilm Addendum, dated 6/25/1914.

24. Burkholder *Ideas* 106.

25. Burkholder *Ideas* 100.

26. Quoted in Burkholder *Ideas* 98.
27. Harmony to Charlie, Uncollected Letters 1/24/1912.
28. Harmony to Charlie, Uncollected Letters 3/4/1914.
29. Harmony to Charlie, Uncollected Letters 3/24/1915. In this letter Harmony also says, "Dad . . . seems more lonely here & easier to manage for he doesn't seem to want to go anywhere or do anything alone."
30. Rossiter presents the thesis that, early on, Ives could have made contact with progressive artists in New York and elsewhere, but was prevented by his Puritan aversion toward Bohemians and the sexually loose. That argument has never convinced me. During the teens there was no thriving *musical* avant-garde that would have welcomed Ives. Such an avant-garde did not develop in the United States until the 1920s, at which point Ives *did* make himself known to them, sexually loose Bohemians and all. Beyond that, Rossiter seems to imply throughout his book that if Ives had been a different and better person, from a different and better country, he would have been a better composer. That is flimsy on the face of it. Ives could not have been a significantly better composer under any achievable circumstances. Certainly if he had been born into the kind of thriving musical milieu Mozart and Beethoven were, he might have developed his comparable talent further. Then, of course, he would not have been Charles Ives or anything resembling him. Rossiter's book remains valuable for its depth of research and for being the first study to detail some of the toll Ives's life took on him, even if one differs with his assertion that Ives had any real choice in how he pursued his musical career.
31. Ives *Memos* 71.
32. This familiar picture—it is on the cover of the *Memos*—usually loses some of the features described here (including the very dim pigeon) in reproduction.
33. There is a University of Illinois doctoral dissertation by John Jeffrey Gibbens called "Debussy's Impact on Ives: An Assessment." It has long been noted that Ives quotes Debussy's *L'aprés-midi*—the opening flute solo—in the song "Grantchester." Gibbens also finds Debussyan influence in works including "The Pond," "Mists,"

"Maple Leaves," and *The Housatonic at Stockbridge*. Ives, while more or less dismissing Debussy as a city slicker in the *Essays,* does manage a kind word for *La Mer.* It seems clear that Debussy was useful to Ives in various ways, but it was also inevitable that the Frenchman's sensuousness would rub Ives the wrong way.
34. Ives *Memos* 96.
35. *An Elegy to Our Forefathers* was originally titled *An Elegy to Stephen Foster.* I have yet to hear a performance of *The Rockstrewn Hills,* the second movement of the Second Set, that convinces me the piece can work. Again, for all the complaints one can more or less justly register against Ives's instrumentation, his orchestral music generally sounds well in his terms, in his fashion. *The Rockstrewn Hills* may be an exception. It seems miscalculated for full orchestra; the string section is too heavy to project the lines and nimble ragtime figures. The same or similar ideas work quite well in the small-orchestra *Ragtime Dances.*
36. Ives *Memos* 98. In Perlis CIR 10–11, Ives's cousin Amelia Van Wyck remembers going to a couple of readings at the East 22nd Street house, and implies that there were others. As noted before, in such informal settings Ives heard his music played much more than is generally recognized—though rarely if ever played well.
37. From Ives's article "Some 'Quarter-Tone' Impressions," in Ives *Essays* 117. Ives's relationship to atonality is such a complex and technical question that it is not addressed extensively here. For a survey see Allen Forte, "Ives and Atonality." Notwithstanding Forte's basic position that "the major part of [Ives's] mature output can be described as atonal" (162), one should add some qualifications. For one thing, many of those same pieces could as well be described as *not* atonal; as Forte notes (163), "melodic lines in Ives tend to be diatonic, chromatic, or whole tone." Ives's attitude to the matter is, as with much else, hard to pin down. But we should remember that for musicians today the word "atonal" carries a good deal of technical and polemical baggage, most of which has little to do with Ives. When he was writing his music Ives did not know the word. He was aware of the concept, in his own terms. As Ives says in the *Memos* (56), he wrote "In the Cage" (1906) "to show that a song does

not necessarily have to be in any one key to make musical sense." (He added sarcastically, from the perspective of the 1930s, "To make music in no particular key has a nice name nowadays—'atonality.' " The melodic line of "In the Cage," however, is whole tone.) The difficulty of placing atonality and polytonality in Ives's music is a subset of the difficulty of defining atonality or polytonality at all. Hindemith in *A Composer's World* denies even the possibility of atonality, because a given sonority can always be related to a central tone. Polytonality can be reasoned out of existence in the same way. In the direction of addressing these issues, a few points may be made. First, there are what we might call an "atonal sound" and a "polytonal sound," which experienced listeners recognize. The "atonal sound" defies definition; it is complex and subjective, though nonetheless real. Ives sounds that way only occasionally, partly because, as Forte says, Ives's leading lines are rarely atonal. When Ives does exhibit an "atonal sound," as in the *Tone Roads,* he seems less Ivesian than, in that case, prophetic of the sound of 1960s music. Similarly, some of the first movement of the Second Quartet arguably sounds as Schoenbergian as Ivesian. The "polytonal sound" is simpler, a matter of emphasized cross-relations between lines or strata. Examples include some of Milhaud's relatively early and lusciously polytonal works such as *Les Choéphores.* As detailed earlier, Ives explored overtly polytonal effects in some of his *Psalms.* Soon, however, his polytonality tended to become so dense that the cross-relations melt into a general sense of chromatic, perhaps "atonal" texture. At the beginning of the *"Saint-Gaudens,"* for example, the string lines can be seen as polytonal—perhaps E minor above A minor, with chromatics obscuring both. The total effect, however, could be called near-atonal, except that the repeated A–C ostinato in the basses tends to create a tonal anchor. There are times, certainly—as in much of the Second Quartet—when the lines take precedence and the harmony more or less takes care of itself (though the quartet is intentionally steadily dissonant). Adding up all these effects, one arrives at a few rules of thumb: Achieving atonality as such was rarely a systematic goal of Ives's, in the way it was with

Schoenberg and his followers. Though Ives used what amount to twelve-tone lines here and there, he showed no favoritism for such lines; they are a technical device equal among many. Nor did Ives develop the kind of systematic procedures for avoiding tonality that the Europeans did—notably the rhetoric of constantly leaping lines, nonstop dissonance, banishment of triads, and so on. No matter how chromatic, leaping, or dissonant Ives got, he still usually saw things as combinations of keys and/or as eventually related to or aiming at a tonality—even if he never quite arrived at that tonality. (The idea of an implicit but never-actually-achieved tonal center would be highly Ivesian. He sometimes explained his idiosyncratic note spellings, for example, with reference to leading tones that never actually lead.) Meanwhile the presence of diatonic tonality in most of his music, however veiled, helped him shift readily between atonal and diatonic effects.

38. The question of style in Ives deserves a book or two to itself and so far has an interesting one: Larry Starr's *A Union of Diversities: Style in the Music of Charles Ives.* The 1974 Ives Festival-Conference revealed that a number of visiting European composers were, at least at that time, unwilling to accept Ives's (to them) incomprehensible stylistic vagaries. Sometimes they seemed outraged by his mixing of style and genre, his meta-style. In the history-obsessed European aesthetic of that time the *Comedy* of Ives's Fourth Symphony was viewed as a revolutionary achievement *in history;* the tonal Fugue that follows it, therefore, could only be seen as a step backward in history, as Ives betraying his own revolution. Thus in a panel discussion among European composers at the Festival-Conference, one excoriated the Fugue at length. There followed some astute ideas from others about the meaning and relevance of the Fugue. At a concert the next day I happened to sit down next to the complaining composer and innocently said, "Well, do you accept the Fugue now?" He got up and stalked out of the hall.

39. As noted before, Ives from early on was a master of novel and effective endings. Much of what is said about his endings in this section applies more to his instrumental, and mainly orchestral, works. Still, in

his instrumentation Ives refused to be limited by the conventions of the medium. Some piano pieces and songs are condensed orchestral music (in fact or in theory), and like a town bandmaster he habitually arranged given pieces for varying combinations. Thus some of his piano works end with a dissonant crash marked *fff* and upward; but a number of them end with diaphanous, lontano effects that strain the limits of piano touch: the *Concord* ends *ppp*, Study No. 22 *pppp*. These are piano versions of his characteristic orchestral fade-out, which in an orchestra can be accomplished relatively easily by putting players offstage or having only a few play. His bell cadences enhance the effect by placing a storm before the whisper. Perhaps someone will do a study of Ivesian endings one of these days; it will reveal as much variety and imagination as any other facet of his work, and a microcosm of his style and philosophy.

40. Ives's "At the River" is listed as ?1916 in *The New Grove*. Composer Michael Carnes once observed to me that so many of the hymns Ives used were lame and cornball until Ives somehow made them great music. I tend to agree. The old tunes of my Southern Baptist childhood—among them "The Sweet By and By," "Just As I Am," "Shall We Gather at the River?"—I now hear as what Ives made of them, not what they used to be. Probably many Ivesians feel the same: he ennobled an American tradition that in itself would seem pale and shallow. Ives's point, of course, is not the quality of the music but rather its meaning to people. That Ives revealed for the first time the human truth and depth in this music is near the heart of what his music is "about."

41. See Hitchcock *Ives* 85. "Ferocious" is his apt word for the Allegro. In its endless-whirlwind effect the Allegro of the *Browning* resembles Beethoven's *Grosse Fuge*—both pieces being examples of composers obsessed with contrapuntal devices and to hell with contrast or breathing room.

42. Wooldridge (282) claims to a find in *Browning* a "golden section" (in the middle Adagio) and Fibbonacci numbers (that section's "vertical constellations"), though he acknowledges that Ives probably knew little about those ideas in the way Bartók did. More poetically, Wooldridge suggests that in *Browning* Ives felt himself tempted,

like Faust, by the devil of serialism. Maybe better: Ives set out to create a work in the image of alchemical mysticism and pulled out all the stops to do it; and a genius like Ives has a lot of stops to pull. But then because of his qualms, Ives didn't give the piece the final going-over it needed. Fortunately, performers can function as Ives's collaborators and provide their own final polish, without destroying the original. We will return to the idea that in many ways Ives demands that we be his co-creators. As an employee said of Ives, "he elevated you."

43. Burkholder "Avant-Gardist/Traditionalist" 37–38.

44. Certainly the emotional qualities described here are hazy and subjective. They are, however, the kinds of terms Romantic composers, and Ives, used themselves, and they at least suggest the difference between one expressive tone and another.

45. Rossiter notes the lack of a tragic sense in Ives (144). That observation, however, is part of Rossiter's accusation that Ives did not face the "obvious gap between his professed altruism and actual system of capitalism and national power to which he gave practical support by his life as a middle-class businessman." Certainly Ives's love of paradox did not extend to moral uncertainties, so he usually gave short shrift, if any, to the darker side of issues. Yet he did perceive and, in his way, address the evils of modern capitalism and imperialism both in and out of business—see chapters before and after this one. If Ives was an accomplice to the sins of capitalism by being a middle-class businessman, so have been millions. At least, unlike most of those millions, Ives did think about the problems and tried to address them.

46. Hitchcock *Ives* 85. Ives may have heard Mahler's music at some point, maybe in 1909–11 when Mahler conducted the New York Philharmonic. Whether there was a direct influence from Mahler to Ives is hard to say, but there is clearly a connection in spirit between them. Ives did say at one point that he came to avoid listening to new composers because they threw him off his stride, as familiar music did not. Still, he heard more new works than he thought, or more than he cared to admit.

47. Ives *Memos* 86.

48. Martin 284–85. Martin says Damrosch was hostile to most European Modernism

beyond roughly Stravinsky's *Petrushka,* though he still performed more advanced pieces now and then.

49. Ives *Memos* 86. Since he knew Damrosch was part Jewish, Ives was careful to append the "mentally, not racially" to his comments on Damrosch's "breed," to avoid any racial stereotyping.

50. In the *New York Times* (3/10/1991) Joseph Horowitz wrote, "Walter Damrosch [was] a mediocrity with impeccable financial and social connections." Ives saw that during the First Symphony reading. Harmony would tell John Kirkpatrick, "He toppled many idols of mine," one of them being Damrosch.

51. Probably with great satisfaction, Ives put pianist/conductor Ossip Gabrilowitsch's obituary in one of his scrapbooks. It says, among other things, "Mr. Gabrilowitsch looked the way musicians are supposed to look in novels, from his long hair to his habit of screwing up one eye while he was talking." He was the sort who thought music had died with Brahms. Harmony Ives, who was president of the Mark Twain Society, apparently didn't care much for Gabrilowitsch's wife Clara, who was Twain's daughter.

52. Ives *Memos* 87.

53. Ives *Memos* 101.

54. Ives's own pre-final drafts of the Second and Third Symphonies survive, which are the versions currently used. Bernard Herrmann told Vivian Perlis he had found the final score of the Second in Damrosch's papers, but if so he lost it again. In June 1915, Damrosch replied to an Ives query about the ink copies of the Second and Third. (Did Ives know then that Mahler had earlier taken a copy of the Third?) Damrosch said he would check for the scores at his other house. He didn't. Ives tried again as late as 1935, with no results. Since Mahler took one copy of the Third we can assume that two professional copies were made.

55. Wooldridge claims to have found an old percussionist who remembered playing Ives's Third under Mahler in Europe. That reading or performance has never come to light, however, and Wooldridge's information is notoriously dicey. I have used his material circumspectly.

56. Morgan passim. Morgan astutely examines many correlations of ways Mahler and Ives recast the forms and tonality of European late Romanticism, while still staying close to the orbit of that world. Both use space as an element in their music, adding offstage ensembles to their orchestral textures (77). Both broke up the traditional approach to a work as an autonomous whole: "The composition is opened up—made permeable as it were, so as to be subject to outside influences. It becomes a more inclusional whole, vulnerable to the ambiguities and contradictions of everyday experience, both musical and otherwise" (78). He concludes, "If the principal currents of musical evolutions during the first half of this century tended to place Mahler and (especially) Ives outside the mainstream, the compositional developments of the past quarter-century have forced them into its forefront." In other words, the more the mainstream of composition turns away from formalism in general and serialism in particular—and in the direction of expressiveness, a new Romanticism, and postmodernism—the more relevant Mahler and Ives become. Their progress in concert and recording life since Morgan's 1978 article seems to confirm that suggestion.

57. Typically for Ives, these three "songs" began in 1911 for three different media—"The Last Reader" a "song without words" for small orchestra, "The New River" for unison chorus and orchestra (these ended up in *114 Songs* arranged for voice and piano), and "Requiem" for voice and piano (not in *114 Songs*).

58. Kirkpatrick Catalogue 60.

59. Kirkpatrick Catalogue 267.

60. Charlie to Harmony, 1/27/1911, Ives Papers Microfilm Addendum.

61. Ives *Memos* 98.

62. Quoted in Cowell and Cowell 96–97.

63. Harmony to Charlie in Uncollected Letters 2/5/1918. The text of Harmony's letter, written from Hartford, shows that she was perfectly willing to disagree with him: "I got your letter this a.m. & it made me laugh very much—you are a killing creature—I dont think Music is life but it expresses things in life better than anything else does—I dont suppose the 'beauty' in it means the same to any two people for when we say beauty we usually mean some concept in our own mind & not Beauty itself of course—all of which is most obvious & trite. I like your music much better than Mozarts anyway!" Here Harmony either echoes shared ideas about beauty or gives her husband some ideas that came out next

year in the *Essays:* "Beauty in music is too often confused with something that lets the ears lie back in an easy chair" (97).

64. A note on the score of "Arguments" says, "from movement S.Q. to make Gustave Bach 'wink'." This Bach was violist of the Kaltenborn Quartet, and Ives had a teasing friendship with him. Ives dedicated the "practice piece" *Holding Your Own* to Gustave. He notes of that piece in the *Memos* (34), "the last time I found *[Holding Your Own]* it seemed quite (or partially) musical, and worth playing."

65. No doubt every Ivesian has blind spots, and the second movement of the Second String Quartet is one of mine. To me it sounds a bit juvenile and not as funny as it purports to be, and the first movement I find more "interesting" than "moving." These thoughts about the first two movements may be buttressed by the manuscripts and by Ives himself. There are no extant sketches for the first two movements and Ives never made his usual fair copy of the score. Only the last movement shows much sign of revision and working-over. Throughout, dynamic and phrasing indications are skimpy—another sign of neglect. Ives did not pull the score out of his drawer until perhaps the 1940s, when copyist George Roberts worked from Ives's rough but mostly readable, mostly two-stave pencil score. As for the last movement, I find it to be one of the more electrifying and inspired movements in the chamber-music repertoire. (It is based on the lost organ work *Memorial Slow March,* written apparently on the death of President McKinley.) The general public's respect for the Second Quartet (it and the First recently won a Grammy for the Emerson Quartet) may stem from the end being so magnificent that it retroactively elevates the whole piece. So it should. Ives, though, seems for a while at least to have turned away from the whole piece. In 1921 violinist Reber Johnson was looking for an American work for his quartet and asked Ives if he had anything. Instead, Ives wrote his old friend Dave Smith, then dean of music at Yale, and suggested Dave send them something because "I have only one [quartet] written several years ago, which I don't want to hear or see again" (CEI to Smith 11/22/1921, Ives Papers 32/6). Here Ives probably means the Second

Quartet, and is ignoring the First entirely.

66. For an exhaustive study of Ives's thematic technique in selected works, see Lora Louise Gingerich, "Processes of Motivic Transformation."

67. Ballantine writes (171), "The final twenty-one measures are a beautiful example of a musical quotation fully in the service of a pregnant association. Situated in a 'visionary' D major with whole-tone-scale underpinnings . . . they symbolize the regular peal of four giant carillons, one for each instrument. The image is made precise and particular by the quotation of 'Westminster Chimes' . . . in the first violin." It is hard to hear the "Westminster Chimes"; one is mainly aware of *Bethany.* It may seem surprising that Ballantine specifically hears "giant" carillons in a string quartet, but that is a testament to the grandiose effect of the end, whose sonority is unique in the quartet literature. Ives did not have the Modernists' obsession with torturing new sounds out of old instruments, and he was not an instrumental colorist on the level of Mahler or Stravinsky, but he produced his share of fresh and expressive sonorities. See Stravinsky's admiring comments on the orchestration of *Decoration Day* in *Themes and Episodes* (16).

68. In *Ives 62,* Hitchcock outlines the musical richness of the Second Quartet: "The wildly varied materials succeed each other abruptly, sometimes violently; sometimes they literally co-exist. Alongside the most radical sort of jagged, wide-spanned, rhythmically disparate, chromatic melody is melody of the simplest stepwise diatonicism. Triadic harmony alternates with fourth- and fifth-chords, chromatic aggregates, and tone clusters. Canons without any harmonic underpinnings follow passages anchored to static harmonic-rhythmic ostinatos. 'Athematic' writing is set side-by-side against passages quoting preexistent melodies in almost cinematic collage. 'Tala' and 'color' repetitions organized serially . . . jostle with diatonic-scale passagework." He points out a number of connections that unify the whole quartet; for example, the opening sonority has implications all the way through, and the cello's whole-tone scale at the end is foreshadowed as early as the ninth bar of the first movement. My sense of the piece has also been helped by an analysis sent me by

composer Larry Moss. In the *Memos* (74) Ives says, "part of a movement was copied out in parts and tried over (at Tam's one day)—it made all the men rather mad. I didn't blame them—it was very hard to play." The fact that he was writing a memo about the Second Quartet in 1932 may indicate that he was no longer rejecting the piece.

69. Kirkpatrick in *The New Grove* 419.
70. Ives on himself in Papers 31/9.
71. Ives *Memos* 64–65.
72. John Kirkpatrick makes this surmise about Halley's Comet being the inspiration for the Fourth Symphony in his article in *The New Grove* (417).
73. Kirkpatrick preface to the Associated Music Fourth Symphony score, p. vii. Both earlier settings of *Watchman* are lost.
74. Charlie to Harmony, Uncollected Letters 10/18/1910.
75. Ives *Memos* 64.
76. Ives *Memos* 63.
77. The *Tone Roads* are analyzed in Nicholls 64–73. With their jagged lines and atonal counterpoint constructed by more or less serial processes, and their entire lack of quotes, the two *Tone Roads* sound startlingly like avant-garde works of the 1960s and 1970s that were arrived at by similar methods. The main difference is that Ivesian formalism is looser, with a manifest warmth, wit, and rhythmic drive that later serialists tend, notoriously, to lack.
78. Unless otherwise noted, sources for this section are James Sinclair's notes on *Three Places* in the preface to the Mercury full-orchestra score; Sinclair's discussion in Hitchcock and Perlis 74–76; and the manuscripts.
79. Ives's final full-orchestra score of *Putnam's Camp*, from 1914, does not have the "mirabile dictu" chord at letter G, or most of the preceding transition that Ives worked out for the 1929 revision. The original score in that spot, says James Sinclair, was a quick dovetail of *Country Band* and "1776" material. The "mirabile dictu" chord sounds remarkably like a similar effect in Stravinsky's *Sacre du printemps*—the eerie string chord that joins the "Adoration De La Terre" and "Danse De La Terre" sections. Could Ives have added his chord after hearing the *Rite* in the twenties? On balance unlikely, but possible. (However, the "mirabile dictu" chord is an inversion of the first chord in

the piece.) There is a record of Ives hearing *The Firebird* (which he hated) and *Chant du Rossignol*, but he said he never heard the *Sacre* as of 1932, and there is nothing to contradict that (see *Memos* 138). The connection is more likely coincidental, just as the similarities of *Thoreau* to late Scriabin are certainly coincidental. (More on the latter issue in a later chapter.)

80. Ives's delightful, slightly surreal lyric for "The Circus Band" was likely added some time after the music was written—probably originally for band—in 1894. It is probably his best march, his closest approach to the level of Sousa (but not all that close—Ives seems to me only a good, not a great, tunesmith in vernacular music). Among the lines: "Horses are prancing, Knights advancing;/ Helmets gleaming, Pennants streaming,/ Cleopatra's on her throne!/ That golden hair is all her own." Copyist George Roberts orchestrated the piano-vocal version for Ives around 1934 (Kirkpatrick note in Ives *Memos* 170).
81. This is the pattern of older American marches such as *Washington Grays*. Newer ones, including Sousa's, do not usually have a da capo. Older marches are often in 4/4 rather than 2/4, but still with a marked *one*-two-*three*-four feel.
82. Genres are rarely invented whole cloth; they tend to arise from some kind of practical situation, whether to be music for dancing, to start off an opera, or the like. Most genres, in other words, begin as *Gebrauchsmusik*. Some remain that, some (like the minuet) spin off into a career as "abstract" music, but preserving some of their original identity. Certainly there are exceptions to this *Gebrauchsmusik* theory—for example the "Pierrot piece," the Modernist genre for voice and chamber group whose history begins with Schoenberg's *Pierrot Lunaire*. (In Boston we call these pieces "for chamber group and agony soprano.") There is a great deal more to be said about the matter and little space to address it. *Putnam's Camp* is here used to show something of Ives's relationship to genre, though one could use a number of other pieces.
83. CEI to Alfred Frankenstein, Ives Papers 29/7.
84. Ives made a piano-vocal sketch of *The Housatonic at Stockbridge* in 1912, but the 1921

piano-vocal version is a different arrangement.

85. This dating of the *Three Places* movements follows James Sinclair's in his full-orchestra score, but the exact years are speculative. Kirkpatrick has slightly different dates in *The New Grove*. Most of the differences are simply uncertainty about when the final scores were made. There is little doubt that most of the essential work on the piece was done between 1911 and 1914. As we will see, when Ives reduced the piece for Nicolas Slonimsky's chamber orchestra in 1929, he revised it somewhat, restoring some of the original complexities and adding more.

86. If it seems that much attention is given to the minutiae of the genesis of the *Housatonic*, the reason will be clear when we get to the appendix on editing, which makes it clear that Maynard Solomon's theories got things backward—Ives did not so much "modernize" his scores after the fact as he restored some of the more radical elements he watered down in earlier versions. As noted earlier, he certainly added dissonances to pieces later—including the *Three Places*—but did not, and could not, change the character of the pieces, make over a conventional piece into a radical one by tricking it out with dissonance and polyrhythm. You can't make a *Fourth of July* out of a "Circus Band" by simply adding dissonances

87. In Hitchcock and Perlis 76, Sinclair calls the missing Price score of *The Housatonic* "a mysterious black hole." The only indication of that score is some memos from Ives to Price, the kind of thing Ives ordinarily did when a piece was being copied. However, those memos were specific enough to be useful to Sinclair in making his edition. Ives could be very thorough at times—and then lose the score that he had been so thorough about. In the same way, he muddied up some of his perfectly clear copies with scribbles.

88. See Sinclair in Hitchcock and Perlis 76. Sinclair's editing of *Three Places*, which attempted to restore the full-orchestra version with some of the advantages of the chamber-orchestra version, was hardest in *Putnam's Camp* because Ives cut up that original score to make patches for the later score (to save copying time). All that remains of the 1914 orchestration of *Putnam's Camp* is, as John Kirkpatrick put it, "lacework." As far as can be seen, though,

there is no indication Ives diluted *Putnam's Camp* in the mid-teens score as much as he did the *Housatonic*.

89. In his preface to the Associated *Fourth of July* score, John Kirkpatrick notes, "The *Holidays* underwent some uncertainty of medium. On a sketch of *Emerson,* Ives wrote: 'Piano Sonata #3, N. E. Holidays.' But the first version of *Decoration Day* (complete, in ink) is for violin and piano . . . and sketches of *Washington's Birthday* seem to betray a violin-and-piano origin. . . . He would have been hard put to arrange *The Fourth of July* for violin and piano." The last sentence deserves a couple of exclamation points.

90. As per Henderson's *Tunebook,* Ives's most-quoted tune is Foster's "Massa's in de Cold, Cold Ground," followed by "Columbia, the Gem." Ives's first use of "Columbia" may have been in the lost *American Woods Overture* from circa 1889, which went into the Second Symphony. His other most-quoted tunes include *Shining Shore,* "The Battle Cry of Freedom," and "Marching Through Georgia."

91. Marshall 23. In this important 1968 article, which first detailed in print how much attention Ives paid to motivic relationships in his borrowed material, Marshall notes (23), "As Ives introduces other popular melodies in *The Fourth of July* he is always concerned with their relationship to the principal source, 'The Red, White and Blue.'" Furthermore, "the chords in fourths [as in 'The Cage'], fifths, and seconds (derived from the intervals in the opening phrase of the patriotic tune) also appear in the strings at the climax of the movement." Ives had discovered, in other words, the principle later basic to twelve-tone technique, that the same interval patterns can function both horizontally/melodically and be turned on end to become harmony. These kinds of relationships presume the "liberation of the dissonance"— Schoenberg's phrase, an Ives assumption early on.

92. Ives *Memos* 104. On p. 105, Ives mentions playing over some of the *Fourth of July* trumpet and piccolo parts himself. He also played a bit of violin. In "Evolution" 447–48, Burkholder notes of the work's melodic relationships, "It is as if Ives shows us the interrelationships among a handful of tunes (or a dozen), arranging them in ways which make the relationships obvious, and

invites us to continue the process for ourselves. . . . Following Ives's dreamlike allu-
sions, we are brought into our own
dreams, as we are reminded of the way we
ourselves think about music and indeed
about life, hearing resemblances, drawing
relationships, confusing similar things and
then sorting them out, noticing and half-
noticing the swirl of experience as it goes
by, and picking new elements out of the
mix each time we rehear it."
93. Ives *Memos* 104n.
94. Ives's occasional use of quick cuts from one
idea to another resembles a cinematic cut
and/or montage. Among his innovations,
then, should be listed these effects, much
like Stravinsky's "block form," which has
been compared to Cubism but may relate
also to the cinema. The thing about Ives,
though, is that he hated movies and all
forms of mass media. Among other things,
he called movies "the great national brain-
softeners." Though presumably he took in
a Nickelodeon or the like at some point—a
good reason to declare movies trivial—one
finds no specific record that Ives ever saw
a film. Moreover, his characteristic jumps
from phrase to phrase go back at least to
the Second Symphony, and film was in its
pre-Griffith infancy when that piece was
written. In short, however cinematic Ives
seems at times, his procedures do not seem
to have been derived from the cinema. It
is another case of Ives sensing a coming
zeitgeist before other artists did. These
kinds of nonlinear formal devices—plus
Ives's distinctive stylistic peregrinations—
anticipate future work by Eliot, Joyce, and
Stravinsky, but also postmodernism in
general.
95. This note was one of several on the *Fourth
of July* score-sketch addressed to George
Price, a Welshman who worked for Tams
Copying Service. According to Gayle Sherwood, Price copied for Ives off and on for
some thirty years, from around 1902–32.
It's amazing they went on that long, given
Price's prickliness and his habit of "correcting" Ives's notes on his own tack. Thus the
exasperated note on *The Fourth of July:*
"Mr. Price: Please don't try to make things
nice! All the wrong notes are right. Just
copy as I have—I want it that way." (Much
of the score-sketch is quite readable,
though it gets messy around the explosions—many additions and revisions.) In
the *Memos* (65), Ives sums up George

Price: "If Wales and the United States
should both wipe each other out, that
wouldn't bother Price—but tell him that
he wasn't perfect and had made a mistake,
and he would be mortally insulted. . . .
What mistakes he made were yours. If
he thought you had put down the wrong
note, he would put it *right* (right or wrong)
and blame you. . . . Then he would get
mad and want to charge you for correcting
your right notes into mistakes. . . . But
his penmanship was as beautiful as a Mi-
chelangelo." Price and some other Ives
copyists—including Hanke—probably
viewed their employer as an amateur and
a nut. (So, of course, do some musicians
today.) So long as Ives was willing to pay,
and he paid well, his copyists did good
work for him.
96. This is from Nelson's description (366–
67) and Ives's outline of the effect in *Memos*
104–6. Ives says he based the *Fourth of July*
final explosion on a similar effect in the old
General Slocum sketch. The 1904 steamboat disaster killed 1020 people. That piece
Ives jotted down to put some feelings
to rest over "this awful catastrophe [that]
got on everybody's nerves. I can give
no other reason for attempting to put
it to music, and I'm glad to look back
and see the sketch is hardly more than a
page."
97. From a conversation with Wayne Shirley,
who edited the Ives Society edition of the
Fourth of July. Regarding the arbitrary al-
teration of serial patterns, Shirley remarked, "Ives wouldn't even submit to his
own rules."
98. Cowell and Cowell 144.
99. For some time I had a theory that the al-
ways-highlighted motive in *Decoration Day*
combines suggestions of *Taps* and the war
song "Over There." Thus it would encompass, as does the whole piece, both the
tragic and the heroic aspects of the holiday. George M. Cohan's war song did, in
fact, become an Ives favorite. The trouble
is that Cohan did not write "Over There"
until 1917, after *Decoration Day* was finished. The motive seems to have been in
the sketches from the beginning, and is
woven into the texture throughout. The
triadic outline of this motive, of *Taps,*
and of Reeves's march in the second half
unites the melodic material of the movement. In fact, the "Over There" motive's
simple triadic outline occurs often in

music. Ives may have picked it up *because* he had already featured it in *Decoration Day.*

100. Ives's use of string glissandi—usually for realistic effects—is another of his anticipations, in this case of the 1960s avant-garde.

101. Stravinsky and Craft 15–16. In his article on *Decoration Day,* Feder concludes that in the music "George is actualized, idealized." One can add, though, that for listeners the music is not *about* George Ives or even about Danbury. To the degree it is the "masterpiece" Stravinsky called it, *Decoration Day* is about all of us, about death and burial and resurrection and remembrance. Stravinsky was moved by the piece, and he cared little about the pro-

gram, about Danbury, or about George Ives. In Western art, at least since the Renaissance, the assumption has often been that one reaches the universal through the personal, the macrocosm through the microcosm.

102. Ives *Essays* 30. Either Ives or editor Howard Boatwright slipped up here, calling the Reeves the *Seventh* rather than *Second Regiment March.* The image of the "vanishing vision" Ives mentions in the *Essays* turns up often in his music—for example in *Hawthorne, Decoration Day, Putnam's Camp,* and the *Comedy* of the Fourth Symphony.

103. Ives *Memos* 97–98.

104. Ives *Essays* 81.

T W E L V E   *That Beautiful Shore*

1. Harmony told John Kirkpatrick (interviews in Ives Papers Microfilm Addendum) that Dave's wife Ella "wasn't right in her mind; she felt we were all against him; so they wanted to get away from us all & went up [to Quebec]."

2. Harmony to Charlie, Uncollected Letters 4/22/1914.

3. Ives Papers 24/8/4.

4. Ives Papers Microfilm Addendum.

5. "Our Book," Ives Papers 45/7.

6. Perlis CIR 83.

7. In his introduction to *Essays Before a Sonata* Howard Boatwright seems to be mistaken when he says (xiv) that the Iveses visited Concord on their 1908 honeymoon—they were across the state in the Berkshires. He also has them visiting Concord in 1916; I have found no indication of that one way or the other. They may well have visited Concord during a weeklong Boston vacation in September 1917, after the *Concord* was finished and Ives was thinking about the *Essays.*

8. Ives Papers Microfilm Addendum, from a 10/1935 CEI letter to John Kirkpatrick.

9. Cowell and Cowell 53.

10. The *Concord's* slow, introspective finale is not entirely unprecedented. Among others, Tchaikovsky's *Pathétique* ends with a slow movement.

11. It is a tribute to Ives's genius and flexibility that the *Concord,* one of his finest works, has relatively few quoted themes and is, at least on the surface, one of his least autobiographical pieces. As we will see, the work does have some resonances in his life,

however. Burkholder in "Evolution" (416n) points out that the programs for the movements may have been added later. There are several printed copies of the *Concord* in which Ives jotted various programmatic ideas, sometimes different ones for the same movement. In a letter of the mid-1930s to John Kirkpatrick, Ives implied that there were no specific stories in the music at all, only general impressions. Such after-the-fact programs are not unusual. Other composers including Liszt wrote pieces before giving them names and/or programs. The most famous program in music, the one for Berlioz's *Symphonie fantastique,* was later disavowed by the composer. Even though Ives generally composed his pieces in "abstract" terms (usually inspired by something concrete) and often developed or changed his programs after the piece was done (as with the First Piano Sonata), he nonetheless remained suspicious of music that did not represent something. Still, the *Concord* is generally as successful in "abstract" terms as the best sonatas traditionally tend to be.

12. Ives *Essays* 36.

13. Struble notes (37) that John Kirkpatrick described *Emerson* as a kind of sonata form. That is a stretch as such, but Ives was certainly thinking in terms of sonata form to some degree—in the tone and the thematic contrast, among other things. Gingerich (276) makes the point that in Ives the development of material is constant, "multidimensional," and "non-chronological," and has little to do with straight-line logic

or with the place of the material in the form. In other words, in Ives's advanced music there is little correlation of development and form, which can make his forms hard to follow. (But by no means is that always the case—his phrase structure, for one thing, is generally quite clear, and that helps to move a piece forward.)

14. Struble (23–24) lists thirteen principal motives, the main ones divided into submotives. Struble's treatment of the themes is confusing, but with the *Concord* it is hard not to be. In the *Essays* (16) Ives lambastes those "partial-wise to the specific," and the *Concord* is made to be difficult to pin down. The subtlety, assurance, and originality of its thematic handling are the result of Ives's years of attention to thematic technique, from college on, which reached great virtuosity in the violin sonatas. In the *Concord,* he surpassed himself.

15. Most of the themes in the *Concord* are interrelated. For example, the "human-faith melody" shares with the Beethoven's Fifth motive (also *Missionary Chant* and *Martyn*) a three-eighth upbeat followed by a descent.

16. Ives *Essays* 11–12. Throughout the *Essays,* some of the material in quotation marks may be literal quotes, but most are likely top-of-the-head paraphrases or entirely Ives's own words, which may or may not be traceable to anything the author wrote. For what was actually said and by whom, so far as it can be known, see Howard Boatwright's expert sleuthing in the footnotes of *Essays Before a Sonata.*

17. This is not to suggest that the *Concord* music was written using ideas from the "Emerson" essay, but rather the other way around: the various points in Ives's essays on Emerson and the other authors may or may not be relevant to the nominal subject, but they are all relevant to the sonata Ives had already composed.

18. Ives *Essays* 16.

19. Ives *Essays* 21.

20. Ives *Essays* 22.

21. Ives *Essays* 23.

22. Ives *Essays* 98–99. The *Emerson Transcriptions* particularly return to some of the complexities of the original *Emerson Overture* sketch.

23. Ives *Memos* 78.

24. James Sinclair suggested this evolution of *Emerson.* Clearly *Emerson* is prophetic of the reflexive, improvisatory, "process" pieces of the 1960s and later avant-garde:

it is a composition about the process of composition.

25. There has been much editorial hair-pulling over the changing versions of the *Concord Sonata,* and that anguish has been fairly public, tending to convince some that Ives could not make up his mind and/or didn't know what he wanted, and/or was an incompetent proofreader of his publications. None of those judgments is accurate (though his proofreading could be erratic). First, in regard to the worrying from John Kirkpatrick and others about the *Concord* and its metamorphoses: around four-fifths of the editorial problems apply only to *Emerson.* Second, as noted in the chapter, that very changeableness was an integral part of the creative concept of *Emerson*—an endless and unresolvable piece of music. (This may not have started off as the concept, but Ives found that the piece simply did not want to finish, and eventually realized how germane that was to the idea.) Third, in all its versions *Emerson* and the entire sonata are essentially the same piece in sound and effect. Compare the original recording (released in 1948) of the 1920 score by John Kirkpatrick with recent recordings using the 1947 Arrow score.

26. Ives *Essays* 42. Struble (33–34) points out some places in the *Essays* where Ives seems to have drawn ideas directly from Billy Phelps's Yale lectures of the 1890s. For example, Struble compares Ives's text on Hawthorne, ". . . Any comprehensive conception of Hawthorne . . . must have for its basic theme something that has to do with the influence of sin upon the conscience," with Phelps's "His great theme, however, is SIN and conscience. . . . He studies with a sad intensity the effect of sin on the heart."

27. Quoted in Struble 45. Kirkpatrick's symmetrical formulation is useful in rationalizing the kaleidoscopic *Hawthorne* up to a point, but the formulation is far tidier than the effect of the music. For one thing, various ideas interpenetrate Kirkpatrick's divisions—ragtime and elements of *Country Band March* mingle in the final "fantasmagoria," for example (it begins on the third system of p. 43 of the Associated score).

28. Ives *Memos* 81.

29. This discussion of the *Concord* sometimes echoes Wilfrid Mellers's admirable essay on Ives (in *Music in a New Found Land*), which influenced my thinking about Ives early on. I disagree, however, with Mellers's ten-

dency to compare Ives unfavorably with Beethoven. Granted, Beethoven is the greater composer and Ives wrote the *Concord* in the spirit of the great Beethoven sonatas, notably the *Hammerklavier*. (Mellers [55] compares *Emerson* to middle-period Beethoven, *Thoreau* to the approach to the sublime in late Beethoven.) But Ives was not a lesser composer, as Mellers implies, in his inability to finally integrate and resolve his pieces. In his lack of resolution Ives was pursuing a vision different from Beethoven's: "Music may be yet unborn," as he puts it in the *Essays*. Ives's vision is equally compelling. Beethoven's edge lies in his craftsmanship, his organic form, his depth and breadth of expression including a powerful sense of tragedy. Ives could not have written, say, the song of thanksgiving in *Fidelio*, when the prisoners emerge from underground. (And these are of course vague and subjective responses—as are Mellers's). One has to compare as well Beethoven's dozens of masterpieces to Ives's, say, something under a dozen. Ives might give different reasons for Beethoven's primacy, but he surely would have agreed in principle. After all, Ives writes in the *Essays*, "In the history of this youthful world, the best product that human beings can boast of is probably Beethoven" (88). As we will see, though, Ives qualifies even that extravagant assertion because "Music may be yet unborn." Ives saw both himself and Beethoven as still part of "this youthful world," assisting in the birth of music, which is a vital part of the true birth of humanity.

30. Ives *Essays* 48.
31. Ives *Essays* 67. Ives explicitly places *Thoreau* in autumn and *Hawthorne* in winter, which suggests an implied four seasons in the *Concord*, as in the *Holidays*. In 1944, while working on the second edition, Ives drafted a letter to Peter Yates including, "Emerson in the 1st Edition—may stand more as under late Autumn or winter landscape & in 2nd [edition] reflecting more of a summer impression." The latter case, anyway, would leave spring, quite appropriately, to *The Alcotts*.
32. Ives *Essays* 67. Feder opines that both Emerson and Thoreau are images of George Ives.
33. Thoreau *Journal* vol. 1, 156.
34. Thoreau *Journal* vol. 1, 251.
35. Thoreau *Journal* vol. 1, 102–3.
36. Thoreau *Journal* vol. 3, 67–68. Thoreau

the loner generally seems to be hearing music from a distance, and to prefer it that way—the bell from town, the piano down the street, distant martial music. He loved the music of silence best of all.

37. There appears to have been a general connection at that time of Debussy, mists, and whole-tone effects. Certainly Debussy had popularized the whole-tone scale. When Bix Beiderbecke wrote his whole-toney imitation of Debussy, he called it "In a Mist." (Meanwhile, the piano Prelude Debussy called "Mists" is *not* whole tone, while "Veils" is.)
38. The texture of *Thoreau* is a bit like the song "Mists," but there is no pure whole-tone writing. Ives specifically notes in the "Thoreau" essay (*Essays* 53) that "it is not the whole tone scale of the Orient but the scale of a Walden morning" (again characteristically mixing technical and poetic ideas). He may have said this exactly because he associated *Thoreau* with the whole-tone song "Mists." Still, a certain whole-tone flavor lingers in *Thoreau*. Feder deals with the connection between "Mists" and *Thoreau* in *Ives* 269–70. He adds another connection: Harmony "used a fragment from Thoreau as setting for another poem (now lost), 'Smoke'. . . . This became the inspiration for the opening measures of . . . *Thoreau*."
39. Ives *Essays* 68.
40. Struble 65.
41. Ives *Essays* 69.
42. This is from the end of Ives's "Thoreau" essay (*Essays* 69), an interweaving of his own words with quotes and near-quotes and quasi-quotes from Thoreau. Besides the added flute in the last movement, there is an added viola in the first. The flute is central to both the program and the musical denouement in the last movement; the brief, inexplicable appearance of the viola in *Emerson* is one of those late off-the-cuff revisions that arguably don't work, while the flute seems to me irreplaceable. (The viola was added in the 1940s—and the later the change, the more suspect.) Naturally some people disagree about both points. In any case, performers don't have to take a both-or-neither approach. Both flute and viola are optional in the score, so one can use the flute and omit the viola. The flute part is often played from offstage, making its entrance both startling and moving.
43. Ives Papers 33/2.

44. Perlis CIR 81.
45. CEI to Moss Ives, 6/3/1914, Ives Papers Microfilm Addendum.
46. For the period between 1900 and 1925—during which there was apparently negligible inflation—one multiplies a dollar by 11.38 to get the 1991 equivalent.
47. Brewster Ives in Perlis Oral History 1/7.
48. "Our Book," Ives Papers 45/7. Ives revised nearly everything, including his daily schedule; there is a pencil draft of this schedule on the reverse.
49. Ives used a condensed version of Lindsay's poem that appeared in *The Independent* on January 12, 1914 (*Memos* 176n). Because of copyright problems with the text, Ives did not include it in the 1922 *114 Songs*. In 1934 he paid John J. Becker to arrange it for solo, chorus, and instruments. Writing to Becker with detailed advice about the arrangement, Ives says in part, "In the old brass-band score both the snare and bass drum kept the 'street-beat' phrase going all through—but the snare drum sounded too loudly for one voice indoors—a bass drum doing this is enough. . . . The strings play the beat all together, in one stroke as the drum. . . . A cornet and trombone an octave apart played with the voice. . . . An 'E' flat alto horn, tenor horn or trombone and euphonium took off that 'street brass-band' stuff. I had it played over this way shortly after it was written. I played the piano and some of the violin part with one trombone and voice, and alto, another trombone and tuba and drums, but it was all too loud for indoors. . . . In the final chorus #96 . . . the brass plays the after-beat chords (as a melodian) with the strings (wood-winds) and R.H. piano above them taking the drum-beat chords. As I remember, this sounded well and quite 'street bandy.' " (This is a typed page, probably from Ives's dictation, now with the *Booth* musical sketches at Yale.) Note the detail with which Ives recalls a lost score from twenty years before. Becker made his arrangement from Ives's voice-and-piano version, incorporating Ives's suggestions.
50. Harmony Ives heard Vachel Lindsay perform *Booth* in Hartford, in 1916, after the song was written.
51. Quoted in Hitchcock *Ives* 24.
52. Hitchcock points out (*Ives* 26) that in *General Booth* Ives sets the line "Are you washed in the blood of the Lamb?" not to the tune usually associated with those words but rather, symbolically, with the tune *Cleansing Fountain:* "There is a fountain filled with blood/ Drawn from Immanuel's veins;/ And sinners, plunged beneath that flood,/ Lose all their guilty stains." That is what happens at the end of the song. Thus the words of the quoted tune are relevant here, and often elsewhere in Ives, as a shadow text. As noted before, that is not always the case—sometimes the tune's relevance is purely "abstract," as part of a melodic pattern. In "Evolution," Burkholder presents (624–28) the idea that in *Booth* the friction between tune and words—they do not match in syllables or accents—is deliberate: "Because the text and the music do not fit together nicely, we become aware of the force of will which Booth must exert to overcome the contradictions in his faith and achieve salvation." The point almost convinces me. At least, I can think of no better reason for the mismatch.
53. Mellers 44.
54. Block 13. It is not clear from Ives's description in *Memos* 98 whether or not the Globe Theater run-throughs of *Washington's Birthday* were public. The barn dance section may have been played as an entr'acte in a stage performance, like other bits and pieces of Ives during the first two decades of the century.
55. Harmony to Charlie, Uncollected Letters, 3/25/1915.
56. Ives *Memos* 92–93.
57. It may not be coincidental that Ives's song "The Masses" (also called "Majority") echoes the title of a socialist newspaper of the day—his text could be a socialist marching song. Ives did not attach his name to "-*isms*" of any stripe, but his personal ideology, as we will see, had a good deal of socialism in it, and at times he used socialist jargon ("proletariat," etc.).

T H I R T E E N *Tom Sails Away*

1. Perlis CIR 100.
2. On the manuscript of that page of *Browning* Ives wrote, "The Forest joins the Services and Lifts its voices and marks its choruses of waving limbs by its many rhythms." The section is a collection of

rhythmic series, like a pondful of frogs (though the effect doesn't sound like that in practice).

3. "Our Book," Ives Papers 45/7.

4. From 1905 Moss Ives served two terms in the Connecticut legislature as a Republican and was a judge advocate-general on the staffs of several governors. Among various other posts he was a lieutenant in the National Guard and after World War I went to Washington for nearly a year to help draw up the army reorganization bill. He made other trips to Washington to promote election reform—probably trying to get rid of the electoral college. As for serving in office, though, Moss ran once unsuccessfully for lieutenant-governor of Connecticut and once for governor, then swore off elective office outside his hometown (Ives Papers 40). Like all his family, and in the style of his mentor Uncle Lyman, Moss loomed large in the life of Danbury. His biography, which his brother helped assemble, appears in the *National Cyclopedia of American Biography*.

5. Perlis CIR 74.

6. Perlis CIR 79.

7. Perlis CIR 84–85. The nephews whom Perlis interviewed, Moss's sons, appear to be characters—real Iveses. Brewster became a successful Manhattan developer and, among other things, managed the Dakota, where John Lennon lived (and was shot). Moss had one daughter, Sarane, who, with Uncle Charlie's financing became a concert pianist. She died relatively young in 1956. Her husband Arthur Hall remembers her working on the *Concord*. Once they visited the town and Sarane played *The Alcotts* on the Alcotts' piano (Perlis CIR 92).

8. In that period there seems to have been a Twichell family crusade to get Deac, in his forties by then, into real life and a real job. He resisted the effort. Harmony wrote Charlie (Uncollected Letters) in February 1917, "Deac is pretty mad at me for my letter [brother] Joe says. Joe has been giving it to him, he says, about 'no work, no play' & thinks the time has come to put it up to him if ever. He says that Deac is going to be unbearable if this keeps on. I feel sick & tired of family all around." Father Joe continued his decline, and probably by then sister Sally's mental illness had settled in for good. Moreover, Dave Twichell's wife had never regained her health and had become paranoid about the Twichells and

Iveses. No wonder Harmony was tired of family in 1917: her father was senile and depressed, Sally ill, Dave estranged, and Deac doing nothing in particular. Charlie, at least, thought Deac fine the way he was.

9. "Our Book," Ives Papers 45/7.

10. Harmony to Charlie, Uncollected Letters from December 1915.

11. "Our Book," Ives Papers 45/7.

12. Harmony to Charlie, Uncollected Letters, 2/29/1916.

13. Uncollected Letters, undated, presumably circa 1917.

14. Ives Papers 31/2.

15. Perlis CIR 48–49.

16. Perlis CIR 64.

17. Years after Edith Ives Tyler's death, her son Charles Ives Tyler received a letter from one of her sisters, asking if she remembered the family. The sister did not know Edie had died.

18. John Kirkpatrick interview 3/1988.

19. Perlis CIR 130.

20. Perlis CIR 116.

21. Ives *Memos* 106.

22. Kirkpatrick transcriptions in Ives Papers Microfilm Addendum.

23. CEI letter of 5/19/1917 in Ives Papers 36/6. The ambulance Ives contributed to the Red Cross cost $1000, which is more than $11,000 in 1991 dollars.

24. Ives *Essays* 134, Boatwright introduction to "Stand By the President."

25. Ives *Essays* 136–38.

26. Ives *Memos* 112.

27. Rossiter 153–54.

28. As usual, in "Flanders Fields" Ives carefully prepares the "surprise" ending from early on in the song—with the drumbeat in measure 7, the melodic and harmonic suggestions at "poppies grow," and in further ways.

29. Ives *Memos* 118. It is possible, as John Kirkpatrick notes in the *Memos* 69n, that Talmadge also played the First Violin Sonata in a private recital. The evidence of that is a mimeographed program note in copyist Emil Hanke's hand, and some vague implications by Ives.

30. Ives *Memos* 121–22. Kirkpatrick observes (*Memos* 131n) that Ives shared his time's prejudice toward Mozart as a sort of china-doll composer, not as serious as the "manly" artists like Beethoven and Brahms.

31. Ives Papers 32/10. In that period another trainee at Camp Upton was Irving Berlin, who there wrote a show with what has to be one of the world's silliest titles: *Yip! Yip!*

Yaphank! The show did, at least, feature the hit "Oh, How I Hate to Get Up in the Morning." Did Irving Berlin hear Charles Ives play?

32. Perlis CIR 82.
33. Perlis CIR 59–60.
34. Scrapbook, Ives Papers 43.
35. MONY Ives file.
36. Uncollected Letters.
37. Ives Papers 34/7.
38. MONY Ives file.
39. Kirkpatrick Chronology in Ives *Memos.*
40. Ives Papers Microfilm Addendum.
41. Ives Papers 34/3.
42. Memo in Ives Papers 25/6.
43. Ives *Essays* 225. A later CEI note on the typescript of the World Union proposal says he wrote it in 1916 rather than 1918—the same kind of dating mistake Ives often made on his music manuscripts. It could not have been 1916 because it refers to Wilson's Fourteen Points, announced in January 1918.

44. Ives Papers 36/9. This recollection of his 1918 physical Ives wrote years later on a Yale class questionnaire. If it is accurate regarding what the doctor said, Ives ignored a virtual death sentence.
45. Ives Papers Microfilm Addendum, 9/4/1918.
46. "Our Book," Ives Papers 45/7.

FOURTEEN *A Fall and a Credo*

1. Perlis CIR 12. During a 1947 interview with the Bridgeport *Post,* Harmony observed, "He wore himself out trying to make FDR . . . see the value of 'baby bonds' " (Ives Papers 54/7).
2. Feder *Ives* 285. Feder says that Ives failed the first physical "for reasons that remain obscure." As Ives details in the letter quoted in the last chapter, the reasons were not the least obscure: the doctor told him the trip to France would be fatal because of heart disease.
3. From John Kirkpatrick interviews with Harmony in Ives Papers Microfilm Addendum.
4. From John Kirkpatrick interviews with Harmony in Ives Papers Microfilm Addendum. She told him relatively little about Charlie's heart attack, saying, "It's like a physical effort recollecting these things—it's like lifting something heavy."
5. Perlis CIR 12.
6. During a February 1991 telephone interview with musicologist, Ives scholar, and diabetes sufferer Howard Boatwright I asked if there were any aspects of Ives that he felt had not been adequately addressed. His response: "Diabetes." He began to describe his own experience with the disease, observing, "I don't know if any of this applies to Ives." Nearly everything he said applied to Ives, as does the literature on the disease. My basic information is from the Columbia University *Complete Home Medical Guide* and from Boston endocrinologist Dr. Richard Spark. Other sources are as cited in the notes and bibliography. All conclusions, of course, are my own. Concerning the illness, Bierman and Toohey write (11), "Diabetes runs in families; so whether you got it as a child or later in life, you still had to have some genes that predisposed you to it. Second, some physical or emotional stresses combined with your hereditary tendency and possibly your environment pushed you over the brink." Ives was under extraordinary stress—personal, familial, professional and physical—in the years before 1918. Write Dolger and Seeman (26): "When diabetes appears in a family it seems to develop earlier in each succeeding generation." George Ives died of a stroke at forty-nine, after what may have been several years of depression and declining health. Charles Ives's devastating attack occurred at age forty-three. (One wonders if George's year off from the army in the war may have been an early flare-up of diabetes or an allied ailment, rather than the ostensible back injury. In his notebook George describes himself as "sick" rather than injured.) Dolger and Seeman (36): "Let us imagine an adult with an inherent susceptibility. . . . Under ordinary circumstances, he may not develop his diabetes until he reaches the age of 50. But . . . under the impact of a series of stresses, his diabetes arrives at the age of 30." Ives's 1906 attack was at age thirty-two. Possible stresses then: the insurance investigation, anxieties over his courtship of Harmony, creative problems, his usual overwhelming schedule. Dolger and Seeman continue: "Then, as treatment is begun and takes hold, there may be an abrupt remission. The diabetes will mysteriously vanish, not to appear again until the age of 50 or thereabouts, when it originally may have been

due. Situations like this do not happen often, but they *do* occur." (This is sometimes called the "honeymoon" period; Ives may have had two of them, after 1906 and after 1918.) Ives seemed relatively healthy for ten years after his marriage in 1908, or convinced himself he was. It is surprising that no one to date has advanced the thesis that diabetes figured all along in Ives's health and heredity. Stuart Feder suggests— though he avoids a definitive statement— that Ives's 1918 breakdown was largely mental rather than physical. As a psychoanalyst, Feder naturally looks for psychological explanations. Perhaps for that reason, he bypasses most of the medical evidence assembled here, including that Ives was specifically warned about a heart attack in his earlier 1918 physical exam. From a position unbiased one way or another, the theory about Ives's breakdown that seems best to suit the evidence is that Ives was certainly diabetic, and he may have suffered from a bipolar disorder that was subclinical for some time, perhaps more serious in later years. Another possibility is that congenital heart disease first triggered the diabetes, which was also congenital. One must confess, though, that Feder's thesis is more poetically satisfying. He believes Ives's collapse was part of an extended mourning for his father, a kind of sympathetic breakdown in which Charlie's final creative demise came at around the age of his father's literal one. Feder the doctor is proposing a literary theory, Swafford the artist is proposing a medical one. Although we will never know the answer for sure, these two seem the most reasonable hypotheses.

7. Current medical wisdom says that some of the impotence experienced by diabetics is psychological, but that wisdom was not current in Ives's day.

8. Perlis CIR 36.

9. Harmony to Charlie, from Uncollected Letters quoted in Chapter 9.

10. On manic-depressive (or bipolar) disorder, see the Columbia University *Complete Home Guide to Mental Health*. Like all conclusions about Ives's health, this one is speculative, but there is much evidence for the illnesses. As Feder notes in passing (259), before his health breakdown in 1918, Ives may have had a milder, chronic form of bipolar disorder called *cyclothymia,* which is less severe in symptoms but more continuous in its up and down swings. (A

substantial minority with cyclothymia go on to develop the more severe bipolar disorder.) Some relevant excerpts from the Columbia *Guide* (119): "The inexhaustibility of manic people can be amazing. They throw themselves into work, social, school . . . activity with hyperactive energy, and they show little need for sleep. . . . Many people invest huge sums in grandiose business schemes . . . or give away their savings." Besides his enormous generosity to friends, family, employees, and social organizations, Ives spent tens of thousands (1991 dollars) publishing his music in 1920–22. That is certainly understandable, likewise perhaps the considerably more he spent paying off Edith's parents during roughly the same period. However, there is at least one outlay harder to comprehend: Ives's 1923 tax records show a bad debt deduction of over $375,000 (1991), some three-quarters of his income that year, made to a lawyer acquaintance who subsequently went bankrupt. The person may have been a good friend, but if so I have not run across his name anywhere else, or any indication Ives was paid back. More from the Columbia *Guide:* "While in a hypomanic phase, individuals with cyclothymia can be unusually creative and productive. Indeed, numerous studies have shown mood disorders, especially the bipolar disorders, to be overrepresented among people in the creative professions" (120). "Loss of a relationship or loved one [is] . . . high on the list [of causes]. Some people, perhaps by virtue of early life experiences, are particularly sensitive to issues of loss and are thus more vulnerable to depression" (124). The disorders seem to be inherited and to run in families, *but to be inherited from the mother rather than the father* (Corsini 364). In that we may find a connection to the hyperbolic personality of the Iveses, to the personality of Charlie's Uncle Joe and especially Uncle Ike, to Aunt Amelia, Grandmother Sarah, and mother Mollie (in contrast to George Ives, who seems to have been ebullient but less extreme than his brothers). Corsini: "Male relatives of bipolar patients are likely to suffer from alcoholism, sociopathy, and depression, while female relatives are likely to suffer from depression." Here could be a clue to the family secretiveness about Mollie Ives, and a nurse she had looking after her in 1894. Medical sources stress that there is a high degree of variability in bipolar disease. Manic phases, for example, tend to be *deceptively* creative and brilliant—but what about a person of genius suffering from the disease? (Handel, for one, may have had a severe case, given his creative frenzies and terrible depressions.) Finally, as Freud noted, even paranoids have enemies. The depressive phases, when a victim feels everyone is against him, were hardly unrealistic in regard to Ives's music. Perhaps with Ives the disease got worse after the heart attack because everything did, because he had more to be depressed about, and because at that point his social, political, and musical ideas fell into a state of grandiosity (a prime symptom of bipolar illness). Ives spent long periods in bed in his later years. This could have resulted from his diabetes and/or heart disease, from depression, or a combination of them. If it is true that these three contrapuntal illnesses were present, Ives and his wife must have had a heartbreakingly miserable time of it.

11. Harmony to Charlie, Uncollected Letters 3/4/1914.
12. Certainly Ives had life insurance, but he probably wanted to leave behind more than that could provide, especially for his still-young daughter and perhaps for his nephews and niece.
13. Of course, it is possible that Ives's decision to self-publish his music preceded the heart attack, but in any case the attack made everything more pressing.
14. In some ways Ives's situation after the Fourth Symphony resembles that of D. W. Griffith in the same period. With *The Birth of a Nation* and *Intolerance,* Griffith stretched his gifts and the creative and technical potential of his medium to the breaking point, and left himself nowhere to go but backward in scope and ambition. Like Griffith, Ives largely completed smaller-scale work in his last creative years (with the exception of one redone movement of the Fourth), but a general retreat in ambition would not have been like him. Griffith appears to have been sunk more by alcohol and by changes in the industry—mainly sound—than by a creative impasse.
15. Perlis CIR 12, and indications from letters in the 1930s.
16. Ives Papers Microfilm Addendum. It is striking that Ives cites his pancreas as a possible "hidden muse." Insulin is produced in

the pancreas—but medicine did not know that in 1919, when he wrote this letter.
17. Kirkpatrick interviews with Harmony in Ives Papers Microfilm Addendum.
18. The list is in Ives Papers 24/11.
19. "Our Book," Ives Papers 45/7.
20. Rossiter, Feder, and others dismiss Ives's ideas cavalierly and dissect his literary and philosophical shortcomings mercilessly. As is clear in the text, Ives's shortcomings are a given, but I dispute that he cannot be taken seriously. Compare Wagner's writings, which while broadly influential are even less coherent than Ives's and are often malevolent and outlandish in what they do manage to convey. (They also have, of course, a good measure of brilliance and insight as well.) Other than in relation to Wagner's prospectus of music drama, what Ives has to say about art and reality is ultimately more fruitful than what Wagner says, and would be that even if Wagner were not the vicious anti-Semite he was. In addition to everything else, Ives was a prophet of modern pluralistic, democratic liberalism.
21. Burkholder (*Ideas* 41): "The whole of his family's tradition and thinking became integrated in Ives's mind through his own reading of Emerson and Thoreau, and his ideas attained their apparent Transcendentalist cast as he [later] refined his childhood influences in Transcendentalist terms. . . . Ives arrived at most of his attitudes about music and his concepts of dualism, idealism, and self-reliance independently of [Emerson], in large part at least, but . . . Emerson's writings played a vital role in the final stages of his development." Burkholder's analysis is convincing, but it should be noted that Ives *did* read Emerson and Thoreau early on and they may have been half-conscious influences all along—perhaps Thoreau more than Emerson, because, as shown, Thoreau was more involved with music than Emerson (who once called musicians "mutilated eunuchs"). One can pick up a book read twenty years ago, barely understood then and apparently forgotten, and discover ideas by which one has lived ever since. One of those books, in my own case, was *Essays Before a Sonata.*
22. Ives *Essays* 8.
23. Quoted in Michael Moran, "New England Transcendentalism" in *The Encyclopedia of Philosophy,* (New York: Macmillan, 1967).

24. MacKinnon 68.
25. Ives *Essays* 57.
26. Ives *Essays* 11–12.
27. Ives *Essays* 16.
28. Ives *Essays* 26: "Emerson is neither a classic or romantic but both—and both not only at different times in one essay, but at the same time in one sentence—in one word." This seems not only inaccurate with respect to Emerson, but flapdoodle in general. Moreover, it contradicts Ives's just-stated claim that "there is no such thing as 'classicism or romanticism.' "
29. From "New England Transcendentalism" in *The Encyclopedia of Philosophy*.
30. Ives *Essays* 25.
31. Emerson wrote, "No object really interests us but man, and in man only his superiorities." At one point in the *Essays* (16) Ives does seem to recognize Emerson's basic elitism, but he quickly fogs it over: "It is occasionally said that Emerson has no vital message for the rank and file. He has no definite message, perhaps, for the literal, but his messages are all vital, as much by reason of his indefiniteness as in spite of it." What was that again?
32. Ives *Essays* 24.
33. Ives's puritanical suspicion of the physical seems puzzling for a sports fan, but that was probably a common Victorian mode of doublethink.
34. Ives *Essays* 28.
35. Ives *Essays* 62.
36. Ives *Essays* 51.
37. Ives *Essays* 67.
38. Ives *Essays* 71.
39. Ives *Essays* 75. Burkholder (*Ideas* 70) shows that Ives probably derived his dichotomy of substance and manner from an article on Debussy by his New Haven choirmaster John C. Griggs, who used the dichotomy "manner" and "content" in his analysis. Surprisingly, Ives's old mentor was not a believer in program music, as we will find Griggs writing in his reply after Ives sent him the *Essays*.
40. Ives *Essays* 76.
41. Ives *Essays* 77.
42. Ives *Essays* 77–79. Ives's hypothetical composer assimilating Apache music is exactly the process Bartók describes for a composer interiorizing folk music. (Ives is likely thinking of Arthur Farwell, though.)
43. Ives *Essays* 77. Ives says he is quoting François Roussel-Despierres, but editor Boatwright could not find the quote. Much of Ives's argument against Wagner amounts to the belief that Wagner's, or anyone's, personal sins inevitably damage their work. This would seem to be a naive and narrowly Victorian point of view, but the idea that the morality of the artist can, and usually does, sully his art seems to be widely embraced by critics and academics these days. Funny how things come around again. Ives's style of moral arguments against Wagner and his music has been turned often enough on himself. Recently a letter writer in the *New York Times* compared Ives's homophobia to Wagner's anti-Semitism and thereby implicitly dismissed Ives's music. I find that idea vastly overstated, but in a sense Ives is simply getting a dose of his own medicine. We will return to the idea that sometimes in his writings Ives can be his own worst enemy.
44. Ives *Essays* 97.
45. Ives *Essays* 101.
46. Rosalie Sandra Perry speculates on Ives's connection to Peirce and James in her chapter "The Middle-Class Conscience," though from different angles than here. Perry does note, interestingly, that James was influenced by the ideas of Helmholtz, as was Ives—though with James it was not Helmholtz's studies of acoustics. As Perry notes, James and Peirce were both influenced by Emerson in the creation of pragmatism. Ives's similarity to contemporary philosophers may have come from some combination of Emersonian extrapolations and the spirit of the age. As said earlier, the zeitgeist is a powerful presence in an artist, regardless of what books that artist has read. This helter-skelter way of picking up things does not make one an expert philosopher or psychologist, but it can provide grist for the mill, and for an artist that's what matters. A major study of Ives's relationship to the American philosophical tradition remains to be done.
47. Menand 32.
48. Peirce, "Pragmatism," in MacKinnon 160.
49. Menand 35.
50. These days the assumption of evolutionary science is that the Worm wants not to become Man but to stay a worm, albeit a happier and more sexually fulfilled one. It may be that when evolutionary science gave up the idea that species always evolve upward and simply want to stay where they are, it was at about the same time as the general decline of belief in progress. Which came first?
51. Quoted in Allen xvii.

52. Ives *Memos* 191–92. Ives approved of performers taking liberties with his scores more in theory than in practice. One of the reasons he rarely kept up with performances of his music in later years was that he usually didn't like them.
53. Quoted in Allen 124.
54. Ives *Essays* 14.
55. Ives *Essays* 22.
56. James letter to his wife of July 1898, quoted in Allen 239–40. It was written from Keene Valley, the little town where Ives would conceive the *Universe Symphony*. In his lecture "Philosophical Conceptions and Practical Results" of August 1898, James begins with a good deal of Adirondack imagery, calling poets and philosophers pathfinders and trail-blazers. In a bleakly ironic parallel with Ives, James's day of epiphany on the mountains strained his heart and he was never healthy again.
57. Perlis CIR 219.
58. Ives *Essays* 96.
59. Ives *Essays* 19.
60. Ives *Essays* 29.
61. Ives *Essays* 30–31.
62. Ives *Essays* 59.
63. Ives *Essays* 31.
64. Ives *Essays* 36.
65. Ives *Essays* 73.
66. Ives *Essays* 88–89.
67. Ives *Essays* 95–96.
68. Ives *Memos* 114.
69. Cowell and Cowell 5.
70. Kirkpatrick in Ives *Memos* 278.

F I F T E E N *Overtures*

1. Ives wrote composer Henry F. Gilbert in May 1920, "It takes longer to correct proofs than I imagined—and besides the mistakes make the music sound so much better (to others) that there are big decisions to make on every page" (Ives Papers 29/11).
2. Feder *Ives* 305.
3. Perlis CIR 64.
4. The material for "The Majority" is in Ives Papers 25/2. An edited final version is in the *Essays*.
5. Ives Papers 40.
6. Ives *Memos* 211, from "George's Adventure."
7. Ives *Essays* 142.
8. Ives *Essays* 148.
9. In a letter to me, Elie Siegmeister compared Ivesian socialism with that of depression-era lefties like himself: "His socialism derived from Emerson, Thoreau, Unitarianism, Whitman, etc. mine from Kropotkin [and] Emma Goldman . . . which I got from my father in my teens, and from Marx in my 20's and '30's, from the left wing movement of the time."
10. Ives *Essays* 181.
11. Ives *Essays* 186.
12. Ives *Essays* 163.
13. Ives *Essays* 169–70. Ives may be right that Beethoven would have composed money or no, but he is entirely wrong about the profit-driven Edison.
14. Ives *Essays* 197.
15. Ives *Memos* 225. Ives mentions in this passage that recruiting agents was a factor in his success, but does not present it as a major factor.
16. Gorer 31–32.
17. Gorer 44.
18. Dickens 245. Obviously, this 1842 observation is still true today.
19. "George's Adventure" is Appendix 9 of the *Memos*. As Kirkpatrick says there, "The Majority" began as a dialogue à la Plato and ended up an essay. "George's Adventure" is a sketch for a short story in the original dialogue form, using some of the "Majority" material. Among other personal items in the essay, Ives shows his disillusionment with liberal New York governor Al Smith: "The thing that makes me sore . . . is that, when I thought I was voting for the new schoolhouse, I was just voting for the Governor and his party. I don't mind being a fool, but I hate to be fooled." Certainly there is much autobiography in the story, and the wife owes something to Harmony Ives, but it should not be seen as sheer biography. In the story George, like Ives, has been ailing, but from a mugging rather than a heart attack. George's wife, quite unlike Harmony, is described as not liking her husband much, and married him at age sixty.
20. The material relating to the Twentieth Amendment is in Ives Papers 25.
21. Cowell and Cowell 92.
22. Several of Ives's political stances and some of his style in expressing them remind one of the contemporary example of Ross Perot. Both were successful businessmen

(Perot far richer) whose success in the marketplace did not necessarily imply a gift for realistic politics.

23. Ives *Essays* 200–201.
24. Ives's amendment is in the *Essays*. In a 6/1988 interview discussing what Ives had in mind with the amendment and his other proposals, John Kirkpatrick, with his usual deliberate thoughtfulness, said, "I think he just saw a problem and proposed a way to address it. It would be like him to want to think through what would happen to the Twentieth—it would be his habit as a businessman. He was beguiled by the excitement of the idea." There were more things going on with Ives then, but there is much in what Kirkpatrick said.
25. The exchange with Darby Day is in Ives Papers 25/4. Day ran one of the biggest Mutual agencies in the country. One has to wonder if Day actually received the Twentieth Amendment broadsides and tacitly refused to distribute them. Ives wrote him, "You may not agree with the 'plan' but you will assume no responsibility by suggesting a distributor."
26. Ives *Essays* 201.
27. Ives Papers 25/4.
28. Ives Papers 37/2.
29. The New Symphony Orchestra was founded in 1919 by Edgard Varèse partly to play avant-garde music, but it was quickly taken away from him and given over to less adventurous programming.
30. Ives Papers 35/4.
31. Ives *Memos* 102–3. Despite the inadequacy of the *Decoration Day* reading, Ives took notes on the score for orchestration revisions.
32. Ives Papers 29/11. Note that this is a *draft* of the letter to Gilbert. Ives often tempered his self-abnegation in the final drafts. One should also remember that most artists have doubts; Ives was simply more honest about them than most. When you strike out into new territory you are always on the verge of getting lost, always uncertain, sometimes frightened. Hemingway said that every artist needs, above all, "a built-in, shockproof crap detector." Hemingway's detector was hardly infallible; nobody's is, as most artists are painfully aware.
33. Ives Papers 31/6.
34. Ives Papers 41.
35. Quoted in Ives *Memos* 256.
36. Ives *Memos* 258.
37. While Schirmer would engrave the music for pay, the publisher was careful to keep its own name off the scores of the *Concord* and the songs. They were probably embarrassed by the music.
38. Ives Papers 27/10.
39. Ives Papers 29/13.
40. Banfield passim. Elizabeth Sprague Coolidge would end up commissioning works from Stravinsky, Bartók, Schoenberg, Prokofiev, and many others. Banfield details that in the 1920s she developed a special connection to British composers including Percy Grainger (originally Australian, to be sure), Cyril Scott, Eugene Goossens, Frank Bridge, and Arnold Bax, and she later became close to Benjamin Britten. This selection of British composers suggests that, even if she commissioned more advanced works on occasion, her basic tastes were conservative. Harmony told Kirkpatrick that in general Charlie couldn't stand Elizabeth Sprague Coolidge, who was probably the model of a music patroness with more money and good intentions than real understanding. There is a story that when Stravinsky accepted a commission from Coolidge Diaghilev complained, "Why are you writing for that rich lady? She has no ear." Replied Stravinsky pointedly to the impresario, "she has no ear, but she *pays*." Certainly, however, Coolidge was considerably more advanced and broad-minded than the usual artistic rich lady, and she had a powerful and salutary effect on music in this century.
41. Ives Papers 27/12. Kirkpatrick guesses that Coolidge's friend in Boston was probably the orientalist composer Henry Eichheim.
42. CEI letter draft to Coolidge in Ives Papers 27/12.
43. Ives Papers 32/13.
44. Most of this information on Whitmer's *Mysteries* is from his printed prospectus for the project, a copy of which is in the Ives Papers. He did extract a ballet from the score, which was played in the 1920s by Stokowski in Philadelphia and in Paris under Francis Casadesus.
45. Ives Papers 32/13.
46. The Ives/Bellamann correspondence is in Ives Papers 27/8.
47. Ives Papers 27/8.
48. Cowell and Cowell 99–100.
49. From material Furness sent to Ives, in Ives Papers.
50. Ives Papers 29/9.
51. Ives Papers 29/9.

S I X T E E N *The Work of Our Hands*

1. Ives *Memos* 127.
2. Bill from Schirmer in Ives Papers 35/11.
3. As per John Kirkpatrick's list of the songs in *The New Grove*, Ives had written 144 when he published *114 Songs*. The final number, according to *New Grove*, is 151, the last ones written after the *114*.
4. Schirmer bills in Ives Papers 35/11.
5. Feder's treatment of the songs in his Chapter 21 is admirable, notwithstanding his claim that "Ives intended the *114 Songs* as a work of autobiography" (311). Feder also calls them a "diary," which does make sense, at least for many of them. Certainly some of the songs are direct responses to his life, of which the courtship songs and the *Housatonic* are one example and the election song "November 2" another. But Ives wrote songs for all sorts of reasons, often with no conscious autobiographical intention. As much as anything, he appears to have written something because a poem grabbed him when he came across it—he took several songs, including *General Booth* and "The Greatest Man," right out of newspapers. There are two specific pieces of evidence that suggest his songs were more occasional or spur-of-the-moment affairs than otherwise. First, Ives rarely wrote "laboratory" songs; when he wanted to try out a technical idea he usually wrote an instrumental piece (and often left it unfinished when he had found what he wanted to know). Second, he wrote little about the songs in the *Memos* or anywhere else. The *Concord* publication merited the whole of the *Essays; 114 Songs* got only the short, oddly contrite Postface.
6. Hitchcock *Ives* 9.
7. Hitchcock *Ives* 13.
8. Joseph W. Reed goes into the issue of Ives and genre in his *Three American Originals*, focusing on the connection of genre in Ives to the films of John Ford, one of his other subjects. Reed's fourth chapter is rich with ideas, such as these: "[Ives] knows that much of genre is machine and although he seems to have nothing much but contempt for that kind of machine, he knows at the same time that this is not to say that genre is formula" (135); and "*At the River* is a hymn to a hymn" (139).
9. While in my opinion Ives's best instrumental pieces are generally the more radical ones, most of the songs I rate highest are more orthodox (*General Booth* being one of

the exceptions). Perhaps that is so because the main thing about a song is its vocal line. Many of Ives's more advanced songs resemble much classical vocal music of this century, in which the voice part is the least interesting feature of the piece. There is one other reason: performances such as Jan de Gaetani's recording of the sentimental "Rather Sad" and Henry Herford's of the 1929 spiritual arrangement "In the Mornin' " reveal how moving some of the conventional songs can be if they are sung wholeheartedly and without irony.
10. Ives *Essays* 130.
11. Ives *Essays* 130–31.
12. The story of Stokowski's firing came from Gunther Schuller, who had it from the violin soloist involved and told it to Tanglewood students as an instructive story.
13. *Musical Courier* 4/21/1921.
14. *Musical Courier* 7/4/1927. The periodical had a special interest in Bartók in the 1920s, perhaps because the Hungarian correspondent was Kodály.
15. Mead *Cowell's New Music* 23.
16. It appears that Bartók's use of tone clusters in the Fourth String Quartet and later works came directly from hearing Henry Cowell's cluster pieces.
17. Here we must part company with Maynard Solomon on another issue: that Ives had a "defensive assertion of his own priority" because of his "rivalrous personality for whom such issues may become an obsessive preoccupation" (453). Ives got defensive about his priority as an innovator mainly when someone accused him of borrowing other composers' ideas and he knew he hadn't. Ives's response may have been exaggerated, but his response to everything was exaggerated. He felt he had made technical discoveries that had advanced the art of music and he wanted credit for that; for that reason he also got steamed when he saw famous composers (which he was not, for a long time) celebrated for inventing things that were old news to him. But in the end innovation was a subsidiary issue for Ives. When in 1949 interviewer Howard Taubman commended his discoveries, Ives waved his hand and said, "That's not my fault." Occasional explosions of resentment aside, that was what he essentially believed all along. It is also odd that Solomon cites (464) Ives's "powerful thirst for public recogni-

tion" as if that were something unscrupulous or unusual for an artist. Ives was writing for the public all along and naturally wanted people to hear his work. He was if anything less self-serving than most artists in how he went about seeking a public—one of the reasons it took him so long to get famous. One should not, however, get the impression that there is nothing valuable in Solomon's article. As I noted in the introduction, it did have the virtue of throwing a spotlight on what Ives was doing in the 1920s after he said he had practically quit composing. Besides that, I find only a few nuances to quarrel with in Solomon's overall summary about Ives's "need to be free of influences, to deny [musical] ancestry, to relieve his guilt over transcendence of his father, to be the unrivalled inventor-creator. Ives somehow came to believe that originality lay in being up-to-date, in the patenting of techniques and procedures." Some caveats about that: Ives's guilt probably stems mainly from George Ives's having died in a period when teenaged Charlie was practically defying him. Ives did not become obsessed with *patenting* innovations so much as he fell into the characteristically Modernist tendency to equate innovation with value, including *his* value.

18. The Furness-Ives correspondence is in the Papers 29/9.
19. Carter "Documents" 300.
20. Carter "The Case of Mr. Ives" 27.
21. Carter "Documents" 300.
22. Cowell and Cowell 100.
23. Ives Papers 29/1.
24. Ives Papers 29/9.
25. Ives Papers 30/12.
26. Ives Papers 31/9.
27. Ives Papers 32/13.
28. Ives Papers 29/13.
29. Ives Papers 27/10.
30. Sousa's note in the Ives Papers is uncatalogued.
31. Quoted in Kirkpatrick Chronology in Ives *Memos*.
32. *Musical Courier* 2/16/1922. That the paper's contributors were not entirely close-minded is seen in the same issue, where a critic says of Schoenberg's epochal Six Piano Pieces, "For concentrated conciseness these six pieces are probably unequalled in the history of art."
33. *Musical Courier* 9/21/1922.
34. Ives Papers 24/11.

35. Cowell and Cowell 90–91.
36. CEI to Madden, Ives Papers 30/17.
37. George Madden was an active voice teacher, but his English was apparently not up to his command of music. Some of his stationery proclaimed a "Scientific Mental Way of Singing," and in 1936 he invited Ives to a performance by saying "you would help trajonically by your presence."
38. Ives Papers 29/13.
39. Ives Papers 29/13.
40. Ives Papers 35/4, a letter of 3/6/1923. From a later, hard-to-read Ives memo on the letter it appears that the *Three Places* score had been sent to the Philharmonic by Sigmund Klein, a pianist associated with the Pro Musica organization (he would play in the premiere of the *Three Quarter-Tone Pieces*). Ives also notes on the memo, "Didn't know it was sent till almost a year later. I dont send score to aural & cissy cowards."
41. Ives *Memos* 248–49. The house was moved again during the 1960s.
42. Cowell and Cowell 101.
43. Rossiter 354n.
44. Perlis *Two Men* 3–10. In conversation with Edison, Schmitz told the inventor that Debussy often said the piano as it currently existed was inadequate for his music. Schmitz and Edison envisioned an electrified piano without the percussive attack of the hammers and capable of crescendos. It is amazing that while distressed at the limitations of the piano Debussy still produced some of the most effective and original pianistic sonorities ever conceived. Maybe you have to be disgusted to come up with something fresh. (On the other hand, if Debussy could have heard some of the late-century synthesized versions of his piano music, he might have been more content with the plain old piano.)
45. Perlis *Two Men* 11–12.
46. Perlis CIR 125.
47. Rossiter 207.
48. Monique Schmitz in Perlis Oral History 3/52.
49. While Schmitz's group officially changed its name to Pro Musica in 1923, it appears that the old name Franco-American Society persisted in various capacities for several years.
50. Ives *Essays* 110.
51. Ives *Essays* 117.
52. Ives *Essays* 118.
53. Ives *Memos* 110.

54. Ives *Memos* 111. Besides downplaying his own quarter-tone studies, Ives was not particularly happy with the other experiments he heard. He wrote in the *Memos,* "I must say that I think Hans Barth went at the matter in the wrong way . . . the concerts he has given and the way he has used the [quarter-tone piano Ives helped finance], to my way of thinking, have done more harm than good in interesting people in quarter tones, or developing a natural sense and use for them. (Besides, I think that new scales . . . will gradually be evolved in a natural way probably, perhaps in centuries, and that their intervals will not be . . . of the whole, half, or quarter tones known or so-called now.)" Despite Alois Hába, Hans Barth, and other composers devoting their lives to the cause in the 1920s, quarter tones did not catch on. To hear Ives's efforts, which are probably better than most in that era, is to get some idea of why.

55. Ives Papers 54/2. Carter writes ("Documents" 302) that Goldstein made a private recording of the Second Sonata, but if so that has not survived. Carter probably remembered incorrectly.

56. HTI interview with Kirkpatrick in Ives Papers Microfilm Addendum. She added that "Charlotte [Ruggles] felt the same way. Charlotte said it was death to hear a performance of Carl's music. But they sat together. Charlotte was braver than I was."

57. Perlis CIR 72–74.

58. Ives Papers 29/1.

59. Ives Papers 29/9. The date is uncertain, but the best guess seems 4/6/1924.

60. Ives Papers 29/9.

61. Elliott Carter in Perlis Oral History 1/14. Again, Carter's memory can be inaccurate. For years he said that he heard *Le sacre du printemps* with Ives, but it was probably *Rossignol* and/or *The Firebird.* Ives lambasted the latter in the *Essays.*

62. Both John Kirkpatrick and Nicolas Slonimsky told me Katherine Heyman's technique was more or less adequate for Scriabin, but not for the *Concord.* Certainly Schmitz had the virtuosity to handle any of Ives's piano music, and he apparently played some of the *Concord* in Paris. But he never really championed Ives's keyboard music.

63. Interview with Nicolas Slonimsky.

64. Edith Ives's diary, Ives Papers 45/D9. In her diary Edie was busy in those days creating her "Lady Beauty" line of fashions and accessories. Lady Beauty's son, also featured in Edie's drawings, i named Prince Rollo. Monique Schmitz and Vivian Perlis that when they played "Sleeping Beauty" Edie would inevitably be the princess. She had long golden hair, like Edith in Longfellow's "Children's Hour"—which Ives set, however, years before Edie was born.

65. David Twichell to HTI, Uncollected Letters, 7/27/1924. One can only wonder, with a shudder, if Harmony and Charlie received Dave's letter in London after getting the cable that Dave had killed himself.

66. HTI interviews with Kirkpatrick in Ives Papers Microfilm Addendum.

67. This is from a CEI memo in Ives Papers 37/5. Ives was not sure of the date of Gershwin's call, but it seems to have been when he was in England. It s unlikely that Ives made up the incident whole cloth, but his account is secondhand, muddled, and probably exaggerated. It includes, "G.G. wanted to see me & thank me for the help my music had been to him—that it had opened up possibilities in rhythm & tonal ways[?] etc.—which had influenced his music and many other composers." Ives speculates that Gershwin attended the performance of the Fourth Symphony movements in 1927. The idea that Ives had some influence on Gershwin is intriguing. Gershwin had broad interest in new music and it would have been like him to play through Ives's scores if they fell into his hands (he may well have been on Ives's mailing list). Ives apparently said nothing against Gershwin. (He probably had little chance to hear Gershwin's music, though.) Ives was willing to compliment composers who were personal friends and whose work he genuinely admired (many Ruggles), but for those who were not friends he mostly indicated his approval by staying silent. Sooner or later he surely saw, and played over, Schoenberg scores, and he may have heard *Wozzeck* in concert in the 1930s. Ives never wrote about Berg's or Schoenberg's music—but, tellingly, neither did he complain about them. As we will see, he did meet Schoenberg on one occasion.

68. Ives Papers 45/D10.

69. Cowell and Cowell 125.

70. HTI interviews with Kirkpatrick in Ives Papers Microfilm Addendum.

71. Ives Papers 45/10.

72. Ives *Memos* 112.

73. Interview with Mutual archivist Charron Fullerton, 6/1991.
74. The discussion of the *Comedy* here is based on Thomas Brodhead's article, which is an outstanding piece of sleuthing. Brodhead edited the Ives Society edition of *The Celestial Railroad*, on which he based most of his ideas. The conclusions about *why* Ives covered up the true date of the *Comedy* are my own. If Maynard Solomon had known Brodhead's conclusions, this matter would likely have been the centerpiece of his article suggesting that Ives lied about his datings to make himself look more the prophet. Since there is no real evidence that Ives was doing that, I have pursued my own explanations for his dating of the *Comedy*. A primary reason why Ives had no need to lie is that he had already written quite a number of prophetic pieces before the *Comedy*, as both his own testimony and the best efforts of manuscript analysis confirm. As the most obvious examples: the *Concord Sonata* and many of the *114 Songs* contain music as advanced as anything Ives wrote, and they were printed in 1920–22. The composer of *The Unanswered Question* in 1906 and *The Fourth of July* in the teens did not need to lie to make himself look like a prophet. Nor, as noted before, did Ives significantly "modernize" originally milder scores. He simply punched up, here and there rather at random, the dissonance in some of his more advanced scores.
75. Ives *Memos* 65–66.
76. Ives *Memos* 82.
77. Ives did make some sort of workable version of the *Celestial Railroad* (pianist Anton Rovinsky played it for years), but that score has not turned up. Brodhead shows that the score-sketch of the *Comedy* followed directly from the *Celestial Railroad* pinned-up draft; after that unusually clear and complete score-sketch came Ives's full score, then one done by Ives's copyist Reis. The latter seems to have been made somewhere between 1923 and 1926, and from that score the *Comedy* was played in early 1927.
78. Brodhead's datings and reconstruction of the order of composition of the *Hawthorne* Concerto and *Hawthorne* in the *Concord* are bound to be speculative, especially since the concerto manuscript is lost except for three pages of sketches. Brodhead accepts Ives's date of August 1913 for the concerto, which is noted on one of those sketch pages—but that would seem to conflict with Kirkpatrick's dating of the *Concord's Hawthorne* as 1911 (the date used earlier in this book); besides, another sketch page has the note, "Pells-Sep-1910." Brodhead or Ives may be wrong about 1913, or Kirkpatrick about 1911 (which is also based on Ives's recollections). Or the piano piece might have preceded the concerto, or both may have been composed in the same period. (Are we sufficiently confused?) As with the *Three Places* muddle, much of the problem results from missing material that might help illuminate the dating (although finding it could just as well confuse things more).
79. This highly speculative chronology is a synthesis of Kirkpatrick and Brodhead. The latter's window for composition of the *Comedy* was 1921 to 1923. Ives probably did little or no work on it in 1921 because he was busy with the *114 Songs,* So my speculative date is 1922–23.
80. Interview with Charron Fullerton 6/1991; Rossiter 113.
81. The information on Ives's income is from his tax records in the Ives Papers.
82. Ives has already been called a hypocrite and will undoubtedly be called that still more after this information about his earnings emerges. But Ives was more honest and honorable than most people, and certainly more so than most artists. Perhaps the real answer is that anybody whose standards are as unrealistically high as Ives's is bound to contradict his ideals in the course of being human—and looking out for his family.
83. Ives Papers Microfilm Addendum.
84. Redding neighbor Will Ryder in Perlis Oral History 1/26. The poem is in Ives Papers 27/7.
85. "On the Antipodes" (Kirkpatrick dates are 1915–23, from earlier sketches) involves elaborate mirror formations suggesting the linked paradoxes of the text: "Nature's relentless;/Nature is kind./Nature is Eternity;/Nature's today! . . ." The accompaniment for piano four hands contains some of Ives's densest and most formalistic keyboard writing. The shockingly ineffective interjection of parodistic harmony on the lines "Sometimes Nature's nice and sweet, as a little pansy" shows how Ives's anger (and homophobia) could overwhelm his aesthetic sense starting in the 1920s. Here is one of the few times that Ives's emotions got the better of him

enough to derail an otherwise interesting piece.

86. The discussion of the music of *Psalm 90* is partly based on Nicholls (80–87) and Hitchcock *Ives* (32–36).

87. Kirkpatrick Preface to the Merion Music score. In *Psalm 90* Ives also quotes, barely detectably, Gottschalk's sentimental "Last Hope." That is a good example of a point Peter Burkholder made, that Ives's quotes often duplicate the mental effects of thought and experience, in which everything happens with stronger or weaker hints of other associations. In the case of *Psalm 90,* Ives's reflection on his and his father's death called up a distant memory of Gottschalk's deathbed weeper.

88. Since the original *90th Psalm* is lost, it is impossible to say if it already contained the chordal sequence from the First Symphony, or which version came first. In either case, Ives appears to have associated this music with his father's death.

89. Kirkpatrick Preface to the score.

90. James Sinclair calls John Kirkpatrick's edition of "Sunrise" "a major excavation job." Ives had written the melodic lines but Kirkpatrick assembled the piano part from rough sketches.

91. 1935 CEI letter to Kirkpatrick, quoted in the Kirkpatrick Catalogue 92.

92. This imagining of the scene is based on Kirkpatrick's note of Harmony Ives's brief recollection, quoted in *Memos* (279): "Not long after they'd moved in—as Harmony recalled—'he came downstairs one day with tears in his eyes, and said he couldn't seem to compose any more—nothing went well, nothing sounded right.'" Ives probably overtaxed himself in the 1920s with his composing and publications and promotion. Instead of the more likely outcome of a fatal heart attack, his mind and body shut down by degrees. His diabetes was getting worse and was not diagnosed and treated until early 1931. His condition improved somewhat for a few years after that, but then he resumed his downward slide.

Entr'acte Three · *Watchman, Tell Us of the Night*

1. Except where otherwise noted, this chapter is based on Jan Johnson (Swafford), "The Second Phase: Compositional Techniques and Form in Ives' Fourth Symphony," unpublished undergraduate thesis. While that tome is largely technical and limited by the age and experience of its author, it still seems to tour the workings of the symphony well. Conversations with conductor Michael Tilson Thomas—during rehearsals for two performances and eventual recording of the Fourth—helped add elements to this chapter that were missed in the theory-focused thesis. Above all, some ideas of Thomas's contributed to my thoughts on the way Ives in general and the Fourth in particular conveyed Ives's sense of community. In the same way, a remark by James Sinclair—"Ives wrote himself right out of reality"—began the development of a major theme in this book.

2. As an example of the thoroughness of motivic work in Ives, the structure of the opening measures, especially of the bass line, will be outlined. As the text notes, the first three pitches in the basses form the Urmotiv, a half step and a minor third. In the second measure the top violin line inverts the motive in "Schoenbergian" fashion:

The trumpet fanfare is a rearranged version of the Urmotiv. The relationship of the bass line to the Urmotiv goes considerably beyond the first three notes. Its three *longest* notes form a descending variant of the Urmotiv, the "major" version as opposed to the opening "minor" version:

This "major" version turns up often (say, as a lyricized and tonalized avatar of the Urmotiv) and defines the connection of the Urmotiv to the distant harp's opening phrase and therefore to *Bethany:*

Altogether, on the first page we hear the Urmotiv and its variants some nine times. The second half of the bass line at the end of the first page is made of interlocking forms:

In its first fourteen notes the bass line includes the entire chromatic scale. It approaches a twelve-tone row then, but rather than functioning that way it more generally prepares the chromaticism heard in later movements. (The first two measures also involve all twelve notes among the parts.) Meanwhile the distant instrumental choir on the first page suggests A major / minor, a hint of the usual dominant tonality of the second theme in sonata form. The opening four measures thereby set up a range of possibilities from diatonic harmony through pandiatonicism to atonality.

Another important element of the opening bass line has to do with rhythm. The implied rhythm of the whole bar is $\frac{6}{4}$ divided 3 + 3. However, the sound of the first four notes is ambiguous; they could be heard as 2 + 2 (thus the $\frac{6}{4}$ ($\frac{3}{2}$) time signature). This suggests a rhythmic duality seen throughout the work—the contrast of *two* and *three*. It sometimes appears as simple duality, other times as ambiguity, other times as conflict. The interaction is carried on both horizontally, as alternation of duple and triple groupings (say, in ragtime rhythms), and vertically in polyrhythmic juxtapositions. The main rhythmic character of the Urmotiv is marchlike; its most common rhythmic form (especially in the *Comedy*) is a dotted figure, say, ♪.♪♩ . Meanwhile the lyric motive tends to have a related dotted figure in a triple context: ♪.♪♩ or ♪♪.♩ . Ives plays with those figures throughout the *Comedy*. The main musical focus of the second movement is on melody and rhythm, of the third movement on harmony and counterpoint. In this context one can do little more than hint at the subtlety of the melodic construction in the Fourth, but it is pervasive. The general idea is to unify a great many borrowed tunes—over fifty in the piece—by means of the simple, ubiquitous structures of the Urmotiv and lyric motive. It is a technique Ives had developed over the years, usually as part of an overall cumulative form; like so many Ives works, the Fourth Symphony

will end with the first plain, extended statement of its most essential theme, *Bethany:* "Nearer, My God, to Thee."

3. The beginning of *Bethany* and "Sweet By and By" (also *Watchman*) are inversions of each other—all a progression of whole steps, the lyric motive. This characteristic Ivesian "punning" is a major element of thematic development in the work. As another example, prominent in the finale are the hymns *Martyn, Missionary Chant,* and *Dorrnance,* all of which begin with three repeated notes and a descent of a third to the tonic (which also suggests the Beethoven Fifth motive—another pun).

4. Kirkpatrick Preface to the Associated score, vii.

5. The second two pages of the published score of the Fourth have always puzzled me. It is not clear why Ives follows the dramatic opening with two quiet pages that sound static and sketchy (though the manuscript shows he worked them over). The explanation may be what is said in the text, that the association of "Sweet By and By" with his father was so strong that for Ives the association made the passage seem stronger than it actually is. In other words, maybe Ives's personal feelings overcame his generally acute sense of form and continuity.

6. I suggest that despite Ives's request the choir should always be included in the Prelude (as it usually has been). Only if all listeners knew the hymn by heart would his "preferably without voices" apply. The audience could be given the words and asked to follow along, but then it would be hard to follow the ways Ives varies and adapts the hymn, cutting words and repeating "Traveller, yes" three times to establish his programmatic theme.

7. Ives recomposes the first verse of *Watchman* to make the effect of two verses. Typically, the second verse is not a literal restatement but a varied one—richer in texture, and with the basses now harmonizing the D-major melody in B minor. Ives generally varies all repetitions, and the second time through a phrase or section is usually more elaborate. In the structural dimension this produces a different effect than literal repetition. In, for example, Debussy's characteristic pattern of literally repeating phrases twice in a row, the first time tends to have more weight: – ⌣ . In

8. In the program notes Ives and Bellamann say the *Comedy* "is not a scherzo." It is one anyway. Its function in the symphony is that of the traditional scherzo, and it has some of the parodistic, grotesque character of some of Mahler's. In fact, until fairly late in the game Ives placed the *Comedy* as third movement, the usual slot for a scherzo.

contrast, Ives builds up the second statement: ⌣ —.

9. In other words, Ives generally approved of the technology that was current in his youth and was suspicious of later inventions such as motion pictures, radio, and phonograph. The main exceptions were the telephone—even though telephones came to Danbury in his childhood, he had something of a phobia about them—and the dictagraph, which he used at work.

10. Either Ives missed, or maybe it amused him, that part of what Hawthorne is satirizing in this passage is the kind of social activism Ives saw the insurance business as promoting: throwing your little quota of virtue into the common pool, and thereby enhancing the virtue of society.

11. More specifically, the theme sections dominated by the Urmotiv in the *Comedy* might be called the allegro / marcato / duple / brassy group, the ones dominated by the lyric motive the slow / lyric / hymnic / triple / string group. While the two groups were presented in relative harmony in the Prelude, they are competitors in the *Comedy*. At the same time, there is a regular exchange of traits between the groups. In general, the melodic genesis of the *Comedy* tends to produce steadily longer and more well-defined themes (most of them variants of familiar melodies). In other words, as is characteristic of Ives, there is a long-range trend toward clarity and extended melodic statement. In the *Country Band* climax at Rehearsal Number 40, both Urmotiv and lyric motive (or variants) are integrated in the main theme.

12. To put it more technically, much of the *Comedy* is in effect *nonharmonic*. Except in some of the interludes, one finds little planning in the vertical sonorities except to keep them chromatic and dense. Musically speaking, the *Comedy* is "about" melody, rhythm, and texture, as the third movement is "about" counterpoint and harmony in the traditional sense.

13. Ives may never have been more subtle in his control of texture than in the *Comedy*. Many of the phrases are defined by shifts of timbre and texture even though the sound on both sides of the shift is equally busy. One example is the striking change at No. 13, which to a casual glance looks hardly different on the page than the previous measure. I also consider the *Comedy* to be one of Ives's, and the century's, most masterful achievements in form. To keep all those notes, and a form so complex, episodic, and unprecedented, moving forward is phenomenal. I would say the same of the finale.

14. After he heard the 1927 performance of the *Comedy* Ives put into the score a system of letters indicating foreground to background lines. Sometimes the letters run from A (the foreground parts) to F. The letters only sometimes clarify matters, however. Occasionally they make little discernible sense, such as the places where Ives skips a letter in the sequence of layers, or when he puts an A on something that can't possibly be heard. On the whole, though, the scoring of the *Comedy* is reasonably practical, in Ivesian terms. Foreground tunes in the denser passages are generally put into trumpets and trombones, who can cut through anything. (Part of the fun of the movement is hearing those instruments get a chance to let it rip as they are rarely allowed to do in the standard repertoire. This helps give the *Comedy* its markedly brass-band effect.) It's harder to figure out why Ives left out oboes and horns in the movement. The rhythmic incisiveness of oboes especially would seem to have come in handy. One guess is that in the winds Ives was sticking close to the makeup of a Danbury-style cornet band, which often lacked French horns and oboes.

15. Ives *Memos* 106.

16. Around the time Ives was composing the *Comedy* he visited his friend T. Carl Whitmer's farm "Dramamount" (see CEI to Whitmer, letter of 9 / 18 / 1923, Ives Papers 32/13). As noted, maybe there he began to imagine the *Universe Symphony* laid out with multiple orchestras and choruses spread around Whitmer's natural amphitheater. The ultimate question is whether Ives's perspective effects in the *Comedy* work at all as intended. I'd say only partially. But a lot of fine works don't function as intended—not Seurat's dots of

color, not Van Gogh's paintings whose pigments have changed color, not Bach's cantatas that were written to be spread through a church service, and for that matter all religious works designed to strengthen a faith which most of its beholders do not share, and most paintings that were intended for the home rather than for a museum. The main thing to stress about the *Comedy*, once again, is that while recording inevitably flattens out the sonic perspective, live performance has a depth of sound that is unique and powerfully effective—even if its complexity does not allow the spacial subtlety of, say, *Hanover Square*.

17. It is remarkable that every page of the Fourth works in its terms today, while much of it was beyond the reach of any orchestra in the first decades of the century. It is only the experience of Modernism that has given orchestras the skills necessary for realizing the Fourth Symphony. Somehow, while allowing the *Universe* to escape reality, Ives was able to keep the Fourth consistently playable *in the future,* even if not at the time he was writing it.

18. Chester Ives recalled (Perlis Oral History 1 / 16) that Uncle Charlie told him the *Comedy* was like sounds on the street.

19. In general, and with detours, the *Comedy* tends to progress, phrase by phrase, from greater complexity in the general direction of clarity. The climax of that process is the arrival toward the end at *Country Band March,* which is the movement's point of greatest *relative* rhythmic and tonal unanimity—except for the brief, full-orchestra rhythmic unison on "Yankee Doodle" just before the music dissolves.

20. Ives described this section—from roughly No. 22—as a "take-off on salon music . . . pink teas in Vanity Fair social life" (quoted in Kirkpatrick Preface to the score). The effect is equally redolent of pianos in barrooms, of which Ives had much experience.

21. Several of the *Comedy's* quiet interludes have a more or less ragtimey, allegro shadow line or two in the background. These lines help smooth the transitions, as do some metric modulations (which might better be called "tempo modulations").

22. As often with lines in the movement, the violin's rhythm in the central adagio is ambiguous, the strong beats of the melody set off from the meter. There is no room to

detail the rhythmic development that runs through the *Comedy*, but I'll try to suggest some of it. The "technique of ambiguity" here mostly applies to the rhythm, at all levels. Ragtime, for example, normally creates syncopation by regrouping the normal stresses of the measure, say, breaking the regular $2 + 2$, $4 + 4$ of $\frac{4}{4}$ time into patterns such as $3 + 3 + 2$. Ives pushes that process further, creating lines that phase in and out of perceivable congruence with the beat and meter, and / or ones forming larger metric patterns outside the written bar lines (and those often involve polyrhythms). Meanwhile he plays games with his basic dotted rhythmic motives. For instance, the march pattern ♩. ♪ ♩ is clearly duple, while the patterns ♪♪♪ ♩ and ♪♪.♪ are triple. But Ives suggests the question: At what point do these become ambiguous, a perceived sense of a duple figure phase into triple or vice versa? In the *Comedy* these questions come to rest in the full-orchestra eruption of "Yankee Doodle" at the end. That pattern of even eighths—two before No. 47—is derived from the preceding percussion patterns in $\frac{6}{8}$: ♪♪♪ ♪♪♪ | ♪♪♪ ♪♪♪. The even eighths of "Yankee Doodle" are in effect created by tying two notes in the triple pattern ♩. ♪♪ to make a duple pattern, ♪♪ . It seems that here Ives is subtly reconciling duple and triple, in a joking way showing that, musically, three can equal two and vice versa. At climactic points there tends to be a general agreement with the actual meter, which is one of the things that make them climactic. One of the large-scale processes in the movement, in fact, is increasing definition of the march-time meter, away from ambiguity and toward clarity. But even in the maximum clarity of the *Country Band* climax, not everybody agrees on the beat. It is characteristic of Ives's mature music to move toward clarity and resolution but never finally to achieve them. That there is always more to be said is a great part of his point.

23. On one sketch of the Fugue Ives notes "for Church Ritual movement."

24. In the Fugue there is more or less a cadence in C major five bars after No. 3, but it sounds unsettled, with its emphasis on the fifth of the chord. At the bottom of page 104 there is a solid cadence in F. Though

that cadence is unemphasized, it does help set up the subdominant as the main secondary key.

25. In the Fugue Ives deliberately subverts the dominant key in the exposition—suggesting it without really modulating—and throughout the movement maintains a preference for the subdominant key of F. (Though the second and fourth entries of the subject are ostensibly on the dominant, he tiptoes around the F♯ that would define the dominant key.) The traditional problem with modulations to the subdominant is that they tend to be ambiguous, because the tonic key is dominant of the subdominant. Ives deliberately exploits that ambiguity. His modulation to F after No. 5 is actually no modulation at all—he never uses the B♭ that defines the new key, but after the hold simply pops into F major as if he had modulated. Adding to the overall equivocation is a habit of sliding around chromatically in parallel sixths. He mostly avoids cadences of any sort. Part of what makes the arrival of the stretto at No. 10 so powerful is that it is the only strong tonic cadence in the piece. Even the final cadence at the end (plagal, as is only logical) is on the fourth beat, held over to the downbeat and quickly cut off. That fourth-beat cadence echoes the main theme, which begins with an upbeat on the tonic. One could argue, in fact, that the harmonic ambiguity of the whole Fugue flows from the opening tonic upbeat of "Greenland."

26. There are several subsidiary themes in the Fugue, notably one that first appears at No. 3 where rising fourths prepare the refrain of "Greenland's Icy Mountains" at the stretto. There is no particular fugal countersubject. One finds Ives's accustomed careful relationships of thematic material throughout. Regarding the texts, the subject of Lowell Mason's "Greenland" is missions. In this as in some other quoted themes in the symphony, the words of the hymn don't appear particularly relevant to the program. Samples of the text that seem irrelevant, if not contradictory to Ives and the program, if not utterly racist: "They call us to deliver / Their land from error's chain . . . every prospect pleases, / And only man is vile. . . . The heathen in his blindness / Bows down to wood and stone." Etc. Again: texts are relevant sometimes in Ives (as with Bethany and "Sweet By and By" in the Fourth) and sometimes

not. A rule of thumb is that if relating the words seems a stretch, they're probably not intended to be part of the discourse. "Greenland" 's connection to the primary musical motives of the symphony involves variants of both Urmotiv and lyric motive.

27. The horns enter "in the manner" of a Bach prelude because the entries are not successive phrases from a single chorale melody, as they would have been in Bach. In Ives's case they are simply another contrapuntal line (sometimes involving a quoted tune) added periodically to the old Fugue. But the effect is distinctly reminiscent of the Bach preludes Ives grew up playing on organ. Perhaps the reason Ives didn't use a single tune is that it would have been hard to weave into the already completed counterpoint, and in this piece he did not want the dissonance that simply tossing a tune into the texture would have created.

28. At No. 13, where the old version of the Fugue picks up after the retransition, the basic harmonic ambiguity is in full cry. Even though there is no B♭ to define the key of F, the harmony comes to a hold on F as if it were a cadence. At that point it is hard to tell whether C or F is the tonic, and the uncertainty remains for several measures. Then, as noted, at the end of the piece Ives undercuts the final C-major cadence by putting it on the weakest beat in the measure, the last—as if it were an upbeat. The idea of a final cadence made into an upbeat is a characteristic bit of Ivesian symbolism.

29. Ives Essays 59.

30. Ives Essays 82.

31. Typically for Ives, in the finale the Battery Unit maintains its own tempo but never settles down to an unvaried pattern for the duration, though some patterns are repeated for several cycles after the initial gearing-up. (Editor Wayne Shirley says Ives calculated the complex relationship between the Battery Unit pulse generally well, but did make some mistakes in alignment.) As we saw in the Essays, by his maturity Ives had come to be suspicious of all literal repeats, reasoning that if life never exactly repeats anything, why should music.

32. Ives's sketches for the finale are dense and voluminous. Interestingly, in earlier drafts the bass line begins on the original D, from the first movement. Only later did Ives de-

cide to withhold the tonic until the coda. He "implies" a base on B in the bass line because the first note is A♯, eventually moving to B. (Before the coda Ives does anticipate its resolution to D major, in a bass line striding down in whole tones from D to D, but that is only a hint to prepare the full cadence.) The ink draft of the movement is fairly clear, with some sloppy spots and later additions. Typically, the title page of Ives's ink draft of the finale dates it as 1910–16, while the first page of the score has it as 1911–16.

33. This section of the finale, from measure 40, is the part based on the lost *Memorial Slow March* for organ, written on the death of McKinley. That music, and its tone of somber nobility, began with a scene Ives observed not unlike the one that led to *Hanover Square:* When the news of the president's assassination came, he watched people at a New York cafe stand up and sing "Nearer, My God, to Thee" (Kirkpatrick Preface vii). The intermediate stage of the idea, as noted before, is the end of the Second String Quartet.

34. The cadence formula that prepares the coda of the finale is, surprisingly enough given how right it sounds in that context, a simple II 6 / 5, I 6 / 4, V in D major, which leads to the downbeat on I in the next measure. The cadence is blurred by various added notes, which is what creates its effect of floating in a mist. This movement, and especially this measure, is an answer to charges that Ives could not orchestrate. In the finale (and in the *Comedy*) Ives remade the orchestra, shaping sounds and textures utterly unprecedented and never heard since. Moreover, each of his other big orchestral phantasmagorias generally "statistical" in effect—*The Fourth of July, Hanover Square, Decoration Day, Browning, Putnam's Camp, The Housatonic,* and the *Comedy*—has a distinctive orchestral sound of its own. These works are more strongly characterized, more individually *orchestrated,* than many "statistical" works of the 1960s and 1970s.

35. Thanks to James Sinclair for this observation, and that the beginning of the Fourth is Ives's only "heroic" opening.

36. Besides the symbolic and metaphysical implications of Ives's endless, open form, there is an abstract musical logic too. His melodic germs are so generalized that they can be found in nearly any tonal tune. It is

therefore impossible to limit the motives, make them into a sum, get to the end of them. Ives takes advantage of that situation to shape open forms that tend to fade in and out, implying that somewhere it is all being said, somewhere all the implications are being followed, though as yet we may only be able to hear a small part of the process. In that idea musical logic and profound symbolism merge.

37. Ives *Essays* 33.

38. Editor Wayne Shirley told me that the idea for the percussion "Battery Unit" of the *Universe Symphony,* and its function and meaning, preceded the Fourth Symphony finale. If so, it is another case of a *Universe* idea being transferred into the Fourth.

39. Some of the *Universe* sketches may have disappeared into the possession of Henry and Sidney Cowell. John Kirkpatrick was never able to find out what happened to them—and access to the Cowell papers has been denied. The surviving sketches have been fascinatingly fleshed out in various versions by composer Larry Austin, but they inevitably contain more Austin than Ives.

40. Cowell and Cowell 201–3. The Cowells' description of the *Universe,* with "several different orchestras, with huge conclaves of singing men and women . . . to be placed about in valleys, on hillsides, and on mountain tops," and which is to be finished by other composers, seems to be the final version of the concept, which had grown steadily over the years since its conception in 1915, and arrived at that hyperbolic form after Ives had visited Whitmer's "Dramamount." The description in the *Memos,* dated from 1932, presents the *Universe* without the mountains and valleys, and at that point Ives still hoped to finish it himself: "I had this fairly well sketched out, but not completed . . . but hope to finish it out completely this summer" (106). How much was actually sketched is impossible to say since so much is lost, and what is left, as Kirkpatrick observes, is "tragically fragmentary."

41. I say Ives's achievement was unique in *Western* history because some of his music and its spirit reminds me, among other things, of the misty mountainscapes of Chinese painting going back over a thousand years. Likely his shaping of ambiguity and suggestiveness would not have been possible without the example of Debussy.

SEVENTEEN *Advances and Retreats*

1. Elliott Carter in Perlis Oral History 1/14.
2. Cowell and Cowell 103.
3. This is from Goossens's 1961 recollection, an interview in Wooldridge (212–13). Though Cowell and Cowell observe (103) that Goossens was not fond of the piece at the time, the conductor professed great admiration in 1961. He also said that Milhaud claimed the bulk of the rehearsal time for the concert, and that the players were miffed that Ives never showed his face in rehearsals. Goossens told Wooldridge that the orchestra ended up liking the *Comedy*. That's hard to believe, in 1927; it's rare enough in the 1990s. Goossens calls Ives "a charming and delightful man when he chose to be—and as shrewd as the devil." He was certainly right about that.
4. Perlis Oral History 2/32.
5. Composer Jerome Moross in Perlis Oral History 1/22.
6. Ives Papers Microfilm Addendum. Ives told the story of the men wishing he were as dead as Debussy to Lucille Fletcher, who began her prospective *New Yorker* piece with it.
7. *New York Times* 1/30/1927.
8. New York *Telegram* 1/31/1927.
9. Scrapbook, Ives Papers 40.
10. Cowell to CEI in Ives Papers 28/1.
11. CEI to Cowell in Ives Papers 28/1.
12. Mead "Amazing Mr. Cowell" 72.
13. Mead "Amazing Mr. Cowell" 65.
14. Letter of Sidney Cowell to Harmony Ives, 7/7/1949, in Ives Collection.
15. Mead *New Music* 20–21.
16. Mead "Amazing Mr. Cowell" 70.
17. Mead "Amazing Mr. Cowell" 69.
18. Cowell to CEI 3/27/1928 Ives Papers 28/1.
19. Mead "Cowell, Ives, and *New Music*" 558. Ives always asked that his donations be kept secret. His generosity was well known in general, but the details were not and may never be. Ives seems to have given away a staggering amount of money, to everyone from relatives and friends to composers he had never met. How secretive he was about it was shown in my 1988 interview with Nicolas Slonimsky: despite their long association Slonimsky had no idea Ives had given money to people including Schoenberg, Varèse, John J. Becker, Lou Harrison, and a long list of others. (That is, Slonimsky knew little of the transactions with which he had not been involved.)
20. Mead "Cowell, Ives, and *New Music*" 541.
21. From Herman Langinger's recollection in Perlis *Two Men* 9. The reason it took so long to find an engraver for the *Comedy* was presumably the music rather than the manuscript. By then the piece was in a clear copy that Goossens had used for the 1927 performance.
22. Quoted in Cowell and Cowell 121.
23. Furness in Ives Papers 4/22/1929. He also wrote in that letter, "[Elliott] Carter and I both agree that your wit (with practical applications) is equal to that of Tristram Shandy."
24. Cowell letter of 6/1/1929 in Ives Papers 28/1.
25. Corelli letter in Ives Papers 27/14.
26. Furness to Ives, Ives Papers 29/10.
27. Heyman in Ives Papers 30/7. She had written astutely before leaving for Paris, "This morning I have just seen through your 'Emerson' . . . I shall have to be a whole orchestra." In a letter from Paris she asks to be remembered to the Lady and the Fairy Child, meaning Harmony and Edith. Ives dispensed funds to Paris and Heyman responded with long, chatty letters. But she played *Emerson* relatively little, and that mostly in the dimly lit gatherings of her circle, which she called "Conferences." It was probably during these that she dispensed her spirit messages from Scriabin. For a while she had considerable success in Paris; Ezra Pound wrote a poem to her. Heyman remained chronically poor, though, and, as she wrote Ives during the thirties, was terrorized for years by a female companion.
28. Kirkpatrick to CEI, 10/7/1927, Ives Papers 30/13.
29. In the Perlis interviews (Oral History 2/32), Kirkpatrick describes his young self as a "spoiled brat." He adds, "It's only fairly recently that . . . I've learned what it is to practice." As performer, curator, and scholar, Kirkpatrick would spend much of his later life in the service of Ives and his music, a rare case of a superlative artist devoting himself to a greater one. But for someone who admired the liberal-unto-socialistic Ives, and who flirted with the occult early on and believed to the end in reincarnation, it is surprising to find that Kirkpatrick ended up on the far fringes of

the right wing. In later years he gave massive contributions to groups including the John Birch Society and the Lyndon Larouch organization. Kirkpatrick was also active in the C. S. Lewis Society and, partly from Lewis principles, resolutely turned away from friends who divorced. Kirkpatrick deserves a book to himself one of these days. Like the artist he championed so selflessly, John Kirkpatrick was quite a piece of work.

30. CEI to Henry Cowell 10/11/1928, Ives Papers 28/1.
31. Ives Papers 32/14.
32. CEI to Whitmer, 6/27/1927 (draft), Ives Papers 32/13.
33. Ives Papers 25/7. It's worth mentioning that in a nineteenth-century context, and in his hyperbolic way, Ives is saying much the same thing about female influence as Ann Douglas says in *The Feminization of American Culture.*
34. Ives Papers 24/13. I have not been able to identify "Prof. Ladd."
35. Gorer 85, 125.
36. CEI to Myrick in Ives Papers 30/18. In his reply Myrick says he doesn't take the pleasure in business that he used to, but he hasn't saved up enough for retirement as Charlie has, so he'll stick it out for a while. Myrick died in the saddle nearly forty years later.
37. Even though he never understood Charlie's music, Mike Myrick noticed his partner's growing reputation. In May 1930 he wrote, "From everything I hear you will go down in posterity not only as being a great insurance man but one of the great American composers so I would much rather have you work on your music than worry about coming down here and if you want to dedicate one of your symphonies to me, I will be much pleased as I would like to travel down that road with you" (Ives Papers 30/18). Thus the dedication of *The Fourth of July* to Myrick.
38. Slonimsky *Perfect Pitch* 113–14.
39. Slonimsky *Perfect Pitch* 116–17.
40. As per Henry Cowell postcard to CEI 5/20/1929 in Ives Papers 28/1.
41. Slonimsky *Perfect Pitch* 118.
42. Ives Papers 32/1.
43. James Sinclair (in Hitchcock and Perlis 75) describes the process of reworking *Three Places:* "New ideas laid right on top of old ones; simple rhythms complicated with rag ideas; single lines now doubled in fourths, now doubled in thirds, now complicated

with new lines on top of that; the bass line obfuscated with a half-step doubling or a major seventh." Elliott Carter observed some of this and later wondered in print when Ives's pieces got "their last shot of dissonance." (Thus Carter, perhaps deliberately, planted a seed of doubt about whether Ives was the prophet he seemed to be.) Meanwhile, since Ives did some of the revisions on old sketches and cut up some of the original fair copies to paste into the new score, he obliterated material that would have made later editors' lives considerably easier. It is often impossible to say which of the changes were new and sometimes debatable additions, and which were restorations of old ideas. (Ives also lost a mid-teen score of *The Housatonic* that apparently restored some of the complexity of the original sketches.)

44. Slonimsky *Perfect Pitch* 119.
45. Bigelow Ives in Perlis CIR 83.
46. CEI to Slonimsky 4/17/1930, Ives Papers 28/1.
47. Zuck 112. Among the most active leftist composers of the 1930s besides Cowell were Charles Seeger, Wallingford Riegger, Elie Siegmeister, and Aaron Copland. Zuck notes that Ruggles was briefly listed on the editorial staff of *New Masses,* but eventually seems to have become something of a reactionary.
48. *Eastern Underwriter* 9/19/1930.
49. CEI to Slonimsky 8/1930, Ives Papers 32/1.
50. Rossiter 224.
51. The Ives/Slonimsky correspondence is in the Ives Papers 32/1–4. It is also published in Slonimsky's *Music Since 1900.*
52. In Perlis CIR 151, Slonimsky says a radio station did broadcast the *Three Places* program. By mail Slonimsky made some last-minute rescoring requests. Speaking as he often did from his experience with theater orchestras, Ives said yes to one idea, but as to a horn doubling: "Perhaps if the violins and piano could pound the waltz out somewhat it might do—I used to find if 2 countertunes in about the same register were played by 2 brass instruments the contrast was sometimes lost. However, the quality of the trumpets seems different today than when I played one. But do anything in this or other places you think advisable [in other words, No]. . . . Will see you tomorrow—come right up."
53. Quoted in Cowell and Cowell 106. In Perlis CIR (150) Slonimsky called the perfor-

mance "excellent." ("Scrambling" is probably the more accurate.)

54. Slonimsky *Perfect Pitch* 120.
55. This is the report of old Poverty Flat roommate George Lewis, in a letter in the Ives Papers 31/4. As usual, Ives sent concert tickets to a collection of friends.
56. From a Lucille Fletcher draft of her article.
57. CEI to Whitmer, 1/13/1931. Ives Papers 32/14.
58. Slonimsky *Perfect Pitch* 120.
59. Slonimsky *Perfect Pitch* 121.
60. Slonimsky *Perfect Pitch* 121–22, and article "Working with Ives."
61. CEI to Slonimsky 5/8/1931, Ives Papers 32/2.
62. Slonimsky *Perfect Pitch* 122–23.
63. Quoted in Rossiter 227–28.
64. Quoted in Ives *Memos* 15.
65. Ives *Memos* 27.
66. Hale quoted in Ives *Memos* 13.
67. Quoted in Ives *Memos* 14.
68. Mead *Cowell's New Music* 135–36.
69. Scrapbook, Ives Papers 41.
70. Slonimsky *Perfect Pitch* 128.
71. Mead *Cowell's New Music* 420n. Bartók didn't hear the Ives set and never spoke of Ives to Slonimsky.
72. Ives Papers 31/11.
73. Ziffrin passim. She notes that Ruggles's bluster hid considerable self-doubts. He asked everyone for advice and probably took too much of it.
74. Article in Ives Papers 54/3.
75. Celebrated conductor Otto Klemperer was present for Slonimsky's Berlin concert and found himself fascinated by Ives. Klemperer tried for years, without success, to secure parts for the *Fourth of July*. Into the 1970s orchestras would be supplied, if they could get parts at all, with the same wretched ones Slonimsky used in the 1930s. (Wooldridge 222–23, 247.)
76. Scrapbook, Ives Papers 41.
77. Quoted in Slonimsky *Perfect Pitch* 130.
78. Scrapbook, Ives Papers 41.
79. The idea that Ives did not intend the *Memos* to be public is my own take on it, but John Kirkpatrick agreed with me.
80. Ives *Memos* 26.
81. Ives *Memos* 30.
82. Ives *Memos* 134–35. Ives was being deliberately ironic and provocative in placing Ruggles above Bach and Beethoven. He knew better, as plenty of his writings attest.
83. Burkholder "Fathers" 10.
84. Ives *Memos* 114.
85. Ives *Memos* 115.

86. CEI to Ruggles 9/8/1939, Ives Papers 31/11.
87. Maynard Solomon and others have accused Ives of creating an "Ives Myth" around himself. They are perhaps seeing Ives too much in contemporary terms, in the Andy Warhol model of the artist as above all a self-promoter and shaper of an Image. That was far from Ives's style. True, he had spent years writing advertising copy in the office and sometimes promoted himself astutely, making liberal use of his reviews. At other times he fled the spotlight in ways that damaged the progress of his music, and deprecated himself more often than he boasted. Anyway, a certain amount of self-mythologizing is universal; artists simply do that more than most, and more effectively, *because* they are artists. As Burkholder has written, Ives misrepresented himself as a self-created composer in the *Memos,* but still there is more in his memos accurate and informative than otherwise. Besides, his potshots at composers whom he knew, and admitted, were greater than he could hardly have been part of a sane and systematic plan to enhance his image. At least some of the potshots were honest differences of taste: Ives ran down Ravel and Stravinsky's *Firebird* because in *his* terms they were indeed "weak, morbid, and monotonous." I find that less provoking than the places where Ives denigrates his own heroes for any reason, neurotic or self-serving.
88. Ives *Memos* 58–59.
89. Ives *Memos* 78.
90. Ives *Memos* 91.
91. Ives *Memos* 78. He ends this section, "Henry Cowell and Gertrude Stein are both labeled modern. I don't call Henry modern because I don't like to nod, but he is—one of the best of them—and I don't call Gertrude Stein modern because she isn't—she's Victorian without the brains. She has something she wants to sell, so perhaps in that she may get in on 'modern.' " That may be the nicest thing Ives ever wrote about Cowell's music, and it isn't much. As to Stein's commercialism: Hemingway made the same point in *A Movable Feast.*
92. Ives *Memos* 239. To John Tasker Howard Ives wrote of the *Essays Before a Sonata,* "those were written some fifteen years ago, and I cannot agree with them all today." As he advised in the *Essays,* he refused to stand pat on ideas, but kept reaching.

E I G H T E E N   *Distant Bells*

1. Henry Bellamann and his wife lived in the Ives's New York house while they were away on the long European trip. After that, though, the friendship seemed to have languished.
2. Ives Papers 32/3.
3. Perlis Oral History 2/44.
4. Bell to Kirkpatrick in 1959, Ives Papers 27/7.
5. Ives Papers 45/11.
6. Ives Papers 32/3. When I interviewed Slonimsky in 1988 he did the same thing that Ives had teased him for in the thirties—pulled his old conducting reviews out of his pocket and showed them to me.
7. Perlis CIR 165.
8. Ives Papers 33/3.
9. Ives Papers 32/4.
10. Ives Papers 37/1.
11. Ives Papers 27/7.
12. Harmony interviews with John Kirkpatrick in Ives Papers Microfilm Addendum.
13. Perlis Oral History 2/45. Flexner's story about Edith and "Eve's apple" was on the interview tape but not in the transcript or in CIR. Edie also told Flexner she had once tried to drown herself in the bathtub, but was stopped by the thought that strangers would see her body. I don't entirely believe that; I suspect it was Edie's Ivesian imagination at work, though certainly she was isolated and often ill and depressed. From childhood on, loneliness was a steady theme in what she said and wrote. She told Flexner that her father "made her miserable by his anxiety when she went out on dates" (CIR 103), but Flexner added that there were no restrictions when he took Edie out. After her teens she returned to being a devoted daughter. (One of the first things she told George Tyler on meeting him was that her father was the greatest American composer.) Edie's charming hand-drawn map of Redding survives, and her paintings on the walls of "Deac's House" in Redding.
14. Ives Papers 28/3. In a short letter of the same month Cowell writes that Horatio Parker's widow had asked for Ives's address. There is no extant letter from Mrs. Parker.
15. Scrapbook, Ives Papers 41.
16. Slonimsky interview 11/16/1988. Slonimsky said E. Robert Schmitz had tried to connect him with the Cincinnati Symphony; a committee from the orchestra came to Boston to interview him for the conductor's position.
17. Slonimsky *Perfect Pitch* 140–41, and in our 1988 interview. Slonimsky told me he was literally yanked from the podium of Hollywood Bowl after the first movement of the Beethoven *Eroica*. I wonder about that. When I observed that it must have been a horrendous experience, he said, "Not at all. I felt I was part of a vanguard marching inexorably into the future." Then he added, with anguish undimmed after nearly sixty years, "*How* could you get reviews like that and not be successful?"
18. Perlis CIR 117.
19. Around the time the Iveses returned from Europe in 1933 there was a reception in New York for Arnold Schoenberg, who had fled the Nazis and come to America to teach. To everyone's surprise Ives showed up for the occasion. Years later Schoenberg recalled how frail Ives looked—and that he had a check in hand (Yates "American Composer"). Perhaps Schoenberg's famous words on Ives that begin "There is a great man living in this country—a composer" have much to do with that occasion, when the obviously ailing Ives appeared to hand the refugee a contribution. In March 1935 Schoenberg conducted his *Kammersymphonie #1* and *Pierrot Lunaire* at a New Music Society concert in San Francisco, and Cowell surely spoke to him of Ives around then. As noted, though, it is not clear exactly how aware of Ives's music Schoenberg was, and it is hard to imagine that he thought much of it. (Schoenberg's famous words begin *great man*, not *great composer*.) Peter Yates recalled sitting next to Schoenberg for a performance of *The Unanswered Question* at some point; Lou Harrison wrote of showing Schoenberg scores by Ives in *New Music* (probably the *Comedy* and/or *Fourth of July*); and Schoenberg probably heard Ives at some of their mutual seventieth-birthday concerts in California during the 1940s. But it seems Schoenberg never said anything publicly about Ives's music as such—nor Ives about his. Ives financed some Schoenberg printing in *New Music* and performances at Evenings on the Roof.
20. Article in Scrapbook, Ives Papers 41.
21. Perlis CIR 166.
22. Elie Siegmeister letter to Swafford, 9/23/1990.

23. Quoted in Zuck 95.
24. Quoted in Rossiter 273. Of course, Aaron Copland's Americana pieces are the most famous of his works but are not the whole spectrum. Toward the end of his life he returned to the severe style of his youth, by way of serial pieces.
25. The Americana composers did concur with Wagner in at least one dimension—as fervent nationalists.
26. Kirkpatrick letter in Ives Papers 27/14.
27. Perlis CIR xv.
28. Perlis CIR 214.
29. Kirkpatrick in Ives *Memos* 249
30. Ives Papers 30/13.
31. Ives Papers 32/4. Besides dealing with the complex notational problems in *Three Places* (when Ives focused in on practical matters he could be quite astute), typical of their exchanges was a conductor's note Slonimsky wanted. He had learned to conduct the polymeters in *Three Places* and similar scores simultaneously, a different tempo in each hand. Being inordinately proud of that (for the rest of his life he would demonstrate at the drop of a hat), Slonimsky wanted a note in the published score to suggest using the technique. Ives patiently replied, "Your conductor's note is 'well put'—for some conductors it will be a help and others it will . . . mix them up so they will 'sidestep' the whole job . . . there are [some] I wouldn't like to have think . . . that I underrate their intelligence—for example Goossens." And so forth, gently and digressively, but being translated indicating: absolutely no to the suggestion. In this period Slonimsky mentioned that Schoenberg told him he had seen Ives scores in *New Music* and wanted to see the *Three Places* proofs. Again, there is no indication of whether he did, or what he thought.
32. Besides arranging for the concert where *Booth* premiered, Cowell supervised the song's engraving for the 1935 *New Music* publication of *Eighteen Songs*. Due to the journal's chronic slapdashedness, that issue actually contained nineteen songs. Later *New Music* would publish *The Gong on the Hook and Ladder* as *Calcium Light Night*.
33. This is from Lou Harrison's description of Pazmor in Perlis Oral History 2/36. She seems to have cut quite a figure. Harrison describes her as "six feet six or seven feet" tall and "really quite beautiful, in a grand and glamorous way." Pazmor regarded the experience with Ives as a high point of her

career (which never really took off). She wrote him in 1946: "Though I may never see you face to face, dear Mr. Ives, I shall always think of you and Mrs. Ives as friends. Have you not brought me untold riches?" (Ives Papers 31/3).
34. Ives Papers 28/4.
35. Again, from Ives's income tax records in the Ives Papers. Harmony had income of her own, probably from investments Ives made in the 1920s, and those returns have not survived. Hers probably added about a third more to their income. Their first joint tax return, from 1948, shows $13,529 before deductions—just over $100,000 1991. For some time Ives refused to take tax deductions for contributions because he considered them every man's duty, but finally his son-in-law persuaded him that taking deductions would provide more money to contribute. Likewise, in later years Ives's demand that publishers charge no royalties gave way to normal contracts, but he usually assigned the royalties to other people (especially Cowell and Harrison) and organizations (especially Arrow Press).
36. As per CEI letter to Cowell 4/30/1934, Ives Papers 28/5.
37. Rossiter 253.
38. Carl Ruggles was not in a forgiving frame of mind in those days. Not long before, Pan-American's Berlin publisher J. C. Adler had been forced out of business by the Nazis (Ziffrin 136). In the confusion, Adler's copy of *Sun-Treader* disappeared. Not caring about the publisher's personal problems, Ruggles wrote Ives a brutal account: "Did you hear about the dreadful time I've had with the Sun-treader? How that damned Jew Adler busted up, and the fine score Henry took over was either lost or stolen" (Ives Papers 31/11 and Mead *Cowell's New Music* 296). As Ruggles doubtless counted on, Ives started sending money for a new score, engraved by Herman Langinger, which Ruggles made far more expensive with his incessant revisions (Ziffrin 138). In the end Ruggles never heard *Sun-Treader,* his masterpiece, played live. There was a nasty streak of anti-Semitism in several Pan-American composers. Ruggles wrote Cowell in that period, "I agree with [Weiss] and Salzedo that it is a great mistake to have that filthy bunch of Juillard [sic] Jews in the Pan American. They are cheap, without dignity, and with little or no talent" (quoted in Ziffrin 136). Appar-

ently Cowell did not disagree. I emphasize
that Ives was not the least anti-Semitic; I
suspect he dealt with Ruggles's prejudices
the same way he dealt with the dirty
jokes—by quietly letting it be known that
he did not like that sort of thing.
39. Rossiter 253–54.
40. Ives Papers 28/5.
41. The demise of the Pan-American Association ended Slonimsky's last real conducting
opportunities. He would go on to a career
of lexicography (long proprietor of *Baker's
Biographical Dictionary of Musicians,* among
other books), occasional composer of musical ironies (including *Möbius Strip Tease*),
occasional theorist (he coined the familiar
technical term "pandiatonicism"), inspiration of John Coltrane (Slonimsky's book
on scale forms was the great saxophonist's
bible) and of Frank Zappa (who was generally amused by the aged but still puckish
Slonimsky). Varèse, after the collapse of
the Pan-American, entered a period of depression and creative fallowness that lasted
into the fifties.
42. Ives Papers 30/13.
43. Ives Papers 28/5.
44. In the month after Ives's melancholic letter
to Cowell, old friend Clifton Furness
wrote, "That was a splendid little visit that
mother and I had with you. . . . Especially
our walk through the woodlot to the beech
tree with you lingers in mind" (Ives Papers
29/10). His father Chalmers, a sort of grizzled flower child of whom Ives had been
fond (and who hit up Ives for money behind his son's back), had recently died. Furness continued in his letter, "Father
mentioned to me particularly about the last
time he was at Redding, that he was so glad
to see the 'Old Boy' Brahms still dancing
on the back of the piano when you played."
He probably means that the picture of
Brahms that hung on the piano shook as
Ives pounded the keys. (If Deac had been
Ives's petit Thoreau, Chalmers Furness was
the petit Bronson Alcott.) Clifton was
wearing out after years teaching in Boston
and living with his mother and working
at his mammoth Whitman biography that
never got finished. Though he and Ives visited rarely these days, they retained their
affection and their memories of what Furness called the "high bold talk and music-
making" of the old days.
45. Perlis CIR 185–86. In January 1936 another Ives entered print when Moss's book

The Ark and the Dove was published. It is a
history of early Catholics in Maryland and
their contribution to religious liberty.
Judge J. Moss Ives may have been more
conservative than his brother, but he
shared the same love of democracy, the
same lack of prejudice, and the same concern for giving people their due. His book
has recently been republished.
46. Ives Papers 30/1.
47. Harrison in Hitchcock and Perlis 81 and
Perlis CIR 198.
48. Both HTI letters to Charlotte Ruggles are
in Ives Papers 31/11.
49. Hicks 95–98. Cowell was never comfortable with his sexuality and refused to seek
moral support from fellow homosexual
composers. At one point he even blamed
his inclinations on his mother's feminism
(Hicks 105). Slonimsky told me Cowell remained homosexual after his marriage,
though presumably expressed it in less
risky forms. One should note that the story
of Cowell's arrest as told in Slonimsky's
Perfect Pitch is probably inaccurate—
Hicks's documentation is more convincing.
50. Lou Harrison in Hicks 105n.
51. In our 1988 interview Slonimsky said, "As
far as I'm concerned, the only blot on Ives's
record is that he deserted Henry after the
trial." I can understand that opinion but
don't agree. Ives's prejudices against homosexuality were not only typical of his
time but deeply tangled in his own insecurities. Aging and ill as he was, in his social
context (by no means Bohemian), and
prudish as he had always been, it is hard to
imagine Ives could have escaped his prejudices more than he did. Besides, Cowell
was guilty of what our age calls sexual
abuse, a matter on which everyone has had
their consciousness raised in recent years.
Given all that, it is astounding that Ives and
Cowell were ever reconciled. It is also true
that Ives did help from early on to get
Henry paroled. In the Ives Papers (31/12)
there is a letter from Wallingford Riegger
to Ives, dated 6/12/1937: "Thank you for
signing the petition. We now have all the
composers that count and a lot of other
prominent names, so that I hope it will
come to something." That petition was
probably an early attempt to get Cowell
out of prison.
52. Ives papers 32/4. It is unlikely Ives sent
this letter to Slonimsky as drafted. There is

no CEI letter from that year published in Slonimsky's collection in *Music Since 1900*. The draft also contained some of Ives's habitual slants on Arturo Toscanini: "that old stop-watch, clicking machine, little metronome 'Arthur Toscaninny'. . . . He makes Beethoven an emasculated lily-pad." (He may have heard Toscanini on radio.) In July Harmony wrote Slonimsky, speaking mildly given her anxiety, "I get a little discouraged about him tho' he got a very good report from the doctor. . . . He has been working over his Browning score . . . & it has been a lot of work to get it in shape even to be copied. He can work only for a short time at a time as his eyes allow little strain. . . . It wasn't lack of audience & appreciation that made Mr. Ives stop composing. It just happened—the War & the complete breakdown in health. He had worked tremendously hard in his quarry all those years & exhausted the vein I suppose. I am always hoping he may open up a new vein & he may—his ideas are by no means exhausted, but there are the physical disabilities to be contended with. He is such a wonderful person—he has such strength of character and will & sense" (Ives Papers 32/4).

53. Quoted in Slonimsky *Perfect Pitch* 165.

54. Hicks 109. By 1940 Cowell's music classes in San Quentin had over 1500 students, and he conducted a band and orchestra. Besides his solo recitals, he concertized with a fellow inmate who was a virtuoso violinist and writer of bad checks.

55. Mead "Cowell, Ives, and *New Music*" 556. Ives, Becker, and others associated with *New Music* joined in 1939 to press cutbacks and reorganization on director Gerald Strang, who finally agreed to drop the expensive Orchestral Series and use the American Music Center in New York to distribute publications.

56. Perlis *Two Men* 23.

57. Characteristic of Becker's letters to Ives in those days is one of 12/2/1937 saying his wife and son are both in the hospital, and thanking Ives for helping with the mortgage. Ives's letters to the Beckers tend to dwell on his miseries as well: 1/26/1938, "Have been on a down slant for most 2 months. I wanted to send a line at Christmas—But haven't been able to write—breathe or get up & do anything right. . . . That g—d— sap! who said you were a defeatist . . . is a musical half-wit . . . you are

a great composer—to Hell with the lily-ears! Please let the enclosed go toward publishing your 'Sonata.' " (Both letters in Ives Papers 27/5.)

58. Ives Papers 30/4. Ives went to a neighbor's house to hear Herrmann's broadcast of the Fugue and afterward wrote thanks. Later the Iveses listened, on their aged record player, to a recording made of the Fugue performance. In a letter to Herrmann Ives explains the difficulty of finding wooden(!) needles for the machine and the hearing distortion that afflicts him when he listens to it. Finally he curtly says, "The fugue was well played." Herrmann arranged and performed both the first and third movements of the Fourth. Despite Herrmann's assurances to Vivian Perlis, years later, that Ives had sanctioned his arrangements, it's hard to imagine Ives was happy about the Hollywood treatment. In theory Ives was all for creative collaboration from his performers; in practice he was rarely pleased with the results. His criticism of friends tended to be so kindly and oblique that it was sometimes taken for praise.

59. Directly after the premiere, Engel's group sang *Psalm 67* on a nationwide CBS broadcast (Kirkpatrick Datebook); their recording of it would come out on Columbia in 1939.

60. In a Kirkpatrick interview (11/1988) he observed that when they first met "Ives seemed to me like a man who had had a couple of strokes"—that from the perspective of a serious stroke of Kirkpatrick's own. It's not clear whether he meant Ives's signs were more physical or mental. Probably both. The only specific symptom he mentioned was that Ives's rhythmic sense at the piano had gone a bit slack (noticeable in Ives's recordings). Once as Kirkpatrick was leaving, Ives "burst out with something like, 'Well, maybe you think I like this kind of idleness, this doing nothing,' and it went on for about three or four minutes, all about how awful it was to be consigned to this inactivity."

61. Perlis CIR 220. Ives never played again for Kirkpatrick either. The pianist indelibly remembered a "deft, flitting kind of playing, often seeming to be all over the keyboard all at once." While Ives ran down his recordings, Kirkpatrick said they sound very much like what he remembered of Ives's playing in person.

62. The final text of the FDR letter and memo-

randum is in Ives *Essays* 217–24. The drafts are in Ives Papers 25/4.

63. HTI to Charlotte Ruggles, Ives Papers 31/1. At that time Carl was in the hospital with a serious prostate flare-up.

64. Kirkpatrick Datebook.

65. Ives Papers 27/5. In London Ives wrote to Sir Norman Angell, winner of the Nobel Peace Prize and prophet of international relations, asking for a meeting. As usual with Ives's approaches to the famous, nothing came of it.

66. Travel diary, Ives Papers 45/12.

67. Perlis CIR 104.

68. Ives Papers 30/15.

69. Ives Papers 27/5.

70. Ives Papers 27/7.

71. From Gilman's obituary, *Herald Tribune* 9/10/1939.

72. Ives Papers 29/12.

73. Kirkpatrick interview 6/1988.

74. *Herald Tribune* 1/21/1939. Nine months after writing the review Lawrence Gilman died. Replying to the Iveses' letter of condolence, his daughter wrote, "You both know, I am sure, that the experience of studying and hearing Mr. Ives' scores was one of the notable events of last winter for father, and you treasure, as I do, the remembrance of his deep enjoyment of it" (Ives Papers 29/12).

75. Rossiter makes the point (283) that if the idiom of the *Concord* did not suit the time, it still had some appeal because of its Americanness. This was the decade when Van Wyck Brooks's *Flowering of New England,* which alerted the country to the Concord literary tradition, became a best-seller.

76. I am perhaps dwelling oppressively on Ives's health, but doing it deliberately for two reasons. First, his health dwelt oppressively on him and is thus part of the story. Second, tracking Ives's state of health and mind bears on how future editors and performers should view his later tinkerings with scores, especially the *Concord.* Yet as his bursts of energy and lucidity in later life show—for example, the *Alcotts* recording—we can't simply dismiss everything Ives did after any given year. Like it or not, we have to decide on things case by case, and allow for different opinions. See the appendix: "Editing Ives."

77. *Time* 1/30/1939.

78. Ives Papers 30/1.

79. Carter, "The Case of Mr. Ives," in *Writings.* As shown, it *is* usually possible to discover when Ives's innovations developed, and

they were quite early on. It surprises me to find Carter hinting what, as a musician, he knew could not be true: that Ives's pieces somehow began relatively conventionally and were "modernized" after the fact by dissonances and polyrhythm. (Carter's words, of course, are the foundation of Maynard Solomon's questioning of Ives's integrity.) Carter observes that it was really the "Romantic flamboyant gestures" of the *Concord* that most irritated him at first hearing. In the original review, though, there is little about that issue at all, but rather an attack on the quality of the music and on Ives's position as a prophet. As late as Perlis's interview in the 1970s, Carter was still taking potshots at Ives's imagination and competence.

80. Carter told Vivian Perlis (Oral History 1/14), "From that time on I never saw him again, because I just felt as though I had treated him in a way that I wouldn't myself ever want to be treated. I felt very badly about that." Sometimes in later years Carter would spot Ives on the New York commuter train and wait to say hello just before his stop.

81. Much of Carter's problem with Ives's music, then and later, was honestly aesthetic. In his younger days Carter was writing neoclassic works, and like much of his generation he found Ives sloppy, overcomplex, incoherent. But even in Carter's celebrated avant-garde period that owed so much to the technical and spiritual influence of Ives, he would continue to alternate admiration with rejection, a peculiar and interesting relationship with the composer who taught him perhaps more than anyone else. Among other things, Carter has never understood or accepted the whole idea of Ives quoting other music.

82. Ives Papers 36/9.

83. During the same period, Bernard Herrmann wrote his cantata *Moby Dick* and dedicated it to Ives. It was premiered in 1940 by the New York Philharmonic. That may have been the zenith of Herrmann's career as a concert composer, though he would remain active as a conductor. Herrmann wrote several classic scores for Hitchcock films, including *Vertigo, North by Northwest,* and *Psycho.* In all Herrmann wrote sixty-one film scores, beginning memorably with *Citizen Kane* in 1940 and ending with Scorsese's *Taxi Driver* in 1976. Little of his film work shows any overt Ivesian influence.

84. Perlis CIR 169.
85. Ives wrote Lucille Fletcher through Edie, "Some of 'his bad habits' father says as cussing the 'old ladies and nice musicians' are usually misunderstood & just as well left out in the cold." (Maybe Harmony had a part in that.) For another change, when Fletcher wrote that Ives was "the beginning of a new cult," Ives changed it to "a new wide & indigenous movement." (He meant a spiritual and political awakening.) Sections of the Cowells' Ives biography are closely based on the Fletcher article, which in its later drafts had a good deal of Ives's own words—not as quotes, but sections that he wrote imitating Fletcher's style. Thus the Cowells' Ives book may contain sentences actually written by Ives himself. It would make an interesting study, certainly beyond this book, to trace material from Ives through Fletcher to the Cowells. Another sidelight: Fletcher wrote a novel based on Ives's life. No publisher was interested.
86. Perlis CIR 170.
87. Charles Ives Tyler told me that when his parents returned to Redding after their honeymoon the tennis court beside the barn had disappeared, and nothing was ever said about it. Probably Charlie and Harmony decided they were too old to cope with grandchildren playing tennis. That nothing was said typifies their Victorian sense of discretion.
88. Perlis CIR 81–82.
89. One of Harmony's several letters to Kirkpatrick prodding him about the *Concord* ends, "Will you please send the copy with Mr. Ives corrections as soon as possible—it really is rather vexatious you know." That's as furious as one ever finds Harmony.
90. Kirkpatrick interview 11/1988. As always, *Emerson* remained the biggest editing problem, since Ives never saw it as a finished work anyway, never played it the same way twice, and so never stopped tinkering with it.
91. Perlis CIR 186.
92. Some highlights of Babitz and Dahl's tragicomic ten-year odyssey attempting to edit the Third Violin Sonata for *New Music:* 11/1940 Ives writes them that he wants no royalties and that they and *New Music* should receive all fees (so far so good); 9/1941 he approves Babitz's editing and bowing, asks him to correct the first set of proofs; 2/1942 Ives and Harmony both

ill, he can't find a sheet with revisions; 8/1943, after an editing process "ten times" harder than expected, Dahl writes Cowell that the "final" score (by a copyist actually named C. Sharpe Minor) is unusable and will have to be redone; 6/1944 the engraver's proofs are ready, but Ives rejects the respellings of his accidentals and demands at least the beginning be redone (which must have made Babitz and Dahl very tired); 12/1946 Frank Wigglesworth of *New Music* writes that the final score is on its way to the engraver; 1/1947 engraver goes broke, score goes to copyist Pagano, who takes until November; the sonata finally emerges from limbo in the Merion Music edition of 1951 (Ives Papers 27/2).
93. Rossiter 292.
94. Mead "Amazing Mr. Cowell" 83.
95. Ives Papers 28/6.
96. Sidney Cowell had a miscarriage in 1942 and they never had children (Feder *Ives* 345).
97. The first Szigeti radio performance of the Fourth Sonata may have been on WQXR on April 15, 1942. It was prefaced by Cowell, who afterward apologized to Ives that he did not get in mention of the People's World Union as Ives had requested (Ives Papers 28/6).
98. Among other things, John Kirkpatrick tried to convince Szigeti to play the fast movements of the Fourth Sonata a little slower, but Szigeti resisted. Ives finally did make himself listen to Szigeti's recording and wrote a letter of thanks: "you caught the spirit of the music & of those outdoor days—wonderfully" (Ives Papers 32/8).
99. Perlis CIR 210.
100. Ives's version of "They Are There!" released in 1974 on Columbia is a splicing of two takes. Mary Howard's recordings are the most serviceable of the surviving ones; many of the others have been damaged or lost. Ives had copies made of some of the Howard material to send out to performers. She remembers Eugene Ormandy was to get one, which probably indicates that Ives sent records to Koussevitzky and other conductors of major orchestras. The effort got him nowhere.
101. I'm guessing here that Ives began work on the "War Song March" before the League of Composers commission, but it could have been the other way around.
102. Ives Papers 24/14. These prose sketches

concerning the "War Song March"/
"They Are There!" overlap with many
from the World War II period about the
People's World Union and other Ivesian
themes.

103. Ives Papers 30/12. This is a CEI draft of
a letter to Koussevitzky. In our interview,
Slonimsky said he went through all Koussevitzky's papers and did not find this letter from Ives, so it may never have been
sent.

104. Ives Papers 36/3.

105. Ives Papers 35/4.

106. There are many brochures and articles
about the United Nations and world government organizations in Ives's papers,
and he contributed to them.

107. Another Ives effort during the war was to
assume honorary presidency of an organization called the Society of Native American Composers. His letter to the mem-
bership in 1942 sounded his political
themes: "Perhaps music can be of help in
giving definite expression to a universal
plan which may be called a 'People's New
Free World.'" (Characteristically, he
kept revising the name of his imaginary
organization.) He soon heard rumors,
though, of racism and anti-Semitism in
the organization. Alarmed, he set to work
on a letter that began, in one draft, "I have
just recently heard that the . . . Society
is . . . against all Jews—and also in some
underneath way is pro Fascist. I can't believe this is so—but if it is, I must send my
resignation as President immediately. . . .
This kind of medieval group prejudices
. . . are among the greatest curses in the
world today. . . . Also, I hear that the Society is prejudiced against the negro composer, which I hope is unfounded—for it
is the concern of a society of music to hear
the 'color' of the composers tones—and
not the color of his skin." Society officers
Henri Lloyd Clement and Adolph Weiss
hastened to write Ives reassuring letters.
Though there was an anti-Semitic under-
tone to those replies, Ives declared himself
satisfied. All the same, his relations with
the Society appear to have ended around
then (Ives Papers 35/5).

108. A typical Ives response to Yates's *Concord*
campaign for his wife is a letter of 11/3/
1944 (Ives Papers 32/18): "Mr I doesn't
know just what he ought to say now. . . .
He is very grateful to Mrs Yates kind &
generous interest in suggesting making
the records. . . . We think one of the de-

lays in Mr K's recording [is his resistance
to the revisions]. . . . Emerson in the 1st
Edition—may stand more as under late
Autumn or winter landscape & in 2nd
reflecting more of a summer impression.
Anyway Emerson is great enough to have
more than one kind of landscape." And
thus Ives dissolves his refusal into a contemplation of the music. Yates was still
angling to get Ives to agree to a Mullen
recording as late as 1950—by then a nine-
year crusade that Ives never did approve.
Far from holding it against Ives, Yates remained a fervent admirer; there is an extensive and important exchange of letters
between them. In 1944, Yates's Evenings
on the Roof mounted a series of Ives and
Schoenberg concerts to mark the seventi-
eth birthdays of both (Schoenberg probably heard some Ives at that point). When
they were planning that season Yates
wrote Ives thinking he was younger than
Schoenberg. The draft reply by Ives,
whom history has assumed knew little of
the musical world: "I am not a year
younger than Mr. Schoenberg—but only
a few days. . . . Mr I says that he has nothing against Schoenberg for beating him
by 37 days."

109. Cowell and Cowell 113.

110. In our interview (11/1988) John Kirkpatrick said that the original Ives Society
of the forties was the idea of John Mc-
Clure at Columbia Records.

111. Ives Papers 27/10. Part of Ives's objection to the Ives Society was, as the letter
implies, a characteristically generous desire to protect the feelings of friends like
Ruggles and Becker, after whom no one
was proposing to name societies.

112. Elliott Carter and critic Paul Rosenfeld
actually planned to write a book on Ives
together, but that idea was ended by Rosenfeld's death in 1946 (Lederman 48).

113. Ives framed the certificate from the National Institute in his study, where it still
resides. The purple-and-gold lapel pin,
however, is currently in the Ives Papers
still attached to its card. The next year he
apparently turned down a medal from the
Institute, his draft letter beginning, "I
don't want any D— gold meddle!" (He
did not, of course, begin the real letter
that way.) He proposed Roy Harris for
the medal instead—probably in gratitude
for Harris seconding Ives's Ruggles nom-
ination (Ives Papers 35/3).

114. As usual when a piece was gearing up for

performance or publication, Ives began to tinker when Harrison picked up the Third Symphony. It was then that Ives recalled the shadow lines in the old score (his memory for manuscripts was extraordinary, even in old age). He wrote Carter, who was helping Harrison with the Third, that "the first way seemed better." That is why editor Kenneth Singleton was obliged to put the shadow lines back in the Third (as optional parts in small notes). As I've said, in my opinion they don't work.

115. Reviews in Ives Papers 54/7.
116. Ives Papers 35/11.
117. The first record of Harrison's breakdown in the Ives Papers (30/3) is a letter from Harrison's friend John Cage, who asks Ives to help pay the hospital bills. Ives had already planned to give Harrison half of the Pulitzer money, but he probably added to it. Harrison got out of the hospital in July 1947. There are a couple of other letters from Cage to Ives, entirely about Harrison and nothing about music. In his famous years Cage occasionally said vaguely positive things about Ives but kept his distance—probably because he saw the Romantic background of Ives's music that despite some surface similarities was far from his own aesthetic.
118. Lang's thoughtful, ambivalent, and interesting review is in *Saturday Review* 6/1/1946. The copy of it in the Ives Papers has sections bracketed in Ives's hand.
119. From Mrs. Burton Twichell in Perlis Oral History 2/40.
120. Harrison in *Listen* 11/1946.
121. Davis to CEI in Ives Papers 29/1.
122. The familiar photo of Ives standing in profile in front of a window was taken during the Bridgeport *Herald* interview after he was awarded the Pulitzer Prize.
123. Ives Papers 31/12. Ives's letter about the Pulitzer shows how concerned he was to protect Ruggles's feelings.
124. Ives to Becker via Edith 9/14/1947: "Daddy says to tell you that the enclosed check is not from him, but from that 'ole Pulitzer feller' " (Ives Papers 26/5).
125. Perlis CIR 205.
126. Cowell and Cowell 133–34.
127. Perlis CIR 43.
128. Interview with Charles Ives Tyler, August 1987.
129. Cowell and Cowell 124.
130. According to John Kirkpatrick, the likely reason Ives trimmed the margins off many of his manuscripts was not, as Maynard Solomon has suggested, that he was trying to hide incriminating dating evidence but simply that he trimmed them to fit into drawers—perhaps the new ones at Redding. Ives did say on one occasion that he had removed marginalia from one page because it might be taken amiss by the complainees.
131. Ives Papers 31/12.
132. Ives Papers 31/12.
133. Cowell and Cowell 218.
134. Ives Papers 27/5.
135. Perlis Oral History 1/27.
136. *New York Times Magazine* 10/23/1949.
137. Harmony to Dr. Joslin, Ives Papers 34/14.
138. Ives Papers 28/7.
139. Perlis CIR 117.
140. Ives Papers 31/12.
141. Cowell and Cowell 128.
142. Cowell and Cowell 135.
143. Cowell and Cowell 135. Harmony wrote Bernstein after the premiere of the Second, "I have been familiar with it—in snatches—for forty years and more and to hear the whole performed at last was a big event in my life. . . . It took him back so to his father and his youth that he had tears in his eyes. [In fact she was not with him then.] You will be interested to know that his comment on the allegro movements was 'too slow'—otherwise he was satisfied. He thanks you from the bottom of his heart" (Ives Papers 28/8).
144. Ives Papers 30/8.
145. Perlis CIR 98.
146. Secretary Christine Loring in Perlis Oral History 2/49.
147. Ives Papers 32/18.
148. Perlis CIR 151.
149. Ives Papers Microfilm Addendum.
150. Kirkpatrick Datebook.
151. Ives Papers 51.
152. Ives Papers 28/7.
153. Kirkpatrick "Envoi" in Catalogue 278–79.
154. Ives Papers 29/5. On the Roosevelt Hospital certificate the cause of death is "pulmonary edema due to arteriosclerotic and hypertensive heart disease with probable myocardial infarction."
155. Cowell and Cowell 207.

Bibliography

Adams, Henry. *The Education of Henry Adams*. Boston: Houghton Mifflin, 1973.

Allen, Gay Wilson, ed. *A William James Reader*. Boston: Houghton-Mifflin, 1971.

Andrews, Kenneth R. *Nook Farm: Mark Twain's Hartford Circle*. Cambridge: Harvard University Press, 1950.

Bailey, James Montgomery. *History of Danbury, Conn. 1684–1896*. New York: Burr Printing House, 1896 (reprint).

Ballantine, Christopher. "Charles Ives and the Meaning of Quotation in Music." *Musical Quarterly* 65, vol. 2 (April 1979):167.

Banfield, Stephen. " 'Too Much of Albion'? Mrs. Coolidge and Her British Connections." *American Music* 4, no. 1 (spring 1986).

Barnes, Don. "As I See It: The Lion in Winter." *Burrelle's*, November 13, 1989.

Baron, Carol K. "Dating Charles Ives's Music: Facts and Fictions." *Perspectives of New Music* 28 (winter 1990).

Bierman, June, and Barbara Toohey. *The Diabetic's Book*. Los Angeles: Jeremy P. Tarcher, 1990.

Block, Geoffrey. *Charles Ives: A Bio-Bibliography*. New York: Greenwood Press, 1988.

Bloom, Dr. Arnold, *Diabetes Explained*. Aylesbury, England: Medical and Technical Publishing Co. Ltd., 1972.

Brodhead, Thomas M. "The Significance of *The Celestial Railroad*, 'Phantasy' for Solo Piano By Charles Ives." Unpublished article, 1993. (Published in *American Music* 12, no. 4 [1994], as "Ives's *Celestial Railroad* and his Fourth Symphony.")

Brooks, Van Wyck. *The Flowering of New England*. New York: E. P. Dutton, 1940.

Burbank, Richard. *Twentieth Century Music*. London: Thames and Hudson, 1984.

Burkholder, Peter. "The Evolution of Charles Ives's Music: Aesthetics, Quotation, Technique." Ph.D. dissertation, University of Chicago, 1983.

———. *Charles Ives: The Ideas Behind the Music*. New Haven: Yale University Press, 1985.

———. "Charles Ives and His Fathers: A Response to Maynard Solomon." *Newsletter* of the Institute for Studies in American Music, 18, no. 1 (November 1988).

———. "Charles Ives the Avant-Gardist, Charles Ives the Traditionalist." In *bericht über das Internationale Symposion "Charles Ives und die amerikanische Musiktradition bis zur Gegenwart" Köln 1988*. Regensburg: Gustav Bosse Verlag, 1990.

Burpee's *The Story of Connecticut—Personal and Family Records*, vol. IV. New York: The American Historical Company, 1939.

Bushman, Richard L. *From Puritan to Yankee: Character and the Social Order in Connecticut 1690–1765*. Cambridge: Harvard University Press, 1967.

Canby, Henry Seidel. *Alma Mater: The Gothic Age of the American College*. New York: Farrar & Rinehart, 1936.

Carter, Elliott. "The Case of Mr. Ives." Reprinted in *"Modern Music* in Retrospect," *Perspectives of New Music* 2, no. 2 (spring–summer 1964).

———. "Documents of a Friendship with Ives." *Parnassus: Poetry in Review*, spring/summer 1975.

Catton, Bruce. Liner notes to Columbia recording of Civil War songs, *The Union*.

Chase, Gilbert. *America's Music: From the Pilgrims to the Present*, rev. 3rd ed. Urbana: University of Illinois Press, 1987.

Clough, Shepard B. *A Century of American Life Insurance: A History of the Mutual Life Insurance Company of New York, 1843–1943.* New York: Columbia University Press, 1946.

Columbia University. *Complete Home Medical Guide.* New York: Crown, 1985.

———. *Complete Home Guide to Mental Health.* New York: Henry Holt, 1992.

Commager, Henry Steele. *The American Mind: An Interpretation of American Thought and Character Since the 1880s.* New Haven: Yale University Press, 1950.

Corsini, Raymond J., ed. *Encyclopedia of Psychology.* New York: John Wiley & Sons, 1994.

Cowell, Henry, and Sidney Cowell. *Charles Ives and His Music.* London: Oxford University Press, rev. paperback ed., 1969 (first ed., 1955).

Davis, Thomas B., Jr. *Chronicles of Hopkins Grammar School 1660–1935.* New Haven: Cunningham Press, 1938.

Devlin, William E. *We Crown Them All: An Illustrated History of Danbury.* Woodland Hills, Calif.: Windsor Publications, 1984.

———. "Danbury News Man." Danbury *News-Times,* August 13, 1987.

———. "Lyman Brewster, The City's Architect." Danbury *News-Times,* September 10, 1986.

Diabetes Mellitus, 7th ed. Indianapolis: Lilly Research Laboratories, 1976.

Dickens, Charles. *American Notes.* New York: Fromm International Publishing, 1985.

Dolger, Henry, M.D., and Bernard Seeman. *How to Live with Diabetes.* New York: Pyramid Books, 1966.

Douglas, Ann. *The Feminization of American Culture.* New York: Anchor Press, 1988.

Durgy, Evelyn S., ed. *As We Were: A Pictorial History of Old Danbury,* 2nd ed. Danbury, Conn.: Scott-Fanton Museum, 1979.

Eiseman, David. "George Ives as Theorist: Some Unpublished Documents." *Perspectives of New Music* 14, no. 1 (fall-winter 1975): 139–47.

Elkus, Jonathan. "Charles Ives and the American Band Tradition: A Centennial Tribute." Exeter, Eng.: American Arts Pamphlet No. 4, American Arts Documentation Centre, University of Exeter, 1974.

Emerson, Ralph Waldo. *Selected Essays.* Edited by Larzer Ziff. New York: Penguin Books, 1982.

Feder, Stuart. "Decoration Day: A Boyhood Memory of Charles Ives." *The Musical Quarterly* 66, no. 2 (April 1980):234–61.

———. *Charles Ives, "My Father's Song": A Psychoanalytic Biography.* New Haven: Yale University Press, 1992.

Fletcher, Lucille. "A Connecticut Yankee in Music." Unpublished and incomplete drafts for a *New Yorker* article preserved in the Ives Collection at Yale. Nearly every page has additions and corrections in Ives's hand, and some passages were actually written by Ives.

Forma, Warren. *They Were Ragtime.* New York: Grosset & Dunlap, 1976.

Forte, Allen. "Ives and Atonality." In H. Wiley Hitchcock and Vivian Perlis, eds., *An Ives Celebration: Papers and Panels of the Charles Ives Centennial Festival-Conference.* Urbana: University of Illinois Press, 1977.

Furnas, J. C. *The Americans: A Social History of the United States.* New York: G. P. Putnam's Sons, 1969.

Gibbens, John Jeffrey. "Debussy's Impact on Ives: An Assessment." D.M.A. dissertation, University of Illinois at Urbana-Champaign, 1985.

Gillespie, Don. "John Becker, the Musical Crusader of St. Thomas College." *Student Musicologists at Minnesota* 6 (1975 / 76).

Ginger, Ray. *Age of Excess: The United States from 1877 to 1914.* New York: Macmillan, 1965.

Gingerich, Lora Louise. "Processes of Motivic Transformation in the Keyboard and Chamber Music of Charles Ives." Ph.D. dissertation, Yale University, 1983.

Gorer, Geoffrey. *The American People: A Study in National Character,* rev. ed. New York: W. W. Norton, 1964.

Hamm, Charles. *Music in the New World.* New York: W. W. Norton, 1983.

Hansen, Chadwick. "One Place in New England: The Fifty-Fourth Massachusetts Volunteer Infantry as a Subject for American Artists." *Student Musicologists at Minnesota* 6 (1975 / 76).

Hazen, Margaret Hindle, and Robert M. Hazen. *The Music Men: An Illustrated History of Brass Bands in America, 1800–1920.* Washington, D.C.: Smithsonian Institution Press, 1987.

Henderson, Clayton W. *The Charles Ives Tunebook.* Warren, Mich.: Harmonie Park Press, 1990.

Hicks, Michael. "The Imprisonment of Henry Cowell." *Journal of the American Music Society* 44, no. 1 (1991).

Hindemith, Paul. *A Composer's World*. Cambridge, Mass.: Harvard University Press, 1952.

Hitchcock, H. Wiley. Introduction to Horatio Parker's *Hora novissima*. New York: Da Capo Press, 1972.

———. *Music in the United States: A Historical Introduction*. New Jersey: Prentice-Hall, 2nd ed., 1974; 3rd ed., 1988. References to Ives directly are from the 3rd ed., to American music generally from the 2nd.

———. *Ives: A Survey of the Music*. London: Oxford University Press, 1977 (2nd ed., 1983).

Hitchcock, H. Wiley, and Vivian Perlis, eds. *An Ives Celebration: Papers and Panels of the Charles Ives Centennial Festival-Conference*. Urbana: University of Illinois Press, 1977.

Hitchcock, H. Wiley, and Noel Zahler. "Just What *Is* Ives's Unanswered Question?" *Notes* 44, no. 3 (March 1988).

Hofstadter, Richard. *The Age of Reform: From Bryan to F.D.R.* New York: Knopf, 1955.

Howard, John Tasker. *Our American Music: A Comprehensive History from 1620 to the Present*. New York: T. Y. Crowell, 4th ed., 1965.

Ives, Charles. *The Amount to Carry—Measuring the Prospect*. Salesmanship edition, 1920. Ives & Myrick publication. (This is a reprint of a long article of that year in *The Eastern Underwriter*.)

———. "A Conductor's Note." Included in the Associated Music score of the Fourth Symphony, New York, 1965.

———. *Essays Before a Sonata and Other Writings*. Edited by Howard Boatwright. New York: W. W. Norton, 1970.

———. *Memos*. Edited by John Kirkpatrick. New York: W. W. Norton, 1972.

———. Papers, New Haven, Yale University Music Library Archival Collection. Citings refer to box and folder numbers in the Ives Collection; for example, "Ives Papers 45 / 9" indicates box 45, folder 9. If there is only one number, it is a box without folders. There is also a Microfilm Addendum with copies of family letters, John Kirkpatrick interview notes with Harmony Ives, and so on.

Ives, Charles, and Harmony Twichell. Uncollected Letters from the collection of John Kirkpatrick.

Jillisky, Joe. "Charles Ives in the Adirondacks." *Adirondack Magazine,* May 1987.

Johnson (Swafford), Jan. "The Second Phase: Compositional Techniques and Form in Ives' Fourth Symphony." Unpublished senior thesis, Harvard College, 1968.

Johnson, Owen. *Stover at Yale,* 6th ed. New York: Frederick A. Stokes, 1912.

Kaplan, Justin. *Mr. Clemens and Mark Twain*. New York: Simon and Schuster, 1966.

Kearns, William K. *Horatio Parker, 1863–1919: His Life, Music, and Ideas*. Metuchen, N.J.: The Scarecrow Press, 1990.

Kirkpatrick, John. "A Temporary Mimeographed Catalogue of the Music Manuscripts and related materials of Charles Edward Ives." Library of the Yale School of Music, compiled 1954–60.

———. Article on Ives in *The New Grove Dictionary of Music and Musicians* (1980) and the slightly revised version in *The New Grove Dictionary of American Music* (1986). Both are called *New Grove* in notes.

———. Liner notes from the RCA recording of the *Robert Browning Overture*.

———. Preface to *The Fourth of July,* for orchestra, 3rd movement (Summer) from *A Symphony: Holidays* (or "New Eng Holidays"), 1904–13. New York: Associated Music Publishers, 1974.

———. Preface to the score of the Fourth Symphony. New York: Associated Music Publishers, 1965.

———. Unpublished and unfinished Ives Datebook. This is a fairly random series of entries in a large account book.

Lambert, J. Philip. "Ives and Counterpoint." *American Music* 9, no. 2 (summer 1991).

Ledbetter, Steven. Liner notes from the Northeastern recording of *The Celestial Country*.

Lederman, Minna. *The Life and Death of a Small Magazine (Modern Music, 1924–1946)*. Brooklyn: Institute for Studies in American Music Monograph, 1983.

Lee, W. Storrs. *The Yankees of Connecticut*. New York: Henry Holt, 1957.

Levy, Alan Howard. *Musical Nationalism: American Composers' Search for Identity*. Westport, Conn.: Greenwood Press, 1983.

Lord, Walter. *The Good Years: From 1900 to the First World War*. New York: Harper & Brothers, 1960.

MacKinnon, Barbara, ed. and commentary. *American Philosophy: A Historical Anthology*. Albany: State University of New York Press, 1985.

Marshall, Dennis. "Charles Ives' Quotations: Manner or Substance?" In Benjamin Boretz and Edward T. Cone, eds., *Perspectives on American Composers*. New York: W. W. Norton, 1971.

Martin, George. *The Damrosch Dynasty*. Boston: Houghton Mifflin, 1983.

Mazzola, Sandy R. "Bands and Orchestras at the World's Columbian Exposition." *American Music* 4, no. 4 (winter 1986).

McCue, George, ed. *Music in American Society 1776–1976*. New Brunswick, N.J.: Transaction Books, 1977.

Mead, Rita H. "Cowell, Ives, and *New Music*." *Musical Quarterly* 66, no. 4 (October 1980).

———. *Henry Cowell's New Music, 1925–1936*. Ann Arbor, Mich.: UMI Research Press, 1981.

———. "The Amazing Mr. Cowell." *American Music* 1, no. 4 (winter 1983).

Mellers, Wilfrid. *Music in a New Found Land: Themes and Developments in the History of American Music*, rev. ed. New York: Oxford University Press, 1987.

Menand, Louis. "An American Prodigy" (C. S. Peirce). *The New York Review of Books*, December 2, 1993.

Moore, Ralph Joseph, Jr. "The Background and the Symbol: Charles E. Ives, a Case Study in the History of American Cultural Expression." Unpublished senior essay in the American Studies Department, Yale College, 1954.

Morgan, Robert P. "Ives and Mahler: Mutual Responses at the End of an Era." *19th-Century Music* 2 (1978).

Morison, Samuel Eliot. *The Oxford History of the American People*. New York: Oxford University Press, 1965.

Morris, Lloyd. *Incredible New York*. New York: Random House, 1951.

Nelson, Mark D. "Beyond Mimesis: Transcendentalism and Processes of Analogy in Charles Ives' 'The Fourth of July.' " *Perspectives of New Music* 22, nos. 1–2 (1984):353.

Nevins, Allan, and John A. Kraut, eds. *The Greater City: New York, 1898–1948* New York: Columbia University Press, 1948.

Nicholls, David. *American Experimental Music 1890–1940*. Cambridge: Cambridge University Press, 1990.

North, Douglas C. "Life Insurance and Investment Banking at the Time of the Armstrong Investigation of 1905–1906." *The Journal of Economic History* 14, no. 3 (summer 1954).

Noss, Luther. *A History of the Yale School of Music 1855–1970*. New Haven: The Yale School of Music, 1984.

Osborne, William. "Charles Ives the Organist." *The American Organist,* July 1990:58–64.

Perlis, Vivian. *Charles Ives Remembered: An Oral History*. New York, W. W. Norton, 1976. (Abbreviated CIR in notes.)

———. *Two Men for Modern Music: E. Robert Schmitz and Herman Langinger*. Brooklyn: Brooklyn College Institute for Studies in American Music, Monograph Number 9, 1978.

———. Catalogue to the Yale University Archival Collection of the Charles Ives Papers.

———. Unpublished Charles Ives Oral History Project. On file at Oral History Research Office, Yale School of Music, New Haven. Citations refer to box and folder number of transcripts: 1 / 2 would mean box 1, folder 2. I often quote from this source rather than the edited and condensed interviews in Perlis's book *Charles Ives Remembered* because the memories are sometimes fuller in the original interview. (Abbreviated Oral History in the notes.)

Perry, Rosalie Sandra. *Charles Ives and the American Mind*. Kent, Ohio: Kent State University Press, 1974.

Pierson, George Wilson. *Yale College: An Educational History 1871–1921*. New Haven: Yale University Press, 1952.

Raymond, Mike. *The Human Side of Diabetes*. Chicago: The Noble Press, 1992.

Reed, Joseph W. *Three American Originals: John Ford, William Faulkner, & Charles Ives*. Middletown, Conn.: Wesleyan University Press, 1984.

Rossiter, Frank. *Charles Ives and His America*. New York: Liveright, 1975.

Sablosky, Irving L. *American Music*. Chicago: University of Chicago Press, 1969.

Schwartz, H. W. *Bands of America*. New York: Doubleday, 1957.

Sears, Marian V. "The American Businessman at the Turn of the Century." *The Business History Review* 30, no. 4 (December 1956).

Sherwood, Gayle. Yale Ph.D. dissertation on dating Ives's music, in progress.

Silber, Irwin. *Songs of the Civil War*. New York: Columbia University Press, 1960.

Sinclair, James B. Preface to the Mercury score of Ives's *Three Places in New England*, full orchestra version. Bryn Mawr, Pa.: Mercury Music Corp., 1976.

———. Preface to the Peer International score of Ives's *Ragtime Dances*. New York: Peer International, 1990.

Slonimsky, Nicolas. *Music Since 1900*, 4th ed. New York: Charles Scribner's Sons, 1971.

———. "Working with Ives." Program booklet of the South Florida Ives Festival, 1974–76.

———. *Perfect Pitch: A Life Story*. Oxford: Oxford University Press, 1988.

Smith, David Stanley. "A Study of Horatio Parker." *The Musical Quarterly* 16 (April 1930).

Solomon, Maynard. "Charles Ives: Some Questions of Veracity." *Journal of the American Musicological Society* 40, no. 3 (fall 1987).

Starr, Larry. *A Union of Diversities: Style in the Music of Charles Ives*. New York: Schirmer Books, 1992.

Stravinsky, Igor. *Poetics of Music, in the Form of Six Lessons*. New York: Vintage Books, no date.

Stravinsky, Igor, and Robert Craft. *Themes and Episodes*. New York: Alfred A. Knopf, 1966.

Strong, Leah A. *Joseph Hopkins Twichell*. Athens: University of Georgia Press, 1966.

Struble, John Warthen. "The *Concord Sonata* of Charles E. Ives: A Reference for Pianists and Scholars." M.A. thesis, University of California at San Diego, 1978.

Swados, Harvey. *Years of Conscience: The Muckrakers*. New York: Meridian Books, 1962.

Thoreau, Henry D. *The Journal of Henry D. Thoreau*. Fourteen volumes bound as two. New York: Dover Publications, 1962.

———. *The Portable Thoreau*. Edited by Carl Bode. New York: Penguin Books, 1982.

Tick, Judith. "Ragtime and the Music of Charles Ives." *Current Musicology* 18 (1974): 105–13.

Tischler, Barbara L. *American Music: The Search for an American Musical Identity*. New York: Oxford University Press, 1986.

Trattner, Walter I. *From Poor Law to Welfare State: A History of Social Welfare in America*, 3rd ed. New York: The Free Press, 1984.

Twain, Mark. *Autobiography*. Two volumes. New York: P. F. Collier and Son, 1925.

Wagenknecht, Edward. *American Profile: 1900–1909*. Amherst: University of Massachusetts Press, 1982.

Walker, Robert H. *Life in the Age of Enterprise*. New York: Capricorn Books, 1971.

Wallach, "The New England Education of Charles Ives." Ph.D. dissertation, Columbia University, 1973.

Warren, Richard, Jr. *Charles E. Ives: Discography*. New Haven: Yale University Library, 1972.

Wiecki, Ronald V. "Two Musical Idealists—Charles Ives and E. Robert Schmitz: A Friendship Reconsidered." *American Music*, spring 1992.

Wise, Arthur, and Francis A. Lord. *Bands and Drummer Boys of the Civil War*. New York: Thomas Yoseloff, 1966.

Wooldridge, David. *From the Steeples and Mountains*. New York: Alfred A. Knopf, 1974.

Yates, Peter. "Charles Ives, an American Composer," *Parnassus: Poetry in Review* 3, no. 2 (spring–summer 1975).

Yellin, Victor Fell. "Review of the First Recording of *The Celestial Country*, by Charles Ives." *The Musical Quarterly* 60, no. 3 (July 1974).

Zelizer, Viviana A. Rotman. *Morals and Markets: The Development of Life Insurance in the United States*. New York: Columbia University Press, 1979.

Ziffrin, Marilyn J. *Carl Ruggles: Composer, Painter, and Storyteller*. Urbana: University of Illinois Press, 1994.

Zuck, Barbara A. *A History of Musical Americanism*. Ann Arbor, Mich.: UMI Research Press, 1980.

Index

Page numbers in *italics* refer to illustrations or musical examples. Endnotes are not indexed, except when they deal substantially with technical points in the music or with questions about Ive's veracity.

D0498508

NO LONGER PROPERTY OF
THE SEATTLE PUBLIC LIBRARY

THE
BOOK
OF
GOTHEL

MARY McMYNE

THE BOOK OF GOTHEL

REDHOOK

This book is a work of fiction. Names, characters, places, and incidents are the product of the author's imagination or are used fictitiously. Any resemblance to actual events, locales, or persons, living or dead, is coincidental.

Copyright © 2022 by Mary McMyne

Cover design by Lisa Marie Pompilio
Cover illustrations by Shutterstock
Cover copyright © 2022 by Hachette Book Group, Inc.

Hachette Book Group supports the right to free expression and the value of copyright. The purpose of copyright is to encourage writers and artists to produce the creative works that enrich our culture.

The scanning, uploading, and distribution of this book without permission is a theft of the author's intellectual property. If you would like permission to use material from the book (other than for review purposes), please contact permissions@hbgusa.com. Thank you for your support of the author's rights.

Redhook Books/Orbit
Hachette Book Group
1290 Avenue of the Americas
New York, NY 10104
hachettebookgroup.com

First Edition: July 2022
Simultaneously published in Great Britain by Orbit

Redhook is an imprint of Orbit, a division of Hachette Book Group.
The Redhook name and logo are trademarks of Hachette Book Group, Inc.

The publisher is not responsible for websites (or their content) that are not owned by the publisher.

The Hachette Speakers Bureau provides a wide range of authors for speaking events. To find out more, go to www.hachettespeakersbureau.com or call (866) 376-6591.

Library of Congress Cataloging-in-Publication Data
Names: McMyne, Mary, author.
Title: The book of Gothel / Mary McMyne.
Description: First edition. | New York, NY : Redhook, 2022.
Identifiers: LCCN 2021054656 | ISBN 9780316393119 (hardcover) |
ISBN 9780316393317 (ebook) | ISBN 9780316425506 (ebook other)
Subjects: LCGFT: Novels.
Classification: LCC PS3613.C58557 B66 2022 | DDC 813/.6—dc23
LC record available at https://lccn.loc.gov/2021054656

ISBNs: 9780316393119 (hardcover), 9780316393317 (ebook)

Printed in the United States of America

LSC-C

Printing 1, 2022

For my mother

THE
BOOK
OF
GOTHEL

PROLOGUE

The cellar was, at least, a cool respite from the murderous heat wave afflicting the Black Forest, though it smelled like a crypt and I nearly broke my trick knee on my way down the crumbling steps. There was no railing, and my knee ached the way it always did when rain was due. Ingrid Vogel took the stairs recklessly, though her long white plait and rheumy eyes betrayed that she was at least four decades older than I am. Apparently, she was one of those lucky octogenarians for whom arthritis was something that happened only to other people.

When she flicked on the light, I followed her through the archway into an ancient stone cellar, startled by how old it seemed. The cellar was faded rock, almost cavernous, built with simple buttresses and curved archways, obviously a remnant of a much older structure than the thatched-roof cottage above. What did this place use to be, I wondered absently, surveying the stacks of parcels and canned goods in the corner. Before I accepted my position at the University of North Carolina, I spent fifteen years in Germany—earning my PhD, doing a postdoc, lecturing—but the nonchalant way Europeans used ancient spaces as basements still felt like sacrilege.

"*Frau Professorin Eisenberg*," she said, addressing me formally despite my repeated requests to call me Gert. She stood beside an uneven stone that had been removed from the cellar floor, holding an ancient lockbox. I knew from our emails that the codex must be inside. "*Hier ist er.*"

Three days earlier, Frau Vogel had emailed to tell me about a

medieval codex she found in her late mother's cellar. She said she'd
attended a talk I gave in Germany, but I had no memory of meeting
her. Her email described what she knew of the manuscript—it was
illuminated, written in Middle High German by a woman—and
asked if I would be interested in the find. Attached were radiocarbon
dating results verifying the manuscript's age, and an image of a single
sample page. The handwritten text was a sinister rhyme about Snow
White in an obscure Alemannic dialect; beneath it was a painstakingly decorated illustration of a wicked fairy dancing on a rose. She
had blood-red lips, deathly pale skin, and a tangle of black hair.

When Frau Vogel's email pinged my inbox, I had been sitting in
my office, prepping syllabi for the fall semester, trying to ignore two
tenured male colleagues who were prattling on about their latest
books in the hall. I couldn't focus. There was a ball of dread in my
throat so large, it felt like it was blocking the flow of oxygen. I was
scheduled to apply for tenure the following year, and the application process at UNC was brutal. I needed a book under contract,
and my study of the treatment of women in medieval German illuminated manuscripts was going nowhere. It was under review at a
solid press, but one of my peer reviewers had dismissed its subject
matter as "domestic minutiae." The criticism made me livid. Centuries of sexist scribes had left huge gaps in what we know about the
lives of medieval women, and I was *trying* to do something about it.

The image of the fairy made me gasp, loudly enough that one
of my colleagues peeked into my office with a question on his face.
I forced a smile, mouthed the words *I'm fine*, and waited for him
to go back to his conversation before I returned my focus to the
screen. The colors of the illustration were jewel-toned, bright;
the fairy's expression could only be described as malicious. My
heart fluttered with a delicious thrill of excitement. Was I looking at some kind of gothic ancestor to the Snow White folktale
as we knew it? The prospect of studying something new—and so
different—made me giddy.

I wrote Frau Vogel back immediately, expressing interest. Her reply was a bizarre request for me to describe my personal religious beliefs. Her prying ruffled me, but I got the distinct impression that she was testing me, so I answered carefully. My religion was complicated. I was raised Catholic, but I hadn't been to church in ages—a fact that, hopefully, Frau Vogel would understand, given my sixty-four hours of graduate credit on the period that brought the Crusades. Whatever her test was, I must have passed, because her next email contained more digital photographs of the manuscript and a request for my assistance reading it. The additional photos were enough to put me on the plane the next day.

Now, crossing the cellar toward Frau Vogel and her lockbox, I felt an eerie shiver of anticipation. My breath caught in my chest, and I thought I sensed a shift in the room's energy, as if I could *feel* the drop in air pressure from the coming storm. The sensation alarmed me, until I recognized the rest of the premonitory symptoms of my too-frequent migraines. The lightbulb hanging from the stone ceiling seemed too bright. My vision was blurry. The dizziness I'd blamed on the twisty drive up the mountain had returned. Of course I would get a migraine *now*, I thought, cursing my luck.

Resolving to take a sumatriptan soon, I peered into the lockbox. Inside was a burnished codex, timeworn. The cover's leather shimmered faintly around the edges, as if it had been painted centuries ago with gold dust. When I saw how ornate it was, a faint gasp escaped my lips: There was an embossed frame decorated with a diamond pattern, and the interior of each shape was decorated with intricate swirls. In the center of it all was a huge design that looked like a sigil. A circle writhing with snakes, large-winged birds, and beasts, at once grotesque and beautiful.

The charged feeling in the air intensified, making me dizzier. I blinked, trying to recover some semblance of professional detachment. The migraine, I thought, it's knocked me off balance.

"*Entschuldigen Sie,*" I said, fumbling in my purse for the bottle of sumatriptan.

Swallowing a pill, I glanced at Frau Vogel, silently asking permission to pick up the codex. She nodded. I picked it up by the edges, trying to get as little oil from my skin on the cover as possible. It was heavy for its size. I could smell the faint musty scent of the leather, feel its age beneath my fingers. I glanced up at my host again, irrationally uncertain about opening the codex, as though she hadn't asked me here precisely for the purpose of reading it.

An amused smile spread across Frau Vogel's face, wrinkling the skin around her lips. "*Es ist alles gut.* It will not bite."

I opened the book, embarrassed. On the first page was a declaration of truth signed by someone named Haelewise, daughter-of-Hedda. My fingers twitched with the urge to trace her signature, though I knew better than to touch the ink. The use of a parent's name as a surname would be unusual for a noblewoman, and I had never seen a mother mentioned instead of a father. Who was this peasant woman who could write, who chose to be known only by her maternal lineage?

I took care not to disturb the pigment, touching only the edges of the pages as I turned them. The ink was surprisingly well preserved for the age of the manuscript, as if it *hadn't* spent centuries under a stone in a cellar floor. The parchment was thin but still flexible to the touch. What I had surmised from the photographs was true: The manuscript was illuminated as if it were a holy book, though the text itself seemed to be a narrative, interrupted occasionally with recipes and verse and what, during the time in which the book was written, could only have been considered heretical prayers.

As I paused to read one, the static electric aura became so pronounced that the hairs on my arms stood on end. Intense vertigo overtook me, strong enough that I wondered if it was a migraine symptom at all. I smothered the thought, telling myself to focus. I had taken the sumatriptan. The aura would pass soon.

The manuscript was decorated with colorful marginalia, faded red and gold initial letters in the style of Benedictine scribes, though none of the text was Latin. There were masterful illustrations; the images were every bit as detailed as those monks painted on prayer books. But the imagery was so out of character for what one would expect to find in an illuminated manuscript from this period. Some of the illustrations were mundane, a mother and daughter in a garden, everyday scenes of births and cooking. Others were the stuff of folktales. On one page, a black-haired woman in a bright blue hood extended her hand, as if to offer the reader the gold-dusted apple in her palm. On another, a ghostly woman in blue knelt in a tangled garden, arms outstretched, psychedelic rays of gilded light radiating from her in every direction. I couldn't help but linger over an image of a beautiful raven-haired young woman lying dead on what appeared to be a stone coffin—her eyes open, her body encased in pale-blue swirls of ice.

"You can read it?" Frau Vogel asked softly. Her voice sounded far away. I had forgotten she was there.

I looked up. Her eyes were fixed on me. "*Ja. Das ist Alemannisch.* I need time."

"How long?"

"All day," I said. "At least."

She met my gaze for a moment, then nodded at the rocking chairs in the corner. "I'll be upstairs," she said, smiling encouragingly. "I want to know everything."

DECLARATION

This is a true account of my life.

Mother Gothel, they call me. I have become known by the name of this tower. A vine-covered spire stretching into the trees, cobbled together from stone. I have become known for the child I stole, little girl, my pretty. Rapunzel—I named her for her mother's favorite herb. My garden is legendary: row after row of hellebore and hemlock, yarrow and bloodwort. I have read many a speculum on the natural properties of plants and stones, and I know them all by heart. I know what to do with belladonna, with lungwort and cinquefoil.

I learned the healing arts from a wise woman, the spinning of tales from my mother. I learned nothing from my father, a no-name fisherman. My mother was a midwife. I learned that from her too. Women come to me from all over to hear my stories, to make use of my knowledge of plants. Traipsing in their boots and lonely skirts through the wood, they come, one by one, with their secret sorrows, over the river, across the hills, to the wise woman they hope can heal their ails. After I give them what they seek and take my fee, I spin my stories, sifting through my memories, polishing the facts of my life until they shine like stones. Sometimes they bring my stories back to me, changed by retelling. In this book, under lock and key, I will set down the truth.

In this, the seventy-eighth year of my earthly course, I write my story. A faithful account of my life—heretical though it may be—a chronicle of facts that have since been altered, to correct the lies being repeated as truth. This will be my book of deeds, written from the famous tower of Gothel, where a high wall encloses the florae and herbs.

—Haelewise, daughter-of-Hedda
The Year of Our Lord 1219

CHAPTER ONE

⁓

W hat a boon it is to have a mother who loves you. A mother who comes to life when you walk into the room, who tells stories at bedtime, who teaches you the names of plants that grow wild in the wood. But it is possible for a mother to love too much, for love to take over her heart like a weed does a garden, to spread its roots and proliferate until nothing else grows. My mother was watchful in the extreme. She suffered three stillbirths before I was born, and she didn't want to lose me. She tied a keeping string around my wrist when we went to market, and she never let me roam.

There were dangers for me in the market, no doubt. I was born with eyes the color of ravens—no color, no light in my irises— and by the time I was five, I suffered strange fainting spells that made others fear I was possessed. As if that wasn't enough, when I was old enough to attend births with my mother, rumors spread about my unnatural skill with midwifery. Long before I became her apprentice, I could pinpoint the exact moment when a baby was ready to be born.

To keep me close, my mother told me the *kindefresser* haunted the market: a she-demon who lured children from the city to drink their blood. Mother said she was a shapeshifter who took the forms of people children knew to trick them into going away with her.

This was before the bishop built the city wall, when travelers still passed freely, selling charms to ward off fevers, arguing about the ills of the Church. The market square was bustling then. You could find men and women in strange robes with skin of every color, selling ivory bangles and gowns made of silk. Mother allowed me to admire their wares, holding my hand tightly. "Stay close," she said, her eyes searching the stalls. "Don't let the *kindefresser* snatch you away!"

The bishop built the wall when I was ten to protect the city from the mist that blew off the forest. The priests called it an "unholy fog" that carried evil and disease. After the wall was built, only holy men and peddlers were allowed to pass through the city gate: monks on pilgrimage, traders of linen and silk, merchants with ox-carts full of dried fish. Mother and I had to stop gathering herbs and hunting in the forest. Father cut down the elms behind our house, so we had room to grow a kitchen garden. I helped Mother plant the seeds and weave a wicker coop for chickens. Father purchased stones, and the three of us built a wall around the plot to keep dogs out.

Even though the town was enclosed, Mother still wouldn't let me wander without her, especially around the new moon, when my spells most often plagued me. Whenever I saw children running errands or playing knucklebones behind the minster, an uneasy bitterness filled me. Everyone thought I was younger than I was, because of my small stature and the way my mother coddled me. I suspected the *kindefresser* was one of her many stories, invented to scare me into staying close. I loved my mother deeply, but I longed to wander. She treated me as if I was one of her poppets, a fragile thing of beads and linen to be sat on a shelf.

Not long after the wall was built, the tailor's son Matthäus knocked on our door, dark hair shining in the sun, his eyes flashing with merriment. "I brought arrows," he said. "Can you come out to the grove, teach me to shoot?"

Our mothers had become friends due to my mother's constant need for scraps of cloth. She made poppets to sell during the cold season, and the two women had spent many an afternoon sorting scraps and gossiping in the tailor's shop as we played. The week before, Matthäus and I had found an orange kitten. Father would've drowned him in a sack, but Matthäus wanted to give him milk. As we sneaked the kitten upstairs to his room, I had racked my brain for something to offer him so we could play again. Mother had taught me everything she knew about how to use a bow. Shooting was one of the few things I was good at.

"Please please please," I begged my mother.

She looked at me, tight-lipped, and shook her head.

"Mother," I said. "I need a friend."

She blinked, sympathetic. "What if you have a spell?"

"We'll take the back streets. The moon is almost full."

Mother took a deep breath, emotions warring on her face. "All right," she sighed finally. "Let me tie back your hair."

I yelped with joy, though I hated the way she pulled my curls, which in general refused to be tamed and which I had inherited from her. "Thank you!" I said when she was finished, grabbing my quiver and bow and my favorite poppet.

Ten was an odd age for me. I could shoot as well as a grown man but had yet to give up childish things. I still brought the poppet called Gütel that Mother made for me everywhere. A poppet with black hair just like mine, tied back with ribbons. She wore a dress of linen scraps dyed my favorite color, madder-red. Her eyes were two shining black beads.

I was a quizzical child, a show-me child—a wild thing who had to be dragged to Mass—but I saw a sort of magic in Mother's poppet-making. Nothing unnatural, mind you. The sort of thing everyone does, like set out food for the Fates or choose a wedding date for good luck. The time she took choosing the right scraps, the words she murmured as she sewed, made that doll alive to me.

On our way out, Mother reminded me to watch for the *kinde-fresser*. "Amber eyes, no matter what shape she takes, remember." She lowered her voice. "You'll want to warn that boy about your spells."

I nodded, cheeks flushing with shame, though Matthäus was too polite to ask what my mother had said under her breath. We hurried toward the north gate, past the docks and the other fishermen's huts. I pulled my hood over my head so the sun wouldn't bother my eyes. They were sensitive in addition to being black as night. Bright light made my head ache.

The leaves of the linden trees were turning yellow and beginning to fall to the ground. As we stepped into the grove, ravens scattered. The grove was full of beasts the carpenters had trapped when the wall was built. It was common to see a family of hares hopping beneath the lindens. If you were foolish enough to open your hand, a raven would swoop down and steal a *pfennic* from your palm.

Matthäus showed me the straw-stuffed bird atop a pole that everyone used for archery practice. I sat Gütel at the base of a tree trunk, reaching down to straighten her cloak. My heart soared as I reached for my bow. Here I was, finally outside the hut without Mother. I felt normal, almost. I felt free.

"Did you hear about the queen?" Matthäus asked, pulling his bow back to let the arrow fly. It went wild, missing the trunk to stray into the sunny clearing.

"No," I called, squinting and shading my eyes as I watched him go after it. Even with the shadow of my hand, looking directly at the sunlight hurt.

He reappeared with the arrow. "King Frederick banished her."

"How do you know?"

"A courtier told my father while he was getting fitted."

"Why would the king banish his wife?"

Matthäus shrugged as he handed me the arrow. "The man said she asked too many guests into her garden."

I squinted at him. "How is that grounds for banishment?" I didn't understand, then, what the courtier meant.

He shrugged. "You know how harsh they say King Frederick is."

I nodded. Since his coronation that spring, everyone called him "King Red-Beard" because his chin-hair was supposed to be stained with the blood of his enemies. Even as young as ten, I understood that men make up reasons to get rid of women they find disagreeable. "I bet it's because she hasn't given him a son."

He thought about this. "You're probably right."

I strung my bow, deep in thought. After the coronation, the now-banished queen had visited with the princess, and Mother had taken me to see the parade. I remembered the pale, black-haired girl who sat with her mother on a white horse, still a child, though her brave expression made her seem older. Her eyes were a pretty hazel with golden flecks. "Did the queen take Princess Frederika with her?"

Matthäus shook his head. "King Frederick wouldn't let her."

I imagined how awful it would be to have my mother banished from my home. Where my mother was protective, my father was cold and controlling. A house without Mother would be a house without love.

I forced myself to concentrate on my shot.

When the arrow pierced the trunk, Matthäus sucked in his breath. At first I thought he was reacting to my aim. Then I saw he was looking at the tree where Gütel sat. A giant raven with bright black hackles was bent over her.

I charged at the bird. "Shoo! Get away from her!"

The bird ignored me until I was right beside it, when it looked up at me with amber eyes. *Kraek*, it said, shaking its head, as it dropped Gütel on the ground. It kept something in its beak, something glittering and black, which flashed as it took off.

On the left side of Gütel's face, the thread was loose. The wool had come out. The raven had plucked out her eye.

A cry leapt from my throat. I fled from the grove, clutching Gütel to my chest. The market square blurred as I ran past. The tanner called out: "Haelewise, what's wrong?"

I wanted my mother and no one else.

The crooked door of our hut was open. Mother stood in the entryway, sewing, a needle between her lips. She had been waiting for me to come home.

"Look!" I shouted, rushing toward her, holding my poppet up.

Mother set down the poppet she was sewing. "What happened?"

As I raged about what the bird had done, Father walked up, smelling of the day's catch. He listened for a while without speaking, his face stern, then went inside. We followed him to the table. "Its eyes," I sobbed, sliding onto the bench. "They were amber, like the *kindefresser*—"

My parents' eyes met, and something passed between them I didn't understand.

Overcome by a telltale shiver, I braced myself, knowing what would happen next. Twice a month or so—if I was unlucky, more—I had one of my fainting spells. They always started the same way. Chills bloomed all over my skin, and the air went taut. I felt a pull from the next world—

The room swayed. My heart raced. I grasped the tabletop, afraid I would hit my head when I fell. And then I was gone. Not my body, but my soul, my ability to watch the world.

The next thing I knew, I was lying on the floor. Head aching, hands and feet numb. My mouth tasted of blood. Shame filled me, the awful not-knowing that always plagued me after a swoon.

My parents were arguing. "You haven't been to see her," Father was saying.

"No," Mother hissed. "I gave you my word!"

What were they talking about? "See who?" I asked.

"You're awake," Mother said with a tight smile, a panicked edge to her voice. At the time, I thought she was upset about my swoon. My spells always rattled her.

My father stared me down. "One of her clients is a heretic. I told your mother to stop seeing her."

My gut told me he was lying, but contradicting him never went well. "How long was I out?"

"A minute," Father said. "Maybe two."

"My hands are still numb," I said, unable to keep the fear out of my voice. The feeling usually came back to my extremities by this point.

Mother pulled me close, shushing me. I breathed in her smell, the soothing scent of anise and earth.

"Damn it, Hedda," Father said. "We've done this your way long enough."

Mother stiffened. As far back as I could remember, she had been in charge of finding a cure for my spells. Father had wanted to take me to the abbey for years, but Mother outright refused. Her goddess dwelt in things, in the hidden powers of root and leaf, she told me when Father was out. Mother had brought home a hundred remedies for my spells: bubbling elixirs, occult powders wrapped in bitter leaves, thick brews that burned my throat.

The story went that my grandmother, whom I hardly remembered, suffered the same swoons. Supposedly, hers were so bad that she bit off the tip of her tongue as a child, but she found a cure for them late in life. Unfortunately, Mother had no idea what that cure was, because my grandmother died before I suffered my first swoon. Mother had been searching for that cure ever since. As a midwife she knew all the local herbalists. Before the wall was built, we had seen wise women and wortcunners, sorceresses who spoke in ancient tongues, the alchemist who sought to turn lead into gold. The remedies tasted terrible, but they sometimes kept my spells away for a month. We had never tried holy healers before.

I hated the emptiness I felt in my father's church when he dragged me to Mass, while my mother's secret offerings actually made me *feel* something. But that day, as my parents argued, it occurred to me that the learned men in the abbey might be able to provide relief that Mother's healers couldn't.

My parents fought that night for hours, their white-hot words rising loud enough for me to hear. Father kept going on about the demon he thought possessed me, the threat it meant to our livelihood, the stoning I would face if I got blamed for the wrong thing. Mother said these spells ran in her family, and how could he say I was possessed? She said he'd promised, after everything she gave up, to leave her in charge of this *one* thing.

The next morning, Mother woke me, defeated. We were going to the abbey. My eagerness to try something new felt like a betrayal. I tried to hide it for her sake.

It was barely light out as we walked to the dock behind our hut. As we pushed our boat into the lake, the guard in the bay tower recognized my father and waved us through the pike wall. Our boat rocked on the water, and Father sang a sailing hymn:

> *"Lord God, ruler of all, keep safe*
> *this wreck of wood on the waves."*

He rowed us across the lake, giving a wide berth to the northern shoreline, where the mist the priests called "unholy" cloaked the trees. "God's teeth," Mother said. "How many times do I have to tell you? The mist won't hurt us. I grew up in those woods!"

She never agreed with the priests about anything.

Pulling our boat ashore an hour later, we approached the stone wall that surrounded the abbey. Elderly and thin with a long white beard and mustache, a kind-looking monk unlocked the gate. He stood between us and the monastery, scratching at the neckline of his tunic, as Father explained why we had come. I couldn't help but notice the fleas he kept squelching beneath his fingers as he listened to my father describe my spells. Why didn't he scatter horsemint over the floor, I wondered, or coat his flesh with rue?

Mother must have wondered the same. "Don't you have an herb garden?"

The monk shook his head, explaining that their gardener died last winter, nodding for Father to finish his description of my spells.

"Something unnatural settles over her," he told the monk, his voice rising. "Then she falls into a kind of trance."

The monk watched me closely, his gaze lingering on my eyes. "Do you suspect a demon?"

Father nodded.

"Our abbot could cast it out," the monk offered. "For a fee."

Something fluttered in my heart. How I wanted this to work.

Father offered the monk a handful of *holpfennige*. The monk counted them and let us in, shutting the heavy gate behind us.

Mother frowned as we followed the monk across the grounds. "Don't be afraid," she whispered to me. "There is no demon in you."

Through a huge wooden door, the monk led us into the main chamber of the minster, a long room with an altar on the far end. Along the aisle, candles flickered below murals. Our footsteps echoed. When we reached the baptismal font, the monk told me to take off my clothes.

Father reached for my hand and squeezed it. He met my eyes, his expression kind. My heart almost burst. It'd been so long since he looked at me that way. For years, he'd seemed to blame me for the demon he thought possessed me, as if some weakness, some flaw in my character had invited it in. If this works, I thought, he'll look at me that way all the time. I'll be able to play knucklebones with the other children.

I stripped off my boots and dress. Soon enough I was barefoot in my shift, hopping from foot to foot on the freezing stones. Six feet wide, the basin was huge with graven images of St. Mary and the apostles. I bent over the edge and saw my reflection in the holy water: my pale skin, the vague dark holes of my eyes, the wild black curls that had come loose from my braids as we sailed. The basin was deep enough that the water would rise to my chest, the water perfectly clear.

When the abbot arrived, he laid his hands on me and said something in the language of clergymen. My heart soared with a desperate hope. The abbot wet his hand and smeared the sign of the cross on my forehead. His finger was ice cold. When nothing happened, the abbot repeated the words again, making the sign of the cross in the air. I held my breath, waiting for something to happen, but there was only the chilly air of the minster, the cold stones under my toes.

The holy water glittered, calling me. I couldn't wait any longer. I wriggled out from under the monk's hands and climbed into the basin.

"*Haelewise!*" my father bellowed.

The cold water stung my legs, my belly, my arms. As I plunged underwater, it occurred to me that if there was a demon inside me, it might hurt to cast it out. The silence of the church was replaced by the roar of water on my eardrums. The water was like liquid ice. Holy of holies, I thought, opening my mouth in a soundless scream. How could the spirit of God live in water so cold?

When I burst out, gasping, the abbot was speaking in the language of priests.

"What do you think you're doing?" my father yelled.

Finishing his prayer, the abbot tried to calm him. "The Holy Spirit compelled her—"

I clambered out of the basin, wondering if the abbot was right. Water rolled down my face in an icy sheet. Hair streamed down my back. I stood up, flinging water all over the floor. My teeth chattered. Mother fluttered around me, helping me wring out my hair and shift, trying to dry me with her skirt.

Father watched while I shivered and pulled on my dress. He looked at the abbot, then Mother, his brow furrowed. "How do you feel?"

I made myself still, considering. Wet and cold, I thought, but no different. Either there had been no demon, or I couldn't tell that it had left. The realization stung. I thought of all the remedies we'd tried so far, the foul-tasting potions, the sour meatcakes and bitter herbs. Who knew what they'd try next?

I met their eyes, making my own grow wide. Then I knelt in my puddle on the stones, making the sign of the cross. "Blessed Mother of God," I said. "I am cured."

CHAPTER TWO

After the exorcism, my spells stayed gone for six blessed weeks, the longest respite from them I'd ever had. When they returned, I tried to hide them from Father. I couldn't bear to disappoint him. Eventually he found out, decreeing that we would only seek healing from holy men and women, since the exorcism had lasted longer than anything we had tried before. By the time I was fifteen, we had visited every church and shrine within two days' travel, and I had become deeply skeptical about the permanence of these cures. Some of these pilgrimages were followed immediately by spells, while others stopped them for a month or so. Mother wouldn't let me leave the house without her. I could only see Matthäus when she took me to the tailor shop.

That summer, Father found an anchoress a full three days south of town who was known for performing miracles. After our pilgrimage, I didn't suffer a swoon for many weeks, and my skepticism began to fade. By the beginning of my third month without a spell, I was deliriously hopeful. Even Mother believed. She began to talk about a time when I would marry, have children, and start seeing my own clients. She started sending me on errands to purchase midwifery supplies and letting me go shooting with Matthäus, though she still warned me to beware the *kindefresser.*

That month, Matthäus stopped by nearly every day after he finished work at the tailor shop. Our friendship flourished. As we practiced our shooting, we talked, gossiping and telling each other stories. He told me secrets—how obsessed his father was with the nobles whose clothes he sewed, how he had nightmares about the beasts in the woods—his head lowered in shame. I confided how distant my father had been before my spells stopped, how badly I wanted his approval.

One late summer evening on our way to the grove, I found myself preoccupied by the way Matthäus's hand kept brushing mine. Is he doing it on purpose, I wondered, watching his expression out of the corner of my eye. He whistled cheerfully, oblivious. My desire for him to take my hand was so strong, I couldn't breathe.

Could he tell how I felt? I wondered. I jerked my hand back, mortified, resolving to stop before he caught on. He could tell when something was bothering me.

"Haelewise," he said.

I cursed inwardly, certain he had read my mind. "Aye?"

He nodded in the direction of the public fountain. The tanner's son was hunched before it, wrapped in a tattered animal skin, growling and menacing his sisters. "Albrecht and Ursilda," Matthäus said under his breath. "Remember when we used to play that game?"

I smiled, relieved. "Behind the tailor shop."

"Ursilda is *mine*. Forever!" the older girl yelled, clutching her younger sister.

"Help me, Father!" the little girl screamed. "The witch keeps me locked in a cage!"

Children had been playing that game as long as I could remember. Supposedly, when I was about five, the wise woman who lived in the forest near Prince Albrecht's castle kidnapped the princess. The story went that she locked Ursilda in her tower, which was protected by a mist that made men blind. To get his daughter back, Prince Albrecht put on a magic wolf-skin so the spell wouldn't affect him. As a wolf, he led his men to the tower and rescued his daughter.

When we played, Matthäus always pretended to be Prince

Albrecht, and I always pretended to be the wise woman. The kitten we'd found behind the tailor shop had fulfilled the role of princess. The memory made me smile.

"We were like brother and sister," Matthäus said fondly.

He meant the statement to be kind, no doubt, but it only high-lighted the inappropriateness of my feelings. My smile faltered.

"By thunder," he said, still watching the children. "The little girl looks *terrified*."

I followed his gaze. He was right. The little girl seemed to have worked herself into some kind of frenzy of belief. "She probably begged to be Ursilda."

As we passed, the little girl shrieked with glee. Her older brother lifted her to his shoulders. Rescued at last. Matthäus grinned at me, gray eyes laughing, sharing in the girl's joy. God's teeth, I thought. When did he get so handsome?

I sped up my pace so his hand wouldn't be in danger of touching mine. Turning his attention from the children, Matthäus hurried to catch up with me. For once, he didn't seem to notice my stiff posture or the awkwardness of my smile. "I wonder what really happened to Ursilda," he said as he fell into step with me. "Did you ever get your mother to talk about it?"

Mother had seen so many clients over the years, she knew every version of every tale. When I asked her about this one, the subject made her uncomfortable. "She got angry whenever I mentioned it. All she would tell me was the story was a lie."

Matthäus looked thoughtful, falling silent until we reached the grove. "Father's been trying to get Prince Albrecht to wear his clothes for years. He says Albrecht is a good Christian and that story is nonsense, but I wouldn't want to be the one to fit him."

"Neither would I be," I said, with a rush of fear for his safety that was stronger than I'd like to admit.

We had arrived at the grove. I smiled at the familiar straw-stuffed bird atop the pole and shrugged off my quiver, relieved to pursue a pastime that would require my full concentration. During the moment I aimed my bow, my mind went blessedly blank.

The act of shooting would distract me from my feelings.

The harder I tried to ignore my feelings for Matthäus, the worse they got. By the end of that month, the third since I had gone to see the anchoress, he was the first thing I thought about in the morning and the last thing I thought about before I slept. I knew that I could tell him anything, that he treasured our friendship, but there wasn't a single sign that he shared my affection. It felt like my mind was tormenting me. I was a fisherman's daughter. Matthäus was the son of a wealthy merchant. There was no reason for the object of my affection to be so unattainable.

Three months to the day after my father took me to see the anchoress, I woke up thinking of him, cursing every god in the heavens who might be responsible for my infatuation. In a foul mood, I pushed my feet into the slippers Mother had made me from scrap yarn. In the front room, which doubled as her workshop, lace and cloth fluttered from the rafters, alongside the dried parsley, sage, and parsnips she grew in the garden. A string of golden glass beads, which my mother used as eyes for her poppets, refracted light as they hung in the window-slot. I squinted, cursing my sensitive eyes. Bright sunlight dappled the straw floor, that buttery color the priests say should remind us of God's love. Yes yes yes, I thought miserably, shading my eyes. Beauty and beauty and joy. We know.

I closed the shutters. The hut dimmed. What was left of last night's embers glowed in the fire. I stamped them. Poppets stared down at me mindlessly from the crooked shelves on the walls, queer little girls with unstuffed arms and half-finished dresses, blank-faced princesses with yarn for hair, a king and queen in motley robes. On the top shelf were the monstrous poppets Father hated. Wild men and women, Mother called them. This year she'd sewn both Lamia and Pelzmärtel dolls, which sold well in winter. At Christmastime, the demon-goddess was said to eat poorly behaved children, and Pelzmärtel was supposed to appear and beat them with sticks. Beside them was the poppet Mother had made in my image. Gütel. She had been waiting years for the glassmaker's wife to give us a matching bead for her missing eye. Her scrap dress was neatly arrayed, her black hair tied with ribbons, her eye-thread still loose. Some trick of the light made her look as if she was peering at me, one-eyed, sad to be left on the shelf.

"Haelewise," Mother called. "Are you up?"

"Yes. Which of the poppets shall we take to market today?"

"The queens."

King Frederick—whose rule now extended over the whole of the Roman Empire—had remarried, and Mother was fascinated with his choice of bride. Queen Beatrice had been orphaned young, Mother said, and raised by her grandmother, a sorceress in Francia who taught her the old ways. Father scoffed when he overheard such talk. Last week, the royal couple had visited the bishop-prince, and Mother had taken me to watch the parade. As the queen passed in her bright blue carriage, Mother had waved fervently, and the queen had been kind enough to wave back. I had been astonished by her ankle-length golden braids, which had glimmered like her crown in the sun. During the parade, the shoe-maker said he caught a glimpse of her whispering an incantation into a hand-mirror, and his story had spread like fire.

The day after the parade, Mother had made three poppets in the new queen's image with long yellow braids. I put them in a sack and followed her out.

The street was dim. The sky was dark, cloud-filled. My favorite weather for market day; the sun wouldn't bother my eyes. The sound of our footsteps disappeared beneath the noise of the crowd. The flower peddler selling her wares, the beggar on the minster steps seeking alms. The only thing wrong with the day was the unlucky direction of the wind, which carried the stench of the tannery. I cleared my throat, deciding to bring up something that had been bothering me. "Do you remember the sorceress we visited when I was ten?"

Mother opened her mouth, then closed it.

"That resin she tried to sell us to speed my progress toward womanhood. Do you think we could go back for it? I'm still about as flat as a tart crust, and there's no sign of my monthlies."

My failure to develop had been on my mind, more and more, as my uncomfortable affection for Matthäus had grown. The probability of attracting his interest was already so small, I wanted to do anything I could to improve my chances with him.

Mother shook her head. "We can't go back to her. You know that. Only holy healers. I gave your father my oath."

The bright blue of her dress was swallowed by the crowd as she hurried toward the square. I didn't move, disappointed by her answer, angry at my father for compelling it. What harm would it do?

A light rain tapped the minster steps. The beggar called, "These are troubling times. What is a king without an heir?" His eyes searched the crowd, then rested on me. "Would that I could flee this land, like you."

I tried to control my expression. Mother had taught me to respect my elders, and his comment made no sense. Still, something about him moved me. His kindly face. His ragged cloak. "Blessings to you," I said, dropping a *holpfennic* in his cup.

"Oh, no." He fished it out. "You'll need this more than I."

As he placed the coin in my palm, I shivered, wondering what he knew that I didn't.

"Haelewise!" I could barely make my mother out, a small dot of blue at the end of the street, as she waved. I hurried after her. One of the prince's physicians, an elderly monk with a perfectly trimmed beard, stumbled out of the apothecary. He nodded at me as he clumsily untangled his robe from where it'd caught on an herb bushel.

Next door, the furrier frowned outside his shop, carving the skin off the palest fox I had ever seen. Normally I tried to avoid him—he was foul-tempered—but the fox's fur was fine and white and soft, the color of snow or stars. As I stopped to watch, a huge raven swooped down to the street beside me. It looked up at me, its amber eyes glittering. I shivered, remembering the amber-eyed bird who stole Gütel's eye. A childish fear knotted my stomach, and I felt a chill. The air snapped taut.

The next thing I knew I was lying crumpled on the stones, devastated by the realization that the anchoress's cure hadn't worked. Someone was holding my head. When I finally opened my eyes—cross-eyed, squinting—I was looking right up the tanner's nose. "Where's your mother?" he said. "I thought you were cured!"

I sat up. A crowd had gathered around us. The furrier's two pimple-faced sons were watching me, eyes narrowed. The physician stood behind them all, his robe untangled from the bushel, frozen in the act of leaving the shop. Outrage filled me as I watched him disappear into the crowd. Clearly, the health of a lowborn girl like me was no concern of his. I was so angry—at him, at my spells for returning—that I muttered an oath my mother only used when Father wasn't around. "*Dyēses linekwmy twe*," I spat, though I didn't know what the words meant.

The tanner pulled back, stricken, as if I had cursed him. A hush fell over the crowd. I sat up, fearing what folks would think: the oath, my swoon.

"Don't meet her eyes," the furrier's elder son hissed. "That's how demons move from one body to the next—"

One of the storekeeps crossed himself. The gesture rippled from one person to the next. The miller's sister made the demon-warding sign, forming a circle with her thumb and forefinger. Those who saw it stepped back, looking at one another, whispering.

My chest tightened. Something dark and mindless settled over the crowd. A voice deep inside urged me to run.

Then I saw Mother, elbowing her way toward me, her face tight with fury. "Leave her alone!" she yelled. The crowd froze. She gave the furrier's elder son a look that would curdle milk. "These spells. St. Mary save us. For generations, they've burdened my kin."

Reaching me, she put her hand on my shoulder. "Thank you," she told the tanner brightly. She met the others' eyes, her voice cold. "We're done here."

Whatever had settled over the crowd seemed to lift. People shook their heads and went back to their business. The tanner blinked and murmured a blessing. The miller's sister hurried into the furrier's shop. The furrier scowled at my mother, following the miller's sister inside. His elder son slammed the door behind them.

Mother's expression was grave as she drew me to her breast. "That was close."

The next morning seemed a day like any other. No raven lit on the windowsill. No bat flew into the house. If there was anything out of the ordinary, it was that the house seemed quieter than usual. The only sounds were those of horses outside, clip-clopping the stones. For a moment, I didn't think of the scene I'd made in the square the day before. And then I did, staring at the dried herbs hanging from the rafters, cursing myself. If my feelings for Matthäus had been difficult before, they were downright impossible now. It was bad enough that I was a fisherman's daughter. His father would never let him marry the girl who cursed the tanner.

I wanted to pull my blanket over my head and pretend the previous day hadn't happened, to go back to sleep and wake up from this horrible dream. But that wasn't going to happen, so I made myself get up. I expected to find Mother—and the comfort she would offer—at the table, putting the finishing touches on a poppet. But the table was empty, the rush lights on the wall beside it unlit. Was

Mother out selling poppets so we could pay the anchoress's fee again?

In the window, a strand of beads she'd obtained from the glass-maker's wife refracted the sun into a gaudy rainbow. God's teeth, I thought, squinting with pain as the light hit my eyes. Sometimes I wished I could sleep all day like an owl.

The sack Mother usually took to market hung by the door.

"Mother?" I brushed by a sack of parsnips in the cupboard, a garlic rope. "Are you home?"

The back shutters were closed, so no sunlight came in from the garden but for the single stripe between them. Mother was asleep, her thick black hair like a thundercloud around her head. Some-thing about the way she lay concerned me. She was like a pile of sticks scattered across the bed. The angles were all wrong. I touched her ankle beneath the wool. She didn't respond. I opened the shut-ters. Sunlight poured in, yellow and pure, bathing the bed. Moth-er's limbs moved, as if she was collecting herself, putting herself aright. Out from the covers she peered, blinking. Nothing seemed out of sorts until she smiled. Then I noticed how tired her eyes were, how bloodshot. She looked like she hadn't slept at all.

"Mother," I asked. "What ails you?"

"What do you mean?" Her voice was all wrong. There was little actual sound to it, like wind whispering through the trees.

Some sixth sense, out of proportion with the details before me, filled me with dread. "You never sleep this late. You look half dead."

She cleared her throat nervously, as if she was surprised about her voice. "I couldn't sleep last night. I went for a walk."

"Where did you go?"

"Only a little way into the forest."

A weight settled on my shoulders. But she refused to say more.

Never before had I seen Mother fall asleep on her feet. Not at the table while she worked, her needle in her mouth. First her jaw slackened and her eyes went soft. Then she dropped the poppet whose cloak she was sewing. When she dropped her prized—her only—needle in the straw, I coaxed her back to bed. She had never missed a day of work before. Even if she and Father argued until late, she got up early. In the mornings, she put on her lucky gloves and gardened. In the afternoons, she visited pregnant women who needed her help. At night she sewed poppets. There had never been an idle moment.

The next week, her forehead burned, and she stopped going out. Gone was the woman who popped up as soon as the sun rose. She slept even after I opened the shutters. Her eyelids would flutter when the sun filled the room, but she wouldn't wake until almost noon. Father tried to get the bishop to send a physician, but his petitions were ignored.

As word spread about Mother's illness, her friends began to bring food. The fishwife who lived next door brought flour so I could make bread in the embers. Matthäus's mother brought over a stew, but her son didn't come with her. When I noted I hadn't seen him in over a week, Mechtilde apologized, saying he was very busy sewing clothes for an upcoming wedding. She shared the sad news about our friend, the tanner, who had fallen ill with a fever while trimming the hide of a bull. His wife found him slumped in front of the lime pit, mumbling nonsense, his face flushed.

I couldn't help but fear my mother had also been stricken thus.

That evening, there was a rapping on our door. The miller's wife was in labor. Her nephew was here to fetch Mother for the birth. When I went into the back to tell her, her eyes fluttered open. "The miller's wife?" It took her a moment to understand. Her expression was pained. I could see her thinking, skin stretched tight around her eyes, which had acquired a yellow tint. Her voice cracked as she said, "Tell them I'm sick."

"What?" I breathed. We had never abandoned a client during her pangs. The miller's wife would be fine; she could send for someone else. But her mother, the baker's wife, knew *everyone*. If we didn't show up, everyone would find out that we'd abandoned a client during her time of need. We'd lose half our clients in a day. "Her mother will tell everyone!"

Mother sighed, her thin voice barely audible. "I can't go. I haven't the strength."

I looked at her. It was true. She could barely muster the energy to speak. There had to be something I could do to help. I'd served as her apprentice for five years, and I was good at our work. "Why don't I go alone?"

Mother looked alarmed. "Haelewise, no. They won't want you."

Her words stung. "I've gone with you to visit her many times. I know about her swollen leg, her preferences in birthing oils."

"I know you *could* do it, and you could do it well. But no one wants a childless midwife, and it's a terrible idea after what happened in the square. If something goes wrong, the baker's wife will tell everyone it's your fault. You'd be putting your life in danger."

Her answer maddened me—she was right, I knew—but her words filled me with self-hate. Why had I spoken that oath in the presence of so many people? Everyone already thought me strange. My thoughts raced. Out the front window, I heard the sound of normal people laughing. A resentment filled me that I couldn't even do this simple thing for her. "Fine," I said bitterly, feeling defeated. "We'll let our practice fall to ruins."

"Thank you," she breathed, too ill to remark on my rancor.

After her eyes fluttered closed, I stared at her for a long time, watching the way the moonlight made her face glow, the sickly yellow of her complexion. Her illness terrified me. How could I let her abandon our livelihood? What would we do when she got better if no one wanted us to attend births?

I braided my hair as quickly as I could. When I opened the door, the boy was still waiting. "Hedda is ill," I whispered. "I will come in her place."

As the boy led me toward the miller's stately cottage, I could hear the millwheel groaning, locked against the river's current. I hesitated at the door, worried that Mother was right. All my life, I had loved attending births. Staying up all night with the expectant mother. Helping a new soul into the world. Whenever I entered a woman's chamber, I could sense an otherworldly weight, a possibility that pulled the child's soul from the next world into this.

I could sense that possibility in the air as soon as I walked into the miller's house. The veil thinning between this world and the next, the pull. Suddenly, I was nervous to face it by myself. During a particularly difficult birth the month before, we had lost both mother and child: the wife of a fisherman and a baby that never made it out of her womb. I'd told my mother when I felt a trembling at the threshold, which she had taught me to recognize as a soul. But the fisherman's wife didn't have the strength to push. Nothing my mother did helped. On the third night, the wife became racked with chills. The pull shifted suddenly in the opposite direction, and the wife's soul was sucked from her breast. What if something like that happened to the miller's wife? If she or her baby died, her family would blame me. My mother was right. It was dangerous for me to be here by myself.

The boy went into the next room to announce me. "Hedda is ill," I heard him saying. "Haelewise has come in her stead."

Voices rose and fell in the next room. Moonlight shone through the window, lighting the tapestries on the wall. The air was full of the spicy scent of the caudle brewing over the fire. "Come back," a voice finally said.

I paused for a moment, gathering my courage. Every midwife has her first birth, I told myself. You're ready.

A sheet had been hung over the doorway that separated the rooms. Pushing it aside, my hand met a dozen or more rope charms, intricate knots of garlic and sage, clay amulets chalked with crosses to ward off demons and death.

Inside the dark room, half a dozen women were gathered around the bed drinking caudle. A tapestry had been drawn over the window to keep out spirits. Candles burned on every surface. The light caught the whites of the women's eyes. No one would meet my gaze. In the corner, the miller's sister made the demon-warding sign. The miller's wife looked up from the birthing stool. She held a crucifix in one hand, a St. Margaret's charm in the other. Her breath was ragged. She was retaining even more water than the last time we visited. Her face was pink and shiny, her fingers puffy and plump, but I could see that she had hours of labor left.

"Send her home!" the miller's sister was saying.

The miller's wife sighed. "She's come with Hedda all this time. She's good at her trade."

"She's never had children," her sister-in-law said. "Her skill is *unnatural*."

The rope charms swayed as she stormed out. The miller's wife looked wary. As soon as her sister was gone, I set about showing her that she'd made the right choice. If I was going to work as a midwife one day, I needed to prove myself.

I helped her up and got her walking. I massaged her swollen leg. Between contractions, I rubbed her back with peppermint oil. Her pangs were still several minutes apart. As she paced, I started a fire to keep the water warm.

With the passing hours, the other women curled up on the floor and slept. From time to time, they woke and watched us, eyes wary. I pretended not to notice their mistrust until sometime after midnight when the wife's contractions subsided, and everyone but her gossipy mother, the baker's wife, fell asleep. I was already worried about the cessation of her pangs. Often, when that happened, it was not a good sign. As I waited for the contractions to return, counting the minutes, the hairs on the back of my neck rose. Out of the corner of my eye, I caught the baker's wife watching me from her pallet, as if she wanted to say something.

I imagined her telling everyone what happened tonight, spreading vicious rumors about me if something went wrong. I tried to ignore the feeling that she was watching me, but the feeling of her gaze upon me didn't subside. After a while, I couldn't bear it. "What?" I whispered, whirling on her, resigning myself to a conversation. "Whatever it is, please, out with it. Say it to my face."

The woman balked at my boldness. "Surely it's common for a client's mother to ask questions. Surely you don't mind answering mine."

"Of course not," I muttered, certain whatever she was about to say wasn't so innocent.

She smiled prettily in the candlelight. "How many times have you attended a birth alone?"

I met her eyes, defiant. "This is my first."

She shifted on her pallet so the darkness hid her face. "Can you really sense death before it happens? I heard you could."

This again. I sighed. "Sometimes."

"Is it here now?"

I couldn't tell if she was being earnest or trying to reveal me as a heretic. "It's not death I sense exactly. Only tension in the air, the trembling of souls. All I can sense now is the possibility, the weight that will eventually pull the child's soul into this world."

"So you don't know if my daughter will live?"

"I'm sorry. That's not how it works."

The baker's wife fell silent, but I could sense her unsettlement from her pallet. She lay there for hours, tossing and turning, waiting for her daughter's pangs to resume in full force. When they did, I could feel the possibility of the birth growing stronger, a shimmering weight in the air. The bells for lauds had just sounded at the abbey down the street when the woman's pangs finally began to come one on top of the next. Then I felt a subtle trembling in the air around us. The soul, ready to enter the child's throat. "It's time," I said, leading the new mother toward the birthing stool while her mother held her hand. She was tired, deathly so, from the difficulty of her labor. The transition to motherhood was always more work than women thought.

"You can do this," I said, willing the statement true, still worried that something was going to go wrong with the birth.

"I can't," the miller's wife said weakly.

"We just have to get you to that stool," I said, guiding her toward it, though the weakness of her voice scared me. Like a new mother underestimating the difficulties of labor, I had underestimated the burden of attending a birth alone. I could feel everyone's eyes on me now, watching me, waiting for me to do what I had come here to do.

Another pang came over the woman before her mother and I got her seated. I cursed myself inwardly. The soul was waiting. I was letting the birth go on too long.

"Can you feel it now, Haelewise?" the baker's wife pleaded. "Is everything going to be all right?"

I waved her away. "Let me focus."

As we finally got the new mother to the stool, the child's soul shook with fierce tremors.

I squeezed the woman's shoulder and smiled at her encouragingly. It occurred to me that my mother always mouthed a prayer before she told a client to push. I had no idea what she said, though, because she only ever crossed herself and moved her lips. I crossed myself, following suit. I had no idea to whom she prayed. St. Margaret? Her goddess? St. Mary? *Let this woman's transition into motherhood be easy*, I settled upon finally, sending up the prayer to whoever was listening. *Help me keep this woman and child safe.*

That settled, I put my hand over the woman's belly and waited for the next contraction. When I felt it stir, I spoke. "Now. When you feel the urge, push!"

The sound the woman made as she pushed was like a growl and scream combined. Her sisters jumped up from the floor, wild-eyed, straightening their skirts. They squeezed her hands, murmuring encouragement, reciting prayers for her and the baby's health.

The possibility in the air was so great. I could feel a powerful weight, pulling the child's soul from the next world into this. It was vibrating wildly at the threshold. I crouched beside the miller's wife, watching the space between her legs. After two pangs, I could see the baby's crown, shiny with mucus and blood. A shoulder emerged with the third. With the fourth, the mother emitted a blood-curdling growl, and the child slid out into my arms.

A fat little boy, hale and silent and stout. I slipped my hand inside his mouth as my mother had taught me, to clear the way for his soul to enter his throat. My arms prickled with goose bumps, as I felt it whoosh by, overeager—a silvery mist—on its way into his mouth. As soon as it entered him, he started crying, so loud and wild I forgot everything else.

And just like that, the weight in the air collapsed. The veil between worlds closed. I swaddled the child, looked into his blue eyes, felt his hunger and fear. It was only a moment before his mother reached for him, but that was long enough for me to fall in love with the need in his eyes. The act of holding him, of answering that need, felt *natural*. He was so small, so helpless. When his mother held out her arms, I didn't want to give him up.

A thought occurred to me, unbidden. Who knew if I would ever get the chance to have a child of my own? I could remedy that, right now, steal away with him and raise him as my own.

I only hesitated a moment, but the miller's wife must've read my expression. "Give him to me!" she said, alarmed.

Her mother narrowed her eyes.

"Sorry," I said quickly, giving him up. "Here you go."

As soon as the babe was in his mother's arms, the baker's wife turned to me. "Thank you very much, Haelewise," she said. "That'll do. I can deliver the afterbirth myself."

Before I knew what was happening, she was putting some coins in my hand and ushering me out. As the door shut behind me, I paused, trying to come to terms with how quickly they'd cast me out. I felt indignant that they had become so irate at my simple desire to hold a baby a bit longer. What woman hadn't felt that? He's the first child I ever delivered, I thought petulantly. Of course I got caught up in the moment.

Let she who is without sin cast the first stone.

CHAPTER THREE

O n my way home from the miller's cottage, I decided to take the
road that went past the tailor's shop. Matthäus was opening the
door for a wealthy client as I passed. It looked like he was going to
come over to talk to me, until his father saw what he was doing and
called him inside. Before Matthäus shut the door, he met my eyes—
an apologetic look on his face—and mouthed the word *sorry*.

The encounter was so humiliating, I tried to put it out of my
mind. When I got home, Father was nowhere to be found. I spent
the next few days cooking and cleaning and trying to nurse my
mother back to health. I couldn't stop thinking about the moment
I held the miller's son, the urge I'd felt to steal him away. Before,
I had simply assumed I would become a mother because it was
expected of me. Now, it was something I *longed* to do.

Every morning, I checked the dock behind our hut for my
father's boat, but he didn't come home until four days later. When
he did, his clothes were filthy, and his face was covered with inexplicable pockmarks, but he came bearing good news. The bishop
had finally granted his petition to send a physician to heal my
mother's illness.

The physician the bishop sent was the same monk who'd deserted
me in the square. When I opened the door and saw his fine robe,
his cold eyes and perfect beard, my outrage rekindled itself.

"Well, look who the bishop sent." I didn't bother to hide my
resentment. "Thank you for humbling yourself enough to visit us."

He stiffened, squinting in the late morning sun. "I go where I'm
told. Someone wrote the bishop on your mother's behalf."

My father must have found someone to write the bishop, somehow, during the four days he was gone.

It took me a moment to master my anger and lead the physician into the back room. As soon as he saw my mother asleep on the cot, he handed me a phial. "Fill this with water from the public fountain," he said, presuming I would do as told.

"We just filled the jug at the well," I said, hesitant to leave her alone with him. "I'll fill it with that."

The physician shook his head. "The water must be from the fountain."

"God's teeth," I swore. "The well water's clean."

On the bed, my mother opened her eyes. "Haelewise," she whispered. "Mind your manners."

The physician met her eyes, then mine, resigning himself to delivering an explanation. "Everything I do, I must do with God's blessing. The well is stagnant, a dozen feet underground. Only the fountain water is clean enough to bless."

"Fine," I said angrily. I took the phial and stomped off toward the fountain, though I suspected the well water was cleaner. The Lord knew it certainly tasted better.

When I brought it back, the physician was sitting by my mother on her cot, peering down at a small chart of inscrutable symbols. "Moon in Libra," he murmured, retrieving a fleam from his bag. With a flick of his wrist, he slit her forearm.

My mother seemed oddly fine with his action.

The physician peered thoughtfully at the droplets of blood on the blade. "Give me the phial," he demanded, holding out his hand.

I practically threw it at him.

He ignored my anger, saying a quick prayer over the phial in the language of priests, then mixing a few drops of water with the blood on the fleam. "Sluggish," he said after a moment, looking up at my mother. "You're too phlegmatic. You need foods flavored with marjoram. More baths and exercise."

Mother smiled a tight smile. "If you say so."

I could tell she was just being polite.

"Before you took ill, did you notice any foul odors in the house?"

Mother shook her head, her smile false.

The physician wrapped his fingers around her arm, pressing the underside of her wrist. I suppressed an urge to swat his hand away. "Have you sins to shrive?"

Mother shook her head. "This is no spiritual sickness, Brother."

My thoughts swung between two extremes. I mistrusted the physician, but I feared for my mother's health. "Tell him where you went the night before you took ill."

"How many times do I have to tell you I only went for a walk?" she snapped.

Something about the look in her eyes told me to stay quiet. It was the same look she gave me when I was little, when she tied the keeping string around my wrist in the market.

The physician peered at her. "Where did you go?"

"Only a little way into the forest."

He raised a brow. "Beyond the north gate? At night?"

Mother nodded, closing her eyes.

"The forest fills with poison vapors at night," the monk pushed. "The mist carries disease."

"The mist does no such thing," Mother snapped, losing her temper. "It's perfectly benign. The stuff of which souls are made—"

The physician looked stunned. "What are you raving about? The mist derives from the filth on the forest floor. Rot and ordure, crawling things and dead leaves. The tanner went hunting in the forest the night before he took ill. The mist was bad that night. I don't know if you heard, but yesterday, he died."

Sorrow clouded my mother's face. Tears stung my eyes. For a moment, the physician looked pleased to have made his point. Then he remembered to bow his head. "God rest his soul."

He waited just long enough to be respectful, then went back to lecturing us about the mist. He called it miasmata: an evil essence of death and disease that rose from the soil. "It's gotten into your blood," he said. "We'll need to do a bloodletting."

Mother's eyes crossed, like they did when Father said something ridiculous, but she held out her forearm. "Mark my words," she said to me. "I'm doing this because of a promise I made to your father. The mist has nothing to do with my illness."

The physician shook his head, eyebrows raised, then told me to light the rush lights and torch. When I returned, he had taken out his leeches, horrid little flat black worms, which he kept in a pot. It took him two hours to place them on my mother's skin, and one more for her to faint. Then she lay still, sweat on her brow, as the leeches worked. I watched her chest rise and fall, eager to see some sign of improvement, but there was none. Only an increasing pallor to her complexion that brought out the faded pink scar on her cheek. The physician touched the scar. "How did she get that?"

"Hunting in the woods. Before the wall was built. At least that's what she says. She's had it as long as I can remember."

He nodded quietly, thinking. "Your mother is stubborn."

I had to laugh at that. The room fell quiet. "Will she live?"

The physician looked into the leech jar. There was movement at the bottom, a small black mass of worms. "If the Lord wills it."

He frowned as he pulled the leeches from her skin, glistening with jewel-drops of blood. When he finished, he told me some patients slept for a while after a bloodletting, and I would need to see that her throat stayed wet. He showed me how to cup the bottom of her jaw to open her lips. He gave me a phial full of a thick red draught, which he said would calm her. "No more than three swallows a day," he said. "It's strong."

I nodded, warming toward him a little.

From his bag, he pulled a censer covered with tiny filigrees and cross after cross after cross. He handed it to me. Inside were several small, sweet-smelling bricks of incense. "Burn these," he said. "They've been blessed by the bishop."

I took the censer, though I knew my mother would be skeptical.

"Hippocrates thought fainting spells were brought on by the phase of the moon. Do yours happen at any particular time of the month?"

I nodded, confused at the change of subject. "More often around the new moon."

"Look here?" He stretched my eyelids open, then brought a candle close to my face. A ball of light exploded across my vision. "Your pupils don't respond to the light at all. That's why your eyes are so dark."

Pain stabbed my temples.

"Did your father ever bring you to get an exorcism?"

"It didn't take."

The physician cleared his throat and stood. "Let me give you some advice. If your mother survives, keep her out of the wood. And you, stay home as much as you can. They just drowned a girl with fits in the next village. There are many who blame you for the fever."

Mother fell into a deep sleep and wouldn't wake. I set the incense burning and opened the shutters, but it didn't do any good. I watched her with my back to the light, taking in her slack expression, the limpness of her black hair. How still she is, I thought, over and over. I brought her water. She slept and slept. Father came home late. His breath smelled of spirits, and he wouldn't look at me while we ate. Not that this was unusual. He drank often, and we had spoken little since my spell in the square.

When he left the next morning, she still hadn't stirred. Her chest rose and fell beneath the blanket, but she did nothing else. All that day, I stood at the edge of her room and watched her breathe. The signs of her illness seemed similar to those of the deadly fever that was going around. I was afraid that the physician was right, that she'd caught it somehow in the woods.

Father came home late again that night, unsteady on his feet, as if he'd spent the day in the tavern. He said no blessing when we sat down for dinner. He didn't carve a cross in the bread. He even forgot to wash his hands with water from the jug. As we shared the tart I'd made from eggs and perch, he complained that the physician had only made things worse.

"How did you convince the bishop to send him, anyway?"

Father's eyes shifted in my direction.

"The physician said someone sent a letter."

"All I did was put in a request."

I met his eyes. "That was weeks ago. He only agreed to come after you went away for four days. Where did you go?"

The rain beat the roof. He picked a fishbone from his teeth. The only answer he made was to say, "It's your fault your mother's ill."

The words were like a knife in my chest. I could scarcely breathe, staring across the table at him. My skin crawled. He took another drink from his tankard. A piece of parsnip fell from his beard. I closed my eyes and swallowed. "How can you say that?"

He glared at me for a moment, then shrugged. His eyes wide, what was left of his blond hair unkempt. "Because it's true."

Guilt clutched at my throat. I ran to the cupboard, pulling my wool blanket over my head. Tears streaked my cheeks as I heard him leaving the house.

That night, I tossed and turned, checking on my mother every hour until my father came home, smelling of drink. The straw itched my back. Outside, dogs howled. I closed my eyes tight, my chest full of an ache I knew no physician could cure.

I woke up before dawn. Mother was still asleep, unmoving, so I went into the garden to finish harvesting the leeks myself. It had been a long time since I was in the garden alone. One of the legs of the wooden bench my father built when we first enclosed it had come loose, so the seat was tilted. The sun had barely risen, and the garden wall was tall, so most of the garden was in shadow. As I knelt in the shade beside the leeks, a thrush hopped down from the tree outside the crumbling wall to catch an earthworm. As he hopped back up to the wall, singing sweetly, I envied his good cheer.

Soil scattered to the grass as I shook off the leeks. The chickens, hearing me work, clucked their way out of their coop. They pecked my skirts. The rooster was nowhere to be seen. Since Mother fell ill, I realized, no one had fed them any leftovers, so he was probably down the street somewhere looking for food.

Resolving to feed them soon, I wondered why my father blamed me for my mother's illness. Did he, like the townspeople, think I caused the fever? Did he think I cursed the tanner too? The idea made me angry. I had been fond of the tanner. He was a kind man, my mother's friend. Some dark urge compelled me to wish that I was what everyone thought I was. It would serve them right if I went to the city gate at twilight—arms out, beneath the full moon—and called the mist down on all of them.

Then I caught myself, and my heart swelled with guilt. I said a brief prayer for forgiveness. When I was finished, I couldn't stop looking at the three pebble-crosses beside the herb garden, which marked the graves of my three elder brothers who'd been born dead. Mother often sang to them while she gardened, a lullaby she said her mother taught her. I saw her in my mind's eye, planting a seed in her lucky gloves full of holes.

As I piled the leeks in my skirt, her song haunted me:

"Sleep until morning, my dear one,
Housos leaves honey and sweet eggs.
Hera brings blooms, blue and red."

I sang the song to myself as I gathered my skirt, my voice catching with sorrow. All I wanted was for Mother to get well.

There was a sound coming from the back of the house, so faint it could've been the wind itself. My mother's voice. *"Haelewise?"*

I rushed through the back door, dropping the leeks all over the floor of her room, hands and knees covered in dirt. Mother had propped herself up on a pillow. Sunlight poured over her arms. "How long was I out?"

"Two days," I said, rushing to hug her. Tears welled in my eyes. "I was worried you wouldn't wake at all."

She tried to swallow. *Water*, she mouthed.

I hurried to the well and drew up a bucket. Much of the liquids I'd given her had dribbled down her chin.

She drank the cup dry three times before she spoke. "I don't even think I dreamed."

"I need to ask you about something Father said."

Her eyes narrowed. "What?'

"He said your illness is my fault."

"No no no. It most certainly is not!"

"I feared it before he said it. If it's not true, then tell me where you went the night before you took ill."

She reached for my hand and squeezed it in an attempt to reassure me. Neither of us spoke. "Your father is like the physician, asking about poison vapors and sins, looking for something to blame. This illness isn't your fault. It's the same illness that took your grandmother."

I had only vague recollections of an older woman, thin and matronly in an apron, with an ample bosom and a full head of dark hair. It was so long ago that I couldn't even picture her face. All I remembered was that she was kind, and her home had been full of pastries and apples. I blinked the memory away and tried to think. "Why does Father blame me, then?"

Mother sighed, sadness glinting in her eyes, then patted the cot beside her. "That's a long story. Have a seat."

I sat cross-legged on the bed, as I had done so many times when I was little. She reached for my hand and squeezed it, meeting my gaze, as if whatever she was about to tell me was important. Sadness glinted in her eyes. "Your father—" she started, then stopped, as if she were measuring her words. "Your father has been angry with me a long time. What have you heard of the wise woman who lives in the tower in the forest?"

I met her eyes, confused. "What does she have to do with this?"

"Give me a moment. Tell me what you know of her."

I thought on everything I knew. "Some say she is an old woman, stooped and hideous; others say she's an ogress. They say she lives in a tower near Prince Albrecht's castle, deep in the darkest part of the forest. They say no man can see inside the stone circle that surrounds the tower, that once men step inside, their vision fills with mist. They say she knows the old ways, how to make a philter to start and stop a belly's swell. They say a lot of things, Mother. There's nothing like a woman who lives alone to get stories going. Supposedly she kidnapped Princess Ursilda, and her father had to wear a wolf-skin to rescue her"—I looked up—"but you said that story was false."

My mother pressed her lips together tight, her face acquiring the strained expression she always wore when I asked about this story, but this time, I could tell she was going to push through whatever kept her silent. When she spoke, her tone was different from the one she usually used when she told a story. Not full of mischief with the act of tale-telling, but clear and matter-of-fact. "The wise woman knows the old ways, that much is true. And Albrecht really did wear a wolf-skin—his son Ulrich has it now, though he acts the Christian at court. But there was no 'rescue.' Ursilda's mother sent her to the tower to learn the old ways herself."

I searched my mother's face. "How do you know all this?"

"I heard it from the wise woman."

"When? What did you go to her for?"

My mother drew a deep breath, refusing to meet my eyes. I got the sense that she was trying to decide how much to tell me. When she finally spoke, her voice was haunted. "Don't tell your father I told you this, but I nearly died birthing the third of your stillborn brothers. After that, your father refused me. I went to the wise woman to get something to put a man to sleep, and something to make sure a living child came from what I did next."

Her admission horrified me. "*That's* how I came to be born?"

She nodded slowly. "The wise woman said that life could only be wrought from life, that there would be a cost. I felt the toll on my body then, but—"

"That's why Father blames me?"

Mother nodded again. "When my belly swelled, I told him what I had done, but he didn't believe me."

Outside, children were playing near the docks. The streets echoed with giddy screams.

"I'm thirsty," she said.

I left her to retrieve another bucket of water from the well. When I came back, she lay very still, white-knuckled, her eyes wild. My hand shook as I held the cup to her lips. The water only dribbled down her chin.

When Father came home, late that night, I was huddled with Mother in her cot. "She can't move," I told him. I couldn't keep the panic out of my voice.

He shrugged, dismissing my concerns, and sent me to bed.

I lay in the cupboard all night, restless, sleep eluding me until just before dawn. When I awoke, broad daylight striped the shutters and I could hear my parents talking softly in the back. I put my ear to the wall and listened.

"I've done what I've done," Mother was saying. "There's no turning back."

"Without consulting me, as usual. Doing whatever devilish thing you want—"

"I want to be buried in the garden," Mother said.

Her words were like a slap in my face. I blinked, my eyes filling with tears. Father cursed, slamming something—his hand, maybe—into the wall. All I could hear was the thud. Then footsteps, approaching the cupboard. He was angry, storming out. I panicked, shrinking into the corner. If he caught me listening, he would strike me, but there was no time for me to lie down and pretend to sleep. I sucked in my stomach and flattened myself against the wall. He will not see me, I told myself, he will not, he will not—

The cupboard walls shook as he passed, inches away in the dark. In the front room, I could hear him grabbing the cloak he wore on the water. The door slammed, and I took a deep breath, my fear subsiding. When I was sure he was gone, I hurried into the back room. Mother looked startled. "You're awake?"

"What did you do?" I asked, my voice catching in my throat. "Why were you talking about where you want to be *buried*?"

"Haelewise," my mother said, her face crumpling. "Come here."

I sat down beside her. She made me look at her.

"It was just a precaution," she said. "In case something happens."

I bit my lip, despondent. I knew she was lying.

The sunrise played tricks on the light, casting weird shadows over the bed. Mother's skin gleamed, pale and thin, stretched tight across her bones. She looked like an old woman, twice her age, her black hair on the pillow streaked with white. "Have I ever told you how your father and I met?"

I shook my head, having difficulty focusing on her words. "Why does it matter? You just told me you're dying."

Mother sighed. Her voice was thin. "Your father used to sell fish in the market. I would see him a few times a year when my mother and I drove our cart here to buy flour and other supplies, rare oils and spices. He was handsome, back then. Broad shoulders and a tapered waist, brooding eyes, beautiful golden hair." She closed her eyes, smiling faintly, as if she were seeing the younger version of my father in her mind's eye. Father was balding now, his belly swollen. "I didn't know, when I followed him into the linden grove that day, how wonderful it would feel to kiss him. Nor did I know how much what happened after that kiss would wreck my life. When I fell pregnant, my mother wanted me to drink a potion, but I married him instead." Her voice shook. "In the end, your brother was born dead."

I made myself breathe, trying to make sense of her story. Why was she telling me this now?

When she spoke again, her voice was so soft I could barely make out the words. "I've given up a lot for your father. We argued fiercely in those first months. He wanted me to be baptized." Her voice was full of regret. "Your father won the argument."

I pitied her. "But you still burn offerings. Visit wortcunners. Serve as a midwife."

She met my eyes. "It's not enough."

I did not ask her *enough for what?* I remembered the night the month before, when we were walking home from the birth in which both the fisherman's wife and her unborn child died. Tears had streamed down my mother's face, and her voice had risen with grief. There were things she could've done to save them, she confessed, if she didn't have to worry about being thought a heretic.

Her voice interrupted my thoughts. "What is Matthäus like?"

The question took me by surprise. "Why?"

"Just tell me."

I sighed. It was difficult to think of anything but the fact that my mother was planning her burial. The shock of it haunted me. And thinking about Matthäus made me sad. Since I saw him outside the tailor shop, he hadn't knocked on our door once. I suspected his father had forbidden him to see me. "Kind," I said finally. "Earnest."

Mother nodded. "That's how he seemed to me. Good. How do you feel about him?"

Her question conjured a lump in my throat. "I don't want to talk about it."

She watched my face carefully, measuring what I had just said. "His mother came by before you woke up. His apprenticeship will be over soon. Mechtilde said he wants to ask for your hand."

Her words knocked the breath out of my chest. The shock was palpable, almost too much for me to bear. I must've gone pale as a ghost.

"Haelewise, are you all right?"

"He what?" I said finally, realizing I had stopped breathing. I closed my eyes and made myself draw a deep breath. "Did you just say Matthäus wants to *marry* me?"

She nodded encouragingly, a delighted look on her face. "You like him."

"God's teeth, yes. I can't stop thinking about him. But his family is so wealthy. I'm pretty sure after what happened in the square, his father forbade him to see me." My voice caught. "I'm about as fertile as the dirt beneath the tanner's barrel. Even my own soul disdains my body, Mother. I dare not think it would interest anyone else."

"Oh, Haelewise—" She took my hand and pulled me close. "You're beautiful. Mechtilde says he's fallen for you. She's trying to convince her husband to allow a love match."

"He'll never agree. Not now."

"There's a cure for your spells, Haelewise. Your grandmother—" Her voice trailed off. She looked thoughtful, almost pensive. Finally she nodded, deciding something. "Bring me some water."

When I returned from the well, she patted the cot. I brought her the water and sat next to her. The cot was warm, the blanket scratchy beneath my legs. She hugged me close, resting her chin on my head. "Did I ever tell you the tale of the golden apple?"

I shook my head.

Mother took a deep breath. "In stories old there was a mother whose daughter was plagued with fevers. The girl burned so hot that the mother nearly died while the girl was in her belly. She burned so hot that when the girl was born, she was born nearly dead. But the mother held the girl to her breast anyway to nurse her. The mother wept tears of joy when the girl began to suckle."

There my mother paused, taking a deep breath. I let my head fall against her shoulder. I closed my eyes, feeling sleepy and comforted, the way I had when she held me as a girl. She put her arms around me, pulling me close. As I waited for her to go on, I breathed in the faint scent of anise and listened to the beat of her heart.

"As the girl grew older," she went on, finally, "her mother sought far and wide for a cure to her fevers. They consulted with every alchemist, every sorceress and physician. They brought the hermit from the hovel by the sea. The priest. The bishop. Nothing worked."

Mother stopped again, for a moment, catching her breath. I couldn't help but wonder if she was making this story up. It seemed too close to her efforts to cure my spells.

Outside, a peddler called out, hawking his wares. The room seemed suddenly chill. I pulled the wool blanket over my legs.

"In the end," Mother went on, finally, "it was not a healer who cured the girl. It was the girl herself who found the cure in a plant that grew just outside their doorstep. This plant bore tiny golden apples that shriveled as winter came, filling the air with a heavenly scent. The day the girl ate one, once and for all, her fevers left."

As she spoke these last three words, her voice rose, slow and steady, like a pack horse ascending a rocky path. Then she swallowed, as if her throat was dry. I handed her the cup of water. "Are you saying we've looked in the wrong places for my cure?"

She shook her head and drank.

"You think the cure has been here all along?"

"I'm only saying, sometimes, the cure grows just outside your door, if you look for it."

"What?"

She set down her cup. "Go get me the aniseed pot. There's something I've been wanting to give you."

Mother kept aniseed in the cupboard to make the seed cakes she ate after dinner. The seeds rattled as I brought the pot to her. She removed the lid and stuck her hand into the seeds. The scent of anise filled the air as she took something out, an old key, then shook her head; it wasn't what she was looking for. "Hold this," she said. She fumbled around inside the pot again, then shook the seeds from a tiny black stone figurine.

"Here." She held it out. "This used to belong to your grandmother."

I examined the figurine. The black stone had been carved into the shape of a woman holding a child, but no one would mistake her for the Blessed Mother. She was a bird-woman, naked with heavy breasts and wide hips. Her face was strangely shaped, grotesque, with protrusions on the sides of her face and wide-set eyes. She had wings and a beak. "What is this?"

"A good-luck charm. Put it somewhere safe. That key too. I don't know what it's for, but you might need it. Don't let your father, or anyone else for that matter, find the charm. They'll tell Father Emich, and he'll call you a heretic."

Mother had impressed upon me young the need to keep her faith secret. I hadn't even told Matthäus about the offerings she burned, the curses she muttered, the incantations to chase away bad luck. She was afraid to tell me much because she didn't want to put me in danger. When I was very small, a Frenchwoman who preached the gospel of Mary Magdalene had been stoned in the street. Mother's faith was far more heretical.

I looked closer at the figurine, carefully shaped from a soft black stone. She felt slippery almost. She had taloned feet like an eagle. Her hands were three-fingered, thumbless. She felt oddly warm to the touch. I met my mother's eyes, awed. "You used to say your goddess dwells in things, in the hidden powers of root and leaf—"

"Haelewise. I've broken my promise to your father a dozen ways today. Please don't ask me to do it again."

I sighed and closed my mouth.

"Everyone goes on about the pleasure of the act," she said, suddenly, as if caught in a separate thought. "And there's truth to that. There is. But the best thing about it is the children who come from it." She put her hand on my chin, turning my face to meet hers.

I nodded, a lump rising in my throat.

"You have brought me such joy, do you know that?"

CHAPTER FOUR

I slipped the key and the bird-mother figurine into my pouch where my father wouldn't find them and examined the charm each night when I laid down to sleep. Sometimes, if I stroked her curves, her black stone warmed under my fingers, and the air seemed heavier than before. She was fascinating to look at, simultaneously hideous and beautiful. Enthralling. She hinted at a world outside the bishop's wall, where Mother's beliefs might be accepted, where my fainting spells might not be seen as evidence that I was possessed.

Each night, I rubbed her curves, whispering prayers for my mother's cure. Not that the prayers did anything. Some nights, as I lay in my cupboard, I confess, my faith faltered. I wondered if my father's and mother's gods were like the *kindefresser*: stories people told to influence other people. But every time I was seized with doubt, I remembered the veil I sensed between worlds, the souls I sensed moving in and out of bodies. There was a secret world that shimmered behind the world we knew. I had felt it. I wrapped my fingers around the bird-woman and felt her power.

As the weeks passed, Matthäus didn't knock on my door. He certainly didn't propose. I began to feel foolish that I'd allowed myself to believe my mother's gossip. She had probably just been trying to make me feel better.

Word must have spread that I attended the birth of the miller's son instead of my mother. No one else came to summon Mother for a birth. As autumn turned colder, she slept more and more. From time to time, she lost the ability to move her limbs. When she was awake, her voice blew through the house, a whisper, a faint breeze. She lost her place in speech, glancing up in confusion.

Father became the thud of boots on the floor. I waited longer, each day, for the tinkling of his *holpfennige* in the jar. He said not a word to me as he came in, though he always put food on the table when he did. Fresh-caught whitefish I seared over the fire and ate in clumps, a hardened half wheel of cheese.

The autumn vegetables ripened. I pulled carrots and cabbage, leeks and onions, and soaked them in brine. I straightened the pebbles on my brothers' graves when they were disturbed by animals.

One afternoon in October, there was a knock on our door. Mother was sleeping, as usual. She didn't stir. When I saw Matthäus at the threshold, my heart fluttered. I hadn't seen him since my mother mentioned his intentions. I caught myself wondering if he was there to propose and quashed the thought, embarrassed.

When I let him inside, he scanned the poppets on the shelves in the front room. He'd never set foot in our house, despite all the times he'd knocked on our door. The rush lights on the table sputtered. A breeze swayed the beads in the window, casting light on the floor. In the corner, a rat twitched its nose. Shoo, I wanted to tell it. Get back in your hole!

"How is your mother?" he asked.

"Not well."

He sighed, pulling a strand of wooden beads from his pouch. "My father doesn't know I'm here. I had to sneak out while he was on an errand."

I tried to hide my disappointment. I had been right all along. His father didn't want him to see me. Why did our mothers think his father would accept me as a daughter-in-law?

"My mother and I wanted to give you something," he went on. He put the beads in my hand and closed my fingers around them, his hands lingering on mine. "They're called paternoster beads. We received several as a gift from the Duke of Zähringen, and we thought you might like one. You use them to pray the paternoster over and over, counting the repetitions. The duke says that God is more often moved by repeated prayers."

His touch made me dizzy. I opened my hand. The beads were beautiful, smooth pearls of wood. They had an unearthly weight. "Are you sure you want to give me these?"

"They're a parting gift of sorts, unfortunately. I have to accompany my father on a trip. He says we won't be back until the beginning of Lent."

"Oh," I said softly. Lent was four months away. "Where are you going?"

"The Duke of Zähringen is giving a feast in Zürich. He wants his whole family fitted with new clothes. Everything kermes-dyed, bright red, embroidered with eagles from his family crest." He took my hands in his. "When we come back, things will be different. I promise. I'll come by more often. I'm going to talk to my father about you on the trip."

Shame filled me. I pulled my hands away. "What will you say?" My voice shook. "What can you?"

He met my eyes, his own full of pain. "The truth," he said softly. "That you are important to me."

I thought again of what my mother said, that he wanted to marry me. A sob rose, unbidden, in my throat. I swallowed it and looked away. The rat was watching us from the corner, flicking its tail.

Matthäus held my gaze. "My mother and I have been working on him, but—" He shook his head. "Well, you know how fathers can be."

I made myself nod.

He embraced me for a long moment, his arms wrapped tight around me. His shoulders had gotten so broad. I longed for him to kiss me. "Get out of here," I said, pushing him away so I would stop thinking about it.

Laughing, he brushed my hair from my forehead. When he saw

the tears in my eyes, he moved to go, not wanting to cause me further pain. "I'll come by as soon as we get back. I promise."

As the door fell shut behind him, the rat scurried back into its hole.

The paternoster beads were an unexpected comfort. I put them in my pouch with the bird-mother charm, which I ignored more and more as the weeks passed. Maybe it was because the beads were a gift from Matthäus. Or maybe it was because, unlike the charm, I didn't have to hide them from my father. I carried the beads with me during the day so I could use spare moments to pray for my mother. Each night in my alcove, I whispered the paternoster, counting repetitions on the beads until I fell asleep.

One morning, Mother was feeling well enough to talk, and I told her about Matthäus's visit. "How did it go?"

I sighed. My troubles would only burden her. I tried to think of a way to explain without upsetting her. "He's going with his father to Zürich. The Duke of Zähringen is hosting a feast. He won't be back until Lent."

"Did he say anything about his intentions with you?"

I avoided her gaze, hoping to change the subject. "He's going to work on his father on their trip. I'll know more when he returns."

She nodded thoughtfully, fingering the blanket. After a moment, she looked up. "If his father won't give you his blessing, did you know you could have a wedding without a priest?"

That got my attention. "How?"

"You hold each other's hands, make a vow. There is power in the words themselves." She took my hands and squeezed them. "Look at me, Haelewise. This is important."

Her gaze was so intense, I wanted to look away.

"Their way is not the only way," she said. "Remember that."

As the weeks passed, Mother's condition worsened. Her forehead burned. She slurred her words. She was always too cold, or coughing when our fire filled the hut with smoke. By December, her skin was yellow all over. Her eyes looked like they would pop out of her skull. She was bloated, cheeks swollen. She couldn't get out of bed. It was clear by then that whatever she was fighting wasn't the fever that was going around, which either passed or killed its victims within days. I prayed fiercely for her recovery, fingering the paternoster beads a dozen times a day. Father petitioned the bishop to send a priest to administer a blessing, but so many people had come down with the fever, there weren't enough priests to see everyone.

One morning, I stood at her cot, wringing my hands, uncertain what to do. She had been unable to move for hours, and her breathing was labored. On the table next to the bed, the calming draught the physician had left us glowed. I poured twice the usual amount into a cup and pressed it to her lips. It was like a balm. In an instant she was calm. Her eyelids drooped. She slept.

When she woke, she could move again. Smiling, she chanted a children's rhyme in her odd little whisper. "*Five, six, witch. Seven, eight, good night.*"

Her eyes wet and bright, she petted a wrinkle in the wool blanket and looked at me. "It's beautiful," she cooed. "Do you see it? A beautiful kitten!"

What could I do but pet it with her, a rift opening in my chest?

That afternoon, she had another spell of paralysis. They seemed to be growing more frequent. Her eyes darted, frightened, around the room. I gave her more draught and she slept.

Hours passed, this time, before she woke. When she did, the kitten was back. I petted it with her, asking what color it was. She told me blue. I thought it strange how much she laughed.

At sunset, she complained that she was hot, though the first snow of the year had fallen that day. By the time darkness fell, it was so cold that the fire in the front room barely kept the back warm. I tamped it down, peeled off her blanket, and opened the shutters to let in the cold. Over the street, the sky was moonless, a mess of stars. The cobblestones were covered with a thin dust of snow. I wet a rag and pressed it to her forehead. At length she slept.

When her eyes opened, the light in them burned. "Haelewise," she whispered, barely able to shape the word. "I'm leaving you something."

When her voice trailed off, I reached for her hand, panicked, wondering if she needed more of the draught.

"You have the gift—" she croaked. She opened her mouth, once, twice, like a fish, trying desperately to finish whatever she had wanted to say. She glanced down at her chest. After a moment, she mouthed two words, slowly, carefully: *the gift*. Her eyes went wide. A familiar tension snapped the air in the room taut. The veil lifted. My breath caught. I squeezed her hand. "Mother."

But she only stared, wide-eyed, at the rafters. Her expression terrified, her small lips pursed in an O. After a moment, her hand went limp in mine.

No. The word repeated itself in my mind. No no no—

I knelt beside her, clutching her hand tight, begging her not to leave me behind. I felt a diminishing, a pull from the next world. I watched my mother's mouth, her chest, praying for her to take another breath.

The dew that rose from her mouth was silvery, the color of water, a whisper-wind. I shivered as it passed through me on its way out of this world. My vision blurred with tears as the tension in the air collapsed. All that was left was the cold coming in through the window and my mother's body on the bed. My mother but not, her body but not. A yellowed face, glassy green eyes, swirls of graying hair.

After a while, my eyes stopped seeing the body before me, and I was aware only of the memories replaying themselves in my head. Everything my mother ever did for me, the songs she sang, the tales she told, the alchemists and healers she sought out. What she taught me about how to tell winter is coming, when the spider returns to its chamber, and how to read the meaning of birdsong in each season. Sometime later—I have no idea how long—I heard a sound behind me. Father stood in the doorway. He'd lit the rush lights in the front room. I could see his shadow-shape, blocking the light. I couldn't be sure how long he'd been there. He stood without moving, his hand on the doorframe. Then he took off his cap and bowed his head.

He knew. Relief poured through me. It would've been horrible to have to tell him. After a moment, he walked in, boots pounding the floor. Up into the rafters he stared, crossing himself. His lips moved, his expression unreadable as he said a prayer. He wouldn't meet my eyes. When he walked out, the front door slamming behind him, a terrible guilt crept into my heart. I remembered his accusation that I was the cause of my mother's illness. Out the front window I could see him moving quickly, with purpose, down the street toward the square.

I closed the shutters, then went to the cupboard to lie down, shivering with cold. I shoved the paternoster beads and the bird-mother charm into my purse, where I wouldn't have to look at them. I knew I was supposed to think my mother's death was part of God's plan, but instead, I felt betrayed. Hundreds of times, I had prayed the paternoster, and every one of those prayers had been ignored. My father's god was no better than my mother's goddess, whose "good-luck" charm, I could not help but think now, was nothing more than a glorified toy.

I didn't expect to sleep. I couldn't stop thinking about my mother's body in the next room. Her last words about leaving me something, about my having a gift. None of it made sense. Hours passed before I slept, but eventually I managed to slip out of myself. I dreamed I was cooking, throwing spice after spice into a cauldron full of ooze that smelled like onions and earth. As I stirred it, I understood it was a magical remedy. I brought a ladle of it to my mother, who still lived in the world of the dream. She drank it and got out of bed.

When I woke, it took me a moment to realize the dream wasn't real. I stared at the ceiling. My eyes burned. My heart pounded in my ears, and the smallest of sounds, a *whoosh* of sadness, strangled itself from my throat.

Time was like an endless ribbon that night. It unspooled, wrapped itself around me. Bound so tightly to each moment, I could scarcely breathe, lying on the straw in the dark cupboard. Even the rats in the walls seemed to have slowed their scrambling.

Years passed, or so it seemed. I paced the front room. Out the window, the sky was black, moonless. Stars fell, outside, in the form of snow. I went half mad before I heard the *thunk* of my father's boots, before I smelled the scent of spirits when he ducked in our door. He didn't say a word to me, but I found that I could sleep with him home.

It was noon before I woke. The house had a sweet smell, like that of some spice mixed with pine. Pushing my feet into my slippers, I tiptoed into the back room to find my mother's body gone. There was no blanket on the cot. Even the mat was stripped from its frame.

In the front room, straw smoldered in the fire ring. The house was uncomfortably warm, the air thick with smoke. My father sat at the table in the same clothes he'd worn the night before, his boots and fingernails caked in mud. There were puddles on the floor. On the table was the physician's censer, in which a single brick of charcoal glowed. A fine powdery smoke rose from it, filling the room with that sweet scent. Father nodded without speaking, his eyes going to the back door. When I looked out, I saw that the snow over the garden was firmly packed.

The sight of that snow, glittering in midday sun, destroyed me. He had buried her without me. "How could you?" I said, coming back to the front room, my voice breaking.

He stared at me, his expression vacant. Too numb, I realized, to reply. I wanted to ask whether he'd found a priest or buried Mother himself. Then I saw that the jar at the door was empty of *holpfennige*.

All this time, he had been saving for her funeral rite.

CHAPTER FIVE

Three weeks after my mother's death, on Christmas Eve, I stared into the empty cupboard. I cursed myself for forgetting to feed the chickens. I hadn't seen them in weeks, and Father had asked me to cook Christmas dinner. It would be so simple to go into the woods beyond the south gate and shoot a pheasant, but the guards would accuse me of poaching if I tried to bring it back through the gate. Mother always used the *pfennige* she earned from selling poppets to buy ingredients for feast days. The thought of selling them without her wrecked me, but so did the idea of eating Christmas dinner alone.

The unfinished poppets leered at me from the shelves, their faces blank orbs of cloth. They would look like hobgoblins if I tried to finish them; I had yet to learn how to use a needle without pricking myself. But Mother had finished a dozen poppets before she fell ill. Selecting a Pelzmärtel doll from one shelf and a princess with a fishnet veil from another, I put them in a sack and paused at the door.

The physician's warning to stay home echoed ominously in my ears. On the peg by the door hung my mother's cloak. Bright blue, dyed her favorite color by a wortcunner that we hadn't seen in years. The dye incorporated several secret ingredients, Mother said, for good luck. Everyone else in town wore the more fashionable dark blues the dyer made. It was tempting to put on her cloak—sometimes I wore it at home, just to be enveloped in her scent—but the blue color would give me away.

Into the cupboard I went to put on my wimple and tattered gray blanket, which would hide my face if I wrapped it around me like a hooded robe. I hated the fact that I had become such a pariah. All I'd wanted since I was little was a simple life—a husband, children to cuddle and tell wonder tales, to work as a midwife. None of it seemed possible anymore.

As I walked to market, my stomach growled. The air smelled of pastry and sweetmeats. Children played in the street, throwing snowballs. Peddlers cried out, selling spice cakes and wine for Christmas Eve. The sun shone, pale and cold on the bright snow, so white it pained my eyes. Beside the stable scene that had been erected in front of the minster, a crowd of marketgoers had gathered to listen to a group of choirboys dressed as shepherds, who were singing in the language of priests. I stopped to listen, keeping my distance so no one could see my face. The song stirred something in me, a blurry memory of a Christmas Eve when my parents and I had stopped to listen to a similar choir. The memory made me so sad, I was startled when the song ended and everyone began to disperse. As the crowd streamed past, I held my breath, hoping no one would recognize me.

"Poppets!" I made myself call in a singsong voice, tugging my hood further down over my face. "Poppets for sale!"

Several children, apparently bored by the performance, came straightaway. Their mothers followed. In no time at all, I sold the dolls. No one saw through my disguise. As I purchased the ingredients for Christmas dinner, I saw a man who looked like my father strolling arm in arm with a blond woman who resembled the widow Felisberta from church. As they drew closer and I became certain it was them, I pulled down my tattered hood. My father didn't notice me as he passed, his bald head glinting in the winter light. The widow and he were drinking something from their tankards, and her three little boys were skipping and eating spice cakes behind them. My stomach turned to see my father walking with someone who wasn't my mother and her children. I hurried away, unable to bear the sight, turning to the spice cake I'd bought for comfort.

Behind the minster, I saw two young wives on the steps, wearing wimples and kirtles. Doves danced at my feet, flapping their wings. "What makes you so sure she could cure the fever?" the first woman was saying to the second.

"She's a holy healer," the second answered. "I heard she's writing a book about the healing properties of plants."

"She would never come this far. All the way down the Rhine."

"Still. I would lay odds that she could do it. They say God works through her. She has visions. She writes them down."

"She sounds like a manly woman."

The second woman laughed. "I heard she's building an abbey herself. A fortress, with a river to carry away ordure and filth. She cured a woman in Bingen with fits."

I nearly choked on my spice cake. "Who are you talking about?"

The women turned to look at me.

"Mother Hildegard," the first wife said, peering at me.

I noticed for the first time their brightly dyed kirtles, the stilted way they spoke *diutsch*. Their long, ribboned braids, which my mother called corpse-braids because they were extended with hair from the dead. They were courtiers' wives. The first woman peered under my hood. "Aren't you the midwife's girl?"

"The one who cursed the tanner?" The other squinted at my face. "It's her. Get back!"

My heart beat in my throat. "I didn't curse anyone!" I shouted as I ran away. My feet pounded the cobblestones. I didn't stop until I ran out of breath in the alley behind the furrier's shop. Hunched and wheezing, I chastised myself. It had been foolish to address the women at all. As I caught my breath, I shivered. The air seemed to thin. Not now, I thought. Not here—

But happen it did. I felt the pull. My soul left my flesh.

When I came to, I was on my back in the slush, my hood fallen from my face. The furrier's sons had seen me faint. "You shouldn't be out," the younger boy sneered, blocking the alleyway, making the same gesture the miller's sister had in the square. "You'll loose your demon on someone else."

I stood, a flurry of fear in my stomach. The elder son leered and nudged his little brother. Following their gaze, I saw the budding swell of my breast, exposed by a rip in my dress. I had been so preoccupied with my grief that I hadn't noticed my own blossoming. I felt myself blush as I covered my chest.

The elder brother advanced on me, his muscles taut, like a snake about to strike. I leapt in the other direction, pushing his little brother out of my way, so that he slipped and fell face-first into the snow. As I fled the alleyway, I saw the blood, a beautiful red bloom on the snow where his nose smacked the stones.

On Christmas Day, Father walked home with me from Mass. As soon as we arrived at the hut, we washed our hands, and I sat down at the kitchen table to chop the ingredients for dinner. Father didn't speak at first. He only stood by the window watching me, the winter sun shining at his back, making a too-bright halo around his scalp.

"You'll be needing a woman's shift soon," Father said, watching me chop. "It's about time. What are you, sixteen now?"

I nodded, embarrassed.

He fished some *holpfennige* from his pouch and set them on the table, then pulled a bag of candied fruit from his pack and set them beside the coins. "I thought we should have something sweet, since it's Christmas."

His thoughtfulness took me by surprise. I noticed the shadows under his eyes, the sadness in his tone. All the sorrow I held inside me threatened to tumble out. "I miss Mother so much," I said suddenly. My voice shook.

Father sighed. "Don't despair, Haelewise. It's ungodly."

"It's only been three weeks."

He looked at me sharply. I racked my brain for something neutral for us to talk about. All day, as I cooked, I had daydreamed about making a pilgrimage to Hildegard's abbey. "What do you know of Mother Hildegard?"

He shook his head derisively. "A woman? Building an abbey, curing disease, writing holy books. She might as well be a character from one of your mother's stories."

"I thought she might be able to cure my fainting spells."

"She damn well might. They say she can do everything else. But Bingen is awful far. How would you get there?"

I sighed. Not how can I help you get there, but how would you do it yourself. "I'm still working that out."

Father sighed, going to the cupboard for the physician's censer. He filled it with charcoal and powder and brought it to the fire. It clattered on the table as he set it down, the crosses carved into its side leaking a familiar fragrant smoke.

"What are you doing?"

"Cleansing the house."

"Of what?"

He frowned. "Your mother's sins."

I couldn't believe my ears. Did he blame my mother for her illness? Did he think God struck her down for her "sins"? I shook my head, trying to shake these thoughts from my mind, but I couldn't. Outrage filled my heart.

Father looked away, watching the smoke swirl from the censer and up through the roof holes.

I thought of what he said about blaming me for my mother's death. I wanted to scream at him. "Would you please tell me why you think me responsible for Mother's illness?"

He pulled his gaze from the smoke, his thoughts clearly elsewhere. After a moment, he opened his mouth, then closed it, as if he were trying for once to measure his words. "What I should have said was I blame your mother for your demon."

I stared at him, waiting for him to explain.

The words tumbled out of him, as if he had wanted to say this for a long time. "You know the upbringing your mother had, deep in the dark forest north of town. Your grandmother whispered wicked incantations. When we first met, there was a darkness, a wildness in your mother. After I asked her to marry me, she vowed to forget all that, but your mother never was one for keeping her word. All those unnatural remedies she got for your spells in secret, the unholy incantations she muttered under her breath. Don't think I didn't hear them. When I stopped sharing her bed, she even broke our wedding vows." He hesitated, watching my face, his eyes going wide. "Mother of God!" he thundered. "Did she tell you everything?"

I shook my head. I didn't want to betray her trust. "I don't know what you mean."

"Damn it, Haelewise." It was clear he didn't believe me. He grabbed my hand across the table. His temper flared, as it always did when I refused to do as told. His fingers pinched my wrist, twisting my arm. "Don't lie to me. What did she tell you?"

My eyes watered. I made myself still, counting the holes in the censer. Its smoke tickled my nostrils. It was pungent like a spice, but impossibly sweet, recalling scents I'd smelled in the market as a girl. Cinnamon and anise, fennel and sage. Whatever he was burning was like none and all of them.

"That she visited the wise woman to get a potion."

He let go of my wrist, looking oddly relieved. "Is that all?"

My chest tightened. I made myself nod. "I swear it."

He sighed with relief, closing his eyes. It was a moment before he spoke, his voice matter-of-fact. "I have something to tell you. Do you remember Felisberta? From church?"

My heart beat in my ears. Felisberta was the name of the blond woman I had seen him with in the square. I nodded, afraid I knew where this was going.

"Her husband died of the fever. She has three sons. Her kin have abandoned her. Father Emich has encouraged me to marry her."

My stomach dropped. I could scarcely breathe. I thought of how much my mother had given up for him.

He couldn't meet my eyes. "I'd ask you to come with me to live with her, but she's afraid of your demon. She has her boys to think of."

His words shocked me. I had endured his fickle feelings for me all my life, but I didn't think he would be *this* cruel. Not only was he replacing my mother, but he was going to leave me behind because his new wife didn't want me in her house? No other girls my age lived by themselves. "Have you given any thought as to what this will mean for me?"

"I'll visit once a week. I'll bring fish and cheese. It won't be much different from the way things are now."

I stared at the wall, with a choked feeling in my throat that lasted all through Christmas dinner. As my father babbled about Felisberta's virtues, my eyes watered. The fish and candied fruit stuck in my throat. I kept thinking of the Frenchwoman who was stoned in the street for preaching the gospel of Mary Magdalene. If my father abandoned me and I had another spell in the square, the townspeople would burn me at the stake.

I spent Christmas night in a sort of stupor, trying to come to terms with his abandonment. I kept wishing stupidly that my mother were still alive to comfort me, or that Matthäus would hurry up and come home.

Father came back the next day with Felisberta, driving a cart hitched to an old gray ass. They took almost everything—all of our chairs and trunks—leaving behind only the earthenware jars in the cupboard, the kitchen table, the pallet where I slept, and my mother's trunk. Felisberta tried to take that too, but when she bent down to sift through it, Father stopped her. "That belonged to Haelewise's mother," he told her, his voice gruff with kindness. "Leave it for her."

Tears stung my eyes. My heart swelled. After everything he'd done, I still wanted his love, even though—or perhaps *because*—I knew how rare it was. As soon as they left, I went through the trunk, eager to find out what my father wanted me to have. It was filled with my mother's old linen dresses and smocks, most of them dyed her favorite shade of blue. My heart broke when I brought the fabric to my nose and breathed in her scent. There was a wimple she had discarded because it was torn. A pair of old boots. And beneath that, a small wooden box carved with a simple pattern. Pulling it out, I tried to open it, then realized it was locked.

A lockbox? I didn't know we had one.

The key from the aniseed pot. When I inserted it into the lock and turned it, the lock clicked. Inside, I found a tarnished gold hand-mirror wrapped in a blue silk cloth, its handle engraved with strange symbols and birds. Awed, I remembered the shoemaker's story about seeing the queen with one of these. Why would my mother have one? How would she own something so expensive?

Unwrapping the cloth, I saw that the looking glass had been smashed.

The lake began to freeze the next week, the tidepools near the docks whitening with thin scrims of ice. The winter before, I'd enjoyed stamping on them on daily walks. But since my run-in with the furrier's sons, I was reluctant to leave the hut. I spent most of my time sitting in the garden and trying to make up recipes for meals from what little food I had available at home. More than once, I heard a nine-killer shriek its hellish song from the garden wall, and I crept up and shot it—though the bird, in truth, was too small to eat.

From time to time, I took out the smashed hand-mirror and wondered how much about my mother there was that I didn't know. I fantasized about traveling to Hildegard's abbey. If Matthäus convinced his father to let him marry me, they might be able to afford to send me to her abbey for a cure. Every time I went to market, I took less-traveled streets, checking frequently that my makeshift hood hid my face. I avoided the street with the furrier's shop, choosing the street with the tailor's shop instead. If I saw Matthäus's father inside, I would know that Matthäus had returned from Zürich. But it was always his mother within. At night I dreamed that he came home and knocked on my door with good news: His father had agreed to a love match. And just like that, all my troubles were gone, that is, until I awoke.

At first, Father kept his promise and visited once a week for dinner. He brought food to share, smelly cheese and salted fish. But as time passed, he began to forget. Sometimes he forgot the cheese, other times he forgot the fish. One day, a few weeks before Lent, he showed up empty-handed and left when I didn't have anything to cook. I realized I'd have to buy ingredients myself if I wanted to eat with him.

The next day, disguised in my old blanket-cloak, I sold another completed doll to buy food. As I was purchasing flour, I saw a new face, a town crier I'd never seen before. A big man, ruddy-faced, his voice too loud as he moved from group to group with a scroll. Each time he moved to a new cluster of people, he spoke to them, eyes flashing, expression animated, too far away for me to hear. Each time he finished his speech, there was an exchange: I saw one woman give him a wineskin; another gave him a kiss. After that, he lowered his voice. The women gasped at what he said next, and the crier moved on. When he approached me, the look on his face turned my stomach. I picked up my things to go.

"Where you hurryin' off to," he slurred, following as I rushed down the street that led from the square. I could smell the wine on his breath. "Don't you want to hear the news from his imperial and royal majesty? I'll read the official decree tomorrow, but you can learn it now, if you earn my favor—"

"I have nothing for you."

"It's about the princess."

Something inside me snapped. Selling the poppets had been nerve-racking; by now, I had no patience left. "Leave me alone."

His expression hardened. He grabbed my arm and yanked me into an alley, twisting it behind my back. Too late, I realized my mistake. The crier expected to get what he asked for or else. As the crier pushed me into the wall, my eyes fell on the seal on his scroll: a golden shield with a pattern of black lions. The king's sigil. When he kissed me, I closed my eyes, wishing my soul would leave my body.

"That's how it works," he sneered. "Favor for information. Understand?"

I nodded, glaring at him. He let go of my arm.

"Princess Frederika has fled the castle," he growled. "She's headed this way. If you see her, King Frederick commands you to report it immediately, on pain of death."

CHAPTER SIX

T he last few weeks before Lent were miserable. I was hungry. I was lonely. I was afraid to go out. But I had to sell my mother's poppets to buy food until the spring vegetables ripened, so go out I did, stealing to the market in my tattered blanket-cloak. I smudged my face and clothes to make myself unattractive to bachelors so I would be dismissed as a beggar or worse. I found out soon enough there was freedom in such a disguise. Once I had sold all of the poppets, no one noticed me. Not nobles, not merchants, not even children playing in the streets.

By Ash Wednesday, there was nothing left on my mother's shelves but Gütel and a few unfinished poppets that wouldn't sell. Dolls without clothes, jesters without arms, blank-faced princesses with half-finished crowns. I would make a mess of them if I tried to finish them by myself. It was barely light out when I tied my hair back, pulled on my blanket, and hurried out to see if Matthäus was back from Zürich. Spring had yet to chase away winter's chill, so early in the morning. Even in the blanket, it was freezing.

My heart fluttered when I turned onto his street. How I prayed he was home. It had been so long since I'd seen him. Maybe he would have good news for me about his father. His house stretched above the tailor shop, its roof piercing the gray sky. Staring up at it, I couldn't help but wonder what it would be like to live there with him. Their house wasn't stone like the houses of nobles, but it had a dignity of its own. The crossbeams, the thatching. It had six large windows, a staircase, and two floors.

As I drew near, the orange cat we'd saved as a kitten—now a

huge tomcat, missing an ear from street fights—pressed himself against my legs, purring. I petted him absent-mindedly, looking for a pebble to throw at the window of the upstairs room where Matthäus and his brothers slept. The pebble clattered against the shutters. My breath puffed up in desperate, frigid clouds. "Hsst."

Nothing happened for a moment, apart from the sleet that fell on my nose. Then the shutters opened and Matthäus leaned out in his nightcap. The sight of him was like a balm. Relief washed through me. My breath caught in my throat.

"Haelewise? Is that you?"

I tried to master my feelings. "Can you come down?"

"Of course." Three smaller faces appeared beside his. I heard his brothers protest as Matthäus told them to get back to bed.

When Matthäus opened the door, my stomach fluttered. Had he been this tall when he left for Zürich? Had I forgotten how good-looking he was? Even disheveled in his nightshirt, brown hair falling into his eyes beneath his cap, he was startlingly handsome. When he smiled at me, my hopes soared. I had missed him so much.

"I wasn't sure it was you," he said, nodding at my clothes.

I looked down. "I didn't want to be recognized."

"I'm so sorry about your mother," Matthäus said. He pulled me to him, his eyes haunted with sorrow. "Mother told me last night."

In his embrace, my grief arose from where it had been lying in wait. My eyes burned, and I felt myself crumple in his arms. I wanted him to hold me like this forever.

"I'm so sorry," he whispered, pulling back to look at me. "I know how close you were. I'm going to miss her too."

I didn't know what to say. There was a knot in my throat. I wiped my face with the blanket, suddenly aware that my nose was running. "When did you get back?"

"Only yesterday."

"I'm sorry to wake you," I said, trying not to sound desperate. "The chickens flew away. I forgot to feed them. I need help finishing the last of my mother's poppets so I can sell them to buy food."

"Your father isn't providing for you?"

"He married the widow Felisberta."

Matthäus's eyes widened with anger. "*Married*—so soon?"

"Aye," I said curtly, my own anger at my father rearing up. "Mother died in December. He moved into her house the day after Christmas. I've been living alone, selling poppets for money."

"He didn't invite you to move with him?"

I shook my head, pressing my lips together tight.

The sympathy on his face was unbearable. Suddenly aware of how wretched I must seem, I lifted my chin. "I wouldn't have gone if he did."

He shook his head. "Let me go tell my father."

As soon as he went inside, I wiped my face carefully with the blanket. I smoothed its cloth, wishing I had worn something more presentable. I'd become so used to leaving the house in this blanket that I hadn't spared a thought for how he would see me.

As I waited for him to come out, the street grew visibly lighter. I thought about how Matthäus had promised to see me as soon as he got back. The fact that he was taking so long, that he hadn't come to see me right away, did not bode well. If he'd fixed things with his father, wouldn't he have come to tell me right away? By the time he came back out, my heart was full of dread.

He'd changed into his day clothes, put on his overshirt, and stuck a needle in his cape. His expression was difficult to read. "Sorry that took so long. It was hard to convince him to give me the morning off."

My heart fluttered. I opened my mouth to ask whether he'd talked to his father, then decided I wasn't ready. His father's reluctance to let him help me this morning was a bad sign.

We started the walk back to my house, our footsteps echoing through the largely empty street. The only other person we saw was a woman emptying a chamber pot.

"I'm sorry I didn't come to see you yesterday," Matthäus said. "I wanted to, but my father was insistent I see someone else first."

"Who?"

"Phoebe of Kürenberg."

I knew of the Kürenbergers. They owned estates in the foothills of the mountains in the northern forest and a beautiful cottage on the banks of the lake.

"Did she need to be fitted?"

He heaved a great sigh. "Unfortunately not."

"Why did your father want you to meet with her?"

He looked pained. Dread knotted my stomach. I had to ask. I couldn't wait any longer. "Matthäus. Did you talk to your father?"

"Haelewise—"

"What aren't you telling me?"

He couldn't meet my eyes. "The conversation didn't go well."

I knew he was going to say something along those lines, but hearing him say it was devastating.

"I'm working on it," he said quickly. "I promise—"

My thoughts whirled. All that hoping I'd done, all that praying. I felt like I was going to be sick.

"Haelewise, I mean it. I'm trying to get through to him. My mother's on my side."

He met my eyes.

I took a deep breath. "Thank you for telling me."

A long moment passed before either of us spoke. Our footsteps echoed on the cobblestones.

"I missed you," he said finally.

The look on my face must've been wretched.

After a moment, he changed the subject. "Did you hear about Princess Ursilda's wedding?"

"No," I admitted, trying hard to keep my voice even.

"Her father finally convinced a prince to marry her," Matthäus went on. "The wedding is next week. Father finished her dress yesterday. He won't stop joking about sewing wolf-fur onto the sleeves to match her brother's coat."

Matthäus kept up a stream of chatter about the wedding, and eventually I regained my faculties enough to pay attention. King Frederick would be attending, and he'd ordered a dress for his runaway daughter in case she turned up. Apparently Ursilda and Frederika were friends, and Frederika had been betrothed to Ursilda's brother, Prince Ulrich, before she fled.

That detail caught my attention. I stopped in my tracks. Prince Ulrich with the wolf-skin? "No wonder Frederika ran off!"

Matthäus nodded. "I know."

"Why would he promise his daughter to Ulrich?"

He sighed. "I can only guess that he doesn't believe the stories."

When we got to the hut, I started a fire, then set out the unfinished poppets on the table with my mother's scraps. Bald princes and princesses whose legs were unstuffed, half-clad dukes in sad little capes and nothing else. We planned out seven poppets and began sewing dresses and trousers, threading yarn into scalps. I kept pricking myself with my needle and cursing. The third time it happened, Matthäus stopped me, putting his hand on mine. "Haelewise, will you grant me a request?"

I looked up at him, hopeful. My skin tingled where our hands touched. The look in his eyes said he felt it too. He opened his mouth, his expression dazed, then closed it. His thoughts were clear on his face. He wanted me, and not only that: He was surprised by the strength of his desire. I took his hand in mine and clasped it tightly, smiling at him, praying his request would have something to do with *us*.

But then, as he looked down at our hands, something shifted inside him. "Give me the needle," he said, pulling his hand back, his expression resigned.

A moan of protest escaped my lips.

"You can't sew," he said, laughing, turning his attention to the task at hand. "Tell me a story instead."

I turned away so he couldn't see my disappointment. You can easily entertain him, I told myself, you're good at this. I forced myself to focus, to think about the kind of story that would be best for this moment. I knew Matthäus liked stories inspired by real-life nobles, stories about illnesses cured and injustice made right. But bitterness poisoned my thoughts. All the ideas that came to mind were tawdry yarns that I knew he wouldn't like. Scandalous stories that ended badly. I wasn't in the mood to please him.

Resigning myself to a story I would enjoy telling, I smirked and began the tale. "In stories old, there was a beautiful young queen who couldn't have children. She shared her husband's bed every night for years, but her belly never swelled."

Matthäus blinked at the reference to sex, freezing in the act of threading his needle.

I leaned in closer toward him, our shoulders almost touching, eyebrows raised, my voice an earthy whisper. "The queen drank the royal healer's teas. She prayed. She tried all the herbs the king's monks gave her, all the tricks the midwives recommended, but her belly stayed as flat as a board. Eventually, she heard rumors the king would seek an annulment. She sent for a witch from the forest who knew the hidden properties of plants. In secret, the queen asked the witch for a draught that would help her conceive. 'Life can only be wrought from life,' the witch told her in her raspy voice. 'There will be a cost.'"

Matthäus sat up perfectly straight. Part of me felt bad. I understood what I was doing. Using my body to remind him of his feelings for me. Intentionally trying to throw him off balance, telling him a tale that would disturb him. And yet, I couldn't make myself stop. I was angry, deep down, that Matthäus hadn't stood up to his father, angry that his father was keeping us apart.

"The queen didn't care," I said, defiant. "There was nothing she wouldn't give up for a child. The witch made her an unnatural elixir. That night, she kept the king awake for many hours."

By this point, Matthäus had gone completely still, his face bright red. There was a part of me that enjoyed it.

"The next winter, her belly swelled big and round. She laughed and sang. She was hot all the time, no matter how cold it was. When her time drew near, it became difficult for her to sleep. She stayed up all night, embroidering tiny dresses, sitting on the sill with the window open, gazing out. One night while she was sewing, she pricked herself. A droplet of blood fell to the snow. The blood spattered, and a flower grew where it landed. Bright red, it was, the most *frightful* rose."

Matthäus watched me, puzzled about where the story was going, but I could see that a part of him was entertained despite himself. A faint smile haunted his lips. I focused on the interested part of him—that part deep inside, which loved stories for their own sake—and spoke to it.

"From the petals of that rose there came a fairy," I pushed on. My voice rose. "A wicked nymph with hair the color of night and skin the color of snow. Her hair was a tangle of black thorns, and her lips were blood-red. She sang a terrible tune:

> *"Life from life! Snow White is my name.*
> *Your child will die in three days' time*
> *unless you make it her name too."*

He looked taken aback at the fairy's threat, setting down his needle. "By thunder," he swore. "What did she do?"

I smiled, triumphant that my tale had grabbed him. "She cried out. Her ladies-in-waiting came running. But the fairy had vanished by the time they arrived, leaving only the rose. Barefoot, distraught, in her nightgown, the queen rushed outside to pluck the flower. Only by the time she got there, the rose was gone. When she returned to her chamber—her toes covered in snow, her breathing labored—she had her first pangs. Her labor lasted three nights before the midwife finally told her to push."

Matthäus leaned forward, waiting for me to continue. I smiled at him, proud that my storytelling had made him so enrapt.

"The queen was so exhausted by the time the baby came that she thought she couldn't go on. When she finally held her daughter in her arms and saw the strangeness of the girl's features—her white skin, her red lips, her black hair—she knew what she had done: traded her own life for that of the girl. She drew the child to her breast to nurse, her eyes full of tears."

Matthäus stared at me, horrified.

I held up my finger. "She called for the king and told him they had to name the child immediately. Snow White, she insisted, so her sacrifice wouldn't be in vain. Then—her heart breaking—she fell into a swoon. She died the next day."

Matthäus dropped the poppet he was holding.

I waited an appropriate time before I went on. I had learned this from my mother, from the bishop's physician. A death is significant, important. A death requires a pause. "The king didn't take his wife's death well. His grief made him weak. Within a month, he was remarried. His new bride, Golden Braids, was a powerful witch who had preyed upon him in his grief. She carried a gold hand-mirror in which she could see the whole of the kingdom. She wore a magic yellow shawl made from her own hair."

I made my eyes widen with the alarm I knew Matthäus would feel at the queen's unnatural magic. Every good story needs a villain of some sort, and I was still angry about Felisberta. I saw no reason not to choose the stepmother for this one.

"As Snow White grew more beautiful, the aging Golden Braids became envious. The girl's lips were red. Roses blushed in her cheeks. She reminded the king of his late wife, whom he still seemed to mourn. When the girl turned twelve, Golden Braids convinced the king to promise Snow White to a wicked prince. Unbeknownst to the king, the prince turned into a wolf on the night of every full moon."

I paused here, overwhelmed, falling into the story, sympathizing with the characters. The grieving king. The fairy daughter. For a moment, I almost sympathized with the queen. "Snow White fled the castle on horseback, black hair twisting behind her. The king asked the queen to use her mirror to find her. But the queen lied to him, saying the mirror only showed mist. In truth, the queen could see Snow White in the mirror: The innocent girl lay in a clearing, fast asleep. After the king went to bed, Golden Braids closed her eyes and murmured a spell that made the night-birds hungry. The evil queen watched in the wonder-mirror, as night-herons and owls flew into the clearing. They hovered above Snow White, landing in the branches of nearby trees. The queen kept chanting the incantation, until there were hundreds of birds in the clearing. She didn't stop until the birds pecked Snow White to death."

Matthäus gasped.

"That's it," I said, my voice flat. "That's the end."

Matthäus paused, sitting up straight. He picked up the poppet he had been sewing and stared at it as if it were a foreign thing. For a long moment, he was silent, examining the poppet. Then he went back to sewing, his voice taking on a thoughtful tone. "Call me a fool. I don't know. Only a fool expects all to turn out well in life. But I prefer tales that give the listener hope."

CHAPTER SEVEN

Matthäus didn't come back to my hut for a long time after that. Whether this was because of his father or my story, I didn't know. I was terribly lonely without him, deeply regretful that my bitterness had gotten the better of me. I turned my story over and over in my mind, wishing I had told it differently.

The blooming of my mother's garden, that spring, nearly brought me to tears. Every time a new stem burst from the earth, my head filled with memories of kneeling beside her, learning how to plant seeds or identify seedlings. Each new stem bore a name she had taught me. Endive and spinach, sprouts and asparagus. Sometimes I heard the music of her voice as she taught me their names, sweetened by a mother's love for her daughter, and my heart broke. Other times, the sight of a new cluster of seedlings infuriated me. How dare they thrive—so steadfast, predictable—after their gardener was plucked from the earth?

These betrayals were closely followed by an uprising of flowers. Bloom after bloom of dainty blue primrose, followed by turnip flowers and frothy yellow lady's mantle. There were new seedlings everywhere, as if turning the earth had inspired old seeds to grow. Turnip and parsnip grew too close to the wall. Each morning, I stood over them, wrapped in my tattered robe, wondering where my father had laid my mother to rest. Was her head beneath the spinach or the primrose? Did the lilies grow over her toes?

One morning, when I went out to weed, I noticed a new plant I didn't recognize among the lilies, a plant for which my mother never taught me a name. A green stem, twisting up from the soil, with a single purple bud on its tip. Within a few weeks, another plant of its kind sprang up beside it. The next week, more appeared. By May there were dozens of them, scattered across the back of the garden. Strange bushes with leaves like wild lettuce, a bouquet of tiny purple buds at their centers. Light-thieves, my mother would've called them. Weeds. I couldn't bring myself to pull them up.

By summer's end, they were everywhere, healthy cabbage-like bushes with huge leaves a foot tall and three feet wide. At the center of each where the flowers once bloomed grew tiny nutlike globes, wild green fruit like none I had ever seen before. As the weeks passed, the berries grew larger, their skins turning yellow.

What happened next should have come as no surprise. Matthäus was over a year older than me, eighteen, nearing the end of his apprenticeship. I hadn't seen him in months. Phoebe of Kürenberg was twenty-one or twenty-two. If her father didn't marry her off soon, it would be too late. When the priest announced Matthäus's betrothal to Phoebe during the marriage banns, I was standing in my usual spot behind the rail at the back of the church, near the beggar who often sought alms on the minster steps, where I wouldn't accidentally sit next to anyone who would recognize me. As soon as the priest said the words *Matthäus, son-of-Heinrich-the-Tailor*, I was struck with the worst headache I'd ever felt.

I clutched the rail, white-knuckled. The beggar met my eyes. "A marriage," he breathed. "Is that what drives you away?"

"Away?" I whispered. "Where would I go?"

He didn't answer.

The priest droned on. The church swam around me. I felt nauseated, as if my body wanted to reject what my ears had heard. Calm down, I told myself. Of course Matthäus is marrying the Kürenberg girl. Did you think that you had mesmerized him, somehow, with your blind-bat eyes and dazzling wit? How could he possibly convince his father to let him marry *you*?

Somehow I made it through the service. Afterward, I saw Matthäus leaving with Phoebe, her wheat-colored plaits wound around her head like a crown. She wore a rich green dress that clung to her hips. She was a woman, much more so than me, that was clear. Never before had I hated anyone so much.

When I got home from church, for the rest of the day, I couldn't eat. I couldn't sleep. There is a limit to the amount of loss one person can take; I had already endured more than my share. It seemed unjust for the world to take Matthäus too. It was as if the gods were testing me to find out the limit of what I could take.

The next morning, exhausted, I went out to the back garden to try to make peace with what had happened. I thought I would sit on the broken bench and say a prayer. I'd hoped sitting outside among the plants and vines and stones would calm me, but instead I found myself haunted with memories of my mother. Sitting on that bench, I remembered a spring day we were turning the earth for planting, when a family of robins jumped down from a nest they had made in the back garden wall. The robins had fluttered down, fluting and warbling, to search the freshly dug earth for worms. One of them landed on her skirt, and Mother's laughter had been brilliant.

Searching the garden wall, now, I saw that the nest was long gone, the robins nowhere to be seen. The garden had never been large or well groomed, but I had let it go wild over the summer now that Mother wasn't here to take care of it. The stones of its wall were covered in moss and vines, and several rocks had come loose. The sod we'd pushed into the gaps between stones each year had eroded, leaving holes through which you could see the docks behind the house. It occurred to me that if I didn't intervene, it was only a matter of years before the wall would succumb to the ravages of time. It appeared that nothing in the world could escape that fate.

As I was contemplating this, I heard a muffled sound: a voice calling my name. "Who's there?" I called over the wall.

"Matthäus."

My chest went tight. The last time I'd seen him, I was wearing a tattered blanket. Here I was again, a mess, my hair unkempt, my boots covered in dirt. I tried to think of a reason to turn him away, but couldn't. I went inside and opened the front door a crack. I could see him on the other side, his dark hair straying into his gray eyes. So handsome, I wanted to jump in the lake.

"I came to explain my betrothal."

"You don't owe me anything."

He met my eyes through the crack, his expression pleading. "My father arranged it."

I narrowed my eyes. "What's she like? Your intended."

"Phoebe has a terrible temper and a cruel laugh. She's pregnant with another man's child."

"She's what?" I opened the door.

He stepped into the front room. "She was engaged to another man, who ran off. Her father made an offer mine couldn't refuse. A title. A cottage on the lake. Favor with the bishop-prince."

I shook my head. "Another man's child?"

"I don't want her." He brushed his hair back from his face, completely unaware of how handsome he was. "I wish it was you instead."

It was the one, the only thing he could have said to win me over. I took a deep breath. We stared at each other, becoming conscious of the space between us. He took my hand and squeezed it, then stepped close enough for me to see the green flecks in his eyes. "When my father demanded I court Phoebe, I was furious. But he said he would disown me, prevent me from working as a tailor altogether, if I didn't go through with it."

Listening to him say all of this now, when he was already betrothed to someone else, was torture. "Why are you telling me this?"

He was quiet for a long time. "You want me to say it?"

I could hardly look at him, it hurt so much. "Whatever it is, yes."

Silence filled the room. When he finally spoke, he looked at his feet, his voice husky with feeling. "I have to marry her, but I want you."

At first I wasn't sure what he meant.

He looked up at me furtively, his embarrassment clear on his face. "I've missed you terribly," he said. "I know my father's plans for me have hurt you, but I can't imagine my life without you. My father said we could provide for you. We met a physician in Zürich who said he could cure your spells."

Provide for me? A physician in Zürich—

I realized, suddenly, what he was offering. He wanted me to be his mistress. The realization was like a bucket of cold water poured over my head. "*What?*"

"My father said he doesn't care what we do, as long as I marry Phoebe. He even spoke to Phoebe's father about it."

I gaped at him, unable to make sense of what he was saying. My lips had gone dry. My thoughts were tangled.

"What does Phoebe think of this arrangement?"

"She couldn't care less. She only needs a husband so her child isn't a bastard."

I stared at him dumbly.

"It's a way for us to be together."

I took a deep breath. "It isn't, though."

"Why not? We could even have children."

A wild anger streaked through me. "I want a *family*, Matthäus. No one would let someone's mistress into their house to attend a birth. Our children would be bastards! Have you thought this through at all?"

My voice was shaking.

He blinked at me. Clearly, he hadn't considered it from my perspective. "No," he admitted. "I'm sorry. I guess I haven't."

"Leave," I said, walking to the door and opening it. "I can't stand the sight of you right now."

He looked positively shattered as he walked out.

The truth was, I didn't want to cry in front of him.

Two weeks later, he knocked on my door again. This time, I made him wait. I washed my face and pulled on one of my mother's shifts from her trunk, a beautiful bright blue kirtle with a ribbon that would emphasize my waist. I pulled my braids out from under my wimple so he could see them. Then I opened the door partway. "What do you want?" I said flatly.

"I'm sorry." He looked miserable, like he hadn't slept since we last talked. There were dark shadows under his eyes; his expression was tortured. "I should've thought more about what I was suggesting."

I glared at him. He deserved a couple sleepless weeks. There was no way he'd had as difficult a time as I had. "You should've."

"I understand that you can't accept, Haelewise. You deserve a proper husband. Unfortunately for me, I can't be that for you."

He waited for me to respond. When I didn't, he went on.

"I made you something."

He shrugged off a pack I hadn't noticed he was wearing, withdrawing two fur boots and a madder-red bundle of cloth. A dress, I realized as he held it up, dyed my favorite color. With an embroidered neck, a petticoat sewn into it, and bell-shaped sleeves with golden trim. Lacing down the sides so it could be tightened to fit my frame. "It's beautiful," I breathed, despite myself, awed. It was like a sunset trapped and shining in cloth.

He smiled nervously. "I worked on it every night, after I finished at the shop. I hardly slept."

My thoughts raced. "Matthäus. I don't understand."

He reached into his pack again and pulled out a madder-red cloak with a deep embroidered hood. He pulled it up so I could see it. The trim of the hood shimmered, golden. So fine, each of its threads seemed to shimmer with magic. I touched the trim, the brooch—I'd never owned a brooch—overwhelmed, suddenly, at the beauty of his gesture.

"Matthäus. Why would you make me a dress?"

"I love you." He said the words simply, matter-of-factly, as if there could be no argument against them. There was no show of emotion, no grand gesture, but there were tears in his eyes. When I saw those tears, for the first time, I understood the torment that gave birth to his proposal. He loved me. Everything stopped when I understood this—my breath, my heart—I swear, even the sun and the moon stopped moving. He wanted me as badly as I wanted him, but he saw no way out of marrying Phoebe.

My anger at him began to thaw. "I love you too," I said softly.

He met my eyes. "Come to the wedding."

I gawked at him. My mouth went dry. "Why would I do that? Why would you want me there? Are you mad?"

His expression was pleading, almost ashamed. "I want to look at you as I speak my vows."

His words hung in the air. Otherwise the hut was silent. My lips parted, and a tiny gasp escaped my mouth. Something inside me cracked open.

He reached for me, but I moved out of his grasp, afraid of what would happen if I let him touch me. I didn't trust myself.

"Come to the wedding," he said again. "Please."

"I don't know if I can bear it," I said, my voice husky with feeling. "Let me think on it."

CHAPTER EIGHT

T he night before the wedding, I went down to the docks to bathe. I was as anxious as I would've been if I were the one getting married. I couldn't stop thinking about Matthäus's offer. On one hand, it was impossible. I couldn't bear to share him with another woman, and I was already such a pariah. There were women in town who lived alone—so-called widows and maidens—who we all knew were anything but. Everyone gossiped. The children sang dirty songs. I would be shunned and called a whore.

On the other hand, I *wanted* to be with him. Deep down, I wanted it more than anything. With my mother dead and my father gone, Matthäus was all I had left. How could I survive by myself with no trade, no way of earning money? Could I really live off the garden and the food my father would forget to bring? He had never even taught me to fish.

At the lakeshore, I peeled off everything but my underthings, thankful the lantern-light was scarce. Mud squished between my toes as I steadied myself on the edge of a dock. Wading in, I cleaned my fingernails to ensure they would be clean. I wet my hair and scrubbed my arms until my flesh was raw. For a moment, I was aware only of the stars, the cold water numbing my skin. Then I remembered what was happening tomorrow. Chills bloomed on my skin, and I felt a pull.

The next thing I knew, I was choking on the muddy lake bottom. I coughed, gasping involuntarily, before I could control my movements enough to stand upright.

Unsteady, I grabbed the dock. My limbs were numb. My lungs

burned. The tide slapped the dock. I closed my eyes, felt the mud between my toes, and thought about how foolish it'd be to try to live alone. I couldn't even bathe without endangering myself.

Back home, I undressed before the fire, then warmed my hands and brushed out my hair. Firelight leapt around the room.

When my shift was dry, I decided to try on the dress and cloak Matthäus had made. I wanted to see myself the way he would see me tomorrow, if I decided to go to the wedding. The linen of the dress sighed as I pulled it over my head. The fabric hugged my small breasts as I laced the sides. I smoothed it down over my belly, then pulled on the cloak, the golden trim glittering on its sleeves. They were tight at the top, with long and beautiful pendant cuffs. I wanted to cry. How could I watch Matthäus marry someone else?

When the door creaked open, I was asking this question of the crackling flames. "I thought I'd check on you—" Father was saying as he turned the latch. He trailed off in midsentence. "Hedda," he breathed as the door clapped shut behind him.

I turned, confused that he had spoken my mother's name. "Father? It's me."

Apart from the firelight, the house was dark. "I know," he said, but there was something about his tone. He stepped into the light, frowning at me, his expression stern. "Where did you get those clothes?"

I looked down at my cloak. He'd called me by Mother's name. When had she ever dressed in fine clothes? I tried to call up my memories of my grandmother's house, but my memories of my grandmother were shadowy flashes. An ample bosom, dark hair. Shiny apples she kept in her apron, a cauldron bubbling with stew. There was no telling how wealthy she was.

"Answer me."

"Tomorrow is Matthäus's wedding. He made this for me to wear."

Father stiffened. "At what cost?"

"As a gesture of friendship," I stammered. "I didn't have any-thing appropriate."

He eyed me, suspicious. "Why would you even want to go? I thought you wanted to marry the boy yourself."

My face grew hot.

Father gave me a knowing look, shaking his head with disap-proval. "What is it the wise women in your mother's stories say? There is always a cost."

I was up so late that night, trying to decide whether to go to the wedding, my body nearly made the decision for me. I slept until the church bells rang, when there was barely enough time to dress. But I knew, as soon as I opened my eyes, that I would go. I wanted to hear Matthäus speak his vows to me. I hurried to get ready, pull-ing my new clothes over my head and pulling back my hair.

Then I rushed down the street toward the minster. Mass had already started. I could see the top of Matthäus's head next to Phoebe's blond braids in the Kürenberg pew. The sight of them together made my heart ache. As the priest droned on, all I could think about was how much I hated her. I found myself unable to do anything but glare at her, beset with hate.

After Mass, I hurried outside. A crowd gathered on the steps to see Matthäus and Phoebe's union blessed. Doves cried out mourn-fully, as if they shared my feelings about the event. Matthäus exited the church first in a fine corded shirt and pants, distracted, his eyes methodically searching the crowd. Phoebe followed him, her dress whipping in the wind, a long gown with an elaborate blue-and-gold-patterned neck and a high, gathered waist that failed to hide her belly's swell. Her pale hair looked thicker than usual, and her cheeks bore an awful salmony glow. I couldn't stop staring at her. That could have been me, a small voice inside me kept saying, that could've been me—an unholy chant—only I would be carrying *his* child.

My hands shook with rage as I watched the priest make his way down the steps toward her. I remembered holding the miller's son, the first child I'd ever delivered, how I wanted to steal him away. If I didn't agree to be Matthäus's mistress, I might never have a child of my own. And if I agreed, our children would be shunned.

As the priest began the ceremony, the crowd fell silent, and Matthäus's expression grew frantic. Soon the priest was asking them to speak their vows. Phoebe made her pledge in a flat voice, as if she was resigned to her match. When the priest asked Matthäus to speak his vows, there was a long pause as he scanned the crowd. When he finally saw me, relief flooded his face. He looked at me as he repeated the vows, despite saying her name. My cheeks grew hot, but I didn't look away.

And then the priest was blessing their union, braiding the traditional blue ribbon around their wrists. A polite cheer went up as the newlywed couple walked together down the steps, their families swarming around them. Matthäus's mother, smiling and laughing, embracing him. His father, slapping his back in a gaudy new coat and tunic, strutting like a rooster. I hated that man so much. I threw myself into the parade of revelers who were heading toward the feast. Down the cobblestone street I went toward the north side of town, reluctantly following the colorful band of revelers in bright clothes, richly dressed.

Matthäus's new estate was the Kürenberg cottage on the banks of the lake near the city gate. Under the dark gray sky, the place looked almost ominous, built of jagged gray stones. The lake glittered behind it. The garden was lined with a high wall made from the same stones as the cottage. Gray rocks of uneven size and shape curved up into an entryway. The wooden door mounted to it was open, but its hinges were heavy. Its face was carved with a portal shaped like the sun.

Following the others inside, I heard the sound of strumming, of laughter and talking, a man's singing voice. In the corner, a young

man not much older than me held a finely crafted lyre. He was
flamboyantly clothed in deep-green velvet. Garb so fine, he looked
like he'd stolen it from a prince. A minnesinger. I had only heard
about them in stories. I had never been at an event fancy enough to
hire entertainment.

I felt uneasy as I surveyed the garden. It was dotted with a dozen
tables bedecked with ostentatious garlands and feathers and wreaths.
Carefully pruned spindle plants lined the walls. Through a porthole
window you could see the waves rolling in off the lake. As I looked
for a seat, a peacock feather drifted to the grass, flashing an outra-
geous blue, and I felt an intense wave of resentment. All this wealth
was what made Phoebe so attractive to Matthäus's father. If I were
this rich, he would've matched his son with me in an instant.

But my stomach was growling, and I could smell the promise
of a colossal feast—sausage, mustard, sage and saffron, sweetbreads
and puddings—so I lined up behind the other revelers at the basin
to wash my hands. Then I found a small table in the corner nearest
the gate and seated myself, immediately setting about tearing one
of the garlands near my seat to angry shreds. It took me a moment
to realize what I was doing, to recognize my anger and force myself
to stop. I reached into my coin-purse and fingered the charm, saying a quick prayer to any god who would listen that I wouldn't
punch anyone in the face before I had something to eat.

My prayer was interrupted by the sound of more music.
Strummed with the minnesinger's quill, the lyre made a rippling
sound that reminded me of leaves in wind. It was maddeningly
beautiful. The voice of the young noblewoman who stood up at
the table beside the minnesinger was pure and clear:

> "I raised a wild falcon with my own two hands
> Strong and gray-feathered, he marked my commands
> Until I removed the stitches from his eyes
> And he soared away to find a new guide."

The minnesinger kept glancing at the newlyweds with a bemused expression. Phoebe and Matthäus looked uncomfortable. Phoebe's hand went to her mouth. A low murmur arose from the crowd, as the singer continued her song. The guest seated next to me, a gray-haired woman in silk, tittered. The blond woman across from her chuckled, her lips twisting up in a smirk. "How many suitors has Phoebe run off now?"

The old woman coughed. "The first disliked her temper. The second discovered the third..."

I smirked. "The minnesinger. Who is he?"

The old woman snorted derisively. "Ludwig of Kürenberg, of course. You must be here for the groom." She adjusted the brooch at her throat and turned to the blond woman. "At least their first-born will have noble blood."

The blond woman laughed. I gritted my teeth and turned toward the music. The next song began with a dying strain that made me sigh before the minnesinger even opened his mouth. I knew the melody from the street performers in the market: It was a common song about lovers who had known each other since childhood. When Matthäus caught my eye from the center table, I realized he must've requested it with me in mind. Tears stung the corners of my eyes. I hid my face in my goblet, taking a long draught of honey-thickened wine to hide my sorrow. The liquid warmed my hands and throat as it went down, tasting of expensive spices and a cheer I did not feel.

By the time the song was over, my goblet was empty, and a woman hurried over from the kitchen to fill it. As I sipped my second cup, other servants began to bring out more food than I had ever seen in one place. A dozen types of sausage with mustard for dipping, roasted goose, venison, candied quail, and even roasted boar. I couldn't help but stare at the poor beast's tusks. There was even roasted peacock, offered with its iridescent blue feathers reattached to its skin, fanning out in a fantastic array. My hunger overtook my envy as the plates were passed, and I quickly set to gorging myself. After the meats came giant bowls of fruit. Pear slices wet with piment, so soft and pulpy they seemed to melt in my mouth. An almond bread pudding, so rich and sticky it was like a delicious glue. As I was devouring my pudding, my mouth so full I must've resembled a squirrel, I caught Matthäus watching me. Embarrassed, I swallowed it as quickly as I could.

As the last dish was passed around, the minnesinger stood and wandered the tables, asking for requests. Just as I sank my teeth into a blackberry tart, he nodded, cleared his throat, and spoke. "I have been asked to sing both a wedding song and a funeral song," he said. A group of men at the next table hooted and slapped their thighs, until the women beside them glared at them. After the conversation I had just overheard about Phoebe, I understood the joke. "Something holy and something wicked. Something innocent and something wise." The minnesinger threw up his hands in mock frustration. "You are a difficult crowd!"

The gray-haired woman beside me laughed.

"There is a song I've been working on that might be all those things except holy." He crinkled his nose, glancing at Matthäus. "It's based on a new tale, never before sung. The groom would not reveal his source."

A murmur issued from the crowd. From the center table, Matthäus caught my eye again, trying to tell me something. Face burning, I buried my face in my cup.

The minnesinger held up his lyre and struck it with his quill, making it hum as he walked back to his place at the garden's edge. "The tale of the runaway princess!"

I nearly choked on my drink. Was this *my* tale? The one I told Matthäus? Did he arrange this for me? Everyone began talking at once. I heard snippets of what the blond woman across the table whispered to the woman beside me: "New song—Princess Frederika—Prince Ulrich—"

When the din died down, the minnesinger struck his lyre again, strumming out a melody both whimsical and sad. It sounded like a love song one moment, and falling snow the next. Folks set down their food, finished what they were eating, and grabbed their drinks. I did the same, gulping the last of my second goblet of wine, confused. Why would Matthäus tell the minnesinger my tale? I thought he hated it.

A hush fell over the garden, as the minnesinger sang the first verse:

"The queen at the window with needle and thread,
Seven years, childless, has shared the king's bed.
In sorrow, she pricks a soft finger against barb.
Into the snow falls a red drop of blood."

When he finished, the garden was quiet but for the distant rolling of thunder. Outside the wall, we could hear the tide washing the lakeshore.

How strange it was to hear my story sung by another. I stopped eating. My hands fell limp in my lap. Matthäus caught my eye again, and this time I grasped the meaning of his glance. He understood why I had told him this story. He understood and forgave all my envy, my hurt. He knew how much I loved telling stories. He'd arranged this performance for me as a gift.

For a brief moment, my thoughts cleared, like a sudden patch of sky on a cloudy day. My spirits lifted. Then the moment passed. What did it matter what he thought of me, when she was the one sitting with him?

With a sigh, I turned my attention back to the minnesinger, who was now singing a verse about the blood-rose fairy. Everyone around me had stopped in the middle of eating, hanging onto his words. The women at my table. The men at the next table who had hooted at the minnesinger's jokes. They gasped when Golden

Braids arranged the princess's marriage to the wolf-prince. They cheered when the princess fled the castle.

Two feelings warred inside me. No one would ever listen to me like that, a poor girl without noble blood. And yet, this was my story everyone was listening to, my story these nobles were waiting to hear with bated breath. I stole a glance at the center table. Phoebe was just as enraptured as everyone else. A secret glee rose up in me that I was going to see how she reacted to my horrific ending. It gave me great pleasure when the night-birds descended on the princess and Phoebe's plump face went white with shock.

My glee was short lived, however, as she turned to Matthäus to whisper something in his ear. Whatever she said, he reacted with contrition. He bowed his head and said something with an apologetic expression, like the dutiful husband I realized he would soon become. Anytime she needed him, he would be there for her. That was just the kind of man he was. How long could he play-act such love before his feelings became real? One year? Two? The thought that he would grow to love her stung.

As the music died, the woman beside me whispered something to her friend about how foolish the real princess had been to flee this match. Since the annulment had made her a bastard, Ulrich was about as good as Frederika could get.

Her friend nodded in agreement. "The rumors about Ulrich are idle peasant talk. I saw him outside the cathedral once, giving alms to a beggar. He's a good Christian."

The minnesinger bowed, and several men lifted their tankards. "Again!"

The minnesinger shook his head and launched into a ballad honoring the men who had just died, far away, in a bloody battle. As he strummed his lyre, Matthäus began walking around, thanking people for coming. When he got to my table, he smiled formally and squeezed my hands. Then he leaned close and whispered in my ear. "Come see me at the shop tomorrow."

I nodded quickly, meeting his eyes, as he moved on to the next table.

Before he could finish making the rounds, the storm clouds opened over the garden. Big fat droplets bounced into my empty goblet. "My dress!" the gray-haired woman next to me snapped suddenly, standing up, looking down at a smear of blue on her skirt. She pulled her coat over her head and hurried away from the bench. I looked down at my new clothes, wondering if I should seek shelter too. It would be an excellent excuse to quit this place.

The drops hit the table with loud smacks. The rest of the revelers began to get up. At the center table, I could see Matthäus helping Phoebe over the bench. I looked away before he could catch me watching and hurried outside. "Forgive me," I muttered to no one in particular, then splashed my way home through the mud and the rain.

CHAPTER NINE

To unravel is not human. It is the nature of poppets and pet-ticoats to come undone. And yet, the night of the wedding, it was as if some unholy seamstress pulled the thread that stitched me together. Lying in my cupboard, I had no idea how to stitch myself together again. Every time I closed my eyes, I saw Matthäus and Phoebe in the garden. I saw him helping her over the bench to get out of the rain. I tried to focus on the way he'd spoken his vows as if to me, the gestures he'd arranged, but I couldn't stop seeing him with her.

Hoping for comfort, I took the bird-mother figurine from my pouch, inspecting her strange curves. I remembered the day my mother gave her to me. How soothing it had been to lay my head on her chest, to listen to her stories, to enjoy the faint scent of anise that always surrounded her. That night, I felt her absence as keenly as the day she died. Matthäus's wedding would have been so much more bearable if I still had her to comfort me.

I didn't sleep, that night, until the sun was almost up. I spent the night dreaming up dark stories. There was one about a violent bridegroom, and another about a wolf in the wood.

When I woke around noon, I was hungrier than I'd been in weeks because of how well I'd eaten the day before. I went into the garden to see if any more of the autumn vegetables had ripened. There were no new vegetables, but the yellow berries on the new plants, the light-thieves that had overtaken the back of the garden, had grown quite large. I wondered if they were edible.

I plucked one of the golden fruit, overripened and shiny with dew. Its sweet scent overwhelmed me. It reminded me of apples. A golden apple, I thought with awe, remembering my mother's tale.

My heart leapt. The small fruit glittered with frost. Her words swam back to me. *I'm leaving you something.* Did she plant these herself?

There was never any question about what I was going to do. My mother had made it clear. The golden apple was a cure for my spells. The fruit was like nothing I'd ever tasted. Sweet and soft and pulpier even than the pears at the wedding feast. I took another bite, then another, shocked at the sweet tang, the softness of its flesh made crisp by frost. I made myself eat slowly, savoring the taste. When I reached the mess of golden seeds at its core, one of them got stuck in my teeth, and I stopped. It tasted terrible.

I inspected the seed-core, struck by how clear my vision had become. I could discern every crystal of frost, every whorl and tangle in its pulp. All around me, the dying plants of the garden sparkled with tiny droplets of frost. I saw detail for the first time in the branching veins of leaves.

Was this fruit a cure for my eyesight too? I turned my gaze to the sky to see if its brightness still made my eyes ache. For once, I didn't feel the urge to squint. My heart soared. I wanted to tell someone.

Matthäus. I was supposed to meet him at the tailor shop. I had almost forgotten. I pulled the cloak Matthäus gave me from its hook. Down the street I hurried toward the market, giddy about the new details I saw in the world. The texture of every dead leaf. The cracks in the cobblestones zigzagging in sharp relief. I was so elated, I forgot to avoid the furrier's shop. As I approached the alley behind it, the furrier's older son swaggered out of the back door. His eyes were bloodshot. A blister marred the side of his mouth.

"Haelewise?" he said with a sneer. "Why are you dressed like that?"

Footsteps, behind me. Turning, I saw the younger brother sauntering around the side of the shop. I noticed, for the first time, his dark lashes, the cold hard blue of his eyes. "That's a fine cloak. Come inside and show us what you did to get it."

I looked down at my outfit and knew what he thought, what anyone would think when they saw these clothes. My cheeks burned that I was actually considering it, that I was on my way to see the married man who had given me this cloak. I clutched the purse at my hip, desperate, praying I would escape from this alley with my virtue intact. And just like that, it happened again. My fingers tingled, and I felt a telltale shiver. The next world drawing close. Not now, I thought. No no no—

But instead of the pull I feared, the balance shifted in the opposite direction. The air grew heavy with possibility, the way it did during a birth. I heard a humming sound, an unearthly woman's voice rushing into my ears. *Use their lust*, she hissed with an almost demonic amusement.

I froze, terrified that the demon my father thought haunted me had finally spoken. The alleyway came back into focus. The younger brother's leering smile. The elder boy's footsteps behind me. Demon or not, I wondered if the advice would work. What other choice do I have, I thought. I made myself smile at the younger brother, trying to hide my nervousness. He eyed me. I adjusted my bodice.

"I would actually love a new fur," I whispered, approaching him, forcing a lascivious smile.

The younger brother smirked, surprised, reaching out to pull me to him. As soon as he did, I twisted. His hand swept empty air, and I ducked behind him out of the alley, scraping my knee against the wall. He cursed as I darted away, my hood falling down around my shoulders. The last thing I saw before I darted into the crowd was the humiliation on his face.

Back in the relative safety of my hut, I couldn't stop thinking about the voice I'd heard in the alleyway. Had eating my mother's apple conjured a demon, or was it my mother's goddess? I wanted it to be my mother's goddess, but I knew so little about her, there was no way to tell. I pulled the bird-mother from my coin-purse and set her on the table, inspecting her for some clue as to her nature. Her breasts, her wings, her talons were so strange. When I closed my eyes, I swear, I thought I could feel the air thickening with possibility around her, as if she were pulling something from the next world. Powerful, whatever she represented, but her nakedness, her *fierceness*, concerned me. What kind of goddess would advise a woman to use men's lust to her advantage? I wanted to trust her— my mother worshipped her, after all—but I was afraid my father was right, and my heresy had summoned a demon. A demon with a hissing voice, who was amused by men's embarrassment.

The idea both attracted and repulsed me, which was unsettling in and of itself. As the hour grew late, I put the figurine back in my coin-purse, deciding against telling Matthäus about the golden apples. How could I tell him about the cure without mentioning the voice it had allowed me to hear? And telling him about the voice would scandalize him. He was much more like my father in his beliefs than I was.

The next morning, I ate the only food available to me for breakfast: golden apples. I fingered the bird-mother figurine in my coinpurse, wishing I knew what god or demon she was connected with. I brooded over Matthäus's offer, hoping he would come to see me since I'd failed to visit his shop the day before. But he didn't come.

Soon enough, I was starving for something other than fruit. I decided to go into town and trade my last poppet for food. I could stop by the tailor's shop on my way back. I stood at the shelf where Gütel sat for a long moment before I took her down. She glared at me, one-eyed, her expression full of scorn. "Don't look at me like that," I told her. "I have no choice."

I smoothed her woolen hair, straightened her ribbons, and picked two brown glass beads from the rope that hung beside the window.

I pulled out the black one that remained on her face and sat down to sew her new eyes on. It took me an hour and several pricked fingers before I was satisfied.

Down the street I walked into town with Gütel in my sack, wrapped in my tattered blanket, simultaneously enthralled and afraid at the new details I saw in the world. The change in my eyesight was even more apparent than it had been the day before. The market square was brighter, finer, more intricate, as I moved warily through it, praying I would remain unrecognized for the time it took to sell Gütel and buy cheese and sausage.

At the edge of the market, the furriers' sons had gathered a small crowd around them: the tanner's sons, the cobbler, the blacksmith, the miller's cousins. The elder brother's words drifted toward me. "A succubus possessed her—" he was saying. "Haelewise begged us to lie with her."

Shock and anger filled my breast. "Liar!" I cried before I could think better of it. "I did no such thing—"

Everyone turned. "It's her," the tanner's son shouted, making the demon-warding sign. The crowd around me parted, giving me a wide berth. The gesture spread from the tanner's son to the people around him, hand to hand to hand.

"She'll curse all of us!" the elder brother shouted.

A darkness animated the crowd, a fear intensified by all the deaths the fever had wrought. The tanner's, my mother's. Terrified, I looked for an opening in the crowd to escape.

A gaunt woman with haunted eyes, the tanner's widow, called out, "Stop her!"

The crowd pressed closer. A bitter-browed man took a step forward, picking up a stone. "The fever is her fault!" he shouted, holding it up.

Folks nodded, searching the ground for stones. If I waited any longer, I knew what would happen. I rushed forward, pushing the tanner's widow out of the way, fleeing as fast as my legs would carry me from the square. Behind me, I could hear people shouting, calling me all manner of names. A thousand footsteps, coming fast. The banging of doors as people rushed outside to join the chase.

I raced home as fast as I could, slamming the door, pushing the table against it so no one could batter their way in. I bolted the shutters, breathing heavily, listening for the sound of the mob I knew would come. And then, as I was pushing my mother's cot against the back door, there it was, a pounding on the front door, the furrier's sons shouting for me to come out and pay for my fur. "Fever-bringer," someone shouted. "Heretic!" A child's voice, thin and high. "*Witch!*"

I crawled under the table and sat with my back to the door, shaking, fighting an irrational urge to put my fingers in my ears and pretend they weren't there. After a moment, I heard an animated conversation taking place outside, some kind of argument. I couldn't make the whole thing out, but I had a sinking feeling based on the few words I could—words like *burn* and *oil*—that someone wanted to smoke me out of my hut. Eventually, a man's voice I didn't recognize ended the argument.

"It's not worth it," he called out. "It could spread to the docks."

The murmurs of agreement were a relief, until I heard what the voice said next. "Let's post a watch. You and you, stay with me. We'll get her the next time she comes out."

For hours, I sat under that table, back against the door, trying to figure out what to do. Should I leave town? Go to Matthäus for protection? Both possibilities seemed far-fetched. I would have to pass the watch they'd posted outside to do either. From time to time I could hear men talking in the street. Barely audible conversations, too faint to tell what they were about.

Eventually I came out from under the table to look for something, anything, I could eat to stop my hunger pangs. I found a handful of aniseed at the bottom of the pot, which I sucked seed by seed, distracting myself with their sweet taste. When night fell, I lit a rush light and sat at the table, watching it burn. I couldn't sleep. I kept peeking through the shutters at the dark street, wondering if the men were still out there. As the hour grew late, my thoughts turned again to the voice that had spoken to me in the alleyway. My mind whirled with fears that it was a demon—one of the lamia or lilit—that my prayers to any deity who would listen had invited into my heart. I didn't fall asleep until late.

When the morning sun shone through the cracks in the shutters, I woke with a new resolve. I had to leave town. I tried to summon the courage to open the shutters and see if there was anyone in the street. It occurred to me that perhaps it would be safer to peer through one of the gaps in the stones of the garden wall. I went to the back door and stood there for a long time. I was afraid one of the men who were watching the house had climbed into the garden. When I finally opened the door, I found a bright autumn day, the pale sun shining quietly over the garden wall. Peering through a tiny gap between stones, I could see two men in the street, watching the house.

Backing slowly away from the gap, I retreated to the bench behind the house. The sound of the lake lapping the docks soothed me, as I tried to figure out how to slip out of town. Should I clamber over the garden wall? Steal a boat? My father had never taught me to row. If only I could fly away on the back of some beast like the witch they thought I was. But even if I could, I had nowhere to go.

At sunset, when the air filled with the smell of bonfires and the festive sound of bells, I heard a group of children come down the street, laughing and singing a Martin song, and I realized it was Martinmas. The memory that swam back to me of singing that song with my father was too painful to dwell on for long. I talked to my mother beneath the earth, her goddess in the beyond, fingering the figurine in my coin-purse. I rubbed her black stone absently, praying desperately for guidance on how to escape.

It must have been around midnight—the moon bright, a few days past full—when the figurine grew warm under my thumb and my skin bloomed with chills. I braced myself for a fainting spell, but instead, I felt the air grow heavy with possibility like it had when I heard the voice behind the furrier's shop. The air trembled, as if something was coming. What, I didn't know. A soul? A voice? Then, ghostly tendrils began to unfurl into existence all around me.

I shivered, watching them drift up like smoke from an invisible fire. They grew thicker, glimmering and whorling, coalescing into the shape of a woman kneeling in the dirt.

My mother. She was straightening one of the golden apple plants, wearing her lucky gloves and the bright blue cloak I'd seen moments before inside on its hook. I rushed to her, calling out, "Mother!"

She looked up from the weeds and beamed at me, her face joyful as she opened her arms. I jumped into her embrace. The ghostly feel of her arms around me was a balm. She murmured my name, over and over, pressing her face into my hair. My eyes teared up, as her scent enveloped me. Earth and anise. After a moment, she pulled back from me and frowned. When her lips began to move, it took me a moment to decipher her voice. It hummed, barely audible, like the low buzzing of bees. "You ate the golden apples," she was saying.

I blinked the tears from my eyes, nodding, overwhelmed by a sudden thought. "Was it you who spoke to me?" My voice was soft with wonder. "I thought it was a demon."

She didn't acknowledge my question. Her voice grew deeper, louder. "You have to leave town." She gave me a warning look—half angry, half afraid—the same expression she wore when she spoke of the *kindefresser*.

I tried to explain, choking back sobs. "The townspeople want to stone me. They're keeping watch for me outside."

Her expression softened. "Don't cry. You have your whole life in front of you." She wiped away my tears. Her smile was gentle. "You're going to have children, tell stories, become a midwife. You're going to find your purpose."

"I will?"

She nodded. The air shimmered around her. The mist had begun to drift into the garden. It swirled around her, moonlit, glowing. "There's a whole world outside the wall."

"How do I get past the watch?"

"There's no one out there now. The Martinmas festivities distracted them."

"But where do I go?"

"Find the wise woman in the forest near Ulrich and Ursilda's castle. She needs an apprentice."

I searched her eyes. She was looking at me with such love.

"Haelewise—" She smiled at me, radiant. "I loved you more than life itself." Her eyes glistened, and her voice caught. Then her smile began to waver with uneasiness. The air snapped taut, and I felt a diminishing, a pull from this world into the next. My mother searched the air, frowning, panicked. She shook her head, once, twice, and reached out.

But before she could pull me into an embrace, all the tension in the air collapsed. The mist rushed back into the next world, taking her with it.

CHAPTER TEN

I fell to my knees, kneeling in the place my mother had knelt in the dirt. My heart sang with relief. The voice that spoke to me was my mother's. She had come back to visit me as a ghost. The world of her stories was filled with such apparitions, but I had never expected to see one in real life.

Reaching out to touch the golden apple plant she'd straightened, I wondered what she meant when she said I'd find my purpose. The leaves of the plant rustled, springing back at my touch. I picked up the bird-mother charm, touching the tiny infant she held in her arms. I remembered how right it felt to hold the miller's son, his weight, the need I felt to take care of him. I felt a sudden longing for the children I would one day have.

When Matthäus married, I thought I'd lost my chance, but I should've known better. I was brokenhearted about losing him, but—of course, *of course*, he wasn't the only path forward. If seeing the wise woman was the first step toward making the life I wanted happen, I would go to her. I would ask to become her apprentice.

Determined, I went inside, put on my new cloak, and packed my things: a comb, a water skin. My quiver and bow. The shattered mirror. The rest of the fruit from the garden. I counted two dozen. I wanted to keep eating it. I picked one of the leaves from the plant so the wise woman could identify it. My sack full, I tied my drinking-horn to my belt, then turned my mind to the problem of how I would make it through the market without being recognized. There was no one outside here, but the market would be different, and how would I get through the gate?

In the back room, I rummaged through my mother's trunk until I found a forgotten pair of britches, a man's tattered tunic, and a cloak at its bottom. At the market, no one looked twice at a boy in ragged clothes. I took off my new dress and cloak and headscarf and pressed them into my sack. I wrapped my small breasts tight with a length of fabric, then pulled on the tunic and britches.

My hair, I thought. I found my comb, untangled my knotted locks, and braided them, thinking I would use my knife to cut the plait. But when I put on my father's cloak, I saw that tucking the braid into my tunic hid it. I didn't really want to cut it.

I hurried outside before the watch returned and set out toward the city gate. In the dark square, I only passed a single group of revelers leaving a tavern. Seeing only a boy in tattered clothes, they didn't even nod. I was beneath their notice.

As I approached the shadowy shape of the Kürenberg cottage, I felt a pang in my chest. I couldn't leave without telling Matthäus goodbye.

The garden gate was unlocked. It creaked as I pushed it open. As I slipped in, the orange tomcat who had apparently followed Matthäus to his new home rubbed his face against my legs. The sight of him made my heart ache. Giving him a pet, I checked both upstairs windows. There were no candles burning, no lights. But it looked like someone was awake downstairs. The shutters were open. In the window, I could see the flicker of candlelight.

I peeked inside, where Matthäus appeared to be sewing, needle in mouth, alone among a sea of scraps. It was simultaneously soothing and heartbreaking to see him like that. My childhood friend, my love, now someone else's husband. From my vantage point, I couldn't see the whole room. I took a deep breath. "*Matthäus,*" I hissed, ducking behind a spindle-plant in case anyone else was in there with him. He didn't react. I said his name again. He came to the window alone, peering out in his nightcap. I stepped out from behind the spindle-plant and waved. At first he looked alarmed.

I pulled down my hood, shaking my head. "It's me."

"Haelewise?" He laughed. "By thunder! What are you wearing? Why didn't you come to the shop yesterday?"

"Come out. I'll explain."

He closed the shutters. The flickering light behind them disappeared. A wave washed the shore behind the house. After a moment, the garden door opened, and he walked out, handsome as ever, holding the candle. But for the first time, looking at him, I saw the life he *couldn't* offer me.

He gestured for me to sit with him at a table and held his candle up to look at me. "Your eyes," he said, his voice full of awe. "They're beautiful."

I didn't understand, then, what he meant.

Nervous, I reached for his hand across the table. He met my gaze, his gray irises bright in the candlelight. Hopeful. I could tell he thought I was going to accept his offer. I looked down at our hands. "I'm leaving town," I said quietly. "I couldn't go without saying goodbye."

He set down his candle. "Leaving? Where will you go?"

"To see the wise woman."

"The one who kidnapped Ursilda?" He looked horrified.

"My mother said she didn't. I heard she wants an apprentice."

"Oh, Haelewise," he said, his eyes glowing with disappointment. "There'll be no convincing you to stay?"

I shook my head, tight-lipped, then felt a perverse need to make him understand. "I was almost stoned yesterday. A mob chased me home."

His eyes widened. "Are you all right?"

"The worst injury was to my pride." I sighed. "I'm going to find somewhere else to live, someplace I'm not despised."

His face fell. "Lord have mercy upon my soul." He stared at me, as if he couldn't decide what to say next. Finally, he sighed. "May I kiss you? Just this once?"

My heart stopped. Part of me wanted to scream at him that he didn't deserve it, but another part wanted that kiss so badly it hurt. "Just this once," I said finally.

His lips were soft, and they tasted of salt. I was startled at the depth of his want. The rest of the world fell away, and I forgot where we were, who I was. There was only *us*, there was nothing but the weight of our shared desire. I don't know how long we kissed. It wasn't until his hand brushed my thigh that I remembered—he was married. His pregnant wife was upstairs. I couldn't do this.

His eyes stayed closed for a long moment after I pulled away. His face was full of longing. Then he looked at me, understanding. He didn't speak as I stood up to go.

When I left the garden, the door creaking behind me, he was still sitting, silent, at the table.

I only looked over my shoulder once. He was watching me go, his eyes flashing with regret. I made myself focus on the road that led to the city gate, ignoring the regret that was rising up inside me to meet his. The sound of the lake lapping the shore mocked my heartache.

As I walked toward the north gate, I made myself focus on the problem before me: I had to get past the city guards. If I spoke to them, my disguise would be ruined. After some thought, I decided to make myself swagger like the furrier's sons. One foot in front of the other, tough, chin up. I nodded as I approached the gate as if our exchange would be an annoyance, my expression carefully nonchalant.

The guard nodded, fooled, and let me pass through the gate. The water glittered with moonlight on either side of the bridge. For hours, I encountered only shadows, the shapes of birds sleeping along the lakeshore. As the night turned gray with the coming dawn, the footpath turned west into the forest, away from the lake.

I paused before I stepped onto the footpath. Mother told so many stories about this part of the woods. It was supposed to hide strange animals and fae, the *kindefresser*, the source of the mist, Prince Albrecht's castle on the cliffs. The wise woman's tower.

I took a deep breath and turned down the trail. Elder ash and tangled oaks huddled over the path where it entered the forest, as if the trees were dancing together, holding hands. Following the path, I was surprised at how quickly the shadows closed around me. The canopy of leaves overhead was thick, almost impenetrable. Very little light filtered through.

I walked that path for so long, I lost track of whether it was night or day. Eventually in what must've been afternoon, I shot and ate a rabbit and slept beneath a firethorn bush.

It wasn't until I woke that night that I saw the giant raven, barely visible, in the branches of a spruce tree. *Kraek*, it called, looking right at me, eyes flashing amber. *Kraek!*

Those eyes, I thought, chilled. I no longer believed in the *kinde-fresser*, but I had been superstitious about amber-eyed ravens since the one in the grove took Gütel's eye. Was this same bird, or were there many? The thing flitted from tree to tree, croaking. I got the sense that it wanted me to follow it.

"Shoo," I told it, my voice shaking. The bird croaked again, then took off down the path. The needles of the fir trees shivered. As the path wound uphill, the backs of my calves began to burn.

Just before dawn, I heard distant noise. The call of a trumpet. The howling and baying of dogs, growing nearer. My mother and I had encountered hunting parties long ago, when we used to walk in the woods. This part of the forest belonged to Prince Albrecht. The only nobles hunting here would be he or his son, Ulrich. I didn't want to meet either of them.

I climbed the tallest tree I could find. Sap stuck to my gloves. Branches snapped beneath my boots. I wrapped my cloak tight about me and looked around.

To the north, I saw the distant shape of the shadowy castle on the cliffs where Prince Ulrich lived, surrounded by the misty bog in the valley that was supposed to be full of fae. The sight of the castle gave me a chill. I thought of what my mother said about Ulrich changing into a wolf when the moon was full. It had seemed far-fetched by the light of day, but now I couldn't help but wonder what moon phase it was. The moon was waning, nearly a half moon now.

East of the castle, the sun was edging the treetops on the horizon with a dim pink. No sign of the source of that noise.

To the west, a blanket of trees spread out green and dark. The dogs howled again, closer than before.

There was movement below. A stag bounding through the mist. An arrow struck my tree with a *thwack*, the green feather at its back vibrating with the force of the shot, and I froze.

Hounds bayed in scattered unison, their sound growing louder. I tightened my knees around the top of the tree trunk, holding my breath. Below, the alaunts flew past—snarling and ravening, so fast they were like gray ghosts—too focused on the stag to notice me. I sighed, relieved. The baying faded as I heard the relaxed clip of hooves on dirt, a low sound, the chatter of men behind them.

Out of the mist two young lords trotted into the clearing. Their horses were thick gray things, well-groomed, legs splattered with mud. Green banners zigzagged over their necks. Behind them, a page boy rode a third horse, carrying a green banner with the wolf that was Albrecht's coat of arms. Prince Ulrich, I realized. One of these men must be him.

There, at the back of the group. Black-haired, broad-shouldered, in a mangy coat of wild gray fur on a jet-black horse. The wolf-skin. His expression was determined, his eyes a cold bright blue. He was striking, with black hair, unlike the monster I'd imagined, but there was something predatory about his eyes. As he drew closer, I recoiled, sensing something very *wrong* in the air around him. I clutched my trunk, holding my breath, willing him not to look up.

Trailing behind him on a dappled horse was a woman several

years older than me. She rode into the clearing, gazing up at the moon, contemplative. She wore a long black mourner's cloak and a modest headscarf that hid her hair except for two red braids. The braids swayed as she rode, and her green eyes glistened with tears that streamed down her freckled cheeks. She was beautiful in an unearthly way. There was an aura of wildness about her. "I shouldn't have let Father talk me into coming out," she said, guiding her horse to catch up to Ulrich, her voice fluttering. She smoothed her cloak over her belly. "I don't feel well."

"Father was enacting the physician's orders," Ulrich snapped. "You're far too melancholy for a woman in your condition. The air will do you good."

She didn't answer for a moment. When she replied, her voice was apologetic. "Yes, brother, of course."

Ulrich turned toward his sister. I couldn't see his face, but his voice was barely audible, his tone condescending. "I understand that *you* are a slave to your womanish whims, but *try* not to allow them to disrupt my hunt. The business with Frederika has me snappish. I need the diversion."

She nodded quickly, her headscarf shifting around her shoulders. When she spoke, her voice fluttered with false cheer. "Perhaps I simply need nourishment."

Ulrich turned to the page boy. "Mark this spot, boy. We'll finish the chase after Ursilda has her meal."

The page jumped down from his horse with a flag.

"The southernmost pavilion is just ahead," he told Ursilda, kind again, as if nothing had happened. In the distance, among the trees, I could make out the faint lines of wooden beams. "Can you make it that far?"

His sister nodded silently and followed him.

They led their horses far enough away that I could no longer see them, but close enough that their voices still carried. The sound traveled so well, I was afraid to climb down until I started to nod off and feared that I would fall. The forest is still dark, I told myself, as the men's voices rose. Slowly, I climbed down, testing my steps as I went. The last branch on the way down snapped.

The men went silent. A horse whinnied, nervous.

I winced.

"Did you hear that?"

"The stag?"

"Come with me." Ulrich's voice, cold. "Both of you."

Twigs snapped on the forest floor. The sounds grew nearer. A torch flickered to life. My heart pounded in my ears.

"You don't think Zähringen has spies all the way out here."

Zähringen? The duke who gave Matthäus those paternoster beads?

"I told you," Ulrich hissed to his man. "Zähringen has been furious ever since the king promised to give me Villa Scafhusun."

Although his voice was low, I could hear satisfaction in it, the pleasure he took at the other man's misfortune.

I heard a twig snap nearby. "Get out of my forest!" Ulrich snarled, so close I froze, holding my breath. "Or I'll tear you limb from limb."

A chill ran down my spine. I bolted, hood falling from my face, braid flying behind me.

I looked back only once to see their surprise. None of them had expected a girl.

CHAPTER ELEVEN

A way from the clearing I fled, ducking under branches, weaving around tree trunks. Twigs leapt out to scratch my arms, my face. I heard the sound of crackling leaves behind me, the sound of Ursilda crying out. "Rika!"

I didn't stop to find out what she meant.

Trees bumped up and down. I ran until I almost ran into that raven again, perched in another spruce. The great bird stared me down, its amber eyes glowing like newly fired glass. The bird flapped its wings, commanding my attention, then took off toward a string of boulders that jutted from the ground like teeth.

The circle of stones that surrounded the wise woman's tower. It had to be. My skin tingled as I drew close. Preparing to pass between two of the stones, I had the distinct impression that I was crossing a threshold. There was a great power zapping from stone to stone. Inside the circle, the next world was so close, I could feel a presence enmeshed with the air. A living shadow. The mist, I thought, that makes men blind.

Through the trees, I could see the raven land atop a large stone wall. Beyond it, a vine-covered tower stood cloaked in silvery tendrils of mist. The tower looked ancient, cobbled together from wood and rock, older than old. The stones that made up its face were huge, weatherworn, crumbling, and covered with vines. Its high roof was a thicket of branches tied with rope, shrouded in mist.

The raven eyed me from its perch, watchful, then circled the tower and flew out of sight. I followed it, shadowing the stone wall, heading toward the tower, my heart beating in my throat. The wall stones were cold against my palm, silent in their pact with the dark. Passing a wood-braced portal, I peered through it into a huge shadowy garden, a dim thicket of bushes and vines and weeds. At its far end, rows of plowed earth sat waiting for spring. In the center, grotesque stone figures danced. Skeletal shrubs twisted. Closer to the tower, a huge birdbath stood. Taking it in, I was overcome with a shiver of fear and familiarity, the hairs on the back of my neck standing on end.

It seemed too quiet as I circled the tower, looking for a door or window, cursing the noise my feet made. The opening I found was narrow and tall, the kind of caged window used in fortifications—a slot made for shooting out, instead of looking in.

Dim firelight flickered within. As I crept nearer, my nostrils tickled with smoke. I saw dozens of talismans hanging inside the window, paper rustling, beside a wicked-looking bone amulet and the dried-out skin of a snake. The sight filled me with fear.

Behind the bars, an old woman dozed beside a dim hearth, head resting on her shoulder, a bit of spittle shining at the edge of her mouth, iron-gray hair pulled back. About twice my mother's age, old enough that her skin hung loose around her neck. Her kirtle was brightly dyed, her bosom large, her dark hair roped loosely into white-ribboned corpse-braids like the courtiers' wives wore.

She's a wealthy midwife, I tried to tell myself. A country noblewoman. There's no reason to be afraid.

Then my foot snapped a twig, and her eyes popped open, glowing a hazy amber. I froze, and my heart skipped a beat.

"Well, what have we here?" the old woman said, standing up from her chair to peer through the bars, pushing the talismans and such aside. Her expression was kindly, but her *diutsch* was stilted, and she drew out her words as if they took great effort to shape. Her eyes glittered that hazy amber, and my chest tightened as she looked at me. I heard my mother's voice in my head. *Don't let the kindefresser snatch you away—*

The prince's trumpet sounded in the distance. The old woman shook her head and moved out of sight. I could hear my heart beating in my ears. Some feet away, a door opened. "Hsst," she said. "Ulrich is hunting. Come inside."

What else could I do but follow her inside, though I couldn't shake the feeling that I was escaping something bad into something worse. The tower was dark. Shadows played on the floor. Our footsteps echoed on the stones. The area around the door was filled with earthenware jugs. Farther in, I could see the rest of a large circular room. Candles guttered along the walls. Furs littered the floor. A manuscript sat on the table next to a vat of ink. The rounded walls were rimmed with shelves of books. I blinked at them, surprised at the display. The only books I'd seen before were the ones the priest used at Mass.

Beneath one of the guttering candles, a grid of eerie phials glowed in a cabinet, a collection even larger than the alchemist's. A giant raven perched beside them, settling his wings. I thought he was the one who led me here until he turned toward me and I saw that his eyes were black. Herbs and dried vegetables, ropes of garlic and onions, hung from the beams of the ceiling. Across the room was a table, a cauldron, a wood oven. Behind that, a shadowy set of winding stairs led to another floor.

Reluctant to leave the doorway, I removed my hood. The running had loosened my braid. She broke into a wide grin, beaming at me. "Well, if it isn't Hedda's girl, Haelewise."

I stopped in my tracks, unsettled, wondering how she knew my name. Mother must've come to see her about my spells. There was no other explanation.

I set the thought aside. "And you, what are you called?"

"Mother Gothel, by most."

"Gothel," I tried. The word tasted odd on my tongue.

"My birth name is Kunegunde, if you prefer. Would you like something to eat?"

As soon as she asked, my stomach growled. I hadn't eaten any-thing the day before but the rabbit. Kunegunde smiled. The faint smell of bread wafted from the oven, as if it had been freshly baked in the middle of the night—as if Kunegunde had *known* I was coming.

The thought made me shiver. A cauldron hung over the glowing hearth.

Kunegunde followed my gaze. "I hope that hasn't burned."

She got up to stir whatever was in the cauldron. As she did, I detected the rich smell of beets, leeks and turnips, garlic and parsnip. Some kind of meat—not fish, but dark, like mutton or venison—and a strange scent, a spice I'd smelled before. That spice. A memory came back to me. Not long before the wall was built, my mother went on a long journey to purchase midwifery supplies. She told my father she needed to buy a rare oil. They had a huge argument about it; he said everything she needed for births could be bought in town. She went on the journey anyway, leaving me with my father for four days. When she came back, she gave me a leaf-wrapped package: a delicious meatcake, a new remedy for my spells. It was one of the few curatives my mother gave me that tasted good, and it'd kept my spells away for a month. It smelled *exactly* like the spice in this caul-dron, an exotic scent I hadn't smelled before or since. She must've purchased that meatcake here.

I remembered how excited my mother was for me to try that meatcake and was overcome by a fresh wave of grief. I had to work to keep my voice calm. "How often did my mother come here?"

"Once or twice, perhaps? Maybe more." Kunegunde stirred whatever was in the cauldron without looking up.

"She died last winter," I whispered. The words caught in my throat.

Kunegunde looked at me then. There was sadness in her eyes, as if she remembered my mother with great fondness. "I heard she was sick."

Tears wet my cheeks. How had she heard that all the way out

here? How many folks came to her? In town everyone thought of her as dangerous, Ursilda's kidnapper. I remembered a merchant who called himself Gothel, a cloth-trader we had met in the tailor shop. "Was Gothel your husband's name?"

She chuckled softly. "I have no husband. Gothel is the name of this place."

She broke the loaf from the wood oven into two crusts and filled them with stew. She didn't bother, I noticed, to carve them with a cross. She placed the food on the table near the fire ring and nodded for me to sit. I did, forcing myself to eat slowly, the bread warming my palms, though I wanted to tear into it. It was the most delicious stew I'd ever tasted. Savory with garlic and herbs, the strong flavor of beets. The meat I'd smelled was rabbit, though it was far more delicious than the animal I'd roasted in the wood. There was a crunch to it, a glaze with bitter hints of that spice.

"Is there something I can help you with?"

I squared my shoulders, gathering my courage, deciding it would be best to state my intent outright. "I came to offer myself as an apprentice."

She laughed, at first—a startled, merry sound—raising her eyes to the heavens in what looked like a prayer of thanks. I smiled, certain that my mother was right and she was going to take me on. But after a moment, Kunegunde's expression changed, and all of the joy faded out of it. She looked at me with a weary sadness. "I'm not sure you would be safe here."

My stomach dropped. "But the tower—the mist. I have nowhere else to go."

"The mist isn't infallible. There are ways around it."

"I was almost stoned in my hometown. I already understand something of the healing arts," I said, hoping that would make me more attractive to her. "My mother was a midwife."

"I know that," she snapped, her mood shifting quickly, as if my assumption that she didn't infuriated her. Her eyes flashed.

I blinked. My surprise must've shown on my face.

She froze, realizing how harsh she had just sounded. "Forgive me. It's just—your mother came to me more than once. I remember my clients. Aren't you tired? There's an extra bedchamber on the second floor. I'm cross when I don't get a full night of sleep. We should talk after both of us rest."

"I would be grateful to sleep here," I said slowly, still startled by her sudden temper.

She led me upstairs, chatting amiably about how dark the room would be with the shutters closed, how comfortable I would find the bed. She spoke quickly, as if she was trying to distract me from her outburst by a steady stream of chatter. "Here you are."

The bedchamber had a tall narrow window, brightened by the gray light of dawn. Against the wall was a luxurious cot with linen sheets, a coverlet, and a feather-stuffed mattress. Never had I slept in such a fine bed. My eyes must have gone as round as coins. "Thank you," I breathed.

Kunegunde nodded and excused herself, saying she needed to lock up downstairs before we slept. "The hunting party."

After she left, I went to the window and looked down over the walled garden. One of the smaller ravens was washing its wings in the birdbath. As I watched, the food I'd eaten and my long journey caught up with me, and I was overcome with a sudden wave of exhaustion. I battened the shutters and lay down, my need for sleep warring with my fear that Kunegunde wouldn't accept me.

I reached into the pouch on my belt and pulled out the bird-mother figurine. Please, I prayed, rubbing her curves. Please let me stay. The figurine grew warm in my palm, thrumming softly, thickening the mist in the air around me. The mist swirled, wrapping itself around me, caressing my arms. I shivered, tears in my eyes—tears of happiness, tears of grief—the same way I'd felt when my mother visited me in the garden. The effect was so soothing, I smiled, drifting off into that space between sleep and waking, a sort of dreamless trance. After a while, I thought I heard my mother's voice. Not demonic this time, but gentle. *Visit the next mountain*, she hummed.

I jolted upright so fast, the bedroom swayed around me. I couldn't tell if I had been awake or dreaming.

CHAPTER TWELVE

Midday light brightened the room. For a moment I didn't know where I was. Then it came back to me—the forest, the stone circle, the tower. The mist I'd sensed early that morning, comforting and beautiful. I could still feel it at the edge of things. Sitting up, I saw two ravens perched on the sill, watching me, their black eyes glittering with intelligence. How long had they been watching me? Had Kunegunde opened the window? A third bird, the larger one—though his eyes seemed to be black now—soared down to perch on the sill alongside them. The way he gazed at me, measuring me up, unsettled me.

"Shoo," I told him. He didn't budge.

The shutters creaked as I closed them on all three birds, pushing them out. Barring the window behind them, I could hear them flapping their wings and croaking. I closed my eyes, enjoying for a moment my renewed privacy. Then I remembered the voice I'd heard before I fell asleep. I must've dreamed it. If I hadn't, my mother's advice puzzled me. Why should I visit the next mountain? I had just gotten here.

Wafting up the stairs was the smell of pig meat, the sound of fat sizzling over a fire. How long had I been asleep? Did Kunegunde have time to slaughter a pig? I found the bird-mother charm in my coverlet, slipped her into my pouch, and went downstairs. On the first floor, Kunegunde stood a few feet away from the fire, keeping an eye on the sizzling meat while she read from a tome. Dark colors leapt off the page. Ruby red, deep blue, a gold so bright it glowed. "I set the table outside," she said without looking up.

"Outside?" The day before had been cold enough to require a cloak.

Kunegunde nodded, putting the book away and flipping pig meat onto a plate. It smelled delicious.

I followed her to the door that led into the garden. The basin where the raven had bathed the night before was encircled by a bed of overgrown thorns. The birds were currently nowhere to be seen. Here and there around the birdbath stood the statues I had seen the night before. A naked woman, her arms covered in vines and dirt. Several chipped grotesques, terrible half-human creatures with snouts and horns. Fearsome things, effigies of heathen gods like my mother's Pelzmärtel dolls—or the figurine, I thought suddenly. Along the back wall I saw the trees I'd noticed earlier, glowing with firebright red apples. The ground beneath them was littered with leaves as gold as coins.

The legs of the table crooked to the cobblestones, knobby, the face of the table whittled smooth. In the center of the table was a basket with half a dozen boiled goose eggs. Before each of our chairs was a bowl of sops. Near the table, a fire pit glowed, blazing with a comfortable warmth. Kunegunde set down the plate she was carrying with slabs of pig, and we sat. Over her shoulder I could see a spider greedily spinning her web. "You make a good lad," she said, nodding at my tunic.

"This smells delicious."

Juice and fat filled my mouth, greasy and salty, as I began to eat. I was ravenous. The meat and eggs in particular were incredibly tasty. We settled into a contented silence, enjoying breakfast. After a while, I smiled at her nervously, gathering my courage to bring up the purpose for my journey here again. "My mother said you want an apprentice. Is that not still so?"

"I do," she said quietly, her expression strained. I could tell she was measuring her words. "I'm sorry I didn't express myself adequately this morning. My last pupil—things didn't end well."

I remembered the story my mother had told me about Ursilda. "No one is going to come after me. My father won't even notice I'm missing for a week."

Her eyes flashed with an anger so intense, it scared me.

"Even if he managed to figure out where I went, he certainly doesn't have a wolf-skin," I joked quickly, trying to lighten her mercurial mood.

"It's not that," she said. She closed her eyes and drew a deep breath, though when she spoke next, her voice was tight. "I would love to take you on as my apprentice, but these woods are dangerous. If you stay here, you have to promise not to leave the stone circle."

"I can do that," I said eagerly. "What trade would I learn?"

She nodded and cleared her throat. "I could teach you wortcunnery, midwifery. I could teach you to read and write. I could teach you the old ways—"

My breath caught. "I would like that very much."

The largest raven soared down suddenly from wherever he'd been hiding in the garden. Croaking, he looked at me with glittering black eyes as he tried to hop up on the table. "Have his eyes changed color?"

"There are three of them." The bird croaked as if in agreement. She laughed. "Erste does what he wants."

After that, we fell silent, enjoying our food. For the rest of the meal, she watched me thoughtfully. It was almost as if she wanted to ask me something, but she kept thinking better of it. I didn't feel comfortable enough to ask her what.

By the time we finished breakfast, there was grease all over my tunic. After I helped her bring the leftover cheese and eggs downstairs to the buttery, Kunegunde suggested I bathe in the brook. Although the sun was stronger than it had been yesterday, she said tomorrow would bring frost. Today might be my last chance to bathe in the stream. She gave me a rag, a clean tunic, and a cake of something she called soap, then held the tower door open. "The brook is over there," she said, pointing north. "Through those trees. There's a pool just this side of the stones."

I nodded, ready at that point to agree to anything.

"I'll be at the window, listening. Call for me if you need me. Rush straight back to the tower if you hear anyone."

"I will."

Outside, shadows played beneath the trees, patches of darkness and sunlight. I weaved in the direction she'd pointed. The trees were thick and tall, the shadows dark even by daylight. As I looked for the stream, I heard movement in the brush around me, unseen animals running from the sound of my feet. My skin tingled as I approached a segment of the stone circle that surrounded the tower, and an unseen force stood my hair on end. Walking along the inside of the circle, I searched for the pool, listening for sounds of the hunting party I'd met the night before. Would they still be about? The only thing I could hear was the she-goat, bleating from the tree by the barn. It was warmer than it had been the day before. I couldn't see my breath in the air. Then I heard the sound of water ahead. The brook.

Soon enough I saw the sun glint, golden, on a stream that ran through a clearing into the trees ahead. The brook was wide, only ankle-deep, bubbling and burbling over a rockbed before it tumbled into the perfect bathing hole. I froze as I approached the waterfall. A mother deer and her child were drinking. The doe looked up at me with big brown eyes, then nudged her spindle-legged child and bounded into the trees.

The pool sparkled, crystal clear. Small fish darted at its bottom. It was the kind of place my mother would've loved. All at once, a memory came back to me of splashing with her in a place like it when I was small. For a moment I was a little girl again, laughing with her in the sun. Then the moment passed, and I found myself standing alone at the edge of the pool, my heart filling with grief. The watersong, idyllic sun, and darting fish did nothing to improve my mood; in fact, they seemed almost to mock it. As if that weren't enough, while I was unraveling my braid, a collared dove lit on the branch of a nearby pine and began to sing, as if I had stumbled into the ballad of some cut-rate minnesinger.

"God's teeth," I groaned, unwrapping the cloth I had stretched around my breasts and removing my underthings, in a hurry to finish my bath.

A brief gust of wind made me shiver as I stepped into the pool. The water was cold. Not so cold that I stopped midstep or winced, but cold enough that I knew I would have to make this quick. The waterfall tinkled, and the sun glittered with a maddening cheer on the water's surface as I waded in. I wet my hair quickly, rubbing myself all over with soap like Kunegunde had told me to do. That task completed, I began to wash my hands. As I worked, I noted how smooth my skin was. Even my fingernails were clean. When I was finished, I used the towel to dry myself, noticing a few wispy hairs on my groin.

Gradually, I became aware of a feeling that I wasn't alone. First there was a shiver on my neck, then the hairs on my arm rose. I stood in my towel at the water's edge, conscious of a faint noise. The distant baying of hounds.

I snatched my clothes and ran back toward the tower. Kunegunde opened the door as she saw me coming, dripping wet, nearly naked. "The hunting party again?"

I nodded. "I think so."

Her eyes widened. "They didn't follow you, did they? Was Albrecht with them?"

I shook my head. "I didn't see them. Last night, it was only Ulrich and Ursilda."

Kunegunde took a deep breath, clearly frustrated. "Only? Ursilda knows how to find the tower. She could've been leading her brother here."

"Have they come back since Ursilda was taken?"

Kunegunde went silent. She pressed her lips together.

"Give me those clothes. I'll wash them for you. There's a dress that should fit you in the trunk, along with a comb you can use to tame that bird's nest of hair."

In the trunk I found the items she described. The dress was sewn from tightly woven linen. It fit almost as perfectly as the dress Matthäus had tailored for me. It took me almost an hour to dress and comb out my hair. As I worked, I realized I should ask Kunegunde about the golden apples. She was known to be an excellent wortcunner; there was a good chance she would be able to identify the plant. If that conversation went well, I thought, I could ask her about the bird-woman next. She had just admitted that she practiced the old ways.

As I went downstairs with my sack, she looked up from the tome she was reading at the table. I asked her if I could get her advice about something. When she nodded, I pulled a golden apple from my sack and held it out. "Do you happen to know the plant that bears this fruit?"

She stiffened. Her eyes went to the fruit and back to my face. I couldn't quite read her expression, but I could tell she was concerned. "Yes," she said. "Where did you find it?"

"Dozens of these plants grew in our garden this year." I set it down in front of her, eager to get more information from her. "The fruit seems to be a curative. Two days ago, I tried one. Afterward, there were changes in my vision, and—I take it you know about my fainting spells?"

She nodded, slowly, as if remembering.

"Since I started eating the fruit, they've changed."

I had her full attention now. She cleared her throat. "How?"

"Usually my soul leaves my body, and I faint. Now, instead, I hear a voice."

Kunegunde closed her eyes, rubbing her temples, as if she had been stricken with a sudden headache. "What does it say?"

"Many things," I said. "Last night, she told me to visit the next mountain."

For a moment she didn't respond.

"Do I need to pay your fee before you'll tell me the plant?"

She shook her head without opening her eyes. "No. Your mother already paid. I never charge twice for the same complaint."

"What is it, then?"

"Set the fruit down," she said without opening her eyes. "Carefully. Try not to get any more on your skin."

Slowly, I did as she asked.

She opened her eyes to confirm that I had. "Don't touch it again. I'll be right back." She disappeared into the entryway and came back with a jug of water, a sack, and the soap. "Wash your hands," she said. "Scrub them. It will clean any residue from the fruit off your skin."

I washed my hands while she retrieved a pair of gloves, putting them on before she picked up the fruit to examine it.

"What is the plant? Is it poisonous?"

"Do you have more?" She nodded at my sack.

Careful not to touch them, I poured the rest of the golden apples onto the table. Two dozen, a bit bruised from the long walk in my sack. Kunegunde's eyes widened as she saw how many there were. "How many of these have you eaten?"

I thought about this, growing nervous. "Several. Is that bad?"

She nodded anxiously. "This fruit can be dangerous in such large quantities. I'm going to give you a draught that will expel the poison." She walked over to the apothecary cabinet, from which she retrieved sysemera, rue, and betony—my mother had used those herbs—and began pounding them with a mortar and pestle. She poured out the resulting juice and told me to drink it.

As I did, she slipped the fruit one by one into her sack. With each fruit she took, I felt a loss. I could hardly stand to watch.

When Kunegunde had put them all in her sack but one, she took off the gloves and used the washing water and soap to clean her hands. My stomach heaved, and I threw up in the chamber pot.

When I was finished emptying my stomach, she went to the shelf to retrieve a tome, which looked like it was going to fall apart any minute. "This is a speculum detailing all the plants of the Roman Empire and their properties."

She opened it to a page that contained an exact replica of the plants that grew in my garden. Someone had carefully illustrated one from leaf to root. There were the faded green leaves Mother had straightened, the violet flowers that bloomed at its center, the small golden apples it bore. All of the colors were faded, as if they had been painted by hands long dead. Beneath the plant, underground, the illustration showed its root, a malformed shape like a man. I looked closer at the book. On the opposite page, the same border swirled around a block of text. "Look here." She pointed to the first word on the page, whose beginning letter looked like two mountains, side-by-side, outlined in black. "This word names the plant. *Mandragora*, although most folks around here call it *alrūne*." She pointed again. "This is a description of its properties. That speaks to the root's ability to bring sleep. This discusses its healing properties, its attractiveness to demons, how much is needed to poison the blood. But this is all about the root."

"It says nothing of the fruit?"

Kunegunde shook her head. "What color are your eyes usually?"

"Black," I said. "Why?"

She left the room. I leaned over the hearth, rubbing my hands over the fire to combat the draft from the window-slot. When she returned, she held a hand-mirror. It was tarnished gold, decorated like the smashed one I had taken from my mother's trunk, but its face was smooth. As Kunegunde held it out for me, the image on the metal changed, the tan of her fingers becoming the burnished brown of the ceiling and then a golden-pink version of my thumb as I touched it. The blurry shape of my reflection stared back at me, my cheeks still red with cold from my bath, my wild black hair curling from my scalp. I turned the mirror this way and that, trying to see my features in more detail. I had never seen my face reflected back at me whole. I resembled my mother a great deal. The only thing that set me apart from her was my eyes. My eyes. I opened them wide with disbelief. There was a faint circle of color around my pupils. "My eyes are golden."

She nodded, putting on the gloves again.

She used a small knife to cleave the golden apple on the table. Untangling a seed from the glistening pulp, she cut it in two. From her apron, she produced a small circle of glass, which she held over the seed-halves. In the glass her eye loomed large. I could see the veins that laced its white, the twitch of her pupil as she looked at the kernel up close. "This fruit is overripe. Having hung on the vine so long, it could've taken on properties of the root." She put the glass circle and fruit away, then glanced back at the book, removing her gloves. Her expression turned dark. "I mentioned the demons the plant attracts earlier. Are you sure the voice you heard is one you want to hear?"

She searched my face, her eyes filled with judgment. Anger reared up in my throat, and I had to work to master my expression. Kunegunde had no way of knowing the voice I heard was my mother's. I hadn't told her. "I'm sure," I said, unable to keep a tremor out of my voice.

She watched my face for a long moment, sizing me up. "Your mother gave you something before she died, didn't she?" She held her thumb and forefinger apart just far enough that the bird-mother would fit between them. "A figurine about this tall."

I stared at her. How did she know? My thoughts whirled. If I told the truth, would she take the figurine away like she did the fruit? "What?" I said, pretending confusion. "No."

Her eyes narrowed, as if she didn't believe me. "You must stop eating the alrūne," she continued after a moment, her tone matter-of-fact.

"Different plants possess different amounts of poisons. If you eat the fruit of the wrong vine—" She shook her head. "I can give you a powder made from dried gooseberries and a few potent herbs, which won't make you susceptible to demons. It'll cure your spells. I could even cure your sensitivity to light—"

"I don't want to stop hearing the voice," I said, interrupting.

She frowned at me. "You don't believe it is demonic."

"No."

Her face fell. "If you like, I could add a touch of alrūne to the powder. A small amount that wouldn't threaten your life."

I thought about this. I needed to trust her. I had nowhere else to go. Her eyes were eager, as if the thought of my safety was important to her. "All right."

She looked relieved, getting up. "I'll make it now."

"Do you think you could add something to the powder to bring on my menses? I'm almost seventeen years old, and I still haven't bled."

She considered. "I can't put anything like that in the powder, but I can concoct an oil that might do the trick."

That night, Kunegunde insisted we lock up the tower. For the months I was there, we would do this every night of the week leading up to and after the full moon. She said Ulrich wore the wolf-skin most often around the full moon when its power was at its strongest. Tonight, like last night, she said it was especially important since we knew the hunting party had been near. She locked the bottom door, barring it shut, and she locked up the garden. The downstairs window-slots were caged, but she carefully barred the upstairs shutters too.

Her fear was contagious. By the time I went to bed, I was afraid to open my bedroom window. I wondered what had happened during Ursilda's "rescue" to make her so paranoid. As I tried to sleep, I listened for the sound of the hunting party, but all I heard was the wind. I wondered how Kunegunde knew my mother gave me a figurine. It must be part of what allowed me to hear my mother's voice. Kunegunde must know how it worked.

I pulled the figurine from my coin-purse, inspecting her. The air seemed weightier around her, just as it had the night before, and the mist seemed to thicken around her. Closing my eyes, I rubbed her until I could feel my mother swirling faintly around me, enveloping me like she had the night before. I thought I smelled the faint scent of anise. The same comfort filled me, the same relief. After a moment, the figurine warmed beneath my fingers, as if she couldn't contain all of the power she drew from the next world. I lay there, perfectly still, basking in my mother's presence.

When my sense of her faded, I looked at the figurine in awe. Who was my mother's goddess? What power allowed my mother's spirit to come to me like this? The bird-mother stared back at me, silent, refusing to answer. Her body language was motherly, compassionate, but she was undeniably fierce too. Her beak, her talons, her wings, the child in her arms, her naked breasts and hips. She seemed foreign from all I'd been taught to think of as holy, so monstrous and so sensual. She embodied aspects of motherhood that I'd never thought of as sacred—mother-greed, fury, the animal urge to protect, and lust. I had fought against those instincts in myself because my father had taught me they were sinful. The bird-mother was no Virgin, that much was clear, but that didn't make her a demon. I rubbed the figurine, willing my mother to coalesce and answer my questions, but my only companion that night was the mist itself.

I must've fallen asleep with the figurine in my hand.

CHAPTER THIRTEEN

On the morning of my second day at Gothel, I awoke to find that my things had been moved. On top of the trunk at the foot of the bed, my sack and pouch were laid out, everything I had brought with me arranged in neat little rows. My bow and arrow. The broken mirror. The sight of the figurine, glistening black in the morning sun, filled me with dread. Kunegunde had found her and moved her. She knew I had lied to her. I sat in bed for what seemed like hours, staring at my things, dreading that Kunegunde would cast me out when I went downstairs.

When I finally got up to get dressed, I found a phial filled with oil and a pouch full of powder laid out neatly beside the other things on the trunk. The remedies Kunegunde had promised. Had she come in to give them to me, only going through my things after she saw the figurine in my bed? I shouldn't have lied to her.

The powder tasted bitter. The oil was umber, like dried blood, and it smelled almost bestial. I smeared it on my groin as she'd instructed me the night before, then pulled on my dress, gathering my courage, and marched myself and the figurine downstairs.

Kunegunde was reading a tome. She looked up and met my eyes, defiant, as if she were daring me to lie to her again.

"Thank you for the curatives." I held the figurine up. "I see you found this. I was afraid to admit to you that I had it. My mother warned me never to show her to anyone."

"Mmm," Kunegunde said, turning a page, her voice cold.

"Do you know what it is? How it works?"

Her expression was indignant. "I don't know why you think

I'm going to be honest with you, when you haven't been honest with me."

"I'm sorry, Kunegunde. I apologize for lying. I didn't want you to take it from me."

"Too little, too late."

"Why does it make you so angry that I have it?"

"It's not that. It's the fact that you lied to me about it." She eyed the figurine in my hand, her expression hurt. "Get that thing out of my sight."

Her tone was so scornful, I turned around immediately to go upstairs and put it away. She barely spoke to me for the rest of that morning, and when she did, her words were full of a frosty reserve. I could tell she was angry, punishing me. I wanted to make my lie up to her, but I didn't know how.

After lunch, when she excused herself for a nap, I decided to slip out of the tower and shoot something for dinner in an effort to make her happy with me again. I hurried with my bow to the bathing pool just inside the stone circle. I hid in a bush beside the clearing, waiting for some unlucky animal to try to quench its thirst.

Soon, a family of swans flew down into the water: a cob, a pen, and three cygnets. I couldn't believe my luck; I hadn't eaten swan since the bishop built the wall. My father had loved it when my mother used to make *schwanseklein*; the soup was delicious, his favorite meal. I knew the recipe.

The swans were so graceful with their long white necks; for a moment, I watched them, transfixed. Then they took off all at once, and I cursed, leaving my hiding place to go after them. I paused at the edge of the stone circle, hesitant, but my desire to make things right with Kunegunde won out over my obedience.

As I crossed the threshold, my limbs tingled and I felt the spell zapping between the stones, but the feeling was more muted than it'd been the day before. The swan family was waddling down the bank a ways off. I let my arrow fly and the cob drooped, the other birds flying away in a terrified cloud of white feathers. I hurried along the bank to retrieve him.

As I was plucking his feathers, I heard Kunegunde calling me from inside the stone circle, her voice panicked. "*Haelewise?!*"

I rushed back through the circle, forgetting all about my plans to surprise her, worried that something had happened. She was standing by the pool, the fear on her face quickly shading into anger as she saw the half-undressed bird in my hand.

Her eyes flashed. "Where did you go?"

"Down the brook a ways."

"Outside the circle?!"

"I'm going to make *schwanseklein* for dinner."

She pressed her lips together tight. I braced myself for her to yell at me. But she was too angry even to raise her voice. She gave me a warning look that reminded me of my mother's expression in the garden when she warned me that I had to leave town. "Come in and get dressed," she hissed. "Now. I don't think you understand the gravity of the situation."

After I put on my clothes, she sat me down at the table. I braced myself for an unhappy discussion. "I'm letting you stay here on two conditions," she said, her voice dripping with condescension. "First, you must tell me the truth. Understand?"

I nodded.

"Second, you can't leave the circle without me. I can't emphasize this enough. I take it you know the story about Princess Ursilda."

I nodded again, eager to win back her trust.

"When Ursilda's mother sent her here, Albrecht was on a campaign with the king. When he returned and found out where she was, he was irate. Not because he's Christian, though he pretends to be at court, but because he knew I would cure the fear he'd beaten into his daughter, that I would help her grow strong enough to defy him. After he took her home, he told the king I kidnapped her and convinced King Frederick to issue a writ for my death."

I must've looked horrified. "That's a harsh punishment for taking someone in with her mother's permission."

"Albrecht is wicked. The wolf-skin has belonged to the men in
his family for centuries. It's warped them." She met my eyes, her
expression pointed, her voice low. "Sometimes, peasants traveling
through these woods go missing."

I swallowed, overwhelmed with two emotions at once—a childish
pride that she wanted to protect me, and fear at what she was saying
about Albrecht. I remembered the *wrongness* I sensed in the air around
Ulrich when I saw him wearing the wolf-skin, and I shivered.

Later that afternoon, when Kunegunde invited me to go for a
walk, the day had been going so terribly, I was thrilled. She said it
was safe if we left the circle together because she would be there to
protect me, and she was out of some important herbs. I followed
her toward the edge of the stone circle, hoping she would take the
walk as an opportunity to talk, but my attempts to strike up a conversation with her were met only with grunts. The sensation of the
spell zapping between the stones as we passed through the circle
seemed even weaker than it had in the morning.

Giving up on conversation with Kunegunde, I tried to content
myself with enjoying the beauty and wildness of the woods outside the stone circle. The mountainside was wilder even than the
dark forest I'd walked through to get here, teeming with foxes and
stags and rabbits, a thousand types of rare and poisonous plants and
mushrooms that grew in the shade. It was as if the mist encouraged
everything it touched to grow.

The sunlight, in the rare instances that we stumbled into it,
didn't bother my eyes much. Although I had eaten no alrūne that
day, the gooseberry powder seemed to treat my sensitivity to light.
Eventually, we came across a mossy tree, and she told me to help
her gather some of the moss. As I put the moss in our basket, she
pointed at a thick stand of fernlike plants my mother had taught me
young not to touch. "What's that?" she asked.

"Poison hemlock," I said quickly, eager to show her what I knew. Hemlock bore pretty blooms earlier in the year, but this late all that was left were a few dried seed heads, which the wind had yet to shake loose.

She nodded. "You know the plant. Even this time of year. Your mother taught you well. Hemlock is useful in tiny doses, but too much can cause vertigo and death. Recite that back."

I smiled hopefully at her and repeated it, though I already knew those facts. As we walked, she continued teaching me the names and uses of plants. Some of what she said that day my mother had already taught me, but there were new lessons too. There were many plants in this part of the forest that I'd never seen before. As we walked, I felt relieved, grateful that her anger with me seemed to be thawing.

CHAPTER FOURTEEN

We fell into a routine during the rest of my first week at Gothel. In the mornings, Kunegunde sent me hunting—as long as I promised to stay inside the stone circle. I shot a hare, a pheasant. One day I even shot a goose. Kunegunde spent hours roasting the birds. I found it odd how much her recipes reminded me of home, but I didn't dwell on it. Each prize I brought back to the tower seemed to make her happier with me; she said she was eating better than she had in years. In the afternoons, she set about teaching me my letters and numbers. As a child, I had never even dreamed that I would have the chance to learn to read. I found it fascinating, how the written letters on the page corresponded to the sounds of speech. I loved reading so much. Soon, while Kunegunde studied, I was sounding out the words of a speculum on local flora, which Kunegunde had written herself using a faint brown ink she made from crushing local vegetation. Kunegunde seemed impressed with my memory for sounds and the pleasure I took in words. While she read, I spent hours turning the pages of that speculum, learning its pictures by heart.

I marveled over Kunegunde's striking illustrations of huszwurtz and wolfsgelena, over the vines that spiraled around the borders of its pages. Vines and thorns and exotic flowers. Monsters and gods that resembled my mother's poppets. I recognized Wodin and Cupid, Pelzmärtel and Lamia.

As the days passed, I stopped noticing the tingling inside the stone circle, the mist in the air. When I rubbed the figurine at night, my sense of my mother grew fainter and fainter, until my heart began to ache with longing and disappointment.

One night, when I had been at Gothel about a week, I rubbed the figurine's curves in bed at night and felt nothing. No thrumming, no mist, no indication whatsoever that the figurine was more than a stone carving. For a heartbreaking moment, I questioned whether there had ever been anything special about her, whether I'd conjured my mother's ghost out of the madness of my grief. But no, Kunegunde had promised she would add enough alrūne to the powder that I would still be able to hear the voice. Perhaps she had forgotten? I tried to think of some way to ask her about it, but I was wary, since the figurine was such a touchy subject.

"Kunegunde," I said as I walked downstairs the next morning. She was working on a manuscript at the table. "May I ask you something?"

She kept writing. "Just a moment." Her quill looped over the parchment, darkening the page with indecipherable symbols like the ones on the hand-mirrors. After a moment, she looked up, clearly irritated that I was disturbing her work. "Yes?"

"I can't feel the mist anymore," I said, working hard to keep my voice even. "The mist that surrounds the tower. When I got here, the air was thin, and it was everywhere. But now, the tower feels like an ordinary place. Can you sense the mist too? Did something change?"

"No," she said, setting her quill down on the table, her agitation growing. I couldn't tell if she was frustrated about being disturbed or about my question itself. She took a deep breath, obviously working to stay calm. When she spoke, her voice had a forced quality. "I can't sense the mist anymore either. Not most days. It comes and goes. Think of it like a scent. Once you smell it for a while, you forget it's there."

I nodded slowly. That seemed like a logical explanation. I thought for a moment, trying to figure out what was still bothering me. "I can't hear the voice anymore either. Did you forget to add the alrūne to my powder?"

"Of course not," she snapped. "I told you I would."

"The figurine is different too," I said tentatively, watching her face, worried that I would upset her by mentioning it. "It used to hum, but now—"

"Same principle," Kunegunde said, a warning note in her tone, the words so clipped I knew she would snap if I pressed. "Nothing to worry about."

The next afternoon, the wind blew so strong it shook the last of the red apples from the tree in the garden, and we put our books away to get ready for the storm. "Batten the shutters," Kunegunde said, putting on her apron to walk outside. "I'll be right back. Tonight will mark the last new moon of autumn. We'll bake apple *strützel* and make an offering. I think we have enough aniseed."

"*Strützel*," I said eagerly. Mother and I had always made *strützel* around this time of year too. She said it was a traditional recipe to celebrate the beginning of the darker half of the year. As Kunegunde went outside, I hurried through the tower, latching the shutters, while Kunegunde gathered the fallen apples from beneath the tree.

When she came back in and handed me a firebright apple from her apron, I realized—all at once—who she was. The dark-haired, ample-bosomed woman from my memory, the grandmother my father had told me was dead.

The apple shone, red, in her palm.

I took it from her dizzily as everything fell into place. The sadness Kunegunde showed when I told her my mother died. The huge garden. The memory of swimming with my mother in that pool. No wonder my mother had told me to come to Gothel.

"What is it, Haelewise?"

The apple rolled out of my hand and under the table.

Kunegunde followed it with her eyes. "Cat got your tongue?"

"You're my—" I wanted to say the word *grandmother*, to run to her and embrace her, but as soon as Kunegunde realized what I was going to say, her eyes flashed.

"*Anasehlan!*" she shouted, raising her hands. Her voice lilted with the rhythm of my mother's voice when she swore in the old language. The spell echoed through the air, snapping with power. My chest collapsed, and a terrible force sucked all of the air out of my lungs. I couldn't breathe. My hands went to my throat.

Seeing my fear, her expression turned regretful and she lowered her hands. The action released me. I gasped for air.

"We can't speak of that," she said. "Your mother made me swear. There is blood-magic involved."

I nodded, slowly, though I was more focused on trying to recover my breath than understanding. Once I could breathe again, I worked to regain my composure, reflecting on what she had said. Outside, the storm raged. Wind whistled unhappily around the tower. "Blood-magic?"

She shook her head fiercely. "You're not anywhere near ready to learn about that. You just got here."

When I was recovered, we set about making the dough for the *strützel*. She seemed truly concerned about my well-being. She kept apologizing, asking me if I felt all right. She smiled at me as we worked the dough, calling me "little one," the same name my mother had called me, and I realized that must've been her pet name for my mother.

I couldn't believe I hadn't noticed their resemblance before. As I watched her braid the dough, I saw shadows of my mother in her—the way she pressed her lips together tight to discourage talk about a subject she didn't like, the way she flicked her wrist when she braided the dough—and I longed to grow close to her like a granddaughter should.

While the *strützel* baked, we made dinner: the goose I had shot that morning, the mushrooms I had picked on the way home. We roasted the goose over the hearthfire and cooked the mushrooms in the cauldron in the goose's fat. We made spiced wine, seasoned with anise and a hundred apple slices. She said the meal needed to be good; the new moon was a time of transition, when the otherworldly weather changed and prayers drifted naturally into the next world, so tonight we would set out food as an offering to the Mother.

I didn't understand what she was saying about the otherworldly weather, but the idea of making an offering to my mother's goddess with my grandmother brought tears to my eyes. I remembered all the times my mother and I had burned offerings back home when my father was out. I wondered if the ritual would allow me to feel the mist again, so my mother would be able to come to me as she had on my first nights here, and I felt a wild stab of hope.

Thunder cracked and boomed while the goose finished roasting, and waves of rain crashed into the shutters. Kunegunde carved a spiral into each of three hollowed-out bread crusts, covering each with goose and apples and cheese and the delicious-smelling mushrooms. In a basket, she set one of the crusts, arranging *strützel* in a pretty ring around it. Then she walked to the door of the tower and set it on the ground outside. I stood behind her, watching, hopeful and eager.

When she bowed her head, I bowed mine too.

"Mother," she said, reaching for my hand. "Everything we do, we do in your name. Take this food as our offering. Bless us with enough firewood to stay warm and enough clients to eat well this winter. Keep the tower safe."

My eyes watered at the simplicity of her prayer, and my heart swelled with hope. For a moment, I thought I could feel the mist gathering, an otherworldly presence, but the sensation was so subtle, I wasn't sure. Then it passed, and my heart broke. I reached out, trying desperately to feel it again, but it was gone. Kunegunde stood silent beside me—eyes closed, back straight—her expression transfixed. Clearly, she felt something that I couldn't. When she opened her eyes, a sob leapt from my throat. The disappointment was too much for me to bear.

"Haelewise. What's wrong?"

I crumpled into myself. "I couldn't feel it. I know you said that happens, that it's like a scent, but I could tell you *did*."

Kunegunde led me over to the chair beside the hearthfire and made me a cup of caudle to settle my stomach. Leaving the food on the table uneaten, she sat in the chair beside me. I sat there for a long time—eyes closed, filled with a sadness so heavy I couldn't even lift a finger. After a while, I knew there were sounds coming out of her mouth, but I couldn't bring myself to make sense of them.

"*Haelewise*," she said again. This time, I snapped out of my trance. "It comes and goes. There's no controlling it. This was supposed to be a happy night. What can I do to cheer you up?"

I thought for a long time. My thoughts were sluggish with disappointment. It took me several sips of caudle to rouse myself from it and recognize that I could use her offer as an opportunity. Groggily, I rummaged through all the questions I had for her, trying to decide which one to ask first so I could best capitalize on her pity. If there was ever a time to ask about the bird-mother, I decided, it was tonight. I made my voice small. "Will you tell me about the figurine? Do you know why my mother had it?"

Kunegunde went very still. For a moment, I was afraid that I had pushed her too far. Then she took a deep breath. When she spoke, her voice was measured. "Your mother, like me, worshipped the ancient Mother, who's been forgotten by a world obsessed with the Father."

"That's who the bird-mother represents?"

Kunegunde nodded.

"Who is she?"

"She has many names. She is worshipped in secret everywhere the dove flies, here and in the East, as far away as Rome and Jerusalem."

"What does it mean to follow her?"

She took a long drink of wine. "To protect women and their knowledge. To hold the natural world sacred. To learn the hidden powers of root and leaf and the creatures of the earth."

"Why does she take the form of a bird?"

Kunegunde leaned back in her chair. "That's a difficult question. I'm not sure if anyone knows for sure, but every effigy I've ever seen of her depicts her as a bird-woman. I've always thought she is more like the mist in the forest, or a living shadow, or the ants that will eat that offering we just set outside."

I nodded, drawing a deep breath, alarmed by her comparison of the goddess to crawling insects. I dismissed the thought, mulling over the rest of what she'd said. She'd ignored the most important part of my question. I needed to know how to use the figurine so I could conjure my mother again. I made my voice childlike, small. "What is the figurine? How does it work?"

For a split second, I thought I saw her wince. Then her expression went blank. "It's just a charm," she said, as if the question was silly. "Something you carry around for good luck."

Frustration filled me. I knew she was lying. The figurine had something to do with why I could hear my mother's voice; otherwise, how would she know I had it? Her refusal to tell me what she knew, what I desperately wanted to know, infuriated me, but I was afraid to confront her after the spell she cast on me earlier. I closed my eyes, deciding to pretend to believe her for now, racking my brain for a way to approach the subject more indirectly. "Are there many who worship the Mother?"

Kunegunde's voice went hard. "Not anymore. We have to worship in secret. The world of men is wicked, Haelewise. Full of royals and clergymen so afraid of losing power, they'll execute anyone who stands up to them."

I waited for her to go on, but she fell quiet. The fire crackled. "The spell on the stones. How does it work?"

Flames leapt in her eyes. "I don't know. It's been here longer than I have. As for how it works, this is a thin place. The spell draws its power from the mist beyond the veil."

"A thin place?" I said, confused. "Like what I feel during births and deaths? But permanently?"

"Yes." She shifted in her chair, still watching the fire.

How could my ability to sense something so powerful fade in and out? It didn't make sense. The sluggish disappointment that I'd felt earlier returned, making my head foggy. Suddenly it was hard for me to think again. I took a deep breath, trying to decide what to ask her next, fighting my mental torpor.

"How does a place become thin?" I asked finally.

It was a long time before she took a sip of her wine and spoke. "The same thing that makes the veil thin anywhere. Births, deaths, the presence of gods or ghosts. In places like this, the veil has thinned so many times that it has become worn. The boundary between this world and the next is permeable."

"What happened here?"

Kunegunde shook her head. "I don't know. Nor did the wise woman who lived here before me—I asked the same question when I first arrived. All I know is those aren't ordinary stones, Haelewise. They're graves. I suspect they belong to women. That whoever cast the spell did so to protect the women who remained."

CHAPTER FIFTEEN

Winter fell soft and quiet over the tower, covering the wood in a great white hush. As the days grew cold, Kunegunde acted more and more as a grandmother would. She began checking that I wore my cloak when we went on walks. She made me more powder and fertility oil when I ran out. From time to time, she called me "little one." These gestures brought tears to my eyes, though her temper was still short and her falsehoods complicated my granddaughterly affection. In early December, when my mother would've told stories about my birth and remarked that I was a year older, Kunegunde said nothing, and I found myself haunted by a great sadness.

That winter would be the coldest I've ever lived through, and I've lived through many a winter in my long life. There was snow and snow and more snow, as if the gods wanted to erase every living thing from the forest, to unmake its capacity for life. The wood turned black and white, an intricate latticework of branches and snow. The birds, aside from the ravens Kunegunde kept, all but disappeared. Snowbanks drifted, and we woke to the hoofprints of stags. Frost edged the leaves of the holly bush. Winter berries ripened, as red as blood. Without the reminder of services, the days blended together. Kunegunde celebrated no saints' days, marking only Yule, the shortest day of the year. Her midwinter ritual involved spiced wine, a roast of lamb, and a hearthfire built of logs smeared with lamb's blood that raged into the night.

On the night of the first full moon after Yule, I woke with the sense that there was someone outside. Opening the shutters to peer down into the garden, I saw Kunegunde bent over the birdbath, chanting over the ice that glistened within it. What in the world is she doing, I thought, remembering the rumors about the queen whispering into her hand-mirror.

Her corpse-braids hung down either side of her waist, white ribbons glowing silver, her expression fixed with intense concentration. She was perspiring, murmuring something under her breath. When her lips stopped moving, the ice flashed with colors that were not a reflection. After a moment, they coalesced into the shape of a giant wolf leaping through a wood. The beast was impossibly large, made of shadow. Everything about it seemed wrong. Even at this distance, I knew immediately what it was. Ulrich, in the wolf-skin.

She was using the birdbath to scry on him.

When I gasped, Kunegunde looked up as if she had heard the noise. I jumped back from the window, resolving to get a closer look at the basin in the morning.

The next day while Kunegunde was working on her manuscript, I slipped into the garden, looking over my shoulder to make sure she hadn't followed. When I was sure I was alone, I walked casually to the birdbath. It was waist-high, carved from faded stone. There were hairline cracks in its walls, not deep enough to let water out. All over the inside of the bowl were faded symbols like the ones on the mirrors and Kunegunde's manuscript. Was my mother's mirror for scrying too? How had it shattered? Had Kunegunde given it to her?

Back inside, Kunegunde was still hard at work illuminating a page of her manuscript. The border was decorated with dozens of images of birds in flight; indecipherable black symbols looped and curled all over the page. Some of the birds were outlined in a faint golden sheen. She was making her way down the page, gilding them. Her quill glistened with a gold leaf suspension, which I had seen her make with stag's glue.

Watching her, it occurred to me that my mother *spoke* this language, that she had probably been able to *read* it. Suddenly I was overwhelmed with an urge to touch the symbols, to feel them under my fingers, to shape them with my tongue.

"Is that the old language?" I breathed. "It's on your mirror and the birdbath. It must be."

Kunegunde was making a thin line of gold down the wing of a bird. "Yes," she said absent-mindedly, without looking up.

"Will you teach it to me?"

"Someday," she said. "When you're ready." But there was a guarded note in her tone, a warning, and I understood she meant that someday was a long time away.

During what must've been one of the first days of February, the ravens began acting strangely during our afternoon reading. All three hopped down from their perches on the shelves and croaked noisily. As we looked up from our books, they headed toward the caged windows and flew out. "Someone is approaching the circle," Kunegunde said.

"Is their hearing so subtle?"

"No, but their sense of smell is." Kunegunde got up to go to the door and look out. "People seldom travel this far in winter. Who-ever this is must be desperate."

The visitor the ravens escorted back was an ashen pregnant woman in motley robes and furs who looked like she must've begged for the two large wheels of cheese and bread loaves she offered us. She kept looking over her shoulder at the ravens as she stood on the threshold, like she was afraid of them.

When we shut the door behind her, she relaxed and explained her situation. She'd experienced no pangs, though she expected to have her child last month. Her midwife couldn't help her. She had begun to feel poorly and was afraid for her life. Kunegunde took her coins and let her in. "How long since you felt the child move?"

"Almost a week. Several days at least."

"When did you last bleed?"

"Late March."

Kunegunde frowned. "That is too long. If the child hasn't died yet, it will soon. From the color of your skin, I'm sorry, I fear it already has."

The woman nodded grimly. "My midwife said as much."

"We'll start with gentle herbs. If that doesn't work, we'll try pennyroyal."

Kunegunde told me to ready the hearth area and make the caudle. I didn't say anything, but I agreed with Kunegunde that this wouldn't go well. I couldn't feel what I usually felt before the birth of a living child, the tension in the air. Either the woman's labor was nowhere near starting, or her time had already passed. I began making the preparations—hanging tapestries over the window-slots, lighting candles on every surface—reliving all the times that I made these preparations with my mother.

My eyes were wet by the time I got the fire going and hung caudle over it to warm. As I watched the fire, trying to collect myself before I turned around, my sadness gave way to a hollow ache, an anger in my breast. My mother should still be here, I thought as the flames crackled. I should be apprenticed to her.

When I told Kunegunde I was finished, she asked me to get the snakeskin I'd seen hanging before the window and a particular paper talisman. She hung the talisman around the woman's neck and tied the snake around her belly as a birthing girdle. Then she told me to rub rose oil on the woman's groin, and get tosh and primrose oil from the cabinet so that she could prepare a draught.

As I handed her what she'd asked for, I couldn't help but feel morose. I had seen my mother use a similar brew to bring on labor, but I doubted it would do much good today. As the woman sipped the concoction, Kunegunde murmured something under her breath—a chant or prayer—and reached under the woman's skirt. I was shocked when she pulled her hand away, her expression turning hopeful. "The babe may only be too cramped to stir."

I turned around so they couldn't see my skeptical expression. I had never attended a live birth when I didn't sense tension in the air. As the hours passed, my pity for the woman grew. I listened to her tell Kunegunde about her past labors as we waited for the draught to take. We drank the caudle. The sun set, the shadows in the tower grew deeper, and my anger at Kunegunde ebbed. As I watched the woman cradle her belly, it occurred to me that Phoebe would've given birth by now. I wondered if Matthäus regretted his choice to obey his father. Did he still hate Phoebe? Did he miss me? The idea that he might be stuck in a loveless marriage pleased me, I confess.

I lit the lanterns on the walls. Midnight came and went, and the skin of the world refused to grow thin. When it was clear the draught and caudle had done no good, Kunegunde gave the woman pennyroyal. Within an hour, her pangs were so intense that her round face shone with sweat. Each time she experienced a pang, I felt terrible for her. Usually by this time in labor, the skin of the world was stretched so tight, it was ready to split open. The only time I had felt nothing like this was before a stillbirth.

I rubbed the woman's back with peppermint oil as my mother had taught me to do, whispering words of comfort. When the woman's water broke, Kunegunde told me to melt some snow. I did as she said, though I was sure there would be no live baby to bathe. As the woman's pangs came faster, Kunegunde told her to bend, rock her hips, and remove her skirt. When she did, I thought I saw the shape of a foot kick the surface of her belly. I watched her skin until I saw movement again, shocked.

"God's teeth," I said, forgetting to hide my disbelief. "You were right."

Kunegunde saw it too. "The child is alive, but breech. We have to turn her."

The woman nodded, a determined look coming over her face.

A terrible alarm filled me. It was one thing not to be able to sense the mist at the edge of things here, but if the child was alive, I should be able to feel possibility in the air or a pull into the next world. I had been able to sense that all my life. Kunegunde set to work massaging the woman's belly with the same technique my mother used. She told me to prepare a bath and get the goat's horn with the cloth teat in case the mother had trouble nursing. I did everything she said to do, unsettled.

It was another hour before Kunegunde said the baby was in position. As the birth drew near, Kunegunde instructed the woman to squat on the floor beside a nest of clean linens and rags. The woman screeched as she pushed the child out into Kunegunde's hands, then crumpled to the floor. The baby was larger than any I'd ever seen with a full head of dark hair. Wriggling, balled-up fists. A girl. I was so startled by her movement that when Kunegunde handed her to me, I froze.

"The throat," she said. "Didn't your mother teach you to clear the throat?"

I nodded. The child opened her eyes, shocked and silent and still. I reached into her mouth, waiting for her soul to whoosh past me as I did. But nothing happened; the air in the room was still. The baby gasped all the same, batting yellow-rimmed eyes as she began to mewl. I could scarcely breathe as I smoothed her fuzzy black hair. Why hadn't I sensed her soul?

"See the yellow eyes, the shallow breath?" Kunegunde asked me from where she squatted next to the crumpled woman. "It's the pennyroyal. Bathe her. Swaddle her, while I bring her mother to. The best remedy for that is mother's milk."

The warm water on the baby's skin made her quiet. Her eyes searched mine, wonder-struck, as I cleaned blood and mucus from her hair. She looked to be an ordinary child with an ordinary will. I was rattled that I couldn't sense her soul. When I pulled her from the water, she screamed. I swaddled her until she calmed again. Rocking her to and fro, humming, swaying my hips, I remembered the way I felt holding the miller's son. I was happy the baby appeared to be healthy, but other than that, I felt *nothing*. Despite the fact that I held a child in my arms, I felt utterly disconnected from the work I had always loved.

The babe started crying again. Be quiet, I wanted to scream.

"She's hungry," I said, irritated, raising my voice so Kunegunde would hear.

My grandmother held a cup of water to the mother's lips without answering.

"Kunegunde—" I said, indignant, trying to catch her attention.

Kunegunde continued to ignore me, focused on helping the woman up.

"Another girl?" the woman said when she was finally upright, eyeing her baby weakly from the pile of rags where Kunegunde had propped her up. She patted her chest.

I brought her the infant, my throat tightening with fear. She settled the girl expertly at her breast and pulled aside her robe. The babe went silent immediately, her small mouth seeking out the nipple. The woman closed her eyes and leaned back, relief on her face. I glanced at Kunegunde, who shook her head and mouthed the word *later.*

"Stay the rest of the night," Kunegunde told the woman, who nodded gratefully. "Both of you need rest."

On the way to bed that night, Kunegunde slipped into my room, shut the door behind her, and sat beside me on my bed. In the other room, I could hear the woman cooing to her baby. Kunegunde lowered her voice. "What upsets you, little one?"

"Did it seem to you that there was something strange about that birth?"

Kunegunde looked puzzled. "Only the child's too-long making in her mother's womb and the pennyroyal. Why do you ask?"

"Can you sense souls?"

Kunegunde cleared her throat. "How do you mean?"

"Usually during a birth, I sense possibility in the air, the trembling of the child's soul. This time, I felt nothing. My ability to sense the next world, the movement of souls. The thing that made me a good midwife. It's vanished."

She watched me steadily. "Ah, yes. That happens sometimes. Like I told you before, it comes and goes. As you grow older, the gift can fade. You can still be a good midwife without it."

"Why would it fade now? It's always been reliable."

"Who knows how these mysteries work?" she said, getting up, squeezing my hand. "You did well tonight, little one. I'm exhausted. Let's talk more later."

There was something strange about her tone, her eagerness to go to bed. I could tell she knew more than she was letting on. "Good night," I said helplessly.

As I listened to the sound of her footsteps going upstairs, I felt powerless. Why was Kunegunde hiding things from me? How could I make her tell me what she knew? I needed to know what was happening to me.

CHAPTER SIXTEEN

That night, I dreamed I was a great black bird with talons, searching for something in the wood. I landed in a tree beside a clearing, where a masked rider sat astride a horse bearing Prince Ulrich's banner. The rider dismounted, unsheathing a silver dagger to menace a black-haired woman in ragged clothes who had fallen in the snow. As he advanced on her, I knew with certainty that he was going to kill her. I dove at him to protect the woman, to peck out his eyes, to tear him apart.

Jolting awake, I could feel a faint voice rushing in from the next world, an indecipherable hiss too faint to hear. I knew that my mother was trying to tell me something, that the dream was an omen. But for some reason, I couldn't hear what she was trying to say. I rubbed the figurine, praying, but nothing happened. I was so frustrated about my inability to understand the message that I couldn't get back to sleep. The sounds of the baby's cries and her mother's feet on the stairs didn't help things.

By the time I came down to breakfast, frazzled from lack of rest, I decided to ask Kunegunde about it. "I had a nightmare," I said, sitting across from my grandmother. There were goose eggs and bread in a basket on the table. The mother had gone home.

"What about?"

"I'm a bird, soaring over the wood, looking for something. Down below, I see a woman being menaced by a rider with Prince Ulrich's banner. He's about to kill her with a silver dagger. I swoop down to tear him apart with my talons."

She watched me steadily, her expression shocked.

"At the end of the dream, I hear the voice that spoke to me before, trying to tell me something."

Her expression darkened. "Tell you what?"

"I don't know. That's what's frustrating. I feel like I'm supposed to do something, but I have no idea what."

She watched me for a moment across the table, very still. Fear flashed on her face, though I could tell she was trying to hide it. "You should pay no attention to such dreams," she said angrily. "I told you, the voice that speaks to you is the voice of a demon."

"I told *you*, I don't believe it is."

She glared at me. "I've been putting a touch of alrūne in your powder like you asked. You remember what I showed you in my speculum. Alrūne attracts demons."

"Forget it," I said, deciding to drop the subject. I was too tired for an argument.

That afternoon, Kunegunde and I went for our daily walk into the forest. The snow was already a foot deep, enveloping the bottom of the stones in the circle as we passed through them. I hadn't felt the spell on the stones in months, and the absence of the sensation made me resentful. Outside the circle, the whole world had gone quiet, an icy hush of powder and wood. As our boots crunched the snow, I thought I heard something—a snap of faraway twig, amplified by the cold. Meeting Kunegunde's eyes, I froze in place. The voices we heard next were distant, echoing across the snow. She held out her arm to stop me from bolting, but there was little danger of that. "Be still," she hissed now, reaching into her satchel to put something in her mouth. She chewed it quickly, swallowed, and chanted under her breath.

"Leek haptbhendun von hzost. Tuid hestu."

Her body crumpled to the snow, and her eyes rolled back in her head.

Looking down at her, I wondered if this was how I looked when I swooned. When I knelt down to shake her, she didn't respond.

After a moment, Erste zoomed down through the canopy of leaves toward us, his eyes flashing amber. He perched before her on the snow—eyes fading to black—and her eyes popped open. "Kingsguard," Kunegunde said dizzily. She reached out to a nearby tree to steady herself. "Princess Frederika must be nearby. Help me back to the tower."

There was snow on her corpse-braids and kirtle. I took her arm, steadying her, so shocked I could barely form words. "What just happened?"

"Let's go," Kunegunde said, a look of worry coming over her face.

"What did you do?" I asked again. "What *was* that?"

"Help me back. Now. I can't risk being seen. Remember what I told you about the writ for my death?"

I started moving toward the tower. "Tell me what you did."

She spoke slowly, breathing heavily as we went, as if it took great effort. "Everything that is done can be undone. Even the placement of soul within flesh. That chant loosed my soul. Once freed it entered Erste, and we flew through the trees to find the source of the noise."

I blinked at her, unable to grasp what she said. "You saw them yourself?"

She glanced uneasily into the trees. "From the branches of a nearby spruce, through his eyes." She nodded at the bird on her shoulder. Wind whistled through the pine needles.

My thoughts raced. If her chant loosed her soul, then I truly had lost the ability to sense the movement of souls. Why not, I thought angrily. I had lost everything else. The ability to hear my mother's voice. The ability to sleep through the night.

I stamped through the snow after her.

We hurried back toward the circle, my mind running through what my mother had said about the *kindefresser*. She could take any form. All the amber-eyed ravens that had come to visit me when

I was a girl. God's teeth. What was it Kunegunde said when I first arrived here? That Erste did what he liked. That bird had led me to her tower. Kunegunde had led me to her tower inside him. "Do you do this often?"

"No," she said, her breath coming in huffs. "You can't go far. You can be killed, just as you can in your own body. It's a risk to inhabit a bird."

When we reached the tower, Kunegunde washed her hands and had me help her upstairs to bed, warning me that she might not wake for a while. That night, I lay in my bed, mulling over what I had learned. My father would've run from what I'd seen that day, or at the very least demanded Kunegunde have an exorcism. I remembered what she said when I first arrived at the tower, that the alrūne would make me susceptible to demons. Was she truly afraid of demons or was she putting on a show to make *me* afraid of them?

My gift had started fading almost as soon as I got here, when I told her I heard a voice, and she started making me take the gooseberry powder. How could I trust that she put any alrūne in my powder at all? What if she put something in it to suppress my gift instead?

I pulled the bird-mother charm from my pouch and ran my hands over her curves, but nothing happened. Nothing had happened in months. I closed my fingers around her in the dark, her stone cool on my palm, and prayed for guidance.

There was no call to breakfast the next morning. I woke to the sound of Erste rapping the shutters. This had happened before when Kunegunde closed the shutters of her window upstairs. I tried to ignore him, burying my head under my pillow. "God's teeth," I said. "Go away."

For a while, the rapping faded. I must've fallen asleep until I woke some time later to the sound of croaking. It sounded like a frog had died and was using dark magic to resurrect himself. I groaned and got up to open the shutters. Erste flew in and soared up the stairs into Kunegunde's room.

The bird gone, I sat on my bed, watching the sunlight pour through the open window. Why had my mother told me to come here, if Kunegunde was the kind of person who would give me something to suppress my gift? What was Kunegunde hiding?

By the time I headed downstairs for breakfast, my chest was tight with frustration and bitterness. As I heated yesterday's rabbit stew, all three ravens descended upon me, flapping around and begging for meat and bones. I tossed them my scraps, disgusted, unable to apprehend why Kunegunde kept such scavengers around.

It took me all morning to complete the chores we usually did together. After Kunegunde's deception, I found myself feeling incredibly resentful about the extra work. By the time I fed the geese cabbage and leftover parsnips—the mother and father honking greedily, the goslings pecking at my hands—I was indignant.

My boots sank in the drifts as I walked back to the tower. I shivered as I opened the door. Then I stomped upstairs to the sloping chamber where Kunegunde slept on the third floor, hell-bent on figuring out what she was hiding.

Beside the bed, Kunegunde's purse bulged with whatever she'd eaten before her soul left her flesh. I tiptoed toward the chair to see what it was. Kunegunde didn't stir. The object in her purse was yellow and wrinkled. So shriveled, it took me a moment to recognize it as the husk of one of my golden apples, which Kunegunde must've set out somewhere to dry in the sun.

I stared at it in disbelief. Kunegunde had sworn the alrūne would make me susceptible to demons. She had told me not to eat it, and then she had eaten it herself? My heart filled with outrage.

She lay still on the bed, asleep, huddled under her blankets. In that moment I hated her, pure and simple. I wanted to hurt her back.

I slipped the alrūne back into her purse so she wouldn't know that I knew. Then I left her room to wash my hands. Afterward, I sat in my bedroom, trying to fathom what this discovery meant. Kunegunde didn't want me to hear what my mother was trying to tell me, enough that she lied about the danger the alrūne represented, and I was pretty certain she was putting something in the powder to suppress my gift. I thought of the way Kunegunde's eyes flashed when she spoke of the world of men. Did she want to keep me here, the way my mother tied a keeping string around my wrist when I was little? Was she afraid my mother would tell me to leave her?

My stomach sank. That had to be it. On my first day here, I'd admitted that my mother told me to visit the next mountain, right before she took the alrūne away.

I spent the rest of that day trying to decide what to do about my newfound knowledge. I wondered what was on the next mountain, if I could go there without Kunegunde knowing. That evening, I picked up the pouch of gooseberry powder that sat on the small table beside my cot. The pouch was small, inconsequential in weight. I remembered a petal-picking song from when I was little. *Will I or won't I*, it went. *Shall I or shan't I?* After a long moment, feeling defiant, I put the powder away, deciding not to mix it with my evening drink.

Kunegunde woke an hour or so later, when she padded downstairs in fur slippers and a heavy robe. Lantern-light leapt along the walls. The fire crackled in its ring. I was sitting at the table, examining a page from her speculum. Before me was a half-drunk cup of wine. As the day drew to a close, my anger had only increased. The effect was tiring. After supper, I had read the labels of the earthenware jugs in the entryway and made some spiced wine to calm myself. By the time she woke, I was on my third cup.

She peered into my drink as she sat down beside me, then poured a cup for herself. "How long was I out?"

"A full day." My voice was clipped.

"Expect it, if I do that again. It takes effort for a soul to settle back into a body. You need rest. Did you feed the ravens?"

I nodded, silent.

"The pigs and geese? The goats?"

"Everything we normally do," I said flatly.

She took a sip. "What's wrong?"

Anger rose in my throat like bile. I wanted to confront her, to call her out on her lies, but I was afraid she would cast me out. I felt trapped. The words tumbled out before I could think better of them. "You know *everything* about me. My parents, my upbringing. My spells, my nightmares. You expect me to trust you, to obey you, to believe everything you say. But I know nothing about you!"

Kunegunde met my eyes. She didn't respond for a long time. For a moment I didn't know if she would. I thought she was going to ignore my grievance completely and drift off to sleep. Then she nodded, once, stretching her hands over the fire, the flames giving her fingers a reddish glow, and met my gaze. "How about I tell you the story of how I came to keep this tower? Would that help?"

I glared at her, my indignance slowly giving way to curiosity. Finally, I nodded.

She smirked, shaking her head at my hesitance. Then she took another sip of her wine and leaned back in her chair, closing her eyes. After a moment, I heard the slow tumble of her voice. "My parents marked me for religious life when I was small. I wasn't their tenth child, but I had spells much like yours, and they thought holy life might keep them in check. When I was ten, they sent me away to live with a devout widow, who immediately set about remedying the holes in my religious education. Also there was a girl who wished to be an anchoress, and another young woman by the name of Hildegard."

After everything else she'd lied about, I was dubious. "You knew Hildegard as a girl."

Kunegunde nodded. She leaned back in her chair, sipping her drink, staring into the flames. "She was like a sister to me. She was often ill, but when she was well, we roamed the countryside, playing in the wild places of the estate. We both felt the world itself was sacred. She was obsessed with what she called its *greenness*, the force that dwells in all living things. She was always so sure about the vows we would take. She said she was destined from birth to be the Lord's servant. I did not share her faith. I found the widow's lessons constricting. The memorization of psalms, the obsession with purity and cleanliness. I preferred to spend my days in the woods, listening to the calls of wild animals and birds. The lessons did nothing to stop my spells, which still struck without rhyme or reason. The widow consulted with healers, giving me remedies. As I grew older, and my body blossomed, I dreamed of escaping the life my parents chose for me, of finding a husband and starting a family. When Hildegard was ill, I spent my days gathering flowers in the forests and fields. I dreamed of running away from the widow's manor. One of my favorite places was a hyssop field with a brook running through it on the edge of the estate. In summer I used to take off my boots and wade in the stream, breathing in the hyssop's bitter mint. It was there that I met a handsome lord from a neighboring estate who would often pass astride his horse on the other side of the stream. When I was alone, he spoke to me. If Hildegard was there, he only waved. He was so handsome, Haelewise. Broad shoulders, laughing eyes, and kind." She met my eyes, her own bright in the firelight, the loose strands of hair around her face glowing silver. For a moment, I could see the young woman she had once been beneath her wrinkled expression—in the wonder that lit her eyes and the wist in her smile. "I loved the way he looked at me, Haelewise, like my body was a holy thing. He worshipped me."

I searched her face, surprised to see her speak of love. The fire crackled between us. She smiled, her eyes faraway, caught up.

"Nearly every day at noon, he would pass on horseback, and Hildegard was often ill. If I was alone and I saw him coming, my spirits would lift. Sitting on opposite sides of the stream, we talked of everything: his father's statecraft, his siblings, how much I missed my family, my doubts about holy life. Something held us there and caught us, making us linger with each other by the stream. Over time, he became all I thought about. I believe that was true for him as well. There is a force, Haelewise, that draws lovers together. I could feel it every time we sat across from each other. A heaviness behind my eyes, a pulling toward him. It felt *right*."

I swallowed a sip of my wine, drawn into the story despite my anger with her.

"The day before we were to leave the estate and take our vows, the widow sent for the healer to examine Hildegard. Hildegard was getting over one of her illnesses, and the widow wanted to confirm she was well enough to travel. While we waited for the physician, I went out to the hyssop field, hoping to meet the lord and say goodbye. I fell asleep while I was waiting for him, as I often did. In that field, sunlight warming my eyelids, I dreamed that we were together." She met my eyes, her own feverishly bright, glistening that uncanny amber. "There was something about this dream, Haelewise. It sprang from deep inside me. Even now, I can't explain it. When I woke, I knew it was holy, a vision that would come to pass. Not long after I woke, he rode up. It was hot. Midsummer. I asked him if he wanted to walk barefoot through the stream to cool ourselves, to search the creekbed for pretty stones. I tied the skirt of my dress up, fully aware that the sight of my bare legs would distract him. I pulled up my hair, showing off the nape of my neck. He took off his boots, rolled up his pants, and took my hand." She paused, her eyes reflecting the firelight. "The widow would've whipped me if she saw me like that. Clothes and hair in disarray, skirt tied up, holding a lord's hand. It was exactly the sort of thing she was supposed to protect me from, but everyone was

always so worried about Hildegard, no one paid me any attention."
She laughed bitterly.

When she took another draught of wine, I had a sip of my own,
my doubts all but forgotten. By then, I was caught up in the suspense of her story, waiting for something to happen between her
and the lord, hanging on to her every word.

"I told him that this was the last time I would see him," she
said, "and he looked at me with such sorrow. I sat on a boulder
that jutted from the water and gestured for him to sit beside me.
When he did, my thoughts became fixed on the place where our
thighs touched. His nearness was like an incantation. It pulled me
to him. When I looked into his eyes, I understood what my body
knew already. I was *supposed* to kiss him. When I did, he went stiff,
surprised, but after a moment he kissed me back. I cannot explain
what happened next except to say that we kissed for an eternity.
And then—"

She stopped there to stare into the fire. Flames leapt in her eyes.
She went silent. I filled her cup, noticing the way the muscles in
her face had relaxed, as if she had kept this secret far too long. She
drank before she spoke again, and I could tell that she wanted to
linger over that moment. "It was beautiful, Haelewise. The most
sacred hour of my life. I don't regret one second of it. I can still see
the field in my mind's eye. Lilac flowers everywhere, humming
with hawk-moths, orange-winged. I pushed him onto that bed of
flowers. I remember the scent of the blooms beneath us, the color
of the sky above. The sky was blue, that day, perfectly clear. When
it was over, we lay together in those flowers for I don't know how
long, breathless. Then we said our goodbyes.

"When he was gone, I pulled the flowers out of my hair. I
cleaned my dress in the brook. I said nothing when I returned to
the manor. I held those moments close. The next day, we began
the journey to the abbey. By the time we arrived and prepared to
take our vows, my menses hadn't come." Kunegunde shook her

head, falling silent. When she spoke again, her voice trembled. "I was so happy when I realized I was with child. It was the perfect reason not to take the veil. The first thing I did was tell Hildegard. I thought—naïvely, of course—that she might be happy for me. But her loyalty to the laws of the Church far outweighed our friendship. She shamed me for my condition. She asked me why I had defiled my body. Mortified, the next morning before dawn, I took my horse from the stables and rode south. I went to see my parents, to confess what had happened, so they could go to the lord's family and offer him the dowry they had set aside for the convent. But when I told them, they shamed me just as Hildegard had, saying the lord wouldn't want to marry me since I had defiled myself."

She met my eyes. "I hated them for that. I still do. Condemning me for the one thing I knew I had done right. I fled, riding south without a destination. I slept outside, in barns, as I wandered the countryside. Female cooks sometimes took pity on me and let me wash dishes in exchange for a room. At one such inn, the cook told me about a Mother Gothel who was a friend to women in my condition. Hoping she would take me in, I set out to find her tower." Kunegunde met my eyes. "It was here that I gave birth."

I blinked, surprised to find that her story had reached its end. The night encircled us, the tower dark. The flames leapt in the hearth. I blinked, finding myself overwhelmed by her story. But as I turned the story over in my mind, all my doubts and suspicions about Kunegunde came rushing back. I thought of the dreams I had been having, the way Kunegunde insisted they were sent by a demon. If Kunegunde could have a holy dream, then so could I. Unable to restrain my bitterness, I frowned. "How did you know the dream was holy? That it wasn't demon-sent?"

Panic flitted across her face. For an instant, her eyes went wide and fearful, like the eyes of an animal caught in a trap. Then she mastered her feelings; her expression went as still as the ice in the birdbath. "I hadn't eaten any alrūne, little one. Remember what I showed you in that book? Alrūne is a spiritual poison. It causes *false* visions."

I only nodded, my anger simmering. There was no doubt now. She was lying to me.

CHAPTER SEVENTEEN

That night, I had the dream again. I woke the next morning unable to shake the vision from my head. When the dream world finally dissipated, I found myself more frustrated than ever that I couldn't hear my mother's voice. She was trying to tell me something, I was convinced, and Kunegunde didn't want me to hear her. I sat up in bed, sunlight pouring through the stripe between the shutters, blanket soft on my legs. The bright light made me squint.

God's teeth, I thought, searching for my mother's shattered hand-mirror. There was a shard large enough at its center for me to see my eyes. When I looked into it, my suspicions were confirmed. The golden color that the alrūne had given my irises had been replaced by a deep red. The gooseberry powder, I realized. And now, the black of my pupils looked like it was starting to swallow the red up. If I continued not taking the powder, my eyes would be completely black soon. How could I hide that from Kunegunde? I would have to avoid her gaze as much as possible and hope she didn't notice.

I remembered what my mother said in the garden: that I would find my purpose. Whatever that meant, it had something to do with her goddess, these dreams I was having, her faith. I resolved to find where Kunegunde hid the alrūne so I could hear my mother's voice again. Eating the alrūne would also make the difference in my eyes less noticeable.

The downstairs room was gloomy enough that I could spend that day shadowing Kunegunde, helping her experiment with a remedy from an ancient tome that she hadn't tried before. I tried to avoid meeting her gaze directly as much as I could. Fire leapt in the hearth, and her ravens roosted on the upper shelves, startling me each time they croaked. I pretended to be interested in wortcunnery, watching carefully whenever Kunegunde opened a drawer in the apothecary cabinet or one of the earthenware jugs near the door. Wherever she had stashed the alrūne, it wasn't in the drawers or jugs she used that day.

By evening, I was exhausted from all the deception and frustrated that I hadn't figured out where she kept it. I did not put the powder in my evening drink. When the ravens started swooping at the shutters to get outside, like they often did when there was someone in the forest, I let them out and volunteered to follow them to see what was there.

"Don't leave the circle," Kunegunde reminded me.

Outside, the sun was sinking over the horizon. The last tendrils of daylight were turning pink. The ravens soared away from the tower, sounding their awful deep-throated cry again and again. I followed them into the forest. The wind bit my face. I fingered the bird-woman in my pouch as I walked into the trees, praying that whatever ill omen their calls predicted would not apply to me.

As I neared the brook, I paused, realizing that I could feel a faint tension, a possibility in the air again. Relief coursed through me. It was as I thought. My gift hadn't vanished. Kunegunde's gooseberry powder had stolen it from me.

As I neared the edge of the stone circle, I slowed, trying to decide whether to break Kunegunde's rule. Then something came over me. At first I didn't recognize the source of the shiver. I thought I was just cold. Then I felt the tension in the air, the pull. My soul lifting from my skin.

I woke on my back in the snow, a dull ache in my head. A fainting spell? Now that I had stopped taking the powder, things were back to the way they had been before. I could sense the next world, but without the alrūne, I couldn't hear the voice. I had to find out where Kunegunde had hidden it so my mother could speak to me again. Was she trying to tell me something now? Did she want me to go see what was out there, like she wanted me to visit the next mountain?

Ice snapped beneath my boots as I rushed to the edge of the circle, my frustration spurring me on. It was a relief to be out from under Kunegunde's watchful eye, though this part of the forest was unnaturally dark. When I passed through the stone circle, my whole body tingled. A wild laugh bubbled from my throat. It was wonderful to feel like myself again, to have these sensations. I hurried into the forest after the birds, boots crunching the snow. Again I felt the trace of a shiver prickling the back of my neck, but when I turned to look over my shoulder, I could see only shadows.

"Who's there?" a feminine voice asked behind me.

I whirled around, surprised, despite the fact that I had suspected someone was out here. A girl about my age, maybe a little younger, stood a few paces away, leading a white horse with a large basket around its neck. She had wild dark curls that refused, like mine, to be tamed by her braids; she was dressed in a faded woman's shift and skirt and wimple under dirty furs. Her face was eerily similar to mine. Her pale skin was covered in dust, but she held her head high, as if she had noble blood. In the twilight, her eyes glinted a pretty hazel with bright golden flecks. There was only one other person I'd seen with eyes that color: back home, years ago, beside her mother on a white horse. Princess Frederika. But the princess was years younger than I was, and this girl seemed about my age. Then I remembered how old, how *brave*, the princess had seemed all those years ago on her mother's white horse, and I knew. It was her. "*Your highness.*"

The princess looked over her shoulder uneasily, lowering her voice. "Surely you mistake me for someone else. Who are you?"

"Haelewise, daughter-of-Hedda-the-Midwife."

She looked skeptical. "You sure are finely dressed for a peasant."

"You sure are humbly dressed for a princess."

She frowned.

I could tell she didn't want to give up the pretense, but I was so certain. "I saw you with your mother at a parade. On this horse!"

She laughed, despite herself, searching my face. "By the breath of the gods. You resemble me so much, it's like staring into a mirror."

I gazed at her. She was right. We were about the same height—I was short, and she was a little tall for her age. The resemblance would've been even more pronounced if I were still eating the alrūne, which would've made my eyes gold. "We could be sisters."

"You wouldn't happen to want to marry Prince Ulrich for me, would you?"

My eyes widened. I shook my head, holding up my hands.

She laughed again—loud and wild—and I realized she was kidding. I had spent so long in Kunegunde's tower, I didn't know how *not* to be suspicious. The princess's horse was near enough now for me to see her big brown eyes. I approached the horse in an attempt to change the subject. "Your horse is beautiful."

"Her name is Nëbel."

The horse sniffed my hand and opened my fist with her muzzle, as if to see whether it held a treat. Her nose was cold against my palm. Her huge pupils glistened, inky black, in the dark. When she discovered that my hand was empty, she let out a nicker of protest. "She's friendly."

"She's known nothing but kindness since she was a foal. I saw to that. She's the finest horse in the kingdom, aside from her fearfulness."

I looked at the horse's broad white chest, her rippling muscles. It was hard to imagine her afraid of anything. The creature snorted, meeting my eyes. I turned to Frederika. "What are you doing in this part of the forest?"

She drew back, her expression instantly mistrustful. "Who sent you to spy on me?"

"No one. I—"

"My father? Ulrich?"

I held up my hands. "I'm an apprentice to a local wise woman. I swear it. Our animals were acting strangely, so I came to see who was out here."

"Do you mean Mother Gothel?"

I nodded.

"I've been searching for her tower for ages." She lowered her voice, looking over her shoulder again into the trees. "It's been two moons since I bled. May I follow you back?"

I hesitated. Frederika was a noble, the daughter of the king who had issued a writ for Kunegunde's death. She was the betrothed of a man my grandmother hated more than anyone else. But the tower was supposed to be a haven for women in Frederika's condition. Kunegunde was such a recluse. What were the chances that she would be able to recognize Frederika in these clothes? And why in the world, with all the secrets Kunegunde was keeping from me, should I worry about being honest with her? The idea of lying to my grandmother filled me with pleasure.

Explaining that we would have to hide her identity, I led Frederika back toward the tower. We could use our likeness to our advantage and introduce her as my cousin. We would call her Ree.

At the edge of the stone circle, Nëbel whinnied, pulling on her reins, eyes wild. "The stone circle," Frederika said. "I'd heard of it, but—" She whispered in the horse's ear, then pulled her inside the circle. "By the devil," she swore. "This place is so thin, it's making her nervous."

Can she feel the thinness herself, I wondered, or is she only commenting on the horse's behavior?

Nëbel pranced anxiously, whinnying and blowing air through her nose. By the time we reached the tower, the horse was calmer. The spell, I thought, the one that zapped between the stones. That was what was making her nervous. I helped Frederika tie the horse outside, then led her into my grandmother's home with her basket.

Kunegunde was so absorbed in her writing, she didn't notice that anyone had come in with me. Only Erste looked in my direction when I opened the door, dark eyes glittering from his perch.

"What was out there? A wolf? A fox?" Kunegunde said without looking up.

Frederika stepped forward, clearing her throat. "Mother Gothel?"

Kunegunde looked up. "Do you know this girl?"

I avoided her eyes, grateful the tower was so dim at night. "This is Ree, my cousin on my father's side. She was wandering the forest, looking for the tower."

Kunegunde looked from Frederika to me and back. "Cousins. You look like sisters. You say she's your father's kin?"

I nodded, perhaps a bit too eagerly.

She shook her head. "Well, girl? Out with it. What do you want?"

"It's been two moons since I bled," Frederika said quietly.

"Ah. What did you bring as payment?"

Frederika peeled back the linen that was covering the basket. Inside were several blocks of goat cheese, a large sack of flour, a walnut bread wrapped in cheesecloth, some quinces, and several pounds of dried blaeberries. "Is it a difficult spell?"

"Everything that is done can be undone," Kunegunde said, her voice matter-of-fact.

She nodded at the basket Frederika offered—it was enough—and gestured for her to set it on the table. Then she retrieved the manuscript she was always working on from its place on the shelf and turned to a page that had yet to be illuminated. She lingered over it for a moment, reading, then excused herself to go downstairs to the cellar.

While she was gone, I inspected the indecipherable symbols on the page, awed, realizing the manuscript Kunegunde had been working on all this time was a spellbook. Frederika settled into the chair by the fire ring, her expression melancholy.

In a moment Kunegunde came back upstairs with a lockbox. She fished out a key from a drawer in the apothecary cabinet, which she used to unlock it.

Inside were about three dozen alrūne fruit, the ones I'd brought to Gothel and more, dried like the one I had found in her pouch so they wouldn't rot. Also within were several misshapen bulbs that looked like the plant's root in the drawing she had shown me.

My heart stopped. There they were. Finally, I knew where she was keeping them. I had to work to keep my breath regular.

Kunegunde took out one of the roots with a rag, closed the box, and locked it. I watched her closely as she put everything back, memorizing the locations—the key in the drawer, the lockbox in the cellar—though I was anxious about the prospect of stealing the fruit back. I would have to be careful how much I took.

Kunegunde caught me watching and raised an eyebrow. "Make yourself useful. We need pennyroyal, lavender, thyme. A cup of snow and some rope."

From her chair, Frederika watched me move around the tower, collecting the items Kunegunde named. When I'd collected all of them, Kunegunde suspended the cup in the ropes above the fire ring. She stoked the flames so the snow would melt. After a while, she called Frederika over. She had her knot the rope around the alrūne root, then drop it into the cup, whispering strange words. "This chant binds the root to the child in your belly," she explained. "You're certain you want this?"

Frederika stared into the cup, measuring her words. "I want the child, but I can't foresee a life where I will be able to care for it."

"Isn't that always the way?"

Frederika looked grim, her expression uncertain.

"The potion has to steep overnight. What if we start the spell now, and you can decide tomorrow whether to finish it? It will cost you either way, mind you. The ingredients—"

Frederika thought for a moment, then nodded.

"Sprinkle in the herbs."

She did as told.

Kunegunde turned to me. "Do you want her to sleep in your room?"

I nodded. The prospect of putting off the spell set Frederika at ease. We talked with Kunegunde awhile, spinning stories about my father's family. We play-acted brilliantly, making up anecdotes about all the times we had played together as youths. Our appearances weren't our only likeness; our minds worked similarly. We had never met before this day, and yet somehow we were able to improvise these stories seamlessly, finishing each other's sentences. It was exhilarating.

As soon as we went upstairs, we shut my bedroom door and stared at each other in awe. It almost felt, by then, that the stories we'd made up were true. I pulled the shattered hand-mirror from the trunk so we could indulge in a moonlight comparison of our faces. She touched the symbols with her fingers, looking at me wordlessly, before she turned her focus to our reflections. It was difficult to see with all the cracks in the glass, but we had the same round face and curly black hair, the same high cheekbones. Our noses were a bit different, as were our eyes—mine were almost fully black now, and hers were that gold-flecked hazel—but apart from that, the resemblance was undeniable. We giggled and called each other cousin for long after we heard Kunegunde go to her room. Eventually, when we settled down in bed, I asked Frederika why she ran away from the castle, and she told me the story. As I suspected, it had all begun when her father promised her to Ulrich.

"Why would he promise you to such a man?"

She shook her head. "He doesn't believe the stories. Hardly anyone noble does. Father says they're wives' tales, peasant talk. Ulrich can be so charming at court. He strutted like a peacock into our castle and convinced my father—*my father*, the king and Holy Roman Emperor—to give him my hand. Ulrich boasted about the safety of his castle, swearing he would protect me with his life.

My stepmother tried to tell my father what he's really like, but my father didn't believe her. He swore it was a good match, since my mother"—Frederika blinked, her voice catching—"since the annulment made me a bastard. He *thanked* Ulrich and promised him Scafhusun for his fealty." She shivered again. "I wish I could stay with Daniel."

"Daniel is the father of your child?"

She nodded, telling me about the boy with whom she had fallen in love, a young Jewish man who lived in a nearby settlement. They had been handfasted in secret months ago.

I was so shocked at her description of Daniel that I had trouble paying attention to what she said next. Nobles sometimes married merchants, as Phoebe had married Matthäus, but a high princess carrying the child of a Jewish peasant was beyond belief. When I was little, the synagogue in the next town had burned down in the middle of the night. Father said God set the fire, but Mother said it was set by wicked men who wanted to drive the Jews out of the city.

"He would make such a good father," Frederika was saying.

"How did you end up in his settlement?"

Her voice was tired. "When the nights grew too cold, I couldn't sleep in the forest anymore. I had to find a place to stay. A place that didn't have any connections to my father. I was following the trade route west, when I met a trader on his way to the Jewish settlement. It seemed perfect. Small. No priests, no princes, and the kingsguard wouldn't think to look for me there."

I looked at Frederika anew, realizing for the first time how clever she was. She would have to be to escape her father. People said he was the same way.

"I didn't mean to fall in love with Daniel." She sighed. "It just happened."

Empathizing, I told her about the woman Matthäus had married, how he wished he could marry me instead, how I'd refused to be his mistress. "I couldn't do it," I said, surprised at the bitterness, the anger in my voice. I sounded like Kunegunde when she spoke of the Church. "I couldn't bear the shame."

She was watching me closely. "You cared for him a great deal."

I went silent for a long time, staring into the dark, all the feelings I had tried to suppress threatening to bubble out. "I did," I admitted, finally, my voice carefully controlled. "But it wasn't enough. I need to be respectable to work as a midwife. I want children, a real family of my own."

Frederika fell silent. I thought on what I'd said, realizing it might be unkind to speak of my longing to be a mother when she was trying to decide whether to end her pregnancy. When I apologized, she went sullen, despairing at the plans her father had made for her. Eventually, she changed the subject to the spell Kunegunde would cast in the morning, which seemed to fascinate her in theory if not in effect. When she confessed that her stepmother had taught her a few incantations, I remembered the rumor about the queen whispering into a hand-mirror, and my breath caught. "You've been learning the old ways?"

Frederika nodded slowly, startled by my eagerness.

I tried to rein it in. "Does your father know?"

"Absolutely not. It was all in secret."

Her boldness inspired me. She had learned the old ways in secret, run from her arranged marriage, hidden from her father in these woods, and here I was afraid to sneak into an old woman's lockbox. "I've got to do something," I said, getting up. "I'll be right back."

"All right." Frederika wrapped herself in the blanket.

Down the stairs I crept, listening for movement above, enjoying the fact that I was defying Kunegunde. The ground floor of the tower was silent apart from my footsteps. Embers glowed in the fire ring below the draught that was steeping in the cup. I went to the apothecary cabinet and opened the drawer where Kunegunde had put the key. Lighting a small candle, I tiptoed downstairs into the cellar. The candlelight flickered and hissed as I passed through the archway into the dark. I surveyed the room. Where would she put the lockbox? I checked behind the barrels in the buttery but found nothing. I checked the crates in the corner with no success. As I was searching the shelves, I stumbled slightly on an uneven stone. Kneeling down to remove it, I found the lockbox buried beneath the floor. I could hear the dried fruit rolling around noisily inside it and swore an oath of joy.

Unlocking it, I took out three dried fruit—hopefully not enough for her to notice—closed the box, and locked it, holding my breath as I put everything back. It was only after I had returned the lockbox to its hiding place in the cellar and the key to its drawer upstairs that I could breathe again. I broke off a piece of the dried alrūne, ate it, and wrapped the rest in a cloth, feeling defiant. Blowing out the candle, I was conscious of the need to wash my hands. I did so as silently as I could, then tiptoed back upstairs, feeling more than a little self-righteous about my theft of what had been mine in the first place.

When I slipped back into the room, Frederika was lying on her side, as if she had fallen asleep. I hid the alrūne in the bottom of my sack and lay down, trying to remember where we were in our conversation. While I was thinking, she turned over to look at me.

"I'm glad you're here," she said. "It's good to have someone to talk to."

I smiled. "You don't have to decide right away whether to cast the spell. I bet Kunegunde would let you stay here longer."

"The kingsguard are closing in. If they find me like this—"

"No man can see inside the circle. You're safe here."

"Ulrich can," she sighed. "If he's with them—"

Moonlight striped the cracks of the shutters with pale light. Her eyes brimmed with tears.

CHAPTER EIGHTEEN

W hen I woke the next morning, Frederika said she had been up all night thinking. Daniel's parents had demanded that she come here, but she didn't think she could go through with the spell without talking to him. If Kunegunde agreed to let her stay another night, she wanted to know if I would be willing to go with her to talk to him. She was afraid she wouldn't be able to find her way back to the tower without my help. When I told her how Kunegunde had forbidden me to leave the circle, Frederika said we could sneak out. It was only an hour or so away on horseback, she said. We could go there and back in one night if the weather was good.

"All right," I said, eager to win her trust. "I will."

She smiled and told me to call her Rika, before we went down-stairs. On my way out of the bedroom, I got out my mother's hand-mirror and checked my eyes. My pupils had stopped enlarging, and the thin circle of red around them was becoming coppery. Close enough to how they looked when I was taking the powder that Kunegunde was unlikely to notice. Thank the gods, I thought. The day before had been exhausting.

For breakfast, Kunegunde was making some sort of pastry with the quinces and cheese Rika had brought. All three ravens were roosting on the ceiling beam above her, greedily watching her cook. They weren't making a sound, but the sight of them filled me with unease. Had they been up there the night before, I won-dered, when I sneaked downstairs? Had Kunegunde been watch-ing through Erste's eyes when I stole back the alrūne?

Following me into the room, Rika inhaled the scent of the sizzling dough, then gagged and put her hand over her mouth. "Sorry," she managed to say, as she scanned the room for an exit. Morning sickness. I led her into the garden, where she expelled the contents of her stomach in a snowdrift.

In a moment, her queasiness passed. "That's been happening more often lately."

"It's most common in early pregnancy. If you decide to keep the child, it'll likely run its course in a couple months."

She laughed ruefully. "I can't wait."

My eye fell on the birdbath a few feet away. I checked over my shoulder to make sure Kunegunde or her birds hadn't followed us out. Then I brushed away the snow that had collected on the bird-bath until the symbols were visible. Gesturing for Rika to come closer, I lowered my voice. "Have you seen anything like this before? These are the same symbols from the hand-mirrors and her spellbook."

She moved closer to inspect the basin. I watched her face for signs of recognition. A moment passed before she looked up at me. Her gaze was steady. "That's a water-*spiegel*."

"Did your stepmother teach you to read those symbols? Where did the old language come from? Who speaks it?"

She pressed her lips tight. "I cannot say."

"Why not?" I said, meeting her eyes, my stomach filling with dread. Was she going to refuse to tell me about the old ways too? The words tumbled out. "Rika, that hand-mirror we used last night was my mother's. She died last winter. I know the symbols are the old language, but Kunegunde says I'm not ready to learn about it. She's hiding something—"

"I'm sorry about your mother," she said, cutting me off, her face a mask. Her reserve was infuriating. "But I can't help you. I feel better now. Let's go in. I'm getting cold."

She headed back for the tower before I could stop her.

I blinked, watching her go, feeling slighted. Why wouldn't she tell me what she knew? She was so sure of herself. It was easy to forget she was the younger of us two. I re-covered the birdbath with snow, wondering how I could get her to trust me. By the time I'd finished and gone inside, Rika was explaining her reticence to Kunegunde. My grandmother was listening, pressing quinces and cheese into dough.

"I understand," she said when Rika went quiet, turning to meet my friend's eyes. "It's a difficult decision."

"Too difficult to make lightly," I said. "Could she stay with us while she decides?"

Kunegunde glanced from me to Rika, her brows furrowed. "There's no reason you have to make a decision today. We can finish the spell tomorrow or in a week. I suppose you can stay here until then."

Frederika looked relieved. "That is gracious of you."

Kunegunde turned back to her cooking, her voice suspiciously gentle. "I was once in a situation much like yours. This place was my haven. I feel obligated to return the favor."

That afternoon, in our room, Rika told me a funny story about the night after she and Daniel were handfasted in secret. They had sneaked away from the settlement, and his mother caught them half-clothed in a cave. Daniel's pants were around his ankles, and I was giggling uncontrollably, when Kunegunde called for us to come down, furious. When we went downstairs, she was sitting stiff at the table before her spellbook. Her voice tight, she told us to go to the clearing near the pool to pull up some rapunzel root for a pottage stew, but I was pretty sure she only wanted us to go because she couldn't focus on her writing due to the volume of our laughter.

Rika acted chastened, probably afraid Kunegunde would cast her out, but I was eager to leave the tower with her.

Rika retrieved Nëbel from the stable so the horse could get some exercise. As soon as we were out of earshot of the tower, she went back to telling her story. I made myself listen carefully as we followed the stream, keeping an eye out for the wilted rapunzel shoots that would mean the root was beneath the surface. The stream was half frozen, a thin scrim of ice around its banks. But the farther we got from the tower, the more difficulty I had focusing on her story. When she finally finished, I scanned the trees to make sure the birds hadn't followed us out. "Please. Rika. Tell me what you know of the old ways."

She froze for a moment, then shook her head. "I would like to, but I cannot. I'm sorry, Haelewise."

Her refusal made me angry. "I won't tell anyone."

"That doesn't matter. I swore an oath of secrecy."

I tried to think of a way to get her to trust me, racking my brain again for some way to prove myself. The bird-mother charm. It had been so important to Kunegunde. Perhaps it would prove to Frederika that I could be trusted. I pulled the figurine from my pouch. "My mother gave me this."

Rika's eyes widened. "Your mother. Who was she again?"

"Hedda-the-Midwife."

Rika shook her head; she didn't recognize the name. "May I hold it?"

When I nodded, she took it from my hand, turning it over in hers. "Haelewise, these are *rare*. The Church destroyed most of them. Have you shown this to anyone?"

I shook my head.

"Don't. They would burn you at the stake." She handed it back. "The only other person I know who has one is Ursilda."

I gazed down at the figurine, her breasts, her wings, her talons. "It's an effigy of the Mother, isn't it?"

Rika met my eyes, again, measuring my expression. After a moment, she nodded.

"My mother made offerings to her in secret," I said. "Please. I want to understand her faith."

Rika sat down on a boulder beside the stream, setting her empty basket on the ice. "How do you not know of the faith when you have a figurine? Do you know what *she* is for?"

I sat down next to her. "My mother called her a bird-mother charm. Once, when I rubbed it, I conjured her ghost."

Her eyes widened. "You have the gift."

"What?"

"The figurine calls the next world close. For those who have the gift, that means the ability to see the dead."

"She spoke to me too."

She looked at me more closely. "You're eating the alrūne."

I nodded. "I need to learn how to use the figurine to conjure my mother. I miss her so badly."

She watched me steadily. "I wish I could help you. All the figurine does for Ursilda is increase the potency of her prayers."

"And what of the alrūne?"

"It allows my stepmother to cast spells, to use the water-*spiegel*."

"For scrying?"

Rika thought for a moment, considering. Finally, she nodded. "A circle of women use them to watch the world."

My breath caught. "Do you think my mother was a member of this circle?"

"If she had one of those—" Rika nodded at the figurine. "She was."

My heart stopped. Ice cracked under my feet. Everything went still. For a moment, the wood was so silent that I thought I could hear the heavens circling the earth. My mother had not practiced her faith alone. There was a circle of women out there who were like her. She must've been a member before she married my father. She had a whole life—a life of meaning and magic—that my father had made her give up.

"*Rika*," I said, my voice wavering with emotion. I tried to control it, but I was angry at my father, at Rika for refusing to answer me. "Tell me what you know about the circle."

"I can't."

"I need to know who my mother was."

"I've never even heard her name."

I stood up, unable to contain the anger that was coursing through me. For a moment, the only sound was that of my footsteps as I paced, back and forth, alongside the stream. Then I whirled on Rika, and the ice split beneath me with a loud *crack*. "Was Kunegunde part of the circle?"

She met my gaze, nodding slowly. "But she left after the king issued a writ for her death."

I thought about this. "You and Ursilda, your stepmother, the three of you, you're part of this circle? And my mother and Kunegunde were too?"

Rika took a deep breath. She stood up. "I'm sorry, Haelewise. I've already said too much. I'm not supposed to say *any* of this to someone who hasn't been initiated. And you have not."

"I've never had the chance. My mother died before she could tell me of her faith. Please."

"Haelewise, I can't say. Stop asking me to break my oath."

Her refusal to answer me was so maddening, I didn't speak to her for the rest of our walk.

I stayed angry at Rika for the rest of that afternoon, outrage cold in my breast. I couldn't stand the fact that she knew something about my mother and wouldn't tell me. I was jeopardizing my livelihood, my home, by lying to Kunegunde about who she was. She owed me as much. As we ate supper that evening, I resolved not to help her anymore until she told me about the circle. It would be foolish to risk angering Kunegunde by sneaking out. I had no place else to go.

That second night, it was late before we heard Kunegunde shuffling to her room. As soon as we heard the door shut, Rika moved as if to get out of bed. "Not yet," I whispered. "She'll catch you leaving."

"Me? Aren't you coming?"

I shook my head. "I've thought better of it."

Rika looked stricken. Her breath hitched. When she spoke, she sounded desperate. "Haelewise. I can't go without you. I won't be able to find my way back."

"I'm sorry," I whispered. "Kunegunde will be furious if she finds out I've left the stone circle. I'm risking enough already."

She looked pained. "Haelewise," she said, her voice breaking. "You don't understand. I would tell you if I could. But I swore a blood-vow. I can only speak of the circle to others who have taken the oath."

Remembering the look on Kunegunde's face when I tried to call her *grandmother*, I felt my resolve begin to falter.

"Haelewise," Rika said, her voice trembling. "Come with me. I'm going to see him, no matter what."

Uncertainty pulled at me. If I didn't go with her, she might not be able to find her way back. She might be forced to have the baby, and who knew what her father would do to her or Daniel if he found out? Guilt nagged at my conscience.

"I need your help," she begged. "Haelewise, please."

I led her downstairs in a resentful silence and slipped on my cloak. Outside, the clearing around the tower was still and quiet, the snow glowing an eerie white. The night was bitter cold, and the rising moon seemed too bright for a waning half. The night seemed to energize Rika, but I hated the romance of the moonlight and gleaming snow. It occurred to me to wonder why the natural world never reflected *my* emotions. I always seemed to be at odds with it.

As she showed me how to mount a horse, I was silent. I climbed atop Nëbel behind her, listening to the hard crunch of her hooves on the snow. Outside the stone circle, we rode in silence. When she finally spoke, she tried to chatter about a neutral subject, asking questions about the herbs Kunegunde used for spellcraft. I answered only with noncommittal grunts.

Eventually we approached a mountain with a well-worn trade

route leading up and around the side of it. When Rika turned Nëbel up the path, my heart stopped, and my breath caught in my throat. This was why my mother told me to visit the next mountain. She wanted me to meet Rika. To learn about the circle.

As we rode up the path, I asked my mother to forgive me for not heeding her advice before.

Nestled partway up the side of the mountain was the settlement: a ramshackle hall and stable, set far enough back from the cliff, you couldn't see them from below. On either side of the hall I could see a drab building I suspected was a makeshift synagogue. Scattered among the trees were dim huts of varying sizes, each of their roofs covered in snow.

We tied Nëbel to a tree just outside the cluster of buildings. There was a scarlet firethorn bush with about half its leaves left near the hall, which Rika asked me gingerly if I would wait behind. I squatted behind that bush, feeling foolish for what felt like hours, though it must have been a half hour at most. While I waited, I thought about all the times people had kept things from me, snapping leaf after leaf from the bush, tearing them into shreds.

When I had torn all the remaining leaves from the part of the bush where I crouched, I reached for the figurine in my coin-purse, praying for my mother to speak to me again. I knew it was probably too soon since I stopped the powder and started the alrūne, but I needed her guidance. I had lost my way.

For a long moment, nothing happened. Then I thought I felt the figurine warming subtly beneath my fingers. I thought I felt the air growing taut, the mist gathering faintly around me. A subtle fog—barely perceptible, dewy. I couldn't tell if I was imagining it.

I closed my eyes, chasing after the sensation. A faint gust of wind tousled my hair, and I imagined it was my mother's hand. After a moment I thought I could feel her presence, smell the faint scent of anise in the air. My eyes brimmed with tears. My anger melted, and everything shifted around me: The stars above shivered with beauty; hoarfrost glittered on the firethorn; the night air rippled with cold. Everything I was upset about melted away.

It was just enough hope to renew my faith. Staring down at the nest of broken leaves I had made, I could feel my determination returning. There had to be a way to convince Rika to tell me what I needed to know.

By the time Rika came back, breathless, I knew what I was going to say. Her hair was mussed, and there were leaves in her hair, her eyes feverish with the desire to talk to me. "Daniel said it's my decision whether I want to have the baby, that a living woman's needs must take precedence over the unborn. He says a child's soul doesn't enter its body until it takes its first breath. He called it the breath of life. Is that how it works? You must know."

I nodded slowly. "That's how it works, yes. A child's soul enters its throat when it takes its first breath. I've seen it."

She nodded, determined. Then she took my hands, looking me in my eyes. "Thank you for coming, Haelewise. You've been so good to me. I don't know what I'd do without you."

Her gratitude brought tears to my eyes. I felt bad for denying her before. "Of course."

"I still don't know what I'm going to do."

"Rika," I said, my voice full of urgency. "Could *I* take that vow? The one you took. The oath."

Her eyes widened. Her whole countenance changed.

My voice shook. "I want to join the circle."

Rika's expression turned solemn. "All right," she said. "I will find a way to make that happen."

I could hardly believe what I had heard. "You will?"

"I swear it. When I leave, you're coming with me. Once you take the vow, I'll tell you everything," she said, speaking the words with such conviction that I believed her.

CHAPTER NINETEEN

A week passed, and I was still waiting for Rika to make her decision. I was getting antsy. On the one hand, I wanted to take
the oath as soon as possible, but on the other, I didn't want to rush
her. I had given up waiting for her each night as she sneaked out
of the tower to see Daniel. Now that I'd led her back once, she
said she could find her own way home to the tower. The clearing
where they met was halfway between the two mountains, so she
didn't have to travel far, but she was always gone hours.

Sometimes, I fell asleep as soon as she left, dreaming my inscrutable dreams. I woke in the middle of the night, my skin itch-
ing with feathers, my mother's voice humming in my ears. Her
message continued to elude me, though the words were becoming
louder and clearer. Other times, while Rika was gone, I couldn't
sleep, and I spent hours brooding over my own feelings. Rika was
right when she said I cared for Matthäus a great deal. Beneath my
bitterness at his marriage was an undeniable wellspring of love. If I
lived outside the Christian world in the forest, perhaps I would be
less ashamed for acting on it. If wherever we went when we left the
tower was close enough, perhaps I would go to him.

Every night, I ate the alrūne. Every morning, I checked my eyes
in the shattered mirror. I was trying to limit the amount I ate so
I could reap the benefits of the fruit without my eyes growing so
bright that Kunegunde would notice. I took care not to get too
close to her or look her straight in the eyes.

Rika and I spent most of our days gathering herbs and plants
for Kunegunde inside the circle. As I went about my chores, I

imagined a time after Rika and I left the tower when I was part of the circle. I would eat the alrūne every night, use the figurine to conjure my mother, and watch the world in a water-*spiegel*.

One night, when Rika had been at Gothel almost two weeks, my head was so full of these thoughts that I was unable to sleep. When Rika came back, I was still awake. "Where will we go when we leave the tower?" I asked her, sitting up in bed.

"I've been trying to figure that out," she said. Her cheeks were flushed from the cold and she was out of breath.

"Have you decided if you're going to have the baby?"

She nodded, taking a deep breath. Her voice shook with feeling. "I love Daniel so much. I want a family with him."

"I could help you with the birth. We just need somewhere to go, somewhere your father and Ulrich can't find us."

Her eyes brightened, and she looked hopeful for the first time in days. "It would have to be a thin place like this so we could cast a spell strong enough to keep my father and Ulrich out."

"Could you cast such a spell?"

"No. But you could once you join the circle. Or you could learn—"

"Do you know of another thin place?"

"No," she said excitedly. "But I know someone who might. Let me think about this."

She must have stayed up for the rest of the night, planning our next step. Before I fell asleep, I watched her for a long time, arms folded, deep in thought. I wondered if she inherited her personality from her father or if it was the product of growing up in a castle; I had never met a young woman as reserved and strategic as she was. Still, she was only human. By the next morning, her lack of sleep over the last two weeks was catching up with her. There were dark circles under her eyes, and she fell asleep at breakfast. I saw Kunegunde watching her closely and panicked. I could tell Kunegunde knew something was up.

That night, Rika said she would talk to Daniel about our plan. After she sneaked downstairs and left the tower, I heard the shuffle of Kunegunde's footsteps. My grandmother peeked around the open doorway into our room and saw me lying alone in our cot. "I thought so."

I blinked up at her, not sure what to say.

"She's putting us at risk, coming and going like this. Ulrich could see her and follow her back."

I closed my eyes. "You and I leave the circle together all the time. Rika is careful. She only goes out at night."

Kunegunde's eyes narrowed. "Rika?"

My anger turned to panic as I realized what I'd just done. Kunegunde wasn't stupid. Rika was too close to Frederika.

"I thought you said her name was Ree."

"That's a nickname I call her."

Kunegunde's expression tightened. She watched me silently from the doorway. Then she chuckled with a perverse amusement and went upstairs.

CHAPTER TWENTY

T hree times, I've tried to chronicle this part of my story. Three times, I've failed and scraped my shame from the page. The language I learned as a girl—this language we all speak—doesn't have the words to describe what happened next. *Diutsch* is a language of things, a song of mud and brick and stones. I'm certain the old language would work better to describe these ill-starred events. It was a language of mist, a song of wind and prayer and smoke. But the old language has only survived in spells and oaths. I have no choice but to write these clumsy words onto this page. This try will have to do, whether I fail or no. May the Mother forgive me. If I scrape the parchment further, there won't be any left.

Rika was so late getting back, the night Kunegunde discovered who she was, that I fell asleep before she did. The next day was the worst of my life, a day I would curse for years to come. That morning, I dreamed I was a bird for the final time. Everything was the same as before. The masked rider. The girl. My urge to protect her. This time, however, when I woke, I could finally hear the words my mother spoke to me: *Protect the princess.*

When I jolted awake, I knew who the girl in the dream was.

The side of the bed where Rika slept was empty. There was only a faint impression in the feather-mattress where she'd lain. I hurried downstairs to find Kunegunde in the kitchen reading. "Where's Ree?" I asked, my voice frantic.

"Gone," Kunegunde said, her voice hard.

"What? Where?"

"She changed her mind. She said she was going back to the next mountain to the father of her child."

The idea made my breath catch, though I didn't believe it. Kunegunde had driven Rika out. I fought to swallow my anger.

"How long ago did she leave?"

"An hour, maybe two."

I rushed to the caged window to look out. A white blanket of snow had already spread itself over Rika's footsteps.

I made myself draw a deep breath. I had to find Rika and warn her. Where would she be? The clearing between the two mountains, where she met Daniel at night. The clearing where my dream took place. "My stomach hurts," I said. "Do we have any hellebore?" I knew we were out. "I could use a purgative."

"No," Kunegunde said through clenched teeth, grabbing her cloak. She was on to me, and she wouldn't let me leave without her.

Outside, the world was a tangle of black and white. The trees at the edge of the clearing were glittering and black, sharp with icicles. The sky had gone as colorless as fear. The wind blew in gusts, scattering the snow. Flakes spun in the air. I tightened my cloak about my neck and pulled on my gloves, preparing myself mentally to run.

As we stepped into the wood, the wind whipped my cloak and cleared our path. "There it is," Kunegunde said, pointing into the shade just inside the tree line where the black hellebore grew. I pretended to look for the cluster of white flowers.

Kunegunde threw out her arm to stop me from moving forward. The same gesture she made weeks before when we heard the kingsguard. I followed her gaze to a stand of spruce where a fox was scurrying up a snowbank. A small red beast, thin-legged, with a pointy nose. There was something strange about its posture, the way it raised its muzzle to sniff the air. Its eyes were wild. "It flees something," Kunegunde said.

The fox leapt, heading east, and I heard a faraway sound. Long and high, piercing. A scream. My heart thudded with panic. It sounded like Rika's voice.

"Be still," Kunegunde hissed. She pulled a dried alrūne from her pouch and took a bite without bothering to hide it. She gave me a stern look, then muttered the same chant she had spoken before. *"Leek haptbhendun von hzost. Tuid hestu."*

As I wondered what the words meant, I felt a numbness in the tips of my fingers. My scalp began to tingle, and I felt my soul trembling in my flesh. God's teeth, I thought with horror, as the spell pulled my awareness, unwilling, from my body. Everything that is done *can* be undone—

For an instant, I was nothing. Or rather I became light and shadow, mist and wind, nothing and everything at once. Then I was soaring over a sea of spruce in the body of that bird, the trees swimming dizzyingly below me. The next mountain rose in the distance, amid an endless sea of trees. At first there were no words in that mind-space, only the buoying currents of wind, the un-settling sensation of soaring on them. Far away, the faint sound of echoing voices. The strong scent below of horses and men.

We dove toward the voices. *We.* It took a moment to understand it, but there was indeed a *we* in that mind-space. It was not only me experiencing these sensations; there were other souls with me inside the bird. Our thoughts and feelings were all mixed up. A disturbing disappointment at the living quality of the horses and men. Erste. It was hard to tell where his thoughts stopped and mine began. Another mind was there with us, too, a third. A more com-plex mind, filled with more complex thoughts and a rage so bright it burned. Kunegunde.

The world jerked and we landed on the lowest branch of a spruce. The clearing where we had landed was covered in snow. At its center, Rika stood in her tattered clothes and braid, clutching an arrow that had pierced her thigh. The bright red feather at its back quivered as she inspected the wound. *Rika,* I screamed, my heart breaking. The word came out of the raven's mouth, transformed into the call of a bird. *Kraek!*

Rika looked up, panicked, the arrow dropping to the snow.

At the edge of the clearing, a masked man looked up in the middle of dismounting his horse. He saw the bird in the spruce tree, then returned his focus to Rika. His horse wore Prince Ulrich's colors, just like it had in my dream: a green and black banner emblazoned with a wolf. He advanced on Rika, eyes blank above his mask. "Faithless girl!" he sneered. "Which of those filthy peasants did you lie with? What village is he from?"

Rika went silent, tears streaking her cheeks.

"We saw you with him. Who is he?" The masked man sounded furious on his master's behalf. "Say his name!"

She shook her head fiercely.

"How dare you betray your husband?"

Rika backed away from him, stumbling into a snowdrift. That was when I noticed it, as the man marched toward her. The tension in the air. As he drew closer to her, so did the next world. When he tore off her necklace, I knew it was time to descend upon him in a whirl of feathers. This was it. The scene from my dream.

But as Erste drew himself up to heed my will, Kunegunde made known her will to stay put. No no no, I thought, correcting her. We have to attack. The world shuddered as the bird shook its head, unable to sort out the two contradictory commands. By the time we could see, the masked man had unsheathed his dagger, a wicked silver thing with an emerald-studded hilt. The raven-mind was fascinated with the blade. He couldn't take his eyes off it.

The man held the dagger over Rika's breast. She tried and failed to stand, to flee. She shivered, her lips moving in prayer. "*Xär dhorns—*"

The scream that filled our mind was mine. A silent thing, at first, pure thought, a wordless expression of horror. Then it became bird-sound. *Kraek!*

The man looked up, Rika's necklace swinging in his hand. For a moment, I worried he would recognize us somehow, that he would grab his bow and shoot at us. But he only turned, shaking his head, and dropped the necklace into his pouch. Returning his full attention to Rika, he plunged his blade into her breast.

Her mouth opened in a soundless scream. Her eyes widened, darting and wild. Her body went limp. Blood trickled from her lips. Grief filled my heart as I watched her soul leave her body, a pale wisp of breath, and dissolve into the next world.

The man inspected Rika's hands, retrieved his dagger, and chopped off a finger. The tension in the air collapsed.

Rika lay dead on the snowdrift, a slow circle of blood seeping from her chest. The only sound, for a moment, was the sound of falling snow. As the man sheathed his dagger, the wolf insignia on its pommel cap glinted in the sun. I tried to turn our gaze toward Rika's body, my grief flowing into that mind-space like a river with no place to go. The bird made a strangled sound, and the image began to twitch from one side of our vision to the other, as Kunegunde made felt her desire to go.

No, I corrected her again. Wait—

The conflict set the bird free to do what he wanted. He dove toward the dagger. The man swatted at us, as Erste used his talons to pull the dagger from its sheath.

And then Kunegunde regained control, lifting us up over the trees toward the bodies we'd left behind, the weight of the blade making our flight far less graceful than before. Horror-struck, I tried without success to turn us around. The next thing I knew we were lurching into the snow beside our crumpled bodies. I could feel Kunegunde pulling herself out of the bird's body, and Erste too, becoming one with the mist. For a terrifying moment, I animated his body alone, before I willed myself out—

When I opened my eyes, I was lying on my side near the stand of spruce, my sack open in the snow. I couldn't move. My arms and legs were numb. Ants seemed to march over my skin. I was filled with such grief that I lay unmoving in the snow, giving myself over to the deadening cold.

When I finally looked up, I saw Kunegunde kneeling a few feet away, wobbling as she tried to support herself. Before her, Erste was splayed out, the dagger forgotten nearby in the snow. When she saw me looking at her, she cried out, her voice slurred. "What have you done?"

I couldn't have answered if I'd wanted to. My tongue was stuck to the roof of my mouth. But her selfishness shocked me. Here she was, mourning a bird, when we had just watched Rika die?

After a moment, I managed to push myself halfway up only to fall back into the snow. I tried again. I felt dizzier than I had ever felt.

"You stopped taking the powder," she mumbled, peering at me. "You stole the alrūne. I should've noticed. Your eyes—"

I shivered, managing slowly to stand and draw a deep breath. Something snapped in my chest, like the ice on the banks of the lake at the beginning of spring.

"How could you run Rika off?" It was becoming easier to form words. My tongue was prickling.

"We were supposed to report seeing her on pain of death. If the king found out we harbored her—"

"She's dead because of what you did."

Kunegunde chuckled softly. "Better her than us."

Her callousness horrified me. I screamed at her. "She's dead, Kunegunde. That man stabbed her in the heart."

"I saw."

"You lied to me about the alrūne. You gave me a powder that stole my gift."

"Your gift? Is that what your mother called it?" Kunegunde's breath puffed in frozen clouds from her lips. "Our souls aren't properly moored in our bodies. That's why our souls leave our flesh. It's why we can sense the next world when it's close. Have you been hearing voices again? Is that why you wanted to attack that man?"

My mouth dropped open. "Yes, but—"

"Demons are notorious meddlers in politics. They don't care

about peasants' lives. That man could've killed us. We were bound in the body of a bird. He had a bow!"

"You take the alrūne yourself!"

Kunegunde opened her mouth to speak, but no sound came out. She closed her eyes, as if willing herself to be calm. When she finally spoke, her voice was tight. "You don't understand how dangerous the world of men is. I'm right to silence that demon until you learn enough to protect yourself. If you enter whatever squabble is happening on the next mountain, you'll get *hurt*."

"It's not a demon," I said flatly. "It's Mother. The voice that speaks to me is Mother."

She stared at me. Her amber eyes glittered in the pale light. There wasn't a single sound in the whole wide wood. "Do you know why your father told you I was dead?"

I blinked at her, stunned. I shook my head.

"That scar your mother had on her cheek. How did she tell you she got it?"

My memory of that scar, the discussion I had about it with the physician, seized me. It felt like I was choking. "A hunting accident."

Kunegunde smiled a tight smile. "There was no hunting accident. Your mother was here when Albrecht came for Ursilda. That scar is a wound he dealt her as she was trying to lift the wolf-skin from his back."

I gaped at her with disbelief. No wonder she didn't like to talk about that story.

"It festered. It took six weeks for me to nurse her back to health. Your father blamed me. He didn't think it was safe for your mother to visit. And the truth is, he's right. It won't be safe here until I find a way to destroy the wolf-skin."

I grabbed my sack. Snow pricked my face. An energy filled me, thawing my blood.

"Haelewise. What are you doing?"

"I'm going for a walk. I need some time to think."

I turned and went quickly; I had to find someplace for that energy to go. The trees stood, skeletal, unmoved by my anguish. I wavered between blaming Kunegunde and myself.

My eyes burned as I walked. I would have to leave Gothel. There was no question about it. But leaving Gothel would put me in a worse position than I had been when I left home. With Rika dead, I had nowhere to go. No way to join the circle.

Despair struck me, so hard I didn't know what to do. I fumbled for the figurine in my pouch, wrapping my fingers around her smooth stone, willing my mother to appear to me again. Mother, I prayed. Guide me.

The words floated up to the sky with the last of my hopes.

For a moment, nothing happened. The world was still. The stone of the figurine stayed cold. Then its stone began to warm and my skin began to bloom all over with chills. I felt a heaviness, a weight in the air. The next world drew close, and I heard a hum.

Seek Hildegard, my mother whispered.

I fell to my knees in the snow, relieved that my mother had finally spoken to me again. I blinked back tears, looking anew at the frozen wood. The firs seemed to sparkle with my gratitude.

But as I thought further on this advice, knees freezing in the snow, my mother's words began to baffle me. Why on earth would she tell me to seek a Christian abbess? How in the world could someone like Mother Hildegard help me find my purpose?

The only purpose I felt now was a desperate need to see Rika's killer punished. Rika, my only true friend. Though we had known each other only briefly, she was like my sister. When I was with her, I had felt *known*. A certainty coursed through me, pure and sharp. I understood what I had to do, my heart full of a cold resolve.

I hurried back to retrieve the wolf-dagger from the snow where Erste had dropped it. I could use it as evidence against Ulrich.

My grandmother was slowly packing the snow atop what I

presumed was Erste's grave. She looked exhausted. Every time she moved, she had to pause to catch her breath. A few feet away, the dagger glittered, its blade glinting silver on a snowdrift. I took a deep breath. "I'm leaving Gothel."

Kunegunde looked incredulous. "Where exactly do you think you will go?"

"To make sure Rika's killer is brought to justice."

Kunegunde's eyes widened. She looked genuinely worried. "Haelewise, no. You're a peasant woman. It'll be your word against Ulrich's. He's a noble. No one will believe you."

It was clear she believed what she said, but I knew she was wrong. I could feel it in my bones. "I must."

"And then?" she scoffed. "Where will you live if not here?"

"I don't know," I said, remembering my mother's advice. The abbey might be the only place that I *could* go. My hands shook. My temple pounded, and my temper flared with anger at Kunegunde, at Ulrich, at the baffling cruelty of the world. Kunegunde understood that cruelty, so she had withdrawn to her tower. But burning in my heart was a new resolve. I wanted to fight it.

"Your mother would want you to stay here with me where you're safe."

"She told me to see Mother Hildegard."

Kunegunde's face went white. "Haelewise, no. A peasant girl like you will never get an audience with her. Everyone talks about how great she is, how wise, how holy, but all she's interested in is power, currying favor with archbishops and kings. She has to abide by the rules of men, the rules of the Church. Your word will mean nothing to her."

"My mother—"

"Haelewise." She met my eyes. "Your mother is dead."

The dagger glittered in the snow between us. For a moment, I fantasized about using it against her. When I spoke, it was through gritted teeth. "I never want to see you again."

I dove for the dagger and ran, the frigid air burning in my lungs. Kunegunde moaned, behind me, trying to follow. Her age seemed to make her more susceptible to the exhaustion that came from the movement of our souls.

I knew I could grab my things and leave before she got back to the tower. Inside, I gathered my belongings: clothes, knapsack, bow and quiver, mirror, the alrūne I had stolen back, a bread crust, a few quinces from the cellar, what was left of the fertility oil. I checked my coin-purse for the figurine—it was there—and filled my drinking-horn with water. I wrapped the murderer's dagger carefully in cloth and tucked it in my sack, hoping it would be useful to prove what Ulrich had done. Then I changed into my own clothes, swiped a few coins from the jar where Kunegunde kept her fees, and hurried into the forest.

As I followed the footpath north, I could hear Kunegunde calling my name. Her voice faint, drifting on the wind. For a moment I felt loss: of the kinship we shared, of the closeness I had once wanted to feel with her. A small voice in the back of my mind made itself heard, the old voice that made a mockery of my every choice. Where will you live, if not at Gothel? I pushed the thought down and continued doggedly north, Kunegunde's warning not to get involved in royal affairs echoing in my head.

Certainty did not, it seemed, belie fear.

After I gathered more evidence against Ulrich, I would make it my goal to see that he was punished. The obvious course was to go to the king, but there was the decree. I would have to lie about the fact that she had been staying at Gothel, not to mention the vantage point from which I witnessed her murder. The king was supposed to be a brilliant diplomat. What if he saw through my lies? Perhaps that was why my mother wanted me to seek Hildegard. If I could get *her* to believe my story, she could help me convince the king to take my word over Ulrich's.

Onward I went, past pine trees and snowdrifts. When the wind blew, the snow was blinding. I chuckled when I realized it had finally happened—for the first time in a long time, the weather matched my mood. As I walked, I began to feel a creeping exhaustion, the sort of tiredness that cannot be ignored. The same tiredness that made Kunegunde sleep for a day the last time she sent her soul into the bird. It was catching up with me.

I didn't even make it to the clearing before I started to fall asleep on my feet. Snow filled the air. Wind whistled through the trees, tempting me to lie down in the snow for what might be my final sleep. But I forced myself to trudge on for Rika's sake. I was relieved when I came upon a hollow in a tree trunk where I wouldn't face the full force of the wind. Wind whistled around it, singing a ghostly song—a faint howl like the faraway cry of a wolf. On another day it would've frightened me, but I was so sleepy, I didn't care. Snow dusted my nose and eyelashes as I crouched down to enter the dark hollow. The sun had set. I could barely keep my eyes open.

Inside, I wrapped myself in my cloak and my tattered blanket. The bark was cold against my back, and my blanket didn't do enough to warm me. I didn't know if the hollow would be safe. Still, I had little choice in the matter. This was better than sleeping in the open, where I might be discovered by hunters or worse.

I thought of Rika in my last conscious moments before sleep.

CHAPTER TWENTY-ONE

The sleep that enfolded me was dark and deep. I woke once, terrified, unable to move my arms or legs. My skin prickled all over, numb again, as if it were crawling with ants. When unconsciousness retook me, I dreamed that my mother was still alive, and I was living with her again in our hut. I don't know how long I slept before I sat up, reaching out, expecting to feel the wall of my cupboard, opening my mouth to call for her. When my fingers touched cold bark, the nightmare of everything that had happened came rushing back.

My mother was dead, and so was Rika. I lay unmoving in that tree for an endless moment, trying to come to terms with those facts. When the world of my dream finally fell away, I pulled out the bird-mother figurine, a lump forming in my throat. "*Mother,*" I whispered aloud. "Are you there?" An eternity passed while I waited for an answer. It must've been an hour or more before I ate a bite of alrūne and crawled out of my hollow.

It was light out, although the gray skies and endless snow made it difficult to tell the time of day. I headed in the direction of the clearing, or where I thought it was. But without a raven's ability to follow a scent, I couldn't be sure. I stumbled upon a couple of clearings, but all of them were empty. Eventually, I realized I would need Daniel's help to find the right one.

The skies had cleared by then, and I could see that the sun was setting. The snowstorm had passed. When I reached the settlement, a woman in a tight headscarf stood atop the hall beside the synagogue, knocking snow off the roof with a broom. I hid my bag under the firethorn bush where I'd waited for Rika, my heart lurching with grief. The woman on the roof stared at me, her expression too far away to read.

I headed toward the hall. As soon as I opened the door, I felt a blessed warmth. A fire crackled near the entrance, the heat warming my hands and cheeks. A festive array of dried vegetables hung from the ceiling around the fire: garlic and parsnips, ginger and turnips, some dried herbs too far away for me to identify. Beyond that were four long tables. Well-worn. Faded decorations swayed from wood beams, the old purple of wild violets, the dark red of wild rose. Rush lights flickered on the walls. In the far corner, a woman in a looser headscarf, brown wool skirt, and tunic was stirring a cauldron over a fire ring, humming softly, her hair in a long auburn braid. Noticing her relaxed posture, suddenly, I dreaded telling her why I'd come.

The door creaked as I let it fall shut behind me. The woman with the auburn braid turned and saw me standing before the door. She backed away, her eyes wide with fear, calling out in a language I didn't understand.

I was puzzled at first, racking my brain for an explanation for her reaction. Then it hit me. Daniel must've found Rika in the clearing while I slept. This woman thought I was a ghost.

It was heartbreaking to be mistaken for Rika now. I held up my hands. "My name is Haelewise, daughter-of-Hedda-the-Midwife," I made myself say. "Rika was staying with Mother Gothel and me on the next mountain. I witnessed her murder."

The auburn-haired woman's eyes widened. She studied my face. "Your eyes are different," she said. "Brighter."

The door opened behind me. The woman with the tight headscarf hurried in, her hair completely hidden beneath it. She gawked at me, then turned to the auburn-haired woman, her face pale.

"It's not her," the auburn-haired woman said. "She's a friend Rika made at Mother Gothel's."

The woman with the tight headscarf walked over to me slowly, her face full of fear. She touched my arm, my cheek, my hair. I didn't move. "Why do you look so alike?" she asked. "Are you kin?"

It took me a moment to answer. "No, but she was like my sister."

The auburn-haired woman poured some ale for me from a barrel. "Stay," she said. "Any friend of Rika's is a friend of ours. Eat with us."

She rang the dinner bell, and the woman in the tight headscarf withdrew to one of the tables, her face pale. The other villagers and their families began to trickle in, helping themselves to the cauldron of stew, sitting down at the tables with their bowls. Many of the men were wearing hats. They stared at me as they passed, murmuring among themselves, giving me a wide berth.

When everyone was seated with their stew, the auburn-haired woman introduced me to everyone as a friend Rika had made on the next mountain. After that, the whispering stopped and the bearded man who sat next to the woman in the headscarf led everyone in a blessing in a language much different from *diutsch* or the language of priests.

It was strange to be eating with so many others. I had become accustomed to eating with Kunegunde or by myself. Back home, no one ate together like this except in taverns, and if I'd gone inside a tavern, I would've been run out.

I tore into my stew. I hadn't eaten in over a day. But I had only finished half of it before a memory of Frederika lying dead in the snow came back to me unbidden. I pushed my bowl away.

The hall around me was a welcome distraction. At the next table, the woman in the tight headscarf—whose name, I learned, was Esther—kept glancing at a handsome boy who was staring into the fire at the back of the hall, his eyes shining and dark. He looked so stricken that I knew he must be Daniel. In Esther's gaze, I recognized a mother's love for her child and felt an ache.

As I watched, Esther stopped eating to bring Daniel a cup of something to drink, but he wouldn't take it. She brushed his hair back from his forehead, but he jerked away, too angry to accept such comfort. No matter who went over to try to talk to him, he wouldn't speak. Several of the villagers tried, but he just sat there, staring into the fire. Eventually, they went to the bearded man seated next to Esther, who had led the prayer over the meal.

"It's time, Shemūel," they said. "We can wait no longer."

Shemūel shook his head, but the men protested further.

"Your son has gone mute. We must decide without him."

"We can't just leave the girl up there without a funeral."

Up there? Where in the world did they put her?

His mother glared at the man who said it, then got up to talk to her son. When she came back, her mouth was tight with resolve. "He won't speak," she told Shemūel. "I suppose they're right. It's time we decide."

Someone passed a jug around our table, and everyone began to refill their cups. I refilled mine, my head swimming with a thousand thoughts. Was Daniel too stricken to lead me to the clearing? Should I leave this place now with the dagger and go to Hildegard without waiting for additional evidence? A few men stepped outside, loosening their pants to relieve themselves. All was quiet, except for the sound of tankards thudding against the table. At the next table, Esther and Shemūel looked at each other. Then Shemūel cleared his throat and stood, straightening his hat. "Frederika was untruthful. She led us all to believe she was someone she wasn't."

A few of the older women at their table nodded.

"She put our community in danger," Shemūel went on. "Hiding here from the king, telling us she was a common orphan. Seducing my son when she was already engaged to a prince. When Daniel told us who she was, I was afraid."

It was difficult for me to hear Frederika spoken of this way. I wanted to stand up, correct him. She didn't seduce him. They were in love. Why were they blaming her?

"Still," one of the men at another table said. "She lived with us for months. She fed and groomed our horses. She had stains on her robes from making our food."

"Aye," the auburn-haired woman said, nodding. "She took Daniel's place in the stables when he rode to market. She was good with the mules. Their eyes sparkled when she went into the barn. They hold their heads high, now. She convinced every one of 'em he was a horse."

Laughter echoed through the crowd.

"But she was not Jewish," Esther said.

"Nor was she Christian," another woman spoke up.

"Let her father decide how to bury her!" Shemūel called.

The whole room was silent then. You could hear the shifting of cloth beneath the tables. All eyes were on Esther and Shemūel. They stayed quiet for a long time. After a while, there was the sound of folks drinking and shifting on the benches.

Shemūel looked deep in thought. "If the king finds out she was living here," he said finally, "we'll all be put to death."

Murmurs rippled through the crowd.

"She was shot with a Zähringer arrow."

"Do you think Zähringen was jealous of Ulrich's betrothal?"

I tried to swallow the sob that leapt from my mouth without much luck. Everyone turned to look at me. I wiped my eyes and stood. "I was there," I said, raising my voice. Rush lights crackled and sputtered on the walls. "Frederika was staying with us at Gothel. Yesterday, I saw a masked man attack her. He used one of Zähringen's arrows, but his horse bore Ulrich's banners, and he cursed her on Ulrich's behalf. He asked for the name of her lover. When she wouldn't tell him, he killed her."

Esther's eyes widened, then fluttered closed, her mouth moving in prayer. People began to nod, murmuring. "That's why her finger was missing. The killer took it as proof to take back to Ulrich."

"Frederika was like my sister," I went on, my voice ringing out. "I want to make sure Ulrich is punished. I have the dagger his man used to kill her. If anyone knows anything more about what happened, I urge you to come forward. I'm going to Mother Hildegard of Bingen for guidance on how to tell the king."

Everyone began talking at once. Then the door opened and a little boy rushed in. "Prince Ulrich comes!"

Esther's eyes went wide. "Loose Nëbel!" she told Daniel, her voice urgent. "Hide!"

Daniel nodded and hurried away. In the silent hall he left behind, I thought I heard the distant whicker of a horse.

The hall emptied as if it were on fire, everyone rushing to hide themselves inside their huts. As I left the hall with everyone else, my anger mixed with fear. It unsettled me, fluttering anxiously in my chest. All around the settlement, lanterns were going out, one by one, and doors were slamming shut. My heart thudded. I looked up at the sky, wondering what form the prince would be in tonight, trying frantically to remember the moon phase.

A waxing half moon shone down, ghostly and white.

Esther stood outside the nearest hut—hers, I guessed—watching the receding form of her son. As the sound of carriage wheels and horses grew louder, she closed her eyes and mouthed a silent prayer, reaching for her husband's hand.

When the groaning cart finally crested the path into town, pulled by Ulrich's great black horse, I could see that it was painted black, as were the terrible spikes that extended from it to the horse pulling it. From a distance it almost looked as if the cart were made of shadow. The only colors were the faint gold and green accents that decorated its joints. As the cart drew closer, I saw Prince Ulrich seated beside the driver, drinking lustily from a horn. He wasn't wearing the wolf-skin tonight. He was dressed in clothes so fine, they would put a duke to shame. A beautiful surcoat dyed deep green and black, the colors of his house. His eyes flashed as he looked up, that cruel blue, and his shining black hair hung around his face.

Behind him sat an older woman and his sister, Princess Ursilda. The princess's face glowed in a wimple and black hooded cloak. Very pregnant, hands resting on her belly, dark circles under her green eyes, her face freckled and gaunt.

A muted excitement flitted through me. Ursilda had a figurine; she was a member of the circle. Then I felt a stab of guilt.

"Frederika!" Ursilda cried when she saw me, her eyes lighting up. The elder woman helped her out of the carriage. "You're alive! We heard you were dead!"

Ulrich whirled around to follow her gaze. When he saw me, his eyes filled with horror and fear. He stared at me, shocked speechless.

The idea that I could cow him made me smile. Let him think I was a ghost.

Ulrich made a small noise, something between a moan and a gasp. I leered at him, taking a perverse satisfaction in his fear.

Behind the carriage, four guards in fine green surcoats brought up the rear on powerful steeds. Their hair was oiled, and they were so well dressed, they looked more like courtiers than strongmen.

"Who—what—how?" Ulrich stammered.

Ursilda stepped into the torchlight, the older woman following her. When she saw me up close, her expression crumpled. "Brother," she sobbed, desolate. "That isn't Frederika."

The older woman accompanying her took her hand. "Ursilda. Calm down. Breathe. For the sake of the child—"

Ulrich searched my face again, relief flooding his expression. He handed his page boy the torch, then walked a circle around me, inspecting me like a farmer inspects cattle, prodding my hips, my face, my hair. His breath smelled sickly sweet, like my father's when he had been drinking. I hated him then with all my heart. His cruel blue eyes, his black eyelashes. Every lock of his shining black hair. "So similar," he smiled. "Who are you? Why are you here?"

I froze. If I opened my mouth, the only possible thing that would come out was an ancient curse. The wind blew a mist of tiny snowflakes. They glittered red in the torchlight.

He turned to Esther, his expression guarded. "Frederika is dead, then, as the message said." He looked closer at Esther, her tight headscarf, her husband's hat. "What the hell was she doing in a Jewish settlement?"

"She wasn't here," Esther said, head bowed. "I found her body yesterday in the wood—with one of Zähringen's arrows in her thigh. We moved it to a cave atop the mountain so her remains would be safe until you got here."

Ursilda cried out and stumbled into the arms of the older woman beside her, a sorrowing sound in her throat. The older woman comforted her, whispering into her ear.

Ulrich's expression darkened. He peered at Esther as if seeing her for the first time. He clenched his fists, and his face went white. "What were you doing in the wood?"

Esther paled. "Looking for herbs. This girl might have more information," she said, nodding at me. "She witnessed the murder."

I whirled on Esther, panicking. Why was she telling him that?

"What did you see?" Ulrich asked me through his teeth.

I swallowed my fear. It would be foolish to admit what I saw to the man who ordered Rika's murder, unless I wanted to be next on his list. I cleared my throat, trying to disguise my loathing and sound subservient. "Very little, your highness. The snow was thick."

Ulrich glared at me, then snarled. "We will speak of what you saw after the body is recovered. Fix the killer's face in your memory. Recall every detail you can."

I made myself nod.

Ulrich turned to Esther. "Take me to her body."

Ursilda's caretaker addressed the prince. "Your highness, I don't think your sister can manage the ride up the mountain."

Ulrich turned to Esther. "Woman. She's right. Get my sister some nourishment and a warm place to rest."

"Yes, your highness," Esther said, bowing, already turning toward the hall. "Of course."

I watched Esther lead Ursilda and the older woman away with apprehension.

My anger returned as the guards escorted me up the winding path on a mule, the valley beneath the settlement stretching out white and silent. I hated every one of Ulrich's men, their banners, the snowflakes glittering on the flanks of their horses.

The night was still as we made our way up the wild mountain path, the only constant sound the scratch of hooves on hardened snow. The half moon hung in the sky, eerie and white. The snow gave the mountain an unearthly glow. From time to time, weapons clinked in the guards' sheaths. Daniel and Esther led the way, followed by Ulrich and his entourage, and me. My mule was a stubborn thing that kept stopping and starting, occasionally refusing to move. The first time this happened, Esther doubled back to coax my mount. A single lock of shining dark hair fell from her headcovering as she worked. She blushed furiously and tucked it back under her scarf.

When the mule was moving again, she made sure Ulrich and Daniel weren't in earshot, then hissed, "Do not speak of Daniel to Ulrich—"

"Why did you tell him what I saw? You put me in a difficult place."

"I wanted to draw his attention away from my son. Forgive me. I didn't think it through. When we found out Frederika was pregnant, and who she was, Shemūel and I ran her out. I was the one who told her to visit Mother Gothel. We had to get her away from him."

I tried to hide my anger but couldn't.

"If the king found out a common boy, a Yehudi boy, got his daughter pregnant—" Esther's face went pale. "I wanted Frederika away from here before she started to show. Please. Say nothing of my son to Ulrich."

"I have no desire to get anyone killed."

She searched my face, desperate for some sign that she could trust me, before she rode away.

The next time my mule stalled, Ulrich doubled back, still drinking from his horn. His eyes flashed as he trotted toward me on his horse. Esther tugged on the reins of her mule, following him—to eavesdrop, I presumed. Ulrich's great black horse looked impatient, hot air fuming from its nostrils.

"Who are you?" the prince said.

I swallowed the hate that rose in my throat. "My name is Haelewise, your highness," I said in the stilted *diutsch* Kunegunde spoke. If I were a noblewoman, he might have mercy on me and let me go. "I grew up south of here. Forgive me. I'm not accustomed to speaking with men of your rank."

"I doubt that very much." He narrowed his eyes, as if he thought my innocence was an act. "What were you doing in my forest— alone—a pretty girl like you?"

I gripped the reins of my mule tight, knuckles white. "I beg your pardon, your highness. I am only a girl who saw trouble in the forest near her family estate."

"What is your house?"

"I am a Kürenberger," I lied, remembering that they had estates in this area.

Ulrich fell silent, his expression dark. I made myself lower my eyes with deference.

"Whoa!" Daniel called out from his horse up ahead. "We're here!"

"We will continue this discussion later."

He kicked his horse's flanks. I caught my breath as he turned toward the cave, all my hatred for him rushing back up. I pulled my cloak tight. The wind was fierce, but it was not responsible for the chill I felt.

The cave that had become Frederika's tomb appeared at first to be nothing more than a deep shadow along a ridge. But as we processed toward it, I began to make out details. Jagged rocks that rose like teeth out of the snow, the behemoth boulder that had been rolled in front of the cave to protect it. As the guards began talking about how to move the boulder, I thought of Father Emich's stories about the miracle of Easter and felt a wild, irrational hope that we would find Frederika inside alive.

As the guards worked to move the boulder, Daniel hung back. I watched Ulrich dismount from his massive black horse, my thoughts racing.

I slid off my mule, nearly losing my footing on the uneven ground, as the villagers pushed the boulder aside. Wind howled into the cave. A bat flew out, alien and black, that most unholy of birds. The villagers ducked, covering their heads.

The bat soared away from the cliff like a tiny demon, disappearing into the star-studded night. I shivered, unable to shake the feeling that its appearance was inauspicious, though I was fairly certain it was neither alite nor oscine.

"Wait here," Ulrich called out sternly, his voice cold. He nodded at Daniel, who was gazing at the cave with a stricken expression. "Except you. Come with me. And bring that torch."

He made Daniel go into the cave first, torch sputtering.

Foreboding filled me as I watched the torchlight disappear into the maw of the cave. I stamped my feet, watching the cave mouth, my heart breaking as I imagined Rika's tomb inside it. Then Ulrich was leaving the cave, his expression grim. I hated him so much.

"Bring her down," he shouted bitterly to the guards, mounting his horse.

Esther stared at him, eyes wild, as he galloped past us down the mountain path.

I turned back toward the cave reluctantly. I wanted to pay my respects before the guards carried away Rika's body, but the cavern seemed ill-omened.

Inside, Daniel was bent over a shadowy, still shape. When I approached, he glanced up at me, eyes flickering red and wide in the torchlight. As my eyes adjusted to the light, Rika's body came into view on the stone at our feet.

Hoarfrost silvered her black braids. Blood and rime flecked her lips. Her hazel eyes were glassy, unseeing. She must've lain in that clearing a long time before Daniel found her. Her body was encased in ice so thick, it looked like glass.

As I looked down at her unmoving body, a terrible guilt overwhelmed me. This is my fault, I thought. I could've stopped this.

The stars spun overhead with the snow as we made our way back down the mountain. Ulrich's guards spoke in hushed tones, watching me, as they carried Rika's body down. I wanted to tell them the truth about Ulrich, but I knew they wouldn't believe me. No man would trust the word of a woman over the word of a prince, even a woman he thought was noble.

Daniel rode beside me in silence for much of the way down, his mule knocking up and down on the path. When the guards fell far enough back to be out of earshot, I lowered my voice. "Could you take me to the clearing tomorrow when the sun is up?"

He looked horrified. "I never want to go back there," he said, too loud.

I glanced behind us. The guards had seen us talking. They were speeding up their pace. I spoke quickly, my voice low. "I want to see if there's any more evidence against Ulrich."

His eyes widened, and he breathed deep. He thought for a long moment and nodded. Then the guards were upon us and we fell silent.

When we arrived at the settlement, the guards loaded Frederika's body onto a cart and ushered me into the hall. They were careful not to let me out of their sight, as if I were a precious object, a jeweled crown or a royal cup that might be carried off. Someone had kept the fire in the hall burning, and the rush lights on the walls were still lit. A group of villagers was clustered at a table, talking in hushed tones. Ulrich was nowhere to be seen. Ursilda was sitting alone by the fire, wrapped in furs. As I approached, she stared into the flames, her expression blank, hands cradling her protruding stomach. Red curls frizzed out from under her wimple.

I sat down next to her, realizing this would probably be my only chance to talk to her alone. It was terrible timing. Too soon. She was grief-stricken.

"You must've loved Frederika very much," I said softly, reluctant to disturb her.

She looked up, her face almost as pale as her wimple. Tears made the freckles on her cheeks glisten. She stared into the flames, not meeting my gaze as she spoke. "Is it true? That she was staying with you at Gothel?"

I cursed inwardly, wondering how she knew that. One of the villagers must've told her. Esther, I realized, remembering who had led her back to the hall. Clearly if I had wanted to keep Frederika's stay at Gothel secret, I shouldn't have told her. Fear knotted my stomach. I made myself nod, hoping Ursilda hadn't told anyone else. "Have you mentioned that to your brother?"

She shook her head. "I haven't seen him."

"Could I beg of you not to tell him? Or anyone else?" I looked down at my feet. "If the king finds out—"

She blinked. "The writ."

"I would be in your debt."

"Ulrich becomes livid when I mention Gothel anyway. Even if you hadn't said anything, I wouldn't have." She went back to staring into the fire.

"Were you and Rika close?" I said, testing the waters.

"I've known her since I was little. I stayed—" Ursilda's voice heaved, and she appeared to choke on the words. When she finally spoke again, her voice was a whisper. "I stayed with her for months when the king first married her stepmother. This is a great loss. My second lately. My husband died last year. When I saw you, I hoped—"

She trailed off, unable to finish the sentence. My heart broke for her. Her own brother had done this, and she had no idea.

"I cared for her too," I said quietly, my voice breaking.

She met my eyes and nodded. "What were her last days like?"

I wanted to tell her about our plans, about Daniel, how happy, how in love she had been. How she seemed to float into our room each night after seeing him. But speaking of that might put Daniel in danger. "She was happy."

Ursilda tried to smile. "I'm so glad to hear that," she said, her voice choked. The flames crackled. She reached out her hands, warming them, then wiped her freckled cheeks with a handkerchief. "I would like to talk further. But the stress of this day—I'm sorry. I must rest. Could we speak again in the morning?"

My heart sank. I wanted to talk to her about the circle now. I couldn't wait. "Ursilda. Forgive me for bringing this up at such a delicate time, but we might not have another chance to speak alone." I took a deep breath, and the words came tumbling out. "Rika told me you follow the old ways. She said you have one of these." I pulled out the figurine. "Could you tell me how to use it?"

Her eyes widened. She whirled around to see if anyone had seen. "Put that away!"

I slipped it back into my pouch.

"Where did you get that?"

"My mother gave it to me."

"Your mother? Who is she?"

I opened my mouth to answer truthfully, then stopped myself, uncertain. It would be more prudent to use the same house name I had given Ulrich in case they talked about me, though I would prefer to be honest. "Hedda of Kürenberg, may she rest in peace."

She looked at me with interest. "I'm sorry for your loss."

"Ursilda. I need to ask you something. Please——" My voice was full of want. The flames leapt in her eyes. They were deep green, the color of spruce trees. I willed her to understand how much this meant to me. "I want to take the oath. Rika had promised to give me a place to live, to help me join the circle. Now I have nowhere to go. My mother was a member, but she died. I used the figurine, once, somehow, to conjure her, but I haven't been able to do it again. I need——"

"This is too much," Ursilda interrupted me. "I'm sorry. I can't do this right now. What is your name again?"

"Haelewise of Kürenberg."

She nodded. "I will send for you in the morning. We can talk further then."

I took a deep breath. Again, I wanted to push, to make her understand *now*. If she didn't send for me tomorrow, I might never have another chance to talk to her. But I couldn't risk it. I had to respect her grief. "Of course," I made myself say. "It can wait until morning. Please don't tell your brother what I told you. The writ——"

"I won't," she promised. Squaring her shoulders, she called out to the woman she had brought with her. "Irmgard, help me to the carriage. I need to lie down."

I watched as the older woman helped her out, praying that Ursilda would call for me tomorrow as she promised. The finely dressed guards stood on either side of the door, glowering, daring me to try to follow them out.

Not long after Ursilda and Irmgard left, Ulrich came in to sit at the table nearest the fire. As I watched him stare into the flames, my heart hardened. My whole body stiffened with hate. I swallowed my anger, reminding myself that I only had to be civil to him this one night. As soon as I talked to Ursilda in the morning, I would ask Daniel to take me to the clearing and leave.

Esther hurried in to offer him a pitcher, the scent of wine filling the air. I watched her curtsy obsequiously. "My deepest apologies, your highness," she said, bowing low. "This wine is the best we've got."

Ulrich sneered, as if he was disgusted by the poverty of his accommodations, but allowed her to fill his tankard. When she finished, he drank from the cup, then wiped his lips with the back of his hand. As soon as he set his tankard down, Esther refilled it. She wants to keep him happy, I realized. She's afraid he knows about Daniel and Frederika. Ulrich took another drink. Seeing me, he signaled for me to come over and sit with him. I swallowed my hatred and went.

He took another deep draught from his cup as I sat down beside him. "Tell me everything you saw."

My eyes went to the silver dagger at his belt; my heart beat faster. The dagger's pommel cap had the same wolf insignia as the one I carried, but accusing him now would do nothing but get me killed.

"How was the killer dressed?"

I made myself meet his eyes. He was testing what I knew to see if he should have me killed. My heart thudded in my throat. "I think he wore a leather jerkin, your highness," I lied, "though I can't be sure. The snow—"

Ulrich watched me, slamming his tankard down on the table, his face red. Liquid splashed over the brim. His eyes flashed, ghastly. "Could you not see the horse's banners?"

"No," I lied. "The snow was too thick."

"Not even their colors?"

My mouth was dry. "Forgive me, your highness. I heard a commotion in the clearing from far away. When I arrived, the killer was leaving. All he left was a Zähringer arrow in her thigh.'

"I don't believe you," Ulrich said. He upended his tankard, drinking deep, until all the liquid inside was gone. He set the tankard down, wiping his mouth with his sleeve, his jaw set.

My thoughts raced. Had my story not been good enough? Was he going to kill me anyway?

Someone cleared their throat. Esther had come by with the pitcher. "More, your highness?"

Ulrich stared at her blankly as if he hadn't heard what she said. Then he nodded, and Esther began to refill his cup. When she was done, he took another long draught. He set his tankard on the table, staring at me. His hatred was red-hot, glowing, like iron worked by a blacksmith.

He grabbed my wrist and twisted it, and the hall was no more. My mind went white.

"You're going to admit what you saw," he said. "Then you're going to give me a list of everyone you told."

I turned to hide my face, terrified. I thought of Kunegunde's warnings about Ulrich and his father, how the wolf-skin had made the men in their family wicked. Nothing in my life had prepared me for this conversation.

Ulrich called to Esther. As she approached, he leered at me, and his dark eyes flashed with a loathing so fierce, I had to look away. "Bring a cup for the girl. No, a whole pitcher. Two. Her tongue needs loosening."

Esther curtsied and went away. I didn't want to drink. I was too afraid. I could slip up, make a mistake. Even in the din of the busy hall, I could hear my heart pounding.

Esther returned with the pitchers, meeting my gaze, apologetic. She filled my cup. Ulrich glared at me. *Drink*, his eyes said.

The wine warmed my throat as it flowed down to my belly. The liquid sloshed, dark, in its cup.

When Ulrich spoke next, his outrage was palpable. "Clear the room," he called to the guards, snapping his fingers.

The sound echoed, and I suddenly wished that I were anywhere else. Before I could move, the door slammed on the other side of the room. We were alone.

Ulrich smiled at me fiercely when he saw my eyes on the door. "Tell me what you know."

I froze. Time seemed to slow. I thought of the dagger I had stowed in my sack, wrapped in cloth. I wanted desperately to stab him with it, but his guards would know I had done it.

"I have, your highness. I'm sorry, I don't understand."

"Very well, then. Drink your wine."

I made myself do as he said.

He pulled me over to the fire where I'd sat with Ursilda earlier. The light from the hearth danced in his blue eyes.

Ulrich stoked the dimming fire with the poker. Orange flames flared from the embers. The hall brightened. The tip of the poker glowed bright red. He stared at the tip, considering it. "Are you afraid of me?"

The sob in my throat hardened, and I shook my head no.

"You should be." He leered, then put the poker down and grabbed my hand. I was too terrified to pull away. "Now. Tell me what you know."

When I didn't answer, he pulled me into his lap. "Perhaps you need persuading," he said. His breath was rancid-sweet, his kiss violent. I could feel his desire for me pressing my leg. I wanted more than anything to escape it. As I tried to wriggle free, my thoughts went to my mother, how desperately she had tried to protect me. I wondered, a strange calm coming over me, if she was watching over me now. Would she be disappointed that I didn't go straight to Hildegard, or proud that I had been brave enough to try to seek evidence?

My mother. The figurine. I reached into my pouch. Mother, I prayed, rubbing the smooth stone desperately. Guide me.

My skin began to tingle, and the next world drew close. *Rōtkupfelīn*, my mother whispered.

Thoughts raced in my head. Rōtkupfelīn was the name of the girl in one of my mother's tales. The story went that she met a werewolf on her way to her grandmother's, who encouraged her to stop to pick flowers along the path. The werewolf beat Rōtkupfelīn to her grandmother's, ate the old woman, and crept into the old woman's bed to wait for her. But when Rōtkupfelīn got there, and the werewolf asked her to get into bed with him, she escaped by telling him she needed to go outside to relieve herself.

I gasped, understanding. If I was coy with him, he might believe that I didn't suspect him. I made myself look into Ulrich's eyes. "You sent them away?" I whispered in a playful voice. "So we could be alone?"

He nodded, confused at my overture. His thoughts were clear on his face. Maybe she *didn't* see anything. My ploy was working. "I did," he said slowly.

I leaned back slightly so I could slip my arms out of my cloak. As the fabric hit the floor, I met his eyes, conscious of the way the dress fell over my small breasts and hips. "The common folk tell stories about you where I'm from."

His gaze slid down from my face to my curves.

"Is that so?" he said. "What do they say?"

I made my eyes wide. The hall was still but for the crackle of the fire. "That you turn into a wolf on the night of the full moon. Are the stories true?"

"Indeed," he said, chuckling, as if he were play-acting.

I forced a smile. Brave, I told myself. Be brave.

He slipped his hand under my shift. I made myself sigh with false desire, then opened my eyes. "I think I've had too much wine," I giggled, wiggling. "I'm so sorry, your highness. I need to go outside to relieve myself."

He shifted on the bench. "Go," he said, irritated. "Come right back."

I straightened my dress, put on my cloak, and went with him to the hall door, my heart pounding in my throat. Ulrich barked at the guards. "The girl has to piss."

I hurried behind the firethorn bush near the hall where I'd hidden my bag. As I crouched out of sight of the guards, gathering my courage to dart into the trees, I heard footsteps. A second later there was movement in the shadows, and I heard Esther's whisper from behind a nearby tree. "Did you tell him about Daniel?"

"Of course not. He's wicked. He—" My voice broke.

Esther met my eyes, her expression full of guilt.

"I tricked him into letting me outside. I'm about to run."

She nodded gravely and pressed something into my palm. "Please. Take this with you. Frederika gave it to Daniel. I'm so sorry I told him you saw the murder."

I peered at the object, a heavy circle of gold. It was a ring, bright and cold, set with a hundred glittering pale jewels. Diamonds. I had never seen one before. "Esther. I can't—"

"Aren't you going to an abbey? To see a powerful abbess?"

I nodded.

"I bet they would take you more seriously if you give them that. Besides, I don't want Ulrich to find it in my hut. He'll know she's been here." She pointed farther into the woods where silver fir trees sagged with snow. "Daniel loosed Frederika's horse back there. Find her, quickly, and ride far away."

I thought of Ursilda, the talk we were supposed to have in the morning. Daniel's promise to take me to the clearing. My heart sank. There was too great a cost to stay.

I grabbed my bag and slipped into the woods. The night was cold. My heart hammered in my throat. It was only a moment before I heard the shouts of Ulrich's guards behind me. I searched the trees frantically for any sign of the horse. In the distance I could see a ghostly equine shape standing next to what had once been a stream, head bent over the ice.

"Nëbel," I hissed, my voice panicked. She looked up, her eyes liquid and warm, her body tense. I fumbled in my sack for one of the quinces I had taken from the cellar at Gothel, holding it out. "Do you remember me?" I whispered in a more soothing tone, approaching slowly, willing myself to ignore the commotion at my back.

The horse stayed put, watching me silently, eyeing the quince. When I was close enough, I fed it to her. She snorted a soft greeting. I reached for her reins, then mounted her as Frederika had taught me. She whinnied in surprise. I squeezed her flanks with my thighs and nearly fell, she took off so fast.

CHAPTER TWENTY-TWO

I rode Nëbel away from the settlement as fast as I could, my heartbeat thudding in my ears. Down the mountain, ducking under
branches and weaving around trees. When Nëbel slowed to pick
her way through a dense thicket, I held my breath. I could see
torchlights bouncing behind me. "Halt!" a deep voice shouted.
"Haelewise of Kürenberg, I order you to halt!"

"What is she riding?" a man shouted.

"Is that Frederika's horse?"

It wasn't until Nëbel took off again that I could breathe As we
neared the bottom of the mountain, I could hear riders getting
closer behind me, see their torches growing brighter. When we
reached the valley, I turned Nëbel to follow the old footpath that
led north into the bog. Nëbel was strong and fast without the trees
to slow her, but the prince's men were better riders than I was.
They were gaining on me.

Desperate, I reached into my coin-purse for the figurine, wishing, praying for safety. I searched the woods for a place to turn, but
there was nowhere the riders wouldn't see my hoofprints and follow me.

And then it happened. The figurine grew warm beneath my
thumb, and I thought I saw a shimmer in the bog below. It was so
faint, I thought I might be imagining it, but peering down into the
trees, I could make out a silvery shape. A ghost-woman, beckoning
me into the trees. My mother.

I turned Nëbel sharply into the bog, pressing the horse's flanks
with my thighs, trying to catch up with her. A lump in my throat,

a wild need to see her after all that had happened. She was so far ahead, I could only see her in glimpses. Now a shadowy figure in the distance, now a luminescent ball of light.

She flew through the bog ahead of me, veering north. No matter how hard I pushed my horse, she always seemed the same distance ahead—shimmering, weaving between trees, leading me deeper and deeper into the forest.

Behind me, blessed snowflakes drifted down, vanishing my trail. No matter how hard I rode, I couldn't catch up. After a while, the noise of galloping horses behind me grew faint. I could only hear a single rider—far behind me—see the light of a single distant torch. I kept going, following the glimmer of my mother. From time to time, I checked behind me.

When I could see the torchlight no more, I searched the forest in front of me, desperate, and realized I could see my mother no longer. She was gone.

A rift opened up in my chest, and something yawned in my throat. A moan so low, so terrible, I didn't think it was my own.

I kicked Nëbel's flanks, urging her forward, refusing to believe my mother was gone. But the light never reappeared. After an hour or so, my arms and thigh muscles began to ache. By dawn, I was too tired to ride any longer. I crept into an abandoned hut and pulled the horse inside so she wouldn't be spotted, closing the shutters of the only window.

I was so tired, I almost forgot to eat the alrūne and smear the fertility oil on my groin, but the pressure of the dried fruits against my hip reminded me. Once upon a time, I had been angry with Kunegunde for taking them from me, but now I was grateful for her foresight. If she hadn't dried them, the fruit would be rotten by now, and I would likely be dead.

As the gray morning sun shone through the holes in the roof, my thoughts turned to the circle I would probably never join, the life my mother left behind. What was it like for her to be a part of that circle? How often had she looked into the water-*spiegel*? Did she learn incantations like the ones Kunegunde spoke? Why would she agree to give that up?

I pulled the figurine from my pouch and stroked her curves. In the gray light, she seemed almost to glow. Father had forbidden Mother from telling me so many things. No wonder she told stories. They were the only way she could tell me the truth. The amber-eyed *kindefresser*, who took strange forms and lured away children—that was my grandmother. The golden apples growing just outside the castle—the alrūne. Her stories were like the words she whispered to me now. They were warnings. They came true.

It was almost midmorning before sleep found me, and what sleep I got was fitful. Terrified that one of Ulrich's riders had caught my trail again, I was awakened often by simple sounds: the call of a bird, snow crunching under the foot of an unknown animal. When I awoke undiscovered at sunset, my fear subsided somewhat, but I didn't by any means feel safe.

Before I left the hut, I wrapped my breasts, put on my boy's rags, and tucked my braid under my tunic so I wouldn't be recognized. Outside, I apologized to Nëbel and darkened her white coat with dirt.

I knew how to find the abbey. Head west through the mountains, then follow the river north. The woods were dark as I searched for the river. The only sounds were those of animals—the calls of owls, the distant yips of foxes, the occasional roars of stags. When I found the river, I decided I wouldn't follow the shoreline in case Ulrich's riders were watching the riverbank. Instead, I would shadow it from inside the trees.

I filled my drinking horn full of river water—it was clear here, there were no towns close by—then hurried back inside the tree line. As I guided Nëbel through the wood that first night, keeping the gleam of the river to my left, I found myself haunted by

Frederika's last moments. I found myself reliving, despite my best efforts, the unwilling kiss I'd suffered the night before. Anger burned in my heart, cold and white, at the man who was responsible for both.

When the gloom over the forest lifted, exhausted from riding, I tied Nëbel and curled up under the leafless boughs of an elderberry bush. Its branches were tangled, as if the horns of a hundred stags had grown from its trunk. Laying my head on my sack, I ate a bite of the alrūne, wondering how to approach Hildegard. If I told her anything close to the truth, she would think I was possessed by a demon like my father and everyone else in Christendom.

I fell asleep before I could reach a decision.

Grief is a funny thing. It comes in fits and starts. As I rode the next evening, all of my grief for my mother, for Rika, came rushing back. Soon enough I was crying into Nëbel's mane, turning the dirt I had smeared on it to mud. I was tired of my hair catching on twigs and branches, tired of hiding from Ulrich and his guards. My skin crawled when I thought of what had almost happened the night before last.

The forest was thick. The moon was waxing toward full, but barely any starlight or moonlight shone through the branches. Shapes leapt out of the dark. The night surrounded me, broken up only by the sounds of night-creatures scurrying away, the sounds Nëbel made as she moved. Hooves on dirt, the flap of a tail, a soft whicker, the windy sound of her breath. She was a good horse, calm and sweet, until she sensed a storm coming just before dawn. Then she became unpredictable, nostrils flaring, wild-eyed until I whispered calming words in her ear.

I had a lot of time to think as I followed the river north. I found myself wondering what Matthäus was doing. I imagined him lying with Phoebe, their babe in a cradle beside their bed. He was so dedicated to doing the right thing, I was sure that he would grow to love Phoebe simply because a man was supposed to love his wife.

Perhaps I had been foolish to turn down his offer. How simple it would have been to live out my days as his mistress. What a comfort it would've been to have someone to love, to not be caught up in the treacherous affairs of wolf-princes and princesses.

Such thoughts thickened my mind-fog, feeding my saturnine mood. I built proverbs in my head in an attempt to distract myself: *Blessed is the snow that hides my path. Blessed is the lie that saves a life. Blessed is the woman who helps her kind.* I repeated them like incantations, in the hopes that they would fill my thoughts.

Seven days into my journey, at sunrise, when I could ride no more, I found a hollow tree in which to rest. The forest was warming quickly, as spring set in and I left the mountains behind. I still hadn't decided what to tell Hildegard. In my most hopeful moments, I wondered if there was another reason my mother wanted me to seek her out. It seemed unlikely that the abbess would know something of the circle, but it wasn't impossible.

Mangled roots pressed my bottom as I unwrapped the band I was still wearing about my breasts. Settling in, I took out the figurine from my coin-purse and prayed, rubbing her curves, but her stone remained cold under my thumb. Since the night I'd escaped from Ulrich, I'd prayed over and over for my ghost-mother to return, but she hadn't. Although I had kept taking the alrūne, it seemed that I was completely alone in the world. After a while, I gave up and wrapped myself in my blanket, my thoughts turning again to Matthäus.

I was wondering what he was doing now—saying his morning prayers, getting dressed to work at the tailor's shop—when I heard a soft melody nearby: *hah-mama, hah-mama.* Looking up, I saw a collared dove peering into my hollow. Was I sitting on her nest? As I felt around for it, I had an idea. I had only ever watched Kunegunde send her soul into a raven, but the dove was relatively large. Nowhere near as big as Erste, but if I ate the alrūne and spoke the right words, I could fly in her body to see Matthäus.

My heart lurched. The urge to see Matthäus welled up inside me. Matthäus, my oldest friend, my love. Even though I wouldn't be able to talk to him—to see the face of someone who loved me would be a balm. Kunegunde had warned me that you couldn't fly far or be gone from your body long, but I was willing to take that risk.

I searched my memory for the words that had loosed Kunegunde's soul. In trying to decipher their meaning, I had learned them by heart. Pulling one of the dried alrūne from my sack, careful not to disturb my avian visitor, I took a nibble of the fruit. Then I stammered the words my grandmother had spoken. "*Leek hapt—*" I started, a tingling in the tips of my fingers. "*Leek haptbhendun von hzost. Tuid hestu.*"

My skin crawled. The air went taut. I could feel my soul beginning to lift from my skin. As before, there was an in-between moment—when I became part of the mist—and then I was inside the dove.

Through her eyes, I could see my body crumpled inside the tree. Being inside the dove was different from being inside a raven—the dove-mind was calmer. I felt only a quiet hunger as she scanned the earth for seeds. I pictured us flying, lifting up out of the forest toward home. And then we were moving, soaring up, with a faint sense of avian surprise that we were doing so. Up, up, up over the greening blanket of the wood, southeast toward the lake glimmering pink with dawn. It should've been enthralling, soaring like that toward home, but I felt only an ache for Matthäus, and a nagging fear that I would see something I didn't want to see.

When the city wall rose up beneath us, I pictured us pulling down. The dove obeyed, floating down over the wooden wall toward the Kürenberg estate. We landed on the garden wall, where a sea of clothes had fallen in the process of drying on the clothesline. Here goes nothing, I thought. I hopped onto the shutters of the room where I had seen Matthäus sewing my last night in town. The shutters were closed. We had to pry them open with our beak.

The sewing room was a mess. Fabric scraps everywhere, pin-cushions, cloth. On the floor was a half-made tunic still attached to an abandoned needle and thread. The trunk he kept by the wall was open and spilling with fabric. It looked like Matthäus had been searching for something, and he hadn't had a chance to clean up.

What had disturbed his work? I wondered, pausing to sense where he was. I heard no movement in the other rooms, sensed no sign of life. Cautiously, I flew through the house. No one was there. Upstairs, I found two rooms with empty beds—one with the cradle and one without.

The whole house looked like it had been ransacked, as if some-one had been desperately searching for something. There were broken dishes in the kitchen, trunks open in each room. Cups on the table, clothes on the bed, a half-empty horn of curdled milk in the cradle. If Matthäus had simply traveled with his father, the house wouldn't be such a wreck.

Something had happened.

Fear overtaking me, I soared as fast as the dove would take me toward his father's shop to find out what. Speeding over roofs and alleyways, I saw the city waking up. Women emptying chamber pots from the night before, opening shutters to let the warmth in, oblivious to the ensorcelled dove passing overhead. I fluttered down to light on the windowsill of Matthäus's parents' room above the tailor's shop. The shutters were open. Inside, his mother sat in bed in her nightcap, eyes red from crying. His father sat next to her, his forehead wrinkled with anxiety. For a long time, they were silent, and I wondered if they would ever say anything.

Then his mother shifted in her seat. "It's been almost a week."

"I don't know what you want me to say. He didn't even tell Phoebe he was leaving."

"It's unlike him to vanish like this. He's been hurt. I know it."

"If he doesn't come back soon, we'll petition the bishop."

"What can the bishop do if the guards took him?"

Guards? I stared at them, shocked. Why would the guards take Matthäus? I waited for them to speak further, but they fell silent as if they had reached a familiar impasse. His mother looked stricken. His father looked irritated. Without thinking, I cursed under my breath. The words came out of the dove—*hah-mama*—catching his mother's attention.

"*Heinrich!*" she breathed, clutching her husband's arm. She pointed at the bird. "Its eyes—"

"Holy father protect us," her husband prayed when he saw, his expression horrified. He jumped out of bed and rushed at us, flapping his blanket. "Shoo! Get out of here!"

I flew back to my hollow quickly, afraid that I had already strayed from my body too long. As I lay there, watching the dove wander dizzily from my den, I couldn't stop thinking about Matthäus's disappearance.

The next night, when I continued my journey to the abbey, I scanned the trees for birds I could use to fly home again. I needed to know why the guards might have taken Matthäus. But I came across no birds large enough, that night, to cast the incantation. Only tits and nightjars. Tiny things.

I resolved to find out what had happened to Matthäus as soon as I went to the king.

Over the next few nights, I planned what I would tell the abbess. I deliberated over every detail, rehearsing my speech as I rode. I must have looked a sight, muttering to myself in my tattered boy's clothes on my muddy horse. I felt ridiculous, talking aloud when there was no one else to hear. Even the foxes seemed to judge me from their dens.

By the twelfth morning, I could see the abbey and the city it overlooked across the river. The sight filled me with foreboding, making me so nervous, I could barely eat the hare I shot and cooked over the fire. I was terrified of entering the city, even disguised as

I was. What if Ulrich's men were looking for me there? What if one of the villagers had told him I was headed to see Hildegard? Hoping my disguise was good enough, I used one of Kunegunde's coins to pay for the ferry across the river.

It was strange to be out and about by daylight. The ferry ride made me queasy. I had become accustomed to my only company being foxes and porcupines, glow-flies and the strange bats that soared from the mountains at night. Now there was laughter and yelling and talking. As we crossed, I watched the wheel of the mill near the abbey slowly turn in the river.

At the wooden city gate, there were merchants shouting their wares. The guards eyed me, suspicious of the oddly feminine peasant boy on his muddy mare, but they allowed me to pass through the city gate.

Inside the city, my heart stopped thudding quite so loudly. Before me I found a wet street lined with narrow rows of houses. Muddy rivulets streamed downhill. Spring had come earlier here. As I rode through the city toward the abbey, a cat streaked by, thin and covered in scabs. Screaming children streamed past, playing at chase. One of them limped. Another's face was covered with boils. All of them were skin and bones. I saw new spring gardens, here and there, the plants wan little buds. Sickly looking hens, half-dead goats. The prices in the market were outlandish: eight *pfennige* for freshly caught pike, five *pfennige* for a wheel of cheese. Even the fishmonger looked desperate.

I wondered who was buying food at these prices, if no one was allowed to leave the city gates here, as was true back home. The woods here were plentiful. It had only taken me an hour to shoot and cook the hare I had for breakfast. As I passed through the market, the spires of the abbey rose up on the other side of a smaller river, pale and glittering, like the spires of an enchanted castle from one of my mother's tales. The red bridge that led across the river was beautiful up close, constructed of red and gray and tan bricks.

Sunlight glinted on the river. Crossing the bridge, I saw a grassy path rutted by cart wheels and hoofprints that led to and from several wealthy-looking estates.

Then I saw them in the distance—two of the guards I'd seen with Ulrich on the mountain. Well-coiffed, hair oiled, in black and green surcoats, Ulrich's colors. My stomach dropped, and all the dread I had been carrying deep inside me returned. They were standing guard halfway between where I stood and the abbey gate, talking, huge swords at their hips—waiting for me. How was I going to get past them?

I thought of the deserted hut where I'd slept a few days before and wanted desperately to turn my horse around and go back. Instead, taking a deep breath, I made myself pull down my hood over my bright eyes and ride nonchalantly toward the abbey gate, already spinning the story I would tell them.

The guards glanced up at me, stepping into the path to stop my progress. "Halt. State your name and business."

My heart pounded. I pulled on Nëbel's reins and cleared my throat, making my voice as low and gruff as I could. "My name is Eckert, sir," I said merrily. "Eckert, son-of-Hildebrand-the-Baker. I'm on my way to the mill."

The taller guard eyed me. The shorter one grunted. "We're looking for a young noblewoman with long black hair and golden eyes. She's riding a white horse. We have reason to believe she's traveling to this abbey. Have you seen her?"

I made myself scoff. "*Golden* eyes, you say?"

"We've seen it ourselves."

I snorted. "What, is she magic? Like the goose who laid golden eggs?"

"Get out of here," the taller guard said dismissively.

I laughed as if I found their assignment uproariously funny and pressed Nëbel's muddy flanks with my thighs. She moved on. Behind me, the taller guard groaned to his partner.

"This is a fool's errand."

"Hardly. She's one of the duke's spies. She's implicated in the murder. If we find her—"

I nearly choked as I rode on and their voices behind me grew faint. Ulrich was telling people I was a spy?

"I wish we could've gone with the body. This is tiresome. At least the others get to meet the king."

I could scarcely breathe. The other guard's answer was finally too low for me to hear. My body was tense, and there was an ache behind my eyes. My teeth hurt, I was gritting them so tight.

When I turned the corner, the porterhouse stood beside the gate. Behind it I could see a stable and a half-built structure that was swarming with stonemasons and carpenters, which looked like the beginnings of a church. The outer abbey was still under construction. Beyond the half church was a dock. In the rapids beyond it was the mill I'd mentioned to Ulrich's men, a ways past the abbey. I kept riding past the porterhouse, as if I were going toward the mill.

When I reached the mill, I kept riding. About half an hour from the abbey, I found a bank where a bend in the river made a relatively secluded pool. Trees grew along the bank, offering a bit of privacy. Shivering in the cool spring air, I led the horse into the water to clean her off first, then ducked underwater to unwrap my breasts and undo my braid. The water was demonically cold, as if it had sprung from some frozen part of hell. As I scrubbed the dirt from my skin, I felt a hatred for Ulrich—his overweening sense of his birthright, his arrogance, his lies.

When both of us were as clean as I could manage, I tied Nëbel to a tree so she could graze and I could put on my shift. I thought of Matthäus as I let the sun dry me, praying that he was alive and well, that nothing had happened to him. When I was dry, I pulled on my fine clothes and tied back my hair beneath my wimple. Then I put on the ring Esther had given me, which I planned to offer when I presented myself. The diamonds glittered brightly in the sun.

I mounted and squeezed Nëbel's flanks with my thighs. Toward the abbey we went, the queasiness that had stricken me earlier returning. My mouth went so dry as I approached the workmen that I had to take a drink of water from my horn. My heart thudded in my throat. I made myself turn as quickly as possible from the river toward the porterhouse so the guards wouldn't see me when I went around the bend.

And then I was inside the gate. The porter looked up, confused. "The lady is traveling alone?"

Noblewomen didn't, I realized. I should've known he would ask about that. I met his eyes, knuckles white against Nëbel's reins, and spoke in stilted *diutsch*. "My escort met misfortune."

"Of what sort, miss, if I might ask?"

I groped for a response. "Robbers. Four days north of here."

His eyes widened, as he nodded. "You've traveled far."

"This ring is all I have left to my name." I showed it to him. "I've come to speak with Mother Hildegard."

His eyes grew large as he inspected the ring, and he bowed his head. "What should I call your ladyship?"

I thought long and hard before I answered. I had labored over the decision whether to be honest about who I was for a week. It was a gamble to use my name, but it was a gamble not to. "Haelewise of Gothel," I said finally, praying he couldn't tell I'd never spoken the words in my life. But they were true, at least. I had lived for over three months at Gothel. I'd played there as a girl. My mother grew up there, and my grandmother lived there still.

The porter nodded, taking Nëbel's reins and tethering them to a nearby pole. "Lady Haelewise," he said, holding out his hand.

I smiled at him, nervous, his gesture catching me off guard. After a moment, I took his hand, dismounted, and followed him inside, where dim stones flickered around a hearth. He nodded at a register on the table. "Do you write, miss?"

I nodded, grateful Kunegunde had taught me how. The date on

the register said in painstaking letters: *March 4, The Year of Our Lord 1158.*

"Would it please you to set down your name?"

Haelewise of Gothel, I wrote in my unpracticed script.

"I'll stable your mount. Then we'll get you upstairs."

I listened to the *clip-clop* of Nëbel's hooves as he led her away. While I waited for him to return, I turned the pages of the register, fear fluttering in my throat. Noble name after noble name cluttered its pages. I swallowed my fear, trying to convince myself I was not at risk, that my mother had told me to come. Then I saw the frontispiece of the register. It was emblazoned with the king's seal.

God's teeth, I thought. I've ridden here on his dead daughter's horse.

CHAPTER TWENTY-THREE

My hands shook as the porter led me over stepping-stones that dotted the muddy ground. I could feel my falsehoods threatening to collapse around me like the roof of a burning building. I might be safe as far as Nëbel went—white mares weren't too uncommon—but I had shown the porter Frederika's ring. For all I knew it could be some famous bauble everyone who was anyone knew about. Following the porter up a narrow stone stairwell to the upper level, I tried my best to swallow my fear. There were no rails. Our boots made a nervous music as the porterhouse and stables and half-built church dropped away below, but I was less afraid that I would fall than I was that someone would see through my disguise.

At the landing, a heavy wooden door prevented trespassers from passing through the upper abbey wall. Its iron knocker had been shaped into a grotesque, winged face. The iron looked black and smooth. The face sneered out—godlike, angry—as if to deter unwanted visitors from entering.

The porter reached for it to knock, the iron sounding loud and heavy against the wood. As we waited for the gatekeeper to answer, the porter cleared his throat. The sun shone hot on my clothes. A dizziness came over me, which I attributed at first to the height at which we stood and the social height I was trying to climb.

A panel slid open above the knocker. Through its bars, a face peered out. I could see only dark eyes, sliding over to the porter. "We are not expecting anyone," a woman said in a muffled accent unlike any I'd heard. "Who is this?"

"Lady Haelewise of Gothel," the porter said. "She seeks an audience with Mother Hildegard."

"Has she brought a letter of commendation?"

The porter looked at me. I shook my head, repeating the story I had told him, adding the detail that my papers were stolen during the attack.

The woman continued routinely. "God bless you and keep you from further ill, but this is a sacred place. We cannot let just anyone in. Are you here on pilgrimage?"

I shook my head. "I seek sanctuary."

"From whom?"

I bit my lip, remembering the king's seal on the register. "I witnessed something terrible. I can only tell my story to Mother Hildegard."

"She brought an offering." He nudged me. "Show her."

I held up the ring, terrified that the gatekeeper would recognize it. Like the porter, her eyes widened at the sight of it. Her face disappeared and the panel slid shut. My heart pounded while I waited to see what she did. I thought I heard the sound of keys jangling on the other side of the door. After a moment, the lock clicked. The door opened just wide enough for her to take the ring. Through the crack, I watched her turn it this way and that with tawny fingers. She opened the door. "It may be days before Mother Hildegard can meet with you, Lady Haelewise," she said. She wore a thin crown with a gauzy veil attached to its back, which cast a beautiful white haze over the black of her hair. Her robes glowed white in the sun, contrasting with her bronze skin. "We have standing orders not to disturb her. But we would welcome you to stay in the guesthouse as you wait."

As the sister let me into the upper abbey, my hair stood on end. The air inside the upper level felt taut. I closed my eyes, reaching out. The air was so thin, I could feel the next world enmeshed with this one, just like I could at Gothel, though I could sense no mist here.

This was a thin place. There was no doubt about it. What this meant for Hildegard and her Christian abbey I had no idea.

The sister, who told me her name was Athanasia, began naming each of the buildings we passed—the residential house, the abbess's tower, the cloister. All the buildings on the upper level, she said, had been completed just last year. The mill had been good to them, and Hildegard had hurried to make them comfortable.

I faded in and out, having difficulty attending to what she was saying. My thoughts kept returning to Ulrich's men on the path below, the king's seal on the register. What would the king think if he discovered me here with his dead daughter's horse?

Athanasia continued her chatter, pointing at a stone building, oblivious to my discomfort. "There is the infirmary. There, the garden." She pointed at a stepping-stone path, on either side of which a huge, healthy garden grew with green leaf-buds, a vast swath of growing nettle and dandelion.

I had never seen a garden so endless.

"The garden of remedies is behind it."

The guest cottage stood between the garden and the upper wall. It had one small window with battened shutters and a thatched roof. She opened the door, inviting me to hang my cloak on the wall. In the corner was a small table for eating or reading or sewing. There was a richly dressed bed where I could sleep, a pipe in the wall with a lever that brought water from the river, and a hearth with a cauldron to heat water for baths. I tried to nod casually, as if I expected such wonders, but in truth I was awestruck by the idea of a lever that could bring water directly into my room.

My expression must've betrayed my feelings. Athanasia laughed. "I always forget what a marvel running water is here. It was more commonplace in the East."

"Is that where you're from?" I asked, then wished I hadn't, fearing that my question would betray my unworldliness.

Athanasia turned toward the wall, her expression sorrowful. "I was born in Constantinople. My mother, God rest her soul, died there. I alone escaped."

I nodded, my breast swelling with sympathy. "God rest her soul," I said, meeting her eyes. "How long has it been? My own mother died not a year and a half ago." My voice trembled.

Athanasia crossed herself. "There are things of which it is best not to speak. Someone will bring dinner shortly. Vespers are in two hours. Do you wish to attend?"

I nodded slowly, wondering if it was expected.

"Very well," she said, moving toward the door, her veil trailing behind her. "When the bell sounds, step outside. Someone will come to escort you into the nuns' chapel. In the meantime, you will find soap and towels beside the tub. If you wish, there is time enough before the service to bathe."

I looked down at the things on the stool by the tub as the door clicked shut behind her. I took my mother's mirror from the sack and brought it to my face. In its metal, the shadow-shape of my reflection stared back at me, divided with cracks. My hair was frizzy beneath my wimple, my face covered with a thin film of river sediment. My eyes looked haunted, unearthly, still the same strange bright gold.

The mirror clattered as I set it on the stool and picked up the soap. It was similar to the cake I'd used at Gothel, but it had a more fragrant smell: like quince with hints of a spice I couldn't place. The hand towel was raw linen, embroidered with a pretty pattern around its edge. Working the pump brought water into the barrel beneath the pipe as if by magic. It felt good to make something happen, pressing the pump down and pulling it up.

I filled the cauldron, brought it to the hearth, and started a fire. While I waited for the water to heat, I thought of Matthäus, praying that he was safe. I couldn't get over his mother's mention of guards. Where had Matthäus gone? Why was his house in such disarray? Matthäus was an innocent tailor. Why in the world would the guards want him?

A possibility I hadn't thought of before occurred to me. What if Matthäus and Phoebe had quarreled, and Matthäus had left her? His father would be upset because they faced the loss of their new status. But why in the world would that involve the guards? I wanted to pull out my hair, it made so little sense. I hoped I could see the king quickly so I could make sure Matthäus was all right.

When the water was hot enough, I poured it into the tub. What a relief it was to sink into that water. The warmth soothed my aching muscles. The soap filled the air with the scent of quince. For a blissful moment, I forgot all of my fears. There was nothing but me and the water.

But as I scrubbed my skin, watching the dirt slough off and cloud the water, I thought of Ulrich, how no amount of soap would ever cleanse me of his touch. I thought of the guards below, who might at any moment realize I was already here.

When the knock sounded, I shot up. Bathwater splashed out of the tub. I slipped on its bottom, steadying myself on its lip—silent, naked, bathwater dripping down—certain that the guards had come for me. I scanned the guesthouse for a place to hide. Could I slip out the window?

"Miss," a muffled voice said from the other side of the door. "I brought the stew."

Feeling foolish, I sank back down into the water. "Come in."

The maid was a lay sister with a sly smile, straw-colored hair, and tan, weathered skin. She wore a traditional habit: simple robes unlike Sister Athanasia's. My stomach growled at the sight of the food tray she carried. "Tell me something," I said, trying to keep my voice calm, to pronounce each sound of each word like Kunegunde. "Are royals allowed up here? Guards and such?"

"Royals, miss?"

"I saw the king's seal on the register."

"The count who protects this abbey is the king's half brother. No men've been allowed on the upper level but Brother Volmar and the priest since construction was completed. Even the porter only takes visitors to the upper gate."

Relief flooded me. I closed my eyes. "Who is he? The porter."

Her voice was rueful. "I don't know. It's a post, miss. They change out every week."

"Why do you keep calling me *miss*?" I asked without thinking, relieved that the porter wouldn't be a close associate of the king.

A puzzled look crossed the lay sister's face.

I realized my mistake. A noblewoman would expect to be treated with such deference. "Please, call me Haelewise. What is your name?"

"Walburga, miss," she said with a curtsy. "I mean, Lady Haelewise. Will it please you to eat this?"

She removed the cover of the food tray. A delicious-smelling stew steamed in a bread bowl. Beef, with carrots and parsnips. Garlic.

It took all my willpower not to jump out and dive for it. "Yes. Thank you so much, Walburga." I was starving.

I hoped the monk wasn't on the upper level then, as I was out of the tub before the door closed behind her. I wolfed down that stew, soaking wet, bathwater dripping down my skin. I didn't even bother to dry off until I was done. After that I dressed, taking the last nibble of one of the dried alrūne, noting that I had only two fruit left. I tied back my hair, pulled on the tunic, and paced, anxious to tell Hildegard what Ulrich had done.

When the bell for vespers rang, I waited for someone to escort me into the cloister. A light rain had passed over the abbey while I bathed. The leaf-buds on the plants in the garden glistened—hearty and green—in the sun. After a while, Sister Athanasia showed up to walk me to the cloister. She shook her head when I greeted her, lips tight. The keys on her ring jangled as she turned the lock.

The heavy door creaked as it opened. The cloister glowed with the pink light of dusk. The church inside was candlelit, painted with murals. One depicted a young man on pilgrimage. Another showed him lying ill, his mother beside his bed. Both were scenes, I would later find out, from the life of the saint who had been buried in the crypt.

Near the altar was a door to the nuns' chapel. The tapers on the wall flickered as I found a seat. No one else was here. Seven stacks of psalters sat on the shelf before my pew. I picked one up, saw it was written in the language of priests, and put it back. Soon the sisters began to file in, all dressed like Sister Athanasia in crowns and veils, the white fabric of their robes whispering as they moved. Two dozen sisters, each carrying a candle, which she placed in the holder on the wall as she passed, lightening the dim room in increments. None of the lay sisters, I noticed, attended the service.

Last in the procession was an elderly nun holding a taper larger than the rest. Mother Hildegard. Recognizing her, I wanted to call out, but I knew better than to interrupt the service. The abbess was silvery haired with bone-white skin, and she wore a white robe and veil similar to the other nuns. In the candlelight, as she placed the taper in its holder, her eyes seemed to flash a very faint gold. The effect was almost ominous. For a moment, I wondered if she ate alrūne. Then she passed back into the shadows, smiling, and her eyes seemed to fade to a more common pale brown. Perhaps I'd imagined the brightness out of sheer hope and desperation.

A priest followed her in, swinging a censer of incense that smelled like my father's church. The smoke floated to the ceiling as he spoke a blessing, then led the sisters in an unfamiliar prayer. When he was finished, Hildegard nodded at her daughters. Everyone reached for their psalters. Looking closer at the words below each stack—*dies Lunae, dies Martis, dies Mercurii*—I realized they were ordered by days of the week. I reached for one from the same stack as the sister beside me and struggled to find the page to which she'd turned.

An eerie instrument played a long tense note from another

room. Mother Hildegard waited for the sound to stop, then opened her mouth to sing. Her voice was like a bell, ringing out, walking up and down invisible stairs. The abbess's face shone in the light of the large taper, her eyes radiant—there it was again, that faint glint of gold—her whole aspect lit with joy. Her daughters began to sing with her, their voices following hers like echoes. After a moment, their faces lit up too, and their voices began to shake with feeling. I wondered if they could feel God's presence, although he was no more apparent to me here than he'd been in my father's church.

The service went on, the sisters alternating between song and prayer in the language of priests, their expressions radiant with joy. Jealous, I closed my eyes, reaching out to see if I could feel whatever they did, but despite the thinness of this place, I sensed nothing. Only an emptiness, the same disturbing *lack* that led me to resent going to church as a girl.

Tears stung my eyes. I had to work to master my emotions. I don't know why I expected to sense something, but the fact that I didn't made me inexplicably upset. The sisters sang on, joyful, turning a page of their psalters in unison, sending a chorus of whispers through the chapel. I set down my psalter, giving up on trying to follow along. Then I fumbled for the figurine in my coin-purse, rubbing her curves, reaching out to my mother. "*Why*," I prayed. "*Why did you lead me here?*"

CHAPTER TWENTY-FOUR

Mother Hildegard didn't send for me the next day or the next.
She passed me sometimes, marching to and from the cloister
gate, a wax tablet under her arm, barely registering my presence.
There was no denying that her eyes had a golden tint outdoors—
they shone a brighter gold in the sunlight—but I couldn't tell if that
was from eating alrūne or just her natural eye color. Sometimes
Brother Volmar, the elderly monk who served as her scribe, walked
with her. I would be lying if I said I never had the urge to interrupt
them, but no one else spoke to Hildegard when she passed, and I
was only a lowly visitor.

I spent most of those first days waiting for Hildegard to call me.
I avoided services, staying in my guesthouse except for meals. At
night, I clutched the figurine, desperate to understand why my
mother had brought me here. I rubbed the figurine, but it didn't
thrum; it seemed to have no power within the abbey walls, despite
the thinness of the air. I began to suspect that a blessing on the
grounds by some high holy man—a bishop or an archbishop—kept
it from working.

The suspicion strengthened my resolve to finish my business at
the abbey as soon as possible. Thoughts of my audience with Hildegard began to possess me during mealtimes, making me too agitated to eat. Though I found them monotonous, I started going to
services, willing the abbess to notice me. Time was passing. Ulrich
was no doubt plotting to get away with what he'd done. My sleep
was plagued with nightmares in which I never escaped him, or his
men stormed the abbey. Nightmares in which the guards found

and killed Matthäus. When I awoke from those, I tried to unravel what might've happened to him, but I failed to make any sense of what I'd heard. I reminded myself that I planned to check on him again as soon as I left court, but it didn't feel like enough.

One afternoon, when Hildegard passed me on her way to the scriptorium, her eyes were so bright, I became certain she was eating alrūne. If she was, it would explain a lot about why I was sent here. I found the garden of remedies Athanasia showed me and began searching its rows for alrūne plants. If Hildegard was eating the fruit, surely she would be growing the plants.

The garden was vast. In one area I recognized a number of seedlings—yarrow, bloodwort, and belladonna, all of which were used, I knew, in the healing of ulcers and wounds. The next patch was full of seedlings that grew into plants that reduced fevers: cinquefoil, watercress. There were pea plants and broad beans, thyme and rapunzel, lungwort and hellebore. In another area, I saw growing java pepper, lettuce, dill—plants that Kunegunde's speculum said tempered the desires of the flesh. Finally, I saw a whole patch of alrūne plants at the edge of the garden, lavender flower buds just beginning to peek out of the center of their cabbage-like leaves, and my heart leapt. There were dozens of plants. She had to be eating them. Why else would she grow so many? Maybe she would know something of the circle after all.

I became even more desperate to speak to her, but she didn't send for me, no matter how many services I attended or how often I tried to catch her eye. I became so frustrated, I wanted to scream at her during services, but I knew it would only hurt my cause. I tried to occupy my mind with puzzling out the language in which the sisters sang during services and read at meals. Unraveling the patterns and rules of the language distracted me. At meals, I asked Sister Athanasia questions about the devotional reading. Our whispers seemed to chafe at the sister who always sat beside Athanasia, a tall woman who wore her black hair tightly coiled beneath her veil, who found frequent reasons to touch Athanasia's hand. She pressed her lips together tightly when I asked Athanasia a question, stabbed her radishes, and sent me withering stares.

Athanasia seemed to enjoy teaching me Latin, nevertheless. After almost a week of mealtime conversation, I asked her to meet me in the afternoon, when her companion wouldn't, I presumed, be disturbed. I thought, perhaps, as the gatekeeper, Athanasia might have a special relationship with Hildegard, and if I impressed her, she might tell the abbess to see me sooner.

One day, Athanasia and I were strolling around the garden, talking about the day's psalms. A lay sister in plain robes knelt nearby in the dirt, humming to herself as she planted seeds in a barren area. "*In media umbrae mortis*," I said, stopping beside a row of cabbages, noticing the mournful sound of the phrase. "You say *umbrae* is shadow? And *mortis* death?"

She nodded, a curious look on her face. "Go on."

"*In media umbrae mortis*. It has a sorrowing sound."

"It does," she said, searching my eyes. "To match its sense."

"*Non timebo mala* is lighter. And *quoniam tu mecum es*—"

"How many times have you heard that psalm before?"

I felt myself flush. "Probably many, in church, before I knew what it meant."

"Have you ever thought of taking vows?"

I stared at her mutely. It never occurred to me that I might make the abbey my permanent home. Practically, holy life would offer me a home and safety from men like Ulrich, but the figurine didn't work here, my mother couldn't reach me, and the bald truth was I would break my vows in an instant for Matthäus.

Athanasia sensed my reluctance. "There is freedom in holy life. You might not think it true, locked up as we are from the rest of the world. But every morning I wake up here, I am freer than I ever was at home." Her voice trembled, and she met my eye.

I nodded, wondering what she meant.

"Hildegard is a forgiving mother superior. This is better, much better than the alternative. *Dominus regit me, et nihil mihi deerit.*" There were tears in the corners of her eyes. "Think on it," she said, with a solemn smile.

I made myself nod, reluctant to alienate her.

During the second week of my stay, a storm blew over the abbey, the clouds bursting as Walburga brought my breakfast. She barely had enough time to close the door behind her before lightning split the sky. As she hurried to batten the shutters, she almost spilled my water. Thunder seemed to shake the earth. Loosened by the sudden deluge, bits of thatch began to slide down the roof of the guesthouse. "Such uproar from the heavens," Walburga said, handing me a cup of rose water, her eyes widening with mock scandal. "Interrupting the construction. It's almost as if the Lord is upset with his architect."

I nearly spilled the draught, I laughed so hard. Everyone knew who had designed every inch of the abbey grounds.

Walburga and I had become friends during my first week at the abbey. Whenever she brought me food, we would gossip about life outside the abbey. She told me about the boy who wanted to marry her. I told her about Matthäus and my slow progress toward womanhood, the phial of fertility oil my grandmother made me that was almost out. Walburga seemed to think Hildegard could help with that, as well as replenishing my alrūne, which I told her I took to control my spells. She spoke of the abbess with an interesting mixture of awe and cynicism.

With everyone else, I took pains to be cautious during conversations. But Walburga was earthy, irreverent. She gossiped and told stories. Her upbringing seemed so similar to my own. Of everyone whom I met at the abbey, she seemed least likely to care if she saw through my disguise.

"What do you know of this place?" I asked her that day at breakfast. "What used to be here before Hildegard built her abbey?"

"Mostly farmland, miss," Walburga said, her voice turning nostalgic. "My parents still live in the farmhouse on the hilltop. There was a wood, thick with oaks and berries and birds. A field covered in dandelions. And here, where she built the upper level, there were the crumblin' ruins of the old abbey that housed St. Rupert's crypt." She looked thoughtful. "It was an eerie place, falling apart, an oak tree growing through the roof. My mother used to tell us to put our ears to the wall so the spirit of the place could whisper to us."

Her words made my hair stand on end. "What spirit is that?"

Walburga's expression turned inward. "I don't know, miss. They say this hill was once home to a Roman citadel. And before that, an ancient meeting place. Who knows what gods live here? There's an ancient shrine near the spring we use for holy water. My mother says Hildegard's plans to disturb it will bring bad luck."

I sat up straight, nibbling at a crust of bread, wondering if the shrine was the reason I was supposed to come here. "Have you ever seen it? This shrine?"

She nodded. "All the time. I used to play there."

"What is it like?"

"Quiet." She shrugged. "Unnaturally so. When I was little, we were afraid to make too much noise when we swam in the spring."

"What is it a shrine to?"

Walburga shrugged. "Some heathen religion. My mother won't speak of it."

That caught my attention. "But Hildegard wants to destroy it?"

Walburga lowered her voice. "Actually she wants to incorporate some of the stones into the cloister."

I blinked at her, surprised. First the alrūne, now this. "Really?"

"No one ever speaks of it except in Hildegard's secret language, but I think the archbishop won't give her permission."

"Secret language?"

"She calls it the *lingua ignota*. Hildegard only teaches it to her most trusted initiates, but I've picked up bits and pieces."

"Why would the abbess teach her initiates a secret language?"

Walburga gave me a look. "I wouldn't want to speculate *too* wildly, miss, but if I had to guess, I would say she has secrets."

I giggled. Thunder rolled, and another bit of thatch tumbled down the roof. "Nëbel," I breathed, remembering. "My horse. She's terrified of storms."

"Should we go down to the stable to check on her?"

"I'm afraid to leave the upper level. There are people looking for me."

Her eyes widened. "I could go for you."

"Would you?" I nodded, grateful.

While I waited for her to return, I pondered the shrine, the alrūne patch. What was Hildegard's relationship to the Mother?

When Walburga returned, her habit was soaking wet, plastered to her face and arms. The rain seemed hell-bent on flooding the garden. "Your horse is fine. The stablehand says she reminded him of a mare he cared for as a boy. He knew *just* how to soothe her, wrapping her in a blanket and tethering her tight."

Her words worried me. Had he tended Nëbel before?

"He said she must belong to someone filthy rich who could afford to be sentimental. Who's up there, he wanted to know. A princess? A duchess? I told him I didn't know your station. He had a good laugh at that, calling you the mysterious princess with the mysterious anxious horse."

My voice was small. "Did you give him my name?"

"Aye," she said, watching my expression. "Shouldn't I have?"

"I wish you hadn't. Is he close to the king?"

"Of course not, miss." Walburga stared at me, her brown eyes wide. "He's a peasant."

I closed my eyes, dread filling my stomach. If the stablehand talked, it was only a matter of time before I was discovered.

Walburga waited for me to explain.

"I need to see Mother Hildegard tonight," I said, meeting her eyes. I could wait no longer. "I witnessed Princess Frederika's murder. The horse you just checked on was hers."

That night, walking back to the guesthouse after supper, I found myself thinking about the shrine again, my belly full of pea soup and uneasiness. If this hill was sacred to the Mother, why didn't the figurine work here? Was the blessing on the grounds really so powerful? If Hildegard incorporated stones from a heathen shrine into the cloister, would that change things?

Someone called to me from across the garden. "Lady Haelewise—"

Approaching me was the lay sister Solange, whom I'd often seen on her knees in the garden, a fleshy woman in a plain habit with ruddy skin, dark eyes, and black hair. The sky behind her was moonless so early in the evening, dark and spattered with stars. An earthy odor accompanied her. "Mother Hildegard will see you now," Solange said.

Relief filled me. Finally. I hurried to retrieve the dagger from the guesthouse. Solange waited for me outside. As I walked out, I checked my reflection in the broken mirror, wrapping my hair in a scarf. My golden eyes flashed with determination.

My heart beat double time as Solange led me to the tower. My need to avenge Rika's death surged, filling me with clarity and purpose. The door opened into a stone hall, undecorated except for a shield leaning against the wall that was painted with the king's family crest.

I must've frowned. Solange laughed. "No love for the king, I see, miss. His half brother, the count, donated that shield a couple years ago when he took over as protector. It was meant for the porterhouse, but Mother Hildegard doesn't want to display it publicly. She says the only house we should show allegiance to is God's." Solange led me toward a winding staircase. "Mother Hildegard is upstairs."

Up the steps we went, our footsteps echoing past the second floor of the tower to the third. The keep was a circular room, sparsely furnished, with opulent arched windows. Two ornamental torches glowed on either side of the room, flickering, casting deep shadows over Hildegard's face. She sat in the center of the room in one of two chairs so richly dressed, they looked like thrones. As I entered the room, she looked up, though it was too dark to read her expression.

She looked smaller and thinner than she did during the Divine Office, as if her holy duties enlarged her. She dismissed Solange with a nod, then gestured for me to sit in the other chair. From my seat, I could see her face a little better, though she was still shrouded in shadows. "Forgive the dimness," she said with an apologetic smile. "I'm fighting a headache."

I nodded, thinking of the pain the light once caused me, and decided to get straight to the point. "I've come to seek your counsel, Mother Hildegard. I witnessed the princess's murder. I've been waiting to speak to you for a week."

The shadows prevented me from seeing her reaction, though I tried. The torchlight lit a halo of silver hair around her ears. "No one mentioned the reason for your pilgrimage to me until tonight."

There was a warning note in her tone. I realized, suddenly, how forward I was being. I closed my eyes, took a deep breath, and cautioned myself to be respectful. "The killer was Prince Ulrich's man, Mother. The arrow he put in her thigh was one of Zähringen's, but it was a ruse, I think, to implicate his enemy."

Hildegard was silent for a moment. I wished I could see her expression. "Why would the betrothed of the princess have her murdered?"

"I don't know," I said impatiently. "Does it matter?" Then I caught myself. I kept letting my anger get the better of me. "Forgive me. I *know* it was him. The killer berated her for betraying Ulrich, and he used a dagger emblazoned with his coat of arms."

I held out the cloth-wrapped dagger for her to inspect.

Hildegard drew a deep breath when she saw the bloodstains on the cloth. She set her jaw, taking the cloth from me. She murmured a prayer before she unwrapped the bloodstained blade and saw the wolf design on its hilt.

"I met Ulrich in the forest, and someone told him I had witnessed the murder. I tried to tell him it was impossible to see in the blizzard. He kept trying to get me to tell him everything."

She inspected the dagger in the torchlight. "But you escaped?"

I drew a deep breath, intending to tell her what happened, but the words wouldn't come. My breath hitched, something caught in my throat, and just like that, my composure shattered into a thousand fragments. The next thing I knew, I had gone to pieces like a clay pot dropped to a floor of stone. "He was going to take my virtue," I sobbed. "He wanted to kill me. I can't stop thinking about it. I have nightmares."

Hildegard wrapped the dagger and set it aside, reaching for my hand. "Would you like me to pray with you?"

I couldn't answer, the sobs were coming out of me so fast.

"*Ave Maria*," she began. Her skin was paper thin. Torchlight danced around us. "*Gratia plena . . .*"

As she said the prayer, I took deep breaths, trying to calm myself, paying attention. Had she chosen the Ave Maria for a reason? It was still too dark for me to read her expression, but she spoke the prayer reverently, with feeling.

Out the windows of the keep, the stars were so bright and so many that I wondered if I was looking at all the souls of heaven as they watched over the earth. I wondered if my mother was one of them. If Rika was one of them, watching, waiting to see if I would avenge her death.

"Mother," I said. "I want to take my story to the king. I want to make sure Ulrich is punished. But he has already gone to the king with a false story that implicates *me*. I need your advice. I have no idea how to get the king to take the word of a woman like me over the word of a prince."

Hildegard's eyes flashed. She massaged her temples. I could tell she sympathized with my plight. She was silent for a long time, longer than I expected would be necessary for her to consider my request, as if she was working something out. I wondered what it was. Finally, she nodded, deciding. "The emperor—you should refer to him as *emperor*—is due to hold court at a nearby palace in three weeks' time. I have an audience with him the week after Easter. I could take you to see him myself."

I took a deep breath. The stars shone over the river outside. "Thank you."

Her posture straightened, and she opened her mouth.

I could tell she was about to dismiss me. This might be the only audience I would have with her for weeks. I needed to find out about the alrūne, the shrine. But I couldn't just come out and ask. I thought fast. "There's another matter on which I would seek your help."

She leaned forward, raising her eyebrows. Her expression was so knowing, I feared she would see right through me to my low birth, my heresy. "And what is that?"

"I've heard you're a great healer. I take two remedies, and I'm almost out of both. One is an oil to bring on my menses. I haven't started them yet. The other is a fruit that stops the fainting spells I've had since birth."

"Fainting spells." She shifted in her seat. "What sort?"

I told her what my spells were like—how the air around me thinned, the next world drew close, and my soul left my skin. She watched me closely, something passing over her face that I couldn't quite read in the dark. I described all the cures my parents tried, all the herbalists and holy healers we'd visited, the prayers and blessings and exorcisms. "It wasn't until after I began to eat a certain fruit, last year, that my spells—" I stopped myself. The word I was going to say was *changed*, but I bit it off at the last minute. If I said *changed*, she might ask how, and I didn't dare mention the figurine or the voice because she might think me possessed by a demon. "That I was cured. The fruit was a cure."

She watched me closely. "What fruit?"

"My grandmother called it alrūne."

Her eyes widened and she leaned forward, checking my eyes. There was an uneasiness in what she said next. "You eat alrūne."

"It's a cure. When I eat it, I don't have fainting spells."

"Do you have it blessed first?"

I shook my head, puzzled. "I didn't know I should."

Hildegard was silent for a long moment, and I saw something pass over her face. This time, I was certain I hadn't imagined it.

I summoned my courage. "Mother," I said. "Forgive my boldness, but do you eat alrūne yourself? I've seen the way your eyes glint sometimes during services."

She sat up straight, alarmed. "Haelewise of Gothel. Who taught you this?"

"The princess." I met her eyes, telling myself to be bold. I had to know. "You didn't answer my question, Mother. *Do* you eat it?"

She was silent for a long moment. Then she laughed, shaking her head, clearly shocked at my forwardness. "From time to time, I do, yes. If you must know. It helps with my headaches. I always have it blessed first."

"Mother—"

She held up a hand. "The cardinal says the alrūne grew from the same earth as Adam. He says it carries the devil's influence. We must destroy the fruit you harvested improperly. If the bishop finds out you're eating it, you'll be excommunicated or worse."

I shook my head with a sudden burst of anger. I wouldn't allow anyone else to take my alrūne away from me. I had already made that mistake. "No," I said. "I won't."

Hildegard looked at me, startled. She watched me long enough that I realized how uncommon it must be for anyone to refuse her. Then she closed her eyes, as if she were listening to distant music.

After a moment, she smiled a sad smile. "What a strong will you have. You remind me of my old friend Richardis."

Her voice hitched, and she bowed her head, overcome. When she finally looked up, I knew from her expression that Richardis was dead.

"I'm sorry for your loss."

She nodded. "It's been years. I thought I could speak of her without—" Her voice caught. "Even after all these years, I am too attached."

The grief on her face was so great, it was difficult to watch. She balled her hand into a fist. Her knuckles went white. I heard the sound of them cracking.

After a moment, she regained her composure. "Your grand-mother. Who is she?"

I drew a deep breath. "You know her, actually. Her given name is Kunegunde."

"Kunegunde. I should've known." She gazed at me steadily, as if she was deciding whether to say more. Then she shook her head, pursuing a separate thought. "You resemble her in more ways than one. What color were your eyes when you were born?"

"Black," I said.

She watched me steadily. "Before you took the alrūne, did you have sensitivity to light?"

"Yes," I said. "How do you know?"

"I have it too," she said simply.

I blinked back at her, shocked.

She walked over to the wax tablet to write something down. She began writing on her tablet, muttering to herself in Latin. "*Oculi nigrim, pallid complexionis.* How old are you?"

"Seventeen."

She made a note.

"Might I ask what you're doing?"

"Cataloging your temperament." She put down her stylus. "I'll prepare an oil to bring on your menses. You're far too old not to have had them. It isn't healthy for all that waste inside you to keep building up. As for the alrūne, we have a number of the plants in our garden. I'll have Solange show you how to harvest them and cleanse them. I'll have her take you to the spring we use for holy water."

The spring? Near the shrine? I took a deep breath, trying to hide my eagerness to see the ruins.

"I'll prepare you a tincture from the root," she was saying. "There are no fruits, unfortunately, this time of year."

I nodded, disappointed. Of course there would be no fruit yet this time of year, but I had hoped they would have some dried. "Will the root have the same effect as the fruit?"

She nodded slowly.

"Does blessing the plant alter its effects?"

She nodded again. "Oh, yes."

"How?"

"You'll see." She smiled. "Forgive me. My headache grows worse. I will pray to He-Who-Is that your sleep tonight is untroubled. I'll send Solange in the morning with the oil."

CHAPTER TWENTY-FIVE

Back in the guesthouse, I stripped down to my shift and began my bedtime ritual—bathing, combing my hair, and getting into my bed, reaching into my sack to take a bite of alrūne. The act had become so habitual, I almost forgot that Hildegard had told me to stop. When I remembered, I sat up in bed, holding the fruit in my palm, trying to decide whether to heed her advice. Tomorrow, I would be leaving the abbey grounds. My mother might be able to speak to me beyond the wall. I went to bed without eating it, but my thoughts raced and I found myself unable to sleep until I took a bite.

The rap at my door as I dressed the next morning startled me. Solange stood outside the guesthouse holding an ampulla, stoppered and filled with a gleaming pink oil. "Here you go," she said, handing me the ampulla. "Mother Hildegard asked me to confiscate the rest of your alrūne to be destroyed."

A fierce possessive feeling surged in my breast, but I mastered myself quickly and made myself nod, going calmly to my sack. Fumbling through it for the alrūne, I decided I was unwilling to part with both of the fruits I had left. I smiled at Solange and handed her one with an obedient smile, leaving the other hidden at the bottom.

Solange told me to meet her after terce so she could show me how to harvest the plants properly and cleanse them at the spring.

As soon as Solange was gone, I lay down on my cot, pulled up my shift, and rubbed the oil onto my skin. The ointment was pungent, filling the air with the essence of crushed rose petals, white dock, and an unfamiliar scent. When my skin was slick, I smoothed

my dress down and stared at the ceiling, a ridiculous hopefulness in
my breast. I had long ago given up hope on Kunegunde's unguent,
though I had been using it for months. To put my faith in another
remedy was a self-deceit I thought I knew better than to indulge.
All my life I had been going to alleged saints and healers whose
miracles never quite came through.

But the heart is a traitorous thing. It wants what it wants. As I lay
among the scent of rose and white dock, I allowed myself to fanta-
size about Matthäus. He and Phoebe had quarreled; he'd left their
cottage in a rush to seek an annulment. When the bishop refused
to grant it, he went to the king. The king was sympathetic, having
sought an annulment from his first wife, Rika's mother. Matthäus
went back home a free man, where I found him in the tailor's shop
after I left court. I entreated him to come with me to my hut so we
could talk in private. Soon, he was holding my hands in the cupboard, kissing me, and more. The rose oil had worked by then, and
when I told him I had come of age, he asked me to marry him. It
was such a pretty delusion, I didn't want to let it go.

On my way to the cloister for terce, I worried Hildegard would
be able to tell I'd eaten the alrūne the night before. Then I realized
I was being foolish. At Gothel, it had taken days for the golden eye
color to fade completely.

When I met Solange in the garden, I pretended not to know
where the alrūne grew. I let her lead me toward the patch. As we
walked, I smelled the faint odor of parsley, the bitter scent of some
impossible-to-identify budding green. Sunlight streamed through
the clouds, glittering on the walking stones.

"The alrūne is over there," Sister Solange said, pointing out the
patch I had seen before.

Remembering Athanasia's comment as we passed the plants that
tempered the desires of the flesh, it occurred to me with amusement that if I wanted to stay at the abbey, I should probably sneak
back out here at night and eat *all* of them.

"We have permission to harvest two plants," Solange said, kneeling before the bed.

The garden was quiet, apart from chattering birds. There was no one around but us. As I knelt beside Solange, squinting, I noticed the patch had a trenchant smell as if its soil had recently been turned with manure.

She nodded at the two largest alrūne plants. "These look like they have the most developed roots. To cleanse them, we'll have to leave the abbey. There's a spring on the other side of the hill. We'll leave the roots in its water for a day and a night so their impurities will be cleansed. Then, we'll have the priest bless them, and Mother Hildegard will make you a tincture."

I peered at the plants suspiciously, reminding myself I still had one dried fruit left if the root tincture didn't work.

When I met Solange's eyes, she smiled at me and pulled a pair of gloves from her bag. "Why gloves?" I asked, thinking about how many times I'd touched the fruit on the way here without wearing any.

"Alrūne is poisonous," Sister Solange said, smoothing the leather fingers of her gloves. So Kunegunde hadn't been lying. "The seeds are the worst."

My heart skipped a beat. "The seeds?"

She nodded.

The walk my mother went on the night before she took ill. Did she go looking for an alrūne patch to harvest wild fruit for their seeds? I remembered the lucky gloves she always wore to garden, how full of holes they were. If my mother handled the seeds when she planted them in our garden, that could have been what made her ill. "What are the symptoms of alrūne poisoning?"

Solange looked grim. "Yellow skin. Fevers. Swelling. A woman came to us, once, who ate the seeds by accident. Hildegard tried everything to flush the poison out. The juice of sysemera, betony, and rue pounded in a mortar, mixed with garden spurge and followed by a draught of hydromel usually works to expel any poison, even arsenic. But the woman was dead within three months. After we buried her in the cemetery, an alrūne patch sprouted from her grave. That's where we got these plants."

My mouth went dry. The earth beneath me began to spin. The sun beat down. Had my mother *eaten* the seeds? I remembered the tale of the golden apple, her request that she be buried in the garden. The alrūne patch that grew there the next spring.

She hadn't planted them. She had—

The truth was too difficult for me to bear.

Sister Solange saw the tears in my eyes and misunderstood. "It's a sad tale. That it is. God rest her soul. Agnes, her name was." A fly buzzed around her head. "It's not true, you know, what they say about the roots. They don't scream when you pull them from the earth."

I wiped my eyes with my shirtsleeve, attempting to get a hold of myself.

"I've harvested dozens. They never make a sound."

The spade she pulled from her bag was iron, the sort of fine tool a blacksmith forged in one piece. As Solange excavated the soil around the first plant's roots, I remembered the spade my mother used. A wooden thing with a knot of rope connecting handle to trowel. With my inner ear, I heard the song she used to sing while she gardened. *Sleep until morning, my dear one. Eostre leaves honey and sweet eggs—*

What would it be like to love someone so much, you would sacrifice yourself?

I must've stared into space for a long time. When I blinked and came awake, the abbey garden came into focus. Sister Solange's digging had exposed a root: a gray, misshapen thing. She reached into the dirt with her gloved hand to uproot the plant. There was no sound apart from the snapping of tendrils and spattering of dirt. The root was less human-shaped than the one in Kunegunde's book, resembling a gray carrot more than a man.

The second plant allowed itself to be harvested in silence too. Squinting, I watched her dust off a more typical specimen of the root with a knotted head, a trunk, tendril-like arms, and carroty legs. Solange met my eyes as she plopped it into her bag. "Is your mount stabled here? The spring is far enough away that we'll want to ride."

I followed her through the gate, swallowing my anxiety about leaving the abbey, trying to summon my earlier excitement that I would get to see the shrine. The next world fell away as we descended the stairs. I fell behind Solange, pulling my hood down over my face to hide not only my identity but also my tears.

We found Nëbel housed in the blessedly dim second stall, nibbling on a bag full of hay. The sight of her made my heart swell. Her whicker was kind, and her large eyes seemed to sympathize with the wreck that my life had become. "Did you miss me, girl?" I whispered.

She nuzzled my hand.

I remembered what Rika told me about how well she had cared for Nëbel. This was probably the longest she's been stabled without exercise, I realized, with a pang of guilt.

"Ho, there, miss," a voice from behind me said. "She's yours?"

I turned and met the eyes of the stablehand, a reedy man with ruddy cheeks.

"Beautiful thing, she," he said. "Anxious, but sweet as clover."

Solange cleared her throat, as if she disapproved of my chatting with him. "Bring us two caparisons and saddle cloths."

The stablehand nodded and disappeared. The caparison he brought for Nëbel was bright white. She stood still for him as he put it on her, followed by a bridle with well-ornamented bosses and reins and a saddle. She made a neighing sound as I stepped into the stirrups, flicking her tail at a fly as we rode out of the barn. Ahead of me, Solange sat astride a chestnut mare.

"The spring is north of here," she called back as we rode, "through the woods and up the hill."

My earlier excitement about the shrine was gone. There was nothing I could do about it. My mother's song echoed in my mind. I was glad Solange had ridden ahead of me so we didn't have to make conversation. I couldn't believe that my mother would take her own life.

I followed Solange through the woods, noting tearfully how the next world drew close as we rode uphill through the dense trees. As we approached the top of the hill, I realized I could sense the mist here, shimmering and soothing, at the threshold. Tears filled my eyes, and I smiled, despite the shock I'd just received.

Not long after I heard the burbling of water up ahead, we passed several stone slabs leaning against the trunk of a tree. Alongside them were stacked some fragmented blocks of stone and a crumbling dais. My hair stood on end as we approached, and I nearly jumped from my horse. I could see faded symbols on the stones. "Wait," I told Solange. She pulled on her reins.

I tethered Nëbel and walked to the stacked stone blocks. Some of them were marked with grooves shaped like birds in flight, which recalled the designs on my mother's mirror and the water-*spiegel* at Gothel. Behind them lay a cracked statuette of a woman. She looked like she'd been struck with a hammer, but her destroyer had been careless. Although her body had been fractured, I could still make out some of its parts. She was naked, and her breasts had once been large. In the rubble, I could make out wings, the remnants of her face. Her forehead and eyes were still intact. Staring into her eyes, I was stricken with anger that someone had smashed her likeness. It was sacrilege.

I turned to Solange, unable to hide my fury. "Who smashed this?"

"Brother Volmar, I believe, although it might have been the archbishop when he came to bless the grounds."

"Does Mother Hildegard really want to incorporate some of these stones into the abbey?"

Solange went pale. "How do you know of that?"

"I overheard a conversation."

"In the *lingua ignota*?"

I closed my eyes. "I've pieced some of it together."

"You just got here, miss!"

"Do you know what her purpose is in incorporating them? Why would she want to do that? She's Christian."

Solange wouldn't answer. She had gone pale as a ghost.

I glared at the smashed effigy of the goddess, outraged at whoever had smashed her likeness. The figurine in my coin-purse thrummed. The air went even more taut. My skin began to tingle.

When I touched the figurine, tendrils of mist began to unfurl into existence in the air around me, silvery whorls that caressed my face and arms. I was filled with the same love I felt when the mist embraced me at Gothel. So great, so wide, I gasped at the weight of it. But swirling beneath that endless love was a cacophony of feeling: outrage and ferocity, pride and power, greed and desire.

Put me back together, the familiar voice commanded, louder than I had ever heard her speak, her voice a furious hum.

The veil slipped shut. I worked to regain my bearings. The chaos of feeling haunted me, like a dream I couldn't shake off.

Put me back together? I thought finally. Me?

Solange was staring at me. I couldn't think, I couldn't speak, I couldn't even breathe, the insight hurt so much. I couldn't deny it any longer. I had been telling myself stories, all this time. The voice that spoke to me wasn't my mother. It was *the* Mother.

A low keen escaped my throat. I felt no joy that the goddess had come to me; instead, I was desolate that my mother hadn't. The apparitions, the voice, the mist, I thought. Was none of it her?

Solange hurried toward me. "Lady Haelewise? Are you all right?"

Sobs racked me, and I doubled over. It was as if my mother had died all over again. Nëbel whinnied, pulling at her tether, wild-eyed. "Whoa." Solange tried to calm her.

Solange reached for my hands, but I pushed her away. After a moment, the wave of grief began to subside. I took a deep breath, trying to master myself. "Forgive me," I told Solange. "I lost my mother not so long ago. My grief is unpredictable."

Solange nodded, her eyes widening. For a moment, I thought I saw a knowing expression, but I couldn't be sure, it passed so quickly. I wondered if she knew something I didn't.

She squeezed my hands and got back on her horse. "The spring isn't far."

Taking a deep breath, I mounted Nëbel and followed Solange, slouched atop my horse. We soon came upon a dense stand of trees where the spring burbled cheerfully, without regard for the terrible ache in my heart. Solange dismounted, then bent over the spring, pulling the alrūne from her bag. Hands still gloved, she tied them together with a small length of rope. Bubbles floated to the surface as she sank the roots down, weighting them with a stone. For some reason, watching the roots disappear, I had to suppress another sob.

"I'll come back tomorrow evening to retrieve them," Solange promised.

I followed her back through the woods, overcome by a desperate sadness.

I spent the next day in the guesthouse except for meals, tossing and turning in my bed. I couldn't stop thinking about my mother. My revelation at the shrine had dredged up my memories of her on her sickbed. The physician's red draught dribbling down her chin, the blue kitten I pretended to pet with her. I wanted desperately to believe it was *she* who'd spoken to me all this time, that *she* had appeared to me in the garden, but I didn't want to delude myself.

I was so sick with grief, I couldn't bear to speak to anyone. When Solange stopped by to let me know the alrūne roots were drying, I made her tell me through the door. I even asked Walburga to leave my meals outside.

When I poked my head out to retrieve my evening meal, the light hurt my eyes. I hadn't eaten alrūne the night before, knowing I'd be stuck in the abbey, where my mother—or *the* Mother— couldn't reach me. I knew my light sensitivity would come back, of course, but I wasn't ready for how upset it would make me. By the time I brought the food inside, I'd lost my appetite.

On the second day after I visited the shrine, my grief ebbed. I didn't feel well enough to leave the guesthouse, but I felt well enough to get out of bed. I spent the day reading a Latin primer Athanasia had given me, trying to make peace with what I'd discovered. Many times that day, I reached for the figurine and prayed to the Mother for comfort. I figured since it was she who'd comforted me all this time, perhaps she could comfort me now, but apparently, the blessing on the abbey grounds still made that impossible.

On the third day, Solange informed me that the roots were blessed and ready to be pulverized. She took me to the infirmary to show me how to pound them into a powder. She filled a phial with a tincture and showed me how much to take. I dissolved the tincture in a cup of water and drank it right away, hopeful that it would fix my sensitivity to light. An hour later, my stomach convulsed, and I had to run back to the guesthouse to use the chamber pot. The tincture restored a faint golden color to my irises, but I was queasy for the rest of the day.

The next morning, I couldn't keep down my breakfast. As I walked to prime, my head spun. The abbey seemed brighter. The air around me had been suffused with a dizzying light.

What happened next shouldn't have surprised me. My new curative was prepared by an abbess, and I was standing in a Christian chapel. But I had become so accustomed to the monotony of services, when I felt the chill, I was startled.

I straightened in my pew. The air felt weighted, tense, like the air before a lightning storm. The presence I sensed at the threshold was powerful, paternal, strong. A vertiginous light filled the chapel, filling me with a love that felt both ancient and welcoming. I knew immediately whose presence I was feeling—the Father—but it set me off-balance.

Help us, he commanded, in a voice as deep as thunder.

CHAPTER TWENTY-SIX

After prime, I felt light-headed, confused. I paced the guesthouse, unable to quell the nervous energy that thudded in my chest. Who did the Father mean when he said, "Help *us*"? My hands shook, and I felt inexplicably afraid, almost *suspicious*, of his presence. I couldn't explain my misgivings, but I couldn't talk myself out of them. The Father was supposed to be benevolent. His presence had seemed loving, kind, but my heart beat too fast when I thought of him, and the walls of the guesthouse seemed nauseatingly close. Instead of ecstatic, I found myself disquieted. The more I thought about it, the more I wondered if my experiences with my earthly father were responsible for my misgivings.

The insight did nothing to relieve my unease. Nor did it fix the nausea brought on by the tincture. By terce, I was so sick, I couldn't leave the guesthouse if I wanted to. Clutching the chamber pot, I tried to distract myself by thinking over what I'd learned about Hildegard, about the shrine. Considering the rapture I saw on the sisters' faces during services and the extent of the alrūne patch in the garden, I began to wonder if Hildegard was giving her daughters the tincture. I wondered how long ago the shrine was built, what the people who built it were like, and what had happened to make this place thin.

By that night, my queasiness had subsided somewhat, and I hoped the next day would be different. As I drifted off to sleep, I clutched the figurine. I still couldn't believe what my mother had done; memories of her continued to plague me. The Father's voice echoed in my head, but I couldn't make sense of his command. I prayed for the Mother to tell me what I was supposed to do at the abbey, how she wanted me to put her back together. Did she mean the broken pieces of her effigy, or something else? I begged her to send me these answers in a dream, since she couldn't reach me in waking life, but no such dreams came. Her silence—her absence here—gutted me. More and more, I wanted to leave the abbey.

The next morning, I poured a smaller amount of the tincture into my cup, but after I took it in my morning draught, the dizziness and nausea came back stronger than ever. The Father's light was no longer limited to the chapel. It was everywhere, unavoidable and vertiginous. It filled the guesthouse, even with the windows closed. A love so holy, so unconditional and accepting, it felt incomprehensible. I lay on my cot, the abbey going round and round, struck by a dizziness so strong I couldn't move.

On the second night after I started taking the tincture, someone knocked on the door of the guesthouse. My vertigo had faded as the sun set, just as it had the night before. I was already in bed, relieved the spinning of the guesthouse had stopped, my mother's figurine in hand. I dressed quickly, putting the bird-mother in my pouch where no one would discover her. Running a brush through my hair, I looked at my dim reflection in the shattered mirror. My eyes were wide. Palest gold. My black hair floated frizzy from my crown.

"Miss?" The door opened. It was Solange.

I put the mirror down.

"Mother Hildegard would see you now."

I put the mirror away and wrapped my head in a scarf. Out the door I followed her through the shadowy garden.

In the keep, Hildegard sat in one of the two chairs before an open window. The room was dark. All of the other shutters were closed. The torches on the wall weren't lit. From the landing of the staircase, I could see the waxing moon through the window. An iron lantern brightened the floor around Hildegard's chair. She looked at me, her face a mess of lantern-shadow. "You've been taking the tincture?"

I took a deep breath. "Yes, Mother."

"Do you feel him?"

I nodded, trying to hide my unease. "He spoke to me."

She broke into a dazzling smile, beaming, her face overflowing with joy and happiness. She patted the chair beside her, and I sat. "What did he say?"

"He asked for my help."

She reached for my hand and squeezed it, leaning into the lantern-light. Her eyes glowed the faintest gold. Her expression was kind, open. She smiled encouragingly. "I have prayed on your arrival here."

"You have?"

She nodded. "The Living Light spoke to me. He told me to take you in. When we go to the king, I will be better able to protect you if I can introduce you as a postulant."

My mouth fell open. Athanasia saying I should take the veil was one thing. Hildegard could actually make it come true. I stared at her, speechless. I was a terrible candidate for holy life. The Father's light unsettled me. I was more comfortable with shadow. I was filled with resentment, the desire for human touch, and revenge. I longed to have children, to join the circle, to live the life my mother couldn't. Offered another path, I found myself even more certain about the one I was following.

My feelings must've shown on my face. Hildegard's expression was disappointed. "You don't want holy life?"

The lantern flickered. I didn't. I knew this clear as day, but I couldn't afford to alienate her. I set the question aside, trying to find a safe way to explain my reservations. "Have you ever eaten *unblessed* alrūne?"

Hildegard fell silent. Her eyes widened.

The shock on her face made me feel defiant. "Why do you want to incorporate the stones from the shrine?"

Hildegard didn't respond. She drew a deep breath. Outside, the waxing crescent moon was bright. There were gossamer clouds drifting past it. After a moment, she sighed and met my eyes, lowering her voice until it was barely audible. "What I'm going to say next is not something I speak of freely. I only speak of it to my most trusted daughters. I'm only telling you now because I want you to trust me. Do you understand?"

I nodded, hopeful that she would finally unravel some of the mysteries that had plagued me here. "I won't tell anyone."

"Good," she sighed. She opened her mouth several times to answer, then closed it, as if deciding against a rhetorical approach. When she finally spoke, her voice was quiet. "I've always sensed a feminine presence at the edge of things, a holy greening power that makes things grow and heal. But that power never spoke to me until a year ago, when I forgot to have my alrūne blessed and started hearing a woman's voice at the shrine. The voice commanded me to incorporate the stones."

My jaw dropped. "You didn't think it was a demon?"

She started to laugh then stopped herself, as if she couldn't quite decide whether she found my question amusing. "That was *exactly* what I thought. Only the Living Light had ever spoken to me before that day. I prayed desperately to He-Who-Is to banish her. But instead of offering me salvation, the Lord struck me down with a grave illness. He punished me for questioning her. During the worst of this illness, while I tossed and turned, he sent me a vision of a woman enthroned in a wild forest. She was shadowy, winged, snakes coiled at her feet. She was clothed in swarms of golden bees. Her expression was almost *beatific* at first. I thought I was seeing St. Mary or the Church." Hildegard's expression turned inward, and then she shuddered slightly. "Then her expression turned *furious*. I understood that whoever—*whatever*—she was, she was the source of the voice I'd heard, and she was angry I wanted to disobey her."

Shadows? Wings? Bees? My mind reeled. My hands felt suddenly cold. I remembered what Kunegunde said about the ants that ate her offering, the buzzing of the voice that spoke to me. I opened my mouth but faltered, afraid to speak my thoughts aloud.

"I have seen many strange things with my inner eye, but that vision is by far the strangest." She shook her head, her eyes full of bafflement. Then she turned to me, her voice hesitant. "My illness persisted until I wrote the archbishop for permission to incorporate the stones. Then it ended, as quickly as it had come. Did a woman's voice speak to you here?"

I thought I heard eagerness in her tone. "At the shrine."

She nodded, once, quick. She had been expecting that answer. "What did she say?"

I drew a deep breath. "She told me to put her back together."

Hildegard's expression turned pensive, almost troubled. The moment stretched out so long, I wondered frantically if she saw something heretical in my answer, if she was going to withdraw her offer to escort me to court. Finally, she drew herself up, deciding something. "My offer still stands," she said, meeting my gaze. Relief coursed through me that I hadn't alienated her. "I was deeply saddened when your grandmother made the decision, so long ago, to—" She paused, searching for the right words, her voice measured. "To follow another path. She was like a sister to me. It is clear you are a seer. There are things I do not know about the history of this place. Perhaps you could help me to understand."

I stared at her dumbly. My certainty that I should reject her offer faltered. It meant something different now. The Mother had spoken to her. If she incorporated the stones, perhaps the Mother would be able to speak to me here. No matter what, I needed Hildegard's protection when I went to the king. My head spun. "May I think on it?"

Hildegard smiled. The wrinkles around her eyes crinkled. "Of course. It is a decision of great magnitude."

I was about to take my leave when I realized I had one more

question for her. Even with her protection, I was intimidated by the prospect of speaking at court. "I'm still uneasy about my audience with the king—or, rather, emperor. Would you consider teaching me how to speak to him so I won't say anything improper?"

A slow smile spread across Hildegard's face. "Of course. That I can do well, whether you choose to join us or not."

I stayed with her in the keep until late, talking about how I should carry myself, how an emperor would expect to be addressed. I told her about my likeness to the princess, and we came up with a plan to use it to my advantage. She made me practice my story over and over, correcting me, asking the questions the king would ask. "Tell the truth," she said, again and again. "Frederick is a brilliant diplomat. He will know if you leave anything out."

I tried not to think too hard about this.

CHAPTER TWENTY-SEVEN

Four days before my visit to the king's court, I found a rust-colored stain in my undergarments. Staring at it, I felt a new kind of vertigo. My stomach lurched with disbelief. The rose oil had worked. When I told Walburga, she squealed and clapped her hands, then offered to get me some blood moss to put in my undergarments. As I waited for her to come back with it, I sat on the edge of my bed, staring at the stained cloth, trying to sort through my feelings. I had been praying for this moment forever. I should've been ecstatic, but the happiness I felt was surprisingly distant.

As the day we planned to travel to see the king drew near, I agonized over my next conversation with Hildegard. I knew she would ask me for my decision about whether I would join the abbey, and I had no idea what I was going to say. My mind told me to agree to become an initiate so she could offer her protection, but my heart knew I wouldn't be satisfied with life at the abbey. Meanwhile, my dizziness and nausea worsened. The Father's light had become so bright, I couldn't see anything else. I began to doubt my ability to travel and tell my story to the king if my dizziness and nausea didn't subside.

The night before my audience, I lay in bed in my shift, agonizing over what to do. Since we were leaving the abbey, I wanted to go back to eating the alrūne from my mother's garden, but I was hesitant to break my word to Hildegard after what happened with Kunegunde. I eyed the tincture, wondering how small an amount I could get away with dissolving in my morning drink, how pointless it all was when the Father made me so uneasy. I thought of the miller's son, his weight in my arms—the way Hildegard had shuddered when she told me about her dream.

The fruit at the bottom of my sack called to me.

The next morning, when the sun peeked through the crack in the shutters, I felt better than I had in weeks. Instead of the Father's dizzying light, I felt only the closeness of the next world, the tension in the air. My only complaint was the nagging unease I felt about what I was going to tell Hildegard. Leaving the tincture untouched on the table, I turned my thoughts to what I would wear for my audience with the king. My best clothes, of course, the dress and cloak from Matthäus. I brushed my hair, counting a hundred strokes like the princesses did in my mother's tales. I wrapped the dagger in my sack and, saying a quick prayer, dropped the dried fruit and figurine in my pouch.

I checked my reflection in my mother's mirror. My brushed black hair was wild, frizzing out from my head in shattered waves. My eyes glowed much brighter than the day before, gold and frantic. In the deep red cloak I looked regal, strange, like the seer I supposed I had become.

When Walburga arrived, moments later, with my breakfast, she beamed when I invited her in. "You're feeling better, miss!" she said happily. "Just in time. Isn't your audience with the king today?"

I nodded, tearing into my food. I was ravenous. I hadn't been well enough to eat in weeks. But halfway through the meal, I was hit with a bout of nervousness that my lie would be found out.

"Lady Haelewise," Walburga said when I stopped eating. "What's wrong? I thought you felt better."

I met her eyes, trying to decide how honest to be. Her expression was open, completely without judgment. I lowered my voice. "I've decided to tell Mother Hildegard I'll take the veil."

"Why does that trouble you?"

"I'm already having second thoughts."

Walburga reached for my hands. Her whisper was almost inaudible. "You are wise to declare that intention before you see the king, no matter what."

I hugged her back. "Thank you for saying so."

She nodded, but her reassurance didn't relieve my unease.

"I'll see you when you get back," she said, hugging me on her way out.

There were tears in her eyes as she left the guesthouse. I watched her go, my own eyes wet. Some sixth sense made me fear I wouldn't see her again.

Grabbing my things, I found Sister Athanasia at her table in the gatehouse, reading an illuminated manuscript. She nodded when I appeared at the doorway, stood, and walked me to the gate. "Mother Hildegard is already downstairs."

The bolts made their solemn noise as she pushed them aside. Her keys jangled as she clicked open the lock. She held the door open, then whispered ardently, "Godspeed."

I hugged her, overcome by another wave of anxiety.

Athanasia must've read my expression. "Mother Hildegard wouldn't let you go if she wasn't certain she could protect you."

I smiled a sad smile, pretending her words gave me comfort, and stepped through the gate. The tension in the air dissolved, and I felt the next world fall away.

As I descended the steps to the lower level, my nervousness returned. On the lower level I was assaulted by the scent of manure emanating from the stable. When I lifted the door-flap, a horse-fly buzzed out, and an even stronger variant of the smell hit my nostrils. I brought my sleeve to my face to mask it. The stable-hand stood before a stall, speaking softly to a dappled horse. "Lady Haelewise?" he said as he looked up. I nodded. "Your horse is ready."

Nëbel's eyes glittered when she saw me. She lifted her muzzle and let out a whicker, nuzzling my palm, snorting hot breath. She pranced, shifting her weight, as if she couldn't stand anymore to be still.

"It's good to see you, girl," I whispered.

She nuzzled me and whinnied again as I untethered her and led her from the stall. There was a nervous kick in her step as I put my bag on her tack and mounted her.

"The procession is waiting," the stablehand said.

His words brought me back to myself. I guided Nëbel through the door-flap. I took a deep breath, grateful for the fresh air. Clopping along the stepping-stones, we passed through the abbey gate.

Outside, four guards in leather jerkins waited on horseback. I smiled, hoping they would protect me if we ran into Ulrich's men. A fine carriage sat beneath the oak with black wooden wheels and golden accents. Draped over the top was a bright white canopy embroidered with a golden cross, darkened only by the shadows of leaves.

The abbey guards turned as we passed through the gate and Nëbel's hooves hit the steps. One of them gestured at the carriage. "Mother Hildegard is waiting."

I slipped off my saddle and handed Nëbel's reins to a guard. She whinnied in protest, tossing her head from side to side, and I was struck with a pang of guilt. I cupped her face with my hand and apologized.

The carriage door-flap rustled as I pulled it aside. Hildegard and Brother Volmar were waiting within. Daylight filtered through the canopy, illuminating the interior of the carriage. I sat on one of the benches, unsettled. Hildegard wore a black habit and scapular with a white wimple and black veil. No jewels, this day, no crown. She smiled at me. "Brother Volmar, this is Haelewise." She reached out to brush a blade of grass from the skirt of my cloak. "Haelewise, Brother Volmar is coming along so that record may be made of my audience with the emperor."

"Blessings to you," he said.

"And to you, Brother," I replied automatically.

"The business I have with the emperor is delicate," Hildegard said when I was settled in my seat. "He is displeased with a letter the pope sent him. He won't take what I have to say well. We're hoping your news will improve his mood. He has been trying to identify his daughter's killer for weeks."

I cleared my throat, wondering whether I'd misheard. "Pardon me, Mother, but did you just say the emperor is displeased with the pope?"

She frowned. "I did, in fact."

"That seems rather bold."

She laughed, a strange little trill. "He's a proud man. Have you made your decision?"

Here it was. I had known this moment was coming, planned for it, but now that it was here, I felt paralyzed by indecision. The moment stretched out. I closed my eyes, summoning my courage.

"I'll take the veil," I said finally, feeling uneasy about the lie even before I finished speaking it.

Hildegard didn't seem to notice, or perhaps she ascribed my anxiety to the weight of my choice. The love in her eyes, the joy, as she smiled at me, seemed almost infinite. "You have no idea how much this gladdens me, daughter."

Daughter. The word brought tears to my eyes, and my breath caught in my throat. Stilling my heart, I smiled back, trying to look as if I felt no guilt.

CHAPTER TWENTY-EIGHT

The towers of the palace cast long shadows as I got out of the carriage. Mother Hildegard climbed out after me, and Brother Volmar followed her, muttering grumpily about his aching bones. On the
ride there, Hildegard had chattered on and on about life at the abbey,
the steps of becoming an initiate. I couldn't stop wondering what she
would do if she found out I'd only agreed to take the veil because I
needed her protection. I fretted over every gesture, every word, every
tiny sigh of acknowledgment, worried that each one might reveal my
plans to flee her protection as soon as it was no longer necessary. By the
time we arrived, the knot in my stomach was so tight, I was relieved
for the excuse to get out of the carriage. The afternoon sun beat down
on my arms as I stretched my legs, grateful. The heat was uncommonly strong, giving the world around me a summery haze.

I took Nëbel's reins, and she whinnied softly. I set my self-loathing
aside, trying to focus on the palace in front of me. Well-armed kingsguard stood watch outside the gatehouse. They eyed us calmly at
first, but a murmur passed through them as we drew near. One of the
guards paled, backing away and crossing himself.

"A ghost!" he said, pointing at me. "Sweet Mother of God, a ghost!"
He reached into his pouch and pulled out a holy cross. "*Pater Noster, qui
es in caelis, sanctificetur normen tuum—*"

I took a deep breath.

Behind us, in hushed voices, two kingsguard began to argue
about the identity of my horse.

The captain and two men left their stations to crowd me. "The
princess!" one of them said, pulling on the fabric of my cloak.

"It can't be," said another. "We buried her over a month ago!"

Beside me, Nëbel brayed, nervous.

I feared for a moment that she might panic. My thoughts raced. Anxiety fluttered in my chest. Then I stilled myself, remembering what I was supposed to say. "My name is Haelewise of Gothel," I called out, my voice echoing, resolute. "I am not the princess, but a seer come to help avenge her death."

The captain paused, looking me up and down. The others quieted, waiting to see what he would do. The captain watched me, crossing himself, his face still pale.

I surveyed the crowd. "I foresaw the princess's murder. I have an audience with his imperial and royal majesty to tell him who killed her."

"The girl speaks truth," Hildegard called from beside me.

The captain nodded slowly, his men following suit. One of them went through the gate and came back with a bald man in dark stockings. The bald man's tunic clung to his round belly. "Mother Hildegard, I presume?"

She nodded, just barely, hands clasped before her.

"Let them in," he said. "The emperor is expecting them."

The captain muttered under his breath but let us pass.

We followed the bald man through the gate.

Grapevines coated the outer palace walls. The courtyard was dotted with statues and pools. Our footsteps echoed ominously on the stones. Atop the outer walls, more guards patrolled. At the end of the courtyard, a rectangular building rose from the stones, a narthex sheltering heavy wooden doors.

Inside, torches blazed, crackling, on either side of a hall. Their flames scattered shadows on the floor, which seemed to dance with a life of their own. On the dais were two thrones on which sat the middle-aged king with the fiery red beard and his golden-haired second wife. Rika's stepmother, one of the circle of women who worshipped the Mother in secret, her eyes bright gold. *Queen Beatrice.* She was here with him.

My heart leapt. Another chance to join the circle, I thought. I just have to find a way to speak to her privately.

Beatrice wore a pale-blue dress, crown, and headscarf. Her golden braids, glittering as bright as her eyes, hung to her ankles. As we approached, I realized the reason the braids shone as they did was that they were interwoven with thread spun from gold. She was far younger than I expected, barely older than me, though she carried herself as if she were older. Laughing at something the king said, she seemed at first like the ideal woman—beautiful, feminine, her face modestly draped with undyed linen—until I looked closer and saw the spark in her eyes, the *defiance*, as if she dared anyone in the world to cross her.

I prayed she would notice my eye color, my eagerness to speak to her. How in the world do I get her alone, I wondered.

The king wore a large golden cross around his neck, a black tunic, and a burgundy cloak with golden stockings. On his head, he wore a huge jeweled crown with a giant sparkling cross at the forehead.

When we reached the front, I knelt as Hildegard had advised. "Your imperial and royal majesty."

The king peered at me. He blinked, once, twice, then bellowed, his voice breaking with emotion. "Is this some kind of trick?!"

Hildegard and Brother Volmar bowed their heads. The abbess took a deep breath. "No, your imperial and royal majesty. This is the seer I wrote you about, Haelewise of Gothel. She came to me with news of your daughter's death. I didn't mention her appearance in my letter because I knew you'd have to see it for yourself. I believe her resemblance to your daughter is a sign from He-Who-Is to heed her words in your quest to avenge Frederika's death."

The hall was still. Behind us, guards shifted their stance uneasily, waiting to see what the king said.

"Look at me," the queen commanded. Something passed over her face when she looked into my eyes. "Her nose is different, Frederick. And her eyes are golden."

Hope surged in me. So strong, I almost forgot why I was there. It took everything I had to lower my eyes and turn to the king, returning to the speech we'd rehearsed. "I apologize for my resemblance, your majesty. I hope it is not too painful that I should come to you so soon after your daughter's death."

I watched through my lashes for his reaction. After a moment, the king nodded. "You may rise."

I stood. His eyes bore into mine. One of the jewels in his crown shone so brightly, it was hard to look at him directly. A dazzling red jewel with a strange white glow.

He shifted in his seat, his knuckles white against the arms of his throne, his jaw clenched.

The queen reached out to put her hand on his. He waved it away. "Tell us what you know," he said, glowering at me.

Bowing my head, I opened my mouth to begin the speech I'd practiced with Hildegard. "Your imperial and royal majesty, I throw myself at the mercy of this court. I am your most humble servant." I could see the king's eyes on me. My heart thudded in my breast. I reached for the figurine in my pouch, praying that I would get this right. "I bring difficult tidings. I dreamed of your daughter's death before she was murdered."

He clutched the arm of his throne. The queen leaned forward, watching closely. I met her eyes. I thought I saw something flit across her face again. A wordless prayer rose in my breast.

Then I turned my attention back to the king, focusing on what Ulrich had done, until I was conscious only of my hatred.

"In my dream, I saw a masked man," I said bitterly. "He stabbed a girl in tattered robes whose face I could not see. Taking the form of a bird of prey, I descended upon him to rip him apart with my talons. I had this dream every night for many weeks."

The queen's expression betrayed nothing.

I drew myself up. "It was not until I was gathering herbs in the woods, one day, near my ancestral home, that I saw the masked man come upon your daughter. Forgive me, your imperial and royal majesty. I didn't recognize her because of her tattered clothing. I understand now that she had disguised herself as a peasant. The masked man, I could see now, was wearing Prince Ulrich's colors. His horse bore Prince Ulrich's banners. I heard him berate her for fleeing the castle, for betraying her betrothal to Prince Ulrich. He shot her with a Zähringen arrow to implicate the duke, but the dagger he used was unquestionably Ulrich's—"

The king stood. "Did Zähringen send you here? We heard about a Haelewise who was rumored to be his spy."

Hildegard put her hand on my shoulder. "Show him."

I pulled out the cloth-wrapped dagger, kneeling and offering it up. "In his hurry to get away, the killer dropped the weapon. I bring it to you as proof."

There was movement behind me. After a moment, a guard took the dagger from my hands and brought it to the king. The throne room was silent as he inspected it. He went white when he saw the insignia on the pommel cap. "The arrow," the king shouted. "Ulrich brought us the killer's *head*—"

"He could've stolen the arrow," the queen said. "Beheaded one of his own men. All he and Albrecht care about is power. I told you!"

"They were betrothed. I promised him Scafhusun. Why would he kill her?"

The king's disbelief shattered me. I had hoped the dagger would be enough evidence. I tried to think of another way to convince him. If I told him that Rika had handfasted another, he would understand why Ulrich had done what he did.

"Rika married a commoner," I said softly, head bowed, apologizing to Rika internally. *Forgive me. Ulrich must be punished.*

"What?!" the king thundered.

I drew a deep breath. If I played this right, I could indict Ulrich and still protect Daniel. "Ulrich found out. He killed both of them, but he only brought you her body."

Hildegard stiffened beside me, alarmed that I had strayed from the story I'd told her.

The king turned from the queen to me. I averted my gaze. When he finally spoke, his voice was controlled, restrained and tight with anger. "Why didn't you mention this before?"

"Your imperial and royal majesty." I bowed my head. "Forgive me. I didn't think it relevant."

"Why did you tell Ulrich you were a Kürenberg?"

"I was afraid to give my real name. I knew he was the killer."

The king glared at me. "Two weeks ago, a Kürenberger came to us to report that Prince Ulrich sent guards to his home. He said they were searching for a Haelewise of Kürenberg, whom they claimed was a Zähringen spy involved in my daughter's murder. He said you were anything but. He wanted to clear your name."

My heart sank. Was *that* why Matthäus's house was in disarray? No, I thought. No no no—

"Where? What happened? Did you take him into custody?" I asked, my voice pitching.

"Why do you care, if you are not a Kürenberg?"

I closed my eyes, trying to swallow my guilt. All I could think about was Matthäus. I made myself focus on what the king had said. He had asked me a question, why I cared. I decided to tell the truth. "I regret that my lie may have caused harm to others."

"You should have come to us earlier. We already issued a writ for Zähringen's death. If he's innocent—"

"I apologize, your majesty," I said with a low bow, feeling a sudden pang for the man who'd given Matthäus the paternoster beads. "My failure to come to you sooner was a mistake."

A long silence ensued.

The king sighed. "Bring me Ulrich!"

As several of the guards hurried out, Hildegard cleared her throat. "Your imperial and royal majesty, I pray that my daughter has been helpful. As you well know, there is another matter about which I would speak to you. Could I beg your attention to it now?"

The king blinked as if he'd forgotten she was there. "We have no time for your sermons now, holy lady. The question of my daughter's murder must be resolved first. Guards!" The guards on either side of the dais stepped forward, awaiting his command.

"Lock her in the west chambers."

My heart fell. I was going to be imprisoned? I turned to Beatrice, desperate. "My queen," I whispered fervently, trying to catch her attention. She met my gaze, her eyes flashing, aureate.

I thought fast, searching for something to say that would pique her interest without revealing my heresy to anyone else. I had to get her attention. My thoughts raced. The stories about her upbringing, the sorceress who raised her. Perhaps Hildegard didn't know them. It seemed that nobles sometimes dismissed such talk.

I smiled at the queen, trying to seem obsequious enough that no one else would know what I was getting at. I curtsied. "It's an honor to meet you. My mother spoke highly of your grandmother."

Beatrice blinked, raising her eyebrows so slightly I couldn't tell if I was imagining it.

Hildegard looked at me quizzically, then shook her head, apparently dismissing my statement as an innocent compliment. She turned to the king. "I would wait with my daughter, your majesty, if that is permissible."

"We will allow that." He turned to his guards. "See that they do not speak alone."

CHAPTER TWENTY-NINE

Two of the kingsguard locked us in the windowless west chambers, a dark and echoing place with a stone floor. As the guards lit the torches that lined the walls, a ridiculously ornate table came into view in the center of the room. It was wood, adorned with intricate engravings, a painting of the king's crest in the middle. Benches lined the walls. There were three doors leading into other rooms, no doubt as richly dressed. I sat on one of the benches, awash in a sea of fear and guilt that I had put Matthäus in danger.

Hildegard sat across from me, her expression frustrated. When she turned to me, her expression was stern. For a split second, I was afraid she was going to ask about my comment to Beatrice, but that wasn't what she wanted to talk about. "Why didn't you warn me that you gave Ulrich the wrong name? We could've prepared."

I blinked at her. That mistake was the last thing on my mind. I shrugged, irritated that she seemed more concerned about losing leverage than anything else. For someone who claimed to serve the house of God alone, she seemed awfully preoccupied with earning the king's approval. But now, more than ever, I needed her protection, so I couldn't afford to show my annoyance. "It slipped my mind. I'm sorry."

"And your story about Frederika's commoner husband." Her voice shook with frustration. "Is *that* true?"

Meeting her gaze, I realized how dangerous that disclosure had been. A holy woman had to be truthful. I nodded, bracing myself.

Her eyes were pleading, confused. "Why didn't you tell me?"

I blinked. Where Kunegunde would've gone silent and cold, the abbess was offering compassion, a plea for understanding. Guilt lurched in my chest. This was nothing. If only she knew all the *other* lies I'd told her. I drew a deep breath, deciding the best course here was to tell the truth. This was the sort of falsehood even a holy woman would condone. "The husband is real," I whispered. "But he's still alive. I'm trying to protect him."

"Oh," Hildegard said, her eyes widening. After a moment, she nodded, once, dismissing the subject, and I knew my deception was forgiven.

After that, I withdrew to one of the bedchambers early, worried that, in my exhaustion and emotional state, I would make a mistake that would further rouse Hildegard's suspicions. As I undressed, I thought over my audience with the king, fretting over how badly it had gone. How long would we be here? Where was Matthäus now? Was he all right? Had my statement piqued the queen's interest?

In bed, I prayed for the Mother to send me guidance, but I heard no voice and received no vision. I rubbed the figurine's curves, desperate to understand why she'd gone silent now, when I most needed her. There was no blessing on these grounds as far as I could tell. I fell asleep worrying feverishly over Matthäus's safety, feeling inexorably lost. Since Rika's death, I had followed the Mother's advice as best I could. What mistake had I made to end up trapped in these chambers? Why had my audience with the king gone so utterly wrong?

We were locked in those chambers for days. Each morning, the guards brought food, and I asked them if Ulrich had been found, but the answer was always no. During breakfast, Hildegard chattered happily about my imminent vows, as if there was no question that I would come back with her. I tried to act eager, but my plummeting mood made it more and more difficult as the days passed for me to keep up the charade.

Hildegard and Volmar spent most of their time at the central table, the monk taking dictation for the speculum Hildegard was working on, which they said was an encyclopedia of the hidden properties of all the elements of God's creation. After the guards brought dinner, Hildegard spent her evenings in her chamber in contemplation. I could hear her muttering prayers beneath the door.

As the days turned to weeks, the queen did not come, and my hope that I had captured her interest faded. I became desolate, unable to keep up the pretense that I wanted holy life. When Hildegard chattered about holy orders, I nodded politely. Hildegard and Volmar became increasingly impatient. One morning, during the third week of our confinement, I overheard them talking in the next room when they thought I was still asleep. Through the door, I heard Hildegard express doubts to the monk about my commitment to my vows. She wanted to know if he had noticed my interest fading. When he said he wasn't sure, she expressed concern that Ulrich hadn't been apprehended yet. She said he must've gone into hiding, and perhaps it was time for them to leave this place. During breakfast, I caught her watching me, her faint golden eyes measuring me up, as if she could decipher my true nature with observation. If she left without me, I wondered, would the king relegate me to some far worse prison? Was she the only thing stopping me from being cast into a dungeon?

For the rest of that day, I renewed my attempts to keep up the charade of my commitment to holy life. I tried to make myself useful to Hildegard and Volmar. I sat with them as they worked on their speculum, asking questions, trying to project an appearance of interest in holy work.

Not long after the evening change of guard, I was sitting on the bench listening to Hildegard describe the qualities of a rose quartz to Volmar when we heard footsteps outside.

A key clicked in the lock.

The queen hurried in, golden braids wrapped around her head like a crown. My heart soared as she turned to the guards. She had come, finally, after all this time. "Go," she said, waving the guards out. "Cast your lots in the hall."

The guards left quickly, no doubt relieved to escape the monotony of their post.

"Forgive me, Haelewise," she said, her eyes proud, regal, gold. "I wanted to come sooner, but I had to wait until both guards were mine. Who are you, really?"

Relief filled my heart. I sent up a quick prayer of thanks. "My name is Haelewise of Gothel, your imperial and royal majesty. I am the daughter of Hedda-the-Midwife and a fisherman whose name I will not say."

"She's a postulant at my abbey," Hildegard added.

The queen met my eyes, her brow furrowed. "But you are one of us—"

Volmar narrowed his eyes, suspicious. "One of who?"

Beatrice ignored him, turning to me and Hildegard. "You eat alrūne. Both of you. I see it in your eyes."

"We take a tincture made from the blessed root," Hildegard corrected her, glancing at the monk.

"I asked you a question," Volmar reminded Beatrice. "Answer me."

Beatrice's laughter tinkled, growing louder as she turned to him, her smile tight. "Let me remind you that you are standing in an imperial palace. I am the queen and empress. I can have you arrested for the pleasure of it."

Volmar turned very red, veins pulsing at his temples.

Beatrice smiled prettily, as if she was satisfied with his mortification. Then she turned to me. "Haelewise, the suspense is torment. Are you one of us or not?"

I drew a deep breath. This was it. My chance. But I couldn't ask to join the circle in front of Hildegard without abandoning my charade. If the queen rejected me, I would be left with nothing.

"Haelewise?" Hildegard asked, concerned. "Why do you pause? What does she mean?"

I closed my eyes, a sudden pressure at my temples. "I'm not one of you," I said, looking up to meet the queen's eyes. My voice echoed. "But I wish to be."

The chamber was quiet for a long moment.

The queen laughed, joyful, her eyes full of delight. "*Mervoillos!* How do you know of us?"

"From Frederika and Ursilda."

"Haelewise?" Hildegard asked, distraught. "What are you saying?"

I sighed a great sigh and reached into my pouch for the figurine, though I feared that to do so would alienate Hildegard once and for all. But I saw no other option, and if the figurine would help me win the queen's trust, it didn't matter what Hildegard thought.

"My mother gave me this," I said, holding it out.

"What is that?" Hildegard said, eyeing the charm in my hand.

Brother Volmar grabbed it, eyeing it with contempt. "It's a heathen abomination, like the one we smashed at the shrine!"

Volmar showed her the figurine. I watched Hildegard's face as she recognized what he was holding. For a second, I thought I saw a very complicated regret. Then Hildegard's face became a mask.

"We must destroy this immediately," Volmar said in a matter-of-fact voice, setting it on the table, looking about—I presumed for something to smash it with.

The queen's eyes widened when she saw what Volmar wanted to destroy. "You most certainly will not," she said, then turned to me. "I *thought* you were one of us," she laughed, a tinkling sound like bells.

"Hildegard," Volmar said suddenly, seething. "Your newest postulant is unfit. She's a heretic."

Beatrice smiled a tight smile. "You have no idea what she is. You think you do, but all you know is your Church's idea of her."

Volmar drew himself up, indignant. "Our God's ideas are all

there is." He gestured at the queen and Hildegard and me. "All of us, the ground we walk on, these gardens, this earth. Even the demon that lives in that *thing*"—he pointed at the figurine—"was created by God to test the faithful. If you deny that fact, then you shall find your place in hell."

Hildegard made a comment in the language of priests, her expression stern. The queen snorted. "*Qui beffe!*"

Before anyone could stop me, I took the figurine back.

Hildegard turned to me, her lips pressed tightly shut. "Heed Brother Volmar's words, Haelewise," she said. "There is truth in them."

Her eyes flitted briefly to mine, then fluttered shut. Volmar's bearing changed entirely as he watched Hildegard, his expression panicked. A split second later, she let out a soft moan and crumpled. He reached out awkwardly to steady her, his eyes flitting around for something to stabilize himself. Small though Hildegard was, Volmar was too frail to hold her upright for long. After a moment, Hildegard recovered, straightening in his arms. She shaded her eyes from the torchlight. She squinted at me, her voice hoarse. "The Living Light commands me to take you in." She glanced at Volmar, the figurine in my hand. "Repent, and you can come back with me to the abbey. Smash that demonic thing, confess, and the Lord your God will forgive."

The queen watched me, raising an eyebrow, the pale golden hairs that had come loose from her braids framing her face.

Hildegard waited to see what I would do. I knew she was trying to save me from being branded a heretic, but smashing the figurine was not an option. I held it tight. "Mother. I can't. My late mother gave it to me."

Hildegard glanced at Volmar, who looked scandalized. She shook her head. "It's the only way, Haelewise. You're being tested."

I stiffened, angry that she would say such a thing. "This is no test, Mother. The voice that speaks to me is no demon. You know as well as I do, there are other gods beside yours—"

Volmar gasped.

"A shadow as well as a light—"

Hildegard opened her mouth, as if my words were a battering ram that had slammed into her throat. Her eyes flitted from Volmar to the corners of the chamber, where shadows fell.

My whole body bloomed with chills. The air went taut. The voice I heard was no whisper, a furious sound like the humming of a thousand bees. *The god is the goddess—*

The queen fell to her knees, her eyes wide. She had heard it.

I could tell by the look that crossed Hildegard's face that she had heard it, too—or at least that she'd sensed some change in the otherworldly weather.

"What?" the monk asked the abbess. "What did I miss?"

Beatrice looked up, shaking her head. "*Une mervoille*, monk. Your demon spoke."

Brother Volmar went pale. He crossed himself.

Hildegard glanced sharply at the queen, her expression poisonous. Then she pressed her lips together tight, drawing herself up with a great deep breath. I will never forget the way she looked at me then, her eyes cold. She knew I'd lied to her, and she was hurt.

"You cannot come back with us now," she said in a heavy voice. "You have shown yourself to be a heretic."

Brother Volmar stormed off toward the door.

Hildegard paused behind him, leaning toward me, her voice low enough that the monk couldn't hear. "You are making a mistake," she whispered, her voice urgent.

I didn't know what to say. I couldn't escape my guilt. "I'm sorry," was all I said finally.

She glanced over her shoulder to make sure Volmar wasn't looking, then clasped my hand and squeezed it. The look on her face was stricken, sorrowful. I felt great sadness, a diminishing sense of possibility, as she walked out.

Tears stung my eyes. Her disappointment weighed like a stone around my neck.

The door closed. I drew myself up, trying to master my emotions. I had to focus my attention on the queen.

Beatrice was watching me, her expression awed. There were tears in her eyes. "That was beautiful."

I opened my hand and stared down at the figurine, her breasts, her wings. "Who is she, really? Sometimes she brings comfort. Other times, she frightens me. I can't understand it."

Beatrice laughed. "Some call her the goddess of death or vengeance. Others link her with love or death. In stories old, she's the wife of the Sun Father, the Moon that chases him through the sky. The truth is she's all of these. She's misunderstood. The Church only allows some of her aspects to surface—in St. Mary, the Holy Spirit—but they allow the Father to be himself, a whole, of love and vengeance and anger."

Her words hung in the air. I felt a chill, remembering what the Mother asked me to do at the shrine. *Put me back together.* All of a sudden it made sense. I looked up at the queen, awed, determined. "I want to take the oath."

The queen raised her eyebrows. "Your grandmother—the one you said you were with in the forest—that was Kunegunde? The Gothel in your name is her tower?"

"Yes." I watched her carefully, trying to decide if I should say more. I needed to win her trust. "I was apprenticed to her this winter."

"I thought so. You're a midwife, then? You know the healing arts?"

"Yes," I said.

She nodded, deciding something. She cleared her throat. "I should apologize for my husband's decision to lock you up so unceremoniously. His judgment has been, how do you say, *impaired*, since Frederika's death. His temper has gotten the better of him."

"Has he found Ulrich yet?"

She shook her head angrily. "When the kingsguard got to his castle, Albrecht told them his son was hunting. They're searching for him in the forest, but he has the wolf-skin."

Anger filled me. "Rika's death can't go unpunished."

Beatrice nodded, her expression guarded. "I will do whatever I can to ensure otherwise, I promise you, but there are limitations."

I shook my head. My whole journey here, my visit to Frederick's court, might be in vain? Something about the queen's guarded expression made me think there was another meaning beneath her words. What was she going to do to see that he was punished? Was that part of what the circle did: right wrongs like this? "Miss—er—your majesty. What should I call you?"

"Beatrice."

"Beatrice." I looked her in the eye, my heart clamoring in my throat. "Admit me to the circle. I beg you. My gift is strong, and I have a fighting spirit. I would like to help right these wrongs, restore the Mother's place on earth."

She stared at me, her expression turning serious. "I do think there is something you can do to help. We should go somewhere more private."

She took my hand and pulled me from the room. The guards bowed as we passed.

She led me through the stone courtyard, which glowed in the bright light of the waxing moon. From there, we walked to the north wing of the palace, where another guard stood beside a locked door. He nodded as the queen pulled out her key ring to unlock it. Inside was a well-decorated hall with a series of doors. The last room had heavy drapes, thrown back so the sunlight could stream in through the shuttered windows. There was a four-post bed with a pale-blue canopy. On the table in the center of the room, a large white basin sat, covered with the same golden symbols that were engraved on the mirrors and birdbath. The queen ushered me to the table and shut the door, locking it behind us.

"The oath is a blood-vow," she said, her voice hushed. "You must make a sacrifice, prove your fealty. And then you must swear an oath of secrecy. Are you willing?"

Her words hung in the air. An uncomplicated relief poured through me, a certainty I could feel in my bones. This was it, my chance to redeem myself, to prove that my mother's gift had not been in vain. My first instinct was to jump at the chance. Then my anxieties rose up. This path had been taken from me before. Don't get your hopes up, a small voice inside me said. You will no doubt fail in this, like you've failed in everything else.

I squelched the thought, pushing it down, refusing for once to be controlled by my pessimism. "Whatever you want me to do, I'll do it."

She met my eyes. "Are you sure?"

"I have never been more sure of anything."

She was silent for a long moment, measuring me up. "Very well," she said finally. "The first thing you need to know is that figurine of yours is powerful. If you rub it, it pulls power from the next world into this. You can use it to improve the sensitivity of your gift."

I nodded, tears in my eyes. "Do you know how I can use it to summon my mother? I called her once with it, or at least I think I did."

"No," she said apologetically. "But someone in the circle will." She pointed at the basin. "Have you seen one of these before?" .

"Kunegunde has one. The symbols. It's the old language?"

"Yes," she said. "They're runes. There was a time we all knew it. I wish we remembered more than we do. There is power in its words."

She gestured for me to close the drapes. When the room was dark, she lit a white candle next to the basin. She took a pitcher from the dresser and poured water into the bowl. Then she gestured for me to come close. As I did, she began to move her lips, muttering a strange incantation. The words were mesmerizing, repetitive, with a lilting rhythm like Kunegunde's chant. "*Roudos, roudos. Ursilda osmi und deiko me.*"

As she spoke, the air went taut, and I felt the water tremble. It rippled, a shiver bubbling up from inside it. For a moment, it shimmered with mist, and colors swirled on its surface. I gasped as an image in the water became clear. Princess Ursilda, now hugely pregnant, lay wild-haired, surrounded by pillows in an extravagant bed. As we watched, a servant-woman gave her a plate of food. Ursilda moaned, pushing it away, cradling her belly. The queen pointed at her, her finger close enough to the water that Ursilda's image rippled. "Princess Ursilda is due to give birth any day now. I just found out today that that woman"—Beatrice pointed at the servant-woman standing near the bed—"is Ursilda's new midwife, secretly sent to her a week ago by my husband."

I raised my eyebrows, concerned at her ominous tone, peering at the innocent-looking servant with blond hair. On the plate was a pile of rumpled-looking leaves.

"The midwife has been poisoning Ursilda and her baby."

I stared at the leaves on the plate in horror. "What? Why?"

"Frederick has lost all reason. He's disconsolate. The midwife's mission"—she gestured at the servant in the basin—"is to kill Ursilda and the child, since he can't get to Ulrich." Her voice broke. "I confronted him earlier today when I found out. I tried to tell him Ursilda had nothing to do with the murder, but Frederick is mad with grief."

I stared at her, incredulous. Ursilda had been so kind to me that night in the hall. My heart went out to her. I could understand the rage a parent might feel over the death of a child, but killing an innocent woman and her *baby* as revenge against the woman's brother evidenced a level of cruelty that seemed incomprehensible. I shook my head, trying to clear it. There was something I didn't understand. "If you can summon images in the basin, why didn't you use it to find Frederika?"

"I did," she said. "But all I could see was that she was living in some sort of settlement on a mountain. And I worried for her safety if Frederick found out whom she was with."

Beatrice met my eyes, and I realized what she meant. She hadn't told him. The image in the basin faded, until all that was left was water rippling over runes.

"Ursilda is like a sister to me. We grew up together. I can't warn her with the water-*spiegel* unless she casts the spell on the other end. I need someone to go to her. I wish I could go myself, but Frederick would notice my absence and send men after me. Your presence here is a boon. As a midwife, you can attend the birth and heal Ursilda, after you get rid of the assassin."

Get rid of the assassin, I thought, drawing a deep breath. That sounded dangerous. But it explained why my audience with the king had gone so poorly. I was meant to be here when Beatrice found out about this threat.

"Do you know the general antidotes for poison?"

I nodded.

"Ursilda will need them."

I thought about what she was saying. Her husband was clearly a dangerous person to cross. "Won't the king expect me to be here?"

"Yes," she sighed. "But he might not call for you for weeks yet. By then, you'll be long gone."

I nodded, considering her plan. I wanted to join the circle—to fulfill the promise that lay dormant inside me—but her husband might well be the most dangerous man in the world. "How could the king betroth his daughter to someone like Ulrich in the first place?"

Her expression darkened. "I've tried to tell him, believe me. But Frederick thinks the wolf-skin is a wives' tale. Ulrich can be deceptively charming."

A laugh spasmed, pure and dark, in my chest.

Beatrice looked at me, puzzled.

I mastered myself. "*Charming* isn't the word I'd use. When we met, he tried to take my virtue." This time, I didn't have trouble saying the words. My voice was hard. The passing weeks had encased my memory of that night in a crystalline ball of rage. "I suppose you could say he was *forceful* with me. I barely escaped with my life."

Beatrice's face crumpled. Tears welled up in her eyes. "Must all men be so—?" Her breath hitched. She didn't finish the sentence. I looked into them and felt her desperation. "I am sorry, Haelewise. It's all a game to them. We are like pawns on a chessboard, which they move at whim."

A wave of sympathy passed through me. For Ursilda, for Rika, for all the women who had been caught up in this game. They had been misrepresented in gossip, in the stories folks spoke beside the fire. It wasn't their fault which men asked for their hands in marriage, which land belonged to their families, which houses their fathers or husbands antagonized. None of us deserved the way we were treated. We were all in danger of being cast aside, like the Mother was cast aside by the Church. "If I warn Ursilda, I'll be able to join the circle?"

Beatrice nodded. "That will be your test."

My head swam. My temple pounded. I tried to think of anything else I needed to ask before I said yes. And then it hit me, with such force that I hated myself for not mentioning it yet. "Do you know if the king apprehended the man who tried to clear my name?"

She nodded slowly. "Frederick locked him in the tower."

"*Matthäus*—" My voice shook. "Is he hurt?"

She paused. "He wasn't when he got here. How do you know his name?"

"I grew up with him." My heart beat in my throat. He had come here on my behalf. He was missing from his house because he came here to clear my name. "I will help Ursilda only on the condition that you set him free."

She nodded slowly, surprised that I had a condition. Just a minute before, I had been desperate. In all truth I was surprised myself. "That is within my power."

I nodded. "I'll do it."

"You'll need to sneak into the castle. The guards are no doubt only letting the royal family in and out. But I'll give you cloaks that will allow you to go unseen. *Tarnkappen*."

My heart filled with awe. "*Tarnkappen*. They exist?"

"There are only four in existence, but there are perks to being empress. I have all of them." She laughed that tinkling laugh again. "When you wear one, it pulls your shape into the next world. You become part of the mist. They'll be useful in the forest. If Ulrich is out there, hunting, you don't want to run into him."

The thought gave me a chill. She was right. "Kunegunde said the wolf-skin worked best at the full moon, which is soon. Will Ulrich be at his most powerful then?"

"Unfortunately. And the *tarnkappen* will be at their weakest." She went silent for a long moment, thinking. "I can give you a hand-mirror to help you watch over Ursilda until you get there. It works like this basin."

"A hand-mirror?" I fumbled in my sack for the one I found in my mother's trunk. "Like this one?"

A look of concern passed over her face when she saw how the glass was shattered. "Where did you get this?"

"It was my mother's."

"What happened to it?"

I thought about this. Not long after Kunegunde nursed my mother back to health, my father had told me she was dead. I could piece together what happened. "My father smashed it."

There was sadness in her eyes, understanding. "Would you like me to make it whole again?"

"Yes," I said, my heart filling with an unexpected gratitude. "Please."

"I assume you know the old language?"

I shook my head. "Only a phrase or two."

"But the Mother speaks to you. I can teach you. That is good luck. Very few have the gift."

CHAPTER THIRTY

Beatrice went to an ornate trunk on the west wall and pulled out a locked book like Kunegunde's, where she'd set down all of the spells she knew. On the front of it was a gilded circular sigil, decorated with stylized birds and slithering snakes. She opened it and turned to the page that bore the incantation for fixing something that was broken. Holding her hands over the shattered mirror, she recited the runes. *Wer zi wer*, she chanted, *bedehrben*. The air went taut. Soon enough the mist and light within the glass surfaced. The mirror shimmered, and the shards went liquid. I watched in amazement as the mirror became whole.

"Thank you," I breathed, turning the now-perfect mirror this way and that. There was no way to tell that it had been broken.

"We need to hurry," she said. "It's long past dark. The king expects me soon."

She set about teaching me the incantation I would need to use the mirror. I was a quick study, as I had been when Kunegunde taught me to read. I understood as soon as she pronounced each rune, the way each word should taste in my mouth. *Roudos, roudos*, the chant began. *Osmi und deiko me*, it ended. The word in the middle varied: the person or place you wanted to see in the reflecting surface. The spell could be cast on a basin, a mirror, or a bowl of water, as long as the reflective surface bore the runes.

The first thing I asked it to show me was my mother's garden. The glass rippled, coalescing into a wild tangle of green. The alrūne had gone wild—the old plants grown large, new plants covering her grave, rooting and spreading their stalks—casting shadows. I stared at them for a long time, reflecting on the woman who made them grow, thanking her for the life she had given me with her own. Her love for me had gone wild like those plants, choking out everything else inside her, even her own desire to live. Her love for me had gone wild, and I had eaten of it, I thought, a sob catching in my throat.

Watching my face, Beatrice waited until I looked up and the image in the mirror disappeared. Then she said we needed to hurry. Someone needed to get to Ursilda as soon as possible.

"Do you have something to protect yourself?" she asked. "What you are about to do will be dangerous."

I nodded. "I keep a knife in my boot."

She scoffed. "I'll find you something better."

She pulled the guard at the door aside—an old man with white hair and dim eyes—and spoke with him. In a moment, he nodded and walked off with purpose.

"Take me to Matthäus," I said.

She led me to another part of the palace with a great stone door. Inside, no windows let any light from outside in. The chamber was lit by a single guttering torch on the wall. Our footsteps echoed on the stones as Beatrice grabbed the torch and led me up narrow stairs, passing small cells with iron bars. The openings were small enough that it was difficult to see into them. Peering into one cell, I understood this was a place the king put people he meant to forget. A chill crept through me as Beatrice led me up the dark stairs. Rats darted, shrieking, as her torchlight lit the steps.

There were small holding cells along the stairs, barely large enough to call rooms. They were closer to the size of my cupboard at home but half as tall, as if they had been built for child-sized prisoners. Most of them were empty, but a few we passed were in use. About halfway up the tower, Beatrice stopped outside one and held up her torch so that we could see in. Inside, a figure sprawled on the floor, wrapped in a filthy cloak. As she bent over his cell, the torchlight lit the grime and dirt on his fingers, which were wrapped around a cup. His hand was outstretched toward the iron bars as if he had been begging for a drink when last awake.

"Matthäus?" I said.

He startled and looked up, blinking. Beatrice unlocked his cell.

As he scrambled out, a terrible guilt filled me that I had brought this imprisonment upon him. I searched his face, pained to see him like this, looking for the man I loved under the soot and grime. His eyes widened at the sight of me. He clasped my shoulders, pressed my face to his chest, and kissed the top of my tangled hair, breathing my name. "*Haelewise.*"

He smelled of sweat and blood and dirt and another scent that brought tears to my eyes, a salty scent that I recognized only as his. I held him tight, almost afraid he'd disappear if I let go. His shoulders had grown even broader in the six months we'd been apart. He had shot up in height, too, as men often do during their eighteenth or nineteenth year. When he turned my face up to look at him, his eyes glistened with tears.

"I thought I'd never see you again," I whispered.

"Your eyes. They're golden, like they were when I last saw you. I thought it was the moon."

I nodded. "I'm taking a curative for my spells. It does something to my eyes as well."

He raised his eyebrows.

Beatrice was watching him watch me, an amused expression on her face. She cleared her throat, lowering her voice. "Haelewise. There is very little time. You can talk in the carriage."

Matthäus looked at her, confused. "Am I being freed?"

She nodded. "Explain it to him. I'll be right back."

As she turned to go down the stairs, I took his hands. "Ulrich killed Frederika. The king is trying to avenge her death. He sent a killer to pose as a midwife for Princess Ursilda. I'm leaving to stop her tonight."

Matthäus blinked, as if he couldn't quite link what I was saying with his notion of me. "You negotiated my release?"

I nodded. "Will you come?"

He met my eyes. "I would go with you anywhere."

Beatrice returned with a bag, which she handed to him. "The things they took from you."

Matthäus took the bag as we followed her downstairs. Hurrying, holding his hand, I was filled with a wicked glee. I should've been concerned for his welfare—he had been *imprisoned*—but all I felt was a selfish delight that we were together again.

When we emerged from the tower, an earthly mist—glistening with the light of the swelling moon—had descended over the palace. A blessing, I thought, a good omen. In the hazy courtyard a black-cloaked driver sat atop a bright blue carriage, the same one Beatrice had ridden into my hometown. The driver was the old man she had spoken with earlier outside the door. Close up, I could see golden accents on the cart and wheels, pale-blue roses painted on its canopy.

Hitched to its front were Nëbel and three other horses dressed in gold and black. I gasped when I saw the great white mare shifting her weight from hoof to hoof, beneath a black caparison inscribed with golden runes. The moon shone down on the cloth, making the rune-threads glitter. Nëbel looked dignified and wild, like something out of a tale. I rushed toward the horse to kiss her forehead, then stopped, turning to Beatrice to ask if it was wise for me to take her.

"My husband ordered her destroyed. She reminds him of his daughter. He cannot stand the sight of her." Beatrice pulled the canopy at the back of the carriage aside so Matthäus could climb in. Inside the cart were two benches, one on each side. Everything was covered with a shining blue cloth—the benches, the canopy, the floor—silk, I thought, though I couldn't be sure. There wasn't a stain anywhere. Anxiety filled me. I thought of the beggar back home who haunted the steps of the minster. How hard my mother worked sewing poppets so we could buy a wheel of cheese.

"The driver will take you far enough down the river that you won't be recognized," she told us as we climbed in. "After that, he has to turn back so no one will notice my carriage is gone. Ride the horses hard after that, and you should be fine. You know how to find Ursilda's castle?" I nodded. "You have the mirror?"

"Aye." I patted my sack. "When will I see you again?"

"Use the mirror to scry on me when all this is over. When I sense you watching, I'll cast the spell on my end so we can talk. May the Mother bless you and keep you safe."

Matthäus and I climbed into the carriage and sat across from each other under its canopy. It bumped into motion, the wheels turning awkwardly over the stones. Out of the back of the carriage, we could see the palace courtyard falling away. We heard the gate open before us and watched it close behind. I breathed a sigh of relief as the palace grew smaller behind us. The carriage bumped. As my eyes adjusted to the moonlight that shone through the back of the carriage flap, I could see that Matthäus's face was darkened with grime and soot.

"How long were you in that cell?" I asked him, feeling terrible about using his wife's family name.

"A month or so? I'm not really sure."

"I'm so sorry I used your name. I didn't think—" My voice broke. "I was a fool."

"Haelewise," he interrupted. The way he looked at me then made my breath catch in my throat. His knees were touching mine. I could feel them pressing my own. "When Phoebe told me Ulrich's guards came looking for you, I set out to find you. I'm here of my own free will."

When he put his hand on mine, it was as if no time had passed at all from the last time we spoke. I remembered our kiss in the garden, how he hadn't wanted me to go.

"How old is the baby now?" I dared to ask.

"I don't know. He was only a week old when I left. One month? Two?"

I stared at him, unable to believe so little time had passed. I cleared my throat, feeling awkward to ask. "Will you and Phoebe have another?"

Matthäus shook his head. He looked as if he wanted to say more, giving me a tortured look. "The marriage is in name alone."

I remembered what I saw when I flew to his estate—two rooms upstairs, one with the cradle and one without.

When I met his eyes, I knew what he wanted to say—that he didn't want her because he wanted me. His unspoken thought was like an elixir, a balm for all my anxieties. It pulled me to him, the way the earth pulls autumn apples from trees. The girl I was before I left home might've given up because he was married to another. She had balked at the idea of becoming another man's mistress, worried about what everyone would think of her. But I had seen enough of the world now that I could fathom another option.

I met his eyes, leaning forward, searching for the right words to make him walk away from the world he knew. "I'm yours, if you'll have me."

The invitation surfaced something in the air between us, a power drawing us together. I could tell by the way his mouth fell open, the want in his eyes, that he felt it too.

"My father," he said, but he didn't sound certain, and he stopped in midsentence, his voice trailing off.

"To hell with your father, Matthäus," I said, laughing. "His opinion doesn't have anything to do with us."

Matthäus stared at me for a moment, wide-eyed, shocked. The carriage around us shifted with shadows. Then he burst into laughter. I could feel his shame and fear leaving him. "Who are you, and what have you done with my Haelewise?" he whispered softly, reaching for my hand.

I let him take it, though his question was a good one. I thought for a moment about how to answer it, as the mist that was settling over the path swirled outside the door-flap. He was right. I wasn't the same girl who had kissed him in the garden. He needed to know what I had become. When I finally spoke, my voice was soft. "I should be honest with you, Matthäus. I am myself, but not. The fisherman's daughter, but not. Since I last saw you, I've been cured of my spells. I've learned incantations. I've been blessed and cursed. The fisherman's daughter you knew might as well be buried in the garden with my mother. I have become someone else."

He stared at me. A finger of mist curled through the door-flap, glistening with light. I couldn't tell whether it was from this world or the next. We heard the sound of the horses outside, their hooves hitting the dirt. He smiled, leaning closer to me across the carriage, his breath quickening. The shadow, the shimmering, between us deepened. It felt a thousand years old.

"What I'm about to do will be dangerous. If you want, we can part ways before we get to the castle." I bit my lip, trying to speak without bitterness. "You can go back to Phoebe and your son."

He cringed. The carriage stopped, teetering to one side. We could hear the driver jump off and start puttering with a wheel that had fallen into a rut. The door-flap fell half open. Bright mist crept into the carriage, swirling and glistening in the air around us. Matthäus shook his head, as if awakening from a strange dream, and squeezed my hand. "I begged my father in Zürich," he said under his breath. "I was desolate the night I brought you that cloak."

I met his eyes. My voice trembled. "Everything that is done can be undone."

Matthäus looked troubled. "Even wedding vows?"

I took a deep breath. The air around us trembled.

"I can't abandon Phoebe, or her son. He isn't mine, but he is. Her family would take care of them, no matter what. But my father—" Matthäus trailed off.

I thought of his father, resolute, in his bedroom. His mother's eyes red from crying. The proud little tailor shop. His world was so small. The carriage tilted upright, rolling out of the rut, and the door-flap fell shut. Outside, we could hear the driver climbing back onto the front of the carriage. The wheels began to turn over the dirt.

"I've been miserable," Matthäus said finally.

I stared across the carriage at him, searching my mind, again, for the right words to say. My mother's advice swam back to me. *Their way isn't the only way. All you have to do is hold hands and speak vows. There is power in the words themselves.* I reached for his hands, clasping them tight, interlacing our fingers. Then I took a deep breath, drawing in the mist that swirled between us. "Run away with me into the forest."

He didn't answer at first. He only watched me from across the carriage. I squeezed his hands, seeing our life together spool out in my mind's eye. The life I'd always wanted. The life my mother wanted for me. A humble hut in the forest with two rooms, one of them the room with our bed. I saw us lying in it, tangled up naked in a blanket, glass beads glinting in the windows, fabric spread out over the table, a pincushion, a thousand needles. My midwifery bag, waiting for me, beside it. Outside, a garden, a water-*spiegel*. Our children darting in and out of the trees.

Matthäus leaned in close enough for me to see his expression. The life *he* was imagining for us written all over his face. The hairs on the back of my neck prickled. The mist and light inside me thrummed to life. My body hummed.

"God's teeth." I looked into his eyes. They were gray and glowing, lit from within. "Do you feel that? Matthäus. Doesn't this feel *right*?"

He nodded, his eyes wet with tears. He was struggling. He wanted all of the same things I did, but he didn't share my certainty that they were within reach. He searched my face, his desire so clear. When he finally spoke, he clasped my hands tighter. The words fell out of him like water through a sieve. "I want you. I always have. I have never wanted anyone else."

I smiled at him, overcome. He pulled me to him, his kiss so hard and desperate I could taste his desire. Salty and earthy and bitter, it coursed through me, pulling us together.

He undid the cloak from around my neck. It fell to the floor of the carriage, pooling at my feet. Moonlight filtered through the canopy, setting the blue silk aglow. Then he kissed me again and all the mist, all the possibility in the world around us, shimmered to life. It was dizzying. An indefinite amount of time passed, which I spent enchanted by his touch. When his hand found the space between my legs, my spirits grew quick within my flesh. I felt a pressure, an earthy pleasure, building up within me. He kept kissing me and touching me until all the possibility, all the moonlight and magic in the carriage exploded, opening me up.

When it was over, I climbed onto his lap, lifting my skirts so we could undo his pants. He unlaced my dress so that he could see my breasts. When he pulled away to look at them, the only sound I could shape was his name: "Matthäus." The word held such a sweet taste on my tongue that I wanted to say it again: "Matthäus." Hearing me say his name like that, twice, did something to him. He let out a shaky breath and guided me to the floor of the carriage. How gentle he was. How tender. How cool and soft the floor-covering was on my back. The wheels of the carriage rattled beneath us as he climbed on top of me, the moonlight and mist glowing in the air around his head. And then he was entering me, filling me up, with the most delicious wantonness.

CHAPTER THIRTY-ONE

When the carriage stopped, hours later, we were sleeping. I woke first, startled at the sight of Matthäus asleep next to me. As the events of the last few hours came flooding back, I smiled. Although we were on a dangerous mission, for a moment, all I could think about was the fact that we were together. A giddy delight filled me, delight mixed with disbelief. When Matthäus woke, he smiled back at me.

Together, we peeked through the door-flap. Moonlight fell over the path that led back to Bingen, lighting the rocks and pebbles that scattered the dirt road. Mist clung to the trees that grew, crooked and tangled, along the path. The driver jumped off the front of the carriage and addressed us. He smirked, and I realized he must've heard us earlier. I smirked back at him. Matthäus blushed.

"You're awake," the driver said kindly, forgoing the opportunity to shame us with a crude comment or wink. "This is as far as I can take you. The queen wants me back at the palace 'afore dawn."

I cleared my throat. "Two of the horses are for us?"

"Aye," the driver said.

He unhitched the white horses from the front of the carriage and saddled them with caparisons and reins. I went immediately to Nëbel, meeting her eyes, patting her forehead. Nëbel nuzzled my hand, prancing nervously, then let out a snort.

"Good girl," I murmured. "Sorry to be so long away."

The driver reached into the front of the carriage and tossed us two packs filled with food and supplies. Then he pulled out two lengths of deep rust-colored fabric. Ancient hooded cloaks, the cuffs of the hood and sleeves embroidered with golden runes, like something out of a story. Awe filled me, as he handed one to Matthäus and the other to me. "The *tarnkappen* the queen promised. The horses have them tied to their reins too. Wear them in the forest, near towns—anywhere you might see anyone—in case Ulrich or the king's men are looking for you. But don't wear them for too long at a time. They'll be at their weakest now, but the longer you wear them, the more undetectable you become. If you wear them too long, the shadow will swallow you up. Especially you." He met my eyes. "Even this time of the month. Beatrice said you have the gift."

I nodded, anxious to learn of this limitation. How would we manage this when we entered the forest around Ursilda's castle?

"Another gift from her majesty, for protection."

He held out a shining silver thing. In the dim light, I didn't recognize what it was. Taking it, I gasped at the familiar weight, the wolf emblem on its hilt. It was the dagger that Ulrich's man used to kill Frederika.

Cleaned and polished, it was ready for use.

Matthäus gaped at the blade, his eyes wide.

I made haste to fasten it to my belt.

The driver handed me a bag filled with rags and herbs and phials. With his other hand he offered a scroll, sealed with blue wax. The sigil with the birds and beasts. "Here is your birth bag and the letter for Princess Ursilda. Once you get inside the castle, find the westmost corridor. Show the letter to the guard named Balthazar at Ursilda's door. He's loyal only to her."

Finally, he pointed at the road that led east. "This road will take you east. From there, you can follow the trade route south. The castle is a three-day ride from here."

The driver turned the carriage around and left us. Matthäus stood beside his white mare, cloak in hand. "*Tarnkappen?*"

I grinned at him. "Like in the stories."

I pulled the heavy hood over my dress, shivering as it fell over my face. The cloth felt like ordinary fabric, a bit heavy, perhaps, but the way my hair stood on end—the pull I felt when I put it on—confirmed that they were *tarnkappen*.

"Haelewise? Where did you go?" Matthäus looked as if he had seen a ghost. "By thunder," he whispered, his voice full of awe.

In our sacks we found two wheels of cheese wrapped in cloth and wineskins. We ate and drank, hoods down so we could see each other, as we rode through the misty night.

Matthäus was fascinated with his cloak, turning it inside out to try to see how it worked. He asked me to tell him what I knew about the runes embroidered on the cuffs. As we rode, I told him about the fruit I'd eaten, the way my mother visited me in the garden, the wise woman to whom I'd apprenticed myself in the woods. I told him about the runes she'd inscribed in her book, the spell she cast to send her soul into a raven, the figurine my mother gave me, the voice that spoke to me when I carried it. I told him about the murder I witnessed, explaining that the dagger the queen gave us was the weapon Ulrich used to kill Frederika. When I told him what Ulrich tried to do to me, he flew into a rage.

"He what?!" It took an hour, after that, to calm him.

After I explained, I showed him my mother's mirror, carved with runes, and told him about the spell Beatrice had taught me to cast. He traced the runes on the mirror with his fingers, then looked at me sideways, as if he couldn't quite believe what I was saying.

I didn't blame him. Speaking the story aloud, I found it difficult to believe myself.

When we drew near a town, we put our food away and drew down our hoods. As soon as we did, Matthäus disappeared and I saw only a riderless white horse at my side. It was the strangest sensation to look down and see only the white of Nëbel's back where my body was. I pulled down her hood and she disappeared too, so that it seemed I was floating over the ground. Matthäus did the same. As we galloped past the city wall, orange lights flickered in the towers. I imagined guards hearing our invisible horses gallop through the pasture. I imagined the ghost story they would tell their wives, voices tinged with disbelief.

We galloped past, riding at a heightened pace far enough along the old trade route that the city was only a shadow at our backs. The mist was thick out there, glistening in the gloom before dawn. There was a rotting wood pole, leaning out at the roadside, which looked as if it was used for hangings. I was just about to ask him to take off his hood so I could see where he was, when we heard distant voices carrying from inside the forest. The sound of fighting. Drunken cheers. "We should keep going," Matthäus said, his voice low. "Men who are still up and drinking at this hour could be dangerous."

Peering into the trees, I fumbled in my pouch for the figurine and prayed for the Mother to protect us. After a while, the voices went quiet. Mist drifted over the path. The horizon was beginning to turn pink with the first fingers of sunrise. When neither of us had heard anything in some time, we removed our hoods and led our horses from the road to look for a place to rest.

After everything that had happened, I wasn't surprised to stumble upon the perfect resting place, a safe distance away from the path. An old wooden hut in an overgrown clearing scattered with saplings. Our journey seemed blessed, this resting place foredestined. A brook babbled through the edge of the clearing, a dozen feet or so from the hut. The hut itself was ancient, with not much more than vines left of the roof. The faint moon was setting on the horizon, only a night or two from full. I smiled at the ruined beauty of our campsite, but Matthäus seemed distant. As we tied our horses by the brook, I could tell something was bothering him.

When he lay down next to me inside the hut, turning on his side to look at me, his expression was serious. "Your father thought you were dead," he said, holding his head up with his hand. "He was shocked when I told him you'd intentionally left the city."

This revelation amused me. It hadn't even occurred to me that Father would notice I was gone. But of course he would've come for supper at some point, to give me news of Felisberta's pregnancy or shame me for not making him a proper dinner. I imagined him walking into our hut, calling my name, then wandering back home, wondering where I had gone. How many times had he come to look for me before he presumed me dead? "How long ago was this?"

"Last autumn. I came over several times to see if you'd returned. When you didn't come back by February, well, I started to fear your father was right. I was overjoyed when Phoebe said the guards came looking for a Haelewise." He turned away, suddenly, so I couldn't see his face.

I wondered again what they'd done to him when he came looking for me at the palace, but I didn't want to press.

After a moment, he shook off whatever was bothering him and turned back to me. He touched the runes on the *tarnkappe* we had pulled up over us to ward off the chill, his eyes gone wide and bright. "Haelewise. It feels like we're in one of your stories. Running an errand for a sorceress, wearing *tarnkappen* and carrying a magic mirror." He burst into uneven laughter, shaking his head. "Frederick's beard, all your stories about wise women and fairies, magic mirrors and wondrous plants. I thought you were making them up. But— Haelewise—" His eyes glowed bright gray, anxious, almost feverish. "They're true, every last one of your stories, aren't they?"

I shook my head. "No."

"Right. Right." He nodded, his hair falling into his eyes. He spoke quickly, his words tumbling each into the next. "I know. I know. They didn't happen word for word. But they speak of an earlier time, a time before this one. What used to be possible—"

"In stories old."

He stared at me, excited. "Yes."

I fumbled in my pouch. Now seemed as good a time as any to show him the figurine. I held her out for him to see. Her black stone glistened. "This is the figurine my mother gave me."

He took it from me, shuddering when he saw her naked breasts, her wings, her claws. His expression clouded. "I don't understand. It looks like a demon."

My heart sank. I needed him to see the figurine as I did.

I told him that my mother had worshipped the Mother in secret, that the voice that had been speaking to me for months belonged to her goddess. I told him what Beatrice said, that the Mother was the ancient wife of the Father, whom everyone had forgotten since the Father became so revered. When I told him about the tincture Hildegard had given me, his eyes widened with awe.

"You met Mother Hildegard?"

I nodded. "The Mother speaks to her too." I didn't mention her uneasiness about this.

He thought for a moment. "Are you talking about the Mother of God?"

I took a deep breath. "Maybe that's one of her names. But the stories the priests tell about her don't make sense. She's no Virgin."

Matthäus looked at the figurine in his hand again, examining her carefully, his expression fearful. "She's—not a saint."

I shook my head.

"And you're sure she's not a demon?" He handed it back, holding the figurine at arm's length.

I returned her to my pouch, which I put in the grass that was my pillow. "She's no demon. I can promise you that. She's a protector, a seeker of justice."

He nodded as if he understood, but he looked uncertain. He went silent for a long time before he gave voice to his thoughts. "How far are you willing to go?"

"What do you mean?"

"Beatrice gave you a dagger. For protection, she said. But the midwife is an assassin. How far are you willing to go to protect Princess Ursilda?"

I remembered how kind Ursilda had been to me at the settlement, how much pain she had already experienced. And the baby. The assassin was supposed to kill her baby too. My memory of holding the miller's son swam back to me. I remembered the innocence, the need in his eyes. Anger filled me that the king would hurt something that helpless, that pure. "As far as I have to, Matthäus. Two *lives* are in danger."

"I know. I know. It's just—" He trailed off, struggling to put his thoughts into words. "I'm a tailor. I never thought I would see someone killed. And—you—this goddess you serve. She's no Virgin. She's fierce—"

"Yes," I said. "And there's nothing wrong with that. A woman doesn't have to be pure to be good. Girls get angry. Mothers fight for their children."

He watched me steadily.

"Matthäus," I said, my voice catching with feeling. "This is my task. You don't have to come with me. I'll understand."

"No!" he said quickly. "I can't leave you. My God, your life will be in danger. I won't be able to live with myself if—" He shuddered, unable to say the words.

"All right. But I warn you. I will do anything I must to keep them safe."

He nodded as if he understood. But he was awake for a long time—restless, staring into the dark—before he went to sleep.

I woke at midday to the sound of twigs snapping. The place where Matthäus had lain beside me was empty. Looking up, I saw him headed into the trees. I crept after him, afraid that his uneasiness about the Mother was driving him away. He stopped a stone's throw from the clearing where the brook turned, forming a pool.

Hiding behind a bush, I watched from behind as he took off his breeches and shirt. There were long, thin cuts on his back, scabbed over with a crust of dried blood. I had to cover my mouth when I realized why he didn't want to talk about his imprisonment: The king's men had tortured him.

The guilt I felt then was overpowering. It brought tears to my eyes, and a terrible regret filled my heart. I averted my eyes from the cuts, watching him wade into the stream, the muscles of his legs and buttocks tight. The water made a rushing sound as it slid around his thighs. Birds chirped. The sun cast a thin veil of light over the pool. He ducked underwater, submerging himself. All was quiet until he emerged, smoothing his hair back, dark and wet. His expression was brooding, and there was a tightness in his shoulders that the water had failed to relax. I stayed behind my bush, heartsick over what he'd endured in order to find me. I watched him splash water beneath his arms and wash his face.

When he turned toward the shore, I saw the cuts on his chest and arms and gasped. How many times had they whipped him? How had I failed to notice them the night before? I thought on our time together. He hadn't taken his shirt off. Feeling sick, I wondered if I'd hurt him when I pulled him to me, when I wrapped my hands tight around his arms.

Then he made his way out of the water, and I crouched behind my tree, praying he wouldn't see me. As he dressed, my eyes wandered to the creature that lived between his legs. It was pinker than I'd imagined, with large stones hanging beneath and a tangled nest of hair. Once he walked past, I circled the clearing to pretend I'd gone into the woods to relieve myself.

When I reached the hut, he was waiting for me. "How do you know the voice you hear isn't the Mother of God?" he asked, his expression solemn. "Or your own mother's ghost?"

"I thought it was my mother's ghost at first. But it isn't—or it's not only that." I tried to think of a way to explain it.

"What do you mean?" Matthäus's voice was quiet. "What has the Mother told you to do?"

"Seek Hildegard. Protect the princess. Protect myself."

He nodded slowly. "That doesn't sound like a demon."

"She wants to be restored to her rightful place beside the Father." I clasped his hands. "Does that help?"

He nodded again. "Actually, yes."

As we made ready to go, I reflected on the journey ahead of me. I had everything I needed to make the life I wanted: a path to join the circle, my love beside me. I reached for the figurine in my coin-purse. Thank you, I prayed, sending the gratitude up, up, up.

Matthäus rode in front of me as we followed the old trade route south. Watching his back, I found myself thinking of him instead of the mess we were riding toward. I remembered what we had done the night before and wished that we could stop and do it again. It was as if I had been enchanted, as if I was in his thrall.

We talked about various things as we rode. Our plan to get into the castle. Our fears about running into Ulrich in the wood. Our relief that we had the *tarnkappen* to keep us hidden. News from home. His mother was pregnant again. She thought this time it might be a girl. The terrain became mountainous as we rode south. Near dinnertime, my stomach began to growl. The sun fell in the sky, and we were surprised, turning a curve in a mountain path, to see a linden grove in the valley below. It reminded me of the linden grove we had practiced shooting in back home. The trees were ancient with tangled branches and deep shadows around each trunk. They were thick-trunked, heavy with leaves. As the last rays of sunlight disappeared, we looked at each other from atop our horses.

"We should stop here for the night," Matthäus said.

I nodded, as eager as he was to eat. We tied our horses in the middle of the grove and gave them their feed sacks. He gathered tinder and stones from the nearby trees and went to work building a fire ring. As he did, I sat down and spoke the spell over the mirror, to see if Ursilda was all right. The mirror showed her sitting up in bed, the midwife hovering. Matthäus watched me warily as I spoke the incantation. He stopped working to look at the mirror over my shoulder, his expression awed and horrified.

I thought he would speak, but he went back to building the fire in silence. Once he got it crackling, we sat down together at the base of a nearby tree to eat. It was too late in spring by then, even with the evening chill, to need the fire for anything more than light. Without discussing it, we settled into similar postures to the ones we had developed as children, sitting with our backs against the trunk but closer than before, our thighs touching, side by side. We devoured our cheese and bread and drank the wine Beatrice had given us. By then, the grove was dark except for the firelight and the moon. Mist began to gather at the edges of the firelight. We sat and ate in comfortable silence. The wine Beatrice had put in my flagon was flavorful and dark.

"That was good," Matthäus said, when we were finished, patting my thigh. It was a natural gesture, friendly. He had probably done it a hundred times when we were children. But just like that, the feeling that there was something between us, drawing us together, returned. He looked at his hand, then back up at me. The firelight was fading.

As his lips drew near mine, I abandoned myself to the kiss. I could feel the rest of the world falling away as the now-familiar enchantment encircled us.

When his lips finally pressed mine, my eyes closed. I was no longer myself. I was no one. I was anyone. I was every woman who has ever been kissed. I felt drowsy, suspended in our desire. Soon enough, we were unlacing our clothes, and I was sitting on his lap at the edge of the firelight. As I pushed into him, the rest of the world fell away, and everything went dark. There was only him and me and our interlocking bodies. There was only the myth of us.

Afterward, we sat together for a long time, intertwined. Then it happened again. We felt the pull. Three times, that night, something pulled us together. After the third time, Matthäus whispered softly that he could never leave me. Then he fell asleep on the grass beside me, a half smile on his face, his skin glistening with sweat. Our bed of grass beneath the linden tree was dark. I took a bite of my alrūne and tried to sleep.

Lying next to him, unclothed, I was filled with a preternatural unease. I put on my underpants and shift and tried to sleep, watching him breathe. But the night closed around me, making me anxious. When I finally fell into an uneasy sleep, the Mother sent me another dream. I was pressed against the wall of Princess Ursilda's chamber, watching a masked man climb through the window. Behind him, a waning half moon hung in the sky. The masked man wore black breeches and a black hood over his head. His blue eyes flashed above his mask. His movements were soundless and liquid as he snuffed the torch and drew a knife from a sheath engraved with the king's seal. Then he drew it across the throat of a sleeping figure on the bed and crept toward the cradle.

I jolted awake, the Mother's voice buzzing through the veil, hissing, furious: *Another assassin.*

As I sat up, the tension in the air collapsed. My heart pounded in my throat. How could I sleep, knowing there would be a second murder I was supposed to prevent after this? I clutched my figurine, stomach knotting, praying I would know what to do to stop both killings. The moon would not be waning like that for another week or so.

When the sky finally began to turn gray at the horizon, I woke Matthäus. He startled awake, a terrified look in his eyes, until he realized where he was. "Sorry," he said, embarrassed at his outburst. "They woke me at all hours in that cell to try to get information."

I waited for him to say more, but that was all he would offer. I reached out and squeezed his hand. "Don't apologize, Matthäus," I said, kissing his forehead. "Please. I'm the one who got you involved."

When he was calm, I told him about my dream and what I thought it meant. As soon as I was finished, we decided to ride the rest of the way as hard as we could.

CHAPTER THIRTY-TWO

We were like ghostly demons speeding down the trade route. My need to succeed at my task pulled me onward. Matthäus rode beside me, sharing in the urgency I felt. When we entered the northern tip of the ancient forest where Ulrich's castle stood, we pulled our hoods down, letting the shadow-world envelop us. There was no telling where Ulrich was hiding—he could be anywhere in that forest. Elder oaks and ash trees held hands over our path, as if they were keeping our passage secret. The only signs of our progress through the woods were sounds—the gentle stutter of our horses' hooves, the sound of our breathing.

We didn't dare speak.

Before that, we'd only pulled the hoods on for short periods at a time, when we approached villages or towns or heard sounds in the distance. By the time we'd ridden two hours without removing them, my fingers and toes were numb like they were after a fainting spell. I remembered the carriage driver's warning that I would need to be careful. How long was it safe for me to wear a *tarnkappe* when the moon was full? "Do you feel that?" I whispered. "The pins and needles?"

"No," Matthäus breathed.

"I think we've worn the *tarnkappen* too long."

I didn't want to stop. The longer we dallied, the greater the chance was that we would be too late. But the horses began acting strangely soon after that, and I realized that if the shadow-world swallowed us, we would *never* arrive. Reluctantly, I searched the wood beside the path for a hiding place where we could uncloak.

Before long, I spied a thorny circle of sweetbriar rosebushes. So tangled, so tall and wild, we could dismount our horses in the center without being seen. "This way," I said, turning off the path. I heard Matthäus follow me.

In the middle of the sweetbriar bushes, surrounded by tangled thorns and the fragrance of their buds, I pulled off my hood. Matthäus did the same, and we set to work uncloaking the horses. We all stood perfectly still, and I was relieved to feel the pins and needles in my limbs gradually fading, as if my soul was settling back into my flesh. It took about half an hour for the sensation to go away. When I felt it no more, I nodded grimly. "Let's go."

We pulled the hoods back on and returned to the path, the gravity of our task pressing down upon us. We stopped to uncloak every couple hours for the rest of the way through the forest, but the closer we got to Ulrich's castle, the harder it was to convince myself to stop. By the time we reached the part of the forest I recognized from my long walks with Kunegunde, my heart was thudding in my ears, and I wanted to push all the way through to the castle.

Just after sunset, as we crested a mountain, we saw the fortress across the valley below, gray walls rising from cliffs, the round moon hanging over it. We slowed slightly, gazing at it without speaking. The night was eerily still. The only sound was the crunch of our horses' hooves.

When my fingers and toes went numb, I was determined not to stop. We were too close. As we rode down into the valley, Nëbel began pulling on her reins and prancing wildly, picking up on some change in the otherworldly weather. Perhaps she could feel the numbness in her extremities too. I winced, knowing whatever sounds she made would carry.

There was no sign of Ulrich as we approached the castle. No howl, no movement in the trees. The forest was eerily quiet. Up the mountain we rode, into the trees cloaked with mist. By the time we grew close to the castle, I could feel the pins and needles creeping up my thighs and into my shoulders. I could no longer feel most of my body. It was as if I was becoming the shadow.

I whispered toward the sound of Matthäus's horse. "We should wait until the last possible moment to uncloak. I'm afraid Ulrich will find us so close to the castle."

"Whatever you think is best," he whispered back.

When we could see the castle gate up ahead in the distance, it was lit up with a hundred torches. The drawbridge was open, as if they were waiting for someone to ride in or out in a hurry, and there were bonfires on either side of the gate, burning bright. I wondered if they expected Ulrich that night, if he came back to the castle secretly from time to time.

I turned into the wood and dismounted, removing Nëbel's hood. I tied her loosely to a tree far enough from the path that no one would see her, and Matthäus did the same for his horse. Then I grabbed Matthäus's hand and led him back to the path.

The only sound we made as we approached the torchlit castle gate was the sound of our breathing. I squeezed Matthäus's hand as we approached, praying Ulrich wasn't around.

Several men were standing guard in leather jerkins, passing around a wineskin. The mist and darkness made it difficult to see how many guards were inside the gatehouse. We could hear them laughing and shouting, casting lots.

By then, the numbness had spread to my breast and my groin. As we approached the gate, I gritted my teeth, moving as silently as possible, hoping we had fallen deep enough into the shadow-world that the *tarnkappen* would swallow the sound of our footsteps too. We would have to pass within six feet of the men outside the gatehouse.

Only one of the men looked up as we passed into the gate, a question on his face. His expression was quizzical, and he scanned the place where we were standing. I held my breath, rubbing the figurine in my pocket, praying the Mother would keep us safe. Seeing nothing, he shook his head, drinking from his wineskin.

We crept through the courtyard to the western wing of the castle, where the driver had told us to go. At its western edge was a vast, torchlit hall with a floor of stone. The westernmost corridor. When we entered it, there was no one around, so I led Matthäus west down the middle of the corridor. We passed unseen through the flickering dark, until we heard a door creaking open at the end of the hall. As light spilled into the corridor, I saw three guards keeping watch at the door. A wild fear filled me that Ulrich would come out.

Two figures walked out, the bright light behind them making them unidentifiable silhouettes. Squeezing Matthäus's hand, I pulled him to the side of the hall so they could pass without bumping into us. We held our breath, pressing our backs against the wall. The closest man had a well-trimmed grizzled beard. "She's weak like her mother," he was saying. "Albrecht will be furious if she dies on our watch."

"The new midwife will take good care of her, surely."

"If she doesn't, this will be the last birth she ever attends."

The other man smirked. "Albrecht will make sure of it."

In a moment they were close enough for us to reach out and touch them—and then they were past. I waited until they had left the corridor to move. When I did, I could barely walk, my legs were so numb.

"Uncloak," I whispered to Matthäus, pulling off my hood. "Now, while the guards aren't looking."

The pins-and-needles feeling began to ebb immediately. The guards came to attention as we approached.

"Balthazar?" I asked, using the name the carriage driver had directed.

One of the guards stepped forward.

I showed him the seal on the scroll. "I am Haelewise, daughter-of-Hedda, and this is my escort. I am a midwife of considerable skill. I have come to assist with the birth."

He looked down at the seal, eyes widening. Then he nodded, fiddling with the key ring at his belt. Taking their cue from Balthazar, the other guards stood aside.

It took Balthazar a minute to find the right key on his ring.

Inside the door was a long hall lit with lanterns. A shadowy tunnel, flickering, with a bone-white floor. I became aware of my boots, the dirt they must be tracking in. I dusted off my cloak and smoothed my hair, wondering how tangled it was, how much like a seer or sorcerer I must look in this rune-hood.

"Irmgard!" Balthazar called.

A woman came out of the farthest door. The same woman I had seen with Ursilda on the mountain. Her freckled face was as drawn as before, her hair pulled up tight in a bun, but her clothes were rumpled. She looked like she hadn't slept in days. As she drew close, I held out the scroll, waiting for her to recognize me or mistake me for Frederika, but she only took the scroll from my hands, distracted, noting the seal.

We waited while she read it.

"I'm glad you've come," she said when she had finished. She met my eyes, her expression uneasy. There was no recognition in her gaze. "Ursilda is not well."

"How long has she been in her chamber?"

"Two days now. The pangs have started, but they are still very far apart."

"Has her water broken?"

"This morning. As soon as she got out of bed."

Irmgard pulled out a key ring and unlocked a door.

She turned to Matthäus. "You cannot come to Ursilda's chambers, of course."

Matthäus squared his shoulders as if he wanted to argue. Then he thought better of it. "Of course not," he said with a bow, but as soon as she turned her back, his expression was fierce. He wasn't going to let me go in alone. He gave me a pointed look, fingering the hood of his cloak.

I nodded to show him I understood, then followed Irmgard out. I felt righteous, as she led me across the square. I felt determined.

The door opened into a garden courtyard, like the one at the Kürenberg cottage, but ten times larger. In the thin moonlight, lilies and gilliflowers glowed. Cracked statuettes like the ones Kunegunde kept in her garden—grotesques with snouts and horns—sneered and danced. A birdbath similar to Kunegunde's stood in the corner, ancient, covered with the same gilded runes. At the center of the courtyard was an ancient linden tree, thick with bright-green leaves. It had to be a thousand years old. A good omen, I thought, for me and my shadow.

The round moon brightened the stones.

Irmgard led me up the stairwell, an interminable series of six-stepped flights. At the last landing we paused at another locked door.

As Irmgard unlocked it, I could feel Matthäus standing behind me, his hand on my shoulder. I hoped he would be all right, that the mist wouldn't swallow him, that the brief break from being cloaked would be enough to keep him in this world.

A looking glass hung on the wall just inside the doorway. I made a show of stopping to check my reflection so he would have time to slip past. My golden eyes glowed in the lantern-light. My face was covered in dust, my hair wild, unkempt. No wonder no one had recognized me here. My mission had transformed me. I didn't look like myself.

Irmgard opened the door into a hall with many adjoining rooms. Fine rugs covered the floor, masking Matthäus's footsteps. Candles glowed in eerie lanterns. Tapestries hung on the walls. They were covered with intricately embroidered images of winged women, forest scenes with owls and nymphs, bees and snakes and beasts edged with golden thread.

A scent assaulted my nostrils: acidic, spicy, peppermint. Several of the doors were dark as Irmgard led us past them. Dim light shone through the keyhole of the door at the end of the hall. As we approached it, the smell of peppermint grew stronger, and I knew we were approaching Ursilda's birthing room. I held my breath as Irmgard unlocked the door, preparing myself to see the room I had seen in the mirror.

Stepping inside, I saw the tapestries hung over the windows. Princess Ursilda lay on the bed in a deep-green robe, curled into herself, her huge belly red and glistening with peppermint oil. Her red hair was coiled in a thick braid around her head. She had grown even more thin and pale. Her face looked almost gaunt.

The blond-haired midwife from the water-*spiegel* stood behind her, massaging her back. She startled as we walked in.

Hatred rose in my throat. The room was surprisingly empty apart from the bed and the fire burning in the hearth. Where were all of Ursilda's relatives? Her mother? Her aunts? The air in the room was tense, the otherworldly weather confusing. It swung furiously with a quick-shifting balance to the next world and back. I couldn't make sense of the feeling at first. Then I realized what it meant.

The presence of strong magic. Matthäus, at the edge of the shadow-world in a *tarnkappe*. The possibility of birth and death.

Irmgard announced us with a curtsy. "Ursilda. Beatrice heard of your troubles. She sent you another midwife." She brought the letter around the bed so that Ursilda could see the seal.

Ursilda continued to moan, barely glancing up at it.

Massaging Ursilda's back, the midwife glanced back at us, her eyes full of what looked like concern. "Thank you for coming. We've been struggling to coax this child out."

Her performance was so convincing that for a moment I almost wondered if Beatrice was wrong about her. Then I noticed how tightly she gripped Ursilda's shoulders, how white the skin was under her fingers. "Careful," I said. "You'll hurt her."

The midwife looked down and loosened her grip. "It's been a long two days," she said, as if she were genuinely embarrassed.

My eye fell upon the water pitcher and plate of rumpled-looking leaves on the bedside table, which I'd assumed were poisonous when Beatrice showed me the room in the bowl. Even through the smell of peppermint oil, I could identify their shape and grassy scent as rapunzel. That plant wasn't poisonous—I would have to work harder to figure out what poison the midwife had used.

The midwife saw me looking at the plate. "She's been craving it."

Ursilda moaned one last time, then looked at me as the pang passed. Her eyes were red and watery, unfocused, her face blotchy and pale. Loose hairs stuck out from her braid. "Haelewise," she breathed, before she succumbed to a pang.

I waited for it to end, sitting down beside her.

"We were to speak in the morning, but you left—"

I folded her hand in mine. "Beatrice sent me here to help with the birth."

Ursilda's eyes went out of focus again. She looked like she was having trouble staying conscious. "Something is wrong," she said helplessly. "The child won't come. I feel terribly ill."

The midwife drew herself up, her eyes beady and treacherous. "Like I said, she's having troubles."

I wanted to stab her right then and there. She was the king's tool, I knew, but I couldn't understand how a woman could hurt another woman in her time of need. What price could possibly be enough to betray your kind?

I tried to help Ursilda from the bed. "You've got to walk during pangs," I told her as my mother had told dozens of women.

Tears streamed down Ursilda's face. Her sobs seemed to bring on a pang. She groaned, curling into herself. "I can't—"

"I've tried to get her to walk, but she's too weak," the midwife said.

"What have you given her?" It sounded more like an accusation than I meant.

The midwife stiffened, then forced herself to meet my eyes. Her voice seemed to tremble with concern. "Only the rapunzel she craves and pennyroyal. Should we try somethin' else?"

The pennyroyal might explain some of the paleness of her skin but not all of it. I cleared my throat and tried not to sound frustrated as I explained the first things my mother had taught me, basic facts that any midwife would know. "We should give her caudle, if you haven't already. It helps with the pain."

"She's right. It's been too long since we made her drink," Irmgard said, looking at the midwife. The midwife shook her head, tight-lipped. "I'll ask the cook."

As Irmgard slipped out, I turned to the midwife. "Irmgard said her pangs are still very far apart?"

The midwife nodded. "She has hours of labor left."

I helped Ursilda out of bed and tried to get her walking. The midwife looked on skeptically. Ursilda collapsed after a single step. "I can't—"

Her legs were too weak to support her. She was probably too weak even to use a birthing stool. I helped her back to the bed, wondering if she could support herself well enough to deliver on her hands and knees. I'd helped my mother deliver several babies in that position, when other labors went on too long. This would be easier if more of her family were here to support her. "The rest of her relatives," I asked the midwife. "Aunts. Her mother. Where are they?"

The midwife gave me a bitter look. "Everyone has left the castle. There is no one else here. His highness," the midwife said, crossing herself, "is accused of murdering Princess Frederika, if you haven't heard. He's gone into hiding. Ursilda's parents have gone into hiding too." The midwife was trying to pretend she was angry on Ursilda's behalf, but the hatred she felt for Ulrich was clear in the way she spat his name. "Ursilda won't tell me where they went, so we have no way of contacting them."

"I don't *know* where they are," Ursilda cried weakly.

The midwife narrowed her eyes at me, lowering her voice. "Ursilda's mother would want to be here for the birth. Perhaps you could get Ursilda to tell you where she is so we could send for her."

I blinked at the midwife, my voice hard. "That won't be necessary."

Irmgard hurried back into the room, followed by the cook, a thick, solicitous-looking woman with a pitcher and mug.

"Add tosh and primrose," I told the cook. The woman did so and brought the mug to Ursilda. The princess drank it quickly. "Give her more."

As the cook complied, I wondered what Matthäus was doing. Probably watching the midwife from a corner. I wondered how he felt, being here, what he thought of these forbidden proceedings. Was he anxious? Was he angry on Ursilda's behalf?

I had Ursilda drink the second mug and asked the midwife to help me make a nest of rags on the floor so she wouldn't hurt her knees.

"Now look here," the midwife said. "I'm the one in charge of this birth. You can't just come in here and take over."

"Oh, but she can," Irmgard said firmly. "I've a letter from the queen that says she will. Do what she says, or you will find yourself dismissed."

The midwife blinked up at her. "As you wish."

Ursilda seemed to come alive, a little, as we helped her get to her nest on the floor. The midwife's mood seemed to have darkened, as if she suspected her time with Ursilda was coming to a close.

"How long has it been since she's eaten?" I asked.

"Too long," the midwife said, turning to Ursilda. "Do you want some more rapunzel, dear? It could help to speed your labor."

Ursilda looked at Irmgard, who looked at me, and I nodded.

That much was true. Ursilda nodded, her expression weirdly ravenous.

I watched the midwife offer her the plate from the bedside table, eyeing the leaves. They all looked and smelled like rapunzel. Perfectly innocent. As Ursilda put a leaf in her mouth, I wondered how the midwife was poisoning her.

"Water," Ursilda said. "I need water."

Instead of using the water pitcher from the bedside table, the midwife went all the way to a table on the other side of the room, where another pitcher sat. She poured a cup of its contents and brought it to Ursilda. Then she rubbed her hands with peppermint oil and began to massage Ursilda's back.

Ursilda drank the water and coughed. Then she got back down on her hands and knees. She was barely able to support herself, her limbs were so weak and trembling. The water, I thought. What's in it?

I coughed myself, then moved toward the pitcher on the other side of the room. "Is there another cup?" I asked the cook. She nodded and brought me one. I poured myself a drink, watching the midwife's expression as I brought the water to my nose to smell it. The midwife watched me coldly. The liquid had no scent at all. I thought back on Ursilda's symptoms: her weakness, her red and watery eyes, how thin she had become. Was the midwife using arsenic?

I set down the glass without drinking from it. "Beatrice decreed that I examine Ursilda in private. I would do so now."

"I can't abandon her during her pangs," the midwife said.

"You can and you will," said Irmgard. "By the queen's decree."

The midwife glared at me, her expression dark. Her eyes darted from me to the princess. "I am here by the order of the king!" Her hand went to her belt. Looking closer I thought I saw an oblong shape there. A knife.

Ursilda looked up in surprise.

I felt the otherworldly weather shifting fast in the opposite direction.

A strong pull into the next world. The possibility of death swirled around—the air going taut—like a snake waiting to strike.

A cacophony of feeling rose up in me. Certainty, that I was supposed to be here. Outrage, at the midwife's intent.

The figurine buzzed in my coin-purse, humming, furious. I knew what I had to do. I threw my body between the midwife and Ursilda.

When the midwife drew her knife, the anger inside me burst.

I was not myself when I pulled the dagger from its hilt. I was my mother, lashing out to protect me. I was the Mother's impulse to protect her daughters on earth. I thought of Rika, how I had failed her. I thought of Ursilda, the child in her belly, as I slit the midwife's throat.

The cut was jagged and deep. Blood seeped from the wound onto her dress. She crumpled to the floor.

I heard a stifled cry behind me.

Blood began to pool, thick and red, beneath the body on the rug. My body sagged with relief. Ursilda was safe. I said a quick prayer for the midwife's soul as I watched it exit this world, a thin breeze that hissed on its way out. When it was gone, the tension in the air didn't collapse. The pull into the next world continued.

The disembodied sound of sobbing filled the room.

Matthäus materialized in front of us, removing his *tarnkappe*. The sobs were his. His expression was shocked; he stared at the midwife's corpse in horror. "God have mercy," he said.

Irmgard gasped: a man, in the birthing chamber. She eyed the spreading pool of blood.

"Princess Ursilda," I blurted. "Forgive us for bringing a man into your chamber. The queen warned us you had been beset by an assassin."

Matthäus nodded, averting his eyes. "I couldn't let her face this alone."

I met his eyes, trying to gauge how he felt about what I'd done.

There was relief in his eyes, but also fear. Despite our conversation on the way here, he wasn't sure what to think. We would have to discuss this later.

I turned to Ursilda. "The midwife was sent here by the king to find out where Ulrich was, or kill you. To punish your family."

"Why?"

I met her eyes, uncertain whether I should upset her further. "Your brother ordered Frederika's murder."

Ursilda's mouth fell open, her face crumpling into a sob. "No." She began to hyperventilate. "My brother?"

I nodded, gritting my teeth. "I'm so sorry."

"Why would he kill Frederika?"

"He found out she was handfasted to someone else. A peasant."

Her face crumpled in horror. "No." She burst into tears. "No—"

Irmgard reached for her hand, trying to comfort her.

Ursilda pushed her away. "Frederika." Her voice shook. She kept shaking her head in denial. "He—*I can't*—"

"I'm sorry, Ursilda. I saw his man do it with my own eyes. He berated her for running away from him."

She stared at me, horrified, a darkness creeping into her green eyes. They narrowed, and I saw an anger there that I knew must've simmered for a very long time.

"Beatrice sent us to warn you. The king—he wants revenge. Since he can't get to your brother, he wants you dead. The midwife has been poisoning you, I suspect, with arsenic."

Ursilda's mouth fell open. "That's why I've felt so weak?"

I turned to the cook. "Is there sysemera, betony, and rue in the garden?" She nodded. "What about hydromel? Garden spurge?"

The cook nodded again, rushing out for the ingredients.

I helped Ursilda away from the blood that was seeping into the rags. She listened as I described the murder I'd witnessed, what happened when I testified against Ulrich at court. When I finished the story, a pang overwhelmed her.

I closed my eyes, taking stock of the otherworldly weather. There was no trembling, no soul at the threshold. The pull into the next world was still strong.

"Breathe," I told her, panicking. "Rock your hips. You've got to stay calm."

She arched her back, moaning with pain. All of the color drained from her face. Her eyes rolled back in her head.

I feared that her soul was about to leave her body. She didn't have the strength to push. When the pang passed, she began to pant with shallow breaths, so quickly I worried she might faint. "Breathe deep," I reminded her.

As we waited for the cook to bring back the ingredients for the antidote, Matthäus asked in a small voice, "Should I wait outside?"

"Yes," I said, meeting his eyes. "Thank you for coming with me."

He searched my eyes, his expression wary, full of fear.

Irmgard looked at him. "There's a sitting room across the hall."

As Matthäus slipped out, I pushed my concerns and fears about him down; I made myself focus on the birth. I instructed Irmgard to massage Ursilda's back. Ursilda wailed, her body going rigid, as the cook hurried in with the herbs.

"Another pang!" Irmgard cried.

I nodded as I began to work on expressing the juice from the plants. "They're coming faster now. It's all the excitement." I turned to Ursilda. "Can you push?"

Ursilda screamed at the top of her lungs, arching her back. Her eyes rolled back in her head, then fluttered shut. She crumpled to her belly in the rags.

I left the nearly finished preparation to lay her on her side, putting my palm to her belly, feeling the contraction roll beneath her skin. The baby was still moving. Alive. I could feel it. Moving my hand over her belly, I could feel the baby's head, deep down in the pelvis. Ursilda's breathing was growing more ragged, more shallow.

I felt for her pulse. It was weak.

The contraction stopped.

"Is she going to live?" Irmgard asked, her voice quavering.

I didn't know how to answer the question. There was no way to know whether the preparation would work. I finished making it, quickly, mixing the juice of sysemera, betony, and rue, with garden spurge. I poured it into a cup. "We have to get her to take this."

Irmgard went to Ursilda and shook her. "Your highness—"

"Be gentle," I warned her.

"Wake up!"

Ursilda would not stir.

Taking a deep breath, I went to the princess, cupping the bottom of her jaw to open her lips, as I had once done for my mother. I poured the mixture into her mouth, pressing her lips tightly shut so the liquid wouldn't leak out. "Give me the hydromel," I told the cook. The woman complied.

Ursilda's belly contracted again. She stirred, moaning softly without opening her eyes. It was worrisome that her pangs weren't waking her up. I waited for the contraction to pass, checking her birth canal to see how far along she was. It was nearly time, but I could still feel no soul at the threshold. The pull still went in the other direction. Ursilda had to wake up soon, or both she and the child would be lost.

When the contraction passed, I opened her mouth again to give her hydromel. She gagged involuntarily on the foam it brought up in her throat, but otherwise she did not stir.

Mother, I prayed, clasping her limp hand in my own. Help me save them. I cannot bear another death on my watch.

Ursilda lay still on her side on the rags on the floor. My heart thudded in my throat.

And then, after a blessed moment, Ursilda began to sputter and cough, as foam leaked from her mouth. I sat her upright so she wouldn't choke. I told the cook to bring the chamber pot.

As the cook held it in front of her, Ursilda's eyes flew open. She threw up a foamy substance, her eyes animal-wild and panicked.

When she was finished, I asked Irmgard to pour her a mug of the caudle. Ursilda drank it down between pangs, as if she suffered from great thirst. I checked between her legs and saw that the birth tunnel had opened enough for her to push. "Do you feel any stronger?"

She shook her head.

"Do you think you could try the birthing stool?"

She stared at it skeptically, shaking her head again.

"She needs more caudle," I said.

The cook hurried to pour her another mug. I held it to her lips.

"Now could you try? Sometimes it helps to change positions."

She hung her head, and I knew that she would, though I worried she simply didn't have the strength to argue. I helped her over to the birthing stool and told her to gather her strength for the next pang. She could barely hold herself up. Her legs trembled violently. Her hands shook. I took her wrist, checking for her pulse. Her heartbeat was weak, irregular. The antidote could only do so much. I motioned for Irmgard and the cook to come over and help hold her up. They did so, murmuring soft words of encouragement. "You can do this. You must."

When the next pang came, Ursilda finally began to push, half growling, half screaming a terrible animal cry.

I could still sense no soul, no trembling at the threshold. I crouched on the floor before her. The babe crowned, a little pink circle emerging from the birth canal, sticky with blood and mucus. Was it going to be born dead?

The pull into the next world was so strong, I felt dizzy. As the veil between worlds opened, Ursilda looked at me, her expression woozy—eyes crossed—and let go of my hand. She slumped on her stool.

"Ursilda?" Irmgard said, her voice trembling.

I felt for her pulse again. For a moment there was nothing. Then I thought I felt a faint, single beat. I moved my fingers to see if I was missing a more regular pulse. The princess slumped on the birthing stool in Irmgard's arms, completely unresponsive. A long moment passed during which I avoided Irmgard's gaze. I was afraid we were too late, that in an instant, I would see a dewy soul lift from her mouth. The poison had been too long in her blood.

I reached for the figurine in my pocket, rubbing it, praying for the otherworldly balance to shift. I heard a shadowy voice from the next world. *Move her*, the Mother hissed.

Suddenly I understood. This position wasn't going to work. Panicking, with all my strength, I began to pull her to her hands and knees. "Help me," I told Irmgard.

Another pang contracted Ursilda's stomach as we moved her. She moaned, her eyes flying open.

And then I felt it: the trembling in the air. The child's soul. "Push," I said, crouching beside her. "Ursilda. It's time. Push!"

The princess started sobbing. She summoned up all the strength she had and pushed, letting out a terrible animal growl.

And then the child was out, an angry pink baby girl with a full head of bright-red hair. She was small for a newborn, but not unhealthily so. A squirming weight in my arms, silent.

The princess craned her neck to see the child, her eyes full of exhaustion. Tears streamed down her face. I wiped my hand on my cloak and reached into the baby's throat to clear it of debris. As I finished, I felt goose bumps. A whisper-wind slipped past me. Her soul, flying to enter her.

Her mewling cries awakened a longing so deep, my breath caught in my throat. Her softness, her weight in my arms. Every-thing about holding her felt *right*. When she looked up at me, I saw her eyes, full of need—and completely black. I gasped, awestruck. This baby was like me. She would have the gift.

I held her tight, looking into those eyes, cooing, the strongest mother-greed I've ever felt choking my heart. When Ursilda reached out to touch her—may I be forgiven—I winced. Ursilda tried to stand from her stool, her legs wobbling, falling backward.

"Let's get you cleaned up first and in bed," I said, smiling, using her weakness as an excuse. My eyes fell on the corpse on the floor, the blood pooling around it. It was a dark thing, to see a body as a nuisance. But that's how I felt, staring down at what was left of the midwife: I cursed the trouble she had made for us. "Could you take care of that?" I asked the cook.

"Aye," the cook said. "I'll go get help."

As the cook left to go find the guards, Irmgard used a rag to wipe Ursilda's legs. I bathed the child, swaddled her bottom, and put her in a pretty white embroidered gown. I rocked her and rocked her, my heart full of a greed so pure, so perfect, I couldn't stand it.

Irmgard helped Ursilda over to the bed. She was so weak, she nearly fell three times before she collapsed on the pillows. I watched Irmgard prop her up, straightening her robe, noticing how pale she still was. The midwife must have been poisoning her for a week. Who knows how much arsenic she had been given and when? I hoped her body had protected the child from the poison. Kunegunde would say the best cure for that was mother's milk, but would Ursilda even be able to nurse?

The child had gone silent in my arms. Her black eyes watching me watch her. When Ursilda was settled, I made myself give her the baby, propping her up with a nest of pillows, a choking sensation in my throat. Mine mine mine, a terrible voice inside me whispered. I cursed that voice when I first heard it, I did.

At first.

Irmgard opened Ursilda's robe, and the child began squirming, healthy, hungry, searching out her first meal. As the baby rooted, I breathed deep, trying to push the horrible voice away. Thank you, Mother, I prayed, for everything you've done so far. I have done everything you commanded. Is there anything more I can do to help?

The child latched onto Ursilda and began to suckle.

By the time the guards came back with the cook to take care of the body, we had covered the pair in blankets. Ursilda's eyes fluttered closed, as the baby tried to coax milk from her breast.

After a moment, the child began to squirm. "Try the other breast."

Irmgard helped her move the child. Ursilda looked worried. Her face was drawn. The shadows beneath her eyes were deep.

She straightened suddenly in bed, her expression panicked, as if something had just occurred to her. "What's to stop the king from sending someone else?" The child squirmed in her arms.

I looked up at her, remembering my dream.

Seeing my expression, Ursilda clutched the baby tighter, rattled. "Tell me what you know."

"The Mother speaks to me," I said quietly. "I have the gift."

The child began to mewl, impatient for milk that wasn't flowing. "We need goat's milk," I told the cook. "Get it yourself. Don't let anyone do it for you."

The cook nodded, understanding, then hurried out.

Ursilda shivered as she looked at Irmgard. The bedroom was still and quiet. Irmgard turned to me. "Tell us everything."

"You can speak freely in front of Irmgard," Ursilda said.

We all stared at one another for a long moment. I drew a deep breath. "As you wish. I am Haelewise, daughter-of-Hedda, a supplicant to the circle of daughters who worship the Mother. Sometimes the Mother sends me dreams. Visions that will come to pass unless I do something about them. I foresaw Princess Frederika's murder but failed to stop it. Last night, the Mother told me in a dream that the king would send another assassin after this attempt failed. A masked man who will creep through that window at the waning half moon to kill both of you." Anger made my voice choke. "I saw the knife he brought to the cradle. It bore the symbol of the king."

Ursilda struggled to control her emotions. She looked down at the baby, tears streaming down her cheeks. "To kill her?"

"I'm afraid so." I sighed, uncomfortable. "It's not safe here for you, for the child, until the king captures Ulrich and forgives the rest of your family. If he ever does—"

Ursilda started to sob quietly. Her breath hitched. "I can't go anywhere while I'm this weak."

She was right. She was too sick to walk. She couldn't even nurse. Her arms were shaking. She was struggling to hold even the smallest newborn in bed. The baby wailed.

The cook interrupted our stalemate, just then, with a bottle of goat's milk and a feeding horn. Irmgard bustled around, warming the milk and filling the horn. Ursilda and I fell silent, watching her work. When she handed Ursilda the horn, the princess offered the child the teat. The child wouldn't latch on.

I took the baby, who quieted at my touch. I showed Ursilda how to hold the horn so she could get a good suck. The baby drank noisily.

The look on Ursilda's face was heartbreaking. "I'm not doing her any good," she breathed. "She doesn't need me."

"Don't be silly," I said, but as soon as the child left my arms, she started crying again.

Beside the bed, Irmgard shook her head in protest. Ursilda looked at me. I could tell what she was thinking. It wasn't safe here, but she didn't have the strength to leave. She didn't even have the strength to hold a horn of milk.

The temptation was too great. It felt *right* to say what I said next. The words were out of my mouth before I had time to think twice.

"We could take her to Gothel."

I knew, as soon as I said the words, that Ursilda would say yes. She was weak, filled with motherly insecurity. I knew I was taking advantage of her. But my suggestion was a good one—the tower was safe— and I didn't want to give this baby up.

"She would be safe at Gothel from the king's assassins. When you recover your strength, you could join us."

Ursilda's eyes shone with hope as she nodded, eager. "Kunegunde is a daughter-of-the-Mother. We've been estranged for almost a decade, but she's still bound by oath to help."

The thought of seeing Kunegunde again filled me with dread—on second thought, I didn't even know if she would let us into the tower—but I wanted that baby so badly, any excuse to take her sounded good. And where else would Matthäus and I go?

"I will remind her of her oath. You can use the water-*spiegel* to keep an eye on her until you recover."

Ursilda nodded. "Thank you."

I held the child up. "Do you want to hold her again?"

"I don't have the strength," Ursilda said, kissing the child's forehead wanly. The baby stared up at her, wide-eyed, having already emptied the goat's horn of milk. "Keep her safe until I join you. But what do I tell my father? Where do I say the baby went?"

I stared at her for a long moment, a story forming in my mind. "Tell him the truth. But tell it like this. The new midwife was a witch. She took the baby from your arms when you were too weak to stop her, then flew away with your child into the night."

CHAPTER THIRTY-THREE

W e rode to Gothel, cloaked, the child sleeping in her sling at my
breast. So soundly, it was as if the Mother had enchanted her.
We didn't talk as we rode, afraid Ulrich would find us, the only
sound the echo of our invisible horses' hooves on the mountain
path. The mist dressed the trees in ghostly lace. I thought about
how I would convince Kunegunde to let a man stay at the tower.
If only I had something to offer her to make it worth her while. I
could only hope her oath to the circle would have weight.

I cradled the babe in my sling as we rode. Until her mother
came to get her, I would be the one to hold her, to nurse her, to
come to her when she cried in her sleep. I clutched her tightly. As I
held her, my sense of self blurred into a thousand shadows. She was
me, and I was my mother and every mother who had ever lived
before her.

Gothel wasn't a long ride from the castle. As we drew close to
the mountain where the tower stood, I could feel an unsettling
presence, an ominous disturbance in the otherworldly weather.
It was coming closer. I pulled on my reins. "Wait," I whispered.
Matthäus stopped beside me.

I reached into my coin-purse with shadowy fingers, but the
bird-mother figurine was cold. I rubbed her and closed my eyes,
praying for the Mother to improve the sensitivity of my gift. After
a moment, the figurine grew warm, and I could sense the shadow-
world with greater precision than ever before. I was already half
in it. Though I couldn't see Matthäus or Nëbel, I could sense their
tarnkappen, two otherworldly rivers flowing, nearby, into the next

world. And in the distance, where I felt the presence, I could feel a river flowing in the opposite direction, into the forest from the shadow-world.

Then I heard it. The distant sound of a howl.

Nëbel spooked, dancing nervously, her muscles tensing beneath me. A chill passed through me as I remembered what Albrecht told the king's men when they arrived at the castle—that Ulrich had gone hunting. God's teeth, I thought. That presence pulling shadow into this world. It's Ulrich, wearing the wolf-skin.

Nëbel snorted, nervous. I closed my eyes, trying to pinpoint Ulrich's location. He was headed this way. My first thought was for the child's safety, then Matthäus's. I clutched Nëbel's reins tight, resolute. The horse danced, and I could tell she was rolling her eyes with fear.

"What was that?" Matthäus asked, his voice small, as if he knew the answer to his question already.

"Ulrich," I said. "He's coming for me."

I patted Nëbel, trying to calm her. He'd been lying in wait for me in the woods around the tower of Gothel. How did he know I would return? I hadn't planned to. My thoughts raced. Maybe he didn't. One of the villagers could've told him that we harbored Rika at Gothel, or one of his guards could've found my name in the register in the porterhouse. There were so many ways he could've known to look for me here, in fact, that I felt foolish for not expecting that he would. The realization brought tears to my eyes. I was so naïve. How was I going to face such a conniving monster?

Nëbel snorted, sensing my anxiety, panicking, beginning to neigh and prance. I closed my eyes again, reaching out to see where Ulrich was now. I almost gasped, he'd closed so much distance so quickly. He was heading straight for us, as if he knew where we were. Maybe I hadn't been hooded long enough. Did the full moon make the wolf-skin stronger than the cloak? Maybe he was tracking my scent. He had a wolf's sense of smell. The *tarnkappen* were at their weakest now.

The child. Matthäus. Who knew what he'd do to them when he found us?

"I'm going to face him," I told Matthäus, working through it as I spoke, "so you and the baby can get away."

"No," he whispered fiercely.

"The child's safety comes first," I said, dismounting, my voice hard. There could be no argument about this. If Ulrich was coming after me, the baby needed to be far away. I fumbled for the place where I could feel Matthäus's *tarnkappe* working, finding his horse's stirrup. "Where are you? Here. Let me give her to you."

"Haelewise—" Matthäus touched my arm. His voice was tender, breaking. "I don't want to leave you."

"He's looking for *me*. I don't want you or the child to be around when I confront him." I found his hand and squeezed it.

He dismounted, arguing. "I won't—" But his protest was interrupted by my lips, fumbling for where I thought his mouth would be. They found his cheek, but he moved, fumbling to press his mouth against mine. It was a strange sensation to kiss when we were half in the shadow-world. My mouth was numb, full of pins and needles. The sensation made me dizzy.

Unwrapping the sling from around my breast, I fitted it around his shoulders, tucking the child into the fabric, pressing her to his chest, making sure she was fitted in tight. When she was settled, I kissed her forehead. She whimpered, a tiny squall.

"Keep your hood on. Ride away. I'm going to loose Nëbel. She's panicking. She'll give away my location."

"What are you going to do?"

"I don't know. I can't think while the child is unsafe."

"Where do I go?"

"It doesn't matter where you go. Just hide. I'll be able to find you as long as you're wearing the cloak."

He made a strangled sound, a final noise of complaint. Then he pulled himself together. "All right. If you see no other way. Godspeed, Haelewise. Be safe. I'll see you soon."

There was a pause. Then I heard the sound of hooves thudding the ground—he was fleeing. I uncloaked Nëbel and slapped her side. She took off after them.

Once they were gone, I found I could concentrate on the situation at hand. I turned it over in my mind, racking my brain for some weakness of Ulrich's that I could exploit. My thoughts were tangled, uncertain. Last time, I'd exploited his lust. Last time—

I reached for the figurine in my coin-purse, rubbing her, praying. Please, I breathed. Mother, please, guide me—

The veil slipped open, and the otherworldly balance tilted briefly toward this world. A buzzing filled my ears, like bees rising up to protect the hive. *Steal the wolf-skin*, a feminine voice buzzed from the next world—outraged—before the balance tilted back.

Certainty coursed through me. I blinked, grateful that I knew what to do. If I took the wolf-skin from Ulrich, it would steal his power. What was more, Kunegunde would be so happy with me, she might not turn Matthäus away. But how could I steal it?

He can't see me, I thought. I'm thinking of this wrong. I don't have to be the hunted. I can be the *huntress*.

I surveyed the woods around me. A nearby juniper tree with a tangled trunk looked like it would be easy enough to climb. I clambered up it, hurrying, finding a place to crouch about halfway up—far enough that I would be out of his reach, but not so far that I couldn't jump. Pulling my hood down, tying my *tarnkappe* as tight about me as I could, I drew my bow.

I could feel him moving closer, monstrous, malignant. As I lay in wait, I thought of the dagger he commanded his assassin to put in Rika's heart, the hand he slipped under my shift, the sickly sweet taste of his vile mouth on mine. Let him come, I thought, nocking an arrow.

And then there he was. The largest wolf I'd ever seen, loping out of the shadows. A terrible thing, *wrong*, with none of the beauty of the natural beast. He was grotesque. His shoulders malformed, bones sticking out, his chest barrel-shaped and huge. His fur rippled like smoke. He moved slowly, lifting his snout to sniff the air, as if he was trying to find my scent.

I smiled. He didn't know where I was. Pulling the cloak tighter about me had helped to obscure my location from him.

He loped closer, snout raised, sniffing the air without stopping to linger on my particular tree. He snarled something, a single sound, a guttural sound, more gnarl than speech. He growled, frustrated, tried again. This time, it was close enough to words that I could make out what he meant. "*Haeeel. I kno' yo' herrrre.*"

I stiffened, afraid. Perhaps my leg moved slightly against the trunk. He looked up, snarled, ears flattening, hackles rising, sniffing the air around my tree. When I saw his face, my stomach turned with revulsion, with hate. Eyes like holes, gaping wide. I would only get one shot at him.

He growled, showing his teeth.

I aimed my arrow at his heart. If my shot killed him, problem solved. But if it didn't—he was so large—better that it lodge someplace difficult to get out. Saying a quick prayer that my aim would be true, I let the arrow fly. It soared down at him, striking him in his barreled chest before he could even flinch, and he let out a canine howl of pain.

"*Haelllll!*" He whined, pawing at the arrow. It had struck deep enough that it would not easily come out. When his paw struck its shaft, he whined in pain. Then his body was shaking, changing, the smoke of his fur beginning to ripple. Tendrils of shadow dissolved into mist where his shoulders had been. His fur disappearing, becoming nothing, leaving a man crumpled on the forest floor in its place, bloodied, moaning, inspecting the arrow in his chest.

As I had expected, he had taken the wolf-skin off so he could use his hands to remove the arrow. He moved to check the wound, squinting. It was so close to his heart, he was afraid to pull it out. The wolf-skin lay beside him, forgotten, a malignant thing. I could feel it pulling shadow from the next world—a cloud dark and stinking, hellish—even without him in it.

I returned my bow to its place on my back, pulled my cloak tight, and dropped from my tree. Everything was going according to my plan. He still couldn't see me.

He flinched at the sound of my feet hitting the ground. "Haele-wise!" he screamed, furious, my name a moan of pain, his eyes wild, searching for me.

"I'm here," I whispered, taking great joy in imagining how the words would seem to him. My voice singsong like a child's, echoing from the shadow as if I were some sort of demon. I moved quickly as soon as I said the words, dancing as it occurred to me what to say next: the words he'd said to me in the hall on the mountain. "Are you afraid of me?"

Ulrich closed his eyes, shuddering, revulsion on his face. I couldn't tell if it was a reaction to pain, or what I'd said, or both.

His body went rigid, and I could see fear warring with anger on his face. The anger was to be expected, it was part of who he was, but the fear surprised me. I took a perverse pleasure in that fear, I confess. I never claimed to be a holy woman.

I laughed inwardly, imagining the world from his perspective, crumpled on the forest floor, arrowshot by the girl he tried to rape and kill.

Ulrich pushed himself up to his hands and knees, then stood, breaking off the part of the arrow that was not sunk in his chest. "No," he said, quietly furious. "I'm not afraid. You're just a girl. A girl who's very confused about the way the world works. You harbored my wife at Gothel. You accused me of murder, when all I did was deliver a punishment that was well within my rights. Frederika was a whore, a faithless wife."

His voice had gone very calm while he spoke, as if he was honestly trying to explain these things to me. He searched the forest around him, trying to ascertain my location. Without the wolf-skin, he had no idea where I was.

By then I was standing behind him, where the wolf-skin lay crumpled, forgotten on the ground. When I crept up to retrieve it as I had been planning, the otherworldly weather went berserk. Power zapped from this world to the next and back, ricocheting, drawn to my invisible hand. It was like being stung by a thousand wasps. I screamed, leaping away, realizing the *tarnkappe* and the wolf-skin couldn't be carried by the same person at once; the mist didn't know which direction to go.

Ulrich turned toward the sound. "There you are," he said, clearly taking pleasure in the sound of my pain, though I could tell he was also trying to decipher the reason for my scream. After a moment, he looked down and saw the wolf-skin.

He smiled and bent down to pick it up.

My heart sank. Dread filled my stomach.

He pulled one of its sleeves over his arm, speaking conversationally, his voice maddeningly calm.

"I'm going to punish you. You've done worse to me than Rika. I'll have to be in hiding forever. My family will live in shame. Did you really think you would be safe at Gothel? When I have *this*?"

He pulled the other sleeve on.

Terrible tongues of shadow began to lick the air around him, covering his body in grotesque sinew. His shoulders grew broader, his figure became bulkier, and shadows sprouted from his skin. His nose sank into his mouth, elongating into a snout. His eyes fell in on themselves. The process was so grotesque, I shuddered. Everything about it was wrong.

He sniffed the air, scenting me out. After a moment, his sunken eyes fixed on the air where I couldn't be seen. He lunged straight for me, snarling, raking a claw across my breast.

I fell beneath him. He pawed at me, pushing my hood to the forest floor. Unhooded, he could meet my eyes. He snarled, leering. His breath was foul. *"I'm goin' to ennnjoyy this."*

He pushed me down, the weight of his claws painful on my chest. They stung, tearing through the fabric of my cloak, my dress. I braced myself, waiting for it to happen. He opened his mouth, his teeth flashing white in the moonlight.

Then the smoke of his fur began to ripple. The sinews of his shoulders began to dissolve into mist. His fur disappearing, he whirled around, clawing at what appeared to be thin air.

I heard a yelp.

"Matthäus!" I screamed, pulling the dagger from my belt. It flashed, silver, as I plunged it into the great wolf's back.

The beast fell. The shadows shriveled and shrank.

Matthäus uncloaked beside the crumpled form of Ulrich, holding the wolf-skin in his hand, grinning a roguish grin. His sleeve had been torn, but it was only slightly bloodied. He followed my eyes. "Don't worry. It isn't bad. Are you all right?"

I looked down at the wounds on my breast. I couldn't feel a thing. My heart was pounding so hard, I had forgotten about them. "The baby," I said. "Where did you put the baby?"

He dropped the wolf-skin and hurried away.

I pushed myself up on my hand to look at Ulrich. He lay on his side, curled up like a child in bed, moaning. The dagger had gone deep into his back, and he was bleeding badly. His eyes were wild, as he looked at me. He knew death was coming.

I gazed at him without speaking, waiting for him to leave this world. I knew we would all be the better for it when he was gone. I felt no pity for him. The balance tilted, and I felt the next world pull.

In a moment, it happened. His soul left his mouth—a stinking thing, clouded. The veil hissed as it swallowed it up.

A few tendrils of shadow slipped out through the fissure toward the wolf-skin. I looked over at the miserable thing. I was revulsed by the way it clawed at the air, the malignant shadow it drew around it. As soon as I showed it to Kunegunde, I decided, we would destroy it. She would need to see it for herself.

Matthäus came back with the child.

"Where did you put her?"

"Forgive me," he said. "I made her a cradle from the sling and hung it from a tree. I needed to be sure you were all right."

Ignoring the pain returning to the wounds in my chest, I took the baby from his arms, wrapping her in the sling, looking into her eyes. She was so perfect, so pure, so unaware of anything that had just happened. For a split second, everything seemed right with the world. I held her tight.

CHAPTER THIRTY-FOUR

W e called our horses back and mounted them, debating whether
to wear our cloaks the rest of the way. We figured we should
in case the king's men should stumble upon us. But if we tried to
carry the wolf-skin cloaked, the otherworldly weather went wild.
In the end, we decided Matthäus and his horse would wear *tarnkappen*, but my horse and I would go uncloaked so we could carry the
wolf-skin in a sack. The tower wasn't far. It was only a little ways
into the forest before we were approaching the circle. Two ravens
dove from the sky to circle us. I heard Matthäus suck in his breath.
I could feel his anxiety beside me, though I couldn't see his face.
When the ravens began diving at him, despite being cloaked, I
squeezed Nëbel's flanks. She stopped, whinnying.

"What is it?" he whispered, his voice filled with dread.

"Animals can sense magic."

As we drew near enough to the tower to see the boulders that
spiked up like teeth, I reminded him about the protective spell that
kept this place hidden from the eyes of men. He nodded, remembering, his expression full of foreboding. I hadn't thought about
what it would be like for him to stay at Gothel. Without his sight,
he would be dependent on me until he learned his way around.

We dismounted our horses and took off their hoods to lead them
through the stone circle. They were spooked—neighing, wild-eyed—
with the ravens flying about and the mist. We wrapped their leads
three times around our arms. The ravens flew back to the tower,
calling out. Their croaks echoed. The baby cried out. I held her tight
and rocked her, swaying my hips. "Hush," I told her, "hush—"

Then I turned to Matthäus. "Remove your hood."

Matthäus shrugged his hood off and reached out, letting me lead him toward the stone circle. The horses pulled on their leads behind us, whinnying, reluctant. The spell snapped through the air between the boulders, eager for the chance to make something happen. The hair on my arms and legs stood on end. The baby went quiet too, as if she could sense the magic. And then, blinking with the insight, I realized that she probably could. She had the gift.

As I bent down to kiss her forehead, everything seemed to fall into place. It felt right to be hurrying toward the tower with the child and Matthäus.

We stepped through the stone circle, clutching each other's hands. Our feet landed in unison. The air around us was thinner than ever.

Up ahead, we could hear the sound of water burbling into the pool where I had once bathed. Through the trees, I could see the water glittering. A family of gray geese and their half-grown yellow goslings were floating on it, fast asleep, beaks tucked under their wings. As we drew close, most of the gray geese flew away in a burst of feathers, but the mother goose stayed behind with her goslings to hiss at us.

Matthäus let out a nervous laugh as we circled the pool, a safe distance away from her. "She's so angry."

The bird Kunegunde called Zweite dove down at Matthäus, until I shooed him away. Matthäus's voice was frightened. "Haelewise. The spell. I can't see."

"I can. Hold my hand," I told him. "Don't let go."

I led him through the trees, the horses following behind us. The baby watched me, wide-eyed, from her sling, more aware than I had ever seen a newborn be. An amber-eyed raven flew back toward us and dove at Matthäus's face. *Kraek*, the bird screamed, as Matthäus threw up his hands. It dove at him again and again, pecking his cheeks, his forehead.

"Go home," I screamed, immediately regretting it. The effort of screaming made the wounds on my breast sting, and the baby started crying. "Give me a chance to explain," I continued more quietly, as I tried to soothe the infant.

The bird dove at Matthäus one more time—a warning—then flew away. Behind me, he cleared his throat, his hands still protecting his face. "Is it gone? Did that bird just *listen* to you?"

"Yes," I said, knowing he wouldn't believe me if I tried to explain it. "Are you hurt? Let me see your face."

He opened his hands, and I saw that his cheeks were covered in pockmarks. They looked just like the ones my father had after he found someone to write a letter to the bishop. He came *here*, I realized. Kunegunde wrote that letter for him.

My mind reeled. "Do they hurt?" I asked after a moment.

"I'll be all right."

Cautiously, we resumed our walk. Soon the tower rose up before us, hazy with thin moonlight, the vine-covered walls of the garden behind it, the stable shadowy and peaceful. The sight of the place made me draw in my breath with a strange mixture of relief and anxiety. On the one hand, with Ulrich dead, we were safer here than we had been fleeing the castle. On the other, there was the matter of Kunegunde and the fact that I had brought a man with me.

I put the horses in the stable, then took off our hoods and led Matthäus slowly toward the tower. Behind me, with his free hand, he fumbled for the paternoster beads in his coin-purse, saying the prayer under his breath.

Kunegunde opened the heavy door when we were a stone's throw away. "Haelewise," she called out in a warning tone, her black and white hair tumbling down over her shoulders in wild tangles. Her golden eyes flashed with warning. "Men are not welcome here."

The baby made a mewling sound at my breast. I clutched Matthäus's hand tighter than ever. He squeezed mine in response, his face stricken with fear. I was glad he couldn't see the look on my grandmother's face. "We had nowhere else to go."

"What have you got in that sling?"

"A child with the gift. The mother, Princess Ursilda, was nearly killed by King Frederick's assassin."

Kunegunde shook her head slowly. "King Frederick—"

"Ursilda says you're still a daughter-of-the-Mother. That you're bound by oath to help us."

"The daughters are enlisting the help of men now?" She looked at Matthäus, sizing him up. "He is of the enemy. Do you not see the beads in his hand? The prayer he invokes?"

"It's the Mother who has been speaking to me all this time. I know you know that. She wants to be restored to her throne, to reunite with the Father on earth—"

"You're going to get yourself killed," Kunegunde said bitterly. She shook her head, then closed her eyes and drew a deep breath.

I met her eyes. "Not if you let us in. Kunegunde, please. This child's life hangs in the balance."

Kunegunde glanced at the baby in my arms. All she could see was the back of its head. "Boy or girl?" she asked, her voice hesitant.

"Girl," I said. "Let us in. This man helped me kill Ulrich!"

"He what?"

"Ulrich is dead. Matthäus took the wolf-skin from his back."

Her eyes widened. "Did he *really*?"

I showed it to her. She took the malignant thing from my hands, her nose crinkling at its stench. Then she gave me a giddy smile. "Oh, Haelewise, thank you. What a gift. We'll burn it tonight!"

"Now please," I said. "We're wounded. Let us inside."

She shook her head, meeting my eyes. "No. This doesn't change anything. You and the baby may stay, but he cannot."

Matthäus straightened, uneasy. The paternoster beads rattled in his hands. "I won't tell a soul what happens here," Matthäus spoke up, his voice pleading. "I swear it. I'd never do anything that would harm Haelewise."

My thoughts raced. How could I convince Kunegunde to let Matthäus stay? I couldn't bear to lose him again. Not after all we'd been through. "Gothel is safe now, Kunegunde. We're handfasted. Matthäus is to me what your lord was to you. I would trust him with my life."

Kunegunde closed her eyes, breathing softly, as if she had grown tired of arguing with us. When she spoke, there was a finality in her tone, a frustration that she needed to explain herself again. "I pity you, Haelewise. In truth, I do. But this is not my law. It's the law of this place. Nothing you say now can change the choice before you. You can protect this baby here, or go with him. If he tries to stay, I'll drive him out."

My stomach dropped. All my plans, the life I'd imagined with Matthäus, the task I was completing for the Mother, began to waver. I loved him with my whole heart, but where would we go if not here? Gothel was the safest place for the child, now that we had the wolf-skin. We couldn't run from the king's assassins indefinitely.

I imagined what it would be like for the three of us to flee the king. We would be like the Holy Family fleeing Herod, crossing rivers and deserts in search of some distant hiding place. A mountain village in Moravia. A cave in Egypt. Everywhere, looking over our shoulders. All because I couldn't bear to be parted from Matthäus.

I looked at Matthäus, saw the shame on his face. He didn't want me to have to make this choice any more than I did.

The baby made a cooing sound, looking up, her black eyes—wide and innocent—watching, waiting.

It wouldn't be fair. I couldn't put her life in danger.

I searched Matthäus's face. Grief ripped through me. I wanted to pull my grandmother limb from limb.

"I'm sorry," I told him quietly. "This is the only safe place."

Kunegunde chuckled. "Finally, you understand—"

"I can't endanger the child for our sake."

Matthäus bowed his head. It took him a moment to answer. "I understand."

"Would you wait for me until Ursilda takes the child back? You could go back to your wife—" I winced. "You could work in your father's shop."

He nodded, quickly, trying to master the hurt that showed clearly on his face.

"I don't know how long it will be, I'll be honest."

"I would wait for you forever."

"What a *sweet* little arrangement you've made," Kunegunde said, a shadow passing over her face, quickly enough that I didn't recognize what it meant. She smiled, as if she were moved by the love we had just shown each other. I thought at first that it was genuine. Then her voice turned monstrous and cold. "You've figured everything out, haven't you, little one. But I'm afraid it isn't enough."

I thought back to what had happened after Albrecht left the tower, the lies he told the king, the writ that had been issued for her death. She wasn't going to let Matthäus leave. "Kunegunde," I said. "Wait—"

Her posture straightened and her eyes snapped up from her feet. She drew up her shoulders and opened her mouth, a sorrowful expression on her face.

"*Xär dhorns,*" she sang, her voice shaking with regret. The words drew the air taut. Something zipped through the air, a power, and my skin prickled with a horripilation of dread. She fumbled in her pouch and uncorked a phial. With a flick of her wrist, a cloud of powder hit Matthäus. His face crumpled. "My eyes!"

The babe began to cry in her sling.

"Kunegunde?" I screamed, my voice rising with desperation. "What are you doing? Please, I'm begging you. Stop!"

When Kunegunde spoke the words she spoke next—words I only heard once but found in her spellbook after she died—the world collapsed in on itself. *"Kord agnator vividvant-svas!"*

All the power her words summoned seemed to hang for a moment in the air around Matthäus. I was sure it was going to kill him, terrified I was going to watch him die. Then it entered him, like a blast of mist against his chest. He stumbled backward, and when he looked up next, his face was blank. Not blank as it had been before due to blindness, but blank due to forgetfulness.

"Matthäus?" I whispered.

He turned toward the sound of my voice. "Who are you? Where am I?" he said, letting go of my hand. "Why can't I see?"

The baby cried louder in her sling. I rocked her, staring in horror at him. "It's me. Haelewise."

"Haelewise?" he said, as if he were repeating the name of a song he hadn't heard.

Kunegunde met my eyes, smiling sadly. "I'm sorry."

"Why doesn't he know who I am?"

"He can't leave here with his memory of you intact. He'll keep coming back, over and over. He'll lead men to us. The place will be crawling with them."

I sobbed. "Kunegunde. What have you done?"

"Everything that is done can be undone."

It took me a moment to understand what she meant. I turned to Matthäus, panicked. "My name is Haelewise," I said, my voice choked. "Your childhood friend, your—"

"Don't listen to her, dear," Kunegunde interrupted. "She'll just confuse you. This will all be over soon. Don't worry. I'll lead you out of this mist and home to your wife."

His eyes widened, searching the mist for the source of her voice. He nodded, slowly, as if remembering. "Phoebe," he said, looking relieved to be sure of something. He turned toward the sound of Kunegunde's voice. "Yes. Please. Take me to her."

I forgot to breathe. The world went white. I went numb with disbelief. It was too much to see his love for me so completely unmade.

I couldn't watch as Kunegunde led him from the tower. My breath hitched, and my shoulders shook. I wanted to run after them, stop Matthäus from going to Phoebe, find a way to break the spell and run away with him and the child into the desert. But I had made my choice.

The child began to wail in my arms. After a while, her cries became more insistent, and I knew she needed to be fed. I found Kunegunde's birth bag and the goat's horn with the cloth teat. Then I walked to the barn and milked a she-goat in her sleep. When the horn was full, I found my way back to the chair where Kunegunde often sat. The baby calmed immediately when I offered her the goat's horn. As she suckled, I cradled her in her sling, rocking her, nursing the ache in my heart.

Tears wet my cheeks.

I don't know how long I sat there, crying. Long after the babe had fallen asleep. The sobs that poured out of me were wretched. The next thing I knew, the shadows in the room had changed, and the baby was crying again in her sling. Had I fallen asleep? How much time had passed? Was she hungry again? Was she wet?

I changed her swaddling. Then back to the barn I went to milk the she-goat. As I sat in the chair with her, the child sucked noisily on the goat's horn, making soft little gasping noises. I rocked her back and forth.

She looked up at me, her eyes hungry and full of gratitude.

For a while, I found myself numb even to the pleasure of nursing her. But when the horn was empty and she threw her head back into the crook of my arm, milk-drunk, the mother in me reawakened. The heft of her, her softness, the smoothness of her skin. She was alive. I had saved her like I was supposed to do. She was a boon, a gift. The only thing that I'd ever done right.

I took solace in the comfort I felt, rocking her as she slept in my arms. I felt my mother's presence inside me, as I sang the lullaby she sang to me and my brothers. *Sleep until morning, my dear one. Eostre leaves honey and sweet eggs—*

With these words, I conjured her, and I understood what all mothers must. The babe looking up at me was a person, a living breathing person, and it was a blessing to be responsible for her.

She needed a name. I needed something to call her.

I thought back to the herb her mother asked for all those times from the midwife. The baby had craved it when she was inside her mother. She was a tough little thing. She had already survived so much.

I held her close and whispered the word in her ear: *Rapunzel.*

CHAPTER THIRTY-FIVE

You have no doubt heard the story Princess Ursilda told her father. It spread like wildfire, took on a life of its own. A witch stole the baby from the castle, locked the girl in a tower, and kept the girl out of greed. The witch let the vines of her garden go wild, snaking their way up the tower, choking the window where the girl looked out, singing. The truth is the girl was there with her mother's permission. After Ulrich's body was found, the grieving Albrecht went mad. Blaming the king for all of it—his son's death, the baby's kidnapping—Albrecht withdrew from court and locked his family in the inner chambers of his castle. He wouldn't come out until thirty years later when King Frederick died.

When Kunegunde returned from escorting Matthäus home, she treated the wounds I'd sustained in the battle with Ulrich. The next day, she burned the wolf-skin in the garden. She tried to make a ritual of it. The fire stank. She offered me spiced wine, but I had no stomach for it. I left the cup untouched, watching the bonfire with Rapunzel in my arms. I wanted more than anything to leave Gothel, but before my wounds had even healed, a pregnant woman brought news that the king had issued a writ for my death. Nowhere else was safe.

I had no choice but to serve as my grandmother's apprentice, isolated from the circle at her insistence. I looked everywhere for the lockbox full of alrūne she'd once kept beneath the stone in the cellar floor, but I never found it. During that first month, we fought every day. I tried to convince her to let me eat the alrūne; when she refused, I railed at her, but there was nothing I could do. I needed to keep Rapunzel safe.

Sometimes, as I was feeding Rapunzel a bottle, the air would shimmer, and I would know Ursilda was watching. In those moments, I was near overcome by the sadness I sensed from the other side of the shimmering. Without alrūne, my attempts to cast the spell to speak with her were hopeless.

I thought of Matthäus every day. Sometimes, when Kunegunde caught me sobbing, wretched, she offered to erase my memory. "Let me make you forget him," she said. I told her no, of course—I treasured my memories—but I never tried to leave the tower to see him. Any attempt to correct his forgetfulness would cause me too much pain.

As the months passed, I resigned myself to a life without him. Even when I grew ill in the mornings. Even when my belly began to swell. For you see, what the stories do not tell is that Rapunzel grew up with a sister. A girl with black eyes and dark curls. I named her after her father: Matthea.

She lived without knowing him for five years.

Then one October, Kunegunde died of a fever. As soon as I buried her, I poured out the gift-taking powder she had been making me take in the wood. I went to gather alrūne fruit from my mother's garden, and soon, I felt the Mother enveloping me, filling me with love and purpose.

I pulled the locked spellbook down from the top shelf where Kunegunde kept it in the kitchen, unlocked it, and started working my way through my grandmother's spells. I stared for a long time at the last spell in the book, a working that was supposed to bless a daughter with great power. When cast on a girl who already had the gift, it dedicated her to the Mother completely. In return, the Mother would grant her love, good health, and a long, full existence. There were only two ingredients to the spell: a dozen alrūne plants, eaten whole, and a human life.

In those first weeks of quiet study, at night, while my daughters slept, I used Kunegunde's books and the water-*spiegel* to reach out to Beatrice and the other daughters-of-the-Mother. I joined the circle and took the oath. Of what came of that, I can say very little. I am bound by blood-magic not to speak or write of it. I can say, however, that we worked to put the Mother back together. Beatrice introduced me to a woman who knew my mother when she was part of the circle. Hedda had been a promising apprentice of startling power, not easily forgotten by anyone who met her, before she married my father. This woman taught me the secret of the figurine. It only worked to conjure a ghost on the first full moon after the autumn equinox and the nights surrounding it.

On the full moon, I used the figurine to conjure my mother's ghost. I still remember the joy I felt when she embraced me again. We talked for hours that night. The spell worked better at Gothel and on the night of the full moon proper so she could stay in this world for longer. She told me why the Mother sent me on the quest that led me back to Gothel. I was needed to keep the tower, to be there for other women who needed the Mother's sanctuary.

She also told me Matthäus might remember me now that Kunegunde was gone. The next night, after I put the girls to bed, I sent my soul into Zweite and flew to Matthäus's cottage, telling myself I was only going to look in on him. But when I got there, I couldn't help myself.

I guided the raven to land on his windowsill and croaked to get his attention. He looked up from his sewing, five years older, a man's beard at his jaw, his eyes tired. There were calluses on his hands. When I flew in to land beside his needle, he mouthed my name, a question on his face. I croaked at him, nervous, dancing this way and that through his sewing room. He grabbed his things, hurried outside, and followed me into the wood, speaking excitedly as he walked. He said his memory had returned to him like the memory of a dream. It had come back over the last few weeks in flashes: our childhood friendship, his imprisonment at the palace, the nights we spent together on our journey, the choice I had made to keep the baby safe. He wanted to find me and ask me about it, but he couldn't find the tower. "Did it all really happen?" he kept asking with an expression of complicated disbelief. "The *tarnkappen*, the mirror, the wolf, the spell that made me forget?"

Kraek was all I could say until we reached the tower and my soul could reenter my flesh. "It was real," I said, running to the edge of the stone circle to meet him. "All of it."

His face crumpled, and he tried to walk into the stone circle to embrace me, but he couldn't see anything but mist inside. That spell hadn't faded when Kunegunde died. I led him back out, and we talked for a long time just outside the stone circle, the spell zapping behind us. He cried when I told him that I had borne him a child.

After a while, I knew he would follow me back to the tower. It wasn't something we discussed. It was just the way he looked at me, the tension in the air. As we stood together in the woods, talking, I got goose bumps. The feeling that there was something between us, drawing us together, returned. I reached for his hand. He was silent, his palm warm against mine, as I led him through the stone circle, toward the tower, upstairs. After five years apart, the thing between us had grown strong enough to speak for both of us. In the chamber that had once been Kunegunde's, we reached for each other. Blind, he ran his hands over the curves of my body, seeing me the only way he could on the bed covered in furs. We cried together that night, holding each other tight, mourning all the time together we'd missed. We didn't sleep at all. He told me about the children Phoebe had borne him. The softness she'd developed toward him. In the morning, after he met the girls, we said goodbye until Yule, when he promised to return. We both understood. I had my life and he had his.

Those first few years, I spent most of my time raising the girls, seeing clients—woodwives with troubled pregnancies, young women in times of great need—saving lives, telling stories, doing the work I was called to do. Ten years after I returned to Gothel, I received a letter from Mother Hildegard, delivered by a trusted nun who had transferred to a nearby monastery. The letter was written in the *lingua ignota*. The nun had to translate it for me.

Mother Hildegard had met a nun from Zweifalten whose dearest sister I'd brought back from death's door. This nun reported that when I laid hands on her sister, I spoke an ancient prayer in a language like none she'd ever heard. Hildegard wondered if this was the same language she'd found engraved on the stones from the shrine. At the bottom of the letter were several columns of runes. She asked me to let the nun teach me the *lingua ignota* so I could write her back and teach her to translate them. It was thus that we struck up our long correspondence.

Between letters and clients, I gathered herbs. I raised my daughters. I wrote in this book. Once a season, Matthäus came to us. Once a season, we were a family. He came four nights a year, without fail, meeting me at the edge of the circle on the night of the solstice or equinox. Holding hands, we walked back to the tower together, the shadow between us drawing us together, as always. After the girls went to sleep, he spent the night with me in perfect darkness, running his hands over my body, seeing me the only way he could.

He didn't stop coming to see me, even when Rapunzel left the tower. He didn't stop coming, even when Matthea married a woodcutter and he could visit her on his own. He didn't stop coming, even when he grew stooped and old. When the solstice passed one winter and he didn't come, I knew he would come no more. I found his grave behind his cottage and worked no magic for a year. The girls grieved him with me. They have children of their own now, whom they've taught the old ways. We're all part of the circle. After Matthäus died, my children and grandchildren began coming to the tower to celebrate solstices and equinoxes with me.

That was ten years ago. I no longer know what to do with myself when I am alone in the tower. I'm lost when there are no visitors to care for, no potions to make. Casting spells no longer fills me with excitement. My mind wanders. My hands shake. I have become an old woman, getting ready to leave behind the world of things. One day soon, the air will grow taut, and my soul will leave my body for the last time. I will find out what the next world is like, the world beyond the veil.

I suspect only my obsession with finishing this manuscript—with writing this story—has kept me here as long as I have stayed. This is the last task the Mother has set before me, to gather her fragments, record these events for a world that has forgotten her. Now that I have reached my story's end, I am hesitant to turn the page. If I call this book finished, what have I to look forward to, except the last journey I will make?

EPILOGUE

I blinked, eyes burning, when I finished the last page of the codex. The parchment sprang under my touch, still flexible after all these years. Closing my eyes, I felt my heart ache for Haelewise and Matthäus and Ursilda. I saw Rapunzel and Matthea dancing in that legendary garden. I saw a saint—unlike any saint ever described by holy scribes—carefully copying down a list of pagan runes. I saw Alemannic words and phrases on the backs of my eyelids, the doodles in the margins of wild men and women, wortcunner's tools, misshapen roots and bright green herbs. In all my years studying Middle High German literature, I had seen nothing like this codex. A translation of it could make my career.

Rubbing my temples, I reached into my purse for the bottle of sumatriptan, which had been my stalwart companion throughout the reading experience, wondering how I would classify the manuscript in my preface. As literature? As visionary text? Or something else?

The cellar spun. My head ached. I had taken three doses of sumatriptan already, one more dose than my physician advised. Every few hours, that bizarre static electric charge would return to the air, and the lightbulb hanging from the ceiling would start to seem too bright, flickering faintly, as if the cellar had electrical problems. About halfway through the manuscript, that static electricity had come on and stayed on, so palpable that it seemed less a symptom than the *cause* of my migraine. I tried to tell myself it was just a shift in the air pressure, a symptom of the rainstorm that was battering the mountain, but after so many hours immersed in the manuscript, my thoughts kept circling another explanation entirely, like an air-craft whose pilot was desperate to put off a landing.

When I read the passage where Haelewise pulled the lockbox from the uneven stone in the floor, I'd looked up at the stone in front of me and seen her do it as clear as day. Haelewise, daughter-of-Hedda, introduced herself as a storyteller. Of course there would be exaggerations, the sort of details that bring a fireside yarn to life, but I couldn't discount the manuscript altogether as a fiction. There was the declaration of truth, and it'd been found in a place mentioned in the manuscript. It had to have some autobiographical elements, didn't it? The cellar where I sat was the inspiration for the actual cellar of the tower in the manuscript. It *had* to be. The architecture was a fit; the buttresses and curved archways were pre-Romanesque, old enough to be built centuries before the signature date.

I closed the book, careful not to put undue pressure on the cover. I stared at the sigil for a long time, giving in, finally, to the urge to trace it with my finger, wondering if Frau Vogel had any idea of the historical significance of this cellar. I put the codex back in the lockbox and headed upstairs, wondering if she would allow me to digitize the manuscript right away. I could write both German and English editions. Two books! The thought filled me with a giddy relief. If I signed a contract before I applied, the promotion and ten-ure committee would have no choice but to accept my application.

Opening the cellar door, I had no idea what time it was. The kitchen was dark. The only sounds were the ticking of a clock, the planks of the ancient wood floor creaking beneath my feet. I called for Frau Vogel, but she didn't answer. Through the large window I could see the moon hanging low in the sky, round and full. I caught myself thinking about what that meant for the otherworldly weather, then chided myself, though even the reluctant pilot in my mind had to admit it would explain the static electricity in the air.

My migraine was about to put me out of commission altogether, despite the sumatriptan, and—if my thoughts on the moon phase were any indication—my sanity was evaporating. I tried to drag my thoughts out of the manuscript and back into the modern world, where I was an academic who *studied* medieval literature instead of *living* it, but the modern world I thought I knew was slipping out of reach.

I felt warm; my face was flushed. Frau Vogel was nowhere to be seen. Since I arrived, I'd only emerged from the cellar a handful of times to use the bathroom or eat the meals she prepared for me, but she had always been waiting for me in the kitchen. When I tried to talk to her about the manuscript, she refused, telling me she would prefer to wait until I had read the whole thing.

The cuckoo clock on the wall said it was half past three. Looking out the window at the tangled yard, I was struck by the sudden desire to see this place anew, now that I understood what it had once been. I set the lockbox on the coffee table and crept outside.

My rental car glowed cherry red in the moonlight. It seemed like a relic of someone else's life entirely.

From the end of the drive, I turned to take in the rambling cottage that had been built over the cellar. It was a typical Black Forest cottage with one of those giant thatched roofs that swept almost all the way down to the ground. The ash trees that shaded it glistened with raindrops, bright and wet. I squinted, trying to imagine the ancient tower that had once stretched up from the cellar, the garden wall that would've enclosed the yard behind it. For a moment, I saw it in my mind's eye, and then it vanished.

"*Frau Professorin?*" Frau Vogel was standing at the door in a long white nightgown. Her hair was loose, falling all the way down her back, glistening an unearthly white. "*Sie sind fertig.*"

I nodded. "I'm done."

She motioned for me to come inside, and I followed her into the living room, where she turned on several lamps. She took the codex from the lockbox and placed it in her lap. She sat in a chair, and I sat beside her. "*Und?*" she asked.

"It's astonishing."

I launched into a description of the contents of the first half of the manuscript: the declaration of truth, Haelewise's early life, her desire to be a mother and midwife, her journey to the wise woman's tower. Frau Vogel listened closely, especially when I talked about the tower's cellar, which so closely resembled the one beneath this cottage. I explained that I thought the tower had once been a real structure. That centuries after this manuscript was written, it could've crumbled, and her cottage built where it stood. That Haelewise, daughter-of-Hedda, could've put that manuscript in that lockbox herself. That the story held some fragments of truth.

She searched my face, her expression solemn. "Do you really think so?"

"I do."

A complicated smile spread over her face. Her eyes watered. She smoothed her nightgown over her lap and nodded for me to go on.

I smiled back at her, tears burning my own eyes. "It would be tempting to classify the manuscript as fiction—a late example of the Middle High German 'flowering time.' Or we might categorize it as mystical literature, notable not least because of its heresy. The wise woman teaches Haelewise to cast incantations, and she claims to witness a murder through the eyes of a bird. But the story also involves real historical characters, details that match up with history."

As I talked, Frau Vogel turned to the illuminations that illustrated the events I referenced. She found them surprisingly quickly, as if she had memorized their locations. As if she had been reading the manuscript for years.

"Frau Vogel," I blurted, professional courtesy be damned. "How long has it been since you found the manuscript?"

She smiled. "My mother showed it to me when I was little. She couldn't read it, but she showed me the pictures, passing down the story her mother told her, and *her* mother before her."

My mouth dropped. "You—"

She waited for me to piece it together.

"You—you're Haelewise's descendant?"

Frau Vogel nodded gently.

I met her eyes, but she didn't elaborate. My head spun. The tick of the cuckoo clock seemed suddenly too loud. Questions buzzed in my brain like a swarm of bees, purposeful, insistent. Why did she pretend she didn't know what the manuscript was? I remembered her question about my religion in email, how long she let me talk about the manuscript just now before she opened up. She had been testing me all this time. But what did she want me to *do* with this information? What did this mean for the manuscript's veracity, for the static electricity I could still feel in the air? The energy buzzed, insistent, demanding that I reckon with it. I cast around in my brain for something coherent to say, trying to decide which question to ask first.

"What do you want from me?" I said finally.

"A translation, of course. Publication. I want you to teach it."

"Why go public with it after all this time?"

Her expression was so pained, my breath caught in my throat.

"I don't have anyone to share it with," she said. "I am childless. I tried to interest my sister and her children, but they're very *orthodox*. They don't want anything to do with it." Her face crumpled, and she turned so that I couldn't see her expression. I could tell she was working hard to keep her composure.

"*Entschuldigung*," she said finally, her voice choked. She got up and stepped into the next room. I heard her moving about the kitchen, opening a cabinet, as if she was looking for something. When she returned, she was holding something, though I couldn't see what it was.

"I want you to teach the codex. Write about it. Spread this story far and wide. I think it's time."

I met her eyes, baffled that she had chosen to approach me, an

American, when there were so many more acclaimed Middle High German scholars here in Germany. "Why me?"

"That talk you gave years ago at the Bücherschiff in Konstanz, about how illuminated manuscripts could reveal forgotten medieval women's lives. I wanted to show it to you then."

I thought back to the talk I gave at the Bücherschiff. It was one of my first lectures after I graduated. An older woman with salt-and-pepper hair had approached me after the talk. Frau Vogel, I realized now, a decade or so younger. Eyes shining, she'd squeezed my hand and whispered that my conclusions were more right than I knew.

We *had* met. The static electricity zapped through the air, suddenly twice as insistent, impossible to ignore. My head pulsed. I blinked, disoriented. Could Frau Vogel feel it too? She was watching me. I thought of Hildegard, the headaches she suffered, which historians now speculate were migraines. The visions that accompanied them. I could feel cracks forming in my carefully cultivated academic skepticism.

The pilot had finally decided to land.

Frau Vogel extended her arm, fingers closed tight around whatever she'd retrieved from the kitchen. She met my eyes, as if she were asking my permission. At first I had no idea what she was holding. And then, suddenly, I did. When I nodded, she opened her fist, and my heart soared with decades of suppressed ecstasy at the sight of it.

It was black soapstone. It had wings.

ACKNOWLEDGMENTS

I am grateful to so many people without whom this book would not exist.

I want to begin by thanking my late mother, who told the most incredible folktales at bedtime with great enthusiasm, and my late father, who filled the bookshelves of our childhood home with books. I want to thank my daughter, whose reactions to the folktales I told at bedtime inspired me to write this novel. And finally, I'm deeply grateful to my husband, David S. Bennett, the love of my life, whose support of my writing career has never wavered, not once. Thank you, thank you, thank you—for giving me the child who inspired this book, for the late-night brainstorming sessions, support, and encouragement when I needed it most. I love you.

In the publishing world, I want to start by thanking Sam Farkas, my wonderful agent, whose brilliant feedback, unwavering belief in this book, and nurturing presence have made the professional side of my writing life an utter joy. Thank you for your friendship and for being such a supportive force. I'm also grateful to the rest of the fantastic team at Jill Grinberg Literary Management; it's a wonder to be represented by such a talented, collaborative agency.

I am deeply indebted to Brit Hvide, my brilliant editor at Orbit/Redhook, whose excellent feedback, advocacy, and enthusiasm for Haelewise and her story have been a dream come true. Thank you for believing in Hael, for your advice on the prologue and epilogue, and for your tip that I wasn't quite done with Ulrich. I am incredibly lucky to get to work with you. I also want to thank Angeline Rodriguez, Bryn A. McDonald, Lisa Marie Pompilio, and the rest of the fantastic team at Orbit, as well as Emily Byron and Nadia Saward at Orbit UK, and Amy J. Schneider. It's been an honor to work with all of you.

I have been incredibly blessed with writing friends, whose support over the years has been invaluable. To Ronlyn Domingue, my writer soulmate—thank you for the decades of emails, phone calls, and manuscript reads. I'm so glad that we ended up in that workshop together, all those years ago, writing our weird speculative stories and dreaming of France. To Carolyn Turgeon and Jeanine Cummins, thank you from the bottom of my heart for your excellent advice, multiple reads of this manuscript, and many years of friendship. To Sally Rosen Kindred, thank you for reading and offering gentle guidance and support when I needed it most. To Sayward Byrd Stuart, thank you for decades of friendship, blue Lycra couches, and excellent advice on the Latinate phrasing of sexist peer reviewers. To Fox Henry Frazier, thank you for reading a late version of the manuscript and providing feedback, laughing with me and live-texting terrible TV during the pandemic, and serving as a contemporary real-life model of a witchy single mother in a tower.

I'm grateful to my teachers: Mara Malone, Jim Bennett, Moira Crone, David Madden, Andrei Codrescu, Rick Blackwood, Chuck Wachtel, and E. L. Doctorow; my colleagues and friends: Chad and Julie Brooks Barbour, Donna Fiebelkorn, and Barb Light; and my students, from whom I've learned so much.

I want to thank the many scholars of history, religion, language, and folklore whose research inspired me during the writing of this book, including the historian David Sheffler at the University of North Florida, who generously offered advice on twelfth-century Germany and Middle High German, and the translator and medieval German–literature scholar Peter Sean Woltemade, who offered expertise on German dialogue and Middle High German literature. All mistakes are my own. The following books were especially instrumental: *Daily Life in the Middle Ages* by Paul B. Newman (McFarland & Company, 2001); *Medieval Germany 1056–1273* by Alfred Haverkamp, translated by Helga Braun and Richard Mortimer (Oxford University Press, 1988); *Practicing Piety in Medieval Ashkenaz: Men, Women, and Everyday Religious Observance* by Elisheva Baumgarten (University of Pennsylvania Press, 2014); *At the Bottom of the Garden: A Dark History of Fairies, Hobgoblins, Nymphs, and Other Troublesome Things* by Diane Purkiss (New York University Press, 2000); *Witchcraft in Europe, 400–1700: A Documentary History* edited by Alan Charles Kors and Edward Peters (University of Pennsylvania Press, 2001); *Hildegard of Bingen: The Woman of Her Age* by Fiona Maddocks (Doubleday, 2001); *Hildegard of Bingen: A Visionary Life* by Sabina Flanagan (Routledge, 1998); *Hildegard of Bingen: Scivias* translated by Mother Columbia Hart and Jane Bishop (Paulist Press, 1990); *Hildegard von Bingen's Physica: The Complete English Translation of Her Classic Work on Health and Healing* translated by Priscilla Throop (Healing Arts Press, 1998); *The Personal Correspondence of Hildegard of Bingen* translated by Joseph L. Baird (Oxford University Press, 2006); *Hildegard of Bingen: On Natural Philosophy and Medicine: Selections from Cause Et Cure* translated by Margret Berger (D. S. Brewer, 1999); *The Chalice and the Blade: Our History, Our Future* by Riane Eisler (HarperCollins, 1988); *The Classic Fairy Tales* edited by Maria Tatar (W. W. Norton & Company, 1999); *The Annotated Brothers Grimm* edited by Maria Tatar (W. W. Norton & Company, 2004); *Breaking the Magic Spell: Radical Theories of Folk and Fairy Tales* by Jack Zipes (University Press of Kentucky, 2002); *Yiddish Folktales* edited by Beatrice Silverman Weinreich, translated by Leonard Wolf (Pantheon, 1988); and *A Middle High German Primer* by Joseph Wright (Oxford University Press, 1944).

Finally, I would like to thank the Sustainable Arts Foundation for the award that enabled me to travel to Germany to research this novel and walk in Haelewise's footsteps, as well as the National Endowment for the Arts and Vermont Studio Center for the parent-artist scholarship that paid for my residency at Vermont Studio Center, providing much-needed time to work on this book.